PSYCHOLOGY

PSYCHOLOGY
Fourth Edition

Lester M. Sdorow
Lafayette College

Boston, Massachusetts   Burr Ridge, Illinois   Dubuque, Iowa
Madison, Wisconsin   New York, New York,   San Francisco, California   St. Louis, Missouri

McGraw-Hill
  A Division of the McGraw-Hill Companies, Inc. All rights reserved.

PSYCHOLOGY

McGraw-Hill

A Division of The **McGraw·Hill** Companies

This book is printed on recycled, acid-free paper containing 10% postconsumer waste.

3 4 5 6 7 8 9 0 WEB/WEB 0 9 8 7 6 5 4 3 2 1 0

ISBN 0-697-25285-X

Publisher: Jane E. Vaicunas
Sponsoring Editor: Meera Dash
Marketing Manager: James Rozsa
Project Manager: Jayne Klein
Production Supervisor: Debra Donner
Designer: LuAnn Schrandt/Wayne Harms
Cover designer: GraphiStock: John Ritter, *Man Carrying Eye*
Photo research coordinator: Carrie Burger
Art Editor: Joyce Watters
The credits section for this book begins on page C-1 and is considered an extension of the copyright page.
Compositor: PC&F, Incorporated
Typeface: 10/12 Goudy
Printer: Quebecor Printing Book Group/Dubuque

Library of Congress Number 97-70799

INTERNATIONAL EDITION
Copyright 1998. Exclusive rights by The McGraw-Hill Companies, Inc. for manufacture and export. This book cannot be re-exported from the country to
which it is consigned by McGraw-Hill. The International Edition is not available in North America.

When ordering this title, use ISBN 0-07-115549-X

www.mhhe.com

BRIEF CONTENTS

C O N T E N T S

CHAPTER 3

Behavioral Neuroscience   64

THE NERVOUS SYSTEM: A MEANS
OF RAPID COMMUNICATION   67

THE NEURON: THE NERVE CELL   68

THE ENDOCRINE SYSTEM: HORMONAL
REGULATION OF BODILY PROCESSES   76

THE BRAIN: WHERE FANCY IS BRED   78

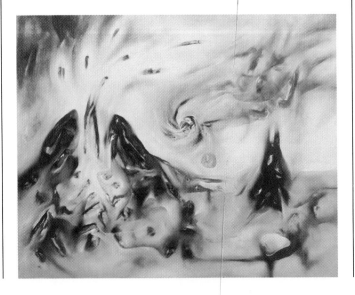

CHAPTER 4

Human Development   104

THE NATURE OF DEVELOPMENTAL PSYCHOLOGY   106

PRENATAL DEVELOPMENT   112

INFANT AND CHILD DEVELOPMENT   115

ADOLESCENT DEVELOPMENT   129

ADULT DEVELOPMENT   134

THINKING ABOUT PSYCHOLOGY

ANATOMY OF A CLASSIC RESEARCH STUDY

ANATOMY OF A CONTEMPORARY RESEARCH STUDY

PREFACE

From psychology's inception as a separate discipline, authors of introductory psychology textbooks have been confronted with the need to convey a broad discipline to students in a book of reasonable length. To accomplish all that I originally intended, this book could easily have been twice as long as it is now. A century ago, William James, disturbed at the length of his now-classic *Principles of Psychology*, gave his own stinging review of it. He called it, among other things, "a bloated tumescent mass." Though this comment may have been written during one of James's frequent bouts with depression, it indicates the challenge of synthesizing a vast quantity of information. Given that psychology has become an even broader discipline and has accumulated an enormous information base, I quickly discovered that I would somehow have to manipulate a kind of intellectual "Rubik's cube" of seven goals to avoid producing a bloated, tumescent mass (or what textbook reviewers often, perhaps euphemistically, refer to as an "encyclopedic" book). My goals could only be achieved by considering each goal in light of the others.

MY SEVEN GOALS

1. Do Justice to the Breadth of Psychology

My students often express amazement at the breadth of psychology. One psychologist might devote a career to studying the relationship between brain activity and schizophrenia; another might devote a career to studying the social factors that promote human love. And while one member of a psychology department studies the perceptual abilities of newborn infants, another studies the language abilities of chimpanzees. Because of this breadth, I was forced to be selective in the topics, studies, and concepts that I included in the book. Nonetheless, I believe the book presents a fair, representative sampling of the discipline.

2. Present Material in Sufficient, but Not Excessive, Detail

Again, compromise was in order. As a teacher and a student, I have disliked textbooks that go to extremes. At one extreme are textbooks that present many topics but only superficial coverage of them. At the other extreme are textbooks that present fewer topics but overwhelm the reader with details. Though my discussions of topics naturally vary somewhat in their extensiveness, I have provided enough information to assure student comprehension, while permitting coverage of a sufficient number of topics to assure a good representation of the entire discipline. The main exceptions to this approach are topics covered in greater depth in the "Thinking About Psychology" sections (discussed below) that end each chapter.

3. Encourage Appreciation of the Research Process

A psychology textbook should provide students with more than theories and research findings. It should discuss "how we know" as well as "what we know." To give students enough background to appreciate the research process, I introduce, in Chapter 2, psychology as a science, the methods of psychological research, and the statistical analysis of research data. The chapter includes a concrete example of the scientific method that shows how it relates to a classic study of interpersonal attraction. The chapter also includes data from a hypothetical health-psychology study on the effect of melatonin on sleep and tells how to calculate descriptive statistics using that data.

In trying to help the student appreciate the research process, I have once again tried to strike a balance throughout the book by discussing research studies in moderate detail. For examples of this, turn to Chapter 9 for the discussion of a study on naturalistic concepts in which nonartists formed concepts of artistic styles from paintings without being able to state the defining features that distinguish one style from another; or turn to Chapter 16 and read the discussion of a study of the use of classical conditioning to suppress the immune system.

4. Promote Critical Thinking

I believe that students should know scientific methodology, research findings, and how to critically evaluate what they read by relying on objective, rational evaluation of empirical evidence. Chapter 2 describes formal steps in thinking critically. Students will find that the ability to think critically benefits them in their daily lives when confronted with claims made by friends, relatives, politicians, advertisers, or anyone else. Almost every page of this book gives the student an opportunity to think about popular claims, provide alternative explanations for research findings, or think of possible implications of research findings. For an example of how I have integrated critical thinking in the textbook, turn to the discussion in Chapter 6 of hypnosis as an altered state of consciousness. Most of the "Thinking About Psychology" sections also provide extended examples of critical thinking.

5. Present Psychology in Context

An article in the *American Psychologist*, dealing with psychology and the liberal arts curriculum, stressed that providing students with the historical context of psychology is an essential goal in undergraduate psychology education. Introductory psychology textbooks should not present psychology as though it developed in "ivory towers" divorced from a historical or personal context. Throughout this book, you will find many ways in which topics are given a historical grounding. For example, Chapter 10 traces the nature/nurture debate regarding intelligence back to the work of Francis Galton and the flood of immigrants in the early twentieth century. And Chapter 11 highlights changing values concerning sexuality by discussing the case of an article submitted to the *Journal of the American Medical Association* in 1899 that was not published until 1983.

I have also taken care to show that psychology is a human endeavor, practiced by people with emotions as well as intellect, and that scientific progress depends on serendipity as well as cool calculation. For example, Chapter 1 discusses William James's effort to have Harvard University grant the doctoral degree to Mary Whiton Calkins, who became an eminent psychologist, but who, as a woman, was denied the degree despite fulfilling the requirements for it. Chapter 3 tells how the first demonstration of the chemical basis of communication between nerve cells came to Otto Loewi in a dream. Chapter 13 describes how psychoanalyst Alfred Adler's concept of the inferiority complex may be rooted in his own sickly childhood.

6. Present a Balanced and Scholarly View of Psychology

This is not only a psychoanalytic book, a behavioristic book, a cognitive book, a humanistic book, or a biopsychological book. It is a bit of each, which reflects my belief that an introductory psychology textbook should introduce students to a variety of perspectives, rather than reflect the author's favored one. Over the decades, the perspectives have waxed and waned in their dominance. Students are introduced to the major psychological perspectives in Chapter 1 and continue to encounter them throughout the book, most obviously in the chapters on personality, psychological disorders, and therapy.

For students to respect psychology as a science, the textbook they use must be scholarly. Though popular examples are sprinkled throughout this text, they are not used as substitutes for evidence provided by scientific research. A perusal of the reference list at the end of the text reveals that it is up-to-date in its coverage of research studies, yet does not slight classic studies.

7. Show the Relevance of Psychology to Everyday Life

I enjoy books that give me a sense of the author by providing "coloration" for the typically sober material that is presented. The examples I use in showing the relevance of psychology to everyday life provides this coloration. The examples come from virtually every area of life, including art, literature, history, biography, entertainment, sport, politics, and student life. Instead of showing the relevance of psychology segregating it in "boxes," I have interwoven the examples into the narrative. For example, Chapter 6 provides research-based suggestions for overcoming insomnia, Chapter 7 discusses how operant conditioning is used to train animals, and Chapter 8 describes ways to improve one's memory and study habits.

SPECIAL FEATURES

Anatomy of a Research Study

The "Anatomy of a Research Study" sections provide unique examinations of research methodology. Beginning with Chapter 2, each chapter features brief expositions of both a classic and a contemporary psychological research study. These sections briefly highlight the rationale, methods, and results of featured studies in an accessible manner for beginning students. These studies are tied directly to the text discussion and emphasize both methodology and critical thinking. Key questions about research findings reinforce the focus on essential and ongoing issues of psychology that appear throughout the book and are highlighted in the "Thinking About Psychology" sections that end each chapter.

Thinking About Psychology

In a senior seminar course I have taught over the years, entitled "Current Issues in Psychology," students read many journal articles and some popular articles on a host of controversial topics, which they then discuss or debate. Because of the success of this course—students enjoy sinking their teeth into controversial issues—I have adapted its rationale for this textbook in many of the topics covered in the "Thinking About Psychology" sections. To provide adequate discussion of each topic, I devote several pages to presenting the status of a particular issue or application.

Many of the topics in these sections illustrate how psychologists think critically about issues such as hemispheric specialization, parapsychology, unconscious influences, ape language, personality consistency, effectiveness of psychotherapy, and Type A behavior. Other "Thinking About Psychology" sections illustrate the connection of research to practical reality, as in the sections discussing biofeedback and motivation and sport. Some of the sections illustrate how scientific issues cannot always be divorced from ethics, values, and politics, including the sections on the ethics of psychological research, the nature-nurture controversy in regard to intelligence, the study of gender differences, the insanity defense, and the effect of pornography on aggression.

For More Information

I believe that the "For More Information on . . ." lists of readings at the end of each chapter are a unique feature of the book. The lists are extensive and are arranged according to the major headings of the chapters. Each list ends with biographical or autobiographical readings about contributors to psychology. The readings provide substantial material for students who are interested in learning more about particular topics or people, or who would like a starting point for writing research papers.

Appendix A: Majoring in Psychology

The appendix "Majoring in Psychology" will prove useful for psychology majors interested in preparing for a career. It might also help other students decide whether or not to major in psychology.

Appendix B: Statistics

The appendix "Statistics" provides an extended discussion and examples of the use of statistics in describing and making inferences from research data.

Appendix C: Industrial/Organizational Psychology

Appendix C surveys industrial/organizational psychology, an important topic for many students who are considering making psychology their career. It was written by Paul Levy, an industrial/organizational psychologist at the University of Akron..

Other Features

Chapter Outline. The outline provides a framework for the content of each chapter.

Margin Glossary. Terms that are printed in boldface are defined in the margins, and these definitions are collected in a page-referenced glossary at the end of the book.

Illustrations. I selected or helped design all of the illustrations in this book. My goal was for each to serve a sound pedagogical purpose. Illustrations were chosen because their visual presentations complemented the material discussed.

Chapter Summary. Each chapter ends with a summary that captures the essential points made in the major sections of the chapter.

Key Concepts. Following the summary is a page-referenced alphabetical list of important concepts which are boldfaced in the text.

Key Contributors. At the end of each chapter is a list of key people who were discussed in the chapter.

CHANGES IN THE FOURTH EDITION

After synthesizing comments from users and reviewers, I found that they considered the third edition scholarly and challenging, yet interesting and clearly written. They particularly appreciated its attention to the historical context of psychology. As many pundits have noted, "If it ain't broke, don't fix it." Nonetheless, I have made some important changes in the fourth edition.

First, the amount of detail covered in the text has been trimmed. Where three or four examples might have been used previously, they have been trimmed to one or two. Prioritizing and condensing examples helps focus a student's attention on what is truly important.

At the end of major topic headings, brief lists of questions called "Staying on Track" have been added to focus student attention where it needs to be directed. These questions help students pinpoint the most essential information from major subject headings and provide a means of seeing if they have absorbed the material they will most need to understand from the chapter. The answers for all of the "Staying on Track" questions have been provided at the end of the book.

The most visible change might be the addition of the appendix devoted to industrial/organizational psychology. Because many instructors cover this important topic in their classes, I wanted to include material on it for this edition. However, because many other instructors do not cover it, and the time limitations within the semester are already severe, I placed it at the end of the book, where those who wish to take advantage of it can do so.

REQUEST FOR COMMENTS

Realizing that the ideal textbook might be approached but never achieved, I welcome your comments about the book and suggestions for improving it. Just as user comments improved the previous editions, more comments will improve the next edition. Please send your correspondence to the following address:

Les Sdorow
c/o Psychology Editor
McGraw-Hill College Division
699 Boylston Street
Boston, MA 02116

SUPPLEMENTS

We've combined a student-oriented textbook with an integrated ancillary package designed to meet the unique needs of instructors and students. Our goal has been to create a teaching package that is as enjoyable to teach with as it is to study from.

The **Instructor's Course Planner** was prepared by Steven A. Schneider of Pima Community College. This flexible instructor's manual and planner provides many useful tools to enhance your teaching. For each chapter, an extended chapter outline, suggestions for teaching, lecture/discussion suggestions, video and film suggestions, and classroom activities are provided.

Two **Test Item Files** will provide ample questions for your tests for as long as you use this book. Test Item File #1 is newly prepared by Grace Galliano of Kennesaw State University. I prepared the Test Item File #2. Both Test Item Files have 100 items per chapter. Each item is classified as Factual, Conceptual, or Applied and referenced to the learning objectives in the Course Success Guide and the textbook page number. The questions in the test item files are also available on **MicroTest III,** a powerful but easy-to-use test-generating program by Chariot Software Group. MicroTest is available for your use in DOS (3.5-inch disks), Windows, and MacIntosh versions. With MicroTest, instructors can easily select questions from the Test Item File and print tests and answer keys. Instructors can also customize questions, headings, and instructions; add or import their own questions; and print tests in a choice of printer-supported fonts.

The **Course Success Guide** is available in printed and electronic versions. For each chapter of the textbook this study guide provides students with learning objectives, a detailed outline of the chapter, a review of terms and concepts, and multiple choice practice tests.

Sixty book-specific transparencies, which match key illustations in the textbook, are available for your classroom presentation.

The Introductory Psychology Transparency Set features over 100 additional transparencies illustrating key concepts in general psychology and accompanying handbook with specific suggestions for classroom use by Susan J. Shapiro of Indiana University East.

The Critical Thinker, second edition, by Richard Mayer and Fiona Goodchild, both of the University of California–Santa Barbara, explicitly teaches strategies for understanding and evaluating material in any introductory psychology textbook.

The AIDS Booklet, third edition, by Frank D. Cox of Santa Barbara City College, is a brief but comprehensive introduction to Acquired Immune Deficiency Syndrome, HIV, and related viruses.

The Encyclopedic Dictionary of Psychology provides easy reference access to the key figures, concepts, movements, and practices of the field of psychology.

Psychology: The Active Learner CD-ROM by Jane Halonen, Marilyn Reedy, and Paul Smith is an innovative interactive product that will help students learn key concepts taught in introductory psychology in a fun and dynamic way. Focusing on concepts that tend to be most difficult for the beginning psychology student, this program contains 15 modules containing tutorial review and critical thinking exercises for biological foundations, sensation and perception, states of consciousness, learning, memory, development, social psychology and more.

The CD-ROM **Explorations in Health and Psychology** by George B. Johnson of Washington University in St. Louis will help students actively investigate processes vital to their understanding of psychology as they should be explored—with movement, color, sound, and interaction. This set of 10 interactive animations on CD-ROM allows students to set and reset variables in each (including modules on Life Span and Lifestyle, Drug Addiction, Nerve Conduction, IDS, Immune Response, and more) and then evaluate those results. In addition to the colorful and precisely labeled graphics and animated illustrations, the CD-ROM also offers narration in English and Spanish, a glossary with written and oral pronunciations, and lists of additional recommended readings.

A large selection of **videotapes** is also available to adopters based on the number of textbooks ordered.

The Brain Modules on Videodisc, created by WNET in New York, Antenne 2 TV/France, the Annenberg/CPB Foundation, and Professor Frank J. Vattano of Colorado State University, is based on the Peabody Award–winning series *The Brain*. Thirty segments, averaging 6 minutes each, illustrate an array of topics in psychology.

The **Reference Disk Set** is available free to adopters. The disks include over 15,000 book references arranged in files by topic. The complete set of five disks is available on IBM (3.5") or MacIntosh disks.

Psych Online is a reference guide that points students and instructors to electronic resources in introductory psychology. Prepared by Dr. Patricia Wallace, Director of Information Technologies and psychologist at the University of Maryland, Psych Online offers useful general help in using the internet. It includes a list of sites for each area of the discipline.

Annual Editions provides convenient, inexpensive access to a wide range of current, carefully selected articles from magazines, newspapers, and journals. Written by psychologists, researchers, and educators, *Annual Editions: Psychology* provides useful perspectives on important and timely topics. *Annual Editions* is updated yearly, and includes a number of features designed to make it particularly useful including a topic guide, annotated table of contents, and unit overviews. For the professor using *Annual Editions* in the classroom, an Instructor's Resource Guide with test questions is available.

Taking Sides: Clashing Views on Psychological Issues is a debate-style reader designed to introduce students to controversies in psychology. By requiring students to analyze opposing viewpoints and reach considered judgments, *Taking Sides* actively develops students' critical thinking skills.

Sources: Notable Selections in Psychology brings together 46 selections including classic articles, book excerpts, and research studies that have shaped the study of psychology. If you want your students to gain greater background knowledge in reading and interpreting first hand from source material, *Sources* collects a diverse array of accessible but significant readings in one place.

ACKNOWLEDGMENTS

In revising this book, I have appreciated the pride and intrinsic interest of the editorial staff at McGraw-Hill in producing textbooks of high quality. I owe special thanks to my long-time editors, Steven Yetter and Linda Falkenstein, and my new editors, Meera Dash and Hayley Wood. My project manager, Jayne Klein, showed her remarkable ability to maintain a cordial demeanor while undergoing the stress of coordinating the many persons who contribute to the creation of a textbook. The beautiful appearance of the book also owes much to the diligence and expertise of book designer Luann Schrandt, art editor Joyce Watters, and photo editor Carrie Burger. I would also like to thank my permissions editor who again made my life easier by her conscientious performance of a tedious task.

A special thanks is owed those who contributed to the ancillaries that are available with this book, including Rick Johnson, Steve Schneider, and Grace Galliano. Also, Paul Levy, who wrote the industrial/organizational psychology appendix, is owed a special thanks.

Any of the good qualities of the textbook owe themselves in great measure to the many reviewers who read drafts of this text in part or in whole. I have valued, seriously considered, and even savored, each of their suggestions.

For their help with the fourth edition, I'd like to thank the following individuals:

Ronald Baenninger, *Temple University*
Robert C. Beck, *Wake Forest University*
John Benjafield, *Brock University*
Linda Brannon, *McNeese State University*
John B. Connors, *Canadian Union College*
Stanley Coren, *University of British Columbia*
Randolph Cornelius, *Vassar College*
Verne C. Cox, *University of Texas at Arlington*
Deanna L. Dodson, *Lebanon Valley College*
Donald K. Freedheim, *Case Western Reserve University*
Ajaipal S. Gill, *Anne Arundel Community College*
Morton G. Harmatz, *University of Massachusetts–Amherst*
Debra L. Hollister, *Valencia Community College*
Daniel Houlihan, *Mankato State University*
Lera Joyce Jonson, *Centenary College*
Stanley K. Kary, *St. Louis Community College at Florrissant Valley*
Richard Lippa, *California State University–Fullerton*
Gerald McRoberts, *Stanford University*
Ralph Miller, *State University of New York–Binghamton*
Joel Morgovsky, *Brookdale Community College*
Ian Neath, *Purdue University*
Brent D. Slife, *Brigham Young University*
Michael D. Spiegler, *Providence College*
George T. Taylor, *University of Missouri, St. Louis*
Benjamin Wallace, *Cleveland State University*
Wilse Webb, *University of Florida–Gainsville*
Ian Wishaw, *University of Lethbridge*

I'd also like to thank my colleagues who reviewed this textbook in its first three editions:

Thomas R. Alley, *Clemson University*
Barbara L. Andersen, *Ohio State University*
Robert C. Beck, *Wake Forest University*
Virginia Wise Berninger, *University of Washington*
Joseph Bilotta, *Vanderbilt University*
Fredda Blanchard-Fields, *Louisiana State University*
J. E. Boggs, *Purdue University*
John P. Broida, *University of Southern Maine*
J. S. Caldwell, *California State University, Chico*
James F. Calhoun, *University of Georgia*
J. B. Clement, *Daytona Beach Community College*

Kenneth Coffield, *University of Alabama*
Richard T. Comstock, *Monroe Community College*
Katherine Covell, *Brock University*
Patricia Crane, *San Antonio College*
Joseph Culkin, *Queensborough Community College*
Duane Cuthbertson, *Bryan College*
George M. Diekhoff, *Midwestern State University*
Paul Doerksen, *University of Saskatchewan*
Thomas Evans, *John Carroll University*
William F. Ford, *Bucks County Community College*
Laura Freberg, *California Polytechnic State University, San Luis Obispo*
Laurel Furomoto, *Wellesley College*
Grace Galliano, *Kennesaw College*
William Glassman, *Ryerson Polytechnical Institute*
Malcolm Grant, *Memorial University of Newfoundland*
Elaine Hatfield, *University of Hawaii*
Richard Haude, *University of Akron*
Susan M. Heidenreich, *Loyola University, New Orleans*
Peter Hill, *Grove City College*
Morton Hoffman, *Metropolitan State College*
Valerye A. Hunt, *University College of the Frazier Valley*
James E. Jans, *Concordia College*
James Johnson, *Illinois State University*
Richmond Johnson, *Moravian College*
Seth Kalichman, *Medical College of Wisconsin*
Cindy Kennedy, *University of Dayton*
Melvyn King, *SUNY-Cortland*
Mindy L. Kornhaber, *Harvard University*
Daniel K. Lapsley, *Brandon University*
Randy J. Larsen, *University of Michigan*
Thomas Hardy Leahey, *Virginia Commonwealth University*
Mark R. Leary, *Wake Forest University*
Fred Leavitt, *California State University, Hayward*
T. C. Lewandowski, *Delaware County Community College*
Inez Livingston, *Eastern Illinois College*
Karen Macrae, *University of South Carolina*
Leonard Mark, *Miami University*
Mark McCourt, *North Dakota State University*
Paul A. Miller, *Arizona State University West*
Jodi A. Mindell, *St. Joseph's University*
Kevin Moore, *DePauw University*
James Mosely, *University of Calgary*
David I. Mostofsky, *Boston University*
Tibor Palfai, *Syracuse University*
W. Stephen Royce, *University of Portland*
Ina Samuels, *University of Massachusetts*
Steven Schneider, *Pima Community College*
Thomas J. Schoeneman, *Lewis & Clark College*
R. Lance Shotland, *Pennsylvania State University*
Dale Simmons, *Oregon State University*
Cheryl L. Sisk, *Michigan State University*

Sara Rader Staats, *Ohio State University, Newark*
Gordon Timothy, *Ricks College*
Frank Vattano, *Colorado State University*
Wayne Viney, *Colorado State University*
Benjamin Wallace, *Cleveland State University*
Deborah Du Nann Winter, *Whitman College*

I also owe special thanks to my colleagues, students, friends, and family. My department chairperson, Susan Basow, at Lafayette College, has provided me with the opportunity to teach in a psychology department that is dedicated to excellence in undergraduate education.

I have benefited from the continued support of my mother, Mildred Sdorow; my brother, Eric Sdorow; my sister-in-law Connie Sdorow; and my cousins Dawna Gold, Ingrid Gold, Larry Gold, Caryn Stark, and Marilyn Vicenzino. I have also received valued support from my friends Gregg Amore, Annette Benert, Martha Boston, Doris Brandes, Jim Buchanan, Phil Curson, Joe Lambert, Charles Olson, Bjorn Polfelt, Jan Witte, and Paul Witte. Special thanks to my friends John Dwyer and Herb Millman at Cockamamie's and Lino and Carla Fuentes at the Duck Soup Cafe in New Hope, who are always there when I need them. And, most of all, to Sue Reffie, who has brought joy and spirituality into my life.

TO THE STUDENT

While writing this introductory psychology textbook, I kept the needs of the student reader in mind. In addition to writing a textbook that has been well-received for being interesting and clearly written, I have included several special features to help you in studying its content, to represent psychology as a science, and to show the relevance of psychology to the "real world." The combination of the special features, the engaging writing style, and concrete and relevant examples of numerous concepts makes the textbook a powerful learning tool for students who are new to psychology.

—Les Sdorow

Chapter Outline

A detailed outline of the topics covered introduces each chapter. By reading the outline before you start the chapter you can quickly glean the major sections that are covered as well as the subsections, which are indented beneath the capitalized headings. The organization of these sections was crafted to present new material in a logical, student-friendly fashion.

Psychology as a Science

SOURCES OF KNOWLEDGE
Everyday Sources of Knowledge
Common Sense: The Role of Lay Psychology
Appeal to Authority: The Role of Expert Opinion
Reasoning: The Role of Logical Thinking
Unsystematic Observation: The Role of Sensory Data
The Scientific Method: Being Objective and Systematic
Assumptions of Science: Determinism and Skepticism
Steps in Conducting Scientific Research
ANATOMY OF A CONTEMPORARY RESEARCH STUDY: Is the Ability to Detect Drunkenness Simply a Matter of Common Sense?
GOALS OF SCIENTIFIC RESEARCH
Description: Noting Observable Characteristics
Prediction: Hypothesizing About Events
Control: Regulating Aspects of Physical Reality
Explanation: Discovering Causes

METHODS OF PSYCHOLOGICAL RESEARCH
Descriptive Research: Systematically Recording Observations
Naturalistic Observation: Making Observations in the Natural World
Case Studies: Studying Individuals in Depth
Surveys: Asking for Responses to Interviews and Questionnaires
Psychological Testing: Obtaining Samples of Behavior
Archival Research: Analyzing Data from Existing Records
Correlational Research: Examining Relationships Between Variables
Experimental Research: Investigating Cause-and-Effect Relationships
Experimental Method: Exploring the Effects of Independent Variables on Dependent Variables
Internal Validity: The Extent to Which Changes in the Dependent Variable Are Attributable to the Independent Variable

ANATOMY OF A CLASSIC RESEARCH STUDY: Can Experimenter Expectancies Affect the Behavior of Laboratory Rats?
External Validity: Generalizing from Experiments
STATISTICAL ANALYSIS OF RESEARCH DATA
Descriptive Statistics: Summarizing Research Data
Correlational Statistics: Finding Relationships in Research Data
Inferential Statistics: Determining Causality Using Research Data
THINKING ABOUT Psychology
What Are the Ethics of Psychological Research?
Ethical Treatment of Human Subjects
Ethical Treatment of Animal Subjects

31

▶ The Ethical Treatment of Animal Subjects
Animal rights activists have picketed meetings of the American Psychological Association to oppose research that uses animals as subjects. Psychologists have responded by pointing out the benefits of animal research and the strict ethical standards they follow in conducting their research with animals.

potential confounding variables that might affect the behavior of an animal. You would be less likely to worry about subject bias effects, for instance, when studying pigeons. Third, developmental changes across the life span can be studied more efficiently in animals. If you were interested in the effects of the complexity of the early childhood environment on memory in old age, you might take 75 years to complete an experiment using human subjects, but only 3 years to complete one using cats.

Fourth, research on animals can generate hypotheses that are then tested using human subjects. B. F. Skinner's research on learning in rats and pigeons stimulated research on learning in human beings. Fifth, research on animals can benefit animals themselves. For example, as described in Chapter 7, psychologists have developed techniques to make coyotes feel nauseated by the taste of sheep; perhaps these can someday be used to protect sheep from coyotes, and coyotes from angry sheep ranchers. Sixth, because of an assumption that animals do not have the same moral rights as human beings (Baldwin, 1993), certain procedures that are not ethically permissible with human subjects are ethically permissible under current standards with animal subjects. Thus, if you wanted to conduct an experiment in which you studied the effects of surgically removing a particular brain structure, you would be limited to the use of animals.

But these reasons have not convinced animal rights advocates of the merits of psychological research on animals. Animal rights advocates argue that the benefits of laboratory research that subjects animals to painful procedures do not outweigh the suffering they induce (Bowd, 1990). During the past decade some animal rights advocates have even vandalized animal research laboratories and stolen animals from their laboratory cages. The vast majority of advocates, however, have been content to lobby for stronger laws limiting animal research or to picket meetings of animal researchers. Prior to the meeting at which he was harassed, Neal Miller (1985) had pointed out that for every dog and cat used in laboratory research, 10,000 are abandoned by their owners, and that, in contrast, few psychology experiments inflict pain or distress on animals. He urged animal rights advocates to spend more time helping the millions of abandoned pets that are killed in pounds, given to death, or die after being struck by motor vehicles.

Miller (1985) has also cited ways in which animal research contributes to human welfare. Findings from animal research have contributed to progress in the treatment of pain; the development of behavior therapy for phobias; the rehabilitation of victims of neuromuscular disorders, such as Parkinson's disease; the understanding of neurological disorders associated with aging, such as Alzheimer's disease; and the development of drugs for

60　　CHAPTER 2

Illustrations

Special care has been taken to ensure that the illustrations and photographs in this book enhance your understanding of the ideas described. There are several clear figures and graphs as well as excellent physiological drawings. I sought photographs that were relevant and related current events to the concepts in the book. Since many topics within the broad spectrum of psychology are controversial, I have reinforced certain issues visually.

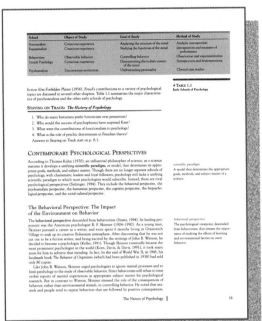

Staying on Track

After each of the major sections per chapter you will find 3 or 4 questions to aid you in reviewing the material you've covered so far. It's a good idea to try to answer these for yourself as you go, to test your own retention of what you've learned and to see what you will need to read again and reinforce. The questions are general and designed to help you understand "the big picture."

Margin Glossary

Key terms with their definitions appear in the margin of the same page on which each term is introduced. This running glossary provides an unobtrusive way to accumulate and learn a psychological vocabulary. These terms are also in the glossary at the end of the book.

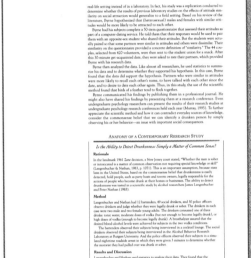

Anatomy of a Contemporary Research Study

Many chapters use this feature to convey how the scientific method can be applied to formulate questions and draw conclusions on current issues that touch most people's lives. Sometimes the findings are surprising and demonstrate the limitations of assumptions that are based on "common sense."

Anatomy of a Classic Research Study

Many key terms and approved approaches to experiments are results of findings from classic research studies. I have included brief synopses of classic studies that are particularly relevant to the ideas, terms, and topics in various chapters. Reading these studies will enhance your conceptual and factual understanding of issues in psychology.

Thinking About Psychology

The last section of each chapter urges you to apply the information you've read or consider a current, controversial issue in psychology about which people have differing opinions. These sections are both provocative and informational; they are great places to start for research topics and class discussions.

Chapter Summary

Each summary recaps the major points in the chapter. The summary is organized by the major sections of each chapter. This feature enables you to get a quick review of the contents and organization of the chapter.

Key Concepts

The terms from the margin glossary are rounded up and organized according to the chapter sections for your review. Because new vocabulary can be daunting and time consuming to learn, it is advisable to take the time to make sure you're keeping current with the new terms as you go.

Key Contributors

The history of the field of psychology is peopled with many interesting figures from different walks of life. I have introduced you to several men and women and their major contributions to psychology in each chapter. To help you keep track of them, I have provided this list for each chapter and the page number on which they first appear.

For More Information on . . .

Each chapter closes with an extensive bibliography to lead you to further reading and research, should a particular topic grab your interest. The bibliography is organized by major topic headings and is both current and extensive. This list of resources is an excellent place to start for a research paper.

CHAPTER 1

▲ CHARLES OLSON
Recognition, 1993

The Nature of Psychology

*C*an brain damage be cured by the transplantation of brain tissue? Do attachment patterns in infancy predict attachment patterns in dating relationships? Do eyewitnesses give accurate testimony? Can chimpanzees learn to use language? Do lie detectors really detect lies? Is there a heart-attack-prone personality? Does pornography incite violence against women? The science that seeks the answers to these—and thousands of other—diverse questions about human and animal behavior and mental processes is psychology.

But what is psychology? The word *psychology* was coined in the sixteenth century from the Greek terms *psyche*, meaning "soul," and *logos*, meaning "the study of a subject." Thus, the initial meaning of *psychology* was "the study of the soul" (La Pointe, 1970). This reflected the early interest of theologians in topics that are now considered the province of psychologists. Psychology has continued to be defined by its subject matter, which has changed over time. By the late nineteenth century, when psychology emerged as a science, it had become "the Science of Mental Life" (James, 1890/1981, Vol. 1, p. 15).

Beginning in the second decade of the twentieth century, many psychologists—believing that a true science can study only directly observable, measurable events—abandoned the study of the mind in favor of the study of overt behavior. This meant that most psychologists moved from studying mental experiences, such as thirst or anger, to studying their observable manifestations, such as drinking or aggression. Consequently, by the 1920s psychology was commonly defined as "the scientific study of behavior." This definition was dominant until the 1960s, when there was a revival of interest in studying the mind. As a result, **psychology** is now more broadly defined as "the science of behavior and mental processes."

What makes psychology a science? Psychology is a science because it relies on the *scientific method*. Sciences are "scientific" because they share a common method, not because they share a common subject matter. Physics, chemistry, biology, and psychology differ in what they study, yet each uses the scientific method. While a chemist might use the scientific method in studying the effects of toxic pollutants, a psychologist might use it in studying the behavior or mental experiences of a person suffering from severe depression. The role of the scientific method in psychology is discussed in Chapter 2.

THE HISTORY OF PSYCHOLOGY

Like any other science, psychology has evolved over time. It has been influenced by developments in other disciplines and by its social, cultural, and historical contexts. To appreciate the state of psychology today, you should understand its origins (Danziger, 1994). But in reading about the history of psychology, or any science, you should seek to achieve a delicate balance between *presentism* and *historicism* (Hilgard, Leary, & McGuire, 1991). **Presentism** is an intellectual approach that sees the past in the context of current knowledge and beliefs, much in the way "Monday-morning quarterbacks" use second-guessing to evaluate the performance of their favorite teams. Presentism at times has the unfortunate effect of demeaning the efforts of some of the greatest minds in history by ridiculing claims that are obviously wrong when seen through hindsight. In contrast, **historicism** is an intellectual approach that considers claims put forth by scientists in the context of the available knowledge, methods, and values of their times. Keep this in mind when you read of some seemingly outrageous proclamation made by an historical contributor to psychology. Even geniuses work under practical constraints.

psychology
The science of behavior and mental processes.

presentism
An approach to history that studies the past in the context of current beliefs and knowledge.

historicism
An approach to history that studies the past for its own sake, in the context of beliefs and knowledge that characterized the period being studied.

CHAPTER 1

◄ **The Scientific Study of Behavior and Mental Processes**
Psychologists from a variety of fields of psychology could provide insight into the behavior of expert skateboarders. A *biopsychology* researcher might study how their brains control their actions. A *learning* researcher might be interested in how they perfect their skills. A *motivation* researcher might explore the reasons why they choose to become competitive skateboarders. A *health psychologist* might assess the effects of skateboarding on their physical and psychological well-being. And a *social psychology* researcher might be interested in the effect of an audience on their performance.

The Roots of Psychology

Psychology's historical roots are in philosophy and science. When scientists of the late nineteenth century began to use the scientific method to study the mind, psychology became an independent scientific discipline. Though scientists and philosophers alike rely on systematic observation and reasoning as sources of knowledge, philosophers rely more on reasoning. For example, a philosopher might use reasoning to argue whether we are ever truly altruistic (that is, completely unselfish) in helping other people, whereas a psychologist might approach this issue by studying the emotional and situational factors that determine whether one person will help another (see Chapter 17).

The Philosophical Roots of Psychology

The philosophical roots of psychology reach back to the philosophers of ancient Greece, most notably Plato (c. 428–347 B.C.) and his pupil Aristotle (384–322 B.C.), who were especially interested in the origin of knowledge. Plato noted that our senses can deceive us, as in illusions like the apparent bending of a straight stick that is partly immersed in a pool of water. Downplaying knowledge gained through the senses, Plato believed that human beings enter the world with inborn knowledge—a position called **nativism.** He also believed that reasoning gives us access to this knowledge, a philosophical approach called **rationalism.**

nativism
The philosophical position that heredity provides individuals with inborn knowledge and abilities.

rationalism
The philosophical position that true knowledge comes through correct reasoning.

empiricism

The philosophical position that true
knowledge comes through the senses.

Though Aristotle, who served as tutor to the future Alexander the Great, accepted the importance of reasoning, he was more willing than Plato to accept sensory experience as a source of knowledge—a philosophical approach called **empiricism.** Yet he recognized the frailty of sensory data, as in "Aristotle's illusion." To experience it for yourself, cross your middle finger over your index finger and run a pen between them. You will feel two pens instead of one. Aristotle contributed to psychology by being one of the first thinkers to speculate formally on psychological topics, as indicated by the titles of his works, including *On Dreams, On Sleep and Sleeplessness, On Memory and Reminiscence,* and *On the Senses and the Sensed.* Scientific research on each of these topics is described in upcoming chapters.

During the early Christian and medieval eras, answers to psychological questions were given more often by theologian philosophers than by secular philosophers like Plato or Aristotle. The dominant Western authority was Saint Augustine (354–430), who lived almost all of his life in what is now Algeria. Augustine wrote of his views on memory, emotion, and motivation in the self-analysis he presented in his classic autobiographical *Confessions.* He anticipated Sigmund Freud in providing insight into the continual battle between our human reason and our animal passions, especially the power of the sex drive (Gay, 1986).

During the Middle Ages, when the Christian West was guided largely by religious dogma, and those who dared to conduct empirical studies risked punishment, scientific investigations became almost solely the province of Islamic intellectuals. The most noteworthy of these was the Persian scientist and philosopher Abu Ibn Sina (980–1037), better known in the West as Avicenna, who kept alive the teachings of Aristotle (Afnan, 1958/1980). With the revival of Western intellectual activity in the late Middle Ages, scholars who had access to Arabic translations of the Greek philosophers rediscovered Aristotle. But most of these scholars limited their efforts to reconciling Aristotle's ideas and Christian teachings.

With the coming of the Renaissance, which extended from the fourteenth to the seventeenth century, Western authorities once again relied less on theology and more on philosophy, to provide answers to psychological questions. The spirit of the Renaissance inspired René Descartes (1596–1650), the great French philosopher-mathematician-scientist. Descartes's ideas regarding the relationship of mind and body are discussed in Chapter 3.

Descartes, the first of the modern rationalists, insisted that we should doubt everything that is not proved self-evident by our own reasoning. In fact, in his famous statement "I think, therefore I am," Descartes went to the extreme of using reasoning to prove to his own satisfaction that he existed. Descartes contributed to the modern intellectual outlook, which opposes blind acceptance of proclamations put forth by authorities, religious or otherwise. Church leaders felt so threatened by Descartes's challenge to their authority that they put his works on their list of banned books.

Other intellectuals, though favoring empiricism instead of rationalism, joined Descartes in rejecting the authority of theologians to provide answers to scientific questions. Chief among these thinkers was the English politician-philosopher-scientist Francis Bacon (1561–1626). Bacon inspired the modern scientific attitude that favors skepticism, systematic observation, and verification of claims by other observers (Hearnshaw, 1985). He was also a founder of applied science, which seeks practical applications of research findings. In support of this, Bacon asserted that "to be useless is to be worthless." Ironically, his interest in the application of scientific findings cost him his life. While studying the possible use of refrigeration to preserve food, he experimented by stuffing a chicken with snow—and caught a severe chill that contributed to a fatal case of pneumonia.

Following in Francis Bacon's empiricist footsteps was the English philosopher John Locke (1632–1704). According to Locke (borrowing a concept from Aristotle), each of us is born a blank slate—or *tabula rasa*—on which are written the life experiences we acquire through our senses. While nativists like Descartes believe that much of our knowledge is inborn, empiricists like Locke believe that knowledge is acquired solely

▲ **Francis Bacon (1561–1626)**
"If a man will begin with certainties, he shall end in doubts; but if he will be content to begin with doubts, he shall end in certainties."

CHAPTER 1

through life experiences. Concern about the relative importance of heredity and life experiences is known as the *nature versus nurture* controversy. Because Locke's views were incompatible with the prevalent belief in the inborn right of certain people to be rulers over others, you can appreciate why Locke's writings helped inspire the American and French Revolutions. The nature-versus-nurture issue, a recurring theme in psychological theory and research, appears in later chapters in discussions about a host of topics, including language, intelligence, personality, and psychological disorders.

A compromise between Descartes's extreme rationalism and Locke's extreme empiricism was offered by the German philosopher Immanuel Kant (1724–1804). Kant was the ultimate "ivory tower" intellectual, never marrying and devoting his life to philosophical pursuits. Despite his international acclaim, he never left his home province—and probably never saw an ocean or a mountain (Paulsen, 1899/1963).

Kant taught that knowledge is the product of inborn mental faculties that organize and interpret sensory input from the physical environment. For example, though the specific language you speak (whether English or another) depends on experience with your native tongue, your ability to speak any language depends on inborn brain mechanisms. If it did not, other animals that can hear speech and that have a vocal apparatus might develop a spoken language when exposed to one.

Despite studying psychological topics, Kant denied that psychology could be a science. He believed this because the mind is not tangible; it cannot be directly observed, measured, or manipulated. Moreover, its contents are in a constant state of flux. And, most important, the very act of examining one's mind alters its contents. For example, suppose that you are asked to report your mental experience while you are angry. The very act of observing your own anger might weaken it, making your verbal report of your anger experience inaccurate. Because of these shortcomings, according to Kant, the study of the mind can never be objective—a prerequisite for any science.

▲ Immanuel Kant (1724–1804)
"Though all our knowledge begins with experience, it by no means follows that all arises out of experience. For on the contrary, it is quite possible that our empirical knowledge is a compound of that which we receive through impressions, and that which the faculty of cognition supplies from itself."

The Scientific Roots of Psychology

By the nineteenth century, scientists were making progress in answering questions about the nature of psychological processes that philosophers were having difficulty with. As a consequence, intellectuals began to look more and more to science for guidance in the study of psychological topics. For example, in the mid nineteenth century, popular belief, based on reasoning, held that nerve impulses travel the length of a nerve as fast as electricity travels along a wire—that is, almost instantaneously—and were too fast to measure. This claim was contradicted by research conducted by the German physiologist Hermann von Helmholtz (1821–1894), arguably the greatest scientist of the nineteenth century.

In studying nerve impulses, Helmholtz found that they took a measurable fraction of a second to travel along a nerve. He demonstrated this in experiments on animal and human subjects. In one experiment, he had human subjects release a telegraph key as soon as they felt a touch on the foot or thigh. A device recorded their reaction time. Subjects reacted slower to a touch on the foot than to a touch on the thigh. Helmholtz attributed this difference in reaction time to the longer distance that nerve impulses must travel from the foot to the spinal cord and then on to the brain. This indicated that nerve impulses are not instantaneous. In fact, Helmholtz found that in human beings they traveled at the relatively slow speed of 50 to 100 meters per second.

Helmholtz's scientific contemporaries made important discoveries about brain functions that could not be discovered by philosophical speculation. The leading brain researcher was the French physiologist Pierre Flourens (1794–1867), who studied the effects of damage to specific brain structures on animal behavior. For example, he found that damage to the cerebellum, a large structure at the back of the brain, caused motor incoordination. This led him to conclude, correctly, that the cerebellum helps regulate the coordination of movements.

Other nineteenth-century scientists were more interested in the scientific study of mental processes, apart from the brain structures that served them. The most notable of these researchers was the German mystic-physician-physiologist-physicist Gustav Fechner

▲ Hermann von Helmholtz (1821–1894)
"I have found that there is a measurable period of time during which the effect of a stimulus consisting of a momentary electrical current applied to the iliac plexus of a frog is transmitted to the calf muscles at the entrance of the crural nerve."

psychophysics
The study of the relationship between the physical characteristics of stimuli and the conscious psychological experiences that are associated with them.

▲ Gustav Fechner (1801–1887)
". . . body and mind parallel each other; changes in one correspond to changes in the other."

differential psychology
The field of psychology that studies individual differences in intellectual, personality, and physical characteristics.

▲ James McKeen Cattell (1860–1944)
"In so far as experiment can be used in the study of mind, scientific progress is assured."

(1801–1887). In his scientific research, Fechner used a technique called **psychophysics,** which had been devised by the German physicist Ernst Weber (1795–1878), whose writings influenced Fechner (Marshall, 1990). Fechner, inspired to do so by a daydream, used psychophysics to quantify the relationship between physical stimulation and mental experience (Narens & Mausfeld, 1992). This accomplishment would have surprised his predecessor Immanuel Kant, who believed it was impossible to study the mind scientifically. Psychophysics considers questions such as these: How much change in the intensity of a light is necessary for a person to experience a change in its brightness? and How much change in the intensity of a sound is necessary for a person to experience a change in its loudness? Psychophysics contributed to psychology's maturation from being a child of philosophy and science to being an independent discipline with its own subject matter, and it has had important applications during the past century. For example, the researchers who perfected television relied on psychophysics to determine the relationship between physical characteristics of the television picture and the viewer's mental experience of qualities such as color and brightness (Baldwin, 1954).

Psychologists of the late nineteenth century were also influenced by the theory of evolution, put forth by the English naturalist Charles Darwin (1809–1882). Darwin announced his theory in *The Origin of Species* (Darwin, 1859/1975), which described the results of research he conducted while studying the plants and animals he encountered during a 5-year voyage around the world on HMS *Beagle*. Though thinkers as far back as ancient Greece had proposed that existing animals had evolved from common ancestors, Darwin (along with fellow English naturalist Alfred Russell Wallace) was the first to propose a process that could account for it. According to Darwin, through *natural selection* physical characteristics that promote the survival of the individual are more likely to be passed on to offspring, because individuals with these characteristics are more likely to live long enough to reproduce.

Darwin's theory had its most immediate impact on psychology through the work of Darwin's cousin, the Englishman Francis Galton (1822–1911). In applying Darwin's theory of evolution, Galton argued that natural selection could account for the development of human abilities. Moreover, he claimed that individuals with the most highly developed abilities would be the most likely to survive. This led him to found the field of **differential psychology** (Buss, 1976), which studies variations among human beings in physical, personality, and intellectual attributes. Galton's impact on the study of intelligence is discussed in Chapter 10.

Differential psychology was introduced to America by the psychologist James McKeen Cattell (1860–1944), who studied with Galton in England. In 1890 Cattell coined the term *mental test,* which he used to describe various tests of vision, hearing, and physical skills that he administered to his students. After being banished from academia for opposing America's entrance into World War I, Cattell started his own business, the Psychological Corporation, which to this day is active in the development of tests that assess abilities, intelligence, and personality. Thus, Cattell was a pioneer in the development of psychology as both a science and a profession (Garfield, 1992).

The Growth of Psychology

James McKeen Cattell was the first psychology professor in the world (that is, he was the first person to hold such a position independent of an academic biology or philosophy department). He began his professorship barely a century ago, a fact that supports a remark made by Hermann Ebbinghaus (1850–1909), a pioneer in psychology: "Psychology has a long past, but only a short history" (Boring, 1950, p. ix). By this, Ebbinghaus meant that though intellectuals have been interested in psychological topics since the era of ancient Greece, psychology did not become a separate discipline until the late nineteenth century.

Psychologists commonly attribute the founding of this new discipline to the German physiologist Wilhelm Wundt (1832–1920). In 1875 Wundt set up a laboratory at the University of Leipzig in a small room that had served as a dining hall for impoverished

◄ Wilhelm Wundt (1832–1920)
Wundt (*third from left*) is shown surrounded by colleagues in his laboratory at the University of Leipzig in 1912. Research conducted in the laboratory in 1879 marked the founding of experimental psychology.

students. Wundt's request for a more impressive laboratory had been rejected by the school's administrators, who did not want to promote a science they believed would drive students crazy by encouraging them to scrutinize the contents of their minds (Hilgard, 1987).

Wundt wrote more than 50,000 pages of books and articles (Bringmann & Balk, 1992), despite being blind in his right eye during the second half of his life. Beginning in 1879 Wundt's laboratory was the site of formal research conducted by many students who later became some of the most renowned psychologists in the world. More than 30 American psychologists took their Ph.D.'s with Wundt (Benjamin et al., 1992). Psychologists recognized Wundt's accomplishment by celebrating 1979 as psychology's centennial year.

The early growth of the new science founded by Wundt was marked by the rise of competing approaches championed by charismatic leaders, who often were trained in both philosophy and science. These approaches were known as *schools* of psychology, and included *structuralism, functionalism, behaviorism, Gestalt psychology,* and *psychoanalysis.* The schools differed in three significant ways: (1) in their object of study (the conscious mind, the unconscious mind, or overt behavior); (2) in their goal of study (analyzing the contents of the mind, examining the functions of the mind, or observing the effect of the environment on behavior); and (3) in their method of study (having subjects report the contents of their minds, or observing overt behavior).

Structuralism: Studying the Elements of the Mind

The first school of psychology—**structuralism**—arose in the late nineteenth century. Structuralists were inspired by the efforts of biologists, chemists, and physicists to analyze matter and categorize it into cells, molecules, and atoms. Following the lead of these scientists, structuralists tried to analyze the mind into its component elements and discover how the elements interact.

Structuralism was named and popularized by Wundt's student Edward Titchener (1867–1927). Titchener, an Englishman, introduced structuralism to the United States after receiving his Ph.D. from Wundt in 1892 and then joining the faculty of Cornell University later that year. To study the mind, Titchener had his subjects use **analytic introspection,** a procedure aimed at analyzing complex mental experiences into what he believed were the three basic mental elements: images, feelings, and sensations (Hindeland, 1971). In a typical study using analytic introspection, Titchener would present a subject with a stimulus (for example, a repetitious sound produced by a metronome) and then ask the subject to report the images, feelings, and sensations evoked by it. As you

structuralism
The early school of psychology that sought to identify the components of the conscious mind.

analytic introspection
A research method in which highly trained subjects report the contents of their conscious mental experiences.

▲ Edward B. Titchener (1867–1927)
"Since all the sciences are concerned with the one world of human experience, it is natural that scientific method, to whatever aspect of experience it is applied, should be in principle the same."

functionalism
The early school of psychology that studied how the conscious mind helps the individual adapt to the environment.

▲ William James (1842–1910)
"Consciousness, then, does not appear to itself chopped up in bits. Such words as *chain* or *train* do not describe it fitly as it presents itself in the first instance. It is nothing jointed; it flows. A *river* or a *stream* are the metaphors by which it is most naturally described. *In talking of it hereafter, let us call it the stream of thought, of consciousness, or of subjective life.*"

know from your own experience, stimuli such as paintings, musical passages, and familiar smells do evoke combinations of images, feelings, and sensations. Based on his research, Titchener concluded that there were more than 40,000 mental elements, the vast majority of them visual in nature (Lieberman, 1979).

Among Titchener's contributions was research that analyzed tastes, which led to the discovery that even complex tastes are mixtures of the four basic tastes of sour, sweet, salty, and bitter (Webb, 1981). Despite Titchener's renown, structuralism became not only the first school of psychology to appear, but the first to disappear. This was caused, in part, by its being limited to the laboratory. In fact, Titchener frowned on psychologists who tried to apply the new science of psychology to everyday life (White, 1994), a practice more in keeping with the scientific approach of Francis Bacon than with that of Titchener's mentor Wilhelm Wundt.

But the demise of structuralism owed more to its reliance on introspection, which limited it to the study of conscious mental experience in relatively intelligent, verbally skillful, adult human beings. Psychologists also found introspection to be unreliable, because introspective reports in response to a particular stimulus by a given subject were inconsistent from one presentation of the stimulus to another. Similarly, introspective reports in response to the same stimulus were inconsistent from one subject to another. And, perhaps most important, the very act of introspecting changed the conscious experience that was being reported—a point that Kant had made many years earlier. Though the shortcomings of analytic introspection made it fade into oblivion, many psychologists today rely on the related research procedure of having their subjects give verbal reports of their mental processes—without necessarily trying to analyze them into their components (Wilson, 1994).

Functionalism: Studying How the Mind Adapts

The American school of psychology called **functionalism** arose chiefly as a response to structuralism. Functionalists criticized the structuralists for limiting themselves to analyzing the contents of the mind. The functionalists preferred, instead, to study how the mind affects what people do. Whereas structuralists might study the mental components of tastes, functionalists might study how the ability to distinguish different tastes affects behavior. This reflected the influence of Darwin's theory of evolution (Taylor, 1990), which stressed the role of inherited characteristics in helping the individual adapt to the environment. The functionalists assumed that the conscious mind evolved because it promoted the survival of individual human beings. Your conscious mind permits you to evaluate your current circumstances and select the best course of action to adapt to them. Recall a time when you tasted food that had gone bad. You quickly spit it out, vividly demonstrating the functional value of the sense of taste.

The most prominent functionalist was the American psychologist and philosopher William James (1842–1910). In his approach to psychology, James viewed the mind as a stream, which, like a stream of water, cannot be meaningfully broken down into discrete elements. Thus, he believed that the mind—or *stream of consciousness*—is not suited to the kind of analytic study favored by structuralists. This led to a rivalry with Wundt. In 1875, the same year that Wundt established his laboratory at Leipzig, James established a psychology laboratory at Harvard University. But, unlike Wundt, James used the laboratory for demonstrations, not for experiments. He urged psychologists, instead, to study how people function in the world outside of the laboratory. James and Wundt were so influential that a recent survey of several major Canadian universities found that 48 percent of their psychology faculty members could trace their intellectual lineage through key faculty members back to James or Wundt (Lubek et al., 1995).

Though he conducted few experiments, James made several contributions to psychology. His classic two-volume textbook *The Principles of Psychology* (1890/1981) highlighted the interrelationship of philosophy, physiology, and psychology. The book is so interesting, informative, and beautifully written that it is one of the few century-old psychology books that is still in print. An abridged version of the book, *Psychology: Brief Edition*, became a leading introductory psychology textbook. William James also contributed a theory of emotion (discussed in Chapter 12) that is still influential today.

As a group, the functionalists broadened the range of subjects used in psychological research by including animals, children, and people suffering from mental disorders. The functionalists also expanded the subject matter of psychology to include such topics as memory, thinking, and personality. And unlike the structuralists, who limited their research to the laboratory, the functionalists, in the tradition of Francis Bacon, applied their research to everyday life. The functionalist John Dewey (1859–1952) applied psychology to the improvement of educational practices. But the functionalist credited with founding the field of applied psychology was Hugo Münsterberg (1863–1916), who became a tragic figure in the history of psychology. Münsterberg had been under extreme stress after being ostracized by his colleagues for trying to promote good relations between America and Germany during the years leading up to World War II (Spillmann & Spillmann, 1993), and he died after suffering a stroke while lecturing in class.

In 1892 William James, tiring of the demands of running the psychology laboratory at Harvard, hired Münsterberg, who had earned his Ph.D. under Wilhelm Wundt in 1885 and had become a renowned German psychologist, to take over the laboratory. Münsterberg quickly gained stature in America. During the first decade of the twentieth century, Münsterberg was second only to James in his fame as a psychologist. Ironically, though he was hired to run the Harvard psychology laboratory, Münsterberg's main contributions were in his role as a founder of applied psychology (Landy, 1992). He conducted research and wrote books describing how psychology could be applied to law, industry, education, psychotherapy, and film criticism.

Because Münsterberg and his fellow functionalists dared to move psychology out of the laboratory and into the everyday world, they felt the wrath of structuralists, such as Titchener, who insisted that psychology could be a science only if it remained in the laboratory. Titchener even held in contempt G. Stanley Hall (1844–1924), a leader of the functionalist school and the founder of the American Psychological Association (Sokal, 1992), for using unorthodox research methods, such as questionnaires, and unorthodox subjects, such as people with mental disorders (Goodwin, 1987). Despite Titchener's criticisms, most psychologists would applaud the functionalists for increasing the kinds of research methods, research subjects, and research settings used by psychologists.

Behaviorism: Studying Overt Behavior

In 1913 a leading functionalist published an article entitled "Psychology as the Behaviorist Views It." It included the following proclamation:

▶ Psychology as the behaviorist views it is a purely objective experimental branch of natural science. Its theoretical goal is the prediction and the control of behavior. Introspection forms no essential part of its methods, nor is the scientific value of its data dependent on the readiness with which they lend themselves to interpretation in terms of consciousness. (Watson, 1913, p. 158)

This bold statement by the American psychologist John B. Watson (1878–1958) heralded the advent of **behaviorism,** a school of psychology that dominated the discipline for half a century. Watson rejected the position shared by structuralists and functionalists that the mind is the proper object of study for psychology. He and other behaviorists were emphatic in their opposition to the study of mental experience. The eminent Russian physiologist and behaviorist Ivan Pavlov (1849–1936) even threatened to fire anyone in his laboratory who dared to use mental terminology (Fancher, 1990). You can read about Pavlov's contributions to psychology in Chapter 7.

To behaviorists like Watson and Pavlov, the proper subject matter for psychological research is observable behavior. Unlike mental experiences, overt behavior can be recorded and subjected to verification by other scientists. For example, some psychologists might study the mental experience of hunger, but behaviorists would prefer to study the observable behavior of eating. Though Watson denied that mental processes could cause behaviors, he did not deny the existence of the mind (Gray, 1980). Thus, he would

▲ **Hugo Münsterberg (1863–1916)**
"The period of pure theoretical psychology is closed. I should neglect my duties if I were not to join and try to lead in the movement toward applied psychology."

▲ **Francis Sumner (1895–1954)**
G. Stanley Hall, a leader of the functionalist movement, made one of his many contributions to psychology by sponsoring the graduate education of Francis Sumner. When he received his doctorate from Clark University in 1920, Sumner, a functionalist, became the first African American to receive a Ph.D. in psychology in the United States. Sumner went on to develop the undergraduate psychology program at Howard University, which has graduated more African Americans who have become psychologists than has any other school. Sumner was also one of the most prolific contributors to *Psychological Abstracts,* the basic library research tool for scholars and students of psychology. Proficient in several languages, he wrote almost 2,000 abstracts of articles written in English, French, Spanish, German, and Russian (Bayton, 1975).

behaviorism
The early school of psychology that rejected the study of mental processes in favor of the study of overt behavior.

▲ John B. Watson (1878–1958)
"Psychology . . . needs introspection as little as do the sciences of chemistry and physics."

▲ Max Wertheimer (1880–1943)
". . . the comprehension of whole-properties and whole-conditions must precede consideration of the real significance of parts."

Gestalt psychology
The early school of psychology that claimed that we perceive and think about wholes rather than simply combinations of separate elements.

phi phenomenon
Apparent motion caused by the presentation of different visual stimuli in rapid succession.

not have denied that human beings have the mental experience called "hunger," but he would have denied that the mental experience of hunger *causes* eating (Moore, 1990). Instead, he would have favored explanations of eating that placed its causes in the body (such as low blood sugar) or in the environment (such as a tantalizing aroma) instead of in the mind (such as feeling famished).

Watson impressed his fellow psychologists enough to be elected president of the American Psychological Association in 1915. Behaviorism later became so popular that Edwin Boring, an early historian of psychology, wrote that "for a while in the 1920s it seemed as if all America had gone behaviorist" (Boring, 1950, p. 645). Watson was an attractive and charismatic person who popularized his brand of psychology by giving speeches and writing books and articles. Though he wrote about both heredity and environment (Todd & Morris, 1992), he placed great faith in the effect of environmental stimuli on the control of behavior, especially children's behavior (Horowitz, 1992). His "stimulus-response" psychology placed him firmly in the empiricist tradition of John Locke and is best expressed in his famous pronouncement on child development:

▶ Give me a dozen healthy infants, well-formed, and my own specified world to bring them up in and I'll guarantee to take any one at random and train him to become any type of specialist I might select—doctor, lawyer, artist, merchant-chief and, yes, even beggarman and thief, regardless of his talents, penchants, tendencies, abilities, vocations, and race of his ancestors. (Watson, 1930, p. 104)

Apparently, no parents rushed to offer their infants to Watson to be trained as specialists. Nonetheless, Watson's views on child rearing became influential. Despite some of their excessive claims, behaviorists injected optimism into psychology by fostering the belief that human beings are minimally limited by heredity and easily changed by experience. In favoring nurture over nature, behaviorists assumed that people, regardless of their hereditary background, could improve themselves and their positions in life. Watson and his fellow behaviorists were more than willing to suggest ways to bring about such improvements. Watson even hoped to establish a utopian society based on behavioristic principles (Morawski, 1982).

As for Watson's influence on psychology, behaviorism dominated psychology through the 1960s (O'Neil, 1995). In fact, from 1930 to 1960 the term *mind* rarely appeared in psychological research articles (Mueller, 1979). But during the past three decades, the mind has returned as a legitimate object of study. The weakened influence of behaviorism is also shown by renewed respect for the constraints that heredity places on learning (a topic discussed in Chapter 7).

Gestalt Psychology: Studying Psychological Processes Holistically

The structuralists' attempt to analyze the mind into its component parts and the behaviorists' view of the human being as a passive responder to environmental stimuli were countered by the German psychologist Max Wertheimer (1880–1943), who founded the school of **Gestalt psychology.** Wertheimer used the word *gestalt*, meaning "form" or "shape," to underscore his belief that we perceive wholes rather than combinations of individual elements. A famous tenet of Gestalt psychology asserts that "the whole is different from the sum of its parts" (Wertheimer & King, 1994). Because of this basic assumption, Wertheimer ridiculed structuralism as "brick-and-mortar psychology" for its attempt to analyze mental experience into discrete elements.

The founding of Gestalt psychology can be traced to a vacation trip taken by Wertheimer in 1912. While aboard a train he daydreamed about the **phi phenomenon**—apparent motion in the absence of actual motion (as in a motion picture). At a stop Wertheimer left the train and bought a toy stroboscope, which, like a motion picture, produces the illusion of movement by rapidly presenting a series of pictures that are slightly different from one another. On returning to his laboratory at the University of Frankfurt, he continued studying the phi phenomenon by using a more sophisticated device called a tachistoscope, which flashes visual stimuli for a fraction of a second. Wertheimer had the tachistoscope flash two lines in succession, first a vertical one and then a horizontal one. When the interval between flashes was just right, a single line appeared to move from vertical to horizontal.

According to Wertheimer, the phi phenomenon shows that the mind does not respond passively to discrete stimuli, but instead organizes stimuli into coherent wholes. Thus, perception is more than a series of individual sensations. This is in keeping with Immanuel Kant's notion of the mind as an active manipulator of environmental input. If the mind responded passively to discrete stimuli, in observing Wertheimer's demonstration you would first see the vertical line appear and disappear and then the horizontal line appear and disappear.

For another example of how the mind can create a whole different from the sum of its parts, consider a melody. A given melody, such as "Yankee Doodle Dandy," can be recognized regardless of whether it is sung, hummed, or whistled; whether it is played on a banjo or by a symphony orchestra; and whether it is played in any of a variety of keys. Thus, a melody is not simply the product of a series of particular sensations produced by a particular source. Instead, a melody depends on the mind's active processing of sensations that may be produced by a variety of sources. Gestalt psychology gave a new direction to psychology by stressing the active role of the mind in organizing sensations into meaningful wholes (Epstein & Hatfield, 1994).

Though founded by Wertheimer, Gestalt psychology was popularized by his colleagues Kurt Koffka (1886–1941), the most prolific and influential writer among the Gestalt psychologists, and Wolfgang Kohler (1887–1967), who promoted Gestalt psychology as a natural science (Henle, 1993) and applied it to the study of problem solving. Koffka and Kohler introduced Gestalt psychology to the United States after fleeing Nazi Germany. Kohler, a Christian college professor, had provoked the Nazis by writing and speaking out against their oppression of his Jewish colleagues (Henle, 1978). He became a respected psychologist and was elected president of the American Psychological Association in 1959. In his presidential address, Kohler (1959) urged Gestalt psychologists and behaviorists to create a psychology that included the best aspects of both of their schools. As you will read later in this chapter, psychologists who favor the cognitive perspective have followed Kohler's advice.

Gestalt psychology also influenced the field of social psychology, mainly through the efforts of the German psychologist Kurt Lewin (Van Elteren, 1992). After studying with Wertheimer, Koffka, and Kohler in Germany, Lewin (1890–1947) emigrated to the United States, where he taught at several universities. He applied Gestalt concepts in his pioneering research on the effects of leadership styles, the principles of small-group behavior, and the best means of resolving social conflicts.

Psychoanalysis: Studying the Unconscious Mind

Unlike Gestalt psychology and the other early schools of psychology, which originated in universities, **psychoanalysis** originated in medicine. Sigmund Freud (1856–1939), the founder of psychoanalysis, was an Austrian neurologist who considered himself "a conquistador of the mind" (Gay, 1988). His theory, which views the human being as first and foremost an animal, owes a debt to Darwin's theory of evolution (Dunn, 1993). Psychoanalysis grew, in part, from Freud's attempts to treat patients suffering from physical symptoms, such as paralyzed legs, inability to speak, or loss of body sensations, that had no apparent physical causes. Based on his treatment of patients suffering from such symptoms of conversion hysteria, Freud concluded that the disorder was the result of unconscious psychological conflicts about sex caused by cultural prohibitions against sexual enjoyment. These conflicts were "converted" into the physical symptoms seen in conversion hysteria, which often provided the patient with an excuse to avoid engaging in the taboo behaviors.

Freud's case studies of patients led him to infer that unconscious conflicts, usually related to sex or aggression, were prime motivators of human behavior. Though Freud's recognition of the importance of unconscious motives was not new, he was the first person to include the unconscious mind in a formal psychological theory. Freud believed that all behavior— whether normal or abnormal—is influenced by psychological motives, often unconscious

psychoanalysis
The early school of psychology that emphasized the importance of unconscious causes of behavior.

▶ **Sigmund Freud (1856–1939)**
Freud is shown here with a group of eminent psychologists during his only visit to the United States, in 1909, when he came to attend the famous Clark University psychology conference. (*Seated, left to right:* Freud, host G. Stanley Hall, and Carl Jung. *Standing, left to right:* Abraham Brill, Ernest Jones, and Sandor Ferenczi.)

▲ "Good morning, beheaded—uh, I mean beloved."
Drawing by Dana Fradon; © 1979 The New Yorker Magazine, Inc.

ones. This belief is called **psychic determinism.** In his book *The Psychopathology of Everyday Life,* Freud (1901/1990) explained how even apparently unintentional behaviors could be explained by psychic determinism. Psychic determinism explains misstatements, popularly known as "Freudian slips," like that of the radio announcer who began a bread commercial by saying, "For the breast in bed . . . I mean, for the best in bread. . . ." As a leading psychologist has noted, the concept of psychic determinism meant that "the forgotten lunch engagement, the slip of the tongue, the barked shin could no longer be dismissed as accident" (Bruner, 1956, p. 465).

In addition to shocking the public by claiming that human beings are motivated chiefly by unconscious—often sexual—motives (Rapp, 1988), Freud made the controversial claim that early childhood experiences were the most important factors in personality development. Freud believed that memories of early childhood experiences stored in the unconscious mind continue to affect behavior throughout life. According to Freud, these unconscious influences explain the irrationality of much human behavior and the origins of psychological disorders.

Freudian psychoanalysis has been so extraordinarily influential that a 1981 survey of chairpersons of graduate psychology departments found that they considered Freud to be the most important figure in the history of psychology (Davis, Thomas, & Weaver, 1982). Nonetheless, psychoanalysis has been the target of severe attacks. Critics have pointed out that the unconscious mind can be too easily used to explain any behavior for which there is no obvious cause. William James had expressed this concern even before Freud's views had become widely known. James warned that the unconscious "is the sovereign means for believing whatever one likes in psychology and of turning what might become a science into a tumbling ground for whimsies" (James, 1890/1981, Vol. 1, p. 166).

Psychoanalysis has also been subjected to criticism for failing to provide adequate research evidence for its claims of the importance of sexual motives, unconscious processes, and early childhood experiences (Hobson, 1985). In fact, Freud never tested his theory experimentally. Instead, he based his theory on notes written after seeing patients, which made his conclusions subject to his own memory lapses and personal biases. Moreover, Freud violated good scientific practice by generalizing to all people the results of his case studies of a relative handful of people with psychological disorders.

Despite these shortcomings, Freud's views have influenced the psychological study of topics as diverse as dreams, creativity, motivation, development, personality, and psychotherapy. Freud's views have also inspired the works of artists, writers, and filmmakers, including Eugene O'Neill's play *Mourning Becomes Electra* (1931) and the classic science

CHAPTER 1

School	Object of Study	Goal of Study	Method of Study
Structuralism	Conscious experience	Analyzing the structure of the mind	Analytic introspection
Functionalism	Conscious experience	Studying the functions of the mind	Introspection and measures of performance
Behaviorism	Observable behavior	Controlling behavior	Observation and experimentation
Gestalt Psychology	Conscious experience	Demonstrating the holistic nature of the mind	Introspection and demonstrations
Psychoanalysis	Unconscious motivation	Understanding personality	Clinical case studies

fiction film *Forbidden Planet* (1956). Freud's contributions to a variety of psychological topics are discussed in several other chapters. Table 1.1 summarizes the major characteristics of psychoanalysis and the other early schools of psychology.

▲ TABLE 1.1
Early Schools of Psychology

STAYING ON TRACK: *The History of Psychology*

1. Why do many historians prefer historicism over presentism?
2. Why would the success of psychophysics have surprised Kant?
3. What were the contributions of functionalism to psychology?
4. What is the role of psychic determinism in Freudian theory?

Answers to Staying on Track start on p. S-1.

CONTEMPORARY PSYCHOLOGICAL PERSPECTIVES

According to Thomas Kuhn (1970), an influential philosopher of science, as a science matures it develops a unifying **scientific paradigm,** or model, that determines its appropriate goals, methods, and subject matter. Though there are no longer separate schools of psychology, with charismatic leaders and loyal followers, psychology still lacks a unifying scientific paradigm to which most psychologists would subscribe. Instead, there are rival psychological perspectives (Salzinger, 1994). They include the *behavioral perspective*, the *psychoanalytic perspective*, the *humanistic perspective*, the *cognitive perspective*, the *biopsychological perspective*, and the *social-cultural perspective*.

scientific paradigm
A model that determines the appropriate goals, methods, and subject matter of a science.

The Behavioral Perspective: The Impact of the Environment on Behavior

The **behavioral perspective** descended from behaviorism (Staats, 1994). Its leading proponent was the American psychologist B. F. Skinner (1904–1990). As a young man, Skinner pursued a career as a writer, and even spent 6 months living in Greenwich Village to soak up its creative Bohemian atmosphere. After discovering that he was not cut out to be a fiction writer, and being excited by the writings of John B. Watson, he decided to become a psychologist (Keller, 1991). Though Skinner eventually became the most prominent psychologist in the world (Korn, Davis, & Davis, 1991), it took many years for him to achieve that standing. In fact, by the end of World War II, in 1945, his landmark book *The Behavior of Organisms* (which had been published in 1938) had sold only 80 copies.

behavioral perspective
The psychological viewpoint, descended from behaviorism, that stresses the importance of studying the effects of learning and environmental factors on overt behavior.

Like John B. Watson, Skinner urged psychologists to ignore mental processes and to limit psychology to the study of observable behavior. Strict behaviorists still refuse to treat verbal reports of mental experiences as appropriate subject matter for psychological research. But in contrast to Watson, Skinner stressed the role of the consequences of behavior, rather than environmental stimuli, in controlling behavior. He noted that animals and people tend to repeat behaviors that are followed by positive consequences.

▲ B. F. Skinner (1904–1990)
"I am a radical behaviorist simply in the sense that I find no place in the formulation for anything which is mental."

psychoanalytic perspective
The psychological viewpoint that is descended from psychoanalysis but places less emphasis on biological motives and more emphasis on the importance of interpersonal relationships.

▲ Melanie Klein (1882–1960)
"The infant's emotional life, the early defenses built up under the stress of the conflict between love, hatred, and guilt, and the vicissitudes of the child's identifications—all these are topics which may well occupy analytical research for a long time to come."

Consider your performance in school. If your studying (a behavior) pays off with an A on an exam (a positive consequence), you will be more likely to study in the future. In Skinner's terms, your behavior has been "positively reinforced."

Skinner, like Watson, was a utopian. In 1948 Skinner—showing that he did, in fact, have the ability to write fiction—published *Walden Two,* a still-popular book that describes an ideal society based on behavioral principles. In Skinner's utopia, society is run by benevolent behaviorists who control its citizens by providing positive consequences for desirable behaviors. The tiny community of Twin Oaks, Virginia, was founded on principles presented in *Walden Two.* Though there is still no behavioral utopia, the behavioral perspective has contributed to improvements in education, child rearing, industrial productivity, and therapy for psychological disorders. These are discussed in later chapters.

Despite Skinner's efforts, the influence of the behavioral perspective has waned in recent years in the face of growing dissatisfaction with the lack of attention that strict behaviorists give to mental processes. This has prompted some behaviorists to study the relationship between mental processes such as thoughts or images, which cannot be directly observed, and overt behavior, which can. These psychologists are called *cognitive behaviorists;* their most influential leader has been Albert Bandura. The views of Skinner and Bandura are discussed further in Chapter 7.

The Psychoanalytic Perspective: Freud's Intellectual Descendants

Like the behavioral perspective, the **psychoanalytic perspective** is a descendant of an early school of psychology—psychoanalysis. The decline of Freudian psychoanalysis began when two of Freud's followers, Carl Jung (1875–1961) and Alfred Adler (1870–1937), developed psychoanalytic theories that contradicted important aspects of Freud's theory. Jung, Adler, and other so-called neo-Freudians placed less emphasis on the biological drives of sex and aggression and more emphasis on the importance of social relationships. Jung developed his own theory of personality, which included the concepts of the inner-directed *introvert* and the outer-directed *extravert.* Adler based his personality theory on his belief that each of us tends to overcompensate for natural childhood feelings of inferiority by striving for superiority, as in the case of daredevils who try to prove their fearlessness by engaging in reckless behaviors.

Other neo-Freudians also contributed to the psychoanalytic perspective. Anna Freud (1895–1982), Sigmund Freud's daughter, was a leader in the field of child psychoanalysis, as was her intellectual rival Melanie Klein (1882–1960), who developed the technique of play therapy. Karen Horney (1895–1952) asserted that the most important factor in personality development is the way we choose to reduce the anxiety caused by the feeling of insecurity that we all experience as weak, dependent infants. Erich Fromm (1900–1980) put forth a similar theory, which explained how the human need for security accounts for the tendency toward social conformity, even to the extent of passively submitting to dictators. Harry Stack Sullivan (1892–1949) was a leader in the application of psychoanalytic techniques to the understanding and treatment of schizophrenia. And Erik Erikson (1902–1994) contributed a theory of development across the life span, with special emphasis on the crises that must be resolved at each stage of the life cycle. The views of the neo-Freudians are discussed in later chapters, particularly in Chapters 4 and 13.

Though the psychoanalytic perspective downplays the importance of biological drives, it accepts the importance of early childhood experiences and the unconscious mind. During the past two decades researchers have devised techniques—some of them ingenious—that permit the scientific study of unconscious mental processes (Hornstein, 1992). (You can read about research on the unconscious mind in Chapter 6.) The success of these techniques supports the claim that "no psychological model that seeks to explain how human beings know, learn, or behave can ignore the concept of unconscious psychological processes" (Shevrin & Dickman, 1980, p. 432).

The Humanistic Perspective: A Positive View of Human Nature

Because it provided the first important alternative to the psychoanalytic and behavioral perspectives (DeCarvalho, 1992), the **humanistic perspective** has been called the "third force" in psychology. It was founded in the 1950s by the American psychologists Abraham Maslow (1908–1970) and Carl Rogers (1902–1987) to promote the idea that human beings have free will and are not merely pawns in the hands of unconscious motives or environmental stimuli. Maslow, who served as president of the American Psychological Association in 1967, had begun as a behaviorist but later rejected behaviorism's narrow focus on observable behavior and the effects of the environment. He stressed the human being's natural tendency toward self-actualization, which was his term for the fulfillment of one's potentials.

Maslow's views were echoed by Rogers. And both assumed that the subject matter of psychology should be the individual's unique subjective mental experience of the world. In favoring the study of mental experience, Maslow and Rogers showed their intellectual kinship to William James. While Maslow and Rogers considered the study of subjective mental experience to be one of several aspects of humanistic psychology, it is the overriding concern of the branch of humanistic psychology called **phenomenological psychology** (Klein & Westcott, 1994). Humanistic psychology's assumption that human beings have free will is central to **existential psychology.** This branch of humanistic psychology favors the study of how human beings respond to the basic givens of reality, including the responsibility of personal freedom, the isolation of one person from another, the need to find meaning in one's life, and the realization that we will eventually die.

Humanistic psychology has been a prime mover in the field of psychotherapy, most notably through the efforts of Carl Rogers (Gendlin, 1988). His *person-centered therapy,* one of the chief kinds of psychotherapy, is discussed in Chapter 15. Though person-centered therapy has been the subject of extensive scientific research, other aspects of humanistic psychology, such as techniques that promote personal "growth experiences" and "consciousness raising," have been criticized for having little scientific support (Wertheimer, 1978). This lack of scientific rigor might be one reason why humanistic psychology has had only a relatively minor impact on academic psychology, a fact lamented by Rogers (1985) near the end of his life. Despite its scientific shortcomings, humanistic psychology has made a valuable contribution in promoting the study of positive aspects of human experience, including love, altruism, and healthy personality development. Moreover, many humanistic psychologists have become more willing to use experimentation to test their theories (Rychlak, 1988).

The Cognitive Perspective: The Individual as an Information Processor

Recent decades have witnessed a so-called cognitive revolution in psychology (Gardner, 1985), leading to the emergence of a **cognitive perspective.** The cognitive perspective combines aspects of Gestalt psychology and the behavioral perspective (Simon, 1995). Like Gestalt psychologists, cognitive psychologists stress the active role of the mind in organizing perceptions, processing information, and interpreting experiences. And like behavioral psychologists, cognitive psychologists stress the need for objective, well-controlled, laboratory studies. Thus, cognitive psychologists infer mental processes from observable responses, without relying on verbal reports alone. But unlike strict behavioral psychologists, who claim that mental processes, such as thoughts, cannot affect behavior, many cognitive psychologists believe that they can (O'Connor, 1981).

The cognitive perspective is illustrated in the work of the Swiss biologist-psychologist Jean Piaget (1896–1980), who put forth a cognitive theory of the child's mental development based on his interviews with children as they solved various problems. Piaget's research is discussed in Chapter 4. The cognitive perspective has also been influenced by the computer revolution of the past three decades, which stimulated research on the human brain as an information processor. A leader in this field has been Herbert Simon, a

humanistic perspective
The psychological viewpoint that holds that the proper subject matter of psychology is the individual's subjective mental experience of the world.

phenomenological psychology
A branch of humanistic psychology primarily concerned with the study of subjective mental experience.

existential psychology
A branch of humanistic psychology that studies how individuals respond to the basic philosophical issues of life, such as death, meaning, freedom, and isolation.

▲ **Abraham Maslow (1908–1970)**
"I suppose it is tempting, if the only tool you have is a hammer [that is, the behaviorist's sole reliance on studying overt behavior], to treat everything as if it were a nail."

cognitive perspective
The psychological viewpoint that favors the study of how the mind organizes perceptions, processes information, and interprets experiences.

psychologist who won the 1978 Nobel Prize in economics, the field in which he worked early in his career (Hilgard, 1993). Some cognitive psychologists use computer programs to create models of human thought processes; others use their knowledge of human thought processes to improve computer programs, like those for computer chess games.

Since about 1980 the cognitive perspective has surpassed the behavioral perspective and the psychoanalytic perspective in its influence on psychology (Robins & Craik, 1994). As you will realize while reading upcoming chapters, the cognitive perspective pervades almost every field of psychology. For example, the cognitive psychologist George Kelly (1905–1967) put forth a theory that has been applied to the study of personality, psychological disorders, and psychotherapy. Kelly believed we are guided by our cognitive intepretations of social reality (see Chapter 13).

The Biopsychological Perspective: The Physiological Bases of Psychological Processes

Though the schools of psychology that appeared in the early twentieth century had their roots in nineteenth-century physiology, there was never a strictly biopsychological school of psychology. In recent decades, growing interest in the biological basis of behavior and mental processes, combined with the development of sophisticated research equipment, has led to the emergence of a **biopsychological perspective.**

Psychologists who favor this perspective are interested in studying the brain, the hormonal system, and the effects of heredity on psychological functions. Though most biopsychology researchers rely on animals as subjects, some of their most important studies have used human subjects. For example, in the course of surgery on the brains of epilepsy victims to reduce their seizures, the Canadian neurosurgeon Wilder Penfield (1891–1976) mapped the brain by using weak electrical currents to stimulate points on its surface. He found that stimulation of particular points on one side of the brain caused movements of particular body parts on the opposite side.

In 1981 the American biopsychologist Roger Sperry (1913–1994) was awarded a Nobel Prize for his studies of the functions of the left and right brain hemispheres of epilepsy victims whose hemispheres had been surgically separated to reduce their seizures. In conducting research on the brain, Sperry and his colleagues found that each hemisphere was superior to the other in performing particular psychological functions. Chapter 3 describes the research of Penfield, Sperry, and other contributors to biopsychology. Because of the increasing influence of this perspective, psychology might be moving toward an even broader definition as "the science of behavior and mental processes, and the physiological processes underlying them."

The Social-Cultural Perspective: Psychology in Context

Though Wilhelm Wundt is most famous for founding psychology as a laboratory science, he stressed the importance of considering social-cultural influences on human psychology (Cahan & White, 1992). In fact, his 10-volume *Folk Psychology*, which was published during the years 1900 to 1920, anticipated the **social-cultural perspective.** This perspective has developed over the past three decades as a reaction against what its proponents believe is the unfortunate tendency to presume that psychological research findings, obtained chiefly from research conducted in Europe and North America, are automatically generalizable to other cultures. As leading social-cultural psychologists have commented:

▶ The typical psychology text contains hundreds of concepts, terms, and theories. . . .
   Most of these abstractions are used as if it has already been established that they are
   applicable everywhere. This is a premature if not dangerous assumption to make. (Lonner &
   Malpass, 1994, p. 2)

Throughout this text you will read about many studies that have attempted to determine whether research findings obtained in one culture are, in fact, applicable to other cultures.

▲ Herbert Simon
"On the American side of the Atlantic Ocean, there was a great gap in research on human thinking from the time of William James almost down to World War II. . . . Cognitive processes . . . were hardly mentioned, and the word *mind* was reserved for philosophers, not to be uttered by respectable psychologists."

biopsychological perspective
The psychological viewpoint that stresses the relationship of physiological factors to behavior and mental processes.

▲ Roger Sperry (1913–1994)
"The new mentalist position of behavioral and cognitive science seems to hold promise, not only as a more valid paradigm for all science but also for all human belief."

social-cultural perspective
The psychological viewpoint that favors the scientific study of human behavior in its social-cultural context.

CHAPTER 1

Harry Triandis (1990), one of the founders of the social-cultural perspective, takes a position that would be favored by functionalists. He suggests that we avoid *ethnocentrism* (viewing other cultures by using ours as the ideal standard of comparison) and instead view each culture as the outcome of attempts by its members to adapt to particular eco-logical niches. Then we would realize that, had we been born in another culture, our views about what is normal and desirable might fit that culture's norms.

What has accounted for the relatively recent surge of interest in the social-cultural perspective? Perhaps the greatest influence has been the "shrinking" of our planet. Today people on opposite sides of the world can communicate instantly with one another using a variety of means, including telephone, radio, television, and computer networks. Other factors include tourism, immigration, and international trade. Thus, it behooves people from different cultures to be less ethnocentric so they can better understand one another.

But there are disagreements among supporters of the sociocultural perspective about how to carry out their research. Some study **cross-cultural psychology.** This approach pre-sumes that culture affects human behavior and mental processes but also that research might discover universal psychological truths. Others believe that human behavior and mental processes are so molded by culture that we should be most concerned with studying how culture affects human behavior and mental processes. They are less inter-ested in searching for universal psychological truths. This approach is known as **cultural psychology** (Shweder & Sullivan, 1993).

Putting the Perspectives in Perspective

To appreciate the differences among the psychological perspectives, consider how each might explain your psychology professor's classroom behavior. Suppose that you find that your pro-fessor is an unusually "happy" person—smiling, cracking jokes, and complimenting students on their brilliant insights. A behavioral psychologist might assume that your professor is happy because she has received positive reinforcement, which might include students who remain alert and interested during lectures. A psychoanalytic psychologist might assume that your professor is happy because she has successfully expressed unconscious aggressive urges in socially acceptable ways, perhaps by playing racquetball or creating extremely difficult exams. A humanistic psychologist might assume that your professor is happy because she has a sense of self-actualization, having reached her potential as a friend, spouse, parent, artist, athlete, and psychology professor. A cognitive psychologist might assume that your professor is happy because she has an optimistic outlook on life, marked by positive thoughts about herself, the world, and the future. A biological psychologist might assume that your professor is happy because she has unusually high levels of brain chemicals associated with positive moods. And a social-cultural psychologist might assume that the factors that make this professor happy in her culture might not have the same effect on persons in other cultures.

While reading the upcoming chapters, you should keep in mind that many psycholo-gists are eclectic—that is, they accept aspects of more than one perspective in guiding their own research or practice. This is in keeping with the wishes of William James, who insisted a century ago that while seeking to unify psychology, psychologists should also revel in its diversity (Viney, 1989).

STAYING ON TRACK: *Contemporary Psychological Perspectives*

1. Why is the humanistic perspective called the "third force"?
2. In what way does the cognitive perspective combine aspects of Gestalt psychology and the behavioral perspective?
3. Why has the social-cultural perspective become influential?

PSYCHOLOGY AS A PROFESSION

As psychology has evolved as a science, its fields of specialization have multiplied and its educational and training requirements have become formalized. Today there are

▲ **Harry Triandis**
"There are myriad cultural differences that can bother us when we interact with people from other cultures. However, we can learn to tol-erate them, and even enjoy them, if we under-stand them better."

cross-cultural psychology
An approach that tries to determine the extent to which research findings about human psychology hold true across cultures.

cultural psychology
An approach that studies how cultural factors affect human behavior and mental experience.

Fields of Specialization of Psychologists
This pie graph presents the percentages of American psychologists working in major fields of specialization. (American Psychological Association, 1995).

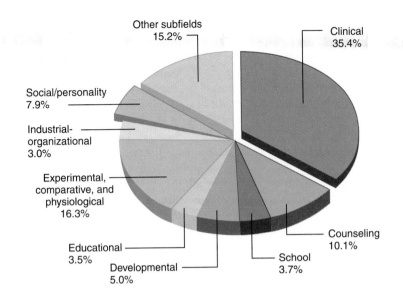

more than 100,000 psychologists in the United States (Stapp, Tucker, & VandenBos, 1985), working in a wide variety of fields in both academic and professional settings (see Figure 1.1). Appendix A discusses the psychology major and ways of pursuing a career as a psychologist, whether academic or professional. The development of psychology has led to the appearance of numerous academic and professional fields of specialization (Bower, 1993). A 1994 report by the U.S. Department of Labor on career outlooks through the year 2005 found that psychology was sixth in its list of the top 10 fastest growing occupations (Burnette, 1994).

Academic Fields of Specialization

Most of the chapters in this book discuss academic fields of specialization in psychology, usually practiced by psychologists working at colleges or universities. In fact, colleges and universities are the main employment settings for psychologists. Because each field of psychology contains subfields, which in turn contain sub-subfields, a budding psychologist has hundreds of potential specialties from which to choose. For example, a psychologist specializing in the field of sensation and perception might be interested in the subfield of vision, with special interest in the sub-subfield of color vision.

Psychology researchers typically conduct either **basic research,** which is aimed at contributing to knowledge, or **applied research,** which is aimed at solving a practical problem. Note that basic research and applied research are not mutually exclusive. Many psychologists conduct both kinds of research, and findings from basic research can often be applied outside of the laboratory (Leibowitz, 1996). For example, basic research findings on learned taste aversions in rats have been applied to preventing cancer chemotherapy patients from becoming nauseated by food, which can make them lose their appetite and, as a result, become weak and emaciated (see Chapter 7).

The largest field of academic specialization in psychology is **experimental psychology.** Experimental psychologists restrict themselves chiefly to laboratory research on basic psychological processes, including perception, learning, memory, thinking, language, motivation, and emotion. Though this field is called experimental psychology, it is not the only field that uses experiments. Psychologists in almost all fields of psychology conduct experimental research. Figure 1.2 shows examples of experimental research involving human and animal subjects.

Consider some of the topics tackled by experimental psychologists that will be discussed in upcoming chapters. Chapter 5 describes how perception researchers determine whether human beings can identify others by their odor. Chapter 8 explains how memory researchers assess the effect of our moods on our ability to recall memories. And

basic research
Research aimed at finding answers to questions out of theoretical interest or intellectual curiosity.

applied research
Research aimed at improving the quality of life and solving practical problems.

experimental psychology
The field primarily concerned with laboratory research on basic psychological processes, including perception, learning, memory, thinking, language, motivation, and emotion.

CHAPTER 1

(a)

(b)

▶ FIGURE 1.2
Psychological Research
Psychologists conduct research on human and animal subjects, such as (*a*) measuring the brain's
response to changing patterns of visual stimulation in infancy, and (*b*) training dolphins to communicate
with human beings.

Chapter 12 discusses how emotion researchers demonstrate the effect of facial expressions on emotional experiences.

Psychologists in the field of **behavioral neuroscience** study the biological bases of behavior and mental processes. Chapter 3 discusses research by behavioral neuroscientists on the effects of natural opiates in the brain, the possibility of using tissue transplants to treat brain damage, and the differences in functioning between the left and right hemispheres of the brain. In Chapter 6 you will learn of research by behavioral neuroscientists on the effects of psychoactive drugs on mind and behavior.

The related field of **comparative psychology** studies similarities and differences in the physiology, behaviors, and abilities of animals, including human beings. Comparative psychologists study motives related to eating, drinking, aggression, courtship, mating, and parenting. Chapter 9 discusses how comparative psychologists even study whether apes can learn to use human language.

The field of **developmental psychology** is home to psychologists who study the factors responsible for physical, cognitive, and social changes across the life span. Chapter 4 presents research showing that infants are born with better perceptual skills than you might assume and that many sex differences might be smaller than is commonly believed.

Personality psychology is concerned with differences in behavior among individuals. As noted in Chapter 13, this field seeks answers to questions such as these: Are our personalities determined more by nature or by nurture? and To what extent do people behave consistently from one situation to another? Personality psychologists also devise tests for assessing personality, such as the famous Rorschach "inkblot test."

Psychologists in the field of **social psychology** study the effects people have on one another. In Chapter 17 you will learn how social psychologists study the factors affecting interpersonal attraction, the problem of "groupthink" in making important decisions, and the reasons why people are often all too willing to follow orders to harm other human beings.

Professional Fields of Specialization

Professional psychologists commonly work in settings outside of college or university classrooms and laboratories. As indicated in Figure 1.1, two of the largest fields of professional psychology are **clinical psychology** and **counseling psychology,** which deal with the

behavioral neuroscience
The field that studies the physiological bases of human and animal behavior and mental processes.

comparative psychology
The field that studies similarities and differences in the physiology, behaviors, and abilities of different species of animals, including human beings.

developmental psychology
The field that studies physical, cognitive, and psychosocial changes across the life span.

personality psychology
The field that focuses on factors accounting for the differences in behavior and enduring personal characteristics among individuals.

social psychology
The field that studies how people affect one another's thoughts, feelings, and behaviors.

clinical psychology
The field that applies psychological principles to the prevention, diagnosis, and treatment of psychological disorders.

counseling psychology
The field that applies psychological principles to help individuals deal with problems of daily living, generally less severe ones than those treated by clinical psychologists.

psychiatry
The field of medicine that diagnoses and treats psychological disorders by using medical or psychological forms of therapy.

school psychology
The field that applies psychological principles to help improve the academic performance and social behavior of students in elementary, junior high, and high schools.

educational psychology
The field that applies psychological principles to help improve curriculum, teaching methods, and administrative procedures.

industrial/organizational psychology
The field that applies psychological principles to improve productivity in businesses, industries, and government agencies.

engineering psychology
The field that applies psychological principles to the design of equipment and instruments.

forensic psychology
The field that applies psychological principles to improve the legal system, including the work of police and juries.

sport psychology
The field that applies psychological principles to help amateur and professional athletes improve their performance.

health psychology
The field that applies psychological principles to the prevention and treatment of physical illness.

environmental psychology
The field that applies psychological principles to help improve the physical environment, including the design of buildings and the reduction of noise.

causes, prevention, diagnosis, and treatment of psychological disorders. Counseling psychologists tend to deal with problems of everyday living related to career planning, academic performance, and marriage and family. In contrast, clinical psychologists typically treat more serious disorders, including phobias, alcoholism, drug abuse, and severe depression. Chapter 15 discusses the various techniques used by clinical and counseling psychologists, as well as research concerning this important question: Is psychotherapy effective?

Clinical psychology and counseling psychology are distinctly different from the medical field of **psychiatry.** A psychiatrist is not a psychologist, but a physician who has served a residency in psychiatry, which takes a medical approach to the treatment of psychological disorders. Because psychiatrists are physicians, they may prescribe drugs or other biomedical treatments. Chapter 15 considers the various biomedical treatments, including drugs to treat schizophrenia, psychosurgery to calm agitated patients, and electroconvulsive therapy to relieve depression.

Psychology has other well-established professional fields. One of the oldest is **school psychology,** founded almost a century ago in part through the efforts of G. Stanley Hall (Fagan, 1992). School psychologists work in elementary schools, junior high schools, and high schools. School psychologists help improve student academic performance and school behavior. For example, school psychologists take part in programs to prevent violence in schools (Li, 1994), to improve reading comprehension (Oakhill, 1993), and to increase homework completion (Olympia et al., 1994).

The allied field of **educational psychology** tries to improve the educational process, including curriculum, teaching, and the administration of academic programs. For example, educational psychologists hope to improve medical education by studying the ways in which medical students acquire their expertise (Schmidt & Boshuizen, 1993). Educational psychologists are usually faculty members at colleges or universities.

Psychologists who practice **industrial/organizational psychology** work to increase productivity in businesses, industries, government agencies, and virtually any other kind of organization. They do so by improving working conditions, methods for hiring and training employees, and management techniques of administrators. Industrial/organizational psychology began in North America, but it has spread to countries as far away as New Zealand (Inkson & Paterson, 1993). Appendix C discusses this important field of psychology.

Specialists in **engineering psychology** are experts in *human factors,* the aspects of human body structure, behavior, and mental processes that must be considered when designing equipment, instruments, and other artificial aspects of the environment. Topics of concern to engineering psychologists include the improvement of warning signs (Wogalter & Laughery,1996) and the design of instrument displays in automobiles (Ward & Parkes, 1994). Like other psychologists, engineering psychologists may need to consider social-cultural differences, as in helping to promote the effective interaction of the many personnel—often from different cultures—responsible for air-flight safety (Maurino, 1994).

Psychologists who practice **forensic psychology** apply psychology to the legal system. The topics they study include the jury deliberation process and the best ways to select jurors. Some forensic psychologists train police to handle domestic disputes, negotiate with hostage takers, and cope with job-related stress. They also help in the development of simulators to teach officers good judgment in the use of firearms (Seymour et al., 1994). Chapter 8 describes another important issue: What is the best way to obtain eyewitness testimony from children? Figure 1.3 illustrates three emerging fields of professional psychology: **sport psychology, health psychology,** and **environmental psychology.**

STAYING ON TRACK: *Psychology as a Profession*

1. What is the difference between basic and applied research?
2. How does psychiatry differ from psychology?

(a)

(b)

(c)

▲ FIGURE 1.3
Emerging Fields of Professional Psychology
In recent years, several new fields of professional psychology have emerged. Professionals in the field of (a) *sport psychology* help amateur and professional athletes, such as slalom skiers, improve their performance. Practitioners of (b) *health psychology* contribute to the prevention of physical illness by promoting adherence to healthy behaviors, including regular aerobic exercise, such as rowing. And (c) *environmental psychology* applies research findings to improve the physical environment, as in designing neighborhoods to reduce noise, crowding, and other sources of stress.

THINKING ABOUT *Psychology*

What Role Did Women Play in the Growth of Psychology?

In 1980 Florence Denmark, then president of the American Psychological Association, remarked that "women have contributed a great deal to the growth and development of the discipline of psychology. . . . For the most part, however, women have been unrecognized, undervalued, and invisible in our recorded history" (Denmark, 1980, p. 1057). Since its founding little more than a century ago, psychology has been more hospitable to women than has any other science, yet obstacles prevented some women from pursuing careers as psychologists, and many women who were pioneers in psychology have not been accorded the degree of recognition they deserve (Bohan, 1993).

EARLY OBSTACLES TO WOMEN IN PSYCHOLOGY

To appreciate the obstacles women faced in the early years of psychology, one must delve into the social and cultural factors that affected them. The chief factor that limited professional opportunities for women was the notion of "separate spheres" for men and women. The primary roles in a woman's sphere included being a good daughter, wife, and mother. In contrast, though a man was expected to be devoted to his family, his sphere included a variety of career choices, including the possibility of becoming a scientist. Women who pursued careers as scientists typically had to forsake (or at least postpone) marriage and parenthood, or faced customs and policies aimed at preventing them from leaving their sphere. This, coupled with beliefs that women simply lacked the personal and intellectual abilities needed to profit from higher education, kept many capable women from entering the sciences, including psychology.

▲ **Florence Denmark**
"The more we study women's history, the more we appreciate the power of society's norms and institutions to affect the development of psychology as well as the career paths of individual psychologists."

▲ **Laurel Furumoto**
"Despite their presence in psychology's past, women psychologists have been a well-kept secret in the history of the discipline."

Moreover, women who wanted to pursue higher education were refused admission by many colleges and universities, were ineligible for financial aid, and were less likely to be offered faculty positions at prestigious universities after graduation. Women also were excluded from professional circles that helped scientists advance in their careers. For example, in 1904 Edward Titchener, appalled at what he believed was the American Psychological Association's movement toward applied psychology, established a psychological research society called the Experimentalists (Goodwin, 1985). Its bylaws excluded women, allegedly to permit men to engage in masculine activities, including smoking and "man talk." Ironically, Titchener's doctoral program in psychology at Cornell University was more hospitable to women than any other doctoral psychology program. In fact, about one-third of his Ph.D. students were women, and he championed their efforts to find academic positions at Cornell and elsewhere. But his banning of women from the Experimentalists prevented them from making the same useful professional connections as their male colleagues—that is, they were blocked from what is known today as "networking."

The leading psychologist who opposed this exclusion was Christine Ladd-Franklin (1847–1930), who studied with Hermann von Helmholtz in Germany and became known for her evolutionary theory of color vision (Furumoto, 1992). For more than two decades, Ladd-Franklin acted as a gadfly, trying unsuccessfully to gain membership for women in the Experimentalists. She even accused Titchener of hypocrisy for admitting males who were not true experimentalists while excluding women who were (Furumoto, 1988). No woman was admitted until 1929, two years after Titchener's death and a year before Ladd-Franklin's.

The first woman member was Margaret Floy Washburn (1871–1939), the leading comparative psychologist of her day and author of the most widely used textbook on animal psychology, *The Animal Mind* (Washburn, 1908). In 1894 she became Titchener's first female doctoral student; in 1921 she became the second female president of the American Psychological Association; and in 1931 she became the first female psychologist elected to the National Academy of Sciences (Goodman, 1980). Washburn, a master at networking, became active in editing journals and in running professional organizations. But perhaps her greatest contribution was the development of the psychology program at Vassar College (Scarborough & Furumoto, 1987).

Despite the roadblocks faced by women, psychology has had a higher proportion of women members than any other science. For example, in the 1920s, when less than 10 percent of other scientists were women, more than 20 percent of psychologists were women. And several women, including Ladd-Franklin and Washburn, became leaders in psychology. But how did women who left their sphere find ways to become pioneers in psychology and other sciences? Oftentimes they had parents who supported education for women and would help them financially. The minority who married typically had supportive husbands. And many were championed by prominent psychologists who helped them advance in their careers. To illustrate several of these factors and to appreciate the accomplishments of women pioneers in psychology, consider Mary Whiton Calkins (1863–1930), arguably the first great woman psychologist.

THE LIFE AND WORK OF MARY WHITON CALKINS

In 1903 Calkins, along with Margaret Floy Washburn and Christine Ladd-Franklin, was listed in a ranking by James McKeen Cattell of the 50 most eminent American psychologists (O'Connell & Russo, 1990). Calkins was one of William James's students. But as pointed out by Laurel Furumoto (1980), an authority on Calkins, being a student of the most renowned psychologist of her time did not guarantee Calkins an easy path to a career as a psychologist.

Calkins, a resident of Newton, Massachusetts, was a descendant of the famous John and Priscilla Alden of Plymouth Colony. Her parents encouraged her to pursue a professional career. In 1885, after earning a bachelor's degree from Smith College, she became a Greek instructor at Wellesley College. In 1890 Wellesley's founder decided to introduce the new science of psychology to the school. Because there were too few psychologists to staff all the psychology departments sprouting up in North America, Calkins, an outstanding teacher, was asked to take graduate courses to prepare her to become Wellesley's first psychology professor.

Calkins sought admission to nearby Harvard University. Though Harvard did not let women enroll in its courses, Calkins's father, a respected minister, convinced Harvard's president to let her audit courses. Despite this initial good fortune, she suffered discrimination throughout her years at Harvard. In her autobiography, Calkins (1930) describes her first course, a seminar offered by William James, from which the other students—all males—withdrew. Given that James was a popular professor and that Harvard students had expressed alarm in the campus newspaper at the possible intrusion of women into their classes (Scarborough & Furumoto, 1987), one is left with the strong suspicion that they withdrew because they disapproved of her presence in the course. As was her custom, Calkins saw the glass as half full rather than half empty and basked in her memories of the time she spent alone with the great William James in front of a library fireplace, discussing psychology and using his just-published *Principles of Psychology* as the textbook.

Calkins also took courses offered by Edmund Clark Sanford, a leading psychologist, at Clark University. They collaborated on one of the earliest experimental studies of dreams, recounted in Chapter 6, which produced findings that have held up remarkably well over the years. In 1891, with Sanford's and James's help, Calkins founded the psychology laboratory at Wellesley College, the first at a women's school (O'Connell & Russo, 1990). By 1895 she had completed the course work and doctoral dissertation necessary for a Ph.D. in psychology. Her dissertation was based on research on memory she had carried out with Hugo Münsterberg; while conducting this research, she invented the paired-associates technique, which became one of the main tools of memory researchers.

In 1895, several eminent members of the Harvard faculty, including William James and Hugo Münsterberg, gave Calkins the customary opportunity to defend her dissertation. James called her performance "the most brilliant examination for the Ph.D. that we have had at Harvard." Münsterberg, her dissertation sponsor, petitioned the Harvard administration to grant her the Ph.D. she had earned. He noted that she was superior to all the male students and was one of the best college professors in America. His request was denied. In 1902 Calkins was offered a Ph.D. from Radcliffe College, Harvard's sister school. She rejected it, insisting that she would not honor Harvard's discriminatory policy by accepting a degree from a school she had not attended. In 1927 several eminent Harvard alumni who had become leading psychologists petitioned Harvard to finally grant Calkins the degree she had earned three decades earlier. Once again, the request was denied (Furumoto, 1980).

The lack of a doctorate did not deter Calkins from becoming a prominent psychologist. In 1905 she became the first woman president of the American Psychological Association. In her presidential speech, she defended her own theoretical creation, self psychology, and put it forth as an alternative to the competing schools of structuralism and functionalism. She urged psychologists to study the conscious mind, the environment (both physical and social), and the relationship between the conscious mind and the environment (Calkins, 1906). She made self psychology the theme of her popular introductory psychology textbook (Calkins, 1901).

Calkins also wrote the first article that criticized John B. Watson's call for a behaviorist approach to psychology (Calkins, 1913). She insisted that ignoring the mind might be fine for the study of animals but was inadequate for the study of human beings. Unlike Watson, who viewed the human being as a passive responder to environmental stimuli, Calkins viewed the human being as active and purposive. Because of the recent cognitive trend in psychology and the reintroduction of the study of the mind, one historian of psychology has suggested that Calkins's relatively unknown self psychology was more prophetic of where psychology is now headed than was Watson's well-known behaviorist theory (Samelson, 1981). The increased attention to theories of the self (see Chapter 13) is in keeping with the direction, if not necessarily the content, of her theory.

Calkins was beloved by her students and colleagues alike. They found her to be a warm, open-minded, and devoutly religious person. She also remained an active champion of women's rights (Furumoto, 1980). At a national suffrage convention in Baltimore,

▲ **Mary Whiton Calkins (1863–1930)**
"I am more deeply convinced that psychology should be conceived as the science of the self, or person, as related to its environment, physical and social."

Calkins gave a speech in favor of granting women the right to vote. She also insisted that allegedly inborn intellectual and personality differences between males and females were more likely the products of sex-role training that begins in infancy and continues throughout life (Scarborough & Furumoto, 1987).

Like her mentor William James, Calkins developed an increasingly active interest in philosophy. In 1918, her fellow philosophers showed their respect for her by electing her president of the American Philosophical Association. In 1929, the year in which women were first admitted to Titchener's society of experimental psychologists, Calkins retired from Wellesley College to write and to care for her mother, only to die of cancer the following year. Though an outstanding psychologist in her day, she, like many other women psychologists, taught at a woman's college that lacked a graduate program. This prevented her theories from being carried forth by graduate-student disciples in their own research, publications, and professional presentations—one of the ways in which psychologists build their reputations.

Calkins would be pleased that women are now at least as likely as men to pursue careers in psychology (Denmark, 1994). A perusal of upcoming chapters will show that women contributors to psychology are more recognized, valued, and visible today than they were when Mary Whiton Calkins fought the odds and became a pioneer in psychology. In fact, the trend in recent years has been for more women than men to earn doctorates in psychology.

STAYING ON TRACK: *What Role Did Women Play in the Growth of Psychology?*

1. What early obstacles faced women in psychology?
2. How were the Experimentalists an illustration of the difficulties faced by women trying to advance their careers in psychology?

 # CHAPTER SUMMARY

THE HISTORY OF PSYCHOLOGY

Psychology is the scientific study of behavior and mental processes. Psychology is a science because it relies on the scientific method; it differs from other sciences in its subject matter, not its basic method. The roots of psychology are in philosophy and science. When nineteenth-century physiologists began to use the scientific method to study psychological processes, psychology emerged as an independent science. The commonly accepted founding date for psychology is 1879, when Wilhelm Wundt established the first formal psychology laboratory.

The late nineteenth century and early twentieth century were associated with the rise of schools of psychology, which differed in their approaches to the study of psychology. Structuralism, led by Edward Titchener, sought to analyze the mind into its component parts by studying conscious mental experiences. Functionalism, led by William James, arose in opposition to structuralism and favored the study of how the conscious mind helps the individual adapt to the environment. Behaviorism, led by John B. Watson, rejected the study of the mind in favor of the study of observable behavior, insisting that a science can study only observable, measurable events. Gestalt psychology, led by Max Wertheimer, favored the study of mental processes and stressed the active role of the mind in perceiving wholes rather than combinations of separate components. And psychoanalysis, led by Sigmund Freud, was an outgrowth of medicine and studied the influence of unconscious sexual and aggressive motives on behavior.

CONTEMPORARY PSYCHOLOGICAL PERSPECTIVES

To date, psychology has no unifying scientific paradigm. Instead, there are competing psychological perspectives. The strict behavioral perspective, championed by B. F. Skinner, rejects the study of mental experiences in favor of the study of observable behavior. But cognitive behaviorists accept the study of mental experiences as long as they are carefully tied to observable behavior. The psychoanalytic perspective, favored by neo-Freudians, places less emphasis on the biological motives of sex and aggression than does traditional psychoanalysis and places relatively more emphasis on the influence of interpersonal relationships. The humanistic perspective, founded by Abraham Maslow and Carl Rogers, arose as a "third force" in opposition to both psychoanalysis and behaviorism. It favors the study of subjective mental experiences and the belief that human beings are not merely puppets controlled by unconscious drives and environmental stimuli. The cognitive perspective, influenced by the work of Jean Piaget and Herbert Simon, views the brain as an active processor of information. The biopsychological perspective, exemplified by the work of Wilder Penfield and Roger Sperry, favors the study of the biological bases of behavior and mental experiences. And the social-cultural perspective, founded by Harry Triandis and like-minded psychologists, insists that psychologists must study the social and cultural factors that influence human behavior.

PSYCHOLOGY AS A PROFESSION

During its century of existence, psychology has seen the emergence of a wide variety of academic and professional fields of specialization. The academic fields of specialization are chiefly concerned with basic research, which aims to add to our fund of knowledge about behavior and mental processes. The major academic fields of specialization include experimental psychology, behavioral neuroscience, comparative psychology, developmental psychology, personality psychology, and social psychology.

The professional fields of specialization are chiefly concerned with applied research, which tries to improve the quality of life. Among the major fields of professional psychology are clinical psychology, counseling psychology, school psychology, educational psychology, industrial/organizational psychology, engineering psychology, and forensic psychology. Emerging fields of professional psychology include sport psychology, health psychology, and environmental psychology.

THINKING ABOUT PSYCHOLOGY: WHAT ROLE DID WOMEN PLAY IN THE GROWTH OF PSYCHOLOGY?

Despite obstacles presented by laws and customs, women contributed to the growth of psychology. Several women psychologists, including Christine Ladd-Franklin and Margaret Floy Washburn, managed to achieve eminence in the early twentieth century. Perhaps the most noteworthy was Mary Whiton Calkins, who contributed to the study of dreams, memory, and personality, and who was the first woman to serve as president of the American Psychological Association.

 KEY CONCEPTS

 KEY CONTRIBUTORS

FOR MORE INFORMATION ON THE NATURE OF PSYCHOLOGY

FOR MORE ON THE HISTORY OF PSYCHOLOGY

General Works

Guthrie, R. V. (1976). *Even the rat was white: A historical view of psychology.* New York: Harper & Row.

Leahey, T. H. (1994). *A history of modern psychology.* (2nd ed.) Englewood Cliffs, NJ: Prentice Hall.

Wright, M. J., & Myers, C. R. (1982). *History of academic psychology in Canada.* Toronto: Hogrefe.

The Roots of Psychology

Philosophical Roots

Robinson, D. N. (1989). *Aristotle's psychology.* New York: Columbia University Press.

Robinson, T. M. (1994). *Plato's psychology.* (2nd ed.) Toronto: University of Toronto Press.

Scientific Roots

Clarke, E., & Jacyna, L. S. (1987). *Nineteenth-century origins of neuroscientific concepts.* Berkeley: University of California Press.

Cowan, R. S., & Rosenberg, C. (Eds.). (1985). *Sir Francis Galton and the study of heredity in the nineteenth century.* New York: Garland.

The Growth of Psychology

Morawski, J. G. (Ed.). (1988). *The rise of experimentation in American psychology.* New Haven, CT: Yale University Press.

Robinson, D. N. (1983). *Toward a science of human nature: Aspirations of nineteenth-century psychology.* New York: Columbia University Press.

Structuralism

Titchener, E. B. (1929/1972). *Systematic psychology: Prolegomena.* Ithaca, NY: Cornell University Press.

Functionalism

Owens, D. A., & Wagner, M. (Eds.). (1992). *Progress in modern psychology: The legacy of American functionalism.* Westport, CT: Greenwood.

Behaviorism

O'Donnell, J. M. (1985). *The origins of behaviorism: American psychology, 1870–1920.* New York: New York University Press.

Gestalt Psychology

Kohler, W. (1947). *Gestalt psychology.* New York: New American Library.

Psychoanalysis

Fine, R. (1987). *The development of Freud's thought.* Northvale, NJ: Aronson.

Contemporary Psychology

Gilgen, A. R. (1982). *American psychology since World War II: A profile of the discipline.* Westport, CT: Greenwood.

Behavioral Perspective

Rachlin, H. (1990). *Introduction to modern behaviorism.* New York: Freeman.

Psychoanalytic Perspective

Fisher, S., & Greenberg, R. P. (1985). *The scientific credibility of Freud's theories and therapy.* New York: Columbia University Press.

Humanistic Perspective

DeCarvalho, R. J. (1990). *The growth hypothesis in psychology: The humanistic psychology of Abraham Maslow and Carl Rogers.* Lewiston, NY: Mellen.

Cognitive Perspective

Gardner, H. (1985). *The mind's new science: A history of the cognitive revolution.* New York: Basic Books.

Biopsychological Perspective

Corsi, P. (Ed.). (1991). *The enchanted loom: Chapters in the history of neuroscience.* New York: Oxford University Press.

Social-Cultural Perspective

Berry, J. W., Poortinga, Y. A., Segall, M. H., & Dasen, P. R. (1992). *Cross-cultural psychology: Research and applications.* New York: Cambridge University Press.

FOR MORE ON PSYCHOLOGY AS A PROFESSION

Fagan, T. K., & VandenBos, G. R. (Eds.). (1993). *Exploring applied psychology: Origins and critical analyses.* Washington, DC: American Psychological Association.

Rheingold, H. L. (1994). *The psychologist's guide to an academic career.* Washington, DC: American Psychological Association.

FOR MORE ON CONTRIBUTIONS OF WOMEN TO THE GROWTH OF PSYCHOLOGY

O'Connell, A. N., & Russo, N. F. (Eds.). (1983). *Models of achievement: Reflections of eminent women in psychology* (Vol. 1). New York: Columbia University Press.

O'Connell, A. N., & Russo, N. F. (Eds.). (1988). *Models of achievement: Reflections of eminent women in psychology* (Vol. 2). Hillsdale, N.J.: Erlbaum.

Scarborough, E., & Furumoto, L. (1987). *Untold lives: The first generation of American women psychologists.* New York: Columbia University Press.

FOR MORE ON CONTRIBUTORS TO PSYCHOLOGY

Contributors to the Roots of Psychology

Philosophical Roots

Brown, P. (1967). *Augustine of Hippo.* Berkeley: University of California Press.

Cranston, M. (1979). *John Locke: A biography.* New York: Oxford University Press.

Gaukroger, S. (1995). *Descartes: An intellectual biography.* New York: Oxford University Press.

Goodman, L. E. (1992). *Avicenna.* New York: Routledge.

Leary, J. E. (1994). *Francis Bacon and the politics of science.* Ames: Iowa State University Press.

Stuckenberg, J. H. (1882/1986). *The life of Immanuel Kant.* Lanham, MD: University Press of America.

Wilbur, J. B., & Allen, H. J. (Eds.). (1979). *The worlds of Plato and Aristotle.* Buffalo, NY: Prometheus.

Scientific Roots

Bowlby, J. (1991). *Charles Darwin: A new life.* New York: W. W. Norton.

Cahan, D. (Ed.). (1993). *Hermann von Helmholtz and the foundations of nineteenth-century science.* Berkeley: University of California Press.

Forrest, D. W. (1974). *Francis Galton: The life and work of a Victorian genius.* New York: Taplinger.

Contributors to the Growth of Psychology

Structuralism

Rieber, R. W. (Ed.). (1980). *Wilhelm Wundt and the making of a scientific psychology.* New York: Plenum Press.

Functionalism

Hale, M., Jr. (1980). *Human science and social order: Hugo Münsterberg and the origins of applied psychology.* Philadelphia: Temple University Press.

Myers, G. E. (1986). *William James: His life and thought.* New York: Columbia University Press.

Ross, D. (1972). *G. Stanley Hall: The psychologist as prophet.* Chicago: University of Chicago Press.

Behaviorism

Babkin, B. P. (1975). *Pavlov: A biography.* Chicago: University of Chicago Press.

Buckley, K. W. (1989). *Mechanical man: John Broadus Watson and the beginnings of behaviorism.* New York: Guilford.

Gestalt Psychology

Harrower, M. (1984). *Kurt Koffka: An unwitting self-portrait.* Gainesville: University Presses of Florida.

Marrow, A. J. (1969). *The practical theorist: The life and work of Kurt Lewin.* New York: Basic Books.

Psychoanalysis

Gay, P. (1988). *Freud: A life for our time.* New York: W. W. Norton.

Rattner, J. (1983). *Alfred Adler.* New York: Frederick Ungar.

Stevens, A. (1990). *On Jung.* New York: Routledge.

Contributors to Contemporary Psychology

The Behavioral Perspective

Bjork, D. W. (1993). *B. F. Skinner: A life.* New York: Basic Books.

Evans, R. I. (1989). *Albert Bandura: The man and his ideas.* New York: Praeger.

The Psychoanalytic Perspective

Coles, R. (1970). *Erik Erikson: The growth of his work.* Boston: Atlantic/Little, Brown.

Grosskurth, P. (1986). *Melanie Klein: Her world and her work.* New York: Knopf.

Knapp, G. P. (1989). *The art of living: Erich Fromm's life and works.* New York: Peter Lang.

Perry, H. S. (1982). *Psychiatrist of America: The life of Harry Stack Sullivan.* Cambridge, MA: Harvard University Press.

Quinn, S. (1987). *A mind of her own: The life of Karen Horney.* New York: Summit.

Young-Bruehl, E. (1988). *Anna Freud.* New York: Summit.

The Humanistic Perspective

Hoffman, E. (1988). *The right to be human: A biography of Abraham Maslow.* Los Angeles: Tarcher.

Kirschenbaum, H. (1979). *On becoming Carl Rogers.* New York: Delacorte.

The Cognitive Perspective

Simon, H. A. (1991). *Models of my life.* New York: Basic Books.

Vidal, F. (1994). *Piaget before Piaget.* Cambridge, MA: Harvard University Press.

The Biopsychological Perspective

Lewis, J. (1982). *Something hidden: A biography of Wilder Penfield.* New York: Doubleday.

CHAPTER 2

JOAQUIN TORRES-GARCIA
Grafismo, 1936

Psychology as a Science

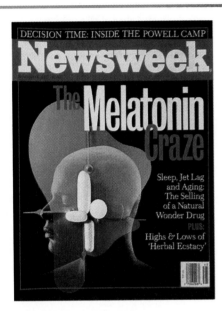

▲ **Science Versus Pseudoscience**
Should we accept media reports as strong evidence for popular claims, such as melatonin's alleged ability to promote sleep, overcome jet lag, and slow the aging process? Scientists require more rigorous standards of evidence than that.

lay psychology
Psychological beliefs based on common sense or folk wisdom.

*I*n November 1995, *Newsweek* magazine published a cover story (Cowley, 1995) about a craze involving the alleged beneficial physical and psychological effects of a "natural wonder drug": the hormone *melatonin*. Melatonin, secreted by the *pineal gland* (located in the center of the brain), was touted in the article as a cure for aging, insomnia, and jet lag. Health-food stores could not keep up with the surge in demand for melatonin pills. When the *Newsweek* article was published, a book praising the effects of melatonin was third on the *New York Times* best-sellers list.

Should readers have accepted the claims about melatonin's amazing effects simply because they appeared in a popular news weekly? Psychologists, being scientists, do not accept such claims unless they are supported by sound scientific research findings. Later in this chapter, you will learn how a psychologist might use the scientific method to conduct an experiment to test the effects of melatonin. But you must first understand the nature of psychology as a science.

In discussing psychology as a science, this chapter will answer questions such as these: Why do psychologists use the scientific method? What are the goals of psychological research? and How do psychologists employ the scientific method in their research? The answers to these questions will help you appreciate the scientific basis of the issues, theories, research findings, and practical applications presented throughout this book.

SOURCES OF KNOWLEDGE

Psychologists and other scientists favor the scientific method as their means of obtaining knowledge, such as knowledge about the effects of melatonin. To appreciate why they do, consider several everyday sources of knowledge—and their shortcomings.

Everyday Sources of Knowledge

Chapter 1 began with a list of questions pertinent to psychology. To find answers to them, you might rely on *common sense, appeal to authority, reasoning,* or *unsystematic observation.*

Common Sense: The Role of Lay Psychology

When you rely on common sense, you assume that if most people share a belief—perhaps because it is a bit of folk wisdom within their culture or it seems to be intuitively obvious—then it must be true. This approach to knowledge is commonly called **lay psychology.** Many college students view psychology as little more than common sense—until they are presented examples of how their commonsense beliefs are false (Osberg, 1993). The photograph of the student changing an answer on a multiple-choice exam provides an example of the shortcomings of common sense that might surprise you.

As another example of the frailty of common sense, consider the practice of calling time-outs during the last few minutes of a close basketball game when an opposing player is about to shoot free throws. This is done to make the player "choke" and miss the shots. The effectiveness of this commonsense strategy was examined in a study of the archival records of 1,237 men's NCAA Division I basketball games from 1977 to 1989. A perusal of the play-by-play records of the games revealed—in accordance with common sense—that when the score became closer and the time remaining decreased, the opposing coaches became more likely to call time-outs when an opposing player was about to shoot free throws. But contrary to common sense, this strategy proved ineffective; in fact, free-throw percentages tended to *increase* after time-outs (Kozar et al., 1993).

◀ **Common Sense**
Should you change your answers on multiple-choice tests? Student common sense would say no. You have probably heard the folk wisdom, "Don't change your answers on exams, because you'll be more likely to change a right answer to a wrong answer than a wrong answer to a right answer." You might be surprised that scientific research has consistently found that students are slightly more likely to change a wrong answer to a right answer than a right answer to a wrong answer (N. F. Skinner, 1983).

But note that scientists do not discount the possibility that commonsense beliefs *might* be true. According to Harold Kelley, a leading researcher on commonsense thinking, "Discarding our commonsense psychology baggage would require us needlessly to separate ourselves from the vast sources of knowledge gained in the course of human history" (Kelley, 1992, p. 22). In other words, common sense may inspire scientific research, even though it cannot substitute for it.

Appeal to Authority: The Role of Expert Opinion

While common sense looks to folk wisdom or lay psychology as a source of knowledge, the *appeal to authority* looks to experts. The *Newsweek* article on melatonin referred to scientific testimony supporting its effectiveness in promoting sleep. This included a reference to a book by a "veteran researcher" that supported the benefits of melatonin. But, as in the case of common sense, authorities can be wrong or contradict one another. For example, another expert quoted in the *Newsweek* article warned that the melatonin craze seemed to be more the product of "hucksterism" than the consequence of good science. Authorities are most credible when their opinions are based on scientific research findings.

Reasoning: The Role of Logical Thinking

Centuries ago, the inadequacies of the appeal to authority as a source of knowledge led René Descartes (1596–1650) to declare that "the first rule [was] never to accept anything as true unless I recognized it to be certainly and evidently such." As you might recall from Chapter 1, Descartes, a rationalist, insisted that true knowledge comes through correct *reasoning,* which involves logical thinking.

Despite Descartes's championing of reasoning, its use does not guarantee correct conclusions. Witness an instance of fallacious reasoning by, of all people, Descartes himself. He reasoned that because thunder sounds like an avalanche, and because an avalanche is caused by snow sliding down a mountainside, then thunder must be caused by snow sliding around inside of clouds (Vrooman, 1970). Modern meteorological research contradicts the conclusion that Descartes reached by reasoning. Despite its fallibility, reasoning is valuable to scientists as a tool in making predictions that they test in their research studies. Thus, psychologists will accept conclusions reached through reasoning when they are supported by scientific research findings (Miller, 1992).

Unsystematic Observation: The Role of Sensory Data

Long before Yogi Berra offered the profound insight that "you can observe a lot just by watchin'," John Locke (1632–1704) countered Descartes' faith in reason. As noted in

▲ **René Descartes (1596–1650)**
"I . . . have had many experiences that have gradually sapped the faith I had in the senses."

Psychology as a Science | **33**

empiricism
The philosophical position that true knowledge comes through the senses.

Chapter 1, Locke insisted, instead, that true knowledge comes through observation—that is, through the senses. Locke's faith in **empiricism** is indicated by his famous statement:

▶ Let us suppose the mind to be, as we say, white paper, void of all characters, without any ideas; how comes it to be furnished? . . . To this I answer, in one word, from EXPERIENCE. In that all knowledge is founded, and from that it ultimately derives itself. (Locke, 1690/1956, p. 42)

Because *unsystematic observation* depends on selective reporting and anecdotal reports unique to particular observers, it is often an inaccurate source of knowledge. Nonetheless, it can spark initial interest in a topic, which will then lead to scientific research on it.

The Scientific Method: Being Objective and Systematic

Because of the weaknesses of common sense, appeal to authority, reasoning, and unsystematic observation as sources of knowledge, scientists prefer the *scientific method*, which is based on certain assumptions and follows a formal series of steps. The fact that the scientific method is the dominant research method in psychology owes much to psychology's origins in nineteenth-century natural science (Polkinghorne, 1992).

Assumptions of Science: Determinism and Skepticism

Albert Einstein was fond of saying, "God does not play dice with the universe." In using the scientific method, psychologists and other scientists share his belief that there is *order* in the universe, meaning that there are lawful, rather than haphazard, relationships among events. In looking for these lawful relationships, scientists also share the assumption of **determinism,** which holds that every event has physical, potentially measurable, causes. This rules out free will and supernatural influences as causes of behavior.

determinism
The assumption that every event has physical, potentially measurable, causes.

Yet, as pointed out a century ago by William James, scientists might be committed to determinism in conducting their research, while being tempted to assume the existence of free will in their everyday lives (Immergluck, 1964). They might succumb to this temptation because, if carried to its logical extreme, the assumption of strict determinism would lead them to unpalatable conclusions—for example, that Mother Teresa does not deserve praise for her work with the poor and that Adolf Hitler did not deserve blame for his acts of genocide, because neither was free to choose otherwise. This also means that strict determinism is incompatible with the legal system, which assumes the existence of free will in order to hold criminals responsible for their actions (Viney, 1990). Despite centuries of philosophical debate, neither side of the determinism versus free will debate has won the battle—this is a controversy that psychologists are probably no more likely than philosophers to resolve (Sappington, 1990).

skepticism
An attitude that doubts all claims not supported by solid research evidence.

Aside from assuming that the universe is an orderly place in which events—including behaviors—are governed by determinism, scientists today, like René Descartes before them, insist that open-minded **skepticism** is the best predisposition when judging the merits of any claim. Open-minded skepticism requires the maintenance of a delicate balance between cynicism and gullibility. As Mario Bunge, a leading philosopher of science, has said, skeptics "do not believe anything in the absence of evidence, but they are willing to explore bold new ideas if they find reasons to suspect that they have a chance" (Bunge, 1992, p. 380). This skeptical attitude requires supportive evidence before accepting any claim. The failure to maintain a skeptical attitude leads to the acceptance of phenomena, such as ESP, that have inadequate empirical support (Alcock, 1991).

Skepticism is important in psychology, because many psychological "truths" are tentative, in part because psychological research findings depend on the times and places in which the research takes place (Scarr, 1985). What is generally true of human behavior in one era or culture might be false in another era or culture. For example, sex differences in behavior in Western cultures have changed dramatically over the past few decades, and sex differences in Western cultures might be unlike those in non-Western cultures. More than two decades before the the social-cultural perspective (see Chapter 1) achieved its current widespread acceptance in North American psychology, Anne Anastasi (1972), in her presidential

Steps in the scientific method

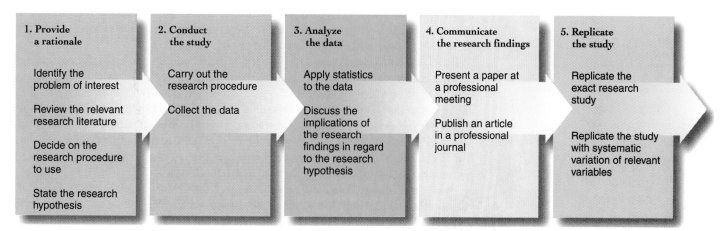

▲**FIGURE 2.1**
The Scientific Method

address to the American Psychological Association, showed foresight in urging psychologists not to confuse their ethnocentric personal beliefs and values with scientific "truths."

Skepticism is valuable not only for scientists, but for all of us in our everyday lives, including in our academic courses (Carlson, 1995). Skepticism is the basis of *critical thinking*—the systematic evaluation of claims and assumptions. The following steps in critical thinking will serve you well as you evaluate claims made in your everyday life. First, you should identify the claim being made. Ask yourself if the claim is based on empirical data (which would be subject to scientific evaluation) or on personal values, opinions, or religious beliefs (which would be less subject to scientific evaluation). Second, examine the evidence in support of the claim. Is the evidence accurate? If so, does it logically support the claim? Third, consider possible alternative explanations of the claim. Perhaps there is a better explanation than the one that has been given.

Steps in Conducting Scientific Research

Because psychologists are skeptical about claims not supported by research findings, they employ the **scientific method** as their means of gaining knowledge. Though scientists vary in their approach to the scientific method (Danziger, 1990), ideally they follow a formal series of steps (as shown in Figure 2.1). The first step is to provide a *rationale* for the study. The scientist identifies the problem, reviews the relevant research literature, decides on the research method to use, and states the research **hypothesis.** A hypothesis (from the Greek word for "supposition") is a testable prediction about the relationship between two or more events or characteristics. The second step is to *conduct* the study. The scientist carries out the research procedure and collects data. The third step is to *analyze* the data, usually by using logical, mathematical techniques called **statistics,** and discussing the implications of the research findings. The fourth step is to *communicate* the research findings. The scientist presents papers at professional meetings and publishes articles in professional journals. In doing so, the scientist includes the rationale for the research, the exact method that was used, the results of the research, and a discussion of the implications of the results. The fifth step is to *replicate* the study. **Replication** involves repeating the study, exactly or with some variation. Successful replications of research studies strengthen confidence in their findings.

These steps were used by psychologist Donn Byrne and his colleagues (Byrne, Ervin, & Lamberth, 1970) in a classic research study of an issue regarding interpersonal attraction: Do opposites attract? Or do birds of a feather flock together? In his study, the problem concerned the relationship between interpersonal similarity and interpersonal attraction. After reviewing the research literature relevant to the problem, Byrne decided to conduct a *field experiment* in which male and female college students were studied in a

scientific method

A source of knowledge based on the assumption that knowledge comes from the objective, systematic observation and measurement of particular variables and the events they affect.

hypothesis

A testable prediction about the relationship between two or more events or characteristics.

statistics

Mathematical techniques used to summarize research data or to determine whether the data support the researcher's hypothesis.

replication

The repetition of a research study, usually with some alterations in its subjects, methods, or setting, to determine whether the principles derived from that study hold up under similar circumstances.

real-life setting instead of in a laboratory. In fact, his study was a replication conducted to determine whether the results of previous laboratory studies on the effects of attitude similarity on social attraction would generalize to a field setting. Based on his review of the literature, Byrne hypothesized that (heterosexual) males and females with similar attitudes would be more likely to be attracted to each other.

Byrne had his subjects complete a 50-item questionnaire that assessed their attitudes as part of a computer-dating service. He told them that their responses would be used to pair them with an opposite-sex student who shared their attitudes. But the students were actually paired so that some partners were similar in attitudes and others were dissimilar. Their similarity on the questionnaire provided a concrete definition of "similarity." The 44 couples, selected from 420 volunteers, were then sent to the student union for a snack. After this 30-minute get-acquainted date, they were asked to rate their partners, which provided Byrne with his research data.

Byrne then analyzed the data. Like almost all researchers, he used statistics to summarize his data and to determine whether they supported his hypothesis. In this case, Byrne found that the data did support the hypothesis. Partners who were similar in attitudes were more likely to recall each other's name, to have talked with each other since the date, and to desire to date each other again. Thus, in this study, the use of the scientific method found that birds of a feather tend to flock together.

Byrne communicated his findings by publishing them in a professional journal. He might also have shared his findings by presenting them at a research conference. Even undergraduate psychology researchers can present the results of their research studies at undergraduate psychology research conferences held each year (Murray, 1995). To further appreciate the scientific method and how it can contradict everyday sources of knowledge, consider the commonsense belief that we can identify a drunken person by simply observing his or her behavior—an issue with important social consequences.

Anatomy of a Contemporary Research Study

Is the Ability to Detect Drunkenness Simply a Matter of Common Sense?

Rationale

In the landmark 1961 *Zane* decision, a New Jersey court stated, "Whether the man is sober or intoxicated is a matter of common observation not requiring special knowledge or skill" (Langenbucher & Nathan, 1983, p. 1071). This is an important assumption, because state laws in the United States, based on the commonsense belief that drunkenness is easily detected, hold people, such as party hosts and tavern owners, legally responsible for the actions of people who become drunk at their homes or businesses. The ability to detect drunkenness was tested in a scientific study by alcohol researchers James Langenbucher and Peter Nathan (1983).

Method

Langenbucher and Nathan had 12 bartenders, 49 social drinkers, and 30 police officers observe drinkers and judge whether they were legally drunk or sober. The drinkers in each case were two male and two female young adults. The drinkers consumed one of three drinks: tonic water, moderate doses of vodka (but not enough to become legally drunk), or high doses of vodka (enough to become legally drunk). A breathalyzer assured that the desired blood-alcohol levels were achieved for subjects in the two vodka conditions.

The bartenders observed their subjects being interviewed in a cocktail lounge. The social drinkers observed their subjects being interviewed in the Alcohol Behavior Research Laboratory at Rutgers University. And the police officers observed their subjects in a simulated nighttime roadside arrest in which they were given 3 minutes to determine whether the motorist they had pulled over was drunk or sober.

Results and Discussion

Langenbucher and Nathan used statistics to analyze their data. They found that the observers correctly judged the drinkers' level of intoxication only 25 percent of the time.

◀ **The Detection of Drunkenness**
Scientific research contradicts the common-sense belief that we can easily detect when someone is legally drunk.

Not a single legally drunk person was identified as such by a significant number of the observers. Of the 91 persons who served as judges, only 5 were consistently accurate—and all of them were members of a New Jersey State Police special tactical unit for the apprehension of drunk drivers. Those 5 police officers had received more than 90 hours of training in the detection of drunkenness. The results implied that without special training even people with extensive experience in observing drinkers may be unable to determine whether a person is legally drunk or sober. The social implication of these findings is that common sense is wrong in assuming that people with experience in observing drinkers can detect whether someone is drunk. We are even more confident in the findings of this study because they were replicated in a different experiment conducted by a different researcher, using different subjects, in a different research setting (Beatty, 1984). Perhaps bartenders, police officers, and habitual party givers should obtain special training similar to that given the 5 police officers who performed well in the study.

▲ ▲ ▲

STAYING ON TRACK: *Sources of Knowledge*

1. What are the basic assumptions of science?
2. What is critical thinking?
3. What are the formal steps in the scientific method?

Answers to Staying on Track start on p. S-1.

GOALS OF SCIENTIFIC RESEARCH

In conducting their research, psychologists and other scientists share common goals. They pursue the goals of *description*, *prediction*, *control*, and *explanation* of behavior and mental experiences (Green & Powell, 1990).

Description: Noting Observable Characteristics

To a scientist, *description* involves noting the observable characteristics of an event, object, or individual. For example, we might note that subjects who take daily doses of melatonin report that they sleep longer. As another example, consider *Type A behavior*, which has been implicated in cardiovascular disease. In describing the actions of people who display this behavior pattern, a psychologist would note that they tend to act in a hostile manner, work under chronic time pressure, and do several things at once.

Psychologists, following in the intellectual tradition of Francis Bacon (1561–1626) (see Chapter 1), are *systematic* in what they describe. Instead of arbitrarily describing everything they observe, they describe only things that are relevant to their research problem. Thus, good observational skills are essential to psychologists (Boice, 1983).

Psychology as a Science | 37

The need to be systematic in what you describe is expressed well in a statement about criminal investigations made by the fictional detective Sherlock Holmes to his friend Dr. Watson:

> ▶ A fool takes in all the lumber [facts] that he comes across, so that the knowledge which might be useful to him gets crowded out, or at best is jumbled up with a lot of other things. . . . It is of the highest importance, therefore, not to have useless facts elbowing out the useful ones. (Doyle, 1930)

In science, descriptions must be more than systematic; they must be precise. Precise descriptions are concrete, rather than abstract. This typically involves **measurement,** the use of numbers to represent events or characteristics. According to Francis Galton, one of the pioneers of psychology, "Until the phenomena of any branch of knowledge have been submitted to measurement . . . it cannot assume the status and dignity of a science" (Cowles, 1989, p. 2). Thus, describing a friend as "generous" would be acceptable in everyday conversation but would be too imprecise for scientific communication.

Scientists solve this problem by using **operational definitions** (Kimble, 1989), which define behaviors or qualities in terms of the procedures used to measure or produce them. Donn Byrne did this when he defined *similarity* according to subjects' responses to a questionnaire in his study of interpersonal attractiveness. More than a century ago, Francis Galton, in studying audience behavior at plays and lectures, operationally defined *boredom* by recording the number of fidgets by audience members. You might operationally define *generous* as "donating more than 5 percent of one's salary to charity." A common operational definition of *drunk* is "a blood-alcohol level of at least 0.1 percent." And a psychologist might operationally define *Type A behavior* as "a score above 5 on the Framingham Type A Behavior Scale." Though operational definitions are desirable, psychologists sometimes find it difficult to agree on acceptable ones. For example, a recent journal article was devoted to a discussion about how best to operationally define *psychological maltreatment* of children by parents (McGee & Wolfe, 1991).

Prediction: Hypothesizing About Events

Psychologists are not content just to describe things. They also make predictions in the form of hypotheses about changes in behavior, mental experiences, or physiological processes. A hypothesis is usually based on a **theory,** which is a set of statements that summarize and explain research findings and from which research hypotheses can be derived. For example, Sigmund Freud's theory of psychoanalysis integrates many observations he had made of the characteristics of people suffering from psychological disorders. Theories provide coherence to scientific research and suggest applications of research findings, making science more than the accumulation of isolated facts (Kukla, 1989). Thus, as Gestalt psychologist Kurt Lewin noted, "There's nothing so practical as a good theory."

Because we cannot know all the factors that affect a person or an animal at a given time, psychologists are never certain about the predictions made in their research hypotheses (Manicas & Secord, 1983). In fact, it would be pointless to conduct a research study whose outcome was certain. Moreover, scientific predictions about human or animal subjects are usually more accurate when applied to many subjects than when applied to a specific subject. For example, your automobile insurance company can more accurately predict the percentage of people in your age group who will have an accident this year than it can predict whether you will have one. Likewise, though melatonin might prove effective in treating insomnia for most people, we would be unable to predict with certainty whether a particular person would benefit from it. Likewise, though you might be correct in predicting that people who exhibit the Type A behavior pattern will be more likely to suffer heart attacks, you cannot predict with certainty whether a given Type A person will suffer a heart attack.

Psychology has nothing to apologize for in being limited to probabilistic prediction, because this situation is no different in the other sciences, which can make predic-

---

measurement

The use of numbers to represent events or characteristics.

operational definition

The definition of behaviors or qualities in terms of the procedures used to measure them.

theory

An integrated set of statements that summarizes and explains research findings, and from which research hypotheses can be derived.

tions only with certain probabilities of being correct (Hedges, 1987). Your physician might prescribe an antibiotic that, based on medical research, is effective 98 percent of the time in treating pneumonia, but she or he cannot guarantee that it will cure *your* pneumonia. Similarly, seismologists know that regions along geological faults are more likely to experience earthquakes, but they cannot accurately predict the day, or even the year, when an earthquake will occur in a given region. For example, the Southern California Earthquake Center estimates that there is an 86 percent chance of a powerful earthquake of at least magnitude 7 on the seismic scale in southern California in the next 30 years (Foote, 1995). But seismologists are far from being able to predict that "a magnitude 7.3 earthquake will strike 18 miles northeast of Los Angeles in the spring of 2014." In the same vein, in regard to interpersonal attraction, people who are similar to each other will probably—but not always—be more attracted to each other than are people who are different from each other. We cannot predict with certainty whether two specific people who are similar to each other will be attracted to each other.

Control: Regulating Aspects of Physical Reality

Psychologists go beyond describing and predicting changes in behavior, mental experiences, and physiological processes. They also try to control them by manipulating factors that affect them. The notion of *control* is used in two ways (Cowles, 1989). First, as you will read in the upcoming discussion of methods of psychological research, control is an essential ingredient in the conduct of experiments. Second, psychologists try to apply their research findings to the control of behavior in everyday life. Thus, a behavior therapy program might help people with Type A behavior change their maladaptive habits, making them less hostile, less intent on working without letup, and more willing to do one thing at a time (Thurman, 1985). Similarly, melatonin might be prescribed to control insomnia by promoting sleep and young adults might be advised to find romance by seeking people who share their values and interests.

Explanation: Discovering Causes

The ultimate goal of psychology is *explanation*—the discovery of the causes of overt behaviors, mental experiences, and physiological processes. We can *control* psychological events without necessarily being able to *explain* them. Likewise, if it is demonstrated that people who ingest melatonin might, in fact, overcome insomnia, the next step might be explaining how melatonin affects the brain to trigger sleep. And even though we know that interpersonal similarity promotes interpersonal attraction, we would still need to explain *why* we prefer people who are similar to us.

A psychologist's favored perspective (see Chapter 1) determines where she or he looks for explanations of psychological events. Psychologists who favor the cognitive, humanistic, or psychoanalytic perspective will look for causes in the mind. Psychologists who favor the behavioral perspective will look for causes in the environment. Psychologists who favor the biopsychological perspective will look for causes in the brain or hormonal system. And psychologists who favor the social-cultural perspective will look for causes in the social-cultural context of the event.

Consider possible explanations for a businesswoman's Type A behavior. A cognitive psychologist might attribute it to her belief that she must be perfect and in control of every aspect of her life. A humanistic psychologist might attribute it to her feelings of inadequacy and a need to live up to standards that are not her own. A psychoanalytic psychologist might attribute it to her unconscious desire to please her parents while repressing hostile feelings toward them. A behavioral psychologist might attribute it to her taking on too many responsibilities and failing to delegate some to other people. A biopsychologist might attribute it to her having an imbalance in brain chemicals that affect moods. And a social-cultural psychologist might attribute it to her living in a culture that rewards achievement at the cost of personal well-being.

Goal	Research Method	Relevant Question
Description	Descriptive	What are its characteristics?
Prediction	Correlational	How likely is it?
Control	Experimental	Can I make it happen?
Explanation	Experimental	What causes it?

STAYING ON TRACK: *Goals of Scientific Research*

1. Why do scientists use operational definitions?
2. In what way are psychology and other sciences probabilistic?
3. What is the nature of scientific explanation in psychology?

METHODS OF PSYCHOLOGICAL RESEARCH

Given that psychologists favor the scientific method as their primary source of knowledge, how do they use it in their research? And once they have collected their data, how do they make sense of it? As shown in Table 2.1, psychologists use research methods that permit them to describe, predict, control, or explain relationships among variables. *Descriptive research* pursues the goal of description, *correlational research* pursues the goal of prediction, and *experimental research* pursues the goals of control and explanation.

Descriptive Research: Systematically Recording Observations

descriptive research

Research that involves the recording of behaviors that have been observed systematically.

Descriptive research is descriptive because the researcher simply records what he or she has systematically observed. Descriptive research methods include *naturalistic observation, case studies, surveys, psychological testing,* and *archival research.*

Naturalistic Observation: Making Observations in the Natural World

naturalistic observation

The recording of the behavior of subjects in their natural environments, with little or no intervention by the researcher.

In **naturalistic observation,** subjects are observed in their natural environment. Researchers who use naturalistic observation study topics as diverse as sex differences in flirtation (McCormick & Jones, 1989) and the ability to recall where one has parked one's car (Lutz, Means, & Long, 1994). To make sure that their observations represent natural behavior, observers refrain as much as possible from influencing the subjects they are observing. In other words, the observer remains *unobtrusive.* If you were studying the eating behavior of students in your school cafeteria, you would not announce your intention over the loudspeaker. Otherwise, your subjects might behave unnaturally; a person who normally gorged on cake, ice cream, and chocolate pudding for dessert might eat jello instead.

In some instances, researchers have devised especially clever unobtrusive ways of observing behavior in natural settings. In a study at Chicago's Museum of Science and Industry, curators determined the most popular exhibit by noting which floor tiles wore out the fastest. They found that the tiles at certain exhibits did not need to be replaced for years, while the tiles at the most popular exhibit—hatching chicks—had to be replaced every 6 weeks (Webb et al., 1966). Had the researchers, instead, walked from exhibit to exhibit carrying clipboards and recording the number of people at each exhibit, they might have increased the number at some, as visitors gathered around, and decreased it at others, as visitors tried to avoid them.

Naturalistic observation is also used in studying animal behavior. Some of the best-known studies employing naturalistic observation have been conducted by Jane Goodall, who has spent more than three decades observing chimpanzees in Gombe National Park in Tanzania. To prevent new chimpanzees from acting unnaturally because of her presence, Goodall spends her initial observation periods letting them get used to her.

◀ Naturalistic Observation
Jane Goodall's naturalistic observations of chimpanzees in the wild have contributed to our understanding of their everyday habits, many of which had never been observed in zoos or laboratories.

The study of animal behavior in the natural environment, as in Goodall's research, is called **ethology.** One of the advantages of an ethological approach is the potential discovery of behaviors not found in more artificial settings, such as zoos and laboratories. Goodall has reported observations of chimpanzee behavior that have not been made in captivity, such as cannibalism, infanticide, and unprovoked killing of other chimpanzees (Goodall, 1990).

ethology
The study of animal behavior in the natural environment.

But researchers who use naturalistic observation, like those who use other research methods, must not be hasty in generalizing their findings. Even the generalizability of Jane Goodall's observations must be qualified. The behavior of the Gombe chimpanzees differs from the behavior of chimpanzees in the Mahali Mountains of western Tanzania. For example, female Mahali chimpanzees hunt more often than female Gombe chimpanzees do (Takahata, Hasegawa, & Nishida, 1984).

Naturalistic observation cannot determine the causes of the observed behavior, because there are simply too many factors at work in a natural setting. So you could not determine *why* female chimpanzees hunt more in one part of Tanzania than in another—is it due to differences in prey, in climate, or in topography, or in another factor, or some combination of factors? It would be impossible to tell just by using naturalistic observation.

Case Studies: Studying Individuals in Depth

Another descriptive research method is the **case study**—an in-depth study of a person, typically conducted to gain knowledge about a particular psychological phenomenon. The case study researcher obtains as much relevant information as possible about a host of factors, including the person's thoughts, feelings, life experiences, and social relationships. The case study is often used in clinical studies of people suffering from psychological disorders. In fact, Sigmund Freud based his theory of psychoanalysis on data he obtained from clinical case studies.

case study
An in-depth study of an individual.

More recently, a best-selling book and a television movie presented the case study of a woman called Sybil, who suffered from the rare psychological disorder known as *multiple personality,* in which the victim shifts from one distinct personality to another. Sybil reportedly had 16 separate personalities, including males and females and adults and children. In seeking help, Sybil attended 2,354 psychotherapy sessions, during which she and her psychiatrist discovered that her disorder was apparently the result of a childhood filled with physical and psychological torture inflicted by her mother.

Because a person's behavior is affected by many variables, the case study method cannot determine the particular variables that caused the behavior being studied. Though

Elephants have been observed swimming from island to island in the Bay of Bengal, at times to pursue a potential mate. They swim up to 20 miles a day, using their trunks as snorkels. This unusual finding shows the advantage of observing animals in their natural habitats rather than in zoos or laboratories.

▲ The Case Study
In the movie *Sybil*, Sally Field portrayed a young woman with sixteen different personalities. The movie was based on the case study of a woman who developed a multiple personality disorder, apparently as a consequence of extreme childhood abuse. This photograph shows Sybil (Field, *wearing glasses*) and her psychotherapist (as portrayed by Joanne Woodward).

survey

A set of questions related to a particular topic of interest administered to a sample of people through an interview or questionnaire.

it might seem reasonable to assume that Sybil's traumatic childhood experiences caused her to defend herself from intense emotional distress by developing multiple personalities, that assumption might be wrong. Other factors, unrelated to how she was treated by her mother, might have caused her disorder. It is even conceivable that Sybil's mother began torturing her only *after* discovering that she had multiple personalities.

Another shortcoming of the case study is that the results of a single case study, no matter how dramatic, cannot be generalized to all people. Even if Sybil's disorder was caused by traumatic childhood experiences, other people with multiple personalities might not have had traumatic childhoods. However, as you will learn in Chapter 14, numerous case studies have shown that people with multiple personalities usually have had traumatic childhoods—making it more likely, but not certain, that a traumatic childhood is a cause of the disorder.

Surveys: Asking for Responses to Interviews and Questionnaires

When psychologists wish to collect information about behaviors, opinions, attitudes, life experiences, or personal characteristics of many people, they use the descriptive research method called the *survey*. A **survey** asks subjects a series of questions about the topic of interest, such as product preferences or political opinions. Surveys deal with topics as varied as the use of condoms to prevent AIDS (Catania, Coates, & Kegeles, 1994) and the factors involved in physical attacks on baseball umpires (Rainey, 1994).

Surveys are commonly in the form of personal *interviews* or written *questionnaires*. You have probably been asked to respond to several surveys in the past year, whether enclosed in the "You May Have Already Won!" offers that you receive in the mail or conducted by your student government association to get your views on campus policies. The prevalence of surveys, and the annoyance they induce, is not new. A century ago, William James (1890/1981) was so irritated by the seeming omnipresence of surveys that he called them "one of the pests of life." Today, the most ambitious of these "pests" is the United States Census, which is conducted every 10 years. Others you might be familiar with include the Gallup public opinion polls and Nielsen television ratings survey.

Good surveys use clearly worded questions that do not bias the respondent to answer in a particular way. But surveys are limited by respondents' willingness to answer honestly and by social desirability—the tendency to give appropriate responses. You can imagine the potential effect of social desirability on responses to surveys on delicate topics such as child abuse, academic cheating, or sexual practices.

Still another issue to consider in surveys is the effect of social-cultural differences between test takers. You are certainly familiar with questionnaires that ask you to respond on a scale from, say, 1 to 7, with 1 meaning "strongly agree" and 7 meaning "strongly disagree." A study of high school students from several countries found that they differed in the degree to which they were willing to use the extreme points on scales like this. Students from Japan and Taiwan were more likely to use the midpoint than were students from Canada and the United States. This finding might be attributable to the greater tendency toward individualism in North American cultures and the greater tendency toward collectivism in East Asian cultures (Chen, Lee, & Stevenson, 1995). Consequently, researchers who use these kinds of scales must consider the cultural backgrounds of their subjects before interpreting their survey findings.

Because of practical and financial constraints, surveys rarely include everyone of interest. Instead, researchers administer a survey to a **sample** of people who represent the target **population.** In conducting a survey at your school, you might interview a sample of 100 students. But for the results of your survey to be generalizable to the entire student population at your school, your sample must be representative of the student body in age, sex, and any other relevant characteristics. This is best achieved by **random sampling,** which makes each member of the population equally likely to be included in the sample.

The need for a sample to be representative of its population was dramatically demonstrated in a notorious poll conducted by the *Literary Digest* during the 1936 United States presidential election. The *Literary Digest*'s presidential poll, based on millions of ballots, had accurately predicted each presidential election from 1916 through 1932. In 1936, based on that poll, the editors predicted that Alf Landon, the Republican candidate, would easily defeat Franklin Roosevelt, the Democratic candidate. Yet Roosevelt defeated Landon in a landslide.

What went wrong with the poll? Evidently the subjects included in the survey were a *biased sample*, not representative of those who voted. Many of the subjects were selected from telephone directories or automobile registration lists, in an era when telephones and automobiles were luxuries to many people and those who had telephones or automobiles tended to be wealthier than those who did not. Because Republican candidates attracted wealthier voters than Democratic candidates did, people who had telephones or automobiles were more likely to favor the Republican, Landon, than the Democrat, Roosevelt.

sample
A group of subjects selected from a population.

population
A group of individuals who share certain characteristics.

random sampling
The selection of a sample from a population so that each member of the population has an equal chance of being included.

Just as biased sampling affected the results of polls on voter preference during the 1936 presidential campaign, it did the same in 1948. The editor of the *Chicago Daily Tribune* had so much confidence in a Gallup poll that placed Thomas Dewey well ahead of Harry Truman that on the night of the election he published an edition proclaiming Dewey the winner. He was more than a little embarrassed when Truman won. The photograph shows Truman gleefully displaying the premature headline after learning that he had won. The Gallup poll was accused of making Dewey's supporters too confident, so that many failed to vote on election day, giving the election to Truman. Criticism that polls can have such an effect on voters has continued to this day.

▲ **Anne Anastasi**
"The test user cannot properly evaluate a test without having some familiarity with the major steps in test construction and some knowledge of the psychometric features of tests, especially as they pertain to norms, reliability, and validity."

psychological test
A formal sample of a person's behavior, whether written or performed.

standardization
1. A procedure assuring that a test is administered and scored in a consistent manner. 2. A procedure for establishing test norms by giving a test to large samples of people who are representative of those for whom the test is designed.

norm
A score, based on the test performances of large numbers of subjects, that is used as a standard for assessing the performances of test takers.

The previous polls did not suffer from this bias because economic differences among voters did not significantly affect their party allegiances until the 1936 election.

Psychological Testing: Obtaining Samples of Behavior

A widely used descriptive research method is the **psychological test,** which is a formal sample of a person's behavior, whether written or performed. The advantage of good tests is that they help us make more unbiased decisions about individuals (Dahlstrom, 1993). There are many psychological tests, including tests of interests, attitudes, abilities, creativity, intelligence, and personality. As noted by Anne Anastasi (1985), who has been an influential authority on psychological testing for the past few decades, a good test reflects important principles of test construction: *standardization, reliability,* and *validity.*

There are two kinds of **standardization.** The first kind assures that the test will be administered and scored in a consistent manner. In giving a test, all test administrators must use the same instructions, the same time limits, and the same scoring system. If they do not, a test taker's score might misrepresent her or his characteristics. The second kind of standardization establishes **norms,** which are the standards used to compare the scores of test takers. Without norms, a score on an intelligence test would be a meaningless number. Norms are established by giving the test to samples of hundreds or thousands of people who are representative of the people for whom the test is designed. If a test is to be used in North America, samples might include representative proportions of males and females; blacks and whites; lower-, middle-, and upper-class individuals; and urban, rural, and suburban dwellers.

The use of testing norms became popular beginning in the early twentieth century, in part because of the introduction of the Stanford-Binet Intelligence Scale in 1916 by Lewis Terman. In one case, Terman (1918) used the scale's norms to prevent the execution of a mentally retarded young man who had committed a heinous murder. Should he have been tried as an adult and, therefore, as responsible for his actions? Or was he so intellectually limited that he should not have been held responsible? The man's score on the Stanford-Binet indicated that his mental age was equivalent to that of a 7-year-old child. Terman testified as a defense witness in opposition to the prosecution's expert witness, who claimed that the young man could perform various activities that only an adult could perform. But he presented no more evidence than his own opinion. Terman convinced the jury, using his intelligence scale's norms as objective evidence, that the activities noted by the prosecution witness could easily be performed by a child of 7 or 8 years of age. The jury, convinced by Terman, accepted that the man was mentally retarded and ruled out the death penalty in his case (Dahlstrom, 1993).

An adequate psychological test must also be *reliable*. The **reliability** of a test is the degree to which it gives consistent results. Suppose you took an IQ test and scored 105 (average) one month, 62 (mentally retarded) the next month, and 138 (mentally gifted) the third month. Because your level of intelligence would not fluctuate that much in 3 months, you would argue that the test is unreliable.

reliability
The extent to which a test gives consistent results.

One way to determine whether a test is reliable is to use the *test-retest method,* in which the same test is given to a group of people on two occasions. The greater the consistency of the scores on the tests from one occasion to the other, the higher the reliability of the test. Intelligence tests typically have high reliability, but personality tests typically have low to moderate reliability. The uses of intelligence testing and personality testing are discussed in Chapters 10 and 13, respectively.

A reliable test would be useless if it were not also valid. **Validity** is the extent to which a test measures what it is supposed to measure. Good tests have *content validity*, meaning that the items they contain are a representative sample of what is being tested. A baking test in which all the questions refer to baking pies would not have content validity, because it would not include questions about other kinds of baking. Similarly, an introductory psychology test on this chapter that asked questions only about this section would not have content validity.

validity
The extent to which a test measures what it is supposed to measure.

Another kind of validity, *predictive validity*, indicates that the test accurately predicts behavior related to what the test is supposed to measure. A test of mechanical ability with predictive validity would accurately predict who would perform better as an automobile mechanic. The behavior or characteristic that is being predicted by a test, whether baking, automobile repair, or academic performance, is called a *criterion*. One of the first studies of the predictive validity of a formal test was conducted by Francis Galton. He collected the civil service exam scores of hundreds of Englishmen who had taken the test in 1861 and compared them to their salaries 20 years later. He found that the exam had good predictive validity, in that those who had scored higher had higher salaries (the criterion) than did those who had scored lower.

A third kind of validity, *construct validity*, is the extent to which the test measures the supposed concept, or *construct*, it is presumed to measure (Messick, 1995). Thus, people who score high on a test of verbal ability should perform better in reading, writing, and vocabulary than do people who score low on the test. This would provide evidence that the test is a valid measure of the construct "verbal ability." As you can see, validity can be assessed in several ways and is essential in psychological testing.

Archival Research: Analyzing Data from Existing Records

The largest potential source of knowledge from descriptive research is **archival research,** which examines collections of letters, manuscripts, tape recordings, video recordings, or similar materials. Archives are valuable sources of historical information. Chiefly through the efforts of John Popplestone and Marion McPherson, the Archives of the History of American Psychology at the University of Akron, which is the main repository of records related to the growth of American psychology, has provided insight into the major issues, pioneers, and landmark events in the history of American psychology (Popplestone & McPherson, 1976).

archival research
The systematic examination of collections of letters, manuscripts, tape recordings, video recordings, or other records.

The uses of archival research are virtually without limit. Is there a home field *disadvantage* in deciding games of the baseball World Series (Baumeister & Steinhilber, 1984)? Do right-handed people live longer than left-handed people (Aggleton, Kentridge, & Neave, 1993)? The answers to these, and other, archival-research questions are presented in upcoming chapters.

Consider the question, Does your signature have psychological implications? An archival study of signatures written in books and on library cards found that the size of the signature increased with the individual's status and self-esteem (Zweigenhaft, 1977). You could conduct a similar study by noting whether the signatures of famous people are larger than those of everyday people. What changes have there been in sex roles? An archival study found that the proportion of acknowledgments in psychology books and journal articles of help given by women increased from 1959 to 1979 (Moore, 1984). This indicates that women may have played a progressively greater role in psychology over that period.

Note that, as is true of all descriptive research, archival research does not permit definite causal statements about the findings. For example, the two archival studies just described do not present enough information to let you determine *why* high-status people had larger signatures or *why* women were mentioned more often in acknowledgments.

Correlational Research: Examining Relationships Between Variables

When psychologists want to predict changes in one variable from changes in another, rather than simply describe something, they turn to **correlational research.** A **correlation** refers to the degree of relationship between two or more *variables*. A **variable** is an event, behavior, condition, or characteristic that has two or more values. Examples of possible variables include age, height, temperature, and intelligence. A **positive correlation** between two variables indicates that they tend to change values in the same direction. That is, as the first increases, the second increases, and as the first decreases, the second decreases. A **negative correlation** between two variables indicates that they tend to change values in opposite directions. For example, as age increases in adulthood, visual acuity decreases. Correlations range in magnitude from zero, meaning that there is no systematic relationship between the variables, to 1.00, meaning that there is a perfect relationship between them. Thus, a perfect positive correlation would be +1.00, and a perfect negative correlation would be –1.00.

Consider the relationship between obesity and exercise. The more people exercise, the less they tend to weigh. This indicates a negative correlation between exercise and body weight: as one increases, the other decreases. But it is essential to realize that when two variables are correlated, one can be used to *predict* the other, but it does not necessarily *cause* the other (Brigham, 1989). That is, *correlation* does not necessarily imply **causation.** Even though it is plausible that exercise causes lower body weight, it is also possible that the opposite is true: Lower body weight might cause people to exercise. Lighter people might exercise more because they find it less strenuous, less painful, and less embarrassing than heavier people do.

As another example, there is a positive correlation between educational level and the likelihood of developing a deadly form of skin cancer called malignant melanoma ("Melanoma Risk and Socio-Economic Class," 1983). This means that as educational level rises, the probability of getting the disease also rises. You would be correct in predicting that people who attend college will be more likely, later in life, to develop malignant melanoma than will people who never go beyond high school.

But does this mean that you should drop out of school today to avoid the disease? The answer is no, because the positive correlation between educational level and malignant melanoma does not necessarily mean that attending college causes the disease. Other variables common to people who attend college might cause them to develop the disease. Perhaps they increase their risk of malignant melanoma by exposing themselves to the sun more than do those who have only a high school education. College students might be more likely to spend spring breaks in Florida, find summer jobs at beach resorts, or go on Caribbean vacations after finding full-time jobs. Instead of dropping out of college to avoid the disease, students might be wiser to spend less time in the sun.

Psychologists are careful not to confuse causation and correlation. They are aware that if two variables are positively correlated, the first might cause changes in the second, the second might cause changes in the first, or another variable might cause changes in both. Because of the difficulty in distinguishing causal relationships from mere correlational ones, correlational research has stimulated controversies in important areas of research. Does televised violence cause real-life aggression? A review of research on that question found a significant positive correlation between watching televised violence and

correlational research
Research that studies the degree of relationship between two or more variables.

correlation
The degree of relationship between two or more variables.

variable
An event, behavior, or characteristic that has two or more values.

positive correlation
A correlation in which variables tend to change values in the same direction.

negative correlation
A correlation between two variables in which the variables tend to change values in opposite directions.

causation
An effect of one or more variables on another variable.

CHAPTER 2

exhibiting aggressive behavior. But this does not indicate that televised violence *causes* aggressive behavior (Freedman, 1984). Perhaps people who are aggressive for other reasons simply prefer to watch violent television programs.

Experimental Research: Investigating Cause-and-Effect Relationships

The research methods discussed so far do not enable you to discover causal relationships between variables. Even when there is a large correlation between variables, you cannot presume a causal relationship between them. To determine whether there is a causal relationship between variables, you must use the **experimental method** (Miller, Chaplin, & Coombs, 1990).

Experimental Method: Exploring the Effects of Independent Variables on Dependent Variables

As in correlational research, the components of an experiment are called variables. Every experiment includes at least one *independent variable* and one *dependent variable*. The **independent variable** is manipulated by the experimenter, which means that she or he determines its values before the experiment begins. The **dependent variable** shows any effects of the independent variable. In terms of cause-and-effect relationships, the independent variable would be the *cause* and changes in the dependent variable would be the *effect*. Thus, in a hypothetical experiment on the effects of drinking on driving, the independent variable of alcohol intake would be the cause of changes in the dependent variable of, say, steering accuracy.

The simplest experiment uses one independent variable with two values (an experimental condition and a control condition) and one dependent variable. A group of subjects, the **experimental group,** is exposed to the experimental condition, and a second group of subjects, the **control group,** is exposed to the control condition. The control condition is often simply the absence of the experimental condition. For example, the experimental condition might be exposure to a particular advertisement, and the control condition might be nonexposure to the advertisement. The dependent variable might be the number of sales of the advertised product. The control group provides a standard of comparison for the experimental group. If you failed to include a control group in the suggested experiment on the effects of advertising, you would be unable to determine whether the advertising accounted for changes in the volume of sales.

experimental method
Research that manipulates one or more variables, while controlling other factors, to determine the effects on one or more other variables.

independent variable
A variable manipulated by the experimenter to determine its effect on another, dependent, variable.

dependent variable
A variable showing the effect of the independent variable.

experimental group
The subjects in an experiment who are exposed to the experimental condition of interest.

control group
The subjects in an experiment who are not exposed to the experimental condition of interest.

Group	Independent Variable	Dependent Variable
(Subjects are randomnly assigned to groups)	(Drug)	(Sleep)
Experimental	Takes melatonin	Hours of sleep
Control	Does not take melatonin	Hours of sleep

▶ **TABLE 2.2**

A Basic Experimental Research Design
Consider a two-group experiment on the effects of melatonin on sleep. Subjects in the experimental group take melatonin nightly for 10 weeks; subjects in the control group do not. The two groups begin roughly equivalent because the subjects have been randomly assigned to them. Given this, the experimenter would assume that a significant difference in average nightly sleep duration between the two groups during the 10 weeks was caused by the experimental group's use of melatonin.

To appreciate the nature of the experimental method, imagine you are a psychologist interested in conducting an experiment on the effect of melatonin on nightly sleep duration. A basic experiment on this topic is illustrated in Table 2.2. Assume that introductory psychology students volunteer to be participants in the study. Members of the experimental group receive the same dose of melatonin nightly for 10 weeks, while members of the control group receive no melatonin. As the experimenter, you would try to keep constant all other factors that might affect the two groups. By treating both groups the same except for the condition to which the experimental group is exposed, you would be able to conclude that any significant difference in average sleep duration between the experimental group and the control group was probably caused by the experimental group's receiving doses of melatonin. Without the use of a control group, you would have no standard of comparison and would be less secure in reaching that conclusion.

In the experiment on melatonin and nightly sleep duration, the independent variable (drug condition) has two values: melatonin and no melatonin. The experimenter is interested in the effect of the independent variable on the dependent variable. The dependent variable in this case is nightly sleep duration, with many possible values: 6 hours and 2 minutes, 7 hours and 48 minutes, and so on.

As an experimenter, you would try to hold constant all factors other than the independent variable, so that the effects of those factors are not confused with the effect of the independent variable. In the melatonin experiment, you would not want differences between the experimental group and the control group in diet, drugs, and other relevant factors to cause changes in the dependent variable that you would mistakenly attribute to the independent variable.

Internal Validity: The Extent to Which Changes in the Dependent Variable Are Attributable to the Independent Variable

An experimenter must do more than simply manipulate an independent variable and record changes in a dependent variable. The experimenter must also promote the **internal validity** of the experiment by *controlling* any extraneous factors whose effects on the dependent variable might be confused with those of the independent variable. Such extraneous factors are called **confounding variables,** because their effects are confused, or *confounded,* with those of the independent variable. A confounding variable might be associated with the procedures, subjects, or experimenters involved in an experiment.

In carrying out the procedure in the melatonin experiment, you would not want any confounding variables to affect nightly sleep duration. You would want the subjects treated the same, except that those in the experimental group would receive the same dose of melatonin nightly over a 10-week period. But suppose that some participants in the experimental group decided to take sleeping pills, to exercise more, or to practice meditation. If, at the end of the study, the experimental group had a longer nightly sleep duration than the control group, the results might be attributable not to the melatonin but to confounding variables—that is, differences between the groups in the extent to which they used sleeping pills, exercised, or practiced meditation.

As an example of the importance of controlling potential confounding procedural variables, consider what happened when the Pepsi-Cola company conducted one of its "Pepsi Challenge" taste tests, an example of *consumer psychology* ("Coke-Pepsi Slugfest," 1976). Coca-Cola drinkers were asked to taste each of two unidentified cola drinks and state their preference. The drinks were Coca-Cola and Pepsi-Cola. The brand of cola was the

internal validity

The extent to which changes in a dependent variable can be attributed to one or more independent variables rather than to a confounding variable.

confounding variable

A variable whose unwanted effect on the dependent variable might be confused with that of the independent variable.

independent variable, and the preference was the dependent variable. To keep the subjects from knowing which cola they were tasting, they were given Pepsi-Cola in a cup labeled M and Coca-Cola in a cup labeled Q. To the delight of Pepsi-Cola stockholders, most of the subjects preferred Pepsi-Cola.

The Pepsi-Cola company proudly—and loudly—advertised this as evidence that even Coca-Cola drinkers preferred Pepsi-Cola. But knowing the pitfalls of experimentation, the Coca-Cola company replicated the experiment, this time filling both cups with Coca-Cola. Most of the subjects still preferred the cola in the cup labeled M. Evidently, the Pepsi Challenge had not demonstrated that Coca-Cola drinkers preferred Pepsi-Cola. It had demonstrated only that Coca-Cola drinkers preferred the letter M to the letter Q. The effect of the letters on the dependent variable (the taste preference) had been confounded with that of the independent variable (the kind of cola).

If you were asked to design a Coke-Pepsi challenge, how would you control the effect of the letter on the cup? Pause to think about this question before reading on. One way to control it would be to use cups without letters. Of course, the experimenter would have to keep track of which cup contained Coke and which contained Pepsi. A second way to control the effect of the letter would be to label each of the colas M on half of the taste trials and Q on the other half. Thus, two ways to control potential confounding procedural variables are to eliminate them or to assure that they affect all conditions equally.

Experimenters must likewise control potential confounding subject variables that might produce effects that would be confused with those of the independent variable. Suppose that in the melatonin experiment the subjects in the experimental group initially differed from the subjects in the control group on several variables, including their nightly sleep duration, psychoactive drug habits, and daily exercise practices. These differences might carry over into the experiment, affecting the subjects' nightly sleep duration during the course of the study and giving the false impression that the independent variable (melatonin versus no melatonin) caused a significant difference on the dependent variable (nightly sleep duration) between the two groups.

Experimenters increase the chance that the experimental group and the control group will be initially equivalent on as many subject variables as possible by relying on *random assignment* of subjects to groups. In **random assignment,** subjects are as likely to be assigned to one group as to another. Given a sufficiently large number of subjects, random assignment will make the two groups initially equivalent on many, though not necessarily all, subject variables.

After randomly assigning subjects to the experimental group and the control group, you would still have to control other subject variables. One of the most important of these is **subject bias,** the tendency of people who know they are participants in a study to behave differently than they normally do. As in the case of naturalistic observation, you might choose to be unobtrusive, exposing people to the experimental condition without their being aware of it. If this were impossible, you might choose to misinform the subjects about the true purpose of the study. (The ethical issues involved in using deception are discussed later in the chapter.)

Experimenters must control not only potential confounding variables associated with the research procedure or the research subjects, but potential confounding variables associated with themselves. *Experimenter effects* on dependent variables can be caused by the experimenter's personal qualities, actions, and treatment of data. Experimenter effects have been studied most extensively by Robert Rosenthal and his colleagues, who have demonstrated them in many studies since the early 1960s (Harris & Rosenthal, 1985). Rosenthal has found that the experimenter's personal qualities—including sex, attire, and attractiveness—can affect subjects' behavior (Barnes & Rosenthal, 1985).

Also of concern is the effect of the experimenter's actions on the recording of data or on the subjects' behavior, as in the **experimenter bias effect.** This occurs when the results are affected by the experimenter's expectancy about the outcome of a study, which is expressed through her or his unintentional actions. The tendency of subjects to behave in accordance with experimenter expectancy is called *self-fulfilling prophecy.* Actions that might promote self-fulfilling prophecy include facial expressions (perhaps smiling at subjects in

▲ Robert Rosenthal

"Recent experiments have shown that an investigator's expectation can . . . come to serve as a self-fulfilling prophecy."

one group and frowning at those in another), mannerisms (perhaps shaking hands with subjects in one group but not with those in another), or tone of voice (perhaps speaking in an animated voice to subjects in one group and speaking in a monotone voice to those in another). Self-fulfilling prophecy is especially important to control in studies of psychotherapy, because therapist expectancies, rather than therapy itself, might affect the outcome of therapy (Harris, 1994).

In a widely publicized study of self-fulfilling prophecy, Rosenthal found that elementary school teachers' expectancies for the performance of their students affected how well the children performed. Students whose teachers were led to believe they were fast learners performed better than students whose teachers were led to believe they were slow learners. Yet the students did not differ in their initial ability (Rosenthal & Jacobson, 1968). This became known as the *Pygmalion effect*, after the story in which an uneducated woman improves herself because of the faith her mentor has in her. The Pygmalion effect can also occur between parents and children, employers and workers, and therapists and patients. The following classic research study demonstrated that experimenter expectancies can even affect the behavior of animals.

ANATOMY OF A CLASSIC RESEARCH STUDY

Can Experimenter Expectancies Affect the Behavior of Laboratory Rats?

Rationale

Robert Rosenthal noted that, in the early twentieth century, Ivan Pavlov had found that each succeeding generation of his animal subjects learned tasks faster than the preceding one. At first he presumed this supported the (since-discredited) notion of the inheritance of acquired characteristics. But he came to believe that the animals' improvement was caused by changes in the way in which his experimenters treated them. Rosenthal decided to determine whether experimenter expectancies could likewise affect the performance of laboratory animals.

Method

Rosenthal and his colleague Kermit Fode had 12 students act as experimenters in a study of maze learning in rats conducted at Harvard University (Rosenthal & Fode, 1963). Six of the students were told that their rats were specially bred to be "maze bright," and 6 were told that their rats were specially bred to be "maze dull." In reality, the rats did not differ in their inborn maze-learning potential. Each student was given five albino rats to run in a T-shaped maze, with one horizontal arm of the maze painted white and the other painted gray. The rats received a food reward whenever they entered into the gray arm. The arms were interchanged on various trials so that the rats had to learn to respond to the color gray rather than to the direction left or right. The students ran the rats 10 times a day for 5 days and recorded how long it took them to reach the food.

Results and Discussion

As shown in Figure 2.2, the results indicated the apparent influence of experimenter expectancy: On the average, the "maze-bright" rats ran faster than the "maze-dull" rats. Because there was no evidence of cheating or misrecording of data by the students, the researchers attributed the results to experimenter expectancy. The students' expectancies apparently influenced the manner in which they trained or handled the rats, somehow leading the rats to perform in accordance with the expectancies. For example, those who trained "maze-bright" rats reported handling them more, and more gently, than did those who trained "maze-dull" rats. Confidence in the experimenter expectancy effect with animal subjects was supported in a replication by a different researcher, using different rats, and involving a different task (Elkins, 1987). This indicates that those responsible for handling animals during an experiment should, if possible, be kept unaware of any presumed differences among the animals.

▲ ▲ ▲

How might experimenter bias affect the results of the melatonin experiment? The experimenter might act more friendly and encouraging toward the subjects in the experimental

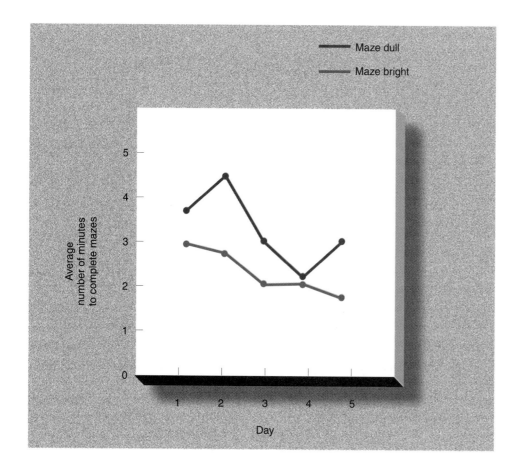

— Maze dull

— Maze bright

Average number of minutes to complete mazes

Day

◀ FIGURE 2.2

Experimenter Bias

The graph shows the results of the Rosenthal and Fode (1963) experiment, which found that allegedly maze-bright rats ran mazes faster than allegedly maze-dull rats.

double-blind technique

A procedure that controls experimenter bias and subject bias by preventing experimenters and subjects from knowing which subjects have been assigned to particular conditions.

placebo

An inactive substance that might induce some of the effects of the drug for which it has been substituted.

external validity

The extent to which the results of a research study can be generalized to other people, animals, or settings.

group, perhaps motivating them to sleep better than they would have otherwise. Subjects with a higher need for social approval would be especially susceptible to experimenter expectancy effects like this (Hazelrigg, Cooper, & Strathman, 1991). One way to control experimenter bias would be to have those who interact with the subjects be unaware of the research hypothesis, eliminating the influence of the experimenter's expectancies on the subjects' performance.

At times both subject bias and experimenter bias might become confounding variables. This might prompt experimenters to use the **double-blind technique,** in which neither the experimenter nor the subjects know the conditions to which the subjects have been assigned. This is a common technique in studies of the effectiveness of drug treatments for psychological disorders. Consider studies of drug treatments for depression. The experimental group would receive the drug and the control group would receive a **placebo**—a similar looking and tasting pill, tablet, or capsule that is inactive. Neither the experimenter nor the recipients would know which individuals were in each group (Lonnqvist et al., 1994). In the melatonin experiment, instead of giving one group melatonin and the other nothing, it would be wise to give one group melatonin and the other a placebo. Neither the experimenter nor the participants would know which subjects received the melatonin and which received the placebo.

External Validity: Generalizing from Experiments

Though experimenters are chiefly concerned with matters of internal validity, they are also concerned with matters of **external validity**—the extent to which they can generalize their research findings to other subjects, settings, and procedures. Because psychology relies heavily on college students as subjects, external validity is an important consideration in psychological research (Sears, 1986). As stressed by David Matsumoto (1994) and other psychologists who favor the social-cultural perspective, the results of a research study done in one culture will not necessarily be generalizable to another culture.

▲ **David Matsumoto**

"Culture can, and does, have dramatic effects on the ways in which we conduct research and analyze data in psychology."

In regard to external validity, an experimenter might ask, "Will the findings of my melatonin experiment with students here at Grimley College hold true for other people? using different doses of melatonin? in other cultures?" The experimenter might also ask, "Will people who suffer from insomnia benefit from melatonin?" and "Will melatonin be more effective in helping subjects fall asleep or in helping them stay asleep?"

Another problem affecting external validity is the use of volunteer subjects. Those who volunteer to take part in a given experiment might differ from those who refuse, possibly limiting the generalizability of the research findings. In a study using volunteer subjects, male and female undergraduates were given the choice of participating in either a study in which they would take a personality test or a study in which they would report their responses to sexual films. The results indicated that, in comparison to those who volunteered to take the personality test, males and females who volunteered for the sexual experiment were more sexually experienced. This means that those who participate in sexual experiments might not be representative of people in general, limiting the confidence with which sex researchers can generalize their findings (Saunders et al., 1985).

Of course, differences between volunteers and nonvolunteers do not automatically mean that the results lack external validity. The best way to determine whether the results of research studies do, in fact, have external validity is to replicate them (Thompson, 1994). Replication also enables researchers to determine whether the results of laboratory studies will generalize to the world outside of the laboratory. Most replications are approximate; they rarely use the same setting, subjects, or procedures. For example, confidence in the Pygmalion effect was strengthened when it was replicated by different researchers, using different teachers, with different students, in a different school (Meichenbaum, Bowers, & Ross, 1969). The ideal would be to replicate studies systematically several times, varying one aspect of the study each time (Hendrick, 1990). Thus, you would be more confident in your ability to generalize the findings of the melatonin experiment if people with insomnia, of a variety of ages, in several different cultures, succeeded in sleeping longer.

Now that you have been introduced to the descriptive, correlational, and experimental methods of research, you should be able to recognize them as you read about research studies described in later chapters. As you read particular studies, try to determine which kind of method was used, as well as its possible strengths and weaknesses—most notably, any potential confounding variables and any limitations on the generalizability of the research findings. You are now ready to learn how psychologists analyze the data generated by their research methods.

STAYING ON TRACK: *Methods of Psychological Research*

1. Why is it important to use unbiased samples in doing surveys?
2. What is validity in psychological testing?
3. What is an independent variable?
4. What is internal validity?

STATISTICAL ANALYSIS OF RESEARCH DATA

How would you make sense out of the data generated by the melatonin experiment? In analyzing the data, you would have to do more than simply state that Jane Rogers slept 9.1 hours, Steve White slept 7.8 hours, Sally Jones slept 8.2 hours, and so on. You would have to identify overall patterns in the data and whether the data support the research hypothesis that inspired the experiment.

As mentioned earlier, to make sense out of their data, psychologists rely on statistics. The term *statistics* was originally used to refer to the practice of recording quantitative political and economic information about European nation-states (Cowles, 1989). Over the past few decades, the use of statistics to analyze research data has become increasingly more prevalent in articles published in psychology journals (Parker, 1990). Psychologists use *descriptive statistics* to summarize data, *correlational statistics* to determine relationships

Experimental Group (Melatonin)				Control Group (No Melatonin)			
Subject	Duration	d	d^2	Subject	Duration	d	d^2
1	9.1	0.2	0.04	1	7.4	−0.5	0.25
2	8.6	−0.3	0.09	2	8.2	0.3	0.09
3	8.6	−0.3	0.09	3	9.5	1.6	2.56
4	8.8	−0.1	0.01	4	8.9	1.0	1.00
5	7.8	−1.1	1.21	5	6.7	−1.2	1.44
6	9.9	1.0	1.00	6	8.9	1.0	1.00
7	8.6	−0.3	0.09	7	7.5	−0.4	0.16
8	9.7	0.8	0.64	8	6.2	−1.7	2.89
9	9.0	0.1	0.01	9	7.8	−0.1	0.01
Sum = 80.1		Sum = 3.18		Sum = 71.1		Sum = 9.40	

Mode = 8.6 hours

Median = 8.8 hours

Mean = $\frac{80.1}{9}$ = 8.9 hours

Range = 9.9 − 7.8 = 2.1 hours

Variance = $\frac{\text{sum of } d^2}{\text{no. of subjects}} = \frac{3.18}{9} = 0.35$

Standard deviation = $\sqrt{\text{Variance}}$
$= \sqrt{0.35}$
$= 0.59$ hours

Mode = 8.9 hours

Median = 7.8 hours

Mean = $\frac{71.1}{9}$ = 7.9 hours

Range = 9.5 − 6.2 = 3.3 hours

Variance = $\frac{\text{sum of } d^2}{\text{no. of subjects}} = \frac{9.40}{9} = 1.04$

Standard deviation = $\sqrt{\text{Variance}}$
$= \sqrt{1.04}$
$= 1.02$

Note: d = deviation from the mean.

◄ **TABLE 2.3**
Descriptive Statistics from a Hypothetical Experiment on the Effect of Melatonin on Average Nightly Sleep Duration

between variables, and *inferential statistics* to test their research hypotheses. Appendix B presents an expanded discussion of statistics and their calculation.

Descriptive Statistics: Summarizing Research Data

You would summarize your data by using **descriptive statistics.** An early champion of the use of descriptive statistics was Florence Nightingale (1820–1910), one of the founders of modern nursing. She urged that hospitals keep medical records on their patients. As a result, she demonstrated statistically that British soldiers during times of war were more likely than the enemy to suffer death from disease and unsanitary conditions. She also was a pioneer in the use of graphs to support her conclusions. Her work led to reforms in nursing and medicine and to her being made a fellow of the Royal Statistical Society and an honorary member of the American Statistical Association (Viney, 1993).

Descriptive statistics include *measures of central tendency* and *measures of variability*. A **measure of central tendency** is a single number used to represent a set of scores. The measures of central tendency include the *mode*, the *median*, and the *mean*. Psychological research uses the mode least often, the median somewhat more often, and the mean most often.

The **mode** is the most frequent score in a set of scores. As shown in Table 2.3, in the melatonin experiment the mode for the experimental group is 8.6 hours and the mode for the control group is 8.9 hours. The **median** is the middle score in a set of scores that have been arranged in numerical order. Thus, in the melatonin experiment the median score for each group is the fifth score. The median for the experimental group is 8.8 hours and the median for the control group is 7.8 hours. You are most familiar with the **mean,** which is the *arithmetic average* of a set of scores. You use the mean when you calculate your exam average, batting average, or gas mileage average. In the melatonin experiment, the mean for the experimental group is 8.9 hours and the mean for the control group is 7.9 hours.

One of the problems in the use of measures of central tendency is that they can be used selectively to create misleading impressions. Suppose you had the following psychology exam scores: 23, 23, 67, 68, 69, 70, 91. The mode (the most frequent score) would be 23,

descriptive statistics
Statistics that summarize research data.

measure of central tendency
A statistic that represents the "typical" score in a set of scores.

mode
The score that occurs most frequently in a set of scores.

median
The middle score in a set of scores that have been ordered from lowest to highest.

mean
The arithmetic average of a set of scores.

the median (the middle score) would be 68, and the mean (the average score) would be 58.7. In this case, you would prefer the median as representative of your performance. But what if you had the following scores: 23, 67, 68, 69, 70, 91, 91? The mode would be 91, the median would be 69, and the mean would be 68.43. In that case, you would prefer the mode as representative of your performance.

Product advertisers, government agencies, and political parties are also prone to this selective use of measures of central tendency, as well as other statistics, to support their claims. But the use of statistics to mislead is not new. Its prevalence in the nineteenth century prompted British Prime Minister Benjamin Disraeli to declare, "There are three kinds of lies: lies, damned lies, and statistics." Even a basic understanding of statistics will make you less likely to be fooled by claims based on their selective use.

To represent a distribution of scores, psychologists do more than report a measure of central tendency. They also report a **measure of variability,** which describes the degree of dispersion of the scores. That is, do the scores tend to bunch together, or are they scattered? Commonly used measures of variability include the *range* and the *standard deviation*. The **range** is the difference between the highest and the lowest score in a set of scores. In Table 2.3 the range of the experimental group is $9.9 - 7.8 = 2.1$ hours, and the range of the control group is $9.5 - 6.2 = 3.3$ hours. But the range can be misleading, because one extreme score can create a false impression. Suppose that a friend conducts a similar experiment and reports that the range of sleep duration among the 15 subjects in his experimental group is 4 hours, with the longest duration being 9.3 hours and the shortest duration being 5.3 hours. You might conclude that there was a great deal of variability in the distribution of scores. But what if he then reported that only one subject slept less than 9.1 hours? Obviously, the scores would bunch together at the high end, making the variability of scores much less than you had presumed.

Because of their need to employ more meaningful measures of variability than the range, psychologists prefer to use the standard deviation. The **standard deviation** represents the degree of dispersion of scores around their mean and is the square root of a measure of variability called the *variance*. The **variance** is a measure based on the average deviation of a set of scores from their group mean. Table 2.3 shows that the standard deviation of the experimental group is 0.59 hours, while the standard deviation of the control group is 1.02 hours. Thus, the distribution of scores in the experimental group has a larger mean, but the distribution of scores in the control group has a larger standard deviation.

Correlational Statistics: Finding Relationships in Research Data

If you were interested in predicting one set of scores from another, you would use a *measure of correlation*. The concept of correlation was put forth in 1888 by Francis Galton, who wanted a way to represent the relationship between parents and offspring on factors, such as intelligence, presumed to be affected by heredity. While the mean and standard deviation are useful in describing individual sets of scores, a statistic called the **coefficient of correlation** is useful in quantifying the degree of association between two or more sets of scores. The coefficient of correlation was devised by the English mathematician Karl Pearson (1851–1926) and is often called *Pearson's r* (with the r standing for "regression," another name for correlation). As you learned earlier, a correlation can be positive or negative, and can range from zero to +1.00 or −1.00. In a *positive correlation* between two sets of scores, relatively high scores on one set are associated with relatively high scores on the other, and relatively low scores on one set are associated with relatively low scores on the other. For example, there is a positive correlation between height and weight and between high school and college grade point averages.

In a *negative correlation* between two sets of scores, relatively high scores on one set are associated with relatively low scores on the other. For example, there is a negative correlation between driving speed and gas mileage. A *zero correlation* indicates that there is no relationship between one set of scores and another. You would find an approximately zero correlation between the intelligence levels of two groups of randomly selected strangers. The types of correlations are illustrated graphically in Figure 2.3.

measure of variability
A statistic describing the degree of dispersion in a set of scores.

range
A statistic representing the difference between the highest and lowest scores in a set of scores.

standard deviation
A statistic representing the degree of dispersion of a set of scores around their mean.

variance
A measure based on the average deviation of a set of scores from their group mean.

coefficient of correlation
A statistic that assesses the degree of association between two or more variables.

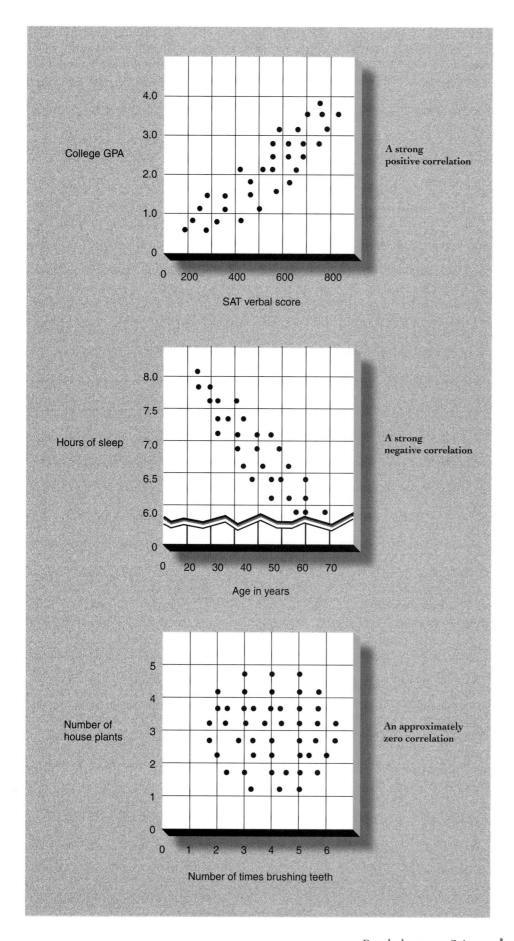

Correlations

In a *positive correlation*, scores on the measures increase and decrease together. An example is the relationship between SAT verbal scores and college grade point average (GPA). In a *negative correlation*, scores on one measure increase as scores on the other measure decrease. An example is the relationship between age and nightly sleep. In a *zero correlation*, scores on one measure are unrelated to scores on the other. An example is the relationship between the number of times people brush their teeth each day and the number of houseplants they have.

The higher the correlation between two variables, the more the scores on one variable will be accurate predictors of scores on the other. For example, suppose you found a correlation of .83 between the number of milligrams of melatonin that people take each night and their nightly sleep duration. This relatively large correlation would make you fairly confident in predicting that as the dose of melatonin increases, the average nightly duration of sleep would increase. If, instead, you found a relatively small correlation of .17, you would have less confidence in making that prediction.

Inferential Statistics: Determining Causality Using Research Data

In the melatonin experiment, the experimental group had a longer average nightly sleep duration than the control group. But is the difference in average nightly sleep duration between the two groups large enough for you to conclude with confidence that melatonin was responsible for the difference? Perhaps the difference happened by chance—that is, because of a host of random factors unrelated to melatonin. To determine whether the independent variable, rather than chance factors, caused the changes in the dependent variable, psychologists use **inferential statistics.** By permitting psychologists to determine the causes of events, inferential statistics help them achieve the goal of explanation. Inferential statistics are "inferential" because they enable experimenters to make inferences from the sample of subjects used in their experiment to the population of individuals they represent.

If there is a low probability that the difference between groups on the dependent variable is attributable to chance (that is, to random factors), the difference is **statistically significant** and is attributed to the independent variable. The concept of statistical significance was put forth by the English mathematician Ronald Fisher (1890–1962) when he sought a way to test a noblewoman's claim that she could tell whether tea or milk had been added to her cup first (Tankard, 1984). Though he never carried out the demonstration, he proposed presenting her with a series of cups in which tea was sometimes added first and milk was sometimes added first. He assumed that if she could report the correct order at a much greater than chance level, her claim would be verified. To rule out simple lucky guessing, she would have to be correct significantly more than 50 percent of the time—the chance level of guessing between two events.

In the melatonin experiment, you would expect that chance factors would account for some changes in the sleep duration of subjects in both groups during the course of the study. As a result, for the difference in average sleep duration between the two groups to be statistically significant, it would have to be significantly larger than would be expected by chance alone. Psychologists usually accept a difference as statistically significant when there is less than a 5 percent (5 in 100) probability that the difference is the product of chance factors—the so-called .05 level.

Nonetheless, even when the analysis of research data reveals statistical significance, the best way to determine whether research findings are generalizable is to replicate them (Cohen, 1994). Two real experiments did, in fact, "replicate" the findings of the imaginary melatonin experiment described earlier. These experiments, which used the double-blind technique, found that subjects who took melatonin slept longer than subjects who took the placebo—regardless of whether the subjects were normal sleepers (Waldhauser, Saletu, & Trinchard, 1990) or insomnia sufferers (MacFarlane et al., 1991). Thus, there is some scientific support for the claims made in the *Newsweek* cover story that opened this chapter.

Still another approach to assessing generalizability is to use the relatively new statistical technique called *meta-analysis*. **Meta-analysis** combines research findings from many, perhaps hundreds, of related studies and goes beyond simply determining statistical significance. It does so by determining the average size of the effect of the independent variable. In Chapter 15, you will read about the results of a massive meta-analysis of 475 research studies that provided support for the effectiveness of psychotherapy (Smith, Glass, & Miller, 1980).

One of the main inferential statistics, the *t test*, is used to determine whether there is a significant difference between the scores of two groups. The *t* test would be used to determine

inferential statistics
Statistics used to determine whether changes in a dependent variable are caused by an independent variable.

statistical significance
A low probability (usually less than 5 percent) that the results of a research study are due to chance factors rather than to the independent variable.

meta-analysis
A technique that combines the results of many similar studies to determine the size and consistency of the effect of a particular kind of independent variable.

CHAPTER 2

whether there was a significant difference in nightly sleep duration between the experimental group and the control group in the melatonin experiment. The t test was invented by statistician and brewmaster William Sealy Gosset (1876–1937) to maintain quality control in the brewing and storage of Guinness Stout, the popular dark, bitter beer. The beverage is still produced by Arthur Guinness, Son and Company, which shows its continued interest in statistics by publishing the *Guinness Book of World Records*.

Gosset compared pairs of batches of stout that he had treated differently in regard to factors such as ingredients, brewing temperature, or storage temperature. He analyzed the data using what became known as Student's t test. It was given this name because the brewery refused to permit its employees to publish anything that might reflect poorly on the company, leading Gosset to take the pseudonym *Student*. The first use of the t test in psychological research was in a paper published by Gosset in 1925, which found that one sleep medication was better than another in the treatment of insomnia.

Another important inferential statistic, the *analysis of variance*, enables researchers to compare two or more groups. The analysis of variance is also called the F test, after Ronald Fisher, who devised it in his research aimed at the improvement of agricultural productivity through the varying of a number of factors, including manure. In fact, the first use of the analysis of variance in a published study was in a 1923 article entitled "The Manuarial Response of Different Potato Varieties." The analysis of variance would be useful in the melatonin experiment if we used three groups: perhaps a melatonin group, a placebo group, and a no-drug group.

As you read the research studies discussed in later chapters, keep in mind that virtually all were analyzed by descriptive statistics, correlational statistics, or inferential statistics. You should also note that statistical significance does not necessarily imply practical significance (Rachman, 1993). For example, a variety of relaxation techniques have been used to treat high blood pressure. Though studies have found that some of these techniques can induce statistically significant decreases in blood pressure, those decreases might not be of practical significance. In other words, they might not be large enough to be considered clinically important.

STAYING ON TRACK: *Statistical Analysis of Research Data*

1. What are measures of central tendency?
2. What are measures of variability?
3. What is statistical significance?

THINKING ABOUT *Psychology*

What Are the Ethics of Psychological Research?

Psychologists must be as concerned with the ethical treatment of their data and subjects as they are with the quality of their research methods and statistical analyses. A serious ethical violation in the treatment of data is falsification. Thus, in the melatonin experiment, you would have to record your data accurately—even if it contradicted your hypothesis. During the past few decades there have been several notorious cases in which medical, biological, or psychological researchers have been accused of falsifying their data. Chapter 10 discusses a prominent case in psychology, in which Sir Cyril Burt, an eminent psychologist, was so intent on demonstrating that intelligence depends on heredity that he apparently misrepresented his research findings. Though occasional lapses in the ethical treatment of data have provoked controversy, there has been even greater concern about the ethical treatment of research subjects, both human and animal.

ETHICAL TREATMENT OF HUMAN SUBJECTS

The first code of ethics for the treatment of human subjects in psychological research was developed in 1953, partly in response to the Nuremberg war crimes trials following World War II (Reese & Fremouw, 1984). The trials disclosed the cruel medical experiments performed by Nazi physicians on prisoners of war and concentration camp inmates. Today, the United States government requires institutions that receive federal research grants to establish committees that review research proposals to assure the ethical treatment of human subjects (McGaha & Korn, 1995).

The American Psychological Association's code of ethics contains specific requirements for the treatment of human subjects. First, the researcher must inform potential subjects of all aspects of the research procedure that might influence their decision to participate. In the melatonin experiment, you would not be permitted to tell subjects they will be given melatonin and then give them a placebo instead, unless they have been informed of the possibility. This requirement, *informed consent*, can be difficult to assure, because subjects might be unable to give truly informed consent. Perhaps the subjects cannot comprehend the language used on informed consent forms (Ogloff & Otto, 1991) or suffer from brain disorders, such as Alzheimer's disease, that make them too impaired to think rationally (High, 1992).

Second, potential subjects must not be forced to participate in a research study, which could become a problem with prisoners or hospitalized patients who fear the consequences of refusing to participate (Rosenthal, 1995). Third, subjects must be permitted to withdraw from a study at any time. Of course, when subjects withdraw, it can adversely affect the study, because those who remain might differ from those who drop out. The loss of subjects can therefore limit the ability to generalize research findings from the subjects who complete the study to the desired target population (Trice & Ogden, 1987).

Fourth, the researcher must protect the subjects from physical harm and mental distress. Again, the use of deception might violate this provision by inducing mental distress. Fifth, if a subject does experience harm or distress, the researcher must try to alleviate it. But some critics argue that it is impossible to routinely determine whether attempts to relieve distress produce long-lasting benefits (Norris, 1978). Sixth, information gained from subjects must be kept confidential. This becomes a major issue in research on sensitive topics, such as AIDS, because laws might force researchers to reveal data that their subjects presumed were confidential (Melton & Grey, 1988).

Despite their code of ethics, psychologists sometimes confront ethical dilemmas in their treatment of human subjects, as in the use of deception to reduce subject bias. Psychologists might fail to inform people that they are subjects in a study or might misinform subjects about the true nature of a study. This is of concern, in part, because it violates the ethical norm of informed consent. Recall that the computer-dating study by Donn Byrne (Byrne, Ervin, & Lamberth, 1970) used deception by falsely claiming that all participants would be matched with partners who shared their attitudes. Today, for this to be considered ethical, the researcher would have to demonstrate to an institutional research review committee that the experiment could not be conducted without the use of deception and that its potential findings are important enough to justify the use of deception (Fisher & Fyrberg, 1994). Moreover, at the completion of the study, the subjects would have to be debriefed. In **debriefing** subjects, the researcher explains the reasons for the deception and tries to relieve any distress that might have been experienced.

Some psychologists worry that deceptive research will make potential subjects distrust psychological research (Sharpe, Adair, & Roese, 1992). And Diana Baumrind (1985), a critic of deceptive research, argues that not even the positive findings of studies that use deception outweigh the distress of subjects who learn that they have been fooled. Arguments against deceptive research have been countered by psychologists who argue that it would be unethical *not* to conduct deceptive studies that might produce important findings (Christensen, 1988).

While some psychologists argue about the use of deception, others try to settle the debate over deceptive research by using the results of empirical research. In one study,

debriefing

A procedure, after the completion of a research study, that informs subjects of the purpose of the study and aims to remove any physical or psychological distress caused by participation.

undergraduates who had been subjects in deceptive experiments rated their experience as more positive than did those who had participated in nondeceptive ones. Moreover, those in deceptive experiments did not rate psychologists as less trustworthy. Any negative emotional effects reported by subjects seemed to be relieved by debriefing. The researchers concluded that debriefing eliminates any negative effects of deception, perhaps because the subjects learn the importance of the research study (Smith & Richardson, 1983).

But this interpretation of the findings has been criticized. You might wish to pause now and see if you can think of an alternative explanation of why subjects in deceptive experiments responded more positively. One possibility is that the procedures used in deceptive experiments are more interesting and enjoyable than those used in nondeceptive ones (Rubin, 1985). Remembering that psychology, as a science, resolves issues through empirical research instead of through argument alone, how might you conduct a study to determine whether this assumption is correct? One way would be to conduct experiments whose procedures have been rated as equally interesting, and use deception in only half of them. If the subjects still rate the deceptive experiments more positively, then the results would support Smith and Richardson (1983). If the subjects rate the deceptive experiments less positively, then the results would support Rubin (1985).

ETHICAL TREATMENT OF ANIMAL SUBJECTS

At the 1986 annual meeting of the American Psychological Association in Washington, D.C., animal rights advocates picketed in the streets and disrupted talks, including one by the prominent psychologist Neal Miller, a defender of the use of animals in psychological research. The present conflict between animal rights advocates and psychologists who study animals is not new. In the early twentieth century, animal rights activists attacked the work of leading psychologists, including John B. Watson and G. Stanley Hall. In 1925, in part to blunt these attacks, the American Psychological Association's Committee on Precautions in Animal Experimentation established a code of regulations for the use of animals in research (Dewsbury, 1990).

Many *animal rights* advocates oppose all laboratory research using animals, regardless of its scientific merit or practical benefits. Thus, they would oppose testing the effects of melatonin on animal subjects. A survey of demonstrators at an animal rights march in Washington, D.C., in 1990 found that almost 80 percent of animal rights advocates valued animal life at least as much as human life, and 85 percent wanted to eliminate all animal research (Plous, 1991). Animal rights advocates go beyond *animal welfare* advocates, who would permit laboratory research on animals as long as the animals are given humane care and the potential benefits of the research outweigh any pain and distress caused to the animals. Thus, they would be more likely to approve the use of animals in testing the effects of melatonin on sleep. Bernard Rollin, an ethicist who has tried to resolve the ethical conflict between animal researchers and animal rights advocates, would permit animal research but urges that, when in ethical doubt, experimenters should err in favor of the animal (Bekoff et al., 1992).

The American Psychological Association's current ethical standards for the treatment of animals are closer to those of animal welfare advocates than to those of animal rights advocates. The standards require that animals be treated with respect, housed in clean cages, and given adequate food and water. Researchers must also subject their animal subjects to as little pain and distress as possible; when it is necessary to kill the animals, researchers must do so in a humane, painless way. Moreover, all institutions that receive research grants from the U.S. government must have committees that judge whether research proposals for experiments using animal subjects meet ethical standards (Holden, 1987). The Canadian government likewise regulates the treatment of research animals in universities, government laboratories, and commercial institutions (Rowsell, 1988).

But with so many human beings available, why would psychologists be interested in studying animals? First, some psychologists are simply intrigued by animal behavior and wish to learn more about it. To learn about the process of echolocation of prey, you would have to study animals like bats rather than college students. Second, it is easier to control

▲ Diana Baumrind
"Deceptive practices do not succeed in accomplishing the scientific objectives that are used to justify such deception any better than methods that do not require deception."

potential confounding variables that might affect the behavior of an animal. You would be less likely to worry about subject bias effects, for instance, when studying pigeons. Third, developmental changes across the life span can be studied more efficiently in animals. If you were interested in the effects of the complexity of the early childhood environment on memory in old age, you might take 75 years to complete an experiment using human subjects, but only 3 years to complete one using rats.

Fourth, research on animals can generate hypotheses that are then tested using human subjects. B. F. Skinner's research on learning in rats and pigeons stimulated research on learning in human beings. Fifth, research on animals can benefit animals themselves. For example, as described in Chapter 7, psychologists have developed techniques to make coyotes feel nauseated by the taste of sheep; perhaps these can someday be used to protect sheep from coyotes, and coyotes from angry sheep ranchers. Sixth, because of an assumption that animals do not have the same moral rights as human beings (Baldwin, 1993), certain procedures that are not ethically permissible with human subjects are ethically permissible under current standards with animal subjects. Thus, if you wanted to conduct an experiment in which you studied the effects of surgically removing a particular brain structure, you would be limited to the use of animals.

But these reasons have not convinced animal rights advocates of the merits of psychological research on animals. Animal rights advocates argue that the benefits of laboratory research that submits animals to painful procedures do not outweigh the suffering they induce (Bowd, 1990). During the past decade some animal rights advocates have even vandalized animal research laboratories and stolen animals from their laboratory cages. The vast majority of advocates, however, have been content to lobby for stronger laws limiting animal research or to picket meetings of animal researchers. Prior to the meeting at which he was harassed, Neal Miller (1985) had pointed out that for every dog and cat used in laboratory research, 10,000 are abandoned by their owners, and that, in contrast, few psychology experiments inflict pain or distress on animals. He urged animal rights advocates to spend more time helping the millions of abandoned pets that are killed in pounds, starve to death, or die after being struck by motor vehicles.

Miller (1985) has also cited ways in which animal research contributes to human welfare. Findings from animal research have contributed to progress in the treatment of pain; the development of behavior therapy for phobias; the rehabilitation of victims of neuromuscular disorders, such as Parkinson's disease; the understanding of neurological disorders associated with aging, such as Alzheimer's disease; and the development of drugs for treating anxiety, depression, and schizophrenia. Nonetheless, Miller's critics accuse him of exaggerating the benefits of animal research (Kelly, 1986).

While reasonable people may disagree about the ethical limits of psychological research on animals, the attention given to such research might be out of proportion to its extent and to the pain and distress it causes. Only 5 percent of psychologists conduct research with animals. Of their animal subjects, 95 percent are mice, rats, and birds; less than 1 percent are dogs, cats, monkeys, and chimpanzees—the kinds of animals to which people feel the greatest kinship (Gallup & Suarez, 1985). Moreover, few psychological studies on animals inflict pain or distress (Coile & Miller, 1984). And despite the special attention that psychological research receives from animal rights advocates, a government report praised the American Psychological Association's ethical standards for the care and use of animals in research as being superior to those of any other science (Fisher, 1986).

No responsible psychologist would condone a cavalier disregard for the pain and suffering of laboratory animals. Nonetheless, it seems that animal rights advocates have been more effective than animal researchers in influencing the public and lawmakers. Thus, it might be wise for animal researchers to communicate more through the popular media to argue that a moderate position on animal research is better than either extreme position (King & Viney, 1992). Moreover, there seems to have been a recent decline in popular interest in the ethics of animal research. An archival study of popular magazine articles found that the number of articles about animal rights peaked in 1990 and declined over the following few years (Herzog, 1995). But others disagree, claiming instead that the animal rights movement might be as influential as ever even if media coverage of it has declined (Rowan & Shapiro, 1996).

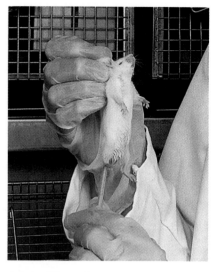

▲ **Animal Research**
Those who favor animal research note the medical and psychological benefits it produces for human beings and, in some cases, animals.

STAYING ON TRACK: *What Are the Ethics of Psychological Research?*

1. Why has the use of deception in research provoked controversy?
2. What is debriefing in psychological research?
3. How do animal rights and animal welfare differ from one other?

 # CHAPTER SUMMARY

SOURCES OF KNOWLEDGE

Psychologists prefer the scientific method to other sources of knowledge, which include common sense, appeal to authority, reasoning, and unsystematic observation. The scientific method is based on the assumptions of order, determinism, and skepticism. In using the scientific method to perform a research study, a psychologist first provides a rationale for the study, then conducts the study, analyzes the resulting data, and, finally, communicates the results to other researchers. Psychologists also try to replicate research studies.

GOALS OF SCIENTIFIC RESEARCH

In conducting research, psychologists pursue the goals of description, prediction, control, and explanation. Scientific descriptions are systematic and rely on operational definitions. Scientific predictions are probabilistic, not certain. Scientists exert control over events by manipulating the factors that cause them. And scientific explanations state the causes of events.

METHODS OF PSYCHOLOGICAL RESEARCH

Psychologists use descriptive, correlational, and experimental research methods. Descriptive research methods pursue the goal of description through naturalistic observation, case studies, surveys, psychological testing, and archival research. Correlational research pursues the goal of prediction by uncovering relationships between variables. In using correlational research, psychologists avoid confusing correlation with causation. Experimental

research pursues the goals of control and explanation by manipulating an independent variable and measuring its effect on a dependent variable.

Experimenters promote internal validity by controlling confounding variables whose effects might be confused with those of the independent variable. These variables might be associated with the experimental procedure itself, the subjects of the experiment, or the experimenter. Random assignment of subjects is used to make the experimental group and control group equivalent before exposing them to the independent variable. Experimenters must also control for subject bias and experimenter bias. Another concern of experimenters is external validity: whether their results are generalizable from their subjects and settings to other subjects and settings. Experimenters rely on replication to determine whether their research has external validity.

STATISTICAL ANALYSIS OF RESEARCH DATA

Psychologists typically make sense of their data by using mathematical techniques called statistics. They use descriptive statistics to summarize data, correlational statistics to determine relationships between variables, and inferential statistics to test their experimental hypotheses. Descriptive statistics include measures of central tendency (including the mode, median, and mean) and measures of variability (including the range and standard deviation). Correlational statistics let researchers use the values of one variable to predict the values of another. And inferential statistics examine whether numerical differences between experimental and control groups are statistically significant. Statistical significance does not necessarily indicate practical significance.

THINKING ABOUT PSYCHOLOGY: WHAT ARE THE ETHICS OF PSYCHOLOGICAL RESEARCH?

American and Canadian psychologists have ethical codes for the treatment of human subjects and animal subjects. In research using human subjects, researchers must obtain informed consent, not force anyone to participate, let subjects withdraw at any time, protect subjects from physical harm and mental distress, alleviate any inadvertent harm or distress,

and keep confidential all information obtained from the subjects. The use of deception in research has been an especially controversial issue.

The use of animals in research has also been controversial. Many animal rights supporters oppose all research on animals, whereas animal welfare supporters approve of research on animals as long as the animals are treated humanely and the potential benefits of the research outweigh any pain and distress caused to the animals. Though relatively few psychologists conduct research on animals, most psychologists support the use of animals in research because of the benefits of such research to both human beings and animals. Moreover, few psychologists treat their research animals in a less than humane way.

KEY CONCEPTS

Sources of Knowledge

lay psychology 32
empiricism 34
determinism 34
skepticism 34
scientific method 35
hypothesis 35
statistics 35
replication 35

Goals of Scientific Research

measurement 38
operational definition 38
theory 38

Methods of Psychological Research

descriptive research 40
naturalistic observation 40

ethology 41
case study 41
survey 42
sample 43
population 43
random sampling 43
psychological test 44
standardization 44
norm 44
reliability 45
validity 45
archival research 45
correlational research 46
correlation 46
variable 46
positive correlation 46
negative correlation 46
causation 46

experimental method 47
independent variable 47
dependent variable 47
experimental group 47
control group 47
internal validity 48
confounding variable 48
random assignment 49
subject bias 49
experimenter bias effect 49
double-blind technique 51
placebo 51
external validity 51

Statistical Analysis of Research Data

descriptive statistics 53
measure of central tendency 53

mode 53
median 53
mean 53
measure of variability 54
range 54
standard deviation 54
variance 54
coefficient of correlation 54
inferential statistics 56
statistical significance 56
meta-analysis 56

What Are the Ethics of Psychological Research?

debriefing 58

KEY CONTRIBUTORS

Sources of Knowledge

Harold Kelley 33
René Descartes 33
John Locke 33
William James 34

Goals of Scientific Research

Francis Bacon 37

Methods of Psychological Research

Jane Goodall 40
Anne Anastasi 44
Lewis Terman 44
Francis Galton 45
John Popplestone 45
Marion McPherson 45
Robert Rosenthal 49

Statistical Analysis of Research Data

Florence Nightingale 53
Karl Pearson 54
Ronald Fisher 56
William Sealy Gosset 57

What Are the Ethics of Psychological Research?

Diana Baumrind 58
Neal Miller 59
Bernard Rollin 59

FOR MORE INFORMATION ON PSYCHOLOGY AS A SCIENCE

FOR GENERAL WORKS ON PSYCHOLOGY AS A SCIENCE

Brannigan, G. G., & Merrens, M. R. (Eds.). (1993). *The undaunted psychologist: Adventures in research.* New York: McGraw-Hill.

Danziger, K. (1990). *Constructing the subject: Historical origins of psychological research.* New York: Cambridge University Press.
Stanovich, K. E. (1992). *How to think straight about psychology* (3rd ed.). New York: HarperCollins.

FOR MORE ON SOURCES OF KNOWLEDGE

Everyday Sources of Knowledge

Fletcher, G. (1996). *The scientific credibility of folk psychology.* Hillsdale, NJ: Erlbaum.

Siegfried, J. (Ed.). (1993). *The status of common sense in psychology.* Norwood, NJ: Ablex.

The Scientific Method

Gower, B. (1997). *Scientific method : A historical and philosophical introduction*. New York: Routledge.

Matsumoto, D. (1994). *Cultural influences on research methods and statistics*. Pacific Grove, CA: Brooks/Cole.

Neuliep, J. W. (Ed.). (1991). *Replication research in the social sciences*. Newbury Park, CA: Sage.

Smith, R. A. (1995). *Challenging your preconceptions: Thinking critically about psychology*. Pacific Grove, CA: Brooks/Cole.

FOR MORE ON THE GOALS OF SCIENTIFIC RESEARCH

Cummins, R. (1983). *The nature of psychological explanation*. Cambridge, MA: MIT Press.

MacDonald, C., & MacDonald, G. (1995). *Philosophy of psychology: Debates on psychological explanation*. Cambridge, MA: Blackwell.

FOR MORE ON METHODS OF PSYCHOLOGICAL RESEARCH

Goodwin, C. J. (1996). *Research in psychology: Methods and design*. New York: Wiley.

Naturalistic Observation

Goodall, J. (1986). *The chimpanzees of Gombe: Patterns of behavior*. Cambridge, MA: Belknap/Harvard.

Case Study Research

Bromley, D. B. (1986). *The case-study method in psychology and related disciplines*. New York: Wiley.

Survey Research

Converse, J. M. (1987). *Survey research in the United States: Roots and emergence, 1890–1960*. Berkeley: University of California Press.

Psychological Testing

Cohen, R. J., Swerdlik, M. E., & Phillips, S. M. (1996). *Psychological testing and assessment: An introduction to tests and measurement* (3rd ed.). Mountain View, CA: Mayfield.

Archival Research

Elder, G. H., Jr., Pavalko, E. K., & Clipp, E. C. (1993). *Working with archival data: Studying lives*. Newbury Park, CA: Sage.

Correlational Research

Kenny, D. A. (1979). *Correlation and causality*. New York: Wiley.

Experimental Research

Levin, I. P., & Hinrichs, J. V. (1995). *Experimental psychology: Contemporary methods and applications*. Madison, WI: Brown & Benchmark.

Orne, M. T. (1991). *On the social psychology of the psychological experiment*. New York: Irvington.

Rosenthal, R. (1976). *Experimenter effects in behavioral research*. New York: Irvington.

FOR MORE ON THE STATISTICAL ANALYSIS OF DATA

Chow, S. L. (1996). *Statistical significance*. Thousand Oaks, CA: Sage.

Cowles, M. (1989). *Statistics in psychology: An historical perspective*. Hillsdale, NJ: Erlbaum.

Holmes, C. B. (1990). *The honest truth about lying with statistics*. Springfield, IL: Charles C Thomas.

Spence, J. T., Cotton, J. W., Underwood, B. J., & Duncan, C. P. (1990). *Elementary statistics* (5th ed.). Englewood Cliffs, NJ: Prentice Hall.

FOR MORE ON THE ETHICS OF PSYCHOLOGICAL RESEARCH

American Psychological Association. (1992). Ethical principles of psychologists and code of conduct. *American Psychologist, 47,* 1597–1611.

Canter, M. B., Bennett, B. E., Jones, S. E., & Nagy, T. F. (1994). *Ethics for psychologists: A commentary on the APA ethics code*. Washington, DC: American Psychological Association.

Miller, D. J., & Hersen, M. (Eds.). (1992). *Research fraud in the behavioral and biomedical sciences*. New York: Wiley.

Pallone, N. J., & Hennessy, J. J. (Eds.). (1995). *Fraud and fallible judgment: Deception in the social and behavioral sciences*. New Brunswick, NJ: Transaction.

Ethical Treatment of Human Subjects

Barnes, J. A. (1979). *Who should know what? Social science, privacy, and ethics*. New York: Cambridge University Press.

Faden, R. R., & Beauchamp, T. L. (1986). *A history and theory of informed consent*. New York: Oxford University Press.

Ethical Treatment of Animal Subjects

American Psychological Association. (1993). *Guidelines for ethical conduct in the care and use of animals*. Washington, DC: Author.

Fox, M. A. (1986). *The case for animal experimentation: An evolutionary and ethical perspective*. Berkeley: University of California Press.

Garner, R. (1997). *Animal rights: Past, present, and future perspectives*. New York: New York University Press.

Regan, T. (1983). *The case for animal rights*. Berkeley: University of California Press.

Rollin, B. E. (1989). *The unheeded cry: Animal consciousness, animal pain, and science*. New York: Oxford University Press.

FOR MORE ON CONTRIBUTORS TO PSYCHOLOGY AS A SCIENCE

Anastasi, A. (1980). Anne Anastasi. In G. Lindzey (Ed.), *A history of psychology in autobiography* (Vol. 4, pp. 1–37). San Francisco: W. H. Freeman.

Cranston, M. (1979). *John Locke: A biography*. New York: Oxford University Press.

Fisher Box, J. (1978). *R. A. Fisher: The life of a scientist*. New York: Wiley.

Forrest, D. W. (1974). *Francis Galton: The life and work of a Victorian genius*. New York: Taplinger.

Gaukroger, S. (1995). *Descartes: An intellectual biography*. New York: Oxford University Press.

Goodall, J. (1990). *Through a window: My thirty years with the chimpanzees of Gombe*. Boston: Houghton Mifflin.

Leary, J. E. (1994). *Francis Bacon and the politics of science*. Ames: Iowa State University Press.

Myers, G. E. (1986). *William James: His life and thought*. New Haven, CT: Yale University Press.

Pearson, E. S. (1938). *Karl Pearson: An appreciation of some aspects of his life and work*. New York: Cambridge University Press.

Pearson, E. S., Plackett, R. L., & Barnard, G. A. (Eds.). (1990). *Student: A statistical biography of William Sealy Gosset*. New York: Oxford University Press.

Tankard, J. W., Jr. (1984). *The statistical pioneers*. Cambridge, MA: Schenkman.

CHAPTER 3

▲ ROBERTO MATTA
Listening to Living, 1941

Behavioral Neuroscience

A disorder, caused by damage to a parietal lobe, in which the individual acts as though the side of her or his world opposite to the damaged lobe does not exist.

The field that studies the relationship between neurological and psychological processes.

▲ **Charles Darwin (1801–1882)**
"I have called this principle, by which each slight variation, if useful, is preserved, by the term Natural Selection."

A clinical case study included the following account:

▶ A 64-year-old, right-handed man was awakened by the sense that there was something strange in his bed. Opening his eyes, he observed to his horror that there was a strange arm reaching toward his neck. The arm approached nearer, as if to strangle him, and the man let out a cry of terror. Suddenly, he realized that the arm had on its wrist a silver-banded watch, which the man recognized to be his own. It occurred to him that the arm's possessor must have stolen his watch sometime during the night. A struggle ensued, as the man attempted to wrestle the watch off of the arm. During the struggle, the man became aware that his own left arm was feeling contorted and uncomfortable. It was then that he discovered that the strange arm in fact was his own. The watch was his, and it was on his own left wrist. He was wrestling with his own arm! (Tranel, 1995, p. 885)

What could account for such bizarre behavior? A stroke had damaged the right side of the man's brain, making him experience the **neglect syndrome,** which typically involves the inability to attend normally to the left side of one's body and one's immediate environment. Such profound effects of brain damage on physical and psychological functioning indicate that abilities we often take for granted require an intact, properly functioning brain. If you have an intact brain, as you read this page your eyes inform your brain about what you are reading. At the same time, your brain interprets the meaning of that information and stores some of it in your memory. When you reach the end of the right-hand page, your brain will direct your hand to turn the page.

But how do your eyes inform your brain about what you are reading? How does your brain interpret and store the information it receives? And how does your brain direct the movements of your hand? The answers to these questions are provided by the field of **behavioral neuroscience,** which studies the relationship between neurological processes (typically brain activity) and psychological functions (such as memory, emotion, and perception).

As we saw in the neglect syndrome, damage to the brain—whether caused by disease or injury—can have devastating effects. In acknowledging this, the U.S. Congress declared the 1990s "The Decade of the Brain" (Cacioppo & Berntson, 1992). Members of Congress hope that researchers in behavioral neuroscience and related fields will increase our knowledge of normal brain functioning and learn more about the causes, treatment, and prevention of brain disorders.

But interest in behavioral neuroscience is not new. A century ago, Sigmund Freud predicted that researchers would one day discover the physiological processes underlying his theory of psychoanalysis (Sulloway, 1979). At about the same time, William James (1890/1981), in his classic psychology textbook, *The Principles of Psychology,* stressed the close association between biology and psychology. James declared, "I have felt most acutely the difficulties of understanding either the brain without the mind or the mind without the brain" (Bjork, 1988, p. 107). Freud and James were influenced by Charles Darwin's (1859/1975) theory of evolution, which holds that individuals who are biologically well adapted to their environment are more likely to survive, reproduce, and thus pass on their physical traits to succeeding generations through their genes.

Thus, the human brain has evolved into its present form because it helped human beings in thousands of earlier generations adapt successfully to their surroundings and

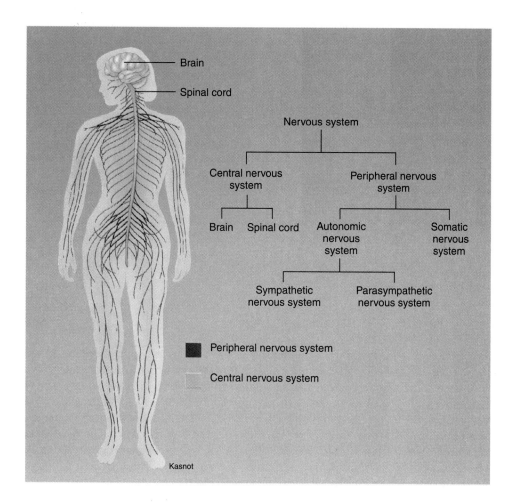

Brain

Spinal cord

Nervous system

Central nervous system — Peripheral nervous system

Brain | Spinal cord | Autonomic nervous system | Somatic nervous system

Sympathetic nervous system | Parasympathetic nervous system

■ Peripheral nervous system

□ Central nervous system

Kasnot

◄ FIGURE 3.1
The Organization of the Nervous System
The nervous system comprises the brain, spinal cord, and nerves.

nervous system
The chief means of communication in the body, which transmits messages along neurons.

neuron
A cell specialized for the transmission of information in the nervous system.

central nervous system
The division of the nervous system consisting of the brain and the spinal cord.

brain
The structure of the central nervous system that is located in the skull and plays important roles in sensation, movement, and information processing.

spinal cord
The structure of the central nervous system that is located in the spine and plays a role in bodily reflexes and in communicating information between the brain and the peripheral nervous system.

peripheral nervous system
The division of the nervous system that conveys sensory information to the central nervous system and motor commands from the central nervous system to the skeletal muscles and internal organs.

nerve
A bundle of axons that conveys information to or from the central nervous system.

somatic nervous system
The division of the peripheral nervous system that sends messages from the sensory organs to the central nervous system and messages from the central nervous system to the skeletal muscles.

autonomic nervous system
The division of the peripheral nervous system that controls automatic, involuntary physiological processes.

sympathetic nervous system
The division of the autonomic nervous system that arouses the body to prepare it for action.

parasympathetic nervous system
The division of the autonomic nervous system that calms the body and performs maintenance functions.

survive long enough to reproduce. Because of its remarkable flexibility in helping us adapt to different circumstances, the brain that helped ancient people survive without automobiles, grocery stores, or electric lights helps people today survive in the arctic, outer space, and New York City.

THE NERVOUS SYSTEM:
A MEANS OF RAPID COMMUNICATION

The brain is part of the **nervous system,** the chief means of communication within the body. The nervous system is composed of **neurons,** cells that are specialized for the transmission and reception of information. As illustrated in Figure 3.1, the two divisions of the nervous system are the *central nervous system* and the *peripheral nervous system.* The **central nervous system** contains the **brain** and the **spinal cord.** The **peripheral nervous system** contains the **nerves,** which provide a means of communication between the central nervous system and the sensory organs, skeletal muscles, and internal bodily organs.

The peripheral nervous system contains the *somatic nervous system* and the *autonomic nervous system.* The **somatic nervous system** includes *sensory nerves,* which send messages from the sensory organs to the central nervous system, and *motor nerves,* which send messages from the central nervous system to the skeletal muscles. The **autonomic nervous system** controls automatic, involuntary processes (such as sweating, heart contractions, and intestinal activity) through the action of its two subdivisions: the *sympathetic nervous system* and the *parasympathetic nervous system.* The **sympathetic nervous system** arouses the body to prepare it for action, and the **parasympathetic nervous system** calms the body to conserve energy.

sensory neuron
A neuron that sends messages from sensory receptors to the central nervous system.

motor neuron
A neuron that sends messages from the central nervous system to smooth muscles, cardiac muscle, or skeletal muscles.

glial cell
A kind of cell that provides a physical support structure for the neurons, supplies them with nutrition, removes neuronal metabolic waste materials, facilitates the transmission of messages by neurons, and helps regenerate damaged neurons in the peripheral nervous system.

reflex
An automatic, involuntary motor response to sensory stimulation.

interneuron
A neuron that conveys messages between neurons in the brain or spinal cord.

soma
The cell body, the neuron's control center.

dendrites
The branchlike structures of the neuron that receive neural impulses.

▲ **Spinal Cord Damage**
A fall from a horse broke the neck and severed the spinal cord of Christopher Reeve, famous for portraying Superman in several movies. The accident left him a quadriplegic, with little or no feeling or voluntary movement in his limbs.

Imagine that you are playing a tennis match. Your sympathetic nervous system speeds up your heart rate to pump more blood to your muscles, makes your liver release sugar into your bloodstream for quick energy, and induces sweating to keep you from overheating. As you cool down after the match, your parasympathetic nervous system slows your heart rate and constricts the blood vessels in your muscles to divert blood for use by your internal organs. Chapter 12 describes the role of the autonomic nervous system in emotional responses, and Chapter 16 explains how chronic activation of the sympathetic nervous system can contribute to the development of stress-related diseases. To appreciate how the autonomic nervous system and all other parts of the nervous system carry out their functions, you need to understand the workings of the neuron.

STAYING ON TRACK: *The Nervous System*

1. What is behavioral neuroscience?
2. What are the divisions of the nervous system?

Answers to Staying on Track start on p. S-1.

THE NEURON: THE NERVE CELL

You are able to read this page because **sensory neurons** are relaying input from your eyes to your brain. You will be able to turn the page because **motor neurons** from your spinal cord are sending commands from your brain to the muscles of your hand. *Sensory neurons* send messages to the brain or spinal cord. *Motor neurons* send messages to the glands, the cardiac muscle, and the skeletal muscles, as well as to the smooth muscles of the arteries, small intestine, and other internal organs. Illnesses that destroy motor neurons, such as *amyotrophic lateral sclerosis* (also known as Lou Gehrig's disease, after the great baseball player struck down by it), cause muscle paralysis (Leigh & Ray-Chaudhuri, 1994).

The nervous system contains 10 times more *glial cells* than neurons. **Glial cells** provide a physical support structure for the neurons (*glial* comes from the Greek word for "glue"). Glial cells also supply neurons with nutrients, remove neuronal metabolic waste, and help regenerate damaged neurons in the peripheral nervous system. Recent research indicates that glial cells might even facilitate the transmission of messages by neurons (Cornell-Bell et al., 1990).

To appreciate the role of neurons in communication within the nervous system, consider the functions of the *spinal cord*, the long, tubelike structure that is enclosed in the protective spinal column and extends from the brain to the tip of the spine. Neurons in the spinal cord convey sensory messages from the body to the brain and motor messages from the brain to the body. You might know people who have suffered a spinal cord injury in a diving or vehicular accident, causing them to lose the ability to move their limbs or feel bodily sensations below the point of the injury.

In 1730 the English scientist Stephen Hales demonstrated that the spinal cord also plays a role in limb **reflexes.** He decapitated a frog (to eliminate any input from the brain) and then pinched one of its legs. The leg reflexively pulled away. Hales concluded that the pinch had sent a signal to the spinal cord, which in turn sent a signal to the leg, eliciting its withdrawal. We now know that this limb-withdrawal reflex involves sensory neurons that convey signals from the site of stimulation to the spinal cord, where they transmit their signals to **interneurons** in the spinal cord (McCrea, 1992). The interneurons then send signals to motor neurons, which stimulate flexor muscles to contract and pull the limb away from the source of stimulation—making you less susceptible to injury.

To understand how neurons communicate information, you should first become familiar with the structure of the neuron. Figure 3.2 presents a drawing of a neuron showing its major structures, and a photograph of neurons, taken with a microscope. The **soma** (or *cell body*) contains the nucleus, which directs the neuron to act as a nerve cell rather than as a fat cell, a muscle cell, or any other kind of cell. The **dendrites** (from the Greek word for "tree") are short, branching fibers that receive neural impulses. The dendrites are covered

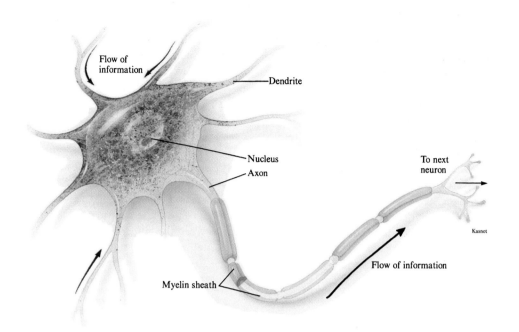

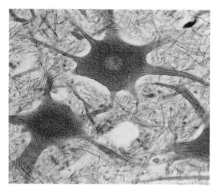

◀ **FIGURE 3.2**
The Neuron
Both the drawing and the photograph show the structure of the motor neuron. Neurons have dendrites that receive signals from other neurons or sensory receptors, a cell body that controls cellular functions, and an axon that conveys signals to skeletal muscles, internal organs, or other neurons.

by bumps called *dendritic spines,* which provide more surface area for the reception of neural impulses from other neurons (Harris & Kater, 1994). The **axon** is a single fiber that sends neural impulses. Axons range from a tiny fraction of an inch (as in the brain) to more than 3 feet in length (as in the legs of a 7-foot-tall basketball player). Just as bundles of wires form telephone cables, bundles of axons form the nerves of the peripheral nervous system. A nerve can contain motor neurons or sensory neurons, or both.

axon

The part of the neuron that conducts neural impulses to glands, muscles, or other neurons.

The Neural Impulse: Sending Messages in the Nervous System

How does the neuron convey information? It took centuries of investigation by some of the most brilliant minds in the history of science to find the answer. Before the neuron was discovered in the nineteenth century, scientists were limited to studying the functions of nerves. In these studies, they typically were influenced by their other research interests.

In the seventeenth century, René Descartes (1596–1650) was intrigued by moving statues in the royal gardens of King Louis XIII, which were controlled hydraulically by fluid-filled tubes that were activated when visitors stepped on hidden levers. For example, when a person approached a statue of a young maiden, she would flee into the bushes. If she was followed, a statue of Neptune would threaten the interloper with his trident. This led Descartes to speculate that the body is controlled in a similar way by fluids, which he called *vital spirits,* flowing through the nerves. He assumed that our limbs move when vital spirits expand the muscles that control them (Wilson, 1967). Descartes was wrong about how muscles function. Though they shorten and thicken when contracted, their overall size remains the same.

The first significant discovery regarding nerve conduction came in 1786, when the Italian physicist Luigi Galvani (1737–1798) gave demonstrations hinting that the nerve impulse is electrical in nature. Galvani found that by touching the leg of a freshly killed frog with two different metals, such as iron and brass, he could create an electrical current that made the leg twitch. He believed he had discovered the basic life force—electricity. Some of Galvani's followers, who hoped to use electricity to raise the dead, obtained the fresh corpses of hanged criminals and stimulated them with electricity. To the disappointment of these would-be resurrectors, they failed to induce more than the flailing of limbs (Hassett, 1978). Not much later, another of Galvani's contemporaries, Mary Shelley, applied what she called "galvanism" (apparently, the use of electricity) to revive the dead in her classic novel, *Frankenstein*.

Though Galvani and his colleagues failed to demonstrate that electricity was the basic life force, they put scientists on the right track toward understanding how neural impulses are conveyed in the nervous system. But it took almost two more centuries of research before scientists identified the exact mechanisms. We now know that neuronal activity, whether involved in hearing a doorbell, throwing a softball, or recalling a childhood memory, depends on electrical-chemical processes, beginning with the *resting potential*.

The Resting Potential: The Quiet Neuron

In 1952, English scientists Alan Hodgkin and Andrew Huxley, using techniques that let them study individual neurons, discovered the electrical-chemical nature of the processes that underlie **axonal conduction,** the transmission of a *neural impulse* along the length of the axon. Hodgkin and Huxley found that in its inactive state, the neuron maintains an electrical **resting potential,** produced by differences between the *intracellular fluid* inside of the neuron and the *extracellular fluid* outside of the neuron. These fluids contain *ions*, which are positively or negatively charged molecules. In regard to the resting potential, the main positive ions are *sodium* and *potassium*, and the main negative ions are *proteins* and *chloride*.

The *neuronal membrane*, which separates the intracellular fluid from the extracellular fluid, is *selectively permeable* to ions. This means that some ions pass back and forth through tiny *ion channels* in the membrane more easily than do others. Because ions with like charges repel each other and ions with opposite charges attract each other, you might assume that the extracellular fluid and intracellular fluid would end up with the same relative concentrations of positive ions and negative ions. But, because of several complex processes, the intracellular fluid ends up with an excess of negative ions and the extracellular fluid ends up with an excess of positive ions. This makes the inside of the resting neuron negative relative to the outside, so the membrane is said to be *polarized*, just like a battery. For example, at rest the inside of a motor neuron has a charge of −70 millivolts relative to its outside. (A millivolt is one thousandth of a volt.)

The Action Potential: The Active Neuron

When a neuron is stimulated sufficiently by other neurons or by a sensory organ, it stops "resting." The neuronal membrane becomes more permeable to positively charged sodium ions, which, attracted by the negative ions inside, rush into the neuron. This makes the inside of the neuron less electrically negative relative to the outside, a process called *depolarization*. As sodium continues to rush into the neuron, and the inside becomes less and less negative, the neuron reaches its *firing threshold* (about −60 millivolts in the case of a motor neuron) and an *action potential* occurs at the point where the axon leaves the cell body.

An **action potential** is a change in the electrical charge across the axonal membrane, with the inside of the membrane becoming more electrically positive than the outside and reaching a charge of +40 millivolts. Once an action potential has occurred, that point on the axonal membrane immediately restores its resting potential through a process called *repolarization*. This occurs, in part, because the sudden excess of positively charged sodium ions inside the axon repels the positive potassium ions, driving many of them out of the axon. This loss of positively charged ions helps return the inside of the axon to its negatively charged state relative to the outside. The restored resting potential is also maintained by chemical "pumps" that transport sodium and potassium ions across the axonal membrane, returning them to their original concentrations. Figure 3.3 illustrates the electrical changes that occur during depolarization and repolarization.

If an axon fails to depolarize enough to reach its firing threshold, no action potential occurs—not even a weak one. If you have ever been under general anesthesia, you became unconscious because you were given a drug that prevented the axons in your brain that are responsible for the maintenance of consciousness from depolarizing enough to fire off action potentials (Nicoll & Madison, 1982). When an axon reaches its firing threshold and an action potential occurs, a neural impulse travels the entire length of the axon at

---

axonal conduction
The transmission of a neural impulse along the length of an axon.

resting potential
The electrical charge of a neuron when it is not firing a neural impulse.

action potential
A series of changes in the electrical charge across the axonal membrane that occurs after the axon has reached its firing threshold.

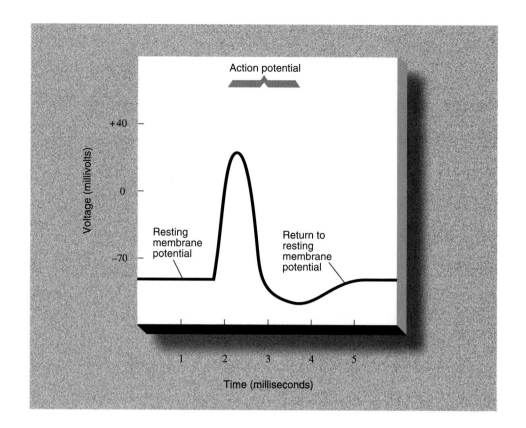

The Action Potential
During an action potential, the inside of the axon becomes electrically positive relative to the outside, but quickly returns to its normal resting state, with the inside again electrically negative relative to the outside.

full strength, as sodium ions rush in at each successive point along the axon. This is known as the **all-or-none law.** It is analogous to firing a gun: If you do not pull the trigger hard enough, nothing happens; but if you do pull the trigger hard enough, the gun fires and a bullet travels down the entire length of its barrel.

Thus, when a neuron reaches its firing threshold, a neural impulse travels along its axon, as each point on the axonal membrane depolarizes (producing an action potential) and then repolarizes (restoring its resting potential). This process of depolarization/repolarization is so rapid that an axon might conduct up to 1,000 neural impulses a second. The loudness of sounds you hear, the strength of your muscle contractions, and the level of arousal of your brain all depend on the number of neurons involved in those processes and the rate at which they conduct neural impulses.

The speed at which the action potential travels along the axon varies from less than 1 meter per second in certain neurons to more than 100 meters per second in others. The speed depends on several factors, most notably whether sheaths of a white fatty substance called **myelin** (which is produced by glial cells) are wrapped around the axon (Miller, 1994). At frequent intervals along myelinated axons, tiny areas are nonmyelinated. These are called *nodes of Ranvier,* after the French anatomist Louis Antoine Ranvier, who first identified them in 1871. In myelinated axons, such as those forming much of the brain and spinal cord, as well as the motor nerves that control our muscles, the action potential jumps from node to node, instead of traveling from point to point along the entire axon. This explains why myelinated axons conduct neural impulses faster than nonmyelinated axons.

If you were to look at a freshly dissected brain, you would find that the inside appeared mostly white and the outside appeared mostly gray, because the inside contains many more myelinated axons. You would be safe in concluding that the brain's *white matter* conveyed information faster than its *gray matter*. Some neurological disorders are associated with abnormal myelin conditions. In the disease *multiple sclerosis*, portions of the myelin sheaths in neurons of the brain and spinal cord are destroyed, causing muscle weakness, sensory disturbances, memory loss, and cognitive deterioration as a result of the disruption of normal axonal conduction (Bennett, Dittmar, & Raubach, 1991).

all-or-none law

The principle that once a neuron reaches its firing threshold, a neural impulse travels at full strength along the entire length of its axon.

myelin

A white fatty substance that forms sheaths around certain axons and increases the speed of neural impulses.

synaptic transmission
The conveying of a neural impulse between a neuron and a gland, muscle, sensory organ, or another neuron.

synapse
The junction between a neuron and a gland, muscle, sensory organ, or another neuron.

neurotransmitters
Chemicals secreted by neurons that provide the means of synaptic transmission.

▲ **Santiago Ramón y Cajal (1852–1934)**
"For all those who are fascinated by the bewitchment of the infinitely small, there wait in the bosom of the living being millions of palpitating cells which, for the surrender of their secret, and with it the halo of fame, demand only a clear and persistent intelligence to contemplate, admire, and understand them."

▲ **Otto Loewi (1873–1961)**
"I got up immediately, went to the laboratory, made the experiment on the frog's heart . . . , and at five o'clock the chemical transmission of nervous impulses was conclusively proved."

To summarize, a neuron maintains a *resting potential* during which its inside is electrically negative relative to its outside. Stimulation of the neuron makes positive sodium ions rush in and *depolarize* the neuron (that is, make the inside less negative relative to the outside). If the neuron depolarizes enough, it reaches its *firing threshold* and an *action potential* occurs. During the action potential, the inside of the neuron becomes electrically positive relative to the outside. Because of the *all-or-none law*, a *neural impulse* is conducted along the entire length of the axon at full strength. Axons covered by a *myelin sheath* conduct impulses faster than other axons. After an action potential has occurred, the axon *repolarizes* and restores its resting potential.

Synaptic Transmission: Communication Between Neurons

If all the neuron did was conduct a series of neural impulses along its axon, we would have an interesting, but useless, phenomenon. The reason why we can see a movie, feel a mosquito bite, think about yesterday, or ride a bicycle is because neurons can communicate with one another by the process of **synaptic transmission**—communication across gaps between neurons.

The Synapse: Neuronal Gaps

The question of how neurons communicate with one another provoked a heated debate in the late nineteenth century. The Italian anatomist Camillo Golgi (1843–1926) led the majority of researchers, who argued that neurons were connected to one another in a network. His rival, the Spanish anatomist Santiago Ramón y Cajal (1852–1934), led the minority, including Sigmund Freud, who argued that neurons were separate from one another (Koppe, 1983). Ramón y Cajal won the debate by using a microscopic technique (ironically, invented by Golgi) to show that neurons do not form a network (Ramón y Cajal, 1937/1966). For their efforts, in 1906 Golgi and Ramón y Cajal shared the Nobel Prize for physiology and medicine. In 1897 the English physiologist Charles Sherrington (1857–1952) had coined the term **synapse** (from the Greek word for "junction") to refer to the gaps that exist between neurons. You should note that synapses also exist between neurons and glands, between neurons and muscles, and between neurons and sensory organs.

As is usually the case with scientific discoveries, the observation that neurons were separated by synapses led to still another question. How could neurons communicate with one another across these gaps? At first, some scientists assumed that the neural impulse simply jumped across the synapse, just as sparks jump across the gap in a spark plug. But the correct answer came in 1921—in a dream.

The dreamer was Otto Loewi (1873–1961), an Austrian physiologist who had been searching without success for the mechanism of synaptic transmission. Loewi awoke from his dream and carried out the experiment it suggested. He removed the beating heart of a freshly killed frog, along with the portion of the *vagus nerve* attached to it, and placed it in a solution of salt water. By electrically stimulating the vagus nerve, he made the heart beat slower. He then put another beating heart in the same solution. Though he had not stimulated its vagus nerve, the second heart also began to beat slower. If you had made this discovery, what would you have concluded? Loewi concluded, correctly, that stimulation of the vagus nerve of the first heart had released a chemical into the solution. It was this chemical, which he later identified as *acetylcholine*, that slowed the beating of both hearts.

Neurotransmitters: The Basis of Synaptic Transmission

Acetylcholine is one of a group of chemicals called **neurotransmitters,** which transmit neural impulses across synapses. Neurotransmitters are stored in round packets called *synaptic vesicles* in the intracellular fluid of bumps called *synaptic knobs* that project from the end branches of axons.

The discovery of the chemical nature of synaptic transmission led to a logical question: How do neurotransmitters facilitate this transmission? Subsequent research revealed the processes involved, which are illustrated in Figure 3.4. First, when a neural impulse

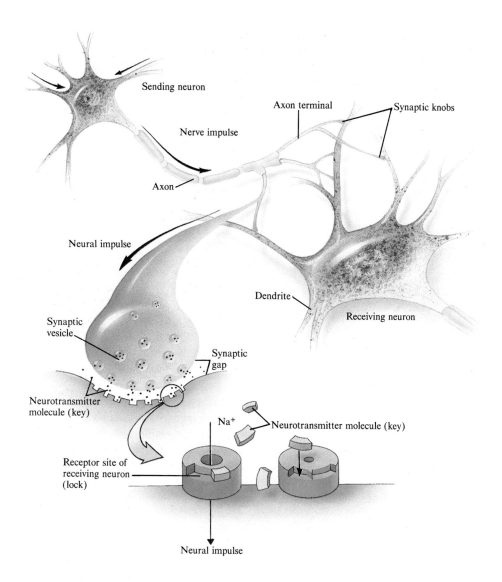

Sending neuron

Nerve impulse

Axon terminal

Synaptic knobs

Axon

Neural impulse

Dendrite

Receiving neuron

Synaptic
vesicle

Synaptic
gap

Neurotransmitter
molecule (key)

Na⁺

Neurotransmitter molecule (key)

Receptor site of
receiving neuron
(lock)

Neural impulse

Synaptic Transmission Between Neurons
When a neural impulse reaches the end of an
axon, it stimulates synaptic vesicles to release
neurotransmitter molecules into the synapse.
The molecules diffuse across the synapse and
interact with receptor sites on another neuron,
causing sodium ions to leak into that neuron.
The molecules then disengage from the receptor
sites and are broken down by enzymes or taken
back into the axon.

reaches the end of an axon, it induces a chemical reaction that makes some synaptic vesicles release neurotransmitter molecules into the synapse. Second, the molecules diffuse
across the synapse and reach the dendrites of another neuron. Third, the molecules attach
to tiny areas on the dendrites called *receptor sites*. Fourth, the molecules interact with the
receptor sites to excite the neuron; this slightly depolarizes the neuron by permitting
sodium ions to enter it. But for a neuron to depolarize enough to reach its firing threshold,
it must be excited by neurotransmitters released by many neurons. To further complicate
the process, a neuron can also be affected by neurotransmitters that inhibit it from depolarizing. Thus, a neuron will fire an action potential only when the combined effects of
excitatory neurotransmitters sufficiently exceed the combined effects of *inhibitory neurotransmitters*. Fifth, neurotransmitters do not remain attached to the receptor sites, continuing to affect them indefinitely. Instead, after the neurotransmitters have done their job,
they are either broken down by chemicals called *enzymes* or taken back into the neurons
that had released them—in a process called *re-uptake*.

　　Of the neurotransmitters, acetylcholine is the best understood. In the peripheral nervous system, it is the neurotransmitter at synapses between the neurons of the parasympathetic nervous system and the organs they control, such as the heart. Acetylcholine also is
the neurotransmitter at synapses between motor neurons and muscle fibers, where it stimulates muscle contractions. *Curare*, a poison that Amazon Indians put on the darts they
shoot from their blowguns, paralyzes muscles by preventing acetylcholine from attaching

▲ **Curare, Acetylcholine, and Hunting**
Natives of the Amazon jungle use curare-tipped
darts to paralyze, and thereby suffocate, their
prey. Curare blocks receptor sites for the neurotransmitter acetylcholine, causing flaccid paralysis of the muscles.

Alzheimer's disease
A brain disorder characterized by difficulty in forming new memories and by general mental deterioration.

Parkinson's disease
A degenerative disease of the dopamine pathway from the substantia nigra, which causes marked disturbances in motor behavior.

endorphins
Neurotransmitters that play a role in pleasure, pain relief, and other functions.

to receptor sites on muscle fibers. The resulting paralysis of muscles, including the breathing muscles, causes death by suffocation.

In the brain, acetylcholine helps regulate memory processes (Fontana, Inouye, & Johnson, 1994). The actions of acetylcholine can be impaired by drugs or diseases. For example, chemicals in marijuana disrupt acetylcholine synapses involved in memory processes, so people who smoke it might have difficulty forming memories (Miller & Branconnier, 1983). **Alzheimer's disease,** a brain disorder common in late adulthood, is associated with the destruction of acetylcholine neurons in the brain. Because Alzheimer's disease is marked by the inability to form new memories, a victim might be able to recall her third birthday party but not what she ate for breakfast this morning. Alzheimer's disease is also associated with severe intellectual and personality deterioration (Karlsson, 1993).

Since the discovery of acetylcholine, dozens of other neurotransmitters have been identified. Your ability to perform smooth voluntary movements depends on brain neurons that secrete the neurotransmitter *dopamine*. **Parkinson's disease,** which is marked by movement disorders, is caused by the destruction of dopamine neurons in the brain (Robertson, 1992). And elevated levels of dopamine activity are found in the serious psychological disorder called *schizophrenia*. Drugs that block dopamine activity alleviate some of the symptoms of schizophrenia (Carlsson, 1988).

Our moods vary with the level of the neurotransmitter *norepinephrine* in the brain. A low level is associated with depression. Many antidepressant drugs work by increasing norepinephrine levels in the brain (Katz et al., 1993). Like norepinephrine, the neurotransmitter *serotonin* is implicated in depression. In fact, people who become so depressed that they try suicide often have unusually low levels of serotonin (Ricci & Wellman, 1990). Drugs that boost the level of serotonin in the nervous system relieve depression (Perry, 1996).

Some neurotransmitters are amino acids. The main inhibitory amino acid neurotransmitter is *gamma aminobutyric acid* (or GABA). GABA promotes muscle relaxation and reduces anxiety. So-called tranquilizers, such as Valium, relieve anxiety by promoting the action of GABA (Breier & Paul, 1990). As discussed in Chapter 7, the main excitatory amino acid neurotransmitter, *glutamic acid,* helps in the formation of memories (Rickard & Ng, 1995).

Another class of neurotransmitters comprises small proteins called *neuropeptides*. The neuropeptide *substance P* has sparked interest because of its apparent role in the transmission of pain impulses, as in migraine headaches (Nakano et al., 1993). During the past few years, neuropeptides called **endorphins** have generated much research and publicity because of their possible roles in relieving pain and inducing feelings of euphoria. The following classic study led scientists to suspect that endorphins existed.

Does the Brain Contain Its Own Opiate Receptors?

Rationale

The endorphin story began in 1973, when Candace Pert and Solomon Snyder of Johns Hopkins University discovered opiate receptors in the brains of animals (Pert & Snyder, 1973). Opiates are pain-relieving drugs (or *narcotics*)—including morphine, codeine, and heroin—derived from the opium poppy. Snyder and Pert became interested in conducting their research after finding hints in previous research studies by other scientists that animals might have opiate receptors.

Method

Pert and Snyder removed the brains of mice, rats, and guinea pigs. Samples of brain tissue were then treated with radioactive morphine and naloxone, a chemical similar in structure to morphine that blocks morphine's effects. A special device detected whether the morphine and naloxone had attached to receptors in the brain tissue.

Results and Discussion

Pert and Snyder found that the chemicals had bound to specific receptors (opiate receptors). If you had been a member of Pert and Snyder's research team, what would you have inferred from this observation? Pert and Snyder inferred that the brain must manufacture its own opiatelike chemicals. This would explain why it had evolved opiate receptors, and it seemed a more likely explanation than that the receptors had evolved to take advantage of the availability of opiates such as morphine, codeine, and heroin in the environment. Pert and Snyder's findings inspired the search for opiatelike chemicals in the brain. The search bore fruit in Scotland when Hans Kosterlitz and his colleagues found an opiatelike chemical in brain tissue taken from animals (Hughes et al., 1975). They called this chemical enkephalin (from Greek terms meaning "in the head"). Enkephalin and similar chemicals discovered in the brain were later dubbed "endogenous morphine" (meaning "morphine from within"). This was then abbreviated into the now-popular term *endorphin*. Endorphins function as both neurotransmitters and *neuromodulators*—neurochemicals that affect the activity of other neurotransmitters. For example, endorphins serves as neuromodulators by inhibiting the release of substance P, thereby blocking pain impulses.

▲ **Candace Pert**
"Our brains probably have natural counterparts for just about any drug you could name."

Once researchers had located the receptor sites for the endorphins and had isolated endorphins themselves, they then wondered, Why has the brain evolved its own opiatelike neurochemicals? Perhaps the first animals blessed with endorphins were better able to function in the face of pain caused by diseases or injuries, making them more likely to survive long enough to reproduce and pass this physical trait on to successive generations (Levinthal, 1988). Evidence supporting this speculation has come from both human and animal experiments.

In one experiment, researchers first recorded how long mice would allow their tails to be exposed to radiant heat from a lightbulb before the pain made them flick their tails away from it. Those mice were then paired with more aggressive mice, who attacked and defeated them. The losers' tolerance for the radiant heat was then tested again. The results showed that the length of time the defeated mice would permit their tails to be heated had increased, which suggests that the aggressive attacks had raised their endorphin levels. But when the defeated mice were given naloxone, which (as mentioned earlier) blocks the effects of morphine, they flicked away their tails as quickly as they had done before being defeated. The researchers concluded that the naloxone had blocked the pain-relieving effects of the endorphins (Miczek, Thompson, & Shuster, 1982). Other studies have found that the endorphins also are associated with pain relief in human beings—including children (Bachiocco, Gentili, & Bartoluzzi, 1995).

Endorphin levels rise in response to vigorous exercise, perhaps accounting for the "exercise high" reported by many athletes, including runners, swimmers, and bicyclists. This was supported by a study that found increased endorphin levels after aerobic dancing (Pierce et al., 1993). Further support came from a study of bungee jumpers. After jumping,

▲ **The Runner's High**
The euphoric "exercise high" experienced by long-distance runners, such as Romanian Anuta Catuna (shown winning the 1996 New York City Marathon), might be caused by the release of endorphins in the brain.

▶ FIGURE 3.5
The Endocrine System
Hormones secreted by the endocrine glands affect metabolism, behavior, and mental processes.

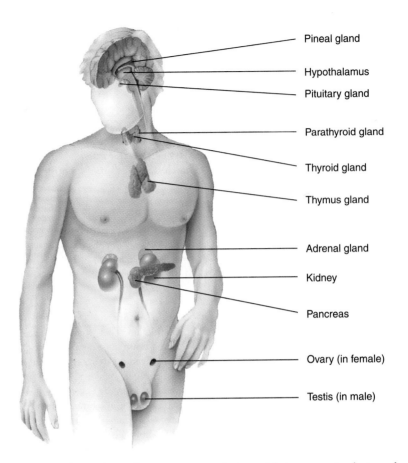

- Pineal gland
- Hypothalamus
- Pituitary gland
- Parathyroid gland
- Thyroid gland
- Thymus gland
- Adrenal gland
- Kidney
- Pancreas
- Ovary (in female)
- Testis (in male)

their feelings of euphoria showed a positive correlation with increases in their endorphin levels (Hennig, Laschefski, & Opper, 1994).

STAYING ON TRACK: *The Neuron*

1. What are the major structures of the neuron?
2. What is the basic process underlying neural impulses?

THE ENDOCRINE SYSTEM: HORMONAL REGULATION OF BODILY PROCESSES

Neurotransmitters are not the only chemical messengers. There are also **hormones,** which are chemicals secreted by glands in the **endocrine system.** The endocrine glands secrete hormones into the bloodstream, which transports them to their sites of action. This contrasts with *exocrine glands*, such as the sweat glands and salivary glands, which secrete their chemicals onto the body surface or into body cavities. Endocrine secretions have many behavioral effects, but exocrine secretions have few. The behavioral effects of exocrine secretions called *pheromones* are discussed in Chapter 5. Figure 3.5 illustrates the locations of several endocrine glands. Hormones can act directly on body tissues, serve as neurotransmitters, or modulate the effects of neurotransmitters.

The Pituitary Gland: The Master Gland

The **pituitary gland,** an endocrine gland protruding from underneath the brain, regulates many of the other endocrine glands by secreting hormones that affect their activity. This is why the pituitary is known as the "master gland." The pituitary gland, in turn, is regulated by the brain structure called the *hypothalamus*. Feedback from circulating hormones stimulates the hypothalamus to signal the pituitary gland to increase or decrease their secretion. Table 3.1 summarizes the functions of some major hormones.

hormones
Chemicals, secreted by endocrine glands, that play a role in a variety of functions, including synaptic transmission.

endocrine system
Glands that secrete hormones into the bloodstream.

pituitary gland
An endocrine gland that regulates many of the other endocrine glands by secreting hormones that affect the secretion of their hormones.

Gland	Hormone	Function
Hypothalamus	Releasing hormones	The hypothalamus is a brain structure that regulates the release of pituitary hormones
Pituitary Anterior (front lobe)	Adrenocorticotropic hormone (ACTH)	Stimulates hormone secretion by the adrenal cortex
	Gonadotropic hormones	Regulate the gonads (testes and ovaries)
	Growth hormone	Stimulates growth
	Prolactin	Stimulates milk production in nursing women
	Thyroid-stimulating hormone	Stimulates hormone secretion by the thyroid gland
Posterior (rear lobe)	Vasopressin	Promotes water retention by the kidneys, and plays a role in the formation of memories
	Oxytocin	Stimulates contractions of the uterus during labor and secretion of milk during nursing
Adrenal Cortex (outer layer)	Aldosterone	Regulates excretion of sodium and potassium
	Cortisol	Regulates metabolism and response to stress
Medulla (inner layer)	Epinephrine and norepinephrine	Contribute to physiological arousal associated with activation of the sympathetic nervous system
Gonads Testes	Testosterone	Regulates development of the male reproductive system, secondary sex characteristics, and sex drive
Ovaries	Estrogens	Regulate development of the female reproductive system and secondary sex characteristics
	Progesterone	Regulates changes in the uterus to maintain pregnancy
Kidneys	Renin	Regulates aldosterone secretion and blood pressure
Pancreas	Insulin	Decreases blood sugar
	Glucagon	Increases blood sugar
Thyroid	Thyroxin	Regulates metabolism and growth
Pineal	Melatonin	Regulates arousal and biological rhythms

▲ TABLE 3.1
Functions of the Major Hormones

Pituitary hormones also exert a wide variety of direct effects. For example, *prolactin* stimulates milk production in nursing women. Because an elevated prolactin level is also associated with both infertility and psychological stress, prolactin might be involved in stress-related infertility. This indicates that women who are highly anxious about their inability to become pregnant might enter a vicious cycle in which their anxiety increases the level of prolactin, which in turn makes them less likely to conceive (Edelmann & Golombok, 1989). This might explain anecdotal reports of couples who, after repeatedly failing to conceive a child, finally adopt a child, only to have the woman become pregnant soon after—perhaps because her anxiety decreased after the adoption.

Growth hormone, another pituitary hormone, aids the growth and repair of bones and muscles. A child who secretes too much growth hormone might develop *giantism*, marked by excessive growth of the bones. A child who secretes insufficient growth hormone might develop *dwarfism*, marked by stunted growth. Giantism and dwarfism do not impair intellectual development. Though it might seem logical to administer growth hormone to increase the height of very short children who are not dwarfs, this is unwise because the long-term side effects are unknown (Tauer, 1994).

Other Endocrine Glands

Among the other psychologically important endocrine glands are the *adrenal glands* and the *gonads.* The **adrenal glands,** which lie on the kidneys, secrete important hormones. The *adrenal cortex,* the outer layer of the adrenal gland, secretes hormones, such as *aldosterone,* that regulate the excretion of sodium and potassium, which contribute to proper neural functioning. The adrenal cortical hormone *cortisol* helps the body respond to stress by stimulating the liver to release sugar. Cortisol also reduces pain from injuries by reducing swelling (Watanabe & Bruera, 1994).

In response to stimulation by the sympathetic nervous system, the *adrenal medulla,* the inner core of the adrenal gland, secretes *epinephrine* and *norepinephrine,* which function as both hormones and neurotransmitters. Epinephrine increases heart rate; as noted earlier, norepinephrine is the neurotransmitter at synapses in the sympathetic nervous system that arouse the body to take action. For example, married people show increases in epinephrine and norepinephrine during conflicts with their spouses (Malarkey et al., 1994).

The **gonads,** the sex glands, affect sexual development and behavior. The **testes,** the male gonads, secrete *testosterone,* which regulates the development of the male reproductive system and secondary sex characteristics. The **ovaries,** the female gonads, secrete *estrogens,* which regulate the development of the female reproductive system and secondary sex characteristics. The ovarian hormone *progesterone* regulates changes in the uterus that maintain pregnancy. The effects of sex hormones, including their possible role in psychological sex differences (Berenbaum & Snyder, 1995), are discussed in Chapters 4 and 11.

Anabolic steroids, synthetic forms of testosterone, have provoked controversy during the past two decades. They have been used by athletes, bodybuilders, and weightlifters to promote muscle development, increase endurance, and boost self-confidence. Yet studies have shown inconsistent effects of steroids on physical strength (VanHelder, Kofman, & Tremblay, 1991). For example, it is unclear whether anabolic steroids directly increase strength or do so through a placebo effect, in which users work out more regularly and more vigorously simply because they have faith in the effectiveness of steroids. Moreover, a dangerous side effect of anabolic steroid use is increased aggressiveness. For example, male weightlifters who go on and off steroids are more verbally and physically abusive toward their wives and girlfriends when they are using steroids than when they are not (Choi & Pope, 1994).

STAYING ON TRACK: *The Endocrine System*

1. What is the difference between exocrine glands and endocrine glands?
2. What are the effects and side effects of anabolic steroids?

THE BRAIN: WHERE FANCY IS BRED

"Tell me, where is fancy bred, in the heart or in the head?" (*The Merchant of Venice,* act 3, scene 2). The answer to this question from Shakespeare's play might be obvious to you. You know that your brain, and not your heart, is your feeling organ—the site of your mind. But you have the advantage of centuries of research, which have made the role of the brain in all psychological processes obvious even to nonscientists. Of course, the cultural influence of early beliefs may linger. Just imagine the response of a person who received a gift of Valentine's Day candy in a box that was brain-shaped instead of heart-shaped.

The ancient Egyptians associated the mind with the heart and discounted the importance of the apparently inactive brain. In fact, when the pharoah Tutankhamen ("King Tut") was mummified to prepare him for the afterlife, his heart and other bodily organs were carefully preserved, but his brain was discarded. The Greek philosopher Aristotle (384–322 B.C.) also believed that the heart was the site of the mind, because when the heart stops, mental activity stops (Laver, 1972). But the Greek physician-philosopher

---

adrenal glands
Endocrine glands that secrete hormones that regulate the excretion of minerals and the body's response to stress.

gonads
The male and female sex glands.

testes
The male gonads, which secrete hormones that regulate the development of the male reproductive system and secondary sex characteristics.

ovaries
The female gonads, which secrete hormones that regulate the development of the female reproductive system and secondary sex characteristics.

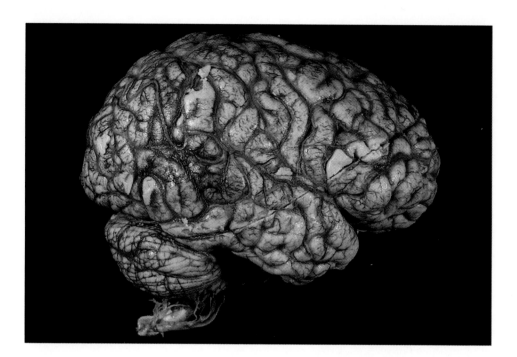

Hippocrates (460–377 B.C.), based on his observations of the effects of brain damage, did locate the mind in the brain:

▶ Some people say that the heart is the organ with which we think and that it feels pain and anxiety. But it is not so. Men ought to know that from the brain and from the brain alone arise our pleasures, joys, laughter, and tears. (quoted in Penfield, 1975, p. 7)

Does this mean that Hippocrates was brilliant and Aristotle foolish? On the contrary, each used the tools available to him—observation and reason—to come to logical, intelligent conclusions. Had subsequent research supported Aristotle's position, we would credit him with the foresight that we now credit to Hippocrates. As noted in Chapter 1, we should be aware of the pitfalls of *presentism* in evaluating the past.

Functions of the Brain

The human brain's appearance does not hint at its complexity. Holding it in your hands, you might not be impressed by either its 3-pound weight or its walnutlike surface. You might be more impressed to learn that it contains billions of neurons. And you might be astounded to learn that any given brain neuron might communicate with thousands of others, leading to an enormous number of pathways for messages to follow in the brain.

As you read this section, you will find that much of what we know about the brain comes from studies of the effects of brain damage, electrical stimulation of the brain, recording of the electricity produced by brain activity, and computer scanning of the brain. As an example, consider the **electroencephalograph (EEG),** which records the patterns of electrical activity produced by neuronal activity in the brain. The EEG has a peculiar history, going back to a day at the turn of the century when an Austrian scientist named Hans Berger fell off a horse and narrowly escaped serious injury. That evening he received a telegram informing him that his sister felt he was in danger.

The telegram inspired Berger to investigate the possible association between *mental telepathy* (the alleged, though scientifically unverified, ability of one mind to communicate with another by extrasensory means) and electrical activity from the brain. In 1924, after years of experimenting on animals and his son Klaus, Berger succeeded in perfecting a procedure for recording electrical activity in the brain. He attached small metal disks called *electrodes* to Klaus's scalp and connected them with wires to a device that recorded changes in the patterns of electrical activity in his brain.

electroencephalograph (EEG)
A device used to record patterns of electrical activity produced by neuronal activity in the brain.

The Structure of the Human Brain
The structures of the hindbrain, midbrain, and forebrain serve a variety of life-support, sensorimotor, and cognitive functions.

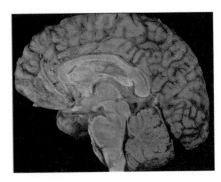

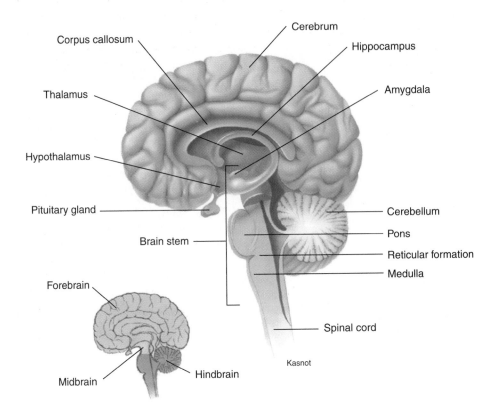

Corpus callosum
Cerebrum
Hippocampus
Thalamus
Amygdala
Hypothalamus
Pituitary gland
Cerebellum
Pons
Brain stem
Reticular formation
Medulla
Spinal cord
Kasnot
Forebrain
Midbrain
Hindbrain

medulla oblongata (medulla)

A hindbrain structure that regulates breathing, heart rate, blood pressure, and other life functions.

Though Berger failed to find physiological evidence in support of mental telepathy, he found that specific patterns of brain activity are associated with specific mental states, such as coma, sleep, and wakefulness (Gloor, 1994). He also identified two distinct rhythms of electrical activity. He called the relatively slow rhythm associated with a relaxed mental state the *alpha rhythm* and the relatively fast rhythm associated with an alert, active mental state the *beta rhythm*. Berger also used the EEG to provide the first demonstration of the stimulating effect of cocaine on brain activity. He found that cocaine increased the relative proportion of the beta rhythm in EEG recordings (Herning, 1985).

Berger's method of correlating EEG activity with psychological processes is still used today. In one study, for example, researchers determined the EEG patterns that accompanied mental fatigue in white-collar workers. The ultimate aim of the researchers was to maximize workers' productivity by determining the optimal length of work periods and rest breaks (Okogbaa, Shell, & Filipusic, 1994). The EEG and other devices have permitted scientists to unlock many of the brain's secrets. Figure 3.6 illustrates the major structures of the *hindbrain, midbrain,* and *forebrain.*

Functions of the Hindbrain

Your ability to survive from moment to moment depends on your hindbrain, located at the base of the brain. The hindbrain includes the *medulla,* the *pons,* the *cerebellum,* and the *reticular formation.*

The Medulla. Of all the hindbrain structures, the most crucial to your survival is the **medulla oblongata** (or, simply, the **medulla**), which connects the brain and spinal cord. At this moment your medulla is regulating your breathing, heart rate, and blood pressure. Because the medulla controls so many vital functions, damage to it can be fatal, as in the 1968 assassination of presidential candidate Robert Kennedy, who was shot through the medulla. When called upon, your medulla also stimulates coughing, vomiting, or swallowing. By inducing vomiting, for example, the medulla prevents people who drink too much alcohol too fast from poisoning themselves.

The Pons. Just above the medulla lies the bulbous structure called the **pons.** As explained in Chapter 6, the pons helps regulate the sleep-wake cycle through its effect on consciousness. Sleep disorders are sometimes associated with abnormal activity in the pons (Culebras & Moore, 1989). And if you have ever been the unfortunate recipient of a blow to the head that knocked you out, your loss of consciousness was caused by the blow's effect on your pons (Hayes et al., 1984).

pons
A hindbrain structure that regulates the sleep-wake cycle.

The Cerebellum. The pons (which means "bridge" in Latin) connects the **cerebellum** (meaning "little brain") to the rest of the brain. The cerebellum controls the timing of well-learned sequences of movements that are too rapid to be controlled consciously, as in running a sprint, singing a song, or playing the piano (Grossberg & Merrill, 1996). As you know from your own experience, conscious efforts to control normally automatic sequences of movements such as these can disrupt them. Pianists who think of each key they are striking while playing a well-practiced piece would be unable to maintain proper timing. Recent research indicates that the cerebellum may even affect the smooth timing and sequencing of mental activities, such as the use of language (Ito, 1993).

cerebellum
A hindbrain structure that controls the timing of well-learned movements.

The Reticular Formation. Passing from the hindbrain through the midbrain and into the forebrain is the **reticular formation,** a diffuse network of neurons that helps regulate vigilance and brain arousal. The role of the reticular formation in maintaining vigilance is shown by the "cocktail party phenomenon," in which you can be engrossed in a conversation but still notice when someone elsewhere in the room says something of significance to you, such as your name. Thus, the reticular formation acts as a filter, letting you attend to an important stimulus while ignoring irrelevant ones.

reticular formation
A diffuse network of neurons, extending from the hindbrain through the midbrain and into the forebrain, that helps maintain vigilance and an optimal level of brain arousal.

Experimental evidence supporting the role of the reticular formation in brain arousal came from a study by Giuseppe Moruzzi and Horace Magoun in which they awakened sleeping cats by electrically stimulating the reticular formation (Moruzzi & Magoun, 1949). Damage to the reticular formation, sometimes caused by drug overdoses, can induce a permanent coma, as may have occurred two decades ago in the widely publicized case of Karen Ann Quinlan, who lived on a respirator—unconscious—for years before her parents won the legal right to remove it.

Functions of the Midbrain

The *midbrain* is a relatively small region in mammalian brains (though it is relatively large in bird, reptile, and amphibian brains). It contains the *tectum* and the *substantia nigra*.

The Tectum. Forming the roof of the midbrain is a structure called the **tectum,** which mediates adaptive, reflexive responses to visual and auditory stimuli. For example, your startle response to a sudden noise is mediated by the tectum (Parham & Willott, 1990), as is your ability to localize sounds (Kelly & Kavanagh, 1994). To appreciate the adaptive function of the tectum, suppose that a hidden prankster throws a snowball at your head. By responding to input from your eyes, the tectum would detect the snowball and prompt you to duck your head before you even realized that the object was a snowball.

tectum
A midbrain structure that mediates reflexive responses to visual and auditory stimuli.

The tectum also helps identify stimuli, even enabling bats to find insects to eat. The bat's sonar system emits sound waves that strike flying insects, creating echoes that differ according to their wingbeat patterns. The tectum then helps the bat identify the insect by analyzing the distinctive pattern of echoes it produces (Pollak, Wenstrup, & Fuzessey, 1986).

The Substantia Nigra. The graceful movements of gymnasts, ballet dancers, and trapeze artists depend on the midbrain structure called the **substantia nigra,** which acts in conjunction with other brain structures to promote smooth voluntary movements. Less-dramatic abilities, such as writing and walking, that require smooth movements also rely on the substantia nigra. Many older adults who suffer from Parkinson's disease, caused by degeneration of dopamine neurons in the substantia nigra, have difficulty performing even these simple acts. Victims of Parkinson's disease tend to have a blank facial expression, walk with a shuffling gait, and exhibit hand tremors when simply holding an object, such as a cup

substantia nigra
A midbrain structure that promotes smooth voluntary body movements.

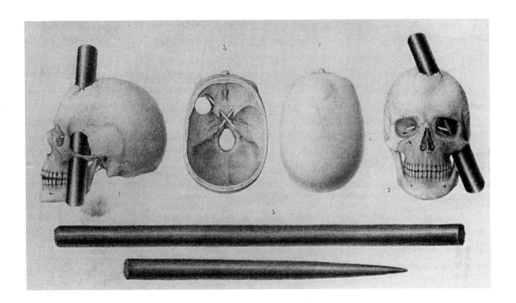

of coffee. They also may have marked difficulty in initiating movements. Because Parkinson's symptoms are caused by a dopamine deficit, the treatment of choice has been administration of the drug *L-dopa*, which is converted into dopamine in the brain (Chase et al., 1995).

Functions of the Forebrain

Above the hindbrain and midbrain is the *forebrain*, which serves the "higher functions" of thinking, learning, memory, emotion, and personality. The forebrain helps you adapt to changes in the environment by integrating information from your senses and your memory. Some of the evidence supporting the importance of the forebrain in emotion and personality has come from case studies of people with damage to it, most notably the case of Phineas Gage (Harlow, 1993). On a fall day in 1848, Gage, the 25-year-old foreman of a Vermont railroad crew laying track, was clearing away rocks. While he was using an iron tamping rod to pack a gunpowder charge into a boulder, a spark ignited the gunpowder. The resulting explosion hurled the rod into Gage's left cheek, through his forebrain, and out the top of his skull.

Miraculously, Gage survived, recuperated, and lived 12 more years, with little impairment of his intellectual abilities. But there were dramatic changes in his personality and emotionality. Instead of remaining the friendly, popular, hardworking man he had been before the accident, he became an ornery, disliked, irresponsible bully. Gage's friends believed he had changed so radically that "he was no longer Gage."

The case study of Phineas Gage implies that the forebrain structures damaged by the tamping rod might be important in emotion and personality. But, as explained in Chapter 2, it is impossible to determine causality from a case study. Perhaps Gage's emotional and personality changes were caused not by the brain damage itself, but instead by Gage's psychological response to his traumatic accident or by changes in how other people responded to him. Nonetheless, the forebrain's importance in emotion and personality has been supported by subsequent scientific research (Stuss, Gow, & Hetherington, 1992). The major structures of the forebrain include the *thalamus*, the *limbic system*, and the *cerebral cortex*.

The Thalamus. Located at the center of the forebrain is the egg-shaped **thalamus.** (The portion of the brain extending from the medulla through the thalamus is called the *brain stem*.) The thalamus functions as a sensory relay station, sending taste, bodily, visual, and auditory sensations on to other areas of the brain for further processing. The visual information from this page is being relayed by your thalamus to areas of your brain that process vision. The one sense whose information is not relayed through the thalamus is smell. Sensory information from smell receptors in the nose goes directly to areas of the brain that process odors.

thalamus

A forebrain structure that acts as a sensory relay station for taste, body, visual, and auditory sensations.

CHAPTER 3

The Limbic System. Surrounding the thalamus is a group of forebrain structures that compose the **limbic system.** The word *limbic* comes from the Latin for "border," indicating that the limbic structures form a border between the left and right halves of the brain (Schiller, 1979). The limbic system interacts with other brain structures to promote the survival of the individual and, as a result, the continuation of the species. Major components of the limbic system include the *hypothalamus,* the *amygdala,* and the *hippocampus.*

Just below the thalamus, on the underside of the forebrain, lies the **hypothalamus** (in Greek the prefix *hypo-* means "below"), a structure that is important to a host of functions. The hypothalamus helps regulate eating, drinking, emotion, sexual behavior, and body temperature. It exerts its influence by regulating the secretion of hormones by the pituitary gland and by signals sent along neurons to bodily organs controlled by the autonomic nervous system.

The importance of the hypothalamus in emotionality was discovered by accident. Psychologists James Olds and Peter Milner (1954) of McGill University in Montreal inserted fine wire electrodes into the brains of rats to study the effects of electrical stimulation of the reticular formation. They had already trained the rats to press a lever to obtain food rewards. When a wired rat now pressed the lever, it obtained mild electrical stimulation of its brain. To the experimenters' surprise, the rats, even when hungry or thirsty, ignored food and water in favor of pressing the lever—sometimes thousands of times an hour, until they dropped from exhaustion up to 24 hours later (Olds, 1956). Olds and Milner examined brain tissue from the rats and discovered that they had mistakenly inserted the electrodes near the hypothalamus and not into the reticular formation. They concluded that they had discovered a "pleasure center." Later research studies showed that the hypothalamus is but one structure in an interconnected group of brain structures that induce feelings of pleasure when stimulated.

The **amygdala** of the limbic system continuously evaluates information from the immediate environment and helps elicit appropriate emotional responses (Aggleton, 1992). If you saw a pit bull dog running toward you, your amygdala would help you quickly decide whether the dog was vicious, friendly, or simply roaming around. Depending on your evaluation of the situation, you might feel happy and pet the dog, feel afraid and jump on top of your desk, or feel relief and go back to studying.

In the late 1930s, Heinrich Klüver and Paul Bucy (1937) found that lesions of the amygdala in monkeys led to "psychic blindness," an inability to evaluate environmental stimuli properly. The monkeys indiscriminately examined objects by mouth, tried to mate with members of other species, and acted fearless when confronted by a snake. Human beings who suffer amygdala damage may also exhibit symptoms of the Klüver-Bucy syndrome, such as a failure to recognize the emotions being conveyed by facial expressions (Adolphs et al., 1994).

In 1966 the amygdala was implicated in the notorious Texas tower massacre (Holmes, 1986), in which a young man named Charles Whitman shot randomly at people on the campus of the University of Texas, killing 16 and wounding 31. He shot most of his victims from the roof of the main administration building before dying in a shoot-out with police. In a diary found after his death, Whitman complained of overwhelming homicidal impulses. An autopsy of his brain discovered that he had a tumor of the amygdala. Were police, physicians, and reporters right in attributing his murderous rampage to this tumor? Possibly; though once again you must be careful not to confuse correlation with causation. Perhaps the presence of the tumor and Whitman's rampage were purely coincidental.

While your amygdala helps you evaluate information from your environment, the limbic system structure that is most important in helping you form memories of that information (including what you are now reading) is the **hippocampus** (Maren & Baudry, 1995). Much of what we know about the hippocampus comes from case studies of people who have suffered damage to it. The most famous study is of a man known as "H. M." (Scoville & Milner, 1957), whose hippocampus was surgically removed in 1953 to relieve his uncontrollable epileptic seizures. Since the surgery, H. M. has formed few new memories, though he can recall events that occurred before his surgery. You can read more about the implications of his case in regard to memory in Chapter 7. Damage to the

limbic system

A group of forebrain structures that, through their influence on emotion, motivation, and memory, promote the survival of the individual and, as a result, the continuation of the species.

hypothalamus

A forebrain structure that, through its effects on the pituitary gland and the autonomic nervous system, helps to regulate aspects of motivation and emotion, including eating, drinking, sexual behavior, body temperature, and stress responses.

amygdala

A limbic system structure that evaluates information from the immediate environment, contributing to feelings of fear, anger, or relief.

hippocampus

A limbic system structure that contributes to the formation of memories.

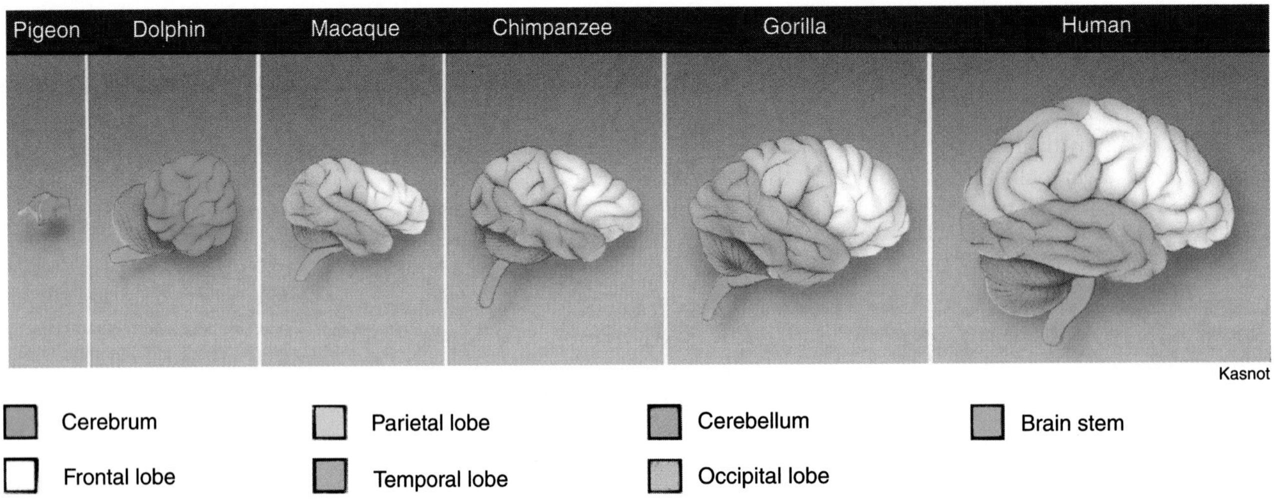

| Pigeon | Dolphin | Macaque | Chimpanzee | Gorilla | Human |

Kasnot

■ Cerebrum ■ Parietal lobe ■ Cerebellum ■ Brain stem

□ Frontal lobe ■ Temporal lobe ■ Occipital lobe

▲ **FIGURE 3.7**
The Evolution of the Brain
Animals that are more cognitively complex have evolved brains that are larger in proportion to their body sizes. Their cerebral cortex is also larger in proportion to the size of their other brain structures, which creates a more convoluted brain surface.

cerebral cortex
The outer covering of the forebrain.

cerebral hemispheres
The left and right halves of the cerebrum.

primary cortical areas
Regions of the cerebral cortex that serve motor or sensory functions.

association areas
Regions of the cerebral cortex that integrate information from the primary cortical areas and other brain areas.

frontal lobe
A lobe of the cerebral cortex responsible for motor control and higher mental processes.

motor cortex
The area of the frontal lobes that controls specific voluntary body movements.

hippocampus has been implicated in the memory loss associated with Alzheimer's disease. Victims of this disease suffer from degeneration of the neurons that serve as pathways between the hippocampus and other brain areas.

Cerebral Cortex. Covering the forebrain is the crowning achievement of brain evolution—the **cerebral cortex.** Cortex means "bark" in Latin. And just as the bark is the outer layer of the tree, the cerebral cortex is the thin, 3-millimeter-thick outer layer of the uppermost portion of the forebrain called the *cerebrum.* The cerebral cortex of human beings and other mammals has evolved folds called *convolutions,* which, as shown in Figure 3.7, give it the appearance of kneaded dough. The convolutions permit more cerebral cortex to fit inside the skull. This is necessary because evolution has assigned so many complex brain functions to the mammalian cerebral cortex that the brain has, in a sense, outgrown the skull in which it resides. If the cerebral cortex were smooth instead of convoluted, the human brain would have to be enormous to permit the same amount of surface area. The brain would be encased in a skull so large that it would give us the appearance of creatures from science fiction movies.

The cerebrum is divided into left and right halves called the **cerebral hemispheres.** Figure 3.8 shows that the cerebral cortex covering each hemisphere is divided into four regions, or *lobes:* the *frontal lobe,* the *temporal lobe,* the *parietal lobe,* and the *occipital lobe.* The lobes have **primary cortical areas** that serve motor or sensory functions. The lobes also have **association areas** that integrate information from the primary cortical areas and other brain areas in activities such as speaking, problem solving, and recognizing objects. The unusually large association areas of the human cerebral cortex provide more area for processing information. This contributes to human beings' greater flexibility in adapting to diverse circumstances (Killackey, 1990).

With the layout of the cerebral cortex in mind, you are ready to begin a tour of its lobes. Your tour begins in 1870, when the German physicians Gustav Fritsch and Eduard Hitzig (1870/1960) published their findings that electrical stimulation of a strip of cerebral cortex along the rear border of the right or left **frontal lobe** of a dog induces limb movements on the opposite side of the body. This is known as *contralateral control.* The area they stimulated is called the **motor cortex.** They were probably the first to demonstrate conclusively that specific sites on the cerebral cortex control specific body movements (Breathnach, 1992).

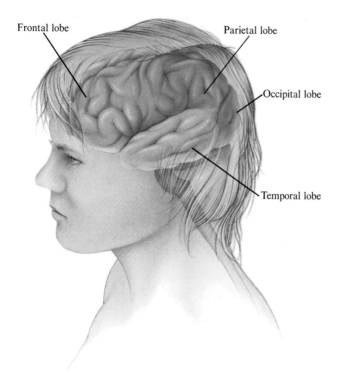

Frontal lobe

Parietal lobe

Occipital lobe

Temporal lobe

◄ FIGURE 3.8
The Lobes of the Brain
The cerebral cortex covering each cerebral hemisphere is divided into four lobes: the frontal lobe, the temporal lobe, the parietal lobe, and the occipital lobe.

Figure 3.9 presents a "map" of the motor cortex of the frontal lobe, represented by a *motor homunculus* (*homunculus* is a Latin term meaning "small human"). Each area of the motor cortex controls a particular contralateral body movement. Certain sites on the motor cortex even show activity merely in anticipation of particular arm movements (Alexander & Crutcher, 1990). Note that the motor homunculus is upside down, with the head represented at the bottom and the feet represented at the top. You might also be struck by the disproportionate sizes of the body parts on the motor homunculus—each body part is represented in proportion to the precision of its movements, not in proportion to its actual size. Because your fingers move with great precision in manipulating objects, the region of the motor cortex devoted to your fingers is disproportionately large relative to the regions devoted to body parts that move with less precision, such as your arms.

The primary cortical areas of the frontal lobes control movements; the primary cortical areas of the other lobes process sensory information. You will notice in Figure 3.9 that the primary cortical area of the **parietal lobes** runs parallel to the motor cortex of the frontal lobes. This area is called the **somatosensory cortex,** because it processes information related to bodily senses such as pain, touch, and temperature. Similarly to the motor cortex, certain sites on it respond when the individual merely anticipates being touched (Drevets et al., 1995). As in the case of the motor cortex, the somatosensory cortex forms a distorted, upside-down homunculus of the body and receives input from the opposite side of the body. Each body part is represented on the *sensory homunculus* in proportion to its sensory precision rather than its size. This is why the region devoted to your highly sensitive lips is disproportionately large relative to the region devoted to your less sensitive back.

How do we know that a motor homunculus and a sensory homunculus exist on the cerebral cortex? We know because of research conducted by neurosurgeon Wilder Penfield (1891–1976), of the Montreal Neurological Institute, in the course of brain surgery to remove defective tissue causing epileptic seizures. Of his many contributions, his most important was the "Montreal procedure" for surgically removing scar tissue that caused epilepsy. In applying the procedure, he made the first use of Hans Berger's EEG, by comparing brain activity before and after surgery to see if it had been successful in abolishing the abnormal brain activity that had triggered his patients' seizures.

parietal lobe
A lobe of the cerebral cortex responsible for processing bodily sensations and perceiving spatial relations.

somatosensory cortex
The area of the parietal lobes that processes information from sensory receptors in the skin.

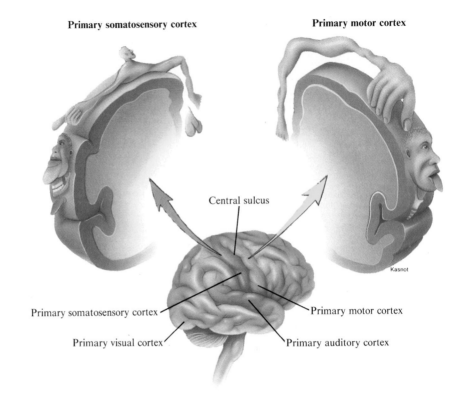

▶ **FIGURE 3.9**
The Motor Cortex and the Somatosensory Cortex
Both the motor cortex and the somatosensory cortex form distorted, upside-down maps of the contralateral side of the body.

Primary somatosensory cortex

Primary motor cortex

Central sulcus

Kasnot

Primary somatosensory cortex

Primary motor cortex

Primary visual cortex

Primary auditory cortex

temporal lobe
A lobe of the cerebral cortex responsible for processing hearing.

auditory cortex
The area of the temporal lobes that processes sounds.

occipital lobe
A lobe of the cerebral cortex responsible for processing vision.

visual cortex
The area of the occipital lobes that processes visual input.

▲ Wilder Penfield (1891–1976)
"The mind remains, still, a mystery that science has not solved."

In using the Montreal procedure, Penfield made an incision through the scalp, sawed through a portion of the skull, and removed a large flap of bone—exposing the cerebral cortex. His patients required only a local anesthetic at the site of the scalp and skull incisions, because incisions in the brain itself do not cause pain. This let the patients remain awake during surgery and converse with him.

Penfield then administered a weak electrical current to the exposed cerebral cortex. He did so for two reasons. First, he wanted to induce an *aura* that would indicate the site that triggered the patient's seizures. An aura is a sensation (such as an unusual odor) that precedes a seizure. Second, he wanted to avoid cutting through parts of the cerebral cortex that serve important functions.

Penfield found that stimulation of a point on the right frontal lobe might make the left forefinger rise, and that stimulation of a point on the left parietal lobe might make the patient report a tingling feeling in the right foot. After stimulating points across the entire cerebral cortex of many patients, Penfield found that the regions governing movement and bodily sensations formed the distorted upside-down maps of the body shown in Figure 3.9. His discovery has been verified by research on animals as well as on human beings. For example, stimulation of points on the cerebral cortex of baboons produces similar distorted "maps" of the body (Waters et al., 1990).

The **temporal lobes** have their own primary cortical area, the **auditory cortex.** The auditory cortex of each lobe receives input from both ears, but more so from the contralateral ear (Geffen & Quinn, 1984). Particular regions of the auditory cortex are responsible for processing sounds of particular frequencies. This enables the temporal lobes to analyze sounds of all kinds, including speech (Binder et al., 1994). When you listen to a symphony, certain areas of the auditory cortex respond more to the low-pitched sound of a tuba, while other areas respond more to the high-pitched sound of a flute.

At the back of the brain are the **occipital lobes,** which contain the **visual cortex.** This region integrates input from your eyes. Because of the nature of the pathways from your eyes to your visual cortex, visual input from objects in your *right visual field* is processed in your left occipital lobe, and visual input from objects in your *left visual field* is processed in your right occipital lobe. Damage to a portion of an occipital lobe can produce a blind spot in the contralateral visual field. In some cases, damage can produce

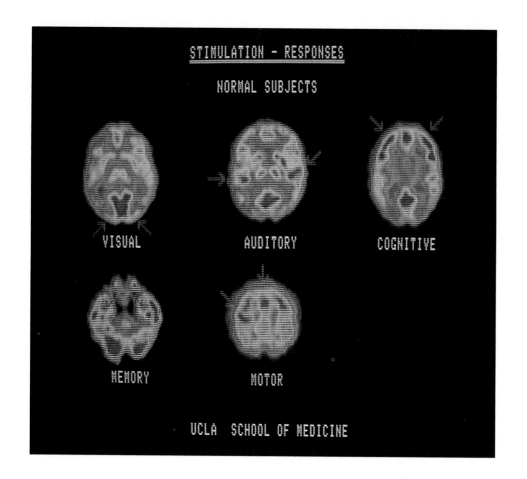

STIMULATION - RESPONSES

NORMAL SUBJECTS

VISUAL   AUDITORY   COGNITIVE

MEMORY   MOTOR

UCLA SCHOOL OF MEDICINE

◄ FIGURE 3.10
The PET Scan
The red areas of these PET scans reveal the regions of the brain that have absorbed the most glucose, indicating that they are the most active regions during the performance of particular tasks (Phelps & Mazziotta, 1985).

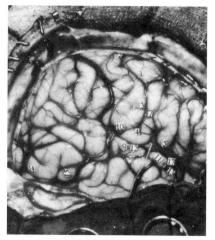

▲ **Mapping the Brain**
Wilder Penfield mapped the cerebral cortex while performing brain surgery on patients with epilepsy. The numbered tags on the exposed brain indicate sites that produced particular movements or mental experiences when electrically stimulated.

positron-emission tomography (PET)
A brain-scanning technique that produces color-coded pictures showing the relative activity of different brain areas.

visual hallucinations, such as the perception of parts of objects that are not actually present (Anderson & Rizzo, 1994).

As stated earlier, our knowledge of the functions of the cerebral cortex and other brain areas comes primarily from studies of brain damage, electrical stimulation of the brain, and EEG recordings of brain activity. In recent years, researchers have added a new tool, the brain scan. Perhaps the most important kind of brain scan to psychologists is **positron-emission tomography (PET)**, which lets them measure ongoing activity in particular regions of the brain. In using the PET scan, researchers inject radioactive glucose (a type of sugar) into a subject. Because neurons use glucose as a source of energy, the most active region of the brain takes up the most radioactive glucose. The amount of radiation emitted by each region is measured by a donut-shaped device that encircles the head. This information is analyzed by a computer, which generates color-coded pictures showing the relative degree of activity in different brain regions. As illustrated in Figure 3.10, PET scans are useful in revealing the precise patterns of brain activity during the performance of motor, sensory, and cognitive tasks (Phelps & Mazziotta, 1985). For example, a study of severe stutterers as they read aloud used the PET scan to identify brain pathways that might be involved in stuttering (Wu et al., 1995).

Two other brain-scanning techniques, which are more useful for displaying brain structures than for displaying ongoing brain activity, are **computed tomography (CT)** and **magnetic resonance imaging (MRI).** The CT scan takes many X rays of the brain from a variety of orientations around it. Detectors then record how much radiation has passed through the different regions of the brain. A computer uses this information to compose a picture of the brain. The MRI scan exposes the brain to a powerful magnetic field, and the hydrogen atoms in the brain align themselves along the magnetic field. A radio signal then disrupts the alignment. When the radio signal is turned off, the atoms align themselves again. A computer analyzes these changes, which differ from one region of the brain to another, to compose an even more detailed picture of the brain.

computed tomography (CT)
A brain-scanning technique that relies on X rays to construct computer-generated images of the brain or body.

magnetic resonance imaging (MRI)
A brain-scanning technique that relies on strong magnetic fields to construct computer-generated images of the brain or body.

Behavioral Neuroscience

Broca's area
The region of the frontal lobe responsible for the production of speech.

▲ **Paul Broca (1824–1880)**
"From the observations (cases) I have collected, and from the large number I have read in the literature, I believe I am justified in advancing the view that the principal lawgiver of speech is to be found in the anterior lobes of the brain."

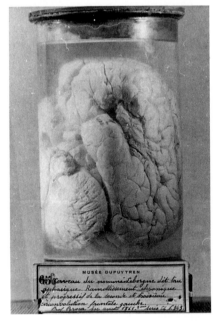

▲ **Tan's Brain**
Tan's brain, preserved for more than a century, shows the damage to Broca's area in the left forebrain that destroyed his ability to speak.

Wernicke's area
The region of the temporal lobe responsible for the comprehension of speech.

Traditional CT and MRI scans have been useful in detecting structural abnormalities. For example, degeneration of brain neurons in living victims of Alzheimer's disease has been verified by CT scans (DeCarli et al., 1990) and MRI scans (Jernigan et al., 1991). In the past few years, a technique called *functional MRI* has joined the PET scan as a tool for measuring ongoing activity in the brain (Cohen & Bookheimer, 1994). This ultrafast version of the traditional MRI detects increases in blood flow to brain regions that are more active at the moment.

In reading about the brain, you might have gotten the impression that each area functions independently of the others. That is far from the truth. Consider the association areas that compose most of the cerebral cortex. These areas combine information from other areas of the brain. For example, the association areas of the frontal lobes integrate information involved in thinking, planning, and problem solving. As in the case of Phineas Gage, damage to the frontal lobes causes emotional instability, inability to plan ahead, and socially inappropriate behavior (Absher & Cummings, 1995). This indicates that the association areas of the frontal lobes are especially important in helping us adapt our emotions and behavior to diverse situations.

The integration of different brain areas underlies many psychological functions. Consider the process of speech, one of the most distinctly human abilities. Speech depends on the interaction of the association cortex of the frontal and temporal lobes. In most left-handed people and almost all right-handed people, the left cerebral hemisphere is superior to the right in processing speech. The speech center of the frontal lobe, **Broca's area,** is named for its discoverer, the French surgeon and anthropologist Paul Broca (1824–1880). In 1861 Broca treated a 51-year-old man named Leborgne, who was given the nickname "Tan" because he had a severe speech disorder that made *tan* the only syllable he could pronounce clearly. After Tan died of an infection, Broca performed an autopsy and found damage to a small area of the left frontal lobe of his brain. Broca concluded that this area controls speech. Tan's speech disorder is now called *Broca's aphasia.* (*Aphasia* is the Greek word for "speechless.")

Though Broca was the first to formalize the relationship between a specific brain site and speech production, he was not the first to note that damage to the left hemisphere is associated with speech disruption. The relationship was noted as long ago as ancient Egypt (Sondhaus & Finger, 1988). Broca's observation was confirmed in later autopsies of the brains of people who had speech disorders similar to Tan's. CT scans have also verified that damage to Broca's area in living people is, indeed, associated with Broca's aphasia (Breathnach, 1989).

What is the nature of Broca's aphasia? Though its victims retain the ability to comprehend speech, they speak in a telegraphic style that can be comprehended only by listeners who pay careful attention. For example, when one victim of Broca's aphasia was asked about a family dental appointment, he said, "Monday . . . Dad and Dick . . . Wednesday nine o'clock . . . doctors and teeth" (Geschwind, 1979, p. 186). The speaker expressed the important thoughts but failed to express the connections between them. Nonetheless, you probably got the gist of the statement.

Speech also depends on a region of the temporal lobe cortex called **Wernicke's area,** named for the German physician Karl Wernicke. In contrast to Broca's area, which controls the production of speech, Wernicke's area controls the meaningfulness of speech. In 1874, Wernicke reported that patients with damage to the rear margin of the left temporal lobe spoke fluently but had difficulty comprehending speech and made little or no sense to even the most attentive listener. This became known as *Wernicke's aphasia.*

Consider the following statement by a victim of Wernicke's aphasia that describes a picture of two boys stealing cookies behind a woman's back: "Mother is away here working her work to get her better, but when she's looking the two boys looking in the other part. She's working another time" (Geschwind, 1979, p. 186). The statement seems more grammatical than the telegraphic speech of the victim of Broca's aphasia, but it is impossible to comprehend—it is virtually meaningless.

The consensus among researchers is that, as diagrammed in Figure 3.11, speech production requires the interaction of Wernicke's area, Broca's area, and the motor cortex

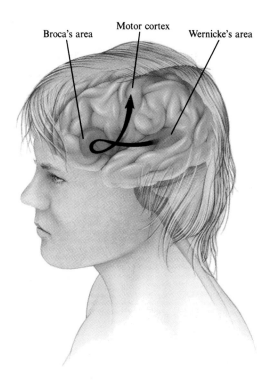

Broca's area Motor cortex Wernicke's area

◀ FIGURE 3.11
Speech and the Brain
Wernicke's area, Broca's area, and the motor cortex interact in producing speech.

(Geschwind, 1979). Wernicke's area selects the words that will convey your meaning and communicates them to Broca's area. Broca's area then selects the muscle movements to express those words and communicates them to the region of the motor cortex that controls the speech muscles. Finally, the motor cortex communicates these directions through motor nerves to the appropriate muscles, and you speak the intended words. As you can see, speaking phrases as simple as *let's go out for pizza* involves the interaction of several areas of your brain.

Localization of Brain Functions

The extent to which psychological functions can be localized in particular areas of the brain has been a controversial issue for the past two centuries. The controversy began when the respected Viennese physician-anatomist Franz Joseph Gall (1758–1828) proclaimed that particular regions of the cerebral cortex control particular psychological functions. Gall's interest in the localization of psychological functions began in his childhood, when he observed that classmates with superior memory ability had protruding eyes. From that limited sample, Gall mistakenly inferred that memory is localized in the cerebral cortex located just behind the eyes. He assumed that the thicker the cerebral cortex in that region, the better the memory and the more the eyeballs would be pushed out of their sockets.

Gall devised a system for associating the bumps and depressions of the skull with intellectual abilities and personality traits. For example, he insisted that the cerebellum (the "amativeness" area of the brain) controlled sexual love (Macklis & Macklis, 1992). He assumed, incorrectly, that the bumps and depressions of the skull reflected the amount of brain tissue lying under them. Thus, the larger the region of the cerebellum, the "sexier" the person. Gall's student Johann Spurzheim popularized this practice as **phrenology** (Greek for "science of the mind"). Figure 3.12 presents an advertisement for Fowlers and Wells, the leading phrenological company of the nineteenth century.

Gall and Spurzheim gave demonstrations of phrenology throughout Europe, and it became popular as far away as Australia (Thearle, 1993). But they and their followers failed to provide adequate scientific support for their claims. On one occasion, prior to a demonstration of phrenology on the preserved brain of a genius, a practical joker replaced that brain with the brain of a mentally retarded person. Despite this exchange, the phrenologist

phrenology

A discredited technique for determining intellectual abilities and personality traits by examining the bumps and depressions of the skull.

Phrenology

Phrenologists such as Gall and Spurzheim developed maps of the head indicating the supposed functions of areas of the brain underlying particular places on the skull. This advertisement for the Fowlers and Wells company shows that phrenology permeated everyday life in the nineteenth century.

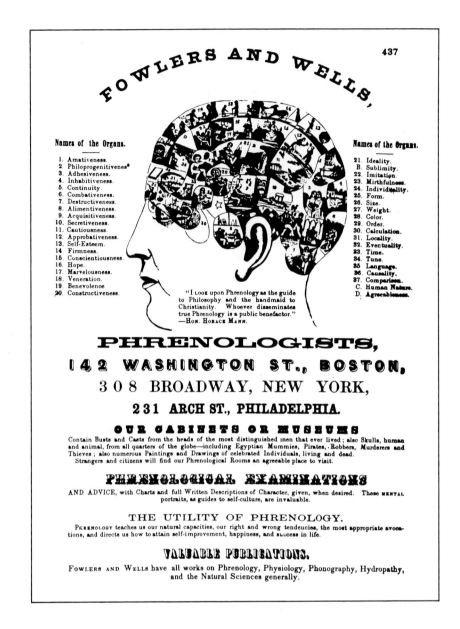

proceeded to praise the intellectual qualities of the brain (Fancher, 1979). You might recognize this as an instance of experimenter bias, discussed in Chapter 2. Though phrenology had its scientific shortcomings, it sparked interest in the localization of brain functions (Miller, 1996).

The practice of phrenology in the nineteenth century was paralleled by research suggesting that psychological functions require the interaction of different areas of the brain. This position was championed by the French physiologist Pierre Flourens (1794–1867) and later by the American psychologist Karl Lashley (1890–1958). Lashley based his belief on experiments in which he trained rats to run mazes to find food and then destroyed specific areas of their cerebral cortex. He found that the destruction of any given area had only a slight effect on their performance. Lashley (1950) concluded that psychological processes, particularly those involved in memory, are not localized in specific areas of the brain but require the interaction of diverse areas. More-recent experiments on rats support Lashley's belief that memory requires the interaction of diverse brain sites (Meyer, Gurklis, & Cloud, 1985).

Today, many behavioral neuroscientists would favor a position between Gall's and Lashley's, viewing the brain as a collection of structures that interact flexibly with one another, according to the demands of the situation. Thus, each psychological function requires the interaction of several brain areas but can be disrupted by damage to one or more of them (Kaas, 1987). The interaction of Wernicke's area, Broca's area, and the motor cortex in the production of speech supports this position.

Even your ability to recognize faces depends on the interaction of association areas running along the underside of the occipital and temporal lobes. Electrical recordings from this region of the brains of sheep and monkeys show that it becomes more active when they are shown the faces of people or animals. For example, certain neurons in this region in sheep brains respond to the faces of sheep, others to the faces of sheepdogs, and still others to the faces of human beings (Kendrick & Baldwin, 1987).

People who have suffered damage to this region exhibit **prosopagnosia,** the inability to recognize faces—even though the ability to see them is unaffected (Ariel & Sadeh, 1996). Imagine a child with prosopagnosia. She might fail to recognize her father's face, yet still recognize his voice. Every time they met, he would have to speak so that she could identify him (Young & Ellis, 1989). Why do you suppose we have evolved cortical association areas devoted to such a narrow function? Perhaps we have done so because the ability to recognize friend from foe has important survival value for us.

Plasticity of the Brain: The Brain as Adaptive

The human brain is remarkable in its ability to learn from experience and to promote adaptive behavior. In doing so, the brain shows **neural plasticity**—that is, it is not completely "hardwired" at birth. Plasticity is shown by the elimination of excess neurons (Kolb, 1989) and synaptic connections (Huttenlocher, 1990) in childhood and the formation of new synaptic connections throughout life (Rosenzweig & Bennett, 1996).

The biggest challenge to the plasticity of the brain is brain damage, whether caused by a stroke, a disease, or a blow to the head. Natural processes in response to brain damage promote a limited degree of recovery. More recently, a technique formerly relegated to science fiction—brain tissue transplantation—has shown promise as a means of encouraging greater recovery from brain damage.

Recovery of Functions After Brain Damage

Brain damage can produce devastating effects, including paralysis, sensory loss, memory disruption, and personality deterioration. But what are the chances of recovering from such damage? It depends on the kind of animal whose brain has been damaged. Certain species of fish and amphibians recover from brain damage by regenerating damaged axons, but mammals, including human beings, do not. Human beings can regenerate damaged axons only in the peripheral nervous system. This regeneration is instigated, in part, by chemical signals sent along damaged axons back to the cell bodies of their neurons (Gunstream, Castro, & Walters, 1995). Glial cells in the peripheral nervous system form tunnels that guide the regrowth of damaged axons. In contrast, glial cells in the brain and spinal cord simply remove dead neurons and might actually block regeneration by forming scar tissue. Human beings and other mammals depend on factors other than the regeneration of neurons for the recovery of lost brain and spinal cord functions.

In mammals, perhaps the most important factor in the recovery of functions that have been lost because of brain damage is the ability of intact brain areas to take over the functions of damaged ones (Bach-y-Rita, 1990). In one experiment, researchers surgically destroyed portions of the somatosensory cortex of monkeys. They found that the somatosensory cortical "map" representing those portions gradually shifted to intact adjacent areas of the parietal lobes, restoring the ability to experience bodily sensations (Fox, 1984). Through **collateral sprouting** (illustrated in Figure 3.13), branches from the axons of nearby healthy neurons grow into the pathways normally occupied by the axons of the damaged neurons. Ideally, the healthy neurons will take over the functions of the damaged ones. The younger the individual, the more likely this is to occur.

Because of **equipotentiality,** more than one area of the brain might be able to control a given function. When the area controlling a function is damaged, another area might gradually take over for it. For example, when a person suffers aphasia as a result of damage

prosopagnosia
The inability to recognize faces, which is typically caused by damage to a region of the temporal and occipital lobes.

neural plasticity
The ability of the brain to alter its neuronal pathways.

collateral sprouting
The process by which branches from the axons of nearby healthy neurons grow into the pathways normally occupied by the axons of damaged neurons.

equipotentiality
The ability of more than one area of the brain to control a given function.

▶ FIGURE 3.13

Collateral Sprouting
When an axon dies and its connections to the dendrites of other neurons degenerate, adjacent axons may sprout branches that form synapses with the vacated sites. The illustration shows (1) input from two axons to a single dendrite; (2) destruction of one of the axons (with anterograde degeneration, which is degeneration of the axon from the point of the injury to the end of the axon); and (3) the intact axon showing collateral branching to the vacated site on the dendrite.

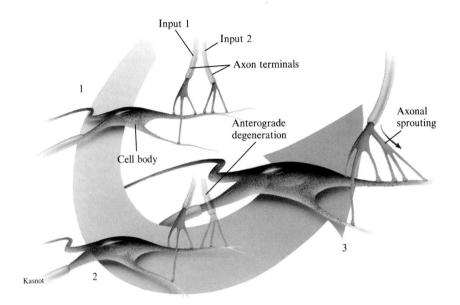

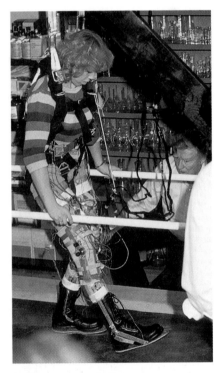

▲ **Bypassing the Spinal Cord**
This woman lost the ability to use her legs after suffering spinal cord damage. She is shown learning to walk with the aid of a computer that sends bursts of electricity to stimulate her leg muscles in a coordinated manner.

hemispherectomy

The surgical removal of an entire cerebral hemisphere, usually to treat uncontrollable epilepsy.

neural grafting

The transplantation of brain tissue or, in some cases, adrenal gland tissue into the brain or spinal cord to restore functions lost because of brain damage.

to the left hemisphere, the right hemisphere and, especially, undamaged areas of the left hemisphere promote the recovery of speech (Gainotti, 1993). Brain plasticity is also shown by the amazing recovery of some children who have had a **hemispherectomy** (the surgical removal of an entire cerebral hemisphere), usually because of uncontrollable epilepsy. The remaining hemisphere might take over the functions of the missing hemisphere. Though such children typically experience some sensory and motor deficits, they may function well intellectually and even go on to succeed in college. This degree of recovery does not occur in adolescents or adults who have had a hemispherectomy, because their brains have less plasticity than younger brains (Ogden, 1989).

Neural Transplantation to Treat Brain Damage

Though plasticity might restore some lost functions, most people who have suffered brain damage—or spinal cord damage—do not recover completely. This has led to research on possible ways to repair damaged brains and spinal cords, including attempts to administer chemicals that promote regeneration of neural connections (Santucci et al., 1993) or to stimulate the same processes that permit axons of the peripheral nerves to regenerate (Bertelli, Orsal, & Mira, 1994). The most widely publicized, and controversial, way has been to use **neural grafting**—the transplantation of healthy tissue into damaged brains or spinal cords (Kimble, 1990).

Though Mary Shelley's vision of transplanting whole brains is still a topic better suited for science fiction, scientists have been studying the use of brain tissue transplants to treat Parkinson's disease (Nikkhah et al., 1994). In an early study, researchers destroyed neurons in the substantia nigra of rats, inducing movement disturbances like those seen in victims of Parkinson's disease. The researchers then transplanted tissue from the substantia nigra of healthy fetal rats into the brains of the brain-damaged rats. After several weeks, the recipients showed a reduction in their symptoms, indicating that the transplanted tissue may have taken over the lost functions of the damaged tissue (Perlow et al., 1979).

More-recent studies have reported a variety of successful applications of neural grafting in animals. Epileptic seizures that have been experimentally induced by surgically created brain damage in rats have been reduced by the transplantation of inhibitory GABA neurons from fetal rat brains (Fine, Meldrum, & Patel, 1990). Even the spinal cord can benefit from tissue transplants. In a study of rats whose spinal cords had been surgically lesioned to cause hindlimb paralysis, grafts of fetal spinal cord cells reduced the severity of their paralysis (Bernstein & Goldberg, 1989). Thus, neural transplants show promise in treating damage to the central nervous system of animals. Researcher Jacqueline Sagen and her colleagues have conducted studies using neural grafts of endorphin-producing adrenal medulla tissue into the brains (Hama & Sagen, 1993) or spinal cords (Sagen, Pappas, & Perlow, 1986) of animals to help relieve pain.

But how do neural transplants achieve their beneficial effects? They appear to do so by secreting neurotransmitters that the damaged region lacks (Becker, Curran, & Freed, 1990), by forming new neural circuits to replace damaged ones (Nunn & Hodges, 1994), and by secreting substances that promote neural regeneration (Lescaudron & Stein, 1990). Before becoming too optimistic about neural transplants, you should realize that many attempts at them have failed (Swenson et al., 1989). And even "successful" transplants might not have the intended effects—the new secretion of neurotransmitters or the new neural circuits can disrupt existing pathways, creating even more functional deterioration (Amemori et al., 1989).

Given the success of some experiments on fetal neural transplants in animals, it is natural to consider the possibility of using such transplants in human beings. Some studies in which fetal brain tissue has been transplanted to human victims of brain damage have produced significant, long-lasting restoration of lost functions. For example, researchers in Sweden have reported success in reducing symptoms of Parkinson's disease by using fetal cell transplants (Lindvall et al., 1990). In the future, if such neural grafts are perfected, brain damage caused by strokes, tumors, diseases, or accidents might be treated by brain tissue transplants. One promising application is the treatment of Alzheimer's disease (Tarricone et al., 1996).

As you might imagine, this possibility has sparked controversy about where we would get tissue to transplant. From animals? From aborted fetuses? From terminally ill patients? Ethicists are already dealing with this issue. In regard to fetal tissue, one set of guidelines that has been offered is to use only dead fetuses, to keep abortion and transplantation decisions separate, and to ban the buying and selling of fetal tissue (Mahowald, 1989). As noted in Chapter 2, scientists must confront ethical, as well as technical, issues in conducting their research.

Because initial efforts to transplant human fetal brain tissue into the brains of victims of Parkinson's disease have met with both technical and ethical problems, researchers have turned to transplanting cells from the brain-damaged person's adrenal glands into his or her own brain. Cells from the adrenal medulla produce dopamine, the neurotransmitter lacking in the brains of victims of Parkinson's disease. In 1982, researchers in Sweden reported disappointing results following the initial adrenal transplants. But 5 years later, researchers in Mexico City announced the first successful use of adrenal transplants. Ignacio Madrazo and his colleagues (1987) observed that symptoms of Parkinson's disease in animals had been relieved by grafting tissue from the adrenal medulla into the brain. They also found that Swedish researchers had technical, though not therapeutic, success with grafts from the adrenal medulla of Parkinson's patients.

Madrazo decided to replicate the Swedish study, hoping to obtain more therapeutic effectiveness. The subjects were a 35-year-old man and a 39-year-old man, both with Parkinson's disease. They received neural grafts of tissue taken from their own adrenal medullas and transplanted into their own brains. Over the next few months, both patients showed marked reduction of their symptoms. They had fewer hand tremors, their facial expressions became more normal, they were able to speak more clearly, and they were able to use their limbs with greater facility. Madrazo attributed the success to the release of dopamine by the neural grafts. Unfortunately, subsequent replications of this study with patients elsewhere failed to produce such dramatic improvements (Lewin, 1988). Though neural grafts have yet to demonstrate their everyday practical worth, researchers may be on the verge of breakthroughs that will restore functions that have been lost as the result of brain or spinal cord damage (Baisden, 1995).

The Mind-Brain Problem: Are Mental Processes Distinct from Brain Activity?

Beyond the issues raised by research on the brain is the question, What is the mind? Descartes favored a position called *dualism*, which views the mind as an immaterial substance, separate from the material brain. He believed that the pineal gland, located at the

▲ Jacqueline Sagen
"The ability to successfully transplant neural tissues into the adult central nervous system (CNS) has opened up the exciting possibility for repair of damaged neuronal circuitry."

center of the brain, was the site where the mind and brain interact. The weakness of such a rationalist approach to knowledge (discussed in Chapter 2) is shown by later research that indicates that the mind can function even if the pineal gland is removed. Other philosophers have favored a position called *monism,* viewing the mind and brain as a single material, or immaterial, substance. Most monists believe that the mind and brain are both matter, with the mind dependent on brain activity for its existence. Behavioral neuroscientist Roger Sperry (1913–1994), who won a Nobel Prize in 1981 for his neuroscience research, favored that view, and claimed that the mind arises from brain activity—yet can affect brain activity, a position he called *emergent interactionism* (Puente, 1995):

▶ In this new synthesis, mental states, as dynamic emergent properties of brain activity, become inseparably interfused with and tied to the brain activity of which they are an emergent property. Consciousness in this view cannot exist apart from the functioning brain. (Sperry, 1993, p. 879)

In contrast, Wilder Penfield, the great brain mapper, favored a position closer to that of Descartes, though he did not implicate the pineal gland. Penfield claimed that the mind is not dependent on the brain for its existence (a view that he used to support his religious belief that the mind survives death):

▶ For my own part, after years of striving to explain the mind on the basis of brain action alone, I have come to the conclusion that it is simpler (and far easier to be logical) if one adopts the hypothesis that our being does consist of two fundamental elements. (Penfield, 1975, p. 80)

Though psychologists have used the scientific method to determine the mental functions of the brain, they have made little progress in determining whether the mind exists apart from the brain—one of the ultimate philosophical issues. The relationship between the mind and the brain is discussed further in Chapter 6.

STAYING ON TRACK: *The Brain*

1. What are the functions of the frontal lobes of the cerebral cortex?
2. What were the weaknesses and contributions of phrenology?
3. How do neural transplants achieve their beneficial effects?
4. What is the mind-brain problem in psychology?

THINKING ABOUT *Psychology*

Do the Cerebral Hemispheres Serve Different Functions?

During the past few years, you may have noted reports in the popular media alleging that the cerebral hemispheres control different psychological functions, leading to the notion of "left-brained" and "right-brained" people. Though most researchers would not assign complete responsibility for any psychological function to just one hemisphere, they have reached agreement on some of the psychological functions for which each hemisphere is primarily responsible. The left hemisphere is *somewhat* superior at performing verbal, mathematical, analytical, and rational functions, and the right hemisphere is *somewhat* superior at performing nonverbal, spatial, holistic, and emotional functions (Springer & Deutsch, 1993). Though each hemisphere has its own strengths, the hemispheres do not work in isolation (Hoptman & Davidson, 1994). For example, the left hemisphere generally controls the production of speech, but the right hemisphere gives speech its appropriate emotional intonation (Hellige, 1993).

PEANUTS reprinted by permission of UFS, Inc.

Because about 90 percent of human beings are right-handed and, as a consequence, the manufactured environment favors right-handers, left-handers have some difficulties functioning in the everyday world. For example, left-handers have difficulty operating control panels designed for righties, especially under stressful conditions that can cause confusion, as in airplane cockpits. Because of this, human-factors engineers must consider left-handed people when designing control consoles (Garonzik, 1989). As in the case of other minorities, left-handers have been the targets of prejudice. For example, negative words such as the French "gauche" and the Latin "sinister" refer to the left side. And you certainly realize that a "left-handed compliment" is far from complimentary.

Because right-handedness is prevalent in virtually all cultures, heredity is evidently more important than life experiences in determining handedness and cerebral lateralization of functions. Additional evidence of this comes from research findings that even newborns show evidence of cerebral lateralization of psychological functions (Fein, 1990). Yet cultural factors can override hereditary tendencies, as revealed in a survey of natives of the Amazon region of Colombia. All of the persons in the survey reported that they were right-handed. The researchers who did the survey concluded that this occurred because those who had been born with initial tendencies toward left-handedness became right-handed as a result of cultural pressures to do so (Bryden, Ardila, & Ardila, 1993).

Perhaps the most controversial issue in recent years regarding handedness is whether right-handed people tend to live longer than left-handed people. There is no controversy about one fact: There are proportionately fewer left-handers among older adults than among younger adults. But as you will soon see, this does not necessarily mean that right-handers live longer. Two of the main proponents of the belief that right-handers do, in fact, live longer have been Stanley Coren and Diane Halpern. The following study by Coren and Halpern (1991) contributed to the debate over handedness and longevity.

ANATOMY OF A CONTEMPORARY RESEARCH STUDY

Is Left-Handedness a Pathological Condition?

Rationale

Coren, a psychologist at the University of British Columbia, and Halpern, a psychologist at California State University at San Bernardino, pointed to earlier studies indicating that the

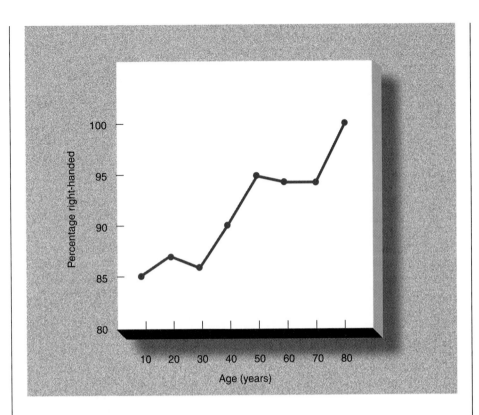

▶ FIGURE 3.14

Handedness and Longevity
As the graph indicates, when comparing different age groups the proportion of right-handers in the population increases as the age of the group increases. While about 85 percent of young adults are right-handers, almost 100 percent of those above age 80 are right-handers. It is unclear whether this decline reflects the greater longevity of right-handers or the forced change from left-handedness to right-handedness in some members of older age groups earlier in their lives.

percentage of right-handers was greater in older age groups (Coren & Halpern, 1991). Figure 3.14 illustrates the drastic change in the percentage of right-handers from younger age groups to older ones (Porac & Coren, 1981). Note that by age 80 there are virtually no left-handers in the population! To assess this handedness effect, Halpern and Coren (1988) conducted an archival study of longevity in professional baseball players, using the *Baseball Encyclopedia* as their source of data on more than 2,000 players. They found that, on the average, right-handers lived eight months longer than left-handers. This inspired them to replicate that study to determine if their findings would generalize to people other than baseball players.

Method

Coren and Halpern sent brief questionnaires to the next of kin of 2,875 persons who had recently died in two counties in southern California. The questionnaires asked questions about the deceased's handedness regarding writing, drawing, and throwing. Each person's age at death was obtained from death certificates. Despite the apparent intrusion of the questionnaires into the lives of grieving relatives, 1,033 questionnaires were returned. Of these, 987 were usable.

Results and Discussion

Coren and Halpern determined whether the deceased had been right-handed or left-handed. They operationally defined them as "right-handed" if they had written, drawn, and thrown with their right hands. They operationally defined them as "left-handed" if they had written, drawn, and thrown with their left hands or if they had shown mixed use of their right and left hands.

The results were startling: right-handers lived an average of 9 years longer than left-handers. Thus, this study found a much larger longevity gap than the study of baseball players found. Coren and Halpern attributed the gap to the earlier deaths of left-handers (the *elimination hypothesis*) rather than to cultural pressures to become right-handed (the *modification hypothesis*) affecting older generations more than younger ones. Coren and Halpern found that the most important factors accounting for this were a greater tendency for left-handers to have accidents, immune disorders, and evidence of neurological defects. For example, a Canadian study of people hospitalized for head injuries caused by automobile accidents found that victims were disproportionately left-handers (MacNiven, 1994).

▲ ▲ ▲

Research findings have not consistently supported Coren and Halpern's findings. Even the allegedly longer life spans of right-handed baseball players have been called into question. A large-scale study of more than 5,000 professional baseball players found that left-handers actually lived an average of 8 months longer than right-handers (Hicks et al., 1994). Coren and Halpern's explanations for the apparent longevity difference favoring right-handers have also been called into question. For example, a study in the Netherlands found no relationship between accident proneness and handedness among undergraduate students (Merckelbach, Muris, & Kop, 1994). Moreover, research has been inconsistent on the relationship between handedness and immune disorders, with some even showing that right-handers are more susceptible to them (Bryden, 1993). And there is conflicting evidence about the greater likelihood of neurological disorders in left-handers (Bishop, 1990).

The strongest response to Coren and Halpern has come from Lauren Harris of Michigan State University, who believes that the modification hypothesis is a better explanation for the decline in left-handers across the life span (Harris, 1993). According to Harris, today's older adults grew up at a time when left-handers were forced to use their right hands or simply chose to conform to a right-handed world. In contrast, over the past few decades left-handedness has lost its stigma, resulting in more left-handers remaining left-handed.

This was supported by a study in Norway. In keeping with Coren and Halpern's findings, the researchers found that about 15.2 percent of 21- to 30-year-olds were left-handed and only 1.7 percent of those more than 80 years old were left-handed. But the researchers found that the apparent decline in left-handedness across the life span was, in reality, due to the fact that many left-handers in earlier generations had switched to being right-handed (Hugdahl et al., 1993). Despite these findings, which contradict their position, Halpern and Coren (1993) insist that most scientifically sound studies support their belief that left-handers tend to die younger.

Several questions remain to be answered, but the main one is this: If we follow groups of young people as they grow older, will the left-handers tend to die sooner than the right-handers? If they do, it would support Coren and Halpern's explanation. If they do not, it would support Harris's explanation. Of course, this would take many decades to determine.

In addition to their interest in handedness, cerebral-laterality researchers study the psychological functions of the left and right hemispheres. They do so by studying the intact brain, the damaged brain, and the split brain.

▲ **Stanley Coren and Diane Halpern**
"The absence of left-handedness in older age groups may be due to the elimination of this set of individuals through selective mortality."

EVIDENCE OF HEMISPHERIC FUNCTIONS
FROM THE INTACT BRAIN

Psychologists interested in hemispheric specialization have devised several methods for studying the intact brain. One of the chief methods has subjects perform tasks while an EEG records the electrical activity of their cerebral hemispheres. Studies have found that people produce greater electrical activity in the left hemisphere while performing verbal tasks, such as solving verbal analogy problems, and greater electrical activity in the right hemisphere while performing spatial tasks, such as mentally rotating geometric forms (Loring & Sheer, 1984).

A more recent approach to studying hemispheric specialization in the intact brain uses the PET scan to create color-coded pictures of the relative activity in regions of the left hemisphere and right hemisphere. Figure 3.15 shows the results of one such study. Another approach, the **Wada test,** studies human subjects in whom a hemisphere has been anesthetized in the course of brain surgery to correct a neurological defect (Loring et al., 1991). This is done by injecting a barbiturate anesthetic into either the right or the left carotid artery, which provides oxygenated blood to the associated cerebral hemisphere. The injection anesthetizes that hemisphere. As you might expect, anesthetization of the left hemisphere, but only rarely of the right hemisphere, induces temporary aphasia—the patient is unable to speak.

Wada test

A technique in which a cerebral hemisphere is anesthetized to assess hemispheric specialization.

The PET Scan and Hemispheric Specialization
The red areas of these PET scans show that the left hemisphere is more active when we listen to speech and the right hemisphere is more active when we listen to music (Phelps & Mazziotta, 1985).

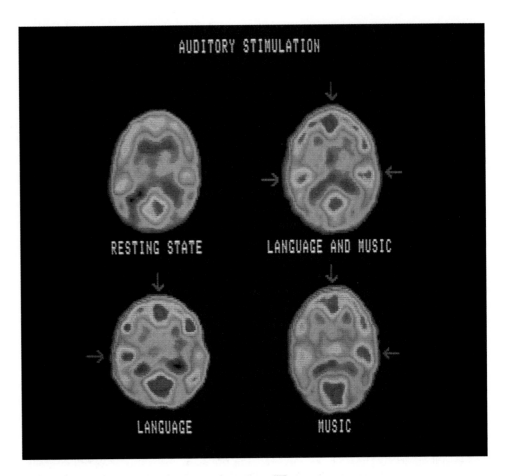

EVIDENCE OF HEMISPHERIC FUNCTIONS FROM THE DAMAGED BRAIN

Case studies of people who have suffered damage to one cerebral hemisphere, often as the result of a stroke, are the oldest sources of evidence on hemispheric specialization. As noted earlier, in the 1860s Paul Broca found that damage to the left hemisphere was associated with the disruption of speech. In the 1880s, the English neurologist John Hughlings Jackson found that damage to the right hemisphere was associated with the disruption of spatial perception, which underlies the ability to read books, draw pictures, or put together puzzles (Levy, 1985).

A profound example of the role of the right hemisphere in spatial perception is the neglect syndrome (introduced at the beginning of this chapter), a disorder typically caused by damage to the right parietal cortex. Victims of this disorder act as though the left side of their world, including their bodies, does not exist (Moscovitch & Behrmann, 1994). A man with this syndrome might shave the right side of his face, but not the left, and might eat the pork chop on the right side of his plate but not the potatoes on the left. Figure 3.16 shows self-portraits painted by an artist who exhibited the neglect syndrome. As in his case, the neglect syndrome is self-limiting, typically lasting weeks or months (Tranel, 1995). Though the neglect syndrome is usually found after right parietal lobe damage, it is sometimes found in people who have suffered left parietal lobe damage; they show neglect for objects in the right half of their spatial world (Mattingley, Bradshaw, & Phillips, 1992).

EVIDENCE OF HEMISPHERIC FUNCTIONS FROM THE SPLIT BRAIN

Studies of damaged brains and intact brains have provided most of the evidence regarding cerebral hemispheric specialization, but the most fascinating approach has

◄ FIGURE 3.16
The Neglect Syndrome
These self-portraits painted by the German artist Anton Raderscheidt were painted over a period of time following a stroke that damaged the cortex of his right parietal lobe. As his brain recovered, his attention to the left side of his world returned (Wurtz, Goldberg, & Robinson, 1982).

been **split-brain research.** This involves people whose hemispheres have been surgically separated from each other. Though split-brain research is only a few decades old, the idea was entertained in 1860 by Gustav Fechner, who was introduced in Chapter 1 as a founder of psychology. Fechner claimed that people who survived the surgical separation of their cerebral hemispheres would have two separate minds in one head (Springer & Deutsch, 1993). Decades later English psychologist William McDougall argued that such an operation would not divide the mind, which he considered indivisible. McDougall even volunteered to test Fechner's claim by having his own cerebral hemispheres surgically separated if he ever became incurably ill.

Though McDougall never had split-brain surgery, it was performed on patients in the early 1960s, when neurosurgeons Joseph Bogen and Phillip Vogel severed the **corpus callosum** of epileptic patients to reduce seizure activity that had not responded to drug treatments. As illustrated in Figure 3.17, the corpus callosum is a thick bundle of axons that provides the means of communication of information between the cerebral hemispheres (Clarke & Zaidel, 1994). Split-brain surgery works by preventing seizure activity in one hemisphere from spreading to the other. Split-brain patients behave normally in their everyday lives, but special testing procedures have revealed an astonishing state of affairs: Their left and right hemispheres can no longer communicate with each other (Hoptman & Davidson, 1994). Each acts independently of the other.

split-brain research
Research on hemispheric specialization that studies individuals in whom the corpus callosum has been severed.

corpus callosum
A thick bundle of axons that provides a means of communication between the cerebral hemispheres, which is severed in so-called split-brain surgery.

Split-Brain Surgery
Severing the corpus callosum disconnects the cerebral hemispheres from each other. Note that in "split-brain" surgery, the entire brain is not split. That would cut through the hindbrain structures that control vital functions, causing immediate death.

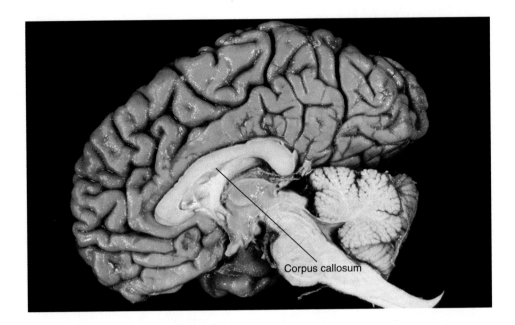
Corpus callosum

▲ **Jerre Levy**
"Although the right hemisphere is nonlinguistic (except in unusual or pathological cases), the evidence is overpowering that it is active, responsive, highly intelligent, thinking, conscious, and fully human with respect to its cognitive depth and complexity."

Roger Sperry (1982) and his colleagues, most notably Jerre Levy and Michael Gazzaniga, have been pioneers in split-brain research. In a typical study of a split-brain patient, information is presented to one hemisphere and the subject is asked to give a response that depends more on one hemisphere than on the other. In one study (Gazzaniga, 1967), a split-brain patient performed a block-design task in which he had to arrange multicolored blocks so that their upper sides formed a pattern that matched the pattern printed on a card in front of him. This is illustrated in Figure 3.18. When the subject performed with his left hand, he did well, but when he performed with his right hand, he did poorly. Can you figure out why that happened?

Because the left hand is controlled by the right hemisphere, which is superior in perceiving spatial relationships, such as those in designs, he performed well with his left hand. And because the right hand is controlled by the left hemisphere, which is inferior in perceiving spatial relationships, he performed poorly with his right hand—even though he was right-handed. At times, when his right hand was having a hard time completing the design, his left hand would sneak up on it and try to help. This led to a bizarre battle for control of the blocks—as if each hand belonged to a different person.

Despite the dramatic findings of split-brain studies, Jerre Levy (1983) believes that researchers, including Gazzaniga (1983), have exaggerated the extent to which each hemisphere regulates particular psychological processes, especially the supposed superiority of the left hemisphere. As always, only additional scientific research will resolve the Levy-Gazzaniga debate, which, you might note, is an example of the continual controversy over the degree to which psychological functions are localized in particular areas of the brain.

STAYING ON TRACK: *Do the Cerebral Hemispheres Serve Different Functions?*

1. What does research indicate about the relative longevity of left-handers and right-handers?
2. What evidence is there for hemispheric specialization based on split-brain research?

► CHAPTER SUMMARY

THE NERVOUS SYSTEM

The field of behavioral neuroscience studies the relationships between physiological processes and psychological functions. The nervous system is composed of cells called neurons and serves as the main means of communication within the body. The nervous system is divided into the central nervous system, which comprises the brain and the spinal cord, and the peripheral nervous system, which comprises the nerves of the somatic nervous system and the autonomic nervous system. The autonomic nervous

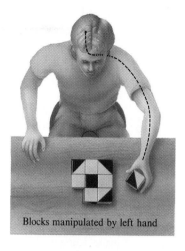

Blocks manipulated by left hand

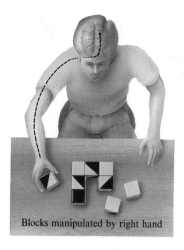

Blocks manipulated by right hand

Pattern to copy

Pattern to copy

◄ FIGURE 3.18
A Split-Brain Study
Gazzaniga (1967) had a split-brain patient arrange multicolored blocks to match a design printed on a card in front of him. The patient's left hand performed better than his right, because the left hand is controlled by the right hemisphere, which is superior at perceiving spatial relationships. You would be able to perform a block-design task equally well with either your right or your left hand, because your intact corpus callosum would let information from your spatially superior right hemisphere help your left hemisphere control your right hand.

system is subdivided into the sympathetic nervous system, which arouses the body, and the parasympathetic nervous system, which conserves energy.

THE NEURON

The nervous system carries information along sensory neurons, motor neurons, and interneurons, as in the limb-withdrawal reflex mediated by the spinal cord. The neuron generally receives signals through its dendrites and sends signals along its axon.

The axon maintains a resting potential during which it is electrically negative on the inside relative to its outside, as a result of a higher concentration of negative ions inside. Sufficient stimulation of the neuron causes the axon to depolarize (become less electrically negative) and reach its firing threshold. This produces an action potential, which causes a neural impulse to travel along the entire length of the axon.

The neural impulses stimulate the release of neurotransmitter molecules into the synapse. The molecules cross the synapse and attach to receptor sites on glands, muscles, or other neurons. These molecules exert either an excitatory or an inhibitory influence. In recent years, the neurotransmitters known as endorphins have inspired research because of their role in pain relief and euphoria.

THE ENDOCRINE SYSTEM

Hormones, secreted into the bloodstream by endocrine glands, also serve as a means of communication within the body. Hormones participate in functions as diverse as sexual development and responses to stress. Most endocrine glands are regulated by hormones secreted by the pituitary gland, which, in turn, is regulated by the hypothalamus.

THE BRAIN

The functions of the brain have been revealed by studies of the effects of brain damage, electrical stimulation of the brain, recordings of the electricity produced by brain activity, and computer scanning of the brain. The brain is divided into the hindbrain (including the medulla, pons, and cerebellum), the midbrain (including the tectum and substantia nigra), and the forebrain (including the thalamus, limbic system, and cerebral cortex). The medulla regulates vital functions, such as breathing; the pons regulates arousal and attention; and the cerebellum controls the timing of well-learned sequences of movements. Extending up from the

hindbrain, through the midbrain, and into the forebrain is the reticular formation, which regulates brain arousal and helps maintain vigilance. The tectum mediates visual and auditory reflexes, and the substantia nigra promotes smooth movements.

The thalamus relays sensory information (except smell) to various regions of the brain for further processing. Within the limbic system, the hypothalamus regulates the pituitary gland, as well as emotion and motives such as eating, drinking, and sex. The amygdala continuously evaluates the immediate environment for potential threats, and the hippocampus processes information into memories.

The cerebral cortex covers the brain and is divided into the frontal, temporal, parietal, and occipital lobes. Well-defined areas of the lobes regulate movements and process sensory information. But most areas of the cerebral cortex—the association areas—are devoted to integrating information from different brain areas, such as those devoted to speech. In the past decade, positron-emission tomography (the PET scan) has contributed to our understanding of the functions of different areas of the brain. Researchers historically have disagreed about the extent to which particular psychological functions are localized in particular areas of the brain.

Neurons in the mammalian central nervous system do not regenerate. Recovery of functions after brain damage demonstrates the brain's plasticity through the ability of undamaged areas to take over the functions of damaged ones. An exciting, and controversial, topic of research is the possibility of using neural grafts to restore brain functions in people who have suffered brain damage.

THINKING ABOUT PSYCHOLOGY: DO THE CEREBRAL HEMISPHERES SERVE DIFFERENT FUNCTIONS?

Each cerebral hemisphere has psychological functions at which it excels, though both hemispheres influence virtually all functions. Studies of the degree of activity in each hemisphere, of the effects of damage to one hemisphere, and of people whose hemispheres have been surgically disconnected show that the left hemisphere is typically superior at verbal tasks and the right hemisphere is typically superior at spatial tasks. Researchers debate whether people with "split brains" literally have two separate minds.

KEY CONCEPTS

KEY CONTRIBUTORS

FOR MORE INFORMATION ON BEHAVIORAL NEUROSCIENCE

FOR GENERAL WORKS ON BEHAVIORAL NEUROSCIENCE

Beatty, J. (1995). *Principles of behavioral neuroscience.* Madison, WI: Brown & Benchmark.

FOR MORE ON THE NERVOUS SYSTEM

Barr, M. L. (1993). *Human nervous system* (6th ed.). Philadelphia: Lippincott.

FOR MORE ON THE

NEURON

Structure of the Neuron

Kuno, M. (1995). *Synapse: Function, plasticity, and neurotrophism.* New York: Oxford University Press.
Shepherd, G. M. (1991). *Foundations of the neuron doctrine.* New York: Oxford University Press.

Neurotransmitters

Chafetz, M. D. (1989). *Nutrition and neurotransmitters: The nutrient basis of behavior.*

Englewood Cliffs, NJ: Prentice Hall.

Classic Neurotransmitters

Fillenz, M. (1990). *The noradrenergic neurons.* New York: Cambridge University Press.
Idzikowski, C., & Cowen, P. J. (Eds.). (1991). *Serotonin, sleep, and mental disorder.* New York: Taylor & Francis.
Steriade, M., & Biesold, D. (Eds.). (1991). *Brain cholinergic systems.* New York: Oxford University Press.

Willner, P., & Scheel-Kruger, J. (Eds.). (1991). *The mesolimbic dopamine system.* New York: Wiley.

Amino Acids

Ascher, P., Choi, D. W., & Christen, Y. (Eds.). (1991). *Glutamate, cell death, and memory.* New York: Springer-Verlag.
Biggio, G., Concas, A., & Costa, E. (Eds.). (1992). *GABAergic synaptic transmission: Molecular, pharmacological, and clinical aspects.* New York: Raven.

Wheal, H., & Thomason, A. (Eds.). (1995). *Excitatory amino acids and synaptic transmission.* San Diego: Academic Press.

Neuropeptides

Crawley, J.N., & McLean, S. (Eds.). (1996). *Neuropeptides: Basic and clinical advances.* New York: New York Academy of Sciences.

Levinthal, C. F. (1988). *Messengers of paradise: Opiates and the brain.* New York: Anchor/Doubleday.

FOR MORE ON THE ENDOCRINE SYSTEM

Nelson, R. J. (1995). *An introduction to behavioral endocrinology.* Sunderland, MA: Sinauer.

Pituitary Gland

Imura, H. (Ed.). (1994). *The pituitary gland* (2nd ed.). New York: Raven Press.

Other Glands

Adashi, E. Y., & Leung, P. C. (Eds.). (1994). *The ovary* (2nd ed.). New York: Raven.

Bliss, M. (1984). *The discovery of insulin.* Chicago: University of Chicago Press.

James, V. H. (1992). *The adrenal gland* (2nd ed.). New York: Raven Press.

McNabb, F. M. (1992). *Thyroid hormones.* Englewood Cliffs, NJ: Prentice Hall.

Nieschlag, E., & Behre, H. M. (Eds.). (1990). *Testosterone: Action, deficiency, and substitution.* New York: Springer-Verlag.

Ritter, M., & Crisp, N. (1992). *The thymus: In focus.* New York: Oxford University Press.

Shafii, M., & Shafii, S. (1990). *Biological rhythms, mood disorders, light therapy, and the pineal gland.* Washington, DC: American Psychiatric Press.

Yesalis, C. E. (Ed.). (1993). *Anabolic steroids in sport and exercise.* Champaign, IL: Human Kinetics.

FOR MORE ON BRAIN FUNCTIONS

The Hindbrain

Hobson, J. A., & Brazier, M. A. (Eds.). (1979). *The reticular formation revisited.* New York: Raven Press.

Klemm, W. R., & Vertes, R. P. (Eds.). (1990). *Brainstem mechanisms of behavior.* New York: Wiley.

Llinas, R., & Sotelo, C. (Eds.). (1992). *The cerebellum revisited.* New York: Springer-Verlag.

The Midbrain

Aitkin, L. (Ed.). (1986). *The auditory midbrain.* Humana.

Tipton, K. F., Glover, V., Stern, G., & Youndim, M. B. H. (Eds.). (1994). *Psychobiology of Parkinson's disease.* New York: Springer-Verlag.

Vanaegas, H. (Ed.). (1984). *Comparative neurology of the optic tectum.* New York: Plenum.

The Forebrain

Thalamus

Steriades, M., Jones, E.G., & McCormick, D.A. (Eds.). (1996). *The thalamus.* New York: Pergamon.

Limbic System

Aggleton, J. P. (1992). *The amygdala.* New York: Wiley.

Cohen, N. J., & Eichenbaum, H. (1993). *Memory, amnesia, and the hippocampal system.* Cambridge, MA: MIT Press.

Doane, B. K., & Livingston, K. E. (Eds.). (1986). *The limbic system: Functional organization and clinical disorders.* New York: Raven Press.

Swaab, D. F. (1992). *The human hypothalamus in health and disease.* New York: Elsevier.

Cerebral Cortex

Peters, A., & Rockland, K. S. (Eds.). (1993). *Cerebral cortex.* New York: Plenum.

Sacks, O. (1985). *The man who mistook his wife for a hat and other clinical tales.* New York: Summit.

Stern, M. B. (1971). *Heads and headlines: The phrenological Fowlers.* Norman: University of Oklahoma Press.

FOR MORE ON THE PLASTICITY OF THE BRAIN AND THE SPINAL CORD

Recovery from Neurological Damage

Finger, S., LeVere, T. E., Almli, C. R., & Stein, D. G. (1988). *Brain injury and recovery: Theoretical and controversial issues.* New York: Plenum.

Oorschot, D. E., & Jones, D. G. (1990). *Axonal regeneration in the mammalian central nervous system.* New York: Springer-Verlag.

Neural Transplantation

Dunnett, S. B., & Bjorklund, A. (Eds.). (1992). *Neural transplantation: A practical approach.* New York: Oxford University Press.

Lindvall, O. (Ed.). (1993). *Restoration of brain function by tissue transplantation.* New York: Springer-Verlag.

The Relationship Between Mind and Brain

Carrier, M. (1991). *Mind, brain, and behavior: The mind-body problem and the philosophy of psychology.* Hawthorne, NY: Walter De Gruyter.

Penfield, W. (1975). *The mystery of the mind.* Princeton, NJ: Princeton University Press.

FOR MORE ON CEREBRAL HEMISPHERIC SPECIALIZATION

Coren, S. (1992). *The left-hander syndrome: The causes and consequences of left-handedness.* New York: Free Press.

Loring, D. W., Meador, K. J., Lee, G. P., & King, D. W. (Eds.). (1991). *Amobarbital effects and lateralized brain function: The Wada test.* New York: Springer-Verlag.

Springer, S. P., & Deutsch, G. (1993). *Left brain, right brain* (4th ed.). New York: W. H. Freeman.

FOR MORE ON CONTRIBUTORS TO BEHAVIORAL NEUROSCIENCE

Goldberg, J. R. (1984, July). The creative mind: Jerre Levy. *Science Digest,* pp. 44–47, 99–92.

Hooper, J. (1982, February). Interview: Candace Pert. *Omni,* pp. 62–65, 110–112.

Koenigsberger, L. (1906/1965). *Hermann von Helmholtz.* New York: Dover.

Lewis, J. (1982). *Something hidden: A biography of Wilder Penfield.* New York: Doubleday.

Loewi, O. (1960). An autobiographic sketch. *Perspectives in Biology and Medicine, 4,* 3–25.

Ramón y Cajal, S. (1937/1989). *Recollections of my life.* Cambridge, MA: MIT Press.

Rose, F. C. (1989). *James Parkinson: His life and times.* New York: Birkhauser.

Schiller, F. (1979). *Paul Broca: Founder of French anthropology, explorer of the brain.* Berkeley: University of California Press.

CHAPTER 4

▲ Edward Potthast
Children at Shore, 1919

Human Development

developmental psychology
The field that studies physical, cognitive, and psychosocial changes across the life span.

maturation
The sequential unfolding of inherited predispositions in physical and motor development.

▲ G. Stanley Hall (1844–1924)
"There is really no clue by which we can thread our way through all the mazes of culture and the distractions of modern life save by knowing the true nature and needs of childhood and adolescence."

Each of us changes markedly across the life span. You are not the same today as you were in infancy or will be in old age. The field of **developmental psychology** studies the physical, perceptual, cognitive, and psychosocial changes that take place across the life span. This chapter addresses questions commonly asked by developmental psychologists, such as these: Are adopted children more similar to their adoptive parents or to their biological parents? Is day care harmful to children? Is adolescence necessarily a period of emotional turmoil? Do parents suffer from an "empty nest syndrome" after their last child has left home? Are there significant psychological sex differences?

THE NATURE OF DEVELOPMENTAL PSYCHOLOGY

Though opinions about the nature of human development can be found in the writings of ancient Greek philosophers, the scientific study of human development did not begin until the 1870s. That decade saw the appearance of the "baby biography," usually written by a parent, which described the development of an infant. Though much of infant development depends on learning, it is also guided by physical **maturation**—the sequential unfolding of inherited predispositions (as in the progression from crawling to standing to walking).

The 1890s saw the beginning of research on child development after infancy (White, 1990), most notably at Clark University by G. Stanley Hall (1844–1924). Hall based his theories on Darwin's theory of evolution, earning him the title "the Darwin of the mind." He applied research findings to the improvement of education and child rearing, and today he is recognized as the founder of *child psychology*. Until the 1950s the study of human development was virtually synonymous with child psychology. During that decade, psychologists began to study human development across the whole life span. The issue of the relative influence of heredity and environment on human development is one of the main concerns of developmental psychologists today, as it was a century ago.

The Influence of Heredity and Environment

To what extent are you the product of your heredity, and to what extent are you the product of your environment? This issue of "nature versus nurture" has been with us since the era of ancient Greece, when Plato championed nature and Aristotle championed nurture. Plato believed we are born with some knowledge; Aristotle believed that at birth our mind is a blank slate (or *tabula rasa*) and that life experiences provide us with knowledge.

In modern times, the argument became even more heated after Charles Darwin (1859/1975) put forth his theory of evolution in the mid nineteenth century. Darwin noted that animals and human beings vary in their physical traits. Given the competition for resources (including food and water) and the need to foil predators (by defeating them or escaping from them), animals and human beings with physical traits best adapted to these purposes would be the most likely to survive long enough to produce offspring, who would likely also have those traits. As long as particular physical traits provide a survival advantage, those traits will have a greater likelihood of showing up in succeeding generations. Darwin called this process *natural selection*. Psychologists, such as Wendy Hill, who champion an evolutionary approach to studying development, employ Darwinian concepts in their research and theorizing.

Behavioral Genetics: The Relative Importance of Heredity and Life Experiences

As noted in Chapter 1, the main proponent of the dominance of nature over nurture was Darwin's cousin Francis Galton. Galton reasoned that if physical traits exist today because they helped our ancestors survive long enough to pass on those traits, then people who are superior on those traits would be the fittest to reproduce. Through his writings and lectures, Galton popularized the phrase *nature versus nurture* (Teigen, 1984). His book *Hereditary Genius* (1869) reveals his bias in favor of nature over nurture. The book traced the family trees of 1,000 reputed geniuses, all males, from 300 families. Given his estimate that genius occurs in only 1 in 4,000 men, Galton concluded, reasonably enough, that genius runs in families. He did not immediately attribute this to heredity, being well aware that environmental similarity goes hand in hand with hereditary similarity. Siblings share not only common hereditary backgrounds but common rearing environments. So, without more information, we have no more right to attribute sibling similarities to their common heredity than to attribute them to their common environment.

After considering the available evidence, Galton concluded that genius is, in fact, produced by nature and not by nurture. One of the pieces of evidence he used to support this conclusion was the fact that the United States did not produce proportionately more geniuses than Great Britain did—despite the more widespread availability of education in the United States. Galton concluded that heredity, not life experiences, accounted for cases of superior intellectual development (Schlesinger, 1985). Those who favored the nurture side of the nature-nurture controversy had their own eminent supporters, including Hermann von Helmholtz, perhaps the greatest scientist of the nineteenth century (Koenigsberger, 1906/1965).

The hereditarian bias of early psychology weakened with the rise of behaviorism in the 1920s. Behaviorists urged psychologists to downplay the importance of heredity and to stress the role of life experiences. The waning of behaviorism since the 1960s has been accompanied by renewed interest in the hereditary basis of human behavior. This has stimulated the growth of **behavioral genetics,** which studies how heredity and life experiences interact in affecting development (Scarr, 1995). Research in behavioral genetics has found evidence of a hereditary basis for characteristics as diverse as divorce (Jocklin, McGue, & Lykken, 1996), empathy (Plomin, 1994), and intelligence (Loehlin, Horn, & Willerman, 1994). The possible role of heredity in human social relationships inspired the following study by evolutionary psychologist David Buss and his colleagues Randy Larsen, Drew Westen, and Jennifer Semmelroth at the University of Michigan (Buss et al., 1992).

▲ Wendy Hill
"Developmental psychobiology might contribute to refinements in evolutionary theory."

behavioral genetics
The study of the effects of heredity and life experiences on behavior.

ANATOMY OF A CONTEMPORARY RESEARCH STUDY

Are Social Relationships Governed by Predispositions Molded by Evolution?

Rationale

Buss believes that evolution has left its mark on human behavior, even in the area of romance. Because women can be sure that their newborns are truly theirs, while men cannot, Buss hypothesized that men would exhibit more sexual jealousy than emotional jealousy. Because prehistoric women were, on the average, physically weaker and more responsible for caring for their children, and depended on men to support them after giving birth, Buss hypothesized that women would exhibit more emotional jealousy than sexual jealousy. He assumes that these differences are the product of thousands of generations of natural selection.

Method

The subjects were 202 male and female undergraduate students. They were asked which of the following two alternatives would distress them more: their serious romantic partner forming a deep emotional attachment to someone else or that partner enjoying passionate sexual intercourse with someone else. The subjects were also asked to respond to a similar dilemma in which their romantic partner either fell in love with another person or tried a variety of sexual positions with that person.

► "Not guilty by reason of genetic determinism, Your Honor."
Drawing by Mankoff; © 1982 The New Yorker Magazine, Inc.

Results and Discussion

The results showed that for the first dilemma 60 percent of the male subjects reported greater jealousy over their partner's potential sexual infidelity. In contrast, 83 percent of the female subjects reported greater jealousy over their partner's potential emotional infidelity. This pattern of responses was repeated in response to the second dilemma. Of course, cultural interpretations of male sexual jealousy and female emotional jealousy are possible. But the researchers pointed to the commonness of intense male sexual jealousy as evidence of its possible hereditary basis.

▲ ▲ ▲

To appreciate behavioral genetics, you should have at least a basic understanding of genetics itself. The science of genetics can be traced to 1866, when the Austrian monk and amateur botanist Gregor Mendel published a paper that described the principles governing the inheritance of physical traits in pea plants. These traits included their size, color, and skin characteristics. Since Mendel's time, we have learned much about the principles of heredity and its physical mechanisms. The cells of the human body contain 23 pairs of *chromosomes*, which are long strands of *deoxyribonucleic acid (DNA)* molecules. (Unlike the other body cells, the egg cell and sperm cell each contains 23 single chromosomes.) DNA molecules are ribbonlike structures composed of segments called *genes*. Genes direct the synthesis of *ribonucleic acid (RNA)*. RNA, in turn, directs the synthesis of proteins, which are responsible for the structure and functioning of our tissues and organs.

Though our genes direct our physical development, their effects on our behavior are primarily indirect (Mann, 1994). There are, for example, no "motorcycle daredevil genes." Instead, physiological factors, such as hormones, neurotransmitters, and brain structures, are influenced by genes. These factors, in turn, make people somewhat more likely to engage in particular behaviors. Perhaps people destined to become motorcycle daredevils inherit a less physiologically reactive nervous system, making them experience less anxiety in dangerous situations. Moreover, given current trends in molecular genetics, behavioral geneticists are on the threshold of identifying genes that affect behavior (Plomin, 1995).

Our outward appearance and behavior might not indicate our exact genetic inheritance. In recognition of this, scientists distinguish between our *genotype* and our *phenotype*. Your **genotype** is your genetic inheritance. Your **phenotype** is the overt expression of your inheritance in your appearance or behavior. For example, your eye color is determined by the interaction of a gene inherited from your mother and a gene inherited from your father. The brown-eye gene is *dominant*, and the blue-eye gene is *recessive*. Dominant genes take precedence over recessive genes. Traits carried by recessive genes show up in phenotypes only when recessive genes occur together. If you are blue-eyed, your genotype includes two blue-eye genes (both recessive). If you have brown eyes, your genotype may include two brown-eye genes (both dominant) or one brown-eye gene (dominant) and one blue-eye gene (recessive).

In contrast to simple traits like eye color, most characteristics are governed by more than one pair of genes—that is, they are *polygenic*. With rare exceptions, this is especially true of genetic influences on human behaviors and abilities. Your athletic, academic, and social skills depend on the interaction of many genes, as well as your life experiences. For example, your muscularity (your phenotype) depends on both your genetic endowment (your genotype) and your dietary and exercise habits (your life experiences).

To appreciate research studies that try to determine the relative contributions of heredity and environment to human development, you should understand the concept of heritability. **Heritability** refers to the proportion of variability in a trait across a population. For example, human beings differ in their intelligence (as measured by IQ tests). To what extent is this variability caused by heredity, and to what extent is it caused by experience? Heritability values range from 0.0 to 1.0. If heritability accounted for none of the variability in intelligence, it would have a value of 0.0. If heritability accounted for all of the variability in intelligence, it would have a value of 1.0. In reality, the heritability of intelligence, as measured by IQ tests, is estimated to be between .50 (Chipuer, Rovine, & Plomin, 1990) and .70 (Bouchard et al., 1990). This indicates that the variability in intelligence is strongly, but not solely, influenced by heredity. Environmental factors also account for much of the variability.

Studies of Relatives: Research on Families, Adoptees, and Reunited Twins

Research procedures that assess the relative contributions of nature and nurture to human development involve the study of relatives. These include family studies and adoption

genotype
An individual's genetic inheritance.

phenotype
The overt expression of an individual's genetic inheritance, which may also show the influence of the environment.

heritability
The extent to which variability in a characteristic within a group can be attributed to heredity.

studies. *Family studies* investigate similarities between relatives with varying degrees of genetic similarity. These studies find that the closer the genetic relationship (that is, the more genes that are shared) between relatives, the more alike they tend to be on a variety of traits. For example, the siblings of a person who has schizophrenia are significantly more likely to have schizophrenia than are the schizophrenic's cousins. Though it is tempting to attribute this to their degree of genetic similarity, one cannot rule out that it is actually due to their degree of environmental similarity.

The best kind of family study is the *twin study*, which compares identical (or *monozygotic*) twins to fraternal (or *dizygotic*) twins. This kind of study was introduced by Galton, who found more similarity between identical twins than between fraternal twins—and attributed this to heredity. Identical twins, because they come from the same fertilized egg, have the same genetic inheritance. Fraternal twins, because they come from different fertilized eggs, do not. They merely have the same degree of genetic similarity as ordinary siblings. Moreover, twins, whether identical or fraternal, are born at the same time and share similar environments. Because research has found that identical twins reared in similar environments are more psychologically similar than fraternal twins reared in similar environments, it is reasonable to attribute the greater similarity of identical twins to heredity. Nonetheless, there is an alternative, environmental explanation. Perhaps identical twins become more psychologically similar because they are reared more alike than fraternal twins are. Identical twins are, in fact, often treated as though they were indistinguishable (Hoffman, 1991).

Superior to family studies are *adoption studies*, which measure the correlation in particular traits between adopted children and their biological parents and between those same adopted children and their adoptive parents. Adoption studies have found that adoptees are more similar to their biological parents than to their adoptive parents in traits such as body fat (Price & Gottesman, 1991), drug abuse (Cadoret et al., 1995), vocational interests (Lykken et al., 1993), and religious values (Waller et al., 1990). These findings indicate that, with regard to such traits, the genes that adoptees inherit from their biological parents affect their development more than does the environment they are provided with by their adoptive parents.

Yet the environment cannot be ruled out as an explanation for the greater similarity between adoptees and their biological parents. As explained later in this chapter, prenatal experiences can affect children's development. Perhaps adoptees are more like their biological parents, not because they share the same genes, but because the adoptees spent their prenatal months in their biological mother's womb, making them subject to their mother's drug habits, nutritional intake, or other environmental influences. Moreover, their experiences with their biological parents in early infancy, before they were adopted, might affect their development, possibly making them more similar to their biological parents.

Perhaps the best procedure is to study *identical twins reared apart*. Research on a variety of traits consistently finds higher positive correlations between identical twins reared apart than between fraternal twins reared together. Because identical twins share identical genes, virtually identical prenatal environments, and highly similar neonatal environments, this provides strong evidence in favor of the nature side of the debate. This has been supported by a widely publicized study conducted at the University of Minnesota, which has examined similarities between identical twins who were separated in infancy and reunited later in life. The study has found some uncanny similarities in the habits, abilities, and physiological responses of the reunited twins (Bouchard et al., 1990). For example, one pair of twins at their first reunion discovered that they "both used Vademecum toothpaste, Canoe shaving lotion, Vitalis hair tonic, and Lucky Strike cigarettes. After that meeting, they exchanged birthday presents that crossed in the mail and proved to be identical choices, made independently in separate cities" (Lykken et al., 1992, p. 1565).

But some of these similarities might be due to coincidence or being reared in similar environments or having some contact with each other before being studied. In fact, research on even unrelated people shows moderately strong similarities in their personality traits (Wyatt, 1993). Moreover, identical twins look the same and might elicit responses from others that indirectly lead to their developing similar interests and personalities. Consider how we treat obese people, muscular people, attractive people, and people with acne. Thus, identical twins who share certain physical traits might become more similar than ordinary siblings who do not share such traits—even when reared in different cultures (Ford, 1993). As you can see, no kind of study is flawless in demonstrating the superiority of heredity over environment in guiding development (Saudino & Plomin, 1996).

Regardless of the influence of heredity on development, behavior genetics researcher Robert Plomin reminds us that life experiences are also important. In one study, personality test scores of identical and fraternal twins were compared at an average of 20 years of age and then at 30 years of age. The conclusion was that the stable core of personality is strongly influenced by heredity but that personality change is overwhelmingly influenced by environment (McGue, Bacon, & Lykken, 1993). Thus, heredity might have provided you with the intellectual potential to become a Nobel Prize winner, but without adequate academic experiences you might not perform well enough even to graduate from college.

▲ **Robert Plomin**
"The evidence from behavioral genetics research indicates that nongenetic factors are at least as important as genetic factors."

Research Methods in Developmental Psychology

Though developmental psychologists often use the same research methods as other psychologists, they also rely on methods that are unique to developmental psychology. These include *longitudinal research, cross-sectional research,* and *cohort-sequential research,* which enable researchers to study age-related changes in their subjects.

Longitudinal Research: Studying Development over Time

Longitudinal research follows the same subjects over a period of time, typically ranging from months to years. The researcher looks for changes in particular characteristics, such as language, personality, intelligence, or perceptual ability. Suppose you wanted to study changes in the social maturity of college students. If you chose to use a longitudinal design, you might assess the social maturity of an incoming class of freshmen and then note changes in their social maturity across their 4 years in college. Longitudinal research has been used to study numerous topics, such as factors associated with risk of divorce in married couples (Karney & Bradbury, 1995) and the effect of day care (Broberg et al., 1997).

Though longitudinal research has the advantage of permitting us to study individuals as they change across their life spans, it has major weaknesses. First, the typical longitudinal study takes months, years, or even decades to complete. This often requires ongoing financial support and continued commitment by researchers—neither of which can be guaranteed. Second, the longer the study lasts, the more likely it is that subjects will drop out. They might refuse to continue or move away or even die. If those who drop out differ in important ways from those who remain, the results of the research might be less generalizable to the population of interest. For example, a 14-year longitudinal study of changes in adult intelligence found that those who dropped out had scored lower on intelligence tests than did those who remained. This made it unwise to generalize the study's findings to all adults. Including only those who remained in the study would have led to the erroneous conclusion that as adults age they show a marked increase in intelligence (Schaie, Labouvie, & Barrett, 1973).

longitudinal research
A research design in which the same group of subjects is tested or observed repeatedly over a period of time.

Cross-Sectional Research: Comparing Different Age Groups

The weaknesses of longitudinal research are overcome by **cross-sectional research,** which compares groups of subjects of different ages at the same time. Each of the age groups is called a **cohort.** If you chose to use a cross-sectional design to study changes in social maturity of college students, you might compare the current social maturity of four cohorts: freshmen, sophomores, juniors, and seniors. A cross-sectional research design was used in a study of changes in male sexuality across adulthood. The researchers compared

cross-sectional research
A research design in which groups of subjects of different ages are compared at the same point in time.

cohort
A group of people of the same age.

samples of men in their thirties through nineties. The stereotypical view of old age as a time of asexuality was countered by the finding that all of the subjects in the oldest groups reported feelings of sexual desire (Mulligan & Moss, 1991).

Like longitudinal research, cross-sectional research has its own weaknesses. The main one is that cross-sectional research can produce misleading findings if a cohort in the study is affected by circumstances unique to that cohort. Thus, cross-sectional studies can identify differences between cohorts of different ages, but those differences might not hold true if cohorts of those ages were observed during another era. Suppose that you conduct a cross-sectional study and find that older adults are more prejudiced against minorities than younger adults are. Does this mean that we become more prejudiced with age? Not necessarily. Perhaps, instead, the cohort of older adults was reared at a time when prejudice was more acceptable than it is today. Members of the cohort might simply have retained attitudes they developed in their youth.

Cohort-Sequential Research: Combining Longitudinal and Cross-Sectional Research

One way to deal with the shortcomings of longitudinal and cross-sectional research is to use **cohort-sequential research,** which begins as a cross-sectional study by comparing different cohorts and then follows the cohorts longitudinally. As an example, consider how a cohort-sequential research design was employed in a study of alcohol use in old age. Healthy cohorts ranging in age from 60 to 86 years old were first compared cross-sectionally. The results showed a decline in the percentage of drinkers with age. The cohorts were then followed longitudinally for 7 years. The results remained the same: as the drinkers aged, they drank less. This made it more likely that the decline in drinking with age was related to age rather than to life experiences peculiar to particular cohorts (Adams et al., 1990).

Longitudinal research, cross-sectional research, and cohort-sequential research have long been staples of developmental research on development from birth to death. Today, technology permits developmental psychologists to study ongoing developmental processes even before birth, during the prenatal period.

STAYING ON TRACK: *The Nature of Developmental Psychology*

1. What have studies of identical twins reared apart discovered about the roles of nature and nurture in human development?
2. What is a cohort-sequential research design?

Answers to Staying on Track start on p. S-2.

PRENATAL DEVELOPMENT

You, Julius Caesar, Oprah Winfrey, and anyone else who has ever lived began as a single cell. The formation of that cell begins the *prenatal period*, which lasts about 9 months and is divided into the *germinal stage*, the *embryonic stage*, and the *fetal stage*. Figure 4.1 illustrates prenatal development.

The Germinal Stage: Development During the First Few Days

The **germinal stage** begins with conception, which occurs when a *sperm* from the male unites with an egg (or *ovum*) from the female in one of her two *fallopian tubes*, forming a one-celled *zygote*. The zygote contains 23 pairs of chromosomes, one member of each pair coming from the ovum and the other coming from the sperm. The chromosomes, in turn, contain genes that govern the development of the individual. The zygote begins a trip down the fallopian tube, during which it is transformed into a larger, multicelled ball by repeated cell divisions. By the end of the second week, the ball attaches to the wall of the uterus. This marks the beginning of the embryonic stage.

cohort-sequential research
Research that begins as a cross-sectional study of different cohorts and then follows the cohorts longitudinally.

germinal stage
The prenatal period that lasts from conception through the second week.

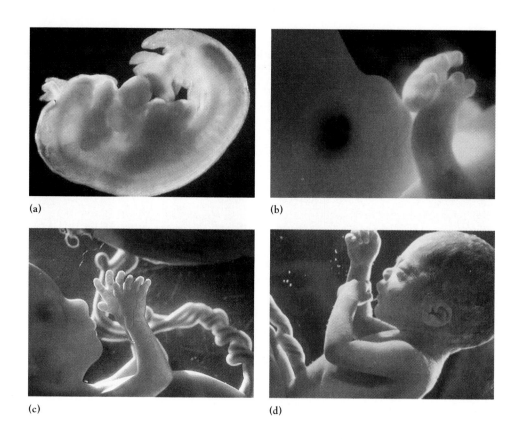

(a)

(b)

(c)

(d)

◀**FIGURE 4.1**
Prenatal Development
Prenatal development is marked by rapid growth and differentation of structures. (a) At 4 weeks, the embryo is about 0.2 inches long, has a recognizable head, arm buds, leg buds, and a heart that has begun beating. (b) At 8 weeks—the end of the embryonic stage—the embryo has features that make it recognizable as distinctly human, including a nose, a mouth, eyes, ears, hands, fingers, feet, and toes. This marks the beginning of the fetal stage. (c) At 16 weeks the fetus is about 7 inches long and makes movements that can be detected by the mother. The remainder of the fetal stage involves extremely rapid growth. (d) At 9 months the fetus is fully formed and ready to be born.

The Embryonic Stage: Development from the Second Through the Eighth Week

The **embryonic stage** lasts from the end of the second week through the eighth week of prenatal development. The embryo, nourished by nutrients that cross the *placenta*, increases in size and begins to develop specialized organs, including the eyes, heart, and brain. What accounts for this rapid, complex process? The development and location of bodily organs is regulated by genes, which determine the kinds of cells that will develop and also direct the actions of *cell-adhesion molecules*. These molecules direct the movement of cells and determine which cells will adhere to one another, thereby determining the size, shape, and location of organs in the embryo (Edelman, 1984). Mutations that affect certain cell-adhesion molecules contribute to mental retardation by interfering with normal brain development (Wong et al., 1995). By the end of the embryonic stage, development has progressed to the point at which the heart is beating and the approximately one-inch-long embryo has facial features, limbs, fingers, and toes.

But what determines whether an embryo becomes a male or a female? The answer lies in the 23rd pair of chromosomes, the sex chromosomes, which are designated X or Y. Embryos that inherit two X chromosomes are genetic females, and embryos that inherit one X and one Y chromosome are genetic males. Near the end of the embryonic period, the primitive gonads of male embryos secrete the hormone *testosterone*, which stimulates the development of male sexual organs.

embryonic stage
The prenatal period that lasts from the end of the second week through the eighth week.

The Fetal Stage: Development from the Ninth Week Through Birth

The presence of a distinctly human appearance marks the beginning of the **fetal stage,** which lasts from the beginning of the third prenatal month until birth. By the fourth

fetal stage
The prenatal period that lasts from the end of the eighth week through birth.

teratogen

A noxious substance, such as a virus or drug, that can cause prenatal defects.

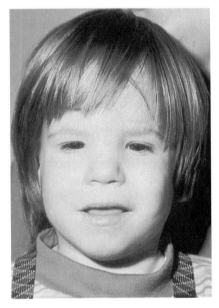

▲ FIGURE 4.2
Fetal Alcohol Syndrome
Prenatal exposure to alcohol can produce fetal alcohol syndrome, which is marked by mental retardation and facial deformities.

fetal alcohol syndrome
A disorder, marked by physical defects and mental retardation, that can afflict the offspring of women who drink alcohol during pregnancy.

month, pregnant women report movement by the fetus. And by the seventh month all of the major organs are functional, which means that an infant born even 2 or 3 months prematurely has a chance of surviving. The final 3 months of prenatal development are associated with most of the increase in the size of the fetus. Premature infants tend to be smaller and less physically and cognitively mature than full-term infants. For example, when an object approaches the eyes of a premature infant, the infant might not exhibit normal defensive blinking (Pettersen, Yonas, & Fisch, 1980).

Though prenatal development usually produces a normal infant, in some cases genetic defects produce distinctive physical and psychological syndromes. For example, the chromosomal disorder called *Down syndrome* (discussed in Chapter 10) is associated with mental retardation and abnormal physical development. Other sources of prenatal defects are **teratogens,** which are noxious substances or other factors that can disrupt prenatal development and prevent the individual from reaching her or his inherited potential. (The word *teratogen* was coined from Greek terms meaning "that which produces a monster.") A powerful teratogen is the X ray. Prenatal exposure to X rays can disrupt the migration of brain cells to their intended targets, causing mental retardation (Schull, Norton, & Jensh, 1990).

Most teratogens affect prenatal development by first crossing the placenta. For example, a potent teratogen is the German measles (rubella) virus, which can cause defects of the eyes, ears, and heart—particularly during the first 3 months of prenatal development. Many popular drugs, both legal and illegal, can cross the placenta and cause abnormal physical and psychological development. These drugs include cocaine (Snodgrass, 1994), nicotine (Day & Richardson, 1994), and marijuana (Fried & Watkinson, 1990). Pregnant women who drink alcohol can afflict their offspring with **fetal alcohol syndrome.** The hallmarks of this disorder are facial deformities and mental retardation (Short & Hess, 1995). Figure 4.2 shows a child who suffers from fetal alcohol syndrome.

STAYING ON TRACK: *Prenatal Development*

1. What are cell-adhesion molecules?
2. What are the symptoms of fetal alcohol syndrome?

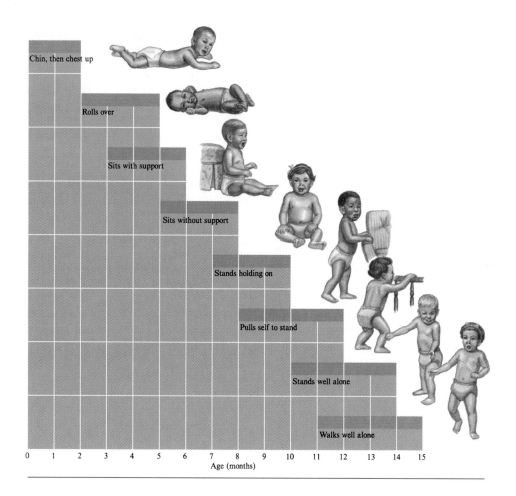

Chin, then chest up

Rolls over

Sits with support

Sits without support

Stands holding on

Pulls self to stand

Stands well alone

Walks well alone

| 0 | 1 | 2 | 3 | 4 | 5 | 6 | 7 | 8 | 9 | 10 | 11 | 12 | 13 | 14 | 15 |

Age (months)

◀ FIGURE 4.3
Motor Milestones
Infancy is a period of rapid motor development.
The infant begins with a set of motor reflexes
and, over the course of little more than a year,
develops the ability to manipulate objects and
move independently through the environment.
The ages at which normal children reach motor
milestones vary somewhat from child to child,
but the sequence of motor milestones does not.

INFANT AND CHILD DEVELOPMENT

Childhood extends from birth until puberty and begins with **infancy,** a period of rapid
physical, cognitive, and psychosocial development, extending from birth to age 2 years.
Many developmental psychologists devote themselves to studying the changes in physical,
perceptual, cognitive, and psychosocial development that occur during childhood.

Physical Development

Newborn infants exhibit reflexes that promote their survival, such as blinking to protect
their eyes from an approaching object and rooting for a nipple when their cheeks are
touched. Through maturation and learning, the infant quickly develops motor skills that
go beyond mere reflexes. The typical infant is crawling by 6 months and walking by 13
months. Though infant motor development follows a consistent sequence, the timing of
motor milestones varies somewhat from one infant to another. Figure 4.3 depicts the
major motor milestones.

Infancy is also a period of rapid brain development, when many connections between
brain cells are formed and many others are eliminated (Huttenlocher, 1990). Though many
of these changes are governed by maturation, research studies by Marian Diamond and her
colleagues over the past few decades have demonstrated that life experiences can affect
brain development (Diamond, 1988). One of these studies determined the effect of enriched
and impoverished environments on the brain development of rats (Camel, Withers, &
Greenough, 1986). A group of infant rats spent 30 days in an enriched environment and

childhood
The period that extends from birth until
the onset of puberty.

infancy
The period that extends from birth
through 2 years of age.

Abilities of Newborn Infants
Newborn infants not only see better than has been traditionally assumed, they can also imitate facial expressions of surprise, sadness, and happiness.

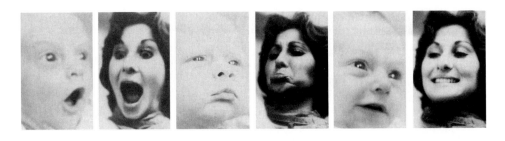

another group spent 30 days in an impoverished environment. In the enriched environment, the rats were housed together in two large, toy-filled cages, one containing water and one containing food, which were attached to the opposite ends of a maze. The pattern of pathways and dead ends through the maze was changed daily. In the impoverished environment, the rats were housed individually in small, empty cages.

Microscopic examination of the brains of the rats found that those exposed to the enriched environment had longer and more numerous dendrites (see Chapter 3) on their brain neurons than did those exposed to the impoverished environment. The increased size and number of dendrites would provide the rats exposed to the enriched environment with more synaptic connections among their brain neurons. The benefits of enriched environments on neural development have been replicated in other studies of animals (Reed, 1993; Wallace et al., 1992).

After infancy, the child's growth rate slows, and most children grow two or three inches a year until puberty. The child's motor coordination also improves. Children learn to perform more-sophisticated motor tasks, such as using scissors, tying their shoes, and riding bicycles. The development of motor skills even affects the development of cognitive skills. For example, children's ability to express themselves through language depends on the development of motor abilities that permit them to speak and to write.

Perceptual Development

A century ago, in describing what he believed was the chaotic mental world of the newborn infant, William James (1890/1981, 1: 462) claimed, "The baby, assailed by eyes, ears, nose, skin, and entrails at once, feels it all as one great blooming, buzzing confusion." But subsequent research has shown that newborn infants have more highly developed sensory, perceptual, and cognitive abilities than James believed. For example, though newborns cannot focus on distant objects, they can focus on objects less than a foot away—as though nature has programmed them to focus at the distance of the face of an adult who might be holding them (Aslin & Smith, 1988).

Ingenious studies have permitted researchers to infer what infants perceive by recording changes in their eye movements, head movements, body movements, sucking behavior, or physiological responses (such as changes in heart rate or brain-wave patterns). For example, infant preferences can be determined by recording which targets they look at longer or by presenting them with a stimulus, waiting for them to *habituate* to it (that is, stop noticing it—as indicated by, for example, a stable heart rate), and then changing the stimulus. If they notice the change, they will show alterations in physiological activity, such as a *decrease* in heart rate.

Studies using these techniques have found that infants have remarkably well developed sensory abilities. Tiffany Field has demonstrated that, as shown in Figure 4.4, infants less than 2 days old can imitate sad, happy, and surprised facial expressions (Field et al., 1982). Nonetheless, other studies have been inconsistent in their findings on neonatal imitation. The most consistent finding has been that neonates will imitate models who stick out their tongues (Anisfeld, 1991). The following study involves the use of the "visual cliff" by Eleanor Gibson and Richard Walk in testing infant depth perception.

▲ Tiffany Field
"We now have evidence for both the discrimination and imitation of facial expressions at an even younger age, shortly after birth."

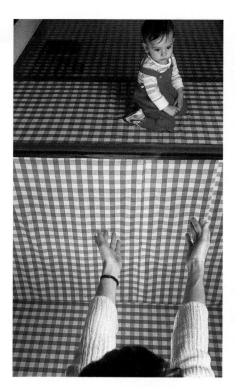

Eleanor Gibson and Richard Walk (1960) developed the *visual cliff* to test infant depth perception. The visual cliff consists of a thick sheet of glass placed on a table: The "shallow" end of the visual cliff has a checkerboard surface just below the glass. The "deep" end of the visual cliff has a checkerboard surface a few feet below the glass. An infant who has reached the crawling stage will crawl from the center of the table across the shallow end, but not across the deep end, to reach his or her mother. This indicates that by 6 months infants can perceive depth. Of course, this does not preclude the possibility that they can perceive depth even before they can crawl.

ANATOMY OF A CLASSIC RESEARCH STUDY

When Do Infants Develop Depth Perception?

Rationale

One of the most important perceptual abilities is depth perception. It lets us tell how far away objects are from us, preventing us from bumping into them and providing us with time to escape from potentially dangerous ones. But how early can infants perceive depth? This was the subject of a classic study by Eleanor Gibson and Richard Walk (1960).

Method

Gibson and Walk used a "visual cliff" made from a piece of thick, transparent glass set about four feet off the ground (see Figure 4.5). Just under the "shallow" side was a red and white checkerboard pattern. The same pattern was placed at floor level under the "deep" side. The sides were separated by a one-foot-wide wooden board. The subjects were 36 infants, aged 6 to 14 months. The infants were placed, one at a time, on the wooden board. The infants' mothers called to them, first from one side and then from the other.

Results and Discussion

When placed on the board, 9 of the infants refused to budge. The other 27 crawled onto the shallow side toward their mothers. But only 3 of the 27 crawled onto the deep side. The remaining ones instead cried or crawled away from it. This indicated that the infants could perceive the depth of the two sides—and feared the deep side. It also demonstrated that depth perception is present by 6 months of age. Replications of the study using a variety of animals found that depth perception develops by the time the animal begins moving about on its own—as early as the first day after birth for chicks and goats. This is adaptive, because it reduces their likelihood of harming themselves.

More recent research on human infants, using decreases in heart rate as a sign that they notice changes in depth, indicates that rudimentary depth perception is present in infants as young as 4 months (Aslin & Smith, 1988). But research indicates that human infants will not fear heights until they have had several weeks of crawling experience. Infants will not avoid the deep side of the visual cliff until they have had 6 to 8 weeks of crawling experience (Bertenthal, Campos, & Kermoian, 1994).

▲ ▲ ▲

Stage	Description	Age Range
Sensorimotor	The infant progresses from reflexive, instinctual action at birth to the beginning of symbolic thought. The infant constructs an understanding of the world by coordinating sensory experiences with physical actions.	Birth–2 years
Preoperational	The child begins to represent the world with words and images; these words and images reflect increased symbolic thinking and go beyond the connection of sensory information and physical action.	2–7 years
Concrete Operational	The child now can reason logically about concrete events and can mentally reverse information.	7–11 years
Formal Operational	The adolescent reasons in more abstract, idealistic, and logical ways.	11–15 years

▲ **TABLE 4.1**
Piaget's Stages of Cognitive Development

Infants also have good auditory abilities, including the ability to localize sounds. Between the ages of 8 and 28 weeks, infants can localize sounds that shift in location by only a few degrees, as indicated by head turns or eye movements in response to the shifts (Morrongiello, Fenwick, & Chance, 1990). Infants can even match the emotional tone of sounds to the emotional tone of facial expressions. In one study, 7-month-old infants were shown a sad face and a happy face. At the same time, they were presented with tones that either increased or decreased in pitch. When presented with a descending tone, they looked longer at a sad face than a happy face, as if they were equating the lower tones with a sad mood and the higher tones with a happy mood (Phillips et al., 1990). As the preceding studies attest, infants are perceptually more sophisticated than William James presumed.

Cognitive Development

Infancy is also a time of rapid cognitive development, during which infants show the unfolding of inborn abilities and their talent for learning. In regard to inborn abilites, for example, newborn infants can distinguish groups of objects that differ in number (Wynn, 1995). In regard to learning, by 4 or 5 months old, an infant's response to the sound of its own name differs from its response to hearing other names (Mandel, Jusczyk, & Pisoni, 1995).

Jean Piaget (1896–1980), a Swiss biologist and psychologist, put forth the most influential theory of cognitive development (Flavell, 1996). Piaget (1952) proposed that children pass through four increasingly sophisticated cognitive stages of development (see Table 4.1). According to Piaget, a child is more than an ignorant adult; the child's way of thinking is qualitatively different from the adult's. Though Piaget assumed that complete passage through one stage is a prerequisite for success in the next one, research suggests that children can achieve characteristics of later stages without completely passing through earlier ones (Berninger, 1988). The issue of whether human cognitive development is continuous (gradual and quantitative) or discontinuous (in stages and qualitative) remains unresolved (Fischer & Silvern, 1985). The stages put forth by Piaget are the *sensorimotor stage, preoperational stage, concrete operational stage*, and *formal operational stage*. Cross-cultural research indicates that children throughout the world tend to pass through these stages in the same order, though the timing varies (Segall et al., 1990).

Sensorimotor Stage

Piaget called infancy the **sensorimotor stage,** during which the child learns to coordinate sensory experiences and motor behaviors. Infants learn to interact with the world by sucking, grasping, crawling, and walking. In little more than a year, they change from being reflexive and physically immature to being purposeful, locomoting, and language-using. By the age of 9 months, for example, sensorimotor coordination becomes sophisticated enough for the infant to grasp a moving object by aiming her or his reach somewhat ahead of the object instead of where the object appears to be at that moment (Hofsten, 1983).

Piaget claimed that experiences with the environment help the infant form **schemas,** which are mental models incorporating the characteristics of persons, objects, events,

▲ **Jean Piaget (1896–1980)**
"As the child's thought evolves, assimilation and accommodation are differentiated and become increasingly complementary."

sensorimotor stage

The Piagetian stage, from birth through the second year, during which the infant learns to coordinate sensory experiences and motor behavior.

schema

A mental model incorporating the characteristics of particular persons, objects, events, or situations.

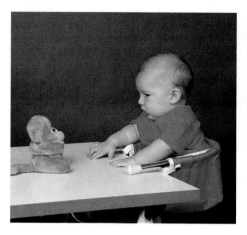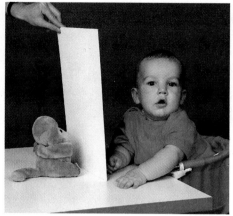

Object Permanence
After young infants see an object being hidden from view, they act as though it no longer exists. This indicates that they lack the concept of *object permanence*—the realization that an object that is no longer in view may still exist.

procedures, or situations. This means that infants do more than simply gather information about the world. Their experiences actively change the way in which they think about the world. Schemas permit infants to adapt their behaviors to changes in the environment. But what makes schemas persist or change? They do so as the result of the interplay between **assimilation** and **accommodation.** We *assimilate* when we fit information into our existing schemas and *accommodate* when we revise our schemas to fit new information.

Young infants, prior to 6 months old, share an important schema in which they assume that the removal of an object from sight means that the object no longer exists. If an object is hidden by a piece of cloth, for example, the young infant will not look for it, even after watching the object being hidden. As illustrated in Figure 4.6, to the young infant, out of sight truly means out of mind. As infants gain experience with the coming and going of objects in the environment, they accommodate and develop the schema of **object permanence**—the realization that objects not in view may still exist. At 8 months infants might look for an object that has been removed, but only at the site where they last saw it. But researchers have questioned Piaget's explanation that young infants fail to search for hidden objects because they lack a schema for object permanence. Perhaps, instead, they simply forget the location of an object that has been hidden from view (Bjork & Cummings, 1984).

After the age of 8 months, most infants demonstrate their appreciation of object permanence by searching at other places for an object they have seen being hidden from view. At this point in their development they can retain a mental image of a physical object even after it has been removed from their sight, and they realize that the object might be elsewhere. This also signifies the beginning of *representational thought*—the use of symbols to stand for physical objects. But Piaget might have placed the development of object permanence too late, because infants as young as 3 or 4 months may show an appreciation of it (Baillargeon & DeVos, 1991).

Preoperational Stage

According to Piaget, when the child reaches the age of 2 years and leaves infancy, the sensorimotor stage gives way to the **preoperational stage,** which lasts until about age 7. The stage is called preoperational because the child cannot perform what Piaget called *operations*—mental manipulations of reality. For example, before about the age of 5 the early preoperational child cannot perform mental addition or subtraction of objects. During the preoperational stage, however, the child improves in the use of language, including a rapid growth in vocabulary and a more sophisticated use of grammar. Thus mental development sets the stage for language development. Unlike the sensorimotor-stage child, the preoperational-stage child is not limited to thinking about objects that are physically present.

During the preoperational stage the child also exhibits what Piaget called **egocentrism,** the inability to perceive reality from the perspective of another person. Egocentrism declines between 4 and 6 years of age (Ruffman & Olson, 1989). Children display egocentrism when they draw a picture of their family but fail to include themselves in the drawing.

assimilation
The cognitive process that interprets new information in light of existing schemas.

accommodation
The cognitive process that revises existing schemas to incorporate new information.

object permanence
The realization that objects exist even when they are no longer visible.

preoperational stage
The Piagetian stage, extending from 2 to 7 years of age, during which the child's use of language becomes more sophisticated but the child has difficulty with the logical mental manipulation of information.

egocentrism
The inability to perceive physical reality from the perspective of another person.

▶ **FIGURE 4.7**
Conservation
During the concrete operational stage, the child develops an appreciation of conservation. The child comes to realize that changing the form of something does not change its amount—for instance, that the containers pictured here can hold the same amount of liquid. In a classic demonstration used by Piaget, a child is shown a tall, narrow container and a short, wide container that can hold equal amounts of a liquid. When the liquid in the short container is poured into the empty tall container, the preoperational child will perceive the tall container as holding more liquid than did the short container. In contrast, the concrete operational child realizes that the tall container now holds the same amount of liquid as did the short container.

concrete operational stage

The Piagetian stage, extending from 7 to 11 years of age, during which the child learns to reason logically about objects that are physically present.

transitive inference

The application of previously learned relationships to infer new relationships.

conservation

The realization that changing the form of a substance does not change its amount.

In some capital criminal cases, lawyers might gain a reduced sentence for a child defendant if they can convince the jury that the child had not progressed beyond egocentrism and therefore was unaware of the effect of the criminal act on the victim (Ellison, 1987).

Concrete Operational Stage

At about the age of 7, the child enters what Piaget calls the **concrete operational stage,** which lasts until about the age of 11. The child learns to reason logically but is at first limited to reasoning about physical things. For example, when you first learned to do arithmetic problems, you were unable to perform mental calculations. Instead, until perhaps the age of 8, you counted by using your fingers or other objects. An important kind of reasoning ability that develops during this stage is the ability to make **transitive inferences**—the application of previously learned relationships to infer new ones. For example, suppose that a child is told that John is taller than Paul, and that Paul is taller than James. A child who can make transitive inferences will correctly conclude that John is taller than James. Though Piaget claimed that the ability to make transitive inferences develops by age 8, research has shown that children as young as 4 can make them—provided they are given age-appropriate tasks (Pears & Bryant, 1990).

By the age of 8, the child in the concrete operational stage also develops what Piaget called **conservation**—the realization that changing the form of a substance or the arrangement of a set of objects does not change the amount. Suppose that a child is shown two balls of clay of equal size. One ball is then rolled out into a snake, and the child is asked if either piece of clay has more clay. The child who has not achieved conservation will probably reply that the snake has more clay because it is longer. Figure 4.7 shows a classic means of testing whether a child has developed the schema of conservation.

The effect of different cultural experiences on the timing of conservation was demonstrated in a study of children in a Mexican village whose parents were pottery makers. The children who normally helped their parents in making pottery learned conservation (at least of mass) earlier than other children did (Price-Williams, Gordon, & Ramirez, 1969). Moreover, certain nonverbal variations of the conservation of liquid volume problem show that children might develop conservation earlier than indicated by studies that have used the traditional verbal demonstration procedure (Wheldall & Benner, 1993). In early adolescence, the concrete operational stage might give way to the formal operational stage, which is discussed in the section of this chapter devoted to adolescent development.

Psychosocial Development

Just as Piaget believed that the child passes through stages of cognitive development, psychoanalyst Erik Erikson (1902–1994) believed that the child passes through stages of psychosocial development. Erikson observed that, across the life span, we go through eight distinct stages. Each stage is marked by a conflict that must be overcome, as described in Table 4.2. Research has supported Erikson's belief that we pass through the stages sequentially—though people differ in the ages at which they pass through them (Vaillant & Milofsky, 1980). Erikson also was one of the first researchers to consider cultural differences in psychosocial development, having studied children in Sioux, Yurok, and other Native American cultures (Coles, 1970).

Age	Conflict	Successful Resolution
First Year	Trust vs. mistrust	The infant develops a sense of security.
Second Year	Autonomy vs. shame and doubt	The infant achieves a sense of independence.
3–5 Years	Initiative vs. guilt	The child finds a balance between spontaneity and restraint.
6 Years–Puberty	Industry vs. inferiority	The child attains a sense of self-confidence.
Adolescence	Identity vs. role confusion	The adolescent experiences a unified sense of self.
Young Adulthood	Intimacy vs. isolation	The adult forms close personal relationships.
Middle Adulthood	Generativity vs. stagnation	The adult promotes the well-being of others.
Late Adulthood	Integrity vs. despair	The adult enjoys a sense of satisfaction by reflecting on a life well lived.

Adapted from *Childhood and Society*, Second Edition, by Erik H. Erikson, by permission of W. W. Norton and Company, Inc. Copyright 1950, © 1963 by W. W. Norton and Company, Inc. Copyright renewed 1978, 1991 by Erik H. Erikson. Also Chatto and Windus, London, England.

Early Attachment: The Importance of a Secure Base

Infants show surprising emotional and social sophistication. They are, for example, capable of expressing three of the basic emotions: fear, surprise, and happiness. In one experiment, infants between 10 and 12 months old were tested in two situations designed to elicit fear (the visual cliff and the approach of a stranger), two designed to elicit surprise (the switching of a toy and the vanishing of an object), or two designed to elicit happiness (a collapsing toy and a game of peek-a-boo). Judges blind to the conditions were asked to assess the infants' emotions based on their facial expressions and behaviors. The judgments of emotions matched what would be expected from each condition, supporting the notion that infants can experience these emotions (Hiatt, Campos, & Emde, 1980).

Erikson found that the major social conflict of the first year of infancy is **trust versus mistrust.** One of the most important factors in helping the infant develop trust is **social attachment,** a strong emotional bond between an infant and a caregiver that develops during the first year. Beginning in the 1930s, British psychiatrist John Bowlby (1907–1990) became interested in the effects of early maternal loss or deprivation on later personality development. Much of his theorizing was based on his study of orphans whose parents were killed in World War II. Bowlby favors an evolutionary viewpoint, suggesting that infants have evolved an inborn need for attachment because their survival depends on adult caregivers (Bowlby, 1988). Thus, infants seek to evoke responses from adults through crying, cooing, smiling, and clinging. Similarly, Sigmund Freud assumed that an infant becomes attached to his or her mother for a functional reason—she provides nourishment through nursing.

Freud's assumption was contradicted by research conducted by Harry Harlow and his colleagues on social attachment in rhesus monkeys. Harlow separated infant monkeys from their parents and peers and raised them for 6 months with two "surrogate mothers." The surrogates were wire monkeys with wooden heads. One surrogate was covered with terry cloth and the other was left bare. Harlow found that the monkeys preferred to cling to the cloth-covered surrogate, even though milk was available only from a bottle attached to the bare-wire surrogate (see Figure 4.8). Harlow concluded that physical contact is a more important factor than nourishment in promoting infant attachment to the mother (Harlow & Zimmerman, 1959).

Harlow's findings from research inspired interest in the possible role of attachment in human psychosocial development. Of course, today's ethical standards would prevent the replication of Harlow's experiment with human infants (and perhaps even with infant monkeys). Much of what we know about attachment in human infants comes from research by Mary Ainsworth (1993) on the mother-infant relationship. She was inspired by her long-time collaboration with Bowlby. Ainsworth conducted her first studies of infant-mother attachment patterns after visiting Uganda (Bretherton, 1992). She and others have found that the mother is more likely to be the primary caregiver across virtually all cultures (Best et al., 1994).

▲ **TABLE 4.2**
Erikson's Stages of Psychosocial Development

trust versus mistrust
Erikson's developmental stage in which success is achieved by having a secure social attachment with a caregiver.

social attachment
A strong emotional relationship between an infant and a caregiver.

▲ **FIGURE 4.8**
Social Attachment
Harry Harlow found that infant monkeys became more attached to a terry-cloth-covered wire surrogate mother than to a bare-wire surrogate mother. Even when fed only from a nipple protruding from the bare-wire surrogate mother, the infant monkeys preferred to cling to the terry-cloth-covered surrogate mother. Harlow concluded that social attachment might depend more on physical contact than on the provision of nourishment (Harlow & Zimmerman, 1959).

Human Development | **121**

▲ **Mary Ainsworth**
"Gaining an understanding of attachment over the whole life span will enrich psychologists' knowledge of human nature."

autonomy versus shame and doubt
Erikson's developmental stage in which success is achieved by gaining a degree of independence from one's parents.

initiative versus guilt
Erikson's developmental stage in which success is achieved by behaving in a spontaneous but socially appropriate way.

industry versus inferiority
Erikson's developmental stage in which success is achieved by developing a sense of competency.

In assessing the mother's influence on the child, Ainsworth makes a distinction between *securely attached* and *insecurely attached* infants. This becomes an especially important issue at about 8 months of age, when infants show a strong preference for their mothers over strangers and show separation anxiety. To test this, Ainsworth developed the Strange Situation: The mother and infant are in a room together; the mother leaves the room, a stranger enters the room, the stranger then leaves and the infant's response to the mother is assessed when she then returns to the room. The securely attached infant seeks physical contact with the mother, yet, despite mildly protesting, freely leaves her to play and explore, using the mother as a secure base. In contrast, the insecurely attached infant clings to the mother, acts either apathetic or highly anxious when separated from her, and is either unresponsive or angry when reunited with her.

An infant whose mother is more sensitive, accepting, and affectionate will become more securely attached. Infants who are insecurely attached tend to show that style of relating in childhood, adolescence, and adulthood (Cassidy & Berlin, 1994). In fact, infant attachment patterns even predict romantic styles later in life (Simpson, 1990).

According to Erikson, during the second year the child experiences a conflict involving **autonomy versus shame and doubt.** The child explores the physical environment, begins to learn self-care skills, such as feeding, and tries out budding motor and language abilities. In doing so, the child develops a greater sense of independence from her or his parents. This might account for the popular notion of the "terrible twos," when the child enjoys behaving in a contrary manner and saying no to any request. Parents who stifle efforts at reasonable independence or criticize the child's awkward efforts will promote feelings of shame and doubt.

At 3 years of age, the child enters the stage that involves the conflict Erikson calls **initiative versus guilt.** The child shows initiative in play, social relations, and exploration of the environment. The child also learns to control his or her impulses, feeling guilt for actions that go beyond limits set by parents. So, at this stage, parents might permit their child to rummage through drawers but not to throw clothing around the bedroom. Thus, the stage of initiative versus guilt deals with the development of a sense of right and wrong.

At about the age of 6, and continuing until about the age of 12, Erikson observed, the child faces the conflict of **industry versus inferiority.** The industrious child who achieves successes during this stage is more likely to feel competent. This is important, because children who feel academically and socially competent are happier than other children (Blechman et al., 1985). A child who develops a sense of inferiority may lose interest in academics, avoid social interactions, or fail to participate in sports.

Parent-Child Relationships: Optimal Parenting

One of the most important factors in psychosocial development is the approach that parents take to child rearing. Psychologist Diana Baumrind distinguished three kinds of parenting: permissive, authoritarian, and authoritative. *Permissive* parents set few rules and rarely punish misbehavior. Permissiveness is undesirable, because children will be less likely to adopt positive standards of behavior. At the other extreme, *authoritarian* parents set strict rules and rely on punishment. They respond to questioning of their rules by saying, "Because I say so!"

Authoritarian parents might also resort to physical discipline. Aside from the potential for injury to the child, child abuse is associated with lasting emotional effects on the target of the abuse. Abused children have poorer self-esteem and are more socially withdrawn (Kaufman & Cicchetti, 1989), they tend to be more aggressive and less empathetic toward children in distress (Main & George, 1985), and they are more likely to become juvenile delinquents (Bowers, 1990).

Of great concern is the vicious cycle in which abused children become abusive parents. However, though most child abusers were abused as children, only 30 percent of abused children become abusers—a far cry from claims that being an abused child automatically makes one a future child abuser (Kaufman & Zigler, 1987). So, if you

CHAPTER 4

were unfortunate enough to have suffered child abuse, you may very well be able to break the vicious cycle when rearing your own children.

Authoritative Parenting. Baumrind has found that the best approach to child rearing is **authoritative parenting** (Baumrind, 1983). Authoritative parents tend to be warm and loving, yet insist that their children behave appropriately. They encourage independence within well-defined limits, show a willingness to explain the reasons for their rules, and permit their children to express verbal disagreement with them. By maintaining a delicate balance between freedom and control, authoritative parents help their children internalize standards of behavior.

Children who have authoritative parents are more likely to become socially competent, independent, and responsible. They are less likely to use drugs (Jackson, Bee-Gates, & Henriksen, 1994), more likely to perform well in school (Steinberg et al., 1992), and more likely to be socially well adjusted (Durbin et al., 1993). But, as cautioned in Chapter 2, be wary of concluding that parenting style causes these effects. Remember that only experimental, not correlational, research permits statements about causality. Perhaps the direction of causality is the opposite of what one would assume. For example, children who behave properly might evoke authoritative parenting.

Research tends to support a positive relationship between authoritative parenting and children's competence. But we still do not know how or why it does so (Darling & Steinberg, 1993). Moreover, we must be aware of cultural differences in child rearing—both between and within societies. For example, authoritative parenting is preferred by educated Kuwaitis more than by less educated Kuwaitis (El-Feky, 1991).

authoritative parenting
An effective style of parenting, in which the parent is warm and loving, yet sets well-defined limits that he or she enforces in an appropriate manner.

Day Care. Another important, and controversial, factor in child rearing is day care. The increase in the number of women who work outside the home in the United States has led to a rise in the number of preschool children who spend their weekdays in day-care centers. The number of American children placed in day care has increased during the 1990s, with about 75 percent of women with school-age children working outside the home (Silverstein, 1991). Today, the mothers of more than half the infants in the United States work outside of the home. Though day care, overall, seems to have neither strong benefits nor strong detrimental effects (Lamb, 1996), research findings are contradictory in regard to the effects of day care on infants. On the negative side are studies finding that infant day care of more than 20 hours a week in the first year of life is associated with insecure attachment during infancy and greater noncompliance and aggressiveness in early childhood (Belsky, 1988) and that children who enter day care before age 2 later perform more poorly in high school than do children who enter day care after age 2 (Ispa, Thornburg, & Gray, 1990). On the positive side are studies finding that infants in day care do not become insecurely attached (Burchinal et al., 1992) and that they later do well in school and act less aggressively than other children do (Field, 1991). These contradictory findings reflect the complex nature of the issue, which involves numerous variables, including the characteristics of the infants, their parents, their caretakers, and their day-care settings.

Because many working parents have no choice but to place their infants in day care, it is reassuring to know that research indicates that high-quality infant day care is probably not harmful (Volling & Feagans, 1995). "High-quality" means that caregivers are well-educated and there is a ratio of about one caregiver for every four children. This provides a safer environment and greater social interaction with the children. Unfortunately, the relatively low salaries and high stress of day-care workers make high-quality day care elusive (Scarr, Phillips, & McCartney, 1990).

Marital Discord. Children are affected not only by parenting and day-care practices but also by the quality of their parents' marital relationships. A meta-analysis of relevant studies (Erel & Burman, 1995) found that parental discord spills over into negative parent-child relationships. Moreover, marital discord can undermine the child's feeling of emotional security and lead to adjustment problems in childhood and marital discord in adulthood (Davies & Cummings, 1994).

In some cases marital discord leads to divorce. Because about half of all marriages in the United States end in divorce, many children spend at least part of their childhood primarily with one parent. More than one third of American children born in the past two decades will experience parental divorce. And they will be more likely to suffer emotional problems, particularly depression (Aseltine, 1996). For example, a study that compared children with divorced parents to children from intact families in Quebec province found that children of divorce exhibit more problem behaviors (Kurtz, 1995).

Because divorce involves so many variables, including the age and economic status of the parents, the age of the children, and the custody arrangements, different combinations of these variables can have different effects on the children. The effects of each combination remain to be determined. It should be noted, however, that children from divorced families have a greater sense of well-being than children from intact families with intense parental conflict (Amato & Keith, 1991). Moreover, it is unclear whether the child's emotional distress is caused mainly by the divorce or by parental conflict prior to the divorce (Furstenberg & Teitler, 1994).

Interaction with Peers: Forming Friendships

Children are affected by their relationships with friends and siblings as well as those with their parents. Friendships provide the context for social and emotional growth (Newcomb & Bagwell, 1995). Few children develop friendships before the age of 3, and 95 percent of childhood friendships are between children of the same sex (Hartup, 1989). Girls tend to have fewer, but more intimate, friendships than boys do (Berndt & Hoyle, 1985). A meta-analysis of children's peer relations found that socially and academically competent children are popular with their peers. In contrast, children who are withdrawn, aggressive, or academically deficient tend to be rejected by their peers (Newcomb, Bukowski, & Pattee, 1993).

Peer relationships in childhood involve play. A classic study (Parten, 1932) found that the interactive play of children gradually increased between 2 and 4 years of age, but that throughout this period children engaged mainly in parallel play, as when two children in a sandbox play separately from each other with pails and shovels. The results of this study have been replicated. For example, a longitudinal study of children from 16 to 32 months

(a)   (b)

◀ **Child's Play**
Young children gradually shift from (a) parallel play to (b) interactive play.

old found a shift from parallel play to interactive play (Eckerman, Davis, & Didow, 1989). There are also cultural differences in play. For example, a study comparing American and Chinese children found that the Americans tended to be more competitive and individualistic (Domino, 1992).

Among our most important peers are our siblings. Sibling birth order is a factor in social development; firstborn children usually are less socially popular than later-born children. This might be because the firstborn interacts more with adults than with siblings, compared to the later-born, who interacts extensively with both parents and siblings. As a consequence, the later-born might be more likely to develop social skills that are well-suited for interacting with peers (Baskett, 1984). As for the only child, the popular belief that she or he suffers because of the absence of siblings is unfounded. For example, an only child is usually superior to all except firstborn children and children from two-child families in intelligence and academic achievement (Falbo & Polit, 1986).

Gender-Role Development: Becoming Male or Female

One of the most important aspects of psychosocial development in childhood is the development of **gender roles,** which are behavior patterns that are considered appropriate for males or females in a given culture. The first formal theory of gender-role development was put forth by Sigmund Freud. He assumed that the resolution of what he called the Oedipus conflict (discussed in Chapter 13) at age 5 or 6 led the child to adopt the gender of the same-sex parent. The Oedipus conflict begins with the child's sexual attraction to the opposite-sex parent. According to Freud, because the child fears punishment for desiring the opposite-sex parent, the child comes to identify with the same-sex parent. But studies of children show that gender identity develops even in children who live in one-parent households. Because of the lack of research support for Freud's theory, most researchers favor more-recent theories of gender-role development.

Social learning theory stresses the importance of observational learning, rewards, and punishment. Thus, social learning theorists assume that the child learns gender-relevant behaviors by observing gender-role models and by being rewarded for appropriate, and punished for inappropriate, gender-role behavior. This process of gender typing begins on the very day of birth. In one study, new parents were interviewed within 24 hours of the birth of their first child. Though there are no observable differences in the physical appearance of male and female newborns whose genitals are covered, newborn daughters were more likely to be described by their parents as cute, weak, and uncoordinated than newborn sons were (Rubin, Provenzano, & Luria, 1974). But an influential review of research on sex differences by Eleanor Maccoby found that parents reported that they did not treat their sons and daughters differently (Maccoby & Jacklin, 1974). Of course, parents might believe they treat their daughters and sons the same, while actually treating them differently. A recent meta-analysis, however, supported Maccoby by finding that gender-role development seems, at best, weakly related to differences in how parents rear their sons and daughters (Lytton & Romney, 1991).

gender roles
The behaviors that are considered appropriate for females or males in a given culture.

social learning theory
A theory of gender-role development that assumes that people learn social behaviors mainly through observation and mental processing of information.

▲ **Eleanor Maccoby**
"Socialization pressures, whether by parents or others, do not by any means tell the whole story of the origins of sex differences."

According to social-learning theory, children learn gender-role behaviors by being rewarded for performing those behaviors and by observing adults, particularly parents, engaging in them.

gender-schema theory

A theory of gender-role development that combines aspects of social learning theory and cognitive-developmental theory.

Traditional gender roles can also be perpetuated by the presence of women and men in stereotypic gender-role positions. For example, as long as women are more likely to be homemakers and men are more likely to be workers outside the home, children will be more likely to view these as appropriate gender-related behaviors. Educational approaches to changing gender roles will have less impact than the increased presence of males and females in nontraditional gender roles (Eagly, 1984). When it comes to gender roles, "Do as I do" is more powerful than "Do as I say."

An alternative to the social learning theory of gender-role development is Sandra Bem's (1981) **gender-schema theory.** Bem's theory holds that social learning leads the child to adopt specific gender-related behaviors that are integrated into a gender schema, which then leads the child to perform behaviors that are consistent with that schema. In essence, the child assimilates and accommodates culture-specific information into the schemas of "male" and "female." Males who hold strong gender schemas of females, for example, are more likely to think of females in stereotypic ways (Hudak, 1993).

Moral Development: Kohlberg's Cognitive Theory

An often-overlooked aspect of life-span development is moral development. According to Sigmund Freud, moral values arise from the resolution of the Oedipus conflict. There is little research support for Freud's view of moral development (Hunt, 1979). Today, the most influential theory of moral development is Lawrence Kohlberg's (1981) cognitive-developmental theory.

Kohlberg's Theory of Moral Development. Kohlberg's theory, formulated in the 1960s, is based on Piaget's (1932) proposal that a person's level of moral development depends on his or her level of cognitive development. Piaget found that children, in making moral judgments, are at first more concerned with the consequences of actions. Thus, a young child might insist that accidentally breaking ten dishes is morally worse than purposely breaking one dish. As children become more cognitively sophisticated, they base their moral judgments more on a person's intentions than on the consequences of the person's behavior. Kohlberg assumed that as individuals become more cognitively sophisticated, they reach more-complex levels of moral reasoning. Research findings indicate that adequate cognitive development is, indeed, a prerequisite for each level of moral reasoning (Walker, 1986).

Kohlberg, agreeing with Piaget, developed a stage theory of moral development based on the individual's level of moral reasoning. Kohlberg determined the individual's level of moral reasoning by presenting a series of stories, each of which includes a moral dilemma. The person must suggest a resolution of the dilemma and give reasons for choosing that resolution.

　　　　CHAPTER 4

Levels	Stages	Moral Reasoning in Response to the Heinz Dilemma	
		In Favor of Heinz's Stealing the Drug	**Against Heinz's Stealing the Drug**
I. Preconventional Level: Motivated by Self-Interest	**Stage 1** *Punishment and obedience orientation:* Motivation to avoid punishment	"If you let your wife die, you will get in trouble."	"You shouldn't steal the drug because you'll be caught and sent to jail if you do."
	Stage 2 *Instrumental relativist orientation:* Motivation to obtain rewards	"It wouldn't bother you much to serve a little jail term, if you have your wife when you get out."	"He may not get much of a jail term if he steals the drug, but his wife will probably die before he gets out, so it won't do him much good."
II. Conventional Level: Motivated by Conventional Laws and Values	**Stage 3** *Good boy–nice girl orientation:* Motivation to gain approval and to avoid disapproval	"No one will think you're bad if you steal the drug, but your family will think you're an inhuman husband if you don't."	"It isn't just the druggist who will think you're a criminal, everyone else will too."
	Stage 4 *Society-maintaining orientation:* Motivation to fulfill one's duty and to avoid feelings of guilt	"If you have any sense of honor, you won't let your wife die because you're afraid to do the only thing that will save her."	"You'll always feel guilty for your dishonesty and lawbreaking."
III. Postconventional Level: Motivated by Abstract Moral Principles	**Stage 5** *Social-contract orientation:* Motivation to follow rational, mutually agreed-upon principles and maintain the respect of others	"If you let your wife die, it would be out of fear, not out of reasoning it out."	"You would lose your standing and respect in the community and break the law."
	Stage 6 *Universal ethical principle orientation:* Motivation to uphold one's own ethical principles and avoid self-condemnation	"If you don't steal the drug, . . . you would have lived up to the outside rule of the law but you wouldn't have lived up to your own standards of conscience."	"If you stole the drug, . . . you'd condemn yourself because you wouldn't have lived up to your own conscience and standards of honesty."

Table "Theory of Moral Development" from *Essays on Moral Development: The Philosophy of Moral Development* (Volume I) by Laurence Kohlberg. Copyright © 1981 by Lawrence Kohlberg. Reprinted by permission of HarperCollins Publishers, Inc.

▲ **TABLE 4.3**
Kohlberg's Theory of Moral Development

The person's stage of moral development depends not on the resolution, but instead on the reasons given for that resolution. What is your response to the following dilemma proposed by Kohlberg? Your reasoning in resolving it would reveal your level of moral development:

▶ In Europe, a woman was near death from a very bad disease, a special kind of cancer. There was one drug that the doctors thought might save her. It was a form of radium that a druggist in the same town had recently discovered. The drug was expensive to make, but the druggist was charging 10 times what the drug cost him to make. He paid 200 dollars for the radium and charged two thousand dollars for a small dose of the drug. The sick woman's husband, Heinz, went to everyone he knew to borrow the money, but he could get together only about one thousand dollars, which was half of what it cost. He told the druggist that his wife was dying and asked him to sell it cheaper or let him pay later. But the druggist said, "No, I discovered the drug, and I am going to make money from it." So Heinz got desperate and broke into the man's store to steal the drug for his wife. (Kohlberg, 1981, p.12)

The levels of moral development represented by particular responses to this dilemma are presented in Table 4.3. Kohlberg has identified three levels: the *preconventional*, the *conventional*, and the *postconventional*. Each level contains two stages, making a total of six stages of moral development. As Piaget noted, as we progress to higher levels of moral reasoning, we become more concerned with the actor's motives than with the consequences of the actor's actions. This was supported by a study of moral judgments about aggressive

▶ **Moral Reasoning**
Lawrence Kohlberg would determine the level of moral development of persons by assessing the moral reasoning that motivated their behavior. This would hold for individuals as diverse as (*a*) Martin Luther King, who urged civil disobedience to unjust laws while leading the civil rights struggle for African Americans in the 1960s, and (*b*) Jack Kevorkian, who has helped many people commit suicide with his "death machine."

(a)   (b)

preconventional level
In Kohlberg's theory, the level of moral reasoning characterized by concern with the consequences that behavior has for oneself.

conventional level
In Kohlberg's theory, the level of moral reasoning characterized by concern with upholding laws and conventional values and by favoring obedience to authority.

postconventional level
In Kohlberg's theory, the level of moral reasoning characterized by concern with obeying mutually agreed upon laws and by the need to uphold human dignity.

▲ **Lawrence Kohlberg (1926–1986)**
"In the study of moral behavior, it is essential to determine the actor's interpretation of the situation and the behavior since the moral quality of the behavior is itself determined by that interpretation."

behavior, which found that high school and college students at higher stages of moral reasoning were more concerned with the aggressor's motivation than were students at lower stages (Berkowitz et al., 1986).

People at the **preconventional level** of moral reasoning, which typically characterizes children up to 9 years old, are mainly concerned with the consequences of moral behavior to themselves. In stage 1, the child has a *punishment and obedience orientation*, in which moral behavior serves to avoid punishment. In stage 2, the child has an *instrumental-relativist orientation*, in which moral behavior serves to get rewards or favors in return, as in "You scratch my back and I'll scratch yours."

People at the **conventional level** of moral reasoning, usually reached in late childhood or early adolescence, uphold conventional laws and values by favoring obedience to parents and authority figures. Kohlberg calls stage 3 the *good boy–nice girl orientation*, because the child assumes that moral behavior is desirable because it gains social approval, especially from parents. Kohlberg calls stage 4 the *society-maintaining orientation*, in which the adolescent views moral behavior as a way to do one's duty, show respect for authority, and maintain the social order. These four stages have even been used to show differences in moral reasoning among members of the United States Congress about political issues (Shapiro, 1995).

At the end of adolescence, some of those who reach Piaget's formal operational stage of cognitive development also reach the **postconventional level** of morality. At this level of moral reasoning, people make moral judgments based on ethical principles that might conflict with their self-interest or with the maintenance of social order. In stage 5, the *social-contract orientation*, the person assumes that adherence to laws is in the long-term best interest of society but that unjust laws might have to be violated. The U.S. Constitution is based on this view. Stage 6, the highest stage of moral reasoning, is called the *universal ethical principle orientation*. The few people at this stage assume that moral reasoning must uphold human dignity and their conscience—even if that brings them into conflict with their society's laws or values. Thus, an abolitionist who helped runaway American slaves flee to Canada in the nineteenth century would be acting at this highest level of moral reasoning.

Criticisms of Kohlberg's Theory. Kohlberg's theory has received mixed support from research studies. Children do appear to proceed through the stages he described in the order he described (Walker, 1989). And a study of adolescents on an Israeli kibbutz found that, as predicted by Kohlberg's theory, their stages of moral development were related to their stages of cognitive development (Snarey, Reimer, & Kohlberg, 1985). But Kohlberg's theory has been criticized on several grounds. First, the theory explains moral reasoning, not moral action. A person's moral actions might not reflect her or his moral reasoning. Yet some research supports a positive relationship between moral reasoning and moral actions. One study found that people at higher stages of moral reasoning tend to behave more honestly and more altruistically (Blasi, 1980).

A second criticism is that the situation, not just the person's level of moral reasoning, plays a role in moral decision making and moral actions. This was demonstrated in a study of male college students who performed a task in which their goal was to keep a stylus above a light moving in a triangular pattern—a tedious, difficult task. When provided with a strong enough temptation, even those at higher stages of moral reasoning succumbed to cheating (Malinowski & Smith, 1985).

Other critics insist that Kohlberg's theory might not be generalizable beyond Western cultures, with their greater emphasis on individualism. This criticism has been countered by Kohlberg and his colleagues. They found that when people in other cultures are interviewed in their own languages, using moral dilemmas based on situations that are familiar to them, Kohlberg's theory holds up well. Moreover, in other cultures, the stages of moral reasoning unfold in the order claimed by Kohlberg. For example, a study of Taiwanese children and young adults found that they progressed through the moral stages in the order and at the rate found in Americans (Lei, 1994). Nonetheless, postconventional moral reasoning is not found in all cultures (Snarey, Reimer, & Kohlberg, 1985).

Still another criticism of Kohlberg's theory is that it is biased in favor of a male view of morality. The main proponent of this criticism has been Carol Gilligan (1982). She points out that Kohlberg's theory was based on research on male subjects, and she claims that Kohlberg's theory favors the view that morality is concerned with detached, legalistic justice (an allegedly masculine orientation) rather than with involved, interpersonal caring (an allegedly feminine orientation).

Thus, Gilligan believes that women's moral reasoning is colored by their desire to relieve distress, while men's moral reasoning is based on their desire to uphold rules and laws. Because Kohlberg's theory favors a male view, women are unfairly considered lower in moral development. The results of a recent study supported Gilligan's claim that males and females differ in their notions of morality. More than 600 undergraduates were asked to write an essay on the experience that was the most important in their moral development. As Gilligan would have predicted, more women than men described experiences related to a care orientation (Barnett, Quackenbush, & Sinisi, 1995).

Another study, based on a controversial and widely publicized legal case of the 1980s, lent only mixed support to Gilligan's position. Undergraduates were asked what they would have decided in the notorious "Baby M" case, in which Mary Beth Whitehead, a surrogate mother, fought over custody with William Stern, the baby's biological father, whose sperm had been used to impregnate Whitehead. The subjects were asked to give the reasons for their decisions. The results indicated that 82 percent of the responses reflected a justice orientation and only 18 percent reflected a care orientation. But, as predicted by Gilligan's viewpoint, more females (23 percent) than males (13 percent) showed a care orientation (Hendrixson, 1989). Despite some research support for Gilligan's position, there does not appear to be a moral chasm between males and females—there are no significant differences between males and females in their use of justice and care orientations (Page & Tyrer, 1996).

▲ Carol Gilligan
"Just as the conventions that shape women's moral judgment differ from those that apply to men, so also women's definitions of the moral domain diverge from that derived from studies of men."

STAYING ON TRACK: *Infant and Child Development*

1. What has research discovered about infant depth perception?
2. What are Piaget's basic ideas about cognitive development?
3. What has research found about the importance of infant attachment to a caregiver?
4. What are the differences between permissive, authoritarian, and authoritative parenting?

ADOLESCENT DEVELOPMENT

Change marks the entire life span, though it is more dramatic at certain stages than at others. Biological factors have a more obvious influence during adolescence and late adulthood than during early and middle adulthood. Social factors exert their greatest

The Adolescent Growth Spurt
The onset of puberty is associated with a rapid increase in height. Note that the growth spurt of females occurs earlier than that of males.

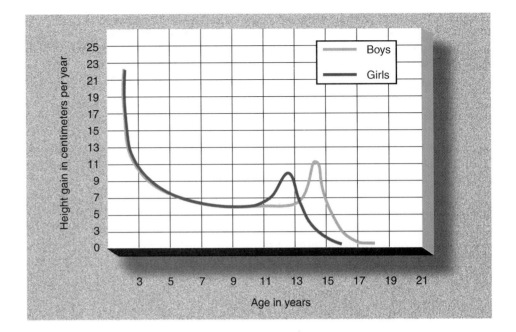

social clock

The major events that typically occur at certain times in the typical life cycle in a given culture.

influence through the **social clock,** which includes major events that occur at certain times in the typical life cycle in a given culture. In Western cultures, for example, major milestones of the social clock include graduation from high school, leaving home, finding a job, getting married, having a child, and retiring from work. Being late in reaching these milestones can cause emotional distress (Rook, Catalano, & Dooley, 1989).

Cultural and historical factors can have different effects on different cohorts. Depending on your cohort, your adolescent and adult experiences might differ from those of other cohorts. Consider an 18-year-old college freshman. College freshmen in the late 1960s and early 1970s were influenced by the turmoil of the divisive Vietnam War, the cynicism generated by the Watergate scandal, the "psychedelic" style and music of groups like the Beatles and Jimi Hendrix, and television programs such as "All in the Family," which broached the formerly taboo topics of racism, sexism, and sexuality.

Today's traditional-age college freshmen, whose childhood spanned the late 1980s and early 1990s, experienced the militarily successful Persian Gulf War, the demolition of the Berlin wall and the downfall of communism, the commercially oriented music of performers like Madonna and M. C. Hammer, and television programs like "The Cosby Show," which portrayed African Americans in a more positive light than earlier programs did. Thus, as you read, keep in mind that although common biological factors and social clocks might make generations somewhat similar in their development, cultural and historical factors that are unique to particular cohorts can make them somewhat different from cohorts that precede or succeed them.

Adolescence is unknown in many nonindustrialized countries. Instead, adulthood begins with the onset of puberty and is commonly celebrated with traditional rites of passage. With the advent of universal free education and child labor laws in Western countries, children, who otherwise would have entered the adult work world by the time they reached puberty, entered a period of life during which they developed an adult body yet maintained a child-like dependence on parents. Formal study of **adolescence,** the transitional period between childhood and adulthood, began with the work of G. Stanley Hall (1904).

adolescence

The transition period lasting from the onset of puberty to the beginning of adulthood.

puberty

The period of rapid physical change that occurs during adolescence, including the development of the ability to reproduce sexually.

Physical Development

Recall your own adolescence. What you might recall most vividly are the rapid physical changes associated with **puberty** (from the Latin word for "adulthood"). As illustrated in Figure 4.9, puberty is marked by a rapid increase in height; girls show a growth spurt between the ages of 10 and 12, and boys show a spurt between the ages of 12 and 14. The

physical changes of puberty also include the maturation of primary and secondary sex characteristics. Primary sex characteristics are hormone-induced physical changes that enable us to engage in sexual reproduction. These changes include growth of the penis and testes in males and the vagina, uterus, and ovaries in females. Secondary sex characteristics are stimulated by sex hormones but are unrelated to sexual reproduction. Pubertal males develop facial hair, deeper voices, and larger muscles. Pubertal females develop wider hips, larger breasts, and more-rounded physiques, caused in part by increased deposits of fat.

These physical changes are triggered by a spurt in the secretion of the female sex hormone estrogen between ages 10 and 11 and the male sex hormone testosterone between ages 12 and 13. Boys generally have their first semen ejaculation between the ages of 13 and 15, typically while asleep (so-called nocturnal emissions). Girls exhibit earlier physical maturation than boys and generally experience **menarche,** their first menstrual period, between the ages of 11 and 13 (Paikoff & Brooks-Gunn, 1991). The average age at menarche is lower than the past; this decline in the age of menarche has been attributed to improved health and nutrition.

Though the dramatic physical changes of puberty are caused by hormonal changes, adolescent mood swings are not necessarily the by-products of hormones run wild. Hormone fluctuations affect the adolescent's moods, but life events have a greater effect (Brooks-Gunn & Warren, 1989). Of course, the physical changes of puberty, including acne, rapid growth, and genital maturation, can themselves produce emotional distress. This is especially true if the adolescent is unprepared for them or is made to feel self-conscious by peers or parents. Males find it difficult enough to deal with scruffy facial hair, unwanted penile erections, and voices that crack, without being made more anxious about those changes. Females, likewise, find it difficult enough to discover suddenly that they have enlarged breasts, experience monthly menstrual flow, and possibly tower several inches above many of their male peers. Adolescents who know what physical changes to expect find puberty less distressing than do those who are not informed; for example, menarche is less stressful for girls who are told about it in advance (Rierdan & Koff, 1990).

Cognitive Development

Adolescent cognitive development is less dramatic, with no obvious surge in mental abilities to match the surge in physical development. According to Piaget's theory, at about 11 years of age some adolescents pass from the concrete operational stage to the **formal operational stage.** A person who reaches this stage is able to reason about abstract, not just concrete, situations. The adolescent who has reached the formal operational stage

menarche
The beginning of menstruation, usually occurring between the ages of 11 and 13.

formal operational stage
The Piagetian stage, beginning at about age 11, marked by the ability to use abstract reasoning and to solve problems by testing hypotheses.

can apply abstract principles and make predictions about hypothetical situations. In contrast, an adolescent still in the concrete operational stage would rely more on blind trial and error than on a formal approach to problem solving.

To appreciate this, imagine that you are given four chemicals and are asked to produce a purple liquid by mixing them—but it is left up to you to discover the proper mixture. People at the concrete operational level would approach this task in an unsystematic manner, hoping that through trial and error they would hit upon the correct combination of chemicals. In contrast, people at the formal operational level would approach it systematically, perhaps by mixing each possible combination of two of the chemicals, then each possible combination of three, and finally all four. Thus, people who reach the formal operational stage perform better on more complex intellectual pursuits. A study of adolescent students found that those in transition between the concrete operational stage and the formal operational stage showed better understanding of abstract concepts presented in a physics textbook than did those still in the concrete operational stage (Renner et al., 1990).

Piaget found that so few people reach the formal operational stage that he gave up his earlier belief that it was universal. Those who reach that stage are more likely to have been exposed to scientific thinking in their academic courses (Rogoff & Chavajay, 1995). Thus, people from cultures that do not stress science in their school curricula are less likely to achieve the formal operational stage.

Psychosocial Development

Erik Erikson noted that psychosocial development continues through adolescence into adulthood and old age. Perhaps the most important psychosocial tasks of adolescence are the formation of a personal identity and the development of healthy relationships with peers and parents.

Identity Achievement: Who Am I?

According to Erikson (1963), the most important feat of adolescence is the resolution of the conflict of **identity versus role confusion.** The adolescent develops a sense of identity by adopting her or his own set of values and social behaviors. Erikson believed this is a normal part of finding answers to questions related to one's identity, such as these: What do I believe is important? What are my goals in life?

Erikson's emphasis on the importance of the identity crisis might reflect, in large part, his own life history. He was born in Germany, the child of a Danish Christian mother and father. Erik's father abandoned his mother while she was pregnant with him. She then married a Jewish physician, Theodore Homburger. Erik was given his new father's surname, making him Erik Homburger. But it was not until Erik reached adolescence that he was told that Homburger was not his biological father (Hopkins, 1995).

Erikson, uncomfortable among Jews and Christians alike, sought to find himself by traveling in European artistic and intellectual circles, as many young adults did in the 1920s. Eventually he met Anna Freud, Sigmund's daughter and an eminent psychoanalyst herself. Erikson underwent psychoanalysis with her almost daily for 3 years. In 1933 Erikson changed his name to Erik Homburger Erikson and left to pursue a career in the United States. His long, rich life was a testament to his success in finding his identity as a husband, writer, teacher, and psychoanalyst.

To appreciate the task that confronts the adolescent in developing an identity, consider the challenge of having to adjust simultaneously to a new body, a new mind, and a new social world. The adolescent body is larger and sexually mature. The adolescent mind can question the nature of reality and argue about abstract concepts regarding ethical, political, and religious beliefs. The social world of the adolescent requires achieving a balance between childlike dependence and adultlike independence. This also manifests itself in the conflict between parental and peer influences. Children's values mirror their parents', but adolescents' values oscillate between those of their parents and those of their peers. Adolescents move from a world guided by parental wishes to a world in which they are

identity versus role confusion
Erikson's developmental stage in which success is achieved by establishing a sense of personal identity.

▲ **Erik Erikson (1902–1994)**
"If ever an identity crisis was central and long drawn out in somebody's life it was so in mine."

CHAPTER   4

confronted by a host of choices regarding sex, drugs, friends, schoolwork, and other things. Erikson's theory of adolescence has received support from longitudinal studies showing that, in fact, adolescents typically move from a state of role confusion to a state of identity achievement (Streitmatter, 1993). Failure to achieve a sense of identity is associated with emotional distress, including feelings of emptiness and depression (Taylor & Goritsas, 1994).

But Carol Gilligan (1982) believes that Erikson's theory applies more to males than to females. She points out that Erikson based his theory on studies of males, who tend to place a greater premium on the development of self-sufficiency than do females, who tend to place a greater premium on intimate relationships in which there is mutual caring. Thus, an adolescent female who fails to develop an independent identity at the same time as her male age peers might unfairly be considered abnormal. Once again, this demonstrates the importance of considering the cultural context of theoretical positions. For example, the Inuit people of Canada see personal identity as inseparable from the physical, animal, and human environments. The Inuits would find it maladaptive if members of their culture formed more individualistic identities (Stairs, 1992).

Social Relationships: The Influence of Peers

Because the adolescent is dependent on parents while seeking an independent identity, adolescence has traditionally been considered a period of conflict between parents and children, or what G. Stanley Hall called a period of "storm and stress." Parents might be shocked by their adolescent's preferences in dress, music, and vocabulary. In trying out various styles and values, adolescents are influenced by the cohort to which they belong. Thus, adolescent males shocked their parents by wearing pompadours in the 1950s, shoulder-length hair in the 1970s, and spiked hairdos in the 1990s. But conformity to parental norms varies across cultures. A survey of adolescents in China, Taiwan, and the United States found that American adolescents were significantly less conforming than those in the other two groups (Zhang & Thomas, 1994).

Despite the normal conflicts between parental values and adolescent behaviors, most adolescents have positive relations with their parents. In general, adolescence is a time of only slightly increased parent-child conflict (Galambos, 1992). Of course, some adolescents adopt negative identities that promote antisocial, or even delinquent, behaviors. This is more common in adolescents whose parents set few rules, fail to discipline them, and do not supervise them (Loeber & Dishion, 1983).

In regard to their friendships, adolescents have more intimate friendships than do younger children, possibly because they are more capable of sharing their thoughts and feelings and understanding those of other people. Adolescent girls tend to have more intimate friendships than do adolescent boys. That is, adolescent girls share more of their private thoughts and feelings. This reflects their greater willingness to trust their friends, apparently because they are less fearful of being ridiculed if they reveal their shortcomings (Berndt, 1992).

Adolescence is associated with an important biologically based psychosocial conflict between the powerful urge to engage in sexual relations and societal values against premarital sex. The proportion of American adolescents engaging in sex increased steadily from the 1930s, when less than 10 percent had premarital sex, to today, when most older

Human Development |

adolescents engage in it. But the sexes differ in their sexual liberality. Adolescent males are more willing to engage in casual sex, while adolescent females are more likely to prefer sex as part of a more intimate relationship (Hendrick et al., 1985).

Though American and European adolescents have similar levels of sexual activity, there are more unwanted pregnancies among Americans. This is attributable in part to the greater ignorance and recklessness of American youth in the use of contraception. This begins from the very first sexual experience, when most American adolescents do not use contraceptives—though the percentage who do use contraceptives increased during the 1980s (Poppen, 1994). Promiscuity and unprotected sex increase the risks of sexually transmitted diseases such as herpes, syphilis, and AIDS. Moreover, irresponsible sexual activity in America leads to thousands of abortions, many fatherless offspring, and inadequate care for resulting offspring (Brooks-Gunn & Furstenberg, 1989).

Adolescence is also a period often involving widespread use of psychoactive drugs, including alcohol, nicotine, cocaine, and marijuana. Peer-group drug use is a factor in the promotion of adolescent drug use. For example, those who take up smoking often do so to become members of peer groups they perceive as desirable (Aloise-Young, Graham, & Hansen, 1994). Today alcohol is the main drug of choice among adolescents in many countries. A survey of more than 2,600 Canadian adolescents found that alcohol use was associated with more problem behaviors than was the use of other drugs (Gfellner & Hundleby, 1994). Fortunately, despite the risks associated with sexual irresponsibility and drug and alcohol abuse, almost all adolescents enter adulthood relatively unscathed.

STAYING ON TRACK: *Adolescent Development*

1. Why should adolescence researchers be concerned with cohort effects?
2. What is the formal operational stage?
3. According to Erikson, how does identity formation manifest itself in adolescents?

ADULT DEVELOPMENT

adulthood
The period beginning when the individual assumes responsibility for her or his own life.

In Western cultures, **adulthood** begins when adolescents become independent of their parents and assume responsibility for themselves. Interest in adult development accelerated in the 1950s after being inspired by Erikson's theory of life-span development (Levinson, 1986) and brought an increased realization that physical, cognitive, and psychosocial changes take place across the entire life span.

Physical Development

Adults reach their physical peak in their late twenties and then begin a slow physical decline that does not accelerate appreciably until old age. Most athletes peak in their twenties, as is shown by the ages at which world-class athletes achieve their best performances (Schulz & Curnow, 1988). Beginning in our twenties, our basal metabolic rate (the rate at which the body burns calories when at rest) also decreases, accounting in part for the tendency to gain weight in adulthood. This makes it especially important for adults to pay attention to diet and exercise, which can also counter the tendency to experience lung, heart, and muscle deterioration in early and middle adulthood. A prime example of this is Kareem Abdul Jabbar, who, by meticulous attention to maintaining a healthy diet and a state of physical fitness, played 20 years of professional basketball.

Aging also brings sexual changes. As men age, they produce fewer and fewer sperm, yet they can still father children into old age. But they might have increasing difficulty in achieving penile erections (Doyle, 1995). Typically beginning in their forties, women experience *menopause*—the cessation of their menstrual cycle. This is associated with a reduction in estrogen secretion, cessation of ovulation, and consequently the inability to become pregnant. The reduction in estrogen can cause sweating, hot flashes, and brittle

(a)

(b)

(c)

◀ **Aging and Physical Well-Being**
These people show that proper diet and exercise can help us maintain our physical well-being as we age: (*a*) By following a strict dietary and exercise routine, 49-year-old Gregg Amore won the 1996 "Mr. U.S.A. Natural" Bodybuilding Championship in both the over 35 and over 45 categories. He did so while caring for his family, running a farm, and serving as director of counseling at Allenstown College. (*b*) Even people in their eighties, such as marathon runner Ruth Rothfarb, can compete in athletics. (*c*) And downhill skiing, too, can be enjoyed by the elderly, including these two men in their seventies.

bones, as well as atrophy of the vagina, uterus, and mammary glands (Greendale & Judd, 1993). Menopause signals an end to the childbearing years, but it does not signal an end to sexuality. Postmenopausal women can still have fulfilling sex lives and social lives. Moreover, a survey of 1,500 Australian women found that health status, not menopausal status, affected the happiness of women in midlife (Dennerstein, Smith, & Morse, 1994).

Middle-aged adults tend to become farsighted and require reading glasses, as evidenced by an increasing tendency to hold books and newspapers at arm's length. But marked changes in physical abilities usually do not occur until late adulthood. The older adult exhibits deterioration in heart output, lung capacity, reaction time, muscular strength, and motor coordination (Maranto, 1984). Old age also brings a decline in hearing, particularly of high-pitched sounds.

Eventually, no matter how well we take care of our bodies, all of us reach the ultimate physical change—death. Though the upper limit of the human life span seems to be about 120 years, few people live to even 100. But why is death inevitable? Death seems to be genetically programmed into our cells by limiting their ability to repair or reproduce themselves (Hayflick, 1980). Animal research indicates that aging can be slowed by the reduction of daily caloric intake, which prevents the buildup of certain metabolic by-products that promote aging. For example, a study of rats found that those who ate a low-calorie diet lived longer (Masoro et al., 1995). The effects of low-calorie diets on human aging and longevity remain unclear.

We do know, however, that the mere act of continuing to work is associated with slower aging. In a study supporting this, elderly people who continued to work or who retired but participated in regular physical activities showed a constant level of cerebral blood flow over a 4-year period. In contrast, elderly people who retired and did not participate in regular physical activities showed a significant decline in cerebral blood flow. Those who continued to work also scored better on cognitive tests than did the inactive retirees (Rogers, Meyer, & Mortel, 1990). There is even evidence that individuals who engage in complex activities can generate new synapses in the brain, partly countering some of the negative effects of aging (Black, Isaacs, & Greenough, 1991). Thus, while physical aging is inevitable, people who maintain an active lifestyle might age at a slower rate. Note that these results do not conclusively demonstrate that activity *causes* a slowing of the effects of aging. Perhaps, instead, people who age more slowly are more likely to stay active.

Cognitive Development

One of the most controversial issues in developmental psychology is the pattern of adult cognitive development, particularly intellectual development. Early studies of this showed that we experience a steady decline in intelligence across adulthood. But this apparent decline is found more often in cross-sectional studies than in longitudinal studies. Longitudinal studies have found that a marked decline in intelligence does not begin until about age 60. This indicates that the decline in intelligence across adulthood found in cross-sectional studies might be a cohort effect (perhaps due to differences in early educational experiences) rather than an aging effect (Schaie & Hertzog, 1983). Moreover, the intellectual decline in old age does not encompass all facets of intelligence. Instead, it holds for fluid intelligence but not for crystallized intelligence (Wang & Kaufman, 1993). **Fluid intelligence** reflects the ability to reason and to process information; **crystallized intelligence** reflects the ability to gain and retain knowledge.

But what accounts for the decline in fluid intelligence in old age? The Seattle Longitudinal Study of 1,620 adults between 22 and 91 years of age conducted by K. Warner Schaie (1989) found that the speed of information processing slows in old age. This has been replicated in other research studies (Bors & Forrin, 1996). This slowing is especially detrimental to short-term memory (Salthouse, 1991), which is the stage of memory that involves the conscious, purposeful mental manipulation of information.

Older adults tend to do more poorly than adolescents and young adults on cognitive tasks. One factor that explains why is that they have been out of school for many years. This was the finding of a study that compared the recall ability of college students of traditional age, their peers not attending college, and older people not attending college. The average age of the younger groups was 22, and the average age of the older group was 69. The three groups were equal in their level of intelligence.

The results showed that the recall ability of the college group was better than that of the other two groups. But there was no difference in the performance of the groups of older persons and younger persons who were not attending college. This indicates that it might be the failure to use one's memory, rather than simply brain deterioration accompanying aging, that accounts for the inferior performance of the elderly on tests of recall. When it comes to the maintenance of cognitive abilities, such as memory, the adage "Use it or lose it" might have some validity (Ratner et al., 1987).

Psychosocial Development

Social development continues through early, middle, and late adulthood. Keeping in mind that these divisions are somewhat arbitrary, assume that early adulthood extends from age 20 to age 40, middle adulthood from age 40 to age 65, and late adulthood from age 65 on. The similarities exhibited by people within these periods are related to the common social experiences of the "social clock." In recent decades, the typical ages at which some of these experiences occur have varied more than in the past. A graduate student might live

fluid intelligence
The form of intelligence that reflects reasoning ability, memory capacity, and speed of information processing.

crystallized intelligence
The form of intelligence that reflects knowledge acquired through schooling and in everyday life.

▲ **Back to School**
The myth that rapid intellectual decline is a normal aspect of aging is countered by the increasing numbers of older adults beginning their undergraduate careers. The older students who might now be in your classes were rare only a decade ago.

| C H A P T E R 4

at home with his parents until his late twenties, a woman working toward her medical degree might postpone marriage until her early thirties, and a two-career couple might not have their first child until they are in their late thirties. Of course, events that are unique to each person's life can also play a role in psychosocial development. Chance encounters in our lives, for example, contribute to our unique development (Bandura, 1982). You might reflect on chance encounters that influenced your choice of an academic major or that helped you meet your current boyfriend, girlfriend, husband, or wife.

Early Adulthood: Love and Work

Though Sigmund Freud paid little attention to adult development, he did note that normal adulthood is marked by the ability to love and to work. Erik Erikson agreed that the capacity for love is an important aspect of early adulthood, and he claimed that the first major task of adulthood is facing the conflict of **intimacy versus isolation** (Gold & Rogers, 1995). Intimate relationships involve a strong sense of emotional attachment and personal commitment. A study of college women supported Erikson's belief that the development of the capacity for intimacy depends on the successful formation of a psychosocial identity in adolescence. Women who were capable of a high degree of intimacy felt more secure and confident as separate individuals and responded with less distress to separations from persons to whom they were attached (Levitz-Jones & Orlofsky, 1985).

intimacy versus isolation
Erikson's developmental stage in which success is achieved by establishing a relationship with a strong sense of emotional attachment and personal commitment.

Marriage. About 95 percent of young adults eventually experience the intimate relationship of marriage. Of course, unlike the decade of the 1950s, there are a variety of kinds of families. No longer is the typical family one with two parents, including a husband who goes to work and a wife who stays home with the children. And at any given time many adults are unmarried—they are either widowed, divorced, not ready, or committed to remaining single. A survey of adults aged 20 to 30 who had never been married found that the women were more motivated to marry than were the men. But while the men were especially concerned with future career considerations, the women were equally concerned with career and family considerations (Inglis & Greenglass, 1989).

Unmarried status is correlated with greater physical and psychological risks, especially for men. A survey of more than 18,000 men conducted in England found that unmarried middle-aged men of all kinds—single, widowed, divorced, or separated—had higher mortality than did married men (Ben-Shlomo et al., 1993). One reason for this is a greater risk of illness in the unmarried, in part because they have less contact with social networks that encourage healthy behavior and medical treatment (Burman & Margolin, 1992).

What characteristics do adults look for in potential spouses? As you might expect, both women and men tend to seek spouses who are kind, loyal, honest, considerate, intelligent, interesting, and affectionate. But men tend to be more concerned than women with the potential spouse's physical attractiveness, and women tend to be more concerned than men with the potential spouse's earning capacity (Buss & Barnes, 1986). As discussed in Chapter 17, psychologists argue whether these preferences reflect the influence of evolution or of cultural norms that differentially affect male and female marital expectations.

What determines whether a marriage will succeed? An important factor is similarity—in age, religion, attitudes, ethnicity, personality, intelligence, and educational level (O'Leary & Smith, 1991). Willingness to talk about problems is another important factor, as found in a 2-year longitudinal study of newlyweds. Those couples who believed that conflicts should be discussed openly reported greater marital happiness than those who believed they should be ignored (Crohan, 1992).

Divorce. Unfortunately, for many couples marital happiness is elusive and they may eventually seek to divorce (Devine & Forehand, 1996). One of the hallmarks of an unhappy marriage is the tendency of the spouses to consistently offer negative explanations for their spouse's behavior (Bradbury & Fincham, 1990). In the United States, about half of first marriages are so unhappy that they end in divorce. In fact, the United States has the highest divorce rate of any industrialized country (O'Leary & Smith, 1991). A study that interviewed over 1,300 persons found that divorce has increased not because marriages were happier in the "good old days," but instead because barriers to divorce (such as conservative values or shared social networks) have fallen and alternatives to divorce (such as a wife's independent income or remarriage prospects) have increased. Thus, the threshold of marital happiness that will trigger divorce is lower than it was several decades ago.

Yet there is evidence that married persons might remain committed to spouses who treat them poorly. You probably have known someone who sticks with a romantic partner who treats that person in a manner that you would not tolerate. Consider a study of 86 pairs of married couples from central Texas, with an average age of 32 years and an average length of marriage of 6 years (Swann, Hixon, & De La Ronde, 1992). The spouses took personality tests measuring their self-concepts. They also measured how the spouses appraised each other and how committed they were to each other. The results revealed that the degree of commitment to one's spouse depended on the degree of congruence between one's self-concept and how one was viewed by one's spouse. That is, those with positive self-concepts felt more committed when their spouses viewed them positively. Likewise, those with negative self-concepts felt more committed when their spouses viewed them negatively.

What could account for this finding, which runs counter to the commonsense notion that we all wish to be admired and treated well? The researchers found that though we might insist on being treated well in casual relationships, we insist on being treated in accordance with our self-concept within the intimacy of marriage. That is, we want our spouses to verify our self-concept so we are not confused about ourselves or about how other people will treat us. In addition, we will trust spouses more who do not try to "snow" us by telling us we're attractive when we feel ugly, intelligent when we feel stupid, and personally appealing when we feel socially inept. Moreover, while people with positive self-concepts might welcome high expectations of them, people with negative self-concepts might fear unrealistically high expectations that they could not meet. The researchers also interpreted their findings as contradicting the popular belief that people with negative self-concepts feel committed to romantic partners who treat them poorly because they hope to win them over and thereby "prove" themselves.

Parenthood. For most couples, parenthood is a major component of marriage. Raising children can be one of the greatest rewards in life, but it can also be one of life's greatest stresses. Because women still tend to be the primary caregiver, their parental responsibilities tend to be especially stressful. But mothers who receive emotional support from their husbands show less distress in regard to parenting (Levitt, Weber, & Clark, 1986). Overall, parenthood brings a modest decline in marital happiness, caused in part by having less time for recreation and more conflict with one's spouse (Belsky & Pensky, 1988). Of course, some couples remain childless. They are not necessarily unhappy. In fact, especially if they are voluntarily childless, they might be more happy than couples with children (Bell & Eisenberg, 1985). This is attributable, in part, to the fact that they do not have the stress that parents experience from money woes, children's illnesses, loss of sleep, and lack of recreational outlets.

But what of single parents? In the 1960s and 1970s, divorce was the chief cause of single parenting. This has been joined by planned or unplanned childbearing outside of marriage. Though single parents are usually women, one in five is male. Many single parents, given social and financial support, are successful in rearing children. But according to the U.S. Bureau of the Census, single-parent families, on the average, suffer disadvantages in regard to income, health, and housing conditions. The most disadvantaged are families consisting of children and a never-married mother (Bianchi, 1995).

Middle Adulthood: Serving Others

In 1850 few Americans lived beyond what we now call early adulthood; the average life span was only 40 years (Shneidman, 1987). But improved nutrition, sanitation, and

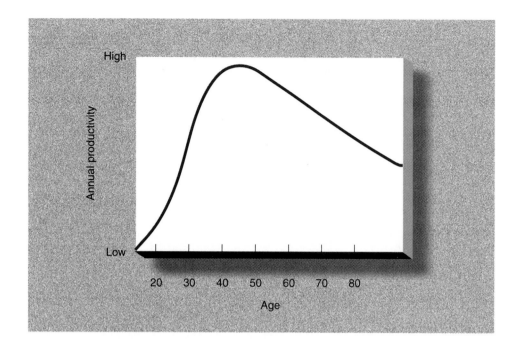

health care have almost doubled that life span. What was the end of the life span more than a century ago is today simply the beginning of middle adulthood. Daniel Levinson (1978) found that during the transition to middle adulthood, men commonly experience a midlife crisis, in which they realize that the "dream" they had pursued in regard to their life goals will not be achieved or, even if achieved, will seem transient in the face of the inevitability of death. This need to resolve the contradiction between the pursuit of one's life dream and the realization of one's mortality is an aspect of Levinson's theory that shows a kinship with existential psychology. Other studies indicate, however, that the midlife crisis is less intense than Levinson found in his research (Fagan & Ayers, 1982). Moreover, the life dreams of women tend to be more complex than the life dreams of men. While men typically focus on their careers, women focus on marriage and children, as well as their careers (Roberts & Newton, 1987).

According to Erik Erikson, the main task of middle adulthood is the resolution of the conflict of **generativity versus stagnation** (Peterson & Stewart, 1996). Those who achieve generativity become less self-absorbed and more concerned about being a productive worker, spouse, and parent. They are also more satisfied with their lives (McAdams, de St. Aubin, & Logan, 1993). One way of achieving generativity is to serve as a mentor for a younger person, as your college professors may do for many of their students. This lets mentors realize their life dreams vicariously and know that their dreams will continue even after their own deaths (Barnett, 1984). In regard to the life dream, as illustrated in Figure 4.10, the transition between early and middle adulthood, from the late thirties to the early forties, is a time when leaders and creative people tend to make their most outstanding contributions to their fields (Simonton, 1988).

generativity versus stagnation
Erikson's developmental stage in which success is achieved by becoming less self-absorbed and more concerned with the well-being of others.

Middle adulthood also brings transitions affected by one's parental status. Couples who have children must eventually face the day when their last child leaves home. You might be surprised to learn that parents become more distressed and experience more marital unhappiness after their first child leaves home than after their last child leaves home. In fact, after the last child has left home, parents tend to be relieved and experience improved marital relations (Harris, Ellicott, & Holmes, 1986). Perhaps the notion of an "empty nest syndrome" (after the last child has left home) should be replaced by the notion of a "partly empty nest syndrome" (after the first child has left home). Moreover, a growing trend in North America is the "crowded nest," caused by the return home of young adults who find it personally or financially difficult to live on their own (Schnaiberg & Goldenberg, 1989).

integrity versus despair
Erikson's developmental stage in which
success is achieved by reflecting back on a
meaningful life.

hospice movement
The movement to provide care for the terminally ill in settings that are as close as
possible to everyday life, and that emphasizes the need to reduce pain and suffering.

Late Adulthood: A Life Well Lived

Now that more people are living into their seventies and beyond, developmental psychologists have become more interested in studying late adulthood. In 1900 only one person
in thirty was over 65. By 2020 one person in five will be over 65 (Eisdorfer, 1983).
Though this increase in the elderly population will create more concern about physical
well-being in old age, it will also create more concern about psychosocial development in
old age. Erikson claimed that the main psychosocial task of late adulthood is to resolve the
crisis of **integrity versus despair** (Hannah et al., 1996). A sense of integrity results from
reflecting back on a meaningful life through a "life review." In fact, Erikson claimed that
pleasurable reminiscing is essential to satisfactory adjustment in old age. This was supported by a study of institutionalized war veterans. Those who frequently reminisced
scored higher on a questionnaire that measured their level of ego integrity (Boylin,
Gordon, & Nehrke, 1976). And old age is not necessarily a time of physical decay, cognitive deterioration, and social isolation. For many, it is a time of physical activity, continued education, and rewarding social relations (Whitbourne & Hulicka, 1990).

Eventually, many adults must confront one of the greatest psychosocial challenges of
old age—the death of a spouse. During the period immediately following the death of
their spouse, bereaved spouses are more likely to suffer depression, illness, or death than
are their peers with living spouses. This increased morbidity and mortality might stem
from the loss of the emotional and practical support previously provided by the
now-deceased spouse. Widowers are usually more devastated than widows, apparently
because widows receive greater social support, particularly from their friends (Stroebe &
Stroebe, 1983).

Though, as Benjamin Franklin observed in 1789, "in this world nothing's certain but
death and taxes," we can at least improve the way in which we confront our own mortality. In old age, successful resolution of the crisis of ego integrity versus despair is associated with less fear of death (Goebel & Boeck, 1987). And a survey of 200 adults found
that those with strong religious convictions and a greater belief in an afterlife have lower
death anxiety (Alvarado et al., 1995).

Prior to the twentieth century, death was accepted as a public part of life. People died
at home, surrounded and comforted by loved ones. Today, people commonly die alone, in
pain, in hospital rooms, attached to life-support systems. One of the most important
developments to counter this approach to death and dying is the **hospice movement,**

(a)

(b)

◀ Accomplishments in Old Age
Old age is not necessarily a time of physical and mental deterioration. (*a*) Anna Mary Moses (1860–1961), better known as "Grandma Moses," began a successful painting career at the age of 75. (*b*) Comedian George Burns continued to be a popular performer into his nineties.

founded in 1958 by the British physician Cicely Saunders. She was motivated to do so by her colleagues' failure to respond sensitively to dying patients and their families. Hospices provide humane, comprehensive care for the dying patient in a hospital, residential, or home setting, with attention to alleviating the patient's physical, emotional, and spiritual suffering (Hayslip & Leon, 1992).

What are the psychological experiences of the dying? The person who sparked interest in studying the experiences of dying persons was the Swiss psychiatrist Elisabeth Kübler-Ross (1969). She saw death and suffering as a young adult as she traveled through France and Poland to help victims of World War II and later when she worked as a physician in the United States (Gill, 1980). Based on her observations of dying patients, she identified five stages commonly experienced by terminally ill patients: denial, anger, bargaining, depression, and acceptance. At first, the patients deny their medical diagnoses, then become angry at their plight, bargain with God to let them live, suffer depression at the thought of dying, and finally come to accept their impending death. Kübler-Ross and others, however, have found that not all terminally ill patients go through all the stages or go through them in the same order (Kübler-Ross, 1974). Though flawed by subjective interpretations and unsystematic recording of patients' reactions to terminal illness, her research has inspired others to study the psychology of dying (Corr, 1993).

▲ Elisabeth Kübler-Ross
"To be with a dying patient makes us conscious of the uniqueness of the individual in this vast sea of humanity, aware of our finiteness, our limited lifespan."

STAYING ON TRACK: *Adult Development*

1. What is the apparent relationship between caloric intake and aging?
2. What does research indicate about changes in intelligence in old age?
3. How do adults successfully resolve Erikson's conflict involving generativity versus stagnation?

THINKING ABOUT *Psychology*

Are There Significant Psychological Sex Differences?

In the nineteenth century, scientific interest in sex differences was stimulated by Darwin's theory of evolution and promoted by Francis Galton, whose views on sex differences were influenced by sexist attitudes of the Victorian era (Buss, 1976). Galton assumed that females and males evolved physical and psychological differences that help them function

in particular roles, and he insisted that they should remain in those roles (Shields, 1975). Views like his were countered by some psychologists, such as Leta Stetter Hollingworth (1886–1939), who insisted that sex differences were due to social factors and did not denote the inferiority of women.

The first major review of sex differences was published by Eleanor Maccoby and Carol Jacklin (1974). They reported that females were superior in verbal abilities and males were superior in spatial and mathematical abilities. They also found that males were more aggressive than females. Nonetheless, they found fewer differences, and generally smaller differences, than were commonly believed to exist. Today, researchers concerned with sex differences are particularly concerned with cognitive differences and psychosocial differences.

COGNITIVE SEX DIFFERENCES

In studying cognitive differences between females and males, researchers have studied differences primarily in three kinds of abilities. They ask, Are there sex differences in verbal abilities? spatial abilities? mathematical abilities?

Verbal Abilities

Research on children supports the popular belief in the verbal superiority of females. Girls tend to be superior to boys in speaking, spelling, vocabulary, and reading comprehension. Yet these differences decrease by adolescence. Overall, sex differences in verbal abilities have declined in size in recent decades until they are virtually negligible (Hyde & Plant,

1995). But what about talkativeness, which the popular stereotype holds to be the province of women? Research indicates that, contrary to the stereotype, men are consistently more talkative than women (Hyde & Linn, 1988).

Spatial Abilities

Though research has tended to find that men are superior in the rotation of mental images, sex differences in other spatial abilities tend to be small and inconsistent (Eagly, 1994). Moreover, a recent meta-analysis of research studies of sex differences in spatial abilities found that the sizes of the differences have decreased in recent years (Voyer, Voyer, & Bryden, 1995). Based on these findings, it seems that sex differences in spatial abilities have little practical impact.

Mathematical Abilities

Perhaps the most strongly established cognitive sex difference is that adolescent and adult males have higher average scores than adolescent and adult females on standardized mathematics tests. A national talent search by Camilla Benbow and Julian Stanley (1983) found that among seventh- and eighth-graders who took the mathematics subtest of the Scholastic Aptitude Test (SAT), the average score for males was higher than the average score for females. In fact, among those scoring higher than 700 (out of 800), males outnumbered females by a ratio of 13 to 1. Could this be attributable to males' having more experience in mathematics? Benbow and Stanley say no, having found little difference in the number of mathematics courses taken by females and males. And because they found no other life experiences that could explain their findings, Benbow and Stanley concluded that heredity probably accounts for the difference. This explanation has received some support from other researchers (Thomas, 1993).

But it has also provoked controversy. Critics argue that the sex differences in mathematical abilities reported by Benbow and Stanley might be attributable to as yet unidentified differences in girls' and boys' experiences with mathematics. Also, boys do not have a higher average score than girls on all measures of mathematical ability. Though boys have higher average scores on mathematics achievement tests, which stress problem solving, girls receive higher grades in mathematics courses (Kimball, 1989). A meta-analysis of more than 3 million subjects in 100 studies found that, aside from higher average male scores on standardized tests, there is no overall gender difference in mathematics ability. If anything, there is a slight superiority in favor of females in abilities such as calculating. Moreover, even male superiority in mathematical problem solving does not appear until adolescence (Hyde, Fennema, & Lamon, 1990). And even this might be attributable to differences in the number of advanced mathematics courses taken by males and females (Hyde & Plant, 1995).

PSYCHOSOCIAL SEX DIFFERENCES

Researchers also study sex differences in social behavior. They have been especially concerned with differences in personality and aggression.

Personality

Meta-analyses of research studies on personality differences have found that males are more assertive and have slightly higher self-esteem, while females are slightly more extraverted and more anxious, trusting, and, especially, tenderminded (that is, more caring and nurturing). These differences tended to be consistent across all ages and educational levels of subjects, as well as across a variety of different cultures (Feingold, 1994).

Researchers have also studied whether the stereotypical view that females are more self-disclosing than males is true. That is, do females reveal more of their private thoughts, feelings, and experiences than males do? Contrary to popular belief, females are only marginally more likely to self-disclose than males are (Dindia & Allen, 1992).

But what of the popular belief that females are more empathetic than males? This apparent sex difference depends on how empathy is measured. When asked to report on their level of empathy, females score higher than males. But when empathy is measured by physiological arousal or overt behavior, sex differences disappear. Evidently, social expectations that females will be more emotionally sensitive than males create differences in their subjective views of themselves but not necessarily in their actual behavior or physiological responses (Eisenberg & Lennon, 1983).

Aggression

Just as females are reputed to be more empathetic than males, males are reputed to be more aggressive than females. Research has found that males are, indeed, more physically aggressive than females are. But Alice Eagly has found that males are only slightly more verbally aggressive (Eagly & Steffen, 1986). Moreover, sex differences in aggression might be the product of gender roles. This was the conclusion of a study in which males and females were tested in the laboratory. When they were singled out as individuals, males were more aggressive than females. When they were deindividuated (that is, made to feel anonymous) males and females did not differ in aggression. The researchers attributed this difference to the power of gender roles: When we feel we are being noticed, we behave according to gender expectations (Lightdale & Prentice, 1994).

EXPLANATIONS FOR POSSIBLE SEX DIFFERENCES

If psychological sex differences exist, what might account for them? Researchers point to physiological factors and social-cultural factors.

Physiological Factors

Because of the obvious physical differences between males and females, researchers have looked to possible physiological factors to explain psychological sex differences. David Buss believes that males and females inherit certain behavioral tendencies as a product of their long evolutionary history. According to Buss, "Men and women differ . . . in domains in which they have faced different adaptive problems over human evolutionary history. In all other domains, the sexes are predicted to be psychologically similar" (Buss, 1995, p. 164). Thus, males are more aggressive and females more nurturing because prehistoric males were more likely to be hunters and prehistoric females were more likely to be homemakers. They do not differ in traits unrelated to their prehistoric roles as males and females.

But how might heredity affect psychological sex differences? Evidence supporting the biological basis of sex differences in social behavior implicates hormonal factors. Girls whose adrenal glands secrete high prenatal levels of testosterone are more likely to become "tomboys" who prefer rough play and masculine activities (though many tomboys do not have this adrenal disorder). These girls' genitals look masculine at birth (though they are usually corrected by surgery), and this might make parents treat them as though they are more masculine, yet parents usually report that they treat these girls the same as parents treat girls without the disorder (Berenbaum & Hines, 1992). There is some evidence, though, for a hormonal basis for cognitive sex differences (Kimura & Hampson, 1994). There also is strong evidence of a hormonal basis for sex differences in play behavior in childhood and fairly strong evidence for its effect on sex differences in aggressiveness (Collaer & Hines, 1995).

A second way that heredity might affect sex differences is through brain development. But efforts to associate specific cognitive differences with differences in brain structures have produced mixed results. In the early 1980s, researchers who examined the brains of deceased men and women created a stir when they reported that a portion of the corpus callosum called the splenium was larger in women than in men (DeLacoste-Utamsing & Holloway, 1982). (As explained in Chapter 3, the corpus callosum provides a means of communication between the left and right hemispheres of the brain.) The researchers concluded that the larger female splenium might explain why females seem to make more equal use of the cognitive abilities associated with the two cerebral hemispheres. But a replication of this study, which used magnetic resonance imaging to examine the brains of living people, found no sex differences in the size of the splenium. Moreover, the relationship, if any, between the size of the splenium and its role in hemispheric communication is unknown (Byrne, Bleier, & Houston, 1988).

Social-Cultural Factors

The possibility that cognitive sex differences are caused more by social-cultural factors than by physiological factors is supported by studies that have found a narrowing of cognitive sex differences between North American males and females during the past 20 years (Hyde & Plant, 1995). This might be explained in part by the cultural trend to provide female and male children with somewhat more similar treatment and opportunities (Jacklin, 1989). Even Camilla Benbow (1988) agrees that environmental, as well as hereditary, factors play an important role in cognitive abilities such as mathematics.

After two decades of extensive research, no sex differences have emerged that are large enough to predict with confidence how particular males and females will behave (Deaux, 1985). This means that decisions concerning the suitability of a given female or male for a specific academic or vocational position should not be influenced by assumptions concerning sex differences in cognitive or social behavior.

This has provoked a controversy about whether we should continue to study sex differences. Some psychologists, such as Roy Baumeister (1988), argue that we should no longer study them. Why study differences that are too few or too small to have practical significance? And why study sex differences when reports of even small differences might support sex discrimination? Baumeister has received support in his opposition to continued research on sex differences (Caplan & Larkin, 1991; Hollway, 1994). But Baumeister's view was countered by sex-difference researchers Sandra Scarr (1988), Alice Eagly (1995), and Diane Halpern (1992), who believe that objective scientific research on sex differences should continue, even if it might find differences that some people would prefer did not exist.

A compromise position has been put forth by Janet Shibley Hyde, who favors studying sex differences but warns against relying on the results of studies that have not been replicated, interpreting sex differences as signs of female deficiencies, and automatically attributing such differences to inherited biological factors. She favors recognizing sex differences but attributes them primarily to social-cultural factors (Hyde & Plant, 1995).

Thus, this chapter ends on the long-standing issue introduced early in the chapter: the relative importance of nature and nurture in human development.

STAYING ON TRACK: *Are There Significant Psychological Sex Differences?*

1. What is the best-established psychological sex difference?
2. Why do psychologists argue about the wisdom of studying sex differences?

CHAPTER SUMMARY

THE NATURE OF DEVELOPMENTAL PSYCHOLOGY

Developmental psychology is the field that studies the physical, perceptual, cognitive, and psychosocial changes that take place across the life span. The field began a century ago with the publication of baby biographies, which gave detailed descriptions of the development of individual infants. An overriding issue in developmental psychology is the relative influence of nature and nurture. The nature view was championed by scientists influenced by Darwin's theory of evolution, including his cousin Francis Galton. The nurture view was championed by followers of behaviorism, founded by John B. Watson. Today, psychologists in the field of behavioral genetics try to determine the extent to which heredity affects human development. The main source of evidence pertinent to this is research on similarities between relatives and research on the effects of enriched environments. Research on relatives includes studies of families, twins, adoptees, and identical twins reared apart. Animals reared in enriched environments show superior development. Research designs typical of developmental psychology include longitudinal research, cross-sectional research, and cohort-sequential research.

PRENATAL PERIOD

The prenatal period is divided into the germinal, embryonic, and fetal stages. Cell-adhesion molecules direct the size, shape, and location of organs in the embryo. Teratogens can impair prenatal development. Women who drink alcohol, a teratogen, during pregnancy might have offspring who suffer from fetal alcohol syndrome.

INFANCY AND CHILDHOOD

Childhood extends from birth until puberty. The first 2 years of childhood are called infancy. Motor development follows a consistent sequence, though the timing of motor milestones varies somewhat among infants. Jean Piaget found that children pass through distinct cognitive stages of development. During the sensorimotor stage, the infant learns to coordinate sensory experiences and motor behavior, and forms schemas that represent aspects of the world. The preoperational stage is marked by egocentrism. In the concrete operational stage, the child learns to make transitive inferences and to appreciate conservation.

Erik Erikson put forth an influential theory of psychosocial development. He believed that the life span consists of eight distinct stages, each associated with a crisis that must be overcome. An important factor in infant development is social attachment, a strong emotional tie to a caregiver. Permissive and authoritarian child-rearing practices are less effective than authoritative ones. Children who receive high-quality day care do not appear to suffer ill effects from being separated from their parents, though this might not be true of infants. Research on the effects of divorce on children has produced inconsistent results, with some studies finding no effects, others finding negative effects, and still others finding positive effects. Though the causes of male and female gender development are still unclear, social learning theory and gender-schema theory try to explain it. The most influential theory of moral development has been Lawrence Kohlberg's cognitive-developmental theory, which is based on Piaget's belief that a person's level of moral development depends on his or her level of cognitive development. Kohlberg proposes that we pass through preconventional, conventional, and postconventional levels of moral development. Carol Gilligan argues that Kohlberg's theory is biased toward a masculine view of morality. Research has provided mixed support for Kohlberg's theory.

ADOLESCENCE

Adolescence is a transitional period between childhood and adulthood that begins with puberty. In regard to physical development, the adolescent experiences the maturation of primary and secondary sex characteristics. In regard to cognitive development, some adolescents enter Piaget's formal operational stage, meaning that they can engage in abstract, hypothetical reasoning. And, in regard to psychosocial development, adolescence is a time of identity formation, an important stage in Erik Erikson's theory of development. The adolescent also is increasingly influenced by peer values, especially in regard to fashions, sexuality, and drug use.

ADULTHOOD

Adulthood begins when adolescents become independent from their parents. In regard to physical development, adults reach their physical peak in their late twenties, at which point they begin a gradual decline that does not accelerate appreciably until old age. Middle-aged women experience menopause, which, contrary to popular belief, is rarely a traumatic event. In regard to cognitive development, though aging brings some slowing of cognitive processes, people who continue to be mentally active show less cognitive decline than do their peers who do not stay active.

In regard to social development, Erik Erikson saw the main task of early adulthood as the establishment of intimacy, typically between a husband and wife. About 95 percent of adults marry, but half of today's marriages will end in divorce. The most successful marriages are those in which the spouses discuss, rather than avoid, marital issues. Erikson saw the main task of middle adulthood as the establishment of a sense of generativity, which is promoted by parenting. After the last child leaves home, parents typically improve their emotional and marital well-being. Erikson saw the final stage of life as ideally promoting a sense of integrity in reflecting on a life well lived. Eventually, all people must face their own mortality. The hospice movement, founded by Cicely Saunders, has promoted more humane, personal, and home-like care for the dying patient. Elisabeth Kübler-Ross stimulated interest in the study of death and dying. She found that dying people typically go through the stages of denial, anger, bargaining, depression, and acceptance.

THINKING ABOUT PSYCHOLOGY: ARE THERE SIGNIFICANT PSYCHOLOGICAL SEX DIFFERENCES?

Research on sex differences has found no consistent differences in male and female brains. Girls and boys differ little in their gross motor abilities until puberty, when boys begin to outperform girls. Females tend to have better verbal abilities, while males tend to have better spatial and mathematical problem-solving abilities. Males also tend to be more physically aggressive than females. Research on sex differences is controversial, because of fears that its findings might be used to promote and legitimate discrimination. Sex differences are based on group averages and are so small that they should not be used to make decisions about individuals.

KEY CONCEPTS

The Nature of Developmental Psychology

developmental psychology 106
maturation 106
behavioral genetics 107
genotype 109
phenotype 109
heritability 109
longitudinal research 111
cross-sectional research 111
cohort 111
cohort-sequential research 112

Prenatal Development

germinal stage 112
embryonic stage 113

fetal stage 113
teratogen 114
fetal alcohol syndrome 114

Infant and Child Development

childhood 115
infancy 115
sensorimotor stage 118
schema 118
assimilation 119
accommodation 119
object permanence 119
preoperational stage 119
egocentrism 119
concrete operational stage 120
transitive inference 120

conservation 120
trust versus mistrust 121
social attachment 121
autonomy versus shame
    and doubt 122
initiative versus guilt 122
industry versus inferiority 122
authoritative parenting 123
gender roles 125
social learning theory 125
gender-schema theory 126
preconventional level 128
conventional level 128
postconventional level 128

Adolescent Development

social clock 130
adolescence 130
puberty 130
menarche 131
formal operational stage 131
identity versus role confusion 132

Adult Development

adulthood 134
fluid intelligence 136
crystallized intelligence 136
intimacy versus isolation 137
generativity versus stagnation 139
integrity versus despair 140
hospice movement 140

KEY CONTRIBUTORS

The Nature of Developmental Psychology

G. Stanley Hall 106
Charles Darwin 106
Wendy Hill 106
Francis Galton 107
Gregor Mendel 108
Robert Plomin 111

Infant and Child Development

Marian Diamond 115
Tiffany Field 116
Eleanor Gibson 116
Jean Piaget 118
Erik Erikson 120
John Bowlby 121
Harry Harlow 121
Mary Ainsworth 121

Diana Baumrind 122
Sigmund Freud 125
Eleanor Maccoby 125
Sandra Bem 126
Lawrence Kohlberg 126
Carol Gilligan 129

Adult Development

K. Warner Schaie 136
Daniel Levinson 139

Cicely Saunders 141
Elisabeth Kübler-Ross 141
Camilla Benbow and Julian
    Stanley 143
Alice Eagly 144
Janet Shibley Hyde 145

FOR MORE INFORMATION ON HUMAN DEVELOPMENT

FOR GENERAL WORKS ON HUMAN DEVELOPMENT

Life-Span Development

Miller, P. H. (1993). *Theories of developmental psychology.* San Francisco: Freeman.
Papalia, D., & Olds, S. W. (1998). *Human development* (7th ed.). Boston: McGraw-Hill.

History of Developmental Psychology

Hogan, J. D. (1996). *A history of developmental psychology in autobiography.* Westview.

Parke, R. D., Ornstein, P. A., Reiser, J. J., & Zahn-Wexler, C. (Eds.). (1994). *A century of developmental psychology.* Washington, DC: American Psychological Association.

Heredity and Environment

Evolution

Badcock, C. (1991). *Evolution and individual behavior: An introduction to human sociobiology.* Cambridge, MA: Blackwell.
Cravens, H. (1988). *The triumph of evolution: The heredity-environment controversy: 1900–1941.*

Baltimore: Johns Hopkins University Press.

Nature-Nurture

Kevles, D. J. (1985). *In the name of eugenics: Genetics and the uses of human heredity.* New York: Knopf.
Plomin, R., McClearn, G. E., & DeFries, J. C. (1995). *Behavioral genetics: A primer* (2nd ed.). New York: W. H. Freeman.

Culture and Human Development

Munroe, R. L., & Munroe, R. H. (1994). *Cross-cultural human development.* Prospect Heights, IL: Waveland Press.
Nsamenang, A. B. (1992). *Human development in cultural context: A third world perspective.* Newbury Park, CA: Sage.

Research Methods in Developmental Psychology

Cozby, P. C., Worden, P. E., & Kee, D. W. (1989). *Research methods in human development.* Mountain View, CA: Mayfield.

Van der Veer, R. (1993). *Reconstructing the mind: Replicability in research on human development.* Norwood, NJ: Ablex.

FOR MORE ON PRENATAL DEVELOPMENT

Abel, E. L. (Ed.). (1996). *Fetal alcohol syndrome: From mechanism to prevention.* Boca Raton, FL: CRC Press.

Kolb, V. M. (Ed.). (1993). *Teratogens: Chemicals which cause birth defects* (2nd ed.). New York: Elsevier.

FOR MORE ON INFANT DEVELOPMENT

General Works

Bremner, J. G. (1994). *Infancy* (2nd ed.). Cambridge, MA: Blackwell.

Field, T. (1990). *Infancy.* Cambridge, MA: Harvard University Press.

Physical Development

Savelsbergh, G. J. (Ed.). (1993). *The development of coordination in infancy.* New York: Elsevier.

Cognitive Development

Colombo, J. (1993). *Infant cognition: Predicting later intellectual functioning.* Newbury Park, CA: Sage.

Yonas, A. (Ed.). (1987). *Perceptual development in infancy.* Hillsdale, NJ: Erlbaum.

Psychosocial Development

Fein, G. G., & Fox, N. (1990). *Infant day care.* Norwood, NJ: Ablex.

Holmes, J. (1994). *John Bowlby and attachment theory.* New York: Routledge.

FOR MORE ON CHILD DEVELOPMENT

General Works

Santrock, J. W., & Yussen, S. R. (1994). *Child development* (6th ed.). Madison, WI: Brown & Benchmark.

Valsiner, J. (Ed.). (1989). *Child development in cultural context.* Toronto: Hogrefe & Huber.

Physical Development

Gallahue, D. L., & Ozmun, J. (1995). *Understanding motor development: Infants, children, adolescents, adults* (3rd ed.). Dubuque, IA: Wm. C. Brown.

Smoll, F. L., Magill, R. A., & Ash, M. (Eds.). (1988). *Children in sport.* Champaign, IL: Human Kinetics.

Cognitive Development

General Works

Feldman, D. H. (1994). *Beyond universals in cognitive development* (2nd ed.). Norwood, NJ: Ablex.

Flavell, J. H., Miller, P. H., & Miller, S. A. (1993). *Cognitive development* (3rd ed.). Englewood Cliffs, NJ: Prentice Hall.

Piaget's Theory of Cognitive Development

Ault, R. L. (1983). *Children's cognitive development: Piaget's theory and the process approach.* New York: Oxford University Press.

Phillips, J. L., Jr. (1981). *Piaget's theory: A primer.* New York: W. H. Freeman.

Psychosocial Development

General Works

Eisenberg, N. (1994). *Social development.* Newbury Park, CA: Sage.

Grusec, J. E., & Lytton, H. (1993). *Social development.* New York: Springer-Verlag.

Erikson's Theory of Psychosocial Development

Evans, R. I. (1967). *Dialogue with Erik Erikson.* New York: Harper & Row.

Gross, F. L., Jr. (1986). *Introducing Erik Erikson: An invitation to his thinking.* Lanham, MD: University Press of America.

Child Rearing

Hetherington, E. M., & Arasteh, J. D. (Eds.). (1988). *Impact of divorce, single parenting, and stepparenting on children.* Hillsdale, NJ: Erlbaum.

Holden, G. (1996). *Parents and the dynamics of child rearing.* Boulder, CO: Westview.

Day Care

Clarke-Stewart, A. (1993). *Daycare* (2nd ed.). Cambridge, MA: Harvard University Press.

LeVine, R. A., Dixon, S., Levine, S., Richman, A., Leiderman, P. H., Keefer, C. H., & Brazelton, T. B. (1994). *Child care and culture: Lessons from Africa.* New York: Cambridge University Press.

Sibling Relationships

Bank, S. P., & Kahn, M. D. (1982). *The sibling bond.* New York: Basic Books.

Cicirelli, V. G. (1995). *Sibling relationships across the life span.* New York: Plenum.

Peer Relationships

Hughes, F. P. (1995). *Children, play, and development* (2nd ed.). Boston: Allyn & Bacon.

Roopnarine, J. L., Johnson, J. E., & Hooper, F. H. (Eds.). (1995). *Children's play in diverse cultures.* Albany: State University of New York Press.

Gender-Role Development

Basow, S. A. (1992). *Gender stereotypes and roles* (3rd ed.). Monterey, CA: Brooks/Cole.

Brannon, L. (1995). *Psychology and gender.* Boston: Allyn & Bacon.

Moral Development

Gilligan, C., Ward, J. V., & Taylor, J. M. (1988). *Mapping the moral domain: A contribution of women's thinking to psychological theory and education.* Cambridge, MA: Harvard University Press.

Kohlberg, L. (1984). *Essays on moral development. Vol. 2: The psychology of moral development.* San Francisco: Harper & Row.

Kurtines, W. M., & Gewirtz, J. L. (Eds.). (1995). *Moral development: An introduction.* Boston: Allyn & Bacon.

FOR MORE ON ADOLESCENT DEVELOPMENT

General Works

Dacey, J. S., & Kenny, M. E. (1997). *Adolescent development* (2nd ed.). Madison, WI: Brown & Benchmark.

Hall, G. S. (1905/1979). *Adolescence.* Salem, NH: Ayer.

Physical Development

Golub, S. (1992). *Periods: From menarche to menopause.* Newbury Park, CA: Sage.

Plant, T. M., & Lee, P. A. (Eds.). (1995). *The neurobiology of puberty.* New York: Blackwell.

Psychosocial Development

Erikson, E. (1963). *Identity: Youth and crisis.* New York: W. W. Norton.

Kroger, J. (1996). *Identity in adolescence* (2nd ed.). New York: Routledge.

FOR MORE ON ADULT DEVELOPMENT

General Works

Cavanagh, J. C. (1998). *Adult development and aging* (3rd ed.). Belmont, CA: Brooks/Cole.

Physical Development

Furman, C. S. (1997). *Turning point: The myths and realities of menopause.* New York: Oxford University Press.

Spence, A. P. (1994). *Biology of human aging* (2nd ed.). Englewood Cliffs, NJ: Prentice Hall.

Cognitive Development

Kausler, D. H. (1994). *Learning and memory in normal aging.* San Diego: Academic Press.

Powell, D. H., & Whitla, D. K. (1994). *Profiles in cognitive aging.* Cambridge, MA: Harvard University Press.

Psychosocial Development

Personality Development

Levinson, D. (1978). *The seasons of a man's life.* New York: Knopf.

McCrae, R. R., & Costa, P. T., Jr. (1990). *Personality in adulthood*. New York: Guilford.

Mercer, R. T., Nichols, E. G., & Doyle, G. C. (1989). *Transitions in a woman's life*. New York: Springer.

Marriage, Parenthood, and Divorce

Guttmann, J. (1993). *Divorce in psychosocial perspective: Theory and research*. Hillsdale, NJ: Erlbaum.

Lauer, R., & Lauer, J. C. (1994). *Marriage and family: The quest for intimacy* (2nd ed). Madison, WI: Brown & Benchmark.

Sperling, M. B., & Berman, W. H. (Eds.). (1994). *Attachment in adults: Clinical and developmental perspectives*. New York: Guilford.

Aging

Belsky, J. K. (1990). *Psychology of aging*. Monterey, CA: Brooks/Cole.

Marshall, V., & McPherson, B. (1994). *Aging: Canadian perspectives*. Peterborough, Ontario: Broadview Press.

Death and Dying

Aiken, L. (1994). *Dying, death, and bereavement* (3rd ed.). Boston: Allyn & Bacon.

Kübler-Ross, E. (1969). *On death and dying*. New York: Macmillan.

Saunders, C. (1990). *St. Christopher's in celebration: Twenty-one years at Britain's first modern hospice*. North Pomfret, VT: Trafalgar Square.

FOR MORE ON SEX DIFFERENCES

Eagly, A. H. (1987). *Sex differences in social behavior: A social-role interpretation*. Hillsdale, NJ: Erlbaum.

Halpern, D. F. (1992). *Sex differences in cognitive abilities* (2nd ed.). Hillsdale, NJ: Erlbaum.

FOR MORE ON CONTRIBUTORS TO THE STUDY OF HUMAN DEVELOPMENT

Ames, L. B. (1989). *Arnold Gesell: Themes of his work*. New York: Human Sciences Press.

Boden, M. A. (1980). *Jean Piaget*. New York: Viking Press.

Bowlby, J. (1991). *Charles Darwin: A new life*. New York: W. W. Norton.

Coles, R. (1970). *Erik Erikson: The growth of his work*. Boston: Atlantic/Little, Brown.

Du Boulay, S. (1984). *Cicely Saunders: Founder of the modern hospice movement*. Albuquerque, NM: Amaryllis Press.

Forrest, D. W. (1974). *Francis Galton: The life and work of a Victorian genius*. New York: Taplinger.

Gill, D. (1980). *Quest: The life of Elisabeth Kübler-Ross*. New York: Harper & Row.

Ross, D. (1972). *G. Stanley Hall: The psychologist as prophet*. Chicago: University of Chicago Press.

CHAPTER 5

▲ GRANT WOOD
Fall Plowing, 1931

Sensation and Perception

▲ Helen Keller (1880–1968)
Because she was deaf and blind, Helen Keller relied on her senses of touch and smell to perceive the world. She used her fingers to read Braille well enough to earn a college degree, and she used her nose to recognize people by their scent.

sensation
The process that detects stimuli from the body or surroundings.

perception
The process that organizes sensations into meaningful patterns.

sensory receptors
Specialized cells that detect stimuli and convert their energy into neural impulses.

sensory transduction
The process by which sensory receptors convert stimuli into neural impulses.

psychophysics
The study of the relationship between the physical characteristics of stimuli and the conscious psychological experiences they produce.

*H*elen Keller (1880–1968), though deaf and blind from infancy, lived a rich, fulfilling life by using her other senses. She became an inspirational figure, finding success as a writer, a lecturer, and an educator. Nonetheless, without vision and hearing she was at greater risk of injury or death, and cut off from many experiences that would have enriched her life. To understand how the senses operate in protecting us and enriching our lives requires an appreciation of *sensory processes.*

SENSORY PROCESSES

As discussed in Chapter 1, because sensory processes are so important to our functioning in everyday life, the first scientific studies by psychologists were concerned with them. Today psychologists distinguish between *sensation* and *perception* (Bloomquist, 1985). The starting point for both processes is a *stimulus* (plural, *stimuli*), a form of energy (such as light waves or sound waves) that can affect sensory organs (such as the eyes or the ears). **Sensation** is the process that detects stimuli from one's body or environment. **Perception** is the process that organizes sensations into meaningful patterns. Visual sensation lets you detect the black marks on this page; visual perception lets you organize the black marks into letters and words. To appreciate the difference between sensation and perception, try to identify the picture in Figure 5.1. Most people cannot identify it, because they sense the light and dark marks on the page but fail to perceive a meaningful pattern.

For a real-life example of the difference between sensation and perception, consider a case study presented by neurologist Oliver Sacks (1985). One of his patients, a music professor he called "Dr. P.," suffered from brain damage that caused him to develop *prosopagnosia,* the inability to recognize faces (see Chapter 3). Dr. P. could recognize his students by the sounds of their voices, but he could not recognize them by sight. His disorder was so severe that he would grab his wife's head, mistaking it for a hat. Yet he was not visually impaired—he could easily see a pin on the floor. Thus, he had visual *sensations* of people's facial features, but he could not organize them into recognizable faces (visual *perceptions*).

Sensation depends on specialized cells called **sensory receptors,** which detect stimuli and convert their energy into neural impulses. This process is called **sensory transduction.** Receptors serve our visual, auditory, smell, taste, skin, and body senses. But some animals have receptors that serve unusual senses. Sharks have receptors that detect the weak electrical fields that emanate from the fish on which they prey (Kalmun, 1982). Whales and dolphins navigate by using receptors that sense variations in Earth's magnetic field; disruption of their magnetic sense might account for some of the periodic strandings of whales and dolphins on beaches (Weisburd, 1984).

Sensory Thresholds: The Detection of Stimuli

How intense must a sound be for you to detect it? How much change in light intensity must occur for you to notice it? Questions like these are the subject matter of **psychophysics,** the study of the relationship between the physical characteristics of stimuli and the corresponding psychological responses to them. Psychophysics was developed more than a century ago by the German scientists Ernst Weber (1795–1878) and Gustav Fechner (1801–1887). Fechner, after the publication of his classic *Elements of Psychophysics*

in 1860, devoted the rest of his life to studying the relationship between physical stimulation and mental experiences (Murray, 1990). Psychophysics has been used to assess, among other things, the perceived slipperiness of floor tiles (Cohen & Cohen, 1994) and the pain judgments of pregnant women in response to labor contractions (Algom & Lubel, 1994).

Absolute Threshold: Detecting a Stimulus

The minimum amount of stimulation that a person can detect is called the **absolute threshold,** or *limen.* For example, a cup of coffee would require a certain amount of sugar before you could detect a sweet taste. Weber used fine bristles to measure touch sensitivity by bending them against the skin. Because the absolute threshold for a particular sensory experience varies, psychologists operationally define the absolute threshold as the minimum level of stimulation that can be detected 50 percent of the time when a stimulus is presented over and over. Thus, if you were presented with a low-intensity sound 30 times and you detected it 15 times, that level of intensity would be your absolute threshold for that stimulus. The absolute thresholds for certain senses are remarkable. For example, you can detect the sweetness from a teaspoon of sugar dissolved in two gallons of water; the odor of one drop of perfume diffused throughout a three-room apartment; the wing of a bee falling on your cheek from a height of one centimeter; the ticking of a watch under quiet conditions at a distance of 20 feet; and the flame of a candle seen from a distance of 30 miles on a clear, dark night (Galanter, 1962).

The absolute threshold is also affected by factors other than the intensity of the stimulus. Because of this, researchers, inspired by Fechner's work, have devised **signal-detection theory** (Johnstone & Alsop, 1996), which assumes that the detection of a stimulus depends on both its intensity and the physical and psychological state of the individual. One of the most important psychological factors is *response bias*—how ready the person is to report the presence of a particular stimulus. Imagine that you are walking down a street at night. Your predisposition to detect a sound would depend partly on your estimate of the probability of being mugged, so you would be more likely to perceive the sound of footsteps in a neighborhood you believe to be dangerous than in a neighborhood you believe to be safe.

Signal-detection researchers study four kinds of reports that a subject might make in response to a stimulus. A *hit* is a correct report of the presence of a target stimulus. A *miss* is a failure to report the presence of a target stimulus that is, in fact, present. A *false alarm* is a report of the presence of a target stimulus that is not, in fact, present. And a *correct rejection* is a correct report of the absence of a target stimulus. Consider these four kinds of reports in regard to walking down a dark street at night. A signal-detection hit would be perceiving

absolute threshold
The minimum amount of stimulation that an individual can detect through a given sense.

signal-detection theory
The theory holding that the detection of a stimulus depends on both the intensity of the stimulus and the physical and psychological state of the individual.

▶ **Sensory Adaptation**
Because of sensory adaptation, our sensory receptors respond less and less to a constant stimulus. These members of the New York Polar Bear Club are taking their traditional New Year's Day dip in cold ocean water. After they enter the water, their skin receptors adapt to the water temperature and they feel less cold.

footsteps when they actually occur. A miss would be failing to perceive footsteps when they actually occur. A false alarm would be perceiving footsteps when they do not occur. And a correct rejection would be failing to perceive footsteps when they do not occur.

Signal-detection theory has important applications to crucial tasks, such as identifying bombs put through airport X-ray machines. Even pain researchers use signal-detection theory to determine the effects of treatments. For example, some procedures for measuring the effectiveness of treatments to relieve pain might affect a person's *response bias* more than they affect his or her *sensitivity* to pain (Lloyd & Appel, 1976). This might lead to the mistaken belief that a new pain medication is effective when, in reality, it is not. The proper application of signal-detection theory might prevent that from happening.

Difference Threshold: Detecting Stimulus Changes

difference threshold
The minimum amount of change in stimulation that can be detected.

In addition to detecting the presence of a stimulus, we must be able to detect changes in its intensity. The minimum amount of change in stimulation that can be detected is called the **difference threshold.** For example, you would have to increase or decrease the intensity of the sound from your compact-disc player a certain amount before you could detect a change in its volume. Like the absolute threshold, the difference threshold for a particular sensory experience varies from person to person and from occasion to occasion. Therefore, psychologists formally define the difference threshold as the minimum change in stimulation that can be detected 50 percent of the time by a given person.

just noticeable difference (jnd)
Weber and Fechner's term for the difference threshold.

Weber's law
The principle that the amount of change in stimulation needed to produce a just noticeable difference is a constant proportion of the original stimulus.

Weber and Fechner referred to the difference threshold as the **just noticeable difference (jnd).** They found that the amount of change in intensity of stimulation needed to produce a jnd is a constant fraction of the original stimulus. This became known as **Weber's law.** For example, because the jnd for weight is about 2 percent, if you held a 50-ounce weight you would notice a change only if there was at least a 1-ounce change in it. But a person holding a 100-ounce weight would require the addition or subtraction of at least 2 ounces to notice a change. Research indicates that Weber's law holds better for stimuli of moderate intensity than for stimuli of extremely low or high intensity.

Sensory Adaptation: Diminished Responding to Stimulation

sensory adaptation
The tendency of the sensory receptors to respond less and less to a constant stimulus.

Given that each of your senses is constantly bombarded by stimulation, why do you notice only certain stimuli? One reason is that if a stimulus remains constant in intensity, you will gradually stop noticing it. For example, on entering a friend's dormitory room, you might be struck by the repugnant stench of month-old garbage. A few minutes later, though, you might not notice it at all. This tendency of sensory receptors to respond less and less to an unchanging stimulus is called **sensory adaptation.**

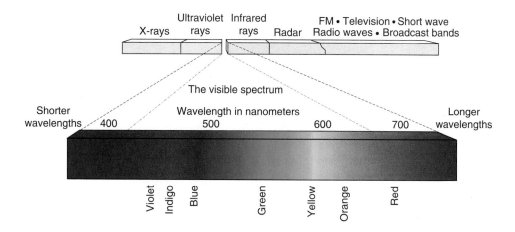

Sensory adaptation lets us detect potentially important changes in our environment while ignoring unchanging aspects of it. For example, when vibrations repeatedly stimulate your skin, you stop noticing them (Hollins, Delemos, & Goble, 1991); and once you have determined that the swimming pool water is cold, it would serve little purpose to continue noticing those stimuli—especially when more important changes might be taking place elsewhere in your surroundings. Of course, you will not adapt completely to extremely intense sensations, such as severe pain or freezing cold. This is adaptive, because to ignore such stimuli might be harmful or even fatal. But research indicates that elderly people adapt faster to odors than young people do and return to normal sensitivity more slowly. This might interfere with their ability to notice dangerous smells, such as the smell produced by a gas leak (Stevens, Cain, & Oatley, 1989).

STAYING ON TRACK: *Sensory Processes*

1. What is the difference between sensation and perception?
2. What is psychophysics?
3. What is sensory adaptation?

Answers to Staying on Track start on p. S-2.

VISION

Because of our reliance on vision, psychologists have conducted more research on it than on all the other senses combined. **Vision** lets us sense objects by the light reflected from them into our eyes. *Light* is the common name for the **visible spectrum,** a narrow band of energy within the *electromagnetic spectrum* (depicted in Figure 5.2). The wavelength of light corresponds to its *hue,* the perceptual quality that we call color. The wavelength is the distance between two wave peaks, measured in nanometers (billionths of a meter). Light varies in wavelength from about 380 nanometers to about 760 nanometers. A light composed of short wavelengths of light appears violet; a light composed of long wavelengths appears red.

Though human beings have visual receptors that sense only the visible spectrum, certain animals have visual receptors that detect other forms of electromagnetic energy. Some fish and insects, as well as birds such as zebra finches (Bennett et al., 1996), have visual receptors that are sensitive to the relatively short wavelengths of *ultraviolet light,* which affects human beings chiefly by causing sunburn. Rattlesnakes have receptors located in pits below their eyes that are sensitive to the relatively long wavelengths of *infrared light,* which conveys heat. This lets rattlesnakes hunt at night by detecting the heat emitted by nearby prey (Newman & Hartline, 1982). Police and military use special infrared scopes and goggles to provide vision in the dark (Rabin & Wiley, 1994).

vision
The sense that detects objects by the light reflected from them into the eyes.

visible spectrum
The portion of the electromagnetic spectrum that we commonly call light.

Sensation and Perception | 155

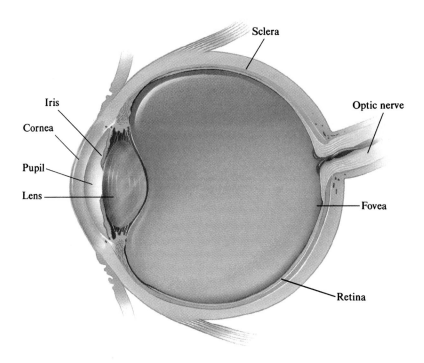

Returning to the visible spectrum, the height, or *amplitude*, of light waves determines the perceived intensity, or *brightness*, of a light. When you use a dimmer switch to adjust the brightness of a lightbulb, you change the amplitude of the light waves emitted by it, thereby changing the brightness of the light you see. The purity of a light's wavelengths determines its *saturation*, or vividness. The narrower the range of wavelengths, the more saturated the light. A highly saturated red light, for example, would seem "redder" than a less saturated one.

The Visual System

Vision depends on the interaction of the eyes and the brain. The eyes sense light reflected from objects and convey this information to the brain, where visual perception takes place. But what accounts for this? Consider what research has discovered about the functions of the eyes.

The Eye

The eye (see Figure 5.3) is a fluid-filled sphere. The "white" of your eye is a tough membrane called the **sclera,** which protects the eye from injury. At the front of the sclera is the round, transparent **cornea,** which focuses light into the eye. Are you blue-eyed? brown-eyed? green-eyed? Your eye color is determined by the color of your **iris,** a donut-shaped band of muscles behind the cornea. At the center of the iris is an opening called the **pupil.** The iris controls the amount of light that enters the eye by regulating the size of the pupil, dilating it to let in more light and constricting it to let in less. Your pupils dilate when you enter a dimly lit room and constrict when you go outside into sunlight.

You can demonstrate the pupillary response to light by first noting the size of your pupils in your bathroom mirror. Next turn out the light for 30 seconds. Then turn on the light and look in the mirror. Notice how much larger your pupils have become and how quickly they constrict in response to the light.

The size of the pupil is also affected by a variety of psychological factors. When we are psychologically aroused, the sympathetic nervous system makes our pupils dilate. Because pupil dilation is a sign of arousal, psychotherapists have used it to monitor the effectiveness of therapy, as in the treatment of snake phobia (that is, an intense

sclera
The tough, white outer membrane of the eye.

cornea
The round, transparent area in the front of the sclera that allows light to enter the eye.

iris
The donut-shaped band of muscles behind the cornea that gives the eye its color and controls the size of the pupil.

pupil
The opening at the center of the iris that controls how much light enters the eye.

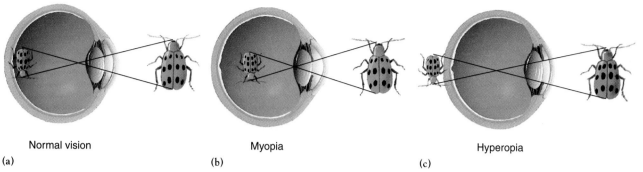

Normal vision
(a)

Myopia
(b)

Hyperopia
(c)

▲ FIGURE 5.4
Visual Acuity
In normal vision, the lens focuses images on the retina. In myopia, the lens focuses images in front of the retina. In hyperopia, the lens focuses images at a point that would fall behind the retina.

fear of snakes that interferes with everyday functioning). As the participants' anxiety decreases, their pupils dilate less when they look at a snake (Sturgeon, Cooper, & Howell, 1989).

Regardless of the psychological phenomena associated with the pupil, its primary function is to regulate the amount of light that enters the eye. After passing through the pupil, light is focused by the **lens** onto the **retina,** the light-sensitive inner membrane of the eye. Tiny muscles connected to the lens control **accommodation,** the process by which the lens increases its curvature to focus light from close objects or decreases its curvature to focus light from more distant objects.

Disruption of normal accommodation has important effects. As we age, the lens loses its elasticity, making it less able to accommodate when focusing on near objects (Fukuda, Kanada, & Saito, 1990). Many adults discover this in their early forties, when they find themselves holding books and newspapers at arm's length to focus the print more clearly on their retinas.

Many people, whether young or old, have conditions that make them unable to focus clear images on the retina. The two most common conditions are illustrated in Figure 5.4. In **myopia,** or *nearsightedness*, the lens focuses images of near objects on the retina, but focuses images of far objects at a point in front of the retina. This occurs because the eyeballs are too long. In **hyperopia,** or *farsightedness*, the lens focuses images of far objects on the retina, but focuses images of near objects at a point that would fall behind the retina. This occurs because the eyeballs are too short. Both of these conditions are easily corrected with prescription eyeglasses or contact lenses.

Today we know that the image cast on the retina is upside down. In the fifteenth century, Leonardo da Vinci (1452–1519) had rejected this possibility, because he could not explain how the brain saw a right-side-up world from an upside-down image. Why, then, do we not see the world upside down? The neural pathways in the brain simply "flip" the image to make it appear right side up.

As shown in Figure 5.5, the retina contains cells called *photoreceptors*, which respond when stimulated by light. The photoreceptors were first identified in the nineteenth century by scientist Heinrich Müller (1820–1864), with the use of a microscope (Riggs, 1985). There are two kinds of photoreceptors, **rods** and **cones,** whose names reflect their shapes. Each eye has about 120 million rods and about 6 million cones. The rods and cones stimulate *bipolar cells*, which in turn stimulate *ganglion cells*. The axons of the ganglion cells form the **optic nerves,** which convey visual information to the brain.

While the rods are especially important in night vision and peripheral vision, the cones are especially important in color vision and detailed vision. Rod vision and cone vision depend on different pathways in the brain (Shapley, 1990). The rods are more prevalent

lens
The transparent structure behind the pupil that focuses light onto the retina.

retina
The light-sensitive inner membrane of the eye that contains the receptor cells for vision.

accommodation
The process by which the thickness of the lens in the eye changes to focus images of objects located at different distances from the eye.

myopia
Visual nearsightedness, which is caused by an elongated eyeball.

hyperopia
Visual farsightedness, which is caused by a shortened eyeball.

rods
Receptor cells of the retina that play an important role in night vision and peripheral vision.

cones
Receptor cells of the retina that play an important role in daylight vision and color vision.

optic nerve
The nerve, formed from the axons of ganglion cells, that carries visual impulses from the retina to the brain.

► **FIGURE 5.5**
The Cells of the Retina
Light must first pass through layers of ganglion cells and bipolar cells before striking the rods and cones. Neural impulses from the rods and cones are transmitted to the bipolar cells, which, in turn, transmit neural impulses to the ganglion cells. The axons of the ganglion cells form the optic nerves, which transmit neural impulses to the brain.

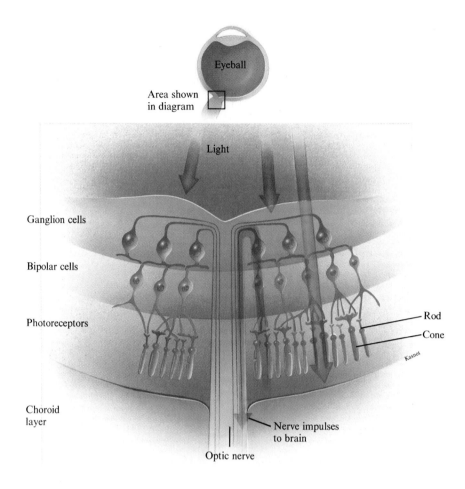

fovea
A small area at the center of the retina that contains only cones and provides the most acute vision.

smooth pursuit movements
Eye movements that track objects.

in the periphery of the retina, and the cones are more prevalent in the center. You can demonstrate this for yourself by taking small pieces of colored paper and selecting one without looking at it. Hold it beside your head, and slowly move it forward while staring straight ahead. Because your peripheral vision depends on your rods and your color vision depends on your cones, you will notice the paper before you can identify its color. Peripheral vision has survival value. For example, we rely on it to help avoid traffic hazards when crossing a street (David, Foot, & Chapman, 1990).

A small area in the center of the retina, the **fovea,** contains only cones. One reason why people differ in their visual acuity is that they vary in the number of foveal cones (Curcio et al., 1987). Because the fovea provides our most acute vision, we try to focus images on it when we want to see fine details. As you read this sentence, words focused on your cone-rich fovea look clear. Meanwhile, words focused on the cone-poor area around your fovea look blurred. One reason foveal vision is more acute is that each cone transmits neural impulses to one bipolar cell. This means that the exact retinal site of input from a given rod is communicated along the visual pathway. In contrast, neural impulses from an average of 50 rods are sent to a given bipolar cell (Cicerone & Hayhoe, 1990). Thus, the exact retinal site of stimulation of a given rod is lost. But in dim light the many rods sending their output to a given bipolar cell help make rod vision more sensitive than cone vision.

To keep objects focused on the foveae, we use two kinds of eye movements: smooth pursuit movements and saccadic movements. **Smooth pursuit movements** help our eyes track moving objects. One of the dangers of drinking and driving is that alcohol disrupts the ocular muscles, which control smooth pursuit movements (Freivalds & Horii, 1994). The following study illustrates how scientists studied these movements in testing an everyday commonsense belief.

Can Batters Really Keep Their Eyes on the Ball?

Rationale

Professional athletes make faster smooth pursuit movements with their eyes than amateurs do (Harbin, Durst, & Harbin, 1989). This is important because, for example, a professional baseball batter might have to track a baseball thrown by a pitcher at more than 90 miles an hour from a distance of only 60 feet. Ted Williams, arguably the greatest hitter in the history of baseball, called hitting a baseball the most difficult single task in any sport. Given this, is there any scientific support for the commonsense suggestion to batters, "Keep your eye on the ball?" Let's look at a study by Terry Bahill and Tom LaRitz (1984), of the University of Arizona, in which they sought the answer to this question.

Method

Bahill and LaRitz rigged a device that propelled a ball toward home plate along a string at up to 100 miles an hour on a consistent path. A photoelectric device recorded the batter's eye movements as he tracked the ball. Several professional baseball players took part in the study.

Results and Discussion

Eye-movement recordings indicated that the batters were able to track the ball until it was about 5 feet from home plate. Over the last few feet they could not keep the ball focused on their foveae—it simply traveled too fast over those last few degrees of visual arc. Thus, the commonsense advice to keep your eye on the ball is well intentioned, but it is impossible to follow the ball's movement all the way from the pitcher's hand to home plate. The reason some hitters, including Ted Williams, claim that they can see the ball strike the bat is that, based on their extensive experience in batting, their brains automatically calculate both the speed and the trajectory of the ball. This allows them to anticipate the point in space where the bat will meet the ball, and make a final eye movement to that exact point.

▲ ▲ ▲

As you scan a scene, such as this page, your eyes make continuous darting movements. These **saccadic movements** bring new portions of scenes into focus on your foveae (Irwin, 1996). After each saccadic movement, the eyes fixate on a target for about 250 milliseconds, a quarter of a second (Rayner, 1993). We pick up visual information only during these fixations, because the saccades, which leap about 8 or 9 letters, are too rapid for us to pick up useful information during them. Golfers who are excellent putters make more-efficient use of saccadic movements while putting than do golfers who are poor putters (Vickers, 1992).

The time needed to make saccadic movements and to extract information during fixations limits even outstanding readers to a maximum of 1,000 words a minute—a phenomenal rate. Yet some "speed-reading" programs claim that they can increase your reading speed to 10,000 words a minute. How do they do so? By teaching you to skim what you read. Though skimming increases the rate at which you turn pages, it also hurts your comprehension of what you read (Homa, 1983).

The retinal images of the words you read, or of any object on which your eyes are focused, are coded as neural impulses sent to the brain along the optic nerves. In the seventeenth century, the French scientist Edmé Mariotte demonstrated the existence of the *blind spot,* the point at which the optic nerve leaves the eye (Riggs, 1985). He placed a small disk on a screen, closed one eye, stared at the disk, and moved his head until the image of the disk disappeared. It disappeared when it fell on the blind spot. The blind spot is "blind" because it contains no rods or cones. To repeat Mariotte's demonstration, follow the procedure suggested in Figure 5.6. We do not normally notice the blind spot because the visual system fills in the missing area (Tripathy et al., 1995).

The Brain

Figure 5.7 traces the path of neural impulses from the eyeballs into the brain. The optic nerves travel under the frontal lobes of the brain and meet at a point called the **optic chiasm.** At the optic chiasm in human beings, axons from the half of each optic nerve

saccadic movements
Continuous small darting movements of the eyes that bring new portions of scenes into focus on the foveae.

optic chiasm
The point under the frontal lobes at which some axons from each of the optic nerves cross over to the opposite side of the brain.

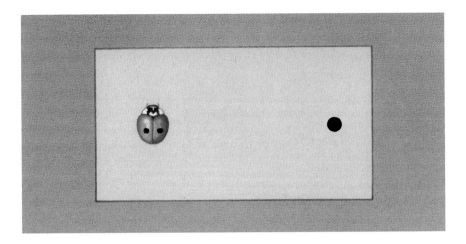

► **Figure 5.6**
Finding Your Blind Spot
Because your retina has no rods or cones at the point where the optic nerve leaves the eye, your retina is "blind" at that spot. To find your blind spot, hold this book at arm's length, close your right eye, and focus your left eye on the black dot. Move the book slowly toward you. When the book is about a foot away, the image of the ladybug should disappear. It disappears when it becomes focused on your blind spot. You do not normally notice your blind spot because your eyes see different views of the same scene, your eyes are constantly focusing on different parts of the scene, and your brain fills in missing details of the scene.

visual cortex
The area of the occipital lobes that processes visual input.

photopigments
Chemicals, including rhodopsin and iodopsin, that enable the rods and cones to generate neural impulses.

toward the nose cross to the opposite side of the brain. Axons from the half of each optic nerve nearer the ears travel to the same side of the brain as they began on. Some axons of the optic nerves go to the *tectum* (see Chapter 3) of the midbrain, which controls visual reflexes like blinking. Most axons of the optic nerves go to the *thalamus* (see Chapter 3), which transmits visual information to the **visual cortex** of the *occipital lobes*. Retinal information about objects in the right visual field is processed in the left occipital lobe, and retinal information about objects in the left visual field is processed in the right occipital lobe. The visual cortex integrates visual information about objects, including their shape and distance (Livingstone & Hubel, 1988), as well as their color (Yoshioka, Dow, & Vautin, 1996), brightness (Rossi et al., 1996), and movement (Li, 1996). Damage to the visual cortex may produce a *scotoma*, a kind of blind spot, in the visual field. But in many cases, the brain fills in the missing detail— even when it is part of a complex wallpaper pattern (Ramachandran, 1992).

Because the visual cortex is covered by a "map" with a point-by-point representation of the retinas, people who have gone blind because of damage to their eyes or optic nerves might someday have their vision restored by devices that directly stimulate the visual cortex. Researchers have invented an electronic system that consists of a video camera connected to a microprocessor, which in turn is connected to a matrix of 64 electrodes attached to the visual cortex. Stimulation of these electrodes produces a pattern of spots of light called *phosphenes* that can be used to represent the outlines of objects seen by the camera. In one experiment, subjects were able to negotiate around walls and objects in a maze using this system (Cha, Horch, & Normann, 1992). Perhaps more sophisticated devices will one day permit blind people to use prosthetic vision to read textbooks, paint pictures, and drive automobiles.

Visual Sensation

People with normal vision can see because of processes taking place in their retinas. Visual sensations depend on chemicals called **photopigments.** Rod vision depends on the photopigment *rhodopsin*, and cone vision depends on three kinds of photopigments called *iodopsin*. Until the late nineteenth century, when the role of photopigments was first discovered, prominent scientists, including Thomas Young, claimed that vision depended on light rays striking the retina, making the optic nerves vibrate (Riggs, 1985).

Today we know that when light strikes the rods or cones it breaks down their photopigments. This breakdown begins the process by which neural impulses are eventually sent along the optic nerves to the brain. After being broken down by light, the photopigments are resynthesized—more rapidly in dim light than in bright light. The cones function better than the rods in normal light, but the rods function better than the cones in dim light. Because of this, in normal light we try to focus fine details on the fovea. But if you were to look directly at a star in the night sky, you would be unable to see it because it would be focused on the fovea. To see the star, you would have to turn your head slightly, thereby focusing the star on the rod-rich periphery of the retina. The photoreceptors are also important in the processes of *dark adaptation* and *color vision*.

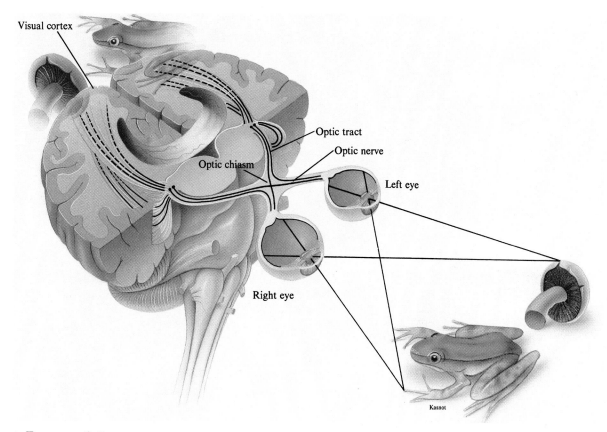

▲ FIGURE 5.7
The Visual Pathway
Images of objects in the right visual field are focused on the left side of each retina, and images of objects in the left visual field are focused on the right side of each retina. This information is conveyed along the optic nerves to the optic chiasm and then on to the thalamus. The thalamus then relays the information to the visual cortex of the occipital lobes. Note that images of objects in the right visual field are processed by the left occipital lobe and images of objects in the left visual field are processed by the right occipital lobe.

Dark Adaptation

When you enter a darkened movie theater, you have difficulty finding a seat because your photoreceptors have been bleached of their photopigments by the light in the lobby. But your eyes adapt by increasing their rate of synthesis of iodopsin and rhodopsin, gradually increasing your ability to see the seats and people in the theater. The cones reach their maximum sensitivity after about 10 minutes of dim light. But your rods continue to adapt to the dim light, reaching their maximum sensitivity in about 30 minutes. So, you owe your ability to see in dim light to your rods. Figure 5.8 illustrates the changes that take place during **dark adaptation,** the process by which the eyes become more sensitive to light. Impaired dark adaptation, which accompanies aging, has been implicated in the disproportionate number of nighttime driving accidents (Mortimer & Fell, 1989) that involve older adults.

The preceding discussion explains why motorists should dim their high beams when approaching oncoming traffic and why passengers should not turn on the dome light to read maps. High beams shining into the eyes or dome lights illuminating the inside of the vehicle bleach the rods, impairing the driver's ability to the see objects that might be ahead. You should also note that the cones are most sensitive to the longer wavelengths of the visible spectrum (which produce the experience of red) and the rods are most sensitive to the medium wavelengths (which produce the experience of green). This explains why at dusk (when we shift from cone vision to rod vision) a red jacket looks dull while a patch of green grass looks vibrant.

dark adaptation
The process by which the eyes become more sensitive to light when under low illumination.

Dark Adaptation
When you enter a dark room, your photoreceptors adapt by becoming more sensitive to light.
The cones reach their maximum sensitivity in
about 10 minutes, and the rods reach their maximum sensitivity in about 30 minutes. Though
the cones adapt to the dark faster than the rods
do, the rods become more sensitive than the
cones. This means that the absolute threshold
of the rods becomes much lower than that of
the cones.

Visible

Cones only

Light intensity

Not
visible

Rods only

0   10   20   30
Time in the dark (minutes)

trichromatic theory
The theory that color vision depends on
the relative degree of stimulation of red,
green, and blue receptors.

▲ **A *Green* Fire Truck?**
Because the rods are more sensitive to the green
region of the visible spectrum than to the red
region, green objects look brighter in dim light
than do red objects. So, though red fire trucks
look bright in the daylight, they look grayish in
dim light. This has led some fire departments to
increase the evening visibility of their trucks by
painting them a yellowish green color.

Color Vision

Color enhances the quality of our lives, as manifested by our concern with the colors of
our clothing, furnishings, and automobiles. Color also contributes to our survival, as
exemplified by the orange or yellow life rafts used at sea that make search and rescue
easier (Donderi, 1994). Primates such as apes, monkeys, and human beings have good
color vision. But human newborns have poor color vision, at least for their first month
after birth (Adams, Courage, & Mercer, 1994). Most other mammals, including dogs, cats,
and cows, have poor color vision. They lack a sufficient number or variety of cones. Most
birds and fish have good color vision. But fish that live in the dark depths of the ocean
lack color vision, which would be useless to them because cones function well only in
bright light (Levine & MacNichol, 1982).

What processes account for color vision? One answer was offered in 1802 when British
physicist Thomas Young presented the **trichromatic theory** of color vision, which was
championed in the 1850s by German scientist Hermann von Helmholtz (1821–1894).
Helmholtz's theories continue to influence research on the senses (Wade, 1994). Young
and Helmholtz found that red, green, and blue lights could be mixed into any color,
leading them to conclude that the input of three receptors was pooled by the brain. Today
the trichromatic theory is also called the *Young-Helmholtz theory*. It assumes that the retina
has three kinds of receptors (which we now know are cones), each of which is maximally
sensitive to red, green, or blue light.

A century after Helmholtz put forth his theory, George Wald (1964) provided evidence
for it in research that earned him a Nobel Prize. Wald found that some cones respond
maximally to red light, others to green light, and still others to blue light (see Figure 5.9).
The colors we experience depend on the relative degree of stimulation of the cones.
Figure 5.10 illustrates the principles of mixing colored lights and mixing colored pigments,
which differ from each other. Mixing colored lights is an additive process: Wavelengths
added together stimulate more cones. For example, mixing red light and green light produces yellow. Mixing pigments is a subtractive process: Pigments mixed together absorb
more wavelengths than does a single pigment. For example, mixing blue paint and yellow
paint subtracts those colors and leaves green to be reflected into the eyes. More recent
research has lent support to the trichromatic theory (Jacobs et al., 1996).

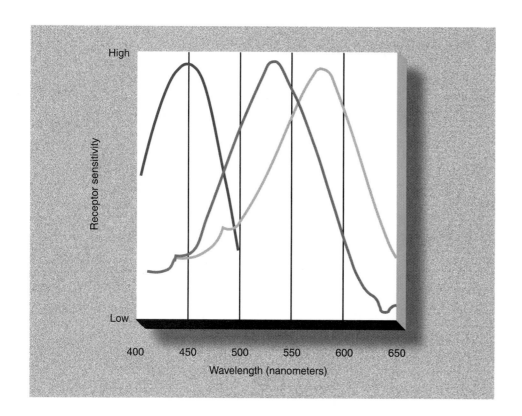

◄ FIGURE 5.9
Relative Sensitivity of the Cones
Each of the three kinds of cones (blue, green, and red) responds to a wide range of wavelengths of light. But each is maximally sensitive to particular wavelengths. The blue cones are maximally sensitive to short wavelengths, the green cones to medium wavelengths, and the red cones to long wavelengths. According to the trichromatic theory, the perceived color of a light depends on the relative amount of activity in each of the three kinds of cones.

In the 1870s, the German physiologist Ewald Hering (1834–1918) proposed an alternative explanation of color vision, the **opponent-process theory.** He did so, in part, to explain the phenomenon of **afterimages**—images that persist after the removal of a visual stimulus. If you stare at a red or blue surface for a minute and then stare at a white surface, you will see an afterimage that is the complementary color. For example, staring at red will produce a green afterimage, and staring at blue will produce a yellow afterimage.

The opponent-process theory assumes that there are *red-green, blue-yellow,* and *black-white* opponent processes (with the black-white opponent process determining the lightness or darkness of what we see). Stimulation of one process inhibits its opponent. When stimulation stops, the inhibition is removed and the complementary color is seen as a brief afterimage. This explains why staring at red leads to a green afterimage and staring at blue leads to a yellow afterimage. It also explains why we cannot perceive reddish greens or bluish yellows: Complementary colors cannot be experienced simultaneously because each inhibits the other.

Psychologist Russell de Valois and his colleagues (1966) provided evidence that supports the opponent-process theory. For example, certain ganglion cells in the retina and certain cells in the thalamus send impulses when the cones that send them input are stimulated by red and stop sending impulses when the cones that send them input are stimulated by the complementary color, green. Other ganglion cells and cells in the thalamus send impulses when the cones that send them input are stimulated by green and stop sending impulses when the cones that send them input are stimulated by red. There is stronger evidence for red-green and blue-yellow opponent processes than for a black-white opponent process (Sokolov & Izmailov, 1988).

The opponent-process theory also explains another phenomenon that the trichromatic theory cannot explain by itself: **color blindness.** People with normal color vision are *trichromats*—they have three kinds of iodopsin (red, blue, and green). Most color-blind people are *dichromats*—they have a normal number number of cones but lack one kind of iodopsin (Cicerone & Nerger, 1989). The most common form of color blindness is the inability to distinguish between red and green. People with red-green color blindness have cones with blue iodopsin, but their red and green cones have the same

opponent-process theory
The theory that color vision depends on red-green, blue-yellow, and black-white opponent processes in the brain.

afterimage
A visual image that persists after the removal of a visual stimulus.

color blindness
The inability to distinguish between certain colors, most often red and green.

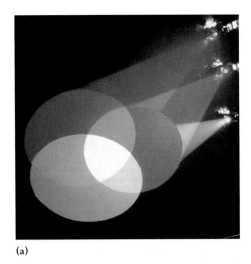

(a)

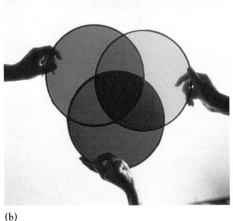

(b)

iodopsin, usually green. Because many people suffer from red-green color blindness, traffic lights always have the red light on top so that color-blind people will know when to stop and when to go.

Because color blindness is a recessive trait carried on the X (female) chromosome, males are more likely than females to be color blind. This means that a male who inherits the trait on his single X chromosome will be color blind. In contrast, a female must inherit the trait on *both* of her X chromosomes to be color blind. Few dichromats have blue-yellow color blindness. And even fewer people are *monochromats*—completely color blind.

But how does color blindness support the opponent-process theory? It does so because, though dichromats cannot distinguish between the complementary colors of red and green or blue and yellow, they never fail to distinguish between red and blue, red and yellow, green and blue, or green and yellow. Today the trichromatic theory and the opponent-process theory are combined in explaining color vision this way (Boynton, 1988): Impulses from the red, green, and blue cones of the retina are sent to the opponent-process ganglion cells and then further integrated in the thalamus and visual cortex.

Visual Perception

Visual sensations provide the raw materials that are organized into meaningful patterns by *visual perception*. Do we have to learn through experience to convert sensations into accurate perceptions? This is the basic assumption of the *constructionist theory* of Hermann von Helmholtz. Or, instead, does visual perception depend mainly on inborn mechanisms that automatically convert sensations into perceptions of stimuli? This is the basic assumption of the *direct perception theory* of James J. Gibson (1904–1979). According to Gibson (1979), evolution has endowed us with brain mechanisms that create perceptions directly from information provided by the sense organs. Thus, we do not need to rely on experience to help us perceive this information properly (Nakayama, 1994). Recent research, discussed in Chapter 4, on the sophisticated inborn perceptual abilities of newborn infants supports Gibson's theory. But most perception researchers believe that we "construct" our perceptions based on what Helmholtz called *unconscious inferences* that we make from our sensations (Cutting, 1987). These inferences are based on our experience with objects in the physical environment.

Form Perception: Distinguishing Figure from Ground

To perceive *forms* (meaningful shapes or patterns), we typically must distinguish a *figure* (an object) from its ground (its surroundings), though there is some evidence that form perception can precede the segmentation into figure and ground (Peterson & Gibson, 1994). Research on the monkey visual cortex has found cells that respond more to a

stimulus when it is perceived as a figure than to a stimulus when it is perceived as a ground (Lamme, 1995). Gestalt psychologist Edgar Rubin (1886–1951) called this **figure-ground perception.** For example, the words on this page are figures against the ground of the white paper. Gestalt psychologists stress that form perception is an active, rather than a passive, process. Your expectancies might affect what you see in an ambiguous figure, for instance (Davis, Schiffman, & Greis-Bousquet, 1990). If you were first shown pictures of pottery and were then shown Figure 5.11, you would be more likely to perceive a vase; if you were first shown pictures of faces, you would be more likely to perceive two profiles. The idea that our expectations impose themselves on sensations to form perceptions (so-called *top-down processing*) runs counter to the idea that we construct our perceptions strictly by mechanically combining sensations (so-called *bottom-up processing*). In fact, subjects do not spontaneously reverse ambiguous figures. They must have experience with reversible figures or be informed that the figures are reversible before they will reverse them (Rock, Gopnik, & Hall, 1994).

Gestalt psychologists, including Max Wertheimer, Kurt Koffka, and Wolfgang Kohler, were the first to study the principles that govern form perception. Research has shown that these principles are more relevant to preceiving complex figures (Gillam, 1992). The principle of *proximity* states that stimuli that are close together tend to be perceived as parts of the same form. The principle of *closure* states that we tend to fill in gaps in forms that we perceive. The principle of *similarity* states that stimuli that are similar to one another tend to be perceived as parts of the same form. And the principle of *continuity* states that we tend to group stimuli into forms that follow continuous lines or patterns. These principles are illustrated in Figure 5.12. The principles have only recently been subjected to experimental research, with initial support for the role of proximity in grouping stimuli into coherent patterns (Kubovy & Wagemans, 1995).

According to Gestalt psychologists, forms are perceived as wholes, rather than as combinations of features. This might prompt you to recall the famous Gestalt saying, mentioned in Chapter 1, that "the whole is different from the sum of its parts." Thus, in Figure 5.13 you see an image of an elephant rather than a bunch of black marks. Though some research findings support the Gestalt position that forms are perceived holistically (Navon, 1974), other research findings suggest that forms can be perceived through the analysis of their features (Oden, 1984).

Consider the letter A. Do we perceive it holistically as a single form, or analytically as a combination of lines of various lengths and angles? Gestalt psychologists would assume that

figure-ground perception
The distinguishing of an object (the figure) from its surroundings (the ground).

▲ **FIGURE 5.11**
Figure-Ground Perception
As you view this picture you will note that it seems to reverse. At one moment you see a vase, and at the next you see the profiles of two faces. What you see depends on what you perceive as figure and what you perceive as ground.

► FIGURE 5.12
Gestalt Principles of Form Perception
These patterns illustrate the roles of (a) closure, (b) proximity, (c) similarity, and (d) continuity in form perception.

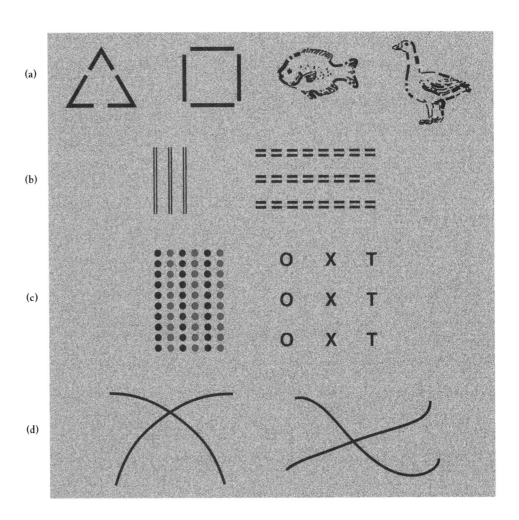

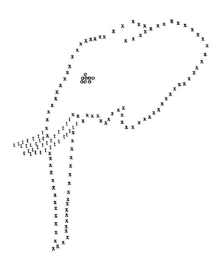

▲ FIGURE 5.13
The Whole Is Different from the Sum of Its Parts
According to Gestalt psychologists, you see a picture of an elephant instead of a random grouping of marks because your brain imposes organization on what it perceives. Your perception of the elephant depends on each of the Gestalt principles of similarity, proximity, closure, and continuity. As discussed later in this chapter, your perception of the elephant also depends on your prior experience. A person from a culture unfamiliar with elephants might fail to perceive the marks as a meaningful form.

feature-detector theory

The view that we construct our perceptions from neurons of the brain that are sensitive to specific features of stimuli.

illusory contours

The perception of edges that do not actually exist, as though they were the outlines of real objects.

spatial frequency filter theory

The theory that visual perception depends on the detection and analysis of variations in patterns of light and dark.

we perceive it holistically. But the **feature-detector theory** of David Hubel and Torsten Wiesel (1979) assumes that we construct it from its components. Hubel and Wiesel base their theory on studies in which they implanted microelectrodes into single cells of the visual cortex of cats and then presented them with lines of various sizes, orientations, and locations. Certain cells responded to specific features of images on the retina, such as a line of a certain length, a line at a certain angle, or a line in a particular location. Hubel and Wiesel concluded that we construct our visual perceptions from activity in such *feature-detector cells*. For their efforts, Hubel and Wiesel won a Nobel Prize in 1981. More-recent studies indicate that while some feature-detector cells respond to component features of forms, others respond to whole forms (Wenderoth, 1994).

Some feature-detector cells in the visual cortex respond to remarkably specific combinations of features. As noted in Chapter 3, different cells in the visual cortex of sheep respond to the faces of sheep, sheepdogs, or human beings (Kendrick & Baldwin, 1987). Feature-detector cells in the visual cortex even provide an anatomical basis for the **illusory contours** shown in Figure 5.14, responding to nonexistent contours as if they were the edges of real objects (Purghe & Coren, 1992).

An alternative to the feature-detector theory of pattern perception is the **spatial frequency filter theory.** It holds that perception depends not on constructing figures from lines, curves, and angles, but rather on the detection and analysis of variations in patterns of light and dark (de Valois & de Valois, 1980). Highly detailed figures will have narrow (high-frequency) bands of light and dark; less-detailed figures will have wider (low-frequency) bands of light and dark. These variations in light and dark bands are called *spatial frequencies* and are illustrated in Figure 5.15. Certain neurons in the visual cortex respond to patterns with wide bands and others respond to patterns with narrow bands (Foley, 1988).

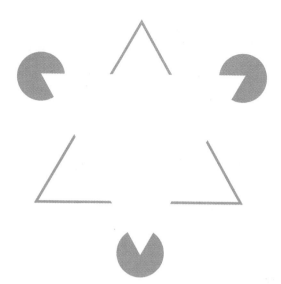

Depth Perception: Perceiving the Distance of Objects

If we lived in a two-dimensional world, form perception would be sufficient. Because we live in a three-dimensional world, we have evolved **depth perception**—the ability to judge the distance of objects. Consider the importance of depth perception to aircraft pilots. In a study conducted by the U.S. Coast Guard, helicopter pilots tried to obtain four target altitudes between 25 and 200 feet without the use of an altimeter. They either ascended from the ground or descended from 500 feet, over both land and water. The pilots tended to be inaccurate, especially when descending. You can imagine the danger this would pose when landing a helicopter or maneuvering it above objects (Ungs & Sangal, 1990).

Given that images on the retina (such as the image of a helicopter landing pad) are two-dimensional, how can we perceive depth? That is, how can we determine the distance of an object (the *distal stimulus*) from the pattern of stimulation on our retinas (the *proximal stimulus*)? Researchers in the tradition of Helmholtz's constructionist theory maintain that depth perception depends on the use of *binocular cues* (which require two eyes) and *monocular cues* (which require one eye).

The two kinds of **binocular cues** involve the interaction of both eyes. One binocular cue is *retinal disparity* (Ichikawa & Saida, 1996), the degree of difference between the images of an object that are focused on the two retinas. The closer the object, the greater the retinal disparity. To demonstrate retinal disparity for yourself, point a forefinger vertically between your eyes. Look at the finger with one eye closed. Then look at it with the other closed. You will notice that the background shifts as you view the scene with different eyes. This demonstrates that the two eyes provide different views of the same stimulus. The "Viewmaster" device you might have used as a child creates the impression of visual depth by presenting slightly different images to the eyes at the same time—mimicking retinal disparity. Retinal disparity is greater when an object is near you than when it is farther away from you. Certain cells in the visual cortex detect the degree of retinal disparity, which the brain uses to estimate the distance of an object focused on the retinas (DeAngelis, Ohzawa, & Freeman, 1995).

The second binocular cue to depth is *convergence*, the degree to which the eyes turn inward to focus on an object. As you can confirm for yourself, the closer the object, the greater the convergence of the eyes. Hold a forefinger vertically in front of your face and move it toward your nose. You should notice an increase in ocular muscle tension as your finger approaches your nose. Neurons in the cerebral cortex translate the amount of muscle tension into an estimate of the distance of your finger (Takagi et al., 1992). Using a computer terminal for hours can induce eye fatigue caused by continuous convergence (Watten, Lie, & Birketvedt, 1994).

depth perception
The perception of the relative distance of objects.

binocular cues
Depth perception cues that require input from the two eyes.

▲ **David Hubel and Torsten Wiesel**
Hubel and Wiesel are shown celebrating the Nobel Prize they won for their research on visual feature detectors in the brain.

Spatial Frequency Analysis
Squint your eyes and focus on the photo on the right. It will look more like the one on the left. Squinting filters out certain high spatial frequencies, leaving lower ones.

monocular cues

Depth perception cues that require input from only one eye.

There are many more monocular cues than binocular cues. **Monocular cues** require only one eye, so even people who have lost the sight in one eye can still have good depth perception. One monocular cue is *accommodation* (Meehan & Day, 1995), which, as explained earlier, is the change in the shape of the lens to help focus the image of an object on the retina. Neurons in the tectum respond so that the greater the accommodation of the lens, the closer the object appears (Judge & Cumming, 1986). But prolonged accommodation can alter your depth perception. For example, if you stare at a near object for a long time and then look at a more distant object, the more distant object will look farther away than it is. This is attributable to the brain's overcompensation for the continuous accommodation of the lens while it was focused on the near object (Fisher & Ciuffreda, 1989).

A second monocular cue is *motion parallax* (Kaiser, Montegut, & Proffitt, 1995), the tendency to perceive ourselves as passing objects faster when they are closer to us than when they are farther away. You notice this when you drive on a rural road, perceiving yourself as passing nearby telephone poles faster than you are passing a distant farmhouse. Infants as young as 3 months old use motion parallax to perceive depth (Hofsten, Kellman, & Putaansuu, 1992). Animal research indicates that particular brain cells might respond to motion parallax. For example, the cat's brain has cells whose firing rate varies with the degree of motion parallax (Mandl, 1985).

The remaining monocular cues, which we use in perceiving depth in everyday life, are often called *pictorial cues* (see Figure 5.16) because artists use them to create depth in their drawings and paintings (Zimmerman, Legge, & Cavanagh, 1995). They include interposition, relative size, linear perspective, elevation, shading patterns, aerial perspective, and texture gradient. Leonardo da Vinci formalized pictorial cues in the fifteenth century in teaching his art students how to use them to make their paintings look more realistic (Haber, 1980).

He noted that an object that overlaps another object will appear closer, a cue called *interposition*. Because your psychology professor overlaps the blackboard, you know that she or he is closer to you than the blackboard is. Comparing the *relative size* of familiar objects also provides a cue to their distance (Higashiyama & Kitano, 1991). If you know that two people are about the same height and one casts a smaller image on your retina, you will perceive that person as farther away.

You probably have noticed that parallel objects, such as railroad tracks, seem to get closer together as they get farther away (and farther apart as they get closer). This pictorial cue is called *linear perspective*. During World War II, naval aviation cadets flying at night sometimes crashed into airplanes ahead of them, apparently because of a failure to judge the distance of those planes. The problem was solved by taking advantage of linear perspective. The traditional single taillight was replaced by two taillights set a standard

◄ **Retinal Disparity and 3-D Movies**
In the 1950s, audiences watched movies in "Natural Vision," which became better known as "3-D." The movie was shot from slightly different angles, mimicking retinal disparity, and then projected on the screen by two projectors through different color filters. Because the lenses of the 3-D spectacles were of different colors, each eye saw only one of the movies. This created a crude three-dimensional image of some scenes. This photograph shows a 1995 audience watching a more technologically sophisticated 3-D movie on an eight story IMAX screen.

distance apart. As a result, when pilots noticed that the taillights of an airplane appeared to move farther apart, they realized that they were getting closer to it (Fiske, Conley, & Goldberg, 1987).

An object's *elevation* provides another cue to its distance. Objects that are higher in your visual field seem to be farther away. If you paint a picture, you can create depth by placing more-distant objects higher on the canvas. *Shading patterns* provide cues to distance (Curran & Johnston, 1994) because areas that are in shadow tend to recede, while areas that are in light tend to stand out. Painters use shading to make balls, balloons, and oranges appear round. *Aerial perspective* refers to the fact that objects that are closer to us seem clearer than more distant ones. A distant mountain will look hazier than a near one.

The final monocular cue, the *texture gradient*, affects depth perception because the nearer an object, the more details we can make out, and the farther an object, the fewer details we can make out. When you look across a field, you can see every blade of grass near you, but only an expanse of green far away from you. Even 7-month-old infants respond to the texture-gradient cue. When presented with drawings that use the texture gradient to make some objects appear to be in the foreground and others in the background, infants will reach for an object in the foreground (Arterberry, Yonas, & Benson, 1989).

Perceptual Constancies: Maintaining Visual Stability

The image of a given object focused on your retina may vary in size, shape, color, and brightness. Yet, because of *perceptual constancy*, you will continue to perceive the object as stable in size, shape, color, and brightness. There is evidence that size and shape constancy are present at birth (Slater, 1992). This is adaptive, because it provides you with a more visually stable world, making it easier for you to function in it. The size of the object on your retina does not, by itself, tell you how far away it is. As an object gets farther away from you, it produces a smaller image on your retina. If you know the actual size of an object, **size constancy** makes you interpret a change in its retinal size as a change in its distance rather than as a change in its size. When you see a car a block away, it does not seem smaller than one that is half a block away, even though the more distant car produces a smaller image on your retina. Size constancy can be disrupted by alcohol. In one study, young adults drank alcohol and were then asked to estimate the size of an object.

size constancy

The perceptual process that makes an object appear to remain the same size despite changes in the size of the image it casts on the retina.

Pictorial Cues to Depth
Artists make use of pictorial cues to portray depth in their drawings and paintings. These cues include (*a*) interposition, (*b*) aerial perspective, (*c*) linear perspective, (*d*) texture gradient, (*e*) elevation, and (*f*) shading patterns.

(a)

(b)

(c)

(d)

(e)

(f)

shape constancy
The perceptual process that makes an object appear to maintain its normal shape regardless of the angle from which it is viewed.

brightness constancy
The perceptual process that makes an object maintain a particular level of brightness despite changes in the amount of light reflected from it.

They consistently underestimated its size. Disruption of size constancy might be one way that alcohol intoxication promotes automobile accidents (Farrimond, 1990).

Shape constancy assures that an object of known shape will appear to maintain its normal shape regardless of the angle from which you view it. Close this book and hold it at various orientations relative to your line of sight. Unless you look directly at the cover when it is on a plane perpendicular to your line of vision, it will never cast a rectangular image on your retinas, yet you will continue to perceive it as rectangular. Shape constancy occurs because your brain compensates for the slant of an object relative to your line of sight (Wallach & Marshall, 1986).

Though the amount of light reflected from a given object can vary, we perceive the object as having a constant brightness. This is called **brightness constancy.** A white shirt appears equally bright in dim light or bright light, and a black shirt appears equally dull in dim light or bright light. But brightness constancy is relative to other objects. If you look at a white shirt in dim light in the presence of nonwhite objects in the same light, it will maintain its brightness. But if you look at the white shirt by itself, perhaps by viewing a large area of it through a hollow tube, it will appear dull in dim light and brighter in sunlight.

Visual Illusions: Misapplication of Visual Cues

In Edgar Allen Poe's story "The Sphinx," a man looks out his window and is horrified by what he perceives to be a monstrous animal on a distant mountain. He learns only later that the "monster" was actually an insect on his window. Because he perceived the animal as far away, he assumed it was relatively large. And because he never had seen such a creature, he assumed that it was a monster. This shows how the misapplication of a visual cue,

(a)

(b)

▲ **FIGURE 5.17**

The Ames Room

(*a*) The "giant" children on the right are actually shorter than the "tiny" adult on the left. (*b*) The floor plan of the Ames room shows that the persons on the left are farther away than the ones on the right, and the floor-to-ceiling height is greater on the left than on the right. The window on the left is also larger than the one on the right. This makes each of the persons seem like they are standing the same distance away from the viewer in a rectangular room. The illusion occurs because the persons on the right fill more of the space between the floor and the ceiling and because we assume that when two objects are the same distance away, the object that produces a smaller image on our retinas is, in fact, smaller.

in this case perceived size constancy, can produce a **visual illusion** (Gregory, 1991). Visual illusions provide clues to the processes involved in normal visual perception (Gordon & Earle, 1992). Figure 5.17 provides an example of a remarkable visual illusion.

As another example, from ancient times to modern times, people have been mystified by the **moon illusion,** illustrated in Figure 5.18, in which the moon appears larger when it is at the horizon than when it is overhead. This is an illusion because the moon is the same distance from us at the horizon as when it is overhead. Thus, the retinal image it produces is the same size when it is at the horizon as when it is overhead. The earliest explanation of the moon illusion was put forth by the Greek astronomer Ptolemy in the second century. His explanation, based on the principle of size constancy, is called the *apparent-distance hypothesis* (Kaufman & Rock, 1962). Ptolemy assumed that we perceive the sky as a flattened dome, with the sky at the horizon appearing *farther* away than it does overhead. Because the image of the moon on the retina is the same size whether the moon is overhead or at the horizon, the brain assumes that the moon must be *larger* at the apparently more-distant location—the horizon. But modern research has found that under certain conditions the sky can look farther away overhead than at the horizon. So, if the apparent-distance hypothesis were correct, the moon would appear larger overhead than it does at the horizon (Baird & Wagner, 1982).

Despite hundreds of studies of the moon illusion, researchers have yet to agree on the best explanation of it, though a modified version of the relative-size hypothesis will probably turn out to be the best candidate (Baird, Wagner, & Fuld, 1990). Moreover, researchers have found that a variety of factors interact to create the moon illusion, so efforts to find a single explanation for it will most likely fail (Plug & Ross, 1994). Figure 5.19 depicts another visual illusion that has stimulated many research studies.

Experience and Perception

As you have just read, visual perception depends on the interaction of the eyes and the brain. But it also depends on life experiences. Even the visual pathways themselves can be altered by life experiences, as demonstrated by the following study.

visual illusion

A misperception of physical reality usually caused by the misapplication of visual cues.

moon illusion

The misperception that the moon is larger when it is at the horizon than when it is overhead.

► FIGURE 5.18
The Moon Illusion
Psychologists have put forth several theories to explain why the moon looks larger when it is at the horizon than when it is high up in the sky.

ANATOMY OF A CLASSIC RESEARCH STUDY

Can Early Experience Affect the Development of the Visual Pathways?

Rationale

As we discussed earlier, David Hubel and Torsten Wiesel found that feature detectors in the visual cortex respond to lines of particular orientations. Other researchers (Hirsch & Spinelli, 1970) reared kittens with one eye exposed to vertical stripes and the other eye exposed to horizontal stripes. When the kittens later were exposed to lines of either orientation with one eye, certain feature-detector neurons in their visual cortexes responded only to lines of the orientation to which that eye had been exposed. But what would occur if kittens were reared in an environment that exposed both eyes to either only vertical or only horizontal stripes? This was the question addressed in a study by Colin Blakemore and Graham Cooper (1970) of Cambridge University in England.

Method

Blakemore and Cooper reared kittens from the age of 2 weeks to the age of 5 months in darkness, except for 5 hours a day in a lighted, large cylinder with walls covered by either vertical or horizontal black and white stripes. Because the kittens also wore large saucer-shaped collars, they could not even see their own legs or bodies. This prevented their being exposed to lines other than the vertical or horizontal stripes.

Results and Discussion

After 5 months the kittens' vision was tested under normal lighting by waving a rod in front of them, sometimes vertically and sometimes horizontally. Kittens that had been exposed to vertical lines swatted at the vertical rod but not at the horizontal rod. And kittens that had been exposed to horizontal lines swatted at the horizontal rod but not at the vertical rod. Recordings of the activity in certain neurons in the visual cortex showed that particular neurons acted as feature detectors by responding to either vertical or horizontal lines, depending on the stripes to which the kittens had been exposed during the previous 5 months (Blakemore & Cooper, 1970). Later studies indicated that neurons in the visual cortex that are responsive to lines of different orientations are present at birth. But in an individual who is not exposed to lines of a particular orientation, the neurons responsive to that orientation will degenerate (Swindale, 1982). A recent study of kittens found that treatment with *nerve growth factor* (a chemical that promotes the growth of neurons) during deprivation might prevent the degeneration of neurons that have been subjected to visual deprivation (Fiorentini, Berardi, & Maffei, 1995).

▲ ▲ ▲

Another source of evidence for the effect of experience on perception comes from studies of people blind from birth who have gained their sense of vision years later. The German physiologist Max von Senden (1932–1960) reviewed all the studies of people who had been born blind because of lens cataracts and who gained their vision after surgical removal of the cataracts. He found that the newly sighted were immediately able to distinguish colors and to separate figure from ground, but had difficulty visually recognizing objects they had learned to identify by touch. They did, however, show gradual improvement in visual object recognition (Dember & Bagwell, 1985).

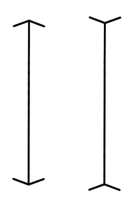

▲ FIGURE 5.19

The Müller-Lyer Illusion

Perhaps the most widely studied illusion was developed a century ago by Franz Müller-Lyer. Note that the vertical line on the right appears longer than the one on the left. If you take a ruler and measure the lines, you will find they are equal in length. Though no explanation has achieved universal acceptance (Mack et al., 1985), a favored one relies on size constancy and the resemblance of the figure on the right to the inside corner of a room and the resemblance of the figure on the left to the outside corner of a building. Given that the lines project images of equal length onto the retina, the line that appears farther away will be perceived as longer. Because an inside corner of a room appears farther away than an outside corner of a building, the line on the right appears farther and, therefore, longer than the line on the left (Gillam, 1980).

Visual perception can also be influenced by life experiences common to one's culture (Akande, 1991). This was confirmed by the anthropologist Colin Turnbull (1961), who studied the Bambuti Pygmies of central Africa. Turnbull drove one of the Pygmies, Kenge, who lived in a dense forest, to an open plain. Looking across the plain at a herd of grazing buffalo, Kenge asked Turnbull to tell him what kind of insect they were. Turnbull responded by driving Kenge toward the herd. As the image of the "insects" got bigger and bigger on his retinas, Kenge accused Turnbull of witchcraft for turning the insects into buffaloes. Because he had never experienced large objects at a distance, Kenge had a limited appreciation of size constancy. To him the tiny images on his retinas could only be insects. Because of his understandable failure to apply size constancy appropriately, Kenge mistook the distant buffalo for a nearby insect (in contrast to the man in Poe's short story, who mistook the nearby insect for a distant monster).

To gain even more appreciation for the possible influence of cultural experience on visual perception, consider the *Ponzo illusion*, illustrated in Figure 5.20. As with most illusions, the Ponzo illusion is caused by the misapplication of perceptual cues. As you read earlier, linear perspective is a cue to depth. Because the train tracks appear to come together in the distance, the horizontal bar higher in the figure appears farther away than the one lower in the figure. If you measure the bars, you will find that they are equal in length. Yet, because the bars produce images of equal length on your retinas, the bar that appears farther away seems to be longer.

Experiences with monocular cues to depth, such as linear perspective, affect responses to the Ponzo illusion. Rural Ugandan villagers, who have little experience with monocular cues in two-dimensional stimuli, are less susceptible to the Ponzo illusion than are Ugandan college students, who have more experience with such cues in art, photographs, and motion pictures (Leibowitz & Pick, 1972). But research finding that infant monkeys

The Ponzo Illusion
(*a*) The two horizontal lines are actually the same length. (*b*) Likewise, the two bars are the same length.

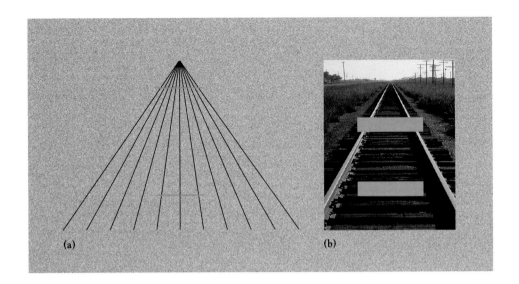

(a)   (b)

respond to pictorial depth cues indicates that learning from exposure to these Western forms of depth representation is not necessary to produce such illusions (Gunderson et al., 1993). Moreover, even pigeons are affected by the Ponzo illusion, making it less likely that it is the product of being exposed to Western art (Fujita, Blough, & Blough, 1993).

STAYING ON TRACK: *Vision*

1. What structures do light waves pass through on their way from the cornea to the retina?
2. What is the trichromatic theory of color vision?
3. What are the Gestalt principles of form perception?
4. What are two binocular cues to depth perception?

HEARING

audition
The sense of hearing.

Like the sense of vision, the sense of hearing (or **audition**) helps us function by informing us about objects at a distance from us. Unlike vision, audition informs us about objects we cannot see because they are behind us, hidden by darkness, or blocked by another object. Sound is produced by vibrations carried by air, water, or other mediums. Because sound requires a medium through which to travel, it cannot travel in a vacuum. (Of course, this has not prevented the *Star Trek* and *Star Wars* movies from enhancing their dramatic effects by including the sounds of massive explosions and roaring rocket engines in the vacuum of outer space.) Sound vibrations create a successive bunching and spreading of molecules in the sound medium. A sound wave is composed of a series of these bunching-spreading cycles. The height of a sound wave is its *amplitude*, and the number of sound-wave cycles that pass a given point in a second is its *frequency*. Sound-wave frequency is measured in *hertz (Hz)*, named for the nineteenth-century German physicist Heinrich Hertz. A 60-Hz sound would have a frequency of 60 cycles a second.

The Auditory System

Sound waves are sensed and perceived by the *auditory system*, which begins at the ear. The structure of the ear is illustrated in Figure 5.21. The ear is divided into an outer ear, a middle ear, and an inner ear. The *outer ear* includes the *pinna*, the oddly shaped flap of skin and cartilage that we commonly call the "ear." Though the pinna plays a small role in human hearing, some animals, such as deer, have large, movable pinnas that help them detect and locate faint sounds. Sound waves gathered by the pinna pass through the

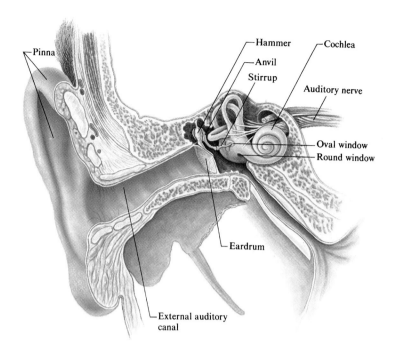

external auditory canal and reach the **tympanic membrane,** better known as the *eardrum*. Sound waves make the eardrum vibrate, and our hearing is responsive to even the slightest movement of the eardrum. If our hearing were any more acute, we would hear the air molecules that are constantly bouncing against the eardrum (Békésy, 1957).

The eardrum separates the outer ear from the *middle ear*. Vibrations of the eardrum are conveyed to the bones, or ossicles, of the middle ear. The ossicles are three tiny bones connected to one another by ligaments. The Latin names of the ossicles reflect their shapes: the *malleus* (hammer), the *incus* (anvil), and the *stapes* (stirrup). Infections of the middle ear must be taken seriously; in children they can produce hearing losses that adversely affect language ability and intellectual development (Roberts & Schuele, 1990).

Connecting the middle ear to the back of the throat are the *eustachian tubes,* which permit air to enter the middle ear to equalize air pressure on both sides of the eardrum. You might become painfully aware of this function during airplane descents, when the pressure increases on the outside of the eardrum relative to the inside. Chewing gum can help open the eustachian tubes and equalize the pressure.

Vibrations of the stapes are conveyed to the *oval window* of the *inner ear*. The oval window is a membrane in the wall of a spiral structure called the **cochlea** (from a Greek word meaning "snail"). Vibrations of the oval window send waves through a fluid-filled chamber that runs the length of the cochlea. These waves set in motion the **basilar membrane,** which also runs the length of the cochlea. The movement of the basilar membrane causes bending of *hair cells* that protrude from it. The bending triggers impulses that travel along the axons of the neurons that form the **auditory nerve.** Auditory impulses eventually reach the thalamus, where some processing takes place (Edeline & Weinberger, 1991). Input to the thalamus is then relayed to the **auditory cortex** of the temporal lobes of the brain, the ultimate site of sound perception. The effects of damage to the auditory cortex depend on the precise location of the damage. Damage that spares the perception of speech and environmental sounds, for example, might profoundly impair the perception of tunes and voices (Peretz et al., 1994).

Auditory Perception

How do vibrations conveyed to the basilar membrane (the proximal stimulus) create a complex auditory experience regarding their source (the distal stimulus)? Your ability to perceive sounds of all kinds depends on *pitch perception, loudness perception, timbre perception,* and *sound localization.*

tympanic membrane
The eardrum; a membrane separating the outer from the middle ear that vibrates in response to sound waves that strike it.

cochlea
The spiral, fluid-filled structure of the inner ear that contains the receptor cells for hearing.

basilar membrane
A membrane running the length of the cochlea that contains the auditory receptor (hair) cells.

auditory nerve
The nerve that conducts impulses from the cochlea to the brain.

auditory cortex
The area of the temporal lobes that processes sounds.

This girl is experiencing the amplification of sounds that large pinnas provide to animals such as deer.

Pitch Perception: The Highs and Lows of Sound

The frequency of a sound is the main determinant of its perceived *pitch*, whether the low-pitched sounds of a tuba or the high-pitched sounds of a flute. When you use the tone control on a CD player, you alter the frequency of the sound waves produced by the vibration of the speakers. This, in turn, alters the pitch of the sound. People with *absolute pitch* can identify and produce tones of a specific pitch. This ability appears to be learned best before the age of 6, and becomes difficult or impossible to develop afterward (Takeuchi & Hulse, 1993).

Human beings and other animals vary in the range of frequencies they can hear. Human beings hear sounds that range from 20 Hz to 20,000 Hz. Because elephants can hear sounds only up to 10,000 Hz, they cannot hear higher-pitched sounds that human beings can hear. Dogs, in turn, can hear sounds up to about 45,000 Hz (Heffner, 1983). Because dog whistles produce sounds between 20,000 and 45,000 Hz, they are audible to dogs but not to human beings.

What accounts for **pitch perception?** In 1863 Hermann von Helmholtz put forth the **place theory,** which assumes that particular points on the basilar membrane vibrate maximally in response to sound waves of particular frequencies. Georg von Békésy (1899–1972), a Hungarian scientist, won a Nobel Prize in 1961 for his research on the place theory. He took the cochleas from the ears of guinea pigs and human cadavers, stimulated the oval window, and, using a microscope, noted the response of the basilar membrane through a hole cut in the cochlea. He found that as the frequency of the stimulus increased, the point of maximal vibration produced by the traveling wave on the basilar membrane moved closer to the oval window. And as the frequency of the stimulus decreased, the point of maximal vibration moved farther from the oval window (Békésy, 1957).

But the place theory fails to explain pitch perception much below 1,000 Hz, because such low-frequency sound waves do not make the basilar membrane vibrate maximally at any particular point. Instead, the entire basilar membrane vibrates equally. Because of this limitation, perception of sounds below 1,000 Hz is explained best by a theory first put forth by the English physicist Ernest Rutherford (1861–1937) in 1886. His **frequency theory** assumes that the basilar membrane vibrates as a whole in direct proportion to the frequency of the sound waves striking the eardrum. The neurons of the auditory nerve will, in turn, fire at the same frequency as the vibrations of the basilar membrane. But because neurons can fire only up to 1,000 Hz, the frequency theory holds only for sounds up to 1,000 Hz.

pitch perception
The subjective experience of the highness or lowness of a sound, which corresponds most closely to the frequency of the sound waves that compose it.

place theory
The theory of pitch perception that assumes that hair cells at particular points on the basilar membrane are maximally responsive to sound waves of particular frequencies.

frequency theory
The theory of pitch perception that assumes that the basilar membrane vibrates as a whole in direct proportion to the frequency of the sound waves striking the eardrum.

Still another theory, the **volley theory** of psychologist Ernest Wever (Wever & Bray, 1937), explains pitch perception between 1,000 Hz and 5,000 Hz. The volley theory assumes that sound waves in this range induce certain groups of auditory neurons to fire in volleys. Though no single neuron can fire at more than 1,000 Hz, the brain might interpret the firing of volleys of particular auditory neurons as representing sound waves of particular frequencies up to 5,000 Hz (Zwislocki, 1981). For example, the pitch of a sound wave of 4,000 Hz might be coded by a particular group of five neurons, each firing at 800 Hz. Though there is some overlap among the theories, the frequency theory best explains the perception of low-pitched sounds, the place theory best explains the perception of high-pitched sounds, and the volley theory best explains the perception of medium-pitched sounds.

volley theory
The theory of pitch perception that assumes that sound waves of particular frequencies induce auditory neurons to fire in volleys, with one volley following another.

Loudness Perception: The Intensity of Sound

Sounds vary in intensity, or *loudness*, as well as pitch. The loudness of a sound depends mainly on the amplitude of its sound waves. When you use the volume control on a CD player, you alter the amplitude of the sound waves leaving the speakers. **Loudness perception** depends on both the number and the firing thresholds of hair cells on the basilar membrane that are stimulated. Because hair cells with higher firing thresholds require more-intense stimulation, the firing of hair cells with higher thresholds increases the perceived loudness of a sound.

loudness perception
The subjective experience of the intensity of a sound, which corresponds most closely to the amplitude of the sound waves composing it.

The unit of sound intensity is the *decibel (dB)*. The decibel is one-tenth of a Bel, a unit named for Alexander Graham Bell, who invented the telephone. The faintest detectable sound has an absolute threshold of 0 dB. For each change of 10 decibels, the perceived loudness doubles. Thus, a 70-dB sound is twice as loud as a 60-dB sound. Table 5.1 presents the decibel levels of some everyday sounds. Exposure to high-decibel sounds promotes hearing loss. Chronic exposure to loud sounds first destroys hair cells nearest the oval window, which respond to high-frequency sound waves. The loss of hair cells continues throughout childhood and into adulthood, as we are repeatedly exposed to loud music, vehicles, and machinery. A study of a sample of audience members at a rock-music concert found that they all displayed a hearing loss immediately after the concert. Three days later, most of them still showed a hearing loss (Danenberg, Loos-Cosgrove, & LoVerde, 1987). Elderly Americans, after a lifetime of exposure to loud sounds, tend to have poor high-frequency hearing. In contrast, the typical 90-year-old in rural African tribes, whose surroundings only occasionally produce loud sounds, has better hearing than the typical 30-year-old North American (Raloff, 1982).

In extreme cases, individuals can lose more than their high-frequency hearing. They can become deaf. In **conduction deafness,** there is a mechanical problem in the outer or middle ear that interferes with hearing. The auditory canal might be filled with wax, the eardrum might be punctured, or the ossicles might be fused and inflexible. Conduction deafness caused by deterioration of the ossicles can be treated by surgical replacement with plastic ossicles. Conduction deafness is more often overcome by hearing aids, which amplify sound waves that enter the ear.

conduction deafness
Hearing loss usually caused by blockage of the auditory canal, damage to the eardrum, or deterioration of the ossicles of the middle ear.

In **nerve deafness,** a problem of the inner ear, the basilar membrane, the auditory nerve, or the auditory cortex is damaged. Victims typically lose the ability to perceive sounds of certain frequencies. Nerve deafness responds poorly to surgery or hearing aids. But *cochlear implants* (pictured in Figure 5.22), which provide electronic stimulation of the neurons leaving the basilar membrane, promise to restore at least rudimentary hearing in people with nerve deafness. Some recipients of cochlear implants hear well enough to perceive simple speech and to produce intelligible speech (Tye-Murray, Spencer, & Woodworth, 1995).

nerve deafness
Hearing loss caused by damage to the hair cells of the basilar membrane or the axons of the auditory nerve.

Timbre Perception: The Quality of Sound

Sounds vary in *timbre*, as well as in pitch and loudness. **Timbre** is the quality of a sound, which reflects a particular mixture of sound waves (Hirsh, 1996). Middle C on the piano has a frequency of 256 Hz, but it has a distinctive timbre because of overtones of varying frequencies. Timbre lets us identify the source of a sound, whether a voice, a musical instrument, or even—to the chagrin of students—a fingernail scratching across a chalkboard. The timbre of that spine-chilling sound is similar to that of the warning cry of

timbre
The subjective experience that identifies a particular sound and corresponds most closely to the mixture of sound waves composing it.

Harmful to Hearing		
	140	Jet engine (25 m distance)
	130	Jet takeoff (100 m away)
		Threshold of pain
	120	Propeller aircraft
Risk Hearing Loss		
	110	Live rock band
	100	Jackhammer/pneumatic chipper
	90	Heavy-duty truck
		Los Angeles, third-floor apartment next to freeway
		Average street traffic
Very Noisy		
	80	Harlem, second-floor apartment
Urban		
	70	Private car
		Boston row house on major avenue
		Business office
		Watts—8 miles from touch down at major airport
	60	Conversational speech or old residential area in L.A.
Suburban and Small Town		
	50	San Diego—wooded residential area
	40	California tomato field
		Soft music from radio
	30	Quiet whisper
	20	Quiet urban dwelling
	10	Rustle of leaf
	0	Threshold of hearing

Reprinted with permission from *Science News*, the weekly newsmagazine of science. Copyright 1982 by Science Service, Inc.

Because the decibel scale is a logarithmic measure of sound intensity, values don't add in the usual way: a 60 = dB sound played atop another 60 = dB sound corresponds to 63 = dB noise. And a 10 = dB difference means one sound is 10 times louder than the other, so that the ratio between 140 dB and 0 dB is roughly 100 trillion to 1. Readings for cities represent levels actually measured by EPA and expressed as a day-night average.

▲ **Rocking His Way to Deafness**
As rock musicians reach middle age and beyond, many will experience hearing loss induced by decades of exposure to loud music.

sound localization

The process by which the individual determines the location of a sound.

macaque monkeys. Perhaps our squeamish response to it reflects an inborn vestigial response inherited from our common distant ancestors who used it to signal the presence of predators (Halpern, Blake, & Hillerbrand, 1986).

Timbre lets us not only identify musical instruments, but evaluate their relative quality. Because musical notes of the same frequency differ in timbre when played on different instruments, no two instruments produce exactly the same sounds. Two instruments playing the same note would also produce different mixtures of accompanying sound waves. This helps you to tell a violin from a guitar and a cheap violin from an expensive one (Hutchins, 1981).

Sound Localization: Discerning the Location of Sounds

We need to localize sounds, as well as identify them. **Sound localization** involves discerning where sounds are coming from. Human beings have an impressive ability to localize sounds, whether of voices at a crowded party or of instruments in a symphony orchestra. Even newborn human infants can localize sounds (Morrongiello et al., 1994). Some animals have especially impressive sound localization ability. A barn owl can capture a mouse in the dark simply by following the faint sounds produced by its movements (Knudsen, 1981).

ufacturers have added animal sex pheromones to perfumes and colognes, hoping to sell them as human aphrodisiacs. But before you run out to purchase a pheromone fragrance, you should note that research findings on the effects of sex pheromones on human beings have been inconclusive. In one study, males and females exposed to animal sex pheromones rated photographs of females as more attractive than did subjects not exposed to them (Maugh, 1982). But a replication of that study, using photographs of males, found no such effect (Filsinger et al., 1984). There is evidence, though not conclusive, that menstrual synchrony (similar menstrual cycles) in women living in dormitories might be promoted by pheromones (Weller & Weller, 1995).

Taste: The Gustatory Sense

Our other chemical sense, taste (or **gustation**), protects us from harm by preventing us from ingesting poisons and enhances our enjoyment of life by letting us savor food and beverages. Taste depends on thousands of **taste buds,** which line the grooves between bumps called *papillae* on the surface of the tongue. The taste buds contain receptor cells that send neural impulses when stimulated by molecules dissolved in saliva (Chaudhari et al., 1996). Taste sensitivity varies with the density of taste buds (Zuniga et al., 1993). Taste buds die and are replaced every few days, so the taste buds that are destroyed when you burn your tongue with hot food or drink are quickly replaced. But because replacement of taste buds slows with age, elderly people may find food less flavorful than they did earlier in life. This means that older adults will prefer foods with more intense flavors (Graaf, Polet, & van Staveren, 1994).

There is more agreement among researchers about the basic tastes than about the basic odors. In the eleventh century, the Arab scientist Avicenna proposed that there were four basic tastes: sweet, sour, salty, and bitter. In 1891 Hjalmar Ohrwall provided support for Avicenna's proposal. Ohrwall tested the sensitivity of the papillae by applying a variety of chemicals, one at a time, to different papillae. Some papillae responded to one taste and some to more than one. But, overall, he found that particular papillae were maximally sensitive to sweet, sour, salty, or bitter substances (Bartoshuk, Cain, & Pfaffman, 1985). Figure 5.23 shows that different areas of the tongue are most sensitive to sweet and salty, the sides are most sensitive to sour and salty, and the back is most sensitive to bitter. All other tastes are combinations of these basic tastes and depend on the pattern of stimulation of the taste receptors (Rogers, 1985).

As in the case of smell, gustation depends, in part, on the shape and size of molecules that stimulate the taste receptors. Taste researchers use this knowledge when they develop artificial sweeteners. Taste receptors in different areas of the tongue are maximally sensitive to molecules of particular shapes.

Do not confuse taste with flavor, which is more complex. While taste depends on sensations from the mouth, flavor relies on both taste and smell, as well as on texture, temperature, and even pain—as in chili peppers (Bartoshuk, 1991). If you closed your eyes and held your nose, you would have trouble telling the difference between a piece of apple and a piece of potato placed in your mouth. Because smell is especially important for flavor, you might find that when you have a head cold that interferes with your ability to smell, food lacks flavor. In fact, people who lose their sense of smell because of disease (a condition known as *anosmia*) find food less appealing (Ferris & Duffy, 1989). And one of the reasons that elderly people may show less interest in food is a decline in their ability to detect and identify odors (Stevens, 1989).

gustation
The sense of taste, which detects molecules of substances dissolved in the saliva.

taste buds
Structures lining the grooves of the tongue that contain the taste receptor cells.

STAYING ON TRACK: *Chemical Senses*

1. What are pheromones?
2. What is the stereochemical theory of smell?
3. Why might a head cold affect your ability to enjoy the flavor of food?

The Basic Tastes
All regions of the tongue are sensitive to each of the four basic tastes, but certain regions are more sensitive to particular ones. (*a*) Sweet receptors line the tip of the tongue; (*b*) sour receptors line the sides; (*c*) salty receptors line the tip and sides; and (*d*) bitter receptors line the back.

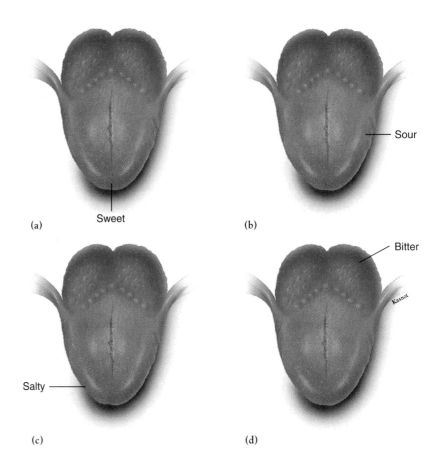

(a) Sweet

(b) Sour

(c) Salty

(d) Bitter

Kasnot

▲ **FIGURE 5.24**
Tactile Sensory Replacement
This man is "seeing" with his skin. Images provided by the video camera on his eyeglasses are impressed onto his skin by tiny vibrating Teflon cones. People who have used this device have been able to identify objects with distinctive shapes (Hechinger, 1981).

skin senses

The senses of touch, temperature, and pain.

somatosensory cortex

The area of the parietal lobes that processes information from sensory receptors in the skin.

SKIN SENSES

We rely on our **skin senses** of touch, temperature, and pain to identify objects, communicate feelings, and protect us from injury. Though there are a variety of receptors that produce skin sensations, there is no simple one-to-one relationship between specific kinds of receptors and specific skin senses. For example, there is only one kind of receptor in the cornea, but it is sensitive to touch, temperature, and pain. The pattern of stimulation of receptors, not the specific kind of receptor, determines skin sensations. Neural impulses from the skin receptors reach the thalamus, which relays them to the **somatosensory cortex** of the brain (see Chapter 3).

Touch: The Cutaneous Sense

Your sense of *touch* lets you identify objects rapidly and accurately even when you cannot see them, as when you find your house key while fumbling with a key chain in the dark. By 8 months of age infants can use touch to identify objects by their shape or texture (Catherwood, 1993). Touch is important in our social attachments, whether between lovers or between parent and child, and in our well-being, as in helping physicians conduct medical examinations (Thompson & Lambert, 1995). Touch sensitivity depends on the concentration of receptors. The more sensitive the area of skin (such as the lips or fingertips), the larger its representation on the somatosensory cortex. Touch sensitivity declines with age, perhaps because of the loss of touch receptors (Gescheider et al., 1994) or alterations in the somatosensory cortex (Spengler, Godde, & Dinse, 1995).

The sense of touch is so precise that it can be used as a substitute for vision. In 1824 a blind Frenchman named Louis Braille invented the Braille system for reading and writing, which uses patterns of raised dots to represent letters. The Braille concept has been extended to provide a substitute for vision, as shown in Figure 5.24. The blind person wears a camera on special eyeglasses and a special computer-controlled electronic vest covered with a grid of tiny Teflon cones. Outlines of images provided by the camera are impressed onto the skin by vibrations of the cones. People who have used the device have been able to identify familiar objects (Hechinger, 1981).

Temperature: The Thermal Sense

In 1927, psychologist Karl Dallenbach "mapped" the temperature receptors of the skin. He drew a grid on the skin and touched each square in the grid alternately with a warm probe and a cold probe. He found that each spot was sensitive to warm or cold, but not both. More-recent research supports this, having found receptors that respond to cold objects and others that respond to warm ones (Sumino & Dubner, 1981). But what of receptors for sensing hot objects? Hot objects stimulate both the cold receptors and the warm receptors. The brain interprets this as hot. Figure 5.25 shows how cold and warm sensations can combine to induce hot sensations.

Since Dallenbach's early study, scientists have discovered that temperature receptors detect changes in temperature: Cold receptors detect decreases in skin temperature, and warm receptors detect increases (Darian-Smith, 1982). Unless the skin is extremely hot or cold, which would induce pain sensations, the temperature receptors adapt, as when you enter a bathtub filled with hot water. At first you feel uncomfortably hot, but your skin quickly adapts to it and you eventually stop noticing it.

In the late seventeenth century, John Locke gave a demonstration of how temperature sensations depend on the detection of changes in skin temperature. To repeat Locke's demonstration, take three bowls and fill one with cold water, one with hot water, and one with lukewarm water. Place one hand in the cold water and the other in the hot water. Keep your hands submerged for a minute to allow temperature adaptation to occur. Then place both hands in the lukewarm water. The water will feel hot to the hand that had been in cold water and cold to the hand that had been in hot water. Thus, the temperature receptors would be responding to the change in temperature, not to the actual temperature of the lukewarm water.

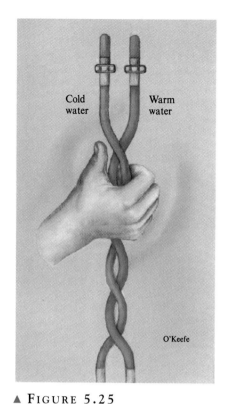

▲ **FIGURE 5.25**
Paradoxical Hot
If cold water circulates through one coil and warm water through the other, a person grasping the coils will feel a hot sensation and quickly let go. This demonstrates that hot sensations are produced by the combined stimulation of receptors responsive to cold and receptors responsive to warmth.

Pain: The Nociceptive Sense

The sense of *pain* (or *nociception*) protects us from injury or even death. People born without a sense of pain, or who lose it through nerve injuries, may harm themselves without realizing it. Because acute pain can be extremely distressing, and chronic pain is severely depressing (Banks & Kerns, 1996), researchers are studying the factors that cause pain and possible ways of relieving it.

Pain Factors

An injury or intense stimulation of sensory receptors induces pain. So, bright lights, loud noises, hot spices, and excessive pressure, as well as cuts, burns, and bruises, are painful. The main pain receptors (or *nociceptors*) are *free nerve endings* in the skin. Two kinds of neuronal fibers transmit pain impulses: *A-delta fibers* carry sharp or pricking pain, and *C fibers* carry dull or burning pain (Mengel et al., 1993). One substance implicated in pain is *bradykinin*, a chemical that accumulates at the site of an injury or inflammation (Dray & Perkins, 1993). Aspirin relieves pain in part by inhibiting the release of bradykinin (Inoki et al., 1978). In the brain, a region called the *periaqueductal gray* is an important pain-processing center (Rosenfeld & Xia, 1993), and pathways to the limbic system might affect emotional responses to pain (Giesler, Katter, & Dado, 1994). Many pain receptor neurons transmit pain impulses by releasing the neurotransmitter *substance P* from their axons. For example, the intensity of arthritis pain varies with the amount of substance P released by neurons that convey pain impulses, and analgesics that reduce levels of substance P reduce arthritis pain intensity (Torri et al., 1995).

gate-control theory
The theory that pain impulses can be blocked by the closing of a neuronal gate in the spinal cord.

▲ **Ronald Melzack**
"Research and observation indicate that a gate-control theory of pain is a better way of understanding pain and approaches to blocking pain."

placebo
An inactive substance that may induce some of the effects of the drug for which it has been substituted.

acupuncture
A pain-relieving technique that relies on the insertion of fine needles into various sites on the body.

transcutaneous electrical nerve stimulation (TENS)
The use of electrical stimulation of sites on the body to provide pain relief, apparently by stimulating the release of endorphins.

The most influential theory of pain is the **gate-control theory** formulated by psychologist Ronald Melzack and biologist Patrick Wall (1965). The theory assumes that pain impulses from the limbs or body pass through a part of the spinal cord that provides a "gate" for pain impulses, perhaps involving substance P neurons (Holland, Goldstein, & Aronstam, 1993). Stimulation of neurons that convey touch sensations "closes" the gate, preventing input from neurons that convey pain sensations. This might explain why rubbing a shin that you have banged against a table will relieve the pain. The closing of the pain gate is stimulated by the secretion of *endorphins* (Taddese, Nah, & McCleskey, 1995), which (as described in Chapter 3) are the brain's natural opiates. Endorphins might close the gate by inhibiting the secretion of substance P (Ruda, 1982). In one study, subjects who exercised showed a negative correlation between pain and endorphin levels: as endorphin levels increased, pain intensity decreased (Droste et al., 1991).

The pain gate is also affected by neural impulses that originate in the brain (Dubner & Bennett, 1983). This might explain why anxiety, relaxation, and other psychological factors can affect pain perception (Melzack, 1993). For example, it might explain the so-called Anzio effect, in which wounded soldiers returning from the fierce World War II battle for control of Anzio, Italy, needed less morphine than did civilians with similar wounds. Perhaps because the soldiers interpreted their wounds as tickets away from the battlefield, they experienced their pain as less intense (Wallis, 1984). Their pain might have been reduced by neural impulses sent from the brain to the spinal cord, closing the pain gate. The Anzio effect also shows that the *reinterpretation* of pain can reduce its intensity (Devine & Spanos, 1990).

Pain Relief

Chronic pain afflicts millions of Americans. Back pain alone torments about 80 percent at some time in their lives (Dolce & Raczynski, 1985). The pain of cancer, surgery, injuries, headaches, and backaches makes pain control an important topic of research in both medicine and psychology (Turk, 1994). The most popular approach to the relief of severe pain relies on drugs such as morphine, which affects endorphin receptors in the brain. Even **placebo** "sugar pills," which are supposedly inactive substances that are substituted for pain-relieving drugs, can relieve pain. One study found that patients with chronic pain who respond to placebos produce higher levels of endorphins than do those who fail to respond (Lipman et al., 1990). But other studies have failed to find a role for endorphins in the placebo effect (Montgomery & Kirsch, 1996).

Other techniques that do not rely on drugs or placebos also relieve pain by stimulating the release of endorphins. For example, the technique of **acupuncture,** popular in China for thousands of years, relies on the insertion of fine needles into various sites on the body. *Naloxone*, a drug that blocks the effects of opiates, inhibits the analgesic effects of acupuncture. This provides evidence for the role of endorphins in acupuncture (Murray, 1995), perhaps by blocking impulses at the pain gate in the spinal cord (Lee & Beitz, 1992).

A similar, more modern technique for pain relief relies on **transcutaneous electrical nerve stimulation (TENS),** which involves electrical stimulation of sites on the body. TENS has proved effective in relieving many kinds of pain, including back pain (Marchand et al., 1993), dental pain (Schwolow, Wilckens, & Roth, 1988), and headache pain (Solomon & Guglielmo, 1985). In one study, which used the double-blind placebo method, subjects had a blood-pressure cuff tightened on their arm until it produced pain caused by cutting off the blood supply. Subjects who received low-frequency TENS reported lower pain levels than those who received placebo treatment, those who received no treatment, and those who received high-frequency TENS (Walsh et al., 1995). As in the case of placebos and acupuncture, TENS might relieve pain by stimulating the release of endorphins because its effects are blocked by naloxone (Wang, Mao, & Han, 1992). TENS might also inhibit activity in the "pain gate" in the spinal cord (Garrison & Foreman, 1994).

Still another technique, hypnosis, has been useful in relieving pain (Holroyd, 1996). For example, it has helped relieve pain experienced by burn victims (Weir, 1990) and cancer victims (Genuis, 1995). But, unlike other pain-relieving techniques, hypnosis does not appear to work by stimulating the release of endorphins. We know this because the pain-relieving effects of hypnosis are not blocked by naloxone. In one study, pain was induced by electrical stimulation of the roots of teeth. Even when given naloxone, hypnotized subjects still experienced pain relief, so endorphins could not account for this effect (Joubert & Van Os, 1989). A recent study found that hypnosis might exert its effects by sending neural impulses that block pain impulses at the spinal cord (Kiernan et al., 1995).

Pain victims can also control their pain by using distracting thoughts or distracting stimuli (Williams & Kinney, 1991). Distracting children with toys, for example, is useful in reducing their distress during blood tests (Vessey, Carlson, & McGill, 1994). You may find it helpful to distract yourself from pain by watching television, listening to music, or imagining pleasant scenes. For this reason, many dentists have music playing as they work on their patients (though the kind of music might induce more distress than it relieves). In a study of dental patients, subjects exposed to music during procedures experienced less pain and distress than did control subjects who were not exposed to it (Anderson, Baron, & Logan, 1991).

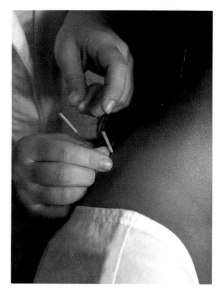

▲ **Acupuncture**
Acupuncture appears to achieve its pain-relieving effects by stimulating the release of endorphins.

STAYING ON TRACK: *Skin Senses*

1. How has the sense of touch been used to provide an electronic substitute for vision?
2. What is the gate-control theory of pain?
3. How is naloxone used to determine whether a pain-relieving technique works by stimulating endorphin activity?

BODY SENSES

While your skin senses let you judge the state of your skin, your body senses tell you the position of your limbs and help you maintain your equilibrium. The body senses—the *kinesthetic sense* and the *vestibular sense*—are often taken for granted and have inspired less research than the other senses have. But they are crucial to everyday functioning.

The Kinesthetic Sense: The Body Movement Sense

The **kinesthetic sense** informs you of the position of your joints, the tension in your muscles, and the movement of your arms and legs. This information is provided by special receptors in your joints, muscles, and tendons. Even with your eyes closed, you can sense the location of your limbs as they move about. Kinesthetic receptors in your muscles let you judge the force as well as the path of your limb movements (Jones, 1986). Limb movements produce activity in specific regions of the somatosensory cortex (Prud'homme, Cohen, & Kalaska, 1994).

If your leg has ever "fallen asleep" (depriving you of kinesthetic sensations) and collapsed on you when you stood up, you realize that the kinesthetic sense helps you maintain enough tension in your legs to stand erect. Your kinesthetic sense also protects you from injury. If you are holding an object that is too heavy, kinesthetic receptors signal you to put it down to prevent injury to your muscles and tendons.

Imagine losing your kinesthetic sense permanently, as happened to a woman described in a case study by Oliver Sacks (1985). This robust, athletic young woman developed a rare inflammatory condition that affected only her kinesthetic neurons. She lost all feedback from her body, making it impossible for her to sit, stand, or walk. Her body became as floppy as a rag doll, and she reported feeling like a disembodied mind. She was able to compensate only slightly by using her sense of vision to regulate her body posture and movements. Thus, our kinesthetic sense, which we usually take for granted, plays an important role in our everyday motor functioning, such as writing (Teasdale et al., 1993). Alcohol intoxication interferes with kinesthetic feedback, impairing movement by disrupting the sense of limb position (Wang et al., 1993).

kinesthetic sense
The sense that provides information about the position of the joints, the degree of tension in the muscles, and the movement of the arms and legs.

▲ **The Body Senses**
The kinesthetic sense and the vestibular sense provide gymnasts, as well as dancers, athletes, and other performers, with exquisite control over their body movements.

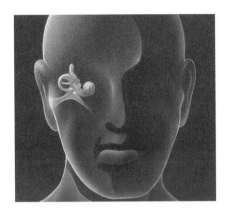

▲ **FIGURE 5.26**
The Semicircular Canals
When your head moves, fluid movement in the semicircular canals stimulates hair cells that send neural impulses to the brain.

vestibular sense
The sense that provides information about the head's position in space and helps in the maintenance of balance.

otolith organs
The vestibular organs that detect horizontal or vertical linear movement of the head.

semicircular canals
The curved vestibular organs of the inner ear that detect movements of the head in any direction.

The Vestibular Sense: The Head Movement Sense

While the kinesthetic sense informs you of the state of your body parts, your **vestibular sense,** which depends on organs in the inner ear, informs you of your head's position in space, helping you maintain your balance and orientation. The **otolith organs** detect horizontal or vertical linear movement of the head and help you orient yourself in regard to gravity. The other vestibular organs are the **semicircular canals,** which are three fluid-filled tubes oriented in different planes. Their location is indicated in Figure 5.26. When your head moves in a given direction, the jellylike fluid in the semicircular canal oriented in that direction at first lags behind the movement of the walls of the canal. This makes hair cells protruding into the fluid bend in the direction opposite to the direction of head movement. The bending of hair cells triggers neural impulses that are relayed to your cerebellum, to help you maintain your balance.

Your semicircular canals also let you keep your eyes fixed on a target even when you are rotating your head. This is aided by the *vestibulo-ocular reflex*, which compensates for rotary head movements by moving the eyes a proportionate amount in the opposite direction. A baseball outfielder tracking a fly ball benefits from this reflex. Alcohol intoxication interferes with this reflex (Post et al., 1994), again demonstrating how alcohol might contribute to motor-vehicle accidents. And a person with damage to the semicircular canals will suffer both impaired balance and disruption of the vestibulo-ocular reflex (Smith & Curthoys, 1989).

Though the vestibular sense helps you maintain your equilibrium, it can also induce motion sickness, including carsickness, airsickness, and seasickness. Fortunately, repeated exposure to situations that induce motion sickness tends to produce tolerance. A study of paratroopers found that two thirds had motion sickness on their first jump, but only one quarter had it on their fifth jump (Antunano & Hernandez, 1989). Moreover, motion sickness is reduced by a sense of control—which might explain why we are less likely to develop motion sickness when we are driving an automobile than when we are passengers in one (Rolnick & Lubow, 1991).

The mechanisms that underlie motion sickness are still debated, but an influential view holds that motion sickness is induced by conflict between visual and vestibular sensations. Suppose you are in a windowless cabin aboard a ship in a rough sea. Your eyes tell you that you are stationary in relationship to one aspect of your environment—your cabin. Yet your vestibular sense tells you that you are moving in relationship to another aspect of your environment—the ocean. But this does not explain *why* conflict between visual and vestibular sensations induces nausea. One hypothesis is that the motion-induced disruption of the normal association between visual and vestibular sensations is similar to that produced by toxins, such as those in spoiled food, that induce nausea. As a result, motion induces nausea (Stern & Koch, 1996).

Drugs that inhibit neural activity in the semicircular canals can reduce motion sickness (Oosterveld, 1987). One of the earliest drug treatments for motion sickness was devised by a Canadian research team led by Wilder Penfield (see Chapter 3) during World War II (Lewis, 1981). In his research on motion sickness, Penfield and his colleagues rode various rides at an amusement park near Montreal until they discovered the kind of motion that best simulated that of a ship at sea. He then built a machine that reproduced this motion. Finally, after testing a variety of drugs, he found one that inhibited the motion sickness sometimes induced by the machine. This discovery helped prevent nausea in sailors on ships and soldiers in landing craft.

Motion sickness can also be reduced by psychological means. Consider sailors below deck. While their vestibular sense tells them that their ship is rolling back and forth, their visual sense tells them that it is not. This can induce nausea. Would providing a means of convincing the eyes that the ship was rolling reduce their nausea? The results of an experiment indicate that the answer is yes. Sailors were tested while performing a series of tasks in a tilting room under each of three conditions. In one condition, the room's window was covered. In the second condition, it was uncovered. In the third condition, the window was covered and an artificial horizon was projected on the wall with a laser beam. The results showed that the subjects felt significantly less nausea and performed better in the second and third conditions. Thus, the provision of a means of reducing the discrepancy between visual and vestibular input might reduce seasickness in sailors who work below deck (Rolnick & Bles, 1989).

STAYING ON TRACK: *Body Senses*

1. What is the kinesthetic sense?
2. What is the role of the vestibular sense in motion sickness?

THINKING ABOUT *Psychology*

Why Do Psychologists Discount ESP?

As you have just read, perception depends on the stimulation of sensory receptors by various kinds of energy. But you have certainly heard claims that support the possibility of perception independent of sensory receptors, so-called **extrasensory perception (ESP).** The field that studies ESP and related phenomena is called **parapsychology** (*para-* means "besides"). The name indicates its failure to gain widespread acceptance within mainstream psychology. Parapsychological abilities are typically called *paranormal.*

Despite scientific skepticism about paranormal abilities, a survey found that more than 99 percent of American college students believed in at least one paranormal ability and that more than 65 percent claimed a personal experience with at least one (Messer & Griggs, 1989). A similar survey likewise found widespread belief in paranormal abilities among New Zealand college students (Clarke, 1991). Moreover, mainstream journals in psychology, philosophy, and medicine periodically publish articles on paranormal abilities (Severi, 1994). Public belief in paranormal abilities was exemplified in a 1986 lawsuit in which a Philadelphia woman who made a living as a psychic sued a hospital, insisting that a CT scan of her head made her lose her ESP abilities. A jury, impressed by the testimony of police officers who claimed that she had helped them solve crimes by using ESP, awarded her $988,000 for the loss of her livelihood (Tulsky, 1986). (The jury's decision was later overturned on appeal.) Despite such widespread public acceptance of paranormal abilities, most psychologists discount it (Bem & Honorton, 1994). Before learning why they do, consider several of the paranormal abilities studied by parapsychologists.

ALLEGED PARANORMAL ABILITIES

More than two decades ago, members of the Grateful Dead rock group had their audiences at a series of six concerts in Port Chester, New York, try to transmit mental images of slides to a person asleep in a dream laboratory miles away at Maimonides Hospital in Brooklyn. When the sleeper awoke he described the content of his dreams. Independent judges rated his dream reports as more similar to the content of the slides than were the dream reports of another person who had not been designated to receive the images (Ullman, Krippner, & Vaughan, 1973). It was reported as a successful demonstration of **mental telepathy,** the alleged ability to perceive the thoughts of others. This was part of a series of ESP-dream studies carried out at Maimonides Hospital (Krippner, 1993).

A study of dream telepathy had a "sender" advertise in a national newspaper that he would send a dream telepathy image between midnight and 10 A.M. on a specified night. Different images were sent every 2 hours. More than 500 readers sent dream reports and

extrasensory perception (ESP)
The ability to perceive events without the use of sensory receptors.

parapsychology
The study of extrasensory perception, psychokinesis, and related phenomena.

mental telepathy
The alleged ability to perceive the thoughts of others without any sensory contact with them.

clairvoyance
The alleged ability to perceive objects or events without any sensory contact with them.

precognition
The alleged ability to perceive events in the future.

déjà vu
The feeling that one has experienced a present experience sometime in the past.

psychokinesis (PK)
The alleged ability to control objects with the mind alone.

▲ J. B. Rhine (1895–1980)
"Good evidence of parapsychological ability is not only more difficult to obtain than that of the whole range of sensorimotor exchange; it is also harder to accept. Therefore, it requires more security in the way of test conditions, perhaps the most of any field."

the times they "received" the images. Judges blind to the target sequence decided whether the reports matched the pictures. Unlike the results of the Grateful Dead demonstration, their assessments provided no support for dream telepathy—the reports did not match the images that were sent (Hearne, 1989).

Related to mental telepathy is **clairvoyance,** the alleged ability to perceive objects or events without any sensory contact with them. You might be considered clairvoyant if you could identify all of the objects in your psychology professor's desk drawer without looking in it. Many colleges host "psychic" entertainers, such as "the Amazing Kreskin," who impress their audiences by giving demonstrations such as "reading" the serial number of a dollar bill in an audience member's wallet. Reports that clairvoyant psychics have solved crimes by leading police to bodies or stolen items are exaggerated. A survey of police departments in the 50 largest American cities found not a single report of a clairvoyant who had solved a crime for them (Sweat & Durm, 1993).

While mental telepathy and clairvoyance deal with the present, **precognition** is the alleged ability to perceive events in the future. An example would be predicting the next spin of a roulette wheel, one of the common ways of measuring precognitive ability (Kugel, 1990–1991). Psychics like the late Jean Dixon make careers of writing tabloid newspaper columns in which they predict events of personal or national interest. Do not confuse precognition with **déjà vu,** an uncanny feeling that you have experienced a present situation in the past and that you can anticipate what will happen in the next few moments. There is no widely accepted explanation of déjà vu (Sno, Schalken, & de Jonghe, 1992).

Closely allied with ESP is **psychokinesis (PK),** the alleged ability to control objects with the mind alone. Our use of "body English" to affect the movements of dice, roulette wheels, baseballs, golf balls, or bowling balls reflects a superstitious belief in PK. PK researchers have even become modern, assessing subjects' ability to influence computer games (Broughton & Perlstrom, 1992). Perhaps you have seen a televised performance by psychic Uri Geller, who gives demonstrations in which he apparently bends spoons, fixes watches, or takes photographs by using mental power alone. Even the military has examined the possibility. But a report by the National Academy of Sciences found no basis for using any kind of paranormal ability (Palmer, Honorton, & Utts, 1989).

PROBLEMS WITH PARANORMAL RESEARCH

Parapsychology has attracted many prominent supporters. Mark Twain, William James, and G. Stanley Hall were members of the Society for Psychical Research, with James serving a term as president and Hall a term as vice president. In 1887 Hall had started the *American Journal of Psychology* (the first English-language psychology journal) using a $500 gift from a man who mistakenly believed he was contributing to the founding of a journal devoted to paranormal research. The man withdrew his support after finding that Hall had attacked psychical research in the very first issue. Credit for making parapsychology a legitimate area of scientific research to some scientists goes to J. B. Rhine (1895–1980) of Duke University, who began a program of experimentation on paranormal phenomena in the 1930s (Matlock, 1991). Several leading British universities have also lent credibility to parapsychology by sponsoring paranormal research. Edinburgh University in Scotland even set up the first faculty chair in parapsychology with a $750,000 grant from the estate of author Arthur Koestler (Dickson, 1984).

Despite the popular acceptance of parapsychology, most psychologists remain skeptical (McConnell & Clark, 1991). One reason is that many supposed instances of paranormal phenomena turn out to be the result of poorly controlled demonstrations. In a case reported by the magician James "The Amazing" Randi, a woman claimed that she could influence fish by PK. Every time she put her hand against one side of an aquarium, the fish swam to the opposite side. Randi responded, "She calls it psychic; I call it frightened fish." He suggested that she put dark paper over a side of the aquarium and test her ability on

◀ "Never mind that—can you bend the spoon?"
Reprinted courtesy Omni Magazine © *1985*.

that side. After trying Randi's suggestion and finding that the fish no longer swam to the opposite side, she exclaimed, "It's marvelous! The power doesn't penetrate brown paper!" (Morris, 1980, p. 106). You might recognize this as an example of Piaget's concept of assimilation (see Chapter 4).

Supporters of parapsychology might also too readily accept chance events as evidence of paranormal phenomena (Diaconis, 1978). For example, at some time you probably have decided to call a friend, picked up the phone, and found your friend already on the other end of the line. Does this mean that mental telepathy made you call each other at the same time? Not necessarily. Perhaps you and your friend call each other often and at about the same time of the day, so on occasion you might call each other at exactly the same moment by mere coincidence.

Another blow against the credibility of parapsychology is that some impressive demonstrations have later been found to involve fraud. In a widely publicized case, the noted psychic Tamara Rand claimed to have predicted the 1981 assassination attempt on U.S. President Ronald Reagan in a videotape made before the attempt and later shown on the "Today" show. This was considered evidence of precognition—until James Randi discovered that she had made the videotape *after* the assassination attempt ("A Psychic Watergate," 1981).

Magic tricks are also often passed off as paranormal phenomena. G. Stanley Hall, after finding little evidence in support of paranormal phenomena, used his outstanding skill as a magician to debunk some alleged psychics by exposing their trickery (Ross, 1972). James Randi, following in the tradition of Hall, sponsored an elaborate hoax that demonstrated the inability of parapsychology researchers to detect magic tricks. In 1979 James McDonnell, chairman of the board of the McDonnell-Douglas corporation, gave $500,000 to Washington University in St. Louis to establish a parapsychology research laboratory. A respected physics professor took charge of the project and invited alleged psychics to be tested there. Randi sent two magicians, aged 17 and 18, to be tested as "psychics." After demonstrating their PK "abilities" during 120 hours of testing over a 3-year period, the two were proclaimed the only subjects with PK ability.

But both had relied on magic—in some instances, beginner's-level magic. For example, they demonstrated PK by moving a clock across a table by using an ultrathin thread held between their thumbs. Because of demonstrations like this, Randi has urged parapsychologists to permit magicians to observe their research so that magic tricks are not mistaken for paranormal phenomena ("Psychic Abscam," 1983). Since 1965 Randi has an ongoing offer of $10,000 to anyone who can demonstrate a true paranormal ability under well-controlled conditions. No one has done so.

Parapsychologists defend their research by insisting that critics often reject positive findings by assuming that they are impossible and therefore must be caused by some other factor, such as poor controls, magic tricks, or outright fraud (Child, 1985). Thus, opposition to paranormal research might reflect the current scientific paradigm as much as it does any methodological weaknesses in paranormal research (Krippner, 1995). Moreover, parapsychologists argue, paranormal abilities might be so subtle that they require highly motivated subjects to demonstrate them. For example, believers in paranormal abilities perform better on paranormal tests than do nonbelievers (Schmeidler, 1985).

But even many parapsychologists agree that, from a scientific standpoint, the main weakness of research studies on paranormal abilities is the difficulty in replicating them. As discussed in Chapter 2, scientists discredit events that cannot be replicated under similar conditions. Yet some parapsychologists insist that positive research findings related to paranormal phenomena have been replicated more often than critics of parapsychology will acknowledge (Roig, 1993) and that meta-analyses show effects that are greater than expected by chance alone (Krippner et al., 1993). This replication is especially true of so-called *ganzfeld studies*, in which external visual stimulation is filtered through table tennis balls cut in half and placed over the eyes and white noise played through headphones (Bem & Honorton, 1994). This removes distracting stimuli. Critics nonetheless have attacked the adequacy of the methodology used in ganzfeld studies (Hyman, 1994).

A final criticism of parapsychology is that there is no satisfactory explanation of paranormal phenomena. Their acceptance might require the discovery of new forms of energy. Evidence for the role of some sort of energy force comes from the finding that research conducted during years with low geomagnetic activity has been asssociated with the most positive ESP research findings (Berger & Persinger, 1991). But attempts to detect any unusual form of energy radiating from people with supposed paranormal abilities have failed (Balanovski & Taylor, 1978).

Parapsychologists point out, however, that failure to know the cause of something does not mean that the phenomenon does not exist (Rockwell, 1979). They remind psychologists to be skeptical rather than cynical, because many phenomena that are now scientifically acceptable were once considered impossible and unworthy of study. For example, scientists used to ridicule reports of stones falling from the sky and refused to investigate them. In 1807, after hearing of a report by two Yale University professors of a stone shower in Connecticut, President Thomas Jefferson, a scientist himself, said, "Gentlemen, I would rather believe that those two Yankee professors would lie than to believe that stones fell from heaven" (quoted in Diaconis, 1978). Today, even young children know that such stones are meteorites and that they, indeed, fall from the sky.

Even William James, perhaps reflecting his being one of the most open-minded of scientists, believed at the end of his life that there was something to psychic phenomena but that he had still not found any convincing evidence of it. Nonetheless, because alleged paranormal abilities are so unusual, seemingly inexplicable, and difficult to demonstrate reliably, even open-minded psychologists will continue to discount them unless they receive more-compelling evidence (Hoppe, 1988). Thus, the extraordinary claims made by parapsychologists will require extraordinary evidence for mainstream psychologists to accept their validity (Grey, 1994).

STAYING ON TRACK: *Why Do Psychologists Discount ESP?*

1. What are the four alleged paranormal abilities?
2. What are the major shortcomings of paranormal research?

► CHAPTER SUMMARY

SENSORY PROCESSES

Sensation is the process that detects stimuli from one's body or environment. Perception is the process that organizes sensations into meaningful patterns. Psychophysics is the study of the relationships between the physical characteristics of stimuli and the conscious psychological experiences they produce. The minimum amount of stimulation that can be detected is called the absolute threshold. According to signal-detection theory, the detection of a stimulus depends on both its intensity and the physiological and psychological state of the receiver. The minimum amount of change in stimulation that can be detected is called the difference threshold. Weber's law states that the amount of change in stimulation needed to produce a just noticeable difference is a constant proportion of the original stimulus. The tendency of our sensory receptors to be increasingly less responsive to an unchanging stimulus is called sensory adaptation.

VISION

Vision lets us sense objects by the light reflected from them into our eyes. Light is focused by the lens onto the rods and cones of the retina. Visual input is transmitted by the optic nerves to the brain, ultimately reaching the visual cortex. During dark adaptation the rods and cones become more sensitive to light, with the rods becoming significantly more sensitive than the cones. The trichromatic theory of color vision considers the interaction of red, green, and blue cones. In contrast, the opponent-process theory assumes that color vision depends on activity in red-green, blue-yellow, and black-white ganglion cells and cells in the thalamus. Color blindness is usually caused by an inherited lack of a cone pigment. The most common kind of color blindness is red-green.

Form perception depends on distinguishing figure from ground. In studying form perception, Gestalt psychologists identified the principles of proximity, similarity, closure, and continuity. Whereas Gestalt psychologists claim that we perceive objects as wholes, other theories claim that we construct objects from their component parts. This is supported by research showing that the visual cortex has feature-detector cells that respond to specific features of objects.

Depth perception lets us determine how far away objects are from us. Binocular cues to depth require the interaction of both eyes. The two main binocular cues are convergence of the eyes and retinal disparity. Monocular cues to depth require only one eye. The monocular cues include accommodation, motion parallax, and various pictorial cues (interposition, relative size, linear perspective, elevation, shading, patterns, aerial perspective, and texture gradient).

Experience in viewing objects contributes to size constancy, shape constancy, and brightness constancy. The misapplication of depth perception cues and perceptual constancies can contribute to visual illusions. Sensory experience and cultural background both affect visual perception.

HEARING

The sense of hearing (audition) detects sound waves produced by the vibration of objects. Sound waves cause the tympanic membrane to vibrate. The ossicles of the middle ear convey the vibrations to the oval window of the cochlea, which causes waves to travel through fluid within the cochlea. The waves make hair cells on the basilar membrane bend,

sending neural impulses along the auditory nerve. Sounds are ultimately processed by the auditory cortex of the temporal lobes.

The frequency of a sound determines its pitch. Pitch perception is explained by the place theory, frequency theory, and volley theory. The intensity of a sound determines its loudness. People may suffer from conduction deafness or nerve deafness. The mixture of sound waves determines a sound's quality, or timbre. Sound localization depends on differences in a sound's arrival time and intensity at the two ears.

CHEMICAL SENSES

The chemical senses of smell and taste detect chemicals in the air we breathe or the substances we ingest. The sense of smell (olfaction) depends on receptor cells on the nasal membrane that respond to particular chemicals. Odorous secretions called pheromones affect the sexual behavior of animals. The sense of taste (gustation) depends on receptor cells on the taste buds of the tongue that respond to particular chemicals. The basic tastes are sweet, salty, sour, and bitter.

SKIN SENSES

Skin senses depend on receptors that send neural impulses to the somatosensory cortex. Touch sensitivity depends on the concentration of receptors in the skin. Though we have separate receptors for cold and warm temperatures, we depend on the simultaneous stimulation of cold and warm receptors to produce hot sensations. Pain depends on both physical and psychological factors. According to the gate-control theory of pain, stimulation of touch neurons closes a spinal "gate," which inhibits neural impulses underlying pain from traveling up the spinal cord. Pain-relieving techniques such as placebos, acupuncture, and transcutaneous electrical nerve stimulation relieve pain by stimulating the release of endorphins. Hypnosis appears to relieve pain by distracting the hypnotized person.

BODY SENSES

Your body senses make you aware of the position of your limbs and help you maintain your equilibrium. The kinesthetic sense informs you of the position of your joints, the tension in your muscles, and the movement of your arms and legs. The vestibular sense informs you of your head's position in space, helping you maintain your equilibrium. The vestibular organs comprise the otolith organs and the semicircular canals.

THINKING ABOUT PSYCHOLOGY: WHY DO PSYCHOLOGISTS DISCOUNT ESP?

Most members of the lay public accept the existence of paranormal phenomena such as extrasensory perception and psychokinesis; most psychologists do not. Psychologists are skeptical because research in parapsychology has been marked by sloppy procedures, acceptance of coincidences as positive evidence, fraudulent reports, use of magic tricks, failure to replicate studies, and inability to explain paranormal phenomena. Supporters of parapsychology claim that their research has been subjected to unfair criticism.

KEY CONCEPTS

 ## KEY CONTRIBUTORS

FOR MORE INFORMATION ON SENSATION AND PERCEPTION

FOR GENERAL WORKS ON SENSATION AND PERCEPTION

Ackerman, D. (1990). *A natural history of the senses.* New York: Random House.
Goldstein, B. E. (1997). *Sensation and perception* (4th ed.). Belmont, CA: Brooks-Cole.

FOR MORE ON VISION

The Eye

Chekaluk, E., & Llewellyn, K. (Eds.). (1992). *The role of eye movements in perceptual processes.* New York: Elsevier.
Janisse, M. P. (1977). *Pupillometry: The psychology of the pupillary response.* New York: Halsted.

Color Vision

Kaiser, P. K., & Boynton, R. M. (1996). *Human color vision* (2nd ed.) Washington: Optical Society of America.
Wasserman, G. S. (1978). *Color vision: An historical introduction.* New York: Wiley.

Visual Perception

Gordon, I. E. (1991). *Theories of visual perception.* New York: Wiley.

Hatfield, G. (1990). *The natural and the normative: Theories of spatial perception from Kant to Helmholtz.* Cambridge, MA: MIT Press.

Visual Illusions

Block, J. R., & Yuker, H. E. (1989). *Can you believe your eyes? Over 250 illusions and other visual oddities.* New York: Gardner Press.

Shepard, R. N. (1990). *Mind sights: Original visual illusions, ambiguities, and other anomalies.* New York: W. H. Freeman.

FOR MORE ON HEARING

Clark, G. (1997). *Advances in cochlear implants for infants and children.* Baltimore: Singular.

Luce, R. D. (1993). *Sound and hearing.* Hillsdale, NJ: Erlbaum.

Moore, B. C. J. (1997). *An introduction to the psychology of hearing* (4th ed.). London: Academic Press.

FOR MORE ON THE CHEMICAL SENSES

Smell

Agosta, W. C. (1992). *Chemical communication: The language of pheromones.* New York: W. H. Freeman.

Tagaki, S. (1988). *Human olfaction: From art to science.* Irvington, NY: Columbia University Press.

Taste

Bolles, R. C. (Ed.). (1991). *The hedonism of taste.* Hillsdale, NJ: Erlbaum.

FOR MORE ON THE SKIN SENSES

Touch

Heller, M., & Schiff, W. (Eds.). (1991). *The psychology of touch.* Hillsdale, NJ: Erlbaum.

Katz, D. (1989). *The world of touch.* Hillsdale, NJ: Erlbaum.

Pain

Kevington, S. M. (1996). *Psychology of pain.* New York: Wiley.

Wall, P. D., & Melzack, R. (Eds.). (1994). *Textbook of pain* (3rd ed.). Edinburgh, Scotland: Churchill Livingstone.

FOR MORE ON THE BODY SENSES

Highstein, S. M., Cohen, B., & Buttner-Ennever, J. A. (Eds.). (1996). *New directions in vestibular research.* New York: New York Academy of Sciences.

FOR MORE ON PARAPSYCHOLOGY

Alcock, J. E. (1989). *Science and supernature: A critical appraisal of parapsychology.* Buffalo, NY: Prometheus.

Randi, J. (1982). *Flim-flam: Psychics, ESP, unicorns, and other delusions.* Buffalo, NY: Prometheus.

FOR MORE ON CONTRIBUTORS TO THE STUDY OF SENSATION AND PERCEPTION

Cranston, M. (1979). *John Locke: A biography.* New York: Oxford University Press.

Koenigsberger, L. (1906/1965). *Hermann von Helmholtz.* New York: Dover.

Myers, G. E. (1986). *William James: His life and thought.* New Haven, CT: Yale University Press.

Randi, J. (1991). *James Randi: Psychic investigator.* London: Boxtree.

Rao, K. R. (Ed.). (1982). *J. B. Rhine: On the frontiers of science.* Jefferson, NC: McFarland.

Reed, E. S. (1988). *James J. Gibson and the psychology of perception.* New Haven, CT: Yale University Press.

CHAPTER 6

▲ HENRI ROUSSEAU
The Sleeping Gypsy, 1897

Consciousness

▲ **Two Hundred Hours Without Sleep**
Peter Tripp experienced emotional, perceptual, and cognitive disturbances during his 200-hour radiothon.

consciousness
The awareness of one's own mental activity, including thoughts, feelings, and sensations.

O n January 21, 1959, a New York disc jockey named Peter Tripp began a radiothon to raise money for the March of Dimes fight against polio. He stayed awake for 200 hours, each night broadcasting his show from an army recruiting booth in Times Square, but as the days passed he developed symptoms of psychological disturbance. After 4 days he experienced hallucinations in which he saw a rabbit run across the booth and flames shooting out of a drawer in his hotel room. On the sixth day he began taking stimulant drugs to stay awake. And on the final day he displayed delusional thinking, including insisting that his physician was about to prepare him for burial. After his ordeal, Tripp slept 13 hours and returned to his customary level of psychological well-being (Segal & Luce, 1966).

Did Tripp's experience demonstrate that we need to sleep to maintain healthy psychological functioning? Possibly—but possibly not. First, his experiences were those of a single subject. Perhaps his reactions to sleep deprivation were unique and not necessarily generalizable to other people. Second, the delusions he displayed near the end of his ordeal might have been caused by the stimulant drugs he took to stay awake rather than by his lack of sleep. As you will learn in this chapter, our knowledge of the effects of sleep deprivation and the effects of stimulant drugs comes from research by psychologists and other scientists interested in the study of consciousness.

THE NATURE OF CONSCIOUSNESS

What is consciousness? In 1690 John Locke wrote that "consciousness is the perception of what passes in a man's own mind" (Locke, 1690/1959, p. 138). Today psychologists share a similar view of **consciousness,** defining it as the awareness of one's own mental activity, including thoughts, feelings, and sensations.

Mind in Flux: The Stream of Consciousness

Two hundred years after Locke offered his definition of consciousness, William James (1890/1981) noted that consciousness is personal, selective, continuous, and changing. Consider your own consciousness. It is *personal* because you feel that it belongs to you— you do not share it with anyone else. Consciousness is *selective* because you can attend to certain things while ignoring other things. Right now you can shift your attention to a nearby voice, the first word in the next sentence, or the feel of this book against your fingers. Consciousness is *continuous* because its contents blend into one another—the mind cannot be broken down into meaningful segments. And consciousness is *changing* because its contents are in a constant state of flux; normally, you cannot focus on one thing more than momentarily without other thoughts, feelings, or sensations drifting through your mind.

Because consciousness is both continuous and changing, James likened it to a stream (Natsoulas, 1995). Your favorite stream remains the same stream even though the water at a particular site is continuously being replaced by new water. Even as you read this paragraph, you might notice irrelevant thoughts, feelings, and sensations passing through your own mind. Some might grab your attention; others might quickly fade away. If you were to write them down as they occurred, a person reading what you had written might think you were confused or even that you were mentally ill. The disjointed nature of stream-of-consciousness writing makes it hard to follow without knowing the context of the story. You can appreciate this by trying to make sense of the opening passage from James Joyce's *A Portrait of the Artist as a Young Man:*

▶ Once upon a time and a very good time it was there was a moocow coming down along the road and this moocow that was coming down along the road met a nicens little boy named baby tuckoo. . . .

His father told him that story: his father looked at him through a glass: he had a hairy face.

He was baby tuckoo. The moocow came down the road where Betty Byrne lived: she sold lemon platt.

> O, the wild rose blossoms
> On the little green place.

He sang that song. That was his song.

> O, the green wothe botheth.

When you wet the bed first it is warm then it gets cold. His mother put on the oilsheet. That had the queer smell.

His mother had a nicer smell than his father. She played on the piano the sailor's hornpipe for him to dance. (Joyce, 1916/1967, p. 171)

As a functionalist, William James believed that consciousness is an evolutionary development that enhances our ability to adapt to the environment. James declared, "It seems reasonable to suppose that, unless consciousness served some useful purpose, it would not have been superadded to life" (quoted in Rieber, 1980, p. 205). Consciousness provides us with a mental representation of the world that permits us to try out courses of action in our mind before acting on them. This makes us more reflective and more flexible in adapting to the world, thereby reducing our tendency to engage in aimless, reckless, or impulsive behavior.

Daydreaming: The Flight of Consciousness

One of the main ways in which we manipulate information about the world is through **daydreaming,** a state of consciousness in which we voluntarily shift our attention from external stimuli to mental fantasies. Daydreaming may occupy a surprisingly large proportion of our waking day, as demonstrated in a study by psychologist Eric Klinger at the University of Minnesota. He provided college students with a pocket alarm to carry all day for several days. The alarm beeped at random times during the day, but on the average beeped every 40 minutes. Whenever the students heard their alarms, they reported their mental activity. The results showed that the students spent one third of their waking day daydreaming (Bartusiak, 1980). This leads to the remarkable conclusion that college students might spend most of each 24-hour day either asleep or daydreaming.

Given that daydreaming occupies so much of our time, what functions might it serve? As William James would agree, daydreaming lets us mentally rehearse alternative courses of action instead of engaging in impulsive behaviors. A second reason why we daydream is to keep mentally aroused when we find ourselves in unstimulating situations—as any student who has sat through a dull lecture knows all too well. A third reason people daydream is to solve problems, both practical and creative. For example, Mark Twain, Edgar Allan Poe, and Robert Louis Stevenson wrote stories inspired by daydreams. A fourth reason to daydream is the pleasure it brings us, as when we fantasize about sex (Purifoy, Grodsky, & Giambra, 1992).

Attention: The Focusing of Consciousness

Today researchers are especially interested in an aspect of consciousness identified by James: its *selectivity.* We refer to the selectivity of consciousness as **attention,** which functions like a tuner to make us aware of certain stimuli while blocking out others. This selectivity is adaptive because it prevents our consciousness from becoming a chaotic

daydreaming
A state of consciousness that involves shifting attention from external stimuli to self-generated thoughts and images.

attention
The process by which the individual focuses awareness on certain contents of consciousness while ignoring others.

▲ Eric Klinger
"Daydreams are so much a part of you that what you experience in them affects what you do in the real world."

▲ **Daydreaming**
We might daydream several hours a day.

jumble of thoughts, feelings, and sensations. For example, while you are reading this paragraph, it would be maladaptive for you to also be aware of irrelevant stimuli, such as the shoes on your feet or people talking. Of course, it would be adaptive to shift your attention if your shoes are too tight or someone yelled "Fire!" outside your room.

Experimental research, as well as everyday experience, illustrates the selectivity of attention. Consider a study in which subjects watched a television screen on which two videotapes were shown simultaneously (Neisser & Becklen, 1975). One videotape portrayed two people playing a hand-slapping game, and the other portrayed three people bouncing and throwing a basketball. The subjects were told to watch one of the games and to press a response key whenever a particular action occurred. Those watching the hand game had to respond whenever the participants slapped hands with each other. Those watching the ball game had to respond whenever the ball was thrown. The results showed that the subjects made few errors. But when they were asked to watch both games simultaneously, using their right hand to respond to one game and their left hand to respond to the other, their performances deteriorated and they made significantly more errors than when they attended to just one of the games.

What determines whether we will attend to a given stimulus? Among the many stimulus factors that affect attention are whether the stimulus is important, changing, or novel. We tend to notice stimuli that are personally *important*. You have certainly experienced this in regard to the "cocktail party phenomenon" (Wood & Cowan, 1995), in which you might be engrossed in one conversation at a party yet notice that your name has been mentioned in another conversation. A *change* in stimulation is likely to attract our attention. When watching television, you are more likely to pay attention to a commercial that is much louder or quieter than the program it interrupts.

Though William James and other psychology pioneers stressed the importance of attention and other aspects of consciousness, interest in these topics declined after John B. Watson published his classic 1913 article proclaiming the behaviorist position. He argued that consciousness, being unobservable, could not be studied scientifically. Watson insisted that "the time seems to have come when psychology must discard all references to consciousness" (Watson, 1913, p. 163). The renewed interest in studying altered states of consciousness during the past few decades (Nelson, 1996) reflects James's observation that "our normal waking consciousness, rational consciousness as we call it, is but one special type of consciousness, whilst all about it, parted from it by the filmiest of screens, there lie potential forms of consciousness entirely different" (James, 1902/1992, p. 388).

STAYING ON TRACK: *The Nature of Consciousness*

1. What psychological topic did William James and James Joyce share an interest in?
2. What is the "cocktail party" phenomenon?

Answers to Staying on Track start on p. S-2.

SLEEP

Perhaps the most obvious alternative to waking consciousness is *sleep*. The daily sleep-wake cycle is one of our **biological rhythms,** which are cyclical changes in physiological processes. Other examples of biological rhythms are the 28-day menstrual cycle in women and the annual cycle of waking and hibernation in bears. Be sure not to confuse biological rhythms, a legitimate topic of scientific research, with "biorhythms," a topic better left to pop psychology. Those who believe in biorhythms claim that each of us is born with physical, emotional, and intellectual cycles that stay constant in length and govern us for the rest of our lives. No scientifically worthy research supports these claims (O'Connor & Molly, 1991).

Biological Rhythms and the Sleep-Wake Cycle

The daily sleep-wake cycle is the most obvious of our **circadian rhythms,** which are 24-hour cycles of changes in physiological processes. The word *circadian* is derived from

biological rhythms
Repeating cycles of physiological changes.

circadian rhythms
Twenty-four-hour cycles of physiological changes, most notably the sleep-wake cycle.

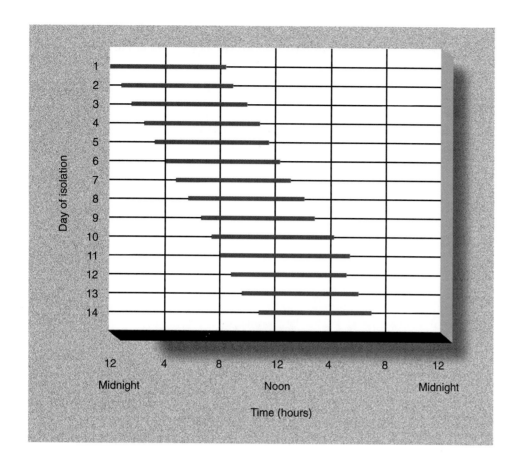

◄ FIGURE 6.1
The Extended Sleep-Wake Cycle
When subjects are kept isolated from cues related to the normal day-night cycle, they gradually adopt a 25-hour cycle. They then go to sleep 1 hour later each day.

the Latin *circa,* meaning "about," and *dies,* meaning "a day." Our circadian rhythm of body temperature parallels our circadian rhythm of brain arousal, with most people beginning the day at low points on both and rising on them through the day. College roommates who are out of phase with each other in their circadian rhythms are more likely to express dissatisfaction with their relationship (Watts, 1982). A student who is a "morning person"—already warmed up and chipper at 7 A.M.—might find it difficult to socialize with a roommate who can barely crawl out of bed at that time.

What governs our circadian rhythms? A chief factor is a part of the hypothalamus called the *suprachiasmatic nucleus* (Amir & Stewart, 1996), which regulates the secretion of the hormone *melatonin* by the **pineal gland,** an endocrine gland in the center of the brain. Melatonin secretion varies with light levels, decreasing in daylight and increasing in darkness (Haimov & Lavie, 1996). As discussed in Chapter 2, because sleepiness increases as levels of melatonin increase, researchers have been studying the possible use of melatonin as a treatment for insomnia. In an experiment on chronic insomniacs, the subjects received a dose of either melatonin or a placebo at 10 P.M. every day for 14 days. Those who had received melatonin reported better nightly sleep than did those who had received the placebo (MacFarlane et al., 1991).

When subjects are cut off from cues related to the day-night cycle, perhaps by living in a cave or a windowless room for several weeks, a curious thing happens. For unknown reasons their sleep-wake cycle changes from 24 hours to 25 hours in length (as shown in Figure 6.1). They go to bed slightly later and get up slightly later each successive day (Webb & Agnew, 1974). You may have experienced this during vacations from work and school. Perhaps you find yourself going to bed later and later and, as a result, awakening later and later.

The natural tendency for the sleep-wake cycle to lengthen might explain why "jet lag" is more severe when we fly west to east than when we fly east to west. The symptoms of jet lag, caused by a disruption of the normal sleep-wake cycle, include fatigue, depressed mood, and poor physical performance. Consider a professional baseball player. Eastbound travel shortens his sleep-wake cycle **(phase advance),** countering its natural tendency to

pineal gland
An endocrine gland that secretes a hormone that has a general tranquilizing effect on the body and that helps regulate biological rhythms.

phase advance
Shortening the sleep-wake cycle, as occurs when traveling from west to east.

phase delay
Lengthening the sleep-wake cycle, as occurs when traveling from east to west.

lengthen. In contrast, westbound travel lengthens his sleep-wake cycle **(phase delay)**, which agrees with its natural tendency to lengthen. So, phase advance requires more adjustment by the athlete. Athletes typically take 3 or 4 days to overcome jet lag and restore their normal physical and mental functioning (Hill et al., 1993).

The one quarter of American workers on rotating shifts, including airplane pilots, police officers, and factory workers, also find their sleep-wake cycles disrupted. Given the natural tendency of the sleep-wake cycle to increase in length, workers on rotating shifts respond better to phase delay than to phase advance. This was demonstrated in a study of industrial workers. Those on a phase-delay schedule moved from the night shift (12 midnight to 8 A.M.) to the day shift (8 A.M. to 4 P.M.) to the evening shift (4 P.M. to 12 midnight). Those on a phase-advance schedule moved in the opposite direction, from the night shift to the evening shift to the day shift. The results showed that workers on a phase-delay schedule had better health, greater satisfaction, higher productivity, and lower turnover (Czeisler, Moore-Ede, & Coleman, 1982).

Another way to counteract the ill effects of rotating shifts (or night shifts) is to expose workers who must work at night to bright lights for at least part of their shifts and to have them wear dark goggles to block out light during the day. This can help reset their circadian rhythms to make them alert at night and sleepy during the day. Workers who have adopted these practices sleep better, feel less fatigued, and maintain better moods (Eastman et al., 1994).

Patterns of Sleep: Sleep as an Active Process

In 1960, four leading introductory psychology textbooks made no mention of sleep, and the most extensive coverage in any introductory textbook was two pages (Webb, 1985). Today, in contrast, all introductory psychology textbooks include (usually extensive) coverage of sleep. This indicates the explosion of scientific interest in studying sleep since the 1960s. Two of the main topics of interest regarding sleep patterns are the sleep cycle and the duration of sleep.

The Sleep Cycle

Imagine that you are a subject in a sleep study. You would first sleep a night or two in a sleep laboratory to get accustomed to the novel surroundings. You would then sleep several nights in the laboratory while special devices recorded changes in your brain waves,

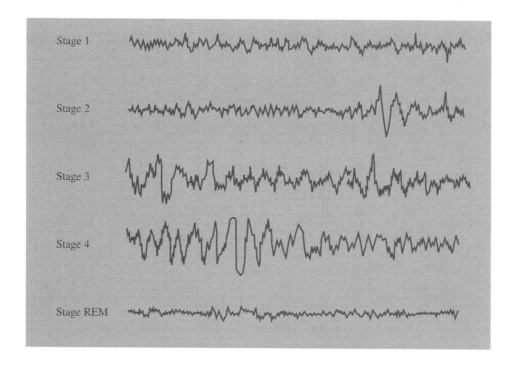

Stage 1

Stage 2

Stage 3

Stage 4

Stage REM

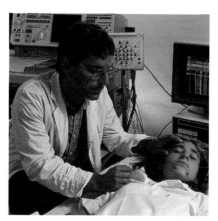

◄ FIGURE 6.2
The Stages of Sleep
Studies of subjects in sleep laboratories have found that the stages of sleep are associated with distinctive patterns of brain-wave activity. As we drift into deeper stages of sleep, our brain waves decrease in frequency and increase in amplitude. When we are in REM sleep, our brain-wave patterns are similar to those in the waking state.

eye movements, heart rate, blood pressure, body temperature, breathing rate, muscle tension, and respiration rate. Your behavior, including any utterances you made, would be recorded on videotape and audiotape.

The physiological recordings would reveal that you do not simply drift into deep sleep, stay there all night, and suddenly awaken in the morning. Instead, they would show that you pass through repeated sleep cycles, which are biological rhythms marked by variations in the depth of sleep, as defined by particular brain-wave patterns. Figure 6.2 illustrates these patterns, which were first identified in the 1930s through the use of the electroencephalograph, or EEG (Loomis, Harvey, & Hobart, 1937).

As you lie in bed with your eyes closed, an EEG recording would show that your brain-wave pattern changes from primarily high-frequency *beta waves* (14 to 30 cycles a second), which mark an alert mental state, to a higher proportion of lower-frequency *alpha waves* (8 to 13 cycles a second), which mark a relaxed, introspective mental state. As you drift off to sleep, you would exhibit slow, rolling eye movements and your brain-wave pattern would show a higher proportion of *theta waves* (4 to 7 cycles a second), which have a lower frequency than alpha waves. You would also exhibit a decrease in other signs of arousal, including heart rate, breathing rate, muscle tension, and respiration rate.

The cessation of the rolling eye movements would signify the onset of sleep (Ogilvie et al., 1988). This initial light stage of sleep is called *stage 1*. After 5 to 10 minutes in stage 1, you would enter the slightly deeper *stage 2*, associated with periodic bursts of higher-frequency (12 to 16 cycles a second) brain waves known as *sleep spindles*. After 10 to 20 minutes in stage 2, you would enter *stage 3*, marked by the appearance of extremely low-frequency (1/2 to 3 cycles a second) *delta waves*. When at least 50 percent of your brain waves are delta waves, you would be in *stage 4*, the deepest stage of sleep. After remaining in stages 3 and 4 for 30 to 40 minutes, you would drift up through stages 3, 2, and 1 until, about 90 minutes after falling asleep, you would reach the *rapid eye movement* stage, better known as **REM sleep.**

REM sleep gets its name from the darting eye movements that characterize it. You have probably seen these movements under the eyelids of sleeping people—or even a sleeping pet dog or cat. Because stages 1, 2, 3, and 4 are not characterized by these eye movements, they are collectively called *non-REM*, or **NREM sleep.** NREM sleep is characterized by slow brain waves, deep breathing, regular heart rate, and lower blood pressure. After an initial 10-minute period of REM sleep, you would again drift down into NREM sleep, eventually reaching stage 4.

REM sleep
The stage of sleep associated with rapid eye movements, an active brain-wave pattern, and vivid dreams.

NREM sleep
The stages of sleep not associated with rapid eye movements and marked by relatively little dreaming.

A Typical Night's Sleep
During a typical night's sleep we pass through cycles that involve stages of NREM sleep and the stage of REM sleep. Note that we obtain our deepest sleep during the first half of the night and that the periods of REM sleep become longer with each successive cycle (Cartwright, 1978).

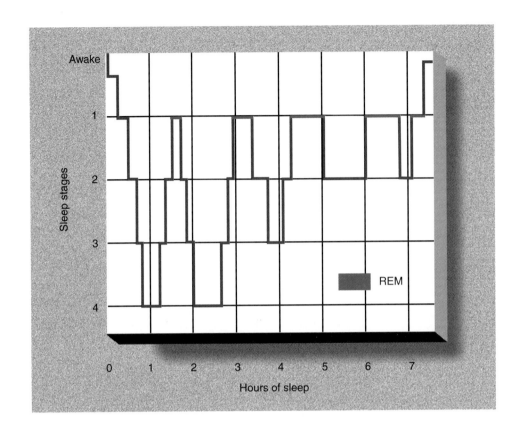

The NREM-REM cycles take an average of 90 minutes, meaning that you pass through four or five cycles in a typical night's sleep. Adults normally spend about 25 percent of the night in REM sleep, 5 percent in stage 1, 50 percent in stage 2, and 20 percent in stages 3 and 4. As shown in Figure 6.3, the first half of your night's sleep has relatively more NREM sleep than the second half, whereas the second half has relatively more REM sleep than the first half. You might not even reach stages 3 and 4 during the second half of the night.

While you are in REM sleep, your heart rate, respiration rate, and brain-wave frequency increase, making you appear to be awake. But you also experience flaccid paralysis of your limbs, making it impossible for you to shift your position in bed. Given that you become physiologically aroused, yet immobile and difficult to awaken, REM sleep is also called *paradoxical sleep*. Because we are paralyzed during REM sleep, sleepwalking (or *somnambulism*) occurs only during NREM sleep, specifically stages 3 and 4. In fact, sleepwalkers spend a greater proportion of their sleep in stages 3 and 4 than nonsleepwalkers do (Blatt et al., 1991). Sleepwalking is also more common in children than in adults. Despite warnings to the contrary, sleepwalkers may be awakened without fear of doing physical or psychological harm to them. Of course, the habitual sleepwalker should be protected from injury by keeping doors and windows locked.

Another characteristic of REM sleep is erection of the penis and clitoris. This occurs spontaneously and is not necessarily indicative of a sexual dream. Sleep clinics use REM erections to determine whether men who are unable to have erections while awake are suffering from a physical or a psychological disorder. If a man has erections while in REM sleep, his problem is psychological, not physical (Gordon & Carey, 1995).

REM sleep is associated with dreaming. We know this because of research conducted in the early 1950s by Eugene Aserinsky and Nathaniel Kleitman (1953) of the University of Chicago. When they awakened sleepers displaying rapid eye movements, the sleepers usually reported that they had been dreaming. In contrast, people awakened during NREM sleep rarely reported that they had been dreaming. Because the longest REM period occurs during the last sleep cycle of the night, you often find yourself in the middle of a dream when your alarm clock wakes you in the morning. You might be tempted to infer that rapid eye movements reflect the scanning of dream scenes, but Aserinsky and his colleagues

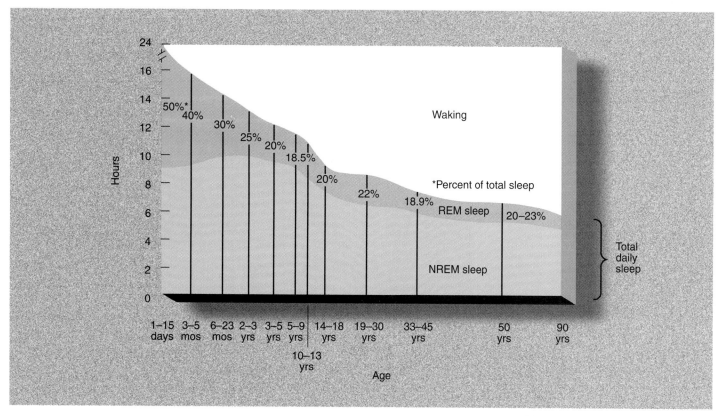

▲ FIGURE 6.4
Sleep Across the Life Span
Our amount of daily sleep declines across the life span, decreasing rapidly in infancy and childhood and more gradually in adulthood. The proportion of time spent in REM sleep also declines across the life span.

(1985) have found that they do not—so if you were dreaming about, say, a tennis match, your rapid eye movements would not have been following the ball's flight.

Researchers are learning more and more about the physiological bases of the sleep cycle. Brain structures that help regulate sleep include the pons, thalamus, hypothalamus, and reticular formation. For example, destruction of the suprachiasmatic nucleus of the hypothalamus in animals disrupts the sleep-wake cycle to the extent that they fall asleep and awaken unpredictably. Neurotransmitters that help regulate sleep include serotonin, which plays a role in triggering NREM sleep, and norepinephrine, which plays a role in triggering REM sleep.

The Duration of Sleep

Sleep is not only cyclical, but varies in duration. Human beings are moderately long sleepers, with young adults averaging 8 hours of sleep a day. In contrast, some animals, such as elephants, sleep as little as 2 hours a day, while other animals, such as bats, sleep as much as 20 hours a day. Efforts to wean human subjects from sleep indicate that it cannot be reduced much below 4 hours without inducing extreme drowsiness and severe mood alterations (Webb, 1985). Figure 6.4 indicates that our daily need for sleep varies across the life span. At one extreme, infants typically sleep 16 hours a day. At the other extreme, elderly people typically sleep 6 hours a day. Of course, you might need to sleep more or less than your age peers. This variability in normal sleep duration among people of the same age appears to have a hereditary basis (Heath et al., 1990).

Regardless of how much sleep they need, North Americans habitually get less than their ideal quota. They might stay awake to watch television, do schoolwork, or perform other activities. You might go to bed when you want to (perhaps after watching the late movie) and awaken when you have to (perhaps in time for an 8 A.M. class), making you chronically sleep deprived. According to sleep researcher William Dement, "Most Americans no longer know what it feels like to be fully alert" (Toufexis, 1990, p. 79).

Difficulty in getting a good night's sleep has been increasing among college students. In a replication of an earlier study, a survey of college students conducted in 1992 found that

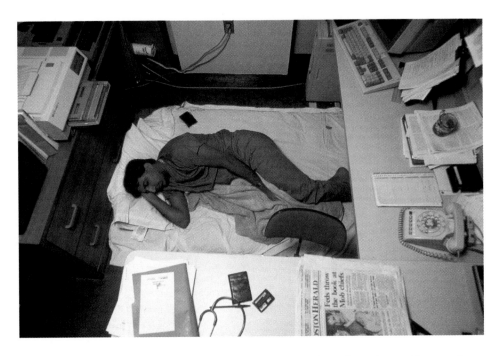

▶ **Sleep Deprivation**
Many workers, especially harried medical residents, must snatch moments of sleep whenever they can. The resulting sleep disruption and deprivation may impair their ability to function well on the job.

they reported sleeping less and being less satisfied with their sleep than college students had reported in a survey conducted in 1978 (Hicks, Johnson, & Pellegrini, 1992). This lack of sleep is associated with daytime sleepiness, mood disturbances, deterioration of performance, and vulnerability to accidents (Carskadon, 1990).

Many people try to overcome the effects of inadequate nighttime sleep by taking daytime naps. Some cultures, typically in regions with hot climates, even incorporate siestas as part of everyday life. Stores and businesses shut down for part of the afternoon so that individuals can rest or nap for an hour or two instead of being worn out by working during the hottest time of the day. Even students and executives in nonsiesta cultures have come to value their "power naps." They are being wise, because an afternoon nap can increase alertness and improve task performance (Horne & Reyner, 1996). Older adults, who sleep less at night and find it more difficult to stay asleep, appreciate the benefits of napping—they nap more than younger adults do (Beh, 1994).

The Functions of Sleep: Why Do We Sleep?

Assuming that you live to be 90, you will have spent about 30 years asleep. Are you wasting one third of your life, or does sleep serve important functions for you? Among the many hypothesized functions of sleep, two are most prominent: *sleep as restorative* and *sleep as adaptive inactivity.*

Sleep as Restorative: Overcoming Daily Wear and Tear

The most commonsense view of sleep holds that it restores the body and the mind after the wear and tear imposed by waking activities. Perhaps sleep repairs body tissues, removes metabolic waste products, and replenishes brain neurotransmitters (Inove, Honda, & Komoda, 1995). One way of testing whether sleep is restorative is to observe the effects of sleep deprivation. The longer we stay awake, the more we crave sleep. In the case of Peter Tripp, sleep deprivation apparently produced hallucinations and delusional thinking, which disappeared after a single night's sleep. In a similar case in 1964, Randy Gardner, a 17-year-old San Diego high school student, stayed awake 264 hours (11 days) to get his name in the *Guinness Book of World Records* (his record has since been broken). He experienced less-severe disturbances than Tripp did, including some fatigue, irritability, and perceptual distortions. On his eleventh day without sleep, Gardner beat William Dement one hundred consecutive times at a pinball game. After 15 hours of sleep, Gardner awoke—like Tripp, restored both physically and mentally (Gulevich, Dement, & Johnson, 1966). Thus, even a single good night's sleep can counteract the negative effects of prolonged sleep deprivation.

Formal, as well as anecdotal, research has provided evidence of the detrimental effects of sleep loss and the restorative effects of sleep. Sleep deprivation is associated with a decline in the ability to perform physical tasks (Rodgers et al., 1995) and mental tasks (Blagrove, Alexander, & Horne, 1995). Moreover, people who experience sleep loss experience temporary impairment of their immune systems (Irwin et al., 1994).

Another source of evidence for the restorative function of sleep is research on the effects of vigorous physical activity on subsequent sleep patterns. Sleep, especially deep sleep, increases on the nights after vigorous exercise (Vein et al., 1991). This was supported by a study of runners who participated in a 57-mile ultramarathon race. They had an increase in the duration of sleep, particularly stage 3 and stage 4, on the first two nights after the race (Shapiro et al., 1981). Though we still do not know exactly what, if anything, sleep restores, one explanation for the increase in deep sleep after vigorous exercise concerns the secretion of growth hormone, which increases during deep sleep. Growth hormone promotes the synthesis of proteins needed for the repair of muscles and other body tissues.

Sleep as Adaptive Inactivity: Self-Protection and Energy Conservation

An alternative view, championed by Wilse Webb (1992), is that sleep evolved because it protected the sleeper from harm and prevented the useless expenditure of energy. Our prehistoric ancestors who slept at night were less likely to gain the attention of hungry nocturnal predators. The limb paralysis accompanying REM sleep may have evolved because it prevented cave dwellers from acting out their dreams, when they might have bumped into trees, fallen off cliffs, or provided dinner for saber-toothed tigers. Evidence for this protective function of REM sleep comes from studies of cats: Destruction of a portion of the pons that normally induces REM paralysis in cats produces stalking and attacking movements during sleep, as though the cats are acting out their dreams (Morrison, 1983).

Further support for the protective function of sleep comes from studies showing that animals with little to fear while asleep (either because they are predators or because they sleep in safe places) sleep for much of the 24-hour day. In contrast, animals that have much to fear while asleep (either because they are prey or because they sleep in exposed places) sleep for relatively little of the 24-hour day. Thus, cats, which are predators, sleep much longer (15 hours) than rabbits (8 hours), which are prey. Likewise, bats, which sleep in caves, sleep much longer (20 hours) than horses (3 hours), which sleep in the open.

Another reason to believe that sleep might be a period of adaptive inactivity is that it conserves energy (Berger & Phillips, 1995). Evidence supportive of this view comes from studies of the food-finding habits of different species. Because the length of sleep for a given species is negatively correlated with how long it takes members of that species to find their daily food, perhaps animals stay awake only long enough to eat sufficient food to meet their energy needs. Animals might have evolved sleep in part to conserve energy the remainder of the time. Thus, the typical young adult human's need for about 8 hours of nightly sleep might mean that our prehistoric ancestors needed about 16 hours to find their daily food (Cohen, 1979).

According to Wilse Webb (1992), both the restorative theory and the adaptive-inactivity theory must be included in an adequate theory of sleep. The restorative theory explains why sleepiness increases as sleep loss increases. The adaptive-inactivity theory explains why sleep follows a circadian rhythm. You have experienced this if you have experienced an "all-nighter" while studying for exams. If you fight your sleepinees and force yourself to stay awake all night, you might be surprised to find yourself less sleepy in the morning (when your circadian rhythm would make you more alert). Later, you would find yourself becoming sleepy when your normal bedtime approaches again.

▲ Wilse Webb
"Natural sleep is when you go to bed when you're sleepy and wake up when you're rested. But the modern system of sleeping is to go to bed when you want to and get up when you have to."

Sleep Disorders: When Sleep Goes Wrong

You might take sleep for granted, but many people do not. They suffer from sleep disorders such as *insomnia*, *sleep apnea*, and *narcolepsy*.

Insomnia: Trouble Falling Asleep or Staying Asleep

Twenty to thirty million Americans suffer from **insomnia** (Roth, 1995), chronic difficulty in sleeping. There are three major forms of insomnia. People who suffer from *sleep-onset insomnia* have trouble falling asleep. You have experienced this if you have ever lain in bed, perhaps for hours, fruitlessly waiting to drift off to sleep. Those who experience *sleep-maintenance insomnia* fall asleep normally but find themselves awakening repeatedly throughout the night. You have encountered *early-morning awakening* if you have slept soundly through the night, only to awaken 2 or 3 hours earlier than you would like.

If you suffer from insomnia, what should you do? Many insomniacs resort to sedative drugs, including alcohol and barbiturates, to fall asleep. Though sedatives will, at least initially, help you fall asleep, they do so at a cost. First, they interfere with the normal sleep cycle, most notably by reducing REM sleep. Second, they eventually lose their effectiveness, leaving you with the same problem you began with. And third, they have harmful side effects, including drug dependence.

The shortcomings of drug-induced sleep have led scientists to search for a natural chemical treatment for insomnia. One promising approach is to use *tryptophan*. This amino acid is a precursor of the neurotransmitter serotonin, which promotes the onset of sleep. Subjects who receive doses of tryptophan do, in fact, fall asleep faster than those who receive doses of a placebo (Spring, Chiodo, & Bowen, 1987).

Instead of turning to sedatives, tryptophan, or other chemical treatments, insomnia victims can use psychological techniques to obtain a good night's sleep (Murtagh & Greenwood, 1995). If you suffer from insomnia, you should reduce your presleep arousal by avoiding exercise and caffeine products too close to bedtime. It is also advisable to avoid napping. If you nap during the day, you might not feel sleepy enough to fall asleep at your desired bedtime. You might even benefit from *paradoxical intention,* in which you try to stay awake while lying in bed. This can, paradoxically, induce sleep by preventing fruitless, anxiety-inducing efforts to fall asleep (Katz, 1984).

Another technique, *stimulus control,* requires arranging your bedtime situation to promote sleep. First, go to bed only when you feel sleepy. Second, to assure that you associate lying in bed with sleep and not with being awake, do not eat, read, watch television, or listen to music while lying in bed. Third, if you toss and turn, get out of bed and return only when you are sleepy (Ladouceur & Gros-Louis, 1986).

Sleep Apnea: The Inability to Sleep and Breathe at the Same Time

sleep apnea

A condition in which a person awakens repeatedly in order to breathe.

Imagine that you stopped breathing hundreds of times every night and awakened each time in order to breathe. You would be suffering from **sleep apnea** (*apnea* means the absence of breathing). Victims of sleep apnea have repeated episodes throughout the night in which they fall asleep and then stop breathing for up to a minute or so. This produces a decrease in blood oxygen that stimulates the brain to awaken them, permitting them to start breathing again. But the renewed breathing is often accompanied by loud snorting sounds as they gasp for air. The spouses of sleep-apnea victims may become so distressed by being repeatedly awakened by these annoying sounds that they take to sleeping in another room. People with sleep apnea typically feel chronically sleepy during the day, yet do not recall their repeated nighttime awakenings.

There are two major causes of sleep apnea. One is the failure of the respiratory center of the brain to maintain normal breathing while the person is asleep. Cases with this cause sometimes respond to drug therapy (Mendelson, Maczaj, & Holt, 1991). The second major cause is the collapse of the breathing passage, which is more common in obese people. An effective treatment in these cases uses a device that pumps a steady flow of air through a breathing mask worn by the sleeper, making the breathing passage resist collapsing (Sforza & Lugaresi, 1995).

Narcolepsy: Falling Asleep Uncontrollably

narcolepsy

A condition in which an awake person suffers from repeated, sudden, and irresistible REM sleep attacks.

While victims of sleep apnea find it impossible to stay asleep at night, victims of **narcolepsy** find it impossible to stay awake all day. If you suffered from narcolepsy, you would experience repeated, irresistible sleep attacks. During these attacks, you would immediately fall into REM sleep for periods lasting from a few minutes to a half hour. Because of its association with REM sleep, narcolepsy is typically accompanied by a loss of muscle tone that causes the victim to collapse. You can imagine how dangerous narcolepsy is for people performing hazardous activities. For example, many people with narcolepsy fall asleep while driving (Aldrich, 1992). Because narcoleptic attacks can be instigated by strong emotions, victims try to maintain a bland emotional life, avoiding both laughing and crying. The resulting inability to experience life to its fullest can lead to chronic depression and even suicide. The cause of narcolepsy is unknown, but given that it runs in families, it might have a genetic basis. Though there is no cure for it, victims might benefit from naps (Mullington & Broughton, 1993) or stimulant drugs (Mitler, Hajdukovic, & Erman, 1993).

STAYING ON TRACK: *Sleep*

1. Why do psychologists discount "biorhythms"?
2. What cycles take place during a typical night's sleep?
3. What evidence supports the view that sleep is a form of adaptive inactivity?
4. What helpful tips would you give to a person suffering from sleep-onset insomnia?

DREAMS

The most dramatic aspect of sleep is the **dream,** a storylike sequence of visual images that commonly evoke strong emotions. Actions that would be impossible in real life may seem perfectly normal in dreams. In a dream, you might find it reasonable to hold a conversation with a dinosaur or to leap across the Grand Canyon. But what are the major characteristics of dreams? This was the question addressed in a classic study conducted a century ago by Mary Whiton Calkins (1893).

dream

A storylike sequence of visual images, usually occurring during REM sleep.

ANATOMY OF A CLASSIC RESEARCH STUDY

What Are the Characteristics of Dreams?

Rationale

Though Sigmund Freud is famous for making the analysis of dreams an important part of psychoanalysis, beginning with the publication of *The Interpretation of Dreams* in 1900, he was not the first person to study them formally. An article published by Mary Whiton Calkins (1893) described a dream study she conducted with her colleague Edmund Clark Sanford. The study is noteworthy because it was referred to by Freud in his book and its findings have held up well. It also shows the transition in late-nineteenth-century psychology from philosophical speculation about psychological topics, such as dreams, to empirical research on them. It is also a landmark study because Sanford presented a paper on it in 1892 at the first meeting of the American Psychological Association.

Method

Calkins recorded her own dreams for 55 nights, and Sanford recorded his for 46 nights. They used alarm clocks to awaken themselves at various times during the night in order to jot down any dreams they were having.

Results and Discussion

Calkins observed dream characteristics that later research has confirmed. One researcher, J. Allan Hobson (1988), credits Calkins with anticipating modern approaches to dream research and pioneering the intensive study of dream subjects over many nights. Her findings included the following:

1. *We dream every night.* On several nights, Calkins believed she had not dreamed—only to find that she had written down several dreams during the night. Ironically, Hugo Münsterberg, who supervised Calkins's doctoral dissertation research on memory,

claimed that he never dreamed (Hale, 1980). Calkins hypothesized that we forget our dreams because of a lack of congruity between dreaming and the waking states of consciousness. This finding anticipated interest in state-dependent memory, which has inspired research studies only in the past few decades and is discussed in Chapter 8.

2. *We have about four dreams a night.* Calkins recorded 205 dreams on 55 nights, and Sanford 170 on 46 nights. This agrees with modern research indicating that we have four or five REM periods on a typical night.

3. *As the night progresses, we are more likely to be dreaming.* Calkins found that most dreams occurred during the second half of the night. This agrees with later research findings, obtained with physiological recording equipment, that successive REM periods increase in length across the night.

4. *Most dreams are mundane and refer to recent life events.* We might not realize that dreams are usually mundane because we tend to recall only the most dramatic ones.

5. *Dreams can incorporate external stimuli.* In one of her dreams Calkins found herself struggling to crawl from an elevator through a tiny opening into an eighth-floor apartment. She awoke to find herself in a cramped position with a heavy blanket over her face.

6. *What Calkins called "real thinking" occurs during sleep.* This finding anticipated research findings that NREM sleep is marked by ordinary thinking, as opposed to the fantastic images and events common to REM dreaming.

7. *We can reason while dreaming and even, to an extent, control our dreams.* This finding anticipated research on lucid dreaming, a serious topic of research only in the past decade that is discussed later in the chapter.

8. *Dreams can disguise their true meaning.* Calkins reported a "romance dream" that included disguised sexual material. This finding anticipated Freud's belief that dreams can use symbols to represent their true—often sexual—meaning.

▲ ▲ ▲

The Content of Dreams: What Do We Dream About?

Human beings have long been intrigued by dreams; references to the content of dreams are found on Babylonian clay tablets dating from 5000 B.C. As just described, Mary Whiton Calkins (1893) found that we tend to dream about mundane personal matters, usually involving familiar people and places. This finding was supported by the research of Calvin Hall (1966), who analyzed the content of thousands of dreams reported by his subjects. A more recent study likewise found that about half of our dreams include material about waking events of the preceding day (Botman & Crovitz, 1989–1990).

The content of some dreams is frightening. These **nightmares** tend to occur when we feel emotionally distressed (Berquier & Ashton, 1992). Consider the apparent effect on nightmares of the major earthquake that struck the San Francisco Bay area of California in 1989. After the earthquake, a study of almost a hundred San Francisco Bay area college students found they had twice as many nightmares as an equivalent group of subjects in Tucson, Arizona. While 40 percent of the San Francisco subjects had nightmares about earthquakes, only 5 percent of the Tucson subjects had them (Wood, Bootzin, & Rosenhahn, 1992).

Do not confuse nightmares, which are frightening dreams that occur during REM sleep, with **night terrors,** which occur during NREM sleep stages 3 and 4. The person experiencing a night terror will suddenly sit upright in bed, feel intense fear, let out a bloodcurdling scream, exhibit a rapid pulse and breathing rate, and speak incoherently. After a night terror, the person typically falls right back to sleep and does not recall the experience the next morning. As a result, a night terror can be more disturbing to the family members who are rudely awakened by it than to the person who has experienced it. Though night terrors are more common in children, they can afflict adults as well (Llorente et al., 1992).

As noted by Mary Whiton Calkins, the content of dreams can be affected by immediate environmental stimuli. Even before Calkins observed this, it was portrayed by Herman Melville in his novel *Moby Dick* in describing the effect of Captain Ahab's peg leg on the dreams of his ship's sailors. Melville wrote, "To his weary mates, seeking repose within six

nightmare
A frightening REM dream.

night terror
A frightening NREM experience, common in childhood, in which the individual may suddenly sit up, let out a bloodcurdling scream, speak incoherently, and quickly fall back to sleep, yet usually fails to recall it on awakening.

inches of his ivory heel, such would have been the reverberating crack and din of that bony step that their dreams would have been of the crunching teeth of sharks." Similarly, you might find yourself dreaming of an ice cream truck ringing its bell, only to awaken suddenly and discover that your dream had been stimulated by the ringing of your telephone.

Such anecdotal reports of the incorporation of stimuli into dreams have inspired laboratory experiments. In one of the first of these, researchers sprayed sleepers with a water mist when they were in REM sleep; on being awakened, many of the subjects reported dreams with watery themes, such as a leaky roof or being caught in the rain (Dement & Wolpert, 1958). Experiments also have found that sleeping subjects who are touched on their bodies (Nielsen, 1993) or rocked in a hammock (Leslie & Ogilvie, 1996) might incorporate that into their dreams. Despite these positive findings, stimuli that we experience when we are asleep are not always incorporated into our dreams. For example, a study of sleep apnea patients found no increase in dream content related to breathing problems (Gross & Lavie, 1994).

You will recall that Mary Whiton Calkins also noted that we might be able to control our ongoing dreams. This is the basis of **lucid dreaming** (Kahan & LaBerge, 1994), an approach, devised by Stephen LaBerge, in which sleeping subjects learn how to be aware while dreaming and how to direct their dreams. Lucid dreamers report an enhanced sense of well-being (Wolpin et al., 1992), though the reasons for this are unclear.

The Purpose of Dreaming: Why Do We Dream?

REM sleep—dream sleep—is important (Mancia, 1995). Subjects who have been deprived of sleep, and then are allowed to sleep as long as they like, show an increase in REM sleep (Dement, 1960). This is known as the *REM rebound effect* and indicates that dream sleep serves certain functions. But what are the functions of dreams? People have pondered this question for thousands of years. The ancient Hebrews, Egyptians, and Greeks believed that dreams brought prophecies from God or the gods, as in the Pharaoh's dream that was interpreted by Joseph in the Old Testament and in dreams described in Homer's *Iliad* and *Odyssey*. But Aristotle, who at first accepted the divine origin of dreams, later rejected this belief, claiming that it is merely coincidental when prophetic dreams come true.

Dreaming as Wish Fulfillment

Sigmund Freud (1900/1990) provided the first formal view of dreaming as wish fulfillment. Freud claimed that dreams function as the "royal road to the unconscious" by serving as safe outlets for unconscious sexual or aggressive impulses that we cannot act on while we are awake because of cultural prohibitions against them. Freud distinguished between a dream's **manifest content,** which is the dream as recalled by the dreamer, and its **latent content,** which is the dream's hidden, underlying meaning. Thus, the manifest content of a dream hides its latent content. But why do we not dream about the latent content directly? If we dreamed directly about emotionally charged sexual or aggressive material, we might repeatedly awaken ourselves from our sleep.

But how can we uncover a dream's latent content from its manifest content? According to Freud, a dream's manifest content consists of symbols that disguise its latent sexual or aggressive content. Thus, in our dreams, trees, rifles, or skyscrapers might act as phallic symbols representing unconscious sexual impulses. The manifest content of a dream reported by a subject is translated into its latent content during the process of psychoanalysis, which is discussed in Chapter 15. Nonetheless, even Freud said that "sometimes a cigar is just a cigar"—meaning that sometimes the manifest content is not symbolic, but instead is the true content of the dream.

Dreaming as Problem Solving

The failure of psychoanalysts to provide convincing research support for dreaming as a form of disguised wish fulfillment (Fisher & Greenberg, 1985) led researchers to study other possible functions of dreams, such as problem solving. Anecdotal reports have long supported the view that dreaming serves the function of problem solving. For example, Elias Howe completed his invention of the sewing machine only after gaining

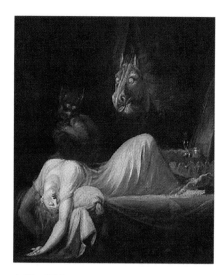

▲ **The Nightmare**
The Nightmare, painted by Henry Fuseli (1741–1825), depicts the fearsome imagery of the typical nightmare.

lucid dreaming
The ability to be aware that one is dreaming and to direct one's dreams.

manifest content
Sigmund Freud's term for the verbally reported dream.

latent content
Sigmund Freud's term for the true, though disguised, meaning of a dream.

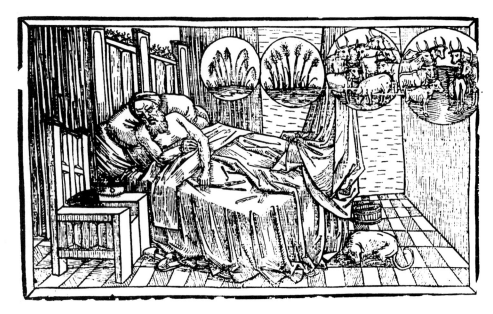

insight from a dream. Rosalind Cartwright (1978), a leading dream researcher, has conducted formal studies of the possible role of dreaming in solving practical and emotional problems. By studying dreams that occur in each of the REM periods across a night's sleep, she concluded that dreamers are concerned with finding possible solutions to personal problems. According to Cartwright, dreaming provides a more creative approach to problem solving because it is freer and less constrained by the more logical thinking of waking life. In a study of people in the process of divorcing their spouse, Cartwright (1991) found that those who dreamed about their relationship with their spouse while they were going through a divorce were less depressed and better adjusted to single life a year later. This was particularly true of those who had highly emotional dreams. Note, however, that this study revealed a positive correlation between dreaming and emotional adjustment. It did not provide evidence that dreaming *caused* better emotional adjustment.

Dreaming as an Aid to Memory

Do you ever stay up all night to study for exams? If so, you might be impairing your ability to memorize the material you have studied. Decades of research indicate that sleep can help you form long-term memories of material you learn during the day. REM sleep appears to be even more beneficial to memory than NREM sleep (Smith, 1996). Consider a study in which undergraduates learned a story during the day and then were awakened periodically to deprive them of equal periods of either REM sleep or stage 4 sleep. The next day they were asked to recall the story they had learned the day before. Subjects who had been deprived of REM sleep showed poorer recall than subjects who had been deprived of stage 4 sleep (Tilley & Empson, 1978).

Additional evidence for the importance of REM sleep comes from research findings that the more REM sleep we have during a night's sleep, the better our memory will be for material learned during the day before. In one study, undergraduates learned Morse code just before bedtime on three consecutive nights. After awakening, they were given a Morse code test. The results revealed a positive correlation between the length of REM sleep and their performance on the test (Mandai et al., 1989). Thus, it seems advisable to get a good night's sleep after studying material you wish to retain in your memory.

Dreaming as the By-Product of Random Brain Activity

Dream theorists traditionally have assumed that dreaming serves psychological functions, such as wish fulfillment or problem solving. In contrast, the **activation-synthesis theory** of J. Allan Hobson and Robert McCarley (1977) holds that dreams are the by-products of

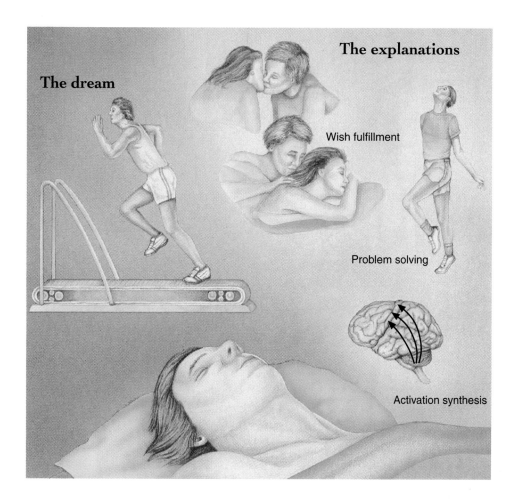

The dream

The explanations

Wish fulfillment

Problem solving

Activation synthesis

◄ **FIGURE 6.5**
One Dream, Three Explanations
The Dream: The dreamer dreams that he is running in place and can neither move from that spot nor stop running.
The Explanations:
1. *Wish Fulfillment*—The manifest content (the dream as reported) would be translated into its latent content (its true meaning). The dream might reflect the conflict between the dreamer's wish for sex (the desire to move from the spot) and guilt feelings about that wish (the desire to stop running).
2. *Problem Solving*—The dreamer has been concerned with recent excessive weight gain, but has been unable to decide on the best course of action for losing weight. Perhaps the dream is directing him to take up aerobic exercise.
3. *Activation Synthesis*—During REM sleep, the pons generates neural impulses that activate random regions of the cerebral cortex. Perhaps it has activated the region of the motor cortex that controls leg and arm movements. Because his limbs are paralyzed during REM sleep, the dreamer might synthesize the cortical arousal and limb paralysis into a dream about running in place without being able to move or stop.

the forebrain's attempt to make sense of activity generated by the brainstem during REM sleep. That is, the forebrain interprets brain *activation* and *synthesizes* it into a dream. As an example, consider a dream in which you are being chased but feel that you cannot run away. According to the activation-synthesis theory, this might reflect the forebrain's attempt to explain the failure of signals from the motor areas of the brain to stimulate limb movements during the paralysis that accompanies REM sleep—paralysis produced by activity in the brainstem. The inability of the forebrain to make logical sense of patterns of random brainstem activity might explain why our REM dreams tend to be more bizarre than our daydreams (Williams et al., 1992).

The activation-synthesis theory does not discount the influence of psychological factors on one's dreams. That is, the theory accepts that the forebrain's interpretation of random brainstem activity presumably reveals something about the personality and experiences of the dreamer. The theory simply assumes that dreams are generated by random brainstem activity, not by unconscious wishes or emotional conflicts. Thus, psychological factors come into play only *after* the onset of brainstem activity (Rittenhouse, Stickgold, & Hobson, 1994).

Despite a century of research, no dream theory has been clearly shown to be superior at explaining the functions of dreams. One of the difficulties in dream research is that the same dream can be explained equally well by different theories. This possibility is illustrated in Figure 6.5.

STAYING ON TRACK: *Dreams*

1. In what ways did Mary Whiton Calkins's 1893 study of dreams anticipate later research findings?
2. What is Freud's theory of dreaming?

Consciousness   ┃   211

HYPNOSIS

While sleep is a naturally occurring state of consciousness, **hypnosis** is an induced state of consciousness in which one person responds to suggestions by another person to alter perception, thinking, feelings, and behavior. Hypnosis originated in the work of the Viennese physician Anton Mesmer (1734–1815), who claimed that he could cure illnesses by transmitting to his patients a form of energy he called *animal magnetism*, a process that became known as *mesmerism*. In the late eighteenth century, Mesmer became the rage of Paris, impressing audiences with his demonstrations of mesmerism (Ellenberger, 1970). Today we still use the word *mesmerized* to describe a person in a trancelike state while engaged in an activity and *animal magnetism* to describe people with charismatic personalities.

Mesmer's flamboyance and extravagant claims, as well as the professional jealousy of other physicians, provoked King Louis XVI to appoint a commission to investigate mesmerism. The commission was headed by Benjamin Franklin and included Antoine Lavoisier (the founder of modern chemistry) and J.I. Guillotin (the inventor of the infamous decapitation device, the guillotine). It completed its investigation in 1784, concluding that there was no evidence of animal magnetism and that the effects of mesmerism were attributable to the power of suggestion and the subjects' active imagination. Mesmer, discredited, moved to Switzerland, where he lived out his life in obscurity. In 1842 the English surgeon James Braid (1795–1860) used mesmerism in his practice as an anesthetic and concluded that it induced a sleeplike state. He renamed mesmerism *hypnotism*, from Hypnos, the Greek god of sleep.

Hypnotic Induction and Susceptibility

How do hypnotists induce a hypnotic state? The process depends less on the skill of the hypnotist than on the susceptibility of the subject. Highly hypnotizable people have more-active fantasy lives and the ability to vividly imagine things suggested to them (Wallace & Kokoszka, 1995). They have a capacity for absorption in what they are doing, whether reading a book, playing a sport, listening to music, or holding a conversation.

Psychologists have developed tests of hypnotizability, such as the Stanford Hypnotic Susceptibility Scale (Weitzenhoffer & Hilgard, 1962). These tests determine the extent to which subjects will comply with hypnotic suggestions after a brief hypnotic induction. A

simple suggestion, to test for some susceptibility, might direct you to hold your hands in front of you and move them apart. A more difficult suggestion, to test for high susceptibility, might direct you to produce handwriting similar to that of a child. Regardless of their susceptibility, people cannot be hypnotized against their will (Lynn, Rhue, & Weekes, 1990).

The aim of hypnotic induction is to create a relaxed, passive, highly focused state of mind. During hypnotic induction the hypnotist might have you focus your eyes on a spot on the ceiling. The hypnotist might then suggest that you notice your eyelids closing, feet warming, muscles relaxing, and breathing slowing—events that would take place even without hypnotic suggestions. You would gradually relinquish more and more control of your perceptions, thoughts, and behaviors to the hypnotist.

Effects of Hypnosis: "Follow My Suggestions"

Many extreme claims about remarkable physical effects of hypnosis have been discredited by experimental research. Perhaps you have heard the claim that hypnotized people who are given the suggestion that their hand has touched red-hot metal will develop a blister—a claim first made two centuries ago (Gauld, 1990). Experiments have shown that such hypnotic suggestions can, at best, merely promote warming of the skin by increasing the flow of blood to it (Spanos, McNeil, & Stam, 1982). Nonetheless, research has demonstrated a variety of impressive perceptual, cognitive, and behavioral effects of hypnosis.

Perceptual Effects of Hypnosis

Stage hypnotists commonly use hypnosis to induce alterations in perception, such as convincing subjects that a vial of water is actually ammonia. The subjects will jerk their heads away after smelling it. But the most important perceptual effect of hypnosis is in pain relief. In the mid nineteenth century, the Scottish surgeon James Esdaile (1808–1859) used hypnosis to induce anesthesia in more than three hundred patients undergoing surgery for the removal of limbs, tumors, or cataracts (Ellenberger, 1970).

Research has supported the effectiveness of hypnotically induced pain relief (Hargadon, Bowers, & Woody, 1995). But how does hypnosis produce its analgesic effects? As discussed in Chapter 5, one way is by using suggestions that help distract sufferers from their pain (Farthing, Venturino, & Brown, 1984). A second way is by sending neural impulses from the brain down the spinal cord, which block the transmission of pain impulses from the body to the spinal cord (Holroyd, 1996). This is in keeping with the gate-control theory of pain (see Chapter 5).

Cognitive Effects of Hypnosis

In 1976, 26 elementary school children and their bus driver were kidnapped in Chowchilla, California, and imprisoned in a buried tractor trailer. The bus driver and two of the children dug their way out and got help. The driver, Frank Ray, had seen the license plate number of the kidnappers' van but was unable to recall it. After being hypnotized and told to imagine himself watching the kidnapping unfold on television, he was able to recall all but one of the digits of the number. This enabled the police to track down the kidnappers (M.C. Smith, 1983).

The Chowchilla case was a widely publicized example of one of the chief cognitive applications of hypnosis—**hypermnesia,** the enhancement of memory. Though many memories retrieved by hypnosis are accurate (Ewin, 1994), hypnosis can also create inaccurate memories, or *pseudomemories* (Spanos & Bures, 1993–1994). Concerns about the possible negative effects of pseudomemories go back to an 1846 murder case in which hypnotically enhanced testimony was admitted in an American court of law. That was also the first time experts testified on the possible unreliability of memory in regard to eyewitness memories (Gravitz, 1995).

One problem is that hypnotized eyewitnesses feel more confident about the memories they recall under hypnosis—regardless of their accuracy (Weekes et al., 1992). In one study, 27 subjects were hypnotized and then given the suggestion that they had been awakened by a loud noise one night during the preceding week. Later, after leaving the hypnotized state, 13 of the subjects claimed that the suggested event had actually occurred. Even after being informed of the hypnotic suggestion, 6 subjects still insisted that they had been awakened by the noise (Laurence & Perry, 1983).

This indicates the potential danger of hypnotically enhanced eyewitness testimony, particularly because juries put more trust in confident eyewitnesses (Sheehan & Tilden, 1983) and hypnotized eyewitnesses (Wagstaff, Vella, & Perfect, 1992). Yet the U.S. Supreme Court has opposed legislation that would eliminate hypnosis-induced hypermnesia in the courtroom, recommending instead that the admissibility of such testimony be determined on a trial-by-trial basis (Watkins, 1989). This makes it essential that psychologists try to discover the factors that determine when hypnotically enhanced memories are accurate and when they are not (McConkey, 1995).

Behavioral Effects of Hypnosis

Hypnosis is effective in treating physical and psychological disorders. For example, hypnosis has helped individuals recuperate after surgery (Blankfield, 1991) and continue to lose weight after treatment for obesity (Kirsch 1996). Hypnotherapists make use of **posthypnotic suggestions,** which are suggestions for subjects to carry out certain behaviors in response to particular stimuli after leaving the hypnosis setting. In one study, posthypnotic suggestions helped collegiate fencers reduce their performance anxiety (Wojcikiewicz & Orlick, 1987).

Though hypnosis can help some people, a century-long debate (Liegois, 1899) has raged about whether hypnosis can be used to induce harmful behavior. Martin Orne and Frederick Evans (1965) demonstrated that hypnotized subjects could be induced to commit dangerous acts. Their study included a group of hypnotized subjects and a group of subjects who simulated being hypnotized. When instructed to do so, subjects in *both* groups plunged their hands into what they were told was a nitric acid solution, threw the liquid in another person's face, and tried to handle a poisonous snake. Of course, the experimenters protected the participants (by immediately washing off the liquid, by actually having them throw water instead of acid, and by stopping them from touching the snake). Because both groups engaged in dangerous acts, the research setting, rather than hypnosis, might have accounted for the results. In any case, there is no evidence that hypnotized subjects become mindless zombies who blindly obey orders to commit harmful acts (Gibson, 1991).

Similarly, some of the effects of stage hypnosis might have less to do with hypnosis than with the setting in which they occur. For example, you might have seen a stage hypnotist direct a hypnotized audience volunteer to remain as rigid as a plank while lying

---

hypermnesia

The hypnotic enhancement of recall.

posthypnotic suggestions

Suggestions directing subjects to carry out particular behaviors or to have particular experiences after leaving hypnosis.

CHAPTER 6

extended between two chairs. But highly motivated, nonhypnotized persons can also perform this "human plank" trick. According to researcher Theodore Barber, even the willingness of hypnotized subjects to obey suggestions to engage in bizarre behaviors, such as clucking like a chicken, might be more attributable to the theatrical "anything goes" atmosphere of stage hypnosis than to the effect of hypnosis itself (Meeker & Barber, 1971). You will appreciate this if you have ever watched contestants on television game shows engage in wacky antics—without their being hypnotized.

The Nature of Hypnosis

In the late nineteenth century, most notably in France, practitioners of hypnosis disagreed whether hypnosis induced an altered, or *trance*, state of consciousness. One group argued that hypnosis induces a trancelike state called **dissociation,** in which parts of the mind become separated from one another and form independent streams of consciousness. This is similar to the practice of many distance runners, who use dissociation to divorce their conscious minds from possibly distressing bodily sensations while still remaining consciously aware of the racecourse ahead of them (Masters, 1992). Another group of French hypnotists argued that hypnosis does not induce a trance state. Instead, they insisted that it just induces a state of heightened suggestibility. This debate lingers on; some researchers view hypnosis as an altered state of consciousness, and others view it as a normal state of waking consciousness.

dissociation
A state in which the mind is split into two or more independent streams of consciousness.

Hypnosis as an Altered State of Consciousness

Today, the main theory of hypnosis as an altered state is the **neodissociation theory.** This theory originated in a classroom demonstration of hypnotically induced deafness by Ernest Hilgard, who directed a hypnotized blind student to raise an index finger if he heard a sound. When blocks were banged near his head, the student did not even flinch. But when asked if some part of his mind had actually heard the noise, his finger rose. Hilgard called this part of the mind the **hidden observer** (Hilgard, 1978). Hilgard helped make hypnosis scientifically legitimate when he founded his laboratory for hypnosis research at Stanford University in 1957 (Bowers, 1994).

Hilgard has used the concept of the hidden observer to explain hypnotically induced pain relief. He relies on the *cold pressor test,* in which subjects submerge an arm in ice water and are asked every few seconds to estimate their degree of pain. Though hypnotized subjects who are told that they will feel less pain report that they feel little or no pain, the hidden observer, when asked, reports that it has experienced intense pain (Hilgard, 1973).

neodissociation theory
The theory that hypnosis induces a dissociated state of consciousness.

hidden observer
Ernest Hilgard's term for the part of the hypnotized person's consciousness that is not under the control of the hypnotist but is aware of what is taking place.

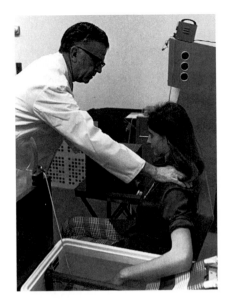

▲ The Hidden Observer
Ernest Hilgard uses the cold pressor test to evaluate the ability of hypnosis to prevent the pain that normally accompanies having an arm immersed in ice water. Though the subject might report little or no pain, the "hidden observer" might report severe pain. The results of the study by Spanos and Hewitt (1980) indicate that the "hidden observer" is not an objective observer but, instead, will report whatever it has been told to expect.

age regression
A hypnotic state in which the individual apparently behaves as she or he did as a child.

Additional evidence in favor of hypnosis as an altered state comes from experiments in which hypnotized subjects experience physiological changes in response to hypnotic suggestions. In one study, hypnotized subjects were given the suggestion that their view of an image on a television screen was blocked by a box. The pattern of electrical activity recorded from their occipital lobes (the site of visual processing in the brain) was similar to what would occur if their view had been blocked by a real box. This indicated that the hypnotic suggestion affected highly specific visual processing in the brain (Spiegel et al., 1985), which is difficult to attribute to mere suggestibility.

A more recent study demonstrated similar findings. Highly hypnotizable subjects learned lists of words and were given posthypnotic suggestions to forget them. Those who reported *posthypnotic amnesia* (their inability to recognize the words they had read) showed changes in components of their brain-wave patterns that are related to attention and recognition. This, again, seems to indicate that posthypnotic amnesia is more than a state of heightened suggestibility (Allen et al., 1995). Research studies also have found distinctive differences in the brain-wave patterns of those who are highly susceptible to hypnosis and those who are not, as well as in the brain-wave patterns of normal waking subjects and hypnotized subjects (Graffin, Ray, & Lundy, 1995; Sabourin et al., 1990–1991).

Hypnosis as a Normal State of Consciousness

The claim that hypnosis is an altered state of consciousness has not gone unchallenged. Critics insist that hypnotically induced effects are only responses to personal factors, such as the subject's motivation, and situational factors, such as the hypnotist's wording of suggestions. By arranging the right combination of factors, the hypnotist increases the likelihood that the subject will comply with hypnotic suggestions (Spanos, Burgess, & Perlini, 1991–1992). Consider the following experiment conducted by Nicholas Spanos and Erin Hewitt (1980) of Carleton University in Ottawa, in which the hidden observer was made to give contradictory reports, depending on the hypnotist's suggestions.

The experiment used undergraduate subjects who scored high on a hypnotizability scale and were then given suggestions for hypnotic analgesia. Two groups of subjects were given contradictory suggestions. One group was told that the hypnotized part of their minds would have little awareness of the pain, while a hidden part would be more aware of the actual intensity of the pain. Another group was told that the hypnotized part of their minds would have little awareness of the pain, while a hidden part would be even less aware of the pain. The subjects were asked to place a forearm in ice water, which induces pain. They were told to have the hypnotized parts of their minds state their level of pain on a scale from 0 to 20 every 5 seconds for 60 seconds. They also were told to hold a forearm in ice water while having their "hidden self" report their level of pain (from 0 to 20) by tapping out a simple code on a response key every 5 seconds for 60 seconds.

When asked to report the intensity of the pain, the hidden observer reported what the subjects had been led to expect. It experienced more pain than the hypnotized part when told it would be more aware and less pain when told it would be less aware. The results are presented in Figure 6.6. Thus, the hidden observer might simply be a result of the subject's willingness to act as though he or she has experienced suggested hypnotic effects. Spanos has found that this is not a case of faking, but probably reflects the well-established ability of subjects to distract themselves from their pain. Moreover, the hidden observer never appears spontaneously—it appears only when explicitly asked to. This study, as well as others by Spanos, indicates that the hidden observer is a product not of the dissociation of consciousness, but, instead, of the subject's willingness to follow the hypnotist's suggestions.

Evidence that hypnosis is a state of heightened suggestibility has also come from studies of hypnotic **age regression,** in which hypnotized subjects are told to return to childhood. A hypnotized adult might use baby talk or play with an imaginary teddy bear. But a published review of research on hypnotic age regression found that subjects do not adopt the true mental, behavioral, and physiological characteristics of children; they just act as though they were children (Nash, 1987). For example, in a classic study, Martin Orne (1951) hypnotized college students and suggested that they regress back to their sixth birthday party. He then asked them to describe the people and activities at the party, which they did in

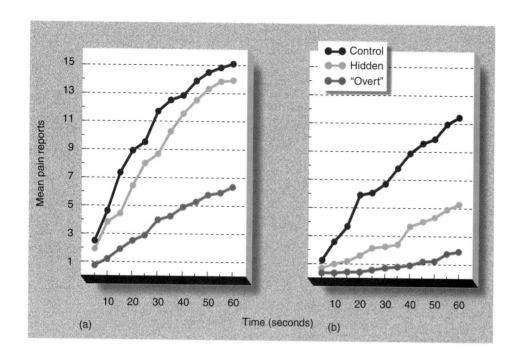

Pain Reports by the Hidden Observer
These two graphs show that the "hidden observer" might merely be the product of hypnotic suggestion, rather than an objective perceiver of reality. (*a*) When told that it will be more aware, the "hidden observer" reports more pain. (*b*) When told that it will be less aware, the "hidden observer" reports less pain.

great detail. When Orne asked the subjects' parents to describe the same birthday party, he found that many of the subjects' "memories" had been fabrications. They reported people and events they presumed would have been at their own sixth birthday party. There was no evidence that they actually reexperienced their sixth birthday party.

Neither side in the debate about the nature of hypnosis has provided sufficient evidence to discount the other side completely. As noted by William James a century ago, both sides might be correct: Hypnosis might be a dissociated state of consciousness that can be shaped by the social context and hypnotic suggestions (Kihlstrom & McConkey, 1990). Today, moreover, hypnosis researchers are less likely to make sharp distinctions between hypnosis as an altered state and hypnosis as a normal state (Kirsch & Lynn, 1995).

STAYING ON TRACK: *Hypnosis*

1. How would you induce a state of hypnosis?
2. What are the benefits and risks of using hypnosis in enhancing the recall of memories?
3. Why do some researchers believe that hypnosis is not an altered state of consciousness?

MEDITATION

Meditation is a procedure that uses mental exercises to achieve a tranquil, highly focused state of consciousness. Traditionally, meditation has been a religious practice aimed at reaching a mystical union with God or the universe. All major religions, including Buddhism, Christianity, Hinduism, Islam, Judaism, and Taoism, include centuries-old formal meditative practices. Since the 1960s, meditation has also gained popularity in North America as a means—often divorced from its religious context—of promoting physical and psychological well-being by reducing stress and inducing relaxation (Kelly, 1996).

Common Meditative Practices: Calming the Mind

The popular forms of meditation share techniques aimed at producing physical relaxation and mental concentration. If you decided to meditate, you would seek a peaceful setting, maintain a comfortable seated position, focus on a sound, an image, an object, or your breathing, and calmly withdraw your attention from any intruding images, feelings, or

meditation
A procedure that uses mental exercises to achieve a highly focused state of consciousness.

The Relaxation Response
Oxygen consumption (blue line) and carbon dioxide elimination (green line) decrease during transcendental meditation. Both of these physiological changes are signs of relaxation.

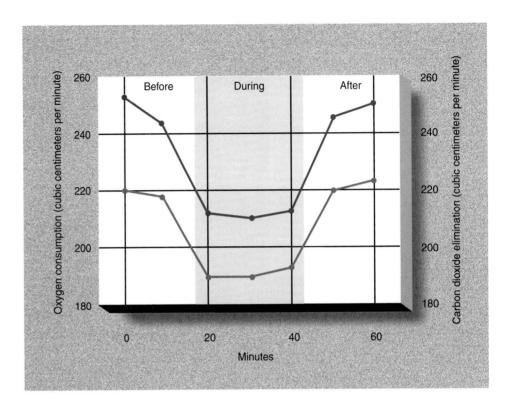

transcendental meditation (TM)
A form of meditation in which the individual relaxes and repeats a sound called a mantra for two 20-minute periods a day.

relaxation response
A variation of transcendental meditation in which the individual may repeat a sound other than a mantra.

▲ **Meditation**
Through meditation, athletes can reduce their mental and physical arousal to help alleviate their precompetitive anxiety.

sensations. Though some forms of meditation promote opening the mind by emptying it of content, popular forms usually involve focusing the mind on one thing.

Meditation was popularized in the West in the late 1960s by Maharishi Mahesh Yogi, an Indian guru, through the influence of his most famous disciples, the Beatles. They promoted a Westernized form of meditation called **transcendental meditation (TM).** In TM, you concentrate on repeating a sound called a mantra (a Sanskrit word such as *Om*) for two 20-minute periods a day. The alternation of *Om* and silence is presumed to represent fulfillment. In the early 1970s, cardiologist Herbert Benson introduced the **relaxation response,** a form of meditation that is identical to TM except that the meditator may mentally repeat a sound other than a mantra, such as the number one or a favorite brief prayer.

Physical and Psychological Effects of Meditation

Benson has promoted meditation as a technique that induces a unique state of physical and mental relaxation by increasing alpha brain waves and decreasing heart rate, respiration rate, oxygen consumption, and carbon dioxide expiration (Wallace & Benson, 1972). (The immediate effects of meditation on physiological arousal are presented in Figure 6.7.) Benson's claim that meditation induces a unique physiological state has not gone unchallenged. For example, some research studies indicate that there is no difference in physiological arousal between subjects who meditate and subjects who merely rest (Holmes, 1984). But other research studies have found that meditation produces a greater reduction in physiological arousal than merely resting does (Alexander et al., 1994). Thus, it remains to be determined under what conditions meditation is, or is not, superior to merely resting in reducing arousal.

Whether or not meditation induces a unique physiological or psychological state, it can produce beneficial physiological and psychological effects. In a recent study (Benson et al., 1994), Benson compared high school students who practiced the relaxation response as part of a wellness curriculum to those who did not. Those who practiced it developed higher self-esteem and a greater sense of control over their lives. Meditation has also proved effective in overcoming insomnia (Jacobs et al., 1993), preventing smoking (Alexander, Robinson, & Rainforth, 1994), and enhancing one's happiness (Smith, Compton, & West, 1995).

1. How would you practice the relaxation response?
2. Why is there controversy over whether meditation induces a unique physiological state?

PSYCHOACTIVE DRUGS

Normal waking consciousness can also be altered by **psychoactive drugs,** which are chemicals that induce changes in mood, thinking, perception, and behavior by affecting neuronal activity. Human beings seem drawn to psychoactive drugs. Many people imbibe beer to reduce social anxiety, take barbiturates to fall asleep, use narcotics to feel euphoric, drink coffee to get going in the morning, or smoke marijuana to enrich their perception of music.

Psychoactive drugs exert their effects by altering synaptic transmission, by either promoting or inhibiting it. But the effects of psychoactive drugs depend on a host of factors. These include their dosage, the user's experience with them, the user's expectations about their effects, and the setting in which they are taken. Individuals typically take their psychoactive drugs by smoking, inhaling, injecting, or swallowing them.

All psychoactive drugs can cause *psychological dependence*—an intense desire to achieve the intoxicated state induced by the drug. Most psychoactive drugs also can cause *physical dependence* (or *addiction*). This means that after people use the drug for a period of time they develop a physiological need for the drug. As people use physically addicting drugs, they develop *tolerance*—a decrease in physiological responsiveness to the drug. As a result, they require increasingly higher doses to achieve the desired effect.

When addicted people stop taking the drug they are addicted to, they experience *withdrawal symptoms*. The pattern and severity of withdrawal symptoms is specific to the kind of drug to which the person is addicted. Common withdrawal symptoms include craving, chills, headache, fatigue, nausea, insomnia, depression, convulsions, and irritability. As shown in Table 6.1, the psychoactive drugs can be divided into three general categories: *depressants, stimulants,* and *hallucinogens*.

Depressants

Depressants reduce arousal by inhibiting activity in the central nervous system. This section discusses several kinds of depressants: *alcohol, barbiturates,* and *opiates*.

Alcohol: Releaser of Inhibitions

Ethyl alcohol, an addictive drug, has been used—and abused—for thousands of years. Even the ancient Romans had to pass laws against drunk driving—of chariots (Whitlock, 1987). Today, in the United States a person with a blood alcohol level of 0.10 percent is considered legally drunk. Canadian provinces are even stricter, setting the limit at 0.08 percent. Drunk drivers are dangerous because they suffer from impaired judgment, perceptual distortions, and motor incoordination. Alcohol is involved in 50 percent of traffic accidents in the United States (Matthews et al., 1996). Alcohol facilitates the actions of the neurotransmitter GABA, which inhibits neuronal transmission in the brain (Korpi, 1994). Given that the typical person metabolizes about one ounce of alcohol an hour, a person who drinks faster than that will become intoxicated. Men metabolize alcohol more efficiently than women do, so a woman might become intoxicated on less alcohol than it would take to intoxicate a man (Frezza et al., 1990).

You have probably seen proper people become sexually indiscriminate, meek people become verbally or physically aggressive, and shy people become the life of the party after a few drinks. Alcohol researcher Claude Steele attributes this to what he calls "alcohol myopia," the inability of intoxicated persons to foresee the negative consequences of their actions and to inhibit behaviors that would normally be inhibited when they are sober. This makes behaviors—both positive and negative—more extreme (Steele & Josephs,

psychoactive drugs
Chemicals that induce changes in mood, thinking, perception, and behavior by affecting neuronal activity in the brain.

depressants
Psychoactive drugs that inhibit activity in the central nervous system.

ethyl alcohol
A depressant found in beverages and commonly used to reduce social inhibitions.

▲ **Claude Steele**
"Sixty-five percent of murders, 88 percent of knifings, 65 percent of spouse beatings, and 55 percent of physical child abuse involve intoxicated participants."

Depressants		
Alcohol	Removes social inhibitions Relieves anxiety Induces sleep Impairs judgment Causes disorientation
Barbiturates	Remove social inhibitions Relieve anxiety Induce sleep Impair judgment Cause disorientation
Inhalants	Create detachment from immediate environment Cause disorientation
Opiates	Induce feelings of euphoria Relieve pain Induce sleep

Stimulants		
Caffeine	Stimulates alertness Promotes wakefulness
Nicotine	Stimulates alertness Relieves anxiety
Amphetamines	Stimulate alertness Promote wakefulness and insomnia Create an overblown sense of confidence Induce feelings of elation May cause symptoms of paranoia
Cocaine	Induces feelings of euphoria Creates an overblown sense of confidence

Hallucinogens		
LSD	Causes visual hallucinations Creates a sense of oneness and timelessness Induces seemingly mystical insights
Cannabis sativa	Induces relaxation Removes social inhibitions Intensifies sensory experience Interferes with memory formation

▲ TABLE 6.1
Psychoactive Drugs

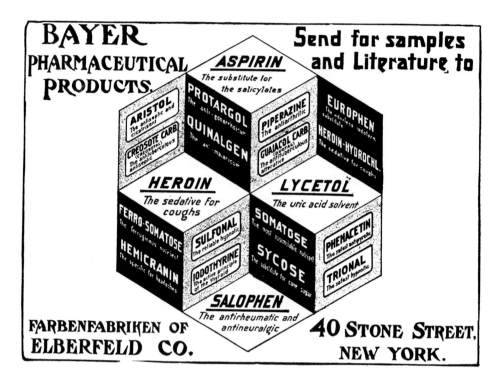

1990). Moreover, because we are aware of alcohol's reputation for removing social inhibitions, we might use it as an excuse for engaging in socially questionable behaviors, such as casual sex (Hull & Bond, 1986). We can then blame our behavior on the alcohol, lessening our guilt and embarrassment.

Barbiturates: Sleeping Pills

Barbiturates are derived from barbituric acid. They produce effects similar to those of alcohol and, likewise, work by facilitating the actions of GABA (Yu & Ho, 1990). The barbiturate Seconal, which acts quickly to induce drowsiness, is used as a sleeping pill. The barbiturate Pentothal is used as a general anesthetic in surgery. Because mild doses of Pentothal induce a drunken, uninhibited state in which the intoxicated person is more willing to reveal private thoughts and feelings, it is popularly known as "truth serum," though it does not guarantee that the information revealed will be true.

barbiturates
Depressants used to induce sleep or anesthesia.

Opiates: Addictive Pain Relievers

The opium poppy is the source of **opiates,** which include opium, morphine, heroin, and codeine. The opiates have been prized since ancient times for their ability to relieve pain and to induce euphoria. Sumerian clay tablets from about 4000 B.C. refer to the opium poppy as "the plant of joy" (Whitlock, 1987). Some nineteenth-century artists and writers used opiates to induce altered states of consciousness. Samuel Taylor Coleridge wrote his famous poem "Kubla Khan" under the influence of opium.

In the early 1860s, physicians used *morphine*, the main active ingredient in opium, to ease the pain of wounded soldiers in the American Civil War. Morphine was named after Morpheus, the Greek god of dreams, because it induces a state of blissful oblivion. In 1898 scientists used opium to derive a more potent drug—*heroin*. Heroin was named after the Greek god Hero, because it was welcomed as a powerful painkiller and cure for morphine addiction. But physicians soon found that heroin simply replaced morphine addiction with heroin addiction. By the early twentieth century, so many Americans had become addicted to opiates that in 1914 Congress passed the Harrison Narcotic Act banning their nonmedical use. Today, morphine, codeine, and the synthetic opiate Demerol are routinely prescribed to relieve severe pain. The euphoric and pain-relieving effects of the opiates are caused by their binding to endorphin receptors, which act to block pain impulses and stimulate the brain's pleasure centers (Levinthal, 1988).

opiates
Depressant drugs, derived from opium, used to relieve pain or to induce a euphoric state of consciousness.

▲ **Cocaine and Coca-Cola**
This late-nineteenth-century advertisement indicates that Coca-Cola was a popular stimulant, which was also cheap, legal, and easily obtained.

Stimulants

Whereas depressant drugs reduce arousal, stimulant drugs increase it. **Stimulants** include *caffeine*, *nicotine*, *amphetamines*, and *cocaine*.

Caffeine: A Mental Pick-Me-Up

Few North Americans go a day without ingesting the addictive drug **caffeine,** which is found in a variety of products, including coffee, tea, soft drinks, chocolate, cold pills, diet pills, and stimulant tablets. The mind-altering effects of caffeine have made it a popular drug for centuries. Chocolate, for example, was considered a gift from the gods by the Aztecs of Mexico, who drank cocoa during their religious rituals. In the late nineteenth century, Americans' use of coffee accelerated after the introduction of the first commercial mix of coffee beans at a Nashville hotel called Maxwell House (Ray, 1983).

Today caffeine is a popular means of maintaining mental alertness, apparently by stimulating the release of the excitatory neurotransmitter glutamate (Silinsky, 1989). But it is important to note that the belief that a cup of coffee will help a drunken person sober up enough to drive home is a folk myth—though it can, to an extent, improve the person's cognitive performance (Hasenfratz et al., 1993). Unfortunately, caffeine's ability to enhance mental arousal can interfere with nightly sleep, even if the coffee is ingested only early in the day (Landolt et al., 1995). Because of its ability to increase alertness, caffeine is beneficial to night-shift workers. In one study, workers received either caffeinated or decaffeinated coffee for several nights during a simulated 8.5-hour night shift. The results showed that the caffeine group had decreased sleepiness and enhanced performance on an assembly-line task (Muehlbach & Walsh, 1995). If you are a habitual caffeine user and suddenly stop using it, you will find that caffeine withdrawal is marked by headaches and drowsiness (Hughes et al., 1991).

Nicotine: The Smoking Scourge

"If you can't send money, send tobacco" read a 1776 appeal from General George Washington (Ray, 1983). Washington's troops actually craved **nicotine,** a powerful addictive drug contained in tobacco. Nicotine works by stimulating certain acetylcholine receptors, which might increase the efficiency of information processing in the brain (Pritchard et al., 1995), a point not lost on students who smoke.

The addictiveness of nicotine is comparable to that of cocaine, heroin, and alcohol (Stolerman & Jarvis, 1995). But why is it that some people get quickly addicted to nicotine, others smoke only occasionally, and still others avoid it totally? There seems to be a genetic basis for this variability. The more responsive users are to nicotine, the more quickly they develop tolerance and become dependent on it (Pomerleau, 1995). You can read more about smoking in Chapter 16.

Amphetamines: The Speed Trap

Amphetamines—including Benzedrine, Dexedrine, and Methedrine—are addictive synthetic stimulant drugs that are popularly known as "speed" and are more powerful than caffeine and nicotine. They exert their effects by stimulating the release of dopamine and norepinephrine and inhibiting their re-uptake by the neurons that secrete them. In the 1930s, truck drivers discovered that amphetamines would keep them alert during long hauls, letting them drive for many hours without sleeping. For several decades college students have used amphetamines to stay awake while cramming for final exams. Amphetamines were even used during Operation Desert Storm by the U.S. Air Force Tactical Air Command to stay alert during the Persian Gulf War against Iraq (Emonson & Vanderbeek, 1995). Because amphetamines also suppress appetite and increase the basal metabolic rate, they are commonly used as diet pills. But chronic users might also experience "amphetamine psychosis," marked by extreme suspiciousness and, sometimes, violent responses to imagined threats (Kokkinidis & Anisman, 1980).

Cocaine: Euphoria at a Price

During the 1980s, **cocaine,** an extract from the coca leaf, became the stimulant drug of choice for those who desired the brief but intense feeling of exhilaration and self-confidence

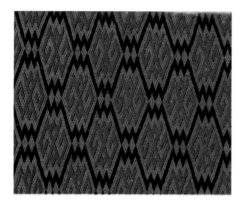

that it induces. Cocaine prevents the re-uptake of dopamine and norepinephrine by the neurons that secrete them (Gawin, 1991) and by facilitating activity at serotonin synapses (Aronson et al., 1995). Users snort cocaine in powdered form, smoke it in crystal form ("crack"), or inject it in solution form.

People of the Andes have chewed coca leaves for more than a thousand years to induce euphoric feelings and to combat fatigue. In the nineteenth century, Sir Arthur Conan Doyle made his fictional character Sherlock Holmes a cocaine user. And Robert Louis Stevenson relied on cocaine to stay alert while taking just 6 days to write two drafts of *The Strange Case of Dr. Jekyll and Mr. Hyde*. In 1886 an Atlanta druggist named John Pemberton contributed to cocaine's popularity by introducing a stimulant soft drink that contained both caffeine and cocaine, which he named Coca-Cola.

Unfortunately, cocaine causes harmful side effects, as discovered by Sigmund Freud, who used it himself. In the 1880s, Freud praised cocaine as a wonder drug for combatting depression, inducing local anesthesia, relieving asthmatic symptoms, and curing opiate addiction. But Freud stopped using and prescribing cocaine after discovering its ability to cause addiction, paranoia, and hallucinations (Freud, 1974). In the early twentieth century, the dangers of cocaine use also led to its removal as an ingredient in Coca-Cola. Cocaine can stimulate the heart (Foltin, Fischman, & Levin, 1995), which may account for instances of sudden death in persons with cardiac dysfunctions.

Hallucinogens

The **hallucinogens** induce extreme alterations in consciousness. Users might experience visual hallucinations, a sense of timelessness, and feelings of depersonalization. It has been difficult to determine whether adverse personality changes associated with hallucinogens are caused mainly by the powerful effects of the drugs or by the tendency of people with psychological instability to use them (Strassman, 1984). The hallucinogens can induce psychological dependence, but there is little evidence that they can induce physical dependence. They exert their effects primarily by affecting serotonin neurons, stimulating some and inhibiting others (Glennon, 1990). The most commonly used hallucinogens include *psilocybin*, a chemical present in certain mushrooms, *mescaline*, a chemical in the peyote cactus, and *phencyclidine*, a synthetic drug better known as "PCP" or "angel dust." But perhaps the best known hallucinogens are *LSD* and *cannabis sativa*.

LSD: The Acid Trip

On April 19, 1943, Albert Hofmann, director of research for the Sandoz drug company in Switzerland, accidentally experienced the effects of a microscopic amount of the chemical lysergic acid diethylamide **(LSD).** He evidently absorbed it through his skin. Hofmann reported that he felt as though he was losing his mind: "in a twilight state with my eyes closed . . . I found a continuous stream of fantastic images of extraordinary vividness and intensive kaleidoscopic colours" (Julien, 1981, p. 151). Hofmann found it a horrifying experience. Because many people in the 1960s and 1970s used LSD recklessly, Hofmann (1983) titled his autobiography *LSD: My Problem Child*.

▲ **Hallucinogens**
The geometric designs in these weavings by the Huichol Indians of Mexico were inspired by visual hallucinations induced by the ingestion of peyote, a cactus that contains the hallucinogen mescaline. LSD and other powerful hallucinogens can induce similar effects.

hallucinogens
Psychoactive drugs that induce extreme alterations in consciousness, including visual hallucinations, a sense of timelessness, and feelings of depersonalization.

LSD
A hallucinogen derived from a fungus that grows on rye grain.

▲ **Albert Hofmann**
"Now, little by little I could begin to enjoy the unprecedented colors and plays of shapes that persisted behind my closed eyes. Kaleidoscopic, fantastic images surged in on me, alternating, variegated, opening and then closing themselves in circles and spirals, exploding in colored fountains, rearranging and hybridizing themselves in constant flux."

synesthesia

The process in which an individual experiences sensations in one sensory modality that are characteristic of another.

LSD seems to exert its effects by affecting brain receptors for serotonin, most likely by inhibiting their activity (Aghajanian, 1994). A dose of LSD induces a "trip" that lasts up to 12 hours. The trip includes visual hallucinations, such as shifting patterns of colors, changes in the shapes of objects, and distortions in the sizes of body parts. Even **synesthesia** is possible. This phenomenon occurs when stimulation of sensory receptors triggers sensory experiences that characterize another sense (Cytowic, 1989). Thus, someone on an LSD trip while listening to music might report seeing the notes as different colors. Users of LSD might also report a sense of timelessness, a feeling of oneness with the universe, and, at times, mystical insights into the meaning of life.

The effects of LSD are so powerful that users can have "bad trips," in which the alteration in their consciousness is so disturbing that it induces feelings of panic (Miller & Gold, 1994). People with unstable personalities, who are not told what to expect, and who are in stressful circumstances, are more likely to have a "bad trip" (McWilliams & Tuttle, 1973). Hofmann (1983), appalled by the indiscriminate use of LSD and the psychological harm it might do, questioned whether the human mind should be subjected to such extreme alteration. After all, the brain evolved to help us function by letting us perceive reality in a particular way, unaffected by hallucinogens like LSD.

Cannabis Sativa: *Marijuana and Its Relatives*

cannabis sativa

A hallucinogen derived from the hemp plant and ingested in the form of marijuana or hashish.

The most widely used hallucinogenic drug is tetrahydrocannabinol (THC), present in the hemp plant **cannabis sativa.** Hemp fibers have traditionally been used in rope making. Hemp has also been popular for two of its other products: *marijuana* and the more potent *hashish*, which many people smoke to induce an altered state of consciousness. Marijuana is a combination of the crushed stems, leaves, and flowers of the plant, and hashish is its dried resin. Marijuana and hashish exert their effects by stimulating THC receptors in the brain (Herkenhahn et al., 1991).

Marijuana has been used for thousands of years as a painkiller; the earliest reference to that use is in a Chinese herbal medicine book from 2737 B.C. (Julien, 1981). In the nineteenth century, marijuana was a popular remedy for the pain of headache, toothache, and stomachache. Today most marijuana smokers use it for its mind-altering effects, which are related to its concentration of THC. Moderately potent marijuana makes time seem to pass more slowly and induces rich sensory experiences, in which music seems fuller and colors seem more vivid. Highly potent marijuana induces visual hallucinations, in which objects may appear to change their size and shape.

In 1937, after centuries of unregulated use, marijuana was outlawed in the United States because of claims that it induced bouts of wild sexual and aggressive behavior. Contrary to its popularity as an alleged aphrodisiac, marijuana at best causes disinhibition of the sex drive, which itself might be a placebo effect caused by its reputation as an aphrodisiac (Powell & Fuller, 1983). Moreover, marijuana does not promote aggression and might even inhibit it (Myerscough & Taylor, 1985).

But it would be unwise to drive or to operate machinery while under the influence of marijuana—or any other psychoactive drug. This is because marijuana impairs coordination (Navarro et al., 1993) and the ability to concentrate on tasks without being distracted (Solowij, Michie, & Fox, 1995). And marijuana can disrupt memory formation (Smith, 1995). This finding should be of special concern to students who combine their studies with marijuana smoking. Marijuana smokers may also exhibit *amotivational syndrome* (Nelson, 1995), in which they prefer doing nothing rather than working or studying. But this raises the issue of causation versus correlation. That is, though marijuana smoking might produce the syndrome, it is just as logical to assume that unmotivated people are drawn to marijuana.

STAYING ON TRACK: *Psychoactive Drugs*

1. What are the symptoms of physical dependency on drugs?
2. What are the effects and side effects of cocaine?
3. What are the effects and side effects of marijuana smoking?

| CHAPTER 6

THINKING ABOUT *Psychology*

Are We Affected by Unconscious Influences?

In the late nineteenth century, William James (1890/1981), in his classic psychology textbook, included a section entitled "Can States of Mind Be Unconscious?" which presented ten arguments answering yes and ten answering no. Today the extent to which we are affected by unconscious influences still provokes animated debate. But the notion of the unconscious involves any of three different concepts: (1) *perception without awareness*, the unconscious perception of stimuli that exceed our normal absolute threshold but that fall outside our focus of attention; (2) *subliminal perception*, the unconscious perception of stimuli that are too weak to exceed the absolute threshold for detection; and (3) the *Freudian unconscious*, a region of the mind containing thoughts and feelings that motivate us without our awareness.

PERCEPTION WITHOUT AWARENESS: WHEN DID I LEARN THAT?

There is substantial evidence that we can be affected by stimuli that are above the normal absolute threshold but to which we are not attending at the time. At the turn of the century, the existence of such **perception without awareness** (Merikle, 1992) led some psychologists to assume that suggestions given to people while they sleep might help children study harder or adults quit smoking (Jones, 1900). But subsequent research has failed to support such sleep learning. Any learning that does take place apparently occurs during brief awakenings (Wood, Bootzin, Kihlstrom, & Schacter, 1992). So, if you decide to study for your next psychology exam by playing an audiotape of class lectures while you are asleep, you will be more likely to disrupt your sleep than to learn significant amounts of material. Though there is no evidence that we can form memories while asleep, there is some evidence that we can form unconscious memories while under general anesthesia during surgery (Kihlstrom & Couture, 1992).

Research on attention also has demonstrated the existence of perception without awareness. Consider studies of *dichotic listening*, in which the subject, wearing headphones, repeats—or "shadows"—a message being presented to one ear while another message is being presented to the other ear (Asbjornsen & Hugdahl, 1995). This is illustrated in Figure 6.8. By shadowing one message, the subject is prevented from consciously attending to the other one. Though subjects cannot recall the unattended message, they might recall certain qualities of it, such as whether it was spoken by a male voice or by a female voice. This demonstrates that our brain can process incoming stimuli that exceed the normal absolute threshold even when we do not consciously attend to them (Cherry, 1953).

Perception without awareness is also supported in studies of brain damage. Consider *prosopagnosia*, the inability to recognize faces. The disorder is caused by damage to a particular region of the cerebral cortex. In one study, two women with prosopagnosia were shown photographs of strangers, friends, and relatives while their galvanic skin response (a measure of arousal based on changes in the electrical activity of the skin) was recorded. Though the women were unable to recognize their friends and relatives from the photographs, they gave larger galvanic skin responses to those photographs than to the photographs of strangers. This indicated that intact visual pathways in the brain had distinguished between the familiar and the unfamiliar faces without the women's conscious awareness of it (Tranel & Damasio, 1985). This phenomenon of *blindsight* indicates that certain unknown retinal pathways process visual information without our conscious awareness (Weiskrantz, 1995).

Of course "awareness" is usually not an all-or-none phenomenon. For example, there is a continuum between *controlled processing* and *automatic processing* of information (Strayer

perception without awareness
The unconscious perception of stimuli that normally exceed the absolute threshold but fall outside our focus of attention.

controlled processing

Information processing that involves conscious awareness and mental effort, and that interferes with the performance of other ongoing activities.

automatic processing

Information processing that requires less conscious awareness and mental effort, and that does not interfere with the performance of other ongoing activities.

subliminal perception

The unconscious perception of stimuli that are too weak to exceed the absolute threshold for detection.

& Kramer, 1990). At one extreme, when we focus our attention on one target, we use **controlled processing,** which involves more conscious awareness (attention) and mental effort, and interferes with the performance of other activities. At the other extreme, when we do one thing while focusing our attention on another, we use **automatic processing,** which requires less conscious awareness and mental effort and does not interfere with the performance of other activities (Schneider & Shiffrin, 1977).

As we practice a task, we need to devote less and less attention to it because we move from controlled processing to automatic processing (Bargh, 1992). Think back to when you first learned to write in script. You depended on controlled processing, which required you to focus your complete attention on forming each letter. Today, after years of practice in writing, you make use of automatic processing. This lets you write notes in class while focusing your attention on the professor's lecture rather than on the movements of your pen.

Automatic processing can, at times, interfere with controlled processing. Consider the Stroop effect (named for its discoverer), illustrated in Figure 6.9. Time how long it takes you to read the words. Then time how long it takes you name the colors of the words. You probably performed the first task faster, presumably because of your extensive experience in reading. But the automaticity of reading words interfered with your ability to name the colors, a task that you are rarely called upon to do (Lindsay & Jacoby, 1994). Thus, even when you try to name the colors and ignore the words, automatic, unconscious processes make it difficult for you not to read the words.

SUBLIMINAL PERCEPTION: AN ADVERTISER'S DREAM?

Research on **subliminal perception** investigates whether subjects can unconsciously perceive stimuli that do not exceed the absolute threshold. In a recent study of subliminal perception conducted on BBC-TV in England, viewers saw a program of an adult playing with two infants. Those in western England saw the program by itself. Those in eastern England saw the program with a woman's smiling face inserted subliminally. Later, viewers were asked to judge the emotion in a neutral, expressionless face. Those who had been exposed to the subliminal smiling face judged the neutral face as more sad than did those who had not been exposed to the smiling face. This contrast effect was attributed

| PINK | RED | BLUE | GREEN | PINK | YELLOW | BLUE | GREEN |
| GREEN | BLUE | YELLOW | BLUE | GREEN | PINK | RED | BLUE |

to subliminal perception (Underwood, 1994). Nonetheless, some research studies have failed to support the existence of subliminal perception (Fox & Burns, 1993).

Assuming that we might be able to perceive subliminal stimuli, could manufacturers make us buy their products by bombarding us with subliminal advertisements? This is the heart of a controversy that arose in the late 1950s after a marketing firm subliminally flashed the words *Eat Popcorn* and *Drink Coca-Cola* during movies shown at a theater in Fort Lee, New Jersey. Though those watching the movies could not detect the messages, after several weeks of this subliminal advertising popcorn sales had increased 50 percent and Coke sales had increased 18 percent (McConnell, Cutter, & McNeil, 1958). Marketing executives expressed glee at this potential boon to advertising, but the public feared that subliminal perception might be used as a means of totalitarian mind control.

Psychologists, however, pointed out that the uncontrolled conditions of the study made it impossible to determine the actual reason for the increase in sales. Perhaps sales increased because better movies, hotter weather, or more appealing counter displays attracted more customers during the period when subliminal advertising was used. Another problem is that the limen (the point at which we consciously perceive a stimulus), by definition, varies from trial to trial for each subject. This makes it difficult to assess when stimulation has truly been subliminal (Miller, 1991). Thus, perhaps moviegoers were, at times, consciously aware of the supposedly subliminal messages about Coke and popcorn. Moreover, there is even evidence that the original study might have been a fabrication created by an overeager advertising executive (Pratkanis, 1992).

More recently, parents of teenagers have expressed concerns about the alleged subliminal messages in rock music recordings, such as Led Zeppelin's "Stairway to Heaven," that supposedly can be heard clearly when the recording is played backward. Despite the lack of evidence that such messages exist, fear that they might cause crime, suicide, satanism, and sexual promiscuity led California and other states to pass laws requiring warnings on recordings that contained subliminal messages. Yet even if recordings (or movies) contain subliminal messages, there is no evidence that listeners will *obey* them like zombies any more than they will blindly obey messages they are aware of (Vokey & Read, 1985). That is, subliminal *perception* should not be confused with subliminal *persuasion*.

But what of the popular subliminal self-help audiotapes that supposedly help you to improve yourself? They, too, have been evaluated scientifically, as in the following experiment.

ANATOMY OF A CONTEMPORARY RESEARCH STUDY

Are Subliminal Self-Help Audiotapes Effective?

Rationale

Manufacturers of subliminal self-help audiotapes claim they can help listeners do everything from smoke less to improve their study habits. People who listen to these audiotapes typically hear soothing music or nature sounds. Messages (such as "Study harder") presented on audiotapes below the auditory threshold supposedly motivate the listener to improve in the desired area. The authors of this study—Anthony Greenwald, Eric Spangenberg, Anthony Pratkanis, and Jay Eskenazi (1991)—decided to test the effectiveness of these audiotapes.

Method

The subjects were 237 adults recruited from a university community. The study used audiotapes that the manufacturers claimed would improve memory or self-esteem. Before beginning the study, the subjects were given tests of their memory ability and self-esteem. A double-blind technique was used, meaning that neither the subjects nor the experimenter knew which subliminal messages subjects were actually listening to. The audible portions of

◀ **FIGURE 6.9**
The Stroop Effect
You will find it easier to read the words than to name their colors. Evidently, after years of daily reading, reading words has become so automatic that you cannot completely inhibit that tendency even when you try. In contrast, naming colors is a more unusual task that requires controlled processing.

▲**Controlled Processing and Automatic Processing**
When we learn a new task, we depend on controlled processing, which makes us focus our attention on each aspect of the task. With experience we depend less on controlled processing and more on automatic processing. Eventually, we may be able to perform the task while focusing our attention on other activities.

the tapes consisted of classical music, popular music, or nature (surf or woodland) sounds. The subjects were given tapes to which a label had been randomly assigned, indicating that it would improve their memory or that it would improve their self-esteem. The subjects listened to the tapes once a day for one month. They were then given memory and self-esteem tests to assess whether they had improved in those areas.

Results and Discussion

Though the results showed that there was a tendency for the subjects to improve in memory and self-esteem, the improvement was not related to the subliminal message on the tape. That is, listening to the memory tape did not improve memory more than listening to the self-esteem tape. Likewise, listening to the self-esteem tape did not improve self-esteem more than listening to the memory tape. Moreover, regardless of which subliminal message they *actually* listened to, subjects' self-reports of improvement tended to reflect the subliminal message they *believed* they had listened to—even if the tapes had been mislabeled. Thus, testimonial reports that subliminal audiotapes are effective might be little more than placebo effects based on subjects' expectations of improvement. This finding has been supported by other research studies (Moore, 1995).

▲ ▲ ▲

THE FREUDIAN UNCONSCIOUS: WHY DID I DO THAT?

During the 1988 National League baseball playoffs between the New York Mets and the Los Angeles Dodgers, relief pitcher Brian Holton of the Dodgers became so nervous that he could not grip the baseball. Suddenly he found himself singing the lyrics to a folk song, "You take the high road and I'll take the low road." This surprised him, because he believed he had never heard the song. Yet, for some reason, singing it relaxed him enough to enable him to

◀ **Subliminal Perception**
In the 1960s certain songs by Bob Dylan and the Beatles supposedly contained subliminal messages. Opponents of rock music even warn that "Stairway to Heaven" by Led Zeppelin contains satanic subliminal messages that can be detected if the song is played backward. But virtually any song will have combinations of sounds that, when played backward, could be interpreted as satanic, sexual, or violent lyrics—especially if you are told what to listen for.

grip the baseball. When he told his mother about this mysterious behavior, she informed him that his father had comforted him by singing the song to him when he was a young child.

Anecdotal reports such as this are used by psychoanalytic theorists to support the influence of the Freudian unconscious. Freud divided consciousness into three levels: the *conscious*, the *preconscious*, and the *unconscious* (see Figure 6.10). As had William James, Freud viewed the **conscious mind** as the awareness of fleeting images, feelings, and sensations. The **preconscious mind** contains memories of which we are unaware at the moment, but of which we can become aware at will. And the **unconscious mind** contains repressed feelings, memories, and response tendencies of which we are unaware (Erdelyi, 1992). Through what Freud called *psychic determinism*, these unconscious factors affect our behavior. Perhaps this explains why we instantly like or dislike someone for no apparent reason, engage in repeated, irrational, self-defeating behavior, or commit a "Freudian slip," in which we replace intended words with sexual or aggressive ones.

Until recently, the Freudian unconscious was considered impossible to study scientifically because evidence of its existence came solely from anecdotal or clinical reports and because it seemingly could not be observed directly. But more sophisticated techniques, though they have not necessarily convinced all psychologists of the existence of the Freudian unconscious, at least make it subject to scientific research (Epstein, 1994). One technique, developed by Lloyd Silverman, is called **subliminal psychodynamic activation** and is based on the assumption that emotionally charged subliminal messages will alter the recipient's moods and behaviors by stimulating unconscious fantasies (Weinberger & Silverman, 1990).

Silverman claimed that unconscious "oneness fantasies" (which express emotional union with one's mother) relieve anxiety and enhance task performance. For example, subjects are typically presented with a oneness phrase, such as *Mommy and I are one*, or a neutral phrase, such as *People are walking*. The messages are presented by a device called a

conscious mind
The level of consciousness that includes the mental experiences that we are aware of at a given moment.

preconscious mind
The level of consciousness that contains feelings and memories that we are unaware of at the moment but can become aware of at will.

unconscious mind
The level of consciousness that contains thoughts, feelings, and memories that influence us without our awareness and that we cannot become aware of at will.

subliminal psychodynamic activation
The use of subliminal messages to stimulate unconscious fantasies.

► FIGURE 6.10

Levels of Consciousness

According to Sigmund Freud, there are three levels of consciousness. The conscious level contains thoughts, images, and feelings of which we are aware. The preconscious level contains memories that we can retrieve at will. And the unconscious level contains repressed motives and memories that would evoke intense feelings of anxiety if we became aware of them.

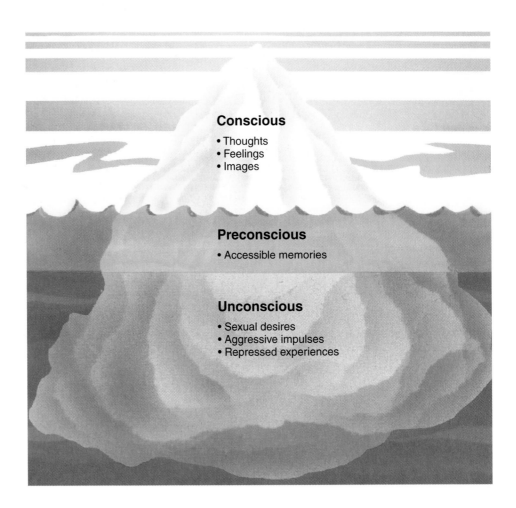

Conscious
- Thoughts
- Feelings
- Images

Preconscious
- Accessible memories

Unconscious
- Sexual desires
- Aggressive impulses
- Repressed experiences

tachistoscope, which flashes visual stimuli too briefly (for only a fraction of a second) to exceed the absolute threshold.

A study of subliminal psychodynamic activation used students who had failed a university mathematics assessment test who then took part in a summer mathematics enrichment program. One group viewed a subliminal oneness message and the other a neutral message. After 20 weeks of the program, the group exposed to the oneness message performed better on a mathematics test than did the group not exposed to it (Hudesman, Page, & Rautiainen, 1992). But other studies have failed to find any effects of subliminal psychodynamic activation (Kothera, Fudin, & Nicastro, 1990). Overall, the results of studies of subliminal psychodynamic activation indicate that it produces small, though statistically significant, effects on moods and behaviors (Hardaway, 1990).

Based on the foregoing discussion of unconscious influences, you should now realize that solid scientific evidence indicates that we can be affected by stimuli of which we are unaware. Some of the more extreme claims for unconscious influences on our moods and behaviors, however, have tainted an otherwise legitimate topic for psychological research.

STAYING ON TRACK: *Unconscious Influences*

1. Should we fear that advertisers will use subliminal stimulation to persuade us to buy their products?

2. How has subliminal psychodynamic activation been used to test Freud's notion of unconscious motivation?

CHAPTER SUMMARY

THE NATURE OF CONSCIOUSNESS

Consciousness is the awareness of one's own mental activity. William James noted that consciousness is personal, selective, continuous, and changing. Consciousness permits us to manipulate mental representations of the world, as in daydreaming. We daydream to rehearse courses of action, to maintain mental arousal, to solve problems, and to experience pleasure. The selectivity of consciousness is the basis of research on attention.

SLEEP

The sleep-wake cycle follows a circadian rhythm. The pineal gland and the suprachiasmatic nucleus help regulate circadian rhythms. The depth of sleep is defined by characteristic brain-wave patterns. REM sleep is associated with dreaming. Our nightly sleep duration and the percentage of time we spend in REM sleep decrease across the life span. The functions of sleep are still unclear. One theory views sleep as restorative. A second theory views it as adaptive inactivity, either because it protects us from danger when we are most vulnerable or because it conserves energy. The major sleep disorders include insomnia, sleep apnea, and narcolepsy.

DREAMS

The most dramatic aspect of sleep is the dream. Though we might fail to recall our dreams, everyone dreams. Most dreams deal with familiar people and situations. REM sleep can be disturbed by nightmares; NREM sleep can be disturbed by night terrors. In some cases we might incorporate into our dreams stimuli from the immediate environment. The major theories of dreaming view it as wish fulfillment, as problem solving, as an aid to memory, or as a by-product of spontaneous brain activity.

HYPNOSIS

Hypnosis is a state in which one person responds to suggestions by another person for alterations in perception, thinking, feeling, and behavior. Hypnosis had its origin in mesmerism, a technique promoted by Anton Mesmer to restore the balance of what he called animal magnetism. Hypnotic induction aims at the creation of a relaxed, passive, highly focused state of mind. Hypnosis is useful in treating pain. Though hypnosis can enhance memory, it might also make subjects more confident about inaccurate memories. Under certain conditions, hypnotized people—like nonhypnotized people—might obey suggestions to perform dangerous acts. The effects of stage hypnosis might result as much from the theatrical atmosphere as from being hypnotized. Researchers debate whether hypnosis is an altered state of consciousness or merely role-playing. Ernest Hilgard has put forth the concept of the "hidden observer" to support his neodissociation theory of hypnosis as an altered state; his theory has been countered by Nicholas Spanos and his colleagues.

MEDITATION

Meditation is a procedure that uses mental exercises to achieve a highly focused state of consciousness. Transcendental meditation and the relaxation response are popular forms of meditation aimed at inducing mental and physical relaxation. As in the case of hypnosis, researchers debate whether meditation produces a unique physiological state.

PSYCHOACTIVE DRUGS

Psychoactive drugs induce changes in mood, thinking, perception, and behavior by affecting neuronal activity. Depressant drugs reduce arousal by inhibiting activity in the central nervous system. The main depressants are alcohol, barbiturates, and opiates. Stimulant drugs, which increase arousal, include caffeine, nicotine, amphetamines, and cocaine. Hallucinogens induce extreme alterations in consciousness, including hallucinations, a sense of timelessness, and feelings of depersonalization. The main hallucinogens are psilocybin, mescaline, phencyclidine, LSD, and *cannabis sativa* (marijuana and hashish).

THINKING ABOUT PSYCHOLOGY: ARE WE AFFECTED BY UNCONSCIOUS INFLUENCES?

The nature of the controversy about whether we are affected by unconscious influences depends on the concept of "unconscious" that is being used. Perception without awareness is the unconscious perception of stimuli that exceed the absolute threshold but fall outside our focus of attention. We might experience perception without awareness whenever we use automatic, rather than controlled, processing of information. Subliminal perception is the unconscious perception of stimuli that are too weak to exceed the absolute threshold for detection. Research has shown that we can be influenced by subliminal stimuli but has not supported fears that we might obey subliminal messages like zombies. The Freudian unconscious is a portion of the mind containing thoughts and feelings that influence us without our awareness. Because the Freudian unconscious deals with unobservable phenomena, it has proven difficult to study it scientifically. Subliminal psychodynamic activation provides one means of doing so.

KEY CONCEPTS

KEY CONTRIBUTORS

The Nature of Consciousness

John Locke 196
William James 196
Eric Klinger 197

Sleep

Eugene Aserinsky 202
Nathaniel Kleitman 202
William Dement 203
Wilse Webb 205

Dreams

Mary Whiton Calkins 207
Calvin Hall 208
Stephen LaBerge 209
Sigmund Freud 209
Rosalind Cartwright 210
J. Allan Hobson 210
Robert McCarley 210

Hypnosis

Anton Mesmer 212
James Braid 212
James Esdaile 213
Martin Orne 214
Ernest Hilgard 215
Nicholas Spanos 216

Meditation

Herbert Benson 218

Psychoactive Drugs

Claude Steele 219
Albert Hofmann 223

Are We Affected by Unconscious Influences?

Sigmund Freud 229
Lloyd Silverman 229

FOR MORE INFORMATION ON CONSCIOUSNESS

FOR GENERAL WORKS ON CONSCIOUSNESS

Nature of Consciousness

Farthing, G. W., Jr. (1991). *Psychology of consciousness.* Englewood Cliffs, NJ: Prentice Hall.

Wallace, B., & Fisher, L. E. (1991). *Consciousness and behavior* (3rd ed.). Newton, MA: Allyn & Bacon.

Daydreaming

Klinger, E. (1990). *Daydreaming: Using waking fantasy and imagery for self-knowledge and creativity.* Los Angeles: Tarcher.

Mavromatis, A. (1990). *Hypnagogia: The unique state of consciousness between wakefulness and sleep.* New York: Routledge.

Attention

Underwood, G. (Ed.). (1994). *The psychology of attention* (2 vols.). New York: New York University Press.

Van Zomeren, A. H., & Brouwer, W. H. (1994). *Clinical neuropsychology of attention.* New York: Oxford University Press.

FOR MORE ON SLEEP

Biological Rhythms

Montplaisir, J., & Godbout, R. (Eds.). (1990). *Sleep and biological rhythms.* New York: Oxford University Press.

Wetterberg, L. (Ed.). (1994). *Light and biological rhythms in man.* New York: Elsevier.

Sleep Processes

Dement, W. (1997). *Sleep.* New York: Viking Penguin.

Webb, W. B. (1992). *Sleep: The gentle tyrant* (2nd ed.). Boston: Anker.

Sleep Disorders

Coren, S. (1996). *Sleep thieves.* New York: Free Press.

Ogilvie, R. D., & Harsh, J. R. (Eds.). (1994). *Sleep onset: Normal and abnormal processes.* Washington, DC: American Psychological Association.

FOR MORE ON DREAMS

Hobson, J. A. (1988). *The dreaming brain.* New York: Basic Books.

Moffitt, A., Kramer, M., & Hoffman, R. (Eds.). (1993). *The functions of dreaming.* Albany: State University of New York Press.

FOR MORE ON HYPNOSIS

Barber, T. X. (1995). *Hypnosis: A scientific approach.* Northvale, NJ: Aronson.

Lynn, S. J., & Rhue, J. W. (Eds.). (1991). *Theories of hypnosis: Current models and perspectives.* New York: Guilford.

FOR MORE ON MEDITATION

Benson, H., & Proctor, W. (1984). *Beyond the relaxation response.* New York: Times Books.

West, M. A. (Ed.). (1987). *The psychology of meditation.* New York: Oxford University Press.

FOR MORE ON PSYCHOACTIVE DRUGS

General Works

Levinthal, C. F. (1996). *Drugs, behavior, and modern society.* Boston: Allyn & Bacon.

Palfai, T., & Jankiewicz, H. (1997). *Drugs and human behavior* (2nd ed.). Madison, WI: Brown & Benchmark.

Depressants

Carroll, C., & Bock, W. (1996). *Alcohol.* Madison, WI: Brown & Benchmark.

Glowa, J. B. (1992). *Inhalants: The toxic fumes.* New York: Chelsea House.

Henningfield, J. E., & Ator, N. (1992). *Barbiturates: Sleeping potions or intoxicants?* New York: Chelsea House.

Levinthal, C. F. (1988). *Messengers of paradise: Opiates and the brain.* New York: Anchor Press/Doubleday.

Stimulants

Gilbert, R. (1992). *Caffeine: The most popular stimulant.* New York: Chelsea House.

Gold, M. S. (1995). *Tobacco.* New York: Plenum.

Lukas, S. E. (1992). *Amphetamines: Danger in the fast lane.* New York: Chelsea House.

Weiss, R. D., Mirin, S. M., & Bartel, R. L. (1993). *Cocaine* (2nd ed.). Washington, DC: American Psychiatric Press.

Hallucinogens

Bakalar, J. B., & Grinspoon, L. (1995). *Marihuana, the forbidden medicine.* New Haven, CT: Yale University Press.

De Rios, M. D. (1991). *Hallucinogens: Cross-cultural perspectives.* Garden City, NY: Avery.

Furst, P. E. (1992). *Mushrooms: Psychedelic fungi.* New York: Chelsea House.

Stevens, J. (1987). *Storming heaven: LSD and the American dream.*

New York: Atlantic Monthly Press.

Stewart, O. C. (1993). *Peyote religion: A history.* Norman: University of Oklahoma Press.

FOR MORE ON UNCONSCIOUS INFLUENCES

General Works

Kelly, W. L. (1991). *Psychology of the unconscious.* Buffalo, NY: Prometheus.

Shevrin, H., Bond, J. A., Brakel, L. A., Hertel, R. K., & Williams, W. J. (1996). *Conscious and unconscious processes: Psychodynamic, cognitive, and neurophysiological convergences.* New York: Guilford.

Perception Without Awareness

Bornstein, R. F., & Pittman, T. S. (Eds.). (1992). *Perception without awareness: Cognitive, clinical, and social perspectives.* New York: Guilford.

Reber, A. S. (1993). *Implicit learning and tacit knowledge: An essay on the cognitive unconscious.* New York: Oxford University Press.

Subliminal Perception

Dixon, N. F. (1971). *Subliminal perception: The nature of a controversy.* New York: McGraw-Hill.

Vokey, J. R., & Read, J. D. (1985). Subliminal messages: Between the devil and the media. *American Psychologist, 40,* 1231–1239.

Freudian Unconscious

Silverman, L. H., Lachmann, F. M., & Milich, R. H. (1982). *The search for oneness.* New York: International Universities Press.

Whyte, L. L. (1978). *The unconscious before Freud.* New York: St. Martin's Press.

FOR MORE ON CONTRIBUTORS TO THE STUDY OF CONSCIOUSNESS

Buranelli, V. (1975). *The wizard from Vienna: Franz Anton Mesmer.* New York: Coward, McCann, & Geohegan.

Calkins, M. W. (1930). Mary Whiton Calkins. In C. Murchison (Ed.), *A history of psychology in autobiography* (Vol. 1, pp. 31–62). Worchester, MA: Clark University Press.

Gay, P. (1988). *Freud: A life for our time.* New York: W. W. Norton.

Hofmann, A. (1983). *LSD: My problem child: Reflections on sacred drugs, mysticism, and science.* Los Angeles: Tarcher.

Leary, T. (1990). *Flashbacks: A personal and cultural history of an era.* Los Angeles: Tarcher.

Myers, G. E. (1986). *William James: His life and thought.* New Haven, CT: Yale University Press.

CHAPTER 7

▲ HENRY O. TANNER
The Banjo Lesson, 1893

Learning

Tying your shoes, writing in script, riding a bicycle, and going out on a date are all activities that at first seemed difficult to you. Yet today you probably perform each of them easily. This indicates the importance of **learning,** which is a relatively permanent change in knowledge or behavior that results from experience. What you learn is relatively permanent; it can be changed by future experience.

This chapter will answer questions about the role of learning in a variety of areas, including these: How can children learn to stop bedwetting? How can children receiving cancer chemotherapy learn to maintain their appetites? How do animal trainers apply learning principles in their work? How might psychological depression depend on learning? How can we learn to exert greater control over our own physiological processes?

Do not confuse learning with reflexes, instincts, or maturation. A reflex is an inborn, involuntary response to a specific kind of stimulus, such as automatically withdrawing your hand after touching a hot pot. An instinct is an inborn complex behavior found in members of a species (such as nest building in birds). And maturation is the sequential unfolding of inherited predispositions (such as walking in human infants). Moreover, because learning is more flexible, it enables us to adapt to ever-changing circumstances.

Psychologists began the scientific study of learning in the late nineteenth century. In keeping with Charles Darwin's theory of evolution, they viewed learning as a means of adapting to the environment. Because Darwin stressed the continuity between animals and human beings, psychologists became interested in studying learning in animals, hoping to identify principles that might also apply to human learning (Purdy, Harriman, & Molitorisz, 1993). As you will read, many of the principles of learning do, indeed, apply to both animals and human beings.

Psychologists have identified three kinds of learning. Classical conditioning considers the learning of associations between stimuli and responses. Operant conditioning considers the learning of associations between behaviors and their consequences. Cognitive learning considers learning as the acquisition of information.

CLASSICAL CONDITIONING: HOW STIMULI CONTROL BEHAVIOR

Classical conditioning grew out of a tradition that can be traced back to Aristotle, who believed that learning depended on contiguity—the occurrence of events close together in time and space (such as lightning and thunder). British philosophers of the seventeenth and eighteenth centuries, most notably John Locke and David Hume, became known as *associationists* because they agreed with Aristotle's view that learning depends on associating contiguous events with one another.

In the early twentieth century, the research of Ivan Pavlov (1849–1936) stimulated worldwide scientific interest in the study of associative learning. Pavlov, a Russian physiologist, won a Nobel Prize in 1904 for his research on digestion in dogs, which attracted the interest of scientists around the world (Windholz & Kuppers, 1990). In his research on digestion, Pavlov would place meat powder on a dog's tongue, which stimulated reflexive salivation. He collected the saliva from a tube attached to one of the dog's salivary glands. He found that after repeated presentations of the meat powder, the dog would salivate in response to stimuli (that is, environmental events) associated with the meat powder. A dog would salivate at the sight of its food dish, the sight of the laboratory assistant who brought

the food, or the sound of the assistant's footsteps. At first Pavlov was distressed by this phenomenon, which he called "psychic reflexes" or "conditional responses," because he could no longer control the onset of salivation by his dogs. But he eventually became so intrigued by the phenomenon that he devoted the rest of his career to studying it.

Pavlov was not alone in discovering this phenomenon. At the annual meeting of the American Psychological Association in 1904, the same year that Pavlov received his Nobel Prize, E. B. Twitmyer, an American graduate student at the University of Pennsylvania, reported the results of a study on the "knee jerk" reflex. As you may know from your last physical examination, when a physician strikes you with a rubber hammer on your patellar tendon just below your bent knee, your lower leg reflexively extends. In his study, Twitmyer rang a bell as a warning that the hammer was about to strike. After repeated trials in which the sound of the bell preceded the hammer strike, the sound of the bell alone caused extension of the lower leg. But, to his disappointment, Twitmyer's presentation was met with indifference. In fact, William James, who chaired Twitmyer's session, was so bored (or hungry) that he adjourned the session for lunch—without providing the customary opportunity for discussion (Coon, 1982). North American psychologists did not begin to take serious note of this kind of learning until John B. Watson described Pavlov's research in his presidential address at the annual meeting of the American Psychological Association in 1914. Because of Pavlov's extensive early research on "conditional responses," the phenomenon earned the name of classical conditioning.

Principles of Classical Conditioning

As Pavlov first noted, in **classical conditioning** a stimulus comes to elicit (that is, bring about) a response (either an overt behavior or a physiological change) that it does not normally elicit. But how does this occur?

Acquisition of the Classically Conditioned Response

To demonstrate classical conditioning (see Figure 7.1), you must first identify a stimulus that already elicits a reflexive response. The stimulus is called an **unconditioned stimulus (UCS)** and the response is called an **unconditioned response (UCR).** You then present several trials in which the UCS is preceded by a neutral stimulus—a stimulus that does not normally elicit the UCR. After one or more pairings of the neutral stimulus and the UCS, the neutral stimulus itself elicits the UCR. At that point the neutral stimulus has become a **conditioned stimulus (CS),** and the response to it is called a **conditioned response (CR).** Pavlov used the UCS of meat powder to elicit the UCR of salivation. He then used a tone as the neutral stimulus. After several trials in which the tone preceded the meat powder, the tone itself became a CS that elicited the CR of salivation. But does the CS directly elicit the CR? On the contrary, research indicates that the CS activates a memory trace representing the UCS, which then elicits the CR (Jacobs & Blackburn, 1995).

classical conditioning
A form of learning in which a neutral stimulus comes to elicit a response after being associated with a stimulus that already elicits that response.

unconditioned stimulus (UCS)
In classical conditioning, a stimulus that automatically elicits a particular unconditioned response.

unconditioned response (UCR)
In classical conditioning, an unlearned, automatic response to a particular unconditioned stimulus.

conditioned stimulus (CS)
In classical conditioning, a neutral stimulus that comes to elicit a particular conditioned response after being paired with a particular unconditioned stimulus that already elicits that response.

conditioned response (CR)
In classical conditioning, the learned response given to a particular conditioned stimulus.

Classical Conditioning
Before conditioning, the unconditioned stimulus of meat elicits the unconditioned response of salivation, and the neutral stimulus of a tone does not elicit salivation. During conditioning, the tone is repeatedly presented before the meat (UCS), which continues to elicit salivation (UCR). After conditioning, the tone becomes a conditioned stimulus (CS) that elicits salivation as a conditioned response (CR).

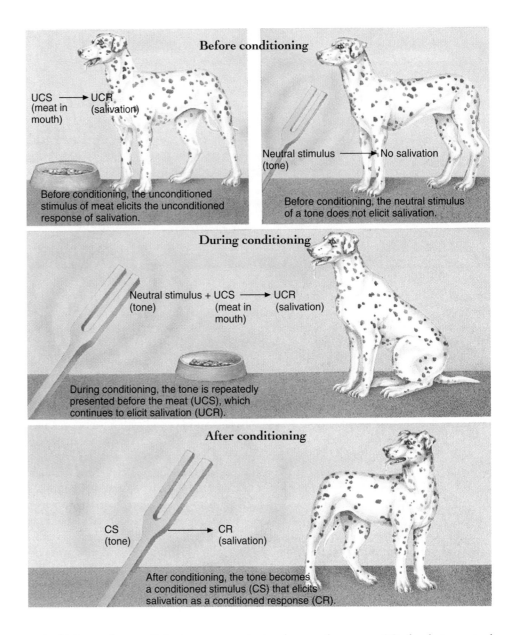

Before conditioning

UCS → UCR
(meat in mouth) (salivation)

Before conditioning, the unconditioned stimulus of meat elicits the unconditioned response of salivation.

Neutral stimulus → No salivation
(tone)

Before conditioning, the neutral stimulus of a tone does not elicit salivation.

During conditioning

Neutral stimulus + UCS → UCR
(tone) (meat in mouth) (salivation)

During conditioning, the tone is repeatedly presented before the meat (UCS), which continues to elicit salivation (UCR).

After conditioning

CS → CR
(tone) (salivation)

After conditioning, the tone becomes a conditioned stimulus (CS) that elicits salivation as a conditioned response (CR).

higher-order conditioning
In classical conditioning, the establishment of a conditioned response to a neutral stimulus that has been paired with an existing conditioned stimulus.

In **higher-order conditioning,** a neutral stimulus may become a CS after being paired with an existing CS. In this case, the existing CS functions like a UCS. If the neutral stimulus precedes the existing CS, it elicits a CR similar to that elicited by the existing CS. This explains how neutral stimuli that have not been paired with a biological UCS such as food can gain control over our behavior. Higher-order conditioning might explain why music in commercials (such as those advertising fast-food restaurants) can affect our attitudes toward the products presented in the commercials (Blair & Shimp, 1992).

Among the most important conditioned stimuli are words. In a clever classroom demonstration of this, a college professor used the word *Pavlov* as a neutral stimulus (Cogan & Cogan, 1984). Student subjects said "Pavlov" just before lemonade powder was placed on their tongues. The UCS of lemonade powder naturally elicited the UCR of salivation. After repeated pairings of *Pavlov* and the lemonade powder, *Pavlov* became a CS that elicited the CR of salivation.

Classical conditioning might account, in part, for the power of words to elicit emotional responses. Perhaps the mere mention of the name of someone with whom you have a romantic relationship makes your heart "flutter." Similarly, if someone repeatedly says something, such as "tickle, tickle," before tickling the sole of your foot, you might eventually learn to jerk away your foot as soon as you hear the words "tickle, tickle" (Newman et al., 1993).

Even bedwetting, or *nocturnal enuresis*, in childhood can be controlled by classical conditioning. An effective technique, devised more than half a century ago (Mowrer & Mowrer, 1938), uses an electrified mattress pad that consists of a cloth sheet sandwiched between two thin metal sheets. The upper metal sheet contains tiny holes. When a drop of urine penetrates that sheet and soaks through the cloth sheet, the moisture completes an electrical circuit between the two metal sheets. This sets off a battery-powered alarm, which wakes the child, who then goes to the toilet. The alarm serves as a UCS, which elicits awakening as a UCR. After repeated trials, bladder tension, which precedes the alarm, becomes a CS, which then elicits awakening as a CR. The child eventually responds to bladder tension by going to the toilet instead of urinating in bed. This technique has become one of the most effective methods of treating nocturnal enuresis (Gustafson, 1993).

What factors affect classical conditioning? In general, the greater the intensity of the UCS and the greater the number of pairings of the CS and the UCS, the greater will be the strength of conditioning. The time interval between the CS and the UCS also affects acquisition of the CR. In delayed conditioning, the CS is presented first and remains at least until the onset of the UCS. An interval of about 1 second between the CS and the UCS is often optimal in delayed conditioning (Rescorla & Holland, 1982), though it varies with the kind of CR. In delayed conditioning using Pavlov's procedure, the tone is presented first and remains on at least until the meat powder is placed on the dog's tongue. Thus, the CS and UCS overlap. In trace conditioning, the CS is presented first and ends before the onset of the UCS. This requires that a memory trace of the CS be retained until the onset of the UCS. In trace conditioning using Pavlov's procedure, the tone is presented and then turned off just before the meat powder is placed on the dog's tongue. In simultaneous conditioning, the CS and UCS begin together. In simultaneous conditioning using Pavlov's procedure, the tone and the meat powder are presented together. And in backward conditioning, the onset of the UCS precedes the onset of the CS. In backward conditioning using Pavlov's procedure, the meat powder is presented first, followed immediately by the tone. In general, delayed conditioning produces strong conditioning, trace conditioning produces moderately strong conditioning, and simultaneous conditioning produces weak conditioning. Backward conditioning generally produces no conditioning, though it is sometimes used successfully (McNish et al., 1997).

Stimulus Generalization and Stimulus Discrimination in Classical Conditioning

In classical conditioning, the CR can occur in response to stimuli that are similar to the CS. This is called **stimulus generalization.** For example, a person who becomes ill after eating chocolate pudding might become repulsed by all chocolate desserts. As another example, a dog conditioned to salivate to a dinner bell (a CS) might also salivate to a doorbell, a telephone bell, or an ice cream truck bell.

stimulus generalization

In classical conditioning, giving a conditioned response to stimuli similar to the conditioned stimulus.

Processes in Classical Conditioning
In classical conditioning, the pairing of the CS and the UCS leads to acquisition of the CR. When the CS is then presented without the UCS, the CR gradually disappears. After extinction and following a rest period, spontaneous recovery of the CR occurs. But extinction takes place again, even more rapidly than the first time.

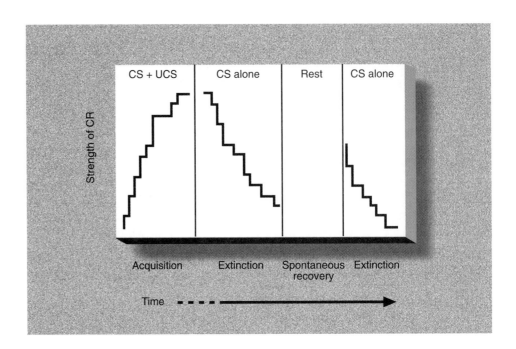

stimulus discrimination
In classical conditioning, giving a conditioned response to the conditioned stimulus but not to stimuli similar to it.

extinction
In classical conditioning, the gradual disappearance of the conditioned response when the conditioned stimulus is repeatedly presented without being paired with the unconditioned stimulus.

spontaneous recovery
In classical conditioning, the reappearance after a period of time of a conditioned response that has been subjected to extinction.

But if the person eats other chocolate desserts without becoming ill, she will eventually become repulsed only by the dessert that made her ill. This would be an instance of **stimulus discrimination,** in which the person or animal responds to the CS but not to stimuli that are similar to the CS. Similarly, the dog might eventually salivate only in response to the dinner bell. This would occur if the dog learns that the other bells are not followed by food.

Extinction in Classical Conditioning

In Pavlov's procedure, will a dog conditioned to salivate in response to a dinner bell do so forever? Not necessarily. If a CS is repeatedly presented without the UCS being presented, the CR will diminish and eventually stop occurring. This process is called **extinction.** A dog that has learned to salivate to a dinner bell (the CS) will eventually stop doing so unless presentations of the dinner bell are periodically followed by presentations of food (the UCS).

But extinction only inhibits the CR, it does not eliminate it (Bouton & Swartzentruber, 1991). In fact, after a CR has been subjected to extinction, it can reappear later if the CS is reintroduced. For example, suppose you produce extinction of the CR of salivation by no longer presenting the dog with food after ringing the dinner bell. If you rang the dinner bell a few days later, the dog might again respond by salivating. This process, by which a CR that has been subjected to extinction will again be elicited by a CS, is called **spontaneous recovery** (Goddard, 1997). In spontaneous recovery, however, the CR is weaker and extinguishes faster than it did originally. Thus, after spontaneous recovery the dog's salivation to the dinner bell will be weaker and subject to faster extinction than it was originally. Figure 7.2 illustrates the acquisition, extinction, and spontaneous recovery of a classically conditioned response.

Applications of Classical Conditioning

In his 1932 novel, *Brave New World,* Aldous Huxley warned of a future in which classical conditioning would be used to mold people into narrow social roles. In the novel, classical conditioning is used to make children who have been assigned to become workers repulsed by any interests other than work. This is achieved by giving them electric shocks (the UCS) in the presence of forbidden objects, such as books or flowers (the CS). Despite such fears of diabolical use, classical conditioning has, in reality, been applied in less ominous, and often beneficial, ways. For example, classical conditioning has been used to explain phobias, drug dependence, and learned taste aversions.

Classical Conditioning and Phobias

Three centuries ago, John Locke (1690/1956) observed that children who had been punished in school for misbehaving became fearful of their books and other stimuli associated with school. Today we would say that these children had been classically conditioned to develop school phobias. A phobia is an unrealistic or exaggerated fear, and a phobia was the subject of a classic study by John B. Watson.

ANATOMY OF A CLASSIC RESEARCH STUDY

Can Classical Conditioning Explain Phobias?

Rationale

The most famous study of a classically conditioned phobia was conducted by John B. Watson and his graduate student Rosalie Rayner (Watson & Rayner, 1920). Their subject was an 11-month-old boy, Albert B., later known as "Little Albert," who enjoyed playing with animals, including tame white rats. Watson and Rayner hoped to provide scientific evidence that emotional responses could be learned by conditioning. This would provide an alternative to the Freudian idea that phobias are symbolic manifestations of unconscious conflicts that arise from early childhood sexual conflicts.

Method

In the study, Albert sat on a mattress. On several trials, just as Albert touched a white rat, Watson made a loud noise behind Albert's head by banging a steel bar with a hammer.

Results and Discussion

Albert responded to the noise (the UCS) with fear (the UCR). He jumped violently, fell forward, and buried his face in the mattress. After seven pairings of the rat and the noise (twice on the first day and five times a week later), Albert responded to the rat (the CS) with fear (the CR) by crying and showing distress in response to it. When tested later, Albert showed stimulus generalization. He responded fearfully to other furlike objects, including a dog, a rabbit, cotton wool, and a sealskin fur coat. Two months later he even showed fear of a Santa Claus mask. He had not shown fear of any of these objects at 9 months. Watson and Rayner hypothesized that pleasurable stimulation paired with a feared object would reduce Albert's phobia. But Albert left before they had the opportunity to try that technique. As discussed in Chapter 15, Watson's student Mary Cover Jones (1924), who became a prominent psychologist, used it a few years later to relieve a child's animal phobia.

Current ethical standards of psychological research (see Chapter 2) would prevent the experimental induction of phobias in children. Attempts to locate Little Albert to determine the long-lasting effects of his experience have failed (Harris, 1979). Though this study was done so haphazardly that it is not a convincing demonstration of a classically conditioned phobia, it led to sounder research studies demonstrating that fears and phobias can, indeed, be learned through classical conditioning (McAllister & McAllister, 1994). For example, a study found that women undergoing chemotherapy for breast cancer responded with anxiety to a distinctive stimulus that had been presented before each session (Jacobsen et al., 1995).

▲ ▲ ▲

Classical Conditioning and Drug Dependence

Classical conditioning might even explain dependence on psychoactive drugs. When a psychoactive drug (the UCS) such as heroin is administered, it produces characteristic physiological effects (the UCR). With continued use, higher and higher doses of the drug are required to produce the same physiological effects. This is known as tolerance, which might be, in part, the product of classical conditioning (Deffner-Rappold, Azorlosa, & Baker, 1996). Stimuli associated with the administration of certain drugs act as conditioned stimuli that elicit conditioned physiological responses opposite to those of the drug. For example, though heroin induces respiratory depression, stimuli associated with its administration

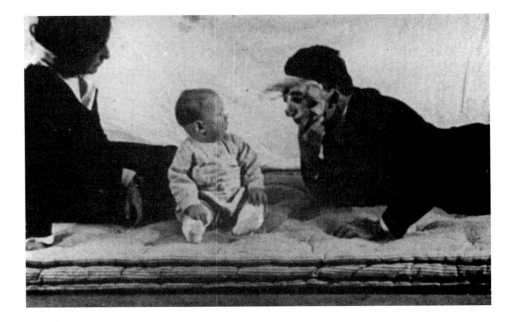

induce respiratory excitation. Why would stimuli associated with drug taking elicit effects opposite to those of the drug itself? Perhaps it is an adaptive, compensatory mechanism that prevents the physiological response to the drug from becoming too extreme.

Consider heroin addiction. Tolerance to heroin might occur because stimuli associated with its administration, such as hypodermic needles and particular settings, can act as conditioned stimuli to counter the physiological effects produced by the drug. This might explain why heroin addicts sometimes die of respiratory failure after injecting themselves with their normal dose of heroin in a setting different from that in which they normally administer the drug. By doing so they remove the conditioned stimuli that elicit conditioned physiological responses that normally counter the unconditioned physiological responses elicited by the drug. As a consequence, tolerance is reduced. This means that the unconditioned physiological responses, particularly respiratory depression, to a normal dose might be stronger than usual—in some cases strong enough to cause a fatal overdose reaction (Siegel et al., 1982).

Classical Conditioning and Taste Aversions

conditioned taste aversion
A taste aversion induced by pairing a taste with gastrointestinal distress.

Have you ever eaten something, by coincidence developed a stomach virus several hours later, become nauseated, and later found yourself repulsed by what you had eaten? If so, you have experienced a **conditioned taste aversion**—the classical conditioning of an aversion to a taste that has been associated with a noxious stimulus. Research on conditioned taste aversion was prompted by the need to determine the effects of atomic radiation, subsequent to the extensive atomic bomb testing of the 1950s. One of the leading researchers in that effort was John Garcia. Garcia and his colleagues exposed rats to radiation in special cages. He found that the rats failed to drink water in the radiation cages, yet drank normally in their own cages. They continued to refrain from drinking in the radiation cages even when they were no longer exposed to radiation in them. Garcia concluded that the plastic water bottles lent a distinctive taste to the water in the radiation cages, which created a conditioned taste aversion after being paired with radiation-induced nausea. Because the water bottles in the rats' own cages were made of glass, the rats did not associate the taste of water from them with nausea (Garcia et al., 1956).

Garcia has also developed useful applications of conditioned taste aversion. In a clever application of this phenomenon, coyotes have been discouraged from killing sheep (Gustavson et al., 1974). Lithium chloride, a drug that causes gastrointestinal distress, is first injected into sheep carcasses. If a coyote eats this tainted meat, it becomes dizzy and nauseated, associates these sensations with eating sheep, and consequently refrains from killing them. This technique might provide a happy compromise between ranchers who want to kill coyotes and conservationists who want to save them. Unfortunately, in some cases it might merely inhibit predators from eating, rather than from killing, their prey (Timberlake & Melcer, 1988). Moreover, sheep ranchers have been reluctant to use the technique, preferring instead to eradicate the coyotes (Reese, 1986). Thus, a procedure that is scientifically feasible is not necessarily one that will be practical.

In responding to Garcia's finding that a taste aversion could be learned even when the taste preceded feelings of nausea by hours, psychologists were at first shocked by this apparent violation of contiguity in classical conditioning (Garcia, 1981). How could the taste of food be associated with nausea that occurs hours later? (Tastes do not linger long enough for that to be an explanation.) Through the persistence of Garcia and his colleagues, who replicated his findings, the conditioning of a taste aversion using a long interval between the CS and the UCS is now an accepted psychological phenomenon. Moreover, there is even evidence that learned taste aversions are more likely to occur when there is a longer interval between the CS and UCS than when there is a shorter interval. For example, a 30-minute interval is superior to a 10-second interval between presentation of a distinctive taste and presentation of a nausea-inducing chemical in the classical conditioning of an aversion to the taste (Schafe, Sollars, & Bernstein, 1995).

Had Garcia been less persistent, we might have been denied a potentially useful tool for combating the nausea-induced loss of appetite experienced by people undergoing cancer chemotherapy. Their loss of appetite makes them eat less and lose weight, weakening them and impairing their ability to fight the disease.

ANATOMY OF A CONTEMPORARY RESEARCH STUDY

Can Classical Conditioning Help Maintain the Appetites of Children Receiving Chemotherapy?

Rationale

Ilene Bernstein (1991), of the University of Washington, has conducted a program of research on taste aversion in chemotherapy patients. In one study, Bernstein (1978) determined whether children receiving chemotherapy would associate a novel taste with the nausea induced by chemotherapy.

Method

Bernstein assigned children receiving chemotherapy to one of three groups. The first group ate "Mapletoff" ice cream, which has a novel maple-walnut flavor, before each chemotherapy session. The second group ate Mapletoff on days when they did not receive chemotherapy. And the third group never ate Mapletoff. From 2 to 4 weeks later the children were given the choice of eating Mapletoff or playing with a game. Later, at an average of 10 weeks after the first session, the children were asked to select Mapletoff or another novel-tasting ice cream.

Results and Discussion

As illustrated in Figure 7.3, when given the option of playing with a game or eating Mapletoff, 67 percent of the children who never ate Mapletoff and 73 percent of the children who ate it only on days when they did not receive chemotherapy chose Mapletoff. In contrast, only 21 percent of the children who ate Mapletoff on days they received chemotherapy chose Mapletoff. When given the option of choosing Mapletoff or another novel ice cream flavor, only 25 percent of those in the Mapletoff-plus-chemotherapy group chose Mapletoff, while 50 percent of the Mapletoff-only group and 66 percent of the no-Mapletoff group chose it. Thus, children exposed to Mapletoff plus chemotherapy developed a taste aversion to Mapletoff.

Based on these findings, and on findings that taste aversion is stronger in response to novel-tasting foods than to familiar-tasting foods (Kimble, 1981), perhaps cancer patients should be given a novel-tasting food before receiving chemotherapy. This might lead them to experience taste aversion in response only to the novel "scapegoat" food instead of to familiar foods, thereby helping them maintain their appetite for familiar, nutritious foods. Bernstein has, in fact, accomplished this with children receiving chemotherapy by using candies with unusual flavors (such as coconut) as "scapegoats" (Broberg & Bernstein, 1987).

▲ ▲ ▲

▲ **Ilene Bernstein**
"The demonstration of taste aversions in children receiving chemotherapy treatments may prove to be of importance to physicians who administer treatments which induce nausea and vomiting."

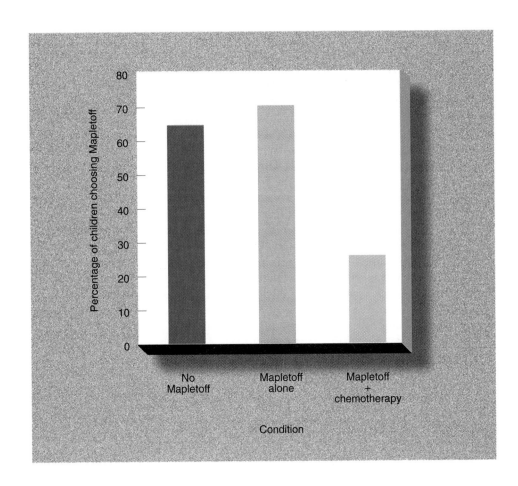

▶ FIGURE 7.3

Chemotherapy and Conditioned Taste Aversion

Ilene Bernstein (1978) found that children undergoing cancer chemotherapy developed conditioned taste aversions to a novel flavor of ice cream (Mapletoff) eaten on the same days as they underwent treatment. The children may have developed the aversion to the flavor because it became associated with the nausea induced by the therapy. As the graph shows, when later given the choice of eating Mapletoff or playing a game, children who had eaten Mapletoff on the days when they received therapy were less likely to choose Mapletoff than were children who had never eaten it or who had eaten it on days when they did not receive therapy.

Limitations on Learning: Biological Constraints on Classical Conditioning

According to Ivan Pavlov (1928, p. 88), "Every imaginable phenomenon of the outer world affecting a specific receptive surface of the body may be converted into a conditioned stimulus." Until the past two decades, learning theorists agreed with Pavlov's proclamation. They assumed that any stimulus paired with an unconditioned stimulus could become a conditioned stimulus. But we now know that there are inherited biological constraints on the ease with which particular stimuli can be associated with particular responses (Kimble, 1981). This was demonstrated in an early study that tried to replicate Watson and Rayner's study on conditioned fear by using an opera glass instead of a white rat. The opera glass did not become a fear-inducing conditioned stimulus after being paired with an unconditioned stimulus that induced fear (Valentine, 1930).

Biological constraints on classical conditioning were more recently demonstrated in a study of classically conditioned taste aversion in which two groups of rats were presented with a CS consisting of three components: saccharin-flavored water, a flash of light, and a clicking sound (Garcia & Koelling, 1966). For one group the CS was followed by a strong electric shock (the UCS) that induced pain (the UCR). For another group the CS was followed by X rays (the UCS) that induced nausea and dizziness (the UCR). The results indicated that the rats that had been hurt by the electric shock developed an aversion to the light and the click but not to the saccharin-flavored water. In contrast, the rats that had been made to feel ill developed an aversion to the saccharin-flavored water but not to the light and the click. This indicates that rats have a tendency, apparently inborn, to associate nausea and dizziness with tastes, but not with sights and sounds, and to associate pain with sights and sounds, but not with tastes. Thus, not all stimuli and responses are equally associable (Weiss, Panlilio, & Schindler, 1993).

STAYING ON TRACK: *Classical Conditioning*

1. How would you use classical conditioning to make a pet cat come running at the sound of a can opener?

2. How does Ilene Bernstein suggest using classical conditioning to help chemotherapy patients retain their appetite for nutritious foods by using "scapegoat" foods?

3. In what way did John Garcia demonstrate biological constraints on classical conditioning?

Answers to Staying on Track start on p. S-3.

OPERANT CONDITIONING: HOW BEHAVIOR IS CONTROLLED BY ITS CONSEQUENCES

In the late 1890s, while Russian physiologists were studying the relationship between stimuli and responses, an American psychologist named Edward Thorndike (1874–1949) was studying the relationship between actions and their consequences. While pursuing a doctoral degree at Harvard University, Thorndike studied learning in chicks by rewarding them with food for successfully negotiating a maze constructed of books. After his landlady objected to Thorndike's raising the chicks in his bedroom, William James, one of his professors, agreed to raise the chicks in his basement—much to the delight of the James children (Thorndike, 1961).

Thorndike left Harvard and completed his studies at Columbia University. At Columbia he conducted research using cats in so-called puzzle boxes (Washburn, Rumbaugh, & Putney, 1994), which were constructed from Heinz wooden shipping crates. In a typical puzzle box study, Thorndike (1898) put a hungry cat in the box and a piece of fish outside of it. A sliding latch kept the door to the box closed. The cat could escape by stepping on a pedal or pulling a string that released the latch. At first the cat performed ineffective actions, such as biting the wooden slats or trying to squeeze between them. Eventually the cat accidentally performed the correct action, thereby releasing the latch, opening the door, and gaining access to the fish. Thorndike repeated this for several trials and found that as the trials progressed the cat took less and less time to escape, eventually escaping as soon as it was placed in the box.

The results of his puzzle box studies led Thorndike to develop the **law of effect,** which states that a behavior followed by a "satisfying" state of affairs is strengthened and a behavior followed by an "annoying" state of affairs is weakened. In the puzzle box experiments, behaviors that let the cat reach the fish were strengthened and behaviors that

▲ **Edward Thorndike (1874–1949)**
"When a certain connection [between a behavior and a consequence] has been followed by a satisfier the connection lasts longer than it does when it has been followed by an annoyer."

law of effect

Edward Thorndike's principle that a behavior followed by a satisfying state of affairs is strengthened and a behavior followed by an annoying state of affairs is weakened.

instrumental conditioning

A form of learning in which a behavior becomes more or less probable, depending on its consequences.

operant conditioning

B. F. Skinner's term for instrumental conditioning, a form of learning in which a behavior becomes more or less probable, depending on its consequences.

Skinner box

An enclosure that contains a bar or key that can be pressed to obtain food or water, and that is used to study operant conditioning in rats, pigeons, or other small animals.

behavioral contingencies

Relationships between behaviors and their consequences, such as positive reinforcement, negative reinforcement, extinction, and punishment.

positive reinforcement

In operant conditioning, an increase in the probability of a behavior that is followed by a desirable consequence.

Premack principle

The principle that a more probable behavior can be used as a reinforcer for a less probable one.

primary reinforcer

In operant conditioning, an unlearned reinforcer, which satisfies a biological need such as air, food, or water.

secondary reinforcer

In operant conditioning, a neutral stimulus that becomes reinforcing after being associated with a primary reinforcer.

discriminative stimulus

In operant conditioning, a stimulus that indicates the likelihood that a particular response will be reinforced.

---

kept it in the box were weakened. Because Thorndike studied the process by which behaviors are instrumental in producing certain consequences, the process became known as **instrumental conditioning.**

Principles of Operant Conditioning

Thorndike's work inspired B. F. Skinner (1904–1990), perhaps the best-known psychologist of the past few decades. In the 1930s Skinner called instrumental conditioning **operant conditioning,** because animals and people learn to "operate" on the environment to produce desired consequences, instead of just responding reflexively to stimuli, as in classical conditioning (Iversen, 1992). Following in Thorndike's footsteps, Skinner used chambers, now known as **Skinner boxes,** to study learning in animals—in particular, rats learning to press levers to obtain food pellets and pigeons learning to peck at lighted disks to obtain grain. Skinner devoted his career to studying the relationships between behaviors and their consequences, which he called **behavioral contingencies:** positive reinforcement, negative reinforcement, extinction, and punishment (Lattal, 1995).

Positive Reinforcement: Increasing the Probability of Behavior

Two centuries ago, while leading a fort-building expedition, Benjamin Franklin increased the likelihood of attendance at daily prayer meetings by withholding his men's rations of rum until they had prayed (Knapp & Shodahl, 1974). This showed his appreciation of the power of reinforcement. A reinforcer is a consequence of a behavior that increases the likelihood that the behavior will occur again. In **positive reinforcement** a behavior (for example, praying) that is followed by the presentation of a desirable stimulus (for example, rum) becomes more likely to occur in the future. Skinner called the desirable stimulus a positive reinforcer. You are certainly aware of the effect of positive reinforcement in your own life. For example, if you find that studying hard for exams earns you high grades, you will be more likely to study hard for exams in the future. Positive reinforcement has even been used to make police officers more courteous (Wilson, Boni, & Hogg, 1997).

A handy approach to determining what will be an effective positive reinforcer is provided by the **Premack principle,** named for its discoverer, David Premack. Premack (1965) pointed out that a behavior that has a higher probability of occurrence can be used as a positive reinforcer for a behavior that has a lower probability. Benjamin Franklin relied on this principle when he used the higher-probability behavior of drinking rum to reinforce the lower-probability behavior of praying. Parents, too, use the Premack principle with their children when they make television a positive reinforcer for the completion of homework. Even animals are trained using the Premack principle. For example, a study using rats as subjects successfully used wheel-running, a higher-probability behavior, as a positive reinforcement for lever pressing, a lower-probability behavior (Iversen, 1993). Keep in mind that, according to the Premack principle, something that is reinforcing to one individual might be less so to another (Timberlake & Farmer-Dougan, 1991). Eating jello might be a positive reinforcer to you, yet repugnant to your friend.

In general, positive reinforcement is strengthened by increasing the magnitude of the reinforcer, decreasing the interval between the behavior and the reinforcer, and increasing the number of pairings of the behavior and the reinforcer. There are two classes of positive reinforcers. A **primary reinforcer** is biological and unlearned, such as oxygen, food, water, warmth, and sleep. In contrast, a **secondary reinforcer** (also known as a conditioned reinforcer) is learned and becomes reinforcing by being associated with a primary reinforcer. This was demonstrated in a classic study in which chimpanzees could obtain grapes by inserting tokens into a vending machine (Wolfe, 1936). After using tokens to obtain grapes from the "chimp-o-mat," the chimps would steal tokens and hoard them. The tokens had become secondary reinforcers. Among the most powerful secondary reinforcers to human beings are praise, money, and success.

Why do behaviors that have been positively reinforced not occur continually? One reason is that behavior is controlled by discriminative stimuli, a process that Skinner calls stimulus control. A **discriminative stimulus** informs an individual when a behavior

◄ "Boy have I got this guy conditioned! Every time I press the bar down he drops in a piece of food."
Source: B. F. Skinner, "A Case History in Scientific Method" in American Psychologist, 11:221–233, 1956.

is likely to be reinforced. You would be silly to dial a telephone number if you did not first hear a dial tone, which acts as a discriminative stimulus to signal you that dialing might result in positive reinforcement—reaching the person whom you are calling. Stimulus control even plays a role in drug abuse. Specific stimuli associated with drug taking make drug taking more likely in their presence (Falk, 1994). This also explains, in part, why drug abusers who have undergone successful treatment often relapse when they return to the people and surroundings associated with their former drug taking.

A second reason that reinforced behaviors do not occur continually is the individual's relative degree of satiation in regard to the reinforcer. Reinforcement is more effective when the individual has been deprived of the reinforcer. In contrast, reinforcement is ineffective when the individual has been satiated by having free access to the reinforcer. So, water is more reinforcing to a thirsty person and praise is more reinforcing to a person who is rarely praised.

Shaping and Chaining. Positive reinforcement is useful in increasing the likelihood of behaviors that are already in an individual's repertoire. But how can we use positive reinforcement to promote behaviors that rarely or never occur? Consider the trained dolphins you have seen jump through hoops held high above the water. How do they learn to perform such a behavior, which is not a part of their natural repertoire? You cannot reinforce a behavior until it occurs. The trainer who simply waits until a dolphin jumps through a hoop held above the water might wait forever; dolphins do not naturally jump through hoops held above the water.

Animal trainers rely on a technique called **shaping** to train rats, dolphins, and other animals to perform actions that they would rarely or never perform naturally. In shaping, the individual is reinforced for successive approximations of the target behavior and eventually reinforced for the target behavior itself. A dolphin trainer might begin by giving a dolphin a fish for turning toward a hoop held underwater and then, successively, for moving toward the hoop, for coming near the hoop, and for swimming through the hoop. The trainer would then gradually raise the hoop and continue to reward the dolphin for swimming through it. Eventually the trainer would reward the dolphin for swimming through the hoop when it was held partly out of the water, then for jumping through the hoop when it was held slightly above the water, and, finally, for jumping through the hoop when it was held several feet above the water. Shaping is also the process by which rats are taught to press levers and

▲ **The Skinner Box**
The computer-controlled stainless steel and Plexiglas Skinner box is a far cry from Thorndike's puzzle box. Rats learn to obtain food by pressing a bar, and pigeons learn to obtain food by pecking a lighted disc.

shaping

An operant conditioning procedure that involves the positive reinforcement of successive approximations of an initially improbable behavior to eventually bring about that behavior.

Natural Shaping
Shaping occurs naturally in the wild. This may explain why wild rats living next to the Po River in Italy will dive to the river bottom to get shellfish to eat, while similar wild rats living next to other rivers will not. The Po River experiences radical changes in depth. *(a)* At times the rats living next to the Po can scamper across exposed areas of its bed to get shellfish. *(b)* As the water rises, the rats wade across the river and submerge their heads to get shellfish. *(c)* Eventually, when the water becomes deeper, they swim across the river and dive to get shellfish. Thus, the natural changes in the depth of the water shape the rats' behavior by reinforcing the rats with shellfish for successive approximations of diving (Galef, 1980).

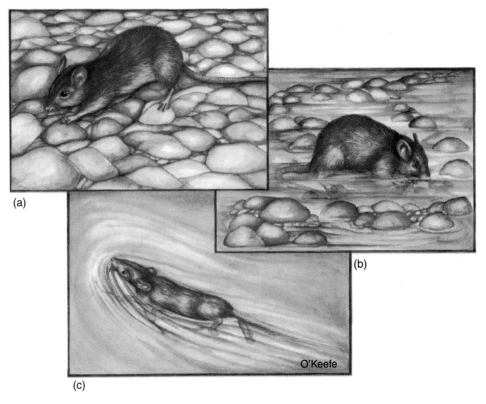

(a)
(b)
(c)

O'Keefe

chaining

An operant conditioning procedure used to establish a desired sequence of behaviors by positively reinforcing each behavior in the sequence.

pigeons to peck at disks in Skinner boxes. Figure 7.4 shows that animal behavior, such as diving for food, can be shaped by nature, not just by human beings (Galef, 1980).

Shaping is not limited to animals. It is also useful in training people to perform behaviors that are not part of their behavioral repertoires. The successful application of what we now call shaping was reported as long ago as the seventh century, when it was used in England to help a mute person learn to speak (Cliffe, 1991). In a much more recent application, shaping was used to train a child with Down syndrome to jump over a hurdle in preparation for the Special Olympics (Cameron & Cappello, 1993). Students can even use shaping to influence the behavior of their teachers. In one demonstration, a college professor asked her psychology students to shape her behavior during the semester (Chrisler, 1988). They were not to tell her what behavior was being shaped or what positive reinforcers were being used. As positive reinforcers, the students used nodding, smiling, eye contact, note taking, and class participation. The students successfully conditioned her to write more often on the chalkboard, to increase eye contact with all members of the class, to move about the classroom more frequently, and to give more examples from her personal life experiences.

What if you wish to teach an individual to perform a series of behaviors, rather than single behaviors? You might use **chaining,** which involves the reinforcement of each behavior in a series of behaviors. For example, in one study chaining was used successfully to train mentally retarded adults to perform the 18 separate steps required to make a corsage (Hur & Osborne, 1993). In forward chaining, a sequence of actions is taught by reinforcing the first action in the chain and then working forward, each time adding a behavioral segment to the chain, until the individual performs all of the segments in sequence. Forward chaining has been successful in areas as diverse as teaching the use of a musical keyboard (Ash & Holding, 1990) and training people with mental retardation to make their beds (McWilliams, Nietupski, & Hamre-Nietupski, 1990).

In backward chaining, a sequence of actions is taught by reinforcing the final action in the chain and then working backward until the individual performs all of the segments in sequence (Hagopian, Farrell, & Amari, 1996). For example, a father could use chaining to teach his child to put on a shirt. The father would begin by putting the shirt on the child, leaving only the top button open. He would then work backward, first reinforcing the

(a) (b)

(c) (d)

◀ **FIGURE 7.5**
The Rat Olympics
Chaining has been used to train animals to perform amazing sequences of actions. Some psychology professors have even instituted so-called Rat Olympics, in which students compete in training rats to perform the longest sequence of actions (Solomon & Morse, 1981). Here, a rat has learned to obtain food by *(a)* pushing a cart to reach a stand, *(b)* climbing onto the cart, *(c)* jumping up to the top of the stand, and *(d)* running up a ramp. Note, however, that the rat learned this chain of behaviors backward, first learning to run up the ramp and finally learning to push the cart.

child for buttoning the top button, then for buttoning the top two buttons, and so on, until the child could perform the sequence of actions necessary for putting on a shirt. Even flight-training programs for pilots are more successful when they have trainees practice individual segments of a chain of actions they are to learn and combine them together through backward chaining (Wightman & Lintern, 1984). Figure 7.5 shows Barnabus, a rat trained to perform a sequence of actions by backward chaining.

Schedules of Reinforcement.

Once an individual has been operantly conditioned to perform a behavior, the performance of the behavior is influenced by its schedule of reinforcement—the pattern of reinforcements given for a desired behavior. In a **continuous schedule of reinforcement,** every instance of a desired behavior is reinforced. A rat in a Skinner box that receives a pellet of food each time it presses a bar is on a continuous schedule of reinforcement. Similarly, candy vending machines put you on a continuous schedule of reinforcement. Each time that you insert the correct change, you receive a package of candy. If you do not receive the candy, you might pound on the machine, but you would, at best, insert coins only one more time. This illustrates another characteristic of continuous schedules of reinforcement—they are subject to rapid extinction when reinforcement stops. Extinction is the decline in the probability of a behavior and its eventual disappearance as a result of its no longer being followed by a reinforcer.

In **partial schedules of reinforcement** (also known as intermittent schedules), reinforcement is given for only some instances of a desired behavior. Because partial schedules produce less-predictable reinforcement, they are more resistant to extinction than are continuous schedules. Skinner (1956) discovered partial schedules by accident when he ran short of food pellets and decided not to reinforce each response but, instead, to reinforce responses only every so often. The rats kept responding and showed resistance to extinction. Partial schedules are further divided into ratio schedules and interval schedules. In a ratio schedule of reinforcement, reinforcement is provided after the individual makes a certain number of desired responses. There are two kinds of ratio schedules: fixed and variable. A **fixed-ratio schedule of reinforcement** provides reinforcement after a specific number of desired responses. A rat in a Skinner box might be reinforced with a pellet of food after every 5 bar presses. Suppose that a garment worker is paid with

continuous schedule of reinforcement
A schedule of reinforcement that provides reinforcement for each instance of a desired response.

partial schedule of reinforcement
A schedule of reinforcement that reinforces some, but not all, instances of a desired response.

fixed-ratio schedule of reinforcement
A partial schedule of reinforcement that provides reinforcement after a set number of desired responses.

Learning | **249**

► Gambling and Schedules of Reinforcement
Gamblers are on variable-ratio schedules of reinforcement, which makes their gambling highly resistant to extinction. This is one of the reasons why compulsive gambling is so difficult to treat. People playing poker, betting on horses, or playing slot machines do not know when they will win, but they do know that they sometimes will. Pool hustlers take advantage of the resistance to extinction of variable-ratio schedules. By letting lesser players win periodically, pool hustlers encourage them to keep playing—and to keep losing several games for each one that they win.

variable-ratio schedule of reinforcement
A partial schedule of reinforcement that provides reinforcement after varying, unpredictable numbers of desired responses.

fixed-interval schedule of reinforcement
A partial schedule of reinforcement that provides reinforcement for the first desired response made after a set length of time.

variable-interval schedule of reinforcement
A partial schedule of reinforcement that provides reinforcement for the first desired response made after varying, unpredictable lengths of time.

▲ Fixed-Interval Schedules of Reinforcement
If you receive your mail at the same time every day, say at exactly 11 A.M., you are on a fixed-interval schedule of reinforcement. You would be reinforced the first time you checked your mailbox after 11 A.M., but you would not be reinforced if you checked it before 11 A.M.

a voucher after every three shirts sewn. That person, too, would be on a fixed-ratio schedule. Fixed-ratio schedules produce high, steady response rates, with a slight pause in responding after each reinforcement.

Unlike a fixed-ratio schedule, a **variable-ratio schedule of reinforcement** provides reinforcement after an unpredictable number of desired responses. The number of responses required will vary around an average. For example, a rat in a Skinner box might be reinforced with a food pellet after an average of 7 bar presses, with the number required varying each time—perhaps 5 presses one time, 10 presses a second time, and 6 presses a third time. People playing slot machines are on a variable-ratio schedule, because they cannot predict how many times they will have to play before they win. Even the archerfish, which hunts insects by spitting water at them as they fly by, continues to hunt that way (despite missing many times) because it is on a variable-ratio schedule of reinforcement (Goldstein & Hall, 1990).

Variable-ratio schedules produce high, steady rates of responding, which are more resistant to extinction than are those produced by any other schedule of reinforcement. In fact, by using a variable-ratio schedule of reinforcement, Skinner conditioned pigeons to peck a lighted disk up to 10,000 times to obtain a single pellet of food. This also explains why compulsive gamblers find it so difficult to quit—they know they will eventually receive positive reinforcement, though they do not know when.

While ratio schedules of reinforcement provide reinforcement after a certain number of desired responses, interval schedules of reinforcement provide reinforcement for the first desired response after a period of time. As in the case of ratio schedules, there are two kinds of interval schedules: fixed and variable. A **fixed-interval schedule** reinforces the first desired response after a set period of time. For example, a rat in a Skinner box might be reinforced with a food pellet for its first bar press after intervals of 30 seconds. Bar presses given during the intervals would not be reinforced.

A fixed-interval schedule produces a drop in responses immediately after a reinforcement and a gradual increase in responses as the time for the next reinforcement approaches. Suppose that you have a biology exam every 3 weeks. You would study before each exam to obtain a good grade—a positive reinforcer. But you would probably stop studying biology immediately after each exam and not begin studying it again until a few days before the next exam.

A **variable-interval schedule** of reinforcement provides reinforcement for the first desired response made after varying periods of time, which vary around an average. For

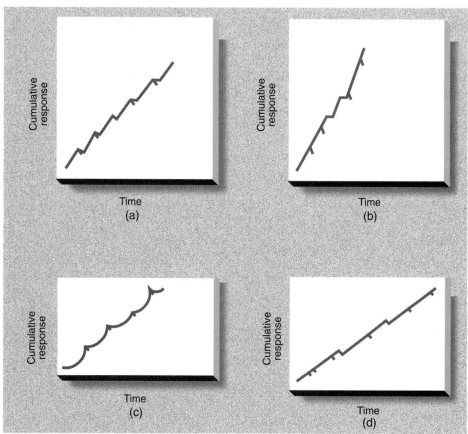

▸ **FIGURE 7.6**
Schedules of Reinforcement
The hash marks show the delivery of reinforcement. Steeper slopes indicate higher rates of responding. *(a)* Pattern of behavior typically produced by a fixed ratio schedule of reinforcement. *(b)* Pattern of behavior typically produced by a variable ratio schedule of reinforcement. *(c)* Pattern of behavior typically produced by a fixed interval schedule of reinforcement. *(d)* Pattern of behavior typically produced by a variable interval pattern of reinforcement.

example, a rat might be reinforced for its first bar press after 19 seconds, then after 37 seconds, then after 4 seconds, and so on, with the interval averaging 20 seconds. When you are fishing, you are on a variable-interval schedule of reinforcement, because you cannot predict how long you will have to wait until a fish bites. Variable-interval schedules produce relatively slow, steady rates of responding, highly resistant to extinction. An individual might continue to fish even if the fish are few and far between. And teachers who give periodic surprise quizzes make use of variable-interval schedules to promote more-consistent studying by their students.

Ratio schedules produce faster response rates than do interval schedules, because the number of responses, not the length of time, determines the onset of reinforcement. Variable schedules produce steadier response rates than do fixed schedules, because the individual does not know when reinforcement will occur. Figure 7.6 illustrates differences in response patterns under different schedules of reinforcement.

Negative Reinforcement: Increasing the Probability of Behavior

In **negative reinforcement** a behavior that brings about the removal of an aversive stimulus becomes more likely to occur in the future. Note that both positive and negative reinforcement increase the likelihood of a behavior. Consider the negative reinforcer known as the boring lecture. Because daydreaming lets you escape from boring lectures, you are likely to daydream whenever you find yourself listening to one. This form of negative reinforcement is called **escape learning**—learning to end something aversive. For example, you can terminate an irritating warning buzzer by putting on your automobile seat belt.

Of course your class might be so boring that you stop attending it. This is a form of negative reinforcement called **avoidance learning**—learning to prevent something aversive. Thus, you can avoid the sound of a warning buzzer by buckling up before you start your automobile engine. And dormitory students at some schools quickly learn to scamper out

negative reinforcement
In operant conditioning, an increase in the probability of a behavior that is followed by the removal of an aversive stimulus.

escape learning
Learning to perform a behavior that terminates an aversive stimulus, as in negative reinforcement.

avoidance learning
Learning to prevent the occurrence of an aversive stimulus by giving an appropriate response to a warning stimulus.

of the shower when they hear a toilet being flushed to avoid being scalded when cold water is diverted to the toilet (Reese, 1986).

But if negative reinforcement involves engaging in a behavior that removes an aversive stimulus, how could avoidance learning (which only prevents an aversive stimulus) be a form of negative reinforcement? That is, what is the aversive stimulus that is being removed? Evidently, what is being removed is an internal aversive stimulus—the emotional distress caused by your anticipation of the aversive event, such as a boring class or a scalding shower. Thus, in escape learning the aversive stimulus itself is removed, while in avoidance learning the emotional distress caused by anticipation of that stimulus is removed (Mowrer, 1947). Even relatively simple animals engage in avoidance learning. For example, bees that get caught in spider webs—and are fortunate enough to escape—may learn to avoid them in the future (Craig, 1994).

Extinction: Decreasing the Probability of Behavior

As in classical conditioning, behaviors learned through operant conditioning are subject to **extinction** (Lerman & Iwata, 1996). Skinner discovered extinction by accident. In one of his early studies, he conditioned a rat in a Skinner box to press a bar to obtain pellets of food from a dispenser. On one occasion he found that the pellet dispenser had become jammed, preventing the release of pellets. Skinner noted that the rat continued to press the bar, though at a diminishing rate, until it finally stopped pressing at all. Extinction might occur when a student who raises her hand is no longer called on to answer questions. Because she is no longer being positively reinforced for raising her hand, she would eventually stop doing so.

When extinction begins, there is typically a burst in the response. This is important in behavior therapy techniques that use extinction, because they might, at first, seem to be ineffective. Experienced therapists realize this and might promote appropriate behavior by reinforcing it while an undesired behavior is undergoing extinction (Lerman & Iwata, 1995).

Also, as with classical conditioning, a behavior that has been subjected to extinction can show **spontaneous recovery**—it might reappear after a period of time. This provides a functional advantage. For example, suppose that wild animals that visit a certain water hole normally obtain positive reinforcement by finding water there. If they visit the water hole on several successive occasions and find that it has dried up, their behavior will undergo extinction; they will stop visiting the water hole. But after a period of time, the animals might exhibit spontaneous recovery, again visiting the water hole—in case it had become refilled with water.

Punishment: Decreasing the Probability of Behavior

Still another way of reducing the probability of behaviors is through **punishment,** in which the consequence of a behavior decreases its likelihood. Do not confuse punishment with negative reinforcement. Negative reinforcement is "negative" because it involves the removal of an aversive stimulus; it does not involve punishment. Negative reinforcement increases the probability of a behavior by removing something undesirable as a consequence of that behavior; punishment decreases the probability of a behavior by presenting something undesirable (*positive punishment*) as a consequence of that behavior or by removing something desirable (*negative punishment*) as a consequence of that behavior. For example, a driver who gets a speeding ticket—an example of positive punishment—is less likely to speed in the future. Likewise, a teenager who is not allowed to use the family car because of speeding—an example of negative punishment—will also be less likely to speed again.

Punishment is useful even in animal, as well as human, societies. For example, social animals punish underlings who threaten group well-being. They use punishment to discipline offspring, promote cooperation, and maintain dominance hierarchies (Clutton-Brock & Parker, 1995). Though punishment can be an effective means of reducing undesirable behaviors, it is often ineffective. Consider some effective and ineffective ways of using punishment to discipline children (Walters & Grusec, 1977). First, punishment for misbehavior should be

extinction
In operant conditioning, the gradual disappearance of a response that is no longer followed by a reinforcer.

spontaneous recovery
In operant conditioning, the reappearance after a period of time of a behavior that has been subjected to extinction.

punishment
In operant conditioning, the process by which an aversive stimulus decreases the probability of a response that precedes it.

Contingency	Behavioral consequence	Probability of behavior	Example
Positive reinforcement	Brings about something desirable	Increases	You study for an exam and receive an A, which makes you more likely to study in the future.
Negative reinforcement	Removes something undesirable	Increases	You go to the dentist to have a cavity filled. This eliminates your toothache, which makes you more likely to visit the dentist in the future when you have a toothache.
Extinction	Fails to bring about something desirable	Decreases	You say hello to a person who repeatedly fails to greet you in return. This leads you to stop saying hello.
Punishment	Brings about something undesirable	Decreases	You overeat at a party and suffer from a severe upset stomach. In the future you become less likely to overeat.

▲ TABLE 7.1
Behavioral Contingencies

immediate so that the child will associate the punishment with the misbehavior. A mother or father should not resort to threats of "wait until your father [mother] gets home," which might separate the misbehavior and punishment by hours. Second, punishment should be strong enough to stop the undesirable behavior but not excessive. You might punish a child for throwing clothes about his room by having him clean the room, but you would be using excessive punishment if you had him clean every room in the house. Punishment that is excessive induces resentment aimed at the person who administers the punishment.

Third, punishment should be consistent. If parents truly want to reduce a child's misbehavior, they must punish the child each time it occurs. Otherwise the child learns only that her parents are unpredictable and that the misbehavior sometimes leads solely to positive reinforcement—that is, the child is on a variable ratio schedule of reinforcement (which is highly resistant to extinction). Fourth, punishment should be aimed at the misbehavior, not at the child. Children who are told that they, rather than their behavior, are "bad" can lose self-esteem. For example, a child who is repeatedly called "stupid" for making mistakes while playing softball might feel incompetent and lose interest in softball and other sports. Fifth, punishing undesirable behavior merely suppresses the behavior in response to a specific discriminative stimulus, such as the parent who administers punishment, and only tells the child what *not to do*. To make sure that the child learns what *to do,* positive reinforcement of desirable behavior should also be used.

One of the main controversies concerning punishment is the use of physical punishment. Children imitate parental models. If they observe that their parents rely on physical punishment, they might rely on it in dealing with their friends, siblings, and, eventually, their own children. Moreover, child abuse is a major problem in the United States, in part because parents might rely on physical punishment rather than on positive reinforcement and nonphysical forms of punishment. Though physical punishment of children can suppress misbehavior in the short run, in the long run it is associated with problems such as juvenile delinquency and adult criminality (Straus, 1991). Being physically punished as a child also is associated with subsequent adult depression, suicidal tendencies, alcohol abuse, wife beating, and physical brutality against children (Straus & Kantor, 1994). Table 7.1 summarizes the differences among the behavioral contingencies of positive reinforcement, negative reinforcement, extinction, and punishment.

▶ **Animal Training**
Animal trainers have used shaping and chaining to train animals to perform amazing behaviors including teaching squirrels to perform stunts while water skiing.
© Gerald Davis/Woodfin Camp & Assoc.

Applications of Operant Conditioning

B. F. Skinner (1986) claimed that many of our everyday problems could be solved by more-widespread use of operant conditioning. As one example, consider the problem of injuries and deaths caused by automobile accidents. As shown in Figure 7.7, operant conditioning is effective in teaching children to use seat belts, thereby reducing their risk of injury (Roberts & Fanurik, 1986). Now consider several other ways in which operant conditioning has been applied to everyday life.

Operant Conditioning and Animal Training

Skinner and some of his colleagues have been pioneers in the use of shaping and chaining to train animals to perform behaviors that are not part of their normal repertoire. Perhaps Skinner's most noteworthy feat in animal training occurred during World War II in "Project Pigeon." This was a secret project in which Skinner (1960) trained pigeons to guide missiles toward enemy ships by training them to peck at an image of the target ship shown on a display to obtain food pellets. Though this guidance system proved feasible, it was never used in combat.

More recently, pigeons have been trained to serve as air-sea rescue spotters in the Coast Guard's "Project Sea Hunt" (Stark, 1981). The pigeons are reinforced with food pellets for

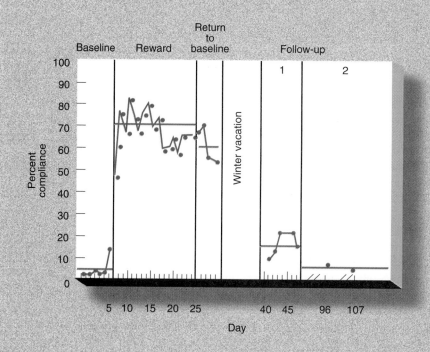

Seat-belt compliance at school 1

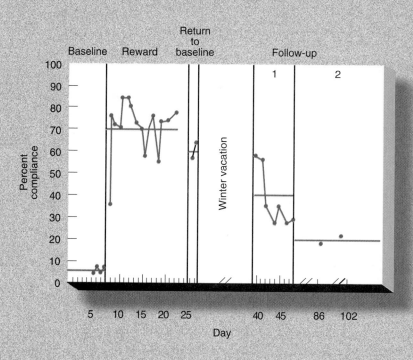

Seat-belt compliance at school 2

◄ FIGURE 7.7
Positive Reinforcement and Seat-Belt Use
Positive reinforcement (reward) is commonly
used to promote adaptive behaviors. These
graphs show the successful use of pizza, bumper
stickers, and coloring books as positive
reinforcers for seat-belt use by students at two
elementary schools. Note that seat-belt use was
higher during the reward phase.

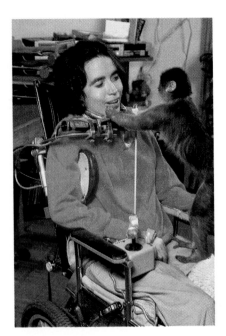

▲ Monkeys as Aides
Psychologists have trained capuchin monkeys to serve as aides to physically disabled persons. An organization called Helping Hands, based in Boston, uses operant conditioning to train the monkeys to respond to one-word commands and a laser pointer. They bring drinks, turn on televisions, and scratch itches. The monkeys are rewarded with edibles, such as sips of fruit juice or licks of peanut butter. The monkeys also help relieve the loneliness of their companions.

token economy
An operant conditioning procedure that uses tokens as positive reinforcers in programs designed to promote desirable behaviors, with the tokens later used to purchase desired items or privileges.

programmed instruction
A step-by-step approach, based on operant conditioning, in which the learner proceeds at his or her own pace through more and more difficult material and receives immediate knowledge of the results of each response.

responding to objects colored red, orange, or yellow—the common colors of flotation devices. Three pigeons are placed in a compartment under a search plane so that they look out of windows oriented in different directions. When a pigeon spots an object floating in the sea, it pecks a key, which sounds a buzzer and flashes a light in the cockpit. Pigeons are superior to human spotters, because they have the ability to focus over a wider area and to scan the sea for longer periods of time without becoming fatigued.

In another beneficial application of operant conditioning, psychologists have trained capuchin monkeys to serve as aides to physically disabled people (Mack, 1981). These monkeys act as extensions of the disabled person—bringing drinks, turning pages in books, changing television channels, and performing a host of other services. The person directs the monkey by using an optical pointer that focuses a beam of light on a desired object.

Operant Conditioning and Child Rearing

In 1945 Skinner shocked the public when he published the article "Baby in a Box," which described how he and his wife had reared an infant daughter in an enclosure called an *air crib*. The air crib filtered and controlled the temperature of the infant's air supply. Instead of diapers, it used a roll of paper that permitted sections to be placed under the baby and discarded when dirty. The parents could even pull down a shade over the front window of the air crib when the baby was ready to go to sleep. Skinner claimed the air crib was a more convenient way to rear infants and allowed more time for social interaction with them. Critics disagreed with Skinner, claiming that his treatment of his daughter was dehumanizing. Over the past few decades, rumors have claimed that Skinner's daughter's experience with the air crib eventually led her to sue her father, to become insane, or to commit suicide. In reality, she had a happy childhood and has pursued a successful career as an artist (Langone, 1983).

The air crib provoked fears of impersonal child rearing, and it was never widely used. Skinner had tried, unsuccessfully, to market the air crib under the clever brand name *Heir Conditioner*. Nonetheless, operant conditioning has proved useful in child rearing. For example, teachers have promoted toothbrushing by positively reinforcing children for having clean teeth by posting their names on the classroom wall (Swain, Allard, & Holborn, 1982). And parents have used extinction to eliminate their child's tantrums. When parents ignore the tantrums, rather than give in to the child's demand for toys, candy, or attention, the tantrums might at first intensify but eventually will stop (Williams, 1959).

Operant Conditioning and Educational Improvement

Teachers have likewise used positive reinforcement to improve their students' classroom performance. For example, verbal praise has been used to increase participation in classroom discussions (Smith et al., 1982), and positive reinforcement in the form of *token economies* has been used to promote desirable classroom behaviors (Swiezy, Matson, & Box, 1992). In a **token economy** teachers use tokens to reward students for proper conduct and academic excellence. The students then use the tokens to purchase items such as toys or privileges such as extra recess time. Token economies have been used to reduce television watching by children (Wolfe, Mendes, & Factor, 1984), increase reading by students (Brown, Fuqua, & Otts, 1986), and improve social skills in adults with mental retardation (Sandford, Elzinga, & Grainger, 1987).

Perhaps the most distinctive contribution that operant conditioning has made to education has been **programmed instruction,** which had its origin in the invention of the *teaching machine* by Sidney Pressey of Ohio State University in the 1920s. His machines provided immediate knowledge of results and a piece of candy to reward correct answers (Benjamin, 1988). But credit for developing programmed instruction is generally given to B. F. Skinner for his invention of a teaching machine that takes the student through a series of questions related to a particular subject, gradually moving the student from simple to more complex questions. After the student answers a question, the correct answer is revealed.

The teaching machine failed to catch on in the 1950s and 1960s because of fears that it would be dehumanizing, that it could teach only certain narrow subjects, and that teachers would lose their jobs. Nonetheless, supporters note that programmed instruction has several advantages over traditional approaches to education (Vargas & Vargas, 1991).

Programmed instruction provides immediate feedback of results (positive reinforcement for correct answers and only mild punishment for incorrect answers), eliminates the need for anxiety-inducing exams, and permits the student to go at her or his own pace. Skinner (1984) claimed that if schools adopted programmed instruction, students would learn twice as much in the same amount of time.

Today's use of **computer-assisted instruction** (Skinner, 1989) in many schools is a descendant of Skinner's programmed instruction. Computer programs take the student through a graded series of items at the student's own pace. The programs even branch off to provide extra help on items that the student finds difficult to master. Though teaching machines and computers have not replaced teachers, they have added another teaching tool to the classroom. Computer-assisted instruction has proved useful with students, whether teaching mathematics to grade-schoolers (Royer, Greene, & Anzalone, 1994), experimental design to college students (Duncan, 1991), or AIDS infection control to physicians (Garrett et al., 1990). Computer-assisted instruction is also useful with special populations, such as deaf students (Mertens & Rabiu, 1992), autistic children (Chen & Bernard-Opitz, 1993), and brain-injury victims (Glisky, 1992).

Operant Conditioning and Psychological Disorders

Operant conditioning has enhanced our understanding of psychological disorders, particularly depression. The concept of **learned helplessness** has gained influence as an explanation for depression through the work of Martin Seligman (see Chapter 14). In his original research, Seligman exposed dogs restrained in harnesses to electric shocks. One group of dogs could turn off the shock by pressing a switch with their noses. A second group could not. The dogs were then tested in a shuttle box, which consisted of two compartments separated by an easily hurdled divider. A warning tone was sounded, followed a few seconds later by an electric shock. Dogs in the first group escaped by jumping over the divider into the other compartment. In contrast, dogs in the second group whimpered but did not try to escape (Seligman & Maier, 1967).

Though replications of various versions of this study have produced inconsistent support for learned helplessness in animals (Klosterhalfen & Klosterhalfen, 1983) and

computer-assisted instruction
The use of computer programs to provide programmed instruction.

learned helplessness
A feeling of futility caused by the belief that one has little or no control over events in one's life, which can make one stop trying and become depressed.

Learning | 257

▶ Computer-Assisted Instruction
Students may benefit from computer-assisted instruction because it permits them to go at their own pace, receive immediate feedback on their progress, and, in some cases, obtain remedial help in areas of weakness.

human beings (Winefield, 1982), the possibility that learned helplessness is a factor in depression has inspired hundreds of studies (Deuser & Anderson, 1995). Depressed people feel that they have less control over obtaining positive reinforcers and avoiding punishments. As a consequence, they are less likely to try to change their life situations—which further contributes to their feelings of depression. You may have seen this in students who study many hours but still do poorly; they might become depressed, stop studying, and even drop out of school.

Operant conditioning has also been used to change abnormal behaviors. This is known as *behavior modification*. For example, token economies have been useful in training mental hospital patients to care for themselves (Morisse et al., 1996). Residents are trained to dress themselves, to use toilets, to brush their teeth, and to eat with utensils. They use the tokens to purchase merchandise or special privileges.

Limitations on Learning: Biological Constraints on Operant Conditioning

Around the turn of the century, Edward Thorndike put forth the concept of *belongingness* to explain why he found it easier to train cats to escape from his puzzle boxes by stepping on a pedal than by scratching themselves. Thorndike observed that animals seemed to inherit tendencies to associate the performance of certain behaviors with certain consequences. Cats are more predisposed to escape by performing actions that affect the environment, such as stepping on a pedal, than by performing actions that affect their bodies, such as scratching themselves.

Thorndike's observation had little influence on his contemporaries, and it was not until the 1950s that psychologists rediscovered what he had observed. Among the first psychologists to make this rediscovery were Keller and Marian Breland, former students of B. F. Skinner who became renowned animal trainers (Bailey & Bailey, 1993). Since its founding in 1947, their Animal Behavior Enterprises in Hot Springs, Arkansas, trained animals to perform in zoos, fairs, movies, circuses, museums, amusement parks, department stores, and television commercials.

Despite their success in training animals, the Brelands were distressed by the tendency of some animals to "misbehave" (Breland & Breland, 1961). Their misbehavior was actually a reversion to behaviors characteristic of their species, which the Brelands called **instinctive drift.** For example, they used operant conditioning to train a chicken to hit a baseball by pulling a string to swing a miniature bat and then run to first base for food. Sometimes, instead, the chicken chased after the ball and pecked at it. This "misbehavior" of animals has distressed animal trainers, but it demonstrates that animals tend to revert back to *species-specific behaviors* even when being reinforced for other behaviors.

After considering instinctive drift and related problems in operant conditioning, psychologist Martin Seligman (1970) concluded that there is a continuum of **behavioral preparedness** for certain behaviors. Behavioral preparedness has been demonstrated in many studies. For example, a hamster more easily learns to dig than to wash its face to obtain positive reinforcement (Shettleworth & Juergensen, 1980). The continuum of behavioral preparedness ranges from *prepared* to *unprepared* to *contraprepared*. Behaviors for which members of a species are *prepared* have evolved because they have survival value for them and are easily learned by members of that species. Behaviors for which members of a species are *unprepared* have no survival value for them and are difficult to learn for members of that species. And behaviors for which members of a species are *contraprepared* have no survival value for them and are impossible to learn for members of that species. For example, human beings are prepared, chimpanzees are unprepared, and dogs are contraprepared to use language. Human beings can learn to speak, read, write, and use sign language. Chimpanzees can learn to use sign language. And dogs cannot learn any of these language skills.

STAYING ON TRACK: *Operant Conditioning*

1. In what way was Edward Thorndike's instrumental conditioning the forerunner of B. F. Skinner's operant conditioning?

2. How would you use shaping to train a child to ride a tricycle?

3. In what ways are positive reinforcement and negative reinforcement similar and in what ways are they different?

COGNITIVE LEARNING: LEARNING THROUGH INFORMATION PROCESSING

Both classical conditioning and operant conditioning have traditionally been explained by the principle of contiguity—the mere association of events in time and space. Contiguity has been used to explain the association of a conditioned stimulus and an unconditioned stimulus in classical conditioning and the association of a behavior and its consequence in operant conditioning. Over the past few decades, the associationistic explanation of learning has been criticized for viewing human and animal learners as passive reactors to "external carrots, whips, and the stimuli associated with them" (Boneau, 1974, p. 308). These critics, influenced by the "cognitive revolution" in psychology, favor the study of cognitive factors in classical conditioning and operant conditioning, as well as the study of learning by observation, which had routinely been ignored by learning researchers (Wasserman, 1997).

Cognitive Factors in Associative Learning

As discussed earlier, the traditional view of classical conditioning and operant conditioning is that they are explained by contiguity alone. But evidence has accumulated that mere contiguity of a neutral stimulus and an unconditioned stimulus is insufficient to produce classical conditioning, and mere contiguity of a behavior and a consequence is insufficient to produce operant conditioning. This evidence has led to cognitive interpretations of associative learning, as in the case of operant conditioning. For

▲ Robert Rescorla

"Simple contiguity of CS and UCS fails to capture the relation required to produce an association."

example, secondary reinforcers have traditionally been thought to gain their reinforcing ability through mere *contiguity* with primary reinforcers. Cognitive theorists believe, instead, that secondary reinforcers gain their reinforcing ability because they have reliably *predicted* the occurrence of primary reinforcers (Rose & Fantino, 1978).

Suppose that you are using dog biscuits as positive reinforcers to train your dog to "shake hands." Just before giving your dog a biscuit, you might offer praise by saying "Good dog!" If you did so every time that your dog shook hands, the words "Good dog!" might become a secondary reinforcer. The traditional view of operant conditioning would claim that the praise became a secondary reinforcer by its mere *contiguity* with food. In contrast, the cognitive view would claim that the praise became a secondary reinforcer because it had become a good *predictor* of the food reward.

Psychologists have also provided cognitive explanations of classical conditioning that rule out mere contiguity as a sufficient explanation. The most influential of these explanations states that classical conditioning will occur only when the conditioned stimulus permits the individual to predict reliably the occurrence of the unconditioned stimulus (Miller, Barnet, & Grahame, 1995). The better the conditioned stimulus is as a predictor, the stronger the conditioning will be. This means that conditioning involves learning relations, or contingencies, among events in the environment (Rescorla, 1988).

This was demonstrated by Robert Rescorla (1968), who favors a cognitive explanation of conditioning. In one experiment, he paired a buzzer (the neutral stimulus) with an electric shock (a UCS), which he administered to rats. All of the rats received the same number of pairings of the buzzer and the electric shock. But some of the rats were given additional shocks not preceded by a buzzer. According to the traditional contiguity-based explanation of classical conditioning, because the buzzer and the electric shock had been paired an equal number of times for all of the rats, the buzzer should have become an equally strong CS, eliciting a CR, for all of them. Yet those for whom the buzzer always preceded the electric shock showed stronger conditioning.

Rescorla would explain this cognitively. The rats who always received an electric shock after the buzzer developed a stronger *expectancy* that the buzzer would be followed by an electric shock than did the rats who sometimes did and sometimes did not receive an electric shock after the buzzer. Consider this explanation in regard to Pavlov's studies of salivation in dogs. The dog learns that a tone is followed by meat powder. The more consistently the tone precedes the meat powder, the more predictable the relationship will be and, as a consequence, the stronger the conditioning will be.

Another source of evidence that supports the cognitive explanation of classical conditioning is the phenomenon of **blocking,** in which a neutral stimulus paired with a CS that already elicits a CR will fail to become a CS itself (Kamin, 1969). Blocking is illustrated in Table 7.2. Suppose that you have conditioned a dog to salivate to the sound of a bell by repeatedly presenting the bell before presenting meat powder. If you then repeatedly paired a light with the bell before presenting the meat powder, the principle of contiguity would make you expect that the light, too, would gain the ability to elicit salivation. But it will not. Instead, the CS (the bell) "blocks" the neutral stimulus (the light) from becoming a conditioned stimulus. According to the cognitive explanation, blocking occurs because the neutral stimulus (the light) adds nothing to the predictability of the UCS (the meat powder). The CS (the bell) already predicts the occurrence of the UCS. Blocking has been demonstrated in animals (Smith, 1997) and human beings (Hinchy, Lovibond, & Ter-Horst, 1995).

Still another source of evidence against a strictly contiguity-based view of classical conditioning comes from research on conditioned taste aversion. As you learned earlier, individuals who suffer gastrointestinal illness hours after eating novel food might avoid that food in the future. This contradicts the notion that events must be contiguous for us to learn to associate those events with each other.

Latent Learning: Learning Without Overt Behavior

The "cognitive revolution" in psychology has also produced a trend in recent decades to view learning less in terms of changes in overt behavior, as in classical or operant conditioning, and

blocking

The process by which a neutral stimulus paired with a conditioned stimulus that already elicits a conditioned response fails to become a conditioned stimulus.

	Phase 1	Phase 2	Phase 3
Experimental group	CS (tone) + UCS (shock)	CS (tone + light) + UCS (schock)	CS (tone) →CR (fear) CS (light) →No CR
Control group	No training	CS (tone + light) + UCS (shock)	CS (tone) CR (fear) CS (light) CR (fear)

▲ **TABLE 7.2**

Blocking

In this example, in phase 1, rats in the experimental group are presented with a tone (the CS) immediately followed by an electric shock (the UCS), while rats in the control group receive neither stimulus. In phase 2, both groups are exposed to a tone and a light, followed by a shock. In phase 3, both groups show fear (the CR) in response to the tone, but only the control group shows fear in response to the light. Because the tone already served as a reliable predictor of the shock for the experimental group, the tone blocked the light from becoming a CS for the rats in that group.

latent learning

Learning that occurs without the reinforcement of overt behavior.

more in terms of the acquisition of knowledge (Greeno, 1980). This means that learning can occur without revealing itself in observable behavior. For example, suppose that after studying many hours and mastering the material for a psychology exam, you fail the exam. Should your professor conclude that you had not learned the material? Not necessarily. Perhaps you failed the exam because the questions were ambiguous or because you were so anxious that your mind "went blank." Your performance on the exam did not reflect how well you had learned the material.

The first psychologist to stress the distinction between learning and performance was Edward Tolman (1932), who pointed out that learning can occur without rewards being given for overt actions, a process that he called **latent learning.** In latent learning, learning is not immediately revealed in performance but is revealed later when a reward is provided for performance. In a classic study, Tolman had three groups of rats run individually through a maze once a day for 10 days. One group received food as a positive reward for reaching the end of the maze, and the other two groups did not. The rewarded rats quickly learned to run through the maze with few wrong turns, while the nonrewarded rats did not. Beginning on the eleventh day, one of the groups of nonrewarded rats was also positively rewarded with food for reaching the end of the maze. As shown in Figure 7.8, the next day that group ran the maze as efficiently as the previously rewarded group did, while the remaining, still nonrewarded group continued to perform poorly. This demonstrated latent learning. The rats that were not rewarded until the eleventh day had learned the route to the end of the maze, but they revealed this learning only when rewarded for doing so (Tolman & Honzik, 1930).

More-recent research has provided additional support for latent learning. In one study, rats given an opportunity to observe a water maze before swimming through it for a food reward performed better than did rats who were not given such an opportunity (Keith & McVety, 1988). This provided evidence that rats can form what Tolman called "cognitive maps"—mental representations of physical reality. But they use their cognitive maps only when rewarded for doing so. Nonetheless, some researchers have found that in similar latent-learning experiments rats might be guided in their swimming not by cognitive maps, but instead by visual cues in their environment (Whishaw, 1991).

Observational Learning: Learning from Models

In the 1960s, research on latent learning stimulated interest in **observational learning,** in which an individual learns a behavior by watching others (models) perform it. That is, learning occurs without any overt behavior by the learner. Observational learning is important to both animals and human beings in a variety of situations, and from early in life. Research on observational learning in animals dates back to at least 1881 (Robert, 1990). Observational learning has also been demonstrated in a variety of animals, including cattle (Veissier, 1993), pigeons (Zentall, Sutton, & Sherburne, 1996), horses (Clarke et al., 1996), and even octopuses (Fiorito & Scotto, 1992). Consider rats. A rat that observes other rats eating foods will be more likely to eat those foods (Galef, 1993), infant rats that observe older rats opening pine cones will learn to do so themselves (Aisner & Turkel, 1992), and rats that observe other rats pushing a joystick in a particular direction to get food will learn to push it in that direction themselves (Heyes, Dawson, & Nokes, 1992).

observational learning

Learning a behavior by observing the consequences that others receive for performing it.

Latent Learning

Rats are capable of latent learning, in which they learn through experience, but they do not reveal this learning in overt behavior until they are reinforced for doing so. As the graph illustrates, in the Tolman and Honzik (1930) study, rats that merely explored a maze once a day for 10 days were given a food reward for reaching the end of the maze on the 11th day. On succeeding days they performed as well as rats that had been rewarded on the first 10 days, while other rats that had never been rewarded continued to perform poorly.

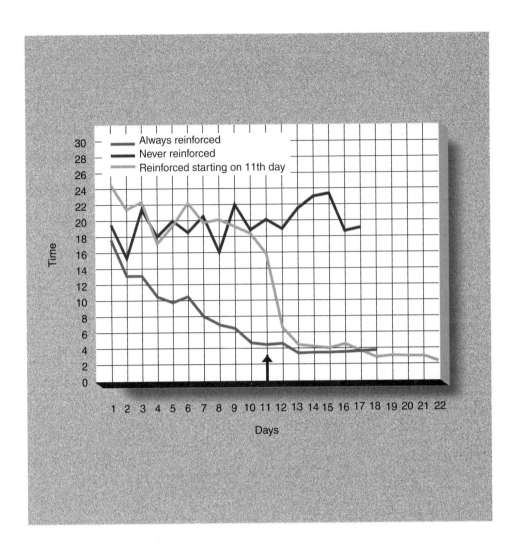

social learning theory

A theory of learning that assumes that people learn social behaviors mainly through observation and mental processing of information.

▲ **Albert Bandura**

"Most human behavior is learned observationally through modeling."

There are numerous examples of human observational learning (Ferrari, 1996). A few examples include infants learning to perform tasks after observing other infants perform them (Hanna & Meltzoff, 1993), ballet dancers learning to perform dance sequences they have seen (Gray et al., 1991), and students learning to behave properly by observing other students doing so (Hallenbeck & Kauffman, 1995).

Observational learning is central to Albert Bandura's **social learning theory,** which assumes that social behavior is learned chiefly through observation and the mental processing of information. What accounts for observational learning? Bandura (1986) has identified four factors: First, you must pay *attention* to the model's actions; second, you must *remember* the model's actions; third, you must have the *ability* to produce the actions; and fourth, you must be *motivated* to perform the actions. Consider a gymnast learning to perform a flying dismount from the uneven bars. She might learn to perform this feat by first paying attention to a gymnast who can already perform it. To be able to try the feat later, the learner would have to remember what the model did. But to perform the feat, the learner must have the strength to swing from the bars. Assuming that she paid attention to the model, remembered what the model did, and had the strength to perform the movement, she still might be motivated only to perform the feat in important competitions.

Observational learning can promote undesirable, as well as desirable, behavior. For example, we can develop phobias vicariously through observing people who exhibit them (Rachman, 1991). In fact, a study of people with spider phobia found that 71 percent traced it to observational learning, 57 percent to classical conditioning, and 45 percent to their knowledge of spiders (Merckelbach, Arntz, & de Jong, 1991). Even

▲ FIGURE 7.9
Observational Learning
Children who observe aggressive behavior being positively reinforced are more likely to engage in it themselves (Bandura, 1965).

monkeys can develop fears through observing other monkeys (Mineka & Cook, 1993). For example, in a study that also found support for the concept of preparedness in the development of phobias through observation, rhesus monkeys watched videotapes of model monkeys showing fear of presumably fear-relevant stimuli (toy snakes or a toy crocodile) or presumably fear-irrelevant stimuli (flowers or a toy rabbit). The monkeys developed fears of the fear-relevant, but not the fear-irrelevant, stimuli (Cook & Mineka, 1989). Perhaps they are prepared by evolution to do so, because such fears have survival value.

In an early study of observational learning in human beings, Bandura (1965) demonstrated the influence of such learning on the aggressiveness of children. Three groups of preschool children watched a film of an adult punching and verbally abusing a blow-up Bobo doll. Each group saw a different version of the film. In the first version the model was rewarded with candy, soda, and praise by another adult. In the second version the other adult scolded and spanked the model. And in the third version there were no consequences to the model. The children then played individually in a room with a Bobo doll and other toys (see Figure 7.9). Those who had seen the model being rewarded for being aggressive were more aggressive in their play than were those who had seen the other two versions of the film. This demonstrated that operant conditioning can occur vicariously, simply through observing others receiving positive reinforcement for engaging in the target behavior. Moreover, observing parents who resort to physical punishment contributes to the vicious cycle of child abuse and aggressiveness (Simons et al., 1991).

Research on observational learning has contributed to concerns about the effects of movies and television on viewers, particularly on children. This concern might be well founded, because children who watch violent programs tend to be more aggressive, while children who watch altruistic programs such as "Mister Rogers' Neighborhood" tend to engage in more positive social behaviors (Huston, Watkins, & Kunkel, 1989). Chapter 17 discusses research on the effects of television on children.

STAYING ON TRACK: *Cognitive Learning*

1. How do experiments on "blocking" support a cognitive interpretation of classical conditioning?

2. In what ways do latent learning and observational learning support a cognitive view of learning?

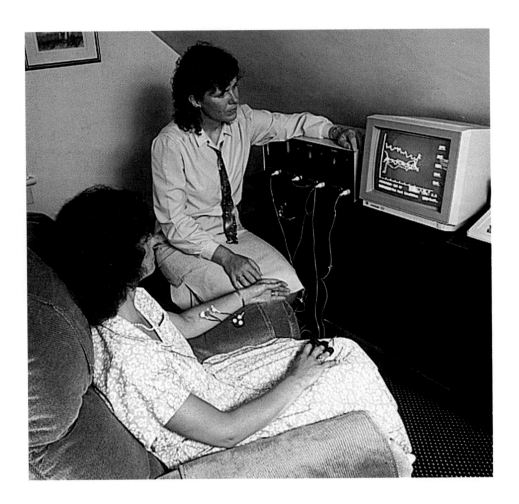

► **Biofeedback**
People provided with feedback on physiological processes may gain some control over normally involuntary ones, such as heart rate, or improved control over normally voluntary ones, such as muscle tension.

THINKING ABOUT *Psychology*

Is Biofeedback an Effective Means for Learning Self-Regulation of Physiological Responses?

biofeedback

A form of operant conditioning that enables an individual either to learn to control a normally involuntary physiological process or to gain better control of a normally voluntary one when provided with visual or auditory information indicating the state of that process.

One day, more than two decades ago, the eminent learning researcher Neal Miller stood in front of a mirror trying to teach himself to wiggle one ear. By watching his ear in the mirror, he eventually was able to make it wiggle (Jonas, 1972). The mirror provided Miller with visual *feedback* of his ear's movement. This convinced him that people might learn to control physiological responses that are not normally subject to voluntary control if they were provided with feedback of those responses. Since the 1960s Miller and other psychologists have developed a technique called *biofeedback* to help people learn to control normally involuntary responses such as brain waves, blood pressure, and intestinal contractions.

THE NATURE OF BIOFEEDBACK

Biofeedback is a form of operant conditioning that enables an individual to learn to control a normally involuntary physiological response or to gain better control of a normally voluntary one when provided with visual or auditory information indicating the state of that response. The feedback acts as a positive reinforcer for changes in the desired direction. How is this accomplished? The first step is to detect changes in electrical activity that reflect changes in the physiological response of interest. This is done by sensors, usually *electrodes*, attached to the body. The second step is to amplify the changes in electrical activity so that they can be recorded and used to generate a feedback signal. The third step is to present the subject with feedback indicating the state of the physiological response. The feedback might be provided by a light that changes in brightness as heart rate changes, a tone that changes in pitch as muscle tension changes, or any of a host of other visual or auditory stimuli that vary with changes in the target physiological response.

HISTORICAL BACKGROUND OF BIOFEEDBACK

Though the term *biofeedback* was not coined until 1969, the ability to gain extraordinary self-control of physiological responses was known long before then. For centuries Indian yogis have demonstrated the ability to gain control over involuntary responses, such as heart rate, that are regulated by the autonomic nervous system. Perhaps the first study of what we now call biofeedback occurred in 1885 when a Russian researcher reported the case of a patient who could control his heart rate when permitted to observe an ongoing polygraph recording of it (Tarchanoff, 1885/1973). But until the 1960s few researchers conducted studies of learned control of normally involuntary physiological responses, in part because influential psychologists such as B. F. Skinner considered it impossible.

Nonetheless, some researchers were undaunted by this pessimistic outlook and continued research on voluntary self-control of physiological responses. Their research bore fruit in the early 1960s with reports of the successful use of physiological feedback in training subjects to control their heart rate (Shearn, 1962) and imperceptible muscle twitches in their hands (Basmajian, 1963). Biofeedback was popularized in the late 1960s by reports of subjects who learned to control their alpha brain-wave patterns (Kamiya, 1969), which, as described in Chapter 6, are associated with a relaxed state of mind. But biofeedback did not become scientifically credible to many psychologists until Neal Miller reported success in training rats to gain voluntary control over physiological responses normally controlled solely by the autonomic nervous system. In his studies, Miller used electrical stimulation of the brain's reward centers (positive reinforcement) or, in some cases, escape or avoidance of shock (negative reinforcement) to train rats to increase or decrease their heart rate, intestinal contractions, urine formation, or blood pressure. Because Miller was an eminent, hard-nosed researcher, serious scientists became more willing to accept the legitimacy of biofeedback. Ironically, for unknown reasons, attempts at replicating his rat studies have generally failed (Dworkin & Miller, 1986).

APPLICATIONS OF BIOFEEDBACK

Disappointment at the failure to replicate Miller's rat studies and of biofeedback to fulfill early promises to induce mystical states of consciousness led to skepticism about its merits. But even though biofeedback has not proven to be an unqualified success, it has not proven to be a failure. Hundreds of studies have demonstrated the effectiveness of biofeedback in helping people learn to control a variety of physiological responses. Clinical applications have included reducing hyperactivity by training children to regulate their own brain waves (Lubar, 1991), promoting relaxation by training anxious people to breathe more regularly (Clark & Hirschman, 1990), and even helping people with painfully cold hands to warm them by increasing blood flow to them (Sedlacek & Taub, 1996).

One of biofeedback's main uses has been in training people to gain better control of their skeletal muscles. Though we normally exert excellent control over our muscles, at times we might want to exert even greater control. For example, biofeedback has been

▲ Neal Miller
"The biofeedback and behavioral medicine techniques already available are preventing unnecessary suffering, correcting disabling conditions, and helping people regain control of their lives."

used to train blind people to adopt more normal-looking facial expressions (Webb, 1977), to train typists to prevent carpal tunnel syndrome by warning them when their wrists are in improper positions (Thomas et al., 1993), and to train headache sufferers to relax their neck muscles (Arena et al., 1995).

In some cases, we want to reduce our level of muscle tension. For example, biofeedback has helped victims of lower-back pain gain relief by relaxing their muscles (Newton, Spence, & Schotte, 1995). In other cases, we might want to increase our level of muscle tension. This is particularly true in physical rehabilitation (Basmajian, 1988). For example, muscle-tension biofeedback has been used to restore use of thigh muscles in patients after total knee-joint replacement (Beckham et al., 1991).

Biofeedback has even been used to help increase muscle strength. In one study, body-builders were randomly divided into two groups. Both groups worked out on a Cybex leg extension machine three times a week for 5 weeks. One group received visual and auditory biofeedback while using the machine; the other group did not. At the end of the training period, the legs of those who had received biofeedback were stronger than the legs of those who had exercised without it. Those who received biofeedback benefited from continuous monitoring of their degree of exertion, which apparently served as positive reinforcement to increase their motivation to exert greater effort (Croce, 1986).

EVALUATING BIOFEEDBACK RESEARCH

Though biofeedback is widely used by psychologists and health professionals, it is not a panacea. In fact, there is controversy about its effectiveness and practicality. To demonstrate the effectiveness of biofeedback, one must show that learned self-regulation of physiological responses is caused by the feedback and not by extraneous factors (Roberts, 1985). For example, early biofeedback studies showed that feedback of alpha brain waves could increase them and induce a state of relaxation. But replications of those early studies showed that the effects were caused by the subjects' sitting quietly with their eyes closed. The brain-wave feedback added nothing (Plotkin, 1979).

Moreover, because biofeedback involves the use of sophisticated, scientifically impressive devices, it has the potential to create powerful placebo effects (Furedy, 1987). To control for such effects, researchers provide some subjects with *noncontingent feedback*, which is recorded feedback of the physiological activity of another subject. If the subjects who receive true feedback and the subjects who receive noncontingent feedback show equal improvement in self-regulation of a physiological response, then the improvement would be considered a placebo effect. But noncontingent feedback might be an inadequate control, because some subjects might realize that the feedback is not accurately reflecting changes in their physiological response. This is most likely true in studies that provide feedback of changes in muscle tension, which is more easily detected without biofeedback than are changes in brain waves, heart rate, or blood pressure (Burnette & Adams, 1987).

Even when the results of a biofeedback study can be attributed to the feedback, the technique might still not be of practical use. Why is this so? First, the typical biofeedback device costs hundreds or even thousands of dollars. Thus, clinicians must decide whether the benefits of biofeedback justify its cost, especially when other equally effective, less expensive treatments are available. For example, simple training in relaxation, requiring no costly apparatus, might be as useful as biofeedback-assisted relaxation (Kluger, Jamner, & Tursky, 1985). Yet, overall, treatment programs that include biofeedback have proved cost-effective in enhancing the quality of life and in reducing physician visits, medication use, medical care costs, hospital stays, and mortality (Schneider, 1987).

Second, laboratory experiments on biofeedback can produce results that are statistically significant (a concept discussed in Chapter 2) and merit being reported but that are too small to be of practical use in clinical settings (Steiner & Dince, 1981). For example, biofeedback might produce a *statistically significant* reduction in blood pressure in hypertensive persons that is too small to be *clinically meaningful*.

Third, biofeedback training in a clinician's office might produce results that do not last much beyond the training sessions. Fortunately, subjects who continue to practice what they have learned in biofeedback therapy sessions will be more likely to retain the benefits. A study of women migraine sufferers found that those who continued to practice handwarming at home showed a decline in headaches while those who did not did not (Gauthier, Cote, & French, 1994). One way to promote the generalization of benefits from clinical training sessions to everyday life is to use portable biofeedback devices (Harrison, Gavin, & Isaac, 1988).

Finally, the results of laboratory studies might not be applicable to the clinical setting. For example, an important factor in any treatment program, including ones that use biofeedback, is an empathetic relationship between the therapist and the client (Duckro, 1991), which would usually not exist between an experimenter and a subject. In addition, unlike experimenters, therapists rarely, if ever, rely solely on a biofeedback device in treating disorders. The therapist who uses biofeedback typically achieves success by combining biofeedback with other therapeutic approaches. Thus, biofeedback does not achieve its clinical effects by itself, as an antibiotic might do in curing a bacterial infection (Green & Shellenberger, 1986). That is, while it would be scientifically sound to compare a psychotherapy-plus-biofeedback group to a psychotherapy-alone group, it would be scientifically unsound to compare a psychotherapy-alone group to a biofeedback-alone group.

STAYING ON TRACK: *Biofeedback*

1. How is noncontingent feedback used to determine whether the results of biofeedback research are merely placebo effects?

2. Why is it important to distinguish between the statistical significance and the practical significance of the results of biofeedback studies?

 # CHAPTER SUMMARY

CLASSICAL CONDITIONING

Learning is a relatively permanent change in knowledge or behavior resulting from experience. As demonstrated by Ivan Pavlov in the kind of learning called classical conditioning, a stimulus (the conditioned stimulus) comes to elicit a response (the conditioned response) that it would not normally elicit. It does so by being paired with a stimulus (the unconditioned stimulus) that already elicits that response (the unconditioned response).

In stimulus generalization, the conditioned response occurs in response to stimuli that are similar to the conditioned stimulus. And in stimulus discrimination, the conditioned response occurs only in response to the conditioned stimulus. If the conditioned stimulus is repeatedly presented without the unconditioned stimulus, the conditioned response diminishes and eventually stops. This is called extinction. But after a period of time the conditioned stimulus again elicits the conditioned response. This is called spontaneous recovery.

Classical conditioning has been applied in many ways, as in explaining phobias, drug dependence, and learned taste aversions. In the past two decades, research has shown that in classical conditioning there are biological constraints on the ease with which particular stimuli can be associated with particular responses.

OPERANT CONDITIONING

While classical conditioning concerns the relationship between stimuli and responses, operant conditioning concerns the relationship between

behaviors and consequences. B. F. Skinner identified four behavioral contingencies to describe the relationship between behaviors and consequences: positive reinforcement, negative reinforcement, extinction, and punishment. In shaping, positive reinforcement is used to increase the likelihood of a behavior that is not in an individual's repertoire. In chaining, positive reinforcement is used to teach an individual to perform a series of behaviors.

In operant conditioning, behavior is affected by schedules of reinforcement. In a continuous schedule, every instance of a desired behavior is reinforced. In partial schedules, reinforcement is not given for every instance. Partial schedules include ratio schedules, which provide reinforcement after a certain number of responses, and interval schedules, which provide reinforcement for the first desired response after a certain interval of time.

In negative reinforcement, a behavior followed by the removal of an aversive stimulus becomes more likely to occur in the future. Negative reinforcement is implicated in avoidance learning and escape learning. When a behavior is no longer followed by reinforcement, it is subject to extinction. But after a period of time the behavior might reappear, in so-called spontaneous recovery—only to be subject to even faster extinction if it is still not reinforced. In punishment, an aversive consequence of a behavior decreases the likelihood of the behavior. To be effective, punishment should be immediate, firm, consistent, aimed at the misbehavior rather than the individual, and coupled with reinforcement of desirable behavior.

Operant conditioning has even more diverse applications than does classical conditioning; these include animal training, child rearing, educational improvement, and understanding and treating psychological disorders. Like classical conditioning, operant conditioning is subject to biological constraints, because members of particular species are more evolutionarily prepared to perform certain behaviors than to perform others.

COGNITIVE LEARNING

Cognitive psychologists have shown that contiguity might not be sufficient to explain learning. Mere contiguity of a neutral stimulus and an unconditioned stimulus is insufficient to produce classical conditioning, and mere contiguity of a behavior and a consequence is insufficient to produce operant conditioning. Instead, for learning to occur, active cognitive assessment of the relationship between stimuli or the relationship between behaviors and consequences appears to be essential. In latent learning, learning is revealed in overt behavior only when reinforcement is provided for that behavior. Albert Bandura's social learning theory considers how individuals learn through observing the behavior of others.

IS BIOFEEDBACK AN EFFECTIVE MEANS FOR LEARNING SELF-REGULATION OF PHYSIOLOGICAL RESPONSES?

Biofeedback is a form of operant conditioning that enables an individual to learn to control a normally involuntary physiological response or to gain better control of a normally voluntary physiological response when provided with visual or auditory feedback of the state of that response. Biofeedback gained scientific credibility through the research of Neal Miller. One of the most successful applications of biofeedback has been in the self-control of skeletal muscle activity, particularly in physical rehabilitation. To demonstrate the effectiveness of biofeedback, researchers must show that learned self-regulation of physiological responses is caused by the feedback and not by other factors, such as placebo effects. Its effects must be of practical, as well as statistical, significance. For biofeedback to be of practical value, its benefits must justify its cost. Moreover, the effects of biofeedback must transfer from the clinical setting to the everyday world for it to be useful in treating disorders.

KEY CONCEPTS

KEY CONTRIBUTORS

FOR MORE INFORMATION ON LEARNING

FOR GENERAL WORKS ON LEARNING

Brislin, R. W., Bochner, S., & Lonner, W. J. (Eds.). (1975). *Cross-cultural perspectives on learning.* New York: Halsted Press.
Malone, J. C. (1991). *Theories of learning: A historical approach.* Belmont, CA: Wadsworth.

Schwartz, B. (1995). *Psychology of learning and behavior* (4th ed.). New York: Norton.
Walker, J. T. (1995). *The psychology of learning: Principles and processes.* Englewood Cliffs, NJ: Prentice Hall.

FOR MORE ON CLASSICAL CONDITIONING

Braveman, N. S., & Bronstein, P. (Eds.). (1985). *Experimental assessments and clinical applications of conditioned food aversions.*

New York: New York Academy of Sciences.

Davey, G. (1987). *Cognitive processes and Pavlovian conditioning in humans*. New York: Wiley.

Gormezano, I., Prokasy, W. F., & Thompson, R. F. (Eds.). (1987). *Classical conditioning*. Hillsdale, NJ: Erlbaum.

Pavlov, I. P. (1927/1960). *Conditioned reflexes*. Mineola, NY: Dover.

FOR MORE ON OPERANT CONDITIONING

Kazdin, A. E. (1977). *The token economy: A review and evaluation*. New York: Plenum.

Larkin, J., Scheftic, C., & Chabay, R. W. (Eds.). (1993). *Computer-assisted instruction and intelligent tutoring systems*. Hillsdale, NJ: Erlbaum.

Peterson, C., Maier, S. F., & Seligman, M. E. P. (1993). *Learned helplessness: A theory for the age of personal control*. New York: Oxford University Press.

Skinner, B. F. (1938). *The behavior of organisms*. New York: Appleton-Century-Crofts.

Skinner, B. F. (1948). *Walden two*. New York: Macmillan.

Thorndike, E. L. (1931/1970). *Human learning*. Cambridge, MA: MIT Press.

Tunick, M. (1992). *Punishment: Theory and practice*. Berkeley: University of California Press.

FOR MORE ON BIOLOGICAL CONSTRAINTS ON LEARNING

Klein, S. B., & Mowrer, R. R. (Eds.). (1989). *Instrumental conditioning theory and the impact of biological constraints on learning*. Hillsdale, NJ: Erlbaum.

Klein, S. B., & Mowrer, R. R. (Eds.). (1989). *Pavlovian conditioning and the status of traditional learning theory*. Hillsdale, NJ: Erlbaum.

FOR MORE ON COGNITIVE LEARNING

Amsel, A. (1988). *Behaviorism, neobehaviorism, and cognitivism in learning theory: Historical and contemporary perspectives*. Hillsdale, NJ: Erlbaum.

Bandura, A. (1986). *Social foundations of thought and action: A social-cognitive theory*. Englewood Cliffs, NJ: Prentice Hall.

Heyes, C. M., & Galef, B. G., Jr. (Eds.). (1996). *Social learning in animals: The roots of culture*. San Diego: Academic Press.

Miller, N. E., & Dollard, J. (1962/1979). *Social learning and imitation*. Westport, CT: Greenwood.

Tolman, E. C. (1932). *Purposive behavior in animals and man*. New York: Appleton-Century-Crofts.

FOR MORE ON BIOFEEDBACK

Basmajian, J. V. (1989). *Biofeedback: Principles and practice for clinicians* (3rd ed.). Baltimore: Williams & Wilkins.

Hatch, J. P., Fisher, J. G., & Rugh, J. D. (Eds.). (1987). *Biofeedback: Studies in clinical efficacy*. New York: Plenum.

Sandweiss, J. H., & Wolf, S. L. (Eds.). (1985). *Biofeedback and sports science*. New York: Plenum.

Schwartz, M. S. (1995). *Biofeedback: A practitioner's guide* (2nd ed.). New York: Guilford.

FOR MORE ON CONTRIBUTORS TO THE STUDY OF LEARNING

Bjork, D. W. (1993). *B. F. Skinner: A life*. New York: Basic Books.

Buckley, K. W. (1989). *Mechanical man: John Broadus Watson and the beginnings of behaviorism*. New York: Guilford.

Evans, R. I. (1989). *Albert Bandura: The man and his ideas—A dialogue*. New York: Praeger.

Gray, J. A. (1979). *Ivan Pavlov*. New York: Viking Press.

Joncich, G. (1968). *The sane positivist: A biography of Edward L. Thorndike*. Middletown, CT: Wesleyan University Press.

Sechenov, I. M. (1935/1973). *I. M. Sechenov: Biographical sketch and essays*. Salem, NH: Ayer.

CHAPTER 8

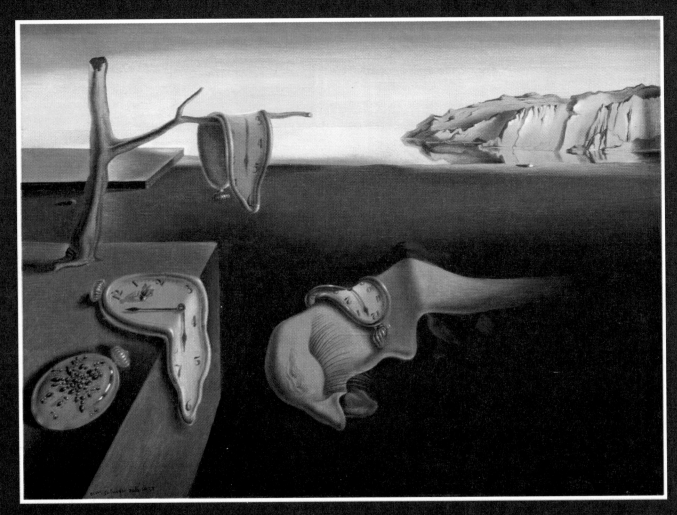

▲ SALVADOR DALI
The Persistence of Memory, 1931

Memory

*I*n 1898 a survey of 179 middle-aged and elderly adults asked, "Do you recall where you were when you heard that Lincoln was shot?" Of those surveyed, 127 claimed they could recall exactly where they were and what they were doing at that moment on April 14, 1865 (Colegrove, 1899). Such vivid, long-lasting memories of important, surprising, emotionally arousing events are called **flashbulb memories** (Brown & Kulik, 1977). People with flashbulb memories of an event might recall who told them about it, where they were, and trivial things that occurred at the time.

Perhaps you have a flashbulb memory of your first kiss or an award you received. You might have a flashbulb memory from January 28, 1986, when the space shuttle *Challenger* exploded shortly after takeoff on live television. Older students might have a flashbulb memory from November 22, 1963, when they heard that President John F. Kennedy had been assassinated. A survey of British college students found that 86 percent formed flashbulb memories of the unexpected resignation of British Prime Minister Margaret Thatcher. In contrast, only 26 percent of students from outside the United Kingdom formed flashbulb memories of that event. This supports research indicating that the formation of a flashbulb memory requires that an event be perceived as both important and surprising (Conway et al., 1994).

What accounts for flashbulb memories? The answer is unclear. Some psychologists believe they are the product of a special brain mechanism that evolved because it assures that we remember important, surprising experiences (Schmidt & Bohannon, 1988). Other psychologists disagree, insisting instead that normal memory processes, such as thinking more often and more elaborately about such experiences, can explain the phenomenon (McCloskey, Wible, & Cohen, 1988).

One psychology professor took advantage of a coincidence to test the common belief that flashbulb memories are more accurate than normal memories. On January 16, 1991, as part of a demonstration regarding flashbulb memories, he had students try to form a vivid memory of an ordinary event. On the same day, as shown on CNN, warplanes attacked Baghdad, beginning the Persian Gulf War. The professor had the students complete questionnaires about their memories for the classroom event and the beginning of the war. They completed them again in April 1991 and January 1992. The accuracy of the students' memories for the two events did not differ significantly. Their level of confidence in their memories, however, did. They were significantly more confident about their memories of the onset of the Persian Gulf War. These results indicate that flashbulb memories might seem special, not because of a special mechanism, but because of the undue confidence we place in them (Weaver, 1993).

The exact nature of flashbulb memories will be discovered by research on **memory,** the process by which information is acquired, stored in the brain, later retrieved, and eventually possibly forgotten. As William James noted a century ago, memory provides our consciousness with its continuity over time. Later in this chapter you will read about a man called "H. M." who suffers from brain damage that has impaired his ability to maintain this continuity of consciousness. Memory also enables us to adapt to situations by letting us call on skills and information gained from our relevant past experiences. Your abilities to drive a car, to perform well on an exam, and to serve as a witness at a trial all depend on memory. Moreover, memory enriches our emotional lives. Your memory lets you reexperience events from your past, such as an uplifting family gathering.

◀ Flashbulb Memories
Memory researchers are searching for explanations of flashbulb memories of momentous events.

In studying memory, psychologists consider several major "how" questions: How are memories formed? How are memories stored? How are memories retrieved? How are brain anatomy and brain chemistry related to memories? How dependable are eyewitness memories? This chapter addresses these questions.

INFORMATION PROCESSING AND MEMORY

During the past three decades, memory research has been driven by the "cognitive revolution" in psychology, which views the mind as an information processor. This is reflected in the most influential model of memory, developed by Richard Shiffrin and Richard Atkinson (1969). Their model assumes that memory involves the processing of information in three successive stages: *sensory memory*, *short-term memory*, and *long-term memory*. **Sensory memory** stores, in *sensory registers*, exact replicas of stimuli impinging on the senses. Sensory memories last for a brief period—from less than 1 second to several seconds. When you attend to information in sensory memory, it is transferred to **short-term memory**, which stores it for about 20 seconds unless you maintain it through mental rehearsal—as when you repeat a phone number to yourself long enough to dial it. Information transferred from short-term memory into **long-term memory** can be stored for up to a lifetime. Your ability to recall old memories indicates that information also passes from long-term memory into short-term memory.

The handling of information at each memory stage has been compared to information processing by a computer, which involves encoding, storage, and retrieval. **Encoding** is the conversion of information into a form that can be stored in memory. When you strike the keys on a computer keyboard, your actions are translated into a code that the computer understands. Similarly, information in your memory is stored in codes that your brain can process. **Storage** is the retention of information in memory. Personal computers typically store information on diskettes or hard disks. In human and animal memory, information is stored in the brain. **Retrieval** is the recovery of information from memory. When you strike certain keys, you provide the computer with cues that make it retrieve the information you desire. Similarly, we often rely on cues to retrieve memories that have been stored in the brain. We are also subject to **forgetting**—the failure to retrieve information from memory. This is analogous to the erasing of information on a diskette. Figure 8.1

sensory memory
The stage of memory that briefly, for at most a few seconds, stores exact replicas of sensations.

short-term memory
The stage of memory that can store a few items of unrehearsed information for up to about 20 seconds.

long-term memory
The stage of memory that can store a virtually unlimited amount of information relatively permanently.

encoding
The conversion of information into a form that can be stored in memory.

storage
The retention of information in memory.

retrieval
The recovery of information from memory.

forgetting
The failure to retrieve information from memory.

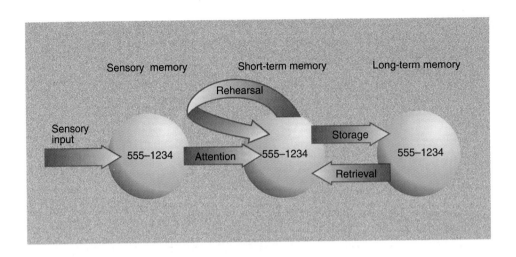

information-processing model
The view that the processing of memories involves encoding, storage, and retrieval.

summarizes this **information-processing model** of memory. Though some psychologists question the existence of separate information-processing stages for sensory memory, short-term memory, and long-term memory, there is strong evidence in support of them (Cowan, 1988).

STAYING ON TRACK: *Information Processing and Memory*

1. What evidence is there that flashbulb memories are not the product of a special brain mechanism?
2. How do sensory memory, short-term memory, and long-term memory differ from one another?

Answers to Staying on Track start on p. S-3.

SENSORY MEMORY: FLEETING TRACES

Think back to the last movie you saw. It was actually a series of frames, each containing a picture slightly different from the one before it. So why did you see smooth motion instead of a rapidly presented series of individual pictures? You did so because of your *visual sensory memory*, which stores images for up to a second. Visual sensory memory is called **iconic memory;** an image stored in it is called an *icon* (from the Greek word for "image"). The movie projector presented the frames at a rate (commonly 24 frames a second) that made each successive frame appear just before the previous one left your iconic memory, making the successive images blend together and create the impression of smooth motion. You can demonstrate iconic memory by rapidly swinging a pen back and forth. Notice how iconic memory lets you see a blurred image of the path taken by the pen. But how much of the information that stimulates our visual receptors is stored in iconic memory? That question inspired the following classic experiment.

iconic memory
Visual sensory memory, which lasts up to about a second.

ANATOMY OF A CLASSIC RESEARCH STUDY

Do We Form Sensory Memories of All the Information That Stimulate Our Sensory Receptors?

Rationale

Though we have a sensory register for each of our senses, most research on sensory memory has been concerned with iconic memory. The classic experiment on this was carried out by a Harvard University doctoral student named George Sperling (1960). Sperling used an ingenious procedure to test the traditional wisdom that sensory memory stores only a small amount of the information that stimulates our sensory receptors.

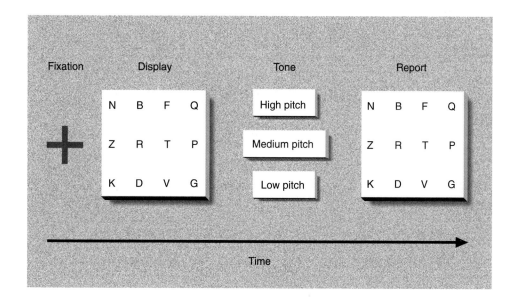

Fixation	Display	Tone	Report
	N B F Q	High pitch	N B F Q
	Z R T P	Medium pitch	Z R T P
	K D V G	Low pitch	K D V G

Time

◄ FIGURE 8.2
Testing Sensory Memory
In Sperling's (1960) study of sensory memory, the subject fixated on a cross on a projection screen. A display of letters was then flashed briefly on the screen. This was repeated with many different displays. At varying times after a display had been flashed, a tone signaled the subject to report the letters in a particular row. This enabled Sperling to determine how many of the letters were stored in sensory memory. By delaying the tone for longer and longer intervals, Sperling was also able to determine how quickly images in sensory memory fade.

Method

Sperling's procedure is illustrated in Figure 8.2. The subjects, tested individually, stared at a screen as Sperling projected sets of 12 letters, arranged in three rows of 4, onto it. Each presentation lasted for only 0.05 second—a mere flash. Sperling then asked the subjects to report as many of the letters as possible. He found that the subjects could accurately report an average of only 4 or 5. The subjects claimed, however, that they had briefly retained an image of the 12 letters, but by the time they had reported a few of them the remaining ones had faded away.

Rather than dismiss these claims, Sperling decided to test them experimentally by using a variation of this task. Instead of using *whole report* (asking the subjects to report as many of the 12 letters as possible), he used *partial report* (asking the subjects to report as many of the 4 letters as possible from a designated row). The task again included displays of 12 letters arranged in three rows of 4. But this time, at the instant the visual display was terminated, a tone was sounded. The pitch of the tone signaled the subject to report the letters in a particular row: a high tone for the top row, a medium tone for the middle row, and a low tone for the bottom row.

Results and Discussion

When subjects gave partial reports, they accurately reported an average of 3.3 of the 4 letters in a designated row. Because the subjects did not know which row would be designated until after the display was terminated, the results indicated that, on the average, 9.9 of the 12 letters were stored in iconic memory. Sperling concluded that virtually all of the information from visual receptors is stored as an image in iconic memory, but, as his subjects had claimed, the image fades rapidly.

This inspired Sperling to seek the answer to another question: How fast does the information in iconic memory fade? He found the answer by repeating his partial-report procedure, but this time delaying the tone that signaled the subject to give a partial report. He varied the period of delay from 0.1 second to 1.0 second. As the delay lengthened, the subject's ability to recall letters in a designated row declined more and more. Sperling found that when the delay reached 1.0 second, the number of letters that could be recalled was about the same as when a whole report was used. Subsequent research has found that the typical duration of iconic memory is closer to 0.3 seconds than to 1.0 second (Loftus, Duncan, & Gehrig, 1992).

▲ ▲ ▲

▲ Sensory Memory
If you walked through Times Square in New York City, your senses would be bombarded by sights, sounds, and smells. An enormous amount of this stimulation would be stored in your sensory memory. But at any given moment you would be consciously aware of only a tiny portion of the stored information. This selectivity of attention prevents your consciousness from being overwhelmed by sensations.

Auditory sensory memory serves a purpose analogous to that of visual sensory memory, blending together successive pieces of auditory information. Auditory sensory memory is called **echoic memory,** because sounds linger in it. Echoic memory stores information longer than iconic memory does, normally holding sounds for 3 or 4 seconds, but perhaps

echoic memory
Auditory sensory memory, which lasts up to 4 or more seconds.

▲ George Sperling

"The fact that observers commonly assert that they can *see* more than they can *report* suggests that memory sets a limit on a process that is otherwise rich in available information."

as long as 10 seconds (Samms et al., 1993). The greater persistence of information in echoic memory lets you perceive speech by blending together successive spoken sounds that you hear (Ardila, Montanes, & Gempeler, 1986). You become aware of your echoic memory when someone says something to you that you do not become aware of until a few seconds after it was said. Suppose that while you are enthralled by a television movie a friend asks, "Where did you put the can opener?" After a brief delay you might say, "What? . . . Oh, it's in the drawer to the left of the sink." Researchers have identified a precise region in the primary auditory cortex that processes echoic memories (Lu, Williamson, & Kaufman, 1992).

Based on Sperling's study, and subsequent research, we know that sensory memory can store virtually all the information provided by our sensory receptors and that this information fades rapidly (though the fade rates vary among the senses). Nonetheless, we can retain information that is in sensory memory by attending to it and transferring it into short-term memory.

STAYING ON TRACK: *Sensory Memory*

1. How did George Sperling demonstrate that iconic memory stores more information than commonly believed?
2. How does the relatively long duration of echoic memory help us perceive speech?

SHORT-TERM MEMORY: WORKING MEMORY

When you pay attention to information in your sensory memory or information retrieved from your long-term memory, the information enters your short-term memory, which has a limited capacity and holds information for about 20 seconds. Because you are paying attention to this sentence, it has entered your short-term memory. In contrast, other information in your sensory memory, such as the feeling of this book against your hands, will not enter your short-term memory until your attention is directed to it. And note that you are able to comprehend the words in this sentence because you have retrieved their meanings from your long-term memory. Because we use short-term memory to think about information provided by either sensory memory or long-term memory, it is also called *working memory* (Hulme & Roodenrys, 1995). Information transferred into short-term memory is represented by one of three codes (H. C. Ellis, 1987): a visual code (images), an acoustic code (sounds), or a semantic code (meanings). We typically encode information as sounds—even when the information is visual. This was demonstrated in a study in which subjects were shown a series of six letters and immediately tried to recall them. The subjects' errors showed that they more often confused letters that sounded alike (for example, T and C) than letters that looked alike (for example, Q and O). This indicated that the letters, though presented visually, had been encoded according to their sounds (Conrad, 1962).

In comparison to sensory memory or long-term memory, short-term memory has a relatively small storage capacity. You can demonstrate this for yourself by performing this exercise: Read the following numerals one at a time, and then (without looking at them) write them down in order on a sheet of paper: 6, 3, 9, 1, 4, 6, 5. Next, read the following numerals one at a time and write them down from memory: 5, 8, 1, 3, 9, 2, 8, 6, 3, 1, 7. If you have average short-term memory storage capacity, you were probably able to recall the 7 numbers in the first set but not the 11 numbers in the second set.

The normal limit of 7 items in short-term memory was the theme of a famous article by psychologist George Miller (1956) entitled "The Magical Number Seven, Plus or Minus Two." Miller noted that short-term memory has, on the average, a capacity of 7 "chunks" of information, with a range of 5 to 9 chunks. His observation has received support from other research studies (Glassman et al., 1994), though some researchers have found that the normal range of capacity is greater than 5 to 9 chunks (Smith, 1992). A *chunk* is a meaningful unit of information, such as a date, a word, or an abbreviation. For example, to a college student familiar with American culture, a list that includes the

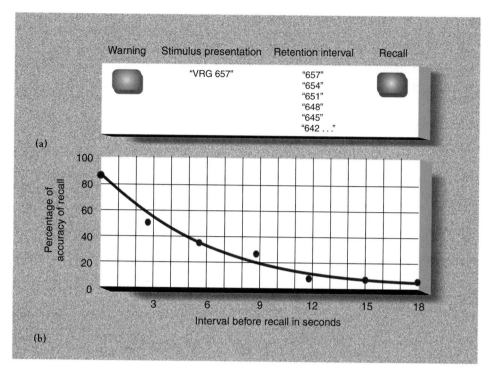

"VRG 657"   "657"
                "654"
                "651"
                "648"
                "645"
                "642 . . ."

(a)

Percentage of accuracy of recall

100
80
60
40
20
0

3   6   9   12   15   18

Interval before recall in seconds

(b)

◄ **FIGURE 8.3**
The Duration of Short-Term Memory
Peterson and Peterson (1959) demonstrated
that the information in short-term memory
lasts no more than 20 seconds. (*a*) A warning
light signaled that a trial was to begin. The
subject then heard a three-letter trigram and a
three-digit number. To prevent rehearsal of the
trigram, the subject counted backward by
threes from the number. After a period of 3 to
18 seconds, a light signaled the subject to recall
the trigram. (*b*) The longer the delay between
presentation and recall of the trigram, the less
likely the subject was to recall it accurately.

meaningful chunks *CBS, NFL,* and *FBI* would be easier to recall than a list that includes the meaningless combinations of letters *JOL, OBS,* and *CWE.*

Miller noted that the ability to chunk individual items of information can increase the amount of information stored in short-term memory (Baddeley, 1994). For example, after a 5-second look at the positions of pieces on a chessboard, expert chess players are significantly better than novice chess players at reproducing the positions of the pieces. This reflects experts' greater ability to chunk chess pieces into familiar configurations (Chase & Simon, 1973). Thus, though chess experts do not store more memory chunks in their short-term memory than novices do, their memory chunks contain more information.

Given that about 7 chunks is the typical amount of information in short-term memory, how long will it remain stored? Without **maintenance rehearsal** (that is, without repeating the information to ourselves), we can store information in short-term memory for no more than about 20 seconds. But if we use maintenance rehearsal, we can store it in short-term memory indefinitely. You could use maintenance rehearsal to remember the items on a short grocery list long enough to select each of them at the store.

Early evidence that unrehearsed information in short-term memory lasts perhaps 20 seconds came from a study conducted by Lloyd and Margaret Peterson (1959) in which they orally presented *trigrams* that consisted of three consonants (for example, *VRG*) to their subjects. Their procedure is presented in Figure 8.3. To distract the subjects and prevent them from engaging in maintenance rehearsal of the trigrams, immediately after a trigram was presented a light signaled the subject to count backward from a 3-digit number by threes (for example, "657, 654, 651, . . ."). Following an interval that varied from 3 seconds to 18 seconds, a light signaled that the subject was to recall the trigram. The longer the interval, the less likely the subjects were to recall the trigram. And when the interval was 18 seconds, the subjects could rarely recall the trigram. Thus, the results indicated that unrehearsed information normally remains in short-term memory for no longer than about 20 seconds.

Information stored in short-term memory is lost primarily by *decay* (the mere fading of information over time) and by *displacement* by new information (Reitman, 1974). The displacement of information from short-term memory was demonstrated in a study in which subjects called a telephone operator for a long-distance number. They showed poorer recall of the number if the operator said "Have a nice day" after giving them the number than if the operator did not. Evidently the cheery message displaced the phone number from short-term memory (Schilling & Weaver, 1983).

maintenance rehearsal
Repeating information to oneself to keep
it in short-term memory.

▲ **Lloyd Peterson and Margaret Peterson**
"Forgetting was found to progress at differential
rates dependent on the amount of controlled
rehearsal of the stimulus."

1. Why do psychologists believe that visual information tends to be stored acoustically in short-term memory?

2. How did Lloyd and Margaret Peterson demonstrate that short-term memories last about 20 seconds?

LONG-TERM MEMORY: MEMORIES FOR UP TO A LIFETIME

As mentioned earlier, information moves back and forth between short-term memory and long-term memory. When functioning at its best, long-term memory can store an enormous amount of information with great accuracy. For example, in the early twentieth century, Hebrew scholars from Poland were able to recall the entire contents of the thousands of pages in the twelve-volume *Babylonian Talmud*, a Hebrew holy book. In fact, when a pin was pushed through the pages of a volume, a scholar could recall each of the words pierced by the pin (Stratton, 1917).

Normal information processing in long-term memory has been compared to the workings of a library. Information in a library is *encoded* in materials such as books or magazines, *stored* on shelves in a systematic way, *retrieved* by using cues given by on-line catalogs, and *forgotten* when it is misplaced or its computer record is erased. Similarly, information in long-term memory is encoded in several ways, stored in an organized manner, retrieved by using cues, and forgotten due to a failure to store it adequately or to use appropriate retrieval cues.

Encoding: Forming Long-Term Memories

William James (1890/1981, Vol. 1, p. 646) noted, "A curious peculiarity of our memory is that things are impressed better by active than by passive repetition." To appreciate James's claim, try to draw the face side of a United States penny from memory. Next, look at the drawings of pennies in Figure 8.4. Which one is accurate? Even if you have handled thousands of pennies over the years and realize that the front of a penny has a date and a profile of Abraham Lincoln, you probably were unable to draw every detail. And even when presented with several drawings to choose from, you might still have chosen the wrong one. If you had difficulty, you are not alone. A study of adult Americans found that few could draw a penny from memory, and less than half could recognize the correct drawing of one (Nickerson & Adams, 1979).

What accounts for our failure to remember an image that is a common part of everyday life? The answer depends in part on the distinction between *maintenance rehearsal* and *elaborative rehearsal*. As noted earlier, in using maintenance rehearsal, we simply hold information in short-term memory without trying to transfer it into long-term memory, as when we remember a phone number just long enough to dial it. In **elaborative rehearsal,** we actively organize information and integrate it with information already stored in long-term memory, as when studying material from this chapter for an exam. Though maintenance rehearsal can encode some information (such as the main features of a penny) into long-term memory (Wixted, 1991), elaborative rehearsal encodes more information (such as the exact arrangement of the features of a penny) into long-term memory (Greene, 1987).

You can experience the benefits of elaborative rehearsal when you are confronted by new concepts in a textbook. If you try to understand a concept by integrating it with information already in your long-term memory, you will be more likely to encode the concept firmly into your long-term memory. For example, when the concept "flashbulb memory" was introduced earlier in this chapter, you would have been more likely to encode it into long-term memory if it provoked you to think about your own flashbulb memories. Elaborative rehearsal also has important practical benefits. In one study, sixth-graders who were taught cardiopulmonary resuscitation showed better retention of what they learned if they used elaborative rehearsal (Rivera-Tovar & Jones, 1990).

elaborative rehearsal

Actively organizing new information to make it more meaningful, and integrating it with information already stored in long-term memory.

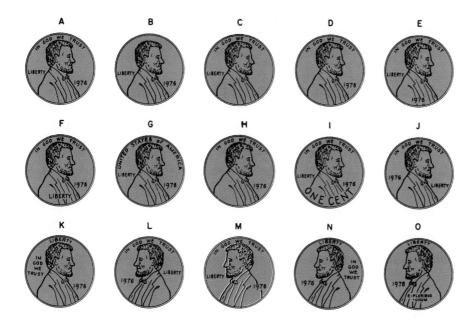

The superior encoding of information through elaborative rehearsal supports the **levels of processing theory** of Fergus Craik and Robert Lockhart (1972), which was originally presented as an alternative to the information-processing model of memory. They believe that the level, or "depth," at which we process information determines how well it is encoded and, as a result, how well it is encoded in memory (Lockhart & Craik, 1990). When you process information at a shallow level, you attend to its superficial, sensory qualities—as when you use maintenance rehearsal of a telephone number. In contrast, when you process information at a deep level, you attend to its meaning—as when you use elaborative rehearsal of textbook material. Similarly, if you merely listen to the sound of a popular song over and over on the radio—a relatively shallow level of processing—you might recall the melody but not the lyrics. But if you listen to the lyrics and think about their meaning (perhaps even connecting them to personally significant events)—a deeper level of processing—you might recall both the words and the melody.

In a study that supported the levels of processing theory, researchers induced subjects to process words at different levels by asking them different kinds of questions about each word just before it was flashed on a screen for a fifth of a second (Craik & Tulving, 1975). Imagine that you are replicating the study, and one of the words is *bread*. You could induce a shallow, *visual* level of encoding by asking how the word *looks*—for instance, "Is the word written in capital letters?" You could induce a somewhat deeper, *acoustic* level of encoding by asking how the word *sounds*—"Does the word rhyme with *head*?" And you could induce a much deeper, *semantic* level of encoding by asking a question related to what the word *means*—"Does the word fit in the sentence *The boy used the _____ to make a sandwich?*" After repeating this with several words, you would present the subject with a list of words and ask him or her to identify which of the words had been presented before. Craik and Tulving (1975) found that the deeper the level at which a word had been encoded, the more likely it was to be correctly identified (see Figure 8.5). Thus, the deeper the level at which information is encoded, the better it will be remembered. This has been supported by research showing that subjects show better recognition of previously presented words when they had attended to their meanings than when they had attended to their sounds (Ferlazzo, Conte, & Gentilomo, 1993).

Storage: Retaining Long-Term Memories

According to influential memory researcher Endel Tulving (1985), we store information in two kinds of long-term memory: **Procedural memory** includes memories of how to perform behaviors, such as making an omelette or using a word processor; **declarative memory**

▲ **Endel Tulving**
"Semantic memory is concerned with the retention and use of general . . . knowledge independent of personal time and space; episodic memory, with the storage and retrieval of information based on particular . . . experiences located in personal time and space."

levels of processing theory
The theory that the "depth" at which we process information determines how well it is encoded, stored, and retrieved.

procedural memory
The long-term memory system that contains memories of how to perform particular actions or skills.

declarative memory
The long-term memory system that contains memories of facts.

Depth of Processing
Craik and Tulving (1975) found that the greater the depth of processing of words, the better will be memory for them. Encoding words according to their meaning produced better recognition of them than did encoding them according to their sound or appearance.

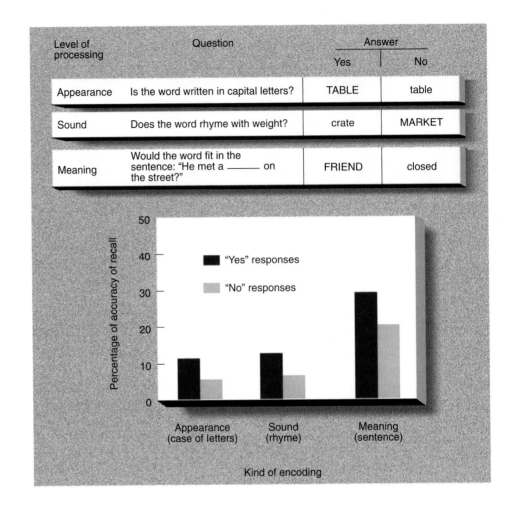

explicit memory
Conscious recollection of general information or personal experiences.

implicit memory
Recollection of previous experiences demonstrated through behavior, rather than through conscious, intentional remembering.

semantic memory
The subsystem of declarative memory that contains general information about the world.

episodic memory
The subsystem of declarative memory that contains memories of personal experiences tied to particular times and places.

includes memories of facts. Declarative memory and procedural memory are also referred to, respectively, as **explicit memory** and **implicit memory** (Schacter, 1992). Tulving (1993) subdivides declarative memory into *semantic memory* and *episodic memory*. **Semantic memory** includes memories of general knowledge, such as the definition of an omelette or the components of a word processor. **Episodic memory** includes memories of personal experiences tied to particular times and places, such as the last time you made an omelette or used a word processor.

Some memory researchers believe that the brain evolved different memory systems for storing these different kinds of memory into declarative memory for facts and events and procedural memory for skills, habits, and conditioned responses (Eichenbaum, 1997). There is evidence that brain-wave activity distinguishes different memory systems. Subjects in one study were presented with a series of pairs of words and had to judge whether members of the pairs were related in meaning (semantic memory) or whether they had been presented with specific pairs before (episodic memory). The semantic-memory task was associated with an abundance of alpha brain waves and the episodic-memory task was associated with an abundance of slower theta brain waves (Klimesch, Schimke, & Schwaiger, 1994).

The main line of evidence in support of multiple memory systems in human beings comes from studies of people with brain damage. For example, either implicit or explicit memory can be intact while the other is impaired (Gabrieli et al., 1995). In a case study (Schacter, 1983), a victim of Alzheimer's disease, a degenerative brain disorder marked by severe memory impairment, was able to play golf (procedural memory) and had good knowledge of the game (semantic memory) but could not find his tee shots (episodic memory). This indicates that though semantic memory and episodic memory are both forms of declarative memory, they may involve different brain systems. Figure 8.6 illustrates the relationship of the different memory systems.

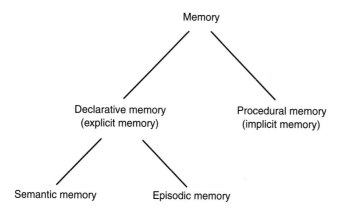

Nonetheless, some theorists believe that the selective loss of procedural, semantic, or episodic memories does not necessarily mean that we have separate memory systems (Horner, 1990). The question that many memory researchers seek to answer is this: Do different brain systems serve the different kinds of memory, or does a single brain system serve all of them? Regardless of how many memory systems we have, long-term memories must be stored in a systematic way. Unlike short-term memory, in which a few unorganized items of information can be stored and retrieved efficiently, long-term memory requires that millions of pieces of information be stored in an organized, rather than arbitrary, manner. Otherwise, you might spend years searching your memory until you retrieved the one you wanted, just as you might spend years searching the Library of Congress for William James's *The Principles of Psychology* if the library's books were shelved randomly. The better we are at organizing our memories, the better our recall of them is (Bjorklund & Buchanan, 1989). For example, a study of a waiter who could take twenty complete full-course dinner orders without writing them down found that he did so by quickly categorizing the items into meaningful groupings. When he was prevented from doing so, he was unable to recall all of the orders (Ericsson & Polson, 1988).

Semantic Network Theory of Long-Term Memory

A theory that explains how semantic information is meaningfully organized in long-term memory is the **semantic network theory,** which assumes that semantic memories are stored as nodes interconnected by links (see Figure 8.7). A *node* is a concept such as "pencil," "green," "uncle," or "cold," and a *link* is a connection between two concepts. More-related nodes have shorter (that is, stronger) links between them. The retrieval of a node from memory stimulates activation of related nodes, so-called *spreading activation* (Collins & Loftus, 1975).

Even young children organize memories into semantic networks. For example, preschool children who enjoy playing with toy dinosaurs and listening to their parents read to them about dinosaurs may organize their knowledge of dinosaurs into semantic networks (Chi & Koeske, 1983). The dinosaurs would be represented as nodes (for example, "Brontosaurus" or "Tyrannosaurus Rex") and their relationships would be represented by links. The retrieval of a dinosaur's name from memory would activate nodes with which it is linked. So, retrieval of *Brontosaurus* would be more likely to activate nodes that contain the names of other plant-eating dinosaurs than nodes that contain the names of meat-eating dinosaurs, such as *Tyrannosaurus Rex.*

semantic network theory
The theory that memories are stored as nodes interconnected by links that represent their relationships.

Schema Theory of Long-Term Memory

An alternative to the semantic network theory of memory organization is the **schema theory,** which is used to explain both episodic memory and semantic memory. The schema theory was put forth decades ago by the English psychologist Frederick Bartlett (1932), who found that long-term memories are stored as parts of schemas. A *schema* is a cognitive structure that organizes knowledge about an event or an object and that affects the encoding, storage, and retrieval of information related to it (Alba & Hasher, 1983). Examples of schemas include "birthday party," "class clown," and "Caribbean vacation."

schema theory
The theory that long-term memories are stored as parts of schemas, which are cognitive structures that organize knowledge about events or objects.

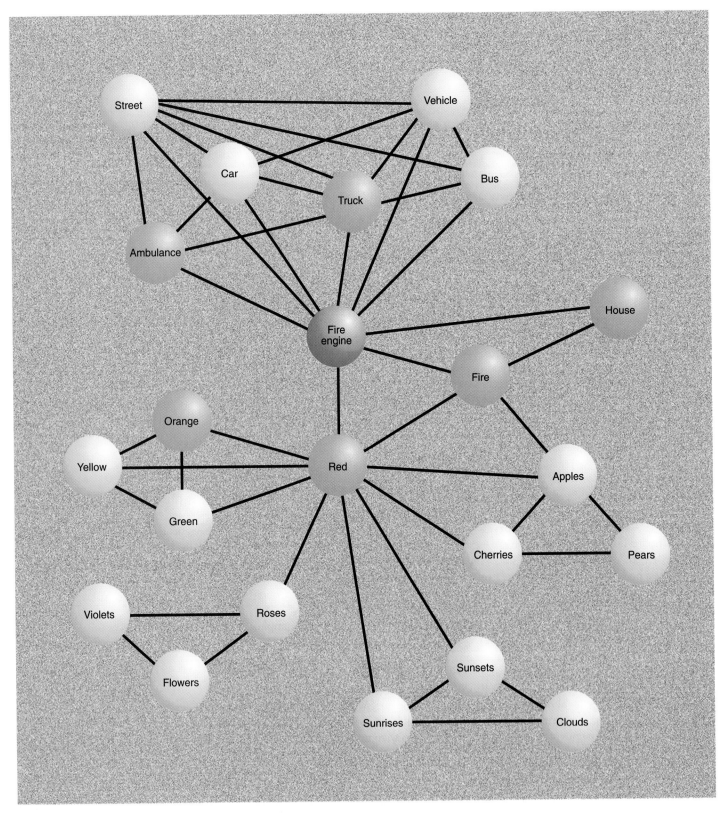

▲ FIGURE 8.7
A Semantic Network
According to Collins and Loftus (1975), our long-term memories are organized into semantic networks in which concepts are interconnected by links. The shorter the link between two concepts, the stronger the association between them. After a retrieval cue has activated a concept, related concepts will also be activated and retrieved from long-term memory.

In a classic study, Bartlett had British college students read a Native American folktale called "The War of the Ghosts," which told about a warrior fighting ghosts, and later write the story from memory. He found that the subjects recalled the theme of the story but added, eliminated, or changed details to fit their own story schemas. For example, the subjects added a moral, left out an event, or altered an aspect (such as changing a canoe to a boat). In a cross-cultural study of memory for stories, American and Mexican college students read brief stories of everyday activities. There were two versions of each story, each consistent with either an American cultural schema or a Mexican cultural schema. A week later, when tested on their recognition of information in the stories, both groups of subjects recognized the stories from the other culture as being more like their own culture than they actually were (Harris, Schoen, & Hensley, 1992). Thus, their recall was influenced by their cultural schemas.

Retrieval: Accessing Long-Term Memories

▶ In short, we may search in our memory for forgotten ideas, just as we rummage our house for a lost object. In both cases we visit what seems to us the probable *neighborhood* of that which we miss. We turn over the things under which, or within which, or alongside which, it may possibly be; and if it lies near them, it soon comes to view. But these matters, in the case of a mental object sought, are nothing but its *associatives*. (James, 1890/1981, Vol. 1, p. 615)

The semantic network theory of memory agrees with William James's statement that the retrieval of memories from long-term memory begins by searching a particular region of memory and then tracing the associations among nodes (memories) in that region, rather than by haphazardly searching through information stored in long-term memory. This is analogous to looking for a book in a library. You would use the on-line catalog to give you a retrieval cue (a book number) to help you locate the book you want. Similarly, when you are given a memory retrieval cue, the relevant stored memories are activated, which in turn activate memories with which they are linked (Anderson, 1983). In keeping with this, advertisers incorporate distinctive retrieval cues in their advertisements for specific products so that the repetition of those cues will evoke recall of those products. For example, a study found that the use of a visual cue helped children recall advertised cereal better and made them more likely to ask their parents to buy the cereal (Macklin, 1994).

To illustrate retrieval from a semantic network, suppose that you were given the cue "sensory memory." If your semantic network were well organized, the cue might activate nodes for "Sperling," "iconic," and "partial report." But if your semantic network were less well organized, the cue might also activate nodes for "amnesia," "chunks," or "Alzheimer's." And if your semantic network were poorly organized, the cue might activate nodes completely unrelated to sensory memory, such as "hallucination," "sensory deprivation," or "extrasensory perception."

In contrast to semantic network theory, schema theory assumes that when we retrieve memories we might alter them to make them consistent with our schemas. An example of the schematic nature of memory retrieval, taken from testimony about the 1972 Watergate burglary that led to the resignation of President Richard Nixon, was provided by the eminent memory researcher Ulric Neisser (1981). Neisser described how a schema influenced the testimony of John Dean, former legal counsel to President Nixon, before the Senate Watergate Investigating Committee in 1973. Dean began his opening testimony with a 245-page statement in which he recalled the details of dozens of meetings that he had attended over a period of several years. Dean's apparently phenomenal recall of minute details prompted Senator Daniel Inouye of Hawaii to ask skeptically, "Have you always had a facility for recalling the details of conversations which took place many months ago?" (Neisser, 1981, p. 1).

Neisser found that Inouye's skepticism was well founded. In comparing Dean's testimony with tape recordings (secretly made by Nixon) of those conversations, Neisser found that Dean's recall of their themes was accurate, but his recall of many of the details was inaccurate. Neisser took this as evidence for Dean's reliance on a schema to retrieve

▲ **Ulric Neisser**
"Constructive recall is the rule, literal recall is the exception."

memories. The schema reflected Dean's knowledge that there had been a cover-up of the Watergate break-in. Neisser (1984) used this to support his conclusion that, in recalling real-life events, we rely on constructive recall more often than literal recall.

What Neisser called **constructive recall** is the distortion of memories by adding or changing details to fit a schema. Schemas in the form of scripts for particular events can even affect eyewitness testimony. For example, the scripts we have for different kinds of robberies can affect our recall of events related to them. We might recall things that did not actually occur during a robbery if they fit our script for that kind of robbery (Holst & Pezdek, 1992). Schemas can even adversely affect the ability of scientists and undergraduates to remember the content of classic research studies they have read (Vicente & Brewer, 1993). But neither the schema theory nor the semantic network theory has yet emerged as the best explanation of the storage and retrieval of long-term memories. Perhaps a complete explanation requires both.

Forgetting: Losing Long-Term Memories

According to William James (1890/1981, Vol. 1, p. 640), "if we remembered everything, we should on most occasions be as ill off as if we remembered nothing." James believed that forgetting is adaptive because it rids us of useless information that might impair our recall of useful information. But as you are sometimes painfully aware of when taking exams, even useful information that has been stored in memory is not always retrievable. The inability to retrieve previously stored information is called *forgetting*.

The first formal research on forgetting was conducted by the German psychologist Hermann Ebbinghaus (1885/1913). Ebbinghaus (1850–1909) made a purposeful decision to do for the study of memory what Gustav Fechner had done for the study of sensation—subject it to the scientific method (Postman, 1985). Ebbinghaus studied memory by repeating lists of items over and over until he could recall them in order perfectly. The items he used were called *nonsense syllables* (consisting of a vowel between two consonants, such as *VEM*) because they were not real words. He used nonsense syllables instead of words because he wanted a "pure" measure of memory, unaffected by prior associations with real words. Despite this effort, he discovered that even nonsense syllables varied in their meaningfulness, depending on how similar they were to words or parts of words.

Ebbinghaus found that immediate recall is worse for items in the middle of a list than for those at the beginning and end of a list (see Figure 8.8). His finding was replicated in the 1890s by Mary Whiton Calkins (Madigan & O'Hara, 1992). This differential forgetting is called the **serial-position effect** (Korsnes, Magnussen, & Reinvang, 1996). The better memory for items at the beginning of a list is called the *primacy effect,* and the better memory for items at the end of a list is called the *recency effect.* Thus, in memorizing a list of terms from this chapter you would find it harder to memorize terms from the middle of the list than terms from the beginning or end of the list.

What accounts for the serial-position effect? The primacy effect seems to occur because the items at the beginning of a list are subjected to more rehearsal as a learner memorizes the list, firmly placing those items in long-term memory. And the recency effect seems to occur because items at the end of the list remain readily accessible in short-term memory. In contrast, items in the middle of the list are neither firmly placed in long-term memory nor readily accessible in short-term memory. Note that this explanation supports Shiffrin and Atkinson's distinction between short-term memory and long-term memory. But the explanation has not received universal support. For example, one study found that the primacy effect occurs even when subjects are prevented from rehearsing items at the beginning of a list that is to be recalled (Wright et al., 1990).

Before Ebbinghaus's work, knowledge of memory was based on common sense, anecdotal reports, and reasoning, with little supporting empirical evidence. Ebbinghaus moved memory from the philosophical realm into the psychological realm, making it subject to scientific research. Ebbinghaus also introduced the **method of savings,** which is commonly called *relearning,* as a way to assess memory. In using the method of savings, Ebbinghaus memorized items in a list until he could recall them perfectly, noting how

constructive recall
The distortion of memories by adding, dropping, or changing details to fit a schema.

serial-position effect
The superiority of immediate recall for items at the beginning and end of a list.

method of savings
The assessment of memory by comparing the time or number of trials needed to memorize a given amount of information and the time or number of trials needed to memorize it again at a later time.

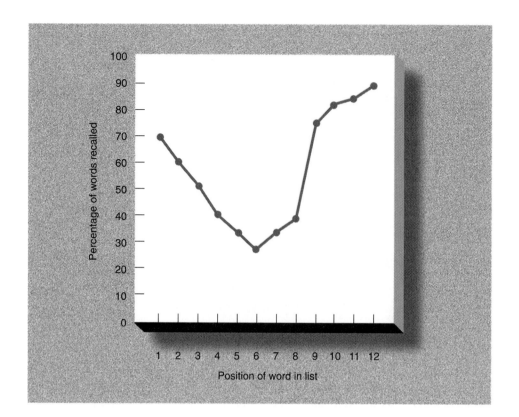

◀ FIGURE 8.8
The Serial-Position Effect
This is a typical serial-position curve, showing
that items in the middle of a list are the most
difficult to recall.

many trials he needed to achieve perfect recall. After varying intervals, during which he naturally forgot some of the items, Ebbinghaus again memorized the list until he could recall it perfectly. The delay varied from 20 minutes to 31 days. He found that it took him fewer trials to relearn a list than to learn it originally. He called the difference between the number of original trials and the number of relearning trials *savings*, because he relearned the material more quickly the second time. The phenomenon of savings demonstrates that even when we cannot recall information, much of it still remains stored in memory, even though it is inaccessible to recall. If it were not still stored, we would take just as long to relearn material as we took to learn it originally.

When you study for a cumulative final exam, you experience savings. Suppose that your psychology course lasts 15 weeks and you study your notes and readings for 6 hours a week to perform at an A level on exams given during the semester. You will have studied for a total of 90 hours. If you then studied for a cumulative final exam, you would not have to study for 90 hours to memorize the material to your original level of mastery. In fact, you would have to study for only a few hours to master the material again. Savings occurs because relearning improves the retrieval of information stored in memory (MacLeod, 1988).

Relearning is a method of testing implicit memory, because it assesses information that has been retained without necessarily being accessible to conscious awareness prior to relearning. As another example of an implicit-memory test, consider the word-stem completion test. Suppose you are exposed in passing to a list of words that includes *telegraph*. Later, despite having no recollection of having seen the word, you would be more likely to take the word stem *tele-* and form the word *telegraph* than if you had not been exposed to that word earlier.

You are more familiar with tests of explicit memory. A *recognition test* measures your ability to identify information that you have been exposed to previously when it is presented again. Recognition tests you might encounter in college include matching, true/false, and multiple-choice exams. A *recall test* measures your ability to remember information without the information being presented to you. Recall tests you might encounter in college include essay and fill-in-the-blanks exams. Ebbinghaus also found that, once we have mastered a list of items, forgetting is initially rapid and then

▲ **Hermann Ebbinghaus (1850–1909)**
"Physical states of every kind, sensations, feelings, ideas, which at one time were present and then disappeared from consciousness, have not absolutely ceased to exist. Although an inward glance may not find them, they are not absolutely denied and annulled, but continue to live in a certain way, retained, as one says, in memory."

► FIGURE 8.9
The Forgetting Curve
The graph at the top presents the results of a
study by Ebbinghaus on memory for nonsense
syllables. The graph shows that forgetting is initially rapid and then levels off.

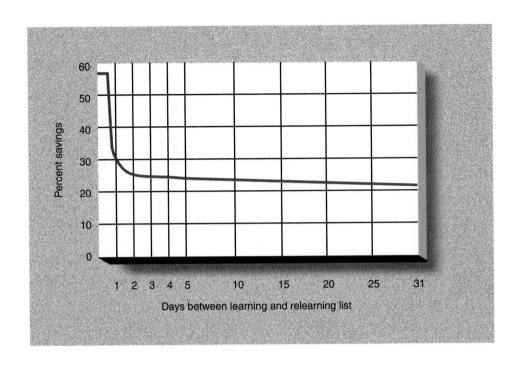

Days between learning and relearning list

forgetting curve

A graph showing that forgetting is initially
rapid and then slows.

decay theory

The theory that forgetting occurs because
memories naturally fade over time.

slows (see Figure 8.9). This phenomenon has been replicated many times (Wixted &
Ebbesen, 1991). So, if you memorized a list of terms from this chapter for an exam,
you would do most of your forgetting in the first few days after the exam. But in
keeping with the concept of levels of processing, meaningless nonsense syllables are
initially forgotten more rapidly than is meaningful material, such as psychology terms.
Ebbinghaus's **forgetting curve,** which shows rapid initial forgetting followed by less
and less forgetting over time, even holds for material learned decades before, as
demonstrated in a cross-sectional study of the retention of Spanish words learned in
high school by groups of subjects ranging from recent graduates to those who had
graduated 50 years earlier. Though some of the subjects had not spoken Spanish in 50
years, they showed surprisingly good retention of some words. Their forgetting was
rapid during the first 3 years after high school, then remained relatively unchanged.
This indicates that after a certain amount of time, memories that have not been forgotten can become permanently held, in a kind of "permastore" (Bahrick, 1984).

Trace Decay and Forgetting

Plato, anticipating the **decay theory,** likened memory to an imprint made on a block of
soft wax: Just as soft-wax imprints disappear over time, memories fade over time. But
decay theory has received little research support, and a classic study provided evidence
against it. John Jenkins and Karl Dallenbach (1924) had subjects memorize a list of 10
nonsense syllables and then either stay awake or immediately go to sleep for 1, 2, 4, or 8
hours. At the end of each period, the subjects tried to recall the nonsense syllables. The
researchers wondered whether sleep would prevent waking activities from interfering with
the memories.

The graph in Figure 8.10 shows that the subjects had better recall if they slept than if
they remained awake. There was some memory loss during sleep, providing modest support
for decay theory, but if decay theory were an adequate explanation of forgetting, the subjects should have shown the same level of recall whether they remained awake or slept.
Jenkins and Dallenbach concluded that the subjects forgot more if they remained awake
because experiences they had while awake interfered with their memories of the nonsense
syllables. In contrast, the subjects had forgotten less after sleeping because they had few
experiences while asleep that could interfere with their memories for the nonsense syllables. The durability of many childhood memories throughout adulthood, such as
high school memories held in "permastore," also provides evidence against the decay theory.

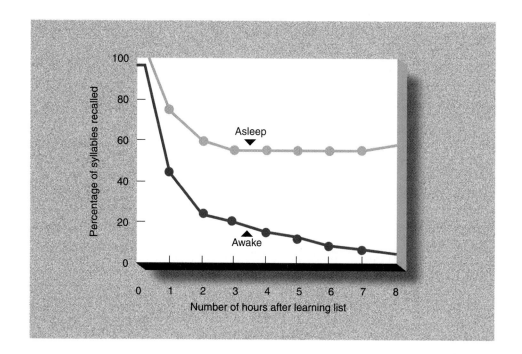

Interference and Forgetting

Since Jenkins and Dallenbach's classic study contradicting decay theory, psychologists have come to favor *interference* as a better explanation of forgetting. **Interference theory** assumes that forgetting results from particular memories' interfering with the retrieval of other memories. This occurs, for example, when trying to recall advertisements for the myriad of products we are exposed to in everyday life (Kent & Allen, 1994). In **proactive interference,** old memories interfere with new memories (if you move to a new home, for instance, your memory of your old phone number might interfere with your ability to recall your new one). Proactive interference has been used to demonstrate that sign language and spoken language may be stored separately in human memory. A study found that there is less proactive interference in memory when old and new materials are each presented in a different language (that is, sign language and spoken language) than if both are presented in the same language (Hoemann & Keske, 1995). In **retroactive interference,** new memories interfere with old ones (your memory of your new phone number might interfere with your memory of your old one). This explains why names of people we meet today may interfere with our ability to retrieve names we learned before (Chandler, 1993). Figure 8.11 illustrates the difference between proactive interference and retroactive interference.

You have certainly experienced both kinds of interference when taking an exam. Material you have studied for other courses sometimes interferes with your memories of the material on the exam. And interference is stronger when the materials are similar. Thus, biology material will interfere more than computer science material with your recall of psychology material. Because of the great amount of material you learn during a semester, proactive interference might be a particularly strong influence on your later exam performance (Dempster, 1985). So it would be best to study different subjects as far apart as possible rather than studying a bit of each every day. Moreover, be sure to study before going to sleep and right before your exam to reduce the effect of retroactive interference on your retrieval of relevant memories during the exam.

Motivation and Forgetting

One day Eileen Franklin-Lipsker looked into her daughter's eyes and was overcome by a horrible memory. Twenty years earlier, as a young child, she had witnessed her father sexually assault and bludgeon to death her 8-year-old friend Susan Nason. Eileen's father warned her that he would kill her if she told anyone about his crime. She was so emotionally overwhelmed that she forgot the event for two decades—until the look in her

interference theory
The theory that forgetting results from some memories' interfering with the ability to remember other memories.

proactive interference
The process by which old memories interfere with the ability to remember new memories.

retroactive interference
The process by which new memories interfere with the ability to remember old memories.

Proactive interference

Old memories interfere with new memories

Retroactive interference

New memories interfere with old memories

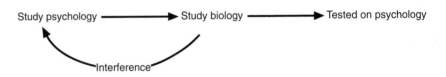

repression

The process by which emotionally threatening experiences are banished from the conscious mind to the unconscious mind.

daughter's eyes evoked the same feelings she had when looking into the eyes of Susan as she was being attacked. Eileen also recalled the general area where her father had buried Susan's body, and she took the police to it. They found Susan's remains, and in 1990 Eileen's father was convicted of murder (MacLean, 1993). Subsequently, because of the potentially leading questioning of Eileen, his conviction was overturned on appeal.

Sigmund Freud might have explained Eileen's amnesia as an instance of motivated forgetting. Freud (1901/1965) claimed that we can forget experiences through **repression,** the process by which emotionally threatening experiences, such as witnessing a murder, are banished to the unconscious mind. Though research findings tend to contradict Freudian repression as an explanation of forgetting (Abrams, 1995), some studies suggest that we are more motivated to forget emotionally upsetting experiences than other kinds of experiences. Yet, other studies find that there is no difference in recall of pleasant or unpleasant experiences (Bradley & Baddeley, 1990).

In an experiment that possibly demonstrated motivated forgetting, subjects were shown one of two versions of a training film for bank tellers that depicted a simulated bank robbery. In one version, a shot fired by the robbers at pursuers hit a boy in the face. The boy fell to the ground, bleeding profusely. In the other version, instead of showing the boy being shot, the bank manager was shown talking about the robbery. When asked to recall details of the robbery, subjects who had seen the violent version had poorer recall of the details of the crime than did subjects who had seen the nonviolent version. One possible explanation is that the content of the violent version motivated subjects to forget what they had seen (Loftus & Burns, 1982). However, in some cases memory of traumatic events will be superior to memory of ordinary events (Christianson & Loftus, 1987).

At times we might be motivated to distort our recall of past events in ways that make the events more consistent with our current circumstances, much as schemas influence our recall of earlier experiences. This possibility was investigated in an experiment in which college students were randomly assigned to a study skills group or to a control group that was put on a waiting list (Conway & Ross, 1984). All subjects began by doing a self-evaluation of their study skills. Three weeks later, the subjects were asked to recall their initial self-evaluations. Members of the study skills group recalled their evaluations as worse than they had actually been, but members of the control group recalled theirs accurately. Members of the study skills group also reported greater improvement in their study skills, and expected better final grades than did those in the control group. But the actual grades of the two groups did not differ. Six months later, members of the study skills group overestimated their academic performance for the period when the program was conducted. The distorted memories of the study skills group might have reflected their desire to have their participation pay off. A more recent study likewise found that

◀ Motivated Forgetting
According to Sigmund Freud, a person (such as the man in this photograph, whose heroic effort to save a friend from a fire was futile) might forget a traumatic event by repressing its memory to the unconscious mind.

college students, when asked to recall their high-school grades, tended to inflate them (Bahrick, Hall, & Berger, 1996).

Though there is some research evidence to support motivated forgetting, the belief that memories of childhood sexual abuse can be repressed and then retrieved years or decades later has been countered by research on false memories, the so-called recovered memory syndrome. Some memory researchers believe that mental-health professionals may be encouraging clients to "recall" nonexistent "repressed memories" of childhood sexual abuse as explanations for their current behavioral and emotional difficulties (Loftus, 1993b). Aside from concern that innocent people might be falsely accused based on such therapist-induced memories, child advocates warn that such cases, when exposed, might undermine support for cases involving survivors of actual childhood sexual abuse (Lindsay, 1994).

Cue Dependence and Forgetting

Because the retrieval of long-term memories depends on adequate retrieval cues, forgetting can sometimes be explained by the failure to have or to use them. For example, odors that we associate with an event can aid our recall of it (Smith, Standing, & de Man, 1992). This is known as *cue-dependence theory*. At times we might fail to find an adequate cue to activate the relevant portion of a semantic memory network. Consider the **tip-of-the-tongue-phenomenon,** in which you cannot quite recall a familiar word—though you feel that you know it (Schwartz & Smith, 1997). As a demonstration, you might induce a tip-of-the-tongue experience by trying to recall the names of the seven dwarfs. You might fail to recall one or two of them, yet still feel that you know them (Miserandino, 1991). The tip-of-the-tongue phenomenon is universal, increases with age, and occurs about once a week for the typical person (Brown, 1991).

A study of the tip-of-the-tongue phenomenon presented college students with the faces of 50 celebrities and asked them to recall their names. The results indicated that the students searched for the names by using cues associated with the celebrities. The students tried to recall their professions, where they usually performed, and the last time they had seen them. Characteristics of the names also served as cues for recalling them. These cues included the first letters of the names, the first letters of similar-sounding names, and the number of syllables in the names (Yarmey, 1973). This study supports the concept of **encoding specificity,** which states that recall will be best when cues that were associated with the encoding of a memory are also present during attempts at retrieving the memory (Tulving & Thomson, 1973).

tip-of-the-tongue phenomenon
The inability to recall information that one knows has been stored in long-term memory.

encoding specificity
The principle that recall will be best when cues that were associated with the encoding of a memory are also present during attempts at retrieving it.

Context-Dependent Memory
Godden and Baddeley (1975) found that words learned underwater were best recalled underwater and that words learned on land were best recalled on land.

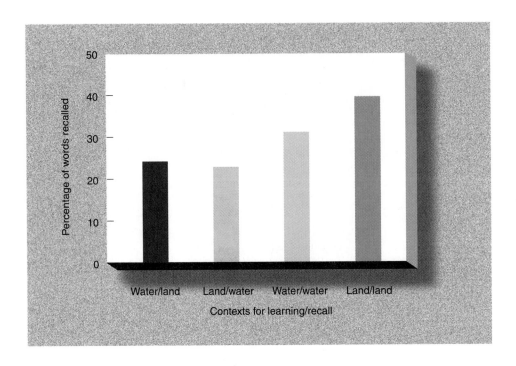

context-dependent memory
The tendency for recall to be best when the environmental context present during the encoding of a memory is also present during attempts at retrieving it.

In an unusual experiment on encoding specificity, scuba divers memorized lists of words while either underwater or on a beach, and then tried to recall the words while either in the same location or in the other location (Godden & Baddeley, 1975). The subjects communicated with the experimenter through a special intercom system. The results (see Figure 8.12) indicated that when the subjects memorized and recalled the words in different locations, they recalled about 30 percent fewer than when they memorized and recalled the words in the same location. This tendency for recall to be best when the environmental context present during the encoding of a memory is also present during attempts at retrieving it is known as **context-dependent memory.** The findings of the study even have practical implications. Instructions given to scuba divers should be given underwater, as well as on dry land, and if divers are making observations about what they see underwater, they should record them there and not wait until they get on dry land (Baddeley, 1982).

When you return to your old school or neighborhood, long-lost memories might come flooding back, evoked by environmental cues that you had not been exposed to for years. This effect of environmental context on recall is not lost on theater directors, who hold dress rehearsals in full costume amid the scenery that will be used during actual performances. Similarly, even your academic performance can be affected by environmental cues. Half a century ago a study found that college students performed worse when their exams were given in classrooms other than their normal ones (Abernethy, 1940). Perhaps you have noticed this when you have taken a final exam in a strange room. If you find yourself in that situation, you might improve your performance by mentally reinstating the environmental context in which you learned the material (Smith, 1984). This mental reinstatement technique is also used in the questioning of eyewitnesses by police.

There is controversy among memory researchers about whether the environmental context is important when *recall* is required, but not when *recognition* is required. This means that your performance on an essay exam might be impaired if you took an exam in a strange room, but your performance on a multiple-choice test would not. Perhaps tasks that require recognition include enough retrieval cues of their own, making environmental retrieval cues relatively less important (Eich, 1980). But some research indicates that even recognition memory is affected by environmental context. In one study, subjects observed a person and were then asked to identify the individual in a photo lineup. Some subjects had to identify the individual under the same environmental context and some under different contexts. Recognition was better under the same contexts. In fact, simply imagining being under the original context improved recognition performance (Smith & Vela, 1992).

◄ State-Dependent Memory
In the movie *City Lights*, a tramp played
by Charlie Chaplin is befriended by a drunken
millionaire. But when the millionaire sobers up,
he considers Chaplin an unwanted intruder and
has him thrown out. When the millionaire gets
drunk again, he once again treats Chaplin as his
good friend. This illustrates so-called alcoholic
blackout, a form of state-dependent memory.

Our recall of memories depends not only on cues from the external environment but
also on cues from our internal states. The effect on recall of the similarity between a
person's internal state during encoding and during retrieval is called **state-dependent
memory.** For example, memories encoded while the person is in a psychoactive drug-
induced state will be recalled better when the person is in that state. A variety of drugs
induce state-dependent memory, a fact first noted in 1835 (Overton, 1991). These drugs
include alcohol (Nakagawa & Iwasaki, 1996), nicotine (Peters & McGee, 1982), Valium
(Roy-Byrne et al., 1987), barbiturates (Kumar, Ramalingam, & Karanth, 1994), nitrous
oxide (Mewaldt et al., 1988), and the Parkinson's disease drug L-dopa (Huber et al., 1989).

In a government-sponsored study on the possible state-dependent effects of marijuana
(Eich et al., 1975), one group of subjects memorized a list of words after smoking marijuana, and a second group memorized the same list after smoking a placebo that tasted like
marijuana. The subjects were "blind"; that is, they did not know whether they were
smoking marijuana or a placebo. Four hours later, half of each group smoked either marijuana or a placebo and then tried to recall the words they had memorized. Recall was
better either when subjects smoked the placebo on both occasions or when they smoked
marijuana on both occasions than when they smoked marijuana on one occasion and the
placebo on the other. You should *not* conclude that marijuana smoking improves memory.
As noted in Chapter 6, marijuana actually impairs memory. And, indeed, in this study the
group that smoked the placebo on both occasions performed *better* than the groups that
smoked marijuana on either occasion or both occasions.

Our internal states also involve our moods, which can play a role in a form of state-
dependent memory called *mood-dependent memory,* in which our recall of information that
has been encoded in a particular mood will be best when we are in that mood again (Eich,
Macaulay, & Ryan, 1994). The mood appears to act as a cue for the retrieval of memories.
Thus, if you have an experience while you are in an angry mood, you might be more likely
to recall details of that experience when you are again in an angry mood. Victims of
crimes might have difficulty recalling details of the crimes because of the radically different moods they are in during the crime and when they are later questioned by police or
lawyers. Closely related to mood-dependent memory is *mood-congruent memory,* which is

state-dependent memory

The tendency for recall to be best when
one's emotional or physiological state is
the same during the recall of a memory as
it was during the encoding of that
memory.

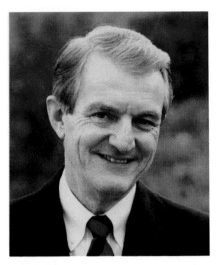

▲ Gordon Bower

"People recall an event better if they somehow reinstate during recall the original emotion they experienced during learning."

the broader tendency to recall memories that are consistent with one's current mood (Watkins et al., 1996). This effect was observed in a study in which moods were induced by having subjects smell either a pleasant odor (almond extract) or an unpleasant odor (the chemical pyridine). The subjects were then asked to recall past experiences. Those in the pleasant odor condition recalled a higher percentage of happy memories than did those in the unpleasant odor condition (Ehrlichman & Halpern, 1988).

Though mood-dependent memory has been demonstrated in a number of studies (Eich, 1995), Gordon Bower, the psychologist who was the first to study it formally, has had difficulty replicating his early research (Bower & Mayer, 1989). Moreover, evidence supporting mood-congruent memory is stronger than that supporting mood-dependent memory (Blaney, 1986). Mood-congruent memory might account for the self-perpetuating nature of depression: the depressed person recalls more depressing memories, and the depressing memories in turn maintain the depression (Matt, Vazquez, & Campbell, 1992).

As you can see, the field of memory research is diverse, fascinating, and filled with promising applications to everyday life. One important application is the improvement of memory, the next topic you will encounter.

STAYING ON TRACK: *Long-Term Memory*

1. How does the superiority of elaborative rehearsal, compared to maintenance rehearsal, support the levels of processing theory of long-term memory encoding?
2. What is the distinction between procedural memory and declarative memory?
3. What is the difference between proactive interference and retroactive interference?
4. What evidence is there to support the notion of state-dependent memory?

IMPROVING YOUR MEMORY

A century ago William James (1890/1981) criticized those who claimed that memory ability could be improved by practice. To James, memory was a fixed, inherited ability and not subject to improvement. He concluded this after finding that practice in memorizing did not decrease the time it took him and other subjects to memorize poetry or other kinds of literature. Regardless of the extent to which memory ability is inherited, we can certainly make better use of the ability we have by improving our study habits and by using *mnemonic devices*.

Using Effective Study Habits: The Techniques of Successful Students

Given two students with equal memory ability, the one with better study habits will probably perform better in school (Sanghui, 1995). To practice good study habits, you would begin by setting up a schedule in which you would do the bulk of your studying when you are most alert and most motivated—whether in the early morning, in the late afternoon, or at some other time. You should also study in a quiet, comfortable place, free of distractions. If you study in a dormitory lounge with students milling around and holding conversations, you might find yourself distracted from the information being processed in your short-term memory, making it more difficult for you to transfer the information efficiently into your long-term memory.

As for particular study techniques, you might consider using the **SQ3R method** (Robinson, 1970). SQ3R stands for Survey, Question, Read, Recite, and Review. This method has proved helpful to students in college (Martin, 1985) and elementary school (Darch, Carnine, & Kameenui, 1986). It requires elaborative rehearsal, in which you process information at a relatively deep level. This is distinct from rote memorization, in which you process information at a relatively shallow level. If you have ever found yourself studying for hours, yet doing poorly on exams, it might be the consequence of failing to use elaborative rehearsal. For example, in one study students used either rote memory,

SQ3R method

A study technique in which the student surveys, questions, reads, recites, and reviews course material.

writing down unfamiliar terms and their definitions, or elaborative rehearsal, writing down how the words might or might not describe them. One week later, students who had used elaborative rehearsal recalled significantly more definitions than did students who had used rote memory (Flannagan & Blick, 1989).

Suppose that you decide to use the SQ3R method to study the final two sections of this chapter. You would follow several steps. First, *survey* the main headings and subheadings to create an organized framework in which to fit the information you are studying. Second, as you survey the sections, ask yourself *questions* to be answered when you read them. For example, you might ask yourself, What is the physiological basis of memory? or Is eyewitness testimony accurate? Third, *read* the material carefully, trying to answer your questions as you move through each section. In memorizing new terms, you might find it especially helpful to say them out loud. A study found that subjects who read terms out loud remembered more of them than did subjects who read them silently, wrote them down, or heard them spoken by someone else (Gathercole & Conway, 1988). Fourth, after reading a section, *recite* information from it to see whether you understand it. Do not proceed to the next section until you understand the one you are studying. Fifth, periodically (perhaps every few days) *review* the information in the entire chapter by quizzing yourself on it and then rereading anything you fail to recall. Asking questions of yourself as you read can increase elaborative rehearsal and the depth of processing, thereby improving your memory for the material (Andre, 1979). You will also find yourself experiencing savings; each time you review the material, it will take you less time to reach the same level of mastery.

You might also wish to apply other principles to improve your studying. First, take advantage of **overlearning.** That is, study the material until you feel you know all of it—and then go over it several more times. A meta-analysis of research studies found that overlearning significantly improves the retention of material (Driskell, Willis, & Cooper, 1992). Overlearning appears to work by making you less likely to forget material you have studied and more confident that you know it (Nelson et al., 1982). This might improve your exam performance by making you less anxious. The power of overlearning is revealed by the amazing ability people show for recognizing the names and faces of their high school classmates decades after graduation. This is attributable to their having overlearned the names and faces during their years together in school (Bahrick, Bahrick, & Wittlinger, 1975).

Second, use **distributed practice** instead of **massed practice.** The advantage of distributed practice over massed practice is especially important in studying academic material (Zimmer & Hocevar, 1994). If you can devote a total of 5 hours to studying this chapter, you would be better off studying for 1 hour on five different occasions than studying for 5 hours on one occasion. You might recognize this as a suggestion to avoid "cramming" for exams. Note how the following explanation by William James for the negative effects of cramming anticipated recent research into the effects of elaborative rehearsal, overlearning, environmental cues, and semantic networks on memory:

▶ The reason why *cramming* is such a bad mode of study is now made clear . . . . Things learned thus in a few hours, on one occasion, for one purpose, cannot possibly have formed many associations with other things in the mind. . . . Speedy oblivion is the almost inevitable fate of all that is committed to memory in this simple way . . . . Whereas on the contrary, the same information taken in gradually, day after day, recurring in different contexts, considered in various relations, associated with other external incidents, and repeatedly reflected on, grow into a fabric, lie open to so many paths of approach, that they remain permanent possessions. (James, 1890/1981, Vol. 1, pp. 623–624)

Even novices who are learning word processing can benefit from distributed practice, as in a study of students in a word-processing seminar. The students were assigned to groups that received either a single 60-minute session or a 60-minute session broken into two segments by a 10-minute break. The students were tested on their speed and accuracy immediately after the training and 1 week later. The group that had received distributed practice performed significantly faster and more accurately on both occasions. The results indicate that those who teach word processing might be wise to divide long sessions into shorter ones (Bouzid & Crawshaw, 1987).

▲ **Overlearning**
In learning a script or a song, actors do not merely memorize it until they recall it perfectly once. Instead, they overlearn it by making sure that they can recall it perfectly several times. This aids their recall of the lines and improves their confidence, thereby improving their performance.

overlearning
Studying material beyond the point of initial mastery.

distributed practice
Spreading out the memorization of information or the learning of a motor skill over several sessions.

massed practice
Cramming the memorization of information or the learning of a motor skill into one session.

► FIGURE 8.13
The Method of Loci
In using the method of loci to recall a shopping list, you would pair each item on the list with a familiar place such as a different room in your house. You would then take a mental tour, retrieving items as you go.

method of loci

A mnemonic device in which items to be recalled are associated with landmarks in a familiar place and then recalled during a mental walk from one landmark to another.

mnemonic devices

Techniques for organizing information to be memorized to make it easier to remember.

Using Mnemonic Devices: The Tricks of the Memory Trade

About 2,500 years ago the Greek poet Simonides stepped outside of the banquet hall where he was to recite a poem in honor of a nobleman. While Simonides was outside, the hall collapsed, killing all the guests and maiming them beyond recognition. Yet, by recalling where each guest had been sitting, Simonides was able to identify each of them. He called this the **method of loci** (*loci* means "place" in Latin), which he recommended to orators because paper and pens were too expensive to waste on writing routine speeches (Bower, 1970). The method of loci is useful for memorizing lists of items. You might memorize concrete terms from this chapter by associating them with places and landmarks on your campus, and then retrieving while taking a mental walk across it. Figure 8.13 provides an example of the method of loci, which has even proved helpful in training older adults to improve their memory for grocery lists (Anschutz et al., 1985). Even the places on a Monopoly board have been used successfully to help students employ the method of loci (Schoen, 1996).

The method of loci is one of several **mnemonic devices,** which are techniques for organizing information and providing memory cues to make it easier to recall, such as learning to associate painters and their paintings in art history courses (Carney & Levin, 1994). These devices are named after Mnemosyne, the Greek goddess of memory. You are familiar with

Step 1	Step 2	Step 3
Memorize pegwords in order	**Pair items with pegwords**	**Create interacting image**

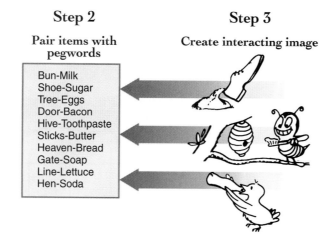

Step 1 — Memorize pegwords in order:
One is a bun
Two is a shoe
Three is a tree
Four is a door
Five is a hive
Six is sticks
Seven is heaven
Eight is a gate
Nine is a line
Ten is a hen

Step 2 — Pair items with pegwords:
Bun-Milk
Shoe-Sugar
Tree-Eggs
Door-Bacon
Hive-Toothpaste
Sticks-Butter
Heaven-Bread
Gate-Soap
Line-Lettuce
Hen-Soda

◀ **FIGURE 8.14**
The Pegword Method
The pegword method can be used to recall a grocery list. Each grocery item is paired with a pegword. Thus, the retrieval of a pegword will cue the retrieval of the associated grocery item.

certain mnemonic devices, such as *acronyms*. An **acronym** is a term formed from the first letters of a series of words. Examples of acronyms include *USA*, *NFL*, and even *SQ3R*. Many students have used the acronym *Roy G Biv* to help them recall the colors of the rainbow. Acronyms have also proved useful to medical students, helping them learn lists of concepts, such as the symptoms that are associated with certain diseases (Wilding et al., 1986).

You are probably familiar with the use of rhymes as mnemonic devices, as in "*I* before *e* except after *c*" and "Thirty days has September . . . ." Though rhymes are useful mnemonic devices, they can sometimes impair memory. In one study, children who listened to stories presented in prose had better recall of them than did children who listened to the stories presented in verse. Evidently, the children who listened to verse processed the stories at a shallow level, as sounds, while the children who listened to prose processed the stories at a deeper level, in terms of their meaning (Hayes, Chemelski, & Palmer, 1982).

A mnemonic device that relies on both imagery and rhyming is the **pegword method,** which begins with memorizing a list of concrete nouns that rhyme with the numbers 1, 2, 3, 4, 5, and so on. For this method to work well, the image of the pegword object and the image of the object to be recalled should interact, rather than just be paired with each other (Wollen, Weber, & Lowry, 1972). Suppose that you wanted to remember the grocery list presented in Figure 8.14. You might imagine, among other things, sugar being poured from a shoe, bees in a hive brushing their teeth, and a hen drinking from a soda bottle. To recall an item, you would simply imagine the pegword that is paired with a particular number, which would act as a cue for retrieving the image of the object that interacted with that pegword. Thus, if you imagined a shoe, you would automatically retrieve an image of sugar being poured from it. The pegword method has proved successful even when used by young children to learn nouns (Krinsky & Krinsky, 1996).

Still another mnemonic device that makes use of imagery is the **link method,** which takes images of the items to be memorized and connects them in sequence. One version of the link method is the *narrative method* (see Figure 8.15), in which unrelated items are connected to one another in a story. In a study that showed its effectiveness, two groups of subjects memorized 12 lists of 10 nouns. One group used the narrative method to memorize the nouns; the other group used ordinary mental rehearsal. Both groups showed nearly perfect immediate recall. But when later asked to recall all of the lists, the narrative group recalled an average of 93 percent of the words, while the mental rehearsal group recalled an average of only 13 percent (Bower & Clark, 1969). More-recent research has replicated the effectiveness of this technique (Hill, Allen, & McWhorter, 1991).

Ironically, despite the usefulness of mnemonic devices, a survey of college professors found that memory researchers were no more likely than other professors to use formal mnemonic devices. Instead, memory researchers and other professors alike recommended that memory be improved by writing things down, by organizing material to be learned, or by rehearsing material to be remembered (Park, Smith, & Cavanaugh, 1990). Like physicians who smoke, memory researchers might not practice what they preach.

acronym
A mnemonic device that involves forming a term from the first letters of a series of words that are to be recalled.

pegword method
A mnemonic device that involves associating items to be recalled with objects that rhyme with the numbers 1, 2, 3, and so on, to make the items easier to recall.

link method
A mnemonic device that involves connecting, in sequence, images of items to be memorized, to make them easier to recall.

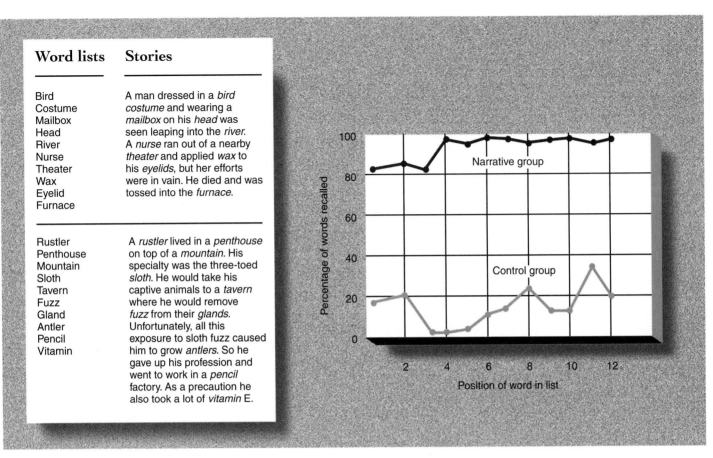

Word lists	Stories
Bird Costume Mailbox Head River Nurse Theater Wax Eyelid Furnace	A man dressed in a *bird costume* and wearing a *mailbox* on his *head* was seen leaping into the *river*. A *nurse* ran out of a nearby *theater* and applied *wax* to his *eyelids*, but her efforts were in vain. He died and was tossed into the *furnace*.
Rustler Penthouse Mountain Sloth Tavern Fuzz Gland Antler Pencil Vitamin	A *rustler* lived in a *penthouse* on top of a *mountain*. His specialty was the three-toed *sloth*. He would take his captive animals to a *tavern* where he would remove *fuzz* from their *glands*. Unfortunately, all this exposure to sloth fuzz caused him to grow *antlers*. So he gave up his profession and went to work in a *pencil* factory. As a precaution he also took a lot of *vitamin* E.

▲ **FIGURE 8.15**
The Narrative Method
In using the narrative method to recall a list of words, you would create a story using each of the words. The graph shows the superior recall of subjects who used the narrative method in a study by Bower and Clark (1969).

STAYING ON TRACK: *Improving Your Memory*

1. What are some suggestions for improving your study habits?
2. How would you use the pegword method to recall lists of objects?

THE BIOPSYCHOLOGY OF MEMORY: THE PHYSICAL BASIS OF MEMORY

Though study habits and mnemonic devices depend on overt behavior and mental processes, they ultimately work by affecting the encoding, storage, and retrieval of memories in the brain. Today, research on the neuroanatomy and neurochemistry of memory is revealing more and more about its biological bases (Rosenzweig, 1996).

The Anatomy of Memory: The Role of the Brain

During the first half of this century, psychologist Karl Lashley (1890–1958) carried out an ambitious program of research aimed at finding the sites where individual memories are stored in the brain (see Chapter 3). Lashley trained rats to run through mazes to obtain food rewards. He then destroyed small areas of their cerebral cortex and noted whether this made a difference in their maze performance. To Lashley's dismay, no matter what area he destroyed, the rats still negotiated the mazes, showing at most a slight decrement in performance. Lashley concluded that he had failed in his lifelong search for the *memory trace* (or **engram**), which he had assumed was the basis of memories (Lashley, 1950).

But many scientists remained undaunted by Lashley's pessimistic conclusion and continued to search for the engram. This persistence paid off decades later when a team of researchers located the site of a specific engram in studies of the sea snail *Aplysia* (Glanzman, 1995). This creature has relatively few neurons, making it a simpler subject of study than animals with complex brains. Researchers have identified a neuronal engram formed when an *Aplysia* is classically conditioned to withdraw its gills in response to the movement of water (Kandel & Schwartz, 1982). This (the unconditioned response) occurs after several trials in which the movement of the water (the conditioned stimulus) has preceded an electric shock (the unconditioned stimulus) that automatically elicits gill withdrawal (the unconditioned response).

Evidence for the localization of engrams in more complex animals comes from research that has identified engrams in the cerebellum (see Chapter 3), a brain structure that plays a role in both memory and the maintenance of equilibrium. The researchers classically conditioned rabbits to blink in response to a tone. Presentations of the tone (the conditioned stimulus) were followed by puffs of air (the unconditioned stimulus) directed at the rabbit's eyes, which elicited blinking (the unconditioned response). After several pairings of the tone and puffs of air, the tone itself elicited blinking (the conditioned response). After conditioning, the researchers found that electrical stimulation of a tiny site in the cerebellum of the rabbit elicited the conditioned eye blink, while destruction of the site eliminated it—but not the unconditioned response. Thus, they had succeeded in locating an engram for a classically conditioned memory (Krupa, Thompson, & Thompson, 1993).

As for human memory, in 1894 Sigmund Freud and Santiago Ramón y Cajal independently speculated that learning produces changes in the efficiency of synaptic connections between neurons, and that these changes might be the basis of memory formation. Their speculation has been supported by research findings that the formation of memories is associated with synaptic changes, including increases in the number of dendritic branches and the number of dendritic spines (protuberances on the dendrites) at certain sites (Stewart et al., 1992). Recent research indicates that memory might also depend on the facilitation of neural impulses across synapses in the brain. The most widely studied phenomenon related to the facilitation of neural impulses is *long-term potentiation,* in which synaptic transmission of impulses is made more efficient by brief electrical stimulation of specific neural pathways. This is viewed as a possible basis for long-term memory, because long-term potentiation induced by specific experiences might strengthen synaptic connections in specific pathways (Martinez & Derrick, 1996).

Researchers who study long-term potentiation are particularly interested in the *hippocampus,* which lies deep within the temporal lobes and helps consolidate memories (Graham & Hodges, 1997). Figure 8.16 illustrates the location of the hippocampus and other brain structures important in memory, including the thalamus (Daum & Ackermann, 1994), the amygdala (Coleman-Mesches & McGaugh, 1995), and, as mentioned earlier, the cerebellum. Long-term potentiation in the hippocampus apparently promotes the storage of new memories but is required for only a limited period of time after a learning experience. Evidence for this comes from animal studies in which the hippocampus is purposely damaged at varying times after learning. The longer the delay before hippocampal damage, the less effect it has on the storage of the new memories (Zola-Morgan & Squire, 1990). More evidence for the importance of the hippocampus in the formation of long-term memories comes from research on Alzheimer's disease, which is marked by degeneration of neural pathways from the hippocampus (Brady & Mufson, 1990). Victims of Alzheimer's disease have a progressively more difficult time forming new long-term memories, particularly declarative memories (Deweer et al., 1994). We know that the hippocampus plays a role in the consolidation of short-term

engram
A memory trace in the brain.

▲ **Karl Lashley (1890–1958)**
"I sometimes feel, in reviewing the evidence on the localization of the memory trace, that the necessary conclusion is that learning just is not possible."

Anatomy of Memory
The brain contains no memory center. Instead, memory depends on the integration of activity in several areas of the brain, including the thalamus, the amygdala, the cerebellum, and, especially, the hippocampus.

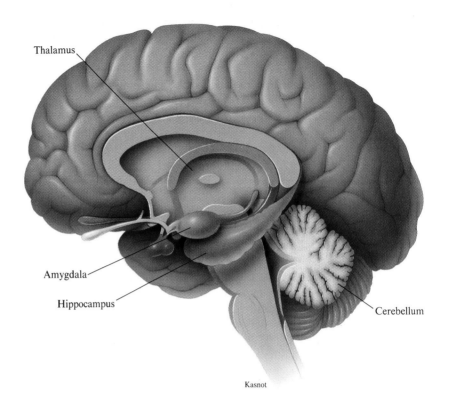

Thalamus

Amygdala

Hippocampus

Cerebellum

Kasnot

memory into long-term memory, but the exact sites of memory storage are unknown—though research findings indicate that they involve the cerebral cortex (McClelland, McNaughton, & O'Reilly, 1995).

The hippocampus might provide an explanation for *infantile amnesia,* the inability to recall declarative memories from early childhood. A study of college students found that their earliest childhood memories were from age 2 for being hospitalized or the birth of a sibling, and from age 3 for the death of a family member or making a family move to a new home. If these events occurred earlier, the students were unable to recall them (Usher & Neisser, 1993). Perhaps infantile amnesia occurs because the hippocampus is too physically immature during infancy to consolidate short-term declarative memories into long-term ones. Note that we show perfectly good retention of procedural memories from infancy. Such memories, which involve skills, habits, and conditioned responses, do not seem to depend on the hippocampus.

The most celebrated single source of evidence for the role of the hippocampus in memory comes from the case study of a man known as "H. M.," who has been studied since the 1950s by Brenda Milner of the Montreal Neurological Institute (Scoville & Milner, 1957). H. M. has formed few new declarative memories since undergoing brain surgery in 1953, when he was 27 years old. The surgery, performed to relieve uncontrollable epileptic seizures, removed almost all of his hippocampus. As a result, H. M. developed anterograde amnesia, the inability to form new long-term declarative memories. Because he cannot recall events after 1953, he feels that each moment of his life is like waking from a dream, as short-term memories continually enter his consciousness and then fade away. H. M. can recall memories from before 1953, but because of his inability to convert short-term memories into long-term memories, he will read the same magazine over and over, without realizing that he has read it before. He will meet the same person on repeated occasions, yet have to be reintroduced each time. Though H. M. cannot form new declarative memories, he can form new procedural memories. For example, he has learned to play tennis since his surgery and has retained that procedural memory—even though he does not recall having taken lessons (Herbert, 1983). Moreover, after undergoing classical conditioning of an eyeblinking response, he retained this procedural memory for 2 years, yet he could not recall the experimenters, instructions, or methodology that had been used to condition the response—each of which involves declarative memory (Woodruff-Pak, 1993).

Additional supporting evidence that the hippocampus is important in the formation of declarative memories but not of procedural memories has come from experiments conducted by neuroscientist Larry Squire and his colleagues. In one study, subjects suffering from the same form of anterograde amnesia as H. M. were trained to read words in a mirror. Though this is a difficult task, they were able to do it and improved their performance over a 3-day period. Despite having the ability to form new procedural memories, the subjects also revealed an inability to form new declarative memories—they failed to recall having ever learned the task (Cohen & Squire, 1980). Squire's finding has been supported by other research demonstrating the role of the hippocampus in the formation of explicit memories—that is, memories for information that has entered conscious awareness (Moscovitch, 1995). This indicates that procedural memories depend on brain structures other than the hippocampus, such as the cerebellum. Regardless of where they are stored, procedural memories are more localized in the brain than are declarative memories, which seem to be stored in several interacting regions of the brain (Thompson, 1991).

▲ **Larry Squire**
"Studies of human amnesia and studies of an animal model of human amnesia in the monkey have identified the anatomical components of the brain system for memory in the medial temporal lobe and . . . this neural system consists of the hippocampus and adjacent anatomically related cortex."

The Chemistry of Memory: The Role of Neurotransmitters and Other Chemicals

In 1959 James McConnell and his colleagues stunned the scientific world by reporting the results of an unusual experiment (McConnell, Jacobson, & Kimble, 1959). They had classically conditioned flatworms to contract their bodies in response to a light by repeatedly pairing presentations of the light with mild electric shocks. They then cut the flatworms in half. Because flatworms can regenerate themselves, both halves grew into whole flatworms. They were then retrained to contract in response to a light. As expected, the flatworms that had regenerated from the head (brain) ends showed memory savings—they took fewer trials to learn to respond to the light than had the original flatworms, which provided evidence that prior learning had been retained by the brain end. But, to the researchers' surprise, the flatworms that had regenerated from the tail ends learned to respond to the light as fast as those that had regenerated from the brain ends. This indicated that the memory of the classically conditioned response may have been encoded chemically and transported to the tail ends.

These findings led to a series of even more unusual experiments by a variety of researchers, which seemed to demonstrate that memories could be transferred from one animal to another. In one study, rats were trained to run to a lighted compartment instead of to a dark compartment (which they would normally favor) by shocking them whenever they entered the dark compartment. When extracts from the brains of these rats were injected into mice, the mice spent less time in the dark compartment than they normally would have. The researchers later isolated the proteinlike substance apparently responsible for this effect, which they called *scotophobin*, meaning "fear of the dark" (Unger, Desiderio, & Parr, 1972).

As you might assume, the results of successful memory transfer studies created controversy, leading 23 researchers to write a letter to the influential journal *Science* in which they reported their failure to produce memory transfer in 18 studies in seven laboratories ("Memory Transfer," 1966). Failure to replicate memory transfer studies became the main reason to reject those that found positive results (Rilling, 1996). But a few years later a published review of the research literature concluded that hundreds of studies of flatworms, goldfish, chickens, mice, rats, and hamsters had demonstrated the transfer of memories (Smith, 1974). Yet, because of the failure of other researchers to replicate those studies and to identify a physiological basis for the chemical transfer of memories, interest in the study of memory transfer has waned. Perhaps interest has declined in part because

▲ Alzheimer's Disease
Because victims of Alzheimer's disease suffer
severe memory impairment, they may benefit
from a "prosthetic environment." Strategically
placed signs enable this woman to locate her personal belongings.

the very notion of memory transfer seems better suited to science fiction than to science.
Scientists in all disciplines, including biology, chemistry, and physics, tend to avoid topics
that appear to violate accepted scientific paradigms (see Chapter 2).

In contrast to the conflict generated by research on the chemical transfer of memories,
there is no controversy about whether neurotransmitters play a role in memory, because
memory processing requires the chemical transmission of neural impulses from one neuron
to another. But the exact relationship between neurotransmitter activity and memory has
only recently begun to reveal itself. The neurotransmitter that is most strongly implicated
in memory processes is *acetylcholine* (Hasselmo & Bower, 1993). Acetylcholine might be
more important in the formation of declarative memories than in the formation of procedural memories. This was implied by the results of a study in which one group of adult subjects received a drug that blocked the effects of acetylcholine, while another group
received a placebo (Nissen, Knopman, & Schacter, 1987). Those who received the active
drug showed a reduced ability to recall and recognize stimuli presented previously (declarative memory) but no reduction in their ability to perform a reaction-time task they had
learned previously (procedural memory).

But the most striking evidence of the role of acetylcholine in memory comes from
studies of victims of Alzheimer's disease. Autopsies of victims of Alzheimer's disease show
degeneration of acetylcholine neurons that connect the hippocampus to other brain areas
(Crews, 1994). In fact, when normal subjects are given drugs that inhibit the activity of
acetylcholine neurons, they show memory losses similar to those seen in victims of
Alzheimer's disease (McKinney & Richelson, 1984).

It would seem logical that treatments aimed at elevating brain levels of acetylcholine
would improve the ability of Alzheimer's victims to form new memories. One approach
has been to administer *choline*—the dietary substance from which acetylcholine is syn-
thesized and that is found in milk and eggs. Unfortunately, administration of high doses
of choline has been only marginally effective in improving the cognitive functioning of
Alzheimer's victims (Davidson et al., 1991). Evidently the degeneration of acetylcholine neurons prevents the additional choline from having a beneficial effect, just as
adding gasoline to the empty tank of a car with no spark plugs would not make it more
likely to start.

Perhaps the most exciting area of current research on the chemical basis of memory
concerns N-methyl-D-aspartate (NMDA) receptors (Steele, Stewart, & Rose, 1995).
NMDA is an amino acid that, when injected into an animal, binds to specific receptors in
the hippocampus and enhances the efficiency of synaptic transmission along particular
neural pathways. Consider a study in which rats learned to respond to a conditioned stimulus that had been paired with an unconditioned stimulus. A drug that blocked NMDA
receptors prevented the formation of a conditioned response, but only if it was given
during conditioning trials. If it was given after them, it had no effect. This supports the
role of NMDA receptors in the acquisition, but not the performance, of a conditioned
response (Kim et al., 1991). Additional support for the role of NMDA receptors in long-
term memory consolidation comes from research on Alzheimer's disease. In the brains of
victims of the disease, neural degeneration occurs in pathways rich in NMDA receptors
(Maragos et al., 1987).

Even hormones play a role in memory formation. The hormone *epinephrine* might have
a special function in assuring that we recall emotionally arousing events (Costa-Miserachs
et al., 1994). For example, in one study subjects were given injections of either an epinephrine blocker or a placebo. An hour later they watched a series of slides accompanied
by a neutral or an emotional story. When tested 1 week later, the subjects who received
the epinephrine blocker had poorer recall of the emotional story than of the neutral story
(Cahill et al., 1994). Given such findings, perhaps, if flashbulb memories are a real phenomenon, epinephrine plays a role in their formation.

Still another topic of research interest regarding the chemical basis of memory is the
effect of blood sugar, glucose. There is a positive correlation between blood glucose levels
and memory performance. For example, studies indicate that college students' performance

on memory tasks is improved more by having a glucose drink than by having a placebo drink (Benton, Owens, & Parker, 1994). Dietary supplements of glucose might also improve memory in the elderly. In one study, adults at least 60 years old received doses of either glucose or saccharin (a placebo) before or after memorizing a brief prose passage. Their recall of the passage was tested 24 hours later. Those who had ingested glucose, before or after memorizing the passage, showed significantly better recall than those who had ingested saccharin. Evidently, the glucose promoted the storage of the prose passages in memory (Manning, Parsons, & Gold, 1992). Injections of insulin, which reduces the level of blood glucose, have impaired memory in laboratory animals (Kopf & Baratti, 1996).

Glucose supplements can even temporarily improve the memory of victims of Alzheimer's disease (Craft, Zallen, & Baker, 1992). But how does glucose improve memory? One way is by increasing the synthesis of acetylcholine in the hippocampus (Messier et al., 1990). Nonetheless, students should not conclude that it would be wise to ingest massive amounts of glucose. On the contrary, the greatest enhancement of memory is produced by moderate doses of glucose (Parsons & Gold, 1992).

As you can see, research on the biopsychology of memory cannot be divorced from the psychology of memory. And biopsychological research promises to discover ways of improving memory. This would be a boon both to people with intact brains and to people with damaged brains.

STAYING ON TRACK: *The Biopsychology of Memory*

1. How did researchers demonstrate the presence of a classically conditioned engram in the cerebellum?
2. How does the case of H. M. support the role of the hippocampus in the consolidation of long-term memories?
3. Why do researchers believe that acetylcholine plays an important role in long-term memory?

THINKING ABOUT *Psychology*

Should We Trust Eyewitness Testimony?

In August 1979, Father Bernard Pagano went on trial for a series of armed robberies. Eyewitnesses had identified him as the so-called gentleman bandit, a polite man who had robbed several convenience stores in Wilmington, Delaware. Father Pagano was arrested after several people who knew him told the police that he resembled published drawings of the bandit. Seven eyewitnesses, who were shown photographs in which Father Pagano wore his clerical collar, identified him as the robber. They might have been influenced by previous police reports that indicated that the perpetrator looked like a clergyman. Fortunately for Father Pagano, while he was on trial, another man, Ronald Clouser, confessed to the crimes (Rodgers, 1982).

There was little resemblance between Father Pagano and Ronald Clouser (see Figure 8.17). The possibility of convicting innocent people or of exonerating guilty people based on inaccurate **eyewitness testimony** has led psychologists to study the factors that affect eyewitness memories. This concern is not new. Hugo Münsterberg (1908), a pioneer in the study of psychology and the law, warned us to consider the imperfections of human memory when evaluating the accuracy of eyewitness testimony. And around the turn of the century, Alfred Binet, who gained fame for developing the first IQ test, championed the scientific study of eyewitness testimony. He introduced the *picture-description*

eyewitness testimony
Witnesses' recollections about events, most notably about criminal activity.

Eyewitness Testimony
Eyewitnesses mistakenly identified Father
Bernard Pagano (*left*) as the perpetrator of a
series of convenience store robberies actually
committed by Ronald Clouser (*right*).

test, which required subjects to examine a picture of a scene and, after varying lengths of
time, to recall as much as possible about the picture or to answer questions about it posed
by an interrogator. Binet found that eyewitness testimony usually included inaccuracies
and that testimony under questioning was less accurate than spontaneous testimony
(Postman, 1985).

During the past three decades, psychologists have conducted many research studies of
the factors that affect the accuracy of eyewitness testimony (Loftus, 1993a). Research on
eyewitness memories shows that they are not like mental tape recordings that record and
play back exactly. Instead, eyewitness recollections are reconstructive, somewhat altering
the events that they represent. Two of the main topics of interest regarding eyewitness testimony are the accuracy of children's eyewitness testimony and the effects of questioning
on eyewitness testimony.

CHILDREN AS EYEWITNESSES: IS CHILDREN'S TESTIMONY AS ACCURATE AS THAT OF ADULTS?

An issue that has concerned psychologists since the beginning of the twentieth century is
whether the testimony of children is trustworthy (Ceci & Bruck, 1993). As first demonstrated by the German psychologist William Stern at the beginning of the twentieth century, children tend to be less accurate than adults in their eyewitness accounts of crimes,
in part because they are more suggestible—that is, they are more susceptible to leading
questions (Bringmann et al., 1989).

Concerns about children as eyewitnesses have been supported by research indicating that misleading information about events can distort children's memories of
them. In an experiment that tested this finding, children 3 to 12 years old listened to
a story about a girl who had a *stomachache* after eating *eggs* too fast. When asked questions about the story, the children answered correctly almost all of the time. But when
asked if they remembered the story of a little girl who got a *headache* because she ate
her *cereal* too fast, the children typically responded that they had. The effect of misleading questions was greater on the younger children than on the older ones (Ceci,
Ross, & Toglia, 1987).

Other studies likewise have found that the younger the children, the less accurate their
testimony tends to be. In one such study, children 3 to 4 years old or 5 to 6 years old were
interviewed about real and fictitious events and were asked whether the events had happened to them. The younger children were more likely than the older ones to claim they
had experienced an event that they had only thought about. This might help explain some

cases in which children have falsely claimed they were sexually abused only after being interviewed in some detail about the alleged abuse. (Ceci, Huffman, & Smith, 1994).

Still another study revealing the fallibility of young children's testimony involved interviewing children 3 to 7 years old immediately after they had undergone a routine physical examination and several weeks later. Younger subjects remembered less information spontaneously and provided fewer details, and there was less consistency between their earlier and their later testimony. Though there was no difference in the accuracy of spontaneously recalled information, the younger children were less accurate in response to specific questions, and only 7-year-olds responded correctly at significantly above the level of chance guessing (Gordon & Follmer, 1994).

Children are also more likely to guess when testifying, as in a study in which kindergartners viewed a slide show of a staged theft and then were asked to identify the perpetrator from a lineup. Many identified a person in the lineup even when the perpetrator was not in the lineup. Moreover, some children who had made correct identifications when the perpetrator was present in the lineup later identified a person in a lineup in which the perpetrator was absent. This is an example of the tendency of children to guess or make up answers when they testify repeatedly about the same event (Beal, Schmitt, & Dekle, 1995).

Not only are young children more fallible in their testimony than older children, children tend to be less accurate in their testimony than adults. One study compared adults and children in the accuracy of their memories for an event they experienced 2 years earlier. The children were less accurate in responding to yes/no questions and open-ended questions, and were more likely to fabricate responses to a question about a man's occupation. This might have an effect on court cases that take a long time to reach trial (Poole & White, 1993).

Of course, especially because of the prevalence of child sexual and physical abuse, courts must achieve a delicate balance between believing children's testimony and being skeptical of it. Fortunately, children can give accurate testimony, provided that they are not given leading questions and provided that the questions are worded so that they can understand them (Brooks & Siegel, 1991). To promote accuracy in children's testimony, the questioning of children should be done by neutral parties rather than by individuals who are biased either toward or against believing the children's stories of abuse. Failure to do so might induce children to testify in a manner consistent with the questioner's personal agenda.

QUESTIONING THE EYEWITNESS: CAN BIASED QUESTIONS ELICIT INACCURATE TESTIMONY?

Though issues regarding the accuracy of children's eyewitness testimony have important social consequences, there has been even more research on the effects of questioning on adult eyewitness testimony. Because jurors attribute greater accuracy to the testimony of eyewitnesses who display confidence, an important factor in eyewitness testimony is how confident eyewitnesses are about their memories. In the 1972 case of *Neil v. Biggers*, the U.S. Supreme Court even ruled that one of the criteria that juries should use in judging the accuracy of an eyewitness's testimony is the degree of confidence expressed by the eyewitness. But this ruling might be misguided, because even though hypnotized eyewitnesses are more confident in the accuracy of their testimony than nonhypnotized eyewitnesses are (Steblay & Bothwell, 1994), eyewitnesses' level of confidence is generally unrelated to the accuracy of their testimony (Wells & Lindsay, 1985). As a consequence, it can be unwise for jurors to assume that a confident eyewitness is necessarily an accurate eyewitness.

One of the main factors regarding eyewitness testimony is the wording of questions. This has been demonstrated in a series of experiments by Elizabeth Loftus, of the University of Washington, and her colleagues. The following study is one of the most influential of her experiments on eyewitness testimony.

Can Leading Questions Influence Eyewitness Testimony?

Rationale

Judges and lawyers are taught to beware of leading questions, which can affect the testimony of eyewitnesses. Nonetheless, clever lawyers use subtle wording to influence testimony. The present study by Elizabeth Loftus and John Palmer (1974) examined the effect of leading questions regarding eyewitness accounts of an automobile accident.

Method

Forty-five undergraduate subjects viewed one of seven driver-education films of two-car automobile accidents lasting 5 to 30 seconds. Some subjects were asked, "About how fast were the cars going when they smashed into each other?" Other subjects were asked a similar question, with the word *smashed* replaced by *contacted, hit, bumped,* or *collided.* In a similar version of the experiment, 150 other undergraduate subjects likewise viewed films of two-car automobile accidents. Subjects in one group were asked, "About how fast were the cars going when they smashed into each other?" and subjects in a second group were asked, "About how fast were the cars going when they hit each other?" A week later, the subjects were asked, "Did you see any broken glass?" To avoid sensitizing the subjects to its purpose, the question was embedded in a list of 10 questions. In reality, there was no broken glass at the accident scene.

Results and Discussion

The subjects' estimates of the speed of the cars in the first part of the study were influenced by the severity of the word used in the question (see Figure 8.18). The average estimates for *contacted, hit, bumped, collided,* and *smashed* were, respectively, 31.8, 34.0, 38.1, 39.3, and 40.8 miles per hour. In the second part of the study, though there had been no broken glass, subjects in both groups recalled seeing some. But subjects who had been given the question containing the word *smashed* were significantly more likely to report having seen broken glass than were subjects who had been given the question containing the word *hit.*

Loftus's findings have been replicated in other studies. In one study, college students were shown a videotaped mock crime. One week later they read a passage that described the crime. The passage contained leading, misleading, or control (no supplemental) information. When asked to recall the crime they had witnessed, the subjects placed more confidence in the biased information presented by the experimenter than in their own memories (Ryan & Geiselman, 1991).

▲ ▲ ▲

Studies like this one demonstrate that the memories of eyewitnesses can be reconstructions, instead of exact replicas, of the events witnessed. This phenomenon was noted in 1846 in a trial that marked the first admission of hypnotically obtained testimony in an American court. Though the defendant was acquitted because of inadequate evidence, testimony by one expert noted that memory is often a reconstruction of events incorporating fact and fantasy (Gravitz, 1995).

Eyewitness memories can be altered by inaccurate information introduced during questioning. That is, "Under some conditions misleading postevent information can impair the ability to remember what was witnessed and can lead people to believe that they witnessed things that they did not" (Lindsay, 1993, p. 86). This also supports the practice of barring leading questions in courtroom proceedings.

Though leading questions can affect the recall of eyewitnesses, research indicates that eyewitnesses might be less susceptible to them than had been suggested by earlier research (Kohnken & Maass, 1988). Eyewitness memory can be improved by relatively simple procedures. One procedure, based on the principle of encoding specificity, improves recall by mentally reinstating the physical setting of the event. In one study, store clerks were asked to identify a previously encountered customer from an array of photographs. The original context was reinstated by providing physical cues from the encounter and by instructing the clerk to mentally recall events that led up to the customer's purchase. As discussed earlier, mentally reinstating the context in which you learned something can improve your

Question	Possible scene recalled	Average estimate of speed
"About how fast were the cars going when they *hit* each other?"		34.0 MPH
"About how fast were the cars going when they *smashed* into each other?"		40.8 MPH

◀ FIGURE 8.18
Leading Questions
The wording of questions can influence the recall of eyewitnesses. As demonstrated in an experiment by Loftus and Palmer (1974), subjects who witnessed a collision between two cars gave different estimates of their speed, depending on the wording of the questions they were asked. The wording may have altered the scenes they recalled.

recall of it. In this study, the reinstatement of the original context led to a significant increase in the accuracy of identifications (Krafka & Penrod, 1985).

We can also prevent misleading information from influencing the memories of eyewitnesses by warning them about that possibility. This was the finding of a study in which subjects were warned just prior to the presentation of misleading information about a simulated crime. The subjects viewed slides of a wallet being snatched from a woman's purse and then read descriptions of the crime. Subjects who had been given warnings showed greater resistance to misleading information in the descriptions (Greene, Flynn, & Loftus, 1982). But some psychologists argue that informing jurors of the unreliability of eyewitness testimony might make already skeptical jurors too skeptical, perhaps leading to the exoneration of guilty persons (McCloskey & Egeth, 1983). This would be particularly distressing in cases of child abuse. Moreover, though Loftus believes that leading questions can encourage eyewitnesses to alter or even overwrite their original memories, other researchers have found that old information in memory is not overwritten by new, misleading information (Pezdek & Greene, 1993).

Regardless of the exact extent to which eyewitness testimony can be influenced by misleading information and the reasons for that influence, Elizabeth Loftus believes that eyewitness testimony is, in fact, too easily affected by such information. She expressed this in a statement that was a takeoff on John B. Watson's claim (quoted in Chapter 1) regarding his ability to condition infants to become any kind of person one desired. Loftus remarked:

▶ Give us a dozen healthy memories, well-informed, and our own specified world to handle them in. And we'll guarantee to take any at random and train it to become any type of memory that we might select—hammer, screwdriver, wrench, stop sign, yield sign, Indian chief—regardless of its origin or the brain that holds it. (Loftus & Hoffman, 1989, p. 103)

STAYING ON TRACK: *Should We Trust Eyewitness Testimony?*

1. What has research discovered about the accuracy of children's eyewitness testimony?
2. What concerns Elizabeth Loftus about the accuracy of eyewitness testimony?

▲ **Elizabeth Loftus**
"One reason most of us, as jurors, place so much faith in eyewitness testimony is that we are unaware of how many factors influence its accuracy."

INFORMATION PROCESSING AND MEMORY

Memory research has been influenced by the cognitive revolution in psychology. The most widely accepted model of memory assumes that memory processing involves the stages of sensory memory, short-term memory, and long-term memory. At each stage the processing of memories involves encoding, storage, retrieval, and forgetting.

SENSORY MEMORY

Stimulation of sensory receptors produces sensory memories. Visual sensory memory is called iconic memory, and auditory sensory memory is called echoic memory. George Sperling found that iconic memory contains more information than had been commonly believed and that almost all of it fades within a second.

SHORT-TERM MEMORY

Short-term memory is called working memory, because we use it to manipulate information provided by either sensory memory or long-term memory. We tend to encode information in short-term memory as sounds. We can store an average of seven chunks of information in short-term memory without rehearsal. Memories in short-term memory last about 20 seconds without rehearsal. Forgetting in short-term memory is caused by decay and displacement of information.

LONG-TERM MEMORY

Memories stored in long-term memory are relatively permanent. Elaborative rehearsal of information in short-term memory is more likely than maintenance rehearsal to produce long-term memories. The levels of processing theory assumes that information processed at deeper levels will be more firmly stored in long-term memory. Researchers distinguish between procedural, semantic, and episodic memories. Semantic network theory assumes that memories are stored as nodes interconnected by links. Schema theory assumes that memories are stored as cognitive structures that affect the encoding, storage, and retrieval of information related to them.

Hermann Ebbinghaus began the formal study of memory by employing the method of savings. He also identified the serial-position effect and the forgetting curve. The main theories of forgetting include decay theory, interference theory, motivation theory, and cue-dependence theory. The main versions of cue-dependence theory are context-dependent memory and state-dependent memory.

IMPROVING YOUR MEMORY

You can improve your memory by practicing good study habits and by using mnemonic devices. A useful study technique is the SQ3R method, in which you survey, question, read, recite, and review. Overlearning and distributed practice are also useful techniques. Mnemonic devices are memory aids that organize material to make it easier to recall. The main mnemonic devices include acronyms, the method of loci, the pegword method, and the link method.

THE BIOPSYCHOLOGY OF MEMORY

Although Karl Lashley failed in his search for the engram, researchers have discovered some of the anatomical and chemical bases of memory. The hippocampus plays an important role in converting short-term memories into long-term memories. Research on NMDA receptors promises to contribute to our understanding of the physiological bases of memory. Neurotransmitters, particularly acetylcholine, play crucial roles in memory formation. Even blood glucose can facilitate memory formation.

SHOULD WE TRUST EYEWITNESS TESTIMONY?

Research by Elizabeth Loftus and her colleagues has shown that eyewitness testimony often can be inaccurate. Of special concern is the need for care in determining the accuracy of children's eyewitness testimony. An important research finding is that eyewitnesses' confidence in their memories is not a good indicator of their accuracy. Another important finding is that leading questions can alter the recall of memories by eyewitnesses.

KEY CONCEPTS

▶ KEY CONTRIBUTORS

▶ FOR MORE INFORMATION ON MEMORY

FOR GENERAL WORKS ON MEMORY

Conway, M. A. (1995). *Flashbulb memories*. Hillsdale, NJ: Erlbaum.

Ebbinghaus, H. (1885/1964). *Memory: A contribution to experimental psychology*. New York: Dover.

Klatzky, R. L. (1995). *Human memory: Structures and processes* (2nd ed.). New York: Freeman.

Schacter, D.S. (1997). *Searching for memory: The brain, the mind, and the past*. New York: Basic Books.

FOR MORE ON SENSORY MEMORY

Cowan, N. (1984). On short and long auditory stores. *Psychological Bulletin, 96*, 343–370.

Sperling, G. (1960). The information available in brief visual presentations. *Psychological Monographs, 74* (No. 498).

FOR MORE ON SHORT-TERM MEMORY

Gathercole, S.E. (1996). *Models of short-term memory*. Hillsdale, NJ: Erlbaum.

Richardson, J. T. (1996). *Working memory and human cognition*. New York: Oxford University Press.

FOR MORE ON LONG-TERM MEMORY

Memory Systems

Graf, P., & Masson, M. E. J. (1993). *Implicit memory: New directions in cognition, development, and neuropsychology*. Hillsdale, NJ: Erlbaum.

Schacter, D. L., & Tulving, E. (Eds.). (1994). *Memory systems*. Cambridge, MA: MIT Press.

Forgetting

Freud, S. (1901/1965). *Psychopathology of everyday life*. New York: W. W. Norton.

Kuiken, D. (Ed.). (1991). *Mood and memory: Theory, research, and applications*. Newbury Park, CA: Sage.

Schacter, D. L., & Coyle, J. T. (Eds.).(1996). *Memory distortion: How minds, brains, and societies reconstruct the past*. Cambridge, MA: Harvard University Press.

FOR MORE ON IMPROVING YOUR MEMORY

Fogler, J., & Stern, L. (1994). *Improving your memory: How to remember what you're starting to forget*. Baltimore: Johns Hopkins University Press.

Herrmann, D., Raybeck, D., & Gutman, D. (1993). *Improving student memory*. Toronto: Hogrefe & Huber.

FOR MORE ON THE BIOPSYCHOLOGY OF MEMORY

Alkon, D. L. (1992). *Memory's voice: Deciphering the mind-brain code*. New York: Harper Collins.

Baudry, M., & Davis, J. L. (Eds.). (1994). *Long-term potentiation* (2 vols.). Cambridge, MA: MIT Press.

McGaugh, J.L., Weinberger, N.M., & Lynch, G. (1995). *Brain and memory: Modulation and mediation of neuroplasticity*. New York: Oxford University Press.

Collingbridge, G. L., & Watkins, J. C. (Eds.). (1995). *The NMDA receptor* (2nd ed.). New York: Oxford University Press.

FOR MORE ON EYEWITNESS TESTIMONY

Children's Testimony

Ceci, S. J., & Bruck, M. (1995). *Jeopardy in the courtroom: A scientific analysis of children's testimony*. Washington, DC: American Psychological Association.

Zaragosa, M. S., Graham, J. R., Hall, G. C., Hirschman, R., & Ben-Porath, Y. S. (Eds.). (1995). *Memory and testimony in the child witness*. Thousand Oaks, CA: Sage.

Questioning the Eyewitness

Loftus, E. F. (1996). *Eyewitness testimony*. Cambridge, MA: Harvard University Press.

Ross, D. F., Read, J. D., & Toglia, M. P. (Eds.). (1994). *Adult eyewitness testimony: Current trends and developments*. New York: Cambridge University Press.

FOR MORE ON CONTRIBUTORS TO THE STUDY OF MEMORY

Allport, S. (1986). *Explorers of the black box: The search for the cellular basis of memory*. New York: W. W. Norton.

Loftus, E. F., & Ketcham, K. (1991). *Witness for the defense*. New York: St. Martin's Press.

Postman, L. (1968). Hermann Ebbinghaus. *American Psychologist, 23*, 149–157.

Thinking and Language

everal years ago, an argument raged in *Sporting News* about whether professional wrestling is an example of the concept "sport." During the past two decades, researchers have found that, contrary to common sense, people who are rewarded for their creativity may become less creative. Researchers in artificial intelligence have developed a computer program capable of defeating a world chess champion. Millions of infants throughout the world are learning to speak their native tongues without any formal training. And several chimpanzees in the United States are communicating through sign language they learned from other chimpanzees.

Each of these topics, which are discussed later in this chapter, falls within the domain of *cognitive psychology*—perhaps the most influential field of psychology in recent years. In fact, the 1950s and 1960s saw a "cognitive revolution" in which strict behaviorism was countered by increased interest in the study of both the mind and behavior (Sperry, 1993). This was inspired by an explosion of interest in the study of computer science, cognitive processes, and language acquisition. **Cognitive psychology** combines William James's concern with mental processes and John B. Watson's concern with observable behavior (Massaro, 1991). Cognitive psychologists accomplish this by using techniques that permit them to infer mental processes from overt behavior.

Thinking and language are different, yet interrelated, cognitive activities. Chapter 8 described the cognitive activity of memory, which permits you to store and retrieve information. Like memory, thinking and language help you profit from experience and adapt to your environment. Your ability to think and to use language will enable you to comprehend the information conveyed in this chapter and to apply some of it, perhaps, in your everyday life.

THINKING: THE COGNITIVE REVOLUTION IN PSYCHOLOGY

Forming concepts. Solving problems. Being creative. Making decisions. Each of these processes depends on **thinking,** which is the purposeful mental manipulation of words and images. Yet in 1925, John B. Watson, the founder of behaviorism, claimed that thinking is not a mental activity. Instead, he insisted that it was no more than subvocal speech—activity of the speech muscles that is too subtle to produce audible sounds. Margaret Floy Washburn (1916), Watson's contemporary, made a similar claim in her *motor theory of thinking*. There is an intuitive appeal to this claim, because you might sometimes find yourself engaging in subvocal speech—perhaps even while reading this chapter. Moreover, physiological recordings of activity in the speech muscles have shown that some people do subvocalize while thinking (McGuigan, 1970).

But this does not necessarily support Watson's claim that subvocal speech *is* thinking. Convincing evidence against Watson's claim came from a study in which a physician, Scott Smith, had himself paralyzed for half an hour by the drug curare (Smith et al., 1947). He did so to assess its possible use in the induction of general anesthesia. Because curare paralyzes the skeletal muscles (see Chapter 3), including the breathing muscles, Smith was put on a respirator. After the curare wore off, he was able to report conversations that had taken place while he had been paralyzed. Because Smith was able to think and form memories while his speech muscles were paralyzed, this showed that thinking does not depend on subvocal speech.

cognitive psychology
The psychological viewpoint that favors the study of how the mind organizes perceptions, processes information, and interprets experiences.

thinking
The mental manipulation of words and images, as in concept formation, problem solving, and decision making.

▲ **Margaret Floy Washburn (1871–1939)**
"The whole of inner life is correlated with and dependent upon bodily movement."

(a)

(b)

◀ Concepts
Concepts refer to events, such as (a) "holidays," or relationships, such as (b) "opposite," as well as to objects, such as "furniture," or qualities, such as "tallness."

Most behaviorists did not equate thinking with subvocal speech, but they agreed with Watson's position that mental processes were not the proper object of study for psychologists. By the 1960s, though, dissatisfaction with the inability of strict behaviorism to explain memory, thinking, and certain other psychological processes contributed to the cognitive revolution. This reintroduced the study of mental processes, or "cognition," to psychology (Pribram, 1985). One of the basic cognitive processes is concept formation, the next topic in this chapter.

STAYING ON TRACK: *Thinking*

1. In what way does cognitive psychology show the influence of William James and John B. Watson?
2. What evidence contradicts the motor theory of thinking?

Answers to Staying on Track start on p. S-4.

Concept Formation: Categorizing Reality

If a biology teacher asked you to hold a snake, you would be more willing to hold a nonpoisonous snake than a poisonous snake. Similarly, you might be willing to eat a nonpoisonous mushroom but not a poisonous mushroom. Your actions would show that you understood the concepts "poisonous" and "nonpoisonous." A **concept** represents a category of objects, events, qualities, or relations whose members share certain features. For instance, poisonous objects share the ability to make you ill or kill you if you ingest them. During your life you have formed thousands of concepts, which provide the raw materials for thinking. Concepts enable us to respond to events appropriately and to store our memories in an organized way (Corter & Gluck, 1992).

concept

A category of objects, events, qualities, or relations that share certain features.

Logical Concepts: Forming Concepts by Identifying Defining Features

How do we form concepts? Consider the case of a **logical concept,** which is formed by identifying the specific features possessed by all things that the concept applies to. "Great Lakes state" is a logical concept. Each of its members has the features of being a state and bordering one or more of the Great Lakes. The book of Leviticus in the Old Testament provides two of the oldest examples of logical concepts. Leviticus distinguishes between

logical concept

A concept formed by identifying the specific features possessed by all things that the concept applies to.

Concept Formation
Laboratory studies of the formation of logical concepts present subjects with a series of examples varying on specific features. The subject's task is to identify the features that compose the concept. The figures in this example can vary in size (small or large), shape (circle or triangle), color (black or magenta), or number (one or two). Given that the odd-numbered cards are members of the concept and the even-numbered cards are not, see how quickly you can identify the concept. (The answer appears at the bottom of this page.)

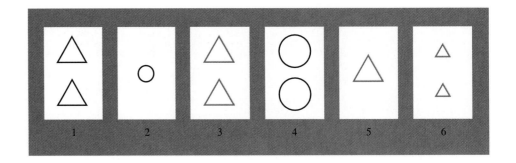

"clean" animals, which may be eaten, and "unclean" animals, which may not. As one example, "clean" sea animals have fins and scales, while "unclean" sea animals do not. This means that bass and trout are "clean" animals, while clams and lobsters are "unclean" animals (Murphy & Medin, 1985).

Logical concepts like those found in Leviticus, which refer to "real-life" concepts, have typically not been the kinds studied in the laboratory. Instead, laboratory studies have generally used logical concepts created by the researcher. The use of logical concepts lets the researcher exert more-precise control over the definitions of particular concepts. An experiment on the formation of a logical concept might present subjects with a series of symbols varying in size, shape, and color. The subject's task is to discover the features that define the concept. For example, a symbol might have to be large, square, and blue to be considered an example of the particular concept. Subjects determine the features of the concept by testing hypotheses about its possible defining features on successive examples that are labeled as either positive or negative instances of it. A positive instance would include the defining features of the concept (in this case, large, square, and blue), while a negative instance would lack at least one of the defining features (for example, large, square, and red). Try to identify the concept presented in Figure 9.1.

Natural Concepts: Forming Concepts Through Everyday Experience

Is baseball a sport? How about table tennis? fishing? shuffleboard? golf? backgammon? bridge? professional wrestling? You have an intuitive sense of how "sportlike" each of these activities is. "Sport" is an example of a **natural concept,** a concept formed through everyday experience rather than by testing hypotheses about particular features that are common to all members of the concept. We might be unable to identify the defining features of natural concepts such as "sport." That is, natural concepts have "fuzzy borders." Such concepts include "truth" (Strichartz & Burton, 1990), "anger" (Russell & Fehr, 1994), "emotion" (Russell, 1991), "personality" (Broughton, 1990), and "romantic jealousy" (Sharpsteen, 1993). Even Saint Augustine, in the fifth century, noted that a natural concept can have fuzzy borders when he remarked, "I know what 'time' is until someone asks me" (Chadwick, 1986, p. 70).

The difficulty in defining natural concepts led psychologist Eleanor Rosch (1975) to propose that they are related to prototypes. A **prototype** is considered to be the best representative of a concept. According to Rosch, the more similarity between an example and a prototype, the more likely we are to consider the example to be a member of the concept represented by the prototype. A robin is a more prototypical bird than a penguin is. Both have wings and feathers and hatch from eggs, but only the robin can fly.

In regard to the concept "sport," baseball is more prototypical than golf, which in turn is more prototypical than backgammon. The "fuzziness" of natural concepts can lead to arguments about whether a particular example is a member of a given concept (Medin, 1989). This was evident in 1988 in a series of letters to the editor of *Sporting News* either supporting or opposing its coverage of Wrestlemania, the Indianapolis 500, and the World Chess Championship. Supporters considered these to be examples of the concept "sport"; opponents did not. Figure 9.2 illustrates how instances of a concept vary in how prototypical they are.

natural concept
A concept, typically formed through everyday experience, whose members possess some, but not all, of a common set of features.

prototype
The best representative of a concept.

Answer to question in Figure 9.1: large triangles.

(a)   (b)

◄ FIGURE 9.2
Prototypes
A prototype is the best representative of a concept. Which do you believe is the more prototypical (a) dog? (b) airplane?

Subsequent research has indicated that we do form concepts by creating prototypes of the relevant objects, events, qualities, or relations (Nosofsky, 1991). In regard to the concept "love," one experiment found that love is better understood from the prototype perspective than from the logical concept perspective. Maternal love was considered most prototypical of "love"; romantic love, love of work, self-love, and infatuation were considered less so (Fehr & Russell, 1991). Reliance on prototypes can also have practical benefits. Medical students learn to diagnose medical disorders better when given prototypes of the disorders than when given an array of specific instances of them (Bordage, 1987).

Influenced by the work of Rosch, psychologists have become more interested in conducting laboratory studies of natural concept formation—the formation of concepts without logically testing hypotheses about their defining features. Consider the following study of the identification of artistic styles (Hartley & Homa, 1981). Subjects who were naive about artistic styles were shown works by the painters Manet, Renoir, and Matisse (see Figure 9.3). Later, the subjects were shown more paintings by these artists and by other artists, without being told the identity of the artists. After viewing the second set of paintings, the subjects accurately matched particular paintings with the styles of the artists whose works they had seen in the first set of paintings. The subjects used the first set to form concepts representing the styles of the three artists: a "Manet," a "Renoir," and a "Matisse." This could not be explained as an example of logical concept formation, because the subjects were unable to identify a set of features that distinguished a Manet from a Renoir from a Matisse.

STAYING ON TRACK: *Concept Formation*

1. What is the difference between a logical concept and a natural concept?
2. In what way do concepts such as "love" and "sport" have fuzzy borders?

Problem Solving: Overcoming Obstacles to Reach Goals

One of the most important uses of concepts is in **problem solving,** the thought process that enables us to overcome obstacles to reach goals. Suppose that your car will not start. In looking for a solution to your problem, you might follow a series of steps commonly used in solving problems (Kramer & Bayern, 1984). First, you *identify the problem:* My car won't start. Second, you *gather information* relevant to the problem: Am I out of gas? Is my

problem solving

The thought process by which an individual overcomes obstacles to reach a goal.

(a)   (b)   (c)

▲ FIGURE 9.3

Artistic Styles as Natural Concepts
We may be able to recognize an artistic style without necessarily being able to specify the characteristics that distinguish it from other styles. Thus, the concepts *(a)* "a Manet," *(b)* "a Renoir," and *(c)* "a Matisse" are natural concepts rather than logical concepts.

battery dead? Are my ignition wires wet? Third, you *try a solution:* I'm not out of gas, so I'll dry off the wires. Finally, you *evaluate the result:* The car started, so the wires were, indeed, wet. If the solution fails to work, you might try a different one: Drying off the wires didn't work, so I'll try a jump start. Problem solving commonly involves one of several strategies, including *trial and error, insight, algorithms,* and *heuristics*.

Trial and Error: Trying Until You Find a Solution

A common strategy for solving problems is **trial and error,** which involves trying one possible solution after another until one works. Ivan Pavlov, though best known for his research on classical conditioning, was one of the first scientists to stress the importance of trial and error (Windholz, 1992). Even the lowly *E. coli* bacterium navigates by trial and error (Marken & Powers, 1989) and spiders pursue prey by using trial and error (Jackson & Wilcox, 1993). For an example of trial and error in human problem solving, imagine that your psychology professor asks you to get a stopwatch from a laboratory and gives you a ring with 10 keys on it. Suppose that on reaching the laboratory you realize that you don't know which key opens the door to the laboratory. You would immediately identify the problem: finding the correct key. After assessing your situation, you would probably decide to use trial and error to solve the problem. You would try one key after another until you found one that opened the door.

Though trial and error is often effective, it is not always efficient. For example, a study of novice computer programmers found that the slower learners relied too much on trial and error (Green & Gilhooly, 1990). If your professor gave you a ring with 50 keys on it, you might find it more efficient to return and ask your professor to identify the correct key rather than waste time trying one key after another. Even worse, imagine learning how to

trial and error
An approach to problem solving in which the individual tries one possible solution after another until one works.

use a word processor by trying various combinations of keystrokes until you hit upon the correct ones to perform desired functions (such as centering a line of text). It might take you years to complete even a brief term paper.

Insight: The Aha! Phenomenon in Problem Solving

In the third century B.C., the Greek physicist Archimedes was asked to solve a problem: Was King Hiero's new crown made of pure gold, or had the goldsmith cheated him by mixing cheap metals with the gold? Archimedes discovered a way to solve this problem when he noticed that if he sat in his bathtub, the water level rose. After shouting "Eureka!" he decided to submerge the crown in water and measure the volume of water it displaced. Reasoning that the volume of water displaced is proportionate to the weight of the object displacing it, he would compare the volume displaced by the crown to the volume displaced by an equal amount of metal that he knew to be pure gold. Archimedes found that the crown was, indeed, pure gold. To make this discovery, he relied on **insight,** an approach to problem solving that depends on mental manipulation of information rather than on overt trial and error.

Insight is also characterized by an "Aha!" experience—the sudden realization of the solution to a problem—as found in research by Janet Metcalfe. In a typical experiment, every 10 seconds Metcalfe asks subjects working on either insight problems or noninsight problems (such as algebra) how "warm" they feel—that is, how close they feel they are to the correct solution. She has found that those working on insight problems are less accurate, indicating that solutions to noninsight problems are incremental and predictable, whereas solutions to insight problems are sudden and unpredictable (Metcalfe & Wiebe, 1987). Nonetheless, her interpretations of her research findings have been countered by Robert Weisberg (1992), who claims that insight is a fiction—what we call insight might seem sudden and unpredictable, but it is the product of the gradual accumulation of knowledge as one works on a problem.

Assuming that insight does exist, can animals use it to solve problems? The classic study of insight in animals was conducted by Gestalt psychologist Wolfgang Kohler (1887–1967) on the island of Tenerife in the Canary Islands during World War I. Kohler (1925) presented a chimpanzee named Sultan with bananas, hanging them from the top of Sultan's cage, well out of his reach (see Figure 9.4). But his cage also contained several crates. After trying fruitlessly to reach the bananas by jumping, Sultan suddenly hit upon the solution. He piled the crates on top of one another, quickly climbed to the top, and grabbed a banana—just as the shaky structure came tumbling down.

The assumption that Sultan displayed insight was challenged more than a half century later by several behaviorists (Epstein et al., 1984). In a tongue-in-cheek study analogous to the one involving Sultan, they used food rewards to train a pigeon to first perform the separate acts of moving a tiny box, standing on the box, and pecking a plastic, miniature banana. When later confronted with the banana hanging out of reach from the top of its cage, the pigeon at first seemed confused but then suddenly moved the box under the banana, climbed on the box, and pecked at the banana to get a food reward. The steps are illustrated in Figure 9.5. According to the researchers, if a pigeon can perform supposedly insightful behavior, then perhaps insight in animals—and even in people—is no more than the chaining together of previously rewarded behaviors.

Algorithms: Guaranteeing Solutions to Problems

If you use the formula *length times width,* you will obtain the area of a rectangle. A mathematical formula is an example of a problem-solving strategy called an algorithm. An **algorithm** is a rule that, when followed step by step, assures that a solution to a problem will be found. Many physicians use algorithms to diagnose diseases, such as sexual dysfunctions, by noting specific combinations of symptoms and personal characteristics of patients (Hatzichristou, Bertero, & Goldstein, 1994). The notion of an algorithm is an offshoot of research in computer science by cognitive psychologists Allen Newell and Herbert Simon (1972). Many computer programs rely on algorithms to process information accurately.

insight
An approach to problem solving that depends on mental manipulation of information rather than overt trial and error, and produces sudden solutions to problems.

▲ Wolfgang Kohler (1887–1967)
"Association theorists know and recognize what one calls insight in man . . . . The only thing that follows for animal behavior is that, where it has an intelligent character, they will treat it in the same way; but not at all that the animal lacks that which is usually called insight in man."

algorithm
A problem-solving rule or procedure that, when followed step by step, assures that a correct solution will be found.

▲ FIGURE 9.4
Insight in Apes
Kohler (1925) demonstrated that chimpanzees can use insight to solve problems. The chimpanzee Sultan found a way to reach bananas hanging out of reach without engaging in mere trial-and-error behavior.

▲ FIGURE 9.5
Insight in a Pigeon?
This pigeon was trained to perform the separate actions of pushing a box to a designated location and climbing on the box to peck a plastic banana. When presented with the box and the banana in separate locations, the pigeon pushed the box under the banana, climbed on the box, and pecked the banana. This showed that an apparent instance of insight might be no more than performing a chain of previously learned behaviors.

But, like trial and error, an algorithm can be an inefficient means of finding the solution to a problem. To appreciate this, imagine that you are in the middle of a chess game. An algorithm for finding your best move would require tracing all possible sequences of moves from the current position. Because there is an average of 35 different moves that can be made in any single position in the middle of a chess game, you would need literally millions of years to find the best move by tracing all possible sequences of moves. Even using an algorithm to follow all possible sequences of just the next 3 moves in the middle of a chess game would require the analysis of an average of 1.8 billion moves (Waltz, 1982). Because a formal chess match has a typical time limit of 5 hours, even world chess champions do not rely on algorithms. Instead, they rely on problem-solving strategies called heuristics.

Heuristics: Rules of Thumb in Problem Solving

A **heuristic** is a general principle, or "rule of thumb," that guides problem solving in everyday life and in scientific fields, such as chemistry (Seroussi, 1995). Unlike an algorithm, a

heuristic
A general principle or "rule of thumb" that guides problem solving, though it does not guarantee a correct solution.

◀ **Heuristics**
If you had unlimited time and patience, you could put together a 1,500-piece jigsaw puzzle by taking a piece and trying one piece after another until you found one that fit that piece. You would continue in a similar manner until you completed the puzzle. But you would perform more efficiently if you relied on heuristics. One heuristic might be, "Separate the pieces into piles of similar colors." A second might be, "Find the corner pieces first." And a third might be, "Complete the edges of the puzzle before proceeding to the center."

heuristic does not guarantee a solution. But a heuristic can be more efficient, because it rules out many useless alternatives before they are even attempted. A chess player might rely on heuristics, such as trying to control the center of the board or trading weaker pieces for stronger ones.

Impediments to Problem Solving: Mental Sets and Functional Fixedness

Before reading on, try to solve the six problems presented in Figure 9.6, in which you must use three jars to measure out exact amounts of water. If you are like most subjects, you could easily solve the first five problems but ran into difficulty with the sixth. In an early study using the water-jar problem, the subjects quickly realized that the solution to the first problem was to fill jar B, pour enough water from it to fill jar A, and then pour enough water from jar B to fill jar C twice. This left the desired amount in jar B. The subjects then found that the same strategy worked for each of the next four problems. But when they reached the sixth problem, two-thirds of them were unable to solve it. Those who failed to solve it had developed a strategy that was effective in solving previous examples but made the simple solution to problem 6 difficult to discover. In contrast, of subjects who were asked to solve only the sixth problem, few had difficulty discovering the simple solution: fill jar A and pour enough water from it to fill jar C, leaving the desired amount in jar A (Luchins, 1946).

This study demonstrated that we sometimes are hindered by a **mental set**, a problem-solving strategy that has succeeded in the past but that can interfere with solving a problem that requires a new strategy. In one study, expert computer programmers and novice computer programmers were given a programming problem that could be solved by using a simple programming strategy that is more often used by novices. The results showed that the novices were more likely to solve the problem, because the experts tried to use a more sophisticated, but ineffective, strategy that they had adopted during their careers as computer programmers. In other words, the experts had developed a mental set that blinded them to the simpler solution (Adelson, 1984).

How can you overcome a mental set? One way is to make assumptions opposite to those you normally make. This approach might have helped the expert computer programmers who were unable to solve the problem that the novices were able to solve. See if you can overcome mental sets by solving the problems in Figure 9.7. Solutions to the problems appear in Figure 9.8.

mental set

A tendency to use a particular problem-solving strategy that has succeeded in the past but that may interfere with solving a problem requiring a new strategy.

Mental Sets
Luchins (1946) asked subjects to use jars with the capacities shown in columns A, B, and C to obtain the amounts required in the right-hand column. The first five problems led subjects to overlook a simpler solution in the sixth problem.

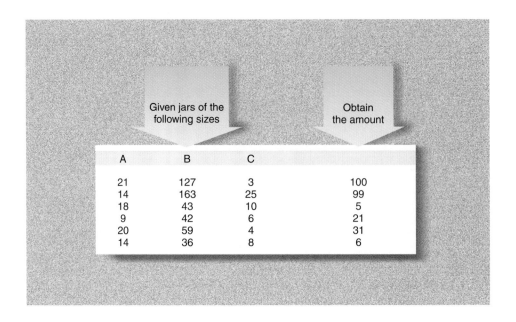

Given jars of the following sizes			Obtain the amount
A	B	C	
21	127	3	100
14	163	25	99
18	43	10	5
9	42	6	21
20	59	4	31
14	36	8	6

functional fixedness

The inability to realize that a problem can be solved by using a familiar object in an unusual way.

Another way in which past experience can impede our ability to solve problems is through **functional fixedness,** the inability to realize that a problem can be solved by using a familiar object in an unusual way. The term *functional fixedness* was coined by Gestalt psychologist Karl Duncker (1903–1940), who was a leader in the study of insight learning (Hilgard, 1987). The role of functional fixedness in problem solving was demonstrated in a classic study (Maier, 1931) in which each subject was asked to perform the simple task of tying together two long strings hanging from a ceiling. The problem was that the two strings were too far apart for the subject to grasp them both at the same time. As shown in Figure 9.9, the room contained a variety of objects, including a table, a chair, an extension cord, and a pair of pliers.

Subjects were given 10 minutes to solve the problem. Each time the subject identified a solution, the experimenter said, "Now do it a different way." One solution was to tie the extension cord to one string, grasp the other string, pull the strings toward one another, and then tie them together. The solution that the experimenter was interested in is illustrated in Figure 9.10. Subjects who discovered that solution tied the pliers to one of the strings and started it swinging like a pendulum. They then grabbed the other string, walked toward the swinging pliers, and tied the two strings together (Maier, 1931). To discover that solution, the subjects had to realize that the pliers could be used as a weight and not solely as a tool. Only 39.3 percent of the subjects discovered this solution on their own. More subjects discovered it when the experimenter provided a hint by subtly setting one of the strings in motion.

As with mental sets, functional fixedness can be overcome. One of the best ways is to change or ignore the names of familiar objects. In a study that used this technique, subjects were given a bulb, some wire, a switch, a wrench, and batteries. The subjects were told to create a circuit that would light the bulb, even though they had too little wire to complete the circuit. The solution was to use the wrench to complete it. Subjects who were told to use nonsense names such as "jod" to refer to the wrench were more likely to solve the problem than were subjects who called the wrench a "wrench" (Glucksberg & Danks, 1968). By using nonsense words to refer to the wrench, the subjects were less likely to think of it as just a mechanical tool.

STAYING ON TRACK: *Problem Solving*

1. Why might heuristics be both superior and inferior to algorithms?
2. How do mental sets hamper problem solving in everyday life?

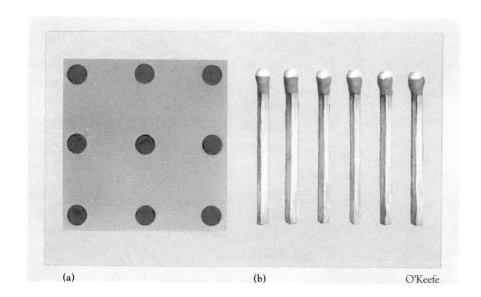

(a)   (b)   O'Keefe

◀ **FIGURE 9.7**
Problem Solving
Test your problem-solving ability on these two brain teasers. (*a*) Connect the nine dots by drawing four straight lines without lifting your pencil. (*b*) Use the six matches to form four equilateral triangles. The solutions are given in Figure 9.8. Did a mental set affect your performance on either problem?

Creativity: Finding Novel Solutions to Problems

In 1950, in his final address as president of the American Psychological Association, creativity researcher J. P. Guilford (1897–1987) expressed disappointment that of the more than 100,000 psychological studies published up until then, fewer than 200 dealt with creativity. Following Guilford's address, and influenced by the cognitive revolution, there was a striking increase in the number of scientific studies of creativity (Barron & Harrington, 1981).

But what is creativity? Like other natural concepts, creativity cannot be defined by a specific set of features—that is, it has "fuzzy borders." We might be able to distinguish between creative and noncreative behavior without being able to identify exactly what makes one example creative and another noncreative. Psychologists generally define **creativity** as a form of problem solving characterized by finding solutions that are novel, as well as useful or socially valued (Mumford & Gustafson, 1988), whether practical, artistic, or scientific.

Of course, the works of many creative geniuses were not socially valued in their time. The exhibition of works by the French artist Paul Cezanne (1839–1906) that toured the world in 1996 drew millions of visitors to museums attracted by the allure of an artist who many authorities believe inspired the development of modern art. Yet in his own time, Cézanne was considered a technically inadequate artist whose paintings had little appeal to critics and lay people alike. What is considered creative in one era or one culture might be considered inept in another.

Thus, in his time, Cézanne's works were considered novel but were not valued—novelty is not sufficient to demonstrate creativity (Epstein, 1991). Said the French mathematician Henri Poincaré (1948, p. 16), "To create consists precisely in not making useless combinations and in making those which are useful and which are only a small minority. Invention is discernment, choice." Thus, if you gave a monkey a canvas, a paintbrush, and a pallet of paint, it might produce novel paintings, but they would not be considered examples of creativity.

Characteristics of Creative People

What characteristics are associated with creativity? Though creative people tend to have above-average intelligence, you do not have to be a genius to be highly creative (Nicholls, 1972). For example, a study of undergraduates found that their scores on a test of intelligence and a test of creative thinking correlated .24, indicating a positive, but small, relationship between the two (Rushton, 1990). And a study of children found a positive

creativity

A form of problem solving that generates novel, socially valued solutions to problems.

▲ **A Picasso of Pachydermia?**
This elephant produces original paintings. But are they examples of creativity?

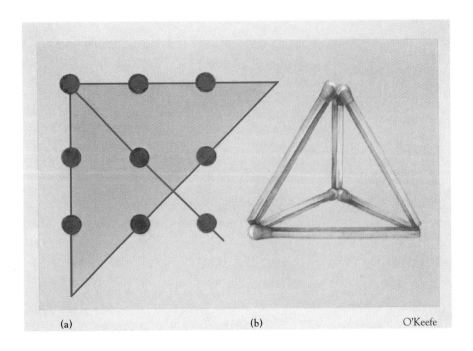

(a)   (b)   O'Keefe

correlation between their intelligence and their creativity up to an IQ of 120 (above average but not in the genius range), but no relationship beyond that level of intelligence (Fuchs-Beauchamp, Karnes, & Johnson, 1993).

Creative people also tend to exhibit certain personality characteristics (Aguilar-Alonso, 1996). They tend to prefer novelty, favor complexity, and make independent judgments (Barron & Harrington, 1981). Moreover, they are able to combine different kinds of thinking, being superior at combining verbal thinking with visual thinking (Kershner & Ledger, 1985) and reality-oriented thinking with imaginative thinking (Suler, 1980). And creative people tend to be more creative when they are engaged in creative behavior for its own sake rather than to obtain some kind of reward.

ANATOMY OF A CONTEMPORARY RESEARCH STUDY

Can Rewarding Creative Behavior Inhibit Creativity?

Rationale

According to creativity researcher Teresa Amabile (1989), creative people are more motivated by their intrinsic interest in creative tasks than by extrinsic factors, such as fame, money, or approval. In fact, when people are presented with extrinsic reasons for performing intrinsically interesting creative tasks, they can lose their motivation to perform them. The present study by Amabile (1985) provided further evidence of this.

Method

Subjects were recruited through advertisements asking for writers to participate in a study of people's reasons for writing. Most of the respondents were undergraduate or graduate students in English or creative writing. All of the subjects were asked to write two brief poems on designated themes (the first on snow, and the second on laughter). Each subject was assigned to one of three groups. After the subjects wrote the first poem, one group completed a questionnaire that focused on intrinsic reasons for writing, such as the opportunity for self-expression, while a second group completed a questionnaire that focused on extrinsic reasons for writing, such as gaining public recognition. The third group served as a control group and was not given a questionnaire. Twelve experienced poets judged the creativity of the poems on a 40-point scale.

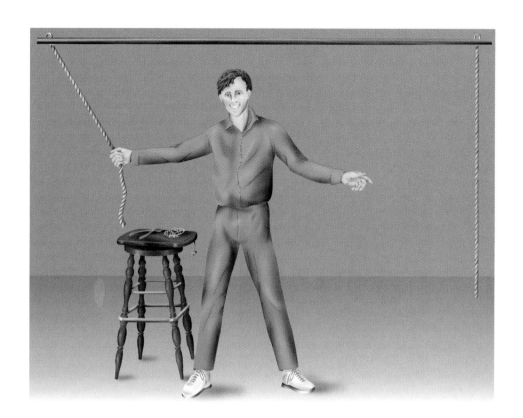

◀ **FIGURE 9.9**
Functional Fixedness
Maier (1931) asked subjects to tie two strings together even though they were too far apart to grasp at the same time. Functional fixedness interfered with finding some of the possible solutions, one of which is illustrated in Figure 9.10.

Results and Discussion

When the first poems were judged for their creativity, the three groups did not differ. However, when the second poems were judged for their creativity, the poems written by the group exposed to the questionnaire that focused on extrinsic reasons for writing were judged less creative than those written by the other two groups; the intrinsic-reasons group and the control group showed no change in creativity from the first poem to the second, but the extrinsic-reasons group showed a significant decrease. Thus, though concentrating on intrinsic reasons for creative writing did not improve creativity, concentrating on extrinsic reasons for creativity impaired it. Even the mere expectation of having one's performance evaluated will hamper creativity (Amabile, Goldfarb, & Brackfield, 1990). These findings agree with the experience of the noted American poet Sylvia Plath, who believed that her persistent writer's block was caused by her excessive concern about an extrinsic reason for writing—the recognition of her work by publishers, critics, and the public. Perhaps, given students who enjoy writing, teachers should avoid pointing out the extrinsic advantages of it, such as obtaining a better job or getting accepted into graduate school. Chapter 11 discusses theories that explain the negative effects of extrinsic motivation.

▲ **Teresa Amabile**
"Intrinsic motivation is conducive to creativity, while extrinsic motivation is detrimental."

Creativity and Divergent Thinking

How many ways can you use a brick? If you could think of only such uses as "to build a house" or "to build a fireplace," you would exhibit convergent thinking. According to Guilford, **convergent thinking** focuses on finding conventional "correct" solutions to problems. If you also thought of less conventional "correct" uses for a brick, such as "to prop open a door" or "to save water by putting it in a toilet tank," you would be engaging in divergent thinking. **Divergent thinking,** a hallmark of creativity (Guilford, 1984), involves freely considering a variety of potential solutions to artistic, literary, scientific, or practical problems. The importance of divergent thinking in creativity was noted as long ago as the mid eighteenth century (Puccio, 1991).

Overemphasis on convergent thinking can impair divergent thinking and, as a result, inhibit creativity (Reddy & Reddy, 1983). One way of inducing divergent thinking is

convergent thinking

The cognitive process that focuses on finding conventional solutions to problems.

divergent thinking

The cognitive process by which an individual freely considers a variety of potential solutions to artistic, literary, scientific, or practical problems.

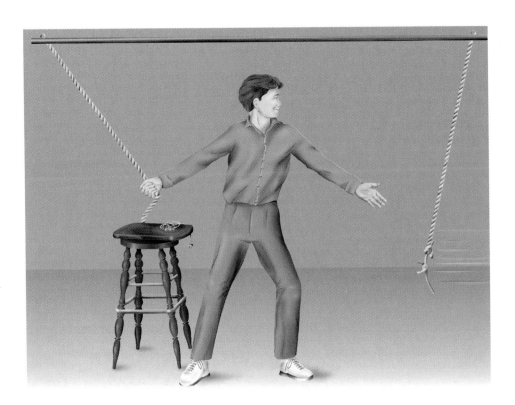

brainstorming, in which thinkers are encouraged to conjure up as many solutions as possible to a problem, though there is no guarantee that the many solutions produced by brainstorming will be superior to those produced by more-focused attempts at problem solving (Buyer, 1988).

To further appreciate the notion of divergent thinking, consider the Remote Associates Test created by Sarnoff Mednick (1962), which presents subjects with sets of three apparently unrelated words. For each set, the subjects are asked to find a fourth word that is related to the other three. To do so, they must use divergent thinking. For example, what word would you choose to associate with the words *piano, record,* and *baseball?* The word *player* would be one possibility. Try testing your ability to find remote associates for the items in Table 9.1. Performance on tests of divergent thinking correlates moderately highly with creative behavior (Runco, 1993). But creative ability in one area, such as writing poetry, might not correlate highly with creativity in another, such as writing stories. That is, divergent thinking might not be a general trait, but might instead be limited to specific creative domains (Baer, 1996).

Divergent thinking can be cultivated. It is promoted by parents who raise their children to be open to a wide variety of experiences (Harrington, Block, & Block, 1987). Even adults can learn to use divergent thinking. This idea is not lost on industrial leaders, many of whom have their employees attend seminars so they can learn to think more creatively by engaging in divergent thinking (Basadur, Wakabayashi, & Takai, 1992). Divergent thinking is also promoted by positive emotional states. When you are angry, anxious, or depressed, you are more likely to engage in convergent thinking. Thus, teachers who evoke positive emotions in their students, and managers who evoke positive emotions in their employees, can encourage creative academic or vocational problem solving. For example, a study of physicians found that when positive emotions were induced in subjects, they became more creative than control subjects (Estrada, Isen, & Young, 1994).

STAYING ON TRACK: *Creativity*

1. What are some personal characteristics associated with creativity?
2. How did Amabile's study demonstrate that extrinsic rewards can impair creativity?

	Given Words		Your Word?
1.	Worker	Boiled	Core	_____
2.	York	World	Born	_____
3.	Base	Foot	Basket	_____
4.	Range	Climber	Grown	_____

Possible responses: (1) hard; (2) new; (3) ball; (4) mountain

Source: Data from S. A. Mednick, "The Associative Basis of the Creative Process" in *Psychological Review* 69: 220–232, American Psychological Association, 1962.

◀ TABLE 9.1
The Remote Associates Test
Items like these are included in the Remote Associates Test (Mednick, 1962). For each of the items, find a word that is associated with all three of the given words.

▲ **Amos Tversky and Daniel Kahneman**
"Most people are . . . very sensitive to the difference between certainty and high probability and relatively insensitive to intermediate gradations of probability."

decision making
A form of problem solving in which one tries to make the best choice from among alternative judgments or courses of action.

representativeness heuristic
In decision making, the assumption that a small sample is representative of its population.

Decision Making: Choosing the Best Alternative

Each of our days is filled with decisions. They can be minor, such as deciding whether to take along a raincoat when leaving home, or major, such as deciding which college to attend. **Decision making** is a form of problem solving in which we try to make the best choice from among alternative courses of action to produce a desired outcome. In making decisions, we weigh two factors: *utility* and *probability*. Utility is the value we assign to a given outcome, and probability is our estimate of the likelihood that a given alternative will lead to a particular outcome. Though we normally prefer outcomes of both high utility and high probability, we might make exceptions. Consider the decision to purchase state lottery tickets to be eligible for a multimillion-dollar payoff. Though such an outcome has a low probability (perhaps one chance in several million), it has high utility (the potential to win millions of dollars), which makes purchasing a ticket an attractive decision to many people. Utility and probability influence decisions in areas as diverse as gambling (Lopes, 1981) and physicians' use of particular diagnostic tests (Moroff, 1986).

Though decision making seems like a simple matter of rationally calculating the utility and probability of particular outcomes, studies in the 1970s found that decision making is also subject to biases that can keep us from making objective decisions. Biases in decision making have been studied most extensively by cognitive psychologists Amos Tversky and Daniel Kahneman. They have found that our decision making is often biased by our reliance on heuristics (Kahneman, 1991). We might even use heuristics in deciding whether to engage in unsafe sex practices (Kaplan & Shayne, 1993).

Heuristics and Decision Making

In using the **representativeness heuristic,** we assume that a small sample is representative of its population (Kahneman & Tversky, 1973). For example, we use the representativeness heuristic when we eat at a fast-food restaurant and assume that other restaurants in the restaurant chain will be that good (or bad). Even young children use the representativeness heuristic (Davidson, 1995). Because a sample might not accurately represent its population, the use of the representativeness heuristic does not guarantee that our decisions will be correct ones. This might account for unwise decisions made under emotional stress, because we are more likely to rely on the representativeness heuristic when we are under stress (Shaham, Singer, & Schaeffer, 1992).

Consider a study of the effect of the representativeness heuristic in regard to the "hot hand" in basketball, in which a player makes several baskets in a row (Gilovich, Vallone, & Tversky, 1985). The study was prompted by a survey, which found that fans and players tend to believe that during a basketball game the chance of making a basket is greater following a made basket than following a miss. The researchers analyzed shooting records of the Boston Celtics and the Philadelphia 76ers. The results indicated that the chance of making a basket after a made basket was no greater than the chance following a miss. Apparently, fans and players alike incorrectly assume that brief runs of successful shooting are representative of a more general tendency to shoot well. The representativeness heuristic guides decisions as varied as choosing a lottery ticket number (Holtgraves &

Skeel, 1992), buying or selling stocks on the stock market (Andreassen, 1988), and judging how entertaining a movie will be based on a brief description (Glass & Waterman, 1988).

To appreciate another kind of heuristic, answer the following question: In English, is the letter *k* more likely to be the first letter or the third letter of a word? Though the letter *k* is more likely to be the third letter, most people decide that it is more likely to be the first. This is explained by what Tversky and Kahneman (1973) call the **availability heuristic,** which is the tendency to estimate the probability of an event by how easily relevant instances of it come to mind. The more easily an instance comes to mind, the more probable we assume the event will be. But the ease with which instances come to mind might not reflect their actual probability. Instead, instances might come to mind because they are vivid, recent, or important. Thus, because it is easier to recall words that begin with *k*, such as *kick* or *kiss*, than words that have *k* as their third letter, such as *make* or *hike*, we conclude that more words have *k* as their first letter than as their third letter. A similar study found that children judged the names of famous human beings and cartoon characters to be more common than they actually are, presumably because they come to mind more easily than other names (Davies & White, 1994).

The practical effect of the availability heuristic was shown in a study in which subjects estimated the prevalence of cheating by welfare recipients. Subjects who first read a vivid case of welfare cheating overestimated its prevalence (Hamill, Decamp, Wilson, & Nisbett, 1980). This reflects our tendency to respond to rare but vivid news reports of instances of welfare recipients living in luxurious comfort by overestimating the likelihood of welfare cheating. In fact, when we lack the information required for making an objective judgment, the availability of even a single instance of an event can make us overestimate the probability of other occurrences of that event (Lewicki, 1985). This holds true when judging the prevalence of drug use (Eisenman, 1993), the probability of product failures (Folkes, 1988), and the likelihood of a person's getting AIDS (Triplet, 1992). It might also explain why New York City, though usually not one of the top 10 American cities in violent crime statistics, has the reputation as the most dangerous American city. Perhaps the national media coverage given to horrible rapes and murders in New York creates, through the availability heuristic, the belief that individuals are more likely to become victims of violent crimes there than they actually are.

Framing Effects and Decision Making

Consider the following statements: "Dr. Jones fails 10 percent of his students" and "Dr. Jones passes 90 percent of his students." Though both statements report the same reality, you might be more inclined to enroll in Dr. Jones's course after hearing the second comment than you would be after hearing the first. This is an example of what Kahneman and Tversky call **framing effects,** biases introduced in the decision-making process by presenting a situation in a particular manner. Judges, lawyers, and prosecutors are aware of the framing effect in the form of "leading questions," which can bias jury decisions.

Framing effects also influence our everyday decisions. In one study (Levin, Schnittjer, & Thee, 1988), undergraduates rated the incidence of cheating at their school higher when told that "65 percent of students had cheated at some time in their college career" than when told that "35 percent of the students had never cheated." The undergraduates were also more likely to rate a medical treatment as more effective, and were more apt to recommend it to others, when they were told it had a "50 percent success rate" than when told it had a "50 percent failure rate." A similar study found that undergraduates rated meat more highly when it was labeled "75 percent lean" than when it was labeled "25 percent fat" (Levin & Gaeth, 1988). Note that in each study both statements present the same fact and differ only in how they frame the information.

To further appreciate the framing effect, consider the following study by Kahneman and Tversky (1982), in which people were asked one of the following two questions: "If you lost a pair of tickets to a Broadway play for which you paid $40, would you purchase two more?" or "If you lost $40 on your way to purchase tickets at the box office, would you still purchase tickets?" Though in each case the subject would be $40 poorer, more

availability heuristic
In decision making, the tendency to estimate the probability of an event by how easily relevant instances of it come to mind.

framing effect
In decision making, biases introduced into the decision-making process by presenting an issue or situation in a certain manner.

subjects answered yes to the second question. Thus, the way in which the questions were framed, not the amount of money the subjects would lose, influenced their decision. Their subjective evaluation was more important than the objective situation. Framing effects influence a variety of kinds of decisions, including the choice of appropriate medical procedures for treating illnesses (Wang & Johnston, 1995) and decisions to engage in healthier behaviors (Rothman & Salovey, 1997).

STAYING ON TRACK: *Decision Making*

1. In what way does decision making depend on utility and probability?
2. What is the availability heuristic?

Artificial Intelligence: Mimicking the Mind with Computer Programs

Almost 200 years ago a Hungarian inventor named Wolfgang von Kempelen toured Europe with the Maezel Chess Automaton, a chess-playing machine. The Automaton defeated almost all the people who dared play against it. One of its admirers was the noted American author Edgar Allen Poe, who wrote an essay speculating—incorrectly—on how it worked. After years of defeating one challenger after another, the Automaton's mechanism was finally revealed. Inside it was a legless Polish army officer named Worouski, who was a master chess player ("Program Power," 1981).

During the past three decades, computer scientists have developed computer programs that actually can play chess. Computer chess programs are the offshoot of studies in **artificial intelligence (AI),** a field founded by Nobel Prize winner Herbert Simon, which integrates computer science and cognitive psychology. Those who study AI try to simulate or improve on human thinking by using computer programs. For example, computer scientists have developed a program that answers political questions as though it were either a politically liberal or a politically conservative person (Abelson, 1981).

Many AI researchers are interested in developing computer programs, so-called **expert systems,** that display expertise in specific domains of knowledge. Computer chess programs have led the way in these efforts—and have contributed to the development of cognitive psychology itself (Charness, 1992). The first computer chess programs were developed in the 1950s at Los Alamos Laboratory in New Mexico and improved steadily during the next two decades until they finally began defeating expert chess players. To date, they have not defeated a world-class player in a multiple-game match.

In 1978 David Levy, the chess champion of Scotland, got a scare when a computer chess program defeated him in the fourth game of a six-game chess match. Levy had made a $2,500 bet that no chess program could defeat him in a match. But Levy won or drew the other five games, and renewed his bet (Ehara, 1980). Despite his victory, Levy and world chess champions appear doomed to eventual defeat by computer chess programs. An ominous sign occurred in 1979 at a backgammon match in Monte Carlo, when a computer program defeated the world backgammon champion, Luigi Villa of Italy. This was the first time a computer program had defeated a human world champion in an intellectual game ("Teaching a Machine the Shades of Gray," 1981).

The computer chess program that finally defeats a world chess champion might be a descendant of the program Belle. In 1981, at the Virginia Open Chess Tournament, Belle took fourth place in competition against master chess players ("Program Power," 1981). The only rating above master is grand master, the level achieved by the best chess players in the world. While other computer chess programs relied on algorithms—searching for all possible sequences of moves, several moves deep—to find the best move in a given position, Belle took a more sophisticated, human approach by using heuristics. Though Belle could follow potential sequences of moves four moves deep, it did not follow each sequence to its conclusion. Instead, Belle stopped following a sequence as soon as it proved inferior to another that had already been identified. This

artificial intelligence (AI)
The field that integrates computer science and cognitive psychology in studying information processing through the design of computer programs that appear to exhibit intelligence.

expert system
A computer program that displays expertise in a specific domain of knowledge.

▲ A Computer Chess Champion
World chess champion Gary Kasparov is shown with Deep Blue, a computer that, because of its powerful chess program (which takes advantage of several processors working in parallel) allows it to examine millions of possible moves each second, is capable of defeating the best chess players in the world. As this textbook went to press, Deep Blue, which had lost to Kasparov in 1996, defeated him in a formal chess match, becoming the first computer chess player to defeat a world champion. Said Kasparov after the first match, "For the first time in the history of mankind I saw something similar to an artificial intellect" (Macklin, 1996, p. B1).

serial processing

The processing of information one step at a time.

parallel processing

The processing of different information simultaneously.

language

A formal system of communication involving symbols—whether spoken, written, or gestured—and rules for combining them.

semanticity

The characteristic of language marked by the use of symbols to convey thoughts in a meaningful way.

made Belle perform faster and examine more potentially effective moves in a given time span than did other computer chess programs (Peterson, 1983). Today, expert computer programs appear to be on the verge of defeating world champion chess players (Hsu et al., 1990).

Though computer chess programs are the best known of expert systems, computer scientists have developed a variety of other systems. Among these expert systems, Mycin has helped physicians diagnose infectious diseases, Prospector has helped mining companies decide where to dig for minerals, and Dipmeter has helped analyze geological data from oil-well drillings (Davis, 1986). Expert systems can also help in the diagnosis and treatment of psychological disorders (Todd, 1996). The program Blue Box helps select the best kind of therapy for depressed people (Gingerich, 1990), and the program Sexpert helps in the assessment and treatment of sexual dysfunctions (Ochs et al., 1994). Expert systems are helpful because, in narrow domains of knowledge, they can analyze data more quickly and more objectively than human experts can.

Despite the speed and objectivity with which computers process certain kinds of information, they will not process information in many everyday situations as efficiently as human beings until there are computer programs that function more like the human brain. Most computer programs perform decision-making processes chiefly serially, meaning that they perform one step at a time. In contrast, the human brain performs decision-making processes both serially and in parallel.

When information is processed in parallel, several decision-making steps occur simultaneously and are then integrated. The human brain can therefore perform many kinds of thinking better than the fastest computers can. For example, AI scientists developed a cart that uses a computerized artificial vision system to find its way around obstacles. Human beings, who use both **serial processing** and **parallel processing** of the size, shape, color, brightness, location, and movement of objects, can quickly find their way around obstacles. In contrast, the cart must stop after moving 3 feet so that its computer program can spend 15 minutes using serial processing just to determine its next movement (Waldrop, 1984). Even human perception of color and form occurs in parallel before being integrated into a single perception of an object (Mordkoff, Yantis, & Egeth, 1990). So, for a computerized cart to rapidly negotiate its way around objects will require a computer program that includes some parallel processing. And it is unlikely that any computer program will defeat human world chess champions until AI researchers develop advanced chess programs that use both serial and parallel processing (Kurzweil, 1985).

STAYING ON TRACK: *Artificial Intelligence*

1. Why are expert systems now capable of defeating the best chess players in the world?
2. What is the difference between serial information processing and parallel information processing?

LANGUAGE: COMMUNICATING THOUGHTS BY USING SYMBOLS

Arguing about politics. Reading a newspaper. Using sign language. Each of these is made possible by **language**, a formal system of communication involving symbols—whether spoken, written, or gestured—and rules for combining them. In using language, we rely on spoken symbols to communicate through speech, written symbols to communicate through writing, and gestured symbols to communicate through sign language. We use language to communicate with other people, to store and retrieve memories, and to plan for the future.

But what makes a form of communication "language"? The world's several thousand languages share three characteristics: semanticity, generativity, and displacement. **Semanticity** is the conveying of the thoughts of the communicator in a meaningful way to

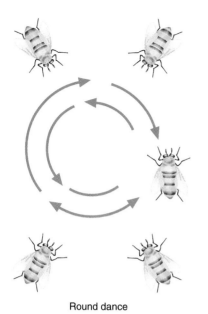

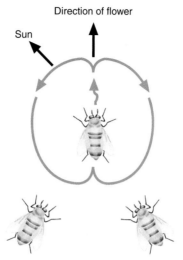

Direction of flower

Sun

Round dance

Tail-wagging dance

◀ FIGURE 9.11
Communication Among Bees
A bee that has found flowers containing nectar will return to its hive and do a circle dance if the nectar is within 50 yards of the hive. If the nectar is more than 50 yards away, the bee will do a waggle dance. The bee moves in a figure eight, with the angle of the straight line in the figure eight relative to the sun indicating the location of the nectar.

those who understand the language. For example, you know that *anti-* at the beginning of a word means being against something and *-ed* at the end of a word means past action. As discussed in Chapter 14, schizophrenics' language often lacks semanticity; it can be meaningless to other people.

Generativity is the combining of language symbols in novel ways, without being limited to a fixed number of combinations. In fact, each day you probably say or write things that have never been said or written by anyone before. This generativity of language accounts for baby talk, rap music, Brooklynese, and the works of Shakespeare.

Displacement is the use of language to refer to objects and events that are not present. The objects and events can be in another place or in the past or future. Thus, you can talk about someone in China, your fifth birthday party, or who will win the World Series next year.

Language is only one form of communication. Many animals, ourselves included, can communicate without using language. For instance, a pet dog can indicate when it is hungry by pacing around its food dish, or indicate when it wants to go out by scratching at the door. But is the dog using language? No, because the only characteristic of language that the dog is displaying is semanticity. Dogs do not exhibit generativity or displacement in their communications.

Other animals also communicate without using true language. A bee can communicate the location of nectar-containing flowers to residents of its hive (see Figure 9.11). When a bee returns to its hive after finding nectar less than 50 yards away, it performs a "circle dance" on the wall of the hive. If the nectar is farther away, the bee does a "waggle dance," moving in a figure-eight pattern. The angle of the straight line in the figure-eight pattern relative to the sun indicates the direction of the nectar, and the duration of the dance indicates the distance of the nectar—the longer the duration, the farther away it is (Frisch, 1974). But these dances are merely a form of communication, not language. They have semanticity and displacement, but they lack generativity—they are not used to indicate anything other than the location of nectar.

Consider also how monkeys use different alarm calls to signal the presence of particular kinds of predators. In one study, researchers presented Vervet monkeys with tape recordings of alarm calls that signified the presence of an eagle, a boa constrictor, or a leopard. The monkeys responded to eagle alarms by looking up, to boa constrictor alarms by looking down, and to leopard alarms by climbing up into trees (Seyfarth, Cheney, & Marler, 1980). Though monkeys use alarm calls to communicate, they do not use true language. Their calls have semanticity because they communicate the presence of a particular

generativity
The characteristic of language marked by the ability to combine words in novel, meaningful ways.

displacement
The characteristic of language marked by the ability to refer to objects and events that are not present.

▲ Language
The ability of human beings to use language makes us much more flexible than any other animal in communicating with one another. We can communicate complex thoughts through written language or sign language, as well as spoken language.

Thinking and Language

kind of predator, but they lack generativity and displacement. Monkeys neither combine their calls in novel ways nor use them to refer to animals that are not present.

In contrast to dogs, bees, and monkeys, human beings use true language. Without language, we would be severely limited in our ability to communicate with one another. You would not even be reading this book; books would not exist. Even the Old Testament book of Genesis recognizes the importance of language. In the story of the Tower of Babel, God punishes human beings for their pride by having them speak different languages—restricting their ability to communicate and engage in cooperative projects, such as building a tower to heaven.

The Structure of Language

English and all other languages have structures governed by rules known as **grammar.** The components of grammar include *phonology, syntax,* and *semantics.*

Phonology: Analyzing the Sounds of Language

All spoken languages are composed of **phonemes**—the basic sounds of a language. The study of phonemes is called **phonology.** Languages use as few as 20 and as many as 80 phonemes. English contains about 40—the number varies with the dialect. Each phoneme is represented by either a letter (such as the *o* sound in *go*) or a combination of letters (such as the *sh* sound in *should*). Words are combinations of phonemes, and each language permits only certain combinations. A native speaker of English would realize that the combination of phonemes in *cogerite* forms an acceptable word in English even though there is no such word. That person would also realize that the combination of phonemes in *klputng* does not form an acceptable word in English.

One language might not include all the phonemes found in another language, and people learning to speak a foreign language might have more difficulty pronouncing the phonemes in the foreign language that are not in their native language. For example, even after extensive conversational practice, native speakers of Japanese who learn English as adults have great difficulty in distinguishing between *r* sounds, as in *rock,* and *l* sounds, as in *lock* (Strange & Dittmann, 1984).

Because children who learn a foreign language have less difficulty pronouncing phonemes not found in their native language, there might be a critical period in childhood after which unused phonemes can no longer be pronounced correctly. Nonetheless, with special training even adults who learn a new language can improve their ability to pronounce unfamiliar phonemes. For example, if you say "the" and "theta," you will notice that there is a subtle difference between the *th* sounds. This distinction is not made by those whose native language is French. Difficulty in perceiving differences between phonemes in a foreign language is accompanied by difficulty in correctly pronouncing those phonemes. But French-speaking Canadians enrolled in a special language-training program quickly learned to distinguish between the *th* sounds in words such as *the* and *theta* (Jamieson & Morosan, 1986).

Individual phonemes and combinations of phonemes form **morphemes,** the smallest meaningful units of language. Words are composed of one or more morphemes. For example, the word *book* is composed of a single morpheme. In contrast, the word *books* is composed of two morphemes: *book,* which refers to an object, and *-s,* which indicates the plural of a word. One of the common morphemes that affect the meaning of words is the *-ing* suffix, which indicates ongoing action. Note that the 40 or so phonemes in English build more than 100,000 morphemes, which in turn build almost 500,000 words. Using these words, we can create a virtually infinite number of sentences. This shows that one of the outstanding characteristics of language is, indeed, its generativity.

Syntax: Arranging Words According to Rules

In addition to rules that govern the acceptable combinations of sounds in words, languages have **syntax**—rules that govern the acceptable arrangement of words in phrases and sentences. Because you know English syntax, you would say "She ate the ice cream"

grammar
The set of rules that governs the proper use and combination of language symbols.

phoneme
The smallest unit of sound in a language.

phonology
The study of the sounds that compose languages.

morpheme
The smallest meaningful unit of language.

syntax
The rules that govern the acceptable arrangement of words in phrases and sentences.

but not "She the ice cream ate" (though poets do have a "license" to violate normal syntax). And syntax varies from one language to another. The English sentence *John hit Bill* would be translated into its Japanese equivalent as *John Bill hit*. This is because the normal order of the verb and the object in Japanese is the opposite of their normal order in English (Gliedman, 1983). As for adjectives, in English they usually precede the nouns they modify, while in Spanish, adjectives usually follow the nouns they modify. The English phrase *the red book* would be *el libro rojo* in Spanish. Therefore, a Spanish-speaking person learning English might say "the book red," while an English-speaking person learning Spanish might say "el rojo libro."

Semantics: Putting Meaning into Language

Not only must words be arranged appropriately in phrases and sentences, they must be meaningful. The study of how language conveys meaning is called **semantics.** Psycholinguist Noam Chomsky has been intrigued by our ability to convey the same meaning through different phrases and sentences. Consider the sentences *The boy fed the horse* and *The horse was fed by the boy.* Both express the same meaning, but they use different syntax. Moreover, the meaning expressed by these sentences can be expressed in French, Chinese, Swahili, and so on, though the sentences used to express it in those languages would be different from the English sentences.

To explain this ability to express the same meaning using different phrases or different languages, Chomsky distinguishes between a language's deep structure and its surface structure. The **deep structure** is the underlying meaning of a statement; the **surface structure** is the word arrangements that express the underlying meaning. Chomsky calls the rules by which languages generate surface structures from deep structures, and deep structures from surface structures, **transformational grammar.** In terms of transformational grammar, language comprehension involves transforming the surface structure, which is the verbal message, into its deep structure, which is its meaning. Thus, the sentences *The boy fed the horse* and *The horse was fed by the boy* are transformed into the same deep structure, or meaning.

The meaning of a statement depends not only on its words and their arrangement but on the social context in which the statement is made. The branch of semantics that is concerned with the relationship between language and its social context is called **pragmatics.** To appreciate the relationship between language and its social context, consider the following statement made by a student about an upcoming meal in the cafeteria: "I can't wait to have dinner tonight." If spoken in an enthusiastic voice during Thanksgiving week, the statement might mean that the student expects to enjoy a delicious turkey dinner. Yet, if spoken in a sarcastic voice during a normal school week, the same statement might mean that the student expects to be confronted by the cafeteria's notorious "mystery meat."

Also consider the following embarrassing incident recounted by Elisabeth Kübler-Ross, the prominent death-and-dying researcher (see Chapter 4). She was reared in Switzerland but lived most of her adult life in the United States. "Last evening I spent 10 minutes trying to understand what a nurse was talking about when she invited me to attend a baby shower! Why should I want to look at a bathroom constructed for infants?" (Gill, 1980, p. 201). The incident is an example of the importance of a fund of cultural knowledge as a basis for language pragmatics (Reeder & Shapiro, 1993).

The importance of pragmatics is also exemplified by the difficulty scientists have had in developing computer programs that comprehend speech (Levinson & Liberman, 1981). A program capable of comprehending speech would have to consider characteristics of the message, the speaker, and the situation. The difficulty in employing pragmatics in developing computer programs that can comprehend speech is illustrated in the following conversation (Gorman, 1985, p. 65) between a news reporter (R) and a computer "therapist" called Eliza (E):

R: Row, row, row your boat

E: What about your own boat?

R: Gently down the stream

semantics
The study of how language conveys meaning.

deep structure
The underlying meaning of a statement.

surface structure
The word arrangements used to express thoughts.

transformational grammar
The rules by which languages generate surface structures from deep structures, and deep structures from surface structures.

pragmatics
The relationship between language and its social context.

E: Why do you say that?

R: Merrily, merrily, merrily, merrily

E: I am not sure I understand you fully

R: Life is but a dream

E: What does the dream suggest to you?

STAYING ON TRACK: *The Structure of Language*

1. What roles do semanticity, generativity, and displacement play in language?
2. What is the relationship between transformational grammar and the deep structure and surface structure of language?

The Acquisition of Language

What accounts for a child's ability to progress from a crying, gurgling infant to a talkative 3-year-old? The process of language acquisition seems to be universal, with infants in all cultures acquiring language in similar ways as they pass through distinct stages (Rice, 1989). Though the timing of the stages can vary among infants, the order does not.

Language Milestones: Stages in Language Acquisition

For the first few months after birth, infants are limited to communicating vocally through cooing, gurgling, and crying, which they use to indicate that they are content, happy, distressed, hungry, or in pain. Between 4 and 6 months of age, infants enter the babbling stage. When infants babble, they repeat sequences of phonemes, such as *ba-ba-ba*. Infants in all cultures begin babbling at about the same age and produce the same range of phonemes, including some that are not part of their parents' language (Roug, Landberg, & Lundberg, 1989). This might account for the prevalence of the words *mama, papa,* and *dada* to refer to parents in a variety of cultures. Even deaf infants begin babbling at the same age as infants who can hear, though their babbling is different from that of hearing infants (Oller & Eilers, 1988). The universality of the onset and initial content of babbling indicates that it is a product of the maturation of an inborn predisposition, rather than a product of experience. Nonetheless, by the age of 9 months, infants begin to show the influence of experience, as they limit their babbling to the phonemes of their family's language.

When infants are about 1 year old, they begin to say their first words. Their earliest words typically refer to objects that interest them. Thus, common early words include *milk* and *doggie.* In using words, older infants exhibit **overextension,** applying words too broadly (Behrend, 1988). Consider an infant who refers to her cat as "kitty." If she also refers to dogs, cows, horses, and other four-legged animals as "kitty," she would be exhibiting overextension. In contrast, if she refers to her cat, but to no other cats, as "kitty," she would be exhibiting **underextension**—applying words too narrowly (Caplan & Barr, 1989). As infants gain experience with objects and language, they rapidly learn to apply their words to the correct objects.

After learning to say single words, infants begin using them in **holophrastic speech,** which is the use of single words to represent whole phrases or sentences. For example, an infant might say "car" on one occasion to indicate that the family car has pulled into the driveway, and on another occasion to indicate that he would like to go for a ride. Between the ages of 18 and 24 months, infants go beyond holophrastic speech by speaking two-word phrases, typically including a noun and a verb in a consistent order. The infant is now showing a rudimentary appreciation of proper syntax, as in "Baby drink" or "Mommy go." Because, in the two-word stage, infants rely on nouns and verbs and leave out other parts of speech (such as articles and prepositions), their utterances are called **telegraphic speech.** To save time and money, telegrams leave out connecting parts of speech yet still communicate meaningful messages.

overextension
The tendency to apply a word to more objects or actions than it actually represents.

underextension
The tendency to apply a word to fewer objects or actions than it actually represents.

holophrastic speech
The use of single words to represent whole phrases or sentences.

telegraphic speech
Speech marked by reliance on nouns and verbs, while omitting other parts of speech, including articles and prepositions.

CHAPTER   9

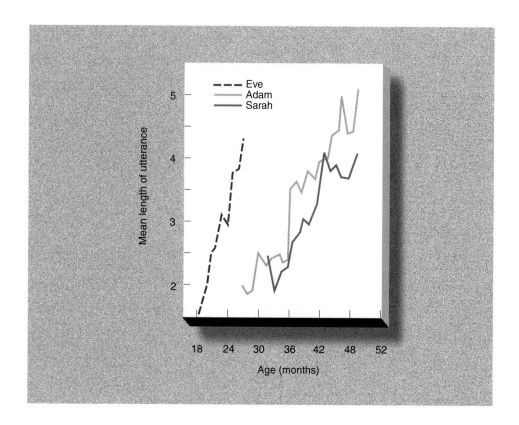

◄ **FIGURE 9.12**
Mean Length of Utterance
Roger Brown (1973) used the mean length of
utterance to assess the language maturity of
children. The graph shows changes in the mean
length of utterance for three children.

Until they are about 2 years old, infants use words to refer only to objects that are located in their immediate environment. At about age 2, children begin speaking sentences that include other parts of speech in addition to nouns and verbs. They also begin to exhibit displacement, as when a 2-year-old asks, "Grandma come tomorrow?" After age 2, children show a rapid increase in their vocabulary and in the length and complexity of their sentences. Psychologist Roger Brown (1973) invented a unit of measurement, the **mean length of utterance (MLU),** to assess children's level of language maturation. The MLU is calculated by taking samples of a child's statements and finding their average length in morphemes. The MLU increases rapidly in early childhood, though there is some variability from one child to another (see Figure 9.12). The MLU is a better predictor of overall language ability at younger ages than in later childhood (Scarborough et al., 1991).

The increased sophistication that young children show in their use of language is partly attributable to their application of language rules, which they learn from listening to the speech of those around them. From the day of their birth, infants are exposed to sophisticated language. In fact, studies have found that, contrary to popular impressions, staff members in hospital nurseries do not rely solely on baby talk and soothing sounds when speaking to newborn infants. Instead, staff members spend much of the time speaking to the infants with normal, though perhaps simple, phrases and sentences (Rheingold & Adams, 1980).

The language rules that children learn are strongly influenced by their mothers' speech (Hoff-Ginsberg, 1986). But English has many exceptions to grammatical rules, which might explain the phenomenon of **overregularization**—the application of grammatical rules without making necessary exceptions (Marcus et al., 1992). For example, at first children using the past tense will, correctly, say words such as *did, went,* and *brought,* which violate the *-ed* rule for forming the past tense. They learn these words by hearing the speech of older children and adults. But as children learn the *-ed* rule, they say words such as *doed, goed,* or *bringed.* Later, when they realize that grammatical rules have exceptions, they learn not to apply the *-ed* rule to irregular verbs, and again say *did, went,* and

mean length of utterance (MLU)

The average length of spoken statements, used as a measure of language development in children.

overregularization

The application of a grammatical rule without making necessary exceptions to it.

▲ **Jean Berko Gleason**
"Theorists of language have been at odds with one another for the last quarter century over questions having to do with the nature of language and the possible prerequisites of its development."

critical period
A period in childhood when experience with language produces optimal language acquisition.

brought (Kolata, 1987). Thus, children tend at first to use correct wording, then begin to overregularize, and finally realize when to follow grammatical rules and when to break them (Marcus, 1995).

How do we know that infants learn rules, rather than a series of specific instances of correct grammar? One source of evidence is a study by Jean Berko (1958), who reasoned that if children use correct grammar when confronted with words they have never heard, then they must be relying on rules, not rote memory. To test her assumption, Berko developed the "Wugs test," which included drawings of imaginary creatures called "wugs." Berko found that children would, indeed, apply grammatical rules to novel words. For example, when shown a picture identified as a "wug" and then a picture with two of them, infants completed the statement "There are two _____" with the word *wugs*. This indicates that they have learned to use the -*s* ending to indicate the plural.

Is There a Critical Period for Language Acquisition?

In 1800 a boy who appeared to be about 12 years old emerged from a forest near Aveyron, France, apparently having survived for many years without human contact (Hunter, 1993). The boy, named Victor by physician Jean Itard, became known as the "Wild Boy of Aveyron." Though Itard made an intensive effort to teach him French, Victor only learned to say "lait" (milk). He could use gestures and comprehend speech and read and write on a basic level. Similar reports have provided evidence of a **critical period** for language acquisition that extends from infancy to adolescence, during which language learning is optimal (Hurford, 1991). If people are not exposed to a language until after childhood, they might never become proficient in speaking it. The critical period also seems to affect the acquisition of sign language (Mayberry & Eichen, 1991).

A more recent and well-documented case described a girl named Genie, who had been raised in isolation. In 1970, 13-year-old Genie was discovered by welfare workers in a room in which her father had kept her restrained in a harness and isolated from social contact—and language—since infancy. He communicated with her by barking and growling, and beat her whenever she made a sound. By 1981, more than a decade after returning to society and undergoing intensive language training, Genie had acquired a large vocabulary but only a limited ability to speak telegraphically, and she was unable to use proper syntax. Like Victor, Genie might have been past her critical period for language acquisition when she joined society (Pines, 1981).

Though the cases of Victor and Genie support the view that there is a critical period for language acquisition, you may recall from Chapter 2 that it is unwise to generalize too freely from case studies. For example, some children who have lived for years in social isolation, such as Kaspar Hauser, who was discovered in Nuremberg, Germany, in 1828 at age 17, have been able to learn language after reaching adolescence (Simon, 1979). Perhaps other factors could account for the findings in the cases of Victor and Genie. For example, suppose that Victor and Genie were born with brain disorders that interfered with their ability to acquire language. Even if they had been reared from birth in normal family settings, they might still have failed to acquire mature language.

Another, perhaps stronger, line of research on critical periods is concerned with adults who learn second languages. Second languages become progressively more difficult to learn as we get older. Support for this came from a study in which older Korean and Chinese immigrants to the United States found it more difficult to learn English than did their younger fellow immigrants—even though the groups were intellectually equal (Johnson & Newport, 1989). Nonetheless, this finding must be viewed with caution in light of the many other factors that could account for differences in the ease with which younger and older immigrants learn a new language.

Theories of Language Acquisition: The Roles of Nature and Nurture

Language researchers debate this question: Is language acquired solely through learning, or is it strongly influenced by the maturation of an inherited predisposition to develop language? Those who favor the learning position assume that if it were possible to raise two infants together with no exposure to language, they would not develop true language. In contrast, those who favor the view that language emerges from an inherited predisposition assume that the two infants might develop a rudimentary form of language marked by semanticity, generativity, and displacement. According to this position, learning normally determines only which language an infant will speak, whether English, French, or Navajo.

B. F. Skinner (1957) claimed that language is acquired solely through learning, chiefly through the positive reinforcement of appropriate speech. For example, a 1-year-old child might learn to say "milk" because her parents give her milk and praise her when she says "milk." Similarly, a 2-year-old child named Jane might be given a cookie and praise for saying "Give Jane cookie" but not for saying "Jane cookie give." As you can see, Skinner assumed that vocabulary and grammar are learned through positive reinforcement. In a study supportive of Skinner's position, two groups of infants between 2 and 7 months old were positively reinforced for producing different phonemes. The infants were reinforced by smiles, *tsk* sounds, and light stroking of the abdomen. One group was reinforced for making vowel sounds, while the other group was reinforced for making consonant sounds. The infants responded by increasing their production of the phonemes that were reinforced. This study showed that positive reinforcement can affect language acquisition (Routh, 1969). Of course, it does not indicate that language is acquired *solely* through learning.

Albert Bandura (1977), the influential cognitive-behavioral psychologist, stresses the role of observational learning in language acquisition. He assumes that children develop language primarily by imitating the vocabulary and grammatical constructions used by their parents and others in their everyday lives. In a study that supported his position, adults replied to statements made by 2-year-old children by purposely using slightly more-complex syntax than they normally would. After 2 months, the children had developed more-complex syntax than did children who had not been exposed to the adult models (Nelson, 1977). Additional support for the effect of modeling comes from findings that 2-year-olds whose parents read to them acquire language more rapidly than do 2-year-olds whose parents do not (Whitehurst et al., 1988). Yet we cannot discount the possibility that other differences between the two groups of parents produced this effect.

The assumption that language is acquired solely through learning has been challenged by Noam Chomsky and his followers (Rondall, 1994). Chomsky insists that infants are born with the predisposition to develop language. He believes they inherit a *language*

▲ **Modeling Language**
The modeling of language by parents is an important factor in the acquisition of a particular language by the child.

▲ **Noam Chomsky**
"We should expect heredity to play a major role in language because there is really no other way to account for the fact that children learn to speak in the first place."

acquisition device—a brain mechanism that makes them sensitive to phonemes, syntax, and semantics. In analyzing the interactions of parents and children, Chomsky has found that children in different cultures progress through similar stages and learn their native languages without formal parental instruction. Children say things that adults never say, and their parents do not positively reinforce proper grammar (or correct improper grammar) in any consistent manner. Modeling, too, cannot explain all language learning, because observations of children show that they vary greatly in the extent to which they imitate what their parents say (Snow, 1981).

What evidence is there to support Chomsky's position? One source of evidence is the universality in the basic features of language and the stages of language acquisition (Miller, 1990), which indicates that the tendency to develop language is inborn. Studies of deaf children support Chomsky's position. One study observed deaf children who were neither rewarded for using sign language nor exposed to a model who used it. Nonetheless, the children spontaneously developed their own gestural system, in which they communicated by using signs with the characteristics of true language (Goldin-Meadow & Mylander, 1983).

Despite the evidence favoring language as innate and contradicting learning as an explanation for language acquisition, research has provided some support for the learning position (Stemmer, 1990). One study tested the claim made by those who favor Chomsky's position that adults typically ignore children's speech errors and fail to correct their ungrammatical statements. The study found that language acquisition does depend in part on feedback provided by adults who correct specific instances of improper grammar. Adults do so by repeating a child's grammatically incorrect statements in grammatically correct form or by asking the child to clarify his or her statements (Bohannon & Stanowicz, 1988).

It seems that the positions of Chomsky, Skinner, and Bandura must be integrated to explain how language is acquired. We appear to be born with a predisposition to develop language, which provides us with an innate sensitivity to grammar. But we might learn our specific language, including its grammar, mainly through operant conditioning and observational learning.

STAYING ON TRACK: *The Acquisition of Language*

1. What are the main characteristics of the stages of language development during infancy?
2. How do the theories of Skinner and Chomsky differ in regard to language development?

The Relationship Between Language and Thinking

In his novel *1984*, George Orwell (1949) envisioned a totalitarian government that controlled its citizens' thoughts by regulating their language. By adding, removing, or redefining words, the government used *Newspeak* to ensure that citizens would not think rebellious thoughts against their leader, "Big Brother." For example, in Newspeak the word *joycamp* referred to a forced labor camp. And the word *free* was redefined to refer only to physical reality, as in *The dog is free from lice*, rather than to political freedom. Even democratic government officials will, at times, resort to euphemisms reminiscent of Newspeak. For example, to reduce public outrage about deceptive government practices, American officials coined the word *misinformation* to replace the word *lying*. Business people also understand the power of language to shape thought, as when used-car dealers refer to their vehicles as *previously owned* instead of *used*.

The Linguistic Relativity Hypothesis: The Effect of Language on Thought

Orwell's view of the influence of language on thought was shared by the linguist-anthropologist Benjamin Lee Whorf (1897–1941), who expressed it in his **linguistic relativity hypothesis,** which assumes that our perception of the world is determined by the particular

CHAPTER 9

language we speak. Whorf (1956) pointed out that Eskimo languages have several words for snow (such as words that distinguish between falling snow and fallen snow), while the English language has only one. According to the linguistic relativity hypothesis, the variety of words for snow in an Eskimo language causes people who speak it to perceive differences in snow in that people who speak English do not.

Critics argue that, on the contrary, thinking determines language. Perhaps the greater importance of snow in their culture led Eskimos to coin several words for snow, each referring to a different kind. Moreover, English-speaking people to whom snow is important, such as avid skiers, use different adjectives to describe different kinds of snow. Their ability to distinguish between crusty, powdery, and granular snow indicates that even English-speaking people can perceive wide variations in the quality of snow. And the number of words for snow in Eskimo languages might have been exaggerated in the early reports that influenced Whorf and other linguistic relativity theorists (Pullum, 1991).

What does formal research have to say about the linguistic relativity hypothesis? In an early study bearing on Whorf's hypothesis (Carmichael, Hogan, & Walter, 1932), subjects were presented with ambiguous drawings of objects that were given either of two labels (see Figure 9.13). When later asked to draw the objects, the subjects drew pictures that looked more like the object that had been named than like the object they had seen. This supported Whorf's hypothesis, at least in that language appeared to influence the subjects' recall of objects. Another topic of interest related to Whorf's hypothesis is the possible influence of language on the perception of colors—the topic of the following classic study.

ANATOMY OF A CLASSIC RESEARCH STUDY

Does Language Influence Our Perception of Colors?

Rationale

Eleanor Rosch (1975) conducted a study to test whether language influences the perception of colors. She hypothesized that if the linguistic relativity hypothesis were correct, people who speak a language that has many color words would perceive colors differently than would people who speak a language with few color words.

Method

Rosch visited the Dani people of New Guinea, who live in a Stone Age culture. She found that the Dani language has two basic color words: *mili* for dark, cool colors, and *mola* for light, warm colors. In contrast, English has eleven basic color words: black, white, red, green, yellow, blue, brown, purple, pink, orange, and gray. To describe these colors, the Dani use relatively long phrases. Rosch wondered whether these differences in language would be associated with differences in the perception of colors. She decided to test this by using "focal" colors, which are considered the best representatives of each of the colors (for example, "fire-engine red" for red), and nonfocal colors.

Method

The subjects, Dani and American, were given a series of trials on which they were first shown a colored plastic chip for 5 seconds. After another 30 seconds, they were asked to select the chip from among 160 colored chips.

Results and Discussion

Both the English-speaking subjects and the Dani subjects performed better when the chip to be recalled was a focal color than when it was a nonfocal color. This contradicted Whorf's hypothesis, because the results indicated that though the Dani use only two color names, they are as capable as English-speaking people of perceiving all the focal colors in the English language. Perhaps we are genetically prepared to perceive these focal colors, regardless of whether our language takes special note of them.

▲ ▲ ▲

▶ FIGURE 9.13

The Effect of Labels on Recall

Subjects were shown the pictures in the middle column with one of two different labels. When later asked to draw what they had seen, the subjects drew pictures that were consistent with the labels, not with the pictures (Carmichael, Hogan, & Walter, 1932). This indicates that language can affect how we think about the world, even though it might not affect how we perceive the world.

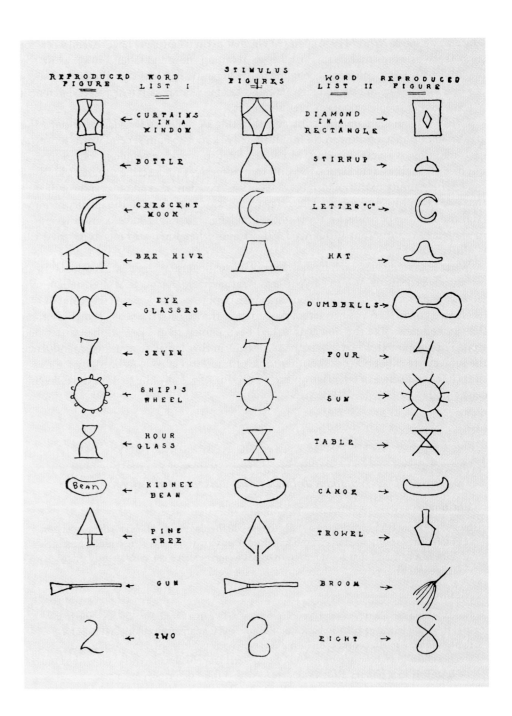

Linguistic Relativity and Sexist Language: Are Masculine Pronouns Truly Neutral?

Though language does not *determine* how we think about the world, it might *influence* how we think about the world (Hoffman, Lau, & Johnson, 1986). This is the basis of the current concern about the traditional use of masculine pronouns, such as *his* and *him*, to refer to persons when no sexual identification is intended (Prentice, 1994). Critics of this practice claim that it makes people think that such statements refer primarily to males (Hyde, 1984). Perhaps repeated exposure to such use of the male pronoun to refer to both males and females promotes the belief that certain sex-neutral activities are more suitable for males than for females.

This assumption has been supported by empirical research. Undergraduates in one study were more likely to assume that the antecedent to the supposedly neutral pronoun *he* was a male (Hamilton, 1988). In another study, students read sentences and described

images that came to mind. When subjects read sentences with the pronoun *he*, they reported a disproportionate number of male images (Gastil, 1990). Because our use of language can affect the way we think about gender roles, as well as other aspects of everyday life, the linguistic relativity hypothesis might have some merit, as long as it is used to recognize that though language influences thinking, it does not determine it (Hunt & Agnoli, 1991).

STAYING ON TRACK: *The Relationship Between Language and Thinking*

1. How does Orwell's concept of Newspeak embody the belief that language affects thought?
2. How are concerns about sexist language related to the linguistic relativity hypothesis?

THINKING ABOUT *Psychology*

Can Apes Use Language?

In the early seventeenth century, the philosopher René Descartes argued that language was the critical feature that distinguished human beings from other animals. Interest in teaching animals cognitive skills, such as language, that normally are associated with human beings was stimulated by the case of "Clever Hans," a horse who impressed onlookers by solving arithmetic problems in Germany in the early twentieth century. Hans was trained to count out the answers to arithmetic problems by tapping one of his hooves until he reached the correct answer. He counted anything present, including persons, hats, or umbrellas. But a psychologist named Oskar Pfungst showed that Hans stopped counting when he noticed tiny movements of his questioner's head, which cued the initiation and termination of counting. When the questioner knew the answer, Hans was correct almost all of the time. But when the questioner did not know the answer, Hans was wrong all of the time. So, Hans might have been clever, but he had no idea how to do arithmetic (Davis & Memmott, 1982).

► Clever Hans
An audience watches Clever Hans perform
arithmetic calculations in Berlin in 1904.

As interest in teaching animals to perform arithmetic waned, interest in teaching them language grew. As you read at the beginning of this chapter, animals as diverse as bees, dogs, and monkeys can communicate in limited, stereotyped ways. But they do not use true language, which is characterized by semanticity, generativity, and displacement. Research on language learning in dolphins (Herman, Kuczaj, & Holder, 1993) and sea lions (Gisiner & Schusterman, 1992) is promising but has yet to provide conclusive findings. A much larger body of research supports the belief that there is at least one kind of nonhuman animal capable of acquiring true language—the ape.

TEACHING CHIMPANZEES TO USE LANGUAGE

More than 50 years ago, Winthrop and Luella Kellogg (1933) published a book about their experiences raising a chimpanzee named Gua with their infant son, Donald. Even after being exposed to speech as a member of the family, Gua could not speak a single word. Another couple, Cathy and Keith Hayes (Hayes, 1951), had only slightly better results with Viki, a chimpanzee they, too, raised as a member of their family. Despite their intensive efforts over a period of several years, Viki learned to say only four words: *mama*, *papa*, *cup*, and *up*. The Hayeses concluded that the vocal anatomy of apes is not designed for producing speech.

In 1925 the primatologist Robert Yerkes, wondering whether apes have lots to say but no way of saying it, suggested teaching them to use sign language instead of speech. His suggestion was not carried out until 1966, when Allen and Beatrix Gardner (1969) of the University of Nevada began teaching American Sign Language (ASL) to a 1-year-old chimpanzee named Washoe. They raised Washoe in a trailer next to their house. To encourage her to use ASL, they never spoke in her presence; instead, they signed to each other and Washoe using simple words about various objects and everyday events (Dewsbury, 1996). They also asked Washoe simple questions, praised her correct utterances, and tried to comply with her requests, just as parents do with young children. After 4 years of training, Washoe had a repertoire of 132 signs, which she used to name objects and to describe qualities of objects. The Gardners later replicated their work with four other apes, teaching each to use sign language (Gardner, Gardner, & Van Cantfort, 1989).

Washoe also displayed the ability to generalize her signs to refer to similar things. For example, she used the sign for *open* to refer to doors on a car, a house, and a refrigerator. Washoe even seemed to show an important characteristic of true language—generativity. On seeing a swan for the first time, Washoe made the sign for *water bird*. And, in a chimpanzee colony in Washington State, Washoe taught ASL to a young chimpanzee named Loulis, whom she had "adopted" (Cunningham, 1985). After 5 years, Loulis had acquired a vocabulary of more than 50 ASL signs, which he could have learned only from Washoe and other chimpanzees, since all human signing was forbidden when Loulis was present (Gardner, Gardner, & Van Cantfort, 1989).

During the past two decades several other apes have been taught to use sign language or other forms of language. Ann and David Premack taught a laboratory chimpanzee named Sarah to use plastic chips of different shapes and colors to represent words (Premack, 1971). Sarah learned to answer questions by arranging the chips in different sequences on a board to form sentences. Duane Rumbaugh taught a chimpanzee named Lana to use a computer to create sentences by pressing large keys marked by lexigrams—geometric shapes representing particular words (Rumbaugh, Gill, & von Glasersfeld, 1973). Lana formed sentences by pressing keys in a particular order. Lana's language was called "Yerkish," in honor of Robert Yerkes. When Lana made grammatically correct requests, she was rewarded with food, toys, music, or other things she enjoyed.

▲ **Washoe**
Allen and Beatrix Gardner taught Washoe to use American sign language. Here Washoe is signing "sweet" in response to a lollipop.

CONTROVERSY ABOUT APE-LANGUAGE RESEARCH

Have Washoe, Sarah, and Lana learned to use true language? Do they exhibit semanticity, generativity, and displacement? That is, can they communicate meaningfully, create novel combinations of signs, and refer to objects that are not present? Columbia University psychologist Herbert Terrace, who once believed that apes can use language, says no (Terrace et al., 1979). Terrace taught a chimpanzee named Nim Chimpsky to use sign language. (Nim was named after Noam Chomsky, who believes that apes cannot learn true language.) After 5 years of training, Nim had mastered 125 signs. At first, Terrace assumed that Nim had learned true language. But after analyzing videotapes of conversations with Nim and videotapes of other apes that had been taught sign language, he concluded that Nim and the other apes did not display true language.

On what did Terrace base his conclusion? He found that apes merely learned to make signs, arrange forms, or press computer keys in a certain order to obtain rewards. In other words, their use of language was no different from that of a pigeon that learns to peck a sequence of keys to get food rewards. No researcher would claim that the pigeon is using language. So, the ability of an ape to produce a string of words does not indicate that the ape has learned to produce a sentence. Terrace also claims that the apparent generativity of ape language might be a misinterpretation of their actions. For example, Washoe's apparent reference to a swan as a "water bird" might have been a reference to two separate things—a body of water and a bird.

As additional evidence against ape language, Terrace claims that many instances of allegedly spontaneous signing by chimpanzees are actually responses to subtle cues from trainers. Terrace found that Nim communicated primarily in response to prompting by his trainer or by imitating signs recently made by his trainer. Thus, he did not use language in an original or spontaneous way, and his signs were simply gestures prompted by cues from his trainer that produced consequences he desired—a kind of operant conditioning (Terrace, 1985).

Terrace's attack has not gone unchallenged. Francine Patterson taught a gorilla named Koko to use more than 300 signs ("Ape Language," 1981). Koko even displays generativity, as in spontaneously referring to a zebra as a "white tiger." Patterson criticized Terrace for basing his conclusions on his work with Nim and on isolated frames he has examined from films of other apes using ASL. She claimed that Nim's inadequate use of language might stem from his being confused by having sixty different trainers, which could account for Nim's failure to use sign language in a spontaneous way. In contrast, Patterson reported that Koko had only one primary trainer and used signs more

▲ **Nim Chimpsky**
According to Herbert Terrace, even his own chimpanzee, Nim Chimpsky, uses sign language only in response to cues from his trainers. The photo shows Nim learning the sign for "drink."

▲ Duane Rumbaugh and Sue Savage-Rumbaugh
"Pygmy chimpanzees may employ a sort of primitive language in the wild."

spontaneously than Nim did. For example, Koko responded to a velvet hat by signing "that soft" (Patterson, Patterson, & Brentari, 1987).

In recent years, the strongest evidence in support of ape language comes from studies by Duane Rumbaugh and Sue Savage-Rumbaugh of Georgia State University and the Yerkes Language Research Center. They trained two chimpanzees, Austin and Sherman, to communicate through Yerkish, the language used earlier by Lana. Austin and Sherman use language in a more sophisticated way than previous chimpanzees. In one study, Austin, Sherman, and Lana were taught to categorize three objects (an orange, a beancake, and a slice of bread) as "edible" and three objects (a key, a stick, and a pile of coins) as "inedible." When given other objects, Austin and Sherman, but not Lana, were able to categorize them as edible or inedible. Perhaps Lana could not learn this task because she had been trained to use language to associate labels with specific objects rather than to understand the concepts to which the labels referred (Savage-Rumbaugh et al., 1980).

Even when housed in different rooms, Austin and Sherman can request objects from each other. This was demonstrated by giving one of the chimpanzees a box from which he could obtain food or drink only by using a tool located in the other chimpanzee's room. The chimpanzee in the room with the food indicated the tool he needed by striking a specific series of keys on a computer keyboard. The chimpanzee in the room with the tools then passed that tool to the other chimpanzee (Marx, 1980).

Sue Savage-Rumbaugh and her colleagues (1986) described their work with two pygmy chimpanzees, Kanzi and Mulika, who have achieved language ability superior to that of previous apes. Kanzi learned Yerkish spontaneously by observing people and other chimpanzees (including his mother) pressing appropriate lexigrams on a keyboard (Savage-Rumbaugh, 1990). He can also identify symbols referred to in human speech. Previous apes depended on their own particular language system to comprehend human communications. Kanzi can even form requests in which other individuals are either the agent or the recipient of action—which reflects his appreciation of syntax (Savage-Rumbaugh et al., 1993). Before, apes such as Nim made spontaneous requests only in which they were the targets of a suggested action. Moreover, Kanzi shows displacement, using lexigrams to refer to things that are not present (Savage-Rumbaugh, 1987).

Perhaps future studies using pygmy chimpanzees will succeed where others have failed in demonstrating convincingly that apes are capable of using true language. But even if apes can use true language, no ape has gone beyond the language level of a 3-year-old child. Is that the upper limit of ape language ability, or is it just the upper limit using current training methods? Research might soon provide the answer. In any case, we do know that apes are capable of more-complex communication than simply grunting to convey crude emotional states.

▲ Kanzi
To date, Kanzi is the ape who has shown the most sophisticated use of language. Here he is using Yerkish, a language consisting of geometric symbols.

STAYING ON TRACK: *Can Apes Use Language?*

1. What evidence is there that apes can exhibit true language, including semanticity, generativity, and displacement?
2. Why do some researchers believe that apes cannot use true language?

 # CHAPTER SUMMARY

THINKING

The past few decades have seen a cognitive revolution in psychology, with increased interest in the study of thinking. Thinking is the purposeful mental manipulation of words and images. Research findings have contradicted the motor theory of thinking.

CONCEPT FORMATION

Thinking depends on concepts, which are categories of objects, events, qualities, or relations whose members share certain features. A logical concept is formed by identifying specific features possessed by all members of the concept. A natural concept is formed through everyday experiences and has "fuzzy borders." The best representative of a concept is called a prototype.

PROBLEM SOLVING

One of the most important uses of concepts is in problem solving, the thought process that enables us to overcome obstacles to reach goals. A basic method of solving problems is trial and error, which involves trying one possible solution after another until finding one that works. The problem-solving strategy called insight depends on the mental manipulation of information. An algorithm is a rule that, when followed step by step, assures that a solution to a problem will be found. A heuristic is a general principle that guides problem solving but does not guarantee the discovery of a solution. A mental set is a problem-solving strategy that has succeeded in the past but that can interfere with solving a problem that requires a new strategy. Our past experience can also impede problem solving through functional fixedness, the inability to realize that a problem can be solved by using a familiar object in an unusual way.

CREATIVITY

Creativity is a form of problem solving characterized by novel solutions that are also useful or socially valued. Creative people tend to have above-average intelligence and are able to integrate different kinds of thinking. Creative people are more motivated by their intrinsic interest in creative tasks than by extrinsic factors. Creativity also depends on divergent thinking, in which a person freely considers a variety of potential solutions to a problem.

DECISION MAKING

In decision making we try to make the best choice from among alternative courses of action. Our decisions are influenced by the factors of utility and probability. In using the representativeness heuristic, we assume that a small sample is representative of its population. In using the availability heuristic, we estimate the probability of an event by how easily relevant instances of it come to mind. We are also subject to framing effects, which are biases introduced in the decision-making process by presenting a situation in a certain manner.

ARTIFICIAL INTELLIGENCE

Artificial intelligence is a field that integrates computer science and cognitive psychology to try to simulate or improve on human thinking by using computer programs. Computer programs called expert systems display expertise in specific domains of knowledge. Computer scientists are trying to develop programs that use parallel information processing, as well as serial information processing.

LANGUAGE

In using language, we rely on spoken symbols to communicate through speech, written symbols to communicate through writing, and gestured symbols to communicate through sign language. We use language to communicate with other people, to store and retrieve memories, and to plan for the future.

THE STRUCTURE OF LANGUAGE

True language is characterized by semanticity, generativity, and displacement. The rules of a language are its grammar. Phonemes are the basic sounds of a language, and morphemes are its smallest meaningful units. A language's syntax includes rules governing the acceptable arrangement of words and phrases. Semantics is the study of how language conveys meaning. Noam Chomsky calls the underlying meaning of a statement its deep structure and the words themselves its surface structure. We translate between the two structures by using transformational grammar. The branch of semantics concerned with the relationship between language and its social context is called pragmatics.

THE ACQUISITION OF LANGUAGE

Infants in all cultures progress through similar stages of language development. They begin babbling between 4 and 6 months of age and say their first words when they are about 1 year old. At first they use holophrastic speech, in which single words represent whole phrases or sentences. Between the ages of 18 and 24 months, infants begin speaking two-word sentences and use telegraphic speech. As infants learn their language's grammar, they may engage in overregularization, in which they apply grammatical rules without making necessary exceptions. There might be a critical period for language acquisition, extending from infancy to adolescence. B. F. Skinner and Albert Bandura believe that language is acquired solely through learning, while Chomsky believes we have an innate predisposition to develop language.

THE RELATIONSHIP BETWEEN LANGUAGE AND THINKING

Benjamin Lee Whorf's linguistic relativity hypothesis assumes that our view of the world is determined by the particular language we speak. But research has shown that though language can influence thinking, it does not determine it.

THINKING ABOUT PSYCHOLOGY: CAN APES USE LANGUAGE?

Researchers have taught apes to communicate by using sign language, form boards, and computers. The most well known of these apes include the gorilla Koko and the chimpanzees Washoe, Sarah, and Lana. Herbert Terrace, the trainer of Nim Chimpsky, claims that apes have not learned true language; instead, they have learned to give responses that lead to rewards, just as pigeons learn to peck at keys to obtain food. Francine Patterson, Duane Rumbaugh, and Sue Savage-Rumbaugh have countered by providing evidence that the apes have, indeed, learned true language characterized by semanticity, generativity, and displacement.

 # KEY CONCEPTS

Thinking

cognitive psychology 310
thinking 310

Concept Formation

concept 311
logical concept 311
natural concept 312
prototype 312

Problem Solving

problem solving 313
trial and error 314
insight 315
algorithm 315
heuristic 316
mental set 317
functional fixedness 318

Creativity

creativity 319
convergent thinking 321
divergent thinking 321

Decision Making

decision making 323
representativeness heuristic 323
availability heuristic 324
framing effect 324

Artificial Intelligence

artificial intelligence (AI) 325
expert system 325
serial processing 326
parallel processing 326

Language

language 326
semanticity 326
generativity 327
displacement 327

The Structure of Language

grammar 328
phoneme 328
phonology 328
morpheme 328
syntax 328
semantics 329
deep structure 329
surface structure 329
transformational grammar 329
pragmatics 329

The Acquisition of Language

overextension 330
underextension 330
holophrastic speech 330
telegraphic speech 330
mean length of utterance (MLU) 331
overregularization 331
critical period 332

The Relationship Between Language and Thought

linguistic relativity hypothesis 334

 # KEY CONTRIBUTORS

Thinking

John B. Watson 310
Wolfgang Kohler 315
Allen Newell 315
Teresa Amabile 320

Amos Tversky and Daniel Kahneman 323
Herbert Simon 325

Language

Noam Chomsky 329
Jean Berko 332

B. F. Skinner 333
Albert Bandura 333
Benjamin Lee Whorf 334
Eleanor Rosch 335
Robert Yerkes 338
Allen Gardner and Beatrix Gardner 338

Ann Premack and David Premack 339
Herbert Terrace 339
Francine Patterson 339
Duane Rumbaugh and Sue Savage-Rumbaugh 340

 # FOR MORE INFORMATION ON THINKING AND LANGUAGE

FOR GENERAL WORKS ON COGNITION

Altarriba, J. (Ed.). (1993). *Cognition and culture: A cross-cultural approach to psychology.* New York: Elsevier.

Gardner, H. (1985). *The mind's new science: A history of the cognitive revolution.* New York: Basic Books.

Medin, D. L., & Ross, B. M. (1997). *Cognitive psychology.* (2nd ed.). San Diego: Harcourt Brace.

FOR MORE ON CONCEPT FORMATION

Harnad, S. (1990). *Categorical perception.* New York: Cambridge University Press.

Lakoff, G. (1987). *Women, fire, and dangerous things*. Chicago: University of Chicago Press.

FOR MORE ON PROBLEM SOLVING

Bransford, J. D., & Stein, B. S. (1993). *The ideal problem solver: A guide to improving thinking, learning, and creativity*. New York: W. H. Freeman.

Mayer, R. E. (1991). *Thinking, problem solving, and cognition* (2nd ed.). New York: W. H. Freeman.

Sternberg, R. J., & Davidson, J. E. (Eds.). (1995). *The nature of insight*. Cambridge, MA: MIT Press.

FOR MORE ON CREATIVITY

Finke, R. A., Ward, T. B., & Smith, S. M. (1992). *Creative cognition: Theory, research, and applications*. Cambridge, MA: MIT Press.

Freeman, M. (1993). *Finding the muse: A socio-psychological inquiry into the conditions of artistic creativity*. New York: Cambridge University Press.

Runco, M. A. (1991). *Divergent thinking*. Norwood, NJ: Ablex.

Weisberg, R. W. (1993). *Creativity: Beyond the myth of genius*. New York: W. H. Freeman.

FOR MORE ON DECISION MAKING

Gilovich, T. (1993). *How we know what isn't so: The fallibility of human reason in everyday life*. New York: Free Press.

Kahnemann, D., Skovic, P., & Tversky, A. (Eds.). (1982). *Judgment under uncertainty: Heuristics and biases*. New York: Cambridge University Press.

Nisbett, R., & Ross, L. (1985). *Human inference: Strategies and shortcomings of social judgment*. Englewood Cliffs, NJ: Prentice Hall.

Plous, S. (1993). *The psychology of judgment and decision making*. New York: McGraw-Hill.

FOR MORE ON ARTIFICIAL INTELLIGENCE

Boden, M. A. (1989). *Artificial intelligence in psychology*. Cambridge, MA: MIT Press.

Crevier, D. (1993). *AI: The tumultuous history of the search for artificial intelligence*. New York: Basic Books.

Levy, D. N., & Newborn, M. (1991). *How computers play chess*. New York: Freeman.

FOR GENERAL WORKS ON LANGUAGE

Carroll, D. W. (1995). *Psychology of language* (2nd ed.). Monterey, CA: Brooks/Cole.

Pinker, S. (1994). *The language instinct: How the mind creates language*. New York: Morrow.

FOR MORE ON LANGUAGE ACQUISITION

Chomsky, N. (1985). *Knowledge of language: Its nature, origin, and use*. New York: Praeger.

Curtiss, S. (1977). *Genie: A psycholinguistic study of a modern-day "wild child."* New York: Academic Press.

Hoff-Ginsberg, E. (1998). *Language development*. Belmont, CA: Brooks-Cole.

Skinner, B. F. (1957). *Verbal behavior*. Englewood Cliffs, NJ: Prentice Hall.

FOR MORE ON THE RELATIONSHIP BETWEEN LANGUAGE AND THINKING

Berlin, B., & Kay, P. (1989). *Basic color terms: Their universality and evolution*. Berkeley: University of California Press.

Lucy, J. A. (1992). *Language diversity and thought: A reformulation of the linguistic-relativity hypothesis*. New York: Cambridge University Press.

Pullum, G. K. (1991). *The great Eskimo vocabulary hoax, and other irreverent essays on the study of language*. Chicago: University of Chicago Press.

Whorf, B. L. (1956). *Language, thought, and reality: Selected writings of Benjamin Lee Whorf* (J. B. Carroll, Ed.). Cambridge, MA: MIT Press.

FOR MORE ON APE LANGUAGE

Patterson, F., & Linden, E. (1981). *The education of Koko*. New York: Holt, Rinehart & Winston.

Premack, D. (1986). *Gavagai! The future history of the ape language controversy*. Cambridge, MA: MIT Press.

Premack, D., & Premack, A. J. (1983). *The mind of an ape*. New York: W. W. Norton.

Savage-Rumbaugh, S., & Lewin, R. (1994). *Kanzi: The ape at the brink of the human mind*. New York: Wiley.

Terrace, H. S. (1986). *Nim: A chimpanzee who learned sign language*. Irvington, NY: Columbia University Press.

FOR MORE ON CONTRIBUTORS TO THE STUDY OF THINKING AND LANGUAGE

Bjork, D. W. (1993). *B. F. Skinner: A life*. New York: Basic Books.

Bruner, J. (1983). *In search of mind: Essays in autobiography*. New York: Harper & Row.

Haley, M. C., & Lunsford, R. F. (1993). *Noam Chomsky*. New York: Macmillan.

Kessel, F. S. (Ed.). (1987). *The development of language and language researchers: Essays in honor of Roger Brown*. Hillsdale, NJ: Erikson.

Ley, R. (1990). *A whisper of espionage: Wolfgang Kohler and the apes of Tenerife*. Garden City, NY: Avery.

Simon, H. A. (1991). *Models of my life*. New York: Basic Books.

Intelligence

▲ The Savant Syndrome
Tom Cruise and Dustin Hoffman are shown in a scene from *Rain Man,* in which Hoffman portrays an autistic savant.

intelligence
The global capacity to act purposefully, to think rationally, and to deal effectively with the environment.

achievement test
A test that measures knowledge of a particular subject.

*I*n the 1988 movie *Rain Man,* which won an Academy Award for best picture, Dustin Hoffman played an autistic man who could perform amazing mental feats, such as recalling the telephone number of anyone in the telephone book. Hoffman portrayed a so-called idiot savant (French for "learned fool"). Idiot savants are now called *autistic savants* to avoid the negative connotation of the word *idiot.* An autistic savant is an autistic person (a person suffering from a disorder that impairs the ability to communicate and to relate to others socially) with below-average intelligence but with an outstanding ability, typically in art, music, memory, or calculating (Cheatham et al., 1995). This phenomenon was first noted in 1751 in an article in a German magazine that described the case of an uneducated farmhand with an extraordinary memory (Foerstl, 1989).

In a much more recent case, a 12–year-old autistic savant could play unfamiliar piano pieces after listening to them once (Young & Nettelbeck, 1995). In another case, an autistic savant could give the day of the week for any date in the twentieth century (Hurst & Mulhall, 1988). He had spent many hours memorizing the day of the week of each date, just as Dustin Hoffman's character spent many hours memorizing the telephone book. Because autistic people tend to be socially aloof and persistent at tasks, they can spend the many hours needed to memorize large amounts of material, such as calendar dates (Howe & Smith, 1988). Their feats are similar to the ability of children to memorize statistics from the backs of hundreds of baseball cards and then recall any statistic for any player. In some cases, instead of memorizing thousands of calendar dates, autistic savants discover the rules of calendar construction and use them to calculate the day of the week for specific dates (O'Connor & Hermelin, 1992).

An autistic savant who memorizes enormous amounts of material is displaying intelligence. You certainly recognize intelligent behavior when you see it: someone getting an A on a calculus exam, or writing a great symphony, or discovering a cure for a disease. Recognizing intelligent behavior, though, is easier than defining intelligence itself. The word *intelligence* comes from the Latin word meaning "to understand," but the concept of intelligence is broader than that. Finding a universally acceptable definition of intelligence is difficult because intelligence is a natural concept. Natural concepts have "fuzzy borders"—they are not easily defined by a distinct set of features (see Chapter 9).

Four decades ago David Wechsler (1958), a leading intelligence researcher, put forth an influential definition of intelligence. He called **intelligence** the global capacity to act purposefully, to think rationally, and to deal effectively with the environment. In other words, intelligence reflects how well we *function.* This definition is in the spirit of the first American school of psychology, functionalism (see Chapter 1), which stressed the importance of adaptive functioning in everyday life. And indeed, intelligent people tend to function better. For example, a study of the children of criminals found that the higher the children scored on intelligence tests, the less likely they were to become criminals themselves. Apparently those with a higher level of intelligence perform better in school, become less alienated, and use their educational success as a means to a socially acceptable career (Kandel et al., 1988).

INTELLIGENCE TESTING: ASSESSING INTELLECTUAL ABILITIES

Modern interest in the study of intelligence began with the development of tests of mental abilities, which include achievement tests, aptitude tests, and intelligence tests. An **achievement test** assesses knowledge of a particular subject. For decades, New York

▲ Galton's Anthropometric Laboratory
Francis Galton measured the physical traits of more than 9,000 subjects in his Anthropometric Laboratory in London.

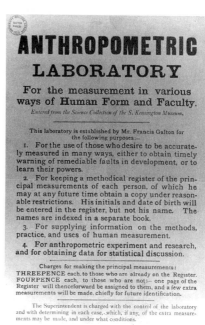

State has required students to pass the Regents Exams, which are achievement tests designed to measure students' knowledge of major academic areas such as English, history, and mathematics. An **aptitude test** predicts your potential to benefit from instruction in a particular academic or vocational setting. Of course, an aptitude test is partly an achievement test—your performance on it depends on your previous experience with the material covered by the test. Aptitude tests are commonly used to screen job applicants and college applicants. For example, a wire-bending aptitude test is a good predictor of the performance of dental students on dental procedures (Kao et al., 1990). In applying to colleges, you may have submitted the results of your performance on either the Scholastic Aptitude Test (SAT), now called the Scholastic Assessment Test, or the American College Test (ACT). These scores help admissions committees determine whether applicants have the potential to succeed in college. An **intelligence test,** the main topic of this section, is a kind of aptitude test that assesses overall mental ability.

The History of Intelligence Testing

Though some psychologists question the strength of the evidence (Bowman, 1989), the use of tests of mental abilities has been traced back to 2200 B.C., when the Chinese appear to have used them to select talented individuals to serve as civil servants (Fox, 1981). But ability testing did not become the subject of scientific study until a century ago, when the English scientist Francis Galton (1822–1911) set up his Anthropometric Laboratory at the 1884 International Health Exhibition in London.

Francis Galton and Anthropometry

The word *anthropometric* means "human measurement." More than 9,000 visitors to Galton's laboratory paid to be measured on a variety of physical characteristics, including head size, grip strength, visual acuity, and reaction time to sounds (Johnson et al., 1985).

aptitude test
A test designed to predict a person's potential to benefit from instruction in a particular academic or vocational setting.

intelligence test
A test that assesses overall mental ability.

▲ David Wechsler (1896–1981)
"Intelligence, operationally defined, is the aggregate or global capacity of the individual to act purposefully, to think rationally, and to deal effectively with his environment."

▲ Francis Galton (1822–1911)
"Social hindrances cannot impede men of high ability from being eminent . . . [and] social advantages are incompetent to give that status to a man of moderate ability."

differential psychology
The field of psychology that studies individual differences in intellectual, personality, and physical characteristics.

▲ Alfred Binet (1857–1911)
"It will be seen that a profound knowledge of the normal intellectual development of the child would not only be of great interest but useful in formulating a course of instruction really adapted to their aptitudes."

Galton was inspired by his cousin Charles Darwin's theory of evolution. According to Darwin, individuals who are the most physically well adapted to their environment are the most likely to survive long enough to produce offspring, who would be likely to also have those physical characteristics. Galton similarly assumed that people with superior physical abilities, especially sensory and motor abilities, are better adapted for survival. He viewed such people as more intelligent than those with average or inferior physical abilities.

Galton's interest in studying physical differences reflected his interest in studying all sorts of individual differences, including the relative beauty of women from different countries. (In a possible instance of experimenter bias, Galton found that the women of England, his home country, were the most beautiful.) His research on individual differences established the field of **differential psychology,** which is concerned with the study of cognitive and behavioral differences among individuals. Galton's anthropometric method was introduced to the United States by James McKeen Cattell (1860–1944), who administered Galton's tests—which Cattell called *mental tests*—to American students (Cattell, 1890).

But anthropometry proved fruitless as a way of measuring general intelligence, because many anthropometric measurements, such as grip strength, proved to have little or no relationship to mental measures of intelligence, such as reasoning ability. Recent research, however, has demonstrated a positive correlation between mental measurements and physical measures such as reaction time. For example, a study of elementary school children found that their reaction time was related to intelligence test scores: Higher test scores were associated with faster reaction times (Lynn & Wilson, 1990). One explanation for this relationship is that intelligence might partially depend on the speed of neural impulse conduction (Barrett, Daum, & Eysenck, 1990). Perhaps one can, indeed, be "quick-witted."

Alfred Binet, Theodore Simon, and the IQ Test

The first formal test of general intelligence—the *Binet-Simon scale*—appeared in 1905. It grew out of an 1881 French law that required all children to attend school even if they could not profit from a standard curriculum (Levine, 1976). This led the French minister of public education to ask psychologist Alfred Binet (1857–1911) to develop a test to identify children who required special classes for slow learners.

Binet collaborated with psychiatrist Theodore Simon (1873–1961) to develop a test that could assess children's ability to perform in school. Binet and Simon began by administering many questions related to language, reasoning, and arithmetic to elementary school children of all ages. Binet and Simon eliminated questions that tended to be answered the same by children of all ages. Questions that were answered correctly by more and more children at each successive age were retained and became the Binet-Simon scale.

The test was administered to children who needed to be placed in school. Each student was assigned a *mental age,* based on the number of test items she or he passed—the greater the number of items passed, the higher the mental age. A student with a mental age significantly below his or her chronological age was considered a candidate for placement in a class for slow learners. Binet urged that his test be used solely for class placement. He disagreed with those who claimed that the test measured a child's inherited level of intelligence or that a child's level of intelligence could not be improved by education.

The Binet-Simon scale proved useful, but the measure of mental age occasionally proved misleading. Suppose that a 10-year-old child had a mental age of 8 and a 6-year-old child had a mental age of 4. Both would be 2 years below their chronological ages, but the 6-year-old would be proportionally farther behind her or his age peers than the 10-year-old would be. This problem was solved by German psychologist William Stern (1871–1938), who recommended using the ratio of mental age to chronological age to determine a child's level of intelligence (Kreppner, 1992). A 10-year-old with a mental age of 8 has a ratio of 8/10 = 0.80, and a 6-year-old with a mental age of 4 has a ratio of 4/6 = 0.67. This indicates that the 6-year-old is relatively farther behind his or her age peers. Stern eliminated the decimal point by multiplying the ratio by 100. Thus, 0.80

becomes 80, and 0.67 becomes 67. The formula (mental age/chronological age) × 100 became known as the **intelligence quotient—(IQ).** As you can see, a child whose mental and chronological ages are the same has an IQ of 100, and a child who has a higher mental than chronological age has an IQ above 100.

intelligence quotient (IQ)
1. Originally, the ratio of mental age to chronological age; that is, MA/CA × 100.
2. Today, the score on an intelligence test, calculated by comparing a person's performance to norms for her or his age group.

Mental Testing in America

The Binet-Simon scale was translated into English and first used in the United States by the American psychologist Henry Goddard (1866–1957) in New Jersey at the Vineland Training School for Feebleminded Girls and Boys. A revised version of the Binet-Simon scale, more suitable for children reared in American culture, was published in 1916 by Stanford University psychologist Lewis Terman (1877–1956). The American version became known as the *Stanford-Binet Intelligence Scale*, which is still used today. Ironically, the Binet-Simon scale was neither widely used nor widely known in France until after the Stanford-Binet had become popular in America (Schneider, 1992). Terman also redesigned the Stanford-Binet to make it suitable for testing both children and adults. (The test has been revised in 1937, 1960, 1972, and 1986.)

Because the Stanford-Binet is given individually and can take an hour or more to administer, it is not suitable for testing large groups of people in a brief period of time. This became a problem during World War I, when the U.S. Army sought a way to assess the intelligence of large groups of recruits. The army wanted to reject recruits who did not have the intelligence to perform well and to identify recruits who would be good officer candidates. The solution to this problem was provided by Terman and his student A. A. Otis. They developed two group tests of intelligence—the *Army Alpha Test* and the *Army Beta Test*. The Army Alpha Test was given in writing to those who could read English, and the Army Beta Test was given orally to those who could not read English. The tests, reflecting their functionalist heritage, viewed intelligence as the ability to adapt to the environment (Mayrhauser, 1989). Descendants of these group intelligence tests include the *Otis-Lennon Mental Abilities Tests* and the *Armed Forces Qualification Test*.

After World War I the Stanford-Binet became the most widely used intelligence test. But the ratio IQ devised by Stern, which was adequate for representing the intelligence of children, proved inadequate for representing the intelligence of adults. Because growth in mental age slows markedly after childhood, the use of the ratio IQ led to the absurdity of people with average or above-average intelligence becoming below average simply because their chronological age increased. For example, consider a 15-year-old girl with a mental age of 20. She would have an IQ of (20/15) × 100 = 133. This would put her in the mentally gifted range (that is, above 130). Suppose that at age 40 she had retained the mental age of 20. She would then have an IQ of (20/40) × 100 = 50. This would put her well within the mentally retarded range (that is, below 70). Yet she might be a successful lawyer, physician, or professor.

This inadequacy of the ratio IQ was overcome by David Wechsler (1896–1981). He replaced Stern's ratio IQ with a *deviation IQ*, which compares a person's intelligence test score with the mean score of his or her age peers. Those who perform at exactly the mean

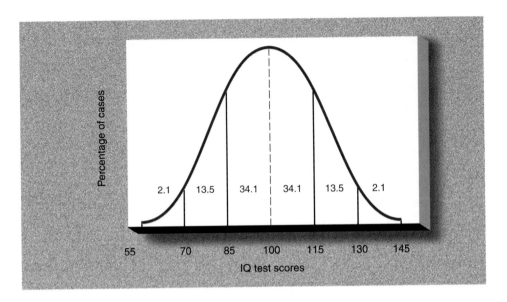

of their age peers receive an IQ of 100; those who perform above the mean of their age peers receive an IQ above 100; and those who perform below the mean of their age peers receive an IQ below 100.

In 1939 Wechsler developed his own intelligence test. While working as chief psychologist at Bellevue Hospital in New York City, he sought a way to assess the intelligence of adult psychiatric patients with low verbal ability. Because the Stanford-Binet stressed verbal ability and was geared toward testing children, it was not suitable for that purpose. This led Wechsler to develop an adult intelligence test that tested nonverbal, as well as verbal, ability, which he called the *Wechsler-Bellevue Intelligence Scale.*

Wechsler later developed versions of his test for use with different age groups, beginning with the *Wechsler Intelligence Scale for Children (WISC)*, for ages 6 to 16; followed by the *Wechsler Adult Intelligence Scale (WAIS)*, for ages from late adolescence through adulthood; and concluding with the *Wechsler Preschool and Primary Scale of Intelligence (WPPSI)*, for ages 4 to 6½. The Wechsler scales have been revised periodically, leading to their current acronyms, *WISC-R, WAIS-R,* and *WPPSI-R.* Each of the Wechsler intelligence scales contains 11 subtests that measure different aspects of verbal and nonverbal intelligence. The test taker receives a verbal IQ, a performance (nonverbal) IQ, and an overall IQ. Research has supported the usefulness of distinguishing, as measured by the Wechsler scales, these three kinds of intelligence (LoBello & Gulgoz, 1991).

Issues in Intelligence Testing

Formal tests must be standardized, reliable, and valid (see Chapter 2). *Standardization* refers to both the establishment of performance norms on a test and uniformity in how the test is administered and scored. When an intelligence test is standardized, the mean performance of the standardization group for each age range is given a score of 100, with a standard deviation of 15. The standard deviation is a measure of how variable a group of scores are around their mean. Figure 10.1 shows that IQ scores fall along a *normal curve.* For the Wechsler scales, this means that about 68 percent of test takers will score between 85 and 115, and about 95 percent will score between 70 and 130. Average intelligence falls between 85 and 115. IQs below 70 fall in the mentally retarded range, and IQs above 130 fall in the mentally gifted range.

The Reliability of Intelligence Tests

You would have confidence in an intelligence test only if it were reliable. The *reliability* of a test is the degree to which it gives consistent results. Suppose you took an IQ test and scored 102 (average) one month, 53 (mentally retarded) the next month, and 146 (mentally gifted) the third month. Because your level of intelligence normally would not fluctuate that much in 3 months, you would argue that the test is unreliable. Because the test-retest reliability correlations for the Stanford-Binet and Wechsler scales are at least .90 (out of a maximum of 1.00), the tests are reliable.

Though standardized IQ tests are reliable in the short run, an individual's IQ score can change over a period of years. The Berkeley Growth Study, conducted at the University of California at Berkeley, contradicted the once-popular belief that intelligence does not change during childhood. The study found that mental ability increases through adolescence and then levels off at about the age of 20 (Bayley, 1955). The nature of intellectual change later in life is discussed in Chapter 4.

The Validity of Intelligence Tests

A reliable test is not necessarily a valid one. A test's *validity* (see Chapter 2) depends on whether the test measures what it is supposed to measure. *Predictive validity* is especially important. Consider the SAT's ability to predict school performance. A published review of research on the SAT reported that the SAT correlated .41 with first-year college grade-point average. This means that the SAT is a moderately good predictor. But high school grade-point average, which correlated .52 with first-year college grade-point average, is an even better predictor. Moreover, the combination of the SAT and high school grade-point average was a still better predictor, correlating .58 with first-year college grade-point average (Linn, 1982).

Claims that students with access to SAT preparation courses have an unfair advantage over others might be unfounded. Such courses produce modest gains. An increase of just 20 to 30 points on the verbal and mathematics subtests would require hours of study almost equivalent to full-time schooling (Messick & Jungeblut, 1981). Of course, because this is based on averages, some students might benefit from extra preparation.

The Stanford-Binet and Wechsler scales correlate between .40 and .75 with school performance, depending on the aspect of school performance being measured (Aiken, 1982). These moderately high correlations indicate that the tests are good, but far from perfect, predictors of school performance. Because the correlations are less than a perfect 1.00, factors other than those measured by the SAT or IQ tests also contribute to school performance. This has made the fairness of intelligence tests one of the most controversial issues in contemporary psychology.

Critics argue that IQ tests and other tests of mental ability might be unfair to minority groups in the United States, most notably African Americans (Bender et al., 1995)—who score an average of 10 to 15 IQ points lower than white Americans on IQ tests (Mackenzie, 1984). Critics of IQ testing allege that because African Americans are less likely to have the same cultural and educational experiences as whites, they tend, on the average, to perform more poorly on IQ tests that assume cultural and educational experiences common to whites (Brooks-Gunn, Klebanov, & Duncan, 1996).

But does this mean that IQ tests are *biased* against African Americans? The issue of the validity of IQ tests for African Americans reached the courts in the 1970s. In 1979 Judge Robert Peckham of the Federal District Court in San Francisco ruled that without court approval California schools could no longer base class placement of African American schoolchildren on IQ tests. His ruling came in the case of *Larry P. v. Wilson Riles* (Riles was the California superintendent of education), which was brought on behalf of six African American children in San Francisco who had been placed in classes for the educable mentally retarded (that is, those with mild mental retardation). After hearing 10,000 pages of testimony from experts and advocates on both sides of the issue, Peckham ruled that the use of IQ tests violated the civil rights of African American children, because a proportionately greater number of these children than white children were being placed in classes for the mentally retarded. His decision convinced school districts in several other states to abandon the use of IQ tests for determining the school placement of African American children (Taylor, 1990).

But Peckham's decision was also met by arguments that IQ tests are not biased against African Americans, because the tests have good predictive validity—they accurately predict the performance of both African American children and white children in elementary

► FIGURE 10.2

Raven Progressive Matrices Test

In this "culture-fair" test, the person is presented with a series of matrices and must complete each by selecting the appropriate symbol from an accompanying group of symbols.

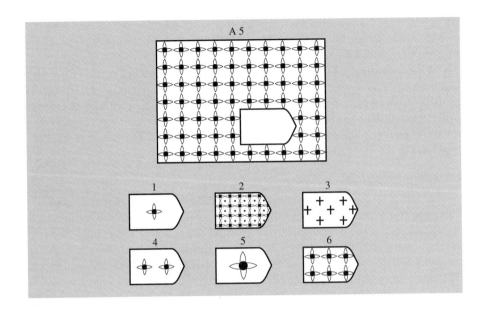

school classes. The differences in IQ scores between the two groups of children might reflect the fact that African American children might be more likely to be reared in socially disadvantaged circumstances that do not provide them with the opportunity to gain experiences that are important in doing well on IQ tests and in school (Lambert, 1981). A committee of scholars from several academic fields reported to the National Academy of Science that standardized tests are accurate predictors of school and job performance for all groups and therefore are not biased against any particular group ("NAS Calls Tests Fair but Limited," 1982). A recent review of research on racial differences in intelligence found no adequate explanation—whether genetic or environmental—for them (Neisser et al., 1996).

Nonetheless, the issue has become as political as it is scientific. On the one side are those, such as Judge Peckham, who believe that biased tests of mental abilities are being used to perpetuate discrimination against African American children by placing more of these children in slower classes and by preventing African American adults from obtaining desirable jobs. Peckham and his supporters favor outlawing the use of such tests. On the other side are those who believe that blaming IQ tests for revealing the negative consequences of deprived upbringings is like killing the messenger who brings bad news. They would favor changing the conditions that contribute to the poorer average IQ test performance of African Americans and many other minority groups (Elliott, 1988).

One possible solution presents a compromise: Use tests that are not affected by the test taker's cultural background. But efforts to develop "culture-free" tests, beginning in the 1940s (Cattell, 1940), and "culture-fair" tests, beginning in the 1950s (Davis & Eels, 1953), produced disappointing results. These tests presented test takers with items that emphasized perceptual and spatial abilities, rather than verbal abilities, and avoided the use of items that would presume an extensive background in a particular culture. Figure 10.2 presents an example of the Raven Progressive Matrices, a nonverbal intelligence test that some have favored over the Stanford-Binet or Wechsler scales (Basu, 1982). But, just like on traditional intelligence tests, people of higher socioeconomic status perform better on these nonverbal tests than do people of lower socioeconomic status (Jensen, 1980). Even the Cattell Culture Fair Intelligence Test, which was designed to reduce cultural bias in testing, appears to contain culturally biased items, as indicated in a study of Indian, American, and Nigerian adolescents who took the test (Nenty, 1986).

Imagine how Alfred Binet would have reacted to the controversy that has arisen over the use of standardized tests, considering that he saw testing as an objective means of assessing students' abilities. In fact, despite the shortcomings of standardized tests, no alternative is as unbiased in assessing individuals without regard to irrelevant characteristics such as sex, race, or ethnic background (Reilly & Chao, 1982). As Richard Weinberg, a leading intelligence researcher, has noted:

▶ In light of the effectiveness of current IQ tests to predict school performance, it is ironic that tests have been outlawed for the very purpose for which they were designed—to prevent subjective judgment and prejudice from being the basis for assigning students to special classes or denying them certain privileges. (Weinberg, 1989, p. 100)

Staying on Track: *Intelligence Testing*

1. What is an autistic savant?
2. How was Galton's view of intelligence influenced by his cousin Charles Darwin's theory of evolution?
3. What was the basis of the case of *Larry P. v. Wilson Riles?*

Answers to Staying on Track start on p. S–4.

EXTREMES OF INTELLIGENCE

Another controversial issue regarding intelligence is the classification and education of people who fall at either extreme of the range of intelligence. As you learned earlier, 95 percent of the population score between 70 and 130 on IQ tests. Of the remaining 5 percent, half score below 70 and half score above 130. Those who score below 70 fall in the mentally retarded range, and those who score above 130 fall in the mentally gifted range—though the classification of a person as mentally retarded or mentally gifted is not based on IQ scores alone.

Mental Retardation

Depending on the criteria used to define **mental retardation,** from slightly more than 3 million to almost 7 million Americans are mentally retarded. The estimate varies because a person's level of adaptive behavior, and not just level of intelligence, needs to be assessed before the person is classified as mentally retarded. In fact, the current trend in classification is to rely more on the person's everyday functioning and less on his or her IQ score (Haywood, Meyers, & Switzky, 1982).

mental retardation
Intellectual deficiency marked by an IQ below 70 and difficulties performing in everyday life.

Classification of Mental Retardation

We have come a long way in our use of terms to classify persons with mental retardation. In the early twentieth century, such persons were sorted into three categories, in terms of increasing degrees of mental retardation: *moron* (from a Greek word meaning "foolish"), *imbecile* (from a Latin word meaning "weak-minded"), and *idiot* (from a Greek word meaning "ignorant"). Fortunately, these terms are no longer used by professionals, but, as you are well aware, they have become terms of disparagement in everyday language.

To be classified as having mental retardation, a person must have an IQ below 70 and, beginning in childhood, difficulties performing in everyday life (Landesman & Ramey, 1989)—including difficulties in self-care (such as eating and dressing), schoolwork (such as reading and arithmetic), and social relationships (such as conversing and developing friendships). Moreover, before a person can be classified as having mental retardation, alternative causes of the person's low IQ score and performance difficulties must be ruled out. These alternative causes include physical illness, impairment of vision or hearing, and coming from a family of people who are not native speakers of the language in which the IQ test was administered.

Today, there are four categories of mental retardation (American Psychiatric Association, 1994). Persons with IQs of 50 to 70 have *mild retardation* and constitute 85 percent of persons with mental retardation. They are able to care for themselves, reach a sixth-grade level of education, hold responsible jobs, be married, and serve as adequate parents. Those with IQs of 35 to 49 have *moderate retardation* and constitute 10 percent of persons with mental retardation. They might be trained to care for themselves, reach a second-grade level of education, and hold menial jobs, often in sheltered workshops, but they have difficulty maintaining social relationships and they rarely marry.

Those with IQs between 20 and 34 have *severe retardation* and constitute 3 to 4 percent of persons with mental retardation. They can learn rudimentary language and work skills but might be unable to care for themselves, benefit from schooling, hold jobs, or maintain normal social relationships. And those with IQs below 20 have *profound retardation* and constitute 1 to 2 percent of persons with mental retardation. They have so few skills that they might spend their lives in institutions that provide them with no more than custodial care.

Causes of Mental Retardation

In 1912 Henry Goddard traced the descendants of a Revolutionary War soldier whom he called Martin Kallikak. The soldier produced two lines of descendants. One line arose from his affair with a tavern maid who had mental retardation. The other line arose from his marriage to a respectable woman of normal intelligence. Goddard found that the descendants of the tavern maid included many derelicts, prostitutes, and persons with mental retardation. In contrast, the descendants of his wife included few such people.

The differences between the two lines of descendants account for Goddard's use of the name *Kallikak*. The name is a combination of the Greek words *kalos* (meaning "good") and *kakos* (meaning "bad"). Goddard concluded that the descendants of the soldier's wife inherited the tendency to be moral and intelligent, while the descendants of the tavern maid inherited the tendency to be immoral and mentally retarded. He discounted the effects of the markedly different sociocultural environments into which the children in each branch of the family were born as the probable causes of the differences.

Controversy has arisen about retouched photographs of the Kallikaks that Goddard (1912) included in a book he wrote. Critics claimed that Goddard (perhaps to show the dire effects of inferior genes) retouched the photographs to make the family members look more mentally retarded and unappealing (Smith, 1988). Others claim that this is much ado about nothing. They insist that Goddard probably retouched the photographs for aesthetic reasons—perhaps to bring out indistinct facial features (Fancher, 1987). This controversy even inspired an empirical study in which adult subjects rated the photographs of the Kallikaks. The subjects generally rated the Kallikaks as "kind" and "very bright" (Glenn & Ellis, 1988). Thus, even if Goddard intended to make them look more ominous, his attempt was not successful.

Today research findings indicate that about 75 percent of cases of mental retardation are caused, not by heredity, but by sociocultural deprivation, so-called **cultural-familial retardation** (Scott & Carran, 1987). In fact, almost all persons with mild retardation come from such backgrounds. Their families might fail to provide them with adequate intellectual stimulation, such as discussing current events with them, encouraging them to read, helping them with homework, and taking them on trips to zoos, museums, and other educational settings. They are also more likely to attend inferior schools, to suffer from malnutrition, and to lack adequate medical care—each of which can impair intellectual growth.

Though most cases of mental retardation are caused by sociocultural deprivation, many cases are caused by brain damage. Pregnant women who ingest drugs can cause brain damage in their offspring. For example, women who drink alcohol while pregnant might give birth to children who suffer from *fetal alcohol syndrome*, marked by physical deformities and mental retardation (Janzen, Nanson, & Block, 1995). Pregnant women who have certain diseases, such as *rubella* (German measles) during the first trimester, also have a greater risk of giving birth to offspring with mental retardation. Women who are infected with the genital *herpes* virus have about a 10 percent chance of producing offspring with mental retardation (Eichhorn, 1982). Women who suffer from severe *malnutrition* while pregnant can produce infants who have mental retardation because of a reduction in the number of their brain cells (Read, 1982). Prenatal exposure to X rays can impair the normal migration of brain cells, increasing the possibility of mental retardation (Schull, Norton, & Jensh, 1990). And a newborn infant who fails to breathe for several minutes after birth will experience *hypoxia*, a lack of oxygen to the brain and the most common cause of perinatal brain damage (Towbin, 1978). Hypoxia can cause **cerebral palsy,** a form of brain damage characterized by movement disorders and often—but not always—accompanied by mental retardation.

cultural-familial retardation
Mental retardation apparently caused by social or cultural deprivation.

cerebral palsy
A movement disorder caused by brain damage and that is sometimes accompanied by mental retardation.

CHAPTER 10

Mental retardation is also caused by genetic defects, such as defects that cause abnormal metabolism, which in turn can lead to brain damage, as in the case of **phenylketonuria (PKU).** PKU is caused by an inherited lack of the enzyme required to metabolize the amino acid *phenylalanine,* which is found in milk and other common foods. This eventually causes brain damage, which leads to mental retardation by the age of 3. Fortunately, routine screening of newborns in the United States and other countries can detect PKU early enough to protect infants from brain damage by putting them on a diet that eliminates almost all of their intake of phenylalanine (Griffiths, Paterson, & Harvie, 1995).

Some cases of mental retardation are caused by genetic defects that cause abnormal development during gestation, as in the case of **Down syndrome.** This disorder is named for the English physician Langdon Down, who identified it in 1866. Human beings normally have 23 pairs of chromosomes, with one member of each pair coming from each parent. A person with Down syndrome has an extra, third chromosome on the 21st pair. The extra chromosome can come from either the mother's egg or the father's sperm. The chances of having a child with Down syndrome increase with age, being more common in middle-aged parents than in younger ones.

Children with Down syndrome usually have moderate retardation and distinctive physical characteristics. These include small ears and hands; short necks, feet, and fingers; protruding tongues; and a fold over the eyes, giving them an almond-shaped, Asian appearance. Because of this, Down syndrome was originally called "Mongolism." This reflected the nineteenth-century Western belief that victims of the disorder failed to develop beyond what was then presumed by Westerners to be the more primitive physical and intellectual level of Asians, such as Mongolians (Gould, 1981).

Education of Persons with Mental Retardation

Over the centuries, people with mental retardation have been treated as everything from children of God, who were believed to bring good luck, to subhumans, who, it was believed, should be locked up as dangerous (Wolfensberger, 1972). Today psychologists interested in persons with mental retardation stress their potential to benefit from education and training. One reason why persons with mental retardation do not perform as well as other people is that they fail to use effective methods of information processing. For example, when persons with mental retardation are given a series of words or pictures to remember, they tend not to rehearse the items or group them into chunks—techniques that are commonly used by people who do not have mental retardation (Campione & Brown, 1979). As explained in Chapter 8, memory is enhanced by the rehearsal and chunking of information.

Today persons with mild retardation are called "educable," and persons with moderate retardation are called "trainable." From the 1950s to the 1970s, persons categorized as being educable mentally retarded were placed in special classes in which they received teaching tailored to their level of ability. But in the 1970s, dissatisfaction with the results of this approach led to *mainstreaming,* which places children with mental retardation in as many normal classes as possible and encourages them to participate in activities with children who do not have retardation. To promote mainstreaming in America, the Education for All Handicapped Children Act of 1975 mandated that children with mental retardation be given instruction in the most normal academic setting that is feasible for them (Sussan, 1990).

The educational needs of individuals with mental retardation are not limited to academic subjects. They might also need training in self-care skills (including eating, toileting, hygiene, dressing, and grooming); home management skills (including home maintenance, clothing care, food preparation, and home safety); consumer skills (including telephone use, money management, and shopping); and community mobility skills (including pedestrian safety and use of public transportation). Behavior modification has been especially useful in teaching self-care to persons with mental retardation. For example, as presented in Table 10.1, behavior modification has been used successfully in training such persons to shower themselves (Matson, DiLorenzo, & Esveldt-Dawson, 1981).

phenylketonuria (PKU)
A hereditary enzyme deficiency that, if left untreated in the infant, causes mental retardation.

Down syndrome
A form of mental retardation, associated with certain physical deformities, that is caused by an extra, third chromosome on the 21st pair.

(a)

(b)

▲ **Down Syndrome**
People with Down syndrome can live rewarding lives, both personally and professionally. *(a)* John Mark Stallings provides emotional support for his father, Gene, the head football coach for the University of Alabama. *(b)* Actor Chris Burke starred in the successful television series "Life Goes On."

Intelligence | 355

► TABLE 10.1
A Step-by-Step Approach for Training People
with Mental Retardation to Shower
Themselves

Task-Analyzed Steps of Showering	
1. Acquire washcloth	15. Wash left leg and foot
2. Turn on the water	16. Wash right leg and foot
3. Adjust temperature	17. Wash back
4. Get wet, then turn water off	18. Wash buttocks
5. Wash hair	19. Rinse off soap
6. Lather cloth	20. Wring out cloth
7. Wash face, ears, and neck	21. Properly dispose of cloth
8. Wash shoulders	22. Get a towel
9. Wash left arm	23. Dry hair
10. Wash under left arm	24. Dry face, ears, and neck
11. Wash right arm	25. Dry remainder of body
12. Wash under right arm	26. Put towel in hamper
13. Wash chest and stomach	27. Apply deodorant
14. Wash genitals	

Reprinted with permission from *Behavior Research and Therapy*, 19, J. L. Matson, T. M. DiLorenzo, and K. Esveldt-Dawson, "Independence Training as a Method of Enhancing Self-Help Skills Acquisition of the Mentally Retarded," pages 399–405. Copyright 1981, Elsevier Science Ltd, The Boulevard, Langford Lane, Kidlington OX5 1GB, UK.

A movement that has paralleled mainstreaming is *normalization*, the transfer of individuals with mental retardation from large institutional settings into community settings so that they can live more normal lives. Given adequate support services, even people with severe and profound retardation can progress in settings other than large, custodial institutions. But in too many instances normalization has simply created smaller custodial settings, rather than ones that truly encourage independent living (Sinson, 1994).

Mental Giftedness

Interest in the study of mental retardation has been accompanied by interest, though less extensive interest, in the study of **mental giftedness.** Francis Galton (1869) began the study of the mentally gifted—or "geniuses"—in the late nineteenth century. Lewis Terman, introduced earlier, considered Galton to be mentally gifted. Terman based his assessment on Galton's early accomplishments, including his ability to recite the alphabet when he was 18 months old and read classical literature when he was 5 years old (Terman, 1917). Today the mentally gifted are considered those with IQs above 130 and with exceptionally high scores on achievement tests in specific subjects, such as mathematics (Fox, 1981).

The special needs of the mentally gifted have traditionally received less attention than those of persons with mental retardation (Reis, 1989). Perhaps the most well-known organization dedicated to meeting the needs of the mentally gifted is Mensa (Serebriakoff, 1985), which limits its membership to those who score in the top 2 percent on a standardized intelligence test. One of the reasons for the traditional lack of interest in the mentally gifted was the belief in "early ripe, early rot." This belief assumed that children who are intellectually precocious are doomed to become academic, vocational, and social failures.

The classic case study in support of this viewpoint was that of William James Sidis (1898–1944). He was named in honor of William James, a colleague of his father, Boris, at Harvard University. Sidis was a mathematically gifted boy who enrolled at Harvard in 1909 at the age of 11 and received national publicity a year later when he gave a talk on higher mathematics to the Harvard Mathematical Club. But constant pressure from his father to excel and the glare of publicity eventually led Sidis to retreat from the world. In his early twenties, Sidis left the faculty position he had taken at Rice Institute in Houston and spent the rest of his life working at menial jobs. Years later, in 1937, James Thurber, writing under a pen name in the *New Yorker*, published a sarcastic article about Sidis entitled "April Fool"

mental giftedness
Intellectual superiority marked by an IQ above 130 and exceptionally high scores on achievement tests in specific subjects, such as mathematics.

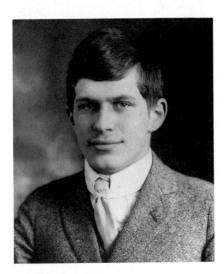

▲ **William James Sidis (1898–1944)**
"He died alone, obscure, and destitute, and he left a troublesome legacy best termed the 'Sidis Fallacy'—that talent like his rarely matures or becomes productive" (Montour, 1977, p. 265).

CHAPTER 10

(Sidis was born on April 1). Thurber wrote that Sidis was a failure, living in a single room in a rundown section of Boston, which Thurber used as evidence of the dire consequences of being too intelligent at too young an age. Sidis sued the *New Yorker* for libel and won a modest settlement shortly before dying—in obscurity—in 1944 (Wallace, 1986).

Terman's Genetic Studies of Genius

Contrary to the case of William James Sidis, mentally gifted children do not tend to become failures. In fact, they tend to be more successful in every area of life and show better adjustment and less emotional disturbance than other people do (Grossberg & Cornell, 1988). This was demonstrated in perhaps the most famous longitudinal study ever conducted, Lewis Terman's Genetic Studies of Genius, which still inspires interest today—more than 70 years after it began (Cravens, 1992).

ANATOMY OF A CLASSIC RESEARCH STUDY

What Is the Fate of Childhood Geniuses?

Rationale

Terman began his study in 1921, and it has continued ever since—even after his death. He hoped to counter the commonsense belief that being too intelligent too early led to later failure.

Method

Terman used the Stanford-Binet Intelligence Scale to identify California children with IQs above 135. He found 1,528 such children between the ages of 8 and 12. Their average IQ was 150. Reports on Terman's gifted children have appeared every decade or two since 1921. After Terman's death in 1956, the study was continued by Robert and Pauline Sears of Stanford University.

Results and Discussion

The Terman Genetic Studies of Genius has shown that mentally gifted children tend to become socially, physically, vocationally, and academically superior adults. They are healthier and more likely to attend college, to have professional careers, and to have happy marriages. The 1972 report on Terman's subjects, then at an average age of 62, found that they were generally satisfied with life, combining successful careers with rewarding family lives (Sears, 1977).

▲ Lewis Terman (1877–1956)
"Children of IQ 140 or higher are, in general, appreciably superior to unselected children in physique, health, and social adjustment; markedly superior in moral attitudes as measured either by character tests or trait ratings; and vastly superior in their mastery of school subjects."

▶ The Mentally Gifted
Children who are mentally gifted, like those who are mentally retarded, benefit from special educational programs to help them develop their abilities.

Of course, Terman's study is not without certain weaknesses. Perhaps the subjects' awareness of being in such an important study affected how they performed in life—a kind of self-fulfilling prophecy. Also, could socioeconomic status, and not solely intelligence, have been a contributing factor? A follow-up study of samples of men from the original study found that the men who maintained better health, had more stable marriages, and pursued more lucrative careers were less likely to come from families in which there was divorce, alcoholism, or other major family problems (Oden, 1968). Evidently, even for geniuses, the family environment is related to their success in life. A less-ambitious replication of the Terman study involved 156 adults (aged 35–50 years) who had graduated from an elementary school for gifted children. As did their counterparts in the Terman study, these gifted individuals showed superior social, physical, and vocational well-being (Subotnik, Karp, & Morgan, 1989).

▲ ▲ ▲

The Study of Mathematically Precocious Youth

Perhaps the best-known recent study of mentally gifted children is the longitudinal *Study of Mathematically Precocious Youth* conducted by Camilla Benbow and Julian Stanley (1983) at Johns Hopkins University. Benbow and Stanley provided special programs for young adolescents who scored above 700 (out of a maximum of 800) on the mathematics subtest of the SAT. The programs offered intensive summer courses in science and mathematics, accelerated courses at universities, and counseling for parents to help them meet the academic and emotional needs of their gifted children. A 10-year follow-up found that subjects in the study had many outstanding educational achievements (Benbow, Arjmand, & Walberg, 1991). And contrary to popular belief, the participants also did not suffer academic burnout from their demanding course work (Swiatek, 1993). Moreover, there is no evidence that these gifted children are prone to the personal and social problems that plagued William James Sidis. In fact, a program such as this might have helped him pursue a rewarding career as a mathematician instead of fading into obscurity.

Staying on Track: *Extremes of Intelligence*

1. What are some possible causes of mental retardation?
2. In what way has Terman's *Genetic Studies of Genius* countered the notion of "early ripe, early rot"?

THEORIES OF INTELLIGENCE: WHAT IS INTELLIGENCE?

Is intelligence a general characteristic that affects all facets of behavior, or are there different kinds of intelligence, each affecting a specific facet of behavior? Today intelligence researchers tend to assume that there are several kinds of intelligence (Sternberg & Wagner, 1993). Consider, for example, a study of men who spent much of their recreational time at racetracks betting on horse races. The results indicated that the men's ability to handicap races accurately was unrelated to their scores on a test of general intelligence. This indicated that handicapping horse races taps a specific kind of mental ability (Ceci & Liker, 1986).

Factor-Analytic Theories of Intelligence

At about the same time as Alfred Binet was developing his intelligence test, the British psychologist Charles Spearman (1863–1945) was developing a theory of intelligence. He considered intelligence a general ability that underlies a variety of behaviors.

Spearman's Theory of General Intelligence

In 1927, after more than two decades of research, Spearman published his conclusions about the nature of intelligence. He developed a statistical technique called **factor analysis,** which determines the degree of correlation between performances on various tasks (Bartholomew, 1995). If performances on certain tasks have a high positive correlation, then they are presumed to reflect the influence of a particular underlying factor. For example, if performances on a vocabulary test, a reading test, and a writing test correlate highly, they might reveal the influence of a "verbal ability" factor.

In using factor analysis, Spearman first gave a large group of people a variety of mental tasks. He found that scores on the tasks had high positive correlations with one another. This meant that subjects tended to score high *or* moderate *or* low on all the tests. This led Spearman to conclude that performance on all of the tasks depended on the operation of a single underlying factor. He called this "*g*"—a general intelligence factor.

But because the correlations between the tasks were less than a perfect 1.00, Spearman concluded that performance on each task also depended, to a lesser extent, on its own specific factor, which he called "*s.*" For example, Spearman explained that scores on vocabulary tests and arithmetic tests tended to have a high positive correlation with each other because vocabulary ability and arithmetic ability are both influenced by a general intelligence factor. But because scores on vocabulary tests and arithmetic tests are not perfectly correlated, each ability must also depend on its own intelligence factor. Nonetheless, Spearman believed that the general intelligence factor was more important than any specific intelligence factor in governing a given ability. The existence of the factor *g* has received some research support (Brodnick & Ree, 1995). It appears to reflect the ability to be precise and flexible in manipulating information in one's short-term memory (Larson & Saccuzzo, 1989).

Thurstone's Theory of Primary Mental Abilities

Like Spearman, Louis Thurstone (1887–1955) used factor analysis to determine the nature of intelligence. But unlike Spearman, Thurstone (1938) concluded that there was no general intelligence factor. Instead, based on a battery of tests that he gave to college students, he identified seven factors, which he called *primary mental abilities:* reasoning, word fluency, perceptual speed, verbal comprehension, spatial visualization, numerical calculation, and associative memory.

Though scores on tests measuring these abilities had moderately high positive correlations with one another, they did not correlate highly enough for Thurstone to assume the existence of a general underlying intelligence factor. Suppose that you took tests to assess your abilities in reasoning, verbal comprehension, and numerical calculation. Thurstone

factor analysis
A statistical technique that determines the degree of correlation between performances on various tasks to determine the extent to which they reflect particular underlying characteristics, which are known as factors.

The Structure of the Intellect
Guilford identified 120 factors underlying intelligence, based on the interaction of five kinds of operations, four kinds of contents, and six kinds of products.

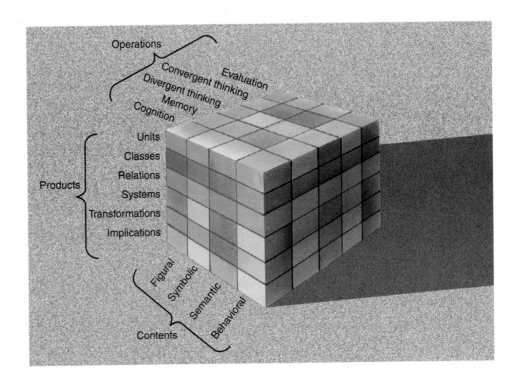

would insist that your performance on any single test would reflect, not the influence of a general intelligence factor, but instead the influence of a specific intelligence factor related to the particular ability assessed by that test.

Guilford's Theory of the Structure of the Intellect

Like Thurstone, J. P. Guilford (1897–1987) rejected the notion of a general intelligence factor (Guilford, 1959). He did so because of the unevenness he observed in children's abilities. Instead of the mere 7 factors in Thurstone's theory, Guilford identified 120 factors through the use of factor analysis (see Figure 10.3). Each of these factors represents the interaction among dimensions that Guilford called *operations* (thought processes, such as memory), *contents* (information that a person is thinking about, such as symbols), and *products* (results of thinking about the information, such as implications). By the end of his life, Guilford (1985) had increased the number of factors to 150, and, ultimately, to 180. Although, given so many factors, it is unlikely that researchers will ever determine the merits of all of them, subsequent research on portions of his structural model have provided some support for it (Chen & Michael, 1993). Before his death, Guilford hoped to help students improve themselves on the factors that he believed composed intelligence (Comrey, Michael, & Fruchter, 1988).

Horn and Cattell's Two-Factor Theory of Intelligence

A recent theory of intelligence based on factor analysis was developed by John Horn and Raymond Cattell (1966), who identified two intelligence factors. **Fluid intelligence** reflects thinking ability, memory capacity, and speed of information processing. Horn and Cattell believe that fluid intelligence is largely inherited, is affected little by training, and declines in late adulthood. The decline of fluid intelligence across adulthood has been supported by other researchers (Bors & Forrin, 1995). Fluid intelligence has much in common with Spearman's notion of a general intelligence factor (Duncan, Burgess, & Emslie, 1995).

Crystallized intelligence reflects the acquisition of skills and knowledge through schooling and everyday experience. Horn and Cattell believe that crystallized intelligence increases or remains the same in late adulthood. Changes in fluid intelligence and crystallized intelligence across the life span are illustrated in Figure 10.4. Special educational programs can enhance fluid and, especially, crystallized intelligence (Stankov & Chen, 1988).

fluid intelligence
The form of intelligence that reflects reasoning ability, memory capacity, and speed of information processing.

crystallized intelligence
The form of intelligence that reflects knowledge acquired through schooling and in everyday life.

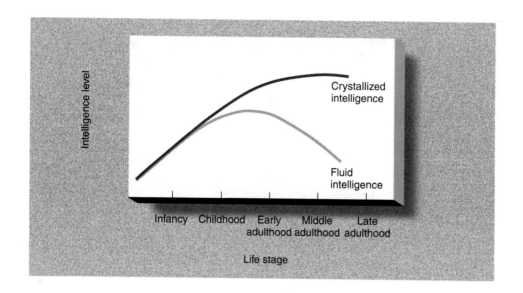

◀ FIGURE 10.4
Life-Span Changes in Intelligence
While fluid intelligence tends to decline in old
age, crystallized intelligence tends to increase
(Horn & Donaldson, 1976).

After reviewing arguments for the existence of fluid and crystallized intelligence, Guilford (1980) insisted that Horn and Cattell had failed to demonstrate the existence of these two factors. It remains for psychologists to determine which, if any, of the factor-analytic theories of intelligence is the best. Perhaps a more telling criticism of factor-analytic theories of intelligence is that they assume that intelligence reflects primarily those cognitive abilities needed to perform in school. A more encompassing theory of intelligence would consider a broader range of abilities (Frederiksen, 1986). Theories proposed by Robert Sternberg and Howard Gardner have done so.

The Triarchic Theory of Intelligence:
Academic, Creative, and Practical Intelligence

As a child, Robert Sternberg performed poorly on IQ tests and suffered from severe test anxiety, yet he later earned a Ph.D. and became a leading researcher in cognitive psychology. This contributed to his belief that intelligence comprises more than the abilities measured by traditional intelligence tests (Trotter, 1986). To determine the views of laypersons on the nature of intelligence, Sternberg and his colleagues (1981) surveyed people reading in a college library, entering a supermarket, or waiting for a train. They were asked to list what they believed were the main characteristics of intelligent people. The results showed that the respondents assumed that intelligent people had good verbal skills, social judgment, and problem-solving abilities.

During the past decade, Sternberg (1994) has developed a **triarchic theory of intelligence,** which claims that intelligence comprises three kinds of abilities similar to those reported by the people in his earlier survey. He bases his theory on his observations of how people process information. *Componential intelligence* is similar to the kind of intelligence considered by traditional theories of intelligence. It primarily reflects our information-processing ability, which helps in academic performance. *Experiential intelligence* is the ability to combine different experiences in insightful ways to solve novel problems based on past experience. In part it reflects creativity, as exhibited by an artist, composer, or scientist. Creative geniuses, such as Leonardo da Vinci and Albert Einstein, have especially high levels of experiential intelligence. *Contextual intelligence* is the ability to function in practical, everyday social situations. It reflects "street smarts," as in negotiating the price of a new car. Though many situations require the use of all three kinds of intelligence, some people are better at using one kind than at using the other two (Sternberg & Clinkenbeard, 1995).

The triarchic theory recognizes that we must be able to function in settings other than school. Sternberg believes that each of the three kinds of intelligence can be improved by special training, and he is developing ways of testing and improving them (Okagaki & Sternberg, 1993). The triarchic theory received some support from a study of intellectually

▲ Raymond Cattell
"Two major forms of intelligence emerge out of development and acculturation: fluid and crystallized."

triarchic theory of intelligence
Robert Sternberg's theory of intelligence, which assumes that there are three main kinds of intelligence: componential, experiential, and contextual.

▲ **The Theory of Multiple Intelligences**
Howard Gardner believes that we have evolved seven kinds of intelligence, which are developed to different extents in each of us. The late Texas Congress person Barbara Jordan's excellent speaking ability exemplifies linguistic intelligence. Basketball star Michael Jordan's superb athletic ability exemplifies bodily-kinesthetic intelligence. Rock musician Neil Young's proficiency in singing, playing, and composing music exemplifies musical intelligence. And physicist Stephen Hawking has used his outstanding logical-mathematical intelligence to contribute to our knowledge of the cosmos—despite being disabled by amyotrophic lateral sclerosis (Lou Gehrig's disease).

gifted adolescent students. They were superior to nongifted adolescent students in the cognitive abilities that are encompassed by componential intelligence. For example, they were more sophisticated and efficient in solving decision-making problems (Ball, Mann, & Stamm, 1994). Though Sternberg's theory goes beyond traditional theories by considering creative intelligence and practical intelligence, as well as academic intelligence, more research is needed to determine its merits.

The Theory of Multiple Intelligences: Expanding the Notion of Intelligence

While Sternberg bases his theory on his study of information processing, Gardner (1983) bases his **theory of multiple intelligences** on his belief that the brain has evolved separate systems for different adaptive abilities that he calls "intelligences." According to Gardner, there are seven types of intelligence, each of which is developed to a different extent in each of us: linguistic, logical-mathematical, spatial, musical, bodily-kinesthetic, intrapersonal, and interpersonal. Gardner assumes that certain brain structures and pathways underly these intelligences and that brain damage interferes with one or more of the intelligences. For example, damage to speech centers interferes with linguistic intelligence, and damage to the cerebellum interferes with bodily-kinesthetic intelligence.

Several of Gardner's kinds of intelligence are assessed by traditional intelligence tests. *Linguistic intelligence* is the ability to communicate through language. If you are good at reading textbooks, writing term papers, and presenting oral reports, you would be high in linguistic intelligence. A person with high *logical-mathematical intelligence* would be good at analyzing arguments and solving mathematical problems. And a person with high *spatial intelligence*, such as a skilled architect or carpenter, would be good at perceiving and arranging objects in the environment.

The remaining kinds of intelligence are assessed little, if at all, by traditional intelligence tests. *Musical intelligence* is the ability to analyze, compose, or perform music. A person with good *bodily-kinesthetic intelligence* would be able to move effectively, as in dancing or playing sports, or to manipulate objects effectively, as in using tools or driving a car. If you have high *intrapersonal intelligence*, you know yourself well and understand what motivates your behavior. For example, emotionally depressed people high in intrapersonal intelligence might be more likely to find ways to relieve their depression. And if you have high *interpersonal intelligence*, you function well in social situations because you are able to understand the needs of other people and to predict their behavior.

▲ **Howard Gardner**
"There is pervasive evidence for the existence of several *relatively autonomous* human intellectual competences, abbreviated . . . as 'human intelligences'."

theory of multiple intelligences
Howard Gardner's theory of intelligence, which assumes that the brain has evolved separate systems for seven kinds of intelligence.

As you have certainly observed in your own life, a person might excel in one or more of Gardner's intelligences while being average or below average in others. In extreme cases, we have the autistic savant who excels in painting but cannot read, the child prodigy who excels in mathematics but cannot dance, the student who excels in science but has no friends, and the athlete who excels in sports but cannot write a coherent sentence. Of course, you may have also encountered the so-called Renaissance person, who excels in several of Gardner's intelligences.

According to Gardner, our ability to succeed in life depends on the degree to which we develop the kinds of intelligence that are needed to function well in our culture. For example, for most people in the United States, success depends more on linguistic intelligence than on musical intelligence. Success in a culture that relies on hunting skills would put a greater premium on spatial intelligence and bodily-kinesthetic intelligence. Gardner's theory is so new that it has yet to generate sufficient research to determine its merits. But it is potentially superior to traditional theories of intelligence in its attention to the kinds of abilities needed to function in both academic and nonacademic settings. Gardner has begun applying his theory to enhancing the intellectual development of children (Krechevsky & Gardner, 1990).

STAYING ON TRACK: *Theories of Intelligence*

1. What is the difference between Spearman's and Thurstone's factor-analytic theories of intelligence?
2. According to Gardner's theory of multiple intelligences, what kinds of intelligence are there?

THINKING ABOUT *Psychology*

Does Intelligence Depend More on Nature or on Nurture?

In the 1983 movie *Trading Places,* two upper-class men argued about whether our social positions are determined more by heredity or by environment. They agreed to settle their argument by manipulating a rich white man (portrayed by Dan Ackroyd) and a poor black

eugenics
The practice of encouraging supposedly superior people to reproduce, while preventing supposedly inferior people from reproducing.

man (portrayed by Eddie Murphy) into trading homes (a mansion versus the street), vocations (big business versus begging), and financial status (wealth versus poverty). This movie illustrate's the popular concern with the issue of *nature versus nurture*.

The phrase *nature versus nurture* was popularized in the 1870s by Francis Galton (Fancher, 1984). As a follower of his cousin Charles Darwin, Galton (1869) concluded that intelligence is inherited after finding that eminent men had a higher proportion of eminent relatives than other men did. This led Galton to champion **eugenics** (Rabinowitz, 1984), the practice of encouraging supposedly superior people to reproduce, while preventing supposedly inferior people from reproducing. Galton's views also influenced the attitudes of psychologists toward immigrants in the early twentieth century.

EARLY STUDIES OF IMMIGRANTS: BIAS IN INTELLECTUAL ASSESSMENT

In 1912 Henry Goddard (1866–1957) became director of testing the intelligence of immigrants arriving at Ellis Island in New York Harbor. Goddard (1917) made the astonishing claim that 79 percent of Italians, 80 percent of Hungarians, 83 percent of Jews, and 87 percent of Russians scored in the "feebleminded" range on the Binet-Simon scale, which today we would call the mildly retarded range. Even after later reevaluating his data, he claimed that an average of "only" 40 percent of these groups were feebleminded (Gelb, 1986). Goddard, following in the footsteps of Galton, concluded that these ethnic groups were, by nature, intellectually inferior.

You probably realize that Goddard discounted possible environmental causes for the poor test performance of immigrants. He failed to consider a lack of education, a long ocean voyage below deck, and anxiety created by the testing situation as causes of their poor performance. Moreover, even though the tests were translated into the immigrants' native languages, the translations were often inadequate. Despite the shortcomings of the tests, low test scores were used as the basis for having many supposedly "feebleminded" immigrants deported. This was ironic, because at the 1915 meeting of the American Psychological Association in Chicago a critic of Goddard's program of intelligence testing reported that the native-born mayor of Chicago had taken an IQ test and had scored in the feebleminded range (Gould, 1981).

Further support for Goddard's position was provided by the army's intelligence-testing program during World War I, which was headed by Robert Yerkes (1876–1956). One of Yerkes's colleagues, Carl Brigham (1923), published the results of the testing program. He found that immigrants scored lower on the IQ tests than American-born whites did. Brigham attributed these differences in IQ scores to differences in heredity. The U.S. Congress passed the Immigration Act of 1924, which restricted immigration from eastern and southern Europe. There is disagreement between those who believe Brigham's findings influenced passage of the act (McPherson, 1985) and those who believe that they did not (Snyderman & Herrnstein, 1983).

Regardless, in 1930 Brigham stated that he had been wrong in assuming that the poorer performance of immigrants was attributable to heredity. He noted that in their everyday lives, immigrants—living in their original cultures—might not have had the opportunity to encounter much of the material in the army IQ tests. To appreciate this, consider the following multiple-choice items from the Army Alpha Test: "Crisco is a: patent medicine, disinfectant, toothpaste, food product [the correct answer];" and "Christy Mathewson is famous as a(n): writer, artist, baseball player [the correct answer], comedian" (Gould, 1981). Similarly, the poorer performance of African Americans on IQ tests was attributed to sociocultural deprivation caused by segregation (Rury, 1988).

RESEARCH ON THE INFLUENCE OF HEREDITY AND ENVIRONMENT

After three decades of relative indifference to it, the issue of nature versus nurture reemerged in the 1960s when President Lyndon Johnson began *Project Head Start*, which provides preschool children from deprived socioeconomic backgrounds with enrichment programs to promote their intellectual development. Head Start was stimulated in part by the finding that African Americans scored lower than whites on IQ tests. Those who supported Head Start attributed this difference to the poorer socioeconomic conditions in which African American children were more likely to be reared.

But in 1969 an article by psychologist Arthur Jensen questioned whether programs such as Head Start could significantly boost the intellectual level of deprived children. Jensen's doubts were based on the notion of **heritability,** the extent to which the variability in a characteristic within a group can be attributed to heredity. Jensen claimed that intelligence has a heritability of .80, which would mean that 80 percent of the variability in intelligence among the members of a group can be explained by heredity. This led him to conclude that the IQ gap between white and African American children was mainly attributable to heredity. But he was accused of making an unwarranted inference. Just because intelligence might have high heritability *within* a group does not mean that IQ differences *between* groups, such as African Americans and white Americans, are caused by heredity. Moreover, research has found that the heritability of intelligence is closer to .50 than to .80 (Casto, DeFries, & Fulker, 1995). Jensen's article led to accusations that he was a racist and to demonstrations against him when he spoke on college campuses, illustrating the tension between academic freedom and social sensitivity.

In the tradition of eugenics, one of Jensen's chief supporters, William Shockley (1972), urged that the federal government pay Americans with below-average IQ scores (who would be disproportionately African American) to undergo sterilization. He recommended paying them $1,000 for each point by which their IQ scores were less than 100. Though Shockley was not a psychologist or even a social scientist, he gained media attention because he had won a 1956 Nobel Prize for inventing the transistor. Shockley and several other Nobel Prize winners even deposited their sperm in a "sperm bank" in California for use by women of superior intelligence who wish to produce highly intelligent offspring ("Superkids?" 1980).

A vigorous response to those who claimed that intelligence is chiefly the product of heredity came from Leon Kamin (1974). Kamin discovered that important data supporting the hereditary basis of intelligence had been falsified. Cyril Burt (1883–1971), a

heritability
The extent to which variability in a characteristic within a group can be attributed to heredity.

(a)

(b)

British psychologist, had reported findings from three studies showing that the positive correlation in IQ scores between identical twins reared apart was higher than the correlation in IQ of fraternal twins reared together. Because identical twins reared apart have the same genes but different environments, yet had a higher correlation in intelligence than did fraternal twins reared together, the data supported the greater influence of heredity on intelligence.

In each of his studies, published in 1943, 1955, and 1966, Burt reported that the correlation in intelligence between identical twins reared apart was .771. But, as Kamin observed, the odds against finding the same correlation to three decimal places in three different studies are so high as to defy belief. Burt's findings were literally too good to be true. Even Burt's official biographer, who began as an admirer and who believed that Burt had not falsified his data, grudgingly concluded that the data were indeed fraudulent (Hearnshaw, 1979). This has not prevented others from coming to Burt's defense, trying to explain away his apparent falsification of data as merely the product of careless data recording (Samelson, 1992). Whatever the explanation, his data are not trustworthy and have no scientific merit (Tucker, 1994). Ironically, less than a decade after Kamin's critique of Burt's research, the Minnesota Study of Twins Reared Apart found that identical twins reared apart had a correlation of .710 in their intelligence—not very different from what Burt had reported (Lykken, 1982).

COMMON GENES VERSUS COMMON EXPERIENCES: FAMILY STUDIES OF INTELLIGENCE

Though the publicity generated by the discovery of Burt's deception struck a blow against the hereditary view of intelligence, other researchers have conducted legitimate family studies of intelligence. As shown in Figure 10.5, the closer the genetic relationship between relatives, the more similar they are in intelligence (Bouchard & McGue, 1981). But the closer the genetic relationship between relatives, the more likely they also are to share similar environments. Consequently, the size of the correlation in intelligence between relatives of varying degrees of genetic similarity is, by itself, inadequate to determine whether this similarity is caused primarily by hereditary factors or by environmental factors.

Perhaps the higher correlation in intelligence between identical twins reared together than between fraternal twins reared together might be attributable to the more-similar treatment received by identical twins. But research findings have provided strong evidence against this interpretation. When identical twins are mistakenly reared as fraternal twins, they become as similar in intelligence as identical twins who are reared as identical twins. Moreover, fraternal twins who are mistakenly reared as identical twins become no more similar in intelligence than do fraternal twins reared as fraternal twins (Scarr & Carter-Saltzman, 1979). These findings indicate that the similarity in intelligence between twins is determined more by their genetic similarity than by their environmental similarity.

CHAPTER 10

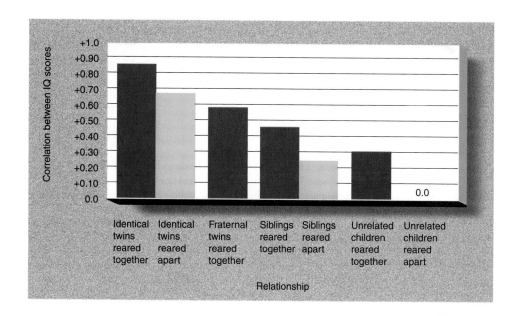

◀ FIGURE 10.5
Heredity Versus Environment
The correlation in IQ between relatives
increases as their hereditary or environmental
similarity increases.

To separate the effects of heredity and environment, researchers have turned to adoption studies. Some of these studies compare the correlation in intelligence between adopted children and their adoptive parents to the correlation in intelligence between adopted children and their biological parents. A published review of adoption studies found that the positive correlation in intelligence between adoptees and their biological parents is larger than the positive correlation between adoptees and their adoptive parents (Loehlin, Horn, & Willerman, 1994). This supports a genetic basis of intelligence; the genes inherited from the natural parents appear to exert a stronger influence on adoptees than does the environment provided by their adoptive parents (Bouchard & McGue, 1981).

Both the Colorado Adoption Project (Coon et al., 1990) and the Texas Adoption Project (Loehlin, Horn, & Willerman, 1994) have provided strong support for a hereditary component in intelligence. The influence of heredity on the variability in intelligence among children *increases* from infancy through childhood. For example, the Colorado Adoption Study has found that the heritability of intelligence is only .09 at age 1 but .36 at age 7 (Fulker, DeFries, & Plomin, 1988). This means that as children spend more years in their home environment, the environment—counter to what common sense would predict—*decreases* in its influence on the variability in intelligence.

In addition to their support for the influence of heredity on intelligence, adoption studies have provided support for the effect of the environment on intelligence. Consider the following study sponsored by the University of Minnesota.

ANATOMY OF A CONTEMPORARY RESEARCH STUDY

What Is the Effect of Adoption on the Intellectual Development of Adopted Children?

Rationale

If nature dominates nurture, then children from lower socioeconomic classes who are adopted by parents from higher socioeconomic classes should show little or no gain in IQ when compared to equivalent children who remain with their biological parents. This possibility was tested by Sandra Scarr and Richard Weinberg (1976) in the Minnesota Adoption Study.

Method

The study included African American children who had been adopted by white Minnesota couples of higher socioeconomic status than the children's biological parents.

Results and Discussion

The study found that the children who had been adopted had an average IQ of 110. This indicated that the environment had a strong effect on their intelligence, because the adoptees scored about 20 points higher than the average IQ of African American children of the same socioeconomic status reared by their biological parents. These findings indicate that nurture, as well as nature, is important in intellectual development, because children adopted into families of higher socioeconomic status have IQs that are higher than those of their biological parents, though lower than those of their adoptive parents (Weinberg, Scarr, & Waldman, 1992).

A study of adopted children in France found that these findings also held for white children. The subjects of the study were 32 white children who had been abandoned at birth by their lower-socioeconomic-class parents and adopted at an average age of 4 months by white professionals. When compared with their siblings who were reared by their biological parents, the adoptees scored an average of 14 points higher in intelligence and were less likely to be left back in school (Schiff et al., 1982).

A more recent study in France included 87 adolescents given up at birth and adopted before 3 years of age into different socioeconomic classes. The results showed a significant negative correlation of .37 between the social class of the adoptive families and the likelihood of repeating a grade in school. That is, as the socioeconomic class of the adoptive families increased, the likelihood of an adoptee's having to repeat a grade decreased. This supported the importance of the environment in determining intellectual performance (Duyme, 1988). Based on their review of adoption studies, Scarr and Weinberg (1983) concluded that intelligence is influenced by both heredity and environment, with neither dominating the other. But other researchers have found that adopted children reared in families of higher socioeconomic status than that of their biological families show a smaller enhancement in intelligence than had been reported in previous studies (Locurto, 1990).

▲ ▲ ▲

▲ Robert Zajonc

"The greater the number of children and the shorter the intervals between successive births, the less mature, on the average, is the intellectual milieu for each child."

confluence model

The view that each child is born into an intellectual environment that is dependent on the intelligence levels of her or his parents and siblings, with the number of children and the interval between births affecting the intelligence of each successive child.

An alternative source of support for the influence of the environment on intelligence comes from family configuration studies. A survey of 400,000 19-year-old men in the Netherlands found that the larger their families and the later they were in the birth order, the less intelligent they tended to be (Belmont & Marolla, 1973). This finding has been explained by Robert Zajonc's (1986) **confluence model,** which assumes that each child is born into an intellectual environment that depends on the intelligence level of his or her parents and siblings. The greater the number of children and the smaller the average interval between births, the lower will be what Zajonc calls the *average intellectual environment* into which a child is born. One of the reasons for this drop may be the inevitable reduction in the attention parents give to each of their children after the birth of another child (Gibbs, Teti, & Bond, 1987).

In a bold gesture, Zajonc (1976) used the confluence model to predict that the decline in SAT scores that had begun in 1963 would stop in 1980 and then begin to rise. Zajonc based his prediction on the fact that high school students who took the SAT between 1963 and 1980 had been born into increasingly larger families during the post–World War II baby boom. But after 1980, high school students who would take the SAT would come from smaller and smaller families. Zajonc's prediction was supported: SAT scores continued to decline until 1980 and then began to rise (see Figure 10.6). Of course, the decline could have a host of other explanations, including greater numbers of academically poor students taking the test (Astin & Garber, 1982).

Though Zajonc (1993) continues to present evidence supporting the confluence model, other researchers present evidence contradicting it (Barbut, 1993). For example, data from a study by the National Institutes of Health, which included 47,000 women and their 53,000 children, failed to find a relationship between the intelligence of the children and the average interval between the births in their families (Brackbill & Nichols, 1982). Moreover, the confluence model has demonstrated, at best, a *correlational*, rather than a *causal*, relationship between family configuration and intelligence. That is, even if the relationship is real, perhaps other unidentified factors account for it (Rodgers, 1988).

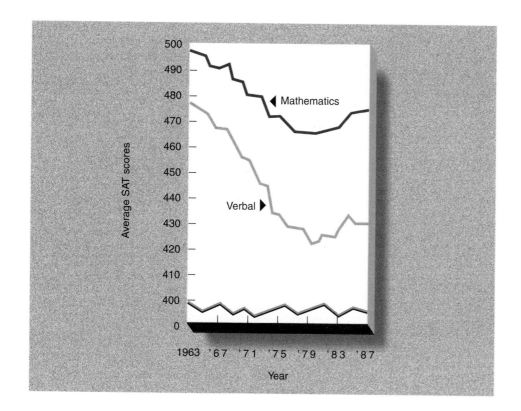

ENHANCING INTELLIGENCE:
INTELLECTUAL ENRICHMENT PROGRAMS

Further support for the influence of the environment on intelligence comes from the finding that the difference between white and African American performance on the SAT narrowed between 1976 and 1983 (Jones, 1984). Moreover, the difference between African American and white children in IQ test scores is declining, possibly because more African American children have gained access to better educational and economic resources (Vincent, 1991). Access to enrichment programs such as Project Head Start might also play a role. Socioeconomically deprived children who attend Project Head Start show an average gain of 10 points in their IQ scores (Zigler et al., 1982) and greater improvement in their cognitive abilities, compared to those not in such programs. This contradicts Jensen's (1969) prediction that Head Start would have no significant effect on intellectual growth. Unfortunately, the gains achieved by children in preschool enrichment programs often decline during grade school (Locurto, 1991), perhaps in part because these children typically attend inferior schools (Lee & Loeb, 1995). This indicates the need to continue enrichment programs beyond the preschool years.

Preschool enrichment programs other than Head Start can also have beneficial effects, as shown in a study of disadvantaged African American children who attended Head Start, other preschool, or no preschool programs. Those in the Head Start and preschool programs showed greater improvement in several intellectual abilities than did those who did not attend either kind of program. This could not be attributed to initial differences in intellectual abilities, because the children were statistically matched on various relevant characteristics (Lee et al., 1990).

Other countries have also found that intellectual enrichment programs can be beneficial. Possibly the most ambitious of all enrichment programs took place from 1979 to 1983 in Venezuela, under its minister of state for the development of intelligence (Gonzalez, 1989). The program provided good prenatal care and infant nutrition, as well as sensory stimulation of preschoolers and special training in cognitive skills. New mothers watched videocassettes on proper child rearing while in their hospital rooms, schoolchildren

attended "learning to think" classes, and television commercials promoted the need to
develop the minds of Venezuelan children (Walsh, 1981). The more than 400 Venezuelan
seventh-graders who participated in a program to teach thinking skills (such as reasoning,
problem solving, and decision making) achieved better academic performance than comparable control students who had not participated (Herrnstein et al., 1986).

Even more evidence of the influence of the environment on intelligence comes from
the finding that IQ scores have increased from 5 to 25 points in fourteen nations during
the past 30 years, apparently because of better nutrition, education, and health care
(Flynn, 1987). And both Galton and Goddard would be surprised to find that today the
Japanese, whom they considered intellectually inferior, score significantly higher than
Americans on IQ tests that have been standardized on Americans. Japanese children score
about 10 points higher than American children (Lynn, 1982). The Japanese increase in
IQ scores parallels that country's increased emphasis on education, with children going to
school more hours, attending school more days, and studying more hours than American
children do. It is difficult to attribute this increase in IQ scores to accelerated evolution of
Japanese brains.

Even the academic achievements of Asian Americans surpass those of white
Americans and African Americans. What might account for this? Stanley Sue, a
cross-cultural psychologist, insists that it is wrong to attribute these achievements to
either an inborn intellectual superiority or a culture that places a high value on education.
Instead, Sue looks to simple adaptive behavior. According to Sue, because Asian
Americans have had cultural and discriminatory barriers to their upward mobility in
careers that place less emphasis on education (such as sports, politics, entertainment, and
corporate leadership), they have sought to pursue careers that provide fewer barriers.
These more accessible alternatives (such as science, mathematics, and engineering) typically place a premium on academic excellence (Sue & Okazaki, 1990). Sue's hypothesis
has not yet been adequately tested.

Some psychologists have suggested that it might not be in our best interest to study the
relative importance of nature and nurture in intellectual development (Sarason, 1984). To
do so might discover little of scientific import, while providing apparent scientific support
for discrimination against racial or ethnic minorities. Instead of examining the relative
importance of nature versus nurture, it might be better to do what Anne Anastasi (1958),
an authority on psychological testing, suggested more than three decades ago: determine

how both achieve their effects (Turkheimer, 1991). The current trend to view intelligence as comprising a variety of abilities and as being improvable by proper education and optimal child rearing might change the focus of some researchers; instead of trying to determine whether particular groups are naturally more intelligent than other groups, they might attempt to discover ways of helping all people approach their intellectual potential.

STAYING ON TRACK: *Does Intelligence Depend More on Nature or on Nurture?*

1. What have adoption studies (especially studies of identical twins reared apart) discovered about the role of nature and nurture in intelligence?

2. What evidence is there supporting and contradicting the confluence model of intelligence?

 # CHAPTER SUMMARY

INTELLIGENCE TESTING

Intelligence is the global capacity to act purposefully, to think rationally, and to deal effectively with the environment. An achievement test assesses knowledge of a particular subject; an aptitude test predicts the potential to benefit from instruction in a particular academic or vocational setting; and an intelligence test is a kind of aptitude test that assesses overall mental ability.

Francis Galton began the study of mental abilities in the late nineteenth century and founded the field of differential psychology. The first formal test of general intelligence was the Binet-Simon scale, which was developed to help place children in school classes. The American version of the test became known as the Stanford-Binet Intelligence Scale. Today that test and the Wechsler Intelligence Scales are the most popular intelligence tests.

Tests must be standardized so that they are administered in a uniform manner and so that test scores can be compared with norms. A test must also be reliable, giving consistent results over time. And a test must be valid, meaning that it measures what it is supposed to measure.

Controversy has arisen over whether intelligence testing is fair to minority groups, particularly African Americans. Those who oppose intelligence testing claim that because African Americans, on the average, score lower on them than whites do, the tests are biased against them. Those who support their use claim that the tests accurately predict the academic performance of both African Americans and whites, and typically attribute the differences in performance to the deprived backgrounds that are more common among African American children. Attempts to develop tests that are not affected by the test taker's cultural background have failed.

EXTREMES OF INTELLIGENCE

To be classified as mentally retarded, a person must have an IQ below 70 and, beginning in childhood, difficulties performing in everyday life. The four categories of mental retardation are mild retardation, moderate retardation, severe retardation, and profound retardation. Though most cases of mental retardation are caused by cultural-familial factors, some are caused by brain damage. Most people with mental retardation can benefit from education and training programs.

To be classified as mentally gifted, a person must have an IQ above 130 and demonstrate unusual ability in at least one area, such as art, music, or mathematics. Lewis Terman's Genetic Studies of Genius have demon-strated that mentally gifted children tend to become successful in their academic, social, physical, and vocational lives. Benbow and Stanley's Study of Mathematically Precocious Youth identifies children with outstanding mathematical ability, provides them with special programs, and counsels their parents about how to help them reach their potential.

THEORIES OF INTELLIGENCE

Theories of intelligence have traditionally depended on factor analysis, a statistical technique for determining the abilities that underlie intelligence. The theories differ in the extent to which they view intelligence as a general factor or a combination of different factors. The most recent factor-analytic theory distinguishes between fluid intelligence and crystallized intelligence.

Robert Sternberg's triarchic theory of intelligence is based on his research on information processing. The theory distinguishes between componential (academic) intelligence, experiential (creative) intelligence, and contextual (practical) intelligence. Sternberg also believes that people can be taught to process information more effectively, thereby increasing their level of intelligence.

Howard Gardner's theory of multiple intelligences is a biopsychological theory, which assumes that the brain has evolved separate systems for different adaptive abilities that he calls "intelligences": linguistic, logical-mathematical, spatial, musical, bodily-kinesthetic, intrapersonal, and interpersonal intelligences. All of us vary in the degree to which we have developed each of these kinds of intelligence.

THINKING ABOUT PSYCHOLOGY: DOES INTELLIGENCE DEPEND MORE ON NATURE OR ON NURTURE?

One of the most controversial issues in psychology has been the extent to which intelligence is a product of heredity or of environment. Early studies of immigrants concluded that many were "feebleminded." The examiners attributed this to hereditary factors rather than to a host of cultural and environmental factors that actually accounted for that finding. Arthur Jensen created a stir by claiming that heredity is a much more powerful determinant of intelligence than environment is. Studies of twins, adopted children, family configuration effects, and enrichment programs indicate that neither heredity nor environment is a significantly more important determinant of intelligence. Moreover, though intelligence might be highly heritable, there is no widely accepted evidence that differences in intelligence between particular racial or ethnic groups are caused by heredity.

KEY CONCEPTS

KEY CONTRIBUTORS

FOR MORE INFORMATION ON INTELLIGENCE

FOR GENERAL WORKS ON INTELLIGENCE

Irvine, S. H., & Berry, J. W. (Eds.). (1988). *Human abilities in cultural context.* New York: Cambridge University Press.

Scarr, S. (1984). Intelligence: What an introductory psychology student might want to know. In A. M. Rogers & C. J. Scheirer (Eds.), *The G. Stanley Hall Lecture Series* (Vol. 4, pp. 59–99). Washington, DC: American Psychological Association.

FOR MORE ON INTELLIGENCE TESTING

Chapman, P. D. (1988). *Schools as sorters: Lewis M. Terman, applied psychology, and the intelligence testing movement, 1890–1930.* New York: New York University Press.

Frank, G. (1983). *The Wechsler enterprise: An assessment of the development, structure and use of the Wechsler tests of intelligence.* New York: Pergamon.

Thorndike, R. M., & Lohman, D. F. (1990). *A century of ability testing.* Chicago: Riverside.

Zenderland, L. (1997). *Measuring minds: Henry Herbert Goddard and the origins of American intellignece testing.* New York: Cambridge University Press.

FOR MORE ON MENTAL RETARDATION

Beirne-Smith, M., Patton, J. R., & Ittenbach, R. (1994). *Mental retardation.* New York: Macmillan.

Dolce, L. (1994). *Mental retardation.* New York: Chelsea House.

Treffert, D. A. (1989). *Extraordinary people: Understanding "idiot savants."* New York: Harper & Row.

Trent, J. W. (1994). *Inventing the feebleminded: A history of mental retardation in the United States, 1840–1990.* Berkeley: University of California Press.

FOR MORE ON MENTAL GIFTEDNESS

Horowitz, F. D., & O'Brien, M. (Eds.). (1985). *The gifted and talented: Developmental perspectives.* Washington, DC: American Psychological Association.

Murray, P. (Ed.). (1989). *Genius: The history of an idea.* New York: Basil Blackwell.

Shurkin, J. N. (1992). *Terman's kids: The groundbreaking study of how the gifted grow up.* Boston: Little, Brown.

Wallace, A. (1986). *The prodigy.* New York: Dutton.

FOR MORE ON THEORIES OF INTELLIGENCE

Gardner, H. (1993). *Multiple intelligences: The theory in practice.* New York: Basic Books.

Spearman, C. (1923/1973). *The nature of "intelligence" and the principles of cognition.* New York: Arno.

Sternberg, R. J. (1984). *Beyond IQ: A triarchic theory of intelligence.* New York: Cambridge University Press.

Thurstone, L. L. (1924/1973). *The nature of intelligence.* Westport, CT: Greenwood.

FOR MORE ON NATURE VERSUS NURTURE

Galton, F. (1869/1972). *Hereditary genius: An inquiry into its laws and consequences.* Magnolia, MA: Peter Smith.

Gould, S. J. (1981). *The mismeasure of man.* New York: W. W. Norton.

Joynson, R. B. (1989). *The Burt affair.* New York: Routledge.

Sternberg, R. J., & Grigorenko, E. (Eds.). (1997). *Intelligence, heredity, and environment.* New York: Cambridge University Press.

Zigler, E., & Valentine, J. (Eds.). (1979). *Project Head Start: A legacy of the war on poverty.* New York: Free Press.

FOR MORE ON CONTRIBUTORS TO THE STUDY OF INTELLIGENCE

Anastasi, A. (1980). Anne Anastasi. In G. Lindzey (Ed.), *A history of psychology in autobiography* (Vol. 7, pp. 1–37). San Francisco: Freeman.

Fancher, R. E. (1985). *The intelligence men: Makers of the IQ controversy.* New York: W. W. Norton.

Forrest, D. W. (1974). *Francis Galton: The life and work of a Victorian genius.* New York: Taplinger.

Hearnshaw, L. S. (1979). *Cyril Burt: Psychologist.* Ithaca, NY: Cornell University Press.

Minton, H. L. (1988). *Lewis M. Terman: Pioneer in psychological testing.* New York: New York University Press.

Wolf, T. H. (1973). *Alfred Binet.* Chicago: University of Chicago Press.

CHAPTER 11

▲ ROMARE BEARDON
Saxaphone Solo, 1987

Motivation

motivation
The psychological processes that arouse, direct, and maintain behavior toward a goal.

instinct
A relatively complex, inherited behavior pattern characteristic of a species.

▲ **Motivation**
Why did Bill Irwin, a blind man, risk hiking the entire Appalachian Trail, which extends from Maine to Georgia? Psychologists rely on the concept of motivation to explain this and other behavior.

*I*n 1972, survivors of an airplane crash in a frigid, isolated region of the Andes mountains of Chile turned to cannibalism, eating the flesh of dead passengers to stay alive (Read, 1974). At the 1988 Olympic Games in Korea, left-handed pitcher Jim Abbott led the United States to a gold medal in baseball, even fielding well, despite being born without a right hand. Why would civilized people eat human flesh? Why would a one-handed person pursue a baseball career when even excellent two-handed athletes often fail?

To explain extraordinary behaviors such as these, as well as everyday behaviors, psychologists employ the concept of **motivation,** which refers to the psychological processes that arouse, direct, and maintain behavior toward a goal. The Andes survivors were motivated by hunger, which aroused them to find food, directed them to eat human flesh, and maintained their cannibalism until they were rescued. Jim Abbott was motivated by his need for achievement, which aroused him to excel as a pitcher, directed him to learn how to play baseball with one hand, and maintained his participation despite periodic failures.

Because we cannot directly observe people's motivation, we must infer it from their behavior. We might infer that a person who drinks a quart of water is motivated by a strong thirst and that a person who becomes dictator of a country is motivated by a strong need for power. The concept of motivation is also useful in explaining fluctuations in behavior over time (Atkinson, 1981). If yesterday morning you ate three stacks of pancakes but this morning you ate only a piece of toast, your friends would not attribute your change in behavior to a change in your personality. Instead, they would attribute it to a change in your degree of hunger—your motivation.

SOURCES OF MOTIVATION

What are the main sources of motivation? In seeking answers to this question, psychologists have implicated *genes*, *drives*, and *incentives*.

Genes: The Hereditary Factors That Motivate Behavior

In the early twentieth century, many psychologists, influenced by Charles Darwin's theory of evolution and led by William McDougall (1871–1938), attributed human and animal motivation to inherited *instincts*. An **instinct** is a complex, inherited (that is, unlearned) behavior pattern characteristic of a species. Instincts are at work when birds build nests, spiders weave webs, and salmon swim upstream to their spawning grounds. But what of human instincts? McDougall (1908) claimed that human beings are guided by a variety of instincts, including instincts for "pugnacity," "curiosity," and "gregariousness." As discussed in Chapter 13, McDougall's contemporary, Sigmund Freud, based his theory of personality on instincts that motivate sex and aggression. And William James (1890/1981) claimed that human beings are motivated by more instincts than any other animal.

In the 1920s, psychologists, influenced by behaviorist John B. Watson, rejected instincts as factors in human motivation. Watson believed that human behavior depended on learning, not heredity. One reason why instinct theorists lost scientific credibility was that they had attempted to explain almost all human behavior as instinctive, in some cases compiling lists of thousands of alleged human instincts (Cofer, 1985). You might say, for example, that people paint because of an "aesthetic instinct" or play sports because of a "competitive instinct."

A second reason why instinct theorists fell out of favor was their failure to *explain* the behaviors they labeled as instinctive. Consider the following hypothetical dialogue about an alleged "parenting instinct":

Why do parents take care of their children?

Because they have a parenting instinct.

But how do you know parents have a parenting instinct?

Because they take care of their children.

Such circular reasoning neither explains why parents take care of their children nor provides evidence of a parenting instinct. Each assertion is simply used to support the other.

Though instinct theory, as applied to human beings, has fallen into disfavor, some scientists believe that human social behavior does, in fact, have a genetic basis (Hoffman, 1995). The chief proponents of this belief work in the field of **sociobiology,** founded by Edward O. Wilson in the 1970s, which studies the hereditary basis of human and animal social behavior (Wilson, 1975). But sociobiology has been criticized for overestimating the role of heredity in human social behavior (Hood, 1995). Critics fear that acceptance of sociobiology would lend support to the status quo, making us less inclined to change what many people believe has been "ordained by God or nature," such as differences in the social status of men and women, blacks and whites, and rich and poor. Nonetheless, research on personality (see Chapter 13) and other topics lends support to some sociobiological notions.

Drives: The "Pushes" That Motivate Behavior

Following the decline of the instinct theory of human motivation, the **drive-reduction theory** of Clark Hull (1884–1952) dominated psychology in the 1940s and 1950s (Webster & Coleman, 1992). According to Hull (1943), a **need** caused by physiological deprivation, such as a lack of food or water, induces a state of tension called a **drive,** which motivates the individual to reduce it. The thirst drive motivates drinking, the hunger drive motivates eating, and the sex drive motivates sexual relations.

Drive reduction aims at the restoration of **homeostasis,** a steady state of physiological equilibrium. Consider your thirst drive. When your body loses water, as when you perspire, receptor cells in your *hypothalamus* (see Chapter 3) respond and make you feel thirsty. Thirst arouses you, signaling you that your body lacks water, and directs you to drink. By drinking, you reduce your thirst and restore homeostasis by restoring your body's normal water level. Undoubtedly we are motivated to reduce drives such as thirst, hunger, and sex, but drive reduction cannot explain all human motivation. In some cases we perform behaviors that do not reduce physiological drives, as in one-handed Jim Abbott's participation in baseball. His behavior shows that we are sometimes motivated by *incentives*.

▲ William McDougall (1871–1938)
"The human mind has certain innate or inherited tendencies which are the essential springs or motive powers of all thought and action."

sociobiology
The study of the hereditary basis of human and animal social behavior.

drive-reduction theory
The theory that behavior is motivated by the need to reduce drives such as sex or hunger.

need
A motivated state caused by physiological deprivation, such as a lack of food or water.

drive
A state of psychological tension induced by a need.

homeostasis
A steady state of physiological equilibrium.

▲ Edward O. Wilson
"The hypothalamus and the limbic system are engineered to perpetuate DNA."

incentive
An external stimulus that pulls an individual toward a goal.

hierarchy of needs
Abraham Maslow's arrangement of needs in the order of their motivational priority, ranging from physiological needs to the needs for self-actualization and transcendence.

▲ Clark Hull (1884–1952)
"The incentive is that substance or commodity in the environment which satisfies a need, that is, which reduces a drive."

Incentives: The "Pulls" That Motivate Behavior

Whereas a drive is an internal state of tension that "pushes" you toward a goal, an **incentive** is an external stimulus that "pulls" you toward a goal. Through experience, we learn that certain stimuli (such as a puppy) are desirable and should be approached, making them *positive* incentives. We also learn that other stimuli (such as elevator music) are undesirable and should be avoided, making them *negative* incentives. Thus, we are pulled toward positive incentives and away from negative ones. Incentives are often used by teachers and employers to motivate students (Kastner et al., 1995) and workers (Loeser et al., 1995).

Incentives are often associated with drives. For example, your thirst drive motivates you to replenish your body's water, but incentives determine what you choose to drink. You could satisfy your thirst by drinking, say, water, lemonade, apple juice, or cherry soda. Your thirst would push you to drink, but your favorite flavor would pull you toward a particular beverage. As with all incentives, your favorite flavor would partly depend on learning, which in this case would depend on your past experience with a variety of flavors. In the case of the Andes survivors, a strong hunger drive made them respond to a weak incentive, human flesh. The opposite can occur in your everyday life. Despite not feeling hungry, you might be motivated to eat in response to a strong incentive, such as an ice cream sundae.

Maslow's Hierarchy of Needs: Some Motives Have Priority over Others

If forced to make a choice, would you prefer enough food to eat or straight A's in school? Would you prefer to have a home or close friends? In each case, though both options are appealing, you would probably choose the first; this shows that some motives have priority over others. The fact that we have such preferences led the humanistic psychologist Abraham Maslow (1970) to develop a **hierarchy of needs** (see Figure 11.1), which ranks important needs by their priority. Maslow used the term *need* to refer to both physiological and psychological motives. According to Maslow you must first satisfy your basic *physiological* needs, such as your needs for food and water, before you will be motivated to meet your higher needs for *safety* and *security,* and so on up the hierarchy from the need for *belongingness and love,* through the need for *esteem,* and ultimately to the needs for *self-actualization* (achievement of all your potentials) and *transcendence* (spiritual fulfillment).

Maslow believed that because few people satisfy all their lower needs, few reach the two highest levels. Nonetheless, success in meeting lower-level needs in the hierarchy is positively correlated with psychological well-being (Lester, 1990). Though Maslow died before conducting much research on people who had reached transcendence, he did study the lives of people he considered self-actualized, including Abraham Lincoln and Eleanor Roosevelt. The characteristics of self-actualized people are listed in Chapter 13. Though research has supported the existence of the needs included in Maslow's hierarchy, it has shown that we do not always place a higher priority on lower-level needs (Goebel & Brown, 1981). For example, martyrs such as Mahatma Gandhi will starve themselves for the sake of others. Now consider the biological motives of *hunger, sex,* and *arousal,* and the social motive of *achievement.*

STAYING ON TRACK: *Sources of Motivation*

1. Why do some scientists criticize sociobiological explanations of human behavioral differences?
2. What are the different levels in Maslow's hierarchy of needs?

Answers to Staying on Track start on p. S-5.

THE HUNGER MOTIVE

The *hunger* motive impels you to eat to satisfy your body's need for nutrients. If you have just eaten, food might be the last thing on your mind. But if you have not eaten for a few days—or even for a few hours—food might be the *only* thing on your mind.

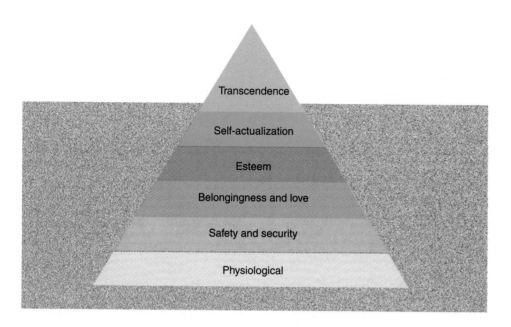

◀ FIGURE 11.1
Maslow's Hierarchy of Needs
Abraham Maslow assumed that our needs are arranged in a hierarchy, with our most powerful needs at the bottom. We will be weakly motivated by higher needs until our lower needs are met.

Factors That Regulate Hunger

What accounts for the waxing and waning of hunger? Hunger is regulated by factors in the body, the brain, and the environment.

Bodily Factors That Regulate Hunger

The main bodily mechanisms that regulate hunger involve the mouth, the stomach, the small intestine, the liver, and the pancreas. Taste receptors in the mouth play a role in hunger by sending taste sensations to the brain, informing it of the nutrient content of the food being tasted (M. G. Miller, 1984). Your brain favors the tastes of foods that contain nutrients you may lack. If you lack protein, you may find yourself craving a steak. If you lack sugar, you may find yourself craving starchy foods such as bread.

Though sensations from your mouth affect hunger, they are not its sole source. The stomach also plays a role in hunger. In 1912, physiologist Walter Cannon had his assistant Arthur Washburn swallow a balloon, which inflated in his stomach (see Figure 11.2). The balloon was connected by a tube to a device that recorded stomach contractions by measuring changes they caused in the air pressure inside the balloon. Whenever Washburn felt a hunger pang, he pressed a key, producing a mark next to the recording of his stomach contractions. The recordings revealed that Washburn's hunger pangs were associated with stomach contractions, prompting Cannon and Washburn (1912) to conclude that stomach contractions cause hunger.

Might they have interpreted their findings another way? Perhaps the opposite was true; Washburn's hunger might have caused the stomach contractions. Or, given that we now know that stomach contractions occur when the stomach contains food, perhaps the balloon itself caused Washburn's stomach contractions, which he misinterpreted as a sign of hunger. Moreover, later research revealed that hunger sensations are not entirely dependent on the stomach; even people whose stomachs have been removed because of cancer or severe ulcers can experience hunger (Ingelfinger, 1944).

Though the stomach is not necessary for the regulation of hunger, it normally plays an important role. Receptor cells in the stomach detect the amount of food it contains. After gorging yourself on a Thanksgiving dinner, you might become all too aware of the stretch receptors in your stomach that respond to the presence of food (Stricker & McCann, 1985). These receptors inform the brain of the amount of food in the stomach by sending neural impulses along the *vagus nerve* to the brain, reducing your level of hunger.

Food stored in the stomach eventually reaches the small intestine, the main site of digestion, where it stimulates the secretion of the hormone *cholecystokinin*, which in turn stimulates the vagus nerve to send neural impulses to the brain, reducing your level of

Cannon's Study of Hunger Pangs
Walter Cannon studied the relationship between stomach contractions and hunger pangs by using the device shown in this drawing. The subject pressed a key whenever he felt a hunger pang. A rotating drum recorded both the hunger pangs and the stomach contractions (Cannon & Washburn, 1912).

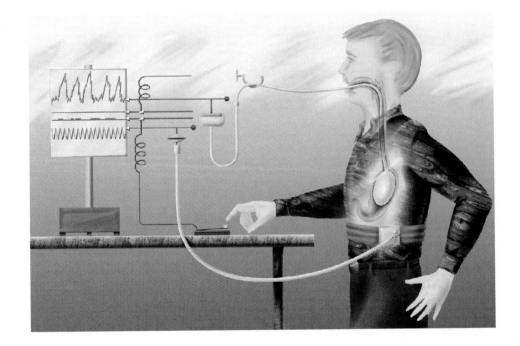

hunger (Gosnell & Hsiao, 1984). In a double-blind study, adult males received daily oral doses of either a placebo or a drug that blocks the effects of cholecystokinin on intestinal receptors. Subjects who received the drug reported greater hunger than did subjects who received the placebo, providing evidence that cholecystokinin does, indeed, reduce hunger (Wolkowitz et al., 1990).

Of special importance in the regulation of hunger is the hormone *insulin*, which is secreted by the pancreas. Insulin helps blood sugar enter body cells for use in metabolism, promotes the storage of fat, and induces feelings of hunger. In fact, hunger depends more on increased levels of insulin than on decreased levels of blood sugar. We know this from studies in which the level of blood sugar has been held constant by a continuous infusion of glucose while insulin levels are permitted to rise. Subjects in those studies reported increased levels of hunger (Rodin, 1985).

Brain Factors That Regulate Hunger

Signals from the body regulate hunger by their effects on the brain. In 1902 Viennese physician Alfred Frohlich reported that patients with tumors of the pituitary gland (see Chapter 3) often became obese. Frohlich concluded that the pituitary gland regulates hunger. But later research found that, in reality, the tumors influenced hunger by affecting the *hypothalamus*, which lies just above the pituitary gland (see Figure 11.3). The neurotransmitter norepinephrine promotes eating by stimulating receptors in the hypothalamus (Towell, Muscat, & Willner, 1989).

Two areas of the hypothalamus are especially important in the regulation of hunger. Electrical stimulation of the *ventromedial hypothalamus (VMH)*, an area at the lower middle of the hypothalamus, inhibits eating, and its destruction induces eating. In the 1940s, researchers demonstrated that rats whose VMH had been destroyed would eat until they became grossly obese and would then eat enough to maintain their new, higher level of weight (Hetherington & Ranson, 1942).

While the VMH has been implicated in reducing hunger, the *lateral hypothalamus (LH)*, comprising areas on both sides of the hypothalamus, has been implicated in increasing it. Research findings indicate that one way in which cholecystokinin inhibits hunger is by enhancing neuronal activity in the LH and suppressing it in the VMH (Shiraishi, 1990). Electrical stimulation of the LH promotes eating, while its destruction inhibits eating. Rats whose LH has been destroyed will stop eating and starve to death even in the presence of food. Only force-feeding will keep them alive long enough for

▲ **Insulin and Hunger**
The mere sight of rich, delicious food can stimulate your pancreas to secrete insulin, making you more hungry and, as a consequence, more likely to eat the food.

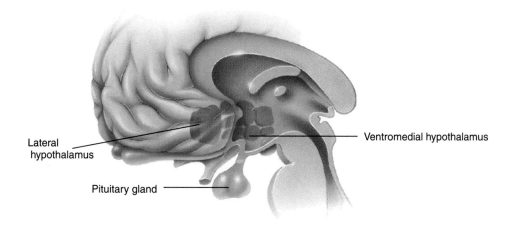

The Hypothalamus and Hunger
The lateral hypothalamus and ventromedial hypothalamus play important roles in regulating hunger.

them to recover their appetite (Anand & Brobeck, 1951). Though early experiments led to the conclusion that the LH acts as our "hunger center" and the VMH acts as our "satiety center," later experiments have shown that these sites are merely important components in the brain's complex system for regulating hunger and eating (Stricker & Verbalis, 1987). There is no simple "on/off" switch for eating.

But how does damage to the hypothalamus affect hunger? It does so in part by altering the body's **set point**—that is, its normal weight. Damage to the LH lowers the set point, reducing hunger and making the animal eat less to maintain a lower body weight. In contrast, damage to the VMH raises the set point, increasing hunger and making the animal eat more to maintain a higher body weight (Keesey & Powley, 1986). While signals from the body regulate changes in hunger from meal to meal, the set point regulates changes in hunger over months or years.

Environmental Factors That Regulate Hunger

Hunger, especially in human beings, is regulated by external, as well as internal, factors. Food can act as an incentive to make you feel hungry. The taste, smell, sight, sound, and texture of food can pull you toward it. Have you ever been watching television, with no appreciable feeling of hunger, only to become hungry after viewing a commercial showing an enticing array of fast-food donuts? But how can the mere sight of food induce feelings of hunger? One way is by increasing the level of insulin in your blood. In fact, even daydreaming about food can stimulate your pancreas to release insulin, making you hungry and possibly sending you on a hunt for cake, candy, or ice cream (Rodin, 1985).

Obesity: The Problem of Being Overweight

Obesity is defined as a body weight more than 20 percent above the norm for one's height and build. Chapter 16 describes the effects of obesity on health and the approaches used to help obese people lose weight. Given the many factors that regulate hunger and eating, why do some people become obese? An important factor in obesity is the body's set point, which reflects the amount of fat stored in the body. Though fat cells can increase in number and can increase or decrease in size, they cannot decrease in number. Once you have fat cells, they are yours forever. This means that obese people can lose weight only by shrinking the size of their fat cells. Because this induces constant hunger, it is difficult to maintain weight loss for an extended period of time (Kolata, 1985).

Another important factor in obesity is the **basal metabolic rate,** the rate at which the body burns calories just to keep itself alive. The basal metabolic rate typically accounts for 65 to 75 percent of the calories that your body ingests (Shah & Jeffery, 1991). This might explain why one of your friends can habitually ingest a milkshake, two hamburgers, and a

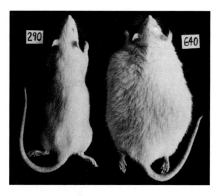

▲ The VMH Rat
Destruction of the ventromedial hypothalamus induces overeating and gross obesity. A rat whose ventromedial hypothalamus has been destroyed may eat until it becomes three times its normal weight.

set point
A specific body weight that the brain tries to maintain through the regulation of diet, activity, and metabolism.

obesity
A body weight more than 20 percent above the norm for one's height and build.

basal metabolic rate
The rate at which the body burns calories just to keep itself alive.

Heredity and Obesity
Data from Danish adoption records indicate that there is a positive relationship between the weight of adopted children and that of their biological parents, but no relationship between the weight of adopted children and that of their adoptive parents. The graph illustrates the relationship between adoptees and their biological and adoptive mothers. The relationship also holds true for adoptees and their biological and adoptive fathers (Stunkard et al., 1986).

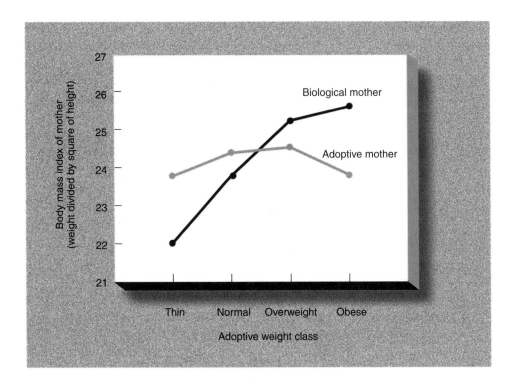

large order of french fries, yet remain thin, while another gains weight by habitually ingesting a diet cola, a hamburger without a bun, and a few french fries. Your first friend might have a basal metabolic rate high enough to burn a large number of calories; your second friend might have a basal metabolic rate too low to burn even a modest number of calories, which forces the body to store much of the ingested food as fat. One way that aerobic exercise promotes weight loss is by elevating the basal metabolic rate (Davis et al., 1992).

Your body alters its basal metabolic rate to defend its set point, increasing the rate if you eat too much and decreasing the rate if you eat too little. But what determines the set point? Thinness (associated with a low set point) and obesity (associated with a high set point) run in families; research findings support a genetic basis for this tendency (Castro, 1993). The role of heredity in obesity has been supported by studies of identical twins. Identical twins who have been reared together show a correlation of .75 in their amount of body fat. Even when identical twins have been reared apart, they show only a slightly lower correlation in their amount of body fat (Price & Gottesman, 1991). Evidence that heredity helps determine the set point was also provided by archival research on Danish adoption records. The results (see Figure 11.4) revealed a strong positive correlation between the weights of adoptees and the weights of their biological parents, but little relationship between the weights of adoptees and those of their adoptive parents. This indicates that heredity plays a more important role in obesity than do habits learned from the family in which one is reared (Stunkard, Stinnett, & Smoller, 1986).

The set point also seems to be affected by early nutrition, as shown by the results of an archival study of 300,000 men who, years earlier, had been exposed to a famine in Holland during World War II. The famine followed a German embargo on food entering Holland as punishment for Dutch resistance to Nazi occupation. Men who had been exposed to the famine during a critical period of development, which encompassed the third trimester of gestation and the first month after birth, were less likely to become obese than were men who had been exposed to the famine at other times during their early development (Ravelli, Stein, & Susser, 1976). The men exposed to the famine during the critical period might have developed lower set points than the other men. Even the results of the study of weight in Danish adoptees (Stunkard, Stinnett, & Smoller, 1986) might be explained by prenatal nutrition rather than by heredity. Perhaps adopted offspring are more similar in body weight to their biological mothers, not because they share their genes, but because they spent their prenatal period in their wombs, where they were subject to environmental influences, such as nutrients provided by their mothers. These prenatal influences might affect their later body weight (Bonds & Crosby, 1986).

Some researchers have also linked obesity to differences in responsiveness to external food cues. Because a series of studies in the 1960s indicated that obese people feel hungrier and eat more in the presence of external food cues, Stanley Schachter (1971) concluded that obese people are more responsive to those cues. Subsequent studies have provided some support for this belief. In one study, which used naturalistic observation, researchers observed people eating in a diner. When a waitress provided an appetizing description of a dessert, obese people were more likely to order it than when she did not. Nonobese people were unaffected by her description of the dessert (Herman, Olmsted, & Polivy, 1983).

Though studies like these support the belief that obese people are more responsive to food cues, the "externality" of obese people does not seem to *cause* their obesity. Instead, their obesity might cause their externality. How? Many obese people are constantly dieting, so they might be in a chronic state of hunger, making them more responsive to food cues. Moreover, obesity researcher Judith Rodin (1981) has found that obese people may have chronically high levels of insulin, making them hungrier and, as a result, more responsive to food cues. This gives the false impression that obese people become obese because they are more external than nonobese people.

Another external factor—stressful situations—can induce hunger and overeating (Greeno & Wing, 1994). You may have suspected this when observing the voracious appetites that some students exhibit during final-exams week. Stressful conditions can induce negative emotions such as anger, boredom, depression, and loneliness, and obese people are more likely than nonobese people to overeat when under stress (Ganley, 1989). But how does stress induce overeating? One possibility is that stress stimulates the brain to secrete *endorphins*. As discussed in Chapters 3 and 5, endorphins are neurotransmitters that relieve pain. They also stimulate eating. In one study, pigs that were given doses of endorphins began to eat more. When the pigs were given naloxone, a drug that blocks the effect of endorphins, they ate less—even when they had been deprived of food (Baldwin, de la Riva, & Ebenezer, 1990). Because their levels increase when we are under stress, endorphins might contribute to stress-related overeating (Morley & Levine, 1980). Perhaps obese people eat more under stress than nonobese people do because stress induces greater increases in their endorphin levels.

Yet stress does not always provoke overeating. Sometimes it inhibits eating. A study of 95 adults who recorded their stress level and eating behavior for 12 weeks found that there was a negative correlation between the two: as stress increased, eating decreased. This was more pronounced in women than in men (Stone & Brownell, 1994). Thus, more research is needed to identify the conditions under which stress provokes overeating and the conditions under which it inhibits it.

Eating Disorders

Are you pleased with the appearance of your body? As revealed by the following study, your answer might depend, in part, on whether you are female or male. Your satisfaction with your body might also influence the likelihood that you will develop an eating disorder.

▲ Judith Rodin
"Almost any overweight person can lose weight; few can keep it off."

ANATOMY OF A CONTEMPORARY RESEARCH STUDY

How Satisfied Are Males and Females with Their Bodies?

Rationale

Some researchers believe that eating disorders, which are more common in females, can be promoted by distorted body images. This inspired researchers April Fallon and Paul Rozin (1985) to examine the issue empirically.

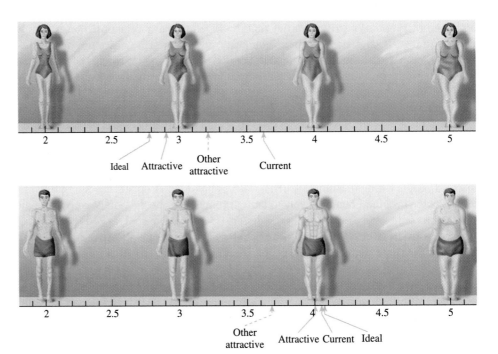

▶ **FIGURE 11.5**

Sex Differences in Body Images

Fallon and Rozin (1985) found that for men (lower illustration) their self-perceived physique ("Current"), the physique they believed was ideal ("Ideal"), and the physique they believed was most attractive to women ("Attractive"), were almost identical. The physique they believed women preferred ("Attractive") was heavier than the one women actually preferred ("Other Attractive"). In contrast, for women (upper illustration), their self-perceived physique ("Current") was heavier than the physique they believed was ideal ("Ideal") and the physique they believed was most attractive to men ("Attractive"). Moreover, the physique they believed men preferred ("Attractive") was thinner than the one men actually preferred ("Other Attractive").

anorexia nervosa

An eating disorder marked by self-starvation.

Method

College students were presented with a set of nine figure drawings that ranged from very thin to very heavy. The subjects were asked to indicate which figures were closest to their current physique, their ideal physique, and the physique they felt was most attractive to the other sex.

Results and Discussion

As shown in Figure 11.5, for men the current, the ideal, and the most attractive physiques were almost identical. For women, the current physique was heavier than the most attractive, and the most attractive was heavier than the ideal. The women also thought men liked women thinner than the men actually reported. Moreover, women tended to be less satisfied with their own physiques than men were with their own physiques.

A study that replicated the essence of these findings found that adolescent girls preferred to be thinner than the average for their age and were more dissatisfied with their own bodies than adolescent males were (Adams et al., 1993). This tendency to have a negative body image might put more pressure on women to lose weight. Perhaps this contributes to women's greater tendency to develop eating disorders marked by excessive concern with weight control, most notably *anorexia nervosa* and *bulimia nervosa*. In fact, people who disparage their own bodies for being fat, whether or not it is objectively true that they are fat, are more likely to develop eating disorders (Hsu & Sobkiewicz, 1991).

▲ ▲ ▲

The ideal that women should be thin permeates Western culture (Weiss, 1995). A study of magazines popular among young adults found that women's magazines contained 10.5 times more articles and advertisements promoting weight loss than did men's magazines (Andersen & DiDomenico, 1992). And a study of personal advertisements, which are used to find romantic partners, found that men tended to seek thin women and women tended to describe themselves as thin—indicating that women's thinness was an important criterion of attractiveness (Andersen et al., 1993). As Western culture exerts greater influence over other cultures, eating disorders among women have increased in those cultures—perhaps because they, too, have adopted the ideal of thinness for their women (Iancu et al., 1994).

Anorexia Nervosa: The Self-Starvation Syndrome

In 1983 the popular singer Karen Carpenter died of heart failure caused by starvation—despite having access to all the food she could want. She suffered from **anorexia nervosa,** a sometimes fatal disorder in which the victim is so desperate to lose weight that he or she goes on a starvation diet and becomes emaciated. As in the case of Karen Carpenter, people who die from anorexia nervosa usually succumb to cardiac disorders caused by electrolyte imbalances (Sharp & Freeman, 1993). People with anorexia nervosa view themselves as fat, even when they are objectively thin (as was Carpenter), and they are preoccupied with food—talking about it, cooking it, and urging others to eat it. Anorexia nervosa is more common in young women; perhaps 5 to 10 percent of cases occur in males (Frasciello & Willard, 1995). Females and males who participate in sports or activities (such as modeling, wrestling, or gymnastics) that stress weight control are more prone to develop eating disorders (O'Connor, Lewis, & Kirchner, 1995).

The causes of anorexia nervosa are unclear. Possible causes include a malfunctioning hypothalamus (Gold et al., 1980), excessive secretion of cholecystokinin (Philipp et al., 1991), a conflict concerning social maturation (Strober & Humphrey, 1987), and a reaction to the tendency to accumulate unwanted body fat during puberty (Attie & Brooks-Gunn, 1989). Anorexia nervosa is also associated with perfectionism (Bastiani et al., 1995) and excessive exercising, such as distance running (Davis et al., 1994).

In regard to conflict about social maturation, the victims' upbringing might provide them with high achievement standards, yet they might feel inadequate to meet the demands of puberty, college, or marriage. Some women victims even become physically childlike; they stop menstruating and lose their mature physiques. Treatment of severe anorexia nervosa commonly begins with the provision of nourishment through intravenous feeding or feeding through a nasogastric tube. Therapists then try to promote more adaptive ways of thinking about food and perceiving one's body (Fernandez et al., 1995).

▲ **Karen Carpenter**
Popular singer Karen Carpenter died from cardiac complications of anorexia nervosa.

Bulimia Nervosa: The Binge-Purge Syndrome

Persons with the related, more common, disorder called **bulimia nervosa,** go on repeated eating binges in which they might ingest thousands of calories at a time—they might eat a half gallon of ice cream, a two-pound box of chocolates, a loaf of French bread, and other high-carbohydrate foods—but they maintain normal weight by then ridding themselves of the food by self-induced vomiting. People with bulimia nervosa think obsessively about food but fear becoming obese. One reason is social disapproval. For example, adolescent girls who become bulimic report that they have been subjected to excessive teasing for being overweight (Thompson et al., 1995). As in the case of anorexia nervosa, most victims of bulimia nervosa are young women; about 10 to 15 percent of victims are males (Carlat & Camargo, 1991). The repeated bouts of vomiting can lead to medical problems, such as dehydration, tooth decay, or ulceration of the esophagus.

The causes of bulimia nervosa are unclear. There is evidence that people with bulimia nervosa have a genetic predisposition to develop the disorder (Hsu, Chester, & Santhouse, 1990). Bulimic people also secrete less cholecystokinin than normal eaters do, thereby reducing one of the main inhibitors of hunger (Brambilla et al., 1995). Another possible cause of bulimia nervosa is a low level of the neurotransmitter serotonin, which is associated with depression (Goldbloom & Garfinkel, 1990). Binge eating of carbohydrates might elevate mood, because certain carbohydrates increase serotonin levels in the brain. This hypothesis is supported by research showing that antidepressant drugs that increase serotonin levels are useful in treating bulimia nervosa. In one study, bulimic women were given fluoxetine (Prozac), an antidepressant that inhibits the re-uptake of serotonin by the neurons that secrete it. While on the drug, the subjects snacked less frequently and ate less at each meal. Moreover, the drug inhibited binge eating (Wilcox, 1990).

Factors other than brain chemistry also play a role in bulimia nervosa. People who pursue activities that emphasize weight control are more likely to develop the disorder. For example, males with bulimia nervosa are often dancers, jockeys, or collegiate wrestlers (Striegel-Moore, Silberstein, & Rodin, 1986). Victims of bulimia nervosa tend to be perfectionistic (Brouwers & Wiggum, 1993) and to come from families that fail to support social independence and emotional expression (Johnson & Flach, 1985). And victims of bulimia nervosa may be *restrained eaters,* people who are continually concerned with controlling their desire for food (Heatherton, Polivy, & Herman, 1990). Our culture has made

bulimia nervosa
An eating disorder marked by binging and purging.

restrained eating especially common among women, because constant dieting has become a normal eating pattern for many of them.

How does restrained eating explain bingeing? When restrained eaters eat a "taboo" food, such as ice cream, they might say to themselves, "I've blown my diet, so I might as well keep eating." In contrast, nonrestrained eaters do not share this all-or-nothing belief. They can ingest a rich food, such as a milkshake, without going on an eating binge (Weber, Klesges, & Klesges, 1988). Restrained eaters might also be less attuned to their internal hunger cues. In one study, restrained and unrestrained eaters were given a placebo that they were told was a vitamin pill. The subjects were told either nothing about how the "vitamin" would affect them or that it would make them feel hungry or full. The results indicated that restrained eaters followed the placebo message. They ate more when given the "hungry" instructions and less when given the "full" instructions. Unrestrained eaters did just the opposite, eating less ice cream under the "hungry" instructions and more under the "full" instructions. Perhaps restrained eaters are underresponsive to internal hunger cues and overresponsive to external hunger cues (Heatherton, Polivy, & Herman, 1989).

What is the treatment for bulimia? One approach has victims attend therapy sessions in which they receive cognitive-behavioral therapy and learn to eat without vomiting (Leitenberg, 1995). Group therapy and individual therapy are equally effective in treating bulimia; abstinence from bingeing and purging is achieved in about 40 percent of those who seek therapy (Cox & Merkel, 1989).

STAYING ON TRACK: *The Hunger Motive*

1. What is the role of the hypothalamus in eating?
2. What evidence is there for a hereditary basis of obesity?
3. What are some possible explanations for the greater incidence of eating disorders among females?

THE SEX MOTIVE

In a typical February, newsstands sell about 2 million copies of a special issue of *Sports Illustrated*, instead of the 100,000 copies they normally sell. The magazine isn't selling 20 times its normal number of copies because the special issue contains fascinating articles about celebrated athletes. The issue is popular because it contains photographs of beautiful women in skimpy bathing suits. This demonstrates both the power of the sex *drive* and the *incentive* value of sexual stimuli. Though some individuals, such as religious celibates, can live long lives without engaging in sexual intercourse, the survival of the species requires that many individuals engage in it. Had sexual intercourse not evolved into an extremely pleasurable behavior, we would have no inclination to seek it. But what factors account for the power of the sex motive?

Physiological Factors in Sexual Behavior

Important physiological factors in sexual motivation are sex hormones secreted by the **gonads,** the sex glands. The secretion of sex hormones is controlled by hormones secreted by the pituitary gland, which in turn is controlled by the hypothalamus. Sex hormones direct sexual development as well as sexual behavior (see Chapter 4).

Though hormones exert a direct effect on human sexual development, they are less influential motivators of sexual behavior in humans than they are in animals. Research indicates that testosterone motivates both male and female sexual behavior (though females secrete less of it than males do) and that estrogen contributes little to the sexual motivation of either females or males. Human males and females who for medical reasons have been castrated before puberty typically show a weak sex drive as adults. In contrast, castration after puberty typically produces only a slight reduction in the human sex drive (Feder, 1984).

gonads

The male and female sex glands—the testes and the ovaries.

Fetishism

A person with a *fetish* gains sexual gratification from inanimate objects such as shoes or panties. In an especially bizarre case, a man obtained brassieres by claiming to be an agent of the Environmental Protection Agency and convincing women to remove their brassieres so that he could administer a "breathing test" to determine whether a local atomic power plant had affected breathing capacities (Duke & Nowicki, 1986).

Transvestitism

A *transvestite* gains sexual gratification from dressing in opposite-sex clothing. Because women in American culture have greater freedom to wear male clothing, almost all transvestites are male. Some transvestites work as female impersonators.

Voyeurism

A *voyeur* gains sexual gratification primarily from watching people who are naked or engaged in sex. According to a popular legend, in A.D. 1057 Lady Godiva rode naked through Coventry, England. Her husband, the Lord of Coventry, had decreed that everyone stay indoors and keep their shutters closed. But Tom, the town tailor, peeked at her and was punished for his voyeuristic act, contributing the name *Peeping Tom* to our language.

Sadomasochism

A *sadomasochist* gains sexual pleasure from giving and receiving pain. In the eighteenth century, the Marquis de Sade, a French nobleman, described the sexual pleasure he obtained from brutalizing women. Thus, a *sadist* gains sexual gratification from inflicting humiliation and pain. In the nineteenth century, Leopold Sacher-Masoch, an Austrian author, wrote novels about men who experienced sexual pleasure from submitting to physical abuse by women. Thus, a *masochist* gains sexual gratification from being forced to submit to bondage, beatings, and humiliation.

▲ **TABLE 11.1**
Paraphilias

Psychological Factors in Sexual Behavior

Many sex researchers study psychological factors in human sexuality. Among the most important are social-cultural factors.

Social-Cultural Factors in Sexual Behavior

Sex hormones are the main motivators of animal sexual behavior, but human sexual behavior depends more on social-cultural factors. Because in most animals sexual motivation is rigidly controlled by hormones, members of a given species will vary little in their sexual behaviors. In contrast, because human sexual motivation is influenced more by social-cultural factors, we vary greatly in our sexual behavior. For example, breast caressing is a prelude to sexual intercourse among the Marquesan islanders of the Pacific but not among the Sirionian Indians of Bolivia (Klein, 1982). In extreme cases, some human beings engage in **paraphilias** (see Table 11.1), which are ways of obtaining sexual gratification that violate cultural norms about proper sexual practices (Levine, Risen, & Althof, 1990).

In Western cultures, acceptable sexual behavior has varied over time. The ancient Greeks viewed bisexuality as normal and masturbation as a desirable way for youth to relieve their sexual tensions. In contrast, most Americans and Europeans of the Victorian era in the nineteenth century believed that all sexual activity should be avoided except when aimed at procreation. The Victorian emphasis on sexual denial led John Harvey Kellogg to invent what he claimed was a nutritional "cure" for masturbation—cornflakes (Money, 1986).

The liberalization of attitudes toward sexual behavior in Western industrialized countries during the twentieth century was shown in 1983 when the *Journal of the American Medical Association* published an article on human sexuality. This would not be noteworthy except that the article had been submitted for publication in 1899, near the end of the Victorian era. The article, based on a paper presented by gynecologist Denslow Lewis (1899/1983) at the annual meeting of the American Medical Association, concerned female sexuality. Lewis described the female sexual response, the need for sex education, the importance of sex for marital compatibility, and techniques for overcoming sexual problems. Lewis even made the radical (for his time) suggestion that wives be encouraged to enjoy sex as much as their husbands did. At the time, the editor of the journal refused to publish the paper, which a prominent physician called "filth" and another editor feared would bring charges of sending obscene material through the mail (Hollender, 1983).

paraphilia

A way of obtaining sexual gratification that violates legal or cultural norms concerning proper sex objects and sexual practices.

▲ Alfred Kinsey (1894–1956)
"The present study was undertaken because the senior author's students were bringing him, as a college teacher of biology, questions on matters of sex. . . . They had found it more difficult to obtain strictly factual information which was not biased by moral, philosophic, or social interpretations."

sexual response cycle
During sexual activity, the phases of excitement, plateau, orgasm, and resolution.

Kinsey's Surveys of Human Sexual Behavior

Denslow Lewis's critics would have been even more upset by research in human sexuality that has taken place in the past few decades, beginning with the post–World War II research of Alfred Kinsey (1894–1956). Kinsey, a biologist at Indiana University, found that he was unable to answer his students' questions about human sexual behavior because of a lack of relevant information. This inspired him to conduct surveys to gather information on the sexual behavior of men (Kinsey, Pomeroy, & Martin, 1948) and women (Kinsey et al., 1953).

Kinsey and his colleagues obtained their data from interviews with thousands of men and women and published their findings in two best-selling books. The books (which contained statistics but no pictures) shocked the public, because Kinsey reported that masturbation, oral sex, premarital sex, extramarital sex, homosexuality, and other sexual behaviors were more prevalent than commonly believed. Among the many findings were that most of the men and almost half of the women engaged in premarital sexual intercourse and most of the women and almost all of the men masturbated.

Scientists warned that care should be taken in generalizing Kinsey's findings to all Americans, because his sample was not representative of the American population; the sample included primarily white, well-educated easterners and midwesterners who were willing to be interviewed about their sexual behavior. Moreover, what is true of people in one generation might not be true of those in another. For example, from the 1950s to the 1980s, premarital sex in the United States increased. Several factors might account for this (Beeghley & Sellers, 1986): Casual sex had been portrayed in a positive light in the media; more effective and more easily obtained forms of contraception made pregnancy less of a risk; modern medicine had reduced the fear of common venereal diseases, such as syphillis and gonorrhea; the "double standard" that prohibited females from being as sexually active as males had weakened; and laws and social norms had become less restrictive in regard to sexual relations between consenting persons. In the 1980s, however, premarital sexual activity with multiple partners tapered off, due to increased fears about incurable venereal diseases, including AIDS, which is fatal, and genital herpes, which is painful and can harm romantic relationships (Gerrard, 1987). The transmission and prevention of AIDS are discussed in Chapter 16.

Changes in sexual behavior since Kinsey's day indicate that sexual norms do, indeed, depend on the time period when they are studied. A recent survey of more than 400 heterosexual American college students found no significant sex differences in age of first intercourse, frequency of intercourse, and participation in oral sex. The study also found that women were more likely than in the past to adopt the traditional male role of initiating sexual activity (Lottes, 1993).

Despite the easing of the "double standard," recent surveys indicate that males and females continue to differ in their sexuality both behaviorally and emotionally. In regard to the decision to lose one's virginity, females place a greater premium on an intimate relationship than do males (Christopher & Cate, 1985). A survey of almost 2,000 men and almost 3,000 women found that males and females even differ in their sexual fantasies—males favoring fantasies of voyeurism and group sex, and females favoring fantasies of committed partners and romantic settings (Wilson, 1987). Males and females also differ in what they perceive as sexually provocative behavior. Males are more likely to perceive friendly behavior by females as sexually flirtatious (Saal, Johnson, & Weber, 1989).

Masters and Johnson's Research on the Human Sexual Response Cycle

The shocked response to Kinsey's surveys was mild compared to that generated in the 1960s by the research of William Masters and Virginia Johnson. Unlike Kinsey, Masters and Johnson were not content with just asking people about their sexual motivation and behavior. Instead, they studied ongoing sexual behavior and recorded physiological changes that accompanied it in hundreds of males and females. To study the female sexual response, they even invented a transparent plastic "penis" through which they could photograph vaginal changes during sexual arousal.

Based on their study of more than 10,000 orgasms experienced by more than 300 men and 300 women, Masters and Johnson (1966) identified four phases in the **sexual response cycle**

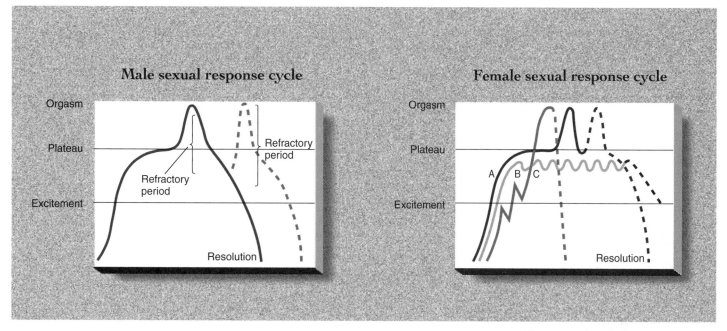

Male sexual response cycle

Orgasm
Plateau
Excitement

Refractory period
Refractory period
Resolution

Female sexual response cycle

Orgasm
Plateau
Excitement

A B C
Resolution

(see Figure 11.6): excitement, plateau, orgasm, and resolution. During the *excitement phase*, mental or physical stimulation causes sexual arousal. In males the penis becomes erect as it becomes engorged with blood. In females the nipples become erect, the vagina becomes lubricated, and the clitoris protrudes as it, too, becomes engorged with blood in response to both direct stimulation and vaginal stimulation (Lavoisier et al., 1995).

During the *plateau phase*, heart rate, blood pressure, muscle tension, and breathing rate increase. In males the erection becomes firmer and the testes are drawn closer to the body to prepare for ejaculation. Drops of seminal fluid, possibly containing sperm (and capable of causing pregnancy), may appear at the tip of the penis. In females the body flushes, lubrication increases, the clitoris retracts, and the breasts swell around the nipples (making the nipples seem to shrink).

The excitement and plateau phases compose the period of sexual foreplay. Males and females differ in the importance they assign to this. A survey of young adults found that women chose foreplay as more important than either intercourse or afterplay, while men chose intercourse as most important. Women also preferred to spend more time on foreplay and afterplay than did men. Women reported more than men did that they enjoyed the verbal and physical affection of sexual behavior (Denney, Field, & Quadagno, 1984).

During the *orgasm phase*, heart rate and breathing rate reach their peak, males ejaculate *semen* (a fluid containing sperm), and both males and females experience intensely pleasurable sensations induced by rhythmic muscle contractions. When females and males are asked to write subjective descriptions of their orgasms, readers cannot distinguish between male and female descriptions (Vance & Wagner, 1976). This indicates that female and male experiences during orgasm are similar. There is evidence that the pleasure induced by orgasm might be caused by the actions of endorphins in the brain (Agmo & Berenfeld, 1990).

Research on heterosexual intercourse shows that the timing of the orgasm is also important to sexual satisfaction. A survey of more than 700 women found that those who experienced orgasm after their partners had experienced it felt less sexually satisfied (Darling, Davidson, & Cox, 1991). This is especially problematic for many women because during sexual intercourse young adult males tend to reach orgasm in just 2 to 3 minutes (Levitt, 1983).

Following the orgasm phase, the person enters the *resolution phase*, as blood leaves the genitals and sexual arousal lessens. This is associated with a *refractory period*, lasting from minutes to hours, during which the person cannot achieve orgasm. For some women, however, continued sexual stimulation can induce multiple orgasms. A survey of 720 women found that 43 percent had experienced multiple orgasms (Darling, Davidson, & Jennings, 1991).

▲FIGURE 11.6
The Human Sexual Response Cycle
Masters and Johnson found that males and females have sexual response cycles comprising four phases: excitement, plateau, orgasm, and resolution. After reaching orgasm, males cannot achieve another orgasm until they have passed through a refractory period. In contrast, pattern A shows that females may experience more than one orgasm during a single cycle. Pattern B shows a cycle during which a female has reached the plateau stage without proceeding to orgasm. Pattern C shows a cycle during which a female has reached orgasm quickly. Males, too, may experience pattern B and pattern C.

▲ **Masters and Johnson**
"Aside from obvious anatomic variants, men and women are homogenous in their physiological responses to sexual stimuli."

Sexual Dysfunctions

After Masters and Johnson had identified the normal phases of the human sexual response cycle, they became interested in studying **sexual dysfunctions,** which are chronic problems at phases in the sexual response cycle. Marital happiness is associated with sexual satisfaction; and male sexual dysfunctions create more discord than do female dysfunctions (Rust, Golombok, & Collier, 1988). Couples with sexual dysfunctions are more likely to have unstable relationships, extramarital affairs, marital conflict, and lack of communication (McCabe, 1994).

Male Sexual Dysfunctions

Among the most common male sexual dysfunctions are erectile dysfunction, premature ejaculation, and retarded ejaculation. About 4 to 9 percent of males suffer from an *erectile dysfunction*—failing either to attain an erection or to maintain it through the arousal phase (Spector & Carey, 1990). A male who exhibits *premature ejaculation* will reach the orgasm phase too fast for his female partner to be sexually satisfied. About one third of all males experience premature ejaculation (Spector & Carey, 1990). Premature ejaculators reach orgasm at lower levels of sexual arousal and have longer periods of abstinence from intercourse (Spiess, Geer, & O'Donohue, 1984).

Female Sexual Dysfunctions

Among women, the most common sexual dysfunctions include orgasmic dysfunction, dyspareunia, and vaginismus. A woman experiencing *orgasmic dysfunction*, present in 5 to 10 percent of women (Spector & Carey, 1990), is unable to reach the orgasm phase. Women who are not orgasmic tend to have greater sexual guilt, difficulty discussing sexual activities that stimulate the clitoris, and more negative attitudes toward masturbation (Kelly, Strassberg, & Kircher, 1990). Women who suffer from *dyspareunia* experience pain during or after sexual intercourse (Meana & Binik, 1994). Those with *vaginismus* have difficulty engaging in sexual intercourse because of muscle spasms around the opening of the vagina (Ogden & Ward, 1995).

Sex Therapy: Treating Sexual Dysfunctions

Based on their research findings, Masters and Johnson (1970) concluded that the psychological causes of sexual dysfunctions are usually sexual guilt, sexual ignorance, or anxiety about sexual performance. A common factor in sexual dysfunction is focusing one's attention on how one is performing instead of on erotic feelings (Barlow, 1986). In treating sexual dysfunctions, Masters and Johnson first have their clients examined by a physician to rule out any physical causes, such as drugs, diabetes, or hormonal imbalances. For example, certain antidepressant drugs, such as Prozac, tend to inhibit sexual responsiveness (Bartlik et al., 1995). Masters and Johnson then counsel their clients to help them overcome their sexual guilt, educate them about sexual anatomy, sexual motivation, and sexual behavior, and teach them specific ways of reducing performance anxiety. Of course, none of these procedures is of much use unless the clients are sexually attracted to each other.

The main technique in Masters and Johnson's sex therapy is **sensate focusing,** in which the partners first participate in nongenital caressing, later proceed to genital stimulation, and finally engage in sexual intercourse. The partners are urged to concentrate on their pleasurable feelings instead of striving for erections and orgasms. They are also instructed to tell each other what kinds of stimulation they enjoy and what kinds they do not enjoy.

Masters and Johnson also teach their clients other techniques. In treating premature ejaculation, they might have the man's partner repeatedly stimulate his penis just to the point before orgasm to teach him to gain control over its timing. This is the treatment of choice in cases of premature ejaculation (St. Lawrence & Madakasira, 1992). They might have a woman with an orgasmic dysfunction practice masturbating to orgasm as a step toward reaching orgasm during sexual intercourse, a more difficult feat. Another technique to promote female orgasm during heterosexual intercourse is to teach the couple ways of

sexual dysfunction

A chronic problem at one or more phases of the sexual response cycle.

sensate focusing

A sex therapy technique that at first involves nongenital caressing and gradually progresses to sexual intercourse.

(a) (b)

aligning their bodies to maximize penile stimulation of the clitoris (Hurlbert & Apt, 1995). One study found that women who received therapy for orgasmic dysfunction went from having orgasms on 9.5 percent of the occasions before therapy to having orgasms on 36.9 percent of the occasions after therapy (Milan, Kilmann, & Boland, 1988).

Masters and Johnson (1970) reported that more than two thirds of their sex-therapy clients showed improvement. But they were criticized for not operationally defining what they meant by "improvement" and for failing to conduct follow-up studies of their clients to determine whether the positive effects of therapy were long-lasting. Masters and Johnson have also been criticized for stressing sexual intercourse as a physical act and for ignoring factors such as love and cultural differences in sexuality (Tiefer, 1994).

Nonetheless, studies of sex therapy by many other therapists have provided convincing evidence of its effectiveness (LoPiccolo & Stock, 1986). A follow-up study of 140 couples who had participated in sex therapy found that, when they were assessed 1 to 6 years after therapy, success was achieved with at least one partner in 75 percent of the cases. Though relapses were common, coping strategies learned in sex therapy helped many couples overcome their relapses (Hawton et al., 1986). A survey of 289 members of the American Association of Sex Educators, Counselors, and Therapists found that success rates were highest in treating premature ejaculation and orgasmic dysfunction. Erectile dysfunction had the lowest success rate (Kilmann et al., 1986).

During the past few decades, Masters and Johnson have also joined with other sex researchers in studying two other major topics in sexuality. These topics are **gender identity** (one's self-perceived sex) and **sexual orientation** (one's erotic interest in persons of one's own sex or of the other sex—or both).

Gender Identity: Do I Feel Like a Male or a Female?

In 1953 Christine Jorgensen shocked the world by announcing that "she" was a man who had undergone surgery and hormone treatments to look more like a woman. Though this procedure had been performed since the 1930s, Jorgensen's case was the first widely publicized instance of **transsexualism,** a *gender-identity disorder* in which a person who is physically a male or female feels psychologically like a member of the other sex. But the transsexual's gender identity does not necessarily indicate his or her sexual orientation (Dickey & Stephens, 1995). The extent to which heredity, hormonal imbalances, or

gender identity
A person's self-perceived sex.

sexual orientation
One's sexual attraction toward persons of either one's own sex or the opposite sex.

transsexualism
A condition in which a genetic male or female has the gender identity of the opposite sex.

(a)

(b)

(c)

(d)

▲ **Sexual Orientation**
Research indicates that your sexual orientation is the outcome of the interaction of biological, psychological, and social factors. While this interaction leads most persons to develop a heterosexual orientation, many persons—such as (a) author Willa Cather, (b) author Oscar Wilde, (c) tennis star Martina Navratilova, and (d) U.S. Representative Barney Frank—develop a homosexual orientation.

homosexuality
A consistent preference for sexual relations with persons of one's own sex.

childhood experiences contribute to transsexualism is unknown—but they all seem to play a role (Money, 1994). Transsexuals might undergo surgery to change the appearance of their sex organs. This is accompanied by hormonal treatments to eliminate physical characteristics of the original sex and to produce those of the other sex (Asscheman & Gorren, 1992). Transsexuals who choose to have surgery might also undergo voice training to adopt a voice quality more in keeping with their new sex (Gunzburger, 1995). Most transsexuals express satisfaction with the results of their sex-change surgery (Snaith, Tarsh, & Reid, 1993). Success depends to a great extent on how well the surgery creates genitals that resemble those of the other sex (Lundstrom, Pauly, & Walinder, 1984). As for sexual performance, the capacity to achieve orgasms tends to increase in female-to-male transsexuals and to decrease in male-to-female transsexuals (Lief & Hubschman, 1993).

Sexual Orientation: Am I Erotically Attracted to Males or Females?

Transsexualism should not be confused with **homosexuality,** a *sexual orientation* that is marked by a preference for sexual relations with persons of one's own sex. Male homosexuals are called *gays*, and female homosexuals are called *lesbians*, after the island of Lesbos, on which the Greek poet Sappho (ca. 620–ca. 565 B.C.) ran a school for women. Sappho killed herself after a student failed to return her love. *Bisexuals* have erotic feelings toward both sexes. A survey of a variety of cultures around the world found that homosexuality is more common than bisexuality (Diamond, 1993). Today, attitudes toward homosexuality and bisexuality vary both among and within cultures. In 1973, in keeping with evidence that homosexuality is not associated with any psychological disorders (Strickland, 1995) and the increasingly liberal attitudes toward homosexuality in the United States, the American Psychiatric Association voted to eliminate homosexuality from its list of mental disorders.

Given that our reproductive anatomy and cultural norms favor heterosexuality, why are an estimated 1 percent of women and 4 percent of men homosexual (Ellis & Ames, 1987)? Theories of homosexuality abound, and none has gained universal acceptance. Biopsychological theories of homosexuality implicate hereditary and physiological factors. Homosexuality runs in families, providing circumstantial evidence for the role of genetic factors. For example, lesbians are more likely than nonlesbians to have lesbians among their sisters, daughters, and nieces (Pattatucci & Hamer, 1995). Of course, it is impossible to determine, based on this evidence alone, whether this pattern is caused more by hereditary similarities or environmental similarities. Likewise, identical twins are more likely to both be homosexual than are fraternal twins, but, again, the extent to which this difference is due to shared genetic or shared environmental influences is unclear (Bailey et al., 1993).

Stronger support for the hereditary basis of homosexuality comes from research showing the following regarding identical twins (who have the same genes) who have been adopted as infants by different families: If one of the twins is homosexual, the other twin has a higher likelihood of also being homosexual than does a nontwin sibling reared together in the same family with a homosexual sibling (Eckert et al., 1986). And a recent study of 40 families in which there were two nontwin homosexual brothers indicated that 26 of the sibling pairs (64 percent) shared a genetic marker on the X chromosome, the sex chromosome inherited from their mother (Hamer et al., 1993). This has been countered by researchers who believe the evidence is not strong enough to connect homosexuality to a specific genetic factor (Risch, Squires-Wheeler, & Keats, 1993). For example, if homosexuality were completely genetically determined, then when one identical twin is homosexual, the other would always be homosexual.

Additional support for the physiological basis of homosexuality comes from research on prenatal hormonal influences—though some researchers warn against concluding that a correlation between prenatal hormonal exposure and later sexual orientation necessarily indicates a causal relationship between the two (Doell, 1995). Females exposed prenatally to excessively high levels of male sex hormones are more likely to become lesbians (Meyer-Bahlburg et al., 1995). Male homosexuality is associated with hormonal activity during a critical period between the second and the fifth month after conception that differs from that of heterosexuals. This might affect the development of the hypothalamus, which helps regulate sexual orientation, in a way that predisposes some males toward a homosexual orientation (Ellis & Ames, 1987).

A controversial study by neuroscientist Simon LeVay (1991) found that a part of the hypothalamus involved in sexual behavior is smaller in homosexual men than in heterosexual men and about the same size as in heterosexual women. The report was based on autopsies of the brains of 19 male homosexuals (all of whom had died of AIDS), 16 male heterosexuals (six of whom had died of AIDS), and six heterosexual women (one of whom had died of AIDS). Even when the brains of the homosexuals were compared to the brains of the heterosexual males who had died of AIDs, the structural difference remained. This made it unlikely that the difference was caused by the effects of AIDS on the hypothalamus. But there is still a possibility that, instead of differences in the hypothalamus causing differences in sexual orientation, differences in heterosexual and homosexual lifestyles cause differences in the hypothalamus.

But what of possible social factors that might account for sexual orientation? The traditional view favored the Freudian notion that male homosexuality is caused by a dominant, overly affectionate mother and an aloof, unemotional father. A survey of psychiatrists found that, though they favored biological theories of sexual orientation, this was their favorite psychological theory (Gallagher, McFalls, & Vreeland, 1993). Though some homosexuals have such backgrounds, others do not. In fact, there is no evidence that any particular pattern of childhood experiences alone causes a person to become a homosexual (Bell, Weinberg, & Hammersmith, 1981). Moreover, according to LeVay (himself a homosexual), it is just as logical to assume that fathers become aloof after noticing that their sons are acting "gay" as it is to assume that aloof fathers cause their sons to become "gay" (Gelman et al., 1992).

A clever theory of homosexuality holds that our sexual orientation, whether heterosexual or homosexual, depends on the sex of the children with whom we are socializing when our sex drive first emerges (Storms, 1981). Reports by homosexuals indicate that their sex drive typically emerges 2 to 3 years before that of heterosexuals, at a time when they are more likely to be socializing exclusively with same-sex peers. Because of this, they might attach their sexual feelings to those children. In contrast, the sex drive of most children emerges later, at a time when they are more likely to be socializing with members of both sexes. This makes them more likely to attach their sex drive to the other sex. Though this theory is provocative, it remains to be adequately tested.

Despite numerous studies on the origins of sexual orientation, none has identified any physiological or social factor that, by itself, explains why one person develops a heterosexual orientation and another develops a homosexual orientation. As suggested by Alfred

Kinsey 50 years ago, it might even be mistaken to view homosexuality and heterosexuality as mutually exclusive categories. This was the finding of a study in which homosexual men and heterosexual men rated their degree of homosexuality-heterosexuality and the size of their penile erections was measured while they watched brief movie clips of nude men and nude women. The men's self-ratings and penile responses showed a positive correlation. As you might expect, the more homosexual their rating, the greater their penile response to nude males; and the more heterosexual their rating, the greater their penile response to nude females. Yet both the homosexual men and the heterosexual men tended to respond at least somewhat both to nude males and nude females (McConaghy & Blaszcynski, 1991).

According to John Money (1987), a leading sex researcher, sexual orientation is affected by biological, psychological, and sociocultural factors, the relative influences of which vary. Money points, as an example, to the Sambia tribe of New Guinea, in which males between the ages of 9 and 19 are encouraged to follow a homosexual orientation to become more manly. At age 19 the males marry and switch to a heterosexual orientation. Thus, a complete explanation of human sexual orientation will probably have to include biological, psychological, and sociocultural factors (Friedman & Downey, 1993).

STAYING ON TRACK: *The Sex Motive*

1. Why were Kinsey's sex surveys controversial, and how has American sexual behavior changed since they were conducted?

2. According to Masters and Johnson, what are the four phases of the human sexual response cycle?

3. What is the difference between gender identity and sexual orientation?

THE AROUSAL MOTIVE

Though the hunger motive and the sex motive seem to dominate North American culture, human beings are also influenced by another biological motive, the **arousal motive.** *Arousal* is the general level of physiological activation of the brain and body. As noted in Chapter 3, the reticular formation regulates brain arousal, and the autonomic nervous system and endocrine system regulate bodily arousal. In 1908 researchers reported that mice learned tasks best at moderate levels of external stimulation, and that the more complex the task, the lower the level of optimal stimulation (Yerkes & Dodson, 1908). Later researchers, led by Donald Hebb (1955) of McGill University in Montreal, showed that human beings perform best at a moderate level of arousal, with performance deteriorating under excessively high or low arousal levels. This relationship between arousal and performance, represented by an inverted U-shaped curve (see Figure 11.7), became known as the **Yerkes-Dodson law,** after the researchers who had conducted the earlier animal study—even though that study dealt with the level of external stimulation rather than with the level of arousal (Teigen, 1994).

Hebb found that optimal arousal is higher for simple tasks than for complex tasks. For example, the optimal level of arousal for doing a simple addition problem would be higher than for doing a complex geometry problem. Hebb also found that optimal arousal is higher for well-learned tasks than for novel tasks. Your optimal level of arousal for reading is higher now than it was when you were first learning to read. Perhaps, when you are bored by studying, you find that playing music in the background helps you raise your level of brain arousal enough for you to maintain your concentration (Patton, Routh, & Stinard, 1986).

But how does arousal level affect performance? According to Hebb, it lets us concentrate and attend to tasks, such as exams. If you are underaroused, your mind might wander to irrelevant details, like when you make careless errors on exams, such as darkening the letter C when you meant to darken the letter B. But if you are overaroused, your focus of attention might become too narrow, reducing your ability to shift to other details that might help you solve a problem, as when you find yourself so anxious that you stare at a particular exam

▲ John Money
"On the issue of the determinants of sexual orientation as homosexual, bisexual, or heterosexual, the only scholarly position is to allow that prenatal and postnatal determinants are not mutually exclusive."

arousal motive
The motive to maintain an optimal level of physiological activation.

Yerkes-Dodson law
The principle that the relationship between arousal and performance is best represented by an inverted U-shaped curve.

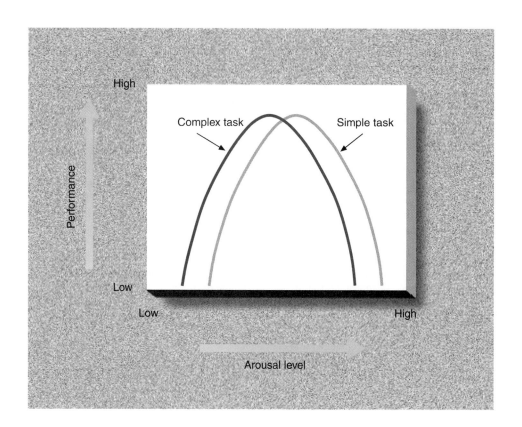

◀ FIGURE 11.7
The Yerkes-Dodson Law
The graph depicts the relationship between arousal level and task performance. Note that the best performance occurs at a moderate level of arousal. Performance declines when arousal is below or above that level. Note that the optimal level of arousal is lower for complex tasks than for simple tasks.

question for several minutes. Overarousal impairs performance in part by interfering with the retrieval of information in short-term memory (Anderson, Revelle, & Lynch, 1989).

Research studies based on the Yerkes-Dodson law have tended to be methodologically flawed and inconsistent in their findings (Baumler, 1994), but many studies have supported the notion of an optimal level of arousal for task performance. In a study of arithmetic performance in third- and fourth-graders under time pressure, low-anxious children performed better than did moderately anxious or high-anxious children (Plass & Hill, 1986). How could the concept of optimal arousal explain these findings? Assume that before performing arithmetic the low-anxious children began *below* their optimal level of arousal, the moderately anxious children began *at* their optimal level, and the high-anxious children began *above* their optimal level. The additional arousal induced by the arithmetic task might have boosted the arousal of the low-anxious children *to* their optimal level and the arousal of the moderately anxious children *above* their optimal level, while the arousal of the high-anxious children might have been boosted even further above their optimal level.

Moreover, for any given task there is no single optimal level of arousal; the optimal level varies from person to person (Ebbeck & Weiss, 1988). So an outstanding math student would have a higher optimal level of arousal for performing arithmetic than would a poor math student. As a consequence, the outstanding math student might have to "psych up" before an exam, and the poor math student might have to relax—each in an effort to reach an optimal arousal level.

Sensory Deprivation: The Effects of Restricted Environmental Stimulation

Though people differ in the amount of arousal they prefer, we require at least a minimal amount for our brains to function properly. Anecdotal reports from Arctic explorers, shipwrecked sailors, and prisoners in solitary confinement made early psychologists aware that human beings require sensory stimulation for proper perceptual, cognitive, and emotional functioning. Today, selection processes for members of Arctic research teams consider who will function best during the *sensory deprivation* that accompanies long periods of isolation (Rothblum, 1990). The following classic study investigated that topic.

ANATOMY OF A CLASSIC RESEARCH STUDY

What Are the Effects of Prolonged Sensory Deprivation?

Rationale

Sensory deprivation is the prolonged withdrawal of normal levels of external stimulation. When people are subjected to sensory deprivation, they may experience delusions, halluci-nations, and emotional arousal caused by the brain's attempt to restore its optimal level of arousal. The experimental study of sensory deprivation began in the early 1950s when the Defense Research Board of Canada asked Donald Hebb to find ways of countering the "brainwashing" techniques that the Chinese communists used on prisoners during the Korean War. During brainwashing, prisoners were deprived of social and physical stimula-tion. This became so unpleasant that it motivated them to cooperate with their captors just to receive more stimulation (Hebb, 1958).

Method

Hebb and his colleagues conducted studies of sensory deprivation in which each subject was confined to a bed in a soundproof room with only the monotonous hum of a fan and an air conditioner. The subjects wore translucent goggles to reduce visual sensations and cotton gloves and cardboard tubes over their arms to reduce touch sensations. They were permitted to leave the bed only to eat or to use the toilet. They stayed in the room for as many days as they could tolerate.

Results and Discussion

After many hours of sensory deprivation, some subjects experienced hallucinations, emo-tional instability, and intellectual deterioration. Though the students who served as vol-unteers for the study were paid $20 a day (a tidy sum at the time) for participating, most quit within 48 hours. They found the lack of sensory stimulation so aversive that they pre-ferred to forego the monetary incentive in favor of sensory stimulation (Bexton, Heron, & Scott, 1954).

Research on sensory deprivation demonstrates that inadequate external stimulation might motivate us to seek external stimulation or to generate our own stimulation through alter-ations in brain activity. This is especially true of people who perform monotonous tasks in relative isolation, such as those who drive long-distance trucking hauls or live for extended periods in outer space. And, as you are certainly aware, even college students seek external stimulation to combat boring classes and dull campus life (Weinstein & Almaguer, 1987).

▲ ▲ ▲

A form of sensory deprivation called flotation restricted environmental stimulation (REST), developed by Peter Suedfeld, has been effective in reducing arousal without causing distress or cognitive impairment (Suedfeld & Coren, 1989). In flotation REST, subjects float in a dark, soundproof tank filled with warm salt water. Flotation REST has proved successful in eliminating the use of drugs, such as nicotine (Suedfeld, 1990). In one study, college students who were heavy social drinkers were assigned either to an experimental group that practiced flotation REST or to a control group that did not. After 2 weeks, the experimental group showed a significant decrease in alcohol intake. This was sustained at a follow-up 6 months after the treatment ended. In contrast, the control group showed an increase in alcohol intake (Cooper, Adams, & Scott, 1988).

Flotation REST has been applied successfully in a variety of other ways, particularly in situations that call for a reduction in arousal. These applications include the relief of chronic tension headache (Wallabaum et al., 1991) and the reduction of high blood pres-sure (McGrady et al., 1987). Though flotation REST produces feelings of relaxation and even euphoria, the exact physiological basis of these effects remains to be determined (Schulz & Kaspar, 1994).

sensory deprivation
The prolonged withdrawal of normal levels of external stimulation.

Sensation Seeking: The Desire to Seek or Avoid Environmental Stimulation

Would you prefer to ride a roller coaster or lie on a beach? Would you prefer to attend a lively party or have a quiet conversation? Your preferences would depend in part on your degree of **sensation seeking,** which is your motivation to pursue sensory stimulation. People high in sensation seeking prefer activities that increase their arousal levels; those low in sensation seeking prefer activities that decrease their arousal. High sensation seekers respond to novel stimuli with greater physiological arousal than do low sensation seekers, who exhibit no change, or even a decrease, in arousal in response to novel stimuli (Zuckerman, 1990). Sensation seeking has a strong hereditary component (Koopmans et al., 1995).

Differences in sensation seeking are apparent in everyday life. A study of British tourists found that those who chose overland adventure holidays scored higher in sensation seeking than did a comparable control group (Gilchrist et al., 1995). Another study found that among students presented with a series of slides depicting paintings in various styles, those high in sensation seeking preferred tense, expressionistic landscapes and those low in sensation seeking preferred calm, pastoral landscapes (Zuckerman, Ulrich, & McLaughlin, 1993).

The concept of sensation seeking might have important practical applications. Consider the potentially dangerous practice of high-speed police pursuits. Police officers who score high in sensation seeking are significantly more likely to engage in such pursuits—endangering themselves and innocent motorists and pedestrians. Perhaps a police officer's score on the scale might be considered when training officers and implementing pursuit policies (Homant, Kennedy, & Howton, 1993).

Sensation seeking is also related to sexual behavior. For example, those who score high in sensation seeking are also more likely to have unprotected sex (Kalichman & Rompa, 1995). A survey of more than 200 male college students found that sensation seeking was positively correlated with their lifetime number of sexual partners, their average number of partners per year, the percentage of their previous relationships that were short-term, and the variety of sexual activities they had experienced (Seto, Lalumiere, & Quinsey, 1995).

> sensation seeking
> The extent to which an individual seeks sensory stimulation.

STAYING ON TRACK: *The Arousal Motive*

1. How would the Yerkes-Dodson law explain poor exam performance by students who are either too relaxed or too anxious?
2. What evidence is there to support the effectiveness of flotation REST?

THE ACHIEVEMENT MOTIVE

Human beings are motivated by social, as well as physiological, needs. Interest in studying social motivation was stimulated in the 1930s and 1940s by the work of Henry Murray (1938), who identified a variety of important social motives, including dominance, achievement, and affiliation. Since Murray's pioneering research, psychologists, led by John Atkinson and David McClelland, have been especially interested in studying the **achievement motive,** which is the desire for mastery, excellence, and accomplishment.

In the context of Maslow's hierarchy of needs, the need for achievement would be associated with one of the higher levels, the need for esteem. This means that the need for achievement would be stronger in cultures, such as Canada and the United States, in which most people have satisfied their lower needs. But even in the United States the relative importance of the need for achievement has changed over time. Figure 11.8 shows the results of a survey of children's readers published between 1800 and 1950; the survey found that the number of achievement themes in the readers increased until about 1890 and then decreased through 1950. This was accompanied by a parallel change in the number of patents issued, indicating that changes in a country's achievement motivation can affect its practical achievements (DeCharms & Moeller, 1962). Nonetheless, it is not certain from the data that changes in achievement motivation *caused* changes in practical

> achievement motive
> The desire for mastery, excellence, and accomplishment.

Achievement Themes and the Patent Index
Between 1800 and 1950, there was a strong positive correlation between the number of achievement themes in children's readers and the number of patents issued by the U.S. Patent Office (DeCharms & Moeller, 1962).

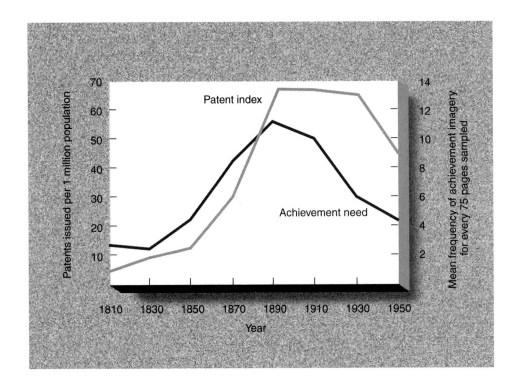

▲ FIGURE 11.9
The Thematic Apperception Test
What is happening in this picture? What led up to it? How does the person feel? How will it turn out? Your responses to several ambiguous pictures like this might contain themes revealing the strength of your need for achievement.

achievements. You will recall that a positive correlation between two variables does not necessarily mean that changes in one *cause* changes in the other. Of course, it does not preclude the possibility of a causal relationship, either.

Changes in the achievement motive over time also differ for males and females. From the late 1950s to the late 1970s, American men showed no change in their achievement motivation, whereas American women showed a marked increase. This has been attributed to the women's movement of the past few decades, which made it more acceptable for women to pursue personal achievement outside of traditional women's domains, such as homemaking (Veroff et al., 1980).

Need for Achievement: The Pursuit of Success

Henry Murray (1938) referred to the achievement motive as the *need for achievement*, which reveals itself in efforts to meet high standards of performance or to compete successfully against other people. How do psychologists measure the need for achievement? The most common means has been the *Thematic Apperception Test (TAT)*, developed by Murray and his colleague Christiana Morgan in the 1930s to assess social motivation (Morgan & Murray, 1935). The TAT is based on the assumption that our fantasies reveal our motives. The test consists of a series of drawings of people in ambiguous situations (see Figure 11.9). The subject is asked to tell what is happening in the picture, what led up to it, how the people feel, and how the situation turns out. The responses are scored for any themes that run through them. Individuals with a high need for achievement will tell stories in which people overcome obstacles, work hard to reach goals, and accomplish great things.

What do we know about people who score high on the need for achievement? Research shows that they persist at tasks in the face of difficulties, delay gratification in the pursuit of long-term goals, and achieve greater success than people with a low need for achievement. They also select moderately difficult challenges, neither so easy that they guarantee success nor so difficult that they guarantee failure (McClelland, 1985). Even psychologists with a high need for achievement become more successful, at least as measured by the recognition accorded their research by fellow psychologists. The published research of psychologists with a high need for achievement is cited more often in journal articles (Helmreich et al., 1980).

The need for achievement varies with the achievement situation. People with a high need for achievement rarely seek success in more than a few areas of life. So, your achievement behavior depends on more than just the strength of your general need for achievement. Your achievement behavior also depends on **incentive value,** the perceived rewards that accompany success in a particular area, and **expectancy,** the perceived probability of success in a particular area (Eccles & Wigfield, 1995). The combination of expectancy and incentive value even affects the choice of a college major by students (Sullins et al., 1995).

Consider your achievement motivation in regard to your achievement behavior in a psychology course. If you are high in achievement motivation, if you find that a good grade in the course has high incentive value for you, and if you expect that studying hard is likely to result in a good grade, you are more likely to work hard in the course. Yet if you are high in achievement motivation but do not value a high grade in psychology (perhaps because it is only an elective course) or believe that you have little chance of success in the course (perhaps because the professor is a notoriously hard grader), you might not work as hard. Your level of achievement motivation might even be associated with where you choose to sit in class. A study of 102 college freshmen who had been given a test of achievement motivation prior to taking their course found that those higher in the need for achievement tended to select seats in the front of the class (Rebeta et al., 1993).

Research has also shown that the need for achievement can interact with arousal to determine a person's performance. As noted earlier, we perform best at our optimal level of arousal for a given task. In an arousing situation, such as giving a speech to a class, a student with a low need for achievement might perform well because the situation raises the student to her optimal level of arousal. In the same situation, a student with a high need for achievement, already at an optimal level of arousal, might perform poorly because the situation raises the student beyond his optimal level (Humphreys & Revelle, 1984).

Goal Setting: Planning for Success

Suppose that you are high in the need for achievement in academics, sports, or some other area. How should you seek to fulfill that need? Hundreds of studies have demonstrated the importance of **goal setting.** Goals increase motivation and improve performance by providing incentives. Your goals focus your attention, increase your effort, maintain your persistence, and encourage you to develop strategies for reaching them. Goal setting has been especially useful in business and industry in stimulating productivity (Nordstrom, Lorenzi, & Hall, 1990). *Management by objectives,* in which employees participate in setting goals, has been especially effective. Of 70 studies included in a review of research on the effectiveness of management by objectives, 68 found that it increased productivity (Rodgers & Hunter, 1991). Goal setting is useful in a variety of other circumstances, as well. These include improving health behavior (Strecher et al., 1995), children's homework performance (Miller & Kelley, 1994), and salespersons' volume of sales (Barrick, Mount, & Strauss, 1993).

But how should you set your goals? Research findings by Edwin Locke and his colleagues provide several suggestions (Locke & Latham, 1985). Specific, challenging goals (such as "I will increase my studying by one hour a night") produce better performance than no goals, vague goals (such as "I will increase the time I spend studying"), easy goals (such as "I will increase my studying by 10 minutes a week"), or mere encouragement to do your best. Feedback on your progress toward a goal (such as keeping a record of how much time you spend studying) will help you reach that goal. And a goal that you set yourself will motivate you more than a goal imposed on you (as when a parent forces a child to stay home and study every day after school).

Another effective technique is to use short-term goals to help you reach long-term ones. This was demonstrated in a program aimed at improving children's arithmetic performance. Children who were given short-term goals did better in arithmetic than did those given long-term goals (Bandura & Schunk, 1981). Suppose you have the long-term goal of owning your own business. You would be wise to have shorter-term goals also.

▲ **Henry Murray (1893–1988)**
Christiana Morgan (1897–1967)
"The strength of a need as a consistently ready reaction system of personality is measured by noting the frequency of its occurrence under given conditions."

incentive value
The perceived rewards that accompany success in a particular area.

expectancy
In achievement situations, the perceived probability of success in a particular area.

goal setting
The establishment of a particular level of performance to achieve in the future.

(a)   (b)   (c)   (d)

▲ **Achievement Motivation**
The need for achievement is demonstrated in the lives of persons who reach the top of their fields, including *(a)* the late Andy Warhol, who championed Pop art; *(b)* Toni Morrison, who won a Nobel Prize for her writing; *(c)* Julia Child, who became a famous television chef; and *(d)* General Colin Powell, who served as head of the U.S. army.

intrinsic motivation
The desire to perform a behavior for its own sake.

extrinsic motivation
The desire to perform a behavior in order to obtain an external reward, such as praise, grades, or money.

▲ **Edwin Locke**
"Goals affect performance by affecting effort, persistence, and direction of attention, and by motivating strategy development."

These might include finding a summer job in your field of interest, earning a bachelor's degree, and gaining an entry-level position after graduation.

Intrinsic Motivation: Performing Activities for Their Own Sake

If you have ever written a term paper just to obtain a grade, you can appreciate William James's distress at having to complete his now-classic 1890 textbook for an extrinsic reason. According to Edward Thorndike (1961, p. 267), "James wrote the *Principles* with wailing and gnashing of teeth to fulfill a contract with a publishing firm." Though James enjoyed writing, he did not enjoy writing for money. He was not unusual, because research has shown that receiving extrinsic rewards for performing intrinsically rewarding activities can reduce the motivation to perform them.

Intrinsic motivation is the desire to perform a task for its own sake. In contrast, **extrinsic motivation** is the desire to perform a task to gain external rewards, such as praise, grades, or money. For example, you might take a psychology course because you find it interesting (an intrinsic reason) or because it is a graduation requirement (an extrinsic reason). Until the 1970s, most psychologists agreed with B. F. Skinner that rewards will increase the probability of behavior or, at worst, have no effect on it. But then research began to show otherwise. In one of the first experiments on intrinsic motivation, children were given a period of time during which they could draw. Some of them were then given a certificate as a reward for having drawn. When given a subsequent chance to draw, students who had been rewarded for drawing spent less time at it than did students who had not been rewarded (Lepper, Greene, & Nisbett, 1973). Fortunately, children who have been trained to stress intrinsic reasons for engaging in creative activities are somewhat immunized against the negative effects of extrinsic rewards (Hennessey & Zbikowski, 1993).

Later studies have also supported the benefits of intrinsic motivation and the possible detrimental effects of extrinsic motivation. Children who are given external rewards for playing with toys later play less with those toys (Margolis & Mynatt, 1986). Among elementary school students, high achievers tend to be more intrinsically motivated and low achievers more extrinsically motivated (Diaz Soto, 1989). And employees governed by extrinsic rewards, such as fringe benefits, are less motivated than are employees governed by intrinsic rewards, such as control over their own work schedule (Notz, 1975). Even the sense of moral obligation can be undermined by extrinsic rewards. This was the outcome of a study in which students who were paid for tape-recording a text for a blind student showed a reduced sense of moral obligation in comparison with those who were not paid for doing so (Kunda & Schwartz, 1983).

Given the everyday observation that extrinsic rewards can increase achievement motivation, especially in people who initially have little or no motivation in a particular area, why do extrinsic rewards sometimes decrease achievement motivation? Two theories provide possible answers. **Overjustification theory** assumes that an extrinsic reward decreases intrinsic motivation when a person attributes his or her performance to the extrinsic reward. The children who were rewarded for drawing might have attributed their behavior to the reward rather than to their interest in drawing. Overjustification occurs when there is high intrinsic interest and the reward is perceived as more than adequate justification for performing the act. In a study of first- and second-graders, children played with an interesting or uninteresting toy and were rewarded or not rewarded. Rewards reduced the motivation to play with the interesting, but not the uninteresting, toy (Newman & Layton, 1984). A meta-analysis that reviewed research findings from many studies found strong support for the overjustification theory (Tang & Hall, 1995).

An alternative theory, **cognitive-evaluation theory,** put forth by Edward Deci, holds that a reward perceived as providing *information* about a person's competence in an activity will increase her or his intrinsic motivation to perform that activity (Deci, Nezlek, & Sheinman, 1981). But a reward perceived as an attempt to *control* a person's behavior will decrease his or her intrinsic motivation to perform that activity. Consider a student whose teacher rewards her for doing well in drawing. If the student believes that the reward is being used to provide information about her competence, her intrinsic motivation to perform that activity may increase. But if she believes that the reward is being used to control her behavior (perhaps to make her spend more time drawing), her intrinsic motivation to perform may decrease. There is strong research support for this theory (Rummel & Feinberg, 1988). So, when you reward people for performing activities that they find intrinsically motivating, you should use rewards as information rather than as controls.

You now have a better appreciation of the influence of motivation, particularly the hunger, sex, arousal, and achievement motives, in your everyday life. To appreciate how motivation affects behavior in an area of life that is important to many people, next consider the role of motivation in sport.

STAYING ON TRACK: *The Achievement Motive*

1. What are some basic rules for the effective use of goal setting?
2. What is the difference between the overjustification theory and the cognitive-evaluation theory in explaining the negative effects of extrinsic motivation?

▲ Edward Deci

"When the controlling aspect of a reward is more salient, it will decrease one's intrinsic motivation . . . . When the informational aspect is more salient (and when the information is positive), it will increase one's intrinsic motivation by initiating the change in perceived competence."

overjustification theory
The theory that an extrinsic reward will decrease intrinsic motivation when a person attributes her or his performance to that reward.

cognitive-evaluation theory
The theory that a person's intrinsic motivation will increase when a reward is perceived as a source of information but will decrease when a reward is perceived as an attempt to exert control.

THINKING ABOUT *Psychology*

What Is the Relationship Between Motivation and Sport?

Just before the turn of the century, Indiana University psychologist Norman Triplett (1898) observed that bicyclists rode faster when competing against other bicyclists than when competing against time. This was perhaps the first study in **sport psychology,** the field that studies the relationship between psychological factors and sport performance. Though Tripplett began the scientific study of sport performance, magazines devoted to sport had advanced the desirability of a psychological approach to sport in the late nineteenth century (King et al., 1995). Today, in studying motivation in sport, researchers are especially interested in the arousal motive and the achievement motive.

sport psychology
The field that applies psychological principles to help amateur and professional athletes improve their performance.

(a)

(b)

(c)

▲ **Arousal and Athletic Performance**
The optimal level of arousal will vary from one sport to another—the more delicate the task, the lower the level of optimal arousal. Thus, (a) professional golfer Nancy Lopez will putt better at a low level of arousal; (b) track star Carl Lewis will jump farther at a more moderate level of arousal; and (c) champion sumo wrestler Konishiki will be better able to push his opponents out of the ring when he is at a high level of arousal.

▲ **Richard Suinn**
"In the past athletes were almost overeducated on physical factors and undereducated on psychological aspects of training and performance."

THE AROUSAL MOTIVE AND SPORT

Your arousal motive, particularly your degree of sensation seeking, influences your choice of sports. People high in sensation seeking prefer more-exciting, more-dangerous sports than do people low in sensation seeking. Thus, participants in whitewater canoeing and kayaking score significantly above average in sensation seeking (Campbell, Tyrrell, & Zingaro, 1993), as do participants in ski jumping and mountain climbing (Rossi & Creatti, 1993). Studies also have found that, in regard to sensation seeking, hang-glider pilots score higher than golfers (Wagner & Houlihan, 1994) and rugby and lacrosse players score higher than rowers and soccer players (Schroth, 1995).

The arousal motive is also important to athletes in regard to their maintaining an optimal level of arousal for their sport performance. If you have ever played a competitive sport, you know what it is to "choke"—to be so anxious that you perform below your normal level of ability. Choking occurs when your anxiety makes you attend to the normally automatic movements involved in playing a sport. If you consciously attend to those movements, they will be disrupted (Baumeister, 1984). Consider foul shooting in basketball. If you attend to each movement of your arm and hand as you shoot foul shots, you will disrupt the smooth sequence of movements that foul shooting requires. Athletes at an optimal level of arousal are less likely to be undermotivated or to choke, as shown in a study of women collegiate basketball players. Those with a moderate level of pregame anxiety performed better than did those with a low or high level (Sonstroem & Bernardo, 1982).

The Yerkes-Dodson law might explain why some athletes perform better during practice than during competition. For example, if you play intramural softball, you might be at your optimal level of arousal during practice, a relatively unstressful situation, but rise above your optimal level during a game, a relatively stressful situation. Similarly, the Yerkes-Dodson law might also explain why some athletes perform better during competition than during practice. In that case, you might be below your optimal level of arousal during practice but rise up to your optimal level during a game.

A good coach will realize which of her athletes must be psyched up and which must be calmed down to achieve an optimal level of arousal during competition. There is no single optimal level of arousal. Each athlete has his own optimal level for a given sport (Raglin & Turner, 1993). Thus, Knute Rockne–style "win one for the Gipper" pep talks might hurt the performance of moderately or highly aroused athletes. Yet such pep talks can be good for athletes who are too relaxed before competition, especially in aggressive sports such as football or weight lifting.

As mentioned earlier, the optimal level of arousal is lower for complex tasks than for simple tasks. This is also true in sports (Gardner, 1986). Your optimal level of arousal while hitting a golf ball (a relatively complex task) would be lower than your optimal level while playing shuffleboard (a relatively simple task). Moreover, the more skillful the athlete, the higher her optimal level of arousal will be. The golfer who makes a putt on the eighteenth green to win the U.S. Open might be so skillful that he has a higher optimal level of arousal than the golfer who "chokes" in the same situation. This also means that when teaching beginners to play golf, to ride a bicycle, or to serve a volleyball, you should try to keep their arousal levels from becoming too high. To avoid excess arousal, beginners should refrain from competition and not practice while being watched by people other than the coach or instructor.

One technique for achieving optimal arousal in athletes is flotation REST. In a study of intercollegiate tennis players, subjects practiced visual imagery alone or combined with flotation REST. Those who practiced both visual imagery and flotation REST showed improved first-serve accuracy, while those who used visual imagery alone did not (McAleney, Barabasz, & Barabasz, 1990). And in a study of the effects of flotation REST on recreational basketball performance, college students who practiced flotation REST reported greater confidence and performed better than control subjects who did not practice it (Suedfeld & Bruno, 1990).

THE ACHIEVEMENT MOTIVE AND SPORT

On June 4, 1986, six weeks after setting the collegiate record for the 10,000-meter run, Kathy Ormsby, running among the leaders, veered off the track midway through the final race at the NCAA championships in Indianapolis. She left the stadium, ran to the nearby White River Bridge, and leaped 50 feet to the river bank. The fall fractured her spine, damaged her spinal cord, and paralyzed her from the waist down. Besides excelling at running, Ormsby had been her high school's valedictorian (with an average of 99 percent), was a premedical student at North Carolina State University, and was dedicated to living up to the strict standards of behavior required by her religious beliefs. As one of her teachers said, "If a human being can be perfect, I would say that Kathy was perfect" (Dwyer, 1986, p. 8-A). Ormsby was certainly high in her need for achievement.

Ormsby had been overcome periodically by anxiety strong enough to force her to drop out of races. Her friends and coaches believed she succumbed to what they called "her will to succeed." Though her high need for achievement certainly motivated her to compete, she apparently succumbed to her fear of failure, finding it more and more difficult to motivate herself to compete against other elite athletes. Kathy Ormsby's tragic story shows that the achievement motive can be a powerful force in athletic competition, as it is in other areas of life.

Athletes with a high need for achievement are motivated to seek competition that provides a fair test of their abilities. Early evidence for this came from a study in which college students played a game of ringtoss. Those with a high need for achievement were more likely to stand at an intermediate distance from the peg, while those with a low need for achievement were more likely to stand either close to the peg or far from it (Atkinson & Litwin, 1960). Similarly, if you were high in your need for achievement in tennis, you would probably choose to play someone of your own ability. Neither playing a 5-year-old child nor playing Monica Seles would be a fair test of your ability. In contrast, a person low in the need for achievement or high in the fear of failure might prefer to play either someone who barely knows how to grip a racket, which would assure success, or a professional tennis player, which would assure that losing would be attributable to the professional opponent's excellence rather than to personal incompetence.

One way in which superior athletes make competition against lesser athletes more motivating is by giving themselves a handicap, making the competition a moderate challenge rather than a guaranteed success (Nicholls, 1984). If you are an excellent table tennis player, you might provide a moderate challenge for yourself by giving a lesser opponent 10 points in a 21-point game. Similarly, in the 1960s Wilt Chamberlain, perhaps the

▲ Kathy Ormsby

▲ Achievement Motivation and Sport
Being physically disabled does not necessarily reduce one's motivation to achieve. Despite being born without a right hand, Jim Abbott has become a successful pitcher. He led the United States to a gold medal in baseball in the 1988 Olympic Games and excelled as a major league pitcher for several years.

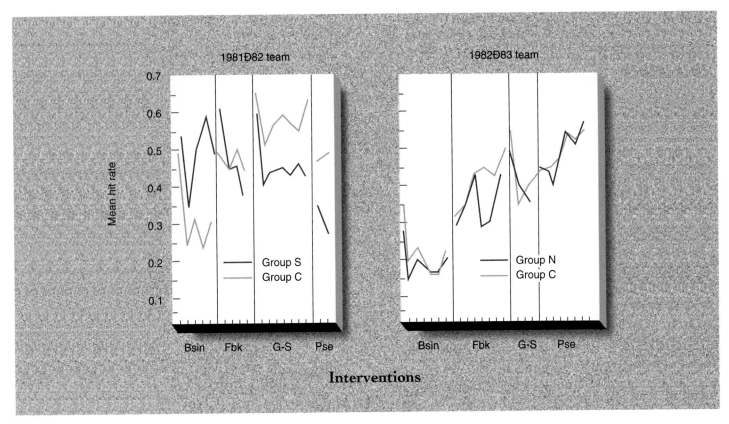

1981Ð82 team

1982Ð83 team

▲ FIGURE 11.10

Goal Setting and Hockey Performance
These graphs show the superiority of goal setting in improving the performance of the University of Notre Dame hockey team by increasing body checking. The *mean hit rate* is the average number of body checks per minute on ice. In regard to interventions, *Bsin* refers to a body-checking baseline period, *Fbk* refers to a body-checking performance feedback, *Goal-set (G-S)* refers to a body-checking goal-setting period, and *Praise (Pse)* refers to a body-checking praise period. In regard to groups, Group S involved talented seniors, Group N involved new players, and Group C involved subjects who played both seasons (Anderson et al., 1988).

most physically imposing athlete in history (who once *averaged* 50 points a game for a whole season in the National Basketball Association), developed a fade-away jump shot to show that he could succeed even when giving up his greatest asset, his ability to score from near the basket because of his great strength and height (7 feet, 1 inch tall). By doing so, he made scoring a moderate, rather than easy, challenge for himself—often to the distress of his coaches.

As in other areas of life, goal setting is important in sport motivation. A survey of more than 300 male and 300 female intercollegiate athletes found that virtually all of them used goal setting to help enhance their performance and that they generally found it effective (Weinberg et al., 1993). In a study of sit-up performance, participants who used specific short-term goals did better more than those who were told only, "Do your best" (Lerner & Locke, 1995). A study of the effect of goal setting on the rifle marksmanship of college students found that those who set specific goals improved more than those who set do-your-best goals (Boyce, 1992). And, as shown in Figure 11.10, members of the University of Notre Dame hockey team successfully used goal setting as part of a motivational program to increase their aggressiveness. They increased their rate of legal body checking and, perhaps as a consequence, improved their team record (Anderson et al., 1988). Because of the many factors involved in sport and goal setting, researchers still must determine what kinds of goals are most effective for specific athletes, performing specific tasks, under specific conditions (Weinberg & Weigand, 1993). For example, it seems that combining short- and long-term goals is especially effective in improving sport performance (Kyllo & Landers, 1995).

Athletes are also more motivated by intrinsic rewards than by extrinsic rewards (Frederick & Ryan, 1995). In a study of college athletes, football players on athletic scholarships reported less intrinsic motivation than did those who were not on scholarships. But among male wrestlers and female athletes, those who were on athletic scholarships reported *more* intrinsic motivation than those who were not. What could account for these findings? Perhaps football coaches use scholarships more as a means of *control*, while wrestling coaches and coaches of female athletes use scholarships more as a means of *informing* athletes about their competence. In terms of the cognitive-evaluation theory, discussed earlier, rewards that are perceived as a means of control can decrease instrinsic motivation, and rewards that are perceived as a means of providing information about competence can increase intrinsic motivation (Ryan, 1980).

As you can see, motivational factors important in other areas of life are also important in sport. Athletes perform best at an optimal level of arousal, which varies with the individual, the sport, and the task. And athletes are influenced by their achievement motive; their level of motivation is enhanced by their need for achievement, proper use of goal setting, and reliance on intrinsic rewards.

STAYING ON TRACK: *What Is the Relationship Between Motivation and Sport?*

1. How does the concept of optimal arousal explain why athletes perform differently in practice and in real competition?

2. Why would an athlete high in the need for achievement prefer an opponent of similar ability, rather than one of much lower or much higher ability?

 # CHAPTER SUMMARY

SOURCES OF MOTIVATION

Motivation is the psychological process that arouses, directs, and maintains behavior. The main sources of motivation include genes, drives, and incentives. Though William McDougall's instinct theory failed to achieve scientific credibility, interest in the hereditary basis of social behavior remains alive today in the field of sociobiology. Instinct theories gave way to the drive-reduction theory of Clark Hull, which assumes that physiological deprivation causes a need, which induces a state of tension called a drive. Drive reduction aims at restoring a steady state of physiological equilibrium called homeostasis. A drive "pushes" you toward a goal, whereas an incentive is an external stimulus that "pulls" you toward a goal. Abraham Maslow categorized human needs in a hierarchy, with the pursuit of higher needs contingent on the satisfaction of lower ones.

THE HUNGER MOTIVE

Hunger impels you to eat to satisfy your body's need for nutrients. Factors that regulate hunger include taste sensations, stretch and nutrient receptors in the stomach, cholecystokinin secreted by the small intestine, glucose receptors in the liver, and insulin secreted by the pancreas. Areas of the hypothalamus regulate hunger by responding to signals from the blood and internal organs. External food-related cues also influence hunger and eating. The most common eating problem is obesity, which is defined as a body weight more than 20 percent above normal for one's height and body build. Obesity depends on one's set point, basal metabolic rate, responsiveness to external cues, chronic level of blood insulin, and reactions to stress. Two of the most prevalent eating disorders are anorexia nervosa and bulimia nervosa.

THE SEX MOTIVE

Sex serves as both a drive and an incentive. Sex hormones direct sexual development and sexual behavior. Unlike in other animals, sexual behavior in human adults is controlled more by sociocultural factors than by sex hormones. Formal research on human sexuality began with surveys on male and female sexual behavior conducted by Alfred Kinsey and his colleagues. Later research by William Masters and Virginia Johnson showed that females and males have similar sexual response cycles.

Masters and Johnson also developed sex therapy techniques that have been successful in helping men and women overcome sexual dysfunctions, which are chronic problems at phases in the sexual response cycle. Human beings vary in their gender identity and sexual orientation. Transsexuals feel trapped in a body of the wrong sex and might seek surgery and hormonal treatments to change their appearance. Homosexuals are sexually attracted to members of their own sex.

THE AROUSAL MOTIVE

Arousal is the general level of physiological activation of the brain and body. The Yerkes-Dodson law holds that there is an optimal level of arousal for the performance of a given task, with the optimal level becoming lower as the task becomes more complex. Studies of sensory deprivation by Donald Hebb and his colleagues show that we are motivated to maintain at least a minimal level of sensory stimulation. Flotation REST has been successful in improving human physical and psychological functioning. People also differ in their degree of sensation seeking, which is the motivation to seek high or low levels of sensory stimulation.

THE ACHIEVEMENT MOTIVE

The achievement motive is the desire for mastery, excellence, and accomplishment. Henry Murray and Christiana Morgan introduced the Thematic Apperception Test as a means of assessing the need for achievement. People with a high need for achievement persist at tasks in the face of difficulties, delay gratification in the pursuit of long-term goals, and achieve greater success than do people with a low need for achievement. They also prefer moderately difficult challenges. Your actual achievement behavior in a given situation depends on the strength of your need for achievement, the incentive value of success for you, and your expectancy of success. Goal setting increases motivation and improves performance by providing incentives. The best goals are specific and challenging, and short-term goals are useful in the pursuit of long-term goals. The intrinsic motivation to engage in an activity can be reduced by extrinsic rewards. Overjustification theory and cognitive-evaluation theory provide different explanations for the detrimental effects of extrinsic rewards.

THINKING ABOUT PSYCHOLOGY: WHAT IS THE RELATIONSHIP BETWEEN MOTIVATION AND SPORT?

Sport psychology is the field that studies the relationship between psychological factors and sport performance, particularly the influence of motivation. In studying motivation and sport, sport psychologists are especially interested in the relationship between arousal and performance. To keep from "choking" during competition, athletes must learn to keep from rising above their optimal level of arousal. Athletic performance is also affected by other motivational factors, including the need for achievement, goal setting, and intrinsic motivation.

KEY CONCEPTS

motivation 376

Sources of Motivation

instinct 376
sociobiology 377
drive-reduction theory 377
need 377
drive 377
homeostasis 377
incentive 378
hierarchy of needs 378

The Hunger Motive

set point 381
obesity 381
basal metabolic rate 381
anorexia nervosa 384
bulimia nervosa 385

The Sex Motive

gonads 386
paraphilia 387
sexual response cycle 388
sexual dysfunction 390
sensate focusing 390

gender identity 391
sexual orientation 391
transsexualism 391
homosexuality 392

The Arousal Motive

arousal motive 394
Yerkes-Dodson law 394
sensory deprivation 396
sensation seeking 397

The Achievement Motive

achievement motive 397

incentive value 399
expectancy 399
goal setting 399
intrinsic motivation 400
extrinsic motivation 400
overjustification theory 401
cognitive-evaluation theory 401

What Is the Relationship Between Motivation and Sport?

sport psychology 401

KEY CONTRIBUTORS

Sources of Motivation

William McDougall 376
Sigmund Freud 376
Clark Hull 377
Abraham Maslow 378

The Hunger Motive

Walter Cannon 379
Stanley Schachter 383
Judith Rodin 383

The Sex Motive

Alfred Kinsey 388

William Masters and Virginia
  Johnson 388
John Money 394

The Arousal Motive

Donald Hebb 394
Peter Suedfeld 396

The Achievement Motive

Henry Murray 397
David McClelland 397
John Atkinson 397
Christiana Morgan 398

FOR MORE INFORMATION ON MOTIVATION

FOR GENERAL WORKS ON MOTIVATION

Badcock, C. (1991). *Evolution and individual behavior: An introduction to human sociobiology.* New York: Basil Blackwell.

Franken, R. E. (1998). *Human motivation* (4th ed.). Belmont, CA: Brooks/Cole.

Senchuk, D. M. (1991). *Against instinct: From biology to philosophical psychology.* Philadelphia: Temple University Press.

FOR MORE ON THE HUNGER MOTIVE

Andersen, A. E. (Ed.). (1990). *Males with eating disorders.* New York: Brunner/Mazel.

Logue, A. W. (1991). *The psychology of eating and drinking* (2nd ed.). New York: W. H. Freeman.

Rodin, J. (1992). *Body traps.* New York: Morrow.

Schlundt, D. G., & Johnson, W. G. (1990). *Eating disorders.* Needham Heights, MA: Allyn & Bacon.

Stunkard, A. J., & Wadden, T. A. (1993). *Obesity: Theory and therapy* (2nd ed.). New York: Raven Press.

FOR MORE ON THE SEX MOTIVE

Docter, R. F. (1988). *Transvestites and transsexuals: Toward a theory of cross-gender behavior.* New York: Plenum.

McWhirter, D. P., Sanders, S. A., & Reinisch, J. M. (Eds.). (1990). *Homosexuality/heterosexuality: Concepts of sexual orientation.* New York: Oxford University Press.

Money, J. (1994). *Interpreting the unspeakable: Sexual motivation in human behavior.* New York: Continuum.

O'Donohue, W., & Geer, J. H. (Eds.). (1993). *Handbook of sexual dysfunction: Assessment and treatment.* Boston: Allyn & Bacon.

Reinisch, J. M. (1990). *The new Kinsey Institute report on sex.* Newbury Park, CA: Sage.

Shainberg, L. W., & Byer, C. O. (1994). *Dimensions of human sexuality* (4th ed.). Dubuque, IA: Wm. C. Brown.

Suggs, D., & Miracle, A. (Eds.). (1993). *Culture and human sexuality.* Belmont, CA: Brooks/Cole.

FOR MORE ON THE AROUSAL MOTIVE

Csikszentmihalyi, M. (1990). *Flow: The psychology of optimal experience.* New York: Harper & Row.

Suedfeld, P., Turner, J. W., & Fine, T. H. (Eds.). (1990). *Restricted environmental stimulation: Theoretical and empirical developments in flotation REST.* New York: Springer-Verlag.

Zuckerman, M. (1994). *Behavioral expression and biosocial bases of sensation seeking.* New York: Cambridge University Press.

FOR MORE ON THE ACHIEVEMENT MOTIVE

Atkinson, J. W., & Feather, N. T. (Eds.). (1966). *A theory of achievement motivation.* New York: Wiley.

Deci, E. L., & Ryan, R. M. (1985). *Intrinsic motivation and self-determination in human behavior.* New York: Plenum.

Locke, E. A., & Latham, G. P. (1990). *A theory of goal setting and task performance.* Englewood Cliffs, NJ: Prentice Hall.

FOR MORE ON MOTIVATION AND SPORT

Roberts, G. C. (Ed.). (1992). *Motivation in sport and exercise.* Champaign, IL: Human Kinetics.

Wann, D. L. (1997). *Sport psychology.* New York: Macmillan.

FOR MORE ON CONTRIBUTORS TO THE STUDY OF MOTIVATION

Benison, S., Barger, A. C., & Wolfe, E. L. (1987). *Walter B. Cannon: The life and times of a young scientist.* Cambridge, MA: Belknap/Harvard.

Cohen, I. B. (Ed.). (1980). *The career of William Beaumont and the reception of his discovery.* New York: Arno.

Coleman, E. (Ed.). (1991). *John Money: A tribute.* Binghamton, NY: Haworth.

Douglas, C. (1993). *Translate this darkness: The life of Christiana Morgan.* New York: Simon & Schuster.

Hoffman, E. (1988). *The right to be human: A biography of Abraham Maslow.* Los Angeles: Tarcher.

Jeffrey, F., & Lilly, J. C. (1990). *John Lilly, so far. . . .* Los Angeles: Tarcher.

Pomeroy, W. B. (1982). *Dr. Kinsey and the Institute for Sex Research.* New Haven, CT: Yale University Press.

Robinson, F. G. (1992). *Love's story told: A life of Henry A. Murray.* Cambridge, MA: Harvard University Press.

Robinson, P. (1988). *The modernization of sex: Havelock Ellis, Alfred Kinsey, William Masters, and Virginia Johnson.* Ithaca, NY: Cornell University Press.

CHAPTER 12

Emotion

emotion

A motivated state marked by physiological arousal, expressive behavior, and mental experience.

*H*ow do you feel? Are you *anxious* about an upcoming exam, *depressed* by a recent loss, in *love* with a wonderful person, *angry* at a personal affront, or *happy* about your favorite team's performance? Such feelings are emotions. The word *emotion* comes from a Latin word meaning "to set in motion," and, like motives (such as sex and hunger), emotions (such as love and anger) motivate behavior that helps us adapt to different situations (Ekman, 1992a). Though it is easy to recognize an emotion, especially one that is a pure, prototypical example (such as extreme anger or intense romantic love), it is difficult to provide a formal definition of the concept itself (Russell, 1991). This led two prominent emotion researchers to observe, "Everyone knows what an emotion is, until asked to give a definition" (Fehr & Russell, 1984, p. 464).

Despite the difficulty of precisely defining the concept of emotion, most psychologists agree that an **emotion** is a motivated state that is marked by physiological arousal, expressive behavior, and mental experience. Emotions also vary in their intensity and pleasantness/unpleasantness (Buck, 1985). Consider an angry man. His heart might pound (a sign of physiological arousal), he might grit his teeth (an expressive behavior), and he might feel enraged (an intense, unpleasant mental experience). In trying to explain emotion, some psychologists prefer to study the biological level (the biopsychology of emotion), others the behavioral level (the expression of emotion), and still others the mental level (the experience of emotion).

THE BIOPSYCHOLOGY OF EMOTION

What are the physiological bases of emotion? To answer this question, psychologists study the autonomic nervous system, the brain, and neurochemicals.

The Autonomic Nervous System and Emotion

Both your emotional expression and your emotional experience depend on physiological arousal, which reflects activity in your *autonomic nervous system*. The system is called "autonomic" because it functions independently, without the need for conscious, voluntary regulation by the brain. Figure 12.1 illustrates the functions of the two branches of the autonomic nervous system: the *sympathetic nervous system* and the *parasympathetic nervous system*. The interplay of these two systems contributes to the ebb and flow of emotions. The sympathetic nervous system relies on the neurotransmitter *norepinephrine* to regulate its target organs; the parasympathetic nervous system relies on the neurotransmitter *acetylcholine* to regulate its target organs.

fight-or-flight response

A state of physiological arousal that enables us to meet sudden threats by either confronting them or running away from them.

Activation of the sympathetic nervous system can stimulate the **fight-or-flight response,** which evolved because it enabled our prehistoric ancestors to meet sudden physical threats (whether from nature, animals, or human beings) by either confronting them or running away from them. After a threat has been met or avoided, the sympathetic nervous system becomes less active and the parasympathetic nervous system becomes more active, calming the body. Yet because the sympathetic nervous system stimulates the secretion of epinephrine and norepinephrine from the adrenal glands into the bloodstream, physiological arousal may last for a while after the threat has disappeared.

The fight-or-flight response is triggered not only by physical threats but also by psychological threats—such as academic demands that we feel inadequate to meet. To appreciate the role of the autonomic nervous system in the emotional response to a psychological

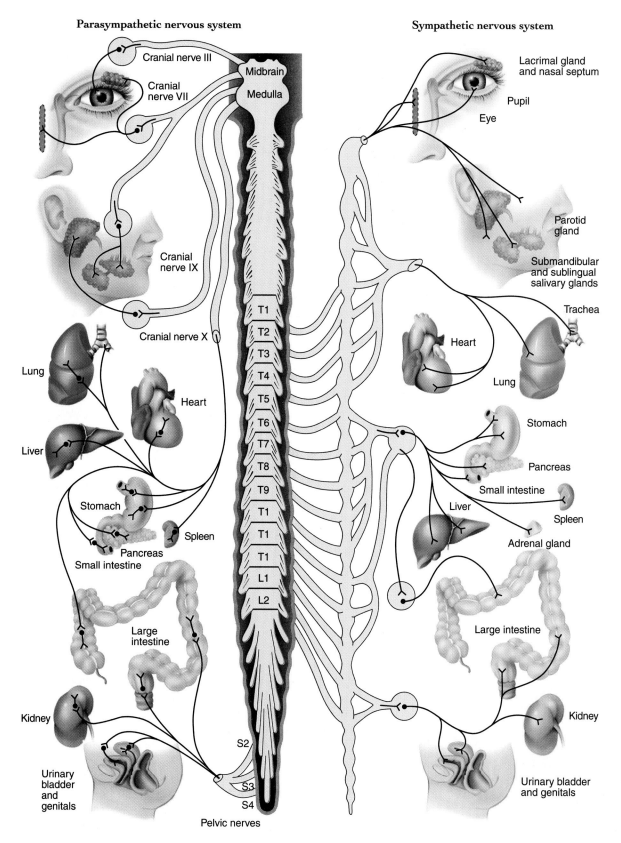

Parasympathetic nervous system

Sympathetic nervous system

Cranial nerve III

Cranial nerve VII

Midbrain

Medulla

Lacrimal gland and nasal septum

Pupil

Eye

Cranial nerve IX

Parotid gland

Submandibular and sublingual salivary glands

Cranial nerve X

T1
T2
T3
T4
T5
T6
T7
T8
T9
T1
T1
T1
L1
L2

Trachea

Lung

Heart

Heart

Lung

Liver

Stomach

Pancreas

Small intestine

Spleen

Stomach

Pancreas

Small intestine

Spleen

Liver

Adrenal gland

Large intestine

Large intestine

Kidney

Kidney

Urinary bladder and genitals

S2

S3

S4

Pelvic nerves

Urinary bladder and genitals

▲ FIGURE 12.1

The Autonomic Nervous System

Emotional responses involve the interplay of the two branches of the autonomic nervous system: the sympathetic nervous system, which tends to arouse us, and the parasympathetic nervous system, which tends to return us to a calmer state.

threat, imagine that you are about to give a classroom speech that you did not prepare adequately. As you walk to your class, you experience anxiety associated with physiological arousal induced by your sympathetic nervous system.

As you enter the classroom, you become more alert and energetic as your circulatory system diverts blood rich in oxygen and other nutrients normally destined for your stomach and intestines to your brain and skeletal muscles. Your energy increases as your liver releases sugar into your bloodstream. Your heart pounds rapidly and strongly in response to epinephrine secreted by your adrenal glands. Your bronchioles dilate to permit more oxygen-rich air to enter your lungs, and you breathe more rapidly as your lungs work harder to expel carbon dioxide. A classmate might notice your pupils dilating, which improves your vision by letting more light into your eyes. And you might notice your mouth becoming dry, goose bumps appearing on your arms, and beads of perspiration forming on your forehead. Your dry mouth reflects a marked reduction in salivation. Your goose bumps are caused by hairs standing on end—a remnant of threat displays made by our furry prehistoric ancestors. And your perspiration provides a means of cooling off your aroused body.

Suppose that as you sit in class in this anxious, aroused state, your teacher announces that a surprise guest speaker will lecture for the entire class period. You immediately feel relieved at not having to give your speech; your arousal subsides partly because of activity in your autonomic nervous system. Your brain becomes less alert, your muscles less energetic, your heartbeat less noticeable, and your breathing more regular. Your pupils constrict to their normal size, your mouth becomes moist again, your goose bumps disappear, and you stop sweating. You might become so profoundly relaxed and relieved that you fall asleep during the guest speaker's lecture.

The Brain and Emotion

Though bodily arousal plays a role in emotionality, the brain is ultimately in control of emotional responses (LeDoux, 1995). As discussed in Chapter 3, autonomic nervous system arousal is regulated by the brain structure called the *hypothalamus*, a component of the *limbic system*, which also includes the *amygdala* and the *septum*. Among other things, the hypothalamus helps control changes in breathing and heart output during the fight-or-flight response (Spyer, 1989). The amygdala prompts us to react emotionally to environmental circumstances, enabling us to respond adaptively (Aggleton, 1993) and to form memories of emotional situations (Cahill et al., 1995). The septum suppresses aversive emotional states. For example, electrical stimulation of the septum in rats reduces their tendency to avoid fear-inducing stimuli (Thomas, 1988). The main limbic system structures are illustrated in Figure 12.2.

Though the limbic system is important in the processing of emotions (Schneider et al., 1995), the *cerebral cortex,* which covers the cerebral hemispheres, is important for our subjective experience of emotion. For example, though the limbic system tends to trigger rapid, automatic emotional reactions to stimuli, the frontal cortex modulates these reactions so that they are not maladaptive (Heller, 1993). Thus, a sudden noise might make you instantly experience fear generated by activity in your limbic system, but if you immediately realize that the noise was produced by your pet dog, your frontal cortex would prevent you from running away screaming or grabbing an object with which to defend yourself.

Research findings suggest that each cerebral hemisphere is specialized to process different emotions, with the left hemisphere more involved in positive emotions and the right hemisphere more involved in negative emotions (Davidson, 1992). But keep in mind that particular emotions are not processed *solely* in one hemisphere or the other.

Much of our knowledge about the role of each hemisphere in emotional experience comes from studies, particularly those conducted by Richard Davidson, that have measured the relative degree of activity in each hemisphere during emotional arousal. For instance, excessive activation of the left hemisphere is associated with euphoria, and excessive activation of the right hemisphere is associated with depression (Flor-Henry,

▲ Richard Davidson

"In adults and infants, the experimental arousal of positive, approach-related emotions is associated with selective activation of the left frontal region, while arousal of negative, withdrawal-related emotions is associated with selective activation of the right frontal region."

CHAPTER 12

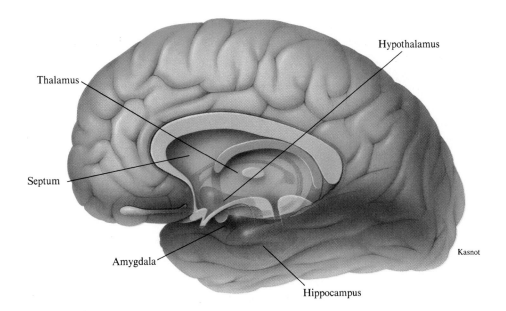

◀ FIGURE 12.2
The Limbic System
Our emotional responses are regulated by
activity in the limbic system.

Thalamus

Septum

Amygdala

Hypothalamus

Kasnot

Hippocampus

1983). One study measured electrical activity while subjects watched emotionally positive or negative film clips to evoke positive or negative emotions in them. Those who experienced positive emotion had higher left-hemisphere activity; those who experienced negative emotion had higher right-hemisphere activity (Wheeler, Davidson, & Tomarken, 1993). A study that recorded electrical activity from the brains of 10-month-old infants found that hemispheric differences in the processing of emotions appear early in life. Greater activation of the left hemisphere was associated with a pleasant facial expression and a tendency to approach people. In contrast, greater activation of the right hemisphere was associated with an unpleasant facial expression and a tendency to withdraw from people (Fox & Davidson, 1988).

The *Wada test*, which involves selective anesthesia of one cerebral hemisphere to determine hemispheric functions (particularly the site of the speech center), has also provided evidence of the lateralization of emotionality. In the Wada test, the anesthetic sodium amobarbital is injected into the left or right carotid artery of patients who are about to undergo brain surgery. Because the carotid arteries supply blood to the brain, injection of sodium amobarbital into one of them will anesthetize the associated hemisphere. Research using the Wada test shows that laughter and elation (positive emotionality) are more frequent after right-hemisphere anesthesia, while crying (negative emotionality) is more frequent after left-hemisphere anesthesia (Lee et al., 1990).

Further evidence that the left hemisphere is more related to positive emotions and the right hemisphere more related to negative emotions has been provided by studies of brain damage. Because each cerebral hemisphere inhibits the emotional activity of the other, we normally experience neither intensely positive nor intensely negative emotions. But damage to one hemisphere can release the other from its inhibition. Damage to the right hemisphere, releasing the left hemisphere from inhibition, leads to laughing, elation, optimism, and other signs of positive emotion. In contrast, damage to the left hemisphere, releasing the right hemisphere from inhibition, leads to crying, worry, pessimism, and other signs of negative emotion (Leventhal & Tomarken, 1986).

The Chemistry of Emotion

When we say that there is "good chemistry" or "bad chemistry" between people, we mean that they have positive or negative emotions in response to each other. Research has shown that our emotional responses do, indeed, depend on chemistry—hormones and neurotransmitters that convey emotion-related impulses from one neuron to

another or between neurons and body organs (Baum, Grunberg, & Singer, 1992). For example, abnormal levels of the neurotransmitters norepinephrine and serotonin have been implicated in mood disorders (see Chapter 14), such as severe depression (Curzon, 1982).

As noted earlier, stressful situations cause the secretion of the hormones epinephrine and norepinephrine, which also serve as neutrotransmitters. In a study of psychologists and physicians, levels of these hormones were measured on a day when the subjects gave a public speech and on a day when they did not. Public speaking was associated with an increase in the level of both epinephrine and norepinephrine. Moreover, there was a rise in blood cholesterol on days when the subjects gave speeches relative to days when they did not. Perhaps stress hormones, by stimulating an increase in low-density lipoproteins (which are implicated in cardiovascular disease), provide one of the mechanisms by which emotional responses to stressful situations contribute to the development of cardiovascular disease (Bolm-Audorff et al., 1989).

Endorphins, a class of neurotransmitters discussed in Chapters 3 and 5, contribute to emotional experiences by providing pain relief and evoking feelings of euphoria. For example, blood levels of endorphins rise markedly after bungee jumping and correlate positively with resulting feelings of euphoria (Hennig, Laschefski, & Opper, 1994). Even the emotional thrill we experience from a music concert, a motion picture, or a dance performance may depend on endorphin activity. This was demonstrated in a study of college students who listened to a musical passage and then received an injection of either naloxone (a drug that blocks the effects of endorphins) or a placebo (in this case, a saline solution that does not block the effects of endorphins). Neither the subject nor the experimenter knew whether the subject had received naloxone or a placebo (you might recognize this as an application of the *double-blind procedure,* which was described in Chapter 2); this prevented subject bias or experimenter bias from affecting the results. After receiving the injection, the subjects again listened to the musical passage. When asked to estimate the intensity of their emotional thrill in response to the music, the subjects who had received naloxone reported a significant decrease in intensity. The subjects who had received a placebo reported no such decrease. Because naloxone blocks the effects of endorphins, but a placebo does not, the findings support the role of endorphins in positive emotional experiences (Goldstein, 1980).

CHAPTER   12

1. What evidence is there that positive and negative emotions are processed primarily in different brain hemispheres?

2. What evidence is there that endorphins are involved in feelings of euphoria?

Answers to Staying on Track start on p. S-5.

THE EXPRESSION OF EMOTION

How do you know how your fellow students feel? Because our emotional experiences are private, they cannot be directly observed by other people. Instead, emotions are inferred from descriptions of them or from expressive behaviors. Behaviors that express emotions include vocal qualities, body movements, and facial expressions. The expression of emotion varies across cultures. For example, people from collectivist cultures, such as Costa Rica, are less comfortable expressing negative emotions than are people from individualistic cultures, such as the United States (Stephan, Stephan, & de Vargas, 1996).

Vocal Qualities and Emotional Expression

When you speak, both your words and your voice convey emotion (Bachorowski & Owren, 1995). The vocal features of speech, other than the words themselves, are called *prosody*. Prosodic features include rate, pitch, and loudness. You can use the same spoken words to express different emotions by simply altering the prosodic features of your speech—the same statement can sound sincere or sarcastic, depending on its vocal qualities. When you are happy, your voice goes up in pitch (just recall the last time you heard the voices of two people greeting each other after a long separation). Changes in vocal qualities indicative of changes in emotion tend to be consistent from one person to another and from one culture to another (Frick, 1985). Perhaps these common vocal patterns evolved in our prehistoric, prelanguage ancestors as a universal means of communicating emotional states in everyday social interaction.

Voice quality also affects social relations. It can sometimes cause social rejection, as in a study in which undergraduates rated depressed or nondepressed fellow undergraduates, who differed in how they spoke. Depressed subjects were more likely to be rejected, in part because they spoke in soft, flat voices, with long pauses. This is an important finding, because unappealing prosodic features can create a vicious cycle in which the depressed person alienates others, thereby reducing the likelihood of positive social interactions that might help the person overcome his or her depression (Paddock & Nowicki, 1986).

The prosodic features of speech are regulated primarily by the right cerebral hemisphere (Gandour et al., 1995), both when we speak (Graves & Landis, 1990) and when we listen to a speaker (Herrero & Hillix, 1990). Evidence for the role of the right hemisphere in prosody comes from studies of stroke victims and patients undergoing the Wada test. Patients with right-hemisphere strokes might retain their ability to speak, but might speak with abnormal emotional tone (Gorelick & Ross, 1987). A study in which the Wada test was given to patients about to undergo brain surgery to relieve their epilepsy found that when the patients received injections of sodium amobarbital in the left carotid artery, they lost their ability to speak. When it was injected in their right carotid artery, they retained their ability to speak but lost the ability to impart emotion to their speech (Ross et al., 1988). In essence, it seems that "the left hemisphere provides the text [words], while the right hemisphere plays the accompaniment [emotional tone]" (Merewether & Alpert, 1990, p. 325).

Body Movements and Emotional Expression

If you have observed the gestures of impatient drivers in heavy traffic on a hot summer day, you know that body movements can convey emotions. Even movements of the whole body can do so. The performance of basketball player Michael Jordan is especially appealing because his movements convey emotions.

► **Conveying Emotions Through Gestures**
Every culture conveys emotions through gestures, though a gesture that has a positive meaning in one culture might have a negative meaning in another (Ekman, Friesen, & Bear, 1984).

But how do we know that we are responding to their movements rather than simply to their facial expressions or physical appearances? The importance of body movements in expressing emotion has been demonstrated in studies that have eliminated other nonverbal emotional cues. In one study (Walk & Homan, 1984), college students watched a videotape of people performing dances that portrayed various emotions. To eliminate the influence of facial expressions and physical appearance, the dancers wore lights on their joints and danced in total darkness. Thus, the subjects saw only the movement of lights. Nonetheless, they accurately identified the emotions represented by the dances. This indicates that the emotional cues provided by body movements are distinct from those provided by facial expressions or physical appearance.

The ability to decode nonverbal behavior is important in social interaction, as exemplified by the following research findings. Females are superior to males in decoding emotional states from body movements (Sogon & Izard, 1987). Elementary school children who are better at decoding nonverbal emotional cues are more popular (Nowicki & Duke, 1992). College roommates rate their relationship more positively when both are high in decoding ability than when one or both are low in it (Hodgins & Zuckerman, 1990). And psychological counselors might be more effective when they are skillful in noting changes in their clients' nonverbal behavior (Hill & Stephany, 1990).

We seem to prefer an optimal level of nonverbal interaction in everyday social interactions. We like people who are neither too nonverbally aloof nor too nonverbally intrusive. In a study that supported this finding, people who were walking on a college campus were asked to respond to a survey. During the brief interaction, they were randomly exposed to one of four conditions related to the interviewer's behavior: (1) eye contact and a momentary touch; (2) eye contact and no touch; (3) no eye contact and a momentary touch; or (4) no eye contact and no touch. At the end of the interaction, the interviewer dropped several folded questionnaires. Subjects in the second or third conditions were more likely to help pick them up than were subjects in the first or fourth. Thus, in agreement with the notion that there is an optimal level of nonverbal communication, the subjects responded more positively to a moderate level of nonverbal interaction (Goldman & Fordyce, 1983).

Facial Expressions and Emotional Expression

Philip D. Chesterfield, an eighteenth-century British statesman, noted that our faces give away our emotions: "Look in the face of the person to whom you are speaking if you wish to know his real sentiments, for he can command his words more easily than his countenance." Chesterfield's observation may explain, in part, how teachers' expectations create the Pygmalion effect (see Chapter 2). Though teachers might believe they are unbiased when speaking to their students, their facial expressions can communicate their true feelings, whether positive or negative, about particular students (Babad, Bernieri, & Rosenthal, 1989). But our recognition of facial expressions might depend on the social context. In one study, subjects who displayed facial expressions of anger while in a frightening situation were judged to be afraid (Carroll & Russell, 1996).

Research has shown that facial expressions convey both the intensity and the pleasantness of our emotional states. Many cardplayers realize this, leading them to maintain an expressionless poker face to avoid revealing the strength of their hands. But cardplayers should note that any judgment of emotions from a person's facial expression depends, in part, on the facial expressions of other people who are present. For example, an expressionless face will seem sad when presented next to a happy face, but it will seem happy when presented next to a sad face (Russell & Fehr, 1987). So, if everyone else maintains a sad face, the person with a poker face will seem happy—as though she or he has a good hand. And if everyone else maintains a happy face, the person with a poker face will seem sad—as though he or she has a poor hand. As in the recognition of emotions from body movements, females are superior to males in recognizing emotions from facial expressions (Giovannini & Ricci Bitti, 1981). Moreover, though males and females tend to respond empathetically by mimicking facial expressions, women do so more demonstratively (Lundqvist, 1995).

Actors who feel the emotions they are portraying facially produce performances that are more emotionally convincing to audiences (Gosselin, Kirouac, & Dore, 1995). Knowledge of the relationship between facial expressions and emotions has enabled researchers to distinguish honest emotional expressions from fake ones. For example, the face reveals when smiles are sincere or false. Sincere smiles include muscular activity around the eyes, causing the skin to wrinkle, and around the mouth, causing the corners of the lips to rise (Frank & Ekman, 1993). This natural smile is called the *Duchenne smile*. In contrast, when people display insincere smiles, perhaps to hide their negative emotional state, the corners of their lips are drawn downward and their upper lip curls up. In one experiment, subjects were more likely to display the Duchenne smile when they watched a pleasant film than when they watched an unpleasant film. They also reported more positive emotions when they exhibited the Duchenne smile, verifying it as a sign of a pleasant emotional state (Ekman, Davidson, & Friesen, 1990).

Charles Darwin (1872/1965) believed that facial expressions evolved because they promoted survival by communicating emotions and helping individuals distinguish friend from foe. For example, the human facial expression of contempt might be a modification of the snarl found in dogs, apes, and our prehistoric ancestors (Izard & Haynes, 1988). Darwin's belief was supported in an experiment that measured how quickly subjects could detect an angry face or a happy face in a crowd (Hansen & Hansen, 1988). The subjects reported that a single angry face seemed to pop out of the crowd faster than a single happy face. The results supported the subjects' impressions. They were able to detect an angry face faster than a happy face. Why might we have evolved the ability to detect angry faces more quickly than other faces? A possible reason is that it promotes our survival by motivating us to take more-immediate action to confront or to escape from a person displaying an angry face.

Research by Carroll Izard (1990a) and his colleagues supports Darwin's view that facial expressions for basic emotions are inborn and universal. One line of research has found that even people who are blind from birth exhibit facial expressions for the basic emotions, including joy, fear, anger, disgust, sadness, and surprise. An early case study involved a 10-year-old girl who had been born deaf and blind. Despite her inability to see normal facial expressions or to receive spoken instructions on how to form them, she displayed appropriate facial expressions for the basic emotions (Goodenough, 1932). Nonetheless, blind infants exhibit a more limited repertoire of facial expressions than do sighted infants (Troster & Brambring, 1992).

A second line of research support for the inborn, universal nature of facial expressions comes from studies showing that young infants produce facial expressions for the basic emotions (Izard et al., 1980). In one study, newborn infants were given solutions of sugar or quinine (which tastes bitter). Despite having no prior experience with those tastes, their facial expressions showed pleasure or displeasure, depending on which solution they had tasted. And the intensity of their facial expressions varied with the strength of the solutions (Ganchrow, Steiner, & Daher, 1983). At 5 months of age, infants react differently to different facial expressions. In one study, infants blinked more in response to angry faces than to happy faces (Balaban, 1995).

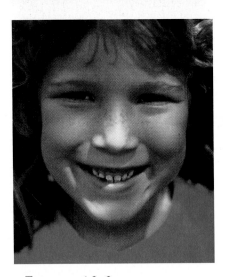

The Universality of Facial Expressions
Support for the inborn, universal nature of facial expressions representing the basic emotions comes from studies showing similar facial expressions in people from different cultures, such as these smiling people from Rwanda, Thailand, and the United States.

Further support for Darwin's evolutionary view of facial expressions comes from studies showing that facial expressions for the basic emotions are universal across cultures (Ekman, 1993), as illustrated in Figure 12.3. The subjects in one study were members of the Fore tribe of New Guinea, who had almost no contact with Westerners prior to the study (Ekman & Friesen, 1971). The tribemembers listened to descriptions of a series of emotion-arousing situations representing joy, fear, anger, disgust, sadness, or surprise. The descriptions included situations such as "He is looking at something that smells bad" and "Her friends have come and she is happy." After each description, the tribemembers viewed a set of three photographs of Western faces expressing different emotions, from which they selected the face portraying the emotion of the person in the description they had just heard.

The tribemembers correctly identified expressions portraying joy, anger, sadness, and disgust but failed to distinguish between expressions portraying fear and surprise. Perhaps the tribemembers' expressions for fear and surprise did not differ because similar situations (such as an enemy or a wild animal suddenly appearing from out of the jungle) evoke both fear and surprise in their culture. This study was replicated, with similar results, in a more recent study of people in ten different cultures from around the world (Ekman et al., 1987). In still another study that supported the universality of certain facial expressions, American, Japanese, and Indonesian subjects agreed on the facial expression that represented the emotion of contempt (Ekman & Heider, 1988). The universality of the contempt expression was supported in a study of Polish, Japanese, Hungarian, and Vietnamese subjects (Matsumoto, 1992). Nonetheless, some researchers question whether research showing cross-cultural consistency in recognition of facial expressions has been sound enough to merit accepting their findings (Russell, 1995). That is, there are cross-cultural differences in the subjective feelings, physiological responses, and expressive behavior associated with emotions (Scherer & Wallbott, 1994).

Regardless of the universality of facial expressions, they play an important role in our everyday lives. In fact, the facial expressions of our favorite television news anchors might affect our preferences for political candidates. A study conducted during the 1984 presidential campaign found that NBC's Tom Brokaw, CBS's Dan Rather, and ABC's Peter Jennings did not show biases in what they said about Republican candidate Ronald Reagan and Democratic candidate Walter Mondale. But Jennings showed a bias in his facial expressions. Unlike Brokaw and Rather, Jennings displayed significantly more positive facial expressions when speaking about Reagan than when speaking about Mondale. A telephone survey found that voters who regularly watched Jennings were significantly more likely to vote for Reagan than were those who watched Brokaw or Rather. The researchers concluded that Jennings's biased facial expressions might have made some viewers more favorable toward Reagan. Of course we must be careful to avoid making hasty inferences about causation (see Chapter 2). Perhaps Jennings's facial expressions did not affect viewers' preferences. The researchers cautioned that, instead, those who already favored Reagan might have preferred to watch Jennings's because he smiled more when talking about him (Mullen et al., 1986).

Staying on Track: *The Expression of Emotion*

1. What are the prosodic features of speech?
2. What evidence is there that certain emotional facial expressions are universal?

THE EXPERIENCE OF EMOTION

Though we have hundreds of words for emotions, there seem to be only a few basic emotions, from which all others are derived. A recent model of emotion, devised by Robert Plutchik (1980), considers joy, fear, anger, disgust, sadness, surprise, acceptance, and anticipation to be the basic emotions. More-complex emotions arise from mixtures of these basic ones (see Figure 12.4).

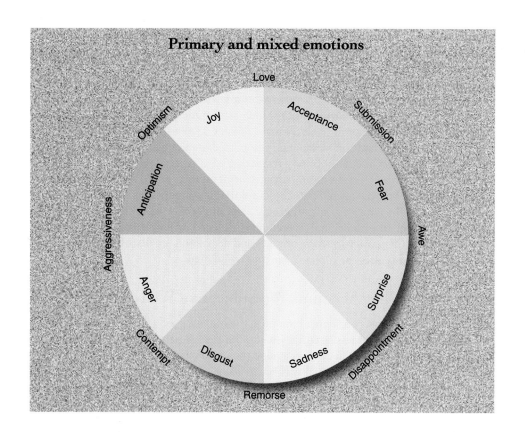

Primary and mixed emotions

Love
Acceptance
Submission
Fear
Awe
Surprise
Disappointment
Sadness
Remorse
Disgust
Contempt
Anger
Aggressiveness
Anticipation
Optimism
Joy

◀ **FIGURE 12.4**
The Emotion Wheel
According to Robert Plutchik (1980), there are eight primary emotions, composed of four pairs of opposites: joy and sadness, acceptance and disgust, fear and anger, and surprise and anticipation. We cannot experience opposites simultaneously. Thus, you could not feel joyful and sad at the same time. The closer together emotions are on Plutchik's emotion wheel, the more similar they are to each other. Mixtures of adjacent emotions produce other emotions. For example, the mixture of joy and acceptance produces love, and the mixture of anger and disgust produces contempt.

Charles Darwin assumed that the basic emotions evolved because they promoted our survival. For example, disgust (which means "bad taste") might have evolved because it prevented our ancient ancestors from ingesting poisonous substances. This might explain why human beings in all cultures exhibit an early feeling of disgust at the sight and smell of feces—the "universal disgust object" (Rozin & Fallon, 1987). Note that disgust involves each of the major aspects of emotion: physiological change (stomach contractions causing nausea), expressive behavior (a contorted face), and mental experience (a feeling of revulsion). And the facial expression of disgust now has a social meaning as well, expressing revulsion at something that someone has said or done.

Folk wisdom holds that just as certain people are prone to experience unpleasant emotions, certain days—particularly so-called blue Mondays—are more likely to induce unpleasant emotions. A study of the "blue Monday effect" had people who insisted that their moods were lowest on Mondays keep daily diaries of their emotional states (Stone et al., 1985). The results indicated that a given person's emotional states tended to be similar on Monday, Tuesday, Wednesday, and Thursday. But, as you might expect, the person's emotional state on weekend days—Friday, Saturday, and Sunday—tended to be more positive than on weekdays. Evidently our "blue Mondays" owe their "blueness" to the contrast of returning to our normal weekday emotional state, rather than to something unique about Mondays. In essence, we might have "blue Mondays," but we also have equally blue Tuesdays, Wednesdays, and Thursdays. We simply notice the contrast between "bright Sunday" and "blue Monday" more.

The experience of emotion varies in both its intensity and its pleasantness. People who tend to experience intensely pleasant emotions (such as elation) also tend to experience intensely unpleasant emotions (such as despair). People who tend to experience mildly pleasant emotions (such as gladness) also tend to experience mildly unpleasant emotions (such as disappointment). This might be one reason why our happiness depends more on the frequency, rather than the intensity, of our positive emotional experiences. A second reason is that intensely positive events can make less-intense positive events seem even less positive. And a third reason is that the happier you are when you succeed at a task, the unhappier you will be when you fail at it (Diener et al., 1991).

▲ **Can a Smile Influence Voters?**
During the 1984 presidential campaign, Peter Jennings showed more positive facial expressions when speaking about Ronald Reagan than when speaking about Walter Mondale. Tom Brokaw and Dan Rather showed no such bias. People who watched Jennings were more likely to vote for Reagan than were people who watched Brokaw or Rather (Mullen et al., 1986). Could those voters have been influenced by Jennings's smiles? What other reasons can you think of that might explain this correlation?

▲ Robert Plutchik

"The history of psychology is so marked with differences as to the meaning of emotion that some psychologists have suggested that the term be eliminated from psychological writings."

▲ Edward Diener

"Women report more negative affect than men but equal happiness as men. . . . Generally, women's more intense positive emotions balance their higher negative affect."

social-comparison theory

The theory that happiness is the result of estimating that one's life circumstances are more favorable than those of others.

adaptation-level theory

The theory that happiness depends on comparing one's present circumstances with one's past circumstances.

Though emotions help us survive and enrich our lives, they can imperil our health. Emotions can impair the immune response, making us more prone to illness. For example, depression has an adverse effect on the immune system (O'Leary, 1990), perhaps even impairing its ability to destroy cancer cells (Levenson & Bemis, 1991). Chapter 16 discusses the mechanisms by which emotions can stimulate or inhibit the immune system.

People tend to view pleasant emotions, such as happiness, as normal and unpleasant emotions, such as depression, as abnormal (Sommers, 1984). Yet, until the past two decades, psychologists had conducted many more studies of unpleasant emotions. In fact, *Psychological Abstracts*, the main library research tool of psychologists, first published in the 1920s, did not include the term *happiness* in its index until 1973 (Diener, 1984). Another perusal of *Psychological Abstracts* found that it contained more emotion-related references under the category of "pathology" than under any other category (Whissell, 1984). To counter the traditional overemphasis placed on unpleasant emotions, and because unpleasant emotions such as anxiety and depression are discussed in later chapters, this chapter discusses the topics of happiness and humor.

Happiness: What Accounts for Subjective Well-Being?

Many philosophers have considered happiness the highest good (Diener, 1984). Thomas Jefferson even made happiness a central issue in the Declaration of Independence. Factors that correlate with happiness in cultures around the world include political systems that promote human rights and societal equality (Diener, Diener, & Diener, 1995). Happiness is also positively correlated with intelligence, social skills, and family support (Diener & Fujita, 1995). Physical attractiveness has a positive correlation with happiness. But this relationship does not necessarily mean that physical attractiveness causes happiness. Perhaps happy people make themselves more physically attractive. For example, happy people are more likely to wear attractive clothing, jewelry, and hairstyles (Diener, Wolsic, & Fujita, 1995).

Our happiness depends on comparisons we make between ourselves and others and between our current circumstances and our past circumstances (Smith, Diener, & Wedell, 1989). Charles Montesquieu, an eighteenth-century French philosopher, noted: "If one only wished to be happy, this could be easily accomplished; but we wish to be happier than other people, and this is always difficult, for we believe others to be happier than they are." One of the most influential theories of happiness—**social-comparison theory**—shares Montesquieu's assumption about the nature of happiness. This theory considers happiness to be the result of estimating that one's life circumstances are more favorable than those of others (VanderZee et al., 1996), as when you discover that your grade is one of the highest in the class. In one study, college students felt happier about themselves when in the presence of another person who was relatively worse off (Strack et al., 1990). Thus, you can make yourself happier with your own life by purposely comparing it with the lives of those who are less fortunate. A factor in social comparison that is less important than commonly believed is wealth. According to happiness researcher Edward Diener (1984), wealthy Americans are no happier than nonwealthy Americans, provided that the nonwealthy people have at least the basic necessities of life, such as a job, home, and family. Though this finding holds true in the United States, it does not hold true in all cultures. For example, a study of people in 39 other countries found a stronger relationship between high income and happiness than in the United States (Diener et al., 1993).

Adaptation-level theory holds that happiness depends not on comparing yourself with other people but with comparing yourself with yourself. Thus, your current happiness depends in part on comparing your present circumstances and your past circumstances. Your present state of happiness is governed more by the most recent events in your life than by the more distant events (Suh, Diener, & Fujita, 1996). But as your circumstances improve, your standard of happiness becomes higher. This can have surprising emotional consequences for people who gain sudden financial success. Life's small pleasures might no longer make them happy—their standards of happiness might become too high, as revealed by a study of Illinois state lottery winners (Brickman, Coates, & Janoff-Bulman, 1978): Despite winning from $50,000 to $1 million, these winners were no happier than

they had been in the past. In fact, they found less pleasure in formerly enjoyable everyday activities, such as watching television, shopping for clothes, or talking with a friend. So, although comparing our circumstances with those of less-fortunate people can make us happier, improvements in our own circumstances might make us adopt increasingly higher standards of happiness—making happiness more and more elusive. Recognizing this, the nineteenth-century clergyman Henry Van Dyke remarked, "It is better to desire the things we have than to have the things we desire."

Humor: What Makes Some Things Funny?

Happiness is enhanced by humor, whether offered by friends, funny movies, situation comedies on television, or stand-up comedians in nightclubs. Psychologists have only recently begun to study humor scientifically. Research findings support the importance of humor in our everyday lives. Humor defuses interpersonal conflicts (McClane & Singer, 1991), contributes to effective teaching (Safford, 1991), and reduces the effects of stress (Martin et al., 1993).

One surprising finding has been that humorous people might not feel as extraverted as they act. Consider the class clown, who sees humor in everything. Though that person might be popular, he might not be as sociable as you might expect; he might, instead, use humor as a way to avoid close personal relationships. For example, a study of humorous adolescents found that they often used humor to maintain their social distance from other people (Prasinos & Tittler, 1981). You may have been frustrated at one time or another by such people, who joke about everything, rarely converse in a serious manner, and never disclose their personal feelings. Evidence that some people use humor to maintain their social distance might explain anecdotal reports that many comedians, who might appear socially outgoing in public performances, are socially reclusive in their private lives. Johnny Carson, who retired in 1992 after 30 years as host of the "Tonight Show," was humorous and engaging on stage but relatively somber and socially aloof off stage.

Granted that humorous people might not be as gregarious as they seem, we are still left with the question: What makes their humor amusing? One factor is the social contexts, such as night clubs, in which humor is expressed. To people who are inebriated, comedians who use blunt, simple humor will seem funnier than comedians who use subtle, complex humor (Weaver et al., 1985). Thus, if you drank a few beers, you would probably find a Three Stooges movie more amusing and a Dennis Miller monologue less amusing.

But what accounts for our responses to humor while in a sober state? The most popular theories are the *disparagement theory*, the *incongruity theory*, and the *release theory* (Berger, 1987). According to C. L. Edson, a twentieth-century American newspaper editor, "We love a joke that hands us a pat on the back while it kicks the other fellow down the stairs." Edson's comment indicates that he favored the **disparagement theory** of humor, first put

▲ Money Does Not Necessarily Buy Happiness
If you buy lottery tickets because you believe that winning the jackpot in your state lottery would make you happy, you may be in for a disappointment should you someday win. Lottery winners often are no happier after they win than they were before. In fact, they might no longer gain satisfaction from many of life's little pleasures.

disparagement theory

The theory that humor is amusing when it makes one feel superior to other people.

(a)

(b)

(c)

▲ **Theories of Humor**
Humor researchers have found that humor is based on disparagement, incongruity, or release. (a) If you have seen Don Rickles hurl insults at his audience or Joan Rivers make critical remarks about prominent people, you have observed performances that support the disparagement theory of humor. (b) The incongruity theory of humor gains support from comedians such as Jay Leno, Carol Leifer, and David Letterman, who play on our sense of the absurd to make us laugh. (c) Comedians such as Eddie Murphy and Buddy Hackett, who rely on sexual humor, exemplify the release theory of humor, which assumes that the sudden release of sexual tension induces a feeling of amusement.

incongruity theory
The theory that humor is amusing when it brings together incompatible ideas in a surprising outcome that violates one's expectations.

release theory
The theory that humor is amusing when it relieves one's sexual or aggressive anxiety.

forth by the seventeenth-century English philosopher Thomas Hobbes. Hobbes claimed that we feel amused when humor makes us feel superior to other people (Nevo, 1985). One study found that humor in which the target is disparaged is perceived as funnier than humor in which the target is uplifted (Mio & Graesser, 1991). Research supporting Hobbes's position has found that we are especially amused when we dislike those to whom we are made to feel superior (Wicker, Barron, & Willis, 1980). Satirists, newspaper columnists, and television commentators take this approach by disparaging certain commonly disliked groups, such as greedy lawyers, crooked politicians, and phony evangelists.

We also like disparaging humor better when we like the person doing the disparaging. Consider David Letterman, host of the Late Show. Why is his disparaging humor perceived as funny? It is funny, in part, because many people find him likable. In a study in which students were presented with examples of Letterman's disparaging humor, those who found him likable rated his humor as funnier (Oppliger & Sherblom, 1992).

In the eighteenth century, the German philosopher Immanuel Kant put forth an alternative theory of humor, the **incongruity theory.** Incongruous humor brings together incompatible ideas in a surprising outcome that violates our expectations (Deckers & Buttram, 1990). Incongruous jokes tend to be perceived as more humorous than other jokes (Hillson & Martin, 1994). The incongruity theory explains why many jokes require timing and may lose something on the second hearing—bad timing or repetition can destroy the incongruity (Kuhlman, 1985). The appreciation of incongruous humor varies with age and conservatism. A study of more than 4,000 subjects aged 14 to 66 found that older people and more-conservative people preferred incongruous humor more, and nonsense humor less, than did younger people and more liberal people (Ruch, McGhee, & Hehl, 1990).

Another theory of humor, **release theory,** is based on Sigmund Freud's claim that humor is a cathartic outlet for anxiety caused by repressed sexual or aggressive energy, as explained in his book *Jokes and Their Relationship to the Unconscious* (Freud, 1905). Humor can raise your level of anxiety—and then suddenly lower it, providing you relief so pleasurable that it can make you laugh (McCauley et al., 1983). Consider a study in which students were told they would be handling or taking blood samples from rats. As they approached the rats, they suddenly discovered they were toys. The students then responded to questionnaires about their reactions to the situation. The more anxious and the more surprised they had been, the funnier they found the situation, thereby supporting the release theory (Shurcliff, 1968). The release theory explains the popularity of humor that plays on our sexual anxieties by weaving a story that ends with a punch line that relieves our tension (Schill & O'Laughlin, 1984).

In a study bearing on the release theory of humor in regard to aggression, high school students were given a frustrating exam. Afterward, they were more likely to respond aggressively to a subsequent frustrating situation. But subjects who were exposed after the exam to a humorous situation that provoked laughter became less likely to respond aggressively to the later frustration. According to the release theory, the subjects' laughter provided a cathartic experience, which released energy that would have provoked later aggression (Ziv, 1987). Despite some research supportive of the release theory, sexual or aggressive humor does not usually reduce the tendency to engage in sex or aggression (Nevo & Nevo, 1983).

The field of humor research is relatively young, and more research is needed to uncover the factors that make people find amusement in one kind of humor but not in another. Such research might explain, for example, why some people (most notably, the French) find Jerry Lewis amusing, while others do not.

Staying on Track: *The Experience of Emotion*

1. What factors are associated with personal happiness?
2. What are the disparagement theory, the incongruity theory, and the release theory of humor?

THEORIES OF EMOTION

How do we explain emotional experience? Theories of emotion vary in their attention to physiology, behavior, and cognition.

Biopsychological Theories of Emotion

Though most theories of emotion recognize the importance of physiological factors, certain theories stress them.

The James-Lange Theory of Emotion

In the late nineteenth century, the American psychologist William James (1884) claimed that physiological changes precede emotional experiences. Because a Danish physiologist named Carl Lange (1834–1900) made the same claim at about the same time, it became known as the **James-Lange theory** (see Figure 12.5). Note that the theory violates the commonsense belief that physiological changes follow emotional experiences.

The main implication of the James-Lange theory is that particular emotional events stimulate specific patterns of physiological changes, each evoking a specific emotional experience (Lang, 1994). According to James (1890/1981, Vol. 2, p. 1065):

> ► Common-sense says, we lose our fortune, are sorry and weep; we meet a bear, are frightened and run; we are insulted by a rival, are angry and strike . . . the more rational statement is that we feel sorry because we cry, angry because we strike, afraid because we tremble.

Your own experience might provide evidence in support of this theory. If you have ever barely avoided an automobile accident, you may have noticed your pulse racing and your palms sweating, and then a moment later found yourself overcome by fear.

The James-Lange theory provoked criticism from the American physiologist Walter Cannon (1927). Consider three of Cannon's main criticisms: First, Cannon noted that we have poor ability to perceive many of the subtle physiological changes induced by the sympathetic nervous system. How could the perception of physiological changes be the basis of emotional experiences when we cannot perceive many of those changes? Second, Cannon noted that different emotions are associated with the same pattern of physiological arousal. How could different emotions be evoked by the same pattern of arousal? And third, Cannon found that physiological changes dependent on the secretion of hormones by the adrenal glands are too slow to be the basis of all emotions. How could a process that takes several seconds account for almost-instantaneous emotional experiences?

In part because of Cannon's criticisms, the James-Lange theory fell into disfavor for several decades. But recent research has lent some support to it. In one study, subjects were directed to adopt facial expressions representing fear, anger, disgust, sadness, surprise, and happiness (Ekman, Levenson, & Friesen, 1983). The subjects were told which muscles to contract or relax but were not told which emotions they were expressing. Recordings of heart rate and skin temperature were taken as they maintained the facial expressions. The results showed that the facial expression of fear induced a large increase in heart rate and a slight decrease in finger temperature, while the facial expression of anger induced a large increase in both heart rate and finger temperature (see Figure 12.6). Finger temperature varies with the amount of blood flow: a decrease in blood flow causes a decrease in temperature, and an increase in blood flow causes an increase in temperature. The presence of different patterns of autonomic activity for different emotions has been replicated in non-Western cultures, such as West Sumatra (Levenson et al., 1992).

Note everyday language: when we are afraid, we have "cold feet," and when we are angry, our "blood is boiling." The difference in the patterns of physiological arousal between fear and anger supports the assumption of the James-Lange theory that particular emotions are associated with particular patterns of physiological arousal. A more recent study lent further support to the specificity of autonomic nervous system responses in different emotions. Subjects followed muscle-by-muscle instructions for constructing facial

James-Lange theory
The theory that specific patterns of physiological changes evoke specific emotional experiences.

James-Lange Theory of Emotion
According to the James-Lange theory, the perception of an event or object induces a specific pattern of physiological changes, which evokes a specific emotional experience.

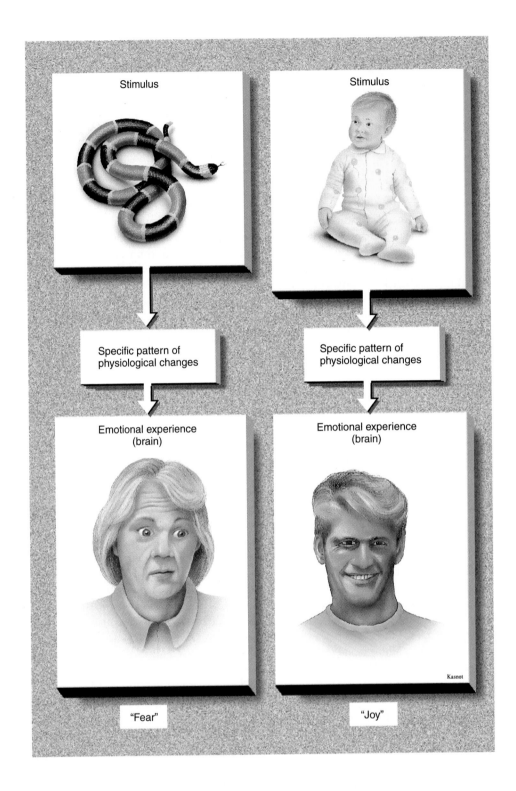

Cannon-Bard theory

The theory that an emotion is produced when an event or object is perceived by the thalamus, which conveys this information simultaneously to the cerebral cortex and the skeletal muscles and autonomic nervous system.

expressions associated with particular emotions and imagined past emotional experiences. The subjects' physiological patterns of response distinguished between the emotions (Levenson et al., 1991).

The Cannon-Bard Theory of Emotion

After rejecting the James-Lange theory of emotion, Walter Cannon (1927) and Philip Bard (1934) put forth their own theory, giving equal weight to physiological changes and cognitive processes. The **Cannon-Bard theory** (see Figure 12.7) claims that an emotion is

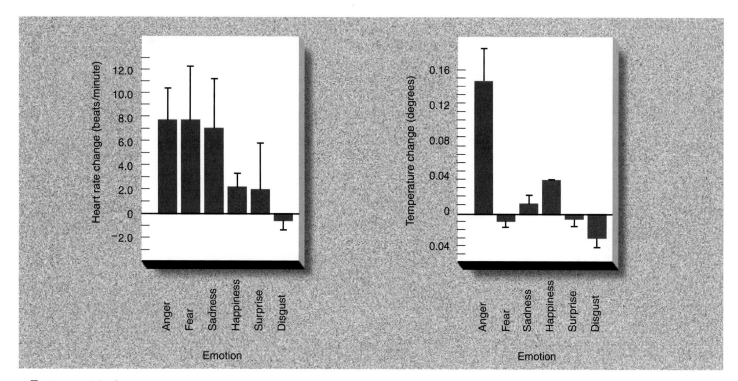

▲ FIGURE 12.6

Specificity of Autonomic Response Patterns

As illustrated in these graphs, heart rate and finger temperature vary between emotions. For example, anger is associated with marked increases in both heart rate and finger temperature, while fear is associated with a marked increase in heart rate and a slight decrease in finger temperature.

produced when an event or object is perceived by the thalamus, the brain structure that conveys this information simultaneously to the cerebral cortex and to the skeletal muscles and sympathetic nervous system.

The cerebral cortex then uses memories of past experiences to determine the nature of the perceived event or object, providing the subjective experience of emotion. Meanwhile, the muscles and sympathetic nervous system provide the physiological arousal that prepares the individual to take action to adjust to the situation that evoked the emotion. Unlike the James-Lange theory, the Cannon-Bard theory assumes that different emotions are associated with the same state of physiological arousal. The Cannon-Bard theory has failed to gain research support, because the thalamus does not appear to play the role the researchers envisioned. But if the theory is recast in terms of the limbic system instead of the thalamus, it *is* supported by research findings. For example, though the thalamus might not directly *cause* emotional responses, it does relay sensory information to the amygdala, which then processes the information. This can occur even when the cerebral cortex is removed; in one study, rats whose visual cortexes had been destroyed still learned to fear visual stimuli associated with pain (LeDoux, Romanski, & Xagoraris, 1989).

Research on victims of spinal cord damage has provided support for the Cannon-Bard theory, while contradicting the James-Lange theory. Studies have found that even people with spinal cord injuries that prevent them from perceiving their bodily arousal experience distinct emotions, often more intensely than before their spinal cord injury (Bermond et al., 1991; Chwalisz, Diener, & Gallagher, 1988). This violates the James-Lange theory's assumption that emotional experience depends on the perception of bodily arousal, while supporting the Cannon-Bard theory's assumption that emotional experience depends on the brain's perception of ongoing events. Of course, as you will learn later, research on victims of spinal cord damage does not rule out sensations from one's own facial expressions as a factor in emotional experience.

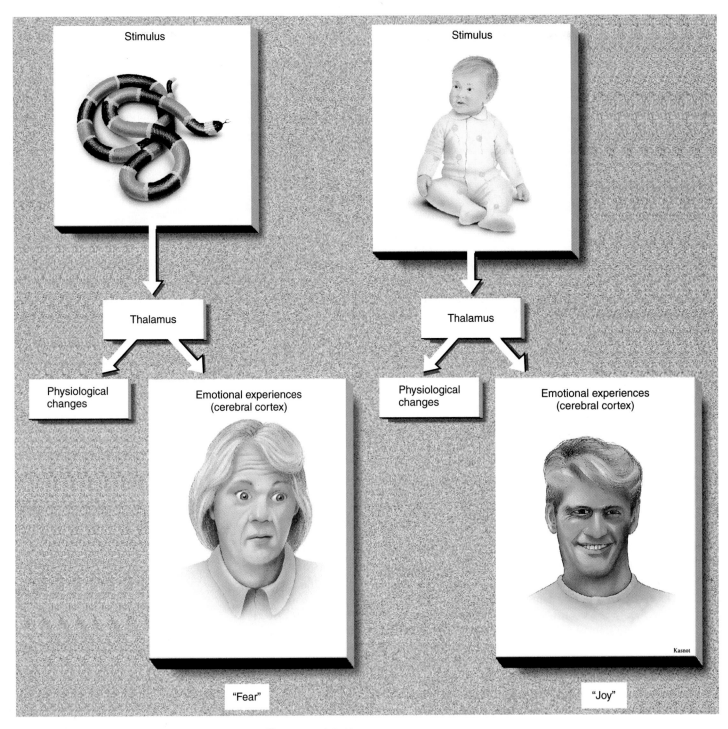

▲ FIGURE 12.7
Cannon-Bard Theory of Emotion
According to the Cannon-Bard theory, when we perceive an event or object, the thalamus activates the skeletal muscles and sympathetic nervous system organs, as well as the cerebral cortex.

The Opponent-Process Theory of Emotion

In anticipating another theory of emotion, Plato, in the *Phaedo*, states:

► How strange would appear to be this thing that we call pleasure! And how curiously it is related to what is thought to be its opposite, pain! The two will never be found together in a man, and yet if you seek the one and obtain it, you are almost bound always to get the other

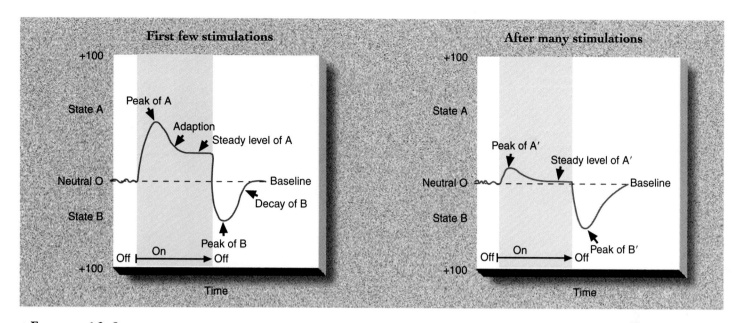

First few stimulations

+100

State A

Peak of A

Adaption

Steady level of A

Neutral O — Baseline

State B

Decay of B

Peak of B

Off | On → Off

+100

Time

After many stimulations

+100

State A

Peak of A'

Steady level of A'

Neutral O — Baseline

State B

Peak of B'

Off | On → Off

+100

Time

▲ **FIGURE 12.8**

Opponent-Process Theory of Emotion

According to the opponent-process theory, when we experience an emotion (A), an opposing emotion (B) will counter the first emotion, dampening the experience of that emotion (as indicated by the steady level of A being lower than the peak of A). As we experience the first emotion (A') on repeated occasions, the opposing emotion (B') becomes stronger and the first emotion weaker, which leads to an even weaker experience of the first emotion (as indicated by the steady level of A' being lower than the peak of A'). For example, the first time you drove on a highway you might have experienced fear, followed by a feeling of relief. As you drove on highways on repeated occasions, your feeling of fear eventually gave way to a feeling of mild arousal (Solomon, 1980).

as well, just as though they were both attached to one and the same head. . . . Wherever the one is found, the other follows up behind. So, in my case, since I had pain in my leg as a result of the fetters, pleasure seems to have come to follow it up.

If Plato were alive today, he might favor the **opponent-process theory** of emotion (see Figure 12.8), which holds that the mammalian brain has evolved mechanisms that counteract strong positive or negative emotions by evoking an opposite emotional response to maintain homeostasis. According to Richard Solomon (1980), who first put forth the theory, the opposing emotion begins sometime after the onset of the first emotion and lasts longer than the first emotion. If we experience the first emotion on repeated occasions, the opposing emotion grows stronger and the emotion that is experienced becomes a compromise between the two opposing emotional states.

Suppose that you took up skydiving. The first time you parachuted from an airplane you would probably feel terror. After surviving the jump, your feeling of terror would be replaced by a feeling of relief. As you jumped again and again, you would feel anticipation instead of terror as you prepared to jump. And your initial postjump feeling of relief might intensify into a feeling of exhilaration.

The opponent-process theory might explain the depression that often follows the joy of childbirth or the euphoria that often follows the anxiety of final-exams week. It might even explain why some blood donors become seemingly "addicted" to donating blood. When a person first donates blood, she might experience fear—but afterward might experience a pleasant feeling known as the "warm glow" effect. If the person repeatedly donates blood, the "warm glow" strengthens, leading the person to donate blood in order to induce that feeling (Piliavin, Callero, & Evans, 1982).

The opponent-process theory implies that our brains are programmed against hedonism, because people who experience intense pleasure are doomed to experience intense displeasure. This provides support for those who favor the "happy medium"—moderation in everything, including emotional experiences.

opponent-process theory

The theory that the brain counteracts a strong positive or negative emotion by evoking an opposite emotional response.

▲ **Richard Solomon (1918–1995)**

"Many hedonic, affective, or emotional states are automatically opposed by central nervous system mechanisms which reduce the intensity of hedonic feelings, both pleasant and aversive."

> ► FIGURE 12.9
> **The Facial-Feedback Theory of Emotion**
> According to the facial-feedback theory of emotion, particular patterns of sensory feedback from facial expressions evoke particular emotions. Thus, sensory feedback from the corrugator muscles, which are active when we frown, may contribute to unpleasant emotional experiences. Similarly, sensory feedback from the zygomatic muscles, which are active when we smile, may contribute to pleasant emotional experiences.

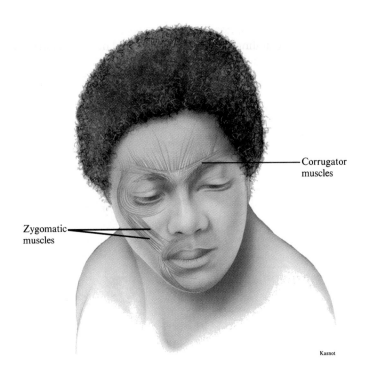

Corrugator muscles

Zygomatic muscles

Kasnot

facial-feedback theory
The theory that particular facial expressions induce particular emotional experiences.

▲ **Fear and Euphoria**
According to the opponent-process theory of emotion, the fear this ski jumper experienced when he first learned to jump eventually gave way to a feeling of euphoria.

Behavioral Theories of Emotion: The Facial-Feedback Theory of Emotion

Benjamin Franklin claimed, "A cheerful face is nearly as good for an invalid as healthy weather." Have you ever received the advice "Put on a happy face" or "Keep a stiff upper lip" from people trying to help you overcome adversity? Both of these bits of advice are commonsense versions of the **facial-feedback theory** of emotion (see Figure 12.9), which holds that our facial expressions affect our emotional experiences. Because it assumes that emotional experience is caused by the perception of physiological changes, the James-Lange theory inspired the facial-feedback theory (Izard, 1990b). As you learned in the discussion of the James-Lange theory, adopting a facial expression characteristic of a particular emotion can induce that emotion (Ekman, Levenson, & Friesen, 1983). But unlike the James-Lange theory, which is primarily concerned with the effects of autonomic nervous system activity on emotion, the facial-feedback theory is limited to the effects of facial expressions.

The facial-feedback theory was put forth in 1907 by the French physician Israel Waynbaum and has recently been restated in various versions. Waynbaum assumed that particular facial expressions alter the flow of blood to particular regions of the brain, thereby evoking particular emotional experiences. For example, smiling might increase the flow of blood to regions of the brain that elevate mood. It remains for research to test Waynbaum's theory, a technically difficult task (Zajonc, 1985).

Contemporary facial-feedback theorists, led by Paul Ekman (1992b), assume that evolution has endowed us with facial expressions that provide different patterns of sensory feedback of muscle tension levels to the brain, thereby evoking different emotions. Support for the theory has come from studies that have found that emotional experiences follow facial expressions rather than precede them, and that sensory neurons convey information from facial muscles directly to the hypothalamus, which plays an important role in emotional arousal (Zajonc, 1985).

But the facial-feedback theory has not received unqualified support. Though there is a positive association between particular facial expressions and particular emotional experiences (Adelmann & Zajonc, 1989), the effect of facial feedback on emotional experience tends to be small (Matsumoto, 1987). Some studies also have found that emotional experience depends more on feedback from autonomic nervous system organs than on feedback from facial muscles (Buck, 1980). Apparently, feedback from facial expressions is just one of several factors that govern our emotional experiences.

Though facial expressions might not be the sole cause of emotions, they can contribute to emotional experience. (Try smiling and then frowning, and note the subtle differences they induce in your mood.) For example, adopting a hostile or friendly facial expression can move one's mood in that direction (Ohira & Kurono, 1993). In one study, female subjects were asked to imagine three pleasant scenes and three unpleasant scenes (McCanne & Anderson, 1987). The three pleasant scenes were "You get a 4.0 grade point average," "You inherit a million dollars," and "You meet the man of your dreams." The three unpleasant scenes were "Your mother dies," "You lose a really close friendship," and "You lose a limb in an accident."

The subjects imagined each scene three times. The first time they simply imagined the scene. The second time they imagined the scene while maintaining increased muscle tension in one of two muscle groups: either muscles that control smiling or muscles that control frowning. Through the use of biofeedback (see Chapter 7), the subjects learned to tense only the target muscles. The third time they imagined the scene, the subjects were instructed to suppress muscle tension in either their smiling muscles or their frowning muscles (see Figure 12.9). On each occasion, the subjects were asked to report the degree of enjoyment or distress they experienced while imagining the scene. The results provided some support for the facial-feedback theory. Subjects reported less enjoyment when imagining pleasant scenes while suppressing activity in their smiling muscles, and they reported less distress when imagining unpleasant scenes while suppressing activity in their frowning muscles.

▲ Paul Ekman
"Autonomic nervous system activity is not the same for all emotions."

Cognitive Theories of Emotion

More recent theories of emotion emphasize the importance of cognition (thinking). They assume that our emotional experiences depend on our subjective interpretation of situations in which we find ourselves.

The Two-Factor Theory of Emotion

Stanley Schachter's **two-factor theory** (see Figure 12.10) views emotional experience as the outcome of two factors: physiological arousal and the attribution of a cause for it.

two-factor theory

The theory that emotional experience is the outcome of physiological arousal and the attribution of a cause for that arousal.

ANATOMY OF A CLASSIC RESEARCH STUDY

Do Emotions Depend on the Attribution of a Cause for Our Physiological Arousal?

Rationale

According to Schachter, when you experience physiological arousal, you search for its source. Your attribution of a cause for your arousal determines the emotion that you experience. For example, if you experience intense physiological arousal in the presence of an appealing person, you might attribute your arousal to that person, and, as a result, feel that you are attracted to him or her.

The two-factor theory resembles the James-Lange theory in assuming that emotional experience follows physiological arousal (Winton, 1990). But it is different from the James-Lange theory in holding, as does the Cannon-Bard theory, that all emotions involve similar patterns of physiological arousal. But the Cannon-Bard theory assumes that emotional experience and physiological arousal occur simultaneously; the two-factor theory assumes instead that emotion follows the attribution of a cause for one's physiological arousal.

Method

The original experiment on the two-factor theory provided evidence that when we experience physiological arousal, we seek to identify its source, and that what we identify as the source in turn determines our emotional experience (Schachter & Singer, 1962). Male college students who served as subjects participated one at a time and were told that they were getting an injection of a new vitamin called "Suproxin" to assess its effect on vision. In reality, they received an injection of the hormone epinephrine, which activates the sympathetic nervous system. The epinephrine caused hand tremors, a flushed face, a pounding heart, and rapid breathing. Some subjects (the informed group) were told to expect these changes. Some subjects (the misinformed group) were told to expect itching, numb feet, and

▲ Stanley Schachter
"Given a state of physiological arousal for which an individual has no immediate explanation, he will label this state and describe his feelings in terms of the cognitions available to him."

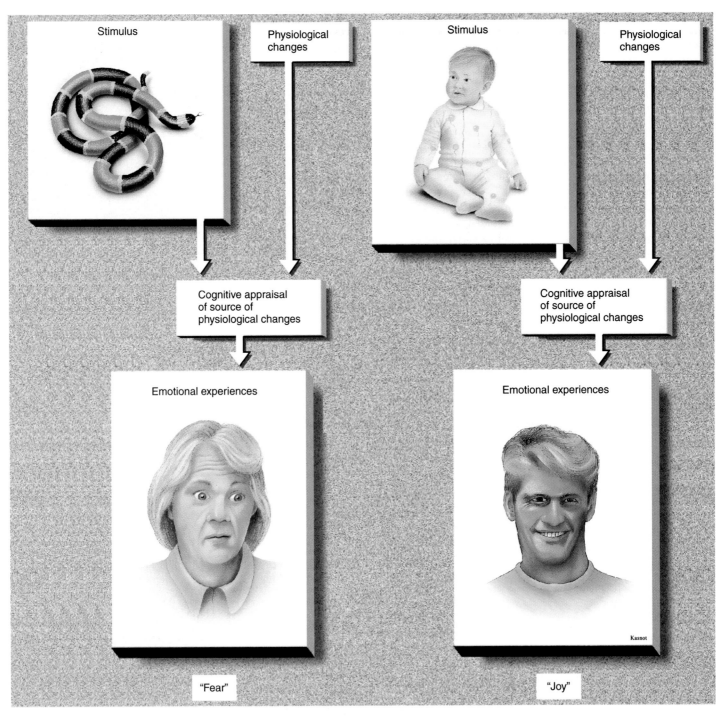

Stimulus

Physiological changes

Stimulus

Physiological changes

Cognitive appraisal of source of physiological changes

Cognitive appraisal of source of physiological changes

Emotional experiences

Emotional experiences

Kasnot

"Fear"

"Joy"

▲ FIGURE 12.10

Two-Factor Theory of Emotion

According to the two-factor theory, when we experience physiological arousal, we seek its source in our immediate situation. The perceived source determines the emotional label we attach to our arousal.

headache, and some (the uninformed group) were told nothing about the effects. Other subjects received a placebo injection of a saline solution instead of an injection of epinephrine and were told nothing about its physiological effects.

The subject then waited in a room with the experimenter's accomplice, a male who acted either happy or angry. When acting happy, the accomplice was cheerful and threw paper airplanes, played with a Hula Hoop, and shot wads of paper into a wastebasket. When acting angry, the accomplice acted upset, stomped around, and complained about a questionnaire given by the experimenter, which included questions about the bathing habits of the respondent's family and the sex life of his mother. The subject's emotional response to the accomplice was assessed by observing him through a one-way mirror and by having him complete a questionnaire about his feelings.

Results and Discussion

The results showed that the informed subjects were unaffected by the accomplice, while the misinformed subjects and uninformed subjects expressed and experienced emotions similar to those of the accomplice. But the placebo group also expressed and experienced situation-appropriate emotions, despite the lack of drug-induced physiological arousal. Schachter concluded that the informed subjects attributed their arousal to the injection and did not exhibit situation-appropriate emotions. In contrast, the misinformed subjects and the uninformed subjects attributed their physiological arousal to the situation they were in, responding positively when the accomplice acted happy and responding negatively when the accomplice acted angry. Schachter assumed that the placebo subjects became physiologically aroused in response to the emotional display of the accomplice and interpreted their own feelings as congruent with those of the accomplice.

Since the original studies of the two-factor theory in the early 1960s, research has produced inconsistent findings. Consider the theory's assumption that unexplained physiological arousal can just as well provoke feelings of joy as provoke feelings of sadness, depending on the person's interpretation of the source of the arousal. This was contradicted by a study in which subjects received injections of epinephrine without being informed of its true effects. The subjects tended to experience negative emotions, regardless of their immediate social environment. Even those in the presence of a happy person tended to experience unpleasant emotions (Marshall & Zimbardo, 1979). A review of research on Schachter's two-factor theory concluded that the only assumption of the theory that has been consistently supported is that physiological arousal misattributed to an outside source will intensify an emotional experience. There is little evidence that such a misattribution will cause an emotional experience (Reisenzein, 1983).

▲ **FIGURE 12.11**
The Cognitive-Appraisal Theory of Emotion
According to the cognitive-appraisal theory, our interpretation of events, rather than the events themselves, determines our emotional experiences. Thus, the same event may evoke different emotions in different people, as in this exhilarated boy and his terrified mother riding on a Ferris wheel.

The Cognitive-Appraisal Theory of Emotion

Though Schachter's two-factor theory has failed to gain strong support, it has stimulated interest in the cognitive basis of emotion. The purest cognitive theory of emotion is the **cognitive-appraisal theory** (see Figure 12.11) of Richard Lazarus (1993a). Unlike the two-factor theory, the cognitive-appraisal theory downplays the role of physiological arousal. Like the two-factor theory, the cognitive-appraisal theory assumes that our emotion at a given time depends on our interpretation of the situation we are in at that time. If we develop inflexible, maladaptive ways of appraising situations, we may develop emotional disorders (Lazarus, 1995). Because cognitive appraisal of specific situations varies across cultures, emotional reactions are culturally dependent (Roseman et al., 1995).

This cognitive view of emotion is not new. In *Hamlet* Shakespeare wrote: "There is nothing either good or bad, but thinking makes it so." Cognitive appraisal can affect your emotions as you prepare for an exam (Abella & Heslin, 1989). For example, you might appraise an impending exam as threatening, while your friend might appraise it as challenging. As a result, you might feel anxious about the exam while your friend feels eager about it. People whose jobs require them to confront human pain, illness, and death find that cognitively reappraising situations, perhaps by finding meaning even in the worst disasters, helps them cope emotionally (McCammon et al., 1988).

An early study by Lazarus and his colleagues supported the cognitive-appraisal theory of emotion (Speisman et al., 1964). The subjects watched a film about a tribal ritual in which incisions were made on adolescents' penises. The subjects' level of emotional arousal was measured by recording their heart rate and skin conductance (an increase in the electrical conductivity of the skin, caused by sweating). Subjects all watched the same film but heard different sound tracks. Those in the *silent group* saw the film without a sound track. Those in the *trauma group* were told that the procedure was extremely painful and emotionally distressing. Those in the *intellectualization group* were told about the procedure in a

cognitive-appraisal theory
The theory that one's emotion at a given time depends on one's interpretation of the situation one is in.

▲ Richard Lazarus
"Appraisal is a necessary as well as sufficient cause of emotion."

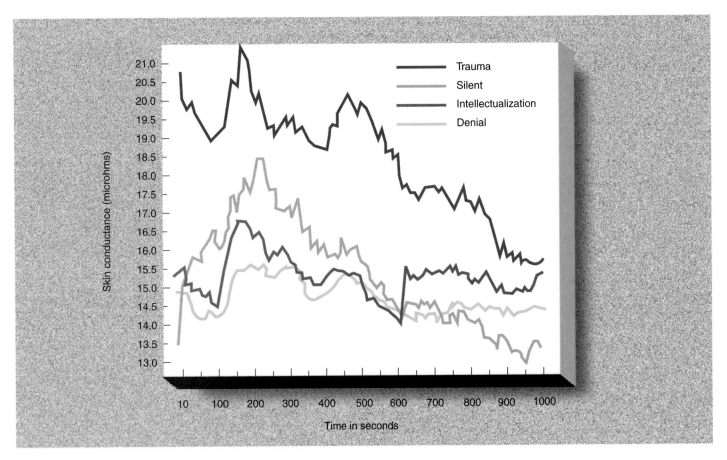

▲ FIGURE 12.12
Cognitive Appraisal and Emotion
The graph shows that the emotional responses of subjects who viewed a film of a ritual in which incisions were made in adolescents' penises depended on the nature of the sound track. Those who heard a sound track that described the procedure as traumatic experienced the greatest emotional arousal (Speisman et al., 1964).

detached, matter-of-fact way, with no mention of feelings. And those in the *denial group* were told that the procedure was not painful and that the boys were overjoyed because it signified their entrance into manhood.

Recordings of the subjects' physiological arousal showed that the trauma group experienced greater arousal than the silent group, which in turn experienced greater arousal than the denial and intellectualization groups (see Figure 12.12). These findings indicate that subjective appraisal of the situation, rather than the objective situation itself, accounted for the subjects' emotional arousal. Lazarus (1993b) has applied his theory of cognitive appraisal in helping individuals cope with stressful situations—a topic discussed in Chapter 16.

Though more recent studies provide additional support for the assumption that your interpretation of a situation affects your emotional state (Smith & Ellsworth, 1985), the cognitive-appraisal theory has been challenged by Robert Zajonc (1984) and others, who insist that cognitive-appraisal is not essential to the experience of emotion. For example, you have probably taken an instant liking or disliking to a person without knowing why. And, as noted in Chapter 6, research findings show that we can respond emotionally to stimuli we are unaware of (Murphy & Zajonc, 1993). This and other evidence indicates that emotional experience can take place without conscious cognitive appraisal (Izard, 1993).

There is even physiological evidence for this, because of the direct pathways from the thalamus (which relays sensory input to other brain regions) to the limbic system (which plays an important role in emotional processing). These pathways bypass the cerebral cortex, the involvement of which seems required for conscious cognitive appraisal. Thus, we can have emotional reactions to stimuli of which we are unaware (LeDoux, 1986).

What can we conclude from the variety of contradictory theories of emotion? The best we can do is to realize that none of them is sufficient to explain emotion, though each describes a process that contributes to it. Moreover, the theories illustrate the importance of the physiological, expressive, and experiential components of emotion.

STAYING ON TRACK: *Theories of Emotion*

1. What evidence is there for and against the James-Lange theory of emotion?
2. How has research supported the facial-feedback theory of emotion?
3. What does research conducted since Schachter and Singer's classic study say about their two-factor theory of emotion?

THINKING ABOUT *Psychology*

Do Lie Detectors Tell the Truth?

As discussed earlier, in everyday life we infer a person's emotional state from his or her expressive behavior. We might even infer whether the person is lying. If you have ever detected a phony smile from a salesperson or politician, you probably noted certain cues indicating that the smile was insincere. Perhaps the smile lasted too long—a sign of insincerity. Or perhaps you noticed that the smile was asymmetrical. Phony expressions, including smiles, will usually be more pronounced on the left side of the face than on the right side (Rinn, 1984). Nonetheless, in everyday life most people are poor at detecting deceit from facial expressions. One exception is U.S. Secret Service agents, who learn to attend to nonverbal cues in their efforts to protect the president from attack (Ekman & O'Sullivan, 1991).

The detection of lies through interpretation of expressive behavior has a long history. The Old Testament describes a case in which King Solomon resolved a dispute between two women who claimed to be the mother of the same infant. Solomon wisely proposed cutting the infant in half, then giving one half to each woman. While one of the women calmly agreed to this, the other pleaded with Solomon to give the infant to her adversary. Solomon reasoned that the pleading woman had to be the real mother, because she was willing to lose the infant rather than see the child killed.

King Solomon inferred lying from expressive behavior, but lie detection has historically been based on the assumption that liars display increased physiological arousal. In the fifteenth century, interrogators for the Inquisition required suspected heretics to swallow pieces of bread and cheese. If the food stuck to the person's palate, he or she was considered guilty. As you will recall, the arousal of the sympathetic nervous system that accompanies emotionality reduces salivation, leading to a dry mouth. A dry mouth would make it more difficult to swallow food. As you can imagine, people brought before the Inquisition would experience increased arousal—whether or not they were heretics—and would be convicted of heresy.

Modern lie detection began in the 1890s with the work of Cesare Lombroso, an Italian criminologist who questioned suspects while recording their heart rate and blood pressure. He assumed that if they showed marked fluctuations in heart rate and blood pressure while responding to questions, they were lying (Kleinmuntz & Szucko, 1984b).

▲ **The Polygraph Test**
The polygraph test assumes that patterns of change in physiological responses, such as heart rate, blood pressure, breathing patterns, and electrodermal activity, will reveal whether a person is lying.

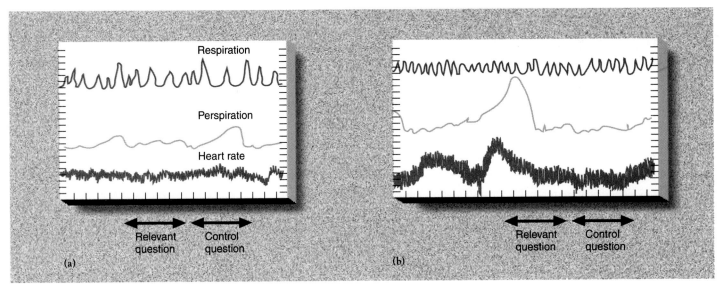

▲ FIGURE 12.13
Relevant Questions Versus Control Questions
The polygraph test compares physiological responses to relevant and control questions. (*a*) This is the record of a person who responded less strongly to a question relevant to a crime than to an emotionally arousing control question not relevant to the crime. Such responses indicate to the examiner that the person is telling the truth. (*b*) This is the record of a person who responded more strongly to a question relevant to a crime than to an emotionally arousing control question not relevant to the crime. Responses such as this indicate to the examiner that the person is lying.

PROCEDURES IN LIE DETECTION: THE POLYGRAPH TEST

polygraph test

The "lie detector" test, which assesses lying by measuring changing patterns of physiological arousal in response to particular questions.

Today the lie detector, or **polygraph test,** typically measures breathing patterns, heart rate, blood pressure, and electrodermal activity. Electrodermal activity reflects the amount of sweating; greater emotionality is associated with more sweating. Though the polygraph test is used to detect lying, no pattern of physiological responses by itself indicates lying. Instead, the test detects physiological arousal produced by activation of the sympathetic nervous system. As David Lykken, an expert on lie detection, has said, "The polygraph pens do no special dance when we are lying" (Lykken, 1981, p. 10).

Given that there is no pattern of physiological responses that indicates lying, how is the recording of physiological arousal used to detect lies? The typical polygraph test given to a criminal suspect begins with an explanation of the test and the kinds of questions to be asked. The subject is then asked *control questions,* which are designed to provoke lying about minor transgressions common to almost everyone. For example, the suspect might be asked, "Have you ever stolen anything from an employer?" It is a rare person who has not stolen at least an inexpensive item, yet many people would answer no, creating an increase in physiological arousal; and even suspects who answer yes to a control question would probably experience some increase in physiological arousal in response to that question.

The subject's physiological response to control questions is compared to her or his physiological response to *relevant questions,* which are concerned with facts about the crime, such as "Did you steal money from the bank safe?" Polygraphers assume that a guilty person will show greater physiological arousal in response to relevant questions and that an innocent person will show greater physiological arousal in response to control questions. Figure 12.13 shows a polygraph printout of differences in arousal in response to the different questions. The typical polygraph test asks about twelve relevant questions, which are repeated three or four times.

ISSUES IN LIE DETECTION: SHOULD YOU TRUST THE LIE DETECTOR?

Polygraph testing has provoked controversy because it is far from being a perfect measure of lying. One difficulty is that the accuracy of the polygraph depends, in part, on the subject's physiological reactivity. People with low reactivity exhibit a smaller difference between their responses to control questions and their responses to relevant questions than do people with high reactivity. This might cause an unemotional criminal to be declared innocent and an emotional innocent person to be declared guilty (Waid, Wilson, & Orne, 1981). Tranquilizers reduce the detectability of lying by reducing physiological arousal (Waid & Orne, 1982).

Criminals are also aware of countermeasures that can make them appear innocent on a polygraph test. Consider the case of Floyd Fay, an innocent man convicted in 1978 of murdering his best friend and sentenced to life in prison after failing a polygraph test that he had taken voluntarily. Two years later a public defender tracked down the real murderer. While in prison, Fay became an expert on lie detection and taught prisoners how to beat the polygraph test. Of 27 inmates who had admitted their guilt to him, 23 passed their polygraph tests (Kleinmuntz & Szucko, 1984a).

What techniques might fool the polygraph machine? One technique uses the properly timed induction of pain. For example, suppose that during control questions you bite your tongue or step on a tack hidden in your shoe. This would increase your level of physiological arousal in response to control questions, thereby reducing the difference between your physiological responses to control questions and relevant questions (Honts, Hodes, & Raskin, 1985).

Though aware that criminals can fool the polygraph machine, critics of the test are more concerned with the possibility that the polygraph will find innocent people guilty. In the 1980s millions of Americans were subjected to polygraph tests in criminal cases, employment screening, employee honesty checks, and security clearances (Kleinmuntz & Szucko, 1984b). In 1983 President Reagan gave an executive order to use the polygraph test to identify federal employees who reveal classified information. But a report commissioned by Congress found that the polygraph test was invalid in the situations favored by Reagan. The report concluded that the only justifiable use of the polygraph test is in criminal cases (Saxe, Dougherty, & Cross, 1985). Though the test might not be valid, it can elicit confessions from suspects who believe in its effectiveness (Simpson, 1986). Thus, the unreliability of the polygraph test makes its use to detect deception questionable (Saxe, 1994).

In June of 1988 President Reagan, confronted with overwhelming opposition to the unrestricted use of polygraph tests, signed the Polygraph Protection Act banning their use for preemployment screening by private employers. But the law still permitted the use of polygraph tests in ongoing investigations of specific incidents. And drug companies, security services, government agencies, and private companies that have contracts with government intelligence agencies were exempted from the ban on using polygraph tests in employment screening (Bales, 1988).

ANATOMY OF A CONTEMPORARY RESEARCH STUDY

How Accurate Are Lie Detectors at Judging Guilt and Innocence?

Rationale

What evidence led to the widespread opposition to the unrestricted use of the polygraph? Supporters of the polygraph test claim accuracy rates of 90 percent or better (Raskin & Podlesny, 1979). But research findings indicate that it is much less accurate than that, as revealed by the following study (Kleinmuntz & Szucko, 1984a).

Method

The polygraph printouts of 50 thieves and 50 innocent people were presented to six highly trained professional polygraphers. They were asked questions about real thefts.

The Validity of Polygraph Testing
A study by Kleinmuntz and Szucko (1984a)
found that the polygraph test is far from fool-
proof in determining guilt or innocence. About
one third of innocent suspects were judged
guilty and about one quarter of guilty suspects
were judged innocent.

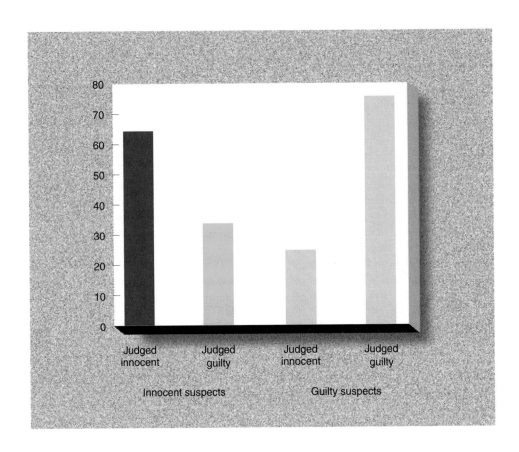

Results and Discussion

The results showed that the polygraphers correctly identified 76 percent of the guilty persons
and 63 percent of the innocent persons (see Figure 12.14). Though their performance was
better than chance, this also meant that they incorrectly identified 24 percent of the guilty
persons as innocent and 37 percent of the innocent persons as guilty. The polygraph test's
high rate of false positives (that is, identifying innocent persons as guilty) can have tragic
consequences for those who are unjustly denied jobs, fired from jobs, or prosecuted for crimes.

▲ ▲ ▲

THE GUILTY KNOWLEDGE TEST:
A PROMISING ALTERNATIVE

Guilty Knowledge Test

A method that assesses lying by measuring
physiological arousal in response to information that is relevant to a transgression
and physiological arousal in response to
information that is irrelevant to that
transgression.

A possible improvement over the polygraph test is the **Guilty Knowledge Test,** developed
by David Lykken (1974). If you have ever played the board game *Clue*, you have some
understanding of the test. In contrast to the polygraph test, Lykken's test assesses knowledge about a transgression, rather than alleged anxiety about it. The Guilty Knowledge
Test is useful only when details of the transgression are known to the transgressor but not
to others who take the test. Consider its use in interrogating suspects in a bank robbery. A
suspect would be asked questions about the victim, the site of the crime, and the commission of the crime. Instead of being asked, "Did you steal money from the bank safe?" the
suspect would be asked, "Was the money stolen from the _____ ?" This question would be
asked several times, each time with different words completing the statement. In this case,
the words might be *bank safe, teller's drawer,* and *armored car.*

 The Guilty Knowledge Test assumes that a guilty person (who knows details of the
crime), but not an innocent person, will show more physiological arousal in response to the
relevant words than in response to the irrelevant words. If a person shows greater physiological reactivity to the relevant words in a *series* of statements (a single positive instance
would be insufficient), that person would be considered guilty. Of course, examiners should

not know any details of the crime. Otherwise, they might affect the suspect's physiological response to relevant words, perhaps by saying those words louder or softer. Researchers are developing a version of the Guilty Knowledge Test that would measure changes in brain-wave patterns to determine when a person has information that he or she is trying to conceal (Bashore & Rapp, 1993).

A laboratory test in which undergraduates committed mock murders supported the assumption that guilt could be detected by differential physiological responses to relevant and irrelevant stimuli (Timm, 1982). In its first use in a study of real criminals, the Guilty Knowledge Test was given to 50 innocent and 48 guilty subjects. The results supported the effectiveness of the test, particularly its ability to avoid false positives. Judges correctly classified 94 percent of the innocent and 65 percent of the guilty (Elaad, 1990). Research findings indicate that the Guilty Knowledge Test is biased toward false negatives, while control-question tests are biased toward false positives (McCauley & Forman, 1988). So, those more interested in protecting the innocent would favor the Guilty Knowledge Test, while those more interested in ferreting out transgressors would favor the control-question test.

Lykken, recognizing the merits of the Guilty Knowledge Test, urges its widespread adoption (Lykken, 1988). But research support for the superiority of the Guilty Knowledge Test has not been universal. Though one study found that it was effective in detecting individuals with knowledge relevant to a crime (Elaad, 1994), another study found that subjects with guilty knowledge might still not be detected reliably (Bradley & Warfield, 1984). Still another study found no difference in the success of the control-question test and Guilty Knowledge Test in detecting lying (Podlesny & Raskin, 1978). So even though the Guilty Knowledge Test is more promising than the control-question test, it has not yet gained sufficient research support to merit complete confidence in it. In fact, there is evidence that use of a Guilty Actions Test (which presents actions that were performed by the perpetrator) might be superior to the Guilty Knowledge Test (Bradley, MacLaren, & Carle, 1996).

▲ **David Lykken**
"Since, in the field, most subjects tend to 'fail' the lie test whether they are truthful or deceptive, the method more often detects lying than it does truthful responding."

STAYING ON TRACK: *Do Lie Detectors Tell the Truth?*

1. What evidence is there to make one cautious about relying on the polygraph test to detect deception?

2. How do the control-question test and the Guilty Knowlege Test differ in their procedures?

 # CHAPTER SUMMARY

THE BIOPSYCHOLOGY OF EMOTION

Emotion is a motivated state marked by physiological arousal, expressive behavior, and mental experience. Emotional arousal depends on activity in the autonomic nervous system and the limbic system. The left cerebral hemisphere plays a greater role in positive emotions; the right cerebral hemisphere plays a greater role in negative emotions. Neurotransmitters, including endorphins, alter our moods by affecting neuronal activity.

THE EXPRESSION OF EMOTION

We express our emotions behaviorally through changes in vocal qualities, body movements, and facial expressions. Charles Darwin believed that facial expressions evolved because they communicate emotions and help individuals distinguish friend from foe. The hereditary basis of facial expressions is supported by research showing cross-cultural consistency in the positive association between particular facial expressions and particular emotions.

THE EXPERIENCE OF EMOTION

Robert Plutchik considers the basic emotions to be joy, fear, anger, disgust, sadness, surprise, acceptance, and anticipation. Emotions vary in their intensity and pleasantness; people who tend to experience intensely pleasant emotions are also likely to experience intensely unpleasant emotions. Psychologists have only recently begun to study pleasant emotions, such as happiness and humor, to the same extent as unpleasant emotions. According to social-comparison theory, happiness is the result of estimating that one's life circumstances are more favorable than those of others. And according to adaptation-level theory, happiness depends on estimating that one's current life circumstances are more favorable than one's past life circumstances. Humor is explained by disparagement theory, incongruity theory, and release theory.

THEORIES OF EMOTION

Psychologists have devised a variety of theories to explain emotional experience. The James-Lange theory assumes that physiological changes precede emotional experiences and that with different patterns of physiological arousal are associated with different emotions. The Cannon-Bard theory claims that the thalamus perceives an event and communicates this information to the cerebral cortex (which provides the subjective experience of emotion) and stimulates the physiological arousal characteristic of emotion. According to the opponent-process theory, the brain has evolved mechanisms that counteract strong positive or negative emotions by evoking an opposite emotional response. If the first emotion is repeated, the opposing emotion gradually strengthens and the first emotion gradually weakens, until a more moderate response becomes habitual.

According to the facial-feedback theory, different emotions are caused by sensory feedback from different facial expressions. The two-factor theory views emotional experience as the consequence of attributing physiological arousal to a particular aspect of one's immediate environment. Cognitive-appraisal theory ignores the role of physiological arousal and considers emotional experience to be solely the result of a person's interpretation of her or his current circumstances.

THINKING ABOUT PSYCHOLOGY: DO LIE DETECTORS TELL THE TRUTH?

The lie detector, or polygraph test, assumes that differences in physiological arousal in response to control questions and relevant questions can be used to determine whether a person is lying. Critics point out that the polygraph can be fooled and that it has poor validity because it finds a large proportion of guilty people innocent and an even larger proportion of innocent people guilty. A promising alternative to the traditional polygraph test is the Guilty Knowledge Test, which depends on the guilty person's physiological arousal to important facts about his or her transgression.

KEY CONCEPTS

emotion 410

The Biopsychology of Emotion

fight-or-flight response 410

The Experience of Emotion

social-comparison theory 420
adaptation-level theory 420
disparagement theory 421
incongruity theory 422
release theory 422

Theories of Emotion

James-Lange theory 423
Cannon-Bard theory 424
opponent-process theory 427
facial-feedback theory 428
two-factor theory 429

cognitive-appraisal theory 431

Do Lie Detectors Tell the Truth

polygraph test 434
Guilty Knowledge Test 436

KEY CONTRIBUTORS

The Biopsychology of Emotion
Richard Davidson 412

The Expression of Emotion

Charles Darwin 417
Carroll Izard 417

The Experience of Emotion

Robert Plutchik 418
Edward Diener 420
Sigmund Freud 422

Theories of Emotion

William James 423
Carl Lange 423
Walter Cannon 423
Richard Solomon 427
Paul Ekman 428

Stanley Schachter 429
Richard Lazarus 431
Robert Zajonc 432

Do Lie Detectors Tell the Truth?

David Lykken 436

FOR MORE INFORMATION ON EMOTION

FOR GENERAL WORKS ON EMOTION

Carlson, J. G., & Hatfield, E. (1992). *Psychology of emotion.* San Diego: Harcourt Brace Jovanovich.

Marcus, H. R., & Kitayama, S. (Eds.). (1994). *Emotion and culture: Empirical studies of mutual influence.* Washington, DC: American Psychological Association.

Plutchik, R. (1993). *Psychology of emotions.* New York: HarperCollins.

FOR MORE ON THE BIOPSYCHOLOGY OF EMOTION

Thompson, J. G. (1988). *The psychobiology of emotions.* New York: Plenum.

Vincent, J. D. (1990). *The biology of emotions.* New York: Basil Blackwell.

Wagner, H. L. (1989). *Social psychophysiology and emotion.* New York: Wiley.

FOR MORE ON THE EXPRESSION OF EMOTION

Collier, G. (1985). *Emotional expression.* Hillsdale, NJ: Erlbaum.

Darwin, C. (1872/1965). *The expression of the emotions in man and animals.* Chicago: University of Chicago Press.

Ekman, P. (1980). *The face of man: Expressions of universal emotions in a New Guinea village.* New York: Garland.

Poyatos, F. (1988). *Cross-cultural perspectives in nonverbal communication.* Lewiston, NY: Hogrefe & Huber.

FOR MORE ON THE EXPERIENCE OF EMOTION

Plutchik, R. (1991). *The emotions.* Lanham, MD: University Press of America.

Scherer, K. R., Wallbott, H. G., & Summerfield, A. B. (Eds.). (1986). *Experiencing emotion: A cross-cultural study.* New York: Cambridge University Press.

FOR MORE ON HAPPINESS

Argyle, M. (1987). *The psychology of happiness*. New York: Routledge.

Eysenck, M. (1990). *Happiness: Facts and myths*. Hillsdale, NJ: Erlbaum.

Myers, D. G. (1992). *Searching for joy: Who is happy and why*. New York: Morrow.

FOR MORE ON HUMOR

Buckman, E. S. (Ed.). (1993). *The handbook of humor: Clinical applications in psychotherapy*. Melbourne, FL: Krieger.

Haig, R. A. (1988). *The anatomy of humor: Biopsychosocial and therapeutic perspectives*. Springfield, MA: Charles C Thomas.

MacHovec, F. J. (1988). *Humor: Theory, history, applications*. Springfield, MA: Charles C Thomas.

Mulkay, M. (1988). *On humor*. New York: Basil Blackwell.

FOR MORE ON THEORIES OF EMOTION

Izard, C. E., Kagan, J., & Zajonc, R. B. (Eds.). (1988). *Emotions, cognition, and behavior*. New York: Cambridge University Press.

Papanicolaou, A. C. (1989). *Emotion: A reconsideration of the somatic theory*. New York: Gordon & Breach.

Plutchik, R., & Kellerman, H. (Ed.). (1980). *Theories of emotion*. San Diego: Academic Press.

FOR MORE ON LIE DETECTORS

Abrams, S. (1989). *The complete polygraph handbook*. New York: Free Press.

Gale, A. (1988). *The polygraph test: Lies, truth, and science*. Newbury Park, CA: Sage.

Lykken, D. T. (1981). *A tremor in the blood: Uses and abuses of the lie detector*. New York: McGraw-Hill.

FOR MORE ON CONTRIBUTORS TO THE STUDY OF EMOTION

Benison, S., Barger, A. C., & Wolfe, E. L. (1987). *Walter B. Cannon: The life and times of a young scientist*. Cambridge, MA: Harvard University Press.

Bowlby, J. (1991). *Charles Darwin: A new life*. New York: W. W. Norton.

Grunberg, N. E., Nisbett, R. E., Rodin, J., & Singer, J. E. (1987). *A distinctive approach to psychological research: The influence of Stanley Schachter*. Hillsdale, NJ: Erlbaum.

Myers, G. E. (1986). *William James: His life and thought*. New Haven, CT: Yale University Press.

Personality

personality
An individual's unique, relatively consistent pattern of thinking, feeling, and behaving.

*B*y now you have probably categorized your fellow students into those with a "good personality," those with a "bad personality," and even some with "no personality." But exactly what is personality? The word *personality* comes from the Latin word *persona,* meaning "mask." Just as masks distinguished one character from another in ancient Greek and Roman plays, your personality distinguishes you from other people. Your **personality** is your unique, relatively consistent pattern of thinking, feeling, and behaving. See if you recognize yourself in the following personality description:

▶ You have a strong need for other people to like and admire you. You have a tendency to be critical of yourself. You have a great deal of unused capacity, which you have not turned to your advantage. . . . Disciplined and controlled on the outside, you tend to be worrisome and insecure inside. . . . At times you are extraverted, affable, and sociable; at other times, you are introverted, wary, and reserved. (Ulrich, Stachnik, & Stainton, 1963)

Study after study has shown that when people are given personality tests and then presented with a mock personality description like this one, they tend to accept the description as accurate. They do so because the description *is* accurate. But it is accurate because it contains traits that are shared by almost everyone; it says nothing that distinguishes one person from another. The acceptance of personality descriptions that are true of almost everyone is known as the "Barnum effect" (Meehl, 1956). This reflects P. T. Barnum's saying "There's a sucker born every minute." We are more likely to succumb to the Barnum effect when the personality description is flattering (Guastello, Guastello, & Craft, 1989).

Astrologers make good use of the Barnum effect (Glick, Gottesman, & Jolton, 1989). In a study of astrological personality descriptions, a researcher placed a newspaper advertisement that offered a free personalized horoscope. Of the 150 persons who responded, 141 (94 percent) said they recognized themselves in the "personalized" description. But each of the respondents had received the same description—the personality profile of a mass murderer from France (Waldrop, 1984). The description simply contained traits that many persons, whether mass murderers or not, have in common. Thus, the Barnum effect demonstrates that useful personality descriptions must distinguish one person from another. You should no more accept a personality description that fails to recognize your distinctive combination of personal traits than you would accept a physical description that merely states that you have a head, a torso, two eyes, ten toes, and other common physical characteristics.

Given that each of us has a unique personality, how do we explain our distinctive patterns of thinking, feeling, and behaving? Personality theorists favor several approaches to this question. In reading about them, you will note that the theorists' own life experiences often color their personality theories (Atwood & Tomkins, 1976; Pearce, 1985; Seeman, 1990). The approaches to the study of personality differ on several dimensions, including the influence of unconscious motivation, the extent to which we are molded by learning, the role of cognitive processes, the importance of subjective experience, and the effects of biological factors.

THE PSYCHOANALYTIC APPROACH TO PERSONALITY

The *psychoanalytic approach* to personality has its roots in medicine and biology. Sigmund Freud, the founder of psychoanalysis, was a physician who hoped to find the biological basis of the psychological processes contained in his psychosexual theory (Knight, 1984).

Freud's Psychosexual Theory

Freud (1856–1939) was born in Moravia to Jewish parents, who moved with him to Vienna when he was 4 years old. Though Freud desired a career as a physiology professor, anti-Semitism limited his choice of professions to law, business, or medicine. He chose medicine and eventually practiced as a neurologist. Freud remained in Vienna until the Nazis began burning his books and threatening his safety. In 1938 he emigrated to England, where he died the following year after suffering for many years from mouth cancer.

Early in his career, Freud became interested in the effects of the mind on physical symptoms. He had studied with the French neurologist Jean Charcot, who demonstrated the power of hypnosis in treating *conversion hysteria*, a disorder characterized by physical symptoms such as deafness, blindness, or paralysis without any physical cause. Charcot used hypnotic suggestion to help his patients regain the use of their lost senses or paralyzed limbs. Freud was also intrigued by a report that psychiatrist Josef Breuer had successfully used a "talking cure" to treat conversion hysteria. Breuer found that by encouraging his patients to talk freely about whatever came to mind, they became aware of the psychological causes of their physical symptoms and, as a result, experienced emotional release, or *catharsis*. This led to the disappearance of the symptoms.

Freud's personality theory reflected his time—the Victorian era of the late nineteenth century. The Victorians valued rationality and self-control of physical drives as characteristics that separated human beings from animals. Freud attributed the symptoms of conversion hysteria to unconscious sexual conflicts, which were symbolized in the symptoms. For example, paralyzed legs might represent a sexual conflict. Freud's claim that sexuality, an animal drive, was an important determinant of human behavior shocked and disgusted many of his contemporaries (Rapp, 1988). Yet, though Freud argued against the extreme sexual inhibitions of his time, he recognized the undesirability of sexual promiscuity (McCarthy, 1981).

Later in his career Freud expanded his theory to include inhibited aggression and inhibited sexuality as important determinants of human behavior. The importance of aggression as a human motive came to him as a result of the carnage of World War I. This led him to claim that we are motivated by both a life instinct, *Eros*, and a death instinct, *Thanatos*. *Eros* and *Thanatos*, as well as many other terms he used, are Greek words, reflecting his fascination with the culture of ancient Greece.

▲ **Sigmund Freud (1856–1939) and Anna Freud (1895–1982)**
After Sigmund Freud's death, his theory was championed by his daughter Anna, who pursued a career as a psychoanalyst.

Levels of Consciousness: The Iceberg Metaphor of Personality

As described in Chapter 6, Freud divided the mind into three levels. The *conscious mind* is merely the "tip of the iceberg," representing a tiny region of the mind. The contents of the conscious mind are in a constant state of flux as feelings, memories, and perceptions enter and leave. Just below the conscious mind lies the *preconscious mind*, which includes accessible memories—memories that we can recall at will. The *unconscious mind*, the bulk of the mind, lies below both the conscious mind and the preconscious mind. It contains material we cannot recall at will.

Freud claimed that threatening thoughts or feelings are subject to *repression*, the banishment of conscious material into the unconscious. Because Freud assumed that unconscious thoughts and feelings are the most important influences on our behavior, he proclaimed: "The theory of repression is the cornerstone on which the whole structure of psychoanalysis rests" (Freud, 1914/1957, p. 16). The notion of repressed thoughts and feelings led to the concept of *psychic determinism*, which holds that all behavior is influenced by unconscious motives. Thus, even apparently mundane or arbitrary behaviors are meaningful. Psychic determinism is exhibited in *Freudian slips*, unintentional statements that might reveal our repressed feelings. For instance, the slip "I loathe you . . . I mean I love you" might reveal repressed hostility.

The Structure of Personality: Id, Ego, and Superego

As illustrated in Figure 13.1, Freud distinguished three structures of personality: the *id*, the *ego*, and the *superego*. The **id** is unconscious and consists of our inborn biological drives. In demanding immediate gratification of drives, most notably sex and aggression, the id obeys the **pleasure principle.** In regard to sex, the id says, "Now!" The word *id* is Latin for "it,"

id
In Freud's theory, the part of the personality that contains inborn biological drives and that seeks immediate gratification.

pleasure principle
The process by which the id seeks immediate gratification of its impulses.

The Structure of Personality
Freud divided the personality into the id, ego, and superego. The id is entirely unconscious and demands immediate gratification of its desires. The ego is partly conscious and partly unconscious. This permits it to balance the id's demands with the external demands of social reality and the moralistic demands of the superego, which is also partly conscious and partly unconscious.

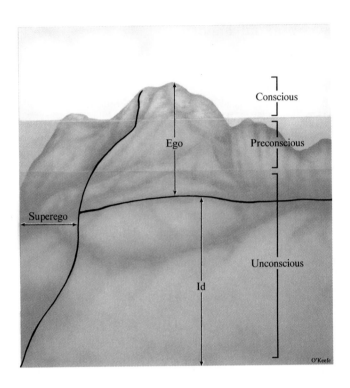

ego
In Freud's theory, the part of the personality that helps the individual adapt to external reality by making compromises between the id, the superego, and the environment.

reality principle
The process by which the ego directs the individual to express sexual and aggressive impulses in socially acceptable ways.

superego
In Freud's theory, the part of the personality that acts as a moral guide telling us what we should and should not do.

defense mechanism
In Freud's theory, a process that distorts reality to prevent the individual from being overwhelmed by anxiety.

reflecting the id's impersonal nature. The classic 1950s science fiction movie *Forbidden Planet* portrays the amoral nature of the id: The id of a mad scientist is transformed into a being of pure energy that runs amok on an alien planet, blindly killing anyone in its path.

Through life experiences we learn that acting on every sexual or aggressive impulse is socially maladaptive. As a consequence, each of us develops an **ego,** Latin for "I." The ego obeys the **reality principle,** directing us to express sexual and aggressive impulses in socially acceptable ways. In regard to sex, the ego says, "Not now, later!" As for aggression, suppose that a teacher refuses to change your grade on an exam that was graded with an incorrect answer key. Your ego would encourage you to argue with the teacher instead of punching him or her.

The **superego** (Latin for "over the I") counteracts the id, which is concerned only with immediate gratification, and the ego, which is concerned only with adapting to reality. The superego acts as our moral guide. It contains the *conscience,* which makes us feel guilty for doing or thinking wrong, and the *ego ideal,* which makes us feel good for doing or thinking right. In regard to sex, the superego says, "Not now, wait until you are married!" Children whose parents do not teach them right from wrong may develop a superego too weak to inhibit aggression. To Freud, your personality is the outcome of the continual battle for dominance among the id, the ego, and the superego.

Defense Mechanisms: Defending Against Anxiety

The ego might resort to **defense mechanisms,** which distort reality, to protect itself from the anxiety caused by id impulses, particularly those of sex and aggression. Table 13.1 summarizes the major defense mechanisms. The ego may also use defense mechanisms to relieve the anxiety caused by unpleasant personal experiences and unacceptable personal characteristics. Each of us uses defense mechanisms to varying extents, which contributes to the distinctiveness of our personalities. Though defense mechanisms can protect us from experiencing anxiety, they can also prevent us from recognizing and dealing with the true source of the anxiety. As noted in Chapter 14, Freudians believe that excessive reliance on defense mechanisms contributes to the development of psychological disorders (Vaillant, 1992).

Because all defense mechanisms involve *repression,* we are not aware when we are using them. The memory of a traumatic event, such as an auto accident, might be repressed to relieve the anxiety that the memory produces. In recent years, the defense mechanism of

Repression
The banishment of threatening thoughts, feelings, and memories into the unconscious mind

Denial
The refusal to admit a particular aspect of reality relevant to oneself

Regression
The displaying of immature behaviors that have relieved anxiety in the past

Rationalization
The providing of socially acceptable reasons for one's inappropriate behavior

Intellectualization
The reduction of anxiety by reacting to emotional situations in a detached, unemotional way

Displacement
The expression of feelings toward a person who is less threatening than the true target of those feelings

Projection
The attribution of one's undesirable feelings to others

Reaction Formation
The tendency to act in a manner opposite to one's true feelings

Compensation
The development of a talent as a response to a personal deficiency

Sublimation
The expression of sexual or aggressive impulses through indirect, socially acceptable outlets

repression has become a popular topic in the mass media because of the rise in reports of adults recalling apparently repressed memories of sexual abuse in early childhood. This topic is discussed in Chapter 8.

We sometimes rely on immature kinds of defense mechanisms. In using *denial*, we simply refuse to admit a particular aspect of reality. For example, terminally ill patients might initially reduce their anxiety by denying they have a fatal disease (Connor, 1986). In resorting to the defense mechanism of *regression*, the individual displays immature behaviors that have relieved anxiety in the past. An adult might respond to job frustrations by crying or throwing temper tantrums.

Other defense mechanisms rely on changing our perception of reality. When we resort to *rationalization*, we provide socially acceptable reasons for our inappropriate behavior. For example, a student whose semester grades include one D and four F's might blame the four F's on studying too much for the course in which he received a D. People who use *intellectualization* reduce anxiety by reacting to emotional situations in a detached, unemotional way. Instead of reacting to the death of a loved one by crying, they might react by saying, "Everyone must die sometime."

In some cases, defense mechanisms direct sexual or aggressive drives in safer directions. A person who fears the consequences of expressing his feelings toward a particular person might express them toward someone less threatening. This is known as *displacement*. For example, a worker who hates his boss, but fears criticizing him, might instead abuse his children with his hostility (Brennan & Andrews, 1990). If we cannot accept our own undesirable feelings, we might resort to *projection*, attributing our undesirable feelings to others. Paranoid people, who are unreasonably suspicious of others, tend to use projection to justify their own hostile feelings (Berman & McCann, 1995).

Reaction formation involves countering undesirable feelings by acting in a manner opposite to them. Samuel Johnson, the eighteenth-century writer and dictionary editor, reported a classic example of reaction formation. A pair of proper ladies who met him at a literary tea commented, "We see, Dr. Johnson, that you do not have those naughty words in your dictionary." Johnson replied, "And I see, dear ladies, that you have been looking for them" (Morris & Morris, 1985, p. 101).

Defense mechanisms can also affect one's lifestyle. In using *compensation,* a person might react to a personal deficiency by developing another talent. Stevie Wonder may have compensated for his blindness by working to become a great singer and composer. According to Freud, the most successful defense mechanism is *sublimation,* the expression of sexual or aggressive impulses through indirect, socially acceptable outlets. The sex drive can be sublimated through creative activities (Kaplan, 1993), such as painting, ballet dancing, or composing music. And the aggressive drive can be sublimated through sports such as football, lacrosse, or field hockey.

Psychosexual Development: The Formation of Personality

Freud assumed that personality development depended on changes in the distribution of sexual energy, which he called **libido,** in regions of the body he called *erogenous zones.* Stimulation of these regions produces pleasure. Thus, he was concerned with stages of *psychosexual development.* Failure to progress smoothly through a particular stage can cause **fixation,** a tendency to continue to engage in behaviors associated with that stage. Freud called the first year of infancy the **oral stage** of development, because the infant gains pleasure from oral activities such as biting, sucking, and chewing. The most important social conflict of this stage is *weaning.* An infant inadequately weaned, because of too much or too little oral gratification, might become fixated at the oral stage. Fixation might lead to an *oral-dependent* personality, marked by passivity, dependency, and gullibility. The person will "swallow anything" and might become a "sucker." Or fixation might lead to an *oral-aggressive* personality, marked by cruelty and sarcastic, "biting" remarks.

At the age of 1 year, children enter the **anal stage.** They now obtain pleasure from defecation and experience an important conflict regarding toilet training. Freud claimed that inadequate toilet training, either premature or delayed, can lead to fixation at the anal stage. The main characters in the play, movie, and television series "The Odd Couple" represent two kinds of anal fixation. Felix represents the *anal-retentive* personality, marked by compulsive cleanliness, orderliness, and fussiness. Oscar represents the *anal-expulsive* personality, marked by sloppiness, carelessness, and informality.

Freud claimed that between the ages of 3 and 5, the child passes through the **phallic stage,** in which pleasure is gained from the genitals. This stage is associated with the **Oedipus complex,** in which the child sexually desires the parent of the opposite sex while fearing punishment from the parent of the same sex. Freud noted this conflict in Sophocles' play *Oedipus Rex,* in which Oedipus, abandoned as an infant, later kills his father and marries his mother—without knowing they are his parents.

Freud believed that the Oedipus story reflected a universal truth—the sexual attraction of each child to the opposite-sex parent. Resolution of the conflict leads to identification with the same-sex parent. The boy gives up his desire for his mother because of his *castration anxiety*—his fear that his father will punish him by removing his genitals. The girl, because of *penis envy,* becomes angry at her mother, whom she believes caused the removal of her penis, and becomes attracted to her father. This is now known as the **Electra complex,** after a Greek character who had her mother killed (Powell, 1993). But, fearing the loss of maternal love, the girl identifies with her mother, hoping to still attract her father. Through the process of *identification,* boys and girls adopt parental values and develop a superego.

Freud called the period between age 5 and puberty the **latency stage.** He was relatively uninterested in this stage because he believed the child experiences little psychosexual development during it. Instead, the child develops social skills and friendships. Finally, during adolescence, the child reaches the **genital stage** and becomes sexually attracted to other people. To Freud, the first three stages are the most important determinants of personality development. He assumed that personality is essentially fixed by the age of 5. Figure 13.2 summarizes these psychosexual stages of development.

---

libido
Freud's term for the sexual energy of the id.

fixation
In Freud's theory, the failure to mature beyond a particular stage of psychosexual development.

oral stage
In Freud's theory, the stage of personality development, between birth and age 1 year, during which the infant gains pleasure from oral activities and faces a conflict over weaning.

anal stage
In Freud's theory, the stage of personality development, between ages 1 and 3, during which the child gains pleasure from defecation and faces a conflict over toilet training.

phallic stage
In Freud's theory, the stage of personality development, between ages 3 and 5, during which the child gains pleasure from the genitals and must resolve the Oedipus complex.

Oedipus complex
In Freud's theory, a conflict, during the phallic stage, between the child's sexual desire for the parent of the opposite sex and fear of punishment from the same-sex parent.

Electra complex
A term used by some psychoanalysts, but not by Freud, to refer to the Oedipus complex in females.

latency stage
In Freud's theory, the stage, between age 5 and puberty, during which there is little psychosexual development.

genital stage
In Freud's theory, the last stage of personality development, associated with puberty, during which the individual develops erotic attachments to others.

Stage	Age	Characteristics
Oral	Birth to 1	Gratification from oral behaviors, such as sucking, biting, and chewing. Conflict over weaning.
Anal	1 to 3	Gratification from defecation. Conflict over toilet training.
Phallic	3 to 5	Gratification from genital stimulation. Resolution of the Oedipus complex.
Latency	5 to puberty	Sexual impulses repressed. Development of friendships.
Genital	Puberty on	Gratification from genital stimulation. Development of intimate relationships.

Adler's Theory of Individual Psychology

Because Freud's intellectual descendants altered his theory, they became known as *neo-Freudians*. Figure 13.3 presents the views of several of the most renowned of them. One of the most influential of Freud's followers was Alfred Adler (1870–1937). In 1902 Adler, a Viennese physician, joined the regular Wednesday evening group discussions of psycho-analysis at Freud's home and became a devoted disciple. But in 1911 Adler broke with Freud, downplaying the importance of sexual motivation and the unconscious mind. Adler (1927)

▲ **Alfred Adler (1870–1937)**
"I began to see clearly in every psychological phenomenon the striving for superiority."

Karen Horney   **Harry Stack Sullivan**   **Erich Fromm**

▶ **FIGURE 13.3**

The Neo-Freudians

The neo-Freudians accepted the importance of unconscious motives, but placed greater emphasis on the ego's relationship to society than on the id's demand for gratification.

Karen Horney (1885–1952)

A German immigrant to the United States, she was the first eminent female psychoanalyst. Horney claimed that the personality develops from the child's attempt to seek security by overcoming the *basic anxiety* caused by feeling isolated and helpless in a potentially hostile world. According to Horney (1937), we try to relieve basic anxiety by socially moving toward, against, or away from people. Normally, this means that we become sociable, competitive, or shy. But in extreme cases we exhibit *neurotic trends*, in which we might relieve basic anxiety by being submissive, aggressive, or reclusive. Horney also criticized Freud's view that women feel inferior to men because of penis envy. Instead, she insisted that women envy men's traditionally superior rights and social status.

Harry Stack Sullivan (1892–1949)

One of the pioneers of modern American psychiatry, he lived a lonely and unhappy life, which may partly account for his theory's emphasis on the importance of healthy social relationships. Sullivan (1953) claimed that human beings have a tendency to either accept or reject their experiences as part of themselves. If we reject our unpleasant experiences and, as a consequence, fail to work at improving the inadequate social relations that cause them, we may become divorced from ourselves and develop maladaptive ways of handling anxiety. Sullivan applied his theory to the process of psychiatry and to possible ways of easing international tensions.

Erich Fromm (1900–1980)

A German immigrant, he is best known for his popular book *The Art of Loving* (1956), which applies psychoanalytic concepts to the understanding of love. Fromm based his theory on the individual's conflict between the need for freedom and the anxiety that freedom brings. In capitalistic societies, people may reduce their anxiety by giving up some of their freedom and developing a *marketing orientation,* in which they alter themselves to please others. We may adopt hairstyles, musical interests, and political beliefs simply to advance our standing with other people. In totalitarian countries, people may reduce the anxiety that freedom brings by letting the government control their social, vocational, and political lives. Fromm (1941) discussed this tendency in his book *Escape from Freedom.*

personal unconscious

In Jung's theory, the individual's own unconscious mind, which contains repressed memories.

developed his own theory, which he called *individual psychology*. The popularity of Adler's theory provoked Freud to complain, "I made a pygmy great" (Hergenhahn, 1984, p. 65).

Adler's childhood experiences inspired his theory of personality. He was a sickly child, crippled by rickets and suffering from repeated bouts of pneumonia. He also saw himself as inferior to his stronger and healthier older brother. Adler assumed that because children feel small, weak, and dependent on others, they develop an *inferiority complex*. This motivates them to compensate by *striving for superiority*—that is, developing certain abilities to their maximum. Perhaps Adler compensated for his childhood frailty by becoming an eminent psychoanalyst.

Adler believed that striving for superiority is healthiest when it promotes active concern for the welfare of both oneself and others, which he called *social interest* (Adler, 1994). For example, both a physician and a criminal strive for superiority, but the physician expresses this motive in a socially beneficial way. Teachers who are high in social interest are more effective in the classroom (Edwards & Kern, 1996). Striving for superiority can lead to *overcompensation,* as in what Adler called *masculine protest*. This means that men (and women) might try to prove themselves by dominating others instead of by developing their own abilities. For example, an Adlerian psychologist might assume that violent "gay bashing" against homosexual men by heterosexual men is an extreme example of masculine protest (Nelson, 1991).

According to Adler, in striving for superiority we develop a *style of life* based on *fictional finalism*, which he referred to as the "guiding self ideal" (Watts & Holden, 1994). This means that we are motivated by beliefs that might not be objectively true. A person guided by the belief that "nice guys finish last" might exhibit a ruthless, competitive style of life. In contrast, a person guided by the belief that "it is more blessed to give than to receive" might exhibit a helpful, altruistic style of life.

Jung's Theory of Analytical Psychology

Freud's favorite disciple was Carl Jung (1875–1961). Though Jung, a native of Switzerland, came from a family in which the men traditionally pursued careers as Protestant pastors, he obeyed a dream that directed him to pursue a career in medicine (Byrne & Kelley, 1981). He later was inspired to become a psychoanalyst after reading Freud's *The Interpretation of Dreams* (1900/1990). Beginning in 1906, Freud and Jung carried on a lively correspondence, and Freud hoped that Jung would become his successor as head of the psychoanalytic movement. But in 1914 they parted over revisions Jung made in Freud's theory, especially Jung's deemphasis of the sex motive. Jung called his version of psychoanalysis *analytical psychology.*

Though Jung agreed with Freud that we each have our own unconscious mind (the **personal unconscious**), he claimed that we also share a common unconscious mind—the **collective unconscious.** Jung held that the collective unconscious contains inherited memories passed down from generation to generation. He called these memories **archetypes,** which are images that represent important aspects of the accumulated experience

The *Star Wars* trilogy has characters that may represent Jungian archetypes. The evil Darth Vader may represent the archetype of the shadow, our animal nature. The elderly Obi-Wan Kenobi may represent the archetype of the wise old man. The adventurer Luke Skywalker may represent the archetype of the hero. And the mysterious Force may represent the archetype of God.

of humankind (see Figure 13.4). Jung claimed that archetypes influence our dreams, religious symbols, and artistic creations.

Jung (1959/1969) even connected the archetype of God to reports of flying saucers. Widespread accounts of flying saucer sightings began in the late 1940s, following the horrors of World War II and the advent of the atomic bomb. According to Jung, these sightings stemmed from the desire of people, inspired by the archetype of God, to have a more powerful force than themselves save humankind from self-destruction. Even the round shape of the flying saucer represented the archetypal image of godlike unity and perfection of the archetype of the *self*. Beginning in the 1950s with the movie *The Day the Earth Stood Still* and continuing on with movies such as *Close Encounters of the Third Kind*, science fiction movies have reflected the Jungian theme of powerful aliens arriving in flying saucers to save us from ourselves.

The archetype of the *mother* is a theme in the novel *Narcissus and Goldmund* (1930/1968), written by Jung's friend Hermann Hesse whom he also psychoanalyzed. The novel describes how the archetype of the mother guides Goldmund in his constant search for the perfect woman and his fondness for images of the Madonna. The *persona* is another archetype related to the self. While the self is the true, private personality, the persona is the somewhat false social "mask" that we wear in public. *Mandalas*, circular paintings found in cultures throughout the world, represent complete congruence of the self and the persona (Musick, 1976). According to Jung, the persona and self of a psychologically healthy individual are fairly congruent. Incongruence between the self and the persona is the theme of the movie *Zelig*, in which Woody Allen plays a human chameleon who alters his persona—and even his physical appearance—to suit the people he is with. This syndrome, in which people too easily adapt a persona that will appeal to those around them, is often observed by psychotherapists in their clients (Moses, 1989).

Jung also distinguished between the *anima*, the feminine archetype in men, and the *animus*, the masculine archetype in women. According to Jung, a psychologically healthy person, whether female or male, must maintain a balance between masculinity and femininity. A "macho" male who acts tough and rarely expresses tender emotions would be unhealthy, as would a "prissy" female who acts passive and has little control over her emotions.

Jung even contributed to our everyday language by distinguishing between two personality types. **Extraverts** are socially outgoing and pay more attention to the surrounding environment; **introverts** are socially reserved and pay more attention to their private mental experiences. Jung applied this concept in his own life, viewing Freud as an extravert and Adler as an introvert (Monte, 1980).

Psychoanalytic Assessment of Personality

A century ago, Sir Arthur Conan Doyle popularized the use of handwriting analysis, or *graphology*, by having his fictional detective Sherlock Holmes use it to solve crimes. Graphology was an ancestor of psychoanalytic personality tests. Graphologists claim that features of one's handwriting, such as the size, shape, and slant of letters, reveal aspects of one's personality. Graphology is based on the assumption that, because all children in a given culture learn to form written letters and words the same way, any deviations from the original prototypes reflect, in part, one's distinctive personality.

collective unconscious

In Jung's theory, the unconscious mind that is shared by all human beings and that contains archetypal images passed down from our prehistoric ancestors.

archetypes

In Jung's theory, inherited images that are passed down from our prehistoric ancestors and that reveal themselves as universal symbols in art, dreams, and religion.

▲ **Carl Jung (1875–1961)**
"While the personal unconscious is made up essentially of contents which have at one time been conscious but which have disappeared from consciousness through having been forgotten or repressed, the contents of the collective unconscious have never been in consciousness, and therefore have never been individually acquired, but owe their existence exclusively to heredity."

extravert

A person who is socially outgoing and prefers to pay attention to the external environment.

introvert

A person who is socially reserved and prefers to pay attention to his or her private mental experiences.

▲ The Mandala
Balanced, circular paintings such as these have been found in cultures throughout history and throughout the world. Jung claimed that this showed the influence of the archetype of the self, which symbolizes unity and wholeness.

projective test
A Freudian personality test based on the assumption that individuals project their unconscious feelings when responding to ambiguous stimuli.

▲ The Rorschach Test
The basic assumption of the Rorschach test is that what we report seeing in a series of inkblots will reveal our unconscious motives and conflicts.

Though professional graphologists can identify successful business persons when comparing samples of their handwriting and samples of handwriting from randomly selected individuals (Satow & Rector, 1995), research findings have questioned the practical usefulness of the technique (Peeples, 1990). A major problem with graphology is that it is subject to the Barnum effect, because people will accept vague, generalized graphological descriptions as accurate portrayals of their personalities (McKelvie, 1990). Given the lack of experimental evidence in support of graphology, few psychologists today use it to assess personality. Graphology has the same rationale as modern psychoanalytic assessment techniques, which are called **projective tests.** They are based on the assumption that we will "project" our repressed feelings and conflicts onto ambiguous stimuli. Today the most popular projective tests are the *Rorschach test* and the *Thematic Apperception Test.*

The Rorschach Test: Responding to Inkblots

Have you ever seen animal shapes in cloud formations? Have you ever argued about images in abstract paintings? If so, you will have some appreciation for the *Rorschach test,* which asks subjects to report what they see in inkblots. This technique was used centuries ago by Leonardo da Vinci, who evaluated the creativity of young artists by having them create meaningful forms from ambiguous figures (Kaplan & Saccuzzo, 1982). The Rorschach test was introduced in 1921 by the Swiss psychiatrist Hermann Rorschach (1884–1922), who died before he was able to conduct much research with it. The test consists of ten bilaterally symmetrical inkblots. Some of the inkblots are in black and white, and the others include colors.

In responding to the inkblots, the person tells what she sees in each one and then reports the features of the inkblot that prompted the response. After scoring each response, based on formal criteria, the examiner uses clinical judgment and one of several available scoring systems to write a profile of the person's motives and conflicts. Such profiles have been used for purposes as diverse as diagnosing psychological disorders (Hilsenroth et al., 1993) and distinguishing between the personalities of murderers and nonviolent criminals (Coram, 1995). A published review of studies of the Rorschach test found that it has moderately high validity (Parker, 1983). This makes it an adequate, though not outstanding, personality test.

The Thematic Apperception Test: Responding to Ambiguous Scenes

The *Thematic Apperception Test (TAT)* (Morgan & Murray, 1935) was created by the American psychoanalyst Henry Murray and his associate Christiana Morgan (Morgan, 1995). The TAT consists of one blank card and nineteen cards containing black-and-white pictures of people in ambiguous situations. The examiner asks several questions about each one: What is happening in the card? What events led up to that situation? Who are the people in the card? How do they feel? How does the situation turn out? Murray and Morgan assumed that subjects' responses would reveal their most important needs, such as the need for sex, power, achievement, or affiliation. The TAT is a moderately good predictor of real-life achievement, such as career success (Spangler, 1992). The TAT has also been used to measure changes in the use of defense mechanisms as a result of psychotherapy, as in a study in which 90 subjects responded to TAT cards before and after 15 months of therapy. The results showed an association between a reduction in the use of defense mechanisms as revealed by the TAT and a reduction in psychological symptoms (Cramer & Blatt, 1990).

Status of the Psychoanalytic Approach to Personality

Of all the psychoanalytic theories of personality, Freud's has been the most influential, but it has received limited support for its concepts (Fisher & Greenberg, 1985). As described in Chapter 6, there is substantial evidence demonstrating the effect of unconscious processes on human behavior (Dixon & Henley, 1991). There is also support for the Freudian view of repression from research showing that people are less likely to recall emotionally unpleasant personal experiences (Hansen & Hansen, 1988), though the notion of total repression of traumatic emotional experiences has received only weak support (Bowers & Farvolden, 1996).

In contrast, there has been little support for some of Freud's other concepts. For example, there is little evidence to support Freud's belief that resolution of the Oedipus complex is essential for gender identity, sexual orientation, and superego development (Schrut, 1994). In fact, research has failed to support the existence of the Oedipus complex (Daly & Wilson, 1990). Adler and Horney saw the Oedipus complex as rooted in cultural, not biological, reality. Adler believed that women envied men's status and power, not their penises. And Horney even speculated that men share "womb envy," because they cannot give birth to children (Horney, 1926/1967).

Perhaps the greatest weakness of Freudian theory is that many of its terms refer to processes that are neither observable nor measurable. Who has ever seen or measured an id? As noted in Chapter 2, we cannot conduct experiments on concepts that are not operationally defined.

Despite the limited support for certain psychoanalytic concepts, the psychoanalytic approach has contributed to our understanding of personality. It has revealed that much of our behavior is governed by motives of which we are unaware, as revealed in dreams, and it has stimulated interest in studying sexual behavior and sexual development. It has demonstrated the importance of early childhood experiences, such as infant attachment; it has contributed to the emergence of formal psychological therapies; and it has inspired research into the effects of psychological factors on illness. It also has influenced the works of artists, writers, and filmmakers.

Adler's theory of personality has influenced cognitive psychology and humanistic psychology through its emphasis on the importance of our subjective experiences of reality. His concept of a style of life that reflects our striving for superiority has an important descendant in the current interest in *Type A behavior*, which is discussed at length in Chapter 16 as a possible factor in coronary heart disease. Type A behavior is marked by hostility, competitiveness, and compulsive activity. Research indicates that, in keeping with Adler's theory, a person who exhibits Type A behavior might be combatting feelings of inferiority (Cooney & Zeichner, 1985). In fact, Meyer Friedman, the cardiologist who first identified the Type A behavior pattern in his patients, reported: "About 70 percent of our sample said they received inadequate parental love and then tried to compensate by being aggressive and overcompetitive" ("Type A," 1984).

Adler's theory has also influenced the development of the humanistic theory of personality, whose cofounders—including Rollo May, Carl Rogers, and Abraham Maslow—studied with him and gave credit to him for inspiring their own views. Of the Adlerian concepts that impressed humanistic psychologists, the most influential were the concepts of social interest, guiding fiction, and style of life (Ansbacher, 1990).

And what of Jung's theory? Jung's concept of personality types has received research support. One study compared the styles of extraverted painters and introverted painters. Extraverted painters tended to use realistic styles, reflecting their greater attention to the external environment. In contrast, introverted painters tended to use abstract styles, reflecting their greater attention to private mental experience (Loomis & Saltz, 1984).

Jung's concept of the archetype has been criticized because it violates known mechanisms of inheritance in its assumption that memories can be inherited. Nonetheless, research findings support the possibility that something at least akin to archetypes affects human behavior (Rosen et al., 1991). Evidence for this comes from research, explained in Chapter 14, showing that we have an inborn predisposition to develop phobias about snakes, heights, and other situations that were dangerous to our prehistoric ancestors. Thus, what Jung called archetypes might be inborn behavioral tendencies rather than inherited memories.

▲ Hermann Rorschach (1884–1922)
"The [ink-blot] test often indicates the presence of latent schizophrenia, neuroses which are barely perceptible clinically, and constitutional mood trends."

STAYING ON TRACK: *The Psychoanalytic Approach to Personality*

1. What does the Barnum effect indicate about the study of personality?

2. What is the relationship between the three structures of personality in Freud's theory?

3. What are the basic tenets of Adler's theory?

4. According to Jung, how do the collective unconscious and its archetypes affect our lives?

Answers to Staying on Track start on p. S–5.

(a)   (b)   (c)

THE DISPOSITIONAL APPROACH TO PERSONALITY

Personality theorists have traditionally assumed that personality is stable over time and consistent across situations. The *dispositional approach* to personality attributes this apparent stability and consistency to relatively enduring personal characteristics called *types* and *traits*.

Type Theories: Categorizing the Kinds of Personality

In his book *Characters*, the Greek philosopher Theophrastus (ca. 372–ca. 287 B.C.) wondered why Greeks differed in personality despite sharing the same culture and geography. He concluded that personality differences arise from inborn predispositions to develop particular personality *types* dominated by a single characteristic. His list of personality types included the Flatterer, the Faultfinder, and the Tasteless Man. Like Theophrastus, some people rely on personality typing when they call certain individuals "nerds" or "jocks." Such people would expect different behavior from a "nerd" than from a "jock."

Today the most influential theory of personality types is Hans Eysenck's *three-factor theory* (Eysenck, 1990). Eysenck (b. 1916), a German psychologist, fled to England after refusing to become a member of Hitler's secret police. Eysenck used the statistical technique of factor analysis (see Chapter 10) in identifying three dimensions of personality. By measuring where a person falls on these dimensions, we can determine his or her personality type.

The dimension of *neuroticism* measures a person's level of stability/instability. Stable people are calm, even-tempered, and reliable; unstable people are moody, anxious, and unreliable. A study of students who began an on-campus exercise program found that a year later those who dropped out had scored higher in neuroticism than had those who remained in the program (Potgieter & Venter, 1995). The dimension of *psychoticism* measures a person's level of tough-mindedness/tender-mindedness. Tough-minded people are hostile, ruthless, and insensitive, whereas tender-minded people are friendly, empathetic, and cooperative. Juvenile delinquents score high in psychoticism (Furnham & Thompson, 1991).

The dimension of *extraversion* measures a person's level of introversion/extraversion. This dimension, first identified by Jung, has stimulated the most research interest. For example, studies have shown that there are proportionately more introverts among expert chess players than in the general population. Because introverted chess champions may be uncomfortable in social situations, they prefer to avoid victory parties, press conferences, and autograph hounds. They might even feel compelled to leave the chess scene itself. In 1972 the American Bobby Fischer generated unprecedented interest in chess with his brilliant play in winning the World Chess Championship, only to retire into seclusion soon after (Olmo & Stevens, 1984). Figure 13.5 illustrates the interaction of the dimensions of introversion/extraversion and stability/instability.

There is evidence that the dimensions in Eysenck's theory have a biological basis. For example, research on twins indicates that neuroticism, psychoticism, and extraversion have a genetic bases. Heredity might explain why introverts are more physiologically reactive than extraverts are (Stelmack, 1990). This might, in turn, explain behavioral differences

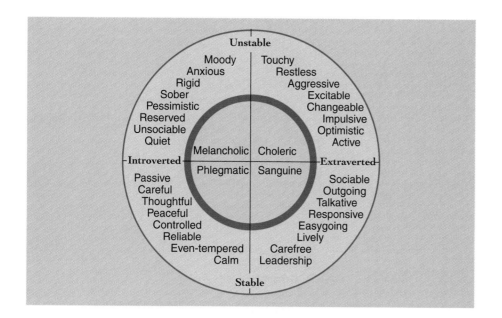

between introverts and extraverts. Because introverts are more physiologically arousable, they might condition easier. This might make introverts more socially inhibited, because they learn more easily to stop performing behaviors that have been punished.

Trait Theories: Determining the Dimensions of Personality

Instead of describing personality in terms of single types, trait theorists describe personality in terms of distinctive combinations of personal dispositions (McCrae & Costa, 1995). A **trait** is a relatively enduring, cross-situationally consistent personality characteristic that is inferred from a person's behavior. Eysenck's theory can be viewed as either a type theory or a trait theory, because the personality types in his theory are products of the interaction of certain trait dimensions. The most influential trait theory is that of Gordon Allport (1897–1967).

Early in his career, Allport had a brief meeting in Vienna with Sigmund Freud that convinced him that psychoanalysis was not the best approach to the study of personality. Confronted with a silent Freud, Allport broke the silence by describing a boy he had met on a train who had complained of dirty people and whose mother had acted annoyed at his behavior. Freud responded, "And was that little boy you?" Based on this meeting, Allport concluded that Freud was too concerned with finding hidden motives for even the most mundane behaviors (Allport, 1967).

Allport began his research by identifying all the English words that refer to personal characteristics. In 1936 Allport and his colleague Henry Odbert, using an unabridged dictionary, counted almost 18,000 such words. By eliminating synonyms and words referring to temporary states (such as *hungry*), they reduced the list to about 4,500 words. Allport then grouped the words into less than 200 clusters of related words, which became the original personality traits in his theory.

Allport distinguished three kinds of traits, the differences depending on how important they are in a given person's life. *Cardinal traits* are similar to personality types, in that they affect every aspect of the person's life. For example, altruism is a cardinal trait in the personality of Mother Teresa. Because cardinal traits are rare, you probably know few people whose lives are governed by them. *Central traits* affect many aspects of our lives but do not have the pervasive influence of cardinal traits. When you refer to someone as kind, humorous, or conceited, you are usually referring to a central trait. The least important traits are *secondary traits*, because they affect relatively narrow aspects of our lives. Preferences for wearing cuffed pants, reading western novels, or eating chocolate ice cream reflect secondary traits.

trait
A relatively enduring, cross-situationally consistent personality characteristic that is inferred from a person's behavior.

▲ Gordon Allport (1897–1967)
"Important—indeed central—to my theoretical position is my own particular conception of 'trait.'"

► **FIGURE 13.6**

The "Iceberg Profile"

Studies using the objective personality test called the Profile of Mood States have consistently found that elite athletes share an iceberg-shaped personality profile. They score higher than average on personal vigor, while scoring below average on negative characteristics: tension (anxiety), depression, anger, fatigue, and confusion. Thus, elite athletes appear to be psychologically healthier than the average person. The graph shows the personality profiles of world-class rowers, wrestlers, and runners (milers and marathoners).

Reprinted with permission from Psychology Today Magazine. Copyright © 1980 (Sussex Publishers, Inc.).

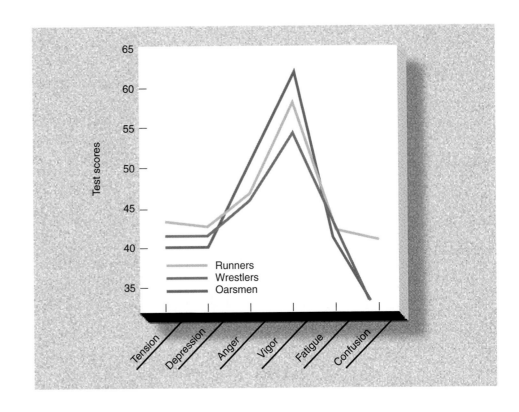

▲ **Cardinal Traits**

Gordon Allport would note that Mother Teresa, who has spent her life helping the poor, exemplifies the cardinal trait of altruism.

Dispositional Assessment of Personality

The dispositional assessment of personality relies on tests of personality types or traits. These are called *objective tests* or *inventories,* because they present subjects with straightforward statements rather than with ambiguous stimuli, as in projective tests. For example, the *Profile of Mood States,* an objective test, has shown that many elite athletes share a particular personality profile, presented in Figure 13.6.

Tests of Personality Types

One of the most popular objective tests is the *Myers-Briggs Type Indicator* (Briggs & Myers, 1943), a dispositional test based on psychoanalytic theory. The test assesses various personality characteristics, including personality types derived from Jung's analytical theory of personality. The subject is presented with pairs of statements and selects the statement in each pair that is closest to how she or he usually acts or feels. A typical item would be "At parties, do you (a) sometimes get bored or (b) always have fun?" An introvert would be more likely to select (a) and an extravert (b). The test has satisfactory validity (J. B. Murray, 1990) and has been used in a variety of research studies. One study found that teaching styles, such as the tendency to incorporate technology into the classroom, are related to specific personality profiles on the test (Smith, Munday, & Windham, 1995).

Tests of Personality Traits

The most widely used of all personality tests is the *Minnesota Multiphasic Personality Inventory (MMPI),* which measures personality traits. The MMPI was developed at the University of Minnesota by psychologist Starke R. Hathaway and psychiatrist John C. McKinley (1943) to diagnose psychological disorders. Hathaway and McKinley used the *empirical method* of test construction, which retains only those questions that discriminate between people who differ on the characteristics of interest. Hathaway and McKinley collected 1,000 statements, which they administered to 700 people, including nonpatients, medical patients, and psychiatric patients. The subjects responded "True," "False," or "Cannot Say" to each statement, depending on whether it was true of them. Hathaway and

CHAPTER 1 3

Scales	Content
Clinical Scales	
Hypochondriasis	Items identifying people who are overly concerned with bodily functions and symptoms of physical illness
Depression	Items identifying people who feel hopeless and who experience slowing of thought and action
Hysteria	Items identifying people who avoid problems by developing mental or physical symptoms
Psychopathic deviate	Items identifying people who disregard accepted standards of behavior and have shallow emotional relationships
Masculinity-femininity	Items identifying people with stereotypically male or female interests
Paranoia	Items identifying people with delusions of grandeur or persecution who also exhibit pervasive suspiciousness
Psychasthenia	Items identifying people who feel guilt, worry, and anxiety and who have obsessions and compulsions
Schizophrenia	Items identifying people who exhibit social withdrawal, delusional thoughts, and hallucinations
Hypomania	Items identifying people who are overactive, easily excited, and recklessly impulsive
Social introversion	Items identifying people who are emotionally inhibited and socially shy
Validity Scales	
Cannot say	Items that are not answered, which may indicate evasiveness
Lie	Items indicating an attempt to make a positive impression
Frequency	Items involving responses that are rarely given by normal people, which may indicate an attempt to seem abnormal
Correction	Items revealing a tendency to respond defensively in admitting personal problems or shortcomings

Source: Data from Minnesota Multiphasic Personality Inventory-2 (MMPI-2), University of Minnesota, 1970.

▲ **TABLE 13.2**
Scales of the MMPI-2

McKinley kept those statements that tended to be answered the same way by people with particular psychiatric disorders. For example, they included the statement "Nothing in the newspaper interests me except the comics" solely because significantly more depressed people than nondepressed people responded "True" to that statement (Holden, 1986).

As shown in Table 13.2, the MMPI has ten clinical scales that measure important personality traits. For example, *hypochondriasis* measures concern with bodily functions and symptoms, and *paranoia* measures suspiciousness and delusions of persecution. The MMPI also has four *validity scales* that test for evasiveness, defensiveness, lying to look good, and faking to look bad. For example, the Lie scale contains statements that describe common human failings to which almost all people respond "True." So, a person who responded "False" to statements such as "I sometimes have violent thoughts" might be lying to create a good impression.

Psychologists commonly use the MMPI to screen applicants for positions in which people with serious psychological disorders might be dangerous, such as police officers or nuclear power plant operators. The MMPI has proved to be a valid means of diagnosing psychological disorders (Parker, Hanson, & Hunsley, 1988). But researchers found that by the 1980s it was diagnosing a higher proportion of people as psychologically disordered than it did when it was first adopted. Did this mean that more people had psychological disorders than in the past? Or did it mean that the MMPI's norms were outdated? The latter seemed to be the case. As one critic noted a decade ago, "Whoever takes the MMPI today is being compared with the way a man or woman from Minnesota endorsed those items in the late 1930s and early 1940s (Herbert, 1983, p. 228).

Because of this, the MMPI was restandardized in the 1980s to avoid comparing people today with the narrow segment of society that served as the standardization group half a century ago—people from farms and small towns with an eighth-grade education and an average age of 35 years (Adler, 1989). The revised 567-item MMPI (the MMPI-2) has added, deleted, or changed many statements. It also has new norms based on a more representative sample of the American population in regard to age, sex, ethnic background, educational level, and region of the country. This makes the MMPI-2, though still imperfect, an improvement over the MMPI (Helmes & Reddon, 1993).

The 16 PF Test

This graph presents personality profiles of writers, creative artists, and airline pilots based on the sixteen personality traits in Cattell's 16 PF Test. The left-hand and right-hand columns present the opposite extremes of each trait. Average scores fall about equidistant between these extremes. Note the differences between the profile of airline pilots and the profiles of the other two groups.

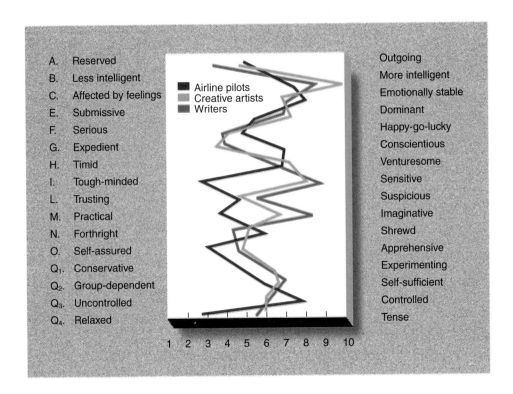

A.	Reserved		Outgoing
B.	Less intelligent		More intelligent
C.	Affected by feelings		Emotionally stable
E.	Submissive		Dominant
F.	Serious		Happy-go-lucky
G.	Expedient		Conscientious
H.	Timid		Venturesome
I.	Tough-minded		Sensitive
L.	Trusting		Suspicious
M.	Practical		Imaginative
N.	Forthright		Shrewd
O.	Self-assured		Apprehensive
Q_1.	Conservative		Experimenting
Q_2.	Group-dependent		Self-sufficient
Q_3.	Uncontrolled		Controlled
Q_4.	Relaxed		Tense

Airline pilots
Creative artists
Writers

1   2   3   4   5   6   7   8   9   10

Early critiques of the MMPI-2 show a diversity of opinions, with some experts stressing its weaknesses (Duckworth, 1991) and others its strengths (Graham, 1991). Empirical studies of the MMPI-2 have produced initially favorable findings. Despite the changes in its content, the MMPI-2 produces profiles comparable to those of the MMPI (Munley & Zarantonello, 1990), though in some cases it does not (Humphrey & Dahlstrom, 1995).

Another popular test for assessing personality traits is the *16 Personality Factor Questionnaire (16 PF)*, which is based on the trait theory of Raymond Cattell. Cattell, a native of England who spent most of his career in the United States, used factor analysis to identify sixteen basic traits, which he called *source traits*. The 16 PF measures the sixteen source traits identified by Cattell (1949).

Psychologists typically use the 16 PF for general personality testing rather than for diagnosing psychological disorders. The 16 PF contains 187 multiple-choice statements. A typical item would be "I feel mature in most things: (a) True, (b) Uncertain, (c) False." The person's scores on the source traits are plotted on a graph to provide a personality profile, which might be used by employers or career counselors to determine whether the profile is similar to those of people who have been successful in particular professions. The 16 PF has been useful in a variety of applications. For example, it has successfully predicted the likelihood that volunteers would remain committed to Big Brother/Big Sister programs (Herman & Usita, 1994). Figure 13.7 presents an example of a 16 PF profile.

Status of the Dispositional Approach to Personality

Though the dispositional approach to personality has been useful in *describing* personality differences, it is less successful in *explaining* those differences. Suppose that the results of testing with the Myers-Briggs Type Indicator reveal that one of your friends is an "extravert." Someone might ask, "Why is she an extravert?" You might respond, "Because she likes to socialize." The person might then ask, "Why does she like to socialize?" To which you might reply, "Because she is an extravert." This circular reasoning would not explain why your friend is an extravert.

One of the few dispositional theories that tries to explain personality is Eysenck's three-factor theory. The existence of the three personality factors identified by Eysenck has been verified by other researchers (Zuckerman, Kuhlman, & Camac, 1988) and it has some cross-cultural support (Eysenck, Barrett, & Barnes, 1993). The introversion/extraversion dimension has received especially strong research support. One of Eysenck's assumptions is that a person's degree of introversion/extraversion depends on his or her customary level of physiological reactivity. As noted earlier, introverts are more physiologically reactive to stimulation than extraverts are. As explained in Chapter 11, we have a tendency to try to adopt a moderate level of arousal. This might explain why introverts avoid stimulation and extraverts seek it. For example, introverted students prefer to work in quieter conditions than extraverted students do (Geen, 1984), and extraverts are more likely than introverts to seek help from others in coping with stress (Amirkhan, Risinger, & Swickert, 1995).

In regard to trait theories, research has reduced the number of basic personality traits from Cattell's sixteen to five (McCrae & Costa, 1995). These are commonly known as "The Big Five." *Extraversion* resembles Eysenck's factor of introversion/extraversion, and *neuroticism* resembles his factor of stability/instability. *Agreeableness* indicates whether a person is warm, good-natured, and cooperative. *Conscientiousness* indicates whether a person is ethical, reliable, and responsible. And *openness to experience* indicates whether a person is curious, imaginative, and interested in intellectual pursuits.

Early research on the *five-factor theory* has found that psychological well-being is negatively correlated with neuroticism and positively correlated with extraversion, agreeableness, and conscientiousness. There is strong support for the five-factor theory (Byravan & Ramanaiah, 1995). For example, individuals who score high on the trait of conscientiousness are less likely to have automobile accidents (Arthur & Graziano, 1996). There is also cross-cultural evidence for it (Paunonen et al., 1996). Moreover, we rely on the five factors when we assess people in our everyday lives (Saucier & Goldberg, 1996). Nonetheless, some leading personality theorists caution that, pending more research, it is premature to accept the five-factor theory as the best approach to personality (Block, 1995; Pervin, 1994).

STAYING ON TRACK: *The Dispositional Approach to Personality*

1. What are the basic characteristics of Allport's trait theory of personality?
2. In what way is the MMPI based on an empirical approach to personality test construction?

THE BEHAVIORAL APPROACH TO PERSONALITY

Those who favor the *behavioral approach* to personality discount biological factors, unconscious influences, and dispositional traits. Instead, they stress the importance of learning and environmental factors (Staats, 1993).

The Operant Conditioning Theory of Personality

To B. F. Skinner (1953), whose *operant conditioning theory* is described in Chapter 7, there is nothing exceptional about personality. He saw no use for concepts invoking biological predispositions, unconscious motives, personality traits, and the like. What we call *personality*, in Skinner's view, is simply a person's unique pattern of behavior, tied to specific situations (Skinner, 1974). You might say that a fellow student has a "gregarious" personality because you have observed the student engage in behaviors such as initiating conversations or going to parties every weekend.

According to Skinner, we are what we do. And what we do in a particular situation depends on our experiences in that situation and similar situations. We tend to engage in behaviors that have been positively or negatively reinforced and to avoid engaging in behaviors that have been punished or extinguished. Thus, Skinner might assume that a gregarious person has a history of receiving attention or anxiety relief for being socially outgoing in a variety of situations. In contrast, a shy person might have a history of being criticized or ignored in a variety of situations for being socially outgoing.

Reciprocal Determinism
Bandura's concept of reciprocal determinism
considers the mutual influence of the person's
characteristics, behavior, and situation. Each of
the three factors can affect the other two.

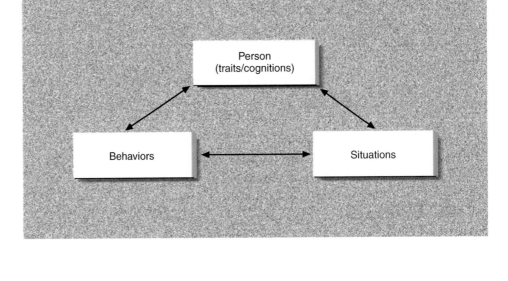

The Social-Cognitive Theory of Personality

Social-cognitive theory builds a bridge between Skinner's strict behavioral approach and
the cognitive approach to personality, which is discussed later in the chapter. Social-cognitive theory is similar to traditional behavioral theories in stressing the role of reinforcement and punishment in the development of personality. But it is different from
traditional behavioral theories in arguing that behavior is affected by cognitive processes.
That is, we are more than robotic responders to environmental stimuli—our interpretation of our own personal characteristics and environmental circumstances affects our
behavior (Bandura, 1989).

Social-cognitive theory was developed by Albert Bandura (b. 1925), who was reared in
Canada but became a professor in the United States and served as president of the
American Psychological Association in 1974. Other social-cognitive theories have been
developed by Julian Rotter and Walter Mischel. Bandura's theory of personality grew out
of his research on observational learning, which is described in Chapter 7. According to
Bandura, we learn many of our behavioral tendencies by observing other people receiving
rewards or punishments for particular behaviors. For example, children learn altruistic
behavior from adults who behave in a selfless manner.

Bandura's (1986) theory of personality also stresses the concept of **reciprocal determinism,** which reflects his belief that neither personal dispositions nor environmental factors can by themselves explain behavior. You will note that this differs from
environmental determinism, which was favored by Skinner, and psychic determinism,
which was favored by Freud. Both of those concepts assume that the person is just a
behavioral pawn. Environmental determinism assumes we are pawns controlled by
external stimuli, and psychic determinism assumes we are pawns controlled by unconscious motives. Instead, as illustrated in Figure 13.8, Bandura assumes that personality
traits, environmental factors, and overt behavior affect one another.

Research studies have found that reciprocal determinism can explain many kinds of
behaviors, such as why depression is so difficult to overcome (Teichman & Teichman,
1990): A depressed person's negative thoughts and emotions might induce gloomy statements, sad facial expressions, and aloof social behavior. This might make other people
avoid or respond negatively toward the depressed person. This social response would promote continued negative thoughts and emotions in the depressed person, thereby completing a vicious cycle that is difficult to break.

According to Bandura, one of the most important cognitive factors in reciprocal determinism is **self-efficacy.** This is the extent to which a person believes that she can perform
behaviors that are necessary to bring about a desired outcome. Self-efficacy determines our

reciprocal determinism
Bandura's belief that personality traits,
environmental factors, and overt behavior
affect each other.

self-efficacy
In Bandura's theory, a person's belief
that she or he can perform behaviors that
are necessary to bring about a desired
outcome.

choice of activities, our intensity of effort, and our persistence in the face of obstacles and unpleasant experiences, in part by reducing the anxiety that might interfere with engaging in the activity (Bandura, Reese, & Adams, 1982). Self-efficacy promotes adherence to physical exercise programs (Fontaine & Shaw, 1995), students' performance in academic courses (Shell, Colvin, & Bruning, 1995), and performance in high school wrestling (Treasure, Monson, & Lox, 1996).

But what determines whether you will have a feeling of self-efficacy in a given situation? The first determinant is *previous success*. You will have a greater feeling of self-efficacy in your psychology course if you have done well in previous courses. The second determinant is *vicarious experience*. You will have a greater feeling of self-efficacy if you know other students who have succeeded in the course. The third determinant is *verbal persuasion*. You will have a greater feeling of self-efficacy if you give yourself pep talks or your advisor convinces you that you have the ability to do well in the course. And the fourth determinant is *physiological arousal*. You will have a greater feeling of self-efficacy if you are at an optimal level of arousal (see Chapter 11). If you are too aroused while making a classroom speech and notice your increased heart rate and irregular breathing pattern, you might become so distracted that you mispronounce words or lose your place.

Behavioral Assessment of Personality

There are two main behavioral approaches to the assessment of personality. One approach examines overt behavior; the other examines cognitions that are closely tied to overt behavior.

Assessment of Overt Behavior

Theorists who favor the examination of overt behavior believe that we should note what people actually do or say they would do in specific situations rather than simply record their responses to personality tests. In *behavioral observation* the subject is observed in real or simulated conditions related to work, school, recreation, or other situations of interest. Behavioral observation is more likely to produce valid findings when it involves several observers who know the person and who on several occasions observe the person in the situation of interest (Moskowitz & Schwarz, 1982). Behavioral observation has been used to assess a variety of personality characteristics in a variety of circumstances—such as psychological disorders (Matese, Matson, & Sevin, 1994) and interactions among family members (Markman et al., 1995).

Another form of behavioral assessment uses the *experience-sampling method*. The subject carries a portable device that beeps at random times, and on hearing the beep the person reports his experiences and behaviors at that time. This reveals relationships between specific situations and the person's thoughts, feelings, and behaviors (Hormuth, 1986). Several studies have demonstrated the practical usefulness of experience sampling, such as studying sex offenders (Hillbrand & Waite, 1994) and clerical workers (Alliger & Williams, 1993). A study of elementary school children assessed their mental self-talk while they worked at their seats. Whenever the children heard a buzzer, they recorded their self-talk. The results showed that children who engaged in positive self-talk had higher academic achievement and more-appropriate social behavior, while children who engaged in negative self-talk had poorer academic achievement and less-appropriate social behavior (Manning, 1990). Of course, only experimental research could determine whether self-talk *causes* differences in academic achievement or social behavior.

Cognitive-Behavioral Assessment

As an example of the *cognitive-behavioral assessment* of personality, consider the *Internal-External Locus of Control Scale*, which was developed by Julian Rotter (1966) to measure what he calls the locus of control. Your *locus of control* is the degree to which you expect that you are in control of the outcomes of your behavior or that those outcomes are controlled by factors such as fate, luck, or chance (Rotter, 1990). In the former case you would have an internal locus of control, and in the latter case you would have an external

▲ **Behavioral Observation**
Behavioral observation is useful in determining how individuals will behave in real-life situations. The responses of astronauts to isolation, weightlessness, and simulated emergencies help determine whether they will be permitted to take part in space flights.

▲ Julian Rotter

"Internal versus external control refers to the degree to which persons expect that a reinforcement or an outcome of their behavior is contingent on their own behavior or personal characteristics versus the degree to which persons expect that the reinforcement or outcome is a function of chance, luck, or fate, is under the control of powerful others, or is simply unpredictable."

locus of control. Rotter's concept of the locus of control has been so influential that his original study is one of the most frequently cited studies in the recent history of psychology (Sechrest, 1984).

The scale contains 29 pairs of statements, including 6 that serve to disguise the purpose of the test. A typical relevant pair would be similar to the following: "The more effort you expend, the more likely you are to succeed" and "Luck is more important than hard work in job advancement." Your responses would reveal whether you have an internal or an external locus of control. Just as your sense of self-efficacy might affect your behavior in everyday life, your locus of control might determine whether you try to exert control over real-life situations.

The locus of control has been used in numerous studies. People with an internal locus of control are less fatalistic, which makes them more likely to seek medical attention for their physical symptoms (Strickland, 1989). An internal locus of control is also associated with better academic achievement, apparently because students with an internal locus of control work harder (Findley & Cooper, 1983). Drivers with an internal locus of control have fewer fatal accidents, perhaps because they are more cautious, attentive, and adept at avoiding dangerous situations (Montag & Comrey, 1987). And people reared in individualistic societies, such as the United States, tend to be higher in their internal locus of control than those from collectivist societies (Rawdon, Willis, & Ficken, 1995).

Status of the Behavioral Approach to Personality

B. F. Skinner's operant conditioning theory of personality has been praised for making psychologists more aware of the influence of learning and environmental factors on personality. But the theory has been criticized by Hans Eysenck (1988) for ignoring the influence of heredity on individual differences in personality. Skinner's theory has also been criticized for viewing the person as a passive responder to the environment and for failing to consider the importance of cognitive factors. The social-cognitive theorists have responded by recognizing the importance of cognitive processes and environmental factors.

Bandura's concept of self-efficacy has been supported by research findings in a variety of areas in addition to those mentioned earlier. One study found that students' feelings of self-efficacy in mathematics affected their anxiety about mathematics and decision whether to major in it (Hackett, 1985). Another study found that people with feelings of self-efficacy for long-distance running are more likely to enter marathon races, train hard for those races, and continue running despite the pain and fatigue they experience (Okwumabua, 1985).

STAYING ON TRACK: *The Behavioral Approach to Personality*

1. How does the social-cognitive theory of personality differ from the operant conditioning theory?
2. What is reciprocal determinism?
3. What are the differences between behavioral observation and experience sampling in the behavioral assessement of personality?

THE COGNITIVE APPROACH TO PERSONALITY

Like the social-cognitive theory, the *cognitive approach* to personality recognizes the influence of thoughts on behavior. But this approach pays more attention to subjective experience and interpretation, and less attention to objective situations, compared to the social-cognitive theory.

The Personal-Construct Theory of Personality

The most influential cognitive theory of personality is the *personal-construct theory* of George Kelly (1905–1967). Kelly, who spent his childhood on a Kansas farm, was educated in both physics and psychology. His background in physics inspired his view of human beings as lay scientists who try to make sense of the world by continually testing and revising hypotheses about social reality. He called these hypotheses **personal constructs** (Kelly, 1963). According to Kelly, your characteristic pattern of personal constructs determines your personality. Thus, instead of being pawns in the hands of heredity, environment, or unconscious motives, we "construe" reality. That is, we actively interpret reality and guide our behavior according to the kind of reality we construe (Cantor, 1990).

Kelly believed that personal constructs are bipolar, meaning that they involve opposite extremes. So people are rated on categories such as *shy/outgoing, safe/dangerous,* or *selfish/generous*. If you hold the personal construct that "strangers are dangerous," you might behave suspiciously toward strangers. Just as scientists retain hypotheses only if they prove accurate, we retain our personal constructs only as long as we believe they are accurate. If you found that elderly strangers are not dangerous, you might revise your personal construct to hold that "young strangers are dangerous." Thus, as children develop, their systems of personal constructs become increasingly more refined and complex.

Kelly called our ability to apply different constructs to a given situation **constructive alternativism,** which he divided into three phases: the circumspection-preemption-control cycle. During the *circumspection phase,* we evaluate constructs that might be relevant to a particular person or situation. During the *preemption phase,* we decide which construct is most relevant to the situation. And during the *control phase,* we follow a course of action based on the chosen construct.

As an example, suppose that someone comes to your door to ask for a contribution to a high school marching band. During the circumspection phase, you would evaluate and choose among several bipolar dimensions to determine which is relevant to the situation. Two might be "honest/dishonest" and "worthy/unworthy." You would consider whether the person seems honest or dishonest and whether the charity seems worthy or unworthy. During the preemption phase, you might determine that the person is honest and that the charity is worthy. During the control phase, these constructs would make you more likely to contribute to it.

Personal-construct theory has been useful in research on many psychological topics, including self-esteem (Forster & Schwartz, 1994), motivation in mathematics courses (Middleton, 1995), and psychological reactions during mourning (Viney, 1991).

Cognitive Assessment of Personality

The chief technique for the cognitive assessment of personality is the *Role Construct Repertory Test (REP Test),* which Kelly derived from his personal-construct theory. The REP Test presents the subject with sets of three persons whom the subject knows. The subject must specify a way in which two of the persons are similar to each other and different from the third. A psychologist might present an individual with sets of three persons who play roles of importance to the subject, such as "father," "best friend," and "disliked teacher." The subject then specifies a way in which two of the persons are similar to each other and different from the third. If you were the subject, you might report that your father and your best friend are both sincere, while the disliked teacher is insincere.

The psychologist repeats this process with several sets of persons. A therapist would take your responses and determine how many constructs you used to distinguish between people. These constructs would be the ones you use to perceive social reality, such as "sincere/insincere." If you relied on too few constructs, you might be inflexible and view people according to stereotypes. In contrast, if you relied on too many constructs, you might be confused and perform poorly in social situations because you would have difficulty predicting people's behavior. In fact, the ability to maintain a relatively stable, yet flexible, set of personal constructs is crucial to psychological well-being (Winter, 1993).

The REP Test has been put to good use in studies of personal constructs. It has, for example, helped career counselors in vocational planning (Neimeyer, 1989). And the REP Test has also found that marital satisfaction is related positively to similarities in the personal-construct systems held by spouses (Neimeyer, 1984).

personal construct
A hypothesis about social reality that is held by a person.

constructive alternativism
The process by which a person applies personal constructs to a given situation.

▲ George Kelly (1905–1967)
"[Personal] constructs are used for prediction of things to come, and the world keeps rolling along and revealing these predictions to be either correct or misleading."

Status of the Cognitive Approach to Personality

fixed-role therapy

A kind of therapy, derived from Kelly's personality theory, that encourages clients to adopt roles that promote new, more adaptive personal constructs.

George Kelly contributed a method of psychotherapy called **fixed-role therapy,** which encourages clients to adopt roles that promote new, more adaptive constructs. It has been used successfully in treating people with social anxiety or social phobias (Beail & Parker, 1991). After Kelly's death, his theory, which has been called "a classic ahead of its time" (Rorer & Widiger, 1983), has been carried on chiefly by a small group of his followers.

The cognitive approach to personality has attracted psychologists who believe that conscious thoughts are more important than unconscious motives or environmental stimuli in determining behavior. But traditional behavioral theorists argue that thoughts do not *cause* behavior. And psychoanalytic theorists criticize cognitive theories for ignoring the irrational, emotional bases of behavior. Nonetheless, there is evidence that we might construct our reality by testing hypotheses, observing behaviors related to the hypotheses, and then trying to reduce any incongruence between our hypotheses and the actual behaviors that we observe by revising our personal constructs (Agnew & Brown, 1989).

STAYING ON TRACK: *The Cognitive Approach to Personality*

1. What is the nature of constructive alternativism?
2. How might a psychotherapist use the REP Test?

THE HUMANISTIC APPROACH TO PERSONALITY

The *humanistic approach* to personality, which emerged in the 1950s, holds that human beings are naturally good. This contrasts with psychoanalytic personality theorists, who believe that human beings are predisposed to be selfish and aggressive, and behavioral personality theorists, who believe that human beings are neither naturally good nor naturally evil.

The humanistic approach also contrasts with the psychoanalytic and behavioral approaches in accepting subjective mental experience *(phenomenological experience)* as its subject matter. This makes the humanistic approach similar to the cognitive approach, though more concerned with emotional experience. Moreover, the humanistic approach assumes that we have free will, meaning that our actions are not compelled by id impulses or environmental stimuli.

The Self-Actualization Theory of Personality

Humanistic theories of personality have some of the flavor of the theories of Jung and Adler in that they view human beings as goal-directed and governed by their subjective views of reality. The first humanistic theory of personality was that of Abraham Maslow (1970), whose theory of motivation is discussed in Chapter 11. Maslow, reared in Brooklyn, was urged by his parents to attend law school. One day he found himself in a course in which he had no interest, and he bolted from the classroom.

self-actualization

In Maslow's theory, the individual's predisposition to try to fulfill her or his potentials.

Maslow never returned to law school. Instead, against his parents' wishes, he decided to pursue a career in psychology. This willingness to fulfill one's own needs, rather than trying to please other people, became a hallmark of humanistic theories of personality. As discussed in Chapter 11, Maslow believed we have a need for **self-actualization,** the predisposition to try to reach our potentials. The concept of self-actualization is a descendant of Adler's concept of striving for superiority (Crandall, 1980).

But who is self-actualized? Maslow presented several candidates, including President Abraham Lincoln, psychologist William James, and humanitarian Eleanor Roosevelt. Table 13.3 presents a list of characteristics shared by self-actualized people. Maslow decided on these characteristics after testing, interviewing, or reading the works of individuals he considered self-actualized. Our psychological well-being is related, in part, to the extent to which we are self-actualized. For example, it seems that one of the reasons why extraverted people tend to be happier than other people is that they are more self-actualized than are more introverted people (Lester, 1990).

- Realistic orientation
- Self-acceptance and acceptance of others and the natural world as they are
- Spontaneity
- Problem-centered rather than self-centered
- Air of detachment and need for privacy
- Autonomous and independent
- Fresh rather than stereotyped appreciation of people and things
- Generally have had profound mystical or spiritual, though not necessarily religious, experiences
- Identification with humankind and a strong social interest
- Tendency to have strong intimate relationships with a few special, loved people rather than superficial relationships with many people
- Democratic values and attitudes
- No confusion of means with ends
- Philosophical rather than hostile sense of humor
- High degree of creativity
- Resistance to cultural conformity
- Transcendance of environment rather than always coping with it

Data from A.H. Maslow, *The Farthest Reaches of Human Nature*, Viking Press, 1971.

The Self Theory of Personality

Carl Rogers (1902–1987) was born near Chicago to a devoutly religious family. His religious upbringing led him to enter Union Theological Seminary in New York City. But Rogers left the seminary to pursue a career in psychology, eventually serving as president of the American Psychological Association in 1946.

Rogers pointed out that self-actualization requires acceptance of one's *self* or *(self concept)*, which is your answer to the question "Who are you?" But each of us experiences some incongruence between the self and personal experience. We might learn to deny our feelings, perhaps claiming that we are not angry or embarrassed even when we are. This might make us feel phony or, as Rogers would say, not genuine. This incongruence between our self and our experience causes us anxiety, which in turn motivates us to reduce the incongruence by altering the self or reinterpreting the experience. Though complete congruence between the self and experience is impossible and would be maladaptive (we would have no motivation to improve the self if we did not experience some incongruence), people who have a great incongruence between the self and experience may develop psychological disorders (see Chapter 14).

How does incongruence between the self and experience develop? According to Rogers, children who do not receive *unconditional positive regard*—that is, complete acceptance—from their parents will develop incongruence by denying aspects of their experience. To gain acceptance from parents, a child might express thoughts, feelings, and behaviors that are acceptable to them. For example, a boy whose parents insist that "boys don't cry" might learn to deny his own painful physical and emotional experiences in order to gain parental approval. Such *conditions of worth* lead children to become rigid and anxious because of a failure to accept their experiences. Instead of becoming self-actualizing, such children may adopt a lifestyle of conformity and ingratiation (Baumeister, 1982). Rogers, like other personality theorists, reveals his own life experiences in his theory. He recalled that as a child he felt that his parents did not love him for himself apart from his accomplishments. That is, he felt that he had not received unconditional positive regard from them (Dolliver, 1995).

Psychologically healthy people have greater congruence between the *actual self* (Rogers's *self*) and the *ideal self* (the person they would like to be). The more self-actualized the person, the less the incongruence between the person's actual self and ideal self

▲ **Carl Rogers (1902–1987)**
"It has been my experience that persons have a basically positive direction."

and, as a result, the greater the person's self-esteem (Moretti & Higgins, 1990). People with a great incongruence between their actual self and their ideal self have more self-doubts and fewer social skills. A study of undergraduates found that as the congruence between their actual and their ideal selves increased, their feelings of happiness increased (Mikulincer & Peer-Goldin, 1991).

One way to protect the actual self is by *self-handicapping,* in which people claim that a task is very difficult or that factors beyond their control might contribute to their less-than-ideal behavior or performance (Deppe & Harackiewicz, 1996). As you have certainly observed, self-handicapping is common among students (Rhodewalt & Hill, 1995). Thus, a student walking into class for a test might remind his classmates that the need to console a friend the night before prevented him from studying enough. Given these excuses, possible failure on the test would be less of a blow to the actual self. And if the student performs well on the test, the actual self would be elevated.

Humanistic Assessment of Personality

How do humanistic psychologists assess personality? Two of the main techniques are the *Personal Orientation Inventory* and the *Q-sort.*

The Personal Orientation Inventory: How Self-Actualized Are You?

Psychologists who wish to assess self-actualization commonly use the *Personal Orientation Inventory (POI)* (Shostrom, 1962). The POI determines the degree to which a person's values and attitudes agree with Maslow's description of self-actualized people, such as being governed by one's own motives and principles. The inventory contains items that force the person to choose between options, such as (a) "Impressing others is most important" and (b) "Expressing myself is most important." A study of undergraduates found that those who scored higher on the POI were more likely to perform independently on a reasoning task in which others tried to influence their performance (Bordages, 1989).

The Q-Sort: How Well Do Certain Personality Characteristics Describe You?

The *Q-sort,* derived from Rogers's self theory, is used to measure the degree of congruence between a person's actual self and her or his ideal self. If you took a Q-sort test, you would be given a pile of cards with a self-descriptive statement on each. A typical statement might be "I feel comfortable with strangers." You would put the statements in several piles, ranging from a pile containing statements that are most characteristic of your actual self to a pile containing statements that are least characteristic of your actual self. You would then follow the same procedure for your ideal self, creating a second set of piles. The greater the degree of overlap between the two sets of piles, the greater the congruence between your actual self and your ideal self. Psychotherapists have used the Q-sort method to determine whether therapy has increased the congruence between a client's actual self and ideal self (Leaf et al., 1992).

Status of the Humanistic Approach to Personality

Research has produced mixed support for Maslow's concept of self-actualization. For example, a study of students who scored low in self-actualization on the POI at the beginning of a university preparatory course found they increased in self-actualization by the end of the course (Fogarty, 1994). But there have been inconsistent findings regarding the assumption that self-actualization increases with age. A cross-sectional study (see Chapter 4) of women aged 19 to 55 found an increase in their sense of autonomy. That is, the subjects became more motivated by their own feelings than by the influence of other people—a characteristic of self-actualized people (Hyman, 1988). Yet a cross-sectional study of faculty members aged 30 to 68 found that their self-actualization did not increase with age (Hawkins, Hawkins, & Ryan, 1989).

There has been relatively more research on the self, per se, than on self-actualization. In fact, there has been a sprouting of a variety of "selves." A view of the self put forth by E. Tory Higgins (1987) considers the relationship between three selves: the *actual self,* the *ideal self,* and the *ought self.* Incongruence between the actual self and the ideal self will make a person feel depressed. This incongruence is expressed in Woody Allen's remark "My only regret in life is that I am not someone else." Incongruence between the actual self and the ought self (which is similar to Freud's ego ideal in representing beliefs about one's moral duties) will make a person feel anxious (Straumann & Higgins, 1988). We are motivated to alleviate our personal distress by reducing the incongruence between these selves (Higgins, 1990).

The humanistic approach has been praised for countering psychologists' tendency to study the negative aspects of human experience by encouraging them to study love, creativity, and other positive aspects of human experience. The humanistic approach has also renewed interest in studying conscious mental experience, which was the original subject matter of psychology a century ago (Singer & Kolligian, 1987). Moreover, the humanistic approach might best reflect popular views of personality. A survey of people in everyday life found that most people believe that others would know them best if others knew their private mental experiences rather than their overt behavior (Andersen & Ross, 1984). The humanistic approach has also contributed to the recent interest in self-development, including the emphasis on improving one's physical appearance. For example, improving one's physique through weight training enhances the self-esteem of both men (Tucker, 1982) and women (Trujillo, 1983).

But the humanistic approach has not escaped criticism. Critics accuse it of divorcing the person from both the environment and the unconscious mind and for failing to operationally define and experimentally test abstract concepts such as the concept of self-actualization (Daniels, 1982). And the assumption of the innate goodness of human beings has been called naive even by the influential humanistic psychologist Rollo May (1982), who believes that innately good human beings would not have created the evil that the world has known.

Maslow and Rogers have been accused of unintentionally promoting selfishness by stressing the importance of self-actualization without placing an equal emphasis on social responsibility (Geller, 1982). They have even been accused of encouraging the alleged "me generation" of Americans that emerged in the 1980s, many of whose members were supposedly more motivated by self-interest than by an interest in contributing to the well-being of others. But this accusation is countered by research showing that people who have developed a positive self-regard tend to have a *greater* regard for others than do people with a negative self-regard (Epstein & Feist, 1988). Thus, we must be careful not to confuse self-regard with self-centeredness.

Though the humanistic approach to personality has received its share of criticism, Rogers has been widely praised for his contributions to the advancement of psychotherapy, which is discussed in Chapter 15. Today, no single approach to personality dominates the others. Each makes a valuable contribution to our understanding of personality.

STAYING ON TRACK: *The Humanistic Approach to Personality*

1. What are the principal characteristics of humanistic theories of personality?
2. What are some of the topics in research on the "self"?
3. How would you use the Q-sort to assess someone's personality?

THE BIOPSYCHOLOGICAL APPROACH TO PERSONALITY

Personality researchers who favor the *biopsychological approach* warn that "any theory that ignores the evidence for the biological underpinnings of human behavior is bound to be an incomplete one" (Kenrick & Dantchik, 1983, p. 302). The biological basis of

temperament

A person's characteristic emotional state, first apparent in early infancy and possibly inborn.

personality has been recognized by ancient and modern thinkers alike. The Greek physician-philosopher Hippocrates (460–377 B.C.) presented an early biological view of personality, which was elaborated on by the Greek physician Galen (A.D. 130–200). Hippocrates and Galen claimed that **temperament,** a person's predominant emotional state, reflects the relative levels of body fluids they called *humors*. They associated blood with a cheerful, or *sanguine*, temperament; phlegm with a calm, or *phlegmatic*, temperament; black bile with a depressed, or *melancholic*, temperament; and yellow bile with an irritable, or *choleric*, temperament. Research has failed to find a humoral basis for personality. But as discussed earlier in the chapter, Hans Eysenck's research supports the existence of these four basic temperaments (Stelmack & Stalikas, 1991).

The humoral theory of personality was dominant until the late eighteenth century, when it was joined by phrenology and physiognomy. As described in Chapter 3, *phrenology* is the study of the contours of the skull. Phrenologists assumed that specific areas of the brain controlled specific personality characteristics and that the bumps and depressions of the skull indicated the size of those brain areas. Those who believed in *physiognomy*, the study of physical appearance, held that personality was revealed by the features of the face.

Research failed to support phrenology and physiognomy. Like astrology, they were subject to the Barnum effect. If you felt the contours of a person's head and wrote a personality description that contained flattering generalities, your subject might place unjustified faith in phrenology (Smith, 1986). Phrenologists did, however, spark interest in the study of the biological bases of personality, particularly the role of heredity (Hilts, 1982). The early twentieth century saw biologically inclined personality researchers begin to study the relationship between physique and personality.

The Relationship Between Physique and Personality

The scientific study of the relationship between physique and personality began with the work of the German psychiatrist Ernst Kretschmer (1888–1964). Kretschmer (1925) measured the physique of hundreds of mental patients and found a relationship between thin physiques and schizophrenia and between rounded physiques and manic depression. But the researcher who did the most to advance the scientific study of the physique–personality relationship was the American physician and psychologist William Sheldon (1898–1977), whose inspiration to become a psychologist came from having William James as his godfather (Hilgard, 1987).

somatotype

A person's body type, whether ectomorphic (thin), mesomorphic (muscular), or endomorphic (fat).

In formulating his *constitutional theory* of personality, Sheldon examined photographs of thousands of young men. He identified three kinds of physiques, which he called **somatotypes.** The *ectomorph* has a thin, frail physique; the *mesomorph* has a muscular, strong physique; and the *endomorph* has a soft, rounded physique. Because Sheldon recognized that few people were pure somatotypes, he rated subjects on a scale of 1 to 7 for each of the three kinds of physiques. Sheldon also administered personality tests to his subjects. He found that each somatotype was associated with a particular temperament. He called the shy, restrained, and introspective temperament of the ectomorph *cerebrotonia*; the bold, assertive, and energetic temperament of the mesomorph *somatotonia*; and the relaxed, sociable, and easygoing temperament of the endomorph *viscerotonia* (Sheldon & Stevens, 1942).

But how might somatotypes affect personality? Sheldon reasoned that their own somatotypes might affect people's behavior and the behavior of others toward them. For example, a mesomorphic person might be more physically imposing, making the person more self-confident and, as a result, more assertive. Moreover, others might find the mesomorph more attractive, further enhancing her or his self-confidence. Sheldon found that mesomorphs were more common among juvenile delinquents, perhaps because they are stronger and more assertive than ectomorphs or endomorphs. Today, though interest in the study of the relationship between body type and personality remains, psychologists who are interested in the biological bases of personality are more likely to study the effects of heredity.

The Relationship Between Heredity and Personality

A century ago Francis Galton insisted that "nature prevails enormously over nurture" (Holden, 1987, p. 598). Today those, like Galton, who believe that heredity molds personality assume that evolution has provided us with inborn behavioral tendencies that differ from person to person (Buss, 1990). The field that studies the relationship between heredity and behavior is called *behavioral genetics* (see Chapter 4). For example, a behavioral genetics study found that the inherited tendency to be highly emotional is an important risk factor in regard to divorce (Jocklin, McGue, & Lykken, 1996). Research in behavioral genetics has shown that even newborn infants exhibit differences in temperament—some are emotionally placid, others are emotionally reactive (Braungart et al., 1992).

How might these initial differences in temperament contribute to the development of differences in personality? They might affect how infants respond to other people and, in turn, how other people respond to them. For example, a placid infant would be less responsive to other people. As a consequence, others would be less responsive to the infant. This might predispose the infant to become less sociable later in childhood, laying the groundwork for an introverted personality.

Biopsychological Assessment of Personality

In general, the closer the genetic relationship between two persons, the more alike they will be in personality characteristics. But this relationship might reflect common life experiences rather than common genetic inheritance. For example, identical twins might respond similarly to personality tests because they are exposed to more-similar environments than fraternal twins are (Schonemann & Schonemann, 1994). Because of the difficulty in separating genetic effects and environmental effects in studies of relatives who share similar environments, researchers have resorted to adoption studies. The Texas Adoption Project (see Chapter 4), found that, in regard to personality, children tend to resemble their biological parents more than their adoptive parents (Loehlin, Horn, & Willerman, 1990). Findings such as these indicate that parent–child personality similarity is influenced more by common heredity than by common life experiences, as supported by the following study.

▶ **Identical Twins Reunited**
When reunited at the age of 39 as part of Thomas Bouchard's study, identical twins Jim Lewis and Jim Springer revealed remarkable similarities even though they had been adopted into different homes at 4 weeks of age. Both liked arithmetic but not spelling, drove Chevrolets, had dogs named Toy, chewed their fingernails to the nub, served as deputy sheriffs, enjoyed vacationing in Florida, married women named Linda, and got divorced and then married women named Betty. Both also enjoyed mechanical drawing and carpentry. The photos show them in their basement workshops, where both had built white benches that encircle trees in their backyards.

ANATOMY OF A CONTEMPORARY RESEARCH STUDY

In Personality, Are Identical Twins Reared Apart More Like Their Adoptive Parents or Their Biological Parents?

Rationale

Since 1979, psychologist Thomas Bouchard of the University of Minnesota has conducted the most comprehensive study of identical twins reared apart and then reunited later in life. He has found amazing behavioral similarities between some of the twins. Consider the case of Oskar Stohr and Jack Yufe, who were born in Trinidad to a Jewish father and a Catholic mother. The twins were separated shortly after birth and reared in vastly different life circumstances. While Oskar was reared in Germany as a Nazi by his maternal grandmother, Jack was reared in Trinidad as a Jew by his father. Decades later, when they arrived at the airport in Minneapolis to take part in Bouchard's study, both Jack and Oskar sported mustaches, wire-rimmed glasses, and two-pocket shirts with epaulets. Bouchard found that they both preferred sweet liqueurs, stored rubber bands on their wrists, flushed the toilet before using it, read magazines from back to front, and dipped buttered toast in their coffee (Holden, 1980). Though there are probably no "flush toilet before using" genes, the men's identical genetic inheritance might have provided them with similar temperaments that predisposed them to develop certain behavioral similarities. In fact, Bouchard and his colleagues have found that the rearing environment has relatively little influence on the development of personality (Bouchard & McGue, 1990).

Studies of identical twins reared apart provide the strongest support for the hereditary basis of personality. Identical twins have 100 percent of their genes in common, while fraternal twins are no more alike genetically than nontwin siblings. This might explain why identical twins who are adopted and reared by different families are more similar in personality than fraternal twins who are reared by their biological parents—even three decades after adoption (Tellegen et al., 1988).

Method

The subjects were participants in the Minnesota Twin Study between 1970 and 1984. There were 217 identical twin pairs reared together and 114 fraternal twin pairs reared together. There were 44 identical twin pairs reared apart and 27 fraternal twin pairs reared apart. The twins who had been reared apart had been separated, on the average, more than 30 years. The subjects were given the Multidimensional Personality Questionnaire, which measures basic personality traits.

Results and Discussion

The results indicated that identical twins reared together and identical twins reared apart were highly similar in intelligence. Identical twins reared apart also were more similar than fraternal twins reared together. Overall, the heritability of personality was .48. (The heritability of personality is the proportion of the variability in personality within a population that is caused by heredity.) Thus, the subjects' personalities were strongly, though not solely, influenced by heredity.

▲▲▲

Status of the Biopsychological Approach to Personality

Research has failed to find the strong relationship between somatotype and personality reported by Sheldon. One of the main problems with Sheldon's research was that *he* rated both the somatotypes and the temperaments of his subjects. This provided room for experimenter bias, perhaps making his ratings support his theory more than they should have. Nonetheless, there is a *modest* relationship between physique and personality. For example, as predicted by Sheldon, mesomorphic males are more extraverted, self-confident, and emotionally stable (Tucker, 1983). But a study in which staff members rated the personalities of children at a day-care center found no relationships between their physiques and their personalities (Lester, Kaminsky, & McGovern, 1993).

▲ **Thomas Bouchard**
"On multiple measures of personality and temperament, occupational and leisure-time interests, and social attitudes, monozygotic twins reared apart seem to be about as similar as monozygotic twins reared together."

Even positive findings do not indicate that physique differences *cause* personality differences. Perhaps, instead, personality differences affect dietary and exercise habits, thereby causing differences in physique. Another possibility is that hereditary factors cause a relationship between physique and personality. For example, a study found that newborn ectomorphic infants were more emotionally responsive than infants with other physiques (Lester & Wosnack, 1990). This supported Sheldon's notion that the same genes might determine both physique and temperament (Sheldon & Stevens, 1942).

Putting aside the question of the relationship between physique and personality, how heritable is personality? Research has been consistent in finding that, though results vary somewhat, the heritability of personality is about .50 (Bouchard, 1994). And what of Bouchard's research on identical twins reared apart? Care must be taken in drawing conclusions from the amazing behavioral similarities in some of the twins he has studied. Imagine that you and a fellow student were both asked thousands of questions (as Bouchard asks his subjects). You would undoubtedly find some surprising similarities between the two of you, even though you were not genetically related. This was demonstrated in a study that found many similarities between pairs of strangers. For example, one pair of women were both Baptists, nursing students, active in tennis and volleyball, fond of English and mathematics, not fond of shorthand, and partial to vacations at historic places (Wyatt et al., 1984). Of course, by comparing twins' performances on formal personality tests, Bouchard does more than simply report selected instances of amazing similarities between certain ones. Given the evidence for both genetic and environmental influences, the best bet is to accept that they both strongly—apparently about equally—affect the development of personality.

STAYING ON TRACK: *The Biopsychological Approach to Personality*

1. What weaknesses are there in research on somatotypes and personality?
2. How do studies of identical twins who have been reunited provide evidence supporting the role of heredity in personality development?

THINKING ABOUT *Psychology*

Is Personality Consistent?

You might recall that the definition of personality includes the word *consistent*. But do people really behave consistently from one situation to another? Professors who write letters of recommendation for students assume that they do, when they refer to their students as "mature," "friendly," and "conscientious." But will a student who has been mature, friendly, and conscientious in college necessarily exhibit those traits in a job or in graduate school? The degree of cross-situational consistency in personality has been one of the most controversial issues in personality research (Siberstein, 1988).

PERSONALITY AS INCONSISTENT

The debate over the consistency of personality began in 1968 with the publication of a book by the social-cognitive theorist Walter Mischel. He reported that personality is much less consistent from one situation to another than was commonly believed. Mischel found that the correlation between any two behaviors presumed to represent the same underlying personality trait rarely exceeded a relatively modest .30. This means that you could not predict with confidence whether a person who scored high on the trait of generosity would behave in a generous manner in a given situation. For example, a person who scored high on a test measuring generosity might donate to the Salvation Army but might not pick up the check in a restaurant—though both behaviors would presumably reflect the trait of generosity. Based on his review of research findings, Mischel concluded that our behavior is influenced more by the situations in which we find ourselves than by our personality characteristics.

Though Mischel stimulated the recent debate over the issue of personality consistency, the issue is not new. Forty years before Mischel published his findings, psychologists reported research showing that children's honesty was inconsistent across situations. A child might cheat on a test but not in an athletic event, or lie at school but not at home (Hartshorne & May, 1928).

If personality is inconsistent across situations, why do we perceive it to be consistent in our everyday lives? First, we might confuse the consistency of behavior in a given situation over time with the consistency of that behavior across different situations (Mischel & Peake, 1982). If a fellow student is consistently humorous in your psychology class, you might mistakenly infer that she is humorous at home, at parties, and in the dormitory. Second, we tend to avoid situations that are inconsistent with our personalities (Snyder, 1983). If you view yourself as "even-tempered," you might avoid situations that might make you lose your temper, such as a discussion about the abortion issue.

Third, our first impression of a person can make us discount later behavior that is inconsistent with it (Hayden & Mischel, 1976). If someone is friendly to you the first time you meet but is rude to you the next time you meet, you might say that he was "not himself" today. And fourth, our perception of cross-situational consistency in others might reflect a powerful situational factor—our presence in their environment (Lord, 1982). If others adapt their behavior to our presence, we might erroneously infer that they are consistent across situations.

PERSONALITY AS CONSISTENT

These attacks on cross-situational consistency have provoked responses from those who claim there is more cross-situational consistency than Mischel and his allies believe (Kenrick & Funder, 1988). First, individuals do show consistency on certain traits. But how do we know *which* traits? One way to find out is to ask. People who claim to be consistent on a given trait tend to exhibit behaviors reflecting that trait across situations (Zuckerman et al., 1988). In one study, students were asked to judge how consistent they were on the trait of friendliness. Those who claimed to be friendly across situations were, in fact, more consistently friendly than were students who did not claim to be—as verified by their peers, parents, and other observers (Bem & Allen, 1974).

Second, cross-situational consistency in behavior depends on whether a person is a *high self-monitor* or a *low self-monitor*. High self-monitors are concerned about how people perceive them and adapt their behaviors to fit specific situations, while low self-monitors are less concerned about how people perceive them and do not adapt their behaviors as much to fit specific situations. This means that low self-monitors show greater cross-situational consistency in their behaviors than do high self-monitors (Gangestad & Snyder, 1985).

Third, many of the studies that Mischel reviewed were guaranteed to find low cross-situational consistency, because they either correlated trait test scores with single instances of behaviors or correlated single instances of behaviors with each other. This would be like trying to predict your exact score on your next psychology test from your score on the Scholastic Assessment Test or from your score on a biology test. The prediction would most likely be wrong, because many factors influence your performance on any given academic test. Similarly, many factors other than a given personality trait influence your behavior in a given situation.

Psychologists have achieved greater success in demonstrating cross-situational consistency by using *behavioral aggregation*. In aggregating behaviors, you would observe a person's behavior across several situations. You would then determine how the person

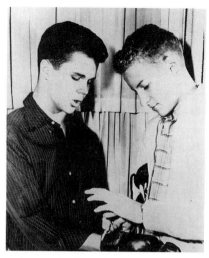

▲ **Personality Consistency**
Perhaps the most controversial issue in personality research during the past two decades has been the extent to which personality is consistent from one situation to another. If you have watched reruns of "Leave It to Beaver," you know that Eddie Haskell is unbearably polite in the presence of Mr. and Mrs. Cleaver, but a wise guy in the presence of Wally and Beaver. Research findings have convinced some personality researchers that our behavior is influenced more by the situation we are in than by the personality characteristics we possess.

▲ **Walter Mischel**
"If human behavior is determined by many interacting variables—both in the person and in the environment—then a focus on any one of them is likely to lead to limited predictions and generalizations."

typically, but not necessarily *always*, behaves—much in the same way that you would find your average on several exams to determine your typical performance in a course. A "humorous" person would be humorous in many, but not all, situations. When we predict how a person will typically behave, instead of how that person will behave in a specific situation, the correlation between traits and behaviors becomes a relatively high .60 or more (Epstein & O'Brien, 1985). For example, a study of college students found that the correlation between their trait of outgoingness and their behaving in an outgoing way was .70 when averaged across a variety of situations (Herringer, 1993). The importance of behavioral aggregation in determining personality consistency was demonstrated in the following classic study.

ANATOMY OF A CLASSIC RESEARCH STUDY

Is Personality Consistent from One Situation to Another?

Rationale

When behavioral aggregation was applied to the Hartshorne and May (1928) study, the correlation between the trait of honesty and behaviors reflecting honesty rose considerably. Consider a similar study by George Dudycha (1936), which examined personality consistency in regard to punctuality.

Method

Dudycha noted that some people have reputations for always being punctual and others for always being late. He decided to study the phenomenon of punctuality in everyday life, rather than set up artificial situations in which punctuality would be measured. The subjects were 307 male and female undergraduates at Ripon College during the 1934–1935 academic year. Their punctuality was assessed on many occasions in six situations: 8 A.M. classes; dinnertime at a dining hall; conference appointments with professors; extracurricular activities (college band and college singers); church services; and entertainment programs (basketball, plays, and concerts). There were a total of 15,360 observations.

Results and Discussion

When correlations were made between any two of these situations, students were inconsistent. This seemed to indicate that the situation, not personality traits, accounted for punctuality. But, as in the Hartshorne and May (1928) study, when behavioral aggregation was applied to the Dudycha study, college students showed much greater cross-situational consistency in their punctuality. Thus, though personality traits might not predict our behavior in particular situations, they might predict our typical behavior across a variety of related situations.

▲ ▲ ▲

The cross-situational consistency debate has died down. The trend is for researchers to agree that the best approach is to consider the interaction of the person and the situation in assessing cross-situational consistency (Murtha, Kanfer, & Ackerman, 1996). Even Gordon Allport, the noted trait researcher, viewed human behavior as the product of those factors, with different traits aroused to different degrees by different situations (Zuroff, 1986). Of course, some situations (such as being in church) are so powerful that almost all people—regardless of their personalities—will behave the same way in them (Monson, Hesley, & Chernick, 1982).

STAYING ON TRACK: *Is Personality Consistent?*

1. Why did Mischel believe that personality is less consistent across situations than was commonly assumed?

2. What evidence is there that personality is more consistent across situations than Mischel believed?

THE PSYCHOANALYTIC APPROACH TO PERSONALITY

Your personality is your unique, relatively consistent pattern of thoughts, feelings, and behaviors. Freud's psychosexual theory emphasizes the conflict between biological drives and social-cultural prohibitions in the development of personality. Freud divided the mind into conscious, preconscious, and unconscious levels. He also distinguished between the personality structures called the id, the ego, and the superego. According to Freud, we progress through oral, anal, phallic, latency, and genital stages of development. These stages depend on changes in the distribution of sexual energy. We may use defense mechanisms to protect us from being overwhelmed by anxiety.

Freud's intellectual descendants altered his theory, generally downplaying the importance of sexuality and emphasizing the importance of social relationships. Alfred Adler's theory of individual psychology assumes that personality develops from our attempts to overcome early feelings of inferiority. Carl Jung's theory of analytical psychology assumes that we are influenced by both a personal unconscious and the archetypes in a collective unconscious. Neo-Freudians such as Karen Horney, Erich Fromm, and Harry Stack Sullivan have made further changes in Freud's theory. In assessing personality, Freudians might use the Rorschach test and the Thematic Apperception Test to uncover unconscious motives and conflicts.

THE DISPOSITIONAL APPROACH TO PERSONALITY

The dispositional approach to personality attributes the consistency we see in personality to relatively enduring personality attributes. Hans Eysenck's three-factor theory sees personality as dependent on the interaction of three dimensions: stability/instability, tough-minded/tender-minded, and introversion/extraversion. In his trait theory of personality, Gordon Allport distinguished three kinds of traits: cardinal traits, central traits, and secondary traits. Raymond Cattell, in his trait theory, identified sixteen source traits. Personality types are measured by tests such as the Myers-Briggs Type Indicator, and personality traits are measured by tests such as the MMPI or the 16 PF.

THE BEHAVIORAL APPROACH TO PERSONALITY

B. F. Skinner's operant conditioning theory assumes that what we call personality is simply a person's unique pattern of behavior. Albert Bandura's social-cognitive theory argues that cognitive processes influence behavior. His concept of reciprocal determinism points out the mutual influence of personality characteristics, overt behaviors, and environmental factors. One of the most important personality characteristics is self-efficacy, the extent to which a person believes that she or he can perform behaviors that are necessary to bring about a desired outcome. Behavioral assessment is accomplished through behavioral observation and the experience-sampling method. Julian Rotter's Internal-External Locus of Control Scale is one of the main cognitive-behavioral assessment techniques.

THE COGNITIVE APPROACH TO PERSONALITY

The most influential cognitive theory of personality is George Kelly's personal-construct theory. Kelly assumed that we continually test hypotheses about social reality. These hypotheses are called personal constructs. We alter our personal constructs through the process of constructive alternativism. The person's unique pattern of personal constructs is measured by the Role Construct Repertory Test.

THE HUMANISTIC APPROACH TO PERSONALITY

Abraham Maslow's self-actualization theory is based on his hierarchy of needs. He assumes that we have a need to develop all of our potentials. Maslow identified the characteristics of eminent people whom he believed were self-actualized. Carl Rogers's self theory holds that psychological well-being depends on the congruence between one's self and one's experience. Other researchers point to the importance of congruence between the actual self, the ideal self, and the ought self. Self-actualization is measured by the Personal Orientation Inventory. Congruence between the actual self and the ideal self is measured by the Q-sort.

THE BIOPSYCHOLOGICAL APPROACH TO PERSONALITY

Closely related to personality is temperament, a person's most characteristic emotional state. Sheldon's constitutional theory holds that different temperaments are associated with different physiques, or somatotypes. Research in behavioral genetics has found evidence of the hereditary basis of temperament and other aspects of personality.

THINKING ABOUT PSYCHOLOGY: IS PERSONALITY CONSISTENT?

In 1968 Walter Mischel stimulated controversy by claiming that situations are more important determinants of behavior than personality traits are. He based this conclusion on studies finding that individuals' behavior is not consistent across different situations. Researchers have spent the past two decades debating whether personality is consistent. The conclusion appears to be that personality is neither as inconsistent as Mischel originally claimed nor as consistent as personality theorists had previously claimed. Our behavior is the product of the interaction between personal characteristics and environmental situations. In some cases, powerful personality characteristics dominate environmental situations. In other cases, powerful environmental situations dominate personality characteristics.

▶ KEY CONCEPTS

personality 442

The Psychoanalytic Approach to Personality

id 443
pleasure principle 443
ego 444

reality principle 444
superego 444
defense mechanism 444
libido 446
fixation 446
oral stage 446

anal stage 446
phallic stage 446
Oedipus complex 446
Electra complex 446
latency stage 446
genital stage 446

personal unconscious 448
collective unconscious 449
archetypes 449
extravert 449
introvert 449
projective test 450

KEY CONTRIBUTORS

FOR MORE INFORMATION ON PERSONALITY

FOR GENERAL WORKS ON PERSONALITY

Hergenhahn, B. R. (1994). *An introduction to theories of personality* (4th ed.). Englewood Cliffs, NJ: Prentice Hall.

Liebert, R. M., & Spiegler, M. D. (1993). *Personality: Strategies and issues* (7th ed.). Belmont, CA: Brooks/Cole.

FOR MORE ON THE PSYCHOANALYTIC APPROACH TO PERSONALITY

Adler, A. (1956). *The individual psychology of Alfred Adler* (H. L. Ansbacher & R. R. Ansbacher, Eds.). New York: HarperCollins.

Fine, R. (1990). *The history of psychoanalysis.* New York: Crossroad.

Fisher, S., & Greenberg, R. P. (1985). *Scientific credibility of Freud's theories and therapy.* New York: Columbia University Press.

Freud, A. (1936/1966). *The ego and the mechanisms of defense.* Madison, CT: International Universities Press.

Freud, S. (1940/1969). *An outline of psychoanalysis.* New York: W. W. Norton.

Fromm, E. (1941). *Escape from freedom.* New York: Holt, Rinehart & Winston.

Horney, K. (1939). *New ways in psychoanalysis.* New York: W. W. Norton.

Jung, C. G. (1958). *The undiscovered self.* New York: Mentor.

Sullivan, H. S. (1953). *The interpersonal theory of psychiatry.* New York: W. W. Norton.

FOR MORE ON THE DISPOSITIONAL APPROACH TO PERSONALITY

Allport, G. W. (1955). *Becoming: Basic considerations for a psychology of personality.* New Haven, CT: Yale University Press.

Eysenck, H. J., & Eysenck, M. W. (1985). *Personality and individual differences.* New York: Plenum.

Graham, J. R. (1990). *MMPI-2: Assessing personality and psychopathology.* New York: Oxford University Press.

FOR MORE ON THE BEHAVIORAL APPROACH TO PERSONALITY

Bandura, A. (1986). *Social foundations of thought and action: A social-cognitive theory.* Englewood Cliffs, NJ: Prentice Hall.

Bellack, A. S., & Hersen, M. (Ed.). (1988). *Behavioral assessment: A practical handbook.* New York: Pergamon.

Schwarzer, R. (Ed.). (1992). *Self-efficacy: Thought control of action.* New York: Hemisphere.

Skinner, B. F. (1953). *Science and human behavior.* New York: Macmillan.

FOR MORE ON THE COGNITIVE APPROACH TO PERSONALITY

Fransella, F., & Thomas, L. (Eds.). (1988). *Experimenting with personal construct psychology.* New York: Routledge & Kegan Paul.

Kelly, G. A. (1963). *A theory of personality: The psychology of personal constructs.* New York: W. W. Norton.

Neimeyer, R. A. (1985). *The development of personal construct psychology.* Lincoln: University of Nebraska Press.

FOR MORE ON THE HUMANISTIC APPROACH TO PERSONALITY

Baumeister, R. F. (Ed.). (1993). *Self-esteem: The puzzle of low self-regard.* New York: Plenum.

Higgins, R. L., Snyder, C. R., & Berglas, S. (Eds.). (1990). *Self-handicapping: The paradox that isn't.* New York: Plenum.

Levin, J. D. (1992). *Theories of the self.* Bristol, PA: Hemisphere.

Rogers, C. R. (1980). *A way of being.* Boston: Houghton Mifflin.

Snyder, M. (1986). *Public appearances—private realities: The psychology of self-monitoring.* New York: W. H. Freeman.

FOR MORE ON THE BIOPSYCHOLOGICAL APPROACH TO PERSONALITY

Kagan, J., Snidman, N., Arcus, D., & Reznick, J. S. (1994). *Galen's prophecy: Temperament in human nature.* New York: Basic Books.

Neubauer, P. B., & Neubauer, A. (1990). *Nature's thumbprint: The new genetics of personality.* Boston: Addison-Wesley.

Sheldon, W. H., & Stevens, S. S. (1942). *The varieties of temperament: A psychology of constitutional differences.* New York: Harper.

FOR MORE ON PERSONALITY CONSISTENCY

Epstein, S., & O'Brien, E. J. (1985). The person-situation debate in historical and current perspective. *Psychological Bulletin, 98,* 515–537.

Mischel, W. (1984). Convergences in the search for consistency. *American Psychologist, 39,* 353–364.

FOR MORE ON CONTRIBUTORS TO THE STUDY OF PERSONALITY

Alexander, F., Eisenstein, S., & Grotjahn, M. (Eds.). (1966). *Psychoanalytic pioneers.* New York: Basic Books.

Allport, G. W. (1967). Autobiography. In E. G. Boring & G. Lindzey (Eds.), *A history of psychology in autobiography,* (Vol. 5, pp. 1–25). New York: Appleton-Century-Crofts.

Bjork, D. W. (1993). *B. F. Skinner: A life.* New York: Basic Books.

Coles, R. (1970). *Erik Erikson: The growth of his work.* Boston: Atlantic/Little, Brown.

Evans, R. I. (1989). *Albert Bandura: The man and his ideas—A dialogue.* New York: Praeger.

Eysenck, H. J. (1990). *Rebel with a cause: The autobiography of Hans Eysenck.* London: W. H. Allen.

Furumoto, L. (1980). Mary Whiton Calkins (1863–1930). *Psychology of Women Quarterly, 5,* 55–68.

Gay, P. (1988). *Freud: A life for our time.* New York: W. W. Norton.

Hoffman, E. (1988). *The right to be human: A biography of Abraham Maslow.* Los Angeles: Tarcher.

Kirschenbaum, H. (1979). *On becoming Carl Rogers.* New York: Delacorte.

Knapp, G. P. (1989). *The art of living: Erich Fromm's life and works.* New York: Peter Lang.

Perry, H. S. (1982). *Psychiatrist of America: The life of Harry Stack Sullivan.* Cambridge, MA: Harvard University Press.

Quinn, S. (1987). *A mind of her own: The life of Karen Horney.* New York: Summit.

Rattner, J. (1983). *Alfred Adler.* New York: Frederick Ungar.

Stevens, A. (1990). *On Jung.* New York: Routledge.

Young-Bruehl, E. (1988). *Anna Freud.* New York: Summit.

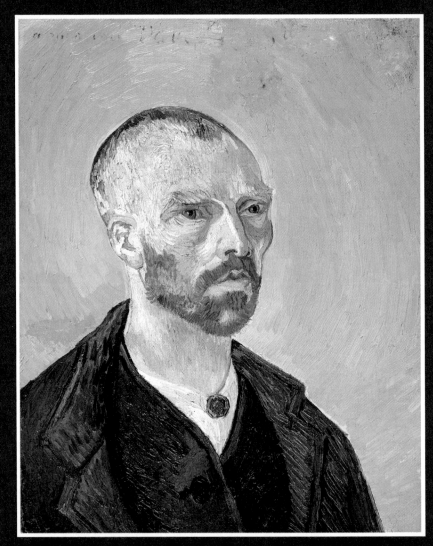

CHAPTER 14

▲ VINCENT VAN GOGH
*Self-Portrait Dedicated to
Paul Gauguin*, 1888

Psychological Disorders

*I*n 1992 former star football player Earl Campbell sat in his car listening to country music when suddenly he felt terrified, his heart racing out of control. After being hospitalized for a week for a suspected heart attack, he was diagnosed, instead, as suffering from *panic disorder*. His fear of having a panic disorder in public led him to stay home, afraid to venture outside even to check his mailbox. He had developed *agoraphobia*.

On January 22, 1987, at a televised news conference, Pennsylvania treasurer R. Budd Dwyer committed suicide by putting the barrel of a pistol in his mouth and pulling the trigger. Dwyer had suffered from *major depression* after his conviction on charges of corruption.

Between 1972 and 1978, a successful, civic-minded Chicago building contractor named John Wayne Gacy murdered 33 boys and young men and buried them under his house. After his capture, Gacy expressed no remorse and, instead, reported that his acts of cold-blooded murder had given him pleasure. Gacy's personal history indicated that he had an *antisocial personality disorder*.

THE NATURE OF PSYCHOLOGICAL DISORDERS

Hardly a week goes by without the news media reporting instances of extreme psychological disorders such as these. But how do we determine whether a person has a psychological disorder? What are the causes of psychological disorders? And how are psychological disorders classified? Answers to these questions are provided by psychologists and others in the field of **psychopathology**—the study of psychological disorders.

Criteria for Psychological Disorders

A recent, ambitious study called the National Comorbidity Survey examined the prevalence of psychological disorders in the United States. The survey of more than 8,000 persons aged 15 to 54 years found that 29 percent had at least one psychological disorder within the past year and 48 percent had at least one during their lifetime (Kessler, 1994). You probably know people whose patterns of moods, thoughts, and actions make you suspect that they, too, suffer from a psychological disorder. But what are the criteria for having such a disorder? The main ones are *abnormality*, *maladaptiveness*, and *personal distress*.

Being Unusual: Abnormality as a Criterion

Abnormal behavior deviates from the behavior of the "typical" person—the *norm*. A norm can be qualitative or quantitative. *Qualitatively* abnormal behavior deviates from culturally accepted standards, perhaps even seeming bizarre. A railroad conductor who announces train stops would be normal; a passenger who announces train stops would be abnormal. *Quantitatively* abnormal behavior deviates from the statistical average. A woman who washes her hands three times a day would be normal, while a woman who washes her hands thirty times a day would be abnormal.

By itself, abnormality is not a sufficient criterion for determining the presence of a psychological disorder. If qualitative abnormality were sufficient, then people who achieve rare accomplishments, such as a Nobel Prize winner, an Olympic decathlon champion, and even your student government president, would be considered psychologically disordered. And if quantitative abnormality were sufficient, then even a physician who washes her hands thirty times a day in the course of seeing patients would be considered psychologically disordered.

psychopathology
The study of psychological disorders.

Thus, the context in which "abnormal" behavior occurs must be considered before deciding that it is symptomatic of a psychological disorder.

Still another problem with using abnormality as the sole criterion in diagnosing psychological disorders is the possibility that nonconformists would be considered psychologically disordered solely for opposing the status quo. Should we view all artistic innovators and political dissidents as victims of psychological disorders?

Functioning Poorly: Maladaptiveness as a Criterion

According to the criterion of *maladaptiveness*, you would have a psychological disorder if your behavior seriously disrupted your social, academic, or vocational life. As an example, consider a person, such as Earl Campbell, with the psychological disorder called *agoraphobia*—fear of being in public places. Such a person might be afraid to leave home, and might consequently alienate friends, fail in school, and lose a job. Similarly, a person who uses drugs or alcohol excessively would be considered psychologically disordered, because such behavior would interfere with everyday functioning. But maladaptive behavior is not always a sign of a psychological disorder. Though cramming for exams, failing to eat fruits and vegetables, and driving 90 miles an hour on a busy highway are maladaptive behaviors, they would not necessarily be symptomatic of a psychological disorder.

Feeling Anguish: Personal Distress as a Criterion

The criterion of *personal distress* assumes that our subjective feeling of anxiety, depression, or another unpleasant emotion determines whether we have a psychological disorder. Nonetheless, personal distress might be neither a necessary nor a sufficient criterion for determining the presence of a psychological disorder (Widiger & Trull, 1991). Some people, like John Wayne Gacy, have psychological disorders without feeling distress.

Behavior that is abnormal, maladaptive, or personally distressing might indicate that a person has a psychological disorder. But there is no single point at which a person moves from being psychologically healthy to being psychologically disordered. Each of us varies

▲ Does This Man Have a Psychological Disorder?
For three decades, the blind poet and musician "Moondog," whose real name was Louis Thomas Hardin, was a fixture on the streets of midtown Manhattan in New York City. Though Moondog certainly deviated from cultural norms, there was no evidence that his behavior was maladaptive. On the contrary, he made enough money to live on by playing homemade instruments and offering copies of his poetry to passersby. And there was no evidence that his behavior caused him personal distress. In fact, he claimed that truly distressed people were those who tried to adapt themselves to the demands of modern society.

Viewpoint	Causes of Psychological Disorders
Biopsychological	Inherited or acquired brain disorders involving imbalances in neurotransmitters or damage to brain structures
Psychoanalytic	Unconscious conflicts over impulses such as sex and aggression, originating in childhood
Behavioral	Reinforcement of inappropriate behaviors and punishment or extinction of appropriate behaviors
Cognitive	Irrational or maladaptive thinking about one's self, life events, and the world in general
Humanistic	Incongruence between one's actual self and public self as a consequence of trying to live up to the demands of others
Diathesis-Stress	A biological predisposition interacting with stressful life experiences

▲ TABLE 14.1
The Major Viewpoints on
Psychological Disorders

on each of the criteria. Thus, there is a degree of subjectivity in even the best answers to the question of how abnormal, maladaptive, or personally distressing a person's behavior must be before we determine that he or she has a psychological disorder.

Viewpoints on Psychological Disorders

Even when psychologists agree on the presence of a particular psychological disorder, they might disagree on its causes. That is, they favor different *viewpoints* regarding the causes of psychological disorders. Since ancient times, people have tried to explain the unusual or distressing behavior patterns that we now call psychological disorders. Many ancient Greek authorities assumed that the gods inflicted psychological disorders on people to punish them for their misdeeds. But the Greek physician Hippocrates (ca. 460–ca. 377 B.C.) argued, instead, that psychological disorders had natural causes.

Despite the efforts of Hippocrates and his followers, supernatural explanations existed alongside naturalistic ones until the nineteenth century. The sixteenth-century Swiss physician Paracelsus (1493–1541) rejected the supernatural viewpoint. Instead of attributing unusual behavior to demons, he attributed it to the moon. Paracelsus called the condition *lunacy* and the people who exhibited it *lunatics*. These terms were derived from the Latin word for "moon." You probably have heard someone say, on an evening when people are acting oddly, "There must be a full moon tonight." But contrary to popular belief, the moon does not affect the incidence of crime, mental illness, or other abnormal behavior (Rotton & Kelly, 1985). Current viewpoints on psychological disorders attribute them to natural factors. As shown in Table 14.1, the viewpoints differ in the extent to which they attribute psychological disorders to biological, mental, or environmental factors.

The Biopsychological Viewpoint

A century ago, Sigmund Freud remarked, "In view of the intimate connection between things physical and mental, we may look forward to a day when paths of knowledge will be opened up leading from organic biology and chemistry to the field of neurotic phenomena" (Taulbee, 1983, p. 45). As a neurologist, Freud might have approved of the *biopsychological viewpoint*, which favors the study of the biological causes of psychological disorders.

Modern interest in the biological causes of psychological disorders was stimulated in the late nineteenth century when researchers discovered that a disorder called *general paresis*, marked by severe mental deterioration, was caused by infection with syphilis. Researchers in the nineteenth century also found that toxic chemicals could induce psychological disorders. In fact, the Mad Hatter in *Alice in Wonderland* exhibits psychological symptoms caused by accidental ingestion of the mercury that was used in making felt hats. This was the origin of the phrase *mad as a hatter* (O'Carroll et al., 1995). Today biopsychological researchers are especially interested in the role of heredity, brain damage, and brain chemistry in the development of psychological disorders.

The Psychoanalytic Viewpoint

The *psychoanalytic viewpoint*, originating in medicine, grew out of the biopsychological viewpoint. But instead of looking for underlying biological causes of psychological disorders, the psychoanalytic viewpoint looks for unconscious causes. As discussed in Chapter 13, Sigmund Freud stressed the continual conflict between inborn biological drives, particularly

sex, which demand expression, and the norms of society that inhibit their expression. According to Freud, conflicts about sex and aggression can be repressed into the unconscious mind, which can lead to feelings of anxiety caused by pent-up sexual or aggressive energy. Freud claimed that we can gain partial relief of this anxiety by resorting to defense mechanisms. If our defense mechanisms are either inadequate or too rigid, we can develop psychological disorders.

Both the biopsychological viewpoint and the psychoanalytic viewpoint support the so-called *medical model*, which assumes that disturbing behavior or unpleasant conscious experience is actually a symptom of underlying processes—whether in the brain or in the unconscious mind. The medical model has contributed a medical vocabulary that is shared by both physicians and many mental health professionals. This includes terms such as *cure, patient, treatment, diagnosis, mental illness,* and *mental hospital.*

The Behavioral Viewpoint

As discussed in previous chapters, the behavioral viewpoint arose in opposition to psychological viewpoints that looked for mental causes of behavior. Those who favor the behavioral viewpoint, in the tradition of B. F. Skinner, look to the environment and to the learning of maladaptive behaviors for the causes of psychological disorders. Psychological disorders might arise in people whose inappropriate behavior is reinforced or whose appropriate behavior is punished or extinguished.

Social-cognitive theorists, such as Albert Bandura, would add that we might develop a psychological disorder by observing other people's behavior. For example, a person might develop a phobia (an unrealistic fear) of dogs after either being bitten by a dog or observing someone else being bitten by a dog.

Those who favor the behavioral viewpoint, with its emphasis on environmental factors, would also be more likely to consider the negative effects of socioeconomic conditions on psychological well-being. For example, poverty is a predisposing factor in a variety of psychological disorders. The results of a survey of residents of New Haven, Connecticut, found that poverty is associated with a higher risk of almost all psychological disorders. This holds true for young and old, men and women, and blacks and whites (Bruce, Takeuchi, & Leaf, 1991).

The Cognitive Viewpoint

The Greek Stoic philosopher Epictetus (A.D. ca. 60–ca. 120) taught that "men are disturbed not by things, but by the views which they take of things." This is the central

▲ Emil Kraepelin (1856–1926)
"Manic-depressive insanity . . . includes on the one hand the whole domain of so-called *periodic and circular insanity* [and] on the other hand *simple mania,* the greater part of the morbid states termed *melancholia.* . . . Dementia praecox consists of a series of states, the common characteristic of which is a peculiar destruction of the internal connections of the psychic personality."

diathesis-stress viewpoint
The assumption that psychological disorders are consequences of the interaction of a biological, inherited predisposition (diathesis) and exposure to stressful life experiences.

neurosis
A general category, no longer widely used, that comprises psychological disorders associated with maladaptive attempts to deal with anxiety but with relatively good contact with reality.

psychosis
A general category, no longer widely used, that comprises severe psychological disorders associated with thought disturbances, bizarre behavior, severe disruption of social relations, and relatively poor contact with reality.

assumption of the *cognitive viewpoint,* which holds that psychological disorders arise from maladaptive ways of thinking about oneself and the world. George Kelly's personal-construct theory (see Chapter 13), the most elaborate cognitive theory of personality, looks to people's personal constructs to determine whether they have psychological disorders. People who fail to maintain a fairly stable, but flexible, set of personal constructs are more likely to suffer from psychological disorders (Button, 1983).

Many cognitive theorists assume that people with psychological disorders hold irrational beliefs that lead to emotional disturbances and maladaptive behaviors. Yet recent studies indicate that people with psychological disorders marked by high levels of anxiety or depression might think *more* rationally and objectively than other people about themselves and the world (Taylor & Brown, 1988). That is, people without psychological disorders might be unrealistically optimistic and view the world through "rose-colored glasses."

The Humanistic Viewpoint

As described in Chapter 13, psychologists who favor the *humanistic viewpoint,* most notably Carl Rogers and Abraham Maslow, stress the importance of self-actualization, which is the fulfillment of one's potential. According to Rogers and Maslow, psychological disorders occur when people fail to reach their potential, perhaps because others, especially their parents, discourage them from expressing their true desires, thoughts, and interests. This *conditional positive regard* can lead the person to develop a public self-image that is favorable to others but markedly different from his or her actual, private self. The distress caused by the failure to behave in accordance with one's own desires, thoughts, and interests can lead to the development of a psychological disorder.

The Diathesis-Stress Viewpoint

No single viewpoint provides an adequate explanation of psychological disorders. This has led to the emergence of the **diathesis-stress viewpoint,** which holds that people differ in their biological predispositions to develop psychological disorders (Fowles, 1992). Such a predisposition is called a *diathesis* and is determined partly by heredity. A person with a strong predisposition to develop psychological disorders might succumb to even relatively low levels of psychological stress. In contrast, a person with a weak predisposition to develop psychological disorders might resist even extremely high levels of psychological stress. Research findings in support of the diathesis-stress model indicate that social stress interacts with physiological predispositions to cause some psychological disorders, including major depression (Monroe & Simons, 1991) and schizophrenia (Fowles, 1992), which are discussed later in this chapter.

Classification of Psychological Disorders

Over the centuries, authorities have distinguished a variety of psychological disorders, each characterized by its own set of symptoms. In 1883 German psychiatrist Emil Kraepelin (1856–1926) devised the first modern classification system (Angst, 1993). Today, the most widely used system of classification of psychological disorders is the fourth edition of the *Diagnostic and Statistical Manual of Mental Disorders (DSM-IV),* published by the American Psychiatric Association.

The DSM-IV: *Categorizing Psychological Disorders*

The *DSM-IV,* which was published in 1994, is a revised version of the *DSM-III,* which was published in 1980 (and revised in 1987 as the *DSM-III-R*). It was preceded by the *DSM-II* in 1968 and the *DSM-I* in 1952. The *DSM-IV* provides a means of communication among mental health practitioners, offers a framework for research on the causes of disorders, and helps practitioners choose the best treatment for particular disorders (Clark, Watson, & Reynolds, 1995).

The *DSM-I* and the *DSM-II,* which were based on psychoanalytic theory, divided disorders into neuroses and psychoses. A **neurosis** involved anxiety, moderate disruption of social relations, and relatively good contact with reality. A **psychosis,** in contrast,

1. **Disorders usually first diagnosed in infancy, childhood, or adolescence** Disorders that appear before adulthood. Examples include stuttering, nocturnal enuresis (bedwetting), attention-deficit/hyperactivity disorder.

2. **Delirium, dementia, and amnestic and other cognitive disorders** Disorders of the brain caused by drugs, toxins, aging, or diseases. Examples include delirium (extreme mental confusion) and dementia (a marked deterioration of the intellect).

3. **Mental disorders due to a general medical condition** Disorders due to a medical condition not classified elsewhere. Examples include catatonic disorder due to . . . , personality change due to . . . , and mental disorder due to. . . .

4. **Substance-related disorders** Disorders that involve dependence on psychoactive drugs to the detriment of everyday functioning. Examples include dependency on cocaine, heroin, alcohol, or marijuana.

5. **Schizophrenia and other psychotic disorders** Disorders associated with marked disorganization of perception, cognition, emotionality, and behavior. Examples include paranoid schizophrenia, catatonic schizophrenia, and disorganized schizophrenia.

6. **Mood disorders** Disorders marked by severe emotional disturbances. Examples include major depression and bipolar disorder.

7. **Anxiety disorders** Disorders associated with extreme anxiety. Examples include phobia, panic disorder, generalized anxiety disorder, obsessive-compulsive disorder, and posttraumatic stress disorder.

8. **Somatoform disorders** Disorders involving physical symptoms, such as paralysis or sensory loss, without a physical cause. Examples include hypochondriasis and conversion disorder.

9. **Factitious disorders** Disorders in which the person fakes symptoms of physical or psychological disorders. Examples include lying about symptoms or inducing symptoms.

10. **Dissociative disorders** Disorders in which conscious awareness is separated from personally relevant thoughts, feelings, and memories. Examples include dissociative amnesia and dissociative fugue.

11. **Sexual and gender identity disorders** Disorders characterized by sexual dysfunctions, paraphilias (culturally disapproved sexual practices), or confusion about one's gender identity. Examples include male erectile disorder, female orgasmic disorder, exhibitionism, sexual masochism, and transsexualism.

12. **Eating disorders** Disorders involving maladaptive eating patterns. Examples include anorexia nervosa and bulimia nervosa.

13. **Sleep disorders** Disorders marked by disruption of the sleep-wake cycle. Examples include insomnia, narcolepsy, hypersomnia, and sleep apnea.

14. **Impulse-control disorders not elsewhere classified** Disorders associated with an inability to resist the impulse to commit certain maladaptive acts. Examples include kleptomania (compulsive stealing), pyromania (fire starting), and pathological gambling.

15. **Adjustment disorders** Disorders in which the person fails to adapt adequately to important stressors. Examples include the inability to adapt well to a divorce or to a financial setback.

16. **Other conditions that may be a focus of clinical attention** Disorders that do not fall within the other categories. Examples include psychological factors affecting medical conditions, relational problems, and problems related to abuse or neglect.

Multiaxial Diagnosis: An Example

Axis I   Alcohol Dependence

Axis II   Antisocial Personality Disorder

Axis III Alcoholic Cirrhosis of the Liver

Axis IV Loss of Job, Threatened Eviction, Separation from Spouse

Axis V   Current Level of Functioning: 40

          Highest Level of Functioning in Past Year: 55

Reprinted with permission from the *Diagnostic and Statistical Manual of Mental Disorders*, Fourth Edition. Copyright 1994 American Psychiatric Association.

▲ TABLE 14.2
The *DSM-IV* Axis I Disorders and Multiaxial Evaluation

involved thought disturbances, bizarre behavior, severe disruption of social relations, and relatively poor contact with reality. *The DSM-III* and the *DSM-IV* dropped this psychoanalytic orientation and instead consider the interaction of biological, psychological, and social factors in diagnosing psychological disorders.

The *DSM-IV* provides five axes for diagnosing psychological disorders. Axis I contains sixteen major categories of psychological disorders. Axis II contains personality disorders and mental retardation. Axis III contains medical conditions that might affect the person's psychological disorder. Axis IV contains social and environmental sources of stress the person has been under recently. And Axis V contains an estimate of the person's level of functioning. The Axis I categories are presented in Table 14.2.

Because the *DSM-IV* is relatively new, there has been much more research on the *DSM-III*. The *DSM-III* was an improvement over previous diagnostic systems, but it met with some criticism (McReynolds, 1989). Research found that, overall, the *DSM-III* diagnostic categories had only modest reliability and validity (Eysenck, Wakefield, &

▲ **David Rosenhan**

"If sanity and insanity exist, how shall we know them?"

Friedman, 1983). The *reliability* of a diagnosis refers to the extent to which different raters reach the same diagnosis. For example, will several clinical psychologists independently agree that a given person has schizophrenia? The *validity* of a diagnosis refers to the extent to which a diagnosis is accurate. For example, does a person who has been diagnosed as schizophrenic truly have schizophrenia?

Note that the creation of categories in the *DSM* is actually an exercise in concept formation. Each category, whether "panic disorder," "major depression," or "antisocial personality," is a concept that is defined by certain characteristics. But concepts of psychological disorders are *natural concepts*, and these have "fuzzy borders" (see Chapter 9). This means that different disorders might share certain characteristics and that a person might exhibit some but not all of the characteristics of a particular disorder. This makes it difficult to achieve high reliability and validity in diagnosis.

Though many American mental health professionals found fault with the *DSM-III*, a survey of mental health professionals in 42 other countries found general approval of it (Maser, Kaelber, & Weise, 1991). *The DSM-IV* has a stronger research base than earlier versions of the *DSM* (Frances et al., 1995), but, like its predecessors, it has been criticized for relying on the medical model (Sanua, 1994).

Criticisms of the Diagnosis of Psychological Disorders

Despite the widespread reliance on the *DSM*, some researchers criticize the potential negative effects of the diagnosis of psychological disorders. This critical attitude was inspired, in part, by a classic study on the effects of diagnosis.

ANATOMY OF A CLASSIC RESEARCH STUDY

Can Sane People Be Recognized in a Mental Hospital?

Rationale

The study was conducted by psychologist David Rosenhan (1973). He wondered whether normal people, complaining of symptoms of schizophrenia, could gain admission to a mental hospital and whether, once they were admitted, the staff would discover their pretense.

Method

Rosenhan had eight apparently normal persons, including himself, gain admission to mental hospitals by calling the hospitals for appointments and then complaining of hearing voices that said "empty, hollow, thud." Hearing imaginary voices is a symptom of schizophrenia.

Results and Discussion

The eight "pseudopatients" were admitted to twelve hospitals in five states; their stays ranged from 7 to 52 days. During their stays, they behaved normally, did not complain of hearing voices, and sometimes wrote hundreds of pages of notes about their experiences in the hospitals. Though no staff members discovered the pseudopatients were faking, several real patients accused them of being journalists or professors investigating mental hospitals. Rosenhan concluded that the diagnosis of psychological disorders is influenced more by preconceptions and by the setting in which we find a person than by any objective characteristics of the person.

But psychiatrist Robert Spitzer, who helped develop the *DSM-III*, claimed that Rosenhan misinterpreted the study's results (Spitzer, 1975). First, the admission of the pseudopatients to the mental hospitals was justified, because people who report hearing imaginary voices might have schizophrenia. Second, people with schizophrenia can go long periods of time without displaying obvious symptoms of the disorder. Thus, the staff members who observed the pseudopatients during their stays had no reason to conclude that they were faking. Nonetheless, the power of the label *mentally ill* to color our judgment of a person was supported by another study. When subjects observed people labeled as mental patients (who actually were not) or similar people not given that label, they were more likely to rate the alleged mental patients as being "unusual" (Piner & Kahle, 1984).

▲ ▲ ▲

The leading critic of diagnostic labels is psychiatrist Thomas Szasz (1960), who has gone so far as to call mental illness, including schizophrenia, a "myth." He believes that the behaviors that become labeled "mental illness" are really "problems in living." According to Szasz, labeling people as mentally ill wrongly blames their maladaptive functioning on an illness. He believes that the notion of "mental illness" is a two-edged sword: it might excuse heinous behavior committed by those labeled "mentally ill," and it might enable governments to oppress nonconformists by labeling them "mentally ill." Szasz's claim that mental illness is a myth has provoked critical responses from other mental health practitioners (Bentall & Pilgram, 1993), as indicated in the following comment:

▶ This myth has a seductive appeal for many persons, especially if they do not have to deal clinically with individuals and their families experiencing the anguish, confusion, and terror of schizophrenia. Unfortunately, informing schizophrenics and their relatives that they are having a mythological experience does not seem to be appreciated by them and is not particularly helpful. (Kessler, 1984, p. 380)

The many mental health professionals who helped create the *DSM-IV* do not view the psychological disorders it discusses as myths. The most important categories of psychological disorders include *anxiety disorders, somatoform disorders, dissociative disorders, mood disorders, schizophrenic disorders,* and *personality disorders.* Figure 14.1 indicates the prevalence of several important psychological disorders.

▲ **Thomas Szasz**
"Mental illness is a myth, whose function it is to disguise and thus render more palatable the bitter pill of moral conflicts in human relations."

STAYING ON TRACK: *The Nature of Psychological Disorders*

1. What are the risks of using abormality as the only criterion in diagnosing psychological disorders?
2. To what does the humanistic viewpoint attribute psychological disorders?
3. Why did Rosenhan's study of patients in mental hospitals provoke controversy?

Answers to Staying on Track start on p. S-6.

ANXIETY DISORDERS: WHEN ANXIETY BECOMES DISRUPTIVE

You certainly have experienced anxiety when learning to drive, taking an important exam, or going on a first date. *Anxiety* is a feeling of apprehension accompanied by sympathetic nervous system arousal, which produces increases in sweating, heart rate, and breathing rate. Though anxiety is a normal and beneficial part of everyday life, warning us about potential threats, in **anxiety disorders** it becomes intense, chronic, and disruptive of everyday functioning. About 10 to 15 percent of adult Americans suffer from anxiety disorders (Robins et al., 1984), which include *generalized anxiety disorder, panic disorder, phobias,* and *obsessive-compulsive disorder.*

anxiety disorder
A psychological disorder marked by persistent anxiety that disrupts everyday functioning.

Generalized Anxiety Disorder: Living with Chronic Anxiety

Though we normally experience anxiety in response to stressful situations, the person with a **generalized anxiety disorder** is in a constant state of anxiety that exists independent of any particular stressful situation. In essence, anxiety becomes one of the individual's cardinal personality traits (Rapee, 1991). The central feature of the generalized anxiety disorder is worry. The person worries constantly about almost everything, including work, school, finances, and social relationships. About 5 percent of the population suffers from generalized anxiety disorder sometime during their life (Wittchen et al., 1994); it is more common in women than in men (Roy et al., 1995).

What accounts for the development of a generalized anxiety disorder? Biopsychological researchers look to heredity, neurochemistry, and brain arousal for answers. The children of victims of anxiety disorders are seven times more likely to develop them than are children whose parents are not victims. Samuel Turner, a leading anxiety researcher, notes that though this hints at a possible genetic basis for anxiety disorders, it does not permit us

generalized anxiety disorder
An anxiety disorder marked by a persistent state of anxiety that exists independently of any particular stressful situation.

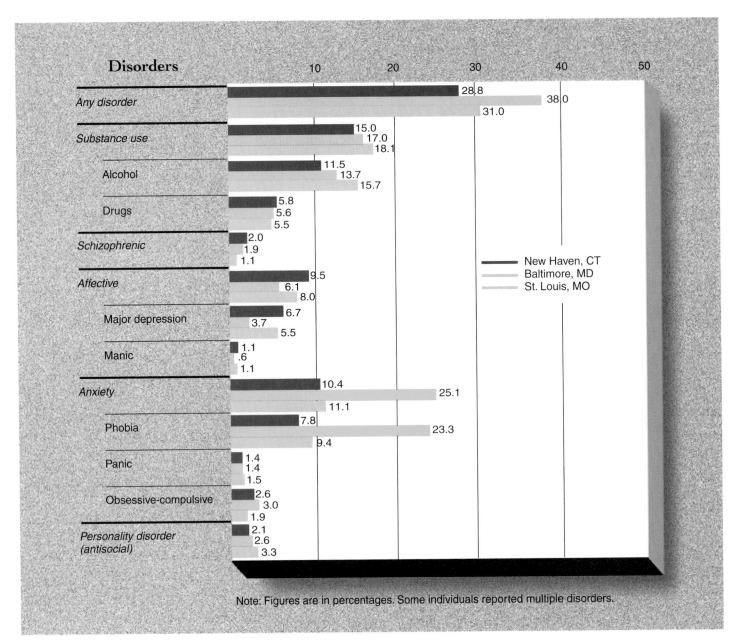

Disorders

	New Haven, CT	Baltimore, MD	St. Louis, MO
Any disorder	28.8	38.0	31.0
Substance use	15.0	17.0	18.1
Alcohol	11.5	13.7	15.7
Drugs	5.8	5.6	5.5
Schizophrenic	2.0	1.9	1.1
Affective	9.5	6.1	8.0
Major depression	6.7	3.7	5.5
Manic	1.1	.6	1.1
Anxiety	10.4	25.1	11.1
Phobia	7.8	23.3	9.4
Panic	1.4	1.4	1.5
Obsessive-compulsive	2.6	3.0	1.9
Personality disorder (antisocial)	2.1	2.6	3.3

Note: Figures are in percentages. Some individuals reported multiple disorders.

▲ **FIGURE 14.1**

Prevalence of Some Major Psychological Disorders

A survey of people in three American cities found that about one-third had experienced one or more *DSM-III* disorders. Note that the prevalence of certain disorders varied markedly from city to city (Robins et al., 1984).

to conclude that anxiety disorders are affected more by common heredity than by common life experiences (Turner, Beidel, & Costello, 1987). Stronger, but also inconclusive, evidence for a hereditary basis of anxiety disorders comes from research that shows a higher concordance rate for identical twins, who share 100 percent of their genes, than for fraternal twins, who are no more similar genetically than nontwin siblings (Torgersen, 1983). The *concordance rate* is the likelihood that a person will develop a psychological disorder given that a particular relative has that disorder.

Whether caused more by heredity or by experience, anxiety is associated with excess activity in serotonin neurons (Eison & Eison, 1994), which is reduced by drugs used to treat anxiety. Positron emission tomography (PET) indicates that anxiety is associated with increased brain arousal. More specifically, PET scans have shown that when subjects are placed in an anxiety-inducing situation, they show increased arousal in their temporal lobes (Reiman et al., 1989).

As for psychological causes, psychoanalysts view generalized anxiety disorder as being the consequence of id impulses threatening to overwhelm ego controls. Cognitive-behavioral theorists find that people with a generalized anxiety disorder exaggerate the number of threatening things in their lives and how threatening they are (Tomarken, Mineka, & Cook, 1989). This places the person in a constant fight-or-flight state of arousal, worrying continually. There is evidence that this worrying might be a way of avoiding thinking about more emotionally distressing topics (Borkovec & Roemer, 1995). Humanistic psychologists have their own point of view. They believe that anxiety arises from a discrepancy between the actual self and the ought self (Strauman & Higgins, 1988), which are described in Chapter 13. This means that we might develop a generalized anxiety disorder when we feel we have failed to live up to desirable standards of behavior.

Panic Disorder: Being Overwhelmed by Anxiety

In describing the motivation for his painting *The Scream,* Norwegian artist Edvard Munch (1863–1944) remarked, "I was walking . . . and I felt a loud, unending scream piercing nature" (Blakemore, 1977, p. 155). Both the painting and the statement indicate that Munch may have suffered a *panic attack,* which is a symptom of **panic disorder,** marked by sudden attacks of overwhelming anxiety, accompanied by dizziness, trembling, cold sweats, heart palpitations, shortness of breath, fear of dying, and fear of going crazy. People experiencing panic attacks might also feel detached from their own bodies or feel that other people are not real. Though panic attacks usually last only a few minutes, they are so distressing that more people seek therapy for panic disorder than for any other psychological disorder (Boyd, 1986). About 1.5 percent of Americans experience panic disorder (Weissman, 1990).

Biopsychological and cognitive theorists disagree about the causes of panic disorder (McNally, 1990). Biopsychological theorists note that panic disorder runs in families, with a concordance rate among family members of about 20 percent (Crowe, 1990). The concordance rate is higher for identical twins than for fraternal twins (Torgerson, 1989). Again, these findings hint at, but do not guarantee, a genetic predisposition for panic disorder (Kendler et al., 1995). PET scans have implicated the temporal lobes, because people with panic disorder show higher activity in the right temporal lobe than in the left, which is not found in other people (Reiman et al., 1984).

According to cognitive theorists, panic disorder results from faulty thinking. For example, people prone to panic disorders engage in catastrophic thinking (Cox, 1996), misattributing physical symptoms of arousal caused by factors such as caffeine, exercise, mild stress, or emotional memories, to a serious mental or physical disorder. Separation anxiety evoked by recalling an important person in one's life whom one has lost is especially likely to instigate a panic attack (Free, Winget, & Whitman, 1993). Catastrophic thinking about minor physical symptoms can induce the overwhelming anxiety that characterizes panic disorder (Agras, 1993). This cognitive explanation of panic has much in common with Schachter's two-factor theory of emotion (see Chapter 12), because it assumes that panic occurs when unexplained arousal is attributed to a catastrophic source.

Phobias: Exhibiting Unreasonable Fears

The word **phobia** comes from *Phobos,* the name of the Greek god of fear, and refers to the experience of excessive or inappropriate fear. The person realizes that the fear is irrational but cannot control it. The phobia might have maladaptive consequences. For example, patients with *claustrophobia* (fear of enclosed places) are sometimes too terrified to undergo diagnostic magnetic resonance imaging, which requires them to lie still in a cylinder for up to an hour or more (Kilborn & Labbe, 1990). Phobias are among the most common psychological disorders, afflicting about 6 percent of Americans (Boyd et al., 1990).

The major classes of phobias are *simple phobias, social phobias,* and *agoraphobia.* A **simple phobia** is an intense, irrational fear of a specific object or situation, such as a spider or heights. People with simple phobias may go to great lengths to avoid the object or situation they fear. Table 14.3 lists common simple phobias.

▲ **Samuel Turner**
"Emerging human and nonhuman primate data suggest that some individuals are likely to be more vulnerable to anxiety than others, and hence are at a greater risk for developing an anxiety disorder."

panic disorder
An anxiety disorder marked by sudden, unexpected attacks of overwhelming anxiety, often associated with the fear of dying or "losing one's mind."

▲ **Panic**
Edvard Munch's painting *The Scream* (1893) conveys the intense anxiety and terror characteristic of a panic attack.

phobia
An anxiety disorder marked by excessive or inappropriate fear.

simple phobia
A phobia of a specific object or situation.

Phobia	Feared Object
Acrophobia	High places
Ailurophobia	Cats
Algophobia	Pain
Aquaphobia	Water
Arachnophobia	Spiders
Astraphobia	Lightning storms
Claustrophobia	Enclosed places
Cynophobia	Dogs
Hematophobia	Blood
Hydrophobia	Water
Monophobia	Being alone
Mysophobia	Dirt
Nyctophobia	Darkness
Ocholophobia	Crowds
Thanatophobia	Death
Triskaidekaphobia	Number 13
Xenophobia	Strangers
Zoophobia	Animals

social phobia
A phobia of situations that involve public scrutiny.

agoraphobia
A fear of being in public, usually because the person fears the embarrassment of a panic attack.

People with a **social phobia** fear public scrutiny, perhaps leading them to avoid playing sports, making telephone calls, or performing music in public (Cox & Kenardy, 1993). There is evidence of neurotransmitter and neurological differences between people with social phobias and people without them (Miner & Davidson, 1995). Social phobia is promoted by increased self-focused attention, which is more likely under conditions of high physiological arousal (Hope, Gansler, & Heimberg, 1989). You have gotten a hint of this experience if you have noticed your mouth becoming dry, your palms sweating, and your heart beating strongly just before making an oral presentation in class. Social phobia seems to have its origins in childhood, with shy children more prone than outgong children to becoming socially phobic adults (Stemberger et al., 1995).

Agoraphobia is the fear of being in public. The word *agoraphobia*, from the Greek term for "fear of the marketplace," was coined in 1871 to describe the cases of four men who feared being in a city plaza (Boyd & Crump, 1991). Agoraphobics typically have a history of panic attacks. They tend to avoid public places because they fear the embarrassment of having witnesses to their panic attacks (Clum & Knowles, 1991). This makes them avoid parties, sports events, and shopping malls. In extreme cases these persons can become prisoners in their own homes—terrified to leave for any reason. Because agoraphobia disrupts every aspect of the victim's life, it is the phobia most commonly seen by psychotherapists.

Certain people have a biological, possibly hereditary, predisposition to develop phobias. One bit of evidence for this is that identical twins have a higher concordance rate than fraternal twins (Kendler et al., 1995). According to Martin Seligman (1971), evolution has biologically prepared us to develop phobias of potentially dangerous natural objects or situations, such as fire, snakes, and heights. Early human beings who were biologically predisposed to avoid these dangers were more likely to survive long enough to reproduce and, as a result, pass on this predisposition to their offspring in their genes. This might explain why phobias that involve potentially dangerous natural objects, such as snakes, are more persistent than phobias that involve usually safe natural objects, such as flowers (McNally, 1987). Though some researchers question the notion of inherited preparedness to fear certain objects or situations (Davey, 1995), there is experimental research supporting that notion. For example, when fear is induced by pairing snakes or houses with electric shocks, fear of snakes lasts longer following the experience (Ohman, Erixon, & Lofberg, 1975). The notion that we are genetically predisposed to fear certain things has some commonality with Jung's concept of archetypes (see Chapter 13).

Psychoanalysts believe that phobias are caused by anxiety displaced from a feared object or situation onto another object or situation. By displacing the anxiety, the person keeps the true source unconscious. The classic psychoanalytic case is that of Little Hans, a 5-year-old boy who was afraid to go outside because of his fear of horses. After listening to the background of the case, Sigmund Freud attributed the phobia to an inadequate resolution of the Oedipus complex. Freud claimed that Hans had an incestuous desire for his mother and a fear of being punished for it by being castrated by his father. Hans displaced his fear of his father to horses, permitting him to keep his incestuous feelings unconscious.

In contrast, behavioral theorists claim that phobias are learned responses to life situations. Phobias develop because of learning, either through personal experience or through observation of phobic people (Ost, 1985). For example, Little Hans's phobia might have been attributable to a horrifying incident he witnessed in which horses harnessed to a wagon fell and then struggled to get to their feet (Stafford-Clark, 1965).

Cognitive-behavioral explanations of phobias implicate self-efficacy (see Chapter 13). Phobic people might believe they lack the ability to cope with stressful situations. Research indicates that a phobic person's feeling of self-efficacy in regard to the feared situation is a more important factor in phobias than is the person's anxiety level or perception of danger (Williams, Turner, & Peer, 1985).

Cognitive explanations of phobias stress the importance of exaggerated beliefs about the harmfulness of the fear-inducing object or situation (Thorpe & Salkovskis, 1995). A study of people with a spider phobia found that they did, indeed, hold more irrational beliefs about what would happen if they confronted a spider, including their reaction to it (Arntz et al., 1993).

Obsessive-Compulsive Disorder: Feeling Compelled to Think Certain Thoughts or Perform Certain Actions

If you have ever been unable to keep an advertising jingle from continually running through your mind, you have experienced a mild *obsession*, which is a persistent, recurring thought. Obsessions can be self-perpetuating, because the very act of trying to suppress a thought will make it more likely to enter consciousness (Wegner et al., 1987). Have you ever repeatedly checked your alarm clock to make sure it was set the night before an

▲ "But that's what you said yesterday—
'Just one more cord'!"
Drawing by Woodman; ©1986 The New Yorker
Magazine, Inc.

obsessive-compulsive disorder
An anxiety disorder in which the person has recurrent, intrusive thoughts (obsessions) and recurrent urges to perform ritualistic actions (compulsions).

somatoform disorder
A psychological disorder characterized by physical symptoms in the absence of disease or injury.

hypochondriasis
A somatoform disorder in which the person interprets the slightest physical changes as evidence of a serious illness.

early-morning exam? If so, you have experienced a mild *compulsion,* which is a repetitive action that you feel compelled to perform. People whose obsessions and compulsions interfere with their daily functioning suffer from **obsessive-compulsive disorder.** This disorder is found in about 3 percent of the population (Rasmussen & Eisen, 1990). The most common compulsions are cleaning and checking. Less common compulsions are counting and hoarding (Ball, Baer, & Otto, 1996).

There might be a hereditary predisposition in those who develop obsessive-compulsive disorder. There is evidence that obsessive-compulsive disorder runs in families (Rasmussen, 1993), and in a study of more than 400 pairs of twins, heredity was found to account for almost half of the variability in obsessional symptoms from one person to another (Clifford, Murray, & Fulker, 1984).

PET scans have found that obsessive-compulsive persons have abnormally high activity in the frontal lobes (Baxter, 1991). Perhaps compulsive behavior is aimed at reducing this overarousal to more comfortable levels. You might have experienced this in a milder form—perhaps you have felt anxious about schoolwork, spent an hour rearranging your room, and as a result felt less anxious.

According to psychoanalysts, obsessive-compulsive disorder is caused by fixation at the anal stage, resulting from harsh toilet training. This causes repressed anger directed at the parents. The child defends against the guilt generated by these feelings of anger and later transgressions by repeating certain thoughts and actions over and over. The obsessions and compulsions often have symbolic meaning, as portrayed in Shakespeare's *Macbeth* when Lady Macbeth engages in compulsive handwashing after murdering King Duncan, illustrating the role of guilt in some cases of obsessive-compulsive disorder (Shafrin, Watkins, & Charman, 1996). Behavioral theorists view obsessions and compulsions as ways of avoiding anxiety-inducing situations. So you might compulsively clean and organize your room to avoid the anxiety of studying for exams.

STAYING ON TRACK: *Anxiety Disorders*

1. What is the difference between an obsession and a compulsion?
2. What is the apparent connection between panic disorder and agoraphobia?

SOMATOFORM DISORDERS: PHYSICAL SYMPTOMS WITHOUT PHYSICAL CAUSES

Somatoform means "bodylike." A **somatoform disorder** is characterized by physical symptoms in the absence of disease or injury. The symptoms are caused, instead, by psychological factors. Do not confuse somatoform disorders with *malingering,* in which the person *purposely* invents symptoms in order to be relieved of certain responsibilities. Persons with a somatoform disorder truly believe they have symptoms of a real physical disorder. Somatoform disorders affect less than 1 percent of the population (Robins et al., 1984). The somatoform disorders include *hypochondriasis* and *conversion disorder.*

Hypochondriasis: Exaggerating Physical Symptoms

A person with the somatoform disorder known as **hypochondriasis** interprets the slightest physical change in her or his body as evidence of a serious illness. Hypochondriacs might go from physician to physician, searching for the one who will finally diagnose the disease that they are sure is causing their symptoms. Some medical students experience a mild form of hypochondriasis in the so-called medical student syndrome, in which a mere cough might convince them they have lung cancer. As you read about the various psychological disorders, you should beware of developing a similar "psychology student syndrome," in which you interpret your normal variations in mood, thinking, and behavior as symptoms of a psychological disorder. Of course, if your symptoms become distressing, prolonged, or disruptive to your life, you should consider seeking professional counseling.

What accounts for hypochondriasis? Psychoanalysts see it as a defense against becoming aware of feelings of guilt or low self-esteem. Behavioral theorists argue that hypochondriacs receive both positive reinforcement, such as being lavished with attention, and negative reinforcement, such as relief from work responsibilities. Cognitivists note that people who develop hypochondriasis fear disease so much that they become overly vigilant about bodily changes, leading them to notice and exaggerate even the slightest ones. A study that compared 60 people with hypochondriasis and 60 people without it found that the hypochondriacs were more likely to interpret physical symptoms as indicative of disease. They seemed to presume that being healthy means being completely symptom-free (Barsky et al., 1993). There is evidence supporting each of these views, but none is clearly superior to the others (Barsky & Klerman, 1983).

Conversion Disorder: Losing Physical Abilities

A person with a **conversion disorder** exhibits loss or alteration of a physical function without any apparent physical cause. In typical cases, the person experiences muscle paralysis, such as difficulty in speaking, or sensory loss, such as an inability to feel an object on the skin. But the apparently lost function is actually intact; a girl who suffered for a year with "paralyzed" legs began using them after simply being given biofeedback that provided her with evidence of activity in her leg muscles (Klonoff & Moore, 1986). Physicians suspect the presence of a conversion disorder when patients display *la belle indifference*—a lack of concern about their symptoms. As illustrated in Figure 14.2, a conversion disorder might also be diagnosed by a physician who notices that a patient's symptoms are anatomically impossible.

Theories explaining conversion disorder have a long, and sometimes bizarre, history. An Egyptian papyrus dating from 1900 B.C. attributed the disorder, which was believed to be limited to women, to a wandering uterus (Jones, 1980). Hippocrates accepted this explanation and called the disorder *hysteria,* from the Greek word for "uterus." Because Hippocrates believed that the uterus wandered when a woman was sexually frustrated, he prescribed marriage as a cure. The wandering-womb view lost credibility with the rise of nineteenth-century science.

Modern biopsychological researchers have found that somatoform disorders run in families. The concordance rate for identical twins is three times greater than for fraternal twins (about 30 percent versus about 10 percent). But it is unclear whether the higher concordance rate for identical twins reflects greater genetic similarity or greater similarity in their life experiences (Torgersen, 1986).

In the late nineteenth century, Sigmund Freud claimed that hysteria resulted from anxiety generated by repressed sexual impulses. The anxiety was converted into symbolic physical symptoms, such as paralyzed legs, that enabled a woman to avoid acting on her sexual impulses. Freud called such disorders *conversion hysteria.* Today, to avoid the implication that the disorder is strictly a female problem, it is called *conversion disorder.* There is evidence that severe psychological trauma, such as sexual abuse, might induce a conversion disorder (Rothbaum & Foa, 1991).

Behavioral theorists assume that somatoform disorders occur because they are reinforced by increased attention or a reduction in responsibilities. Children might become prone to somatoform disorders after they observe other members of their family being reinforced for their physical symptoms (Mullins & Olson, 1990). Explanations consistent with humanistic psychology see somatoform disorders as ways to protect the self through *self-handicapping.* People with hypochondriasis are more likely to complain of symptoms when they know they are going to be evaluated (Smith, Snyder, & Perkins, 1983). For example, a person who complains of a sore throat before a threatening speaking engagement might not be blamed for a poor performance.

STAYING ON TRACK: *Somatoform Disorders*

1. How would you determine whether a person was displaying malingering or hypochondriasis?
2. What is "la belle indifference" in regard to conversion disorder?

conversion disorder

A somatoform disorder in which the person exhibits motor or sensory loss or the alteration of a physiological function without any apparent physical cause.

Conversion Disorder
(a) A person with "glove anesthesia" will complain of numbness in the hand from the wrist to the tips of the fingers. This is easily diagnosed as a conversion disorder because damage to the sensory nerves of the hand will not produce this pattern of sensory loss. Different areas of the hand are served by the ulnar, radial, and median nerves. If a given nerve is injured, there will be numbness in only a portion of the hand. For example, (b) damage to the ulnar nerve produces numbness along the outer edge of the hand.

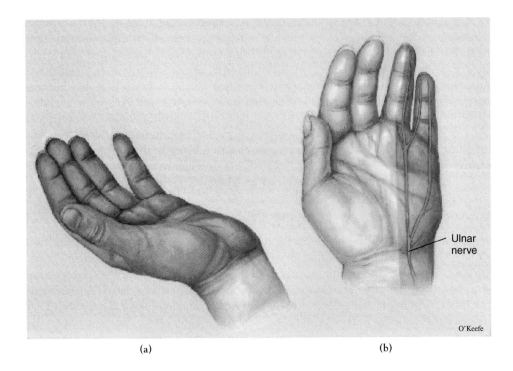

Ulnar nerve

O'Keefe

(a)   (b)

dissociative disorder
A psychological disorder in which thoughts, feelings, and memories become separated from conscious awareness.

psychogenic amnesia
A dissociative disorder marked by the inability to recall personally significant memories.

psychogenic fugue
A dissociative disorder marked by the memory loss characteristic of psychogenic amnesia, the loss of one's identity, and fleeing from one's home.

DISSOCIATIVE DISORDERS: THE SPLITTING OF CONSCIOUSNESS

In a **dissociative disorder,** the person's conscious mind loses access to certain of his or her thoughts, feelings, and memories. The dissociative disorders include *psychogenic amnesia, psychogenic fugue,* and *multiple personality.* Early trauma, such as sexual, physical, or emotional abuse, may be a predisposing factor (Kluft, 1987).

Psychogenic Amnesia: Forgetting Important Memories

While being interrogated about his assassination of Robert F. Kennedy in 1968, Sirhan Sirhan was unable to recall the incident (Bower, 1981). He apparently suffered from **psychogenic amnesia,** the inability to recall personally significant memories (Coons & Milstein, 1992). The lost memories are usually related to a traumatic event, such as witnessing a catastrophe. Victims of psychogenic amnesia typically regain the lost memories hours or days later. The psychoanalytic viewpoint assumes that the repression of painful memories causes psychogenic amnesia. This was supported by a study in which people who viewed slides of normal and disfigured faces accompanied by verbal descriptions had poorer recall of the descriptions associated with the disfigured faces (Christianson & Nilsson, 1984).

Psychogenic Fugue: Fleeing from One's Identity

In September 1980, a young woman was found wandering in Birch State Park, Florida. She could not recall who she was or where she was from. After a nationally televised appearance on a morning television show, she was reunited with her family in Illinois. She suffered from **psychogenic fugue,** which is marked by the memory loss characteristic of psychogenic amnesia, the loss of one's identity, and fleeing from one's home. (The word *fugue* comes from the Latin word meaning "to flee.") The person may adopt a new identity, only to emerge from the fugue state days, months, or years later, recalling nothing that had happened during the intervening period (Kopelman et al., 1994). In one case a 15-year-old girl assumed a new identity, spoke a foreign language she had learned in school, adopted new dress and grooming habits, and showed new skills, interests, and personality traits for 6 days (Venn, 1984).

(a)

(b)

(c)

(d)

Dissociative Identity Disorder: Displaying Multiple Personalities

In 1812 Benjamin Rush, the founder of American psychiatry, reported the following case involving a minister's wife:

▶ In her paroxysms of madness she resumed her gay habits, spoke french, and ridiculed the tenets and practices of the sect to which she belonged. In the intervals of her fits she renounced her gay habits, became zealously devoted to the religious principles and ceremonies of the Methodists, and forgot everything she did and said during the fits of her insanity. (Carlson, 1981, p. 668)

This was one of the first well-documented cases of a *multiple personality disorder* (now technically known as **dissociative identity disorder**), in which a person has two or more distinct personalities that alternate with one another, as in the story of Dr. Jekyll and Mr. Hyde (Garcia, 1990). The multiple personalities might include males and females, children and adults, and moral and immoral persons. A quiet, retiring middle-aged man might alternate with a flamboyant, promiscuous young man. Each personality might have its own way of walking, writing, and speaking, and some might even be animals (Hendrickson, McCarty, & Goodwin, 1990).

You are probably familiar with two cases of multiple personality that were made into popular movies: the story of Chris Sizemore, portrayed by Joanne Woodward in *The Three Faces of Eve,* and the story of Sybil Dorsett, portrayed by Sally Field in *Sybil.* At the height of her disorder, Sizemore had 22 distinct personalities. Her personalities were finally integrated in 1975, and she went on speaking tours to discuss her experiences (Sizemore & Huber, 1988).

dissociative identity disorder
A dissociative disorder, more commonly known as multiple personality disorder, in which the person has two or more distinct personalities that alternate with one another.

Psychological Disorders | **493**

People who develop multiple personalities almost always have had traumatic experiences in early childhood, typically including sexual and physical abuse, leading them to escape into their alternate personalities (MacGregor, 1996). A study of 71 patients with multiple personality disorder in the Netherlands found that 94.4 percent had a history of childhood sexual and physical abuse (Boon & Draijer, 1993). As a child, Chris Sizemore witnessed a man drown, observed the bloody body parts of a man who had been cut to pieces in a sawmill, and was forced to kiss her grandfather's corpse. Sybil Dorsett's mother locked her in closets and sexually tortured her.

Because of a marked increase in reported cases of multiple personality in the 1980s, some researchers believe multiple personalities are being overdiagnosed and are simply the product of role-playing, just as the "hidden observer" in hypnosis (see Chapter 6) might be a case of role-playing. This possibility was demonstrated in a study in which students were hypnotized and asked to reveal, as a self hidden in themselves, the personality of an accused multiple murderer called "Harry Hodgins" or "Betty Hodgins." Eighty percent did so. This indicates that at least some reputed cases of multiple personality disorder might be no more than role-playing, whether intentional or not (Spanos, Weekes, & Bertrand, 1983).

STAYING ON TRACK: *Dissociative Disorders*

1. What kinds of life experiences are common among people who develop multiple personalities?
2. Why do some psychologists doubt the existence of multiple personalities?

MOOD DISORDERS: BEING DOMINATED BY EMOTIONAL EXTREMES

We all experience periodic fluctuations in our emotions, such as becoming briefly depressed after failing an exam or briefly elated after getting an A. But people with **mood disorders** experience prolonged periods of extreme depression or elation, often unrelated to their current circumstances, that disrupt their everyday functioning. The mood disorders include *major depression* and *bipolar disorder*.

Major Depression: Feeling Too Depressed to Function

We normally feel depressed after personal losses or failures; the frequency and intensity of depressive episodes vary from person to person. Since World War II, depression has become ten times more common among Americans (Seligman, 1989), and it is now considered the common cold of psychological disorders. Depression is so prevalent and distressing that, when advice columnist Ann Landers offered a pamphlet on depression to her readers, 250,000 persons wrote for it (Holden, 1986).

People with **major depression** experience extreme distress that disrupts their lives for weeks or months at a time. They might express despondency, helplessness, and loss of self-esteem. Their depression is usually worse in the morning (Graw et al., 1991). They might also be unable to fall asleep or to stay asleep, and they might lose their appetite or overeat, feel constantly fatigued, abandon good grooming habits, withdraw from social relations, lose interest in sex, find it difficult to concentrate, and fail to perform up to their normal academic and vocational standards. About 2 to 3 percent of men and about 5 to 9 percent of women suffer from major depression (American Psychiatric Association, 1994).

Norman Rosenthal and his colleagues have identified a form of depression called **seasonal affective disorder** (Schwartz et al., 1996). Victims suffer from extreme depression during certain seasons, typically in the winter. Seasonal affective disorder might be caused by an inability to adjust physiologically to seasonal changes in light levels. Winter seasonal affective disorder is treated by extending the day by exposing victims to artificial bright light before sunrise or after sunset. The most common method is to expose the person to a large, bright fluorescent light for 2 hours daily or to an even

---

mood disorder

A psychological disorder marked by prolonged periods of extreme depression or elation, often unrelated to the person's current situation.

major depression

A mood disorder marked by depression so intense and prolonged that the person may be unable to function in everyday life.

seasonal affective disorder

A mood disorder in which severe depression arises during a particular season, usually the winter.

◀ **Seasonal Affective Disorder**
Some people experience seasonal bouts of severe depression, typically in the winter. Research shows that such victims of seasonal affective disorder may gain relief if their day is artificially extended by exposing them to extra light before dawn or after sunset.

brighter one for half an hour daily (Tam, Lam, & Levitt, 1995). This treatment has been successful in relieving the depression associated with seasonal affective disorder. The exact mechanism is unknown, though there is evidence that the beneficial effects involve increased serotonin activity (Lam et al., 1996).

People who suffer from major depression are more susceptible to suicide (Petronis et al., 1990). Though some suicides are done for honor, as in the Japanese ritual of hara-kiri, or to escape intolerable pain, as in some cases of terminal cancer, most are associated with major depression. There are more than 200,000 suicide attempts each year in the United States, with more than 25,000 fatalities. Though some suicide victims leave notes explaining why they killed themselves, the vast majority do not (O'Donnell, Farmer, & Catalan, 1993).

Who commits suicide? Roy Baumeister (1990), a leading researcher on disorders of the self, believes that people commit suicide when their self-image becomes so negative that it is too painful for them to bear. Sex, race, and age are also factors. In most countries, females are much more likely than males to attempt suicide, yet many more males than females succeed. This is because males tend to use means that are more lethal, such as gunshots to the head, while females tend to use means that are less lethal, such as overdoses of depressant drugs. Widowed and divorced people are more likely to commit suicide than single or married people (Canetto & Lester, 1995). Whites and Native Americans commit suicide more often than African Americans do (Ellis & Range, 1989). Suicide rates are higher for elderly people than for younger age groups (Moscicki, 1995). Though suicide rates are lower for high school and college students than for older people, suicide is one of the most common causes of death for 15- to 24-year-olds. Adolescent suicide is often associated with a dysfunctional family (Husain, 1990) and drug or alcohol abuse (Rivinus, 1990). Because even young children commit suicide (Lester, 1995), parents and school personnel should be aware of the possibility in depressed, withdrawn children.

During your lifetime, you will probably know people you suspect are contemplating suicide. According to Edwin Shneidman (1994), a leading authority, at least 90 percent of people who attempt suicide give verbal or behavioral warnings before their attempts. This makes it important to take threats seriously and to take appropriate actions to prevent suicide attempts. A study of high school students found that few knew the major

▲ **Norman Rosenthal**
"There is agreement among clinical researchers that seasonal affective disorder is a common condition and that in a large percentage of cases the symptoms of winter depression respond well to treatment with bright environmental light."

► **Kurt Cobain**
Even fame, youth, wealth, and talent may not be enough to prevent suicide, as in the case of Kurt Cobain, lead singer and guitarist of Nirvana. Cobain committed suicide after a long battle with depression and drug abuse.

warning signs and appropriate responses to suicide threats by their peers (Norton, Durlak, & Richards, 1989). Major warning signs include changes in moods and habits associated with severe depression, such as emotional apathy, social withdrawal, poor grooming habits, loss of interest in recreational activities, giving away cherished belongings, tying up loose ends in their lives, and outright suicide threats (Shaughnessy & Nystul, 1985).

Shneidman suggests that because suicide attempts are usually cries for help, the simple act of providing an empathetic response may reduce the immediate likelihood of an actual attempt. Just talking about a problem can reduce its apparent dreadfulness and help the person realize that other solutions than suicide are possible and that her or his options include more than a choice between death and a hopeless, helpless life. You might have the person make a list of options and then rank them in order of preference. Suicide might no longer rank first. An immediate goal should be to relieve the person's psychological pain by intervening, if possible, with those who might be contributing to the pain, whether friends, lovers, teachers, or family members. You should also encourage the person to seek professional help, even if you have to make the appointment for the person and accompany him or her to it. Many cities have 24-hour suicide hotlines or walk-in centers to provide emergency counseling.

To prevent suicides, professionals have devised formal suicide awareness programs. In some programs, college resident assistants are trained to recognize verbal, behavioral, and situational warning signs of suicide. They are also taught how to respond to suicide threats, how to make referrals to professional counselors, and how to support those who seek therapy (Grosz, 1990). A study of Canadian suicide prevention centers found that volunteers found it important to tailor their responses to the callers, being directive with some and nondirective with others (Daigle & Mishara, 1995). There is evidence that suicide prevention centers are modestly effective. In the United States, the presence of suicide centers in a state is associated with a lowering of suicide rates (Lester, 1993).

(a)

(b)

(c)

Bipolar Disorder: The Manic-Depressive Cycle

A biblical story describes how King Saul stripped off his clothes in public, exhibited alternating bouts of elation and severe depression, and eventually committed suicide. Though the story attributes his behavior to evil spirits, psychologists might attribute it to a bipolar disorder. **Bipolar disorder,** formerly called *manic depression,* is characterized by days or weeks of mania alternating with longer periods of major depression, typically separated by days or weeks of normal moods.

Mania (from the Greek term for "madness") is characterized by euphoria, hyperactivity, grandiose ideas, incoherent talkativeness, unrealistic optimism, and inflated self-esteem. Manic people are sexually, physically, and financially reckless. They might also overestimate their own abilities, perhaps leading them to make rash business deals or to leave a sedentary job to train for the Olympics. At some time in their lives, about 1 percent of adults have bipolar disorder, which is equally common in males and females (American Psychiatric Association, 1994).

bipolar disorder
A mood disorder marked by periods of mania alternating with longer periods of major depression.

mania
A mood disorder marked by euphoria, hyperactivity, grandiose ideas, annoying talkativeness, unrealistic optimism, and inflated self-esteem.

Causes of Mood Disorders

What accounts for mood disorders? Each of the major viewpoints offers its own explanation.

The Biopsychological Viewpoint

Mood disorders have a biological basis, apparently influenced by heredity (Merikangas, 1993). Identical twins have higher concordance rates for major depression (Allen, 1976) and bipolar disorder (Mitchell, Mackinnon, & Waters, 1993) than do fraternal twins. Because identical twins have the same genetic inheritance, while fraternal twins are no more genetically alike than nontwin siblings, this provides evidence of a hereditary predisposition to develop mood disorders.

Evidence supportive of a hereditary basis for bipolar disorder was provided by a study of the Amish community in Lancaster County, Pennsylvania. Because the Amish have an isolated community that includes descendants from only 30 ancestors in the eighteenth century, only marrying among themselves, they provide an excellent opportunity to study the influence of heredity on psychological disorders. The study was conducted by Janice Egeland and her colleagues (1987).

Egeland studied the families of people with bipolar disorder. She used blood tests to examine their chromosome structures. Egeland found that Amish people who suffer from bipolar disorder share a defective gene on the 11th chromosome. But because only 63 percent of those with this defect develop the disorder, perhaps differences in life experience also play a role. But similar studies of families in which bipolar disorder follows a hereditary pattern have failed to find a genetic marker for it on the 11th chromosome. These

Brain Activity in Bipolar Disorder
These PET scans show the brain activity of a rapid-cycling bipolar patient. The patient cycled between mania and depression every 24 to 48 hours. The top and bottom sets of scans were obtained during periods when the patient was depressed. The middle set of scans was obtained during a manic period. Note that the red areas indicate significantly higher brain activity during the manic period (Phelps & Mazziotta, 1985).

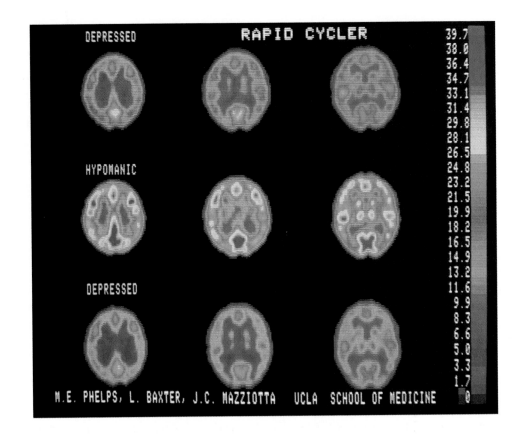

include a study of two Australian families (Mitchell et al., 1991) and a study of three Icelandic families (Kelsoe et al., 1993). This reinforces the importance of research replication, which was stressed in Chapter 2. Of course, it is possible that some cases of bipolar disorder are linked to the 11th chromosome while others are linked to other chromosomes (Ewald et al., 1995).

The hereditary predisposition to develop mood disorders may manifest itself by its effect on neurotransmitters. Major depression is related to abnormally low levels of *serotonin* or *norepinephrine* in the brain (McNeal & Cimbolic, 1986). One study measured levels of a chemical by-product of serotonin in the cerebrospinal fluid of depressed people who had tried suicide. Of those with above-average levels, none subsequently committed suicide. Of those with below-average levels, 20 percent subsequently did (Traskman et al., 1981). Antidepressant drugs, often prescribed for suicidal people, act by increasing levels of serotonin (Baldwin & Rudge, 1995) and norepinephrine (Schildkraut et al., 1995).

Serotonin seems to moderate norepinephrine's relationship to both mania and major depression. Depression is associated with a combination of low levels of both serotonin and norepinephrine, while mania is associated with a combination of low levels of serotonin and high levels of norepinephrine. Figure 14.3 shows that mania is also associated with unusually high levels of brain arousal, perhaps related to these neurotransmitter levels. Moreover, studies using the PET scan have found that victims of major depression tend to have relatively less left-hemisphere activity than right-hemisphere activity (Martinot et al., 1990).

The Psychoanalytic Viewpoint

The traditional psychoanalytic view holds that the loss of a parent or rejection by a parent early in childhood predisposes the person to experience depression whenever she or he suffers a personal loss, such as a job or a lover, later in life. Because such children feel it is unacceptable to express anger at the lost or rejecting parent, they learn to turn their anger on themselves, creating feelings of guilt and self-loathing (Freud, 1917/1963). But research studies have found that this cannot explain all cases of depression. For example, both depressed and nondepressed adults are equally likely to have suffered the loss of a parent in childhood (Crook & Eliot, 1980).

The Behavioral Viewpoint

Behavioral explanations of depression stress the role of learning and environmental factors. One of the most influential of these explanations is Peter Lewinsohn's *reinforcement theory*, which assumes that depressed people lack the social skills needed to gain normal social reinforcement from others and might instead provoke negative reactions from them. For example, depressed people stimulate less smiling, fewer statements of support, more unpleasant facial expressions, and more negative remarks from others than do nondepressed people (Gotlib & Robinson, 1982). Lewinsohn points out that the depressed person is caught in a vicious cycle in which reduced social reinforcement leads to depression and depressed behavior further reduces social reinforcement (Youngren & Lewinsohn, 1980).

An influential cognitive-behavioral theory of depression is based on Martin Seligman's notion of *learned helplessness*, which results from experiences that indicate one has little control over the events in one's life. Because perceived lack of control does not always lead to depression, Seligman and his followers, in a reformulated version of his theory, now explain depression in terms of the attributions we make for events in our lives. Depressed people attribute negative events in their lives to stable, global, and internal factors (Abramson, Seligman, & Teasdale, 1978). A *stable factor* is unlikely to change. A *global factor* affects almost all areas of one's life. And an *internal factor* is a characteristic of one's self rather than of the environment. Research on learned helplessness and depression has tended to find that, as predicted, depressed people make internal, stable, and global attributions for negative events in their lives (Sweeney, Anderson, & Bailey, 1986). For example, college freshmen who attribute their poor academic performance to internal, stable, and global factors—such as intelligence—become more depressed than do those who attribute their own poor academic performance to external, unstable, and specific factors—such as being assigned difficult teachers (Peterson & Barrett, 1987). The reformulated learned-helplessness hypothesis for depression has also been supported in some non–North American cultures, such as Turkey (Aydin & Aydin, 1992).

A 5-year longitudinal study identified the development of this pessimistic explanatory style in children who became prone to depression. Early in the study, children's depression was predicted by negative events and not by their explanatory style. Later, both negative events and a pessimistic explanatory style predicted children's depression. Eventually children who had developed pessimistic explanatory styles maintained them even after their depression had subsided. This made them more susceptible to future bouts of depression (Nolen-Hoeksema, Girgus, & Seligman, 1992).

The Cognitive Viewpoint

Research inspired by George Kelly's personal-construct theory has found that depressed people hold more-negative personal constructs about themselves than do nondepressed people (Neimeyer, 1983). But the most influential cognitive view of depression is Aaron Beck's (1967) *cognitive theory*. Beck has found that depressed people exhibit what he calls a *cognitive triad:* They have a negative view of themselves, their current circumstances, and their future possibilities (Anderson & Skidmore, 1995). The cognitive triad is common among depressed psychiatric patients, but it is not common among other psychiatric patients. This indicates that the triad is specific to depression (Giles & Shaw, 1987). The cognitive triad is maintained by the tendency of depressed people to overgeneralize from negative events. For example, depressed people tend to assume that a single failure means they are incompetent (Carver & Ganellen, 1983).

As mentioned earlier in the chapter, people with psychological disorders might have more-objective beliefs about themselves and the world than do people without such disorders. Depression researcher Lauren Alloy and her colleagues have found that this is especially true of depressed people. Nondepressed people overestimate the likelihood that positive events, and underestimate the likelihood that negative events, will happen to them (Crocker, Alloy, & Kayne, 1988). They tend to be overly cheerful and optimistic

▲ **Peter Lewinsohn**
"Depressed persons, as a group, are less socially skillful than nondepressed individuals."

▲ Lauren Alloy

"Whereas nondepressives exhibit a self-enhancing bias in which they underestimate their probability of failure relative to that of similar others, depressives do not succumb to either positive or negative social comparison biases in prediction."

(Margo et al., 1993). This leads to the surprising conclusion that if you are not depressed, it might mean that you have an unrealistically positive view of yourself and the world. Depressed people, in contrast, are painfully accurate in their view of their reality—so-called *depressive realism* (Haaga & Beck, 1995). Nonetheless, some researchers have failed to find this difference between depressed and nondepressed people (Dobson & Pusch, 1995).

Another cognitive view of depression, put forth by Susan Nolen-Hoeksema, implicates continual rumination about one's plight. People who constantly think about the sad state of their lives experience more severe and more chronic depression than do people who take action to improve their lives or who distract themselves by pursuing enjoyable activities (Nolen-Hoeksema, 1994). Nolen-Hoeksema believes that this may explain why after age 15 females are about twice as likely as males to be depressed (Nolen-Hoeksema & Girgus, 1994). She has found that depressed females tend to ruminate about their depression, while depressed males tend to distract themselves from it (Nolen-Hoeksema, Morrow, & Fredrickson, 1993). In fact, she found that among college undergraduates, rumination was the single most important predictor of how long depression would last. Because female undergraduates tended to ruminate more than male undergraduates, depressed females tended to have longer-lasting bouts of depression (Butler & Nolen-Hoeksema, 1994). Nolen-Hoeksema's *rumination theory* was tested in the following study.

ANATOMY OF A CONTEMPORARY RESEARCH STUDY

Are People Who Ruminate About Their Problems More Likely to Become Depressed?

Rationale

Finding an association between rumination and depression does not guarantee that there is a causal relationship between them. This prompted Nolen-Hoeksema and Morrow (1993) to conduct an experiment to find out whether rumination does, in fact, affect depression.

Method

Nolen-Hoeksema and Morrow randomly assigned 24 nondepressed and 24 mildly to moderately depressed undergraduates to spend 8 minutes focusing their attention on their current feelings and personal characteristics (the *rumination condition*) or on descriptions of geographic locations and objects (the *distraction condition*).

Results and Discussion

Nolen-Hoeksema and Morrow found that depressed subjects in the rumination condition became significantly more depressed. In contrast, depressed subjects in the distraction condition became significantly less depressed. Moreover, rumination and distraction did not affect the moods of nondepressed subjects. Thus, the results supported her contention that depressed people who ruminate are prone to more intense depression, making them take longer to return to a normal mood. The results also supported her contention that depressed people who try to distract themselves become less depressed, enabling them to return to normal moods faster.

Nolen-Hoeksema has found that one of the difficulties in overcoming rumination, however, is that depressed people who ruminate do so to gain insight into their feelings and problems. Thus, they do not feel motivated to take action to distract themselves or to lighten their moods, possibly because they fear that it would prevent them from gaining a better understanding of themselves (Lyubomirsky & Nolen-Hoeksema, 1993). Evidently, it is one thing to know that rumination promotes depression, and another thing to stop it.

▲ ▲ ▲

As noted earlier, one problem with cognitive theories of depression is the difficulty in determining whether the patterns of thought that characterize depressed people are the *cause* of their depression or the *result* of their depression. To determine this in real life requires prospective studies, which follow people over a period of time, to determine whether depressed thinking styles precede, accompany, or follow the onset of depression.

Because there is more evidence that depressed thinking styles accompany or follow the onset of depression, they might not be its cause (Brewin, 1985).

This conclusion was supported by an experiment in which groups of depressed people received either daily doses of antidepressant drugs or twice-weekly psychotherapy sessions. Both groups showed decreases in depression and more-positive views of themselves and the world. Because even those who received only drugs showed cognitive improvement, perhaps nondepressed styles of thinking are simply a consequence of feeling good and depressed styles of thinking are simply a consequence of feeling bad (Simons, Garfield, & Murphy, 1984).

The Humanistic Viewpoint

Those who favor the humanistic viewpoint attribute depression to the frustration of self-actualization. More specifically, depressed people suffer from incongruence between their actual self and their ideal self (Strauman & Higgins, 1988). The actual self is the person's subjective appraisal of her or his own qualities. The ideal self is the person's subjective judgment of the person she or he would like to become. If the actual self has qualities that are too distinct from those of the ideal self, the person becomes depressed.

STAYING ON TRACK: *Mood Disorders*

1. What are Edwin Shneidman's suggestions for preventing someone from committing suicide?
2. How does the reformulated theory of learned helplessness explain depression?
3. How does rumination affect depression?

SCHIZOPHRENIA: THE CANCER OF PSYCHOLOGY

In middle age, Edvard Munch, the founder of modern expressionist painting, began acting in odd ways. He became a social recluse, believed his paintings were his children, and claimed they were too jealous to be exhibited with other paintings (Wilson, 1967). Munch's actions were symptoms of **schizophrenia,** a severe psychological disorder characterized by impaired social, emotional, cognitive, and perceptual functioning. Because it can be so devastating, schizophrenia is considered the "cancer" of psychology.

The modern classification of schizophrenia began in 1860 when the Belgian psychiatrist Benedict Morel used the Latin term *demence precoce* (meaning "premature mental deterioration") to describe the behavior of a brilliant, outgoing 13-year-old boy who gradually withdrew socially and deteriorated intellectually. The term was popularized by German psychiatrist Emil Kraepelin in his diagnostic system as *dementia praecox*. In 1911 the Swiss psychiatrist Eugen Bleuler (1857–1939) coined the term *schizophrenia* (from the Greek terms for "split mind") to refer to the disorder. This reflected his belief that schizophrenia involved a splitting apart of the normally integrated functions of perceiving, feeling, and thinking. About 1 percent of the population become victims of schizophrenia, which is equally prevalent among males and females. Schizophrenic patients occupy half of the beds in American mental hospitals and cost the American economy billions of dollars each year.

schizophrenia
A class of psychological disorders characterized by grossly impaired social, emotional, cognitive, and perceptual functioning.

Characteristics of Schizophrenia

To be diagnosed as schizophrenic, a person must display symptoms for at least 6 months (American Psychiatric Association, 1994). People with schizophrenia typically experience *hallucinations,* which are sensory experiences in the absence of sensory stimulation. Schizophrenic hallucinations are usually auditory, typically voices that ridicule the person or order the person to commit harmful, perhaps violent, acts (Zisook et al., 1995). Hallucinations seem to result from the failure of the cognitive mechanism that normally lets us distinguish between experiences generated by the mind and experiences evoked by

▶ **The Paintings of Louis Wain**
Wain (1860–1939) was a British artist who gained acclaim for his paintings of cats in human situations. But, after developing schizophrenia, he no longer painted with a sense of humor. Instead, his paintings revealed his mental deterioration, becoming progressively more fragmented and bizarre.

external stimuli (Bentall, 1990). Researchers are beginning to identify the regions of the brain that become active during auditory hallucinations (Silbersweig et al., 1995).

Schizophrenia is also characterized by cognitive disturbances. Schizophrenic people are easily distracted by irrelevant stimuli (Mirsky et al., 1995). This inability to focus attention might account for the cognitive fragmentation that is a hallmark of schizophrenia. Because this fragmentation is also evident in schizophrenic language, you might find it frustrating to converse with someone who is schizophrenic. A schizophrenic person's speech might include invented words called *neologisms*, as in "The children have to have this 'accentuative' law so they don't go into the 'mortite' law of the church" (Vetter, 1969, p. 189). The schizophrenic person's speech might also include a meaningless jumble of words called a *word salad,* as in "The house burnt the cow horrendously always" (Vetter, 1969, p. 147).

Among the most distinctive cognitive disturbances in schizophrenia are delusions. A *delusion* is a belief that is held despite compelling evidence to the contrary, such as Edvard Munch's belief that his paintings were his children and were jealous of other paintings. The most common delusions are delusions of influence, such as the belief that one's thoughts are being beamed to all parts of the universe *(thought broadcasting)*. Less common are *delusions of grandeur*, in which the person believes that she or he is a famous or powerful person. The fascinating book *The Three Christs of Ypsilanti* (Rokeach, 1964/1981) describes the cases of three men in a mental hospital who had the same delusion of grandeur—each claimed to be Jesus Christ; the workings of the schizophrenic mind are vividly illustrated when these men meet and each tries to explain why he is Jesus and the others merely impostors.

Delusions vary from culture to culture. For example, a large-scale study of German and Japanese schizophrenic patients found that Germans were more likely to have delusions of direct persecution, such as delusions of being poisoned, and that Japanese were more likely to have delusions of reference, such as delusions of being slandered (Tateyama et al., 1993).

Schizophrenic people typically have flat or inappropriate emotionality. Emotional flatness is shown by an unchanging facial expression, a lack of expressive gestures, and an absence of vocal inflections. For example, people with schizophrenia are less facially responsive to emotional films than other people are (Blanchard, Kring, & Neale, 1995). Emotional inappropriateness is shown by bizarre outbursts, such as laughing when someone is seriously injured. Schizophrenia is also associated with unusual motor behavior, such as tracing patterns in the air or holding poses for hours. And, as in the case of Edvard Munch, schizophrenic people are usually socially withdrawn, with few, if any, friends. This might first appear in childhood.

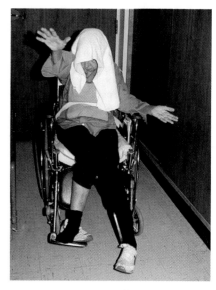

▲ **Catatonic Schizophrenia**
A person with catatonic schizophrenia might maintain bizarre postures.

Kinds of Schizophrenia: Disorganized, Paranoid, and Catatonic

Diagnosticians distinguish several kinds of schizophrenic disorders. Cases that do not fall neatly into any one of the major categories of schizophrenia are commonly lumped into a category called **undifferentiated schizophrenia.** People with **disorganized schizophrenia** show personality deterioration, speak gibberish, dress outlandishly, perform ritualized movements, and engage in obscene behavior. Odd, inappropriate laughter is a hallmark of the disorder (Black, 1982). The bizarreness of their behavior and the incoherence of their speech can make it impossible for them to maintain normal social relationships.

Catatonic schizophrenia is characterized by unusual motor behavior, often alternating between catatonic excitement and catatonic stupor. In *catatonic excitement* the person paces frantically, speaks incoherently, and engages in stereotyped movements. In *catatonic stupor* the person may become mute and barely move, possibly freezing in positions for hours or days. People with catatonic schizophrenia might even exhibit "waxy flexibility," in which they can be moved from one frozen pose to another. Nonetheless, even when in a catatonic stupor, the individual typically remains aware of what is happening in the immediate environment (Ratner et al., 1981).

Paranoid schizophrenia is characterized by hallucinations, delusions, suspiciousness, and argumentativeness. This disorder was portrayed in the World War II movie *The Caine Mutiny*, in which Captain Queeg (played by Humphrey Bogart) developed paranoid delusions in the face of wartime stress. He accused his crew of conspiring against him, and even conducted a full-scale investigation to determine who stole strawberries from the ship's kitchen. In more extreme cases, paranoid schizophrenic persons may feel so threatened that they become violent.

undifferentiated schizophrenia
A catchall category for cases that do not fall neatly into any single kind of schizophrenia.

disorganized schizophrenia
A type of schizophrenia marked by severe personality deterioration and extremely bizarre behavior.

catatonic schizophrenia
A type of schizophrenia marked by unusual motor behavior, such as bizarre actions, extreme agitation, or immobile stupor.

paranoid schizophrenia
A type of schizophrenia marked by hallucinations, delusions, suspiciousness, and argumentativeness.

Causes of Schizophrenia

No single viewpoint can explain all causes of schizophrenia or why some people with certain risk factors develop schizophrenia and others do not. Note that even when a risk factor is identified it might be unclear whether the factor causes schizophrenia, schizophrenia causes the factor, or other factors cause both the apparent risk factor and schizophrenia.

Psychological Disorders | 503

Heredity and the Risk of Schizophrenia
The concordance rates for schizophrenia between people become higher as their genetic similarity becomes greater. This provides evidence supportive of the hereditary basis of schizophrenia, but cannot by itself rule out the influence of the degree of similarity in life experiences (Gottesman & Shields, 1982).

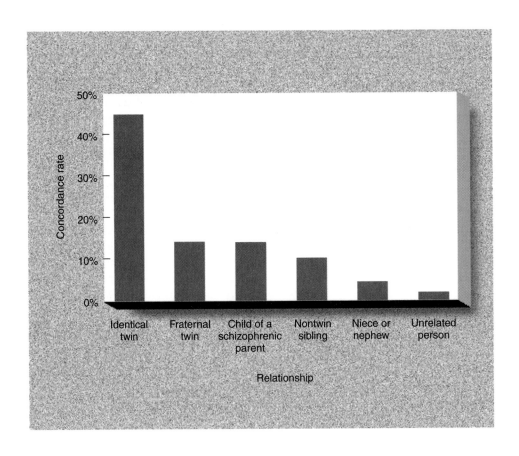

The Biopsychological Viewpoint

Biopsychological theories of schizophrenia emphasize genetic, biochemical, and neurological factors. There are several biological factors, but no single one is specific for schizophrenia (Szymanski, Kane, & Lieberman, 1991). It seems that schizophrenia is best explained by the diathesis-stress viewpoint, which sees it as the outcome of the interaction between a genetic predisposition and stressful life experiences. For example, children who have both a genetic predisposition to become schizophrenic and the stress of losing their father are more likely to develop schizophrenia than are children with only one of those factors (Walker et al., 1981). A review of research found that schizophrenic patients are more vulnerable to stressors, but that they typically have not been exposed to unusually high levels of stress (Norman & Malla, 1993).

Schizophrenia runs in families—the closer their genetic relationship to a schizophrenic, the more likely persons are to become schizophrenic (Kety et al., 1994). Figure 14.4 shows that the concordance rates for schizophrenia appear to have a strong hereditary basis. A recent study found a concordance rate of 48 percent for identical twins and only 4 percent for fraternal twins (Onstad et al., 1991). Yet the higher concordance rate for identical twins might be caused by the more similar treatment that identical twins receive, rather than by their identical genetic endowment.

To assess the relative contributions of heredity and experience, researchers have turned to adoption studies. Many of these studies have been conducted in Denmark, where the government maintains excellent birth and adoption records. The studies support the genetic basis of schizophrenia. For example, schizophrenia is more common in the biological relatives of schizophrenic adoptees than among their adoptive relatives; children adopted from schizophrenic parents have a greater risk of schizophrenia than do children adopted from normal parents; and children of normal parents adopted by schizophrenic parents do not show an increased risk of schizophrenia (Buchsbaum & Haier, 1983).

Given the apparent hereditary basis of schizophrenia, what biological differences might exist between people who develop schizophrenia and those who do not? Studies have found a relationship between schizophrenia and brain chemistry, most notably high levels of activity at synapses that use the neurotransmitter *dopamine*. What evidence is there of a dopamine basis for schizophrenia? First, drugs that are used to treat schizophrenia work by blocking dopamine receptors (Brunello et al., 1995). Second, drugs such as amphetamines, which increase dopamine levels in the brain, can induce schizophrenic symptoms in normal people. Third, *L-dopa,* a drug used to treat Parkinson's disease because it increases dopamine levels in the brain, can induce schizophrenic symptoms in Parkinson's victims (Nicol & Gottesman, 1983).

Biopsychological researchers are struck by one of the best-replicated findings regarding schizophrenia: a disproportionate number of victims are born in the winter (Franzek & Beckmann, 1996). This has been found in countries throughout the world, including Taiwan (Tam & Sewell, 1995), France (d'Amato et al., 1994), Holland (Pallast et al., 1994), and Switzerland (Modestin, Ammann, & Wurmle, 1995). This finding has inspired a search for a possible connection to influenza viruses that might have infected the brains of schizophrenics prenatally—perhaps during the second trimester, when brain development accelerates.

Many studies have investigated the relationship between a worldwide influenza epidemic in 1957 and the development of schizophrenia in people born shortly afterward. Unfortunately, findings have been inconsistent. Some studies have found that people exposed to influenza prenatally, especially during the second trimester, have higher rates of schizophrenia (Mednick, Huttunen, & Machon, 1994). But other studies have found that they do not (Erlenmeyer-Kimling et al., 1994). And still other studies have found that the effect holds only for females (Kunugi et al., 1995). Moreover, efforts to find viruses in the brains of schizophrenics have had little success (Taller et al., 1996), though this does not mean they do not exist. Perhaps they are viruses that do their damage and then are destroyed by the immune system (Sierra-Honigmann, Carbone, & Yolken, 1995).

If there is a viral basis for schizophrenia, it might explain why identical twins do not have a 100 percent concordance rate for schizophrenia. For example, identical twins that share the same placenta have a higher concordance rate for schizophrenia than do identical twins with separate placentas. It is reasonable to surmise that if one twin is infected by a virus, the other twin will be more likely to become infected if it shares the same placenta (Davis & Phelps, 1995).

If viral infections play a role in schizophrenia, they would do so by affecting the brain. PET scans have shown that schizophrenia is often associated with unusual brain activity. Schizophrenic people tend to have lower activity in their frontal lobes when performing cognitive tasks than other people do (Buchsbaum, 1990). As discussed in Chapter 3, the frontal lobes are important in thinking, planning, attention, and problem solving, each of which is usually deficient in schizophrenia.

As illustrated in Figure 14.5, some schizophrenics have atrophy of brain tissue, creating enlargement of the cerebral ventricles, the fluid-filled chambers inside the brain (Syvalahti, 1994). Because this enlargement may exist in people who have exhibited schizophrenic symptoms for only a brief time, it is not the consequence of drug treatments or other factors associated with ongoing schizophrenia (Nopoulos et al., 1995).

Particular kinds of brain dysfunctions might be associated with particular sets of schizophrenic symptoms. According to schizophrenia researcher Nancy Andreasen, there are two kinds of schizophrenic syndromes, characterized by either positive symptoms or negative symptoms (Andreasen & Flaum, 1991). *Positive symptoms* are active symptoms that include hallucinations, delusions, thought disorders, and bizarre behaviors. People with positive symptoms experience acute episodes, show progressively worsening symptoms, respond well to drug treatment, have increased numbers of dopamine receptors, and reveal no brain structure pathology. In contrast, *negative symptoms* are passive symptoms that include mutism, apathy, flat affect, social withdrawal, intellectual impairment, poverty of speech, and inability to experience pleasure. People with negative symptoms respond poorly to drug treatment and often have enlarged brain ventricles, atrophy of the cerebral cortex, and less activity in the frontal lobes (Rubin, 1994).

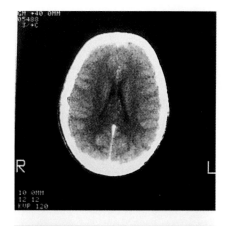

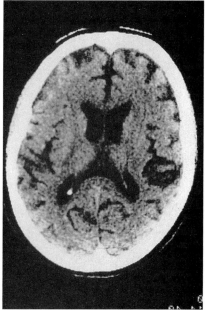

▲ **FIGURE 14.5**

Schizophrenia and Neurological Dysfunctions
CAT scans of the brains of people with schizophrenia often show atrophy and enlarged ventricles. Notice that the ventricles (the dark areas) in the schizophrenic brain (*below*) are much larger than those in the normal brain (*above*).

▲ Nancy Andreasen
"Patients with ventricular enlargement tend to have a preponderance of negative symptoms, while patients without ventricular enlargement tend to have a preponderance of positive symptoms."

More recently, Andreasen and her associates have reported that negative symptoms are not consistently associated with ventricular enlargement (Andreasen et al., 1990). Moreover, it might be premature to divide schizophrenia into just two categories associated with either positive or negative symptoms. The evidence is stronger for a syndrome of negative symptoms than for a single syndrome of positive symptoms (Andreasen et al., 1995).

The Psychoanalytic Viewpoint

According to the psychoanalytic viewpoint, people who become schizophrenic have failed to overcome their dependence on their mothers and, as a result, have become fixated at the oral stage. This gives them a weak ego that fails to defend them against the anxiety caused by unconscious id impulses and external stressors. Instead, they cope with anxiety by resorting to behaviors characteristic of the oral stage, including fantasy, silly actions, incoherent speech, and irrational thinking.

Recent research, in the spirit of the psychoanalytic viewpoint, has found that parents high in what is known as *expressed emotion* might contribute to the maintenance or relapse of schizophrenia in their child. Parents who are high in expressed emotion criticize their child and become emotionally overprotective. Because of the impact of expressed emotion, schizophrenic children who avoid contact with their families tend to have better psychological adjustment than schizophrenic children who maintain contact with them (Cole & Kazarian, 1993).

The Behavioral Viewpoint

Behavioral theories of schizophrenia, which stress the role of learning, assume that schizophrenics are rewarded for behaving in bizarre ways (Ullmann & Krasner, 1975). This was portrayed in the 1974 movie *A Woman Under the Influence*, in which a wife (played by Gena Rowlands) makes bizarre sounds to be rewarded with attention from her boorish husband (played by Peter Falk). Even on her return from a mental hospital, her husband urges her to make the same sounds—in front of a houseful of people at a welcome-home party. Behavioral theorists also assume that a person who engages in bizarre behavior provokes social rejection from others, which in turn contributes to the suspiciousness and social withdrawal characteristic of schizophrenia.

The Cognitive Viewpoint

Proponents of the cognitive viewpoint emphasize disturbances of attention and thinking as the main factors in schizophrenia. As the noted schizophrenia researcher Eugen Bleuler observed earlier this century, people with schizophrenia seem "incapable of holding the train of thought in the proper channel" (Baribeau-Braun, Picton, & Gosselin, 1983). Children exposed to parents who communicate in confusing, irrational ways are predisposed to develop the disturbed cognitive activity of schizophrenia (Doane et al., 1981).

Research inspired by personal-construct theory has found that the disordered thinking of schizophrenia is found in people who use either too few or too many personal-construct dimensions in perceiving social reality. People with an optimal number of personal-construct dimensions would respond to interpersonal events in a more flexible, appropriate way than schizophrenic people do (Phillips, 1981).

The Humanistic Viewpoint

According to the humanistic viewpoint, schizophrenia is caused by extreme incongruence between the public self and the actual self. R. D. Laing (1967) claimed that schizophrenia results when a person develops a false public self to confront an intolerable life situation. This retreat from reality permits the person to experience her or his actual self. The schizophrenic person's bizarre thinking, language, and behavior are indicative of this retreat from reality. In contrast to other humanistic psychologists, Laing recommended that family, friends, and professionals permit the schizophrenic person to go on what he called a "voyage of self-discovery" into his or her actual self, and not interfere with that process by administering drugs or committing the schizophrenic to a mental hospital.

Laing's critics claim that he romanticized schizophrenia, in the same way that nineteenth-century poets romanticized tuberculosis, by implying that it is somehow noble to have a serious psychological disorder. One of Laing's chief critics is Mark Vonnegut, son of novelist Kurt Vonnegut. Mark had been a follower of Laing's until he suffered several episodes of schizophrenia, as described in his autobiography *The Eden Express* (Vonnegut, 1975). When Mark recovered, he did not describe a voyage of self-discovery. Instead, he related a horrifying experience that he would have been better off without. Mark's disillusionment with Laing's view of schizophrenia led him to write a commentary for *Harper's* magazine entitled "Why I Want to Bite R. D. Laing" (Vonnegut, 1974).

STAYING ON TRACK: *Schizophrenia*

1. What are the major symptoms of schizophrenia?
2. What evidence is there that dopamine plays a role in schizophrenia?
3. How do positive symptoms and negative symptoms of schizophrenia differ?

PERSONALITY DISORDERS: WHEN NORMAL TRAITS BECOME EXTREME

Axis II of *DSM-IV* includes the **personality disorders,** which are long-standing, inflexible, maladaptive patterns of behavior. People with personality disorders exhibit certain personality traits to an inappropriate extreme. In essence, personality disorders are negative examples of what Alfred Adler called a "style of life" (see Chapter 13). Table 14.4 summarizes the personality disorders. Though life experiences play important roles in their development, some personality disorders seem to have genetic bases (Nigg & Goldsmith, 1994).

The personality disorder that is currently of greatest interest to researchers is *borderline personality disorder,* perhaps because it is prevalent, extremely disruptive, and a great challenge for therapists to treat successfully. People with borderline personality disorder tend to have inconsistent self-images and are extremely unstable in their moods. It is hard to predict how they will behave socially from one occasion to the next. They can be smiling and trusting at one moment and surly and attacking the next. They might seek intense intimacy, only to run away when they find it. Nonetheless, the personality disorder of greatest interest to the general public has been *antisocial personality disorder,* perhaps because it has been implicated in many notorious criminal cases.

personality disorder
A psychological disorder characterized by enduring, inflexible, maladaptive patterns of behavior.

Antisocial Personality Disorder: The Absence of a Conscience

Antisocial personality disorder is found in about 3 percent of American males and less than 1 percent of American females. In the nineteenth century it was called *moral insanity,* and for most of this century it was called *psychopathy* or *sociopathy.* **Antisocial personality disorder** is characterized by maladaptive behavior beginning in childhood. This includes lying, stealing, truancy, vandalism, fighting, drug abuse, physical cruelty, academic failure, and early sexual activity. Adults with an antisocial personality might not conform to social norms. They might fail to hold a job, to honor financial obligations, or to fulfill parental responsibilities. They are also more likely than other people to become compulsive gamblers (Blaszczynski & McConaghy, 1994).

Because people with an antisocial personality can be charming, lie with a straight face, and talk their way out of trouble, they might pursue careers as shyster lawyers, crooked politicians, or phoney evangelists. Two hallmarks of the antisocial personality are impulsive behavior, such as reckless driving or promiscuous sexual relations, and a remarkable lack of guilt for the pain and suffering they inflict on others (Rogers et al., 1994). Such persons behave as though they cannot tell moral right from moral wrong (Blair et al., 1995).

antisocial personality disorder
A personality disorder marked by impulsive, manipulative, often criminal behavior, without any feelings of guilt in the perpetrator.

Disorders	Symptoms
Disorders Characterized by Odd or Eccentric Behavior	
Paranoid personality disorder	Unrealistic mistrust and suspiciousness of people
Schizoid personality disorder	Problems in forming emotional relationships with others
Schizotypal personality disorder	Oddities of thinking, perception, communication, and behavior not severe enough to be diagnosed as schizophrenia
Disorders Characterized by Dramatic, Emotional, or Erratic Behavior	
Antisocial personality disorder	Continually violating the rights of others, being prone to impulsive behavior, and feeling no guilt for the harm done to others
Borderline personality disorder	Instable in mood, behavior, self-image, and social relationships
Histrionic personality disorder	Overly dramatic behavior, self-centered, and craving attention
Narcissistic personality disorder	Grandiose sense of self-importance, an insistence on being the center of attention, and lacking empathy for others
Disorders Characterized by Anxious or Fearful Behavior	
Avoidant personality disorder	Hypersensitive to potential rejection by others, causing social withdrawal despite a desire for social relationships
Dependent personality disorder	Failure to take responsibility for own life, instead relying on others to make decisions
Obsessive-compulsive personality disorder	Preoccupation with rules, schedules, organization, and trivial details, and inability to express emotional warmth

▲ Table 14.4
Personality Disorders

▲ The Antisocial Personality
Charles Manson was born to a teenage prostitute, raised first by her, then by an aunt and uncle, and again by her. He left home at 14, repeatedly ran afoul of the law, and escaped from numerous juvenile detention centers. In the late 1960s he used his charismatic personality to develop a cult following in California. In August 1969, he convinced his followers to invade an exclusive area of Los Angeles and murder and mutilate pregnant actress Sharon Tate and five other persons. Since his imprisonment, Manson has expressed no remorse for his crime. He is an extreme example of a person with an antisocial personality disorder. He behaved impulsively, failed to learn from punishment, enjoyed harming other people, and expressed no guilt concerning his actions.

In extreme cases, people with an antisocial personality engage in criminal activities and fail to change their behavior even after being punished for it. Criminals with an antisocial personality violate the conditions of their release more than comparable prisoners without an antisocial personality (Hart, Knapp, & Hare, 1988). Robert Hare, a noted researcher on antisocial personality disorder, has found that, fortunately for society, criminals with an antisocial personality tend to "burn out" after age 40 and commit fewer crimes than other criminals do after that age (Hare, McPherson, & Forth, 1988).

Causes of Antisocial Personality Disorder

Antisocial personality disorder has been subjected to more research than other personality disorders, and studies have provided evidence of a physiological predisposition underlying it (Paris, 1996). Thomas Bouchard's University of Minnesota study of identical twins who were separated in infancy and then reunited years later (see Chapter 13) indicates that the antisocial personality has a genetic basis (Grove et al., 1990). Heredity seems to provide people who develop an antisocial personality with an unusually low level of physiological reactivity to stress, most notably physical punishment (Arnett et al., 1993). As discussed in Chapter 11, we try to maintain an optimal level of physiological arousal. Perhaps the unusually low level of arousal of people with an antisocial personality motivates them to engage in behaviors that increase their level of arousal (L. Ellis, 1987). While some people seek to increase their arousal by engaging in auto racing and similar socially acceptable activities, those with an antisocial personality might learn to do so by committing bank robberies and similar antisocial activities.

But what makes one person with a low level of physiological arousal seek thrills through auto racing and another seek thrills through robbing banks? In explaining antisocial personality disorder, psychoanalysts stress the influence of abusive parents or physically absent parents, who make the child feel rejected. Because such children have no emotional ties to their parents, they fail to develop an adequate superego, including a conscience. Behaviorists believe that antisocial personality disorder is caused by parents who reward, or fail to punish, their children for engaging in antisocial behaviors such as lying, stealing, or aggression. There is some evidence that people with antisocial personalities, perhaps because of their

▲ Robert Hare
"Psychopaths seldom commit violent crimes colored by intense emotional arousal."

low physiological reactivity, are less likely to learn from punishment for misdeeds. They do not show the normal increase in anxiety when exposed to punishment (Eysenck, 1982).

STAYING ON TRACK: *Personality Disorders*

1. What is the most likely reason antisocial personality disorder was once called "moral insanity"?
2. What seems to be the relationship between emotional arousal and antisocial personality disorder?

THINKING ABOUT *Psychology*

Should We Retain the Insanity Defense?

More than 2,000 years ago, Plato argued that "[if] someone may commit an act when mad or afflicted with disease . . . let him pay simply for the damage; and let him be exempt from other punishment" (quoted in Carson & Butcher, 1992, p. 32). Today, Plato would face opposition from those who argue against the insanity defense. Spurred by the successful insanity plea of John Hinckley, Jr., following his attempted assassination of President Ronald Reagan, many people have criticized the insanity defense as a miscarriage of justice. But what is insanity?

THE NATURE OF THE INSANITY DEFENSE

Insanity is a legal, not a psychological or psychiatric, term attesting that a person is not responsible for his or her own actions. In criminal cases, this is usually determined by a jury. The insanity defense was formalized in 1843 in the case of Daniel M'Naghten, a paranoid schizophrenic man who had tried to murder the English prime minister Robert Peel, who he believed was persecuting him. But M'Naghten killed Peel's secretary Edward

insanity

A legal term attesting that a person is not responsible for his or her own actions, including criminal behavior.

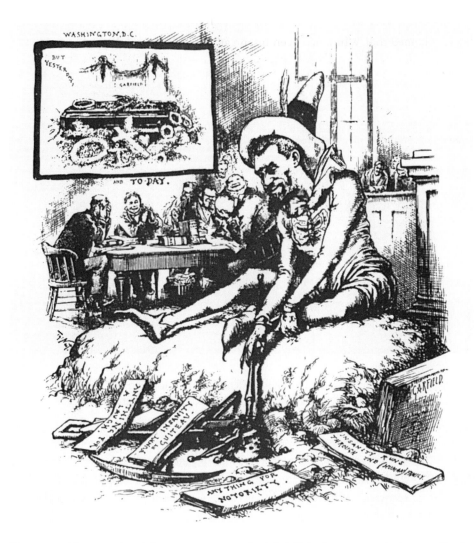

Drummond by mistake. After a controversial trial, M'Naghten was ruled not guilty by reason of insanity and was committed to a mental hospital.

Queen Victoria was so upset by this verdict that she asked the House of Lords to review the case. It upheld the decision, and the M'Naghten rule became a guiding principle in English law. The rule states that a person is not guilty if, at the time of a crime, the person did not know what she or he was doing or did not know that it was wrong.

Today the most widely used standard for determining insanity in the United States is that of the American Law Institute. The standard comprises two rules. The *cognitive rule*, similar to the M'Naghten rule, says that a person was insane at the time of a crime if the person did not know what he or she had done or did not know that it was wrong. The *volitional rule*, which presumes the reality of free will, says that a person was insane at the time of a crime if the person was not in voluntary control of her or his behavior. As described in Chapter 3, an autopsy performed on Charles Whitman, the so-called Texas Tower killer, revealed that he had a brain tumor of the limbic system, a region of the brain that helps control aggression. Had Whitman gone to trial, he might have used the volitional rule as his defense, claiming that the tumor made him unable to control his behavior.

CONTROVERSY CONCERNING THE INSANITY DEFENSE: CAN EATING JUNK FOOD PROVOKE MURDER?

In recent decades, several cases involving the insanity defense, including that of John Hinckley, Jr., have provoked controversy. In 1979, in a widely publicized case, former San Francisco city supervisor Dan White murdered popular mayor George Moscone and city supervisor Harvey Milk, the first openly gay person to hold that post. White's lawyer claimed that White had been insane at the time of the killings because eating junk food had so raised his blood sugar level that it made him lose voluntary control over his behavior. This became known as the "Twinkie defense." A compromise verdict was reached, and White was sentenced to 7 years for manslaughter. After his early release, White committed suicide. White's use of the insanity defense was considered an injustice by critics of the "not guilty by reason of insanity" plea, including Thomas Szasz (1980).

Despite outrage over alleged abuses of the insanity defense, it is rarely used in felony crimes and is rarely successful (Silver, Cirincione, & Steadman, 1994). Thus, the outrage in response to the case of John Hinckley is apparently an example of the availability heuristic (see Chapter 9). In a noteworthy case, Kenneth Bianchi, the so-called Hillside Strangler who raped and murdered at least ten women in California in 1977, pleaded insanity. His defense lawyer claimed that Bianchi had a multiple personality disorder, and that another personality, of whom he was unaware, had committed the murders. In a 1984 Public Broadcasting System documentary, psychiatrists debated whether Bianchi truly had multiple personalities. Some of those who examined Bianchi under hypnosis found that a personality known as "Steve" admitted to the killings (Watkins, 1984).

Those who believed that Bianchi was faking his disorder noted that he had a collection of psychology textbooks that contained descriptions of cases of multiple personality. Moreover, his personal history and pattern of behavior provided no evidence that he had suffered from inexplicable changes in identity and behavior. Psychiatrist Martin Orne contradicted Bianchi's diagnosis and successfully argued that Bianchi was, instead, a clever person with antisocial personality disorder (Orne, Dinges, & Orne, 1984). When it appeared that his insanity plea would fail, Bianchi agreed to a plea bargain and was sentenced to life in prison (Fisher, 1984). There has been a recent trend for more defendants to use multiple personality disorder as an insanity defense, but court decisions have been inconsistent in accepting it (Appelbaum & Greer, 1994).

▲ **Martin Orne**
"The content, boundaries, and number of [Kenneth Bianchi's] personalities changed in response to cues about how to make the conditions more believable, and his response to hypnosis appeared to reflect conscious role playing."

A PROPOSED ALTERNATIVE: GUILTY BUT MENTALLY ILL

The notoriety of cases such as those of John Hinckley, Dan White, and Kenneth Bianchi prompted a reevaluation of the insanity defense by state legislatures and professional organizations. Some states have abandoned the insanity defense entirely, while others have adopted a rule of *guilty but mentally ill*. This requires that an insane person who committed a crime be placed in a mental hospital until she or he is no longer mentally ill, at which time the person would serve the remainder of the sentence in prison. There is also a trend toward placing the burden on the defendant to prove that she or he was insane at the time of the crime, rather than placing it on the prosecutor to prove that the defendant was sane.

The American Psychiatric Association, the American Psychological Association, and the American Bar Association have their own positions regarding the insanity defense. The American Psychiatric Association was so embarrassed by the contradictory testimony of psychiatrists in the Hinckley trial that it published its first opinion ever on the insanity defense. The opinion states that the insanity defense is a legal and moral question, not a psychiatric one, and that psychiatrists should testify only about a defendant's mental status—not about a defendant's responsibility for a crime (Herbert, 1983).

The American Psychological Association has taken a more cautious approach, calling for research on the effects of the insanity defense before deciding to eliminate it or replace it with a plea of guilty but mentally ill (Mervis, 1984). The past few years have, in fact, seen a series of studies on the insanity defense. An archival research study found that legislation passed in 1982 in California to make it more difficult to invoke the insanity defense produced no change in the rate of insanity pleas or acquittals over the next 3 years

(McGreevy, Steadman, & Callahan, 1991). In an experiment on the effect of the guilty-but-mentally-ill verdict option, undergraduates participated as jurors in a mock trial. They then answered questions about the case. Subjects who were given the guilty-but-mentally-ill verdict option showed a two-thirds reduction in the verdicts of either guilty or not guilty by reason of insanity when compared to subjects not given that option (Poulson, 1990).

The American Bar Association would retain the cognitive rule, but would eliminate the volitional (that is, free will) rule, in the insanity defense. A person who did not know what he or she was doing could still use the insanity defense. As the American Bar Association explains:

▶ Someone who knowingly stole a radio, for example, would be legally responsible even if he believed it was issuing instructions to him from Mars. Mental illness would only be a defense if a person were so psychotic that he thought he was squeezing an orange when he was strangling a child. (Holden, 1983, p. 994)

The volitional rule has come under especially strong attack because it might be impossible to determine whether a person has acted from free will or from an irresistible impulse. For example, in 1994 Lorena Bobbitt, in a celebrated case in which she cut off her husband Wayne's penis, was ruled not guilty by reason of insanity. Though she claimed she had been driven to it after years of physical abuse, the prosecution claimed she should still be held criminally responsible for her act.

It remains to be seen whether legislatures will completely overturn our long tradition of not holding people with severe psychological disorders responsible for criminal actions. Science and politics together will determine the outcome of this issue, reflecting the battle between empiricism and emotionalism in regard to the insanity defense (Rogers, 1987).

STAYING ON TRACK: *Should We Retain the Insanity Defense?*

1. What is the difference between the cognitive rule and the volitional rule in regard to the insanity defense?
2. How did the case of John Hinckley, Jr., contribute to the institution of the "guilty but mentally ill" verdict?

▶ CHAPTER SUMMARY

THE NATURE OF PSYCHOLOGICAL DISORDERS

Researchers in the field of psychopathology study psychological disorders. The criteria for determining the presence of a psychological disorder include abnormality, maladaptiveness, and personal distress. The major viewpoints on the causes of psychological disorders include the biopsychological, psychoanalytic, behavioral, cognitive, and humanistic viewpoints. The more recent diathesis-stress viewpoint sees psychological disorders as products of the interaction between a biological predisposition and stressful life experiences. The *Diagnostic and Statistical Manual of Mental Disorders—Fourth Edition (DSM-IV)*, published by the American Psychiatric Association, is the accepted standard for classifying psychological disorders. But the reliability and validity of the *DSM* have been questioned. Some authorities, such as psychiatrist Thomas Szasz and psychologist David Rosenhan, have noted the dangers involved in diagnosing psychological disorders.

ANXIETY DISORDERS

Anxiety disorders are associated with anxiety that is intense and disruptive of everyday functioning. A generalized anxiety disorder is a constant state of anxiety that exists independently of any particular stressful situation. A panic disorder is marked by sudden attacks of overwhelming anxiety, accompanied by dizziness, trembling, cold sweats, heart palpitations, shortness of breath, fear of dying, and fear of going crazy.

Phobias are excessive or inappropriate fears. A simple phobia involves a specific object or situation. A social phobia involves fear of public scrutiny. And agoraphobia involves fear of being in public places. People whose obsessions and compulsions interfere with their daily functioning suffer from an obsessive-compulsive disorder. An obsession is a persistent, recurring thought, and a compulsion is a repetitive action that one feels compelled to perform.

SOMATOFORM DISORDERS

The somatoform disorders are characterized by physical symptoms in the absence of disease or injury. The symptoms are caused, instead, by psychological factors. A person with hypochondriasis interprets the slightest physical changes in his or her body as evidence of a serious illness. A person with a conversion disorder exhibits loss or alteration of a physical function without any apparent physical cause.

DISSOCIATIVE DISORDERS

In dissociative disorders, the person's conscious awareness becomes separated from certain of her or his thoughts, feelings, and memories. A person with psychogenic amnesia is unable to recall personally significant memories. A person with psychogenic fugue suffers from psychogenic amnesia and loss of identity and flees from home. And a person with a dissociative identity disorder (multiple personality disorder) has two or more distinct personalities that vie for dominance.

MOOD DISORDERS

Mood disorders involve prolonged periods of extreme depression or elation, often unrelated to objective circumstances. People with major depression experience depression that is so intense and prolonged that it causes severe distress and disrupts their lives. In such cases, suicide is always a concern. People who attempt suicide usually give warnings, so suicidal threats should be taken seriously. A person with bipolar disorder alternates between periods of mania and periods of major depression. Mania is characterized by euphoria, hyperactivity, grandiose ideas, annoying talkativeness, unrealistic optimism, and inflated self-esteem.

SCHIZOPHRENIA

Schizophrenia is characterized by a severe disruption of perception, cognition, emotionality, behavior, and social relationships. The most serious kind of schizophrenia is disorganized schizophrenia, marked by a complete collapse of the personality and the intellect. Catatonic schizophrenia is marked by unusual motor behavior. Paranoid schizophrenia is marked by hallucinations, delusions, suspiciousness, and argumentativeness.

PERSONALITY DISORDERS

Personality disorders are long-standing, inflexible, maladaptive patterns of behavior. Of greatest concern is antisocial personality disorder, which is associated with lying, stealing, fighting, drug abuse, physical cruelty, and failure to take responsibility for one's own actions. Persons suffering from this disorder also behave impulsively, fail to learn from punishment, and express no remorse for the pain and suffering they inflict on others.

THINKING ABOUT PSYCHOLOGY: SHOULD WE RETAIN THE INSANITY DEFENSE?

Insanity is a legal term attesting that a person is not responsible for his or her own actions. The insanity defense was first used in 1843 in the case of Daniel M'Naghten. Today the insanity defense is based on two rules. The cognitive rule says that a person was insane at the time of a crime if the person did not know what she or he did or that it was wrong. The volitional rule says that a person was insane at the time of a crime if the person was not in voluntary control of his or her behavior. The successful use of the insanity defense by John Hinckley, Jr., the would-be assassin of President Ronald Reagan, has sparked debate over the merits of the insanity defense. Despite this controversy, the insanity defense is rarely used and is even more rarely successful.

KEY CONCEPTS

KEY CONTRIBUTORS

FOR MORE INFORMATION ON PSYCHOLOGICAL DISORDERS

FOR GENERAL WORKS ON PSYCHOLOGICAL DISORDERS

Alloy, L. B., & Acocella, J. (1997). *Abnormal psychology: Current perspectives.* Boston: McGraw-Hill.

Weckowicz, T. E., & Liebel-Weckowicz, H. (1990). *A history of great ideas in abnormal psychology.* New York: Elsevier.

FOR MORE ON THE VIEWPOINTS ON PSYCHOLOGICAL DISORDERS

Castillo, R. L. (1998). *Culture and mental illness.* Belmont, CA: McGraw-Hill.

Hollandsworth, J. G., Jr. (1990). *The physiology of psychological disorders.* New York: Plenum.

Masling, J. M., & Bornstein, R. F. (Eds.). (1993). *Psychoanalytic perspectives in psychopathology.* Washington, DC: American Psychological Association.

Taylor, S. E. (1989). *Positive illusions: Creative self-deception and the healthy mind.* New York: Basic Books.

FOR MORE ON CLASSIFICATION OF PSYCHOLOGICAL DISORDERS

American Psychiatric Association. (1994). *Diagnostic and statistical manual of mental disorders—IV.* Washington, DC: American Psychiatric Press.

Robins, L., & Regier, D. A. (Eds.). (1991). *Psychiatric disorders in America.* New York: Free Press.

Spitzer, R. L., Williams, J. B. W., & Skodol, A. E. (Eds.). (1983). *International perspectives on DSM-III.* Washington, DC: American Psychiatric Press.

Szasz, T. S. (1984). *The myth of mental illness.* New York: Harper & Row.

FOR MORE ON ANXIETY DISORDERS

Agras, S. (1995). *Panic: Facing fears, phobias, and anxiety.* New York: Freeman.

Nardo, D. (1992). *Anxiety and phobias.* New York: Chelsea House.

Rapee, R. M., & Barlow, D. H. (Eds.). (1991). *Chronic anxiety: Generalized anxiety disorder and mixed anxiety-depression.* New York: Guilford.

Taylor, C. B., & Arnow, B. (1988). *The nature and treatment of anxiety disorders.* New York: Free Press.

Wegner, D. (1989). *White bears and other unwanted thoughts.* New York: Viking Penguin.

FOR MORE ON SOMATOFORM DISORDERS

Baur, S. (1988). *Hypochondria: Woeful imaginings.* Berkeley: University of California Press.

Slavney, P. R. (1990). *Perspectives on hysteria.* Baltimore: Johns Hopkins University Press.

FOR MORE ON DISSOCIATIVE DISORDERS

Klein, R., & Doane, B. (Eds.). (1992). *Psychological concepts and dissociative disorders.* Hillsdale, NJ: Erlbaum.

Kluft, R. P., & Fine, C. G. (Eds.). (1993). *Clinical perspectives on multiple personality disorder.* Washington, DC: American Psychiatric Press.

Schreiber, F. (1974). *Sybil.* New York: Warner.

Sizemore, C. C., & Pitillo, E. S. (1977). *I'm Eve.* New York: Jove/Harcourt Brace Jovanovich.

FOR MORE ON MOOD DISORDERS

Goodwin, F. K., & Jamison, K. R. (1990). *Manic-depressive illness.* New York: Oxford University Press.

Kleinman, A., & Good, B. (Eds.). (1985). *Culture and depression: Studies in anthropology and cross-cultural psychiatry of affective disorders.* Berkeley: University of California Press.

Paykel, E. S. (Ed.). (1992). *Handbook of affective disorders.* New York: Guilford.

Rosenthal, N. E. (1993). *Winter blues: Seasonal affective disorder—What it is and how to overcome it.* New York: Guilford.

Shneidman, E. (1993). *Suicide as psyche: A clinical approach to suicidal behavior.* Northvale, NJ: Aronson.

Styron, W. (1990). *Darkness visible: A memoir of madness.* New York: Random House.

Tsuang, M. T., & Faraone, S. V. (1990). *The genetics of mood disorders.* Baltimore: Johns Hopkins University Press.

FOR MORE ON SCHIZOPHRENIA

Gottesman, I. I. (1991). *Schizophrenia genesis: The origins of madness.* New York: W. H. Freeman.

Howells, J. G. (1991). *The concept of schizophrenia: Historical perspectives.* Washington, DC: American Psychiatric Press.

Kay, S. R. (1991). *Positive and negative syndromes in schizophrenia.* New York: Brunner/Mazel.

Leff, J., & Vaughn, C. (1985). *Expressed emotion in families: Its significance for mental illness.* New York: Guilford.

Rokeach, M. (1964/1981). *The three Christs of Ypsilanti.* New York: Columbia University Press.

FOR MORE ON PERSONALITY DISORDERS

Bornstein, R. F. (1993). *The dependent personality.* New York: Guilford.

Cauwels, J. M. (1992). *Imbroglio: Rising to the challenges of borderline personality disorder.* New York: W. W. Norton.

Cleckley, H. (1976). *The mask of sanity: An attempt to clarify some issues about the so-called psychopathic personality.* St. Louis: Mosby.

Costa, P. T., Jr., & Widiger, T. A. (Eds.). (1993). *Personality disorders and the five-factor model of personality.* Washington, DC: American Psychological Association.

Horowitz, M. J. (1991). *Hysterical personality style and the histrionic personality disorder.* Northvale, NJ: Aronson.

Kantor, M. (1993). *Distancing: A guide to avoidance and avoidant personality disorder.* Westport, CT: Greenwood.

Masterson, J. F. (1981). *The narcissistic and borderline disorders: An integrated developmental approach.* New York: Brunner/Mazel.

Parsons, R. D., & Wicks, R. J. (Eds.). (1983). *Passive-aggressiveness: Theory and practice.* New York: Brunner/Mazel.

Turkat, I. D. (1990). *The personality disorders.* New York: Pergamon.

FOR MORE ON THE INSANITY DEFENSE

Maeder, T. (1985). *Crime and madness: The origins and evolution of the insanity defense.* New York: Harper & Row.

Steadman, H. J., McGreevy, M. A., Morrissey, J. P., Callahan, L. A., Robbins, P. C., & Cirincione, C. (1993). *Before and after Hinckley: Evaluating insanity defense reform*. New York: Guilford.

Torrey, E. F. (1984). *The roots of treason: Ezra Pound and the secrets of St. Elizabeth's*. London: Sidgwick & Jackson.

FOR MORE ON CONTRIBUTORS TO THE STUDY OF PSYCHOLOGICAL DISORDERS

Gay, P. (1988). *Freud: A life for our time*. New York: W. W. Norton.

Hirschmuller, A. (1978). *The life and work of Josef Breuer: Physiology and psychoanalysis*. New York: New York University Press.

Hoffman, E. (1988). *The right to be human: A biography of Abraham Maslow*. Los Angeles: Tarcher.

Kirschenbaum, H. (1979). *On becoming Carl Rogers*. New York: Delacorte.

Laing, R. D. (1985). *Wisdom, madness, and folly: The making of a psychiatrist*. New York: McGraw-Hill.

Vatz, R. E., & Weinberg, L. S. (1982). (Eds.). *Thomas Szasz: Primary values and major contentions*. Buffalo, NY: Prometheus.

CHAPTER 15

▲ GAYLE RAY
The Armour

Therapy

▲ **Trephining**
These skulls show the effect of trephining, in which sharp rocks were used to chip holes in the skull. Some authorities believe this was to let out evil spirits that supposedly caused bizarre thinking and behavior. The growth of new bone around the holes in some trephined skulls indicates that many people survived the surgery.

*I*n everyday life, when we feel anxious or depressed, or behave in a maladaptive way, we can usually rely on our own resources to carry us through. We might analyze the causes of our distress or our ineffective behavior and try to change our environment, our thinking, or our behavior. By doing so, we might relieve our distress and function better. Occasionally we might seek the advice of friends, relatives, or acquaintances such as bartenders and hairdressers. Nonetheless, at some time in your life you might become so overwhelmed that you develop a psychological disorder that leads you to seek professional help. The treatment of psychological disorders has come a long way since its ancient origins.

THE HISTORY OF THERAPY

If you visit the Smithsonian Institute in Washington, D.C., you will encounter a display of Stone Age skulls with holes cut in them. The holes were produced by **trephining,** in which sharp stones were used to chip holes in the skull. Some authorities believe this was done to release the demons that some ancients believed caused abnormal behavior. Of course, without written records there is no way to know if this was the true reason (Maher & Maher, 1985). Perhaps, instead, trephining was performed for some unknown medical purpose. If trephining was in fact performed to banish demons, it followed logically from the presumed cause of the abnormal behavior. From ancient times until today, the kinds of therapy used in the treatment of psychological disorders have been based on the presumed causes of those disorders.

The Greek philosopher Hippocrates (460–377 B.C.) turned away from supernatural explanations of psychological disorders, which attributed them to demons or punishment from the gods, in favor of more naturalistic explanations. Hippocrates believed that many psychological disorders were caused by imbalances in fluids that he called "humors," which included blood, phlegm, black bile, and yellow bile. This led him to recommend treatments aimed at restoring their balance. For example, because Hippocrates believed that an excess of blood caused the agitated state of mania, he treated mania with bloodletting. As you would expect, people weakened by the loss of blood became less agitated.

During the early Christian era, such naturalistic treatments existed side by side with supernatural ones. But by the late Middle Ages, treatments increasingly involved physical punishment—literally attempts to "beat the devil out of" a person. This inhumane treatment continued into the Renaissance, which also saw the advent of *insane asylums.* Though some of these institutions were pleasant communities in which residents received humane treatment, most were no better than prisons in which the inmates lived in deplorable conditions. The most humane asylum was the town of Geel in Belgium, where people with mental disorders lived in the homes of townspeople, moved about freely, and worked to support themselves. Geel continues today to provide humane care for 800 individuals who live with 600 families (Godemont, 1992).

Few Renaissance asylums were as pleasant as Geel. The most notorious one was St. Mary's of Bethlehem in London, a nightmarish place where inmates were treated like animals in a zoo. On weekends, families would go on outings to the asylum, pay a small admission fee, and be entertained by the antics of the inmates. Visitors called the male inmates of St. Mary's "Tom Fools," contributing the word *tomfoolery* to our language (Morris & Morris, 1985). And the asylum became known as "Bedlam" (Hattori, 1995),

reflecting the cockney pronunciation of Bethlehem. The word *bedlam* came to mean any uproarious scene.

In 1792, inhumane conditions in French insane asylums and the positive model of Geel spurred the physician Philippe Pinel (1745–1826) to institute what he called **moral therapy** at the Bicetre asylum in Paris (Weiner, 1992). Moral therapy was based on the premise that humane treatment, honest work, and pleasant recreation would promote mental well-being. Pinel had the inmates unchained, provided with good food, and treated with kindness. He even instituted the revolutionary technique of speaking with them about their problems. The first inmate released was a giant, powerful man who had been chained in a dark cell for 40 years after killing a guard with a blow from his manacles. Onlookers were surprised (and relieved) when he simply strolled outside, gazed up at the sky, and exclaimed, "Ah, how beautiful" (Bromberg, 1954, p. 83).

Pinel's moral therapy spread throughout Europe. It was introduced to the United States by Benjamin Rush (1745–1813), the founder of American psychiatry. As part of moral therapy, Rush prescribed work, music, and travel (Farr, 1994). He also prescribed physical treatments that with hindsight we might view as barbaric, but he believed they had therapeutic value (see Figure 15.1). For example, because Rush assumed that depressed people had too little blood in their brains, he whirled them around in special chairs to force blood from their bodies into their heads. One can imagine that this induced a temporary feeling of elation, much as an amusement park ride can do today.

In the 1840s Dorothea Dix (1802–1887), a Massachusetts schoolteacher, shocked the U.S. Congress with reports of the brutal treatment of the inmates of insane asylums. Due to her efforts, many state mental hospitals were built throughout the United States, often in rural settings, that provided good food, social activities, and employment on farms. Dix also influenced Canadian reforms, including the establishment of the first mental hospital in Nova Scotia (Goldman, 1990). Unfortunately, over time many of these mental hospitals became human warehouses, providing custodial care and little else, contradicting the humane treatment Dix had envisioned (Viney & Bartsch, 1984).

In the early twentieth century, public concern about the deplorable conditions in state mental hospitals grew after the publication of *A Mind That Found Itself* by a Yale

◀ **Bedlam**
This engraving by William Hogarth (1697–1764) depicts the asylum of St. Mary's of Bethlehem (better known as "Bedlam") in London, notorious for the inhumane treatment of its residents. Even Shakespeare referred to the bedlam of Bedlam in *King Lear* (act 2, scene 3):
> The country gives me proof and precedent
> Of Bedlam beggars, who, with roaring voices,
> Strike in their numb'd and mortified bare arms
> Pins, wooden pricks, nails, sprigs of rosemary;
> And . . .
> Sometimes with lunatic bans,
> sometimes with prayers,
> Enforce their charity.

▲ **Pinel Unchaining the Inmates of an Asylum**
Philippe Pinel shocked and frightened many of his fellow French citizens by freeing the inmates of insane asylums and providing them with humane treatment. When opponents asked, "Citizen, are not you yourself crazy, that you would free these beasts?" Pinel replied, "I am convinced that these *people* are not incurable if they can have air and liberty" (Bromberg, 1954, p. 83).

▲ **Benjamin Rush (1745–1813)**
"Madness has been exclusively in the mind. I object to this opinion . . . because the mind is incapable of any operations independently of impressions communicated to it through the medium of the body."

moral therapy
An approach to therapy, developed by Philippe Pinel, that provided mental patients with humane treatment.

▲ **Dorothea Dix (1802–1887)**
"Were I to recount the one hundreth part of the shocking scenes of sorrow, suffering, abuse, and degradation to which I have been witness— searched out in jails, in poorhouses, in pens and block-houses, in caves, in cages and cells, in dungeons and cellars; men and women in chains, frantic, bruised, lacerated, and debased, your souls would grow sick at the horrid recital."

▲ **Clifford Beers (1876–1943)**
"Is it not, then, an atrocious anomaly that the treatment often meted out to insane persons is the very treatment which would deprive some sane persons of their reason?"

psychotherapy
The treatment of psychological disorders through psychological, as opposed to bio-medical, means, generally involving verbal interaction with a professional therapist.

  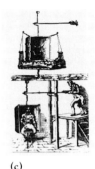

(a) (b) (c)

▲ **FIGURE 15.1**
Nineteenth-Century Treatment Devices
Benjamin Rush invented (*a*) the "tranquilizing chair" to calm manic patients. Other devices that were popular in the nineteenth century included (*b*) the "crib," which was used to restrain violent patients, and (*c*) the "circulating swing," which was used to restore balance to allegedly out-of-balance body fluids.

University graduate named Clifford Beers (Beers, 1908/1970). The book described the physical abuse he suffered during his 3 years in the Connecticut State Hospital. Beers (1876–1943) founded the mental health movement, which promotes the humane treatment of people with mental disorders. The mental health movement has seen mental hospitals joined by group homes, private practices, and counseling centers as alternative treatment sites for psychological disorders.

Today, specially trained professionals offer therapy for psychological disorders. Psychological therapy, or **psychotherapy,** involves the therapeutic interaction of a professional therapist with one or more persons suffering from a psychological disorder. Though there are many approaches to psychotherapy, most psychotherapists favor an *eclectic orientation,* in which they select techniques from different kinds of therapy that they believe will help particular clients (Smith, 1982). This indicates that the practice of therapy is as much an art as it is a science. The first orientation toward the practice of psychotherapy was the psychoanalytic orientation, the topic of the next section.

STAYING ON TRACK: *The History of Therapy*

1. Does the existence of trephined skulls necessarily mean that trephining was performed to release evil spirits?
2. What were some of the basic techniques used in moral therapy?

Answers to Staying on Track start on p. S-6.

THE PSYCHOANALYTIC ORIENTATION: INSIGHT AND CATHARSIS AS CURATIVE

From 1880 to 1882 the Austrian physician Joseph Breuer (1842–1925) treated a young woman he called Anna O., who had symptoms of conversion hysteria (see Chapter 14). She suffered from impaired vision, paralyzed legs, and difficulty swallowing, without any physical causes. Breuer found that when Anna O. spoke freely about her condition, her symptoms disappeared. She called this her "talking cure" or "chimney sweeping." As she spoke freely, she often recalled distressing childhood experiences. By talking about them, she obtained emotional release, followed by a reduction in her physical symptoms. Breuer called this process of emotional release **catharsis.** After she recovered, Anna O., under her real name of Bertha Pappenheim (1859–1936), became a a founder of the social work profession (Swenson, 1994). Breuer's treatment of her marked the beginning of modern psychotherapy.

▲ **The Mental Hospital**
Many of the mental hospitals built through the efforts of Dorothea Dix are still used today.

▲ **Joseph Breuer (1842–1925)**
"In 1880 I had observed a patient suffering from a severe hysteria, who in the course of her illness displayed such peculiar symptoms as to convince me that here a glimpse was being offered into deeper layers of psychopathological processes."

The Nature of Psychoanalysis

After Breuer related the case of Anna O. to him, and after observing similar conditions in some of his own patients, Sigmund Freud turned from medicine to the treatment of psychological disorders. Freud found that childhood emotional conflicts repressed into the unconscious mind instigate the use of defense mechanisms. The excessive or inadequate use of defense mechanisms causes the symptoms of psychological disorders, including conversion hysteria. Freud's aim was to make his clients gain insight into their repressed conflicts, thereby inducing catharsis and relieving the underlying conflict (Jackson, 1994). This led Freud to develop the form of therapy known as **psychoanalysis.**

Traditional Freudian psychoanalysis takes place with the client reclining on a couch and the therapist sitting nearby, just out of sight. Freud claimed that this arrangement relaxes the client, thereby reducing inhibitions about discussing emotional topics. Traditional Freudian psychoanalysts might see clients three to five times a week for years. Though Freudian psychoanalysis does not always take years, at $100 or more a session it is beyond the financial reach of most people.

Techniques in Psychoanalysis

An important goal of psychoanalytic techniques is to make the client's unconscious conflicts conscious. To accomplish this, the therapist actively *interprets* the significance of what the client says. The process by which clients use a therapist's interpretations of what they say to gain insight into the unconscious conflicts that are causing their problems is called *working through*, which should lead to emotional and behavioral improvement (Smith, 1995). The therapist's interpretations are based on the analysis of *free associations, resistances, dreams,* and *transference*.

The main technique of psychoanalysis is the **analysis of free associations,** which has much in common with Anna O.'s "talking cure." In free association, the client is urged to report any thoughts or feelings that come to mind—no matter how trivial or embarrassing they seem. Freud assumed, based on the principle of psychic determinism (see Chapters 1,

▲ **Psychoanalysis Today**
Though most psychotherapists now favor seated, face-to-face interaction with their clients, some psychoanalytic psychotherapists still sit out of sight of the client, who reclines on a couch.

catharsis
In psychoanalysis, the release of repressed emotional energy as a consequence of insight into the unconscious causes of one's psychological problems.

psychoanalysis
A type of psychotherapy, developed by Sigmund Freud, aimed at uncovering the unconscious causes of psychological disorders.

analysis of free associations
In psychoanalysis, the process by which the therapist interprets the underlying meaning of the client's uncensored reports of anything that comes to mind.

analysis of resistances

In psychoanalysis, the process by which the therapist interprets client behaviors that interfere with therapeutic progress toward uncovering unconscious conflicts.

13, and 14), that free association would unlock meaningful information (Busch, 1994). This assumption was not new, because free association was used as long ago as ancient Greece. In Aristophanes' play *The Clouds,* Socrates uses free association to help a man gain self-knowledge.

In the **analysis of resistances,** the psychoanalyst notes behaviors that interfere with therapeutic progress toward self-awareness (Renik, 1995). Signs of resistance include arriving late, missing sessions, and talking about insignificant topics. The client holds on dearly to resistances to block awareness of painful memories or conflicts. By interpreting the meaning of the client's resistances, the therapist helps the client uncover the unconscious conflicts that provoke them. Suppose a client changes the topic whenever the therapist asks him about his father. The therapist might interpret this as a sign that the client has unconscious emotional conflicts about his father. But resistances might also indicate that the client does not trust the therapist's approach to therapy (Rennie, 1994).

analysis of dreams

In psychoanalysis, the process by which the therapist interprets the symbolic, manifest content of dreams to reveal their true, latent content to the client.

Freud believed that the **analysis of dreams** was the "royal road to the unconscious" (see Chapter 6). He claimed that dreams symbolized unconscious sexual and aggressive conflicts. Freud relied on his own dreams, as well as those of his clients, to illustrate his theory (Mautner, 1991). Having the client free-associate about the content of a series of dreams allows the psychoanalyst to interpret the symbolic, or *manifest,* content of the client's dreams to reveal the true, or *latent,* content—their true meaning.

analysis of transference

In psychoanalysis, the process by which the therapist interprets the feelings expressed by the client toward the therapist as being indicative of the feelings typically expressed by the client toward important people in his or her personal life.

The key to a psychoanalytic cure is the **analysis of transference** (Abend, 1993). Transference is the tendency of the client to act toward the therapist in the way she or he acts toward important people in everyday life, such as a boss, spouse, parent, or teacher. Transference can be positive or negative. In *positive transference* the client expresses feelings of approval and affection toward the therapist. In *negative transference* the client expresses feelings of disapproval and rejection toward the therapist—such as criticizing the therapist's skill. By interpreting transference, the therapist helps the client gain insight into the interpersonal origins of his or her current emotional problems.

Traditional Freudian psychoanalysis inspired many offshoots. Freud's students Carl Jung and Alfred Adler broke with him and developed their own versions of psychoanalysis. During succeeding decades, neo-Freudians such as Karen Horney, Melanie Klein, Erich Fromm, Harry Stack Sullivan, Jacques Lacan, and Heinz Kohut developed their own versions. Nonetheless, psychoanalysis, in its various forms, went from being the choice of most therapists in the 1950s to being the choice of about 15 percent in the 1980s (Smith, 1982). One of the main reasons for this declining trend is that other, less costly and less lengthy, therapies are at least as effective as psychoanalysis (Fisher & Greenberg, 1985). Today few therapists are strict Freudians. Instead, many practice what is called *psychodynamic therapy,* which employs aspects of psychoanalysis in face-to-face, once-a-week therapy lasting months instead of years. Psychodynamic therapists also rely more on discussions of past and present social relationships than on trying to uncover hidden emotional conflicts. Psychodynamic therapy has proved effective in the treatment of a variety of psychological disorders (Goldfried, Greenberg, & Marmar, 1990).

STAYING ON TRACK: *The Psychoanalytic Orientation*

1. How do psychoanalysts employ the analysis of free associations?
2. How do psychoanalysts employ the analysis of resistances?

THE BEHAVIORAL ORIENTATION: LEARNING MORE-ADAPTIVE BEHAVIOR

behavior therapy

The therapeutic application of the principles of learning to change maladaptive behaviors.

In 1952 British psychologist Hans Eysenck coined the term **behavior therapy** to refer to treatments that favor changing maladaptive behaviors rather than providing insight into unconscious conflicts. According to Eysenck, simply knowing why you are depressed and experiencing catharsis will not necessarily make you less depressed. Unlike traditional psychoanalysts, behavior therapists ignore unconscious conflicts, emphasize present behavior, and assume that therapy can be accomplished in weeks or months rather than in years. To behavior therapists, abnormal behavior, like normal behavior, is learned and therefore can be unlearned.

Psychoanalytic therapists responded to the challenge of this new form of therapy by insisting that the elimination of maladaptive behaviors without dealing with the supposed underlying, unconscious causes would produce *symptom substitution*—the replacement of one maladaptive behavior with another. But studies have shown that directly changing maladaptive behaviors is not followed by the substitution of other maladaptive behaviors (Kazdin, 1982). Behavior therapists change maladaptive behaviors by applying the principles of classical conditioning, operant conditioning, and social learning theory. In practice, behavior therapists often combine various behavioral techniques in their practices (Turner et al., 1994).

Classical-Conditioning Therapies

According to classical conditioning, a stimulus associated with another stimulus that elicits a response may itself come to elicit that response (see Chapter 7). Therapies based on classical conditioning stress the importance of stimuli in controlling behavior. The goal of these therapies is the removal of the stimuli that control maladaptive behaviors or the promotion of more-adaptive responses to those stimuli.

The classical-conditioning technique of **counterconditioning** replaces unpleasant emotional responses to stimuli with pleasant ones, or vice versa. The procedure is based on the assumption that we cannot simultaneously experience an unpleasant feeling, such as anxiety, and a pleasant feeling, such as relaxation. Counterconditioning was used in the following classic study.

counterconditioning
A behavior therapy technique that applies the principles of classical conditioning to replace unpleasant emotional responses to stimuli with more pleasant ones.

Anatomy of a Classic Research Study

Can Phobias Be Eliminated by Counterconditioning?

Rationale

Therapeutic counterconditioning was introduced by John B. Watson's student Mary Cover Jones (1896–1987). Watson had conditioned a boy he called Little Albert to fear a white rat by pairing the rat with a loud sound (see Chapter 7). Watson proposed that the fear could be eliminated by pairing the rat with a pleasant stimulus, such as pleasurable stroking (Watson & Rayner, 1920).

Method

While working at Columbia University, Jones (1924) took Watson's suggestion and, under his advisement, tried to rid a 3-year-old boy named Peter of a rabbit phobia he had developed. Jones used what she called "direct conditioning," which is now known as counterconditioning. Jones presented Peter with candy and then brought a caged rabbit closer and closer to him. This was done twice a day for 2 months.

Results and Discussion

At first Peter cried when the rabbit was within 20 feet of him. Over the course of the study, he became less and less fearful of it. On the last day he asked for the rabbit, petted it, tried to pick it up, and finally played with it on a windowsill. Evidently, the pleasant feelings that Peter experienced in response to the candy gradually became associated with the rabbit. This reduced his fear of the rabbit. Jones cautioned, however, that this was a delicate procedure. If performed too rapidly, it could produce the opposite effect—fear of the candy. More recently, counterconditioning has been used to reduce distress in children undergoing painful medical procedures, such as lumbar punctures (Slifer, Babbitt, & Cataldo, 1995).

▲ ▲ ▲

systematic desensitization

A form of counterconditioning that trains the client to maintain a state of relaxation in the presence of imagined anxiety-inducing stimuli.

Systematic Desensitization: Overcoming Phobias by Using Relaxation and Mental Imagery

Today the most widely used form of counterconditioning is **systematic desensitization,** developed by Joseph Wolpe (1958) for treating phobias. Systematic desensitization involves three steps. The first step is for the client to practice *progressive relaxation,* a technique developed in the 1930s by Edmund Jacobson to relieve anxiety. To learn progressive relaxation, clients sit in a comfortable chair and practice successively tensing and relaxing each of the major muscle groups—including those of the head, arms, body, and legs—until they gain the ability to relax their entire body.

The second step is the construction of an *anxiety hierarchy* (see Table 15.1), consisting of a series of anxiety-inducing scenes related to the person's phobia. The client lists 10 to 20 scenes, rating them on a 100-point scale from least to most anxiety inducing. A rating of zero would mean that the scene induces no anxiety; a rating of 100 would mean that the scene induces abject terror. Suppose that you have *arachnophobia*—a spider phobia. You might rate a photo of a spider a 5, a spider on your arm a 60, and a spider on your face an 85.

Systematic desensitization has been successful in treating a wide variety of phobias. These include fear of blood (Elmore, Wildman, & Westefeld, 1980), dentists (Klepac, 1986), hypodermic needles (Rainwater et al., 1988), public speaking (Rossi & Seiler, 1989–1990), and magnetic resonance imaging chambers (Klonoff, Janata, & Kaufman, 1986). What accounts for the effectiveness of systematic desensitization?

ANATOMY OF A CONTEMPORARY RESEARCH STUDY

Do Endorphins Mediate the Effect of Systematic Desensitization on Phobias?

Rationale

Might systematic desensitization exert its effects through the actions of endorphins? Perhaps pleasurable feelings induced by endorphins can counter phobic anxiety. This was the rationale behind the present study (Egan et al., 1988).

Method

The subjects all suffered from simple phobias (see Chapter 14), such as fear of heights, dogs, or elevators. The subjects were randomly assigned into two groups. Prior to sessions of systematic desensitization, 6 subjects (the experimental group) received intravenous infusions of naloxone, a drug that blocks the effect of endorphins, and 5 subjects (the control group) received intravenous infusions of a placebo, a saline solution with no specific effects. Because the study used the double-blind procedure, neither the subjects nor the experimenter knew which subjects received naloxone and which received the placebo. This controlled for any subject or experimenter biases. The subjects received eight sessions over a period of 4 weeks.

Initial Rating of Distress	Fear-Inducing Scene
0	Registering for next semester's courses
5	Going over the course outline in class
20	Hearing the instructor announce that the midterm exam will take place in three weeks
30	Discussing the difficulty of the exam with fellow students
45	Reviewing your notes one week before the exam
50	Attending a review session three days before the exam
60	Listening to the professor explain what to expect on the exam the day before it
65	Studying alone the day before the exam
70	Studying with a group of students the night before the exam
75	Overhearing superior students expressing their self-doubts about the exam
80	Realizing that you are running out of study time at 1:00 A.M. the night before the exam
90	Entering the class before the exam and having the professor remind you that one third of your final grade depends on it
95	Reading the exam questions and discovering that you do not recognize several of them
100	Answering the exam questions while hearing other students hyperventilating and muttering about them

◄ **TABLE 15.1**
A Test-Anxiety Hierarchy

Results and Discussion

The results indicated that the subjects who received the placebo experienced a significant decrease in the severity of their phobias, while those who received naloxone did not. Because naloxone blocks the effects of the endorphins, the results support the possible role of endorphins in the effects of systematic desensitization. The pleasant feelings produced by the endorphins might become conditioned to the formerly fear-inducing stimuli.

Of course, the ultimate test of systematic desensitization is the ability to face the actual source of your phobia. One way of assuring such success is to use in vivo desensitization, which physically exposes the client to successive situations on the client's anxiety hierarchy. In vivo desensitization has been successful in treating claustrophobia (Edinger & Radtke, 1993), flying phobia (McCarthy & Craig, 1995), and many other kinds of phobias. In one case, a woman who had chronic nightmares about snakes was relieved of them by an in vivo procedure that had her move closer and closer to a live, harmless snake (Eccles, Wilde, & Marshall, 1988).

Aversion Therapy: Making Appealing Behaviors Unappealing

In a sense, **aversion therapy,** a form of counterconditioning, is the opposite of systematic desensitization. The goal of aversion therapy is to make a formerly pleasurable, but maladaptive, behavior unpleasant. In aversion therapy, a stimulus that normally elicits a maladaptive response is paired with an unpleasant stimulus, leading to a reduction in the maladaptive response. Aversion therapy was introduced in the 1930s to treat alcoholism by administering painful electric shocks to alcoholic patients in the presence of the sight, smell, and taste of alcohol. Today aversion therapy for alcoholism uses drugs that make the individual feel deathly ill after drinking alcohol. The drugs interfere with the metabolism of alcohol, leading to the buildup of a toxic chemical that induces nausea and dizziness.

A follow-up study of more than 400 alcoholic patients who underwent treatment programs that included aversion therapy found that 60 percent were abstinent a year later (Smith & Frawley, 1993). In treating alcoholism, aversion therapy with drugs is superior

▲ **In Vivo Desensitization**
A phobia sufferer may gain relief through in vivo desensitization, which involves gradual exposure to more and more anxiety-inducing situations related to the phobia. This man, suffering from a fear of heights (acrophobia), may have begun therapy by simply looking out of a first-floor window. He has progressed to the point that he is able to walk onto the roof of a tall building. But note that he still holds tightly to the ledge. He should eventually be able to peer over the ledge without having to grasp it.

in vivo desensitization
A form of counterconditioning that trains the client to maintain a state of relaxation in the presence of anxiety-inducing stimuli.

aversion therapy
A form of behavior therapy that inhibits maladaptive behavior by pairing a stimulus that normally elicits a maladaptive response with an unpleasant stimulus.

to aversion therapy with electric shocks (Cannon & Baker, 1981). This supports the concept of *behavioral preparedness* (see Chapters 7 and 14). We seem to have an inborn tendency to associate stomach distress with tastes such as alcohol rather than with external sources of pain such as electric shocks. Aversion therapy has also been used to treat a variety of other behavioral problems, including smoking, bedwetting, overeating, and sexual abuse of children.

Operant-Conditioning Therapies

Treatments based on operant conditioning change maladaptive behaviors by controlling their consequences. This is known as **behavior modification** and is based on the work of learning theorist B. F. Skinner. Popular forms of behavior modification rely on the behavioral contingencies of positive reinforcement, punishment, and extinction.

Positive Reinforcement: Promoting Adaptive Behavior by Positively Reinforcing It

One of the most important uses of positive reinforcement has been in treating patients in mental hospitals. Residents of mental hospitals have traditionally relied on the staff to take care of all their needs. This often leads to passivity, a decrease in self-care, and a general decline in dignified behavior. But "talking therapies," such as psychoanalytic therapy, have been ineffective in improving the behavior of hospitalized patients suffering from schizophrenia.

The development of the "token economy" (Ayllon & Azrin, 1968) provided a way to overcome this problem. The **token economy** provides tokens (often plastic poker chips) as positive reinforcement for desirable behaviors (Morisse et al., 1996), such as making beds, taking showers, or wearing appropriate clothing. The patients use the tokens to purchase items such as books or candy and privileges such as television or passes to leave the hospital grounds. The use of token economies has proved successful, for example, in reducing aggressiveness by mental hospital patients (Dickerson et al., 1994). Token economies are also employed in grade-school classes and in programs for the mentally retarded. In one study, a token economy motivated mentally retarded participants to adhere to an exercise program (Croce, 1990).

Punishment: Reducing Maladaptive Behavior by Punishment

Though less desirable than positive reinforcement, punishment can also be effective in changing maladaptive behaviors. In fact, sometimes it is the only way to prevent inappropriate, or even dangerous, behavior. In using punishment, the therapist provides aversive consequences for maladaptive behavior. A controversial application of punishment has been the use of mild electric shocks to reduce self-biting, head banging, and other self-destructive behaviors in children with autism, who do not respond to talking therapies (see Figure 15.2). *Autism* is a disorder marked by social withdrawal and language difficulties. Before using punishments such as mild electric shocks, therapists must first present their rationale and gain approval from parents and fellow professionals. Once the self-injurious behavior has stopped, the therapist uses positive reinforcement to promote more appropriate behaviors. The combination of punishment and positive reinforcement has been effective in improving the behavior of children with autism (Lovass, 1987).

Extinction: Reducing Maladaptive Behavior by Removing Positive Reinforcement

If a person is not reinforced for a behavior, whether adaptive or maladaptive, it will become extinguished. The technique of *flooding* takes advantage of this in the elimination of intense fears and phobias. While systematic desensitization trains the client to relax and experience a graded series of anxiety-inducing situations, **flooding** exposes the client to a situation that evokes intense anxiety. In *imaginal flooding*, the client is asked to hold in mind an image of the feared situation; in *in vivo flooding*, the client is placed in the actual feared situation. As clients experience the situation mentally or in reality, their anxiety diminishes because they are prevented from escaping and thereby negatively reinforcing their flight behavior through fear reduction. Of course, care must be taken to protect the

---

behavior modification
The application of the principles of operant conditioning to change maladaptive behaviors.

token economy
An operant conditioning procedure that uses tokens as positive reinforcers in programs designed to promote desirable behaviors, with the tokens later used to purchase desired items or privileges.

▲ **FIGURE 15.2**
Punishment and Autism
This autistic child wears a device developed at Johns Hopkins University called the Self-Injurious Behavior Inhibiting System, which delivers a mild electric shock to his leg whenever he bangs his head. This and similar devices have been used with success to reduce self-injurious behavior by autistic children. As you can imagine, the use of such devices has sparked controversy (Landers, 1987).

flooding
An extinction procedure in which a phobic client is exposed to a stimulus that evokes intense anxiety.

client from being overwhelmed by fear. A study that used flooding with 20 social-phobic clients demonstrated a significant decrease in their anxiety levels and heart rate, indicating extinction of their phobias (Turner et al., 1992). Flooding also has helped clients overcome anxiety disorders such as agoraphobia (Jansson & Ost, 1982), noise phobia (Houlihan et al., 1993), and panic disorder (Fava et al., 1991).

You should note that in about one third of cases in which extinction is the sole technique used to alter behavior, the removal of positive reinforcement induces an initial, paradoxical burst in the target behavior (Lerman & Iwata, 1995). This burst is usually temporary and does not necessarily mean that the attempt to alter the behavior has failed. For example, if you try to extinguish a child's tantrums by ignoring them, the tantrums will most likely increase at first. If you can stand the emotional distress that the tantrums induce in you, the tantrums will eventually stop.

Social Learning Therapies

In treating Peter's rabbit phobia, Mary Cover Jones (1924) sometimes let Peter observe children playing with a rabbit. By doing so, Jones made use of social learning (see Chapter 7). Therapists who use social learning have their clients watch other people model adaptive behaviors either in person or on videotape. Clients learn to acquire social skills or to overcome phobias by performing the behavior that is being modeled (see Figure 15.3). Therapists might also use **participant modeling,** in which the therapist models the desired behavior while the client watches. The client then tries to perform the behavior. Participant modeling has been successful in helping individuals overcome their fears, including fears of surgery (Faust, Olson, & Rodriguez, 1991), harmless snakes (Hughes, 1990), dogs and cats (Ladouceur, 1983), and performing gymnastics (McAuley, 1985). It has even been used successfully to overcome a common fear among undergraduate psychology students: handling laboratory rats. This fear tends to decrease when students observe other students handle rats without negative consequences (Barber, 1994).

participant modeling
A form of social learning therapy in which the client learns to perform more-adaptive behaviors by first observing the therapist model the desired behaviors.

STAYING ON TRACK: *The Behavioral Orientation*

1. How would you use systematic desensitization to treat a student who is terrified of making oral presentations in class?
2. How would you use a token economy to improve spelling and arithmetic performance by third-graders?

THE COGNITIVE ORIENTATION: CHANGING IRRATIONAL THINKING

The Greek Stoic philosopher Epictetus (A.D. ca. 60–ca. 120) noted that irrational people tend to become emotionally upset. This indicates the kinship between Stoic philosophy and the cognitive orientation in psychotherapy (Montgomery, 1993). Cognitive therapists believe that events in themselves do not cause maladaptive emotions and behaviors. Instead, these are due to our interpretation of events. Given this assumption, cognitive therapists believe that changes in thinking can produce changes in maladaptive emotions or behaviors. Because cognitive therapies can include aspects of behavior therapy, they are commonly called *cognitive-behavioral therapies*. They have been effective in treating many kinds of disorders, including social phobia (Marks, 1995) and panic disorder (Pollack et al., 1994).

A version of cognitive-behavioral therapy called **stress-inoculation training,** introduced by Donald Meichenbaum (1985), helps clients change their pessimistic thinking into optimistic thinking when they are in stressful situations. In one study, subjects were assigned to one of three conditions. The first condition combined stress-inoculation training with writing instruction; the second condition combined writing instruction with interpersonal attention; and the third condition (the control group) involved no

stress-inoculation training
A type of cognitive therapy, developed by Donald Meichenbaum, that helps clients change their pessimistic thinking into more positive thinking when in stressful situations.

► FIGURE 15.3

Modeling and Phobias

People may learn to overcome their phobias by observing other people either handle objects they are afraid to handle or perform in situations in which they are afraid to perform. The graph shows the results of a study comparing the effectiveness of three kinds of therapy for snake phobia. The control group received no therapy. As you can see, all three therapies produced more approaches to the snakes than did the control condition. But participant modeling produced more improvement than did symbolic modeling (in which subjects watched models on film) or systematic desensitization (Bandura, Blanchard, & Ritter, 1969).

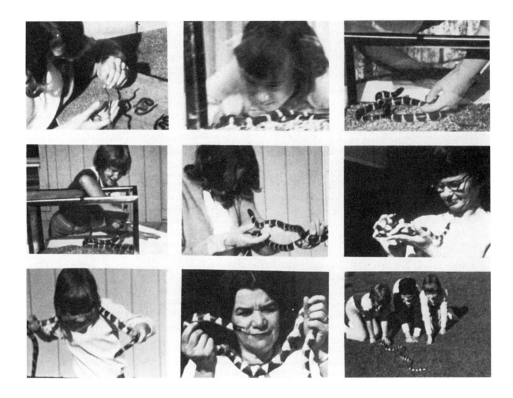

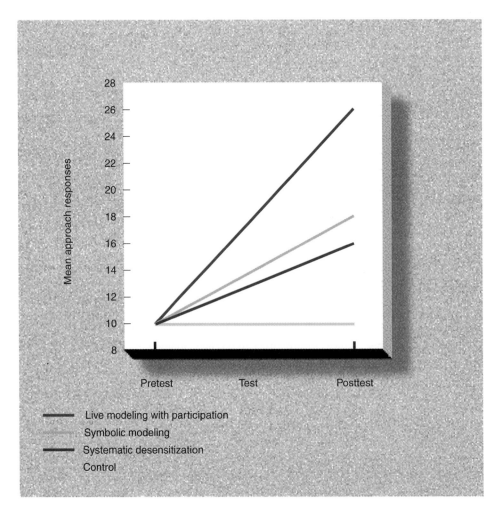

1. It is a dire necessity for an adult to be loved or approved by virtually every other significant person in his or her community.
2. One should be thoroughly competent, adequate, and achieving in all possible respects if one is to consider oneself worthwhile.
3. Certain people are bad, wicked, or villainous and should be severely blamed and punished for their villainy.
4. It is awful and catastrophic when things are not the way one would very much like them to be.
5. Human unhappiness is externally caused and people have little or no ability to control their sorrows and disturbances.
6. If something is or may be dangerous or fearsome one should be terribly concerned about it and should keep dwelling on the possibility of its occurring.
7. It is easier to avoid than to face certain life difficulties and self-responsibilities.
8. One should be dependent on others and need someone stronger than oneself on whom to rely.
9. One's past history is an all-important determiner of one's present behavior, and because something once strongly affected one's life, it should indefinitely have a similar effect.
10. One should become quite upset over other people's problems and disturbances.
11. There is invariably a right, precise, and perfect solution to human problems and it is catastrophic if this perfect solution is not found.

From A. Ellis, *Reason and Emotion in Psychotherapy.* Copyright © 1962 Lyle Stuart, Inc., Secaucus, NJ. Reprinted with permission.

treatment. Subjects in the first two groups reported reductions in their anxiety levels that were greater than those reported by subjects in the control group, but only the combination of stress-inoculation training and writing instruction improved writing quality—and significantly more of those in that group were able to pass a college freshman English equivalency examination (Salovey & Haar, 1990). Stress-inoculation training has also been sucessful in treating anxiety disorders (Saunders et al., 1996) and helping athletes during rehabilitation from injuries (Ross & Berger, 1996). Stress-inoculation training promises to become as influential as the leading forms of cognitive-behavioral therapy: *rational-emotive behavior therapy* and *cognitive therapy*.

Rational-Emotive Behavior Therapy: Challenging Irrational Beliefs

Albert Ellis (1962), who was formerly a psychoanalytic psychotherapist, developed the first cognitive therapy, which he called *rational-emotive therapy (R-E-T)*. He recently renamed it **rational-emotive behavior therapy (R-E-B-T)** to emphasize that it is aimed not only at changing maladaptive thinking but also, ultimately, at changing maladaptive behavior (Corsini, 1995). A survey of therapists found that in recent decades Ellis has been second only to Carl Rogers in his influence on the field of psychotherapy (Smith, 1982). Ellis's therapy is based on his *A-B-C theory* of emotion, in which A is an activating event, B is an irrational belief, and C is an emotional consequence. Ellis points out that most of us believe that A causes C, when in fact B causes C. Imagine that you fail an exam (A) and experience depression (C). Ellis would attribute your depression not to your failure but to an irrational belief you hold, such as a belief (B) that you must be perfect. Thus, your irrational belief, not your failure, causes your depression—and the behaviors it produces. Table 15.2 lists common irrational beliefs that Ellis claims guide many of our lives.

Though therapists who use R-E-B-T might develop warm, empathetic relationships with their clients, Ellis himself is more interested in demolishing, sometimes harshly, the irrational ideas of his clients. After identifying a client's irrational beliefs, Ellis challenges

rational-emotive behavior therapy (R-E-B-T)

A type of cognitive therapy, developed by Albert Ellis, that treats psychological disorders by forcing the client to give up irrational beliefs.

This transcript illustrates how the rational-emotive therapist (T) challenges the client (C) to change irrational beliefs. The client is a 23-year-old young woman experiencing intense feelings of guilt for not living up to her parents' strict standards.

C: Well, this is the way it was in school, if I didn't do well in one particular thing, or even on a particular test—and little crises that came up—if I didn't do as well as I had wanted to do.

T: Right. You beat yourself over the head.

C: Yes.

T: But why? What's the point? Are you supposed to be perfect? Why the hell shouldn't human beings make mistakes, be imperfect?

C: Maybe you always expect yourself to be perfect.

T: Yes. But is that *sane*?

C: No.

T: Why do it? Why not give up that unrealistic expectation?

C: But then I can't accept myself.

T: But you're saying, "It's shameful to make mistakes." *Why* is it shameful? Why can't you go to somebody else when you make a mistake and say, "Yes, I made a mistake"? Why is that so awful? . . .

C: It might all go back to, as you said, the need for approval. If I don't make mistakes, then people will look up to me. If I do it all perfectly—

T: Yes, that's part of it. That, is the erroneous belief; that if you never make mistakes everybody will love you and that it is necessary they do. That's right. That's a big part of it. But is it true, incidentally? Suppose you never did make mistakes—*would* people love you? They'd sometimes hate your guts, wouldn't they?

From Science & Behavior Books, Inc., Palo Alto, California, 1971. Reprinted by permission.

▲ Albert Ellis

"It is my contention . . . that all effective psychotherapists, whether or not they realize what they are doing, teach or induce their patients to reperceive or rethink their life events and philosophies and thereby to change their unrealistic and illogical thought, emotion, and behavior."

cognitive therapy

A type of therapy, developed by Aaron Beck, that aims at eliminating exaggerated negative beliefs about oneself, the world, or the future.

the client to provide evidence supporting them. Ellis then contradicts any irrational evidence, almost demanding that the client agree with him. Table 15.3 presents a verbatim transcript illustrating the use of R-E-B-T.

A meta-analysis of research studies found that R-E-B-T is more effective than placebo treatment and as effective as other therapies (Engels, Garnefski, & Diekstra, 1993). It has helped people overcome social phobia (Mersch, Emmelkamp, & Lips, 1991), obsessive-compulsive disorder (Emmelkamp & Beens, 1991), and a host of other disorders.

Cognitive Therapy: Learning to Think More Rationally

Psychiatrist Aaron Beck assumes that depression is caused by negative beliefs about oneself, the world, and the future (Beck et al., 1979). Thus, depressed people tend to blame themselves rather than their circumstances for misfortunes, attend more to negative events than to positive events, and have a pessimistic view of the future (see Chapter 14). Depressed people also overgeneralize from rare or minor negative events in their lives. The goal of Beck's **cognitive therapy** is to change such exaggerated beliefs in treating psychological disorders, most notably depression.

Beck is less directive in his approach than Ellis is. Beck employs a Socratic technique, in which he asks clients questions that lead them to recognize their negative beliefs. He has clients keep a daily record of their thoughts and urges them to note their negative beliefs and replace them with positive ones. A client who claims, "I am an awful student and will never amount to anything," might be encouraged to think, instead, "I am doing poorly in school because I do not study enough. If I change my study habits, I will graduate and pursue a desirable career." To promote positive experiences, Beck might begin by giving the client homework assignments that guarantee success, such as having a client who feels socially incompetent speak to a close friend on the telephone. Cognitive therapy has been especially successful in treating depression, which was its original purpose (Gaffan, Tsaousis, & Kemp-Wheeler, 1995). Nonetheless, it is also effective in treating other disorders, such as generalized anxiety disorder (Sanderson, Beck, & McGinn, 1994).

STAYING ON TRACK: *The Cognitive Orientation*

1. What are the basic assumptions and techniques of Ellis's rational-emotive behavior therapy?
2. What are the basic assumptions and techniques of Beck's cognitive therapy?

THE HUMANISTIC ORIENTATION: PROMOTING SELF-ACTUALIZATION

About 10 percent of psychotherapists practice some form of *humanistic therapy*, making it one of the most popular approaches to therapy (Smith, 1982). Unlike the psychoanalytic orientation, the humanistic orientation stresses the present rather than the past, and conscious, rather than unconscious, experience. Unlike the behavioral orientation, the humanistic orientation stresses the importance of subjective mental experience rather than objective environmental circumstances. And unlike the cognitive orientation, the humanistic orientation encourages the expression of emotion rather than its control.

Person-Centered Therapy: The Promotion of Self-Actualization

The most popular kind of humanistic therapy is **person-centered therapy,** originally called *client-centered therapy*. It was developed in the 1950s by Carl Rogers (1902–1987), a former psychoanalytic psychotherapist, as one of the first alternatives to psychoanalysis. As noted earlier, a survey of therapists found that Rogers has been the most influential of all contemporary psychotherapists (Smith, 1982). Whereas the rational-emotive therapist is *directive* in challenging the irrational beliefs of clients, the person-centered therapist is *nondirective* in permitting clients to find their own answers to their problems and thereby proceed toward self-actualization (Bozarth & Brodley, 1991). This is in keeping with the humanistic concept of self-actualization (Rogers, 1951) and reminiscent of the Socratic method of self-discovery.

If person-centered therapists give no advice, how do they help their clients? Their goal is to facilitate the pursuit of self-actualization, not by offering expertise but by providing a social climate in which clients feel comfortable being themselves (Bozarth & Brodley, 1991). They do so by promoting self-acceptance. Humanistic psychologists assume that psychological disorders arise from an incongruence between a person's public self and her or his actual self (see Chapter 14). This makes the person distort reality or deny feelings, trying to avoid the anxiety caused by failing to act in accordance with those feelings. The goal of person-centered therapy is to help individuals reduce this incongruence by expressing and accepting their true feelings. Perhaps cathartic experiences generated in psychoanalysis work, not because they release pent-up emotions, but because, as humanistic therapists insist, they put people in touch with their true feelings (Nichols & Efran, 1985).

The person-centered therapist promotes self-actualization through reflection of feelings, genuineness, accurate empathy, and unconditional positive regard (Rogers, 1957). Note that a close friend or relative whom you consider a "good listener" and valued counselor probably exhibits these characteristics, too. *Reflection of feelings* is the main technique of person-centered therapy. The therapist is an active listener who serves as a therapeutic mirror, attending to the emotional content of what the client says and restating it to the client. This helps clients recognize their true feelings. By being *genuine*, the therapist acts in a concerned, open, and sincere manner rather than in a detached, closed, and phony

▲ **Aaron Beck**
"The depressed person has a global negative view of himself, the outside world, and the future."

person-centered therapy
A type of humanistic therapy, developed by Carl Rogers, that helps clients find their own answers to their problems.

manner. This makes clients more willing to disclose their true feelings. During his career, Rogers increasingly stressed the importance of genuineness (Bozarth, 1990), as have others (Quinn, 1993).

The client also becomes more willing to share feelings when the therapist shows *accurate empathy*, which means that the therapist's words and actions indicate a true understanding of how the client feels (Meissner, 1996). Because accurate empathy is important even in everyday informal counseling, psychologists have tried to train people to be more empathetic. In one study, undergraduates were assigned to special empathy training groups or to a no-training control group. The program lasted 4 weeks. The subjects were then observed on videotape as they discussed common student problems with their peers. Students who had received the training were more empathetic in their responses than students who had not received training. These findings held even when the trainees were reassessed a year later (Kremer & Dietzen, 1991).

Perhaps the most difficult task for the person-centered therapist is the maintenance of *unconditional positive regard*—acting in a personally warm and accepting manner. The therapist must remain nonjudgmental no matter how distasteful she or he finds the client's thoughts, feelings, and actions to be. This encourages clients to freely express and deal with even the most distressing aspects of themselves. It does not, however, mean that the therapist must approve of the client's behavior, only that the therapist must accept the client's personal experiences. Thus, if a client says "I hate my children!" the therapist encourages dealing with the feelings and doesn't scold the client for harboring ill will toward his or her offspring.

The personal warmth conveyed by unconditional positive regard is a key aspect of therapy. A study of clients at a university counseling center found that the therapist's personal warmth was one of the most important factors in their willingness to stay in therapy (Hynan, 1990). And a survey of more than 500 therapists found that even they considered personal warmth to be one of the most important factors in selecting their own therapists (Norcross, Strausser, & Faltus, 1988). Table 15.4 presents a verbatim transcript that illustrates the use of person-centered therapy.

Though Rogers urged therapists to be nondirective, even he was unable to fulfill that ideal. A study of films and audio recordings of therapy sessions involving Rogers showed that he was nondirective as long as the client was expressing insight into his or her problems. He became less so when the client failed to express insight. At times, Rogers even became directive (Truax, 1966), which is more characteristic of the form of humanistic therapy called *Gestalt therapy*.

Gestalt Therapy: Encouraging People to Become "Real"

Imagine a therapy that combines aspects of psychoanalysis, R-E-B-T, and client-centered therapy, and you might conceive of **Gestalt therapy.** According to Fritz Perls (1893–1970), a former psychoanalytic psychotherapist and the founder of Gestalt therapy, "The idea of Gestalt therapy is to change paper people to real people" (Perls, 1973, p. 120). To Perls, "paper people" are out of touch with their true feelings and therefore are living "inauthentic lives." Like psychoanalysis, Gestalt therapy seeks to bring unconscious feelings into conscious awareness (Cole, 1994). Like person-centered therapy, Gestalt therapy tries to increase the client's emotional expressiveness. And like rational-emotive behavior therapy, Gestalt therapy might be confrontational in forcing clients to change maladaptive ways of thinking and behaving.

Despite its name, Gestalt therapy is not derived from Gestalt psychology (Henle, 1978), which is discussed in Chapter 1, except in stressing the need to achieve wholeness of the personality—meaning that one's emotions, language, and actions should be congruent with one another (Polster & Polster, 1993). Gestalt therapists insist that clients take responsibility for their own behavior, rather than blame other people or events for their problems, and that clients live in the here and now, rather than be concerned about events occurring at other places and times. Gestalt therapists also assume that people who are aware of their feelings can exert greater control over their reactions to events. The

Gestalt therapy

A type of humanistic therapy, developed by Fritz Perls, that encourages clients to become aware of their true feelings and to take responsibility for their own actions.

This transcript illustrates how the person-centered therapist (T) acts as a psychological mirror, reflecting back the feelings expressed in statements by the client (C). The client feels anxious about taking responsibility for her life. Notice how the therapist is less directive than the one in the transcript of rational-emotive therapy in Table 15.3.

C:	Um-hum. That's why I say . . . (*slowly and very thoughtfully*) well, with that sort of foundation, well, it's really up to me. I mean, it seems to be really apparent to me that I can't depend on someone else giving me an education. (*very softly*) I'll really have to get it myself.
T:	It really begins to come home—there's only one person that can educate you—a realization that perhaps nobody else can give you an education.
C:	Um-hum. (*long pause—while she sits thinking*) I have all the symptoms of fright (*laughs softly*).
T:	Fright: That this is a scary thing, is that what you mean?
C:	Um-hum. (*very long pause—obviously struggling with feelings in herself*)
T:	Do you want to say any more about what you mean by that? That it really does give you the symptoms of fright?
C:	(*laughs*) I, uh . . . I don't know whether I quite know. I mean . . . Well, it really seems like I'm cut loose (*pause*), and it seems that I'm very—I don't know—in a vulnerable position, but, I, uh, I brought this up and it, uh, somehow it almost came out without saying it. It seems to be . . . it's something I let out.
T:	Hardly a part of you.
C:	Well, I felt surprised.
T:	As though, "Well for goodness sake, did I say that?" (*both chuckle*).

Rogers, Carl R., *On Becoming a Person.* Copyright © 1961 by Houghton Mifflin Company. Reprinted by permission.

Gestalt therapist notes any signs that clients are not being brutally honest about their feelings, at times by observing clients' nonverbal communication—posture, gestures, facial expressions, and tone of voice. For example, a client who denies feeling anxious while tightly clenching his fists would be accused of lying about his emotions.

One way that Gestalt therapists help clients develop emotional awareness is through a variety of psychological exercises. In the *two-chair exercise,* the client alternately sits in one chair and then another, with each chair representing an aspect of herself, such as the critical-self "topdog" and the real-self "underdog" (Douglas, 1993). The client carries on a dialogue between the two aspects. The two-chair exercise has proved effective in relieving emotional distress (Greenberg & Dompierre, 1981) and in making important decisions (Clarke & Greenberg, 1986).

But Perls has been criticized for promoting self-centeredness and emotional callousness, as in his "Gestalt prayer" (Perls, 1972, p. 70):

▶ I do my thing and you do your thing. I am not in this world to live up to your expectations. And you are not in this world to live up to mine. You are you and I am I. And if by chance we find each other, it's beautiful. If not, then it can't be helped.

This outlook has been accused of endangering the fabric of society by promoting social aloofness, self-centeredness, and indifference to the well-being of others (Cadwallader, 1984). Moreover, there have been few experimental studies on the effectiveness of Gestalt therapy. In one of the few, prisoners who participated in it improved in their sense of personal responsibility more than prisoners who did not take part in it (Serok & Levi, 1993).

Existential Therapy: Addressing Major Issues in Living

Another kind of humanistic therapy, **existential therapy,** takes a more philosophical approach than either person-centered therapy or Gestalt therapy. Existential therapists assume that emotional and behavioral problems are symptoms of an inability to come to

▲ **Fritz Perls (1893–1970)**
Fritz Perls, the founder of Gestalt therapy, was a refugee from Nazi Germany. Loyal followers were attracted to his center at Esalen Institute in Big Sur, California, in the 1960s in the hope of becoming "authentic people." Perls was a charismatic person who thought as highly of himself as did his followers, claiming, "I believe I am the best therapist for any type of neurosis in the States, maybe in the world" (Prochaska, 1984, p. 128).

existential therapy
A type of humanistic therapy that helps the client overcome emotional or behavioral problems by dealing with major philosophical issues in life, including death, freedom, isolation, and meaning.

▲ **Victor Frankl**
"Life holds a potential meaning under any conditions, even the most miserable ones."

logotherapy
A form of existential therapy, developed by Victor Frankl, that helps the client find meaning in life.

grips with the ultimate issues of life (Halling & Nill, 1995). Irvin Yalom (1980), a leading existential therapist, points to four issues that each of us must face: the inevitability of *death*, our *responsibility* for our own choices, the *isolation* of each person from all others, and the need to find *meaning* in life. For example, a person who has not developed an adequate philosophy of death might anesthetize himself against facing this issue through excessive use of drugs, promiscuous sexual behavior, or working relentlessly without taking a day off. Existential therapy has been used to help victims of AIDS find meaning in their lives (Milton, 1994).

A form of existential therapy called **logotherapy** is especially concerned with helping clients find meaning in their lives. Victor Frankl, the psychiatrist who created logotherapy, used it successfully during World War II in one of the most stressful situations imaginable—Nazi concentration camps. Frankl prevented many of his fellow inmates from collapsing emotionally by helping them find meaning in their suffering, such as surviving to bear witness and gain justice (Gerwood, 1994). He also convinced his fellow inmates that meaning could be found in maintaining their human dignity no matter what was done to them (Frankl, 1961).

Today, logotherapists continue to believe that one of the most important goals of their practice is to help their clients find meaning in their lives. For example, suppose that a woman who finds meaning in her life only through her work loses her job. She might become particularly vulnerable to anxiety or depression. In such a case, the logotherapist would try to help her find new meaning in her life apart from the kind of work she does (Greenlee, 1990). Logotherapy has been used to help parents deal with the death of a child (Berti & Berti, 1994) and to help schoolchildren deal with severe personal problems (Wilson, 1994). Unfortunately, most research on logotherapy comes from clinical case studies, making the role of logotherapy in reports of client improvement impossible to determine.

STAYING ON TRACK: *The Humanistic Orientation*

1. What are the basic characteristics of client-centered therapy?
2. What are the basic issues in existential therapy?

THE SOCIAL-RELATIONS ORIENTATION: TRYING TO IMPROVE INTERPERSONAL RELATIONS

The therapeutic orientations that have been discussed so far involve a therapist and a client. In contrast, the *social-relations orientation* assumes that, because many psychological problems involve interpersonal relationships, additional people must be brought into the therapy process.

Group Therapy: Therapy Involving More Than One Client

In 1905 Joseph Pratt, a Boston physician, found that his tuberculosis patients gained relief from emotional distress by meeting in groups to discuss their feelings. This marked the beginning of group therapy (Allen, 1990). But group therapy did not become an important form of therapy until World War II, when a limited number of therapists found themselves faced with more people in need of therapy than they could see individually (Hersen, Kazdin, & Bellack, 1983). Because group therapy allows a therapist to see more people (typically six to twelve in a group) in less time, more people can receive help at less cost per person. Group therapy provides participants with a range of role models, encouragement from others with similar problems, feedback about their own behavior, assurance that their problems are not unique, and the opportunity to try out new behaviors. Group therapy has been used to improve the emotional well-being of people dealing with things as varied as alcoholism (Solomon, 1982), cancer (Harman, 1991), and bereavement (Zimpfer, 1991).

Psychoanalytic Group Therapies

Group therapies derived from psychoanalysis emphasize insight and emotional catharsis. In 1910 Jacob Moreno (1892–1974), a Romanian psychiatrist, introduced the psychoanalytic group therapy called *psychodrama*, and in 1931 he coined the term *group therapy*. **Psychodrama** aims at achieving insight and catharsis through acting out real-life situations, which can lead to changes in thought, emotion, and behavior. The therapist functions as a director, making observations and offering suggestions. One technique of psychodrama is *role reversal*, in which a participant plays the role of a family member or other important person. This provides insight into the other person's motives and empathy for that person's feelings. Psychodrama has been used to improve the emotional adjustment of prison inmates (Stallone, 1993) and adolescents (Ozbay et al., 1993). Psychodrama is about as effective as other kinds of group therapy (Garfield, 1983).

A more recent form of group therapy inspired by psychoanalysis is **transactional analysis (TA),** popularized in the 1960s by psychiatrist Eric Berne (1910–1970) in his best-selling book *Games People Play* (1964). Berne claimed that we act according to one of three roles: child, parent, or adult. These resemble the Freudian personality structures of id, superego, and ego, respectively. The *child*, like the id, acts impulsively and demands immediate gratification. The *parent*, like the superego, is authoritarian and guides moral behavior. And the *adult*, like the ego, promotes rational and responsible behavior.

Each role is adaptive in certain situations and maladaptive in others. For example, acting childish is appropriate at parties but not at job interviews. According to Berne, our relationships involve *transactions*—social interactions between these roles. *Complementary transactions*, in which both individuals act according to the same role, are usually best. *Crossed transactions*, as when one person acts as a child and the other acts as an adult, are maladaptive. Figure 15.4 presents examples of complementary and crossed transactions.

The goal of TA is to analyze transactions between group members. These are the "games" that people play, which reflect our *life scripts*—the pervasive themes that we follow in our social relations. For example, a person might have a life script that supports his feelings of worthlessness and continually play games that provoke responses from others that support that script. TA has been used to enhance self-esteem (Wissink, 1994), help battered women (Gard, 1993), and treat borderline personality disorder (Sterrenberg & Thunnissen, 1995).

Behavioral Group Therapies

Psychologists who favor behavioral group therapies assume that changes in overt behavior will bring relief of emotional distress. A popular form of behavioral group therapy, also used in individual therapy, is **social-skills training** (Greca, 1993). Its goal is to improve social relationships by enhancing social skills, such as cultivating friendships or carrying on conversations. Participants are encouraged to rehearse new behaviors in the group setting. Members of the group may model more effective behaviors. And shaping (see Chapter 7) may be used to gradually develop more effective behaviors.

Social-skills training has helped people with mental retardation improve their social competence (Margalit, 1995), alcoholic people cope better with stress (Monti, Gulliver, & Myers, 1994), and schizophrenic people improve their functioning in everyday life (Smith, Bellack, & Liberman, 1996). A major review of research on the use of social skills training with socially isolated children found that it significantly improved their social relations (Erwin, 1994).

A form of social-skills training called **assertiveness training** (Salter, 1949) helps people learn to express their feelings constructively in social situations. Many people experience poor social relations because they are unassertive. They are unable to ask for favors, to say no to requests, or to complain about poor service. By learning to express their feelings, formerly unassertive people relieve their anxiety and have more-rewarding social relations.

Members of assertiveness-training groups try out assertive behaviors in the group situation. The therapist typically models assertive behaviors, aggressive behaviors, and passive behaviors to permit group members to distinguish between them. *Assertive* people

▲ **Eric Berne (1910–1970)**
"At any given moment each individual in a social aggregation will exhibit a Parental, Adult, or Child ego state and . . . individuals can shift with varying degrees of readiness from one ego state to another."

Transactional Analysis
According to Eric Berne (1964), our social relationships involve transactions in which we act as parent, adult, or child. In a complementary transaction, two persons act according to the same role. In a crossed transaction, two persons act according to different roles.

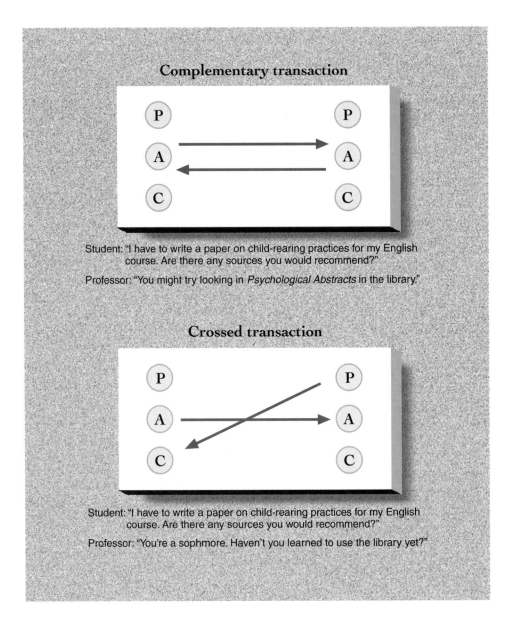

Complementary transaction

Student: "I have to write a paper on child-rearing practices for my English course. Are there any sources you would recommend?"

Professor: "You might try looking in *Psychological Abstracts* in the library."

Crossed transaction

Student: "I have to write a paper on child-rearing practices for my English course. Are there any sources you would recommend?"

Professor: "You're a sophomore. Haven't you learned to use the library yet?"

▲ **Encounter Groups**
Encounter group therapy promotes the expression and acceptance of strong emotions, whether positive or negative. The growth of encounter groups in the 1960s prompted Carl Rogers to claim: "The Encounter Group is perhaps the most significant social invention of this century. The demand for it is utterly beyond belief. It is one of the most rapidly growing social phenomena in the United States. It has permeated industry, is coming into education, is reaching families, professionals in the helping fields, and many other individuals" (Rogers, 1968, p. 3).

express their feelings directly and constructively. *Aggressive* people express their feelings directly but with a hostile edge. And *passive* people express their feelings indirectly, as in pouting.

One assertiveness-training technique is the *broken record,* in which those who have trouble saying "no" practice repeating brief statements that reject requests. The therapist and group members critique each participant's attempts at assertive behaviors. Assertiveness training has improved the communication skills and self-esteem of people as diverse as nurses in Taiwan (Lee & Crockett, 1994) and adults with physical disabilities (Glueckauf & Quittner, 1992).

Humanistic Group Therapies

The humanistic group therapies encourage awareness and acceptance of emotional experiences. In the late 1940s, studies of small-group relationships carried out at the National Training Laboratories in Bethel, Maine, led to the development of sensitivity-training groups. The early sensitivity groups, called *training groups* (or *T-groups*), helped business people improve their relationships with workers and colleagues. Today sensitivity groups are also popular with the clergy, police, educators, and other professionals.

Sensitivity groups typically have twelve to twenty members. Participants explore their own feelings and become aware of how their actions affect the feelings of others. They learn to rely on reason and cooperation instead of coercion and manipulation. But a study of the effectiveness of sensitivity groups found that social-skills training was superior to sensitivity training in improving social skills and reducing social anxiety (Monti et al., 1980). A review of research on sensitivity training found that larger groups and more frequent meetings were associated with greater effectiveness (Faith, Wong, & Carpenter, 1995).

A relative of sensitivity training is the **encounter group,** an offshoot of the *human potential movement* that arose in the 1950s and declined in the early 1970s (Finkelstein, Wenegrat, & Yalom, 1982). Encounter groups may involve people who have had little or no prior contact with one another. The groups meet for hours or days. Compared with sensitivity groups, encounter groups are more concerned with the open expression of emotions than with improving social relationships. Encounter groups promote crying, cursing, and verbal abuse. They might also encourage physical touching as a means of overcoming social isolation. Encounter groups have been used to resolve conflicts among college faculty members (Herrick, Kvale, & Goodykoontz, 1991) and to reduce anxiety among American college students in a study-abroad program in Austria (Rabinowitz, 1994).

But studies of encounter groups indicate that their slight beneficial effects can be temporary (Kilmann & Sotile, 1976) and that they might attract people ill-suited for intense emotional confrontations. Some participants are even emotionally harmed by their experiences (Hartley, Roback, & Abramowitz, 1976). This is especially true of encounter groups in which the leader tries to break down individual selves, hoping to cause the participants to subject themselves to the group—similar to initiations into cults (Cushman, 1989). The potential danger of encounter group participation is made even greater by the fact that people who join the groups tend to be more distressed than their peers who do not (Klar et al., 1990).

The encounter group movement did lead to the emergence of typically less confrontational *self-help groups* for drug abusers, phobia sufferers, and others with specific shared problems. The groups are conducted by people who have experienced those problems. For example, self-help groups for divorced persons would be run by divorced people (Byrne, 1990).

Family Therapy: Improving Social Interactions Within Families

Group therapy usually brings together unrelated people; **family therapy** brings together members of the same family. The basic assumption of family therapy is that a family member with problems related to her or his family life cannot be treated apart from the family. The main goals of family therapy are the constructive expression of feelings and the establishment of rules that family members agree to follow. In family therapy, one of the family members—known as the *identified patient*—is generally assumed to bear the brunt of the family's problems. Typically, the family is brought together for family therapy after that person has entered individual psychotherapy. Family therapy tries to improve communications and relationships among family members, who learn to provide feedback and to accept feedback from each other. The therapist helps family members establish an atmosphere in which no individual is blamed for all of the family's problems.

Family therapists, such as the late Virginia Satir, who favor a *systems approach* might have family members draw diagrams of their relationships and discuss how certain of the relationships are maladaptive (Satir, Bitter, & Krestensen, 1988). Perhaps the family is too child-oriented, or perhaps a parent and child are allied against the other parent. The goal of the therapist is to have the family replace these maladaptive relationships with more-effective ones.

A popular form of family therapy is *structural family therapy,* developed by Salvadore Minuchin (1974). Minuchin emphasizes the emotional "boundaries" between family members. Boundaries that are too rigid create inadequate emotional contact between family members, and boundaries that are too diffuse create intrusive familiarity between family members. What is needed is to establish a flexible family that can shift

encounter group
A derivative of humanistic group therapy in which group members learn to be themselves by openly expressing their true feelings to one another.

▲ **Family Therapy**
In family therapy, family members gain insight into their maladaptive patterns of interaction and learn to change them into healthier ones.

family therapy
A form of group therapy that encourages the constructive expression of feelings and the establishment of rules that family members agree to follow.

▲ **Virginia Satir (1916–1988)**
"Any individual's behavior is a response to the complex set of regular and predictable 'rules' governing his family group, though these rules may not be consciously known to him or the family."

boundaries when the circumstances call for it (Yaccarino, 1993). Family therapy involving parents and adolescents, in particular, aims at achieving a balance between enmeshment and disengagement between parent and child (Perosa & Perosa, 1993).

Family therapy is about as effective as individual therapy. A review of family therapy studies found that people who have been in family therapy are better off than 76 percent of those who have received no treatment or an alternative treatment other than individual therapy (Markus, Lange, & Pettigrew, 1990).

One of the many offshoots of family therapy is *marital therapy*, which tries to improve relationships between married people. Because many committed couples are not married, marital therapy has been joined by *couples therapy*. Though there are several approaches to these kind of therapies, reviews of the research literature find that the major approaches are equally effective in both marital therapy (Dunn & Schwebel, 1995) and couples therapy (Boddington & Lavender, 1995) .

STAYING ON TRACK: *The Social-Relations Orientation*

1. What are the basic assumptions and techniques of transactional analysis?
2. What is the goal of Minuchin's structural family therapy?

THE BIOPSYCHOLOGICAL ORIENTATION: ALTERING BRAIN ACTIVITY TO TREAT PSYCHOLOGICAL DISORDERS

Though Sigmund Freud practiced psychoanalysis, he predicted that, as science progressed, therapies for psychological disorders would become more and more biological (Trotter, 1981). During the past few decades, the *biopsychological orientation* has, indeed, become an important approach to therapy. It is based on the assumption that psychological disorders are associated with brain dysfunctions and consequently will respond to treatments that alter brain activity. Because they involve medical procedures, biopsychological treatments can be offered only by psychiatrists and other physicians. The biopsychological treatments include *psychosurgery, electroconvulsive therapy,* and *drug therapy.*

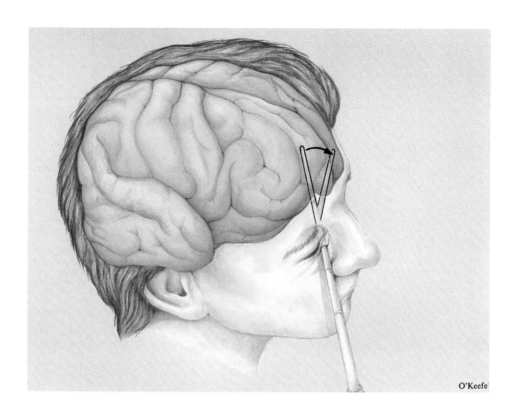

Transorbital Leucotomy
In the form of psychosurgery called transorbital leucotomy, a surgeon uses a mallet to drive a surgical pick through the thin bone of the eye socket into the brain. The surgeon then levers the pick back and forth, severing portions of the frontal lobes from the rest of the brain.

O'Keefe

Psychosurgery: Using Brain Surgery to Affect Behavior

While attending a professional meeting in 1935, Portuguese neurologist Egas Moniz was impressed by a report that agitated chimpanzees became calmer after undergoing brain surgery that separated their frontal lobes from the rest of their brain. Moniz wondered whether such **psychosurgery** might benefit agitated mental patients. Moniz convinced neurosurgeon Almeida Lima to perform a *prefrontal leucotomy* (also known as a *prefrontal lobotomy*) on anesthetized patients. Lima drilled holes in the patient's temples, inserted a scalpel through the holes, and cut away portions of the frontal lobes. Moniz reported many successes in calming agitated patients (Moniz, 1937/1994). As a result, he won a Nobel Prize in 1949 for inventing psychosurgery, which was considered a humane alternative to the common practice of locking agitated patients in padded rooms or restraining them in straitjackets (Valenstein, 1980).

Psychosurgery was introduced to the United States in 1936 by neurosurgeon Walter Freeman and psychiatrist James Watts. They favored a technique called *transorbital leucotomy* (see Figure 15.5). The patient's eyesocket (the *orbit*) is anesthetized (the brain itself is insensitive to pain), and a mallet is used to drive a surgical pick into the frontal lobe. The pick is then levered back and forth to separate portions of the lobe from the rest of the brain.

By 1979, psychosurgery had been performed on about 35,000 mental patients in the United States. But the use of psychosurgery declined markedly. One reason was its unpredictable effects (Swayze, 1995)—some patients improved, others became apathetic, still others became violent, and a small percentage died. A second reason for its decline was the advent in the 1950s and 1960s of drug therapies that provided safer, more effective, and more humane treatment (Weinberger, Goldberg, & Tamminga, 1995). And a third reason was public opposition to what seemed to be a barbaric means of behavior control.

Today, psychosurgery is rarely used in the United States; when it is used, it more often involves the use of electrodes inserted into the brain's limbic system. A direct current is sent through the electrodes, heating and thereby destroying small amounts of tissue in precise areas of that brain region. This technique has achieved some success in treating cases of obsessive-compulsive disorder that have not responded to other treatments (Baer et al., 1995).

psychosurgery

The treatment of psychological disorders by destroying brain tissue.

Electroconvulsive Therapy
In electroconvulsive therapy, the patient receives a series of treatments in which a brief electric current is passed through the brain, inducing a brain seizure that relieves the person's depression through mechanisms that are still unclear.

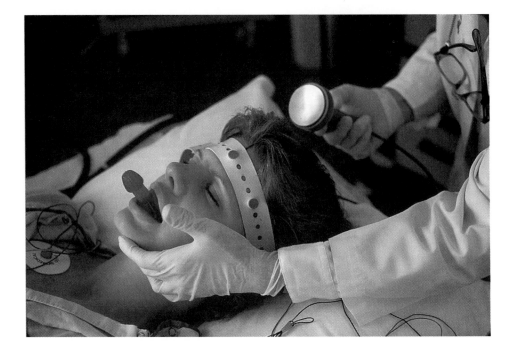

electroconvulsive therapy (ECT)
A biomedical therapy that uses brief electric currents to induce brain seizures in victims of major depression.

Electroconvulsive Therapy: Inducing Brain Seizures to Relieve Severe Depression

Modern "shock therapy" began in 1935 with almost simultaneous reports of its use by the Hungarian psychiatrist Ladislas von Meduna and the Austrian physician Manfred Sakel (Fink, 1984). Sakel found that schizophrenic patients showed improvement following convulsions induced by insulin overdoses. Von Meduna noted that schizophrenia and epilepsy rarely occurred in the same person. He inferred that the induction of brain seizures might relieve the symptoms of schizophrenia. Von Meduna used the drug camphor to induce seizures, but he found that, though the treatments relieved some patients' symptoms, they harmed or even killed other patients.

In 1938, on a visit to a slaughterhouse, Italian psychiatrist Ugo Cerletti watched pigs being rendered unconscious by electric shocks. Cerletti reasoned that electric shock might be a safe alternative to drug-induced shock therapy in calming agitated schizophrenic patients. This inspired Cerletti and his fellow psychiatrist Lucio Bini to introduce **electroconvulsive therapy (ECT)** (Endler, 1988). ECT uses a brief electrical current to induce brain seizures. Though ECT was originally used for treating agitated patients, it proved more successful in elevating the mood of severely depressed patients who had failed to respond to drug therapy.

As shown in Figure 15.6, a psychiatrist administers ECT by attaching electrodes to one or both temples of a patient who is under general anesthesia and who has been given a muscle relaxant. The muscle relaxant prevents injuries that might otherwise be caused by violent contractions of the muscles. A burst of electricity of 70 to 150 volts is passed through the brain for about half a second. This induces a brain seizure, which is followed by a period of unconsciousness lasting up to 30 minutes. The patient typically receives three treatments a week for several weeks.

A major published review of the research literature found that it is unclear whether ECT or antidepressant drugs is best in the treatment of major depression (Piper, 1993). But because ECT produces improvement more rapidly than antidepressant drugs, which can take several weeks, it is the treatment of choice for depressed people in imminent danger of committing suicide (Persad, 1990). And a study found that a maintenance program of ECT was effective in significantly reducing the likelihood of rehospitalization in patients who were unresponsive to other treatments (Schwarz, Loewenstein, & Isenberg, 1995).

But ECT's mechanism of action is unclear. For example, its antidepressant effect is unrelated to its induction of seizures (Sackeim, 1994). Because depression is associated with low levels of norepinephrine, a logical, though unconfirmed, explanation is that ECT stimulates an increase in the level of norepinephrine in the brain (Masserano, Takimoto, & Weiner, 1981). Other studies, using animals, have found that ECT might lift depression by raising the level of endorphins in the brain (Alexopoulos et al., 1983). This has yet to be demonstrated in human beings (Jackson & Nutt, 1990).

Despite the effectiveness of ECT in relieving major depression, there has been controversy about its safety and effectiveness. In the past, the violence of the convulsions induced by ECT often broke bones and tore muscles. Today, muscle relaxants prevent such damage. But ECT still causes *retrograde amnesia*—the forgetting of events that occurred from minutes to days prior to the treatment. In 1982 the potential side effects of ECT and fears that ECT could be used to control people against their will led Berkeley, California, to ban its use. But citizens who argued that this violated the rights of those who might benefit from ECT convinced a California superior court judge to remove the ban (Cunningham, 1983). The debate about the desirability of using ECT is as much emotional and political as it is scientific.

Drug Therapy: Regulating Brain Chemistry to Modify Emotion and Behavior

Since its introduction in the 1950s, drug therapy has become the most widely used form of biomedical therapy. It has been responsible for freeing patients from restraints and padded rooms and permitting many more to live outside of mental hospitals. Some psychological disorders are associated with abnormal levels of neurotransmitters in the brain (see Chapter 14). Drug therapies generally work by restoring neurotransmitter activity to more normal levels. But a common criticism of drug therapies is that they may relieve symptoms without changing the person's ability to adjust to everyday stressors. This means that concurrent psychotherapy is desirable to help clients learn more adaptive ways of thinking and behaving. Of course, for many people the relief of their emotional suffering is sufficient to demonstrate a drug's effectiveness. The following discussion uses well-known brand names for drugs, with their generic names in parentheses.

Antianxiety Drugs

Because of their calming effect, the **antianxiety drugs** were originally called *tranquilizers*. Today the most widely prescribed are the *benzodiazepines*, such as Xanax (alprazolam), Valium (diazepam), and Librium (chlordiazepam). In fact, the prevalence of anxiety disorders has made the antianxiety drugs the most widely prescribed psychoactive drugs. Antianxiety drugs are effective in treating panic disorder. In a double-blind study, subjects received either Xanax or a placebo. Those who received Xanax showed a significantly greater reduction in their panic attacks than did those who received a placebo (Alexander, 1993). The benzodiazepines work by stimulating special receptors in the brain that enhance the effects of the neurotransmitter GABA (Greenblatt, Shader, & Abernethy, 1983), which inhibits brain activity. The benzodiazepines can also produce side effects, including drowsiness, depression, and dependence.

antianxiety drugs
Psychoactive drugs, commonly known as minor tranquilizers, that are used to treat anxiety disorders.

Antidepressant Drugs

The first **antidepressant drugs** were the MAO *inhibitors*, such as Nardil. Originally used to treat tuberculosis, they were prescribed as antidepressants after physicians noted that they induced euphoria in tuberculosis patients. The MAO inhibitors work by blocking enzymes that normally break down the neurotransmitters serotonin and norepinephrine. This increases the levels of those neurotransmitters in the brain, elevating the patient's mood.

But the MAO inhibitors fell into disfavor because they can cause dangerously high blood pressure in patients who eat foods (such as cheeses) or drink beverages (such as beer) that contain the amino acid tyramine. The MAO inhibitors have largely been replaced by the

antidepressant drugs
Psychoactive drugs that are used to treat major depression.

tricyclic antidepressants, such as Elavil (amitriptyline), Tofranil (imipramine), and Anafranil (clomipramine). The tricyclics increase the levels of serotonin and norepinephrine in the brain by preventing their re-uptake by brain neurons that release them. Though the tricyclics are effective in treating depression (Perry, 1996), they take 2 to 4 weeks to have an effect. This means that suicidal patients treated with these antidepressants must be watched carefully during that period.

More recently, drugs known as *serotonin re-uptake inhibitors* have been added to the arsenal of antidepressants. These drugs relieve depression by preventing the re-uptake of serotonin by neurons that release it—thus elevating the level of serotonin in the brain. Among the most popular of these drugs are Zoloft (sertraline), Paxil (paroxetine), and most notably Prozac (fluoxetine). Prozac was popularized in the media and in best-selling books as a wonder drug for the treatment of depression. Though there were early reports that Prozac sometimes increased suicidal thinking and, perhaps, suicidal behavior (Teicher, Glod, & Cole, 1990), there is little scientific evidence to support those claims (Crundell, 1993). Though antidepressant drugs are effective, psychotherapy is usually superior to them in producing lasting relief from depression (Steinbrueck, Maxwell, & Howard, 1983).

Antimania Drugs

In the 1940s, Australian physician John Cade observed that the chemical lithium calmed agitated guinea pigs. Contrary to his belief that lithium worked by affecting their brains, it apparently worked by making them feel sick. Cade tried lithium on human patients and found that it calmed those suffering from mania—apparently, in those cases, because of its effect on the brain. Psychiatrists now prescribe the **antimania drug** *lithium carbonate* to prevent the extreme mood swings of bipolar disorder (Keck & McElroy, 1993). It is important for patients taking this drug to stay on it; of those who discontinue its use, 50 percent relapse within 3 months (Baker, 1994). Psychiatrists must also vigilantly monitor patients taking lithium because it can produce dangerous side effects, including seizures, brain damage, and irregular heart rhythms (Honchar, Olney, & Sherman, 1983).

Antipsychotic Drugs

For centuries, physicians in India prescribed the snakeroot plant for calming agitated patients. Beginning in the 1940s, a chemical derivative of the plant, *reserpine,* was used to reduce symptoms of mania and schizophrenia. But reserpine fell into disfavor because of its tendency to cause depression and low blood pressure. The 1950s saw the development of safer **antipsychotic drugs** called *phenothiazines,* such as Thorazine (chlorpromazine), for treating people with schizophrenia. French physicians had noted that the drug, used to sedate patients before surgery, calmed psychotic patients.

The phenothiazines relieve the positive symptoms of schizophrenia, but not the negative ones (Killian et al., 1984). Positive symptoms include hallucinations, disordered thinking, and bizarre behavior, while negative symptoms include emotional apathy and social withdrawal (see Chapter 14). The phenothiazines work by blocking brain receptor sites for the neurotransmitter dopamine (Sternberg et al., 1982). Unfortunately, long-term use of antipsychotic drugs can cause the bizarre motor side effects that characterize *tardive dyskinesia,* which include grimacing, lip smacking, and limb flailing (Latimer, 1995). A newer antipsychotic drug, Clozaril (clozapine), produces fewer tardive dyskinesia symptoms while effectively treating many cases of schizophrenia that have not responded well to the phenothiazines (Meltzer, 1995).

STAYING ON TRACK: *The Biopsychological Orientation*

1. Why has the use of ECT been controversial?
2. How do the tricyclic antidepressants produce their results?

antimania drugs
Psychoactive drugs, most notably lithium carbonate, that are used to treat a bipolar disorder.

antipsychotic drugs
Psychoactive drugs, commonly known as major tranquilizers, that are used to treat schizophrenia.

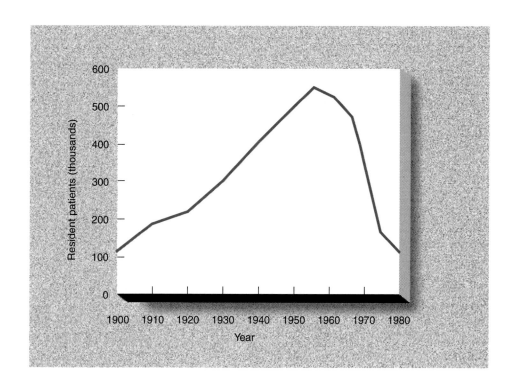

COMMUNITY MENTAL HEALTH: COMMUNITY APPROACHES TO PREVENTING PSYCHOLOGICAL DISORDERS

As discussed earlier, for most of the nineteenth and twentieth centuries, state mental hospitals served as the primary sites of treatment for people with serious psychological disorders. But since the 1950s there has been a movement toward **deinstitutionalization,** which promotes the treatment of people in community settings instead of in mental hospitals. As shown in Figure 15.7, the number of patients in mental hospitals declined from a high of 559,000 in 1955 to fewer than 140,000 in the early 1980s (Bassuk, 1984).

What accounts for this trend? First, new drug treatments made it more feasible for mental patients to function in the outside world. Second, mental hospitals had become underfunded, understaffed, and overcrowded; many were little more than human warehouses, full of patients wasting away with no hope of improvement. Community-based treatment seemed to be a cheaper, superior alternative. Third, increasing concern for the legal rights of mental patients made it more difficult to have people committed to mental hospitals and to keep them there. And fourth, the Community Mental Health Centers Act of 1963, sponsored by President John F. Kennedy, mandated the establishment of federally funded mental health centers in every community in the United States. These centers were to provide services to prevent and treat psychological disorders, further reducing the need for mental hospitals.

Despite its noble intentions, deinstitutionalization has worked better in theory than in practice (Lamb, 1993). Communities too often provide inadequate aftercare for discharged mental patients (Dennis et al., 1991). Even when funding is available for treatment facilities, such as halfway houses, homeowners often oppose the placement of such facilities in their neighborhoods (Turkington, 1984). As a consequence, former mental hospital patients who lack family support might have little choice but to live on the street. About one third of the homeless people on the streets of major cities are former residents of mental hospitals (Slagg et al., 1994). And regardless of whether they are former residents of mental hospitals, many homeless people have symptoms of psychological

deinstitutionalization

The movement toward treating people with psychological disorders in community settings instead of mental hospitals.

disorders. Of course, their disorders might be either causes or consequences of their home-lessness (Lemere, 1993). Some critics, frustrated by the inadequacy of services for former mental hospital patients, urge that deinstitutionalization be more limited, reasoning that people would be better off confined in mental hospitals than living in cardboard boxes (Thomas, 1981).

The potential benefits of adequate support for deinstitutionalization are evident in the results of a study that compared community care for former mental hospital patients in the comparable cities of Portland, Oregon, and Vancouver, British Columbia. At the time of the study, Portland provided few community mental health services, while Vancouver provided many private and public services. One year after their discharge, formerly hospitalized schizophrenics in Vancouver were less likely than those in Portland to have been readmitted and more likely to be employed and to report a greater sense of psychological well-being. Because the two groups were initially equivalent, the greater progress of the Vancouver group was attributed to community mental health services rather than to pre-existing differences between the groups (Beiser et al., 1985).

Community mental health centers provide a variety of services. Outpatient counseling permits people to receive therapy while living and working in the community. Short-term inpatient treatment allows a person experiencing major depression to spend a brief period of time in a local center, receiving drug therapy, counseling, and practical assistance, instead of being committed to a state hospital possibly hours from home. The 24-hour emergency care services might include a suicide hotline, a refuge for battered wives, and a shelter for runaways. Consultation and education are provided to courts, police, and public welfare agencies; for example, a trained counselor might present a program on drug-abuse prevention to schoolchildren. Though community mental health centers provide valuable services, they have failed to completely fulfill their original intent, because they are taxed beyond their resources by increasing social problems, such as family disintegration, drug and alcohol abuse, and urban violence (Ray & Finley, 1994).

Community mental health centers have three main goals in the prevention of psychological disorders. *Primary prevention* helps prevent psychological disorders by fostering social support systems, eliminating sources of stress, and strengthening individuals' ability to deal with stressors (Dalton, Elias, & Beck, 1994). This might be promoted, for example, by reducing unemployment and making low-cost housing available. Canada has instituted a community-based primary prevention program called "Better Beginnings, Better Futures" to prevent physical, cognitive, emotional, and behavioral problems in children from economically disadvantaged families (Peters, 1994).

Secondary prevention provides early treatment, sometimes through *crisis intervention,* for people at immediate risk of developing psychological disorders. Community mental health centers often go into action following disasters in which people are killed or communities are ravaged. Secondary prevention has been used in a special program in England to prevent suicide by adolescents who have made prior attempts (Cotgrove et al., 1995).

Tertiary prevention helps keep people who have full-blown psychological disorders from getting worse or having relapses after successful treatment. Tertiary prevention has been used in a Canadian program to prevent abusive parents from continuing to abuse their children. The program involves home visits by specially trained nurses who provide emotional support, education in proper child-rearing practices, and assistance in helping parents obtain help from other human services (MacMillan & Thomas, 1993). The main community approaches to tertiary prevention include community residences, or *halfway houses,* that provide homelike, structured environments in which former mental hospital patients readjust to independent living.

Consider primary, secondary, and tertiary prevention of anorexia nervosa (see Chapter 11) on a college campus: Primary prevention would be aimed at those at risk in the college community. Secondary prevention would provide treatment for those who have developed symptoms. And tertiary prevention would involve the treatment of advanced cases and the prevention of relapses (Crisp, 1986). An ambitious program in Norway uses primary, secondary, and tertiary prevention to reduce the prevalence of eating disorders among youths (Greskoo & Karlsen, 1994).

▲ **The Crisis Intervention Center**
The community mental-health system is aided by crisis intervention centers. These centers handle emergencies such as rape cases, physical abuse, suicide threats, or other problems that require immediate help. This photograph shows an emergency telephone for use by those who contemplate jumping from a bridge that has been the site of many suicides.

1. What brought about the deinstitutionalization movement?
2 How do community mental health centers provide primary prevention?

THE RIGHTS OF THE THERAPY CLIENT

Does a resident of a mental hospital have the right to refuse treatment? Does a resident of a mental hospital have the right to receive treatment? Is what a client reveals to a therapist privileged information? These questions have generated heated debate during the past three decades.

The Rights of Hospitalized Patients: The Right to Refuse Treatment and the Right to Receive Treatment

In the United States, people who are committed to mental hospitals lose many of their rights, including their rights to vote, marry, divorce, and sign contracts. Revelations about past psychiatric practices in the former Soviet Union show the extent to which the commitment process can be abused. Soviet psychiatrists used diagnoses such as "reformist delusions" and "schizophrenia with religious delirium" to commit political or religious dissidents to mental hospitals (Faraone, 1982).

Ideally, only people who are judged to be dangerous to themselves or others can be involuntarily committed to mental hospitals. The need to demonstrate that people are dangerous before they can be committed was formalized by the United States Supreme Court in 1979 in *Addington v. Texas* (Hays, 1989). Commitment typically requires that two psychiatrists document that the person is dangerous. During the commitment process, the person has the right to a lawyer, to call witnesses, and to a hearing or a jury trial. The final decision on commitment is made by a judge or jury, not a psychiatrist.

Court decisions have also ruled that people committed to mental hospitals have a right to receive treatment. In 1975, in *Donaldson v. O'Connor,* the U.S. Supreme Court ruled that mental patients have a right to more than custodial care. If they are not given treatment, are not dangerous, and can survive in the community, they must be released. The case was brought by Kenneth Donaldson, who had been confined for 15 years in a Florida mental hospital without treatment. But the court ruling in his case might be difficult to put into practice in particular cases. For example, it is difficult to predict whether a person will be dangerous if released from custodial care (Bernard, 1977). Legal decisions such as this contributed to the deinstitutionalization movement by making it more difficult to keep mental patients hospitalized against their will.

In 1983, in *Rogers v. Commissioner of Mental Health*, the Massachusetts Supreme Court ruled that mental patients also have a right to *refuse* treatment, unless a court judges them to be incompetent to make their own decisions (Hermann, 1990). A person committed to a mental hospital is not automatically considered incompetent. When the Rogers case was in court, critics claimed that such a ruling would merely give mental patients the right to "rot with their rights on" (Appelbaum & Gutheil, 1980). In reality, the decision appears to have had little influence. A Massachusetts study found that few cases of involuntary treatment were reviewed in court, and the ones that were reviewed were usually decided in favor of those who had prescribed treatment for a patient who had refused it (Veliz & James, 1987). Recent legal cases have expanded the right to refuse treatment in Canada as well (Gratzer & Matas, 1994).

The Right to Confidentiality: The Duty to Warn

But what of the rights of individuals receiving therapy? One of the most important is the right to confidentiality. In general, therapists are ethically, but not always legally, bound to keep confidential the information revealed by their clients. The extent to which this information is privileged varies from state to state. There are also fears, based on the movement to control costs, that third-party payers might demand more and more information that has traditionally been confidential (Corcoran & Winsalde, 1994).

In recent decades, the most significant legal decision concerning confidentiality was the *Tarasoff* decision, a ruling by the California Supreme Court that a therapist who believes that a client might harm a particular person must protect or warn that person. The ruling came in the case of Prosenjit Poddar, who murdered his former girlfriend, Tatiana Tarasoff. In 1969 Poddar had informed his therapist at the counseling center of the University of California at Berkeley that he intended to kill Tarasoff. The therapist reported the threat to the campus police, who ordered Poddar to stay away from Tarasoff. Two months later Poddar murdered her, leading her parents to sue the therapist, the police, and the university. In 1976 the court ruled in favor of the parents; the therapist should have directly warned Tarasoff about Poddar's threat (Mangalmurti, 1994). The duty to warn has also become an issue in other countries, including Canada (Birch, 1992) and Australia (Milne, 1995).

This decision upholding the *duty to warn* influenced similar decisions in other states and has provoked concern among therapists for several reasons. First, no therapist can reliably predict whether a threat made by a client is a serious one (Rubin & Mills, 1983). If a student in a moment of anger about an unfair exam says to a therapist, "I could just *kill* my psychology professor," should the therapist immediately warn the professor?

Second, it can be impractical to warn potential victims. In one case, a client threatened to kill "rich people." He then murdered a wealthy couple. Considering the duty to warn, this prompted a therapist to ask whether a sign should have been posted reading, "All rich people watch out!" (Fisher, 1985). Moreover, the spread of AIDS has exacerbated the conflict between confidentiality and the duty to warn. Should a therapist warn the potential sex partners of clients who have the AIDS virus (Stanard & Hazler, 1995)? Critics of the duty to warn also wonder why therapists should be required to reveal confidential information when the same legal jurisdiction might not require laypersons to do so (Wallace, 1988).

Third, the duty to warn might keep people from discussing hostile feelings or even seeking therapy at all (Roback & Shelton, 1995). This possibility was the basis of a 1988 ruling by the Court of Appeals in North Carolina in the case of *Currie v. United States*. The court ruled that psychiatrists did not have a duty to commit people to mental hospitals for threatening acts of violence. The case concerned a 1982 murder in which a man, who was under the care of Veterans Administration psychiatrists, shot a fellow IBM employee after making threats against IBM. The victim's relatives sued, claiming that the psychiatrists should have committed the man after he made threats against IBM. The court ruled that such a duty would prevent psychiatrists and clients from discussing hostile feelings, perhaps *increasing* the probability of violence (Bales, 1988). The implications of the *Tarasoff* decision continue to perplex therapists, who must balance the need to serve their clients while protecting themselves from potential lawsuits if third parties are harmed by them (Monahan, 1993).

STAYING ON TRACK: *The Rights of the Therapy Client*

1. What are the possible ramifications of the right to refuse treatment and the right to receive treatment?
2. Why has the *Tarasoff* decision been controversial?

SELECTING A THERAPIST

At times in your life, you or someone you know might face psychological problems that require more than friendly advice. When personal problems disrupt your social, academic, or vocational life, or when you experience severe and prolonged emotional distress, you might be wise to seek the help of a therapist. You could receive therapy from a psychologist, a psychiatrist, or a variety of other kinds of therapists (see Table 15.5).

Clinical Psychologist	A clinical psychologist has earned a doctoral degree in clinical psychology, including training in both research and clinical skills, and has served a one-year clinical internship. Clinical psychologists typically work in private practice, counseling centers, or mental hospitals.
Counseling Psychologist	A counseling psychologist has either a master's degree or a doctoral degree in counseling psychology. Counseling psychologists tend to have less training in research skills and tend to treat less severe or more narrow problems than do clinical psychologists. Thus, counseling psychologists might limit their counseling to families, married couples, or college students. Counseling psychologists typically work in private practice, mental-health centers, or college counseling centers. In fact, college counselors are more likely to be counseling psychologists, while hospital psychologists are more likely to be clinical psychologists (Watkins et al., 1986).
Pastoral Counselor	A pastoral counselor is a layperson or a member of the clergy who has earned a master's degree in pastoral counseling. Pastoral counselors combine spiritual and psychological counseling in their work in settings such as prisons, churches, hospitals, or counseling centers. Some people prefer seeing a pastoral counselor, because they find it less stigmatizing than seeing a clinical or counseling psychologist (Bales, 1986).
Psychiatrist	A psychiatrist is a physician who has served a three- or four-year residency in a mental hospital or a psychiatric ward of a general hospital. Though psychiatrists often rely on biomedical therapies, particularly drug therapy, some restrict their practices to psychotherapy. Psychiatrists usually work in private practice, psychiatric wards, or mental hospitals. A psychoanalyst is a psychiatrist (or, sometimes a psychologist) with special training in psychoanalytic psychotherapy. Psychoanalysts receive their training at psychoanalytic institutes and almost always work in private practice.
Psychiatric Nurse	A psychiatric nurse is a registered nurse who has a master's degree (M.S.N.) in nursing and specialized training in psychiatric care. Psychiatric nurses usually work under the supervision of psychiatrists in psychiatric wards or mental hospitals.
Psychiatric Social Worker	A psychiatric social worker has a master's degree (M.S.W.) in social work and training in the counseling of individuals and families. Psychiatric social workers work in hospitals, private practice, human service agencies, and mental-health centers.
Paraprofessional	A paraprofessional may lack an advanced degree—or anything more than a high school diploma—but has special training in counseling people with certain problems, such as obesity, drug abuse, or criminal conduct. Paraprofessionals are often people who have overcome the problem that they treat and who work under professional supervision in mental-health centers or in self-help groups.

Just as there is no single way to find a physician, there is no single way to find a therapist. As discussed later in the chapter, in general the personal qualities of the therapist matter more than the kind of therapy she or he practices. You also should remember that most therapists have an eclectic orientation (Jensen, Bergin, & Greaves, 1990), selecting their techniques from a variety of approaches to therapy. Perhaps the best-known eclectic therapy is Arnold Lazarus's *multimodal therapy* (Lazarus & Lazarus, 1986). Lazarus believes that the therapist should be free to combine techniques related to what he calls *BASIC ID*. The letters of this acronym stand for *behavior, affect, sensation, imagery, cognition, interpersonal,* and *drugs*. This technique has been used in treating a variety of people, including those with a borderline personality disorder (Proeve, 1995) and survivors of sexual abuse (Zahn & Schug, 1993). But critics of the eclectic approach argue that it is illogical to combine techniques that are based on different outlooks on the causes of psychological disorders (Patterson, 1989).

How might you find a therapist, eclectic or otherwise? Your college counseling center might be a good place to start. You may have a friend, relative, or professor who can recommend a therapist or counseling center to you. Other potential sources of help or referral include community mental health centers, psychological associations, and mental health associations. You can find many of these organizations, as well as private practitioners, listed in the Yellow Pages.

After finding a therapist, try as best you can to assess her or his credentials, reputation, therapeutic approach, and interpersonal manner. Does the therapist have legitimate academic and clinical training? For example, is the therapist licensed or certified? Do you know anyone who will vouch for the therapist's competence? Does the therapist's approach make sense for your problem? Do you feel comfortable talking with the therapist? The therapist should be warm, open, concerned, and empathetic. Therapy clients prefer therapists whom they find to be helpful and likable (Alexander et al., 1993).

If you find that you lack confidence in the therapist even after discussing your doubts and examining your own possible resistances to dealing with distressing feelings, feel free to seek help elsewhere. Once you are in therapy, do not expect instant miracles; but if you make little progress after a reasonable length of time, feel free to end the relationship.

STAYING ON TRACK: *Selecting a Therapist*

1 What are the major kinds of psychotherapists?
2. What are some good ways to go about seeking a psychotherapist?

THINKING ABOUT *Psychology*

Is Psychotherapy Effective?

In 1952 Hans Eysenck published an article that sparked a debate on the effectiveness of psychotherapy that has continued to this day. Based on his review of twenty-four studies of psychotherapy with neurotics (people suffering from disorders involving moderate anxiety or depression), Eysenck concluded that about two thirds of those who received psychotherapy improved. This would have provided strong evidence in support of the effectiveness of psychoanalysis (then the dominant kind of psychotherapy), had Eysenck not also found that about two thirds of control subjects who had received *no* therapy also improved. He called improvement without therapy **spontaneous remission** and attributed it to beneficial factors that occurred in the person's everyday life. Because those who received no therapy were as likely to improve as those who received therapy, Eysenck concluded that psychotherapy is ineffective.

Eysenck's article provoked criticisms of its methodological shortcomings. One shortcoming was that many of the untreated people were under the care of physicians who prescribed drugs for them and provided informal counseling. Another shortcoming was that the treated and untreated groups were not equivalent, differing in educational level, socioeconomic status, and motivation to improve. This meant that the control group might have had a better initial prognosis than the treatment group had. Still another

spontaneous remission
The improvement of some persons with psychological disorders without their undergoing formal therapy.

shortcoming was that Eysenck overestimated the rate of spontaneous remission, which other researchers have found is closer to 40 percent than to 65 percent (Bergin & Lambert, 1978). Nonetheless, Eysenck (1994) still insists that psychotherapy does not produce improvement at a rate superior to that of spontaneous remission.

EVALUATION OF PSYCHOTHERAPY

During the decades since Eysenck's article, hundreds of studies have assessed the effectiveness of psychotherapy. But this is a difficult scientific endeavor. For one thing, the definition of "effective" varies with the aim of therapy. Should therapy aim to restore normality? change maladaptive behavior? relieve personal distress?

The aims also will vary with the orientation to therapy. A psychoanalytic therapist might look for insight into unconscious conflicts that originate in childhood and result in cathartic release of repressed emotions. A behavioral therapist might look for changes in maladaptive behaviors. A rational-emotive behavior therapist might look for sound changes in thinking. And a person-centered therapist might look for greater acceptance of oneself, personal warts and all.

Moreover, who is to judge whether these changes have occurred? Certainly clients' self-reports of changes in their symptoms and self-concept are important (Connolly & Strupp, 1996). A survey of client satisfaction with psychotherapy found that about three quarters of those who responded said that they were "satisfied" (Lebow, 1982). But clients, as well as therapists, can be biased in favor of reporting improvement. To avoid bias, friends, family members, teachers, or employers might also be asked for their assessment of the client. This provides cross-validation of client and therapist reports of improvement.

What has been found by the admittedly imperfect research on the effectiveness of psychotherapy? The general conclusion drawn from research conducted since Eysenck issued his challenge is that both psychotherapy and placebo therapy are more effective than no therapy and that psychotherapy is superior to placebo therapy. Placebo effects in psychotherapy are caused by factors such as the client's faith in the therapist's ability and the client's expectation of success (Critelli & Neumann, 1984).

Mary Lee Smith and her colleagues (Smith, Glass, & Miller, 1980) published a comprehensive meta-analysis that combined the results of 475 studies on the effectiveness of psychotherapy. They found that, on the average, the typical psychotherapy client is better off than 80 percent of untreated persons. And there is little overall difference in the effectiveness of the various approaches to therapy (see Figure 15.8). So psychotherapy does work, but no single kind stands out as clearly more effective than the others (Stiles, Shapiro, & Elliott, 1986).

More recently, results of an ambitious $10 million study sponsored by the National Institute of Mental Health have lent further support to the effectiveness of psychotherapy. The study, which involved the University of Pittsburgh, the University of Oklahoma, and George Washington University, randomly assigned 239 severely depressed adult subjects to four groups. One group received Beck's cognitive therapy. A second group received interpersonal psychotherapy (a form of psychoanalytic therapy). A third group received the antidepressant drug Tofranil plus a minimal amount of social support from a therapist. And a fourth group received a placebo treatment (an inactive pill) plus a minimal amount of social support from a therapist.

The participants were assessed after 16 weeks of therapy and again at a follow up 18 months later. As expected, all of the groups had improved by the end of the 16 weeks; the three forms of active therapy eliminated depression in more than 50 percent of the subjects, and the placebo therapy eliminated depression in 29 percent of the subjects. There were no differences in effectiveness between the three active forms of therapy. Though drug therapy relieved symptoms more quickly, the two psychotherapies eventually caught up in their effectiveness (Mervis, 1986). But the follow-up study found that many of the subjects relapsed, indicating that 16 weeks of therapy might be insufficient to produce lasting improvement (Shea et al., 1992).

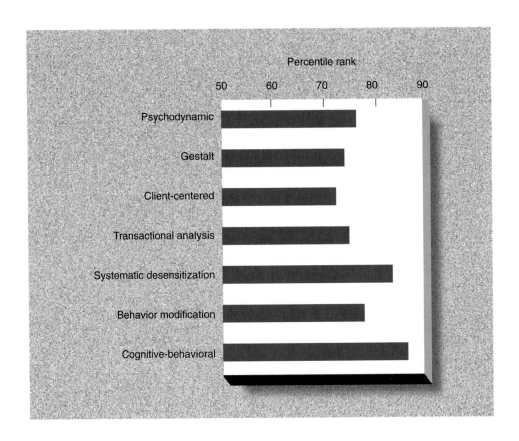

The Effectiveness of Psychotherapy
Research has found that psychotherapy is effective, but that no approach is consistently better than any other approach. This graph shows the effectiveness of different kinds of therapy relative to no treatment. Overall, people given psychotherapy show, on the average, significantly greater improvement than about 80 percent of untreated people (Smith, Glass, & Miller, 1980).

▲ **Lester Luborsky**
"Researchers have reached the consensus opinion that the evidence strongly supports the positive conclusion that most patients *will* benefit from psychotherapy."

FACTORS IN THE EFFECTIVENESS OF PSYCHOTHERAPY

Given the consensus that psychotherapy is usually effective and that no approach is significantly more effective than any other approach, researchers are faced with the question, What factors account for the effectiveness of psychotherapy? In trying to answer this question, researchers study the characteristics of therapies, clients, and therapists.

Therapy Characteristics

One of the first comprehensive reviews of therapy, client, and therapist factors, carried out by Lester Luborsky and his colleagues (1971), found that the poorest predictor of success in therapy was the nature of the therapy itself. More recent research studies have likewise found that the major kinds of therapy are equally effective (Shapiro, 1995). The only important therapy characteristic seems to be the number of therapy sessions—the more sessions, the greater the improvement. A review of fifteen studies of psychotherapy using more than 2,400 clients found that 50 percent of clients improved by the end of 8 weekly sessions and 75 percent improved by the end of 26 weekly sessions (see Figure 15.9). Additional sessions added little to the therapeutic outcome, indicating that most clients gain maximum benefit from relatively brief psychotherapy (Howard et al., 1986).

Brief psychotherapy, sometimes with a time limit put into a contract between the therapist and the client, has grown in popularity. Depending on the agreement between the therapist and the client, brief therapy will last less than 6 months. Arnold Lazarus (1989) believes that brief psychotherapy will become more popular as more people who seek therapy lack the funds to pay for lengthy therapy. Fortunately, brief psychotherapy can be effective (Shefler, Dasberg, & Ben-Shakhar, 1995).

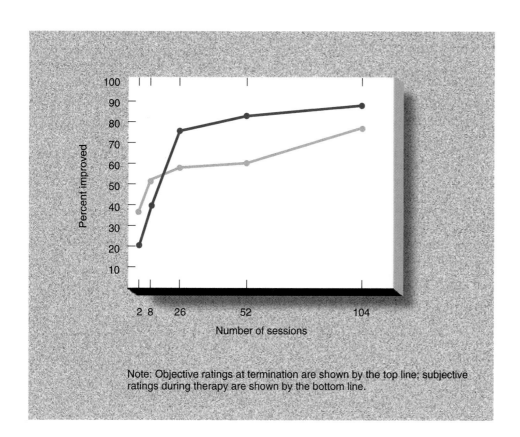

The Length of Therapy and Therapy Effectiveness
As the number of therapy sessions increases, the percentage of clients who improve increases. But after the 26th session, additional sessions help relatively few clients. Note the slight difference between objective ratings of improvement given by therapists and subjective ratings given by the clients themselves, though the general trend is similar for both (Howard et al., 1986).

Note: Objective ratings at termination are shown by the top line; subjective ratings during therapy are shown by the bottom line.

Client Characteristics

The classic review by Luborsky and his colleagues (1971) found that therapeutic success was related to client characteristics. Clients were more likely to improve if they were higher in education, intelligence, and socioeconomic status. Improvement was also greatest in those with less severe disorders and disorders of recent onset. Other factors that promoted therapeutic success were a more adequate personality and greater motivation to change. Client factors that can impair therapy include being poorly motivated or expecting therapy to be painless (Mohr, 1995). Unfortunately, no client characteristics have been documented that can serve as a basis for the selection of a particular treatment (Dance & Neufeld, 1988).

Therapist Characteristics

Therapy is an intense, intimate, vulnerable relationship between human beings. So the kind of therapy is generally less important than the qualities of the therapist (Lambert, 1989). Though it might be logical to assume that therapy would be best when the client and therapist are similar, there is little evidence that similarity in their sex (Redfern, Dancey, & Dryden, 1993), race (Atkinson, 1983), or personality (Rinaldi, 1987) has a consistent impact on therapeutic outcomes.

Just what therapist characteristics *are* important, then? The client's perception of therapist empathy has been consistently identified as an important factor in the effectiveness of psychotherapy (Free et al., 1985). In fact, one of the main factors in negative effects of pychotherapy is a lack of empathy in the therapist (Mohr, 1995). The importance of accurate empathy was first championed by Carl Rogers. In fact, Rogers began the formal study of the therapy process by taping his therapy sessions and analyzing his interactions with clients (Gendlin, 1988). As noted earlier, though personal warmth and genuineness cannot be taught, empathy can (Ju, 1982). Perhaps students who intend to become therapists should have their degree of personal warmth and genuineness, in addition to their academic credentials, assessed as part of the application process for admission to graduate school. Personal warmth has been found to be a factor that differentiates successful and unsuccessful therapists (Najavits & Strupp, 1994). But empathy is not enough. A meta-analysis found that highly trained therapists are more successful than less well trained therapists, particularly in having fewer clients drop out of therapy (Stein & Lambert, 1995).

Researchers, particularly those who favor an eclectic approach (Beutler & Consoli, 1993), are refining their methods to study more-precise questions: What kind of therapy, offered by what kind of therapist, is helpful for what kind of client, experiencing what kind of problem, in what kind of circumstances? We must wait for future studies testing interactions among these factors to determine the most effective combinations. Currently, the best we can do is determine the effectiveness of two factors at a time, such as the kind of therapy and the kind of problem. For example, cognitive therapy is superior to other therapies in the treatment of depression (Gaffan, Tsaousis, & Kemp-Wheeler, 1995), and behavior therapy is superior to other therapies in the treatment of phobias (Goisman, 1983) and for treating children and adolescents (Weisz et al., 1995). We can only look forward to the day when we can make more-precise declarations, such as: "Systematic desensitization offered by an empathetic psychologist will prove superior for a middle-aged college student with a public-speaking phobia when addressing strangers."

STAYING ON TRACK: *Is Psychotherapy Effective?*

1. Why did Eysenck claim that psychotherapy produces no better results than spontaneous remission?
2. Are any therapist factors important in the effectiveness of psychotherapy?

CHAPTER SUMMARY

THE HISTORY OF THERAPY

People with psychological disorders might seek professional therapy. Modern therapy has come a long way since ancient times. In trephining, holes were cut in the skull, possibly to release evil spirits that were alleged to cause abnormal behavior. Hippocrates introduced a more naturalistic form of treatment, including procedures to restore the balance of body "humors." The Renaissance saw the appearance of insane asylums; some, such as Bedlam, were awful places, but others, such as Geel, provided humane treatment. Near the end of the eighteenth century, Philippe Pinel released asylum inmates and championed moral therapy. Moral therapy was introduced to America by Benjamin Rush, who also used unusual devices for treating certain disorders. Through the efforts of Dorothea Dix, state mental hospitals were built throughout the United States. But they became crowded and deteriorated into mere human warehouses. In the early twentieth century, a book by Clifford Beers, describing his horrible experiences in a mental hospital, led to the founding of the mental health movement, which promotes the prevention and humane treatment of psychological disorders.

THE PSYCHOANALYTIC ORIENTATION

After hearing Joseph Breuer's report of the benefits of catharsis in the case of Anna O., Sigmund Freud developed psychoanalysis. Psychoanalysis principally involves the analysis of free associations, dreams, resistances, and transference. The goal of these analyses is for the client to gain insight into unconscious conflicts and experience catharsis.

THE BEHAVIORAL ORIENTATION

The behavioral orientation emphasizes the importance of learning and environmental influences. Two of the main kinds of behavioral therapy based on classical conditioning are systematic desensitization, which is useful in treating phobias, and aversion therapy, which makes formerly pleasurable but maladaptive behavior unpleasant. One of the main applications of the operant conditioning principle of positive reinforcement is the use of a token economy in institutional settings. The operant conditioning principle of punishment is useful in eliminating behaviors, such as self-injurious behavior in children with autism. Albert Bandura's social learning theory has contributed participant modeling as a way to overcome phobias.

THE COGNITIVE ORIENTATION

The cognitive orientation assumes that thoughts about events, rather than events themselves, cause psychological disorders. Donald Meichenbaum uses stress-inoculation training to help people be more optimistic when in stressful situations. In Albert Ellis's rational-emotive behavior therapy, the client learns to change irrational thinking. Aaron Beck developed cognitive therapy to help depressed people think less negatively about themselves, the world, and the future.

THE HUMANISTIC ORIENTATION

The humanistic orientation emphasizes the importance of being aware of one's emotions and feeling free to express them. Carl Rogers's person-centered therapy, a form of nondirective therapy, helps clients find their own solutions to their problems. In contrast, Fritz Perls's Gestalt therapy is more directive in making clients face their true feelings and act on them. Existential therapy aims at helping the client develop a personal philosophy that can address the basic issues of life.

THE SOCIAL-RELATIONS ORIENTATION

The social-relations orientation assumes that people cannot be treated as isolated individuals. In group therapy, people, usually strangers, are brought together for therapy. Group therapy derived from the psychoanalytic approach includes psychodrama and transactional analysis. Group therapy derived from the behavioral approach includes social-skills training and assertiveness training. And group therapy derived from the humanistic approach includes sensitivity groups and encounter groups. In family therapy, family members gain insight into their unhealthy patterns of interaction and learn to change them. Offshoots of family therapy include marital therapy and couples therapy.

THE BIOPSYCHOLOGICAL ORIENTATION

The biomedical orientation uses medical procedures to treat psychological disorders. The main procedures include psychosurgery (rarely used today), electroconvulsive therapy for depression, and drug therapy. Psychiatrists might prescribe antianxiety drugs, antidepressant drugs, antimania drugs, and antipsychotic drugs.

COMMUNITY MENTAL HEALTH

The community mental health movement was stimulated by deinstitutionalization, the treatment of people in community settings instead of in mental hospitals. Commmunity mental health centers aid in both prevention and treatment of psychological disorders. The failure to provide adequate housing and services for former mental hospital patients has contributed to the growing problem of homelessness.

THE RIGHTS OF THE THERAPY CLIENT

Laws require that formal procedures be followed before a person is committed to a mental hospital. Once in a mental hospital, patients have the right to refuse treatment and the right to receive treatment. What clients reveal in therapy sessions is normally confidential, but legal cases, most notably the *Tarasoff* decision, have led to the concept of the duty to warn.

SELECTING A THERAPIST

There are many kinds of therapists, including both professionals and paraprofessionals. Most professional therapists have an eclectic orientation. You should be as careful in selecting a therapist as you are in selecting a physician.

IS PSYCHOTHERAPY EFFECTIVE?

In 1952 Hans Eysenck challenged psychotherapists by claiming that people who received psychotherapy improved no more than did people who received no therapy. Subsequent research has shown that psychotherapy is better than no therapy and better than placebo therapy. But no single kind of therapy stands out as clearly superior to the rest. More sophisticated research is required to determine the ideal combinations of therapy, therapist, and client factors for treating specific disorders.

▶ KEY CONCEPTS

KEY CONTRIBUTORS

The History of Therapy

Hippocrates 518
Philippe Pinel 519
Benjamin Rush 519
Dorothea Dix 519
Clifford Beers 520

The Psychoanalytic Orientation

Joseph Breuer 520
Bertha Pappenheim (Anna O.)
    520
Sigmund Freud 521

The Behavioral Orientation

Mary Cover Jones 523
Joseph Wolpe 524

The Cognitive Orientation

Donald Meichenbaum 527
Albert Ellis 529
Aaron Beck 530

The Humanistic Orientation

Carl Rogers 531
Fritz Perls 532
Irvin Yalom 534
Victor Frankl 534

The Social-Relations Orientation

Jacob Moreno 535
Eric Berne 535
Virginia Satir 537
Salvadore Minuchin 537

The Biopsychological Orientation

Egas Moniz 539
Ugo Cerletti 540

Is Psychotherapy Effective?

Hans J. Eysenck 548

FOR MORE INFORMATION ON THERAPY

FOR GENERAL WORKS ON THERAPY

Patterson, C. H. (1990). *Theories of counseling and psychotherapy* (4th ed.). New York: Harper & Row.

Sue, D. W., & Sue, D. (1990). *Counseling the culturally different.* New York: Wiley.

Yalom, I. D. (1989). *Love's executioner and other tales of psychotherapy.* New York: Basic Books.

Zeig, J. K., & Munion, W. M. (Eds.). (1990). *What is psychotherapy?* San Francisco: Jossey-Bass.

FOR MORE ON THE HISTORY OF THERAPY

Reisman, J. M. (1976). *A history of clinical psychology.* New York: Irvington.

Whiteley, J. M. (Ed.). (1980). *The history of counseling psychology.* Pacific Grove, CA: Brooks/Cole.

Zeig, J. K. (Ed.). (1987). *The evolution of psychotherapy.* New York: Brunner/Mazel.

Zeig, J. K. (Ed.). (1992). *The evolution of psychotherapy: The second conference.* New York: Brunner/Mazel.

FOR MORE ON THE PSYCHOANALYTIC ORIENTATION

Fisher, S., & Greenberg, R. P. (1985). *The scientific credibility of Freud's theories and therapy.* New York: Columbia University Press.

Kris, A. O. (1987). *Free association.* New Haven, CT: Yale University Press.

Luborsky, L., & Crits-Christoph, P. (1990). *Understanding transference.* New York: Basic Books.

Reik, T. (1952). *Listening with the third ear: The inner experience of a psychoanalyst.* New York: Farrar, Straus.

Strean, H. S. (1990). *Resolving resistances in psychotherapy.* New York: Brunner/Mazel.

FOR MORE ON THE BEHAVIORAL ORIENTATION

Boudewyns, P. A., & Shipley, R. H. (Eds.). (1983). *Flooding and implosive therapy: Direct therapeutic exposure in clinical practice.* New York: Plenum.

Hadley, N. H. (1985). *Foundations of aversion therapy.* New York: Luce.

Kazdin, A. E. (1977). *The token economy: A review and evaluation.* New York: Plenum.

Thorpe, G. L., & Olson, S. L. (1997). *Behavior therapy* (2nd ed.). Boston: Allyn & Bacon.

FOR MORE ON THE COGNITIVE ORIENTATION

Beck, J. S. (1995). *Cognitive therapy: Basics and beyond.* New York: Guilford.

Dalton, P., & Dunnett, G. (1992). *A psychology for living: Personal construct theory for professionals and clients.* New York: Wiley.

Ellis, A., & Dryden, W. (1997). *The practice of rational emotive behavior therapy.* Boston: Allyn & Bacon.

Meichenbaum, D. (1985). *Stress-inoculation training.* New York: Pergamon.

Gabriel, M. A. (1997). *Group psychotherapy.* New York: Free Press.

FOR MORE ON THE HUMANISTIC ORIENTATION

Frankl, V. E. (1959/1992). *Man's search for meaning: An introduction to logotherapy.* Boston: Beacon Press.

Harman, R. L. (1990). *Gestalt therapy: Discussions with the masters.* Springfield, MA: Charles C Thomas.

Mearns, D., & Thorne, B. (1988). *Person-centered counseling in action.* Newbury Park, CA: Sage.

Yalom, I. D. (1980). *Existential psychotherapy.* New York: Basic Books.

FOR MORE ON THE SOCIAL-RELATIONS ORIENTATION

Blatner, A., & Blatner, A. (1988). *Foundations of psychodrama: History, theory, and practice.* New York: Springer.

Clarkson, P. (1991). *Transactional analysis psychotherapy: An integrated approach.* New York: Routledge.

Minuchin, S., & Nichols, M. P. (1992). *Family healing: Tales of hope and renewal from family therapy.* New York: Free Press.

Yalom, I. D. (1985). *The theory and practice of group psychotherapy.* New York: Basic Books.

FOR MORE ON THE BIOPSYCHOLOGICAL ORIENTATION

Abrams, R. (1997). *Electroconvulsive therapy* (3rd ed.). New York: Oxford University Press.

Fisher, S., & Greenberg, R. P. (Eds.). (1989). *The limits of biological treatments for psychological distress.* Hillsdale, NJ: Erlbaum.

Lickey, M. E., & Gordon, B. (1995). *Drugs for mental illness.* New York: Freeman.

Valenstein, E. S. (1986). *Great and desperate cures: The rise and decline of psychosurgery and other radical treatments for mental illness.* New York: Basic Books.

FOR MORE ON COMMUNITY MENTAL HEALTH

Dear, M. J., & Wolch, J. R. (1992). *Landscapes of despair: From deinstitutionalization to homelessness.* Princeton, NJ: Princeton University Press.

Isaac, R. J., & Armat, V. C. (1990). *Madness in the streets: How psychiatry and the law abandoned the mentally ill.* New York: Free Press.

Johnson, A. B. (1990). *Out of bedlam: The truth about deinstitutionalization.* New York: Basic Books.

Mosher, L., & Burt, L. (1994). *Community mental health: A practical guide.* New York: W. W. Norton.

FOR MORE ON THE RIGHTS OF THE THERAPY CLIENT

Appelbaum, P. S., Lidz, C. W., & Meisel, A. (1987). *Informed consent: Legal theory and clinical practice.* New York: Oxford University Press.

Donaldson, K. (1976). *Insanity inside and out: The personal story behind the landmark Supreme Court decision.* New York: Crown.

Lakin, M. (1988). *Ethical issues in the psychotherapies.* New York: Oxford University Press.

VandeCreek, L., & Knapp, S. (1993). *Tarasoff and beyond: Legal and clinical considerations in the treatment of life-endangering patients.* Sarasota, FL: Professional Resource Press.

FOR MORE ON THE SELECTION OF A THERAPIST

Pies, R. W. (1997). *A consumer's guide to choosing the right therapist.* Northvale, NJ: Aronson.

FOR MORE ON THE EFFECTIVENESS OF PSYCHOTHERAPY

Garfield, S. L., & Bergin, A. E. (Eds.). (1986). *Handbook of psychotherapy and behavior change.* New York: Wiley.

Luborsky, L., Crits-Christoph, P., Mintz, J., & Auerbach, A. (1988). *Who will benefit from psychotherapy? Predicting therapeutic outcomes.* New York: Basic Books.

Mahoney, M. J. (1991). *Human change processes: The scientific foundations of psychotherapy.* New York: Basic Books.

Smith, M. L., Glass, G. V., & Miller, T. I. (1980). *The benefits of psychotherapy.* Baltimore: Johns Hopkins University Press.

FOR MORE ON CONTRIBUTORS TO THE STUDY OF THERAPY

Burston, D. (1991). *The legacy of Erich Fromm.* Cambridge. MA: Harvard University Press.

Clarkson, P., & Mackewn, J. (1993). *Fritz Perls.* Newbury Park, CA: Sage.

Dain, N. (1980). *Clifford Beers: Advocate for the insane.* Pittsburgh: University of Pittsburgh Press.

Evans, R. I. (1989). *Albert Bandura: The man and his ideas: A dialogue.* Westport, CT: Praeger.

Gay, P. (1988). *Freud: A life for our time.* New York: W. W. Norton.

Gollaher, D. (1994). *A voice for the mad: The life of Dorothea Dix.* New York: Free Press.

Grosskurth, P. (1986). *Melanie Klein: Her world and her work.* New York: Knopf.

Hawke, D. F. (1971). *Benjamin Rush: Revolutionary gadfly.* New York: Irvington.

Hirschmuller, A. (1978). *The life and work of Josef Breuer: Physiology and psychoanalysis.* New York: New York University Press.

Jorgensen, E. W., & Jorgensen, H. I. (1984). *Eric Berne: Master gamesman—A transactional biography.* New York: Grove-Weidenfeld.

Kirschenbaum, H. (1979). *On becoming Carl Rogers.* New York: Delacorte.

Perry, H. S. (1982). *Psychiatrist of America: The life of Harry Stack Sullivan.* Cambridge, MA: Harvard University Press.

Quinn, S. (1987). *A mind of her own: The life of Karen Horney.* New York: Summit.

Rattner, J. (1983). *Alfred Adler.* New York: Frederick Ungar.

Sayers, J. (1991). *Mothers of psychoanalysis: Helene Deutsch, Karen Horney, Anna Freud, and Melanie Klein.* New York: W. W. Norton.

Stevens, A. (1990). *On Jung.* New York: Routledge.

Walker, C. E. (1991). *The history of clinical psychology in autobiography* (Vol. 1). Pacific Grove, CA: Brooks/Cole.

Walker, C. E. (1992). *The history of clinical psychology in autobiography* (Vol. 2). Pacific Grove, CA: Brooks/Cole.

Weishaar, M. (1992). *Aaron Beck.* Newbury Park, CA: Sage.

Wiener, D. N. (1988). *Albert Ellis: Passionate skeptic.* Westport, CT: Praeger.

Young-Bruehl, E. (1988). *Anna Freud.* New York: Summit.

CHAPTER 16

▲ ERIC ISENBURGER
Summer

Psychology and Health

▲ Behavioral Causes of Illness and Death
Half of the mortality from the leading causes of death in the United States is influenced by unhealthy or dangerous behaviors, such as overeating, failing to exercise, and overexposing oneself to the sun.

health psychology

The field that applies psychological principles to the prevention and treatment of physical illness.

stress

The physiological response of the body to physical and psychological demands.

stressor

A physical or psychological demand that induces physiological adjustment.

o you overeat, smoke cigarettes, drive recklessly, exercise rarely, drink excessive amounts of alcohol, fail to follow your physician's medical recommendations, or respond inefficiently to stressful situations? If you engage in any of these maladaptive behaviors, which are among the leading causes of death in the United States, you might be reducing your life span. According to the National Academy of Sciences, half of the mortality from the ten leading causes of death in the United States is strongly influenced by personal lifestyle (Hamburg, 1982).

This statement would not have been true at the turn of the century, when most North Americans died from infectious diseases such as influenza, pneumonia, and tuberculosis. But the development of vaccines and antibiotics, as well as improved hygiene and public sanitation practices, led to a decline in infectious diseases as causes of illness and mortality. This was accompanied by a surge in the relative importance of noninfectious diseases, especially those caused by dangerous or unhealthy behaviors. A century ago, cancer and cardiovascular disease, which are promoted by unhealthy lifestyles pursued over a span of decades, were relatively uncommon causes of death among Americans. Today they are the two most common causes. We now are more likely to become ill or die because of our own actions than because of viruses or bacteria that invade our bodies. The role of psychological factors in the onset and prevention of cancer, cardiovascular disease, and other illnesses that are affected by lifestyle is one of the main problems studied by psychologists who do research in *health psychology*.

Health psychology is the field that studies the role of psychological factors in the promotion of health and the prevention of illness. Health psychology has grown so rapidly that even clinical psychologists, traditionally concerned primarily with the treatment of psychological disorders, now conduct more research in health psychology than in any other area (Sayette & Mayne, 1990). Health psychologists favor a *biopsychosocial model* of health and illness, which emphasizes the interaction of biological, psychological, and social factors. In contrast, the traditional *biomedical model* emphasizes biological factors and neglects psychological and social ones. The chief topics of interest to health psychologists are the relationship between stress and illness, the modification of health-impairing habits, and the promotion of adaptive reactions to illness.

STRESS AND ILLNESS

In the 1960s, undergraduates at Penn State University, recognizing their isolation in rural, peaceful State College, Pennsylvania, dubbed the town and its surroundings "Happy Valley." The students were vindicated in 1988, when California psychologist Robert Levine reported the results of his survey of living conditions in the United States. He concluded that State College had the distinction of being the least stressful place to live in America (Rossi, 1988).

But what is *stress?* According to Canadian endocrinologist Hans Selye (1907–1982), the founder of modern stress research, **stress** is the physiological response of the body to physical and psychological demands. Such demands are known as **stressors.** Though stress has been implicated as a factor in illness, some degree of stress is normal, necessary, and unavoidable. As Selye noted, "complete freedom from stress is death" (Selye, 1980, p. 128). Stress motivates us to adjust our behavior to meet changing demands, as when we study for an upcoming exam, wear a sweater in cold weather, or seek companionship when

◄ **Stress**
The physical and psychological demands on this worker will induce what Hans Selye called "stress."

lonely. Stress can even be pleasurable, as when we attend a party, play a game of Scrabble, or shoot river rapids on a raft. Selye called unpleasant stress *distress* and pleasant stress *eustress* (from the Greek for "good stress").

Psychological Stress and Psychological Stressors

Health psychologists study several major types of stressors. They also study the kinds of stress produced by stressors.

Types of Stress: Frustration, Pressure, and Conflict

There are three general categories of psychological stressors. They are *frustration*, *pressure*, and *conflict*.

Frustration. You experience **frustration** when you are blocked from reaching a goal. Minor frustrations include waiting in line at a movie theater or performing poorly on an exam. Major frustrations include losing one's job or flunking out of school. Work is a common source of frustration. For example, a study of professional word processors found that those who worked on computer systems with slow response times felt more frustrated and experienced more physical discomfort than those who worked on faster systems (Schleifer & Amick, 1989).

frustration
The emotional state induced when one is blocked from reaching a goal.

Pressure. You experience **pressure** when you face demands that tax your abilities to meet them, such as writing a research paper or working to pay your tuition. Even great athletes experience pressure during competition, which can lead to "choking"—that is, playing below one's normal standards when a good performance is needed. In recent years there has been controversy about whether, contrary to popular belief, home teams in professional baseball and basketball are more likely to *lose* in deciding games of championship series. This possibility was raised by an archival study of baseball World Series records from 1924 through 1982 and National Basketball Association championship records from 1967 through 1982. The home teams retained their home-field advantage in nondeciding games, but had a home-field *disadvantage* in deciding games (Baumeister & Steinhilber, 1984).

pressure
The emotional state induced when one is confronted by personal responsibilities that tax one's abilities.

What could explain the difference in home-team performance between early games and deciding games? The researchers attributed this to the increased *pressure* of playing important games before home fans. This pressure makes home-team players more self-conscious. As a result, they pay attention to the performance of skilled movements that they normally perform automatically with little or no conscious awareness. The home-team players become less fluid in their movements and more prone to perform below their normal level of ability. For example, in the World Series, the home team makes significantly more errors in seventh games than in earlier games.

This supposed home-field disadvantage has been countered by other researchers who reanalyzed the original data and added data from more recent championship competitions. These critics have found that the home team wins as often in deciding games as in early games of championships series (Schlenker et al., 1995). Thus, though pressure can promote choking in both home and visiting players, it does not seem to create the home-field disadvantage in deciding games reported in the original research study. This also supports the importance of replication in psychological research—a scientific essential (see Chapter 2).

Conflict. You experience a **conflict** when you are torn between two or more potential courses of action. Gestalt psychologist Kurt Lewin (1935) identified three major kinds of conflicts: *approach-approach, avoidance-avoidance,* and *approach-avoidance.* In an **approach-approach conflict,** you are torn between two desirable courses of action. This might occur when one friend invites you to attend a party, another invites you to attend a concert, and you can't do both because they're scheduled at the same time. This is usually the least stressful kind of conflict, because both options are desirable. But the pursuit of two desirable, yet conflicting, options can induce intense distress—as is experienced by many adults, especially women, who pursue both a career and parenthood (Lewis & Cooper, 1983). Job demands can lead to neglect of parental duties, and caring for a sick child can lead to neglect of job responsibilities. Both scenarios induce stress. While some parents avoid the conflicting demands of work and parenthood by pursuing only one of them, others find that remaining in the conflict is necessary.

In an **avoidance-avoidance conflict,** you are forced to choose between two unpleasant courses of action, such as going to the dentist or suffering with a toothache. Though you might delay making a choice for as long as possible, the conflict is resolved when one option forces you to choose it as the lesser of two evils. An unbearable toothache would eventually make you go to the dentist. But some people caught in an avoidance-avoidance conflict find both courses of action intolerable. This might lead them to seek the artificial solace of drugs or alcohol. Animal research provides support for this possibility. Moderate doses of alcohol weaken avoidance-avoidance conflicts in laboratory rats (Mansfield, 1979). Perhaps research will find that human beings who use alcohol to relieve their stress sometimes use it to weaken their avoidance-avoidance conflicts.

In an **approach-avoidance conflict,** you are simultaneously drawn to and repelled by the same goal. College seniors might experience this when they consider their upcoming graduation, which has both desirable and undesirable aspects. Dieters might be attracted by a luscious dessert and repulsed by the thought of added body fat. The approach-avoidance conflict is also at the heart of Freudian theory. For example, in the Freudian interpretation, conversion disorder (see Chapter 14), in which a person experiences motor or sensory loss without any physical cause, is the outcome of a conflict between the desire to approach sex and the desire to avoid guilt for engaging in it (O'Neill & Kempler, 1969).

As first noted by psychologist Neal Miller, a person in an approach-avoidance conflict (such as a conflict over sexual behavior) vacillates, sometimes moving toward the goal and sometimes moving away from it (Dollard & Miller, 1950). When you are far from the goal, both your approach tendency and your avoidance tendency are relatively weak, with your approach tendency typically being stronger than your avoidance tendency. This motivates you to approach the goal. As you move toward the goal, both

conflict
The emotional state induced when one is torn between two or more potential courses of action.

approach-approach conflict
A conflict in which one must choose between two desirable courses of action.

avoidance-avoidance conflict
A conflict in which one must choose between two undesirable courses of action.

approach-avoidance conflict
A conflict in which one is faced by a course of action that has both desirable and undesirable qualities.

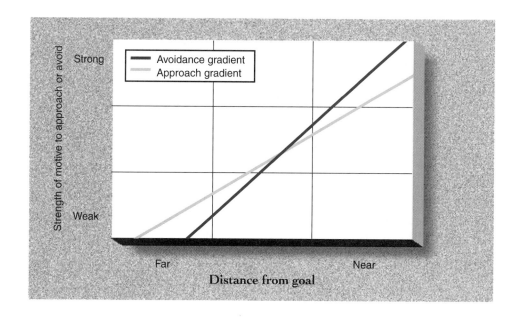

Approach-Avoidance Conflict
In an approach-avoidance conflict, the approach and avoidance tendencies both increase in strength the closer you get to a goal. But the avoidance tendency increases more rapidly. Vacillation between approach and avoidance will be greatest at the point where the two tendencies are of about equal strength. In the graph, this is the point where the approach and avoidance gradients cross.

your approach tendency and your avoidance tendency intensify. But your avoidance tendency increases faster than your approach tendency. If the avoidance tendency eventually surpasses the approach tendency, you may fail to reach the goal. This is illustrated in Figure 16.1.

Consider engaged couples, who commonly experience an approach-avoidance conflict. When they get engaged, their approach tendency is much stronger than their avoidance tendency. But as they approach the wedding day, they might develop "cold feet" as they think more about the negative aspects of marriage. In extreme cases, the avoidance tendency can become so strong that the bride or groom fails to appear at the wedding ceremony.

Types of Stressors: Life Changes and Everyday Hassles

Frustration, pressure, and conflict are often the results of life events. These include *life changes* and *daily hassles*.

Life Changes. Throughout life each of us must adjust to life changes, both pleasant ones (such as moving into a new home) and unpleasant ones (such as the death of a loved one). Interest in the relationship between life changes and illness began when Thomas Holmes and Richard Rahe (1967) developed the *Social Readjustment Rating Scale*. Holmes and Rahe asked medical patients to report positive and negative life changes they had experienced during the months before they became ill. This generated the list of 43 kinds of life changes in Table 16.1.

Members of another sample were then asked to rate, on a 100-point scale, the degree of life change, or *adjustment*, required by each of the 43 kinds of life changes. Each was rated relative to getting married, which Holmes and Rahe gave the arbitrary value of 50. Note that the death of a spouse has the highest rating—100 points. Minor violations of the law have the lowest rating—11 points. Also note that the scale includes both negative events, such as foreclosure on a mortgage or loan, and positive events, such as Christmas.

Your *life change score* is the sum of the scores for your life changes that occurred in a given period of time, generally the past year. Holmes and Rahe found that people who had a total life-change score of more than 300 points in the preceding year were more than twice as likely to become ill as people who had a total of less than 300 points. Similarly, a recent survey of elderly people found that the more life changes they had experienced in the past 6 months, the more illnesses they had experienced (Bieliauskas, Counte, & Glandon, 1995).

▲ **Richard Rahe**
"By use of a life chart, which chronologically documents a person's major life events and concomitant health status over his or her life span, a fuller understanding can be reached regarding why an individual becomes ill at a particular time."

Psychology and Health |

An important weakness of the Social Readjustment Rating Scale is that its very content might cause researchers to overestimate the relationship between life changes and illness. The scale contains some life changes that might be either causes *or* effects of illness (Zimmerman, 1983). The most obvious examples are "Change in eating habits," "Change in sleeping habits," and "Personal injury or illness." Thus, a positive correlation between life changes and illness indicates only that there *might* be a causal relationship between the two. But there have been experiments that provide evidence supporting the causal effect of life events on illness. One of these studies exposed 17 volunteers to a rhinovirus (which causes the common cold) and then isolated them individually for 5 days. The twelve subjects who developed colds had experienced significantly more life changes in the previous year than had the five subjects who did not (Stone et al., 1992). An explanation for this finding is provided by research studies showing that the greater the number of life changes one has experienced in the past year, the weaker one's immune response (Birmaher et al., 1994).

Though Holmes and Rahe assumed that adjustment to life changes—whether the changes are positive or negative—induced stress, subsequent research has shown that it is the nature of the change, rather than change itself, that induces stress. Negative life changes induce more stress than neutral or positive life changes (Monroe, 1982). This agrees with Selye's distinction between distress and eustress.

Traumatic events, such as wars or disasters, are particularly stressful and can lead to **posttraumatic stress disorder** (Brewin, Dalgleish, & Joesph, 1996), which can appear months or years after the event. The disorder is marked by a variety of symptoms. Emotional symptoms include anxiety, emotional apathy, and survivor guilt. Cognitive symptoms include hypervigilance, difficulty concentrating, and flashbacks of the event. Behavioral symptoms include insomnia and social detachment. Posttraumatic stress disorder is especially common among victims of rape. They initially experience intense anxiety and depression, which tend to diminish gradually over the first year. Nonetheless, 20 percent of rape victims have severe, long-lasting emotional scars (Hanson, 1990).

Though posttraumatic stress disorder can occur following any of a variety of traumas, including rape, earthquake, kidnapping, and airplane crash, it was first widely publicized in regard to Vietnam War veterans who developed it years after returning to the United States. Veterans who were exposed to combat are more likely to develop posttraumatic stress disorder (Fontana & Rosenheck, 1994). At least 15 percent of American veterans of the Vietnam War developed posttraumatic stress disorder (McGuire, 1990). The rate among Canadian veterans of the Vietnam War is even higher, in part because of differences in social support available to the two groups. Canadian veterans have tended to receive even less recognition for their service, and to have fewer options for obtaining professional help to relieve their distress (Stretch, 1991).

posttraumatic stress disorder

A syndrome of physical and psychological symptoms that appears as a delayed response after exposure to an extremely emotionally distressing event.

Life Event	Mean Value	Life Event	Mean Value
Death of spouse	100	Son or daughter leaving home	29
Divorce	73	Trouble with in-laws	29
Marital separation	65	Outstanding personal achievement	28
Jail term	63	Spouse begins or stops work	26
Death of close family member	63	Begin or end school	26
Personal injury or illness	53	Change in living conditions	25
Marriage	50	Revision of personal habits	24
Fired at work	47	Trouble with boss	23
Marital reconciliation	45	Change in work hours or conditions	20
Retirement	45	Change in residence	20
Change in health of family member	44	Change in schools	20
Pregnancy	40	Change in recreation	19
Sex difficulties	39	Change in church activities	19
Gain of new family member	39	Change in social activities	18
Business readjustment	39	Mortgage or loan for lesser purchase (car, TV, etc.)	17
Change in financial state	38	Change in sleeping habits	16
Death of close friend	37	Change in number of family get-togethers	15
Change to different line of work	36	Change in eating habits	15
Change in number of arguments with spouse	35	Vacation	13
Mortgage or loan for major purchase (home, etc.)	31	Christmas	12
Foreclosure on mortgage or loan	30	Minor violations of the law	11
Change in responsibilities at work	29		

Reprinted with permission from *Journal of Psychosomatic Research*, 11: 213–218, T. H. Holmes and R. H. Rahe, "The Social Readjustment Rating Scale," 1967, Elsevier Science Ltd., Pergamon Imprint, Oxford, England.

▲ TABLE 16.1
Social Readjustment Rating Scale

Posttraumatic stress disorder is also associated with an increased risk of physical illness. For example, in 1980 a natural disaster struck the state of Washington—the eruption of the Mount Saint Helens volcano in the Cascade Mountains. Though more than 100 miles from the volcano, the town of Othello was covered by volcanic ash. Residents of that farming community suffered the distress of their fields being covered with ash, the fear of the effects of the ash on their health, and the dread that the volcano would erupt again. During the first 6 months after the disaster, a local medical clinic reported an almost 200 percent increase in stress-related illnesses among the residents of Othello. There also was an almost 20 percent increase in the local death rate (Adams & Adams, 1984).

Daily Hassles. Though major life changes are important stress-inducing events, they are not the sole ones. Richard Lazarus and his colleagues have found other important, though less dramatic, stress-inducing events: the *hassles* of everyday life (Kanner et al., 1981). A typical day can be filled with dozens of hassles, such as forgetting one's keys, being stuck in traffic, or dealing with a rude salesperson. People who experience the cumulative effect of many daily hassles are more likely to suffer from health problems (Nelson, Karr, & Coleman, 1995), including headaches, sore throats, and influenza.

Life changes can promote illness indirectly by increasing daily hassles (Pillow, Zautra, & Sandler, 1996). Some studies have even found that there is a stronger association between hassles and illness than between life changes and illness (Ruffin, 1993). For example, a study that examined 930 victims of a devastating hurricane found that the stress they experienced was due less to the hurricane itself and more to the chronic physical, family, and financial hassles it created for them (Norris & Uhl, 1993).

Likewise, consider a person who gets divorced—a major life change. The stress she or he experiences might be a product not only of the divorce process itself but also of the need to cope with new daily hassles. Perhaps the person must now take on all of the responsibilities that had been shared during the marriage, including grocery shopping,

▶ **Posttraumatic Stress Disorder**
The bombing of the federal building in Oklahoma City in 1995 shocked Americans across the country, and left survivors with physical and psychological damage that they might never overcome completely. Survivors of disasters like this often experience posttraumatic stress disorder.

▲ **Hans Selye (1907–1982)**
"Even prehistoric man must have recognized a common element in the sense of exhaustion that overcame him in conjunction with hard labor, agonizing fear, lengthy exposure to cold or heat, starvation, loss of blood, or any kind of disease."

meal preparation, house cleaning, and child care. The person's adrenal glands might respond by increasing their secretion of the hormones cortisol, epinephrine, and norepinephrine. Though these hormones help us adapt to stressors, they also impair the immune system's ability to protect us from illness (Cacioppo, 1994). And increases in daily hassles are, indeed, associated with impairment of the immune response (Brosschot et al., 1994).

Most research on the relationship between daily hassles and illnesses makes it difficult to determine whether they are just correlated with each other or whether hassles actually promote illness. This is because few *prospective* studies have been conducted on the relationship between hassles and health. A prospective study would investigate whether a person's current level of hassles is predictive of his or her future health. This contrasts with *retrospective* studies, which simply find that people who are ill report more hassles in their recent past.

One of the few prospective studies of the effects of daily hassles found that hassles do, in fact, promote illness. On two occasions, adolescent girls who served as subjects in the study were asked to indicate, for each of twenty commonly experienced circumstances, whether it had occurred in their lives and whether they rated its occurrence as positive or negative. They also completed an illness symptoms checklist and a personality test measuring depression. The results indicated that negative circumstances were associated with depression and poor health. But this was true only when the girls also reported low levels of positive circumstances, or *uplifts*. Apparently, uplifts can buffer the effects of hassles, making them have fewer negative effects (Siegel & Brown, 1988).

This, again, is in keeping with Selye's distinction between distress (such as hassles) and eustress (such as uplifts). In fact, the immune system response might be stronger during periods of eustress than during periods of distress. This was demonstrated in a study in which healthy university students were exposed to an *antigen* (that is, a substance that evokes an immune response). Three weeks later, those who had experienced more "good stress" had higher lymphocyte proliferation than those who had experienced more "bad stress" (Snyder, Roghmann, & Sigal, 1993). This indicates that during times of maximum hassles, such as the last few weeks of a semester, students might do well to seek compensatory uplifts, such as attending a movie, going to a party, or visiting a friend.

The Biopsychology of Stress and Illness

Whether it is caused by life changes or daily hassles, stress is marked by physiological arousal and, in some cases, diminished resistance to disease. In the nineteenth century, English physician Daniel Hack Tuke wrote one of the first books on the physiological effects of psychological stressors, *Illustrations of the Influence of the Mind on the Body* (Weiss, 1972). Today, Tuke's intellectual descendants study the effects of both physical and psychological stressors on physiological arousal. As explained in Chapter 12, physical and psychological stressors evoke the *fight-or-flight response,* first described by physiologist Walter Cannon (1915/1989). The fight-or-flight response involves activation of the sympathetic nervous system and secretion of stress hormones (cortisol, epinephrine, and norepinephrine) by the adrenal glands.

The General Adaptation Syndrome

Cannon's work influenced that of Hans Selye. Selye (1936) had hoped to discover a new sex hormone. As part of his research, he injected rats with extracts of ovarian tissue and found that the rats developed stomach ulcerations, enlarged adrenal glands, and atrophied spleens, lymph nodes, and thymus glands. Selye later observed that rats displayed this same response to a variety of stressors, including heat, cold, injuries, and infections. This indicated that his initial findings were not necessarily caused by a sex hormone.

Selye also found that animals and people, in reacting to stressors, go through three stages, which he called the **general adaptation syndrome.** During the first stage, the *alarm reaction,* the body prepares to cope with the stressor by increasing activity in the sympathetic nervous system and adrenal glands (the fight-or-flight response). For example, medical students experiencing the stress of a series of academic exams respond with an increase in the stress hormone cortisol (Malarkey et al., 1995). Selye noted that during the alarm stage different stressors produced similar symptoms, such as fatigue, fever, headache, and loss of appetite.

If the body continues to be exposed to the stressor, it enters the *stage of resistance,* during which it becomes more resistant to the stressor. The stage of resistance is like the second wind you might experience while playing a sport or studying for a final exam. During a second wind, your initial fatigue gives way to a feeling of renewed energy and well-being. However, during the stage of resistance your resistance to disease might decline. During final-exams week you might be able to cope well enough to study for all your exams, but soon after finals are over you might come down with the flu. Selye called stress-induced illnesses "diseases of adaptation." If you succumb to disease, you may have entered the *stage of exhaustion.* At this point, the person's resistance to disease collapses; in extreme cases, death can follow.

Stress and Noninfectious Diseases

The fight-or-flight response evolved because it helped animals and human beings cope with periodic stressors, such as wildfires or animal attacks. Unfortunately, in twentieth-century industrialized countries, we are subjected to continual, rather than periodic, stressors. The infrequent attack by a saber-toothed tiger has been replaced by rush-hour traffic jams, three exams on one day, and threats of muggers on city streets. The repeated activation of the fight-or-flight response takes its toll on the body, possibly causing or aggravating diseases, both infectious and noninfectious ones. Stress-affected noninfectious diseases include asthma (Moran, 1991), headaches (Andrasik, 1990), diabetes (Fisher et al., 1982), gastric ulcers (Young et al., 1987), and essential hypertension (Nyklicek, Vingerhoets, & Van Heck, 1996). Such diseases have traditionally been called *psychosomatic,* based on the assumption that they are caused or worsened by emotional factors, such as unconscious conflicts.

Of all the diseases that might be affected by stress, coronary heart disease has received the most attention from health psychologists. Coronary heart disease is caused by **atherosclerosis,** which is promoted by cholesterol deposits in the coronary arteries (see Figure 16.2). Even the

general adaptation syndrome
As first identified by Hans Selye, the body's stress response, which includes the stages of alarm, resistance, and exhaustion.

atherosclerosis
The narrowing of arteries caused by the accumulation of cholesterol deposits.

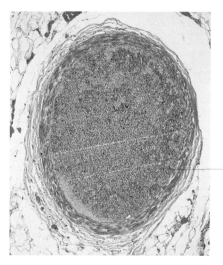

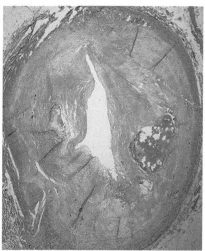

▲ **FIGURE 16.2**
Atherosclerosis
Diets high in cholesterol contribute to atherosclerosis, which narrows coronary arteries and predisposes the person to heart attacks. The top photograph shows a cross section of a healthy artery, and the bottom photograph shows a cross section of an atherosclerotic artery.

Bereavement and the Immune Response
During the first 2 months after the death of
their wives, widowers show a decrease in the
proliferation of lymphocytes in response to
doses of antigens (Schleifer et al., 1983).

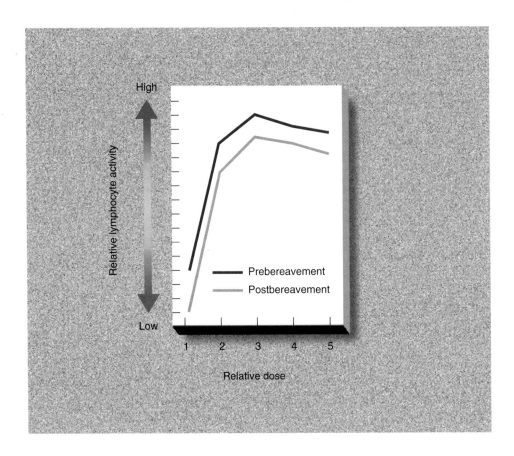

stress of everyday college life can affect the level of cholesterol in your blood. In fact, college students who merely anticipate an upcoming exam show significant increases in their
levels of blood cholesterol (Van Doornen & van Blokland, 1987). Stress can also promote
coronary heart disease by elevating heart rate and blood pressure, as well as stimulating
the release of stress hormones. This can damage the walls of the coronary arteries by
increasing blood turbulence and levels of stress hormones in the blood, making the walls
of the coronary arteries more susceptible to the buildup of cholesterol plaques (Krantz &
Manuck, 1984).

Stress and Infectious Diseases

In 1884 a physician reported in a British medical journal that the depression experienced
by mourners at funerals predisposed them to develop illnesses (Baker, 1987). A century
later, a research study provided a scientific basis for this observation (see Figure 16.3). The
study found that men whose wives had died of breast cancer showed impaired functioning
of their immune systems during the first 2 months of their bereavement (Schleifer et al.,
1983). This agrees with research showing that depression is associated with suppression of
the immune system (Zisook et al., 1994).

   The realization that stressful events, such as the death of a loved one, can impair the
immune system led to the emergence of **psychoneuroimmunology,** the interdisciplinary
field that studies the relationship between psychological factors and illness, especially
the effects of stress on the immune system (Kiecolt-Glaser & Glaser, 1995). This field
recognizes that stress affects the immune system through the mediation of the brain and
the endocrine system. Though many of the mechanisms by which stress suppresses the
immune system remain to be determined, one mechanism is well established (see Figure
16.4). Stress prompts the hypothalamus to secrete a hormone that stimulates the pituitary gland to secrete adrenocorticotropic hormone (ACTH), which then stimulates the
adrenal cortex to secrete corticosteroids. The hypothalamus also increases activity in

psychoneuroimmunology

The interdisciplinary field that studies the
relationship between psychological factors
and physical illness.

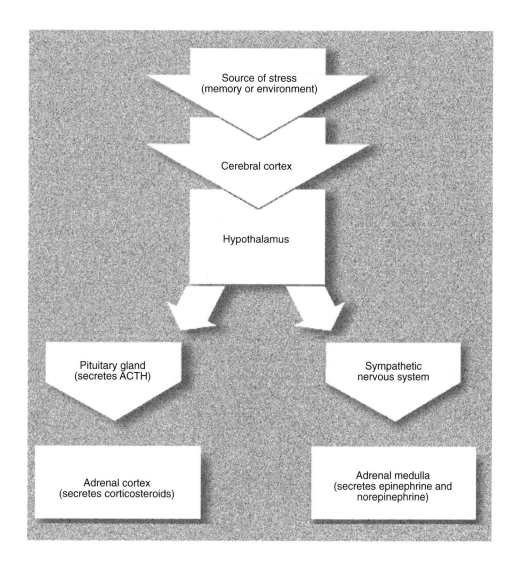

◀FIGURE 16.4
Stress Pathways
When the cerebral cortex processes stressful memories or stressful input from the immediate environment, it stimulates a physiological response by way of the endocrine system and the sympathetic nervous system. Both pathways involve the hypothalamus. The hypothalamus signals the pituitary gland, which secretes adrenocorticotropic hormone (ACTH). ACTH, in turn, stimulates the adrenal cortex to secrete corticosteroid hormones, which mobilize the body's energy stores, reduce tissue inflammation, and inhibit the immune response. The hypothalamus also sends signals through the sympathetic nervous system to the adrenal medulla, which in turn stimulates the release of epinephrine and norepinephrine. These hormones contribute to the physiological arousal characteristic of the "fight or flight" response.

the sympathetic nervous system, which stimulates the adrenal medulla to secrete the hormones epinephrine and norepinephrine. As noted earlier, though adrenal hormones might make us more resistant to stressors, they can also impair our immune systems (Kiecolt-Glaser & Glaser, 1995).

The cells chiefly responsible for the immunological response to infections are white blood cells called B-lymphocytes and T-lymphocytes. *B-lymphocytes* attack invading bacteria, and *T-lymphocytes* attack viruses, cancer cells, and foreign tissues. The immunosuppressive effects of stress hormones might explain why Apollo astronauts, after returning to Earth from stressful trips to the moon, had impaired immune responses (Jemmott & Locke, 1984). But you do not have to go to the moon to experience stress-induced suppression of your immune response, as revealed in a study of college students. After the students had given speeches that were evaluated for their merit, they showed impairment of their immune response (Marsland et al., 1995).

Additional support for the adverse effect of academic stress on the immune system came from a study of dental students (Stone et al., 1987). The students recorded their daily mood three times a week for 8 weeks. On each occasion a sample of their saliva was taken and mixed with an antigen. The results showed that their B-lymphocyte response to the antigen was stronger on days when they were in a good mood (eustress) than on days when they were in a bad mood (distress). Given that the immune system is affected by stressful life experiences, is it conceivable that the immune response could be altered by learning? This question inspired the following experiment.

Conditioned Immunosuppression
When Ader and Cohen (1982) paired saccharin-sweetened water with cyclophosphamide, a drug that suppresses the immune response, they found that the sweet-tasting water itself came to elicit immunosuppression. (See Chapter 7 for a discussion of the relationship between the UCS, UCR, CS, and CR.)

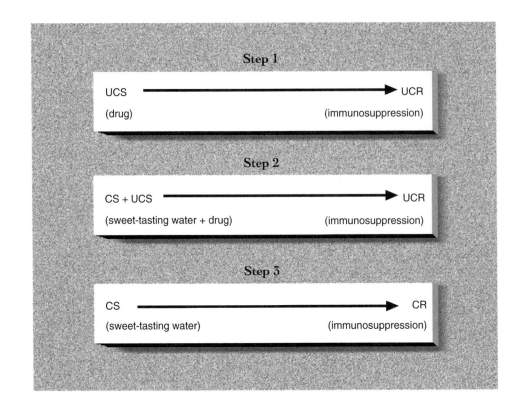

Step 1

UCS ————————————————————→ UCR
(drug)   (immunosuppression)

Step 2

CS + UCS ————————————————→ UCR
(sweet-tasting water + drug)   (immunosuppression)

Step 3

CS ————————————————————→ CR
(sweet-tasting water)   (immunosuppression)

ANATOMY OF A CONTEMPORARY RESEARCH STUDY

Can the Immune Response Be Altered by Classical Conditioning?

Rationale

Certain chemicals can enhance or suppress the immune response. Researcher Robert Ader wondered whether such a chemical could be used as the basis for classically conditioning the immune response. He reasoned that a neutral stimulus paired with the chemical might come to have the same effect on the immune response. This possibility inspired him to test his hypothesis experimentally.

Method

Ader and his colleague Nicholas Cohen (1982) used the drug cyclophosphamide, which suppresses the immune system, as the unconditioned stimulus. When mice were injected with the drug, they experienced both nausea and immunosupression—dual effects of the drug. Ader and Cohen used saccharin-flavored water as the neutral stimulus. They hoped that if the mice drank it before being injected with the drug, the taste of sweet water would suppress their immune response to an antigen.

Results and Discussion

As Ader and Cohen expected, the mice developed an aversion to sweet-tasting water, because they associated it with nausea caused by the drug. But when some of the them were later forced to drink sweet-tasting water, several developed illnesses and died. Ader and Cohen attributed this to conditioned suppression of the mice's immune response, with the sweet-tasting water having become a conditioned stimulus after being paired with the drug (see Figure 16.5). Many subsequent studies have provided additional evidence that the immune response is subject to classical conditioning (Markovic, Dimitrijevic, & Jankovic, 1993). Animal research indicates that conditioned immunosuppression might be mediated by the effects of epinephrine and norepinephrine on the immune system (Lysle, Cunnick, & Maslonek, 1991).

▲▲▲

Perhaps classical conditioning will one day be applied clinically to enhance immune responses in people who have low resistance to infections, such as those at risk for *acquired immune deficiency syndrome (AIDS)*, which is caused by the *human immunodeficiency virus (HIV)*. AIDS victims experience stress induced by both their illness and hostile social reactions to them. Such stress might further impair the functioning of their immune systems, making them even more vulnerable to infections that often prove fatal (Ironson et al., 1994).

Classical conditioning might also be used to suppress undesirable immune responses, such as those that occur in *autoimmune diseases*, in which the immune system attacks a person's own body tissues as though they were foreign. One candidate for such treatment might be rheumatoid arthritis, which is affected by stress (McFarlane & Brooks, 1990). Preliminary research indicates that another beneficial application of conditioned immunosuppression might be in preventing the rejection of transplanted tissues and organs. In one study, skin grafts in rats were less likely to be rejected when the rats had been conditioned to suppress their immune response (Gorczynski, 1990).

Stress and Cancer

In the second century, the Greek physician Galen noted that depressed women were more likely than happy women to develop cancer. An association between emotion and cancer has received support from modern research. Consider a study of medical students who had been given personality tests in medical school and were assessed 30 years later: Of those who had been emotionally expressive, less than 1 percent had developed cancer. Those who had been loners, and presumably more emotionally controlled, were 16 times more likely to develop cancer than were those who were emotionally expressive (Shaffer et al., 1987). Other studies have supported the relationship between the tendency to suppress emotions and the development of cancer (Anderson, Kiecolt-Glaser, & Glaser, 1994); apparently the suppression of emotions is associated with suppression of the immune response (Eysenck, 1994).

Assuming that our emotions can affect the progress of cancer, what mechanisms might account for this? Stress might indirectly promote cancer by encouraging cancer-promoting behaviors, such as smoking tobacco, eating high-fat foods, and drinking too much alcohol; stress might also directly interfere with the immune system's ability to defend against cancer (Delahanty et al., 1996). In fact, during periods when they are under intense academic pressure, medical students exhibit a reduction in the activity of *natural killer cells*, the lymphocytes responsible for detecting and destroying cancer cells. This appears to be the result of a decrease in the production of *interferon*, a chemical needed for the proper functioning of natural killer cells (Glaser et al., 1986). A review of relevant research studies found that depression is consistently associated with large decreases in natural killer cell activity (Herbert & Cohen, 1993). As you reflect on the link between psychological factors and cancer, note that though stress can *impair* the immune system's ability to destroy cancer cells, there is little evidence that stress can directly *cause* normal cells to become cancerous (Levenson & Bemis, 1991).

Scientific support for psychological effects on resistance to cancer has come from animal research that has demonstrated both conditioned suppression and conditioned enhancement of natural killer cell activity. In one study, mice were classically conditioned by pairing saccharin-flavored water as the conditioned stimulus with an injection of either an immunosuppressing drug or an immunoenhancing drug as the unconditioned stimulus. Conditioning occurred after just one pairing of the saccharin flavor and the drug. Subsequent exposure to the saccharin led to either enhancement or suppression of natural killer cell activity, depending on the drug that had been used as the unconditioned stimulus (Hiramoto et al., 1987). Conditioned enhancement of natural killer cell activity seems to be mediated by interferon, which apparently provides a chemical link between the central nervous system and the immune system (Solvason, Ghanta, & Hiramoto, 1993).

1. Why are cancer and cardiovascular disease the most common causes of death today but not a century ago?
2. What is posttraumatic stress disorder?
3. Why do some researchers believe that life changes create stress through their effects on daily hassles?
4. What evidence is there that the immune response can be classically conditioned?

Answers to Staying on Track start on p. S-7.

FACTORS THAT MODERATE THE STRESS RESPONSE

More than 2,000 years ago, Hippocrates recognized the relationship between individual factors and physiological responses when he observed that it is more important to know what sort of person has a disease than to know what sort of disease a person has (Rees, 1983). Because of variability among individuals, a given stressor will not evoke the same response in every person. Our reactions to stress are moderated by a variety of factors. These include *physiological reactivity, cognitive appraisal, explanatory style, feeling of control, psychological hardiness,* and *social support.*

Physiological Reactivity and Stress

People differ in their pattern of physiological responses to stressors (Walsh, Wilding, & Eysenck, 1994). Your physiological reaction to being trapped in rush-hour traffic might differ markedly from your best friend's reaction. **Physiological reactivity** refers to increases in heart rate, blood pressure, stress hormone secretion, and other physiological activity in response to stressors. In one study, men with mild hypertension played a video game while their heart rate and blood pressure were measured. Those who displayed greater increases in heart-rate and blood pressure also had higher levels of blood cholesterol. This may help explain why people with greater physiological reactivity have a higher risk of atherosclerosis (Jorgensen et al., 1988). Males and females tend to differ in their physiological reactivity. For example, males show greater increases in both cardiovascular activity and secretion of stress hormones in response to stressors. This might contribute to the greater vulnerability of males to coronary heart disease (Stoney, Davis, & Matthews, 1987).

Cognitive Appraisal and Stress

Though Hans Selye believed that all stressors produce similar patterns of physiological responses, more-recent research indicates that different stressors may produce different patterns (Krantz & Manuck, 1984). Your physiological response to rush-hour traffic might be different from your physiological response to a job interview. Richard Lazarus, whose work on daily hassles was discussed earlier in the chapter, believes that one of the reasons different stressors can produce different responses in the same person is that the person interprets the two stressors differently. This is known as **cognitive appraisal** (Lazarus, 1993), which Lazarus also uses as the basis of his theory of emotions (see Chapter 12).

Cognitive appraisal involves two stages: primary appraisal and secondary appraisal. In *primary appraisal* you judge whether a situation requires a coping response. If you judge that a situation does require a coping response, you then engage in *secondary appraisal* by determining whether you have the ability to cope with the situation. The greater the perceived controllablity of a stressful situation, the lower its perceived stressfulness (Peeters, Buunk, & Schaufeli, 1995). Consider final exams. Students who perceive them to be highly demanding and who lack confidence in their ability to perform well on them experience greater stress than students who perceive their upcoming exams as moderately demanding and are confident of their ability to perform well. This view has

---

physiological reactivity
The extent to which a person displays increases in heart rate, blood pressure, stress hormone secretion, and other physiological activity in response to stressors.

cognitive appraisal
The subjective interpretation of the severity of a stressor.

been supported by research finding lower levels of physiological reactivity to stressors in people who are high in *self-efficacy* (Bandura, 1982), a concept (see Chapter 13) that has much in common with the notion of secondary appraisal.

The importance of cognitive appraisal in affecting our physiological response to stressors was demonstrated in a replication of a study (see Chapter 12) by Lazarus and his colleagues on reactions to a stressful film (Lazarus et al., 1985). In the replication, two groups of college students viewed a film depicting three factory accidents. Before viewing the film, one group heard a statement that simply told them the content of the film, and the other group heard a statement that urged them to adopt a detached, analytical attitude while watching the film. The latter group, which used intellectualization as a means of cognitive appraisal, displayed less physiological arousal than the former group (Dandoy & Goldstein, 1990). Thus, the physiological response of the subjects depended on their cognitive appraisal of the film, not the objective content of the film.

Explanatory Style and Stress

Depressed people tend to have a pessimistic **explanatory style** (see Chapter 14). They attribute unpleasant events to *stable, global,* and *internal* characteristics of themselves. In other words, depressed people attribute unpleasant events to their own unchanging, pervasive, personal characteristics—such as a lack of intelligence. A pessimistic explanatory style is also associated with poorer health. For example, a study of Turkish undergraduates found that students who used a pessimistic explanatory style were more likely to have symptoms of physical illness (Aydin, 1993).

The possible role of a pessimistic explanatory style in the promotion of illness was also supported by a retrospective study of 99 graduates of the Harvard University classes of 1942–1944. Graduates who had used a pessimistic explanatory style at the age of 25 (based on questionnaires they had completed at that time) became less healthy between the ages of 45 and 60 than graduates who had not used a pessimistic explanatory style at age 25. All of the graduates had been healthy at age 25 (Peterson, Seligman, & Vaillant, 1988). The researchers hypothesized that a negative pessimistic style might make people less likely to take actions to counter the effects of negative life events, leading to more severe stress in their lives. A pessimistic explanatory style might increase susceptibility to illness by leading to poor health habits, suppression of the immune system, and withdrawal from sources of social support. Each of these factors can promote illness. Fortunately for many people, as demonstrated by health psychologist Shelley Taylor (1989), people with a more optimistic outlook on life—even a somewhat unrealistically positive one—are less susceptible to illness.

Feeling of Control and Stress

In a best-selling book describing his recovery from a massive heart attack, Norman Cousins, former editor of the *Saturday Review,* claimed that his insistence on taking personal responsibility for his recovery—including devising his own rehabilitation program—helped him regain his health. In contrast, as Cousins noted in his book, "good patients" (patients who remain passive) discover that "a weak body becomes weaker in a mood of total surrender" (Cousins, 1983, p. 223). Research findings have supported his anecdotal report by converging on a **feeling of control** over stressors as one of the most important factors moderating the relationship between stress and illness. A feeling of control over stressors reduces their perceived stressfulness (Paterson & Neufeld, 1995). People who work at demanding jobs and feel they have little control over job stressors are more likely to develop coronary heart disease (Krantz et al., 1988). And consider the person whom Cousins called the "good patient" in the hospital, who adopts a passive, compliant role—leaving his or her recovery up to nurses and physicians. The poorer recuperative powers of such patients are associated with **learned helplessness**—the feeling that one has little control over events in one's life.

explanatory style
The tendency to explain events optimistically or pessimistically.

▲ **Shelley Taylor**
"Mentally healthy people exhibit positive illusions."

feeling of control
The degree to which a person feels in control over life's stressors.

learned helplessness
A feeling of futility caused by the belief that one has little or no control over events in one's life, which can make one stop trying and become depressed.

People in all walks of life benefit from a sense of control over the stressors that affect them. Residents of retirement homes who are given greater responsibility for self-care and everyday activities live longer and healthier lives than residents whose lives are controlled by staff members, in part because residents who feel greater control over their daily lives maintain stronger immune responses. People who feel a lack of control tend to secrete more adrenal hormones in response to stress, which in turn can impair their immune systems (Rodin, 1986). In fact, people who perceive themselves as lacking control over their lives show reduced natural killer cell activity in response to stressors (Reynaert et al., 1995). As discussed earlier in the chapter, natural killer cells provide a defense against cancer.

A perceived lack of control might even adversely affect the health of astronauts. When the Apollo astronauts returned to Earth after their trip to the moon in 1969, they displayed impaired immune responses. Though this might have been a result of other stressful factors related to their trip, it might also have been a result of their being forced to remain passive during their highly stressful journey of almost half a million miles. In *The Right Stuff*, Tom Wolfe points out the importance of a feeling of control for test pilots and the resulting problems this caused in the recruitment of test pilots to become astronauts:

▶ The pilot's, particularly the hot pilot's, main psychological bulwark under stress was his knowledge that he controlled the ship and could always do something. . . . This obsession with active control, it was argued, would only tend to cause problems on Mercury [space] flights. What was required was a man whose main talent was for doing nothing under stress. (Wolfe, 1979, p. 151)

Psychological Hardiness and Stress

Psychologist Suzanne Kobasa was puzzled by the fact that while some people can work under chronic, intense pressure and remain healthy, others cannot. She wondered whether this might be related to personality differences. To test this possibility scientifically, she gave a group of business executives a battery of personality tests and then conducted a 5-year, prospective study during which she periodically recorded their health status. She found that those who were illness-resistant tended to have a set of personality characteristics not shared by those who were illness-prone (Kobasa, Maddi, & Kahn, 1982).

Kobasa called this set of personality characteristics *psychological hardiness*. She has found that people high in **psychological hardiness** are more resistant to stressors and, possibly as a result, are less susceptible to stress-related illness. This has been supported by other researchers, as well. For example, a study of police officers—whose jobs are among the most stressful—found that those who scored high in psychological hardiness missed fewer work days than those who scored low in it (Tang & Hammontree, 1992).

What characteristics are shared by people high in hardiness? Kobasa found that hardy people face stressors with a sense of commitment, challenge, and control (see Table 16.2). People with a sense of *commitment* are wholeheartedly involved in everyday activities and social relationships, rather than being alienated from them. Thus, even though college is stressful, hardy students remain committed to their course work rather than being alienated from it. People with a sense of *challenge* view life's stressors as opportunities for personal growth rather than as burdens to be endured. Hardy students view term papers as chances to improve their knowledge, thinking, and writing, rather than as just unpleasant demands on their time. And people with a sense of *control* believe they have the personal resources to cope with stressors, rather than being helpless in the face of them. Hardy students believe that their abilities and efforts will lead to academic success, rather than believing that nothing they do will make a difference.

But how does hardiness reduce susceptibility to illness? One way is by making hardy individuals less physiologically reactive to stressors, as demonstrated in a study of patients who were awaiting dental surgery (Solcova & Sykora, 1995). Another way is by affecting

▲ **Suzanne Kobasa**
"Hardiness has an active emphasis in that it predisposes persons to interact more intensely with stressful events in order to transform them into less stressful forms."

psychological hardiness
A personality characteristic marked by feelings of commitment, challenge, and control that promotes resistance to stress.

Commitment (versus alienation)
Hardy person: "Even though I'm not majoring in them, I would like to learn all I can from my courses in English, psychology, and other subjects."
Nonhardy person: "I don't know why I have to waste time taking courses that are not in my major."

Challenge (versus threat)
Hardy person: "My statistics course is difficult, but if I can master it, I can do well in any course."
Nonhardy person: "Statistics is too hard. Maybe I should drop the course."

Control (versus helplessness)
Hardy person: "The Spanish teacher wants us to present our term papers orally. I suppose that if I practice enough, I should be able to do it."
Nonhardy person: "I can't believe the Spanish teacher wants us to give oral reports. No matter what I do, I'll just sound stupid."

◀ **TABLE 16.2**
Psychological Hardiness
People who score high in psychological hardiness have a feeling of commitment, challenge, and control instead of a feeling of alienation, threat, and helplessness.

health habits. People high in personal hardiness, compared to people low in it, are more likely to maintain good health habits in the face of stress (Wiebe & McCallum, 1986). Thus, hardy students may be more resistant to illness because they are more likely to eat well, take vitamins, exercise more, and seek medical attention for minor ailments even when confronted by social, academic, and vocational stressors.

Social Support and Stress

Misery may indeed love company. People who have **social support** are less likely to become ill (Uchino, Cacioppo, & Kiecolt-Glaser, 1996). For example, a lack of social support is a key factor in the "broken-heart phenomenon": the tendency of some bereaved spouses to die sooner than others. Those who die sooner tend to not remarry, to live by themselves, to feel more lonely, and to have no one to talk to (Stroebe, 1994). Thus, a network of friends and relatives can buffer bereaved spouses against stress-related illness.

Social support can be tangible, in the form of money or practical help, or intangible, in the form of advice or encouragement about how to remove or tolerate stress. Social support promotes health by reducing the effects of stressful life events, promoting recovery from illness, and increasing adherence to medical regimens (Heitzmann & Kaplan, 1988). Even the social support provided by a beloved pet animal reduces physiological responses to stressors (Allen et al., 1991).

People who have recently been diagnosed as being HIV-positive experience less distress when they have social support (Schlebusch & Cassidy, 1995), and social support is associated with a stronger immune response in AIDS patients (Theorell et al., 1995). This is important, because HIV-positive individuals show reductions in natural killer cell activity and certain other lymphocytes when facing stressful life events (Evans et al., 1995).

But what experimental evidence is there that social support boosts the immune response? In one study, samples of saliva were taken from healthy college students 5 days before their first final exam, during the final-exams period, and 14 days after their last final exam. The samples were analyzed for the level of immunoglobulin A, an antibody that provides immunity against infections of the upper respiratory tract, gastrointestinal tract, and urogenital system. Salivary concentrations of immunoglobulin A after the final-exams period were lower than before it. But students who reported more-adequate social support during the pre-exam period had consistently higher immunoglobulin A

social support

The availability of support from other people, whether tangible or intangible.

Psychology and Health |

concentrations than did their peers who reported less-adequate social support (Jemmott & Magloire, 1988). This indicates that social support may promote health by strengthening the immune response.

STAYING ON TRACK: *Factors That Moderate the Stress Response*

1. What are the components of psychological hardiness?
2. How does social support moderate the stress response?

COPING WITH STRESS

Given that stress is unavoidable and often harmful, coping with stress is an important part of everyday life. Coping with stress has much in common with St. Francis of Assisi's "Serenity Prayer," which asks God for the wisdom to know the difference between what one can change and what one cannot. Similarly, one approach to coping divides it into task-oriented, emotion-oriented, and avoidance-oriented coping (Higgins & Endler, 1995). For example, suppose you find it distressing to make oral presentations. You might engage in task-oriented coping by preparing carefully for them; emotion-oriented coping by cognitively reappraising the possible negative consequences of peer responses to your presentations; or avoidance-oriented coping by not enrolling in courses that require oral presentations.

Of course, some people pursue more formal ways of coping with stress. Among the most common of these are formal stress-management programs (Kerr & Goss, 1996), such as stress-inoculation training (see Chapter 15). Two other approaches to coping with stress are aerobic exercise and relaxation training.

Exercise and Stress

Three decades ago, President John F. Kennedy, a physical fitness proponent, observed that "the Greeks knew that intelligence and skill can only function at the peak of their capacity when the body is healthy and strong—that hearty spirits and tough minds usually inhabit sound bodies" (Silva & Weinberg, 1984, p. 416). Kennedy would approve of the recent trend toward greater concern with personal fitness among adults. The only way to achieve fitness is to maintain a program that includes regular aerobic exercise (exercise that markedly raises heart rate for at least 20 minutes). The beneficial effect of aerobic exercise was demonstrated in a longitudinal study (Brown & Siegel, 1988), which found that adolescents under high levels of stress who exercised regularly had a significantly lower incidence of illness than did adolescents who exercised little (see Figure 16.6). People who exercise benefit because they become less physiologically reactive to stressors (Rejeski et al., 1991) and more confident in their ability to cope with them (Steptoe et al., 1993). There is also evidence that exercise can enhance the functioning of the immune system (Smith, 1995). Because high physical fitness is associated with lower absenteeism (Tucker, Aldana, & Friedman, 1990), employers have increasingly promoted employee physical fitness programs.

Relaxation and Stress

Because stress is associated with physiological arousal, health psychologists emphasize the importance of relaxation training. Several techniques have proved effective in reducing psychological or physiological arousal. These include hypnosis (Leung, 1994), meditation (Janowiak & Hackman, 1994), biofeedback (Tyson & Sobschak, 1994), deep rhythmic breathing (Fried, 1990), and restricted environmental stimulation, or REST (Schulz & Kaspar, 1994). Hypnosis and meditation are discussed in Chapter 6, biofeedback in Chapter 7, and REST in Chapter 11.

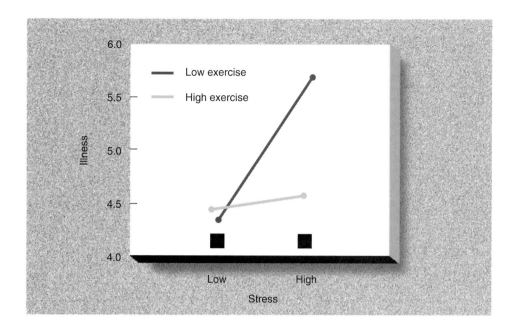

◀ FIGURE 16.6
Exercise and Illness
A study of the relationship between exercise
and illness found that adolescents who exercised little and adolescents who exercised regularly did not differ in their incidence of illness
when under low levels of stress. In contrast,
when under high levels of stress, those who
exercised regularly had a significantly lower
incidence of illness than did those who exercised little (Brown & Siegel, 1988).

▲ **Edmund Jacobson (1888–1983)**
"To be excited and to be fully relaxed are physiological opposites. Both states cannot exist . . .
at the same time."

progressive relaxation

A stress-reducing procedure that involves
the successive tensing and relaxing of each
of the major muscle groups of the body.

The most basic relaxation technique is **progressive relaxation,** which was developed
decades ago by Edmund Jacobson (1929/1974). To practice progressive relaxation, successively tense and relax each of the major muscle groups of your body. By doing so, you learn
to distinguish muscle tension from relaxation and, eventually, to relieve anxiety by immediately relaxing your muscles. This will reduce activity in your sympathetic nervous
system, as well. Progressive relaxation has been effective in reducing high blood pressure
(Broota, Varma, & Singh, 1995).

Progressive relaxation can even enhance the immunological response (Hewson-Bower
& Drummond, 1996). Consider the following experiment that involved medical students,
conducted by Janice Kiecolt-Glaser, a leading researcher on psychoneuroimmunology.
Blood samples were taken from students 1 month before midterm exams and then on the
day of the exams. Half of the students were randomly assigned to participate in regular
relaxation practice during the month between the two measurement days. The students
who were not assigned to practice relaxation, compared to the students who were, displayed a significantly greater decrease in natural killer cell activity between the first and
second measurements (Kiecolt-Glaser et al., 1986). You will recall that natural killer cells
are one of the body's main defenses against cancer cells.

STAYING ON TRACK: *Coping with Stress*

1. What did the study of adolescents by Brown and Siegel (1988) conclude about the
   relationship between exercise and health?
2. What did the study by Kiecolt-Glaser et al. (1986) find about the relationship
   between relaxation and the immune response?

HEALTH-IMPAIRING HABITS

Habits as varied as smoking, overeating, avoiding exercise, and failing to wear seat belts
sharply increase the chances of illness, injury, or death. Yet a study found that college students tended to have an "it can't happen to me" attitude. Their estimate of the probability
that their own risky behaviors would lead to illness or injury underestimated the actual
probability. Because of our inability to estimate the true riskiness of our behaviors, such as
the risk of getting skin cancer from sun exposure (Eiser et al., 1995), programs aimed at

▲ **Janice Kiecolt-Glaser**
"The possible enhancement of immune function by behavioral strategies has generated con-
siderable interest."

changing health-impairing habits must not only point out risky behaviors but also make participants realize that those habits make them more susceptible to unhealthy consequences than they might believe (Weinstein, 1984). An ambitious community program in New Zealand called Superhealth Basic used brief group sessions to help participants improve their behaviors related to sleep, stress, weight, smoking, drinking, exercise, and nutrition. Participants showed significant improvements in their mental health, physical health, management of stress, and sense of well-being (Raeburn et al., 1994).

One of the most important factors that determine whether people are motivated to engage in health-promoting behavior is their feeling of self-efficacy (Kelly, Zyzanski, & Alemagno, 1991). People high in self-efficacy feel that their actions will be effective. People with a high sense of self-efficacy in regard to health-promoting behaviors are more likely to see the benefits of such behaviors and to downplay barriers to performing them (Alexy, 1991). Feelings of self-efficacy are positively related to important health-promoting behaviors, including maintenance of smoking cessation, control of diet and body weight, and adherence to preventive health behaviors (O'Leary, 1985). The most important health-impairing habits include unsafe sexual practices, lack of exercise, smoking tobacco, and poor nutrition.

Unsafe Sexual Practices: The Plague of AIDS

Today many health psychologists have turned their attention to unsafe sexual practices that contribute to the spread of venereal diseases, including AIDS, syphilis, gonorrhea, and genital herpes. But because it is inevitably fatal, AIDS has become of greatest interest to them. AIDS kills its victims by impairing their immune systems, making them eventually succumb to cancer or opportunistic infections—that is, infections that rarely occur in people with healthy immune systems. Since 1981, when it was first identified, AIDS has spread through much of the world with alarming rapidity. No group is safe from it today. AIDS afflicts people of all ages, sexes, races, and sexual orientations. A survey found that Irvin "Magic" Johnson's announcement that he had contracted HIV from unprotected, promiscuous sexual behavior made many people more aware of the risk to heterosexuals (Brown & Basil, 1995). Nonetheless, heterosexuals still tend to underestimate the risk of contracting HIV from unprotected sex (Kusseling et al., 1996).

HIV is spread by infected blood or semen (Catania et al., 1990). Some victims, most notably hemophiliacs, have acquired the virus in transfusions of contaminated blood. One of the most widely publicized cases in which this occurred was that of young Ryan White. Heroin addicts can acquire HIV by sharing hypodermic needles with infected addicts. The virus can also be transmitted through sexual activity, including anal sex and vaginal sex. Even infants born to mothers with AIDS are at high risk of developing the disease. Transmission of the virus from infected dental or medical personnel to their patients, or from infected patients to dental or medical personnel, is much less likely. Nonetheless, the case of Kimberly Bergalis, who was infected by her dentist, gained national attention. There is no evidence that the virus is spread by kissing, simple touching, food handling, or other casual kinds of contact.

People infected with HIV can take up to 10 years or more to develop full-blown AIDS. But because there is no cure for AIDS, its prevention is crucial. One of the primary means of prevention is educating people to avoid risky behaviors. Foremost among the suggestions has been to practice "safe sex" (or at least "safer sex"). In regard to AIDS, the safest sex is abstinence or limiting oneself to one uninfected partner. Many people choose not to abstain, however, and might have a series of sexual partners, so the next-best suggestions are to use latex condoms and limit the number of one's sex partners.

Efforts to reduce risky behaviors have achieved some success. Though elsewhere in the world AIDS is more prevalent among heterosexuals, in North America it has been more prevalent among homosexual men. This has been attributed to the common practice among homosexual males of unprotected anal sex. The 10 percent of heterosexuals who practice anal sex are also at increased risk of contracting AIDS (Voeller, 1991). Because it has so ravaged the North American homosexual community, the earliest anti-AIDS programs have

(a)

(b)

(c)

(d)

been aimed at homosexuals. Cities with large homosexual populations have instituted workshops on AIDS prevention for homosexual and bisexual men. For example, a survey of homosexual men in San Francisco, where there is a high level of AIDS education, found a significant increase in their use of condoms (Catania et al., 1991).

Lack of Exercise: Fitness and Health

People who exercise regularly are healthier and live longer than those who do not. Exercise promotes health and longer life, in part by boosting the immune system and reducing physiological reactivity (Senkfor & Williams, 1995). For example, subjects who had tested positive for the AIDS virus showed enhanced immunological responses after participating in an aerobic exercise program (Antoni et al., 1991).

There is especially strong evidence for the effectiveness of exercise in preventing obesity and cardiovascular disease (Labbate et al., 1995). Aerobic exercise (such as running, swimming, bicycling, brisk walking, or cross-country skiing) combats obesity by burning calories, raising the basal metabolic rate, and inhibiting the appetite. Aerobic exercise also reduces the cardiovascular risk factors of elevated cholesterol and high blood pressure (Martin & Dubbert, 1985).

The health risks of physical inactivity and the health benefits of exercise have led many sedentary people to start exercising. Even employers, who see the benefits of having a healthy workforce, have instituted employee fitness programs. Research findings indicate that these are successful in reducing absenteeism, turnover, and health-care costs (Gebhardt & Crump, 1990). Unfortunately, of those who begin formal exercise programs, about 50 percent will drop out within 6 months. According to Rod Dishman, an authority on exercise adherence, people who are obese or who have symptoms of cardiovascular disease—the very people who might benefit most from exercise—are the least likely to exercise (Dishman & Gettman, 1980).

One of the reasons for failing to adhere to exercise programs is low self-efficacy—that is, a lack of confidence in one's ability to fulfill the requirements of the program. One study measured the self-efficacy of participants in an 8-week step-aerobics exercise class. There was a positive relationship between their self-efficacy levels and their attendance (Fontaine & Shaw, 1995). Common reasons for failing to adhere to exercise programs are a lack of time and a lack of motivation (McAuley et al., 1990).

▲ Exercise
People who exercise are more stress resistant and disease resistant than people who do not. The well-publicized benefits of exercise account for the popularity of exercise "gurus" such as Jane Fonda, Jack LaLanne, and Richard Simmons.

The failure of people to maintain exercise programs has prompted health psychologists to study ways of increasing exercise adherence (Godin et al., 1995). One of the best ways to improve the motivation to exercise is to make exercising enjoyable (Wankel, 1993). Perhaps this explains the popularity of dance aerobics classes and similar approaches to exercise. But some programs aimed at increasing adherence are more formal. In one study, groups of people engaged in jogging, aerobic dancing, or conditioning for skiing for 10 weeks. Some of the participants in each of the three groups also took part in a special program to increase their motivation to exercise. The program made participants more aware of obstacles to exercise and taught them how to cope with periodic exercise lapses, instead of having an all-or-none attitude. Rather than give up after exercise lapses, exercisers were urged to return immediately to their exercise programs. The results showed that those who participated in the adherence program, compared to those who did not, were indeed more likely to adhere to their exercise programs (Belisle, Roskies, & Levesque, 1987).

Smoking Tobacco: The Most Deadly Habit

During the 1996 presidential campaign, Senator Robert Dole provoked controversy when he declared that smoking was not addictive. Dole's proclamation went against an enormous amount of evidence that smoking tobacco is addictive and perhaps the single worst health-impairing habit (Klesges, Ward, & DeBon, 1996). Despite the harmful effects of smoking, governments permit it—and even profit from it. In 1565 King James I of England, though viewing smoking as a despicable habit, chose to tax cigarettes rather than ban them, a practice governments still follow today (Whitlock, 1987).

The Effects of Smoking

Contrary to Dole's claim, smokers can become addicted to the nicotine in tobacco—though a small minority of smokers remain "chippers" who are able to smoke intermittently without becoming addicted (Shiffman et al., 1995). Though many addicted smokers insist they smoke to relieve anxiety or to make them more alert, they actually smoke to avoid the unpleasant symptoms of nicotine withdrawal, which include irritability, hand tremors, heart palpitations, and difficulty concentrating. Thus, addicted smokers smoke to regulate the level of nicotine in their bodies (Parrott, 1995). Smoking is especially difficult to stop because it can become a conditioned response to many everyday situations, as in the case of smokers who light a cigarette when answering the telephone, after eating a meal, or upon leaving a class.

Smoking produces harmful side effects through the actions of tars and other substances in cigarette smoke. Smoking causes fatigue by reducing the blood's ability to carry oxygen, making smoking an especially bad habit for athletes. But, more important, smoking contributes to the deaths of more than 300,000 Americans each year from stroke, cancer, emphysema, and heart disease. Thus, its prevention is paramount.

The Prevention of Smoking

The ill effects of smoking make it imperative to devise programs to prevent the onset of smoking. Children are more likely to start smoking if their parents and peers smoke. Many smoking-prevention programs are based in schools and provide information about the immediate and long-term social and physical consequences of smoking. Students learn that, in the short run, smoking causes bad breath, yellow teeth and fingers, and weakened stamina. They also learn that, in the long run, smoking causes cancer, emphysema, and cardiovascular disease. But simply providing children with information about the ill effects of smoking is not enough to prevent them from starting. Smoking-prevention programs must also teach students how to resist peer pressure and advertisements that encourage them to begin smoking. Overall, smoking-prevention programs have been effective, reducing the number of new smokers among participants by 50 percent (Flay, 1985). Such programs have been especially effective in black communities (see Figure 16.7).

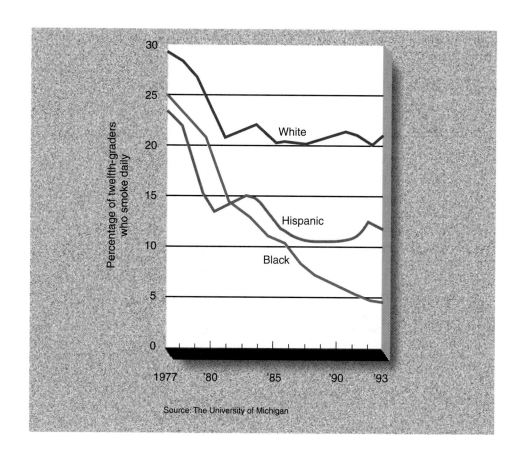

◄FIGURE 16.7

The Decline in Smoking Among Youth
The movement against smoking in American society has dramatically reduced smoking among teenagers. The graph shows the results of a study sponsored by the University of Michigan of changes in smoking by twelfth-graders between 1977 and 1993. The most striking finding is the precipitous decline in smoking among black teenagers—while about 25 percent smoked in 1977, less than 5 percent smoked in 1993. This has been attributed to black communities' mobilization against cigarette advertising directed specifically at black youth. This also shows the influence of cultural factors on smoking behavior. Smoking is considered highly undesirable by the vast majority of black youths, while it is considered "cool" and rebellious by a large minority of white youth.

The Treatment of Smoking

Though programs to prevent the onset of smoking are important, techniques to help people stop smoking are also essential. But quitting is difficult. A major University of Minnesota study followed 802 smokers for 2 years. Of those smokers, 62 percent tried to quit, but only 16 percent succeeded and 9 percent became "chippers" (Hennrikus, Jeffery, & Lando, 1995). Those who do quit find it difficult to resist relapsing. Two thirds of those who quit—whether on their own or with formal treatment—relapse within 3 months (Carmody, 1993).

Health psychologists use a variety of techniques to help those who cannot quit on their own. Subjects are taught to expect the symptoms of nicotine withdrawal—which begins 6 to 12 hours after smoking cessation, peaks in 1 to 3 days, and lasts 3 to 4 weeks (Hughes, Higgins, & Bickel, 1994). Even smoking nonnicotine (placebo) cigarettes reduces withdrawal symptoms (possibly because of classical conditioning) and might be useful in the transition period to total abstinence (Butschky et al., 1995). But certain consequences of quitting, including hunger, weight gain, and nicotine craving, might persist for 6 months or more (Hughes et al., 1991). Nicotine prevents weight gain by reducing hunger and increasing metabolism (Winders & Grunberg, 1989). Thus, many smokers rightly fear that quitting will lead to weight gain. But weight gain is not a necessary consequence of smoking cessation (Talcott et al., 1995).

Because most of the harmful effects of smoking are caused by tars and other chemicals in tobacco rather than by the nicotine, some treatments aim at preventing smoking by providing subjects with safer ways of obtaining nicotine. These nicotine replacement techniques prevent some of the relapse caused by the desire to avoid weight gain (Nides et al., 1994) or withdrawal symptoms (Levin et al., 1994).

Nicotine replacement therapy has proved successful. The two most common techniques use *nicotine chewing gum* (Fortmann & Killen, 1995) or a *nicotine patch* that provides nicotine through the skin (Cinciripini et al., 1996). A meta-analysis of well-controlled experiments found that of subjects who used a nicotine patch, 22 percent abstained from smoking after 6 months. Moreover, those who used a nicotine patch smoked less than those who used a placebo patch—that is, a patch without nicotine (Fiore et al., 1994). Smokers who use the nicotine patch and chew nicotine gum have more success in quitting than those who use either technique alone (Fagerstrom, Schneider, & Lunell, 1993). A recent addition to the nicotine replacement arsenal is nicotine nasal spray (Perkins et al., 1996).

Of course, though replacement therapy reduces the health risks of smoking, it does not help smokers overcome their *addiction* to nicotine. Those who wish to overcome their addiction do better if they are high in two of the factors that appear repeatedly as health promoters: a feeling of self-efficacy (Nicki, Remington, & MacDonald, 1984) and the presence of social support (Nides et al., 1995). But a study of 3,610 smokers found that social support was more important in quitting for men than for women (Murray et al., 1995).

For those who are motivated to overcome their addiction, *nicotine fading* is useful. This technique gradually weans smokers off nicotine by having them use cigarettes with lower and lower nicotine content until it has been reduced to virtually zero (Becona & Garcia, 1993). A more extreme technique is *rapid smoking,* a form of aversion therapy in which the smoker is forced to take a puff every 6 to 8 seconds for several minutes. This induces feelings of nausea and dizziness, and after several sessions the person might develop an aversion to smoking. Like nicotine fading, rapid smoking has proved effective (Tiffany, Martin, & Baker, 1986).

Another approach to smoking cessation involves *self-management programs* that use behavior modification to promote smoking cessation. The programs encourage smokers to avoid stimuli that act as cues for smoking, such as coffee breaks, alcoholic beverages, and other smokers. A potentially powerful way of teaching smokers self-management skills is to have their physicians educate them about how to quit. An ambitious study in England involved 1,200 heavy smokers and their primary-care physicians. They received brief advice from their physician, a booklet on how to quit smoking, and nicotine patches or placebo patches they wore for 16 hours a day for 18 weeks. A 1-year follow-up found that the nicotine patch was twice as effective as a placebo patch in promoting abstinence: 9.6 percent versus 4.8 percent, respectively (Stapleton et al., 1995).

Poor Nutrition: The Fatty Diet

Health psychologists recognize the importance of diet in health and illness. They are especially concerned with the relationship between diet and cardiovascular disease. A high-fat diet is one of the main risk factors in cardiovascular disease. High-fat diets contribute to high blood pressure and high levels of cholesterol in the blood, which promote atherosclerosis by the buildup of plaque deposits that narrow the arteries. The narrowing of cerebral arteries and coronary arteries reduces blood flow, promoting strokes and heart attacks. Health psychologists have developed programs that combine nutritional education and behavior modification to help people reduce their risks of cardiovascular disease by adopting healthier eating habits. For example, programs that reduce fat intake produce significant reductions in blood pressure in participants with elevated blood pressure (Jacob, Wing, & Shapiro, 1987).

A high-fat diet also contributes to obesity—an important risk factor in illness for both men and women. Yet in Western cultures a leaner figure has been stylish for women only since the early twentieth century, and a muscularly toned figure only in the past decade or two. For the preceding 600 years, cultural standards favored a more rounded figure (Bennett & Gurin, 1982). You have probably seen this in Renaissance paintings that depict the ideal woman as being plump. Figure 16.8 depicts changes in cultural views concerning the ideal female figure. Even today some cultures favor rotund women. Thus, body weight is regulated by cultural, as well as biological and behavioral, factors (Brownell & Wadden, 1991).

But current Western standards of beauty, and concern with the health-impairing effects of obesity, make weight loss a major North American preoccupation. Weight reduction seems deceptively easy: You simply make sure that you burn more calories than you ingest.

The Ideal Female Figure
In Western cultures the ideal female figure has changed over time. The ideal has at times been represented by the plump Rubenesque nude of the early seventeenth century, the voluptuous actress Marilyn Monroe of the 1950s, and the muscular athlete Florence Griffith-Joyner of the 1980s.

Yet, as noted by obesity researcher Kelly Brownell (1982), less than 5 percent of obese people maintain their weight loss long enough to be considered "cured." Some obesity researchers argue that this pessimistic figure represents only people who have been in formal weight-loss programs. In contrast, most people who try to lose weight on their own succeed. Perhaps those who seek treatment for obesity are a select group of people who are the least likely to succeed (Schachter, 1982). In fact, negative results typically come from university-based treatment programs. A small percentage of people in these programs lose weight—but they differ from the general population of obese people. They tend to be more overweight, more likely to engage in binge eating, and more prone to psychological disorders (Brownell, 1993).

Because of the great cultural variability in perceptions of ideal body types and the difficulty obese people have in maintaining weight loss, some critics believe it might be better to help obese people learn to accept their body type. There are group counseling programs that try to accomplish this. Participants discuss ways of maintaining their self-respect and social relationships despite being fat in a culture that frowns on fat people (Tenzer, 1989). In keeping with this approach, some authorities believe it would be better to promote weight control as a way to improve health rather than as way to achieve a particular body weight (Foreyt & Goodrick, 1994).

Though many people do, in fact, desire to lose weight for health reasons, others desire to do so for social or aesthetic reasons. But how can people control their weight? A common but ineffective approach is dieting. People who diet may drastically reduce their caloric intake for weeks or months. Unfortunately, as dieters lose weight, their basal metabolic rate slows (Foreyt, 1987), forcing them to diet indefinitely to maintain their lower level of weight—an impossible feat. Because dieting cannot last for a lifetime, dieters eventually return to the same eating habits that contributed to their obesity. Moreover, dieting is unhealthy; 25 percent of diet-induced weight loss consists of lean body tissue, including skeletal muscle (Brownell, 1982).

Failing to change their eating habits, obese people often resort to diet pills, usually amphetamines. These stimulant drugs produce weight loss by their effects on the hypothalamus, though the exact mechanism is unknown (Paul, Hulihan-Giblin, & Skolnick, 1982). Amphetamines eventually lose their effectiveness, though, and can cause insomnia, high blood pressure, and symptoms of paranoid schizophrenia.

Formal psychological approaches to weight loss rely on behavior therapy in conjunction with aerobic exercise. In behavior therapy programs, participants monitor their eating behaviors, change maladaptive eating habits, and correct their misconceptions about eating. Aerobic exercise promotes weight loss not only by burning calories during the exercise but by raising the metabolic rate for hours afterward. This counters diet-induced decreases in the basal metabolic rate. Weight loss through aerobic exercise is also healthier than weight loss through dieting alone, because only 5 percent of the weight lost will be lean tissue (Brownell, 1982). Despite the effectiveness of aerobic exercise in weight control, half of

those who enroll in formal exercise programs drop out within a few months (McMinn, 1984). Moreover, it is difficult for many obese people to maintain the intensity of exercise necessary to produce significant weight loss (Blix & Blix, 1995).

People who wish to lose weight are often impatient. But rapid weight loss does not guarantee long-term weight loss. This was the finding of a study of 49 obese women randomly assigned to a 52-week behavior-modification program combined with either moderate or severe restrictions on their daily caloric intake. Subjects in the moderate diet condition were limited to 1,200 calories a day throughout the study. Those in the severe diet condition were limited to a 420-calorie liquid diet for 16 weeks and a 1,200-calorie diet for the remaining 36 weeks.

During the first 26 weeks, those in the strict diet condition lost almost twice as much weight as those in the moderate diet condition. But by the end of a 26-week follow-up after the study, those who had been in the strict diet condition had gained so much weight that their net weight loss was slightly less than those who had been in the moderate diet condition (Wadden, Foster, & Letizia, 1994). And though the past three decades have demonstrated the short-term effectiveness of behavior modification in helping mildly or moderately obese people lose weight, no program has been able to halt the inevitable return to obesity by the great majority of participants (Wilson, 1994).

STAYING ON TRACK: *Health-Impairing Habits*

1. What behaviors can transmit HIV from one person to another?
2. What are the beneficial effects of regular aerobic exercise?
3. Why is it unwise to try to lose weight strictly by dieting?

REACTIONS TO ILLNESS

Despite your best efforts to adapt to stress and to live a healthy lifestyle, you will periodically suffer from illness. Health psychologists study ways to encourage people to seek treatment for symptoms of illness, to reduce patient distress, and to increase patient adherence to medical regimens.

◄ *Losing the Weight Is the Easy Part*
Talk-show host Oprah Winfrey has gained attention for her repeated efforts to lose weight and keep it off. Her difficulty in doing so is shared by millions of people.

Seeking Treatment for Medical Problems

What do you do when you experience a headache, nausea, diarrhea, dizziness, constipation, or nasal congestion? Your reaction would depend on your interpretation of the symptoms. This would depend, in turn, on your past experience with these symptoms, information you have received about them, their intensity, and their duration. Some people inappropriately seek medical attention for the most minor symptoms. However, many others deny, ignore, or misinterpret their symptoms, which might make them fail to seek help; as a consequence, many people let minor ailments become serious, or delay treatment of serious ailments that might be cured by early treatment. Victims of heart attacks have a much better prognosis for recovery if they seek help within an hour of experiencing symptoms. But victims typically wait several hours from the time they first notice symptoms until they seek help (Dracup et al., 1995).

The importance of seeking appropriate medical care has inspired health psychologists to study factors that motivate people to seek treatment. An important factor is social support. People with social support might be encouraged to seek treatment, might be referred to appropriate medical personnel, and might feel less anxious about seeking treatment (Roberts, 1988). Even one's explanatory style can affect the decision to seek medical treatment. A study of undergraduates found that those with a pessimistic explanatory style were less likely than optimistic students to seek medical treatment. Thus, the finding that pessimistic people are usually less healthy than optimistic ones might reflect their greater passivity in the face of disease (Lin & Peterson, 1990).

One of the main factors in seeking treatment for symptoms is how one interprets them. A study of 366 older adults (average age 62 years) found that when they had ambiguous symptoms of illness, those who had experienced a stressful life event in the preceding 3 weeks were less likely to seek treatment than were those who had not experienced one. Evidently, those who did not seek treatment attributed their symptoms to the stress instead of to an illness. When the symptoms were not ambiguous, there was no difference in the likelihood of seeking treatment (Cameron, Leventhal, & Leventhal, 1995).

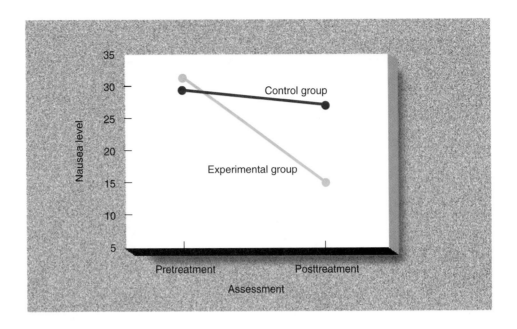

► FIGURE 16.9
Controlling Patient Distress
Children who played video games while undergoing cancer chemotherapy (the experimental group) showed a marked reduction in nausea. In contrast, children who did not play video games while undergoing cancer chemotherapy (the control group) showed little change in nausea (Redd et al., 1987).

Relieving Patient Distress

Illness, especially chronic illness or illness that requires surgery or painful procedures, induces distress in patients. Patients differ in their ability to cope with illness or stressful medical procedures. An important factor is their degree of self-efficacy. For example, patients high in self-efficacy cope better with painful dental procedures (Litt, Nye, & Shafer, 1995).

Some patients can also benefit from psychological techniques that encourage effective coping with pain or stressful procedures. These patients include cancer sufferers (Telch & Telch, 1985), children who undergo prolonged hospitalizations (Yap, 1988), and burn victims who must undergo excruciatingly painful skin debridement (Wisely, Masur, & Morgan, 1983). A meta-analysis found that psychological preparation for surgery is effective in reducing pain, distress, and length of stay. Informing surgery patients about the procedures they will undergo is especially effective (Johnston & Vogele, 1993).

Modeling has been a useful technique for reducing patient distress during unpleasant medical procedures (O'Halloran & Altmaier, 1995). In keeping with this, observing a patient who has undergone successful surgery can be beneficial to a patient about to undergo surgery. Patients waiting to undergo coronary bypass surgery who have a hospital roommate who has just undergone successful surgery of any kind are less anxious before surgery, walk more after surgery, and go home sooner than similar patients who have a roommate who is about to undergo surgery. Apparently, simply observing a person who has survived surgery has a calming effect on patients anticipating surgery. Moreover, people who have undergone surgery can reduce the distress of patients about to undergo surgery by letting them know what to expect and suggesting ways to cope with the situation (Kulik & Mahler, 1987).

In some cases, relatively simple procedures can reduce illness-related distress. In a study of children undergoing chemotherapy for cancer, the experimental group played video games during their chemotherapy and a control group did not. As shown in Figure 16.9, children in the experimental group reported less anxiety and nausea. The children who played video games were apparently distracted from the unpleasant sensations caused by the chemotherapy (Redd et al., 1987).

There has been increasing interest in another factor related to patient distress: the quality of the relationship between the patient and the medical practitioner. A study found a negative correlation between the perceived empathy of nurses and patient anger, anxiety, and depression (Olson, 1995). Patients who perceive a lack of empathy in their physicians are more likely to sue them for malpractice (Frankel, 1995). Findings like these have prompted some health psychologists to suggest that health-care professionals receive education on how to interact better with their patients, including learning how to prepare patients for stressful medical and surgical procedures, as well as how to communicate with worried family members (Wilson-Barnett, 1994).

Promoting Adherence to Medical Regimens

Recovery from illness often depends on following a medical regimen recommended by a physician. This might include a prescription drug, a restricted diet, or an exercise program. Adherence is important in medical regimens aimed at controlling diabetes (DiMatteo et al., 1993), treating obesity (Brownell & Cohen, 1995), relieving arthritis pain (Taal et al., 1993), and lowering high blood pressure (Dunbar-Jacob, Dwyer, & Dunning, 1991). One of the main reasons patients fail to follow treatment regimens is that they do not understand the physician's instructions (Glen & Anderson, 1989). The patient's personality also is a factor. A study relating the five-factor theory of personality (see Chapter 13) to patience adherence found that patients who scored high on the factor of conscientiousness were more likely to adhere to medication regimens (Christensen & Smith, 1995).

As is the case in the relief of patient distress, the relationship between the patient and the physician plays a key role in adherence to medical regimens (Clark et al., 1995). Patients are more likely to adhere to regimens prescribed by physicians they like. One of the most important factors determining whether a patient will be satisfied with a physician is the physician's emotional warmth during consultations. A physician who acts more like an automobile mechanic fixing a car than a health-care provider helping a suffering human being will evoke negative reactions from patients. A study that used videotaped consultations between patients and other physicians supported this. The results indicated that the most important determinant of patient satisfaction with consultations was the emotional expressiveness of the physician (Bensing, 1991).

Sometimes patients abandon their medical regimens prematurely because they no longer notice any symptoms. Consider a patient with essential hypertension (marked by chronic high blood pressure) who must take medication, watch her diet, and follow an exercise program. Because we have, at best, only a slight ability to sense the level of our blood pressure (Pennebaker & Watson, 1988), the patient might assume, incorrectly, that because she does not feel like she has high blood pressure, she actually does not have high blood pressure—and abandon her prescribed medical regimen. This again points to the importance of adequate communication between the physician and the patient. Physicians need to communicate the risks and benefits of treatment and the specific details of the medical regimen (DiMatteo, Reiter, & Gambone, 1994).

Even the simple act of asking patients to adhere to medical regimens can be effective. In one study, patients were put on 10-day antibiotic regimens to treat bacterial infections. The patients were divided into an experimental group and a control group. Those in the experimental group made oral and written commitments to adhere to the regimen. Those in the control group did not. The results showed that those in the experimental group were more likely than those in the control group to adhere to the regimen (Putnam et al., 1994).

As you have just read, health psychologists have demonstrated that we play an active role in maintaining our health, succumbing to disease, and recovering from illness. Though some diseases and injuries are unavoidable, we can no longer view ourselves as simply the passive victims of viruses, bacteria, or carcinogens. By learning to adapt effectively to stressors, eliminate risky behaviors, and adopt health-promoting behaviors, we can greatly reduce our chances of illness, injury, and death. For example, the way in which you adapt to everyday stressors may affect your risk of developing coronary heart disease, as exemplified by research on Type A behavior—the topic of the next section.

1. What are some factors that affect seeking treatment for symptoms of illness?
2. What role does the relationship between patient and health practitioner play in medical treatment?

THINKING ABOUT *Psychology*

Does Type A Behavior Promote Coronary Heart Disease?

▲ Mike Ditka and Type A Behavior
When Mike Ditka, the intense, aggressive former head coach of the Chicago Bears, suffered a heart attack during the 1988 football season, his only risk factor was a Type A behavior pattern.

Type A behavior
A syndrome—marked by impatience, hostility, and extreme competitiveness—that is associated with the development of coronary heart disease.

On November 2, 1988, "Iron Mike" Ditka, the tough head coach of the Chicago Bears football team, was hospitalized with a mild heart attack. In a televised interview on ESPN, Ditka's physician reported that Ditka had none of the common physical risk factors for coronary heart disease, such as smoking, obesity, or lack of exercise. His only risk factor was a psychological one: *Type A behavior.* A published review of research on Type A behavior in middle-aged men (such as Mike Ditka) found that Type A behavior was present in 70 percent of those with coronary heart disease, and in only 46 percent of those who were healthy (Miller et al., 1991). Thus, Type A behavior is associated with an increased risk of coronary heart disease—though its presence does not guarantee coronary heart disease and its absence does not guarantee freedom from it.

CHARACTERISTICS OF TYPE A BEHAVIOR

What are the characteristics of Type A behavior? They were first described in the following classic research study.

ANATOMY OF A CLASSIC RESEARCH STUDY

Is There a Relationship Between Behavior and Heart Disease?

Rationale

In the late 1950s, San Francisco cardiologist Meyer Friedman noticed that his waiting room chairs were worn along the front edges. He interpreted this as a sign of the impatience of his patients, who spoke rapidly and interrupted frequently during conversations. The patients were also easily angered, highly competitive, and driven to do more and more in less and less time. Friedman, with his colleague Ray Rosenman, called this syndrome of behaviors **Type A behavior.** In contrast, *Type B behavior* is characterized by patience, an even temper, and willingness to do a limited number of things in a reasonable amount of time. The Type A person might also show time urgency by changing lanes to advance a single car length, chronic activation by staying busy most of every day, and *multiphasic activity* by reading, eating, and watching television at the same time. This lifestyle means that the Type A person is in a constant state of fight or flight. Would this lifestyle be associated with a greater risk of heart disease? Let's look at the method that Friedman and Rosenman (1959) used to answer this question.

Method

Friedman and Rosenman asked managers and supervisors of large companies to identify colleagues who fit the description of the Type A and Type B behavior patterns. They identified 83 men, including many executives, who fit each pattern. No women were included because at the time there were relatively few women in executive positions. The subjects were interviewed about their medical history and behavioral tendencies, such as being driven to succeed, feeling highly competitive, and feeling under chronic time pressure. They were observed for body movements, tone of voice, teeth clenching, and any observable signs of impatience. Based on the interview, 69 of the men were labeled pure Type A and 58 of the men were labeled pure Type B. The subjects also kept diaries of their food and alcohol intake for 1 week, and their blood cholesterol levels were measured.

Results and Discussion

Friedman and Rosenman found that the Type A subjects had significantly higher levels of blood cholesterol than the Type B subjects. More important, 28 percent of the Type A subjects had symptoms of coronary heart disease, but only 4 percent of the Type B subjects had such symptoms. Before leaping to the conclusion that the study definitely demonstrated that Type A behavior promotes heart disease, note two other findings. First, the Type A subjects smoked much more than Type B did. Today we know that smoking is a major risk factor in heart disease. Second, the Type A subjects' parents had a higher incidence of coronary heart disease than did the Type B subjects' parents. Perhaps the Type A subjects inherited a genetic tendency to develop heart disease. Of course, there could just as well be a genetic tendency toward Type A behavior, which in turn might promote heart disease. In any case, Friedman and Rosenman contributed one of the first formal studies demonstrating a possible link between behavior and heart disease.

Later, based on subsequent research findings, Friedman and Rosenman boldly concluded:

▶ In the absence of Type A Behavior Pattern, coronary heart disease almost never occurs before 70 years of age, regardless of the fatty foods eaten, the cigarettes smoked or the lack of exercise. But when this behavior pattern is present, coronary heart disease can easily erupt in one's thirties or forties. (Friedman & Rosenman, 1974, p. xi)

▲▲▲

▲ **Multiphasic Activity**
The Type A behavior pattern is associated with multiphasic activity, in which the person engages in several activities at once as part of a continual effort to do more and more in less and less time.

In 1975 Friedman, Rosenman, and their colleagues (Rosenman et al., 1975) reported the results of a study on coronary heart disease that began in 1960 and lasted 9 years—the Western Collaborative Group Study. They studied more than 3,000 middle-aged men who were free of heart disease at the beginning of the study. Each of the men was categorized as Type A or Type B, based on an interview. The subjects answered questions related to Type A behavior, and the examiner noted behavioral manifestations of Type A behavior during the interview, such as rapid speech, hostile comments, or interrupting the examiner. The results indicated that during the period of the study, the men classified as Type A were more than twice as likely to develop coronary heart disease as were the men classified as Type B (Rosenman et al., 1975). The pattern of behavior shown by the Type A subjects indicates that they are overconcerned with controlling their environment. This leads to repeated physiological arousal when other people, time constraints, or personal responsibilities threaten their sense of control.

Type A behavior is not just a style of responding to the environment; it can induce the very environmental circumstances that evoke it. This was illustrated in a study that compared Type A and Type B police radio dispatchers during work shifts. Type A's generated more job pressures by initiating extra work tasks for themselves and attending to multiple tasks at the same time. Moreover, perhaps following the adage "If you want something done, give it to a busy person," their coworkers and supervisors looked to them when there were additional tasks to be performed. So, Type A people can help create work conditions that help maintain their driven, time-urgent, impatient behavioral style (Kirmeyer & Biggers, 1988).

In keeping with this, a Type A student might take a course overload, work at a full-time job, serve on several student committees, and participate in intramural sports—all at the same time. In fact, Type A students report both more daily hassles and more daily uplifts than Type B's do (Margiotta, Davilla, & Hicks, 1990). Even when under the intense time pressure caused by their lifestyle, Type A's will usually continue to perform their organizational duties (Organ & Hui, 1995).

▲ Redford Williams
"Research evaluating the relationship between hostility and coronary heart disease suggests that higher levels of anger toward others coupled with difficulty in expressing that anger form a key neurotic conflict in the predisposition to coronary heart disease."

But the role of Type A behavior in coronary heart disease was brought into question by the results of a 22-year follow-up of participants in the Western Collaborative Group Study, which found no relationship between Type A behavior and coronary heart disease mortality (Ragland & Brand, 1988). In fact, Type A's who had suffered a heart attack had a somewhat *lower* risk of a second heart attack. Of course, this might have been a result of other factors, such as greater medical attention given to Type A than to Type B heart-attack victims.

Though this study indicated that the *overall* pattern of Type A behavior is unrelated to coronary heart disease, research findings have been converging on a specific component of the Type A behavior pattern, *cynical hostility*, as the factor most related to coronary heart disease. Cynical hostility is marked by rude, condescending behavior (Dembroski & Costa, 1988).

EFFECTS OF TYPE A BEHAVIOR

Regardless of whether cynical hostility or some other aspect of Type A behavior promotes coronary heart disease, how might it do so? One way might be by inducing chronic stress responses. In fact, people who display cynical hostility are more physiologically reactive to stressors, including competitive tasks (Felsten & Leitten, 1993) and interactions in which they must disclose personal information (Christensen & Smith, 1993).

High physiological reactivity might unleash harmful effects through the actions of stress hormones. This was confirmed in a study in which Redford Williams and his colleagues (1982) had Type A and Type B male college students perform the stressful task of counting aloud backward by 17s from 7,683. The first to finish would win a prize. The results indicated that the Type A's displayed a significantly greater increase in levels of the adrenal gland stress hormones cortisol, epinephrine, and norepinephrine. These stress hormones promote the buildup of cholesterol plaques on the walls of arteries, narrowing them and increasing the risk of heart attacks due to atherosclerosis (Fava, Littman, & Halperin, 1987).

Perhaps, in everyday life, Type A's induce similar physiological responses in themselves by their eagerness to subject themselves to stressful competitive situations. For example, a study found that when playing competitive computer games, Type A's displayed greater heart-rate increases than Type B's (Griffiths & Dancaster, 1995). But reviews of the research are contradictory in regard to whether people displaying Type A behavior are (Lyness, 1993) or are not (Myrtek, 1995) more physiologically reactive to stressors.

Another possible factor mediating the effect of Type A behavior on coronary heart disease is the tendency of Type A people to ignore symptoms of illness. Before being hospitalized with his heart attack, Mike Ditka had ignored pain earlier in the week; at a team workout shortly before the heart attack, his assistant coaches forced him to seek medical attention. His job meant more to him than his health. This tendency of Type A's to discount illness first appears in childhood. Type A children are less likely to complain of symptoms of illness, and Type A children who have surgery miss fewer days of school than Type B's who have surgery (Leikin, Firestone, & McGrath, 1988).

DEVELOPMENT OF TYPE A BEHAVIOR

Once researchers identified the characteristics of Type A behavior and its possible harmful effects, they became interested in studying how Type A behavior develops. Though there is only weak evidence of a hereditary basis for Type A behavior, there is strong evidence that the pattern runs in families. In a study of male and female adolescents, those who scored high on the hostility component of Type A behavior and also had a parent suffering from essential hypertension showed a greater elevation in blood pressure in response to stressful tasks than did subjects who had a parent with essential hypertension but who did not score high on hostility (McCann & Matthews, 1988).

Karen Matthews, a leading researcher on Type A behavior, points to child-rearing practices as the primary origin of Type A behavior. Parents of Type A children encourage them to try harder even when they do well and offer them few spontaneous positive comments.

Type A children might be given no standards except "Do better," which makes it difficult for them to develop internal standards of achievement. They might then seek to compare their academic performance with the best in their class. This might contribute to the development of the hard-driving component of the Type A behavior pattern (Matthews & Woodall, 1988). You probably know fellow students who want not only an A on an exam but the highest grade in the class. In keeping with this are research findings that Type A behavior is associated with perfectionism (Flett et al., 1994).

MODIFICATION OF TYPE A BEHAVIOR

Because of the possible association between Type A behavior and coronary heart disease, its modification might be wise. But a paradox of Type A behavior is that Type A persons are not necessarily disturbed by their behavior. Why change a behavior pattern that is rewarded in competitive Western society? Programs to modify the Type A behavior of those who are willing to participate try to alter specific components of the Type A behavior pattern, particularly impatience, hostility, and competitiveness. For example, a program using flotation REST (see Chapter 11) reduced hostility in people displaying the Type A behavior pattern (Forgays & Forgays, 1994).

▲ **Karen Matthews**
"Type A children's awareness of high standards . . . may maintain their struggle to strive after everescalating goals."

Another treatment program has been successful in reducing Type A behavior in people who are especially prone to it—college teachers. Teachers received cognitive behavior modification and assertiveness training in eight 2-hour group sessions. The participants learned to modify their maladaptive beliefs and attitudes related to anger, impatience, hostility, and competitive drive. They also learned to express themselves assertively, rather than passively or aggressively. A follow-up found that the participants displayed less impatience and less hostility a year later (Thurman, 1985). More recently, rational-emotive behavior therapy has been used sucessfully to reduce Type A behavior, especially its time urgency component (Moller & Botha, 1996).

As you can see, though the worn edges of Friedman's waiting-room chairs have inspired much research, many questions about Type A behavior as a risk factor in coronary heart disease remain to be answered. Which aspects of the Type A behavior pattern promote coronary heart disease? What physiological mechanisms account for the relationship between Type A behavior and coronary heart disease? Why do some people adopt the Type A behavior pattern while others adopt the Type B pattern? What protects certain Type A people from coronary heart disease? How can we best modify the Type A behavior pattern?

STAYING ON TRACK: *Does Type A Behavior Promote Coronary Heart Disease?*

1. What is the Type A behavior pattern?
2. What have researchers on Type A behavior discovered about cynical hostility?
3. What childhood factors are associated with the development of the Type A behavior pattern?

▶ CHAPTER SUMMARY

STRESS AND ILLNESS

Health psychology is the field that studies the role of psychological factors in the promotion of health and the prevention of illness and injury. One of the main topics of interest to health psychologists is stress, the physiological response of the body to physical and psychological demands. The main psychological kinds of stress are frustration, pressure, and conflict. They are associated with stressors involving life changes and daily hassles.

Hans Selye identified a pattern of physiological response to stress that he called the general adaptation syndrome, which includes the alarm reaction, the stage of resistance, and the stage of exhaustion. Stress has been linked to noninfectious disease, infectious disease, and cancer. The field that studies the relationship between psychological factors and illness is called psychoneuroimmunology.

FACTORS THAT MODERATE THE STRESS RESPONSE

The relationship between stress and illness is mediated by a variety of factors. These include physiological reactivity, cognitive appraisal, explanatory style, feeling of control, personal hardiness, and social support.

COPING WITH STRESS

Health psychologists use stress-management programs to help people learn to cope with stress. Other formal methods of coping with stress include aerobic exercise and relaxation training.

HEALTH-IMPAIRING HABITS

Most deaths in the United States are associated with unhealthy habits, including unsafe sexual practices, lack of exercise, smoking tobacco, and poor nutrition. Programs aimed at changing these habits hold promise for reducing the incidence of illness and death.

REACTIONS TO ILLNESS

Health psychologists study aspects of how people cope with illness, including seeking treatment, patient distress, and adherence to medical regimens. The patient-practitioner relationship is an important factor in adherence.

THINKING ABOUT PSYCHOLOGY: DOES TYPE A BEHAVIOR PROMOTE CORONARY HEART DISEASE?

People who display Type A behavior are easily angered, highly competitive, and driven to do more and more in less and less time. They also show time urgency, chronic activation, and multiphasic activity. Research indicates that at least some components of the Type A behavior pattern, particularly cynical hostility, are related to the development of coronary heart disease.

Type A behavior might increase the risk of coronary heart disease by increasing blood pressure and levels of stress hormones such as cortisol, epinephrine, and norepinephrine. Type A behavior originates in childhood and is associated with parents who constantly encourage their children to improve without providing clear standards of achievement. Programs aimed at reducing the risk of coronary heart disease by altering the Type A behavior pattern show promise, but their effect on the incidence of coronary heart disease remains to be determined.

KEY CONCEPTS

health psychology 558

Stress and Illness

stress 558
stressor 558
frustration 559
pressure 559
conflict 560

approach-approach conflict 560
avoidance-avoidance conflict 560
approach-avoidance conflict 560
posttraumatic stress disorder 562
general adaptation syndrome 565
atherosclerosis 565
psychoneuroimmunology 566

Factors That Moderate the Stress Response

physiological reactivity 570
cognitive appraisal 570
explanatory style 571
feeling of control 571
learned helplessness 571
psychological hardiness 572
social support 573

Coping with Stress

progressive relaxation 575

Is There a Relationship Between Behavior and Heart Disease?

Type A behavior 586

KEY CONTRIBUTORS

Stress and Illness

Hans Selye 558
Kurt Lewin 560
Thomas Holmes 561
Richard Rahe 561
Richard Lazarus 563
Walter Cannon 565

Robert Ader 568
Nicholas Cohen 568

Factors That Moderate the Stress Response

Suzanne Kobasa 572

Coping with Stress

Edmund Jacobson 575
Janice Kiecolt-Glaser 575

Health-Impairing Habits

Rod Dishman 577
Kelly Brownell 581

Is There a Relationship Between Behavior and Heart Disease?

Meyer Friedman 586
Ray Rosenman 586
Redford Williams 588
Karen Matthews 588

FOR MORE INFORMATION ON PSYCHOLOGY AND HEALTH

FOR GENERAL WORKS ON PSYCHOLOGY AND HEALTH

Dasen, P. R., Berry, J. W., & Sartorius, N. (Eds.). (1988). *Health and cross-cultural psychology.* Newbury Park, CA: Sage.

Sarafino, E. P. (1994). *Health psychology: Biopsychosocial interaction.* New York: Wiley.

Taylor, S. E. (1991). *Health psychology* (2nd ed.). New York: McGraw-Hill.

FOR MORE ON STRESS AND ILLNESS

Psychological Stress and Psychological Stressors

Goldberger, L., & Breznitz, S. (Eds.). (1993). *Handbook of stress: Theoretical and clinical aspects.* New York: Free Press.

Holmes, T. H., & David, E. M. (Eds.). (1989). *Life change, life events, and illness: Selected papers.* Westport, CT: Praeger.

Lipton, M. I. (1994). *Posttraumatic stress disorder.* Springfield, IL: Charles C Thomas.

Biopsychology of Stress and Illness

Buckingham, J. C., Gillies, G., & Cowell, A. M. (1997). *Stress, stress hormones, and the immune system*. New York: Wiley.

Cooper, C. L., & Watson, M. (Eds.). (1991). *Cancer and stress*. New York: Wiley.

Goldstein, D. S. (1995). *Stress, catecholamines, and cardiovascular disease*. New York: Oxford University Press.

Rice, P. L. (1992). *Stress and health* (2nd ed.). Belmont, CA: Brooks/Cole.

Selye, H. (1956). *The stress of life*. New York: McGraw-Hill.

Shorter, E. (1992). *From paralysis to fatigue: A history of psychosomatic illness in the modern era*. New York: Free Press.

FACTORS THAT MODERATE THE STRESS RESPONSE

Buchanan, G., & Seligman, M. E. (Eds.). (1994). *Explanatory style*. Hillsdale, NJ: Erlbaum.

Cousins, N. (1989). *Head first: The biology of hope*. New York: Dutton.

Friedman, H. S. (1991). *The self-healing personality: Why some people achieve health and others succumb to illness*. New York: Henry Holt.

Lazarus, R. S. (1991). *Stress and coping* (3rd ed.). New York: Columbia University Press.

Maddi, S. R., & Kobasa, S. (1984). *Hardy executive: Health under stress*. Belmont, CA: Brooks/Cole.

Peterson, C., Maier, S. F., & Seligman, M. E. P. (1993). *Learned helplessness: A theory for the age of personal control*. New York: Oxford University Press.

Sarason, B. R., Sarason, I., & Pierce, G. R. (Eds.). (1990). *Social support: An international view*. New York: Wiley.

Seligman, M. E. P. (1991). *Learned optimism*. New York: Knopf.

Taylor, S. E. (1989). *Positive illusions: Creative self-deception and the healthy mind*. New York: Basic Books.

COPING WITH STRESS

Fried, R. (1990). *The breath connection*. New York: Human Sciences Press.

Pennebaker, J. (1990). *Opening up: The healing power of confiding in others*. New York: Morrow.

Schiraldi, G. R. (1994). *Stress management strategies* (2nd ed.). Dubuque, IA: Wm. C. Brown.

Willis, J. D., & Campbell, L. F. (1992). *Exercise psychology*. Champaign, IL: Human Kinetics.

FOR MORE ON HEALTH-IMPAIRING HABITS

Dishman, R. K. (1994). *Advances in exercise adherence*. Champaign, IL: Human Kinetics.

Manning, W. G., Keeler, E. B., Newhouse, J. P., Sloss, E. M., & Wasserman, J. (1991). *The costs of poor health habits*. Cambridge, MA: Harvard University Press.

Mermelstein, R. J. (1990). *Smoking cessation: A biopsychosocial approach*. New York: Pergamon.

Polivy, J., & Herman, C. P. (1983). *Breaking the diet habit: The natural weight alternative*. New York: Basic Books.

Temoshok, L., & Baum, A. (Eds.). (1990). *Psychosocial perspectives on AIDS*. Hillsdale, NJ: Erlbaum.

FOR MORE ON REACTIONS TO ILLNESS

Blacker, R. S. (1987). *The psychological experience of surgery*. New York: Wiley.

Cramer, J. A., & Spilker, B. (1991). *Patient compliance in medical practice and clinical trials*. New York: Raven Press.

Fisher, S., & Todd, A. D. (1992). *The social organization of doctor-patient communication*. Norwood, NJ: Ablex.

Gregg, C. H., Robertus, J. L., & Stone, J. B. (1989). *The psychological aspects of chronic illness*. Springfield, MA: Charles C Thomas.

FOR MORE ON TYPE A BEHAVIOR

Friedman, M. (1997). *Type A behavior: Its diagnosis and treatment*. New York: Plenum.

Houston, B. K., & Snyder, C. R. (Eds.). (1988). *Type A behavior pattern: Research, theory, and intervention*. New York: Wiley.

Roskies, E. (1987). *Stress management for the healthy Type A: Theory and practice*. New York: Guilford.

Siegman, A. W., & Smith, T. W. (Eds.). (1993). *Anger, hostility, and the heart*. Hillsdale, NJ: Erlbaum.

Williams, R. (1989). *The trusting heart: Great news about Type A behavior*. New York: Random House.

FOR MORE ON CONTRIBUTORS TO THE STUDY OF PSYCHOLOGY AND HEALTH

Benison, S., Barger, A. C., & Wolfe, E. L. (1987). *Walter B. Cannon: The life and times of a young scientist*. Cambridge, MA: Belknap/Harvard.

Selye, H. (1979). *The stress of my life: A scientist's memoirs*. New York: Van Nostrand Reinhold.

Social Behavior

social psychology

In the 1890s, bicycle racing was a major spectator sport in North America. As noted in Chapter 11, Norman Triplett (1898) observed that those who raced against other riders rode faster than those who raced against time. He decided to study this phenomenon experimentally by having boys spin fishing reels as fast as they could while competing against either time or another boy. He found that those who competed against another boy performed faster. This, the first experimental study of the relationship between psychological factors and sport performance (Davis, Huss, & Becker, 1995), was possibly the first experiment in *social psychology*.

Social psychology is the field that studies behavior in its interpersonal context—that is, how people affect one another's thoughts, feelings, and behaviors. Though social-psychological research was conducted before the turn of the century and the first social-psychology textbooks were published in 1908 (Pepitone, 1981), social psychology did not become an important field of study until after World War II, when many psychologists became interested in the formal study of social behavior. The major topics of interest to social psychologists include *social cognition, interpersonal attraction, attitudes, group dynamics, prosocial behavior,* and *aggression.*

SOCIAL COGNITION: THE PROCESSING OF SOCIAL INFORMATION

Psychologists who study **social cognition** are concerned with how we perceive, interpret, and predict social behavior. As you will read, though social cognition is usually accurate (Jussim, 1991), biases and subjectivity can distort it. Two of the main topics in social cognition are *causal attribution* and *person perception.*

Causal Attribution: Judging the Causes of Behavior

As first noted in the 1940s by social psychologist Fritz Heider (1944), when we engage in **causal attribution** we determine the extent to which a person's behavior is caused by the person or by the person's circumstances. When you decide that the person is primarily responsible for his or her behavior, you are making a *dispositional attribution.* That is, you would be attributing the behavior to personal qualities, such as emotions, abilities, or personality traits. When you decide that circumstances are primarily responsible for a person's behavior, you are making a *situational attribution.* Consider explanations given for poverty. Two research studies, one using university students and one using nonstudents, found that political liberals and political conservatives tended to make different attributions for it (Zucker & Weiner, 1993). Liberals tended to make situational attributions for poverty (blaming it on factors such as discrimination and lack of opportunities), and conservatives tended to make dispositional attributions (blaming it on factors such as a lack of effort or ability).

Principles of Causal Attribution

There was so much research on causal attribution in the 1970s that it became known as "the decade of attribution theory in social psychology" (Weiner, 1985b, p. 74). The most influential attribution theorist of that decade was Harold Kelley; he identified factors that determine when we make either dispositional attributions or situational attributions.

social psychology

The field that studies how people affect one another's thoughts, feelings, and behaviors.

social cognition

The process of perceiving, interpreting, and predicting social behavior.

causal attribution

The cognitive process by which we infer the causes of both our own and other people's social behavior.

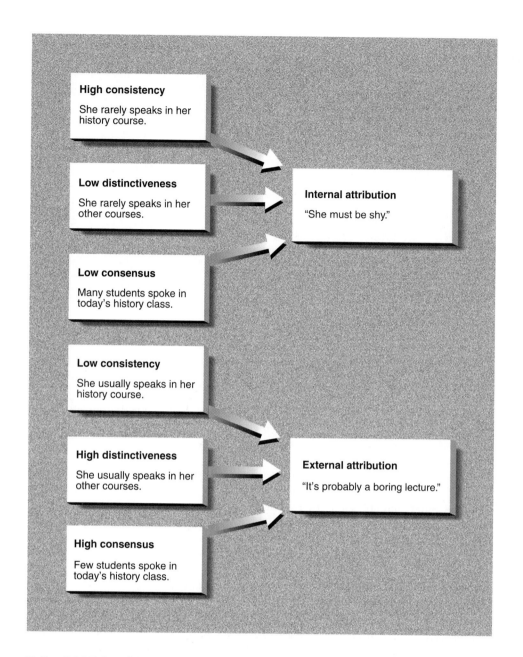

High consistency

She rarely speaks in her history course.

Low distinctiveness

She rarely speaks in her other courses.

Low consensus

Many students spoke in today's history class.

Internal attribution

"She must be shy."

Low consistency

She usually speaks in her history course.

High distinctiveness

She usually speaks in her other courses.

High consensus

Few students spoke in today's history class.

External attribution

"It's probably a boring lecture."

◀ FIGURE 17.1

Dispositional and Situational Attribution
In deciding why a student did not speak today in a history class, Kelley (1973) would have us consider the factors of consistency, distinctiveness, and consensus. These are only two of the many possible combinations of the three factors. Though low consistency is normally associated with situational (external) attributions, high consistency can be associated with either situational or dispositional (internal) attributions.

▲ Harold Kelley
"Individuals, in making attributions for behavior, expect to encounter information patterns indicating . . . person or circumstance causation. Each of these patterns is characterized by certain levels of consensus, distinctiveness, and consistency."

Kelley (1973) found that causal attribution depends on *consistency*, *distinctiveness*, and *consensus*. **Consistency** is the extent to which a person behaves in the same way in a given situation over time. How consistent are you in participating in your introductory psychology class? **Distinctiveness** is the extent to which a person behaves in the same way across different situations. Do you participate to the same extent in other courses as in your introductory psychology course? And **consensus** is the extent to which, in a given situation, other people behave the same as the person being observed. Do other students participate to the same extent as you do in your introductory psychology course?

These factors played a role in a study of college students who were manipulated into either cheating or not cheating during an experiment. When asked to explain their behavior, those who had cheated made situational attributions for their actions and those who had not cheated made dispositional attributions. Cheaters noted the high distinctiveness, high consensus, and low consistency of their actions. Noncheaters noted the low distinctiveness, low consensus, and high consistency of their actions. The cheaters' attributions helped them maintain a positive self-image, and the noncheaters' attributions helped them enhance their self-image (Forsyth, Pope, & McMillan, 1985). Figure 17.1 illustrates these two patterns of causal attribution.

consistency

The extent to which a person behaves in the same way in a given situation on different occasions.

distinctiveness

The extent to which a person behaves in the same way across different situations.

consensus

The extent to which, in a given situation, other people behave in the same way as the person being observed.

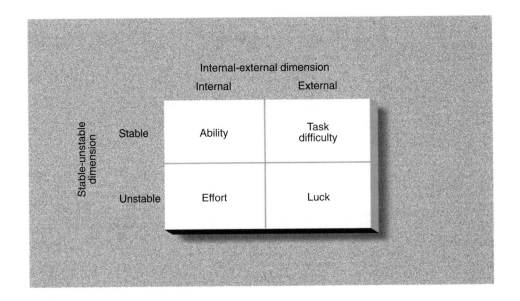

▲ **Bernard Weiner**
"A variety of sources of information are used to reach causal inferences in achievement-related contexts. The primary perceived causes of success and failure are ability and effort."

fundamental attribution error
The bias to attribute other people's behavior to dispositional factors.

actor-observer bias
The tendency of observers to make dispositional attributions for the behavior of others but to make situational attributions for their own behavior.

Dimensions of Causal Attribution

Kelley's theory of attribution was soon joined by one devised by Bernard Weiner (1985a) to explain our successes and failures. Weiner and his colleagues found that estimating the relative impact of dispositional and situational factors is important but cannot by itself account for causal attribution. Weiner identified three dimensions that govern causal attribution. The *internal-external dimension* is akin to Kelley's distinction between dispositional and situational attribution. The *stable-unstable dimension* refers to the degree to which we attribute a behavior to a factor that is stable or unstable. And the *controllable-uncontrollable dimension* indicates the extent to which we attribute a behavior to a factor that is controllable or uncontrollable. Weiner has found that people in a variety of cultures around the world use these dimensions in making attributions for success and failure (Schuster, Forsterling, & Weiner, 1989). Figure 17.2 illustrates the interaction of two of Weiner's attributional dimensions.

Werner's three attributional dimensions are commonly used by students in explaining their performance in academic courses (Anazonwu, 1995). In fact, students might use the dimensions in making excuses that both maintain their self-esteem and prevent professors from becoming angry with them (Weiner, Figueroa-Munoz, & Kakihara, 1991). Suppose you wanted to make an excuse for submitting a term paper late. Your excuse would be more effective if you attribute your behavior to external, unstable, and uncontrollable factors, such as a family emergency, than if you attribute it to internal, stable, and controllable factors, such as a difficulty in budgeting your time effectively.

Biases in Causal Attribution

If human beings were as rational and objective as Mr. Spock in "Star Trek," the causal attribution process would be straightforward. But being somewhat irrational and subjective, we exhibit biases in the causal attributions we make. One bias is the tendency to attribute other people's behavior to dispositional factors. This is known as the **fundamental attribution error** (Nisbett & Ross, 1980). A survey of advice columns, including "Dear Abby" and "Ann Landers," found that people who write for advice tend to attribute their own problems to situational factors and other people's problems to dispositional factors (Schoeneman & Rubanowitz, 1985). Thus, in explaining why other people are unemployed, we might commit the fundamental attribution error by considering it the product of their laziness. Yet if we find ourselves unemployed, we might attribute it to a bad economy. This tendency for observers to make dispositional attributions for the behavior of others but situational attributions for their own behavior is called the **actor-observer bias.**

Why are we subject to the actor-observer bias? One explanation is that we usually have greater knowledge of the circumstances that influence our own behavior than of those

◀ **The Actor-Observer Bias**
If you were the driver of the red car, which struck the car on the right, you would probably blame the accident on situational factors, such as a bad road. Yet if you saw someone else have the accident, you would probably blame it on dispositional factors, such as carelessness.

that influence other people's behavior. As an example, suppose that a student is consistently absent from her introductory psychology course. Her professor might attribute the absences to her unreliable nature. In contrast, the student might attribute her absences to dull lectures. Thus, the greater awareness that the student has of the circumstances affecting her behavior might lead her to make a situational attribution for her absences. In contrast, the professor, being aware only of the student's behavior, might be biased in favor of making a dispositional attribution for her absences (Eisen, 1979).

We are also subject to a **self-serving bias,** which is the tendency to make dispositional attributions for our own positive behaviors and situational attributions for our own negative behaviors. The self-serving bias is prevalent among college students, who will take credit for their academic successes but deny responsiblity for their failures (McAllister, 1996). A study of college students found that those who received A's or B's tended to make dispositional attributions for their own performance, attributing their success to their own efforts and abilities. In contrast, students who received C's, D's, or F's tended to make situational attributions, attributing their lack of success to bad luck and difficult tests (Bernstein, Stephan, & Davis, 1979). The self-serving bias is in keeping with evidence (see Chapter 13) that psychological well-being is associated with the maintenance of a somewhat unrealistically positive self image (Taylor & Brown, 1988).

self-serving bias
The tendency to make dispositional attributions for one's successes and situational attributions for one's failures.

Person Perception: Judging Other People

In addition to making attributions about the causes of behavior, we spend a great deal of our time making judgments about the personal characteristics of people. Such **person perception** is often based on superficial characteristics. For example, people who wear glasses are perceived as more intellectual than those who do not (Hellstrom & Tekle, 1994).

person perception
The process of making judgments about the personal characteristics of others.

Impression Management: Putting Your Best Foot Forward

Do you know a fellow student who is considered "phony" by other students? The students might be reacting to that student's obvious attempt to convey an impression that is at odds with his or her true self. Such deliberate attempts to control the impressions that others form of us is called **impression management** (Leary & Kowalski, 1990). Impression management is a normal part of everyday social relations. Job applicants use impression managment when they write their resumes (Knouse, 1994) and during job interviews (Stevens & Kristof, 1995).

A common technique that we use in impression management is self-handicapping (see Chapter 13). When we self-handicap, we let others know that we are performing under a handicap. If we then do well, we look good to others. If we do poorly, others will attribute our poor performance to our "handicap." Consider a student who announces that he was anxious during an exam. Success on the exam would reflect well on his ability; others would attribute failure on the exam to his anxiety rather than to lack of ability—thereby protecting his self-esteem. We would not be so lenient in judging his performance if he claimed he had not tried hard (Rhodewalt et al., 1995).

impression management
The deliberate attempt to control the impression that others form of us.

social schema

A cognitive structure comprising the presumed characteristics of a role, an event, a person, or a group.

stereotype

A social schema that incorporates characteristics, which may be positive or negative, supposedly shared by almost all members of a group.

Social Schemas: Models of Social Reality

College professor. Rock concert. Bill Cosby. Eskimo. Each of these concepts involves a **social schema,** which comprises the presumed characteristics of a role, event, person, or group. Social schemas bring order to what might otherwise be a chaotic social world by permitting us to interpret and predict the behavior of others. A social schema can have powerful effects on our social perception. Think of the labels *spokesperson* and *mouthpiece*. Would you expect different behaviors from individuals described by these terms? The social schema for *mouthpiece* includes negative characteristics that the social schema for *spokesperson* does not. The possible negative impression created by the label *mouthpiece* was the basis of a lawsuit on behalf of Frank Sinatra's attorney against *Barron's Business and Financial Weekly*, which referred to the attorney as "Sinatra's mouthpiece." The results of a survey sponsored by Sinatra's attorney showed that the term *mouthpiece* created a negative impression in the minds of readers. This was introduced as evidence in court. Though the judge accepted the validity of this evidence, *Barron's* won the case on the grounds of freedom of the press (Kramer et al., 1985).

Social Stereotypes: Overgeneralizing About Others

If you believe that almost all members of any social group—men, women, blacks, whites, Jews, Christians, and so on—share a set of characteristics that is unique to that group, you are guilty of stereotyping. A **stereotype** is a social schema that includes characteristics, which can be positive or negative, that supposedly belong to almost all members of a group (Krueger, 1996). Thus, stereotypes are based partly on our tendency to view members of our own group (our *in-group*) as more variable than members of another group (an *out-group*). For example, a study of college sorority members found that they judged members of their own sorority as being more diverse than those of another sorority (Park & Rothbart, 1982). The more variability we believe exists within a group, the less likely we are to stereotype individual members of that group (Ryan, Judd, & Park, 1996).

Stereotypes are used to make predictions about the behavior of group members. We are likely to rely on stereotypes in making decisions about others' behavior when we have little else but their group memberships on which to base our decisions. Of course, few people who hold stereotypes assume that *all* members of an out-group share the same characteristics. Thus, when confronted with someone who violates a stereotype, they simply assimilate that person into their out-group schema as an exception to the rule (Hewstone, Johnston, & Sird, 1992).

First Impressions: The Primacy Effect

When we first meet a person, we might have little information about the individual other than her or his sex, race, apparent age, and physical appearance. Each of these might activate a particular social schema, which in turn will create a first impression of that person. A first impression functions as a social schema to guide our predictions of a person's behavior and our desire to interact with that person. First impressions are important in many situations; for example, they can determine whether college roommates will become friends (Berg, 1984).

A classic experiment by Harold Kelley (1950) demonstrated the importance of a first impression on our evaluation of a stranger. Undergraduates were given a written description of a guest lecturer as "a rather warm person, industrious, critical, practical, and determined" or the same description with the word *warm* replaced by the word *cold*. After the lecture, which provided the opportunity for questions and discussion, the students were asked for their impressions of the lecturer. Students who had been told that the lecturer was warm rated him as more informal, sociable, and humorous than did those who were told he was cold. Those who had been told the lecturer was warm also asked more questions and participated in more discussions with him. This indicated that the students assimilated the lecturer's behavior into the schema they had been given. This study has been replicated successfully using similar methodology (Widmeyer & Loy, 1988).

Self-Fulfilling Prophecy: How Our Expectations Can Influence Other People's Behavior

One of the important effects of first impressions is the **self-fulfilling prophecy,** which is the tendency for one person's expectations to make a second person behave in accordance with them (Dvir, Eden, & Banjo, 1995). This occurs because the social schema we have of the other person will make us act in a certain way toward that person, which in turn will make the person respond in accordance with our expectations (Darley & Fazio, 1980). Thus, if you expect a person to be unfriendly and, as a result, to act cold and aloof, you might elicit unfriendly behavior from that person—even if he or she would normally be inclined to be friendly.

A classic experiment, which showed how first impressions can create self-fulfilling prophecies, investigated the influence of teachers' expectations on the performance of schoolchildren. The teachers were told that a new intelligence test indicated that certain students were "late bloomers" and would show a marked increase in intelligence by the end of the school year. The experimenters assigned the label *late bloomer* randomly to about 20 percent of the students, and at the end of the school year the "late bloomers" showed a significantly greater increase in IQ scores than did the students who were not given that label. Apparently, the teachers' expectations led them to treat the "late bloomers" differently than they treated the other students, thereby creating a self-fulfilling prophecy (Rosenthal & Jacobson, 1968).

▲ **First Impressions**
Do these women bring different thoughts and feelings to mind? Your first impressions of them might determine how you initially act toward them.

self-fulfilling prophecy
The tendency for one person's expectations to influence another person to behave in accordance with them.

STAYING ON TRACK: *Social Cognition*

1. What is self-serving bias?
2. How do we use self-handicapping for impression management?
3. How can a first impression create a self-fulfilling prophecy?

Answers for Staying on Track start on p. S–8.

INTERPERSONAL ATTRACTION: LIKING AND LOVING

While forming impressions of other people, we also develop *interpersonal attraction* toward some of them. By this point in the semester, you have probably become friendly with certain students; you might even have developed a romantic relationship with someone in particular. Social psychologists interested in interpersonal attraction seek answers to questions like these: Why do we like certain people more than others? What is the nature of romantic love?

Liking

Think of the students you have met this semester. Which ones do you like? Which ones do you not like? Among the factors that determine which ones you like are *proximity, familiarity, physical attractiveness, similarity,* and *self-disclosure.*

Proximity: Nearness Makes the Heart Grow Fonder

You are more likely to develop a liking for someone who lives near you, works with you, or attends the same classes as you. Research has consistently supported the importance of *proximity* in the development of friendships, as in a classic study of the residents of apartments in a housing project for married students at the Massachusetts Institute of Technology. The closer students lived to one another, the more likely they were to become friends. In fact, 41 percent of the students reported that their best friends lived next door. Because the students had been randomly assigned to apartments, their initial degree of liking for one another could not explain the findings (Festinger, Schachter, & Back, 1950).

Familiarity: Does It Breed Contempt?

Proximity makes us more familiar with certain people. But contrary to the popular saying, familiarity tends to breed liking, not contempt. As explained in Chapter 6, the more familiar we become with a stimulus—whether a car, a painting, or a professor—the more we will like it. So, in general, the more we interact with particular people, the more we tend to like them (Moreland & Zajonc, 1982). Of course, this tendency, called the *mere exposure effect,* holds only when the people do not behave in negative ways. The effect of familiarity on liking is not lost on politicians, who enhance their popularity by making repeated television appearances. The more familiar we are with public figures (assuming they do nothing scandalous), the more we tend to like them (Harrison, 1969).

▲ **Physical Attractiveness**
Romantic couples tend to be similar in their
level of physical attractiveness.

The mere exposure effect was supported by a clever experiment that used female college students as subjects. For each subject, two photographs of the subject were presented to the subject and to a friend. One photograph was a direct image of the subject; the second was a mirror image—what the subject would see when looking at herself in a mirror. Mirror images and normal photographic images differ because our faces are not perfectly symmetrical—the left and right sides look different. Subjects and friends were asked to choose which of the two photographs was preferable. Friends were more likely to choose the direct image, while subjects were more likely to choose the mirror image. This was evidence for the mere exposure effect, because the friends were more familiar with the direct image, while the subjects were more familiar with their own mirror image (Mita, Dermer, & Knight, 1977).

Physical Attractiveness: What Is Beautiful Seems to Be More Likable

Proximity not only lets us become familiar with people, it also lets us note their appearance. We tend to like physically attractive people more than physically unattractive ones. Sensitivity to physical attractiveness begins early in life; infants as young as 4 months prefer to look at attractive faces instead of unattractive ones (Samuels et al., 1994). This bias can have practical benefits for attractive people. For example, physically attractive people are perceived as more intelligent (Jackson, Hunter, & Hodge, 1995) and more socially competent (Hope & Mindell, 1994). They also are more likely to be hired for jobs than unattractive applicants with equivalent qualifications (Marlowe, Schneider, & Nelson, 1996). Physically attractive defendants are less likely to be convicted of crimes and, if convicted, less likely to be severely punished (Mazzella & Feingold, 1994). Even mothers of attractive infants are more playful with them and affectionate toward them than mothers of less attractive infants (Langlois et al., 1995).

Judgments of facial attractiveness have strong cross-cultural consistency. In one study, native-born white Americans and newly arrived Asian and Hispanic students rated the attractiveness of photographs of black, white, Asian, and Hispanic women. The correlation in ratings, .93, was almost perfect. Exposure to Western media had no effect on the ratings. In a companion study, black and white American men rated the attractiveness of photos of black women. Ratings of facial attractiveness correlated .94, but blacks and whites differed in their judgments of body attractiveness (Cunningham et al., 1995).

Physical attractiveness is an important factor in dating relationships. In an early experiment on the effect of physical attractiveness, freshmen at the University of Minnesota took part in a computer dating study. They completed personality and aptitude tests and were told that they would be paired based on their responses. In reality, they were paired randomly. Independent judges rated the physical attractiveness of each student. The couples then attended a dance that lasted several hours and rated their partners on a questionnaire. The results showed that physical attractiveness was the most important factor in determining whether subjects liked their partners and whether they desired to date them again (Walster et al., 1966).

Though we might prefer to have relationships with highly attractive people, social sorting usually leads us to have friends (Cash & Derlega, 1978) and romantic partners (Folkes, 1982) who are similar to us in physical attractiveness. That is, though we might prefer more attractive people, they might reject us—just as we might reject people who are less attractive than we are. This leaves us in relationships with people whose level of attractiveness is similar to our own.

Similarity: Likeness Promotes Liking

Though we tend to develop relationships with people who are similar to us in physical attractiveness, do we seek people who are similar to us in other ways? Do opposites attract? Or do birds of a feather flock together? You may recall the experiment discussed in Chapter 2 that showed we are more attracted to people whose attitudes are similar to our own (Byrne, Ervin, & Lamberth, 1970). The findings of that classic study have been replicated in many research studies, including recent experiments (Lancaster, Royal, & Whiteside, 1995). But this interpretation has been challenged by research showing that we are likely to associate with people who hold similar attitudes simply by default, because we are *repulsed* by those who have dissimilar ones. Life's circumstances simply put us in religious, political, recreational, and educational settings where we are likely to associate with people who share our attitudes (Rosenbaum, 1986).

But the results of recent research studies indicate that attitude similarity plays a more important role in interpersonal attraction than attitude dissimilarity does in preventing it (Drigotas, 1993; Tan & Singh, 1995). And other research indicates that we like people who share our activity preferences even more than we like people who share our attitudes (Lydon, Jamieson, & Zanna, 1988). Thus, you might enjoy playing sports or going to music concerts with someone whose sexual, religious, and political values differ from yours.

Self-Disclosure: To Know You Is to Like You

To determine whether we share similar attitudes and interests with someone else, we must engage in *self-disclosure,* in which we reveal our beliefs, feelings, and experiences. Reciprocation of self-disclosure is important, because we tend to like people more if they have disclosed personal information to us and if we have disclosed personal information to them (Collins & Miller, 1994). In social relationships, self-disclosure is best if it is gradual. When people disclose highly personal information to us too early in a relationship, we may become uneasy, suspicious, and less attracted to them. If you have ever been regaled by someone you have just met with his or her whole life story, including intimate details, you might have felt uncomfortable and uninterested in pursuing the relationship. Moreover, we must consider the cultural background of the person with whom we are interacting. For example, a study found that American college students preferred to engage in more self-disclosure than Taiwanese college students did (Chen, 1995).

Romantic Love

Love might make the world go round, but there were few scientific studies of romantic love until the 1970s. Since then, the findings of such research have been used to help prevent and relieve the emotional and physical suffering that is produced by unhappy romantic relationships, including spouse abuse, child abuse, and divorce. What have researchers discovered about the nature of romantic love? For one thing, the concept of love has "fuzzy boundaries" (see Chapter 9). That is, we know love when we see it or experience it, but we cannot define it by a single set of features without finding that there are exceptions to any definition we put forth (Fehr & Russell, 1991).

Theories of Love

Elaine Hatfield, undaunted by earning the first Golden Fleece Award for the research she conducted with her colleague Ellen Berscheid, distinguishes between passionate love and companionate love (Hatfield, 1988). **Passionate love,** commonly known as sexual love, involves intense emotional arousal, including sexual feelings. **Companionate love** involves feelings of affection and commitment to the relationship. Over time, romantic relationships tend to decline in passionate love and increase in companionate love.

More research has been conducted on passionate love than on companionate love. According to Berscheid and Hatfield, passionate love depends on three factors. First, the culture must promote the notion of passionate love. Passionate love has been important in Western cultures only for a few centuries, and even today some cultures have no concept of it. Second, the person must experience a state of intense emotional arousal. Third, the emotional arousal must be associated with a romantic partner (Berscheid & Walster, 1974).

Berscheid and Hatfield's theory of romantic love incorporates aspects of Stanley Schachter's two-factor theory of emotion. As explained in Chapter 12, Schachter's theory assumes that you will experience a particular emotion when you perceive that you are physiologically aroused and attribute that arousal to an emotionally relevant aspect of the situation in which you find yourself. The two-factor theory assumes that romantic love is the result of being physiologically aroused in a situation that promotes the labeling of that arousal as romantic love.

The two-factor theory of romantic love was supported by a clever experiment that took place on two bridges in Vancouver, British Columbia (Dutton & Aron, 1974). One, the Capilano River Bridge, is 5 feet wide, 450 feet long, and 230 feet above rocky rapids. It has low handrails and is constructed of wooden boards attached to wire cables, making it prone to wobble back and forth, inducing fear-related physiological arousal in those who walk across it. The other bridge, over a tiny tributary of the Capilano River, is wide, solid, immobile, and only 10 feet above the water. These characteristics make that bridge less likely to induce arousal in those who walk across it.

In the experiment, whenever a man walked across one of the bridges, he was met by an attractive woman who was the experimenter's accomplice. The woman asked each man to participate in a psychology course project about the effects of scenic attractions on creativity. Each man was shown a picture of a man and a woman in an ambiguous situation and was asked to write a brief dramatic story about the picture. The woman then gave the man her telephone number in case he wanted to ask her any questions about the study. The results showed that, compared with the men on the other bridge, the men who were on the bridge that induced physiological arousal wrote stories with more sexual content and were more likely to call the woman later.

According to the two-factor theory of romantic love, the men on the bridge that induced arousal had attributed their arousal to the presence of the attractive woman, leading them to experience romantic feelings toward her. But this interpretation of the results has been rejected by some researchers, who offer an alternative interpretation that assumes that the presence of the woman reduced the men's fear of the bridge, which, as a consequence, conditioned them to find her more attractive (Riordan & Tedeschi, 1983). Nonetheless, results of studies similar to the Capilano River study have supported the two-factor theory of romantic love. In one such study, men who were physiologically aroused by exercise while in the presence of an attractive woman were more attracted to that woman than were men who were not physiologically aroused (White, Fishbein, & Rutstein, 1981).

Another prominent theory of love has been put forth by Robert Sternberg (1986). His *triangular theory of love* presumes that the experience of love depends on the interaction of three components. *Passion* encompasses drives that lead to romance, physical attraction, and sexual relations. *Intimacy* encompasses feelings of closeness, bondedness, and connectedness. And *decision/commitment* encompasses, in the short term, the decision that one loves another, and, in the long term, the commitment to maintain that love. The intensity of love depends on the individual strengths of these three components, while the kind of love that is experienced depends on the strengths of the three components relative to one another. For example, strong passion combined with little intimacy and weak decision/commitment is associated with infatuation, while strong passion and great intimacy combined with weak decision/commitment is associated with romantic love. Though the

▲ **Ellen Berscheid** (*above*) **and Elaine Hatfield**
The evidence suggests that most individuals docilely accept the prescription that beauty and sexual and romantic passion are inexorably linked.

▲ **Companionate Love**
For romantic love to last after passionate love has waned somewhat, romantic partners must maintain the deep affection that characterizes companionate love.

triangular theory of love has been with us for more than a decade, it has inspired surprisingly little empirical research to test its merits. Thus, it remains a theory that is interesting but has, at best, only inconsistent support (Acker & Davis, 1992).

Promoting Romantic Love

What factors promote romantic love? As in the case of personal liking, similarity is an important factor. We tend to date and to marry people who are similar to us in attractiveness (Murstein, 1972), as well as in age, race, religion, ethnic background, and educational level (Buss, 1985). A survey found that when females and males were asked to rate the factors that would make someone attractive as a romantic partner, a sense of humor was the most important one (Buss, 1988). We also prefer romantic partners who are similar to us in sensation seeking (see Chapter 11). Thus, couples, whether dating or married, in which one member is a "homebody" and the other is a "party animal" are less likely to be satisfied (Schroth, 1991). A study of 18-year-old dating couples found that those who engaged in mutual self-disclosure early in the relationship were more likely to be together 4 months later (Berg & McQuinn, 1986).

Another important factor in romantic relationships is equity, the belief that each partner is contributing equally to the relationship, which promotes contentment and commitment (Winn, Crawford, & Fischer, 1991). Even the mere promise of equity might be important in promoting romantic relationships. This has been shown in archival research on personal advertisements. A survey of 800 advertisements placed by individuals seeking romantic partners found that the advertisers tended to seek equitable relationships. But women and men differed in complementary ways in the rewards they sought and offered. Men tended to seek attractive women, while offering financial security in return. In contrast, women tended to seek financially secure men, while offering physical attractiveness in return (Harrison, 1977). These findings have been replicated in a laboratory experiment (Sprecher, 1989) and in more-recent archival research studies (Cicerello & Sheehan, 1995). These findings hold across cultures, as in a study of the marital preferences of more than 1,500 college students in Japan, Russia, and the United States (Hatfield & Sprecher, 1995).

Sociobiologists would claim that these findings are not surprising because they reflect millions of years of evolution. According to the sociobiological interpretation of these findings, men prefer younger, physically attractive women because they would be more likely to have the ability to bear children and, as a result, pass on the men's genes. Similarly, women prefer men of higher financial status—especially those with personalities that are kind, caring, and loyal—because they would probably be more able and willing to care for them and their offspring (Greenlees & McGrew, 1994). Of course, like most sociobiological viewpoints, this is an after-the-fact explanation for behaviors that might be explained just as well by learned cultural differences in female and male sex roles.

STAYING ON TRACK: *Interpersonal Attraction*

1. What evidence is there that the mere exposure effect contributes to liking?
2. What are some rules for the adaptive use of self-disclosure in social relationships?
3. How do personal avertisements for romantic partners support equity as a factor in romantic relationships?

ATTITUDES: WHAT ARE YOUR OPINIONS?

What are your opinions about the insanity defense? surprise parties? abstract art? sorority members? Your answers to these questions would reveal some of your attitudes. **Attitudes** are evaluations of ideas (such as the insanity defense), events (such as surprise parties), objects (such as abstract art), or people (such as sorority members). In the 1930s, the noted psychologist Gordon Allport claimed that the concept of attitude was the single most important concept in social psychology. It no longer maintains such a lofty position, but it is still one of the most widely studied concepts in social psychology.

attitude
An evaluation, containing cognitive, emotional, and behavioral components, of an idea, event, object, or person.

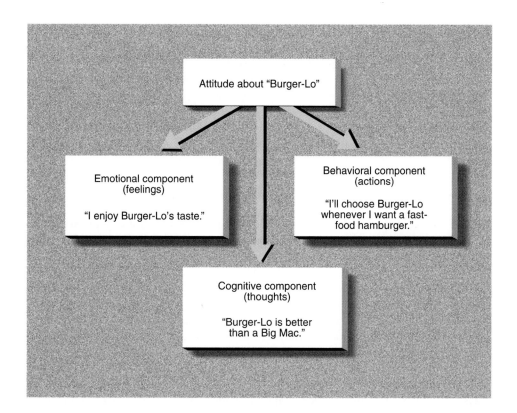

As shown in Figure 17.3, attitudes have emotional, cognitive, and behavioral components (Breckler, 1984). To appreciate this, imagine that you have been asked to participate in a market research survey of attitudes toward a new low-cholesterol, fast-food hamburger called "Burger-Lo." The market researcher would determine your attitude toward Burger-Lo by measuring one or more of the three components of your attitude. Your *emotional* response might be measured by a questionnaire asking you to rate your feelings about Burger-Lo's taste, aroma, texture, and appearance. Your *cognitive* response might be measured by asking you to describe the thoughts that Burger-Lo brings to mind, such as "It's better than a Big Mac." And your *behavioral* response might be measured by observing whether you choose Burger-Lo over several other fast-food hamburgers in a blind taste test.

The Formation of Attitudes

How are our attitudes formed? Some are learned through *classical conditioning* (see Chapter 7) by the pairing of something desirable or undesirable with the object of the attitude (Cacioppo et al., 1992). If Burger-Lo tastes good, you will associate that experience with Burger-Lo and develop a positive attitude toward it. Research indicates that our food preferences are, in fact, influenced by classical conditioning (Rozin & Zellner, 1985). Advertisers of foods and other products take advantage of classical conditioning by pairing them with stimuli that are already desirable (Allen & Janiszewski, 1989). Thus, advertisers often try to sell automobiles to men by associating them with beautiful women.

Attitudes can also be formed through *operant conditioning,* as in an experiment conducted at the University of Hawaii (Insko, 1965). Undergraduates, contacted by telephone, were asked whether they agreed or disagreed with statements that favored or opposed a proposed "Springtime Aloha Week." The caller positively reinforced certain statements by saying "good." For half of the telephone calls, the caller said "good" whenever the student agreed with a statement favoring the proposal. For the other half, the caller said "good" whenever the student agreed with a statement opposing the proposal. One week later the students were given a "local issues questionnaire." Among the items in the questionnaire was a question asking whether they favored or opposed the proposed Springtime Aloha Week. The responses to that question showed that students who earlier had been reinforced for making statements that favored the Springtime Aloha Week were more likely to favor it, while students who earlier had been reinforced for making statements that opposed it were more likely to oppose it.

According to *social learning theory*, many of our attitudes are learned through observing others—particularly our parents, our peers, and characters on television shows—being punished or positively reinforced for expressing particular behaviors (Kanekar, 1976). Even our attitudes toward the use of drugs are affected by social learning. For example, adolescents have a more positive attitude toward the use of alcohol if they have consistently seen their peers, parents, and siblings drinking it (Ary et al., 1993).

The Art of Persuasion

In 1956, Edward Schein published an article that described the results of his interviews with United Nations soldiers who, as prisoners during the Korean War, had been subjected to so-called brainwashing, which in some cases made them express sympathy for the North Koreans and antipathy toward the United States. Publicity about brainwashing, and fears that it could be used by totalitarian governments to control citizens, stimulated further interest in studying factors that affect persuasion and resistance to it. **Persuasion** is the attempt to influence the attitudes of other people. Today researchers have less interest in studying brainwashing than in studying the everyday use of persuasion, whether by friends, relatives, advertisers, or politicians.

According to the **elaboration likelihood theory** of Richard Petty and John Cacioppo (1981), persuasive messages can take a *central route* or a *peripheral route*. A message that takes a central route relies on clear, explicit arguments about the issue at hand. This encourages active consideration of the merits of the arguments. In contrast, a message that takes a peripheral route relies on factors other than the merits of the arguments, such as characteristics of the source or the situational context. The more elaborately we think about the merits of an argument, the more lasting will be any attitude change that occurs. The central and peripheral routes are related to the main factors in persuasion: the *source*, the *message*, and the *audience*. These three factors were first studied more than 2,000 years ago by Aristotle. He found that persuasion was most effective when the source had good character, the message was supported by strong evidence, and the audience was in a receptive frame of mind (Jones, 1985).

The Source and Persuasion

One of the important peripheral factors in persuasion is the source of the message. The greater the *credibility* of the source, the greater the persuasiveness of the message. Politicians realize this and gain votes by having credible supporters praise their merits and criticize their opponents' faults (Calantone & Warshaw, 1985). But what determines a source's credibility? Perhaps the most important factor is the source's *expertise*. A meta-analysis of 114 studies on the effects of source characteristics on persuasion found that expertise was the single most credibility-enhancing source characteristic (Wilson & Sherrell, 1993).

Another important factor in promoting source credibility is *trustworthiness*. When we perceive sources as trustworthy, we are less likely to critically scrutinize their message. This makes us more likely to be persuaded by the message (Priester & Petty, 1995). We perceive sources as especially trustworthy when their message is not an obvious attempt at persuasion, particularly when the message is contrary to the source's expected position (Wood & Eagly, 1981). For example, as noted in Chapter 10, Sir Cyril Burt's biographer concluded that Burt had fabricated data supporting a strong genetic basis for intelligence. The author of an article that discussed Burt's biography claimed, "The conclusion carries more weight because the author of the biography, Professor Leslie Hearnshaw, began his task as an admirer" (Hawkes, 1979, p. 673). If Hearnshaw had been a critic of Burt's work, his conclusion would have been less credible.

Sources that are *attractive*, because they are likable or physically appealing, are also more persuasive. Advertisers take advantage of this by having attractive actors appear in

persuasion

The attempt to influence the attitudes of other people.

elaboration likelihood model

A theory of persuasion that considers the extent to which messages take a central route or a peripheral route.

▲ The Power of Persuasion
Attempts at persuasion pervade our everyday lives, as in this confrontation between pro-life and pro-choice abortion protesters.

their commercials (Shavitt et al., 1994). Even the appeal of politicians is affected by their attractiveness. Richard Nixon's unattractive appearance during a debate with John F. Kennedy may have cost him the 1960 presidential election. Nixon's five-o'clock shadow and tendency to perspire made him less attractive to voters who watched the debate on television. Surveys found that those who watched the debate on television rated Kennedy the winner, while those who listened to it on the radio rated Nixon the winner (Weisman, 1988). Having learned from Nixon's mistake, today's politicians make sure that they appear as attractive as possible on television.

▲ **The Appeal to Fear**
Persuasive appeals that rely on fear can be effective if the supposed threat is severe, its likelihood is high, and we can do something to prevent or eliminate it. For example, a study of public service announcements about AIDS found that fear-evoking messages were especially effective in convincing sexually active people that they should use condoms (Struckman-Johnson, Struckman-Johnson, & Gilliland, 1994).

The Message and Persuasion

It might surprise you to learn that it is not always desirable to present arguments that support only your position. Simply acknowledging the other side of an issue, while strongly supporting your own, is at times more effective. A meta-analysis of research studies found that two-sided messages are generally more effective than one-sided messages in changing attitudes (Allen, 1993). This was discovered by social psychologist Carl Hovland and his colleagues in the waning days of World War II, following the surrender of Germany (Hovland, Lumsdaine, & Sheffield, 1949). The military asked Hovland for advice on how to convince soldiers that the war against Japan would take a long time to win. The researchers presented soldiers with a 15-minute talk that presented either one-sided or two-sided arguments. In the one-sided argument, they presented only arguments about why the war would not be over soon, such as the fighting spirit of the Japanese. In the two-sided argument, they presented both that argument *and* arguments explaining why the war might end earlier, such as Allied air superiority. Before and after the message, the subjects were given surveys that included questions about how long they believed the war would last.

The results showed that those who originally believed the war would take a long time to win were more influenced by the one-sided argument and became more extreme in their attitudes. But those who originally believed there would be an early end to the war were more influenced by the two-sided argument. As you can see, if the listener already favors your position or has no counterarguments handy, arguments that favor your position alone will be more persuasive. But if the listener opposes your position, arguments that acknowledge both sides of the issue will be more persuasive. Two-sided arguments are effective, in part, because they enhance the credibility of the source and decrease counterarguing by the listener (Kamins & Assael, 1987).

The Audience and Persuasion

Persuasion depends on the audience, as well as the message and its source. An important audience factor is intelligence, because it determines whether a message will be more effective using the central or the peripheral route. People of relatively high intelligence are more likely to be influenced by messages supported by rational arguments—the central route. People of relatively low intelligence are more likely to be influenced by messages supported by factors other than rational arguments—the peripheral route (Eagly & Warren, 1976). Overall, people of lower intelligence are more easily influenced than people of higher intelligence (Rhodes & Wood, 1992).

Another important audience factor is whether the audience finds the message personally important (Zuwerink & Devine, 1996). A message's importance for a particular audience determines whether the central route or the peripheral route will be more effective (Petty & Cacioppo, 1990). When a message has high importance to an audience, the central route will be more effective. When a message has low importance, the peripheral route will be more effective. This was the finding of a study that measured student attitudes toward recommended policy changes at a university. The changes would be instituted either the following year (high importance) or in 10 years (low importance). Students who were asked to respond to arguments about policy changes of high importance were influenced more by the quality of the arguments (central route) than by the expertise of the source (peripheral route). In contrast, students who were asked to respond to arguments about policy changes of low importance were influenced more by the expertise of the source than by the quality of the arguments (Petty, Cacioppo, & Goldman, 1981).

Attitudes and Behavior

Common sense tells us that if we know a person's attitudes, we can accurately predict her or his behavior. But the relationship is not that simple. For one thing, our behavior might not always agree with our attitudes. Perhaps more surprisingly, our behavior can sometimes affect our attitudes.

The Influence of Attitudes on Behavior

Until the late 1960s, most social psychologists accepted the commonsense notion that our behavior is consistent with our attitudes. But since then researchers have found that attitudes are not as consistent with behavior as previously believed (Scott & Willits, 1994). You have seen this exhibited dramatically, for example, by television evangelists who preach sexual denial while themselves engaging in extramarital sexual relations.

Though widespread interest in the inconsistency between attitudes and behaviors is only two decades old, evidence supporting the inconsistency between attitudes and behaviors appeared as early as the 1930s, when sociologist Richard LaPiere (1934) traveled with a young Chinese couple for 10,000 miles throughout the United States. They ate at 184 restaurants and stayed at 66 hotels, motels, and other places. Though anti-Chinese feelings were strong at that time, only 1 of the 250 establishments refused them service. Six months after the journey, LaPiere wrote to each of the establishments, asking whether they would serve Chinese people. Of the 128 that replied, 118 (92 percent) said they would not. LaPiere concluded that this showed that our behaviors do not always agree with our attitudes. But the study had a major flaw. The people who served them (waiters and desk clerks) might not have been the same people who responded to LaPiere's letter (owners and managers). Nonetheless, LaPiere's study stimulated interest in research on the ability of attitude questionnaires to predict real-life behavior (Dockery & Bedeian, 1989).

But what determines whether our attitudes and behaviors will be consistent? Attitudes that are strongly held (Kraus, 1995) or personally important (Crano & Prislin, 1995) are better predictors of behavior. Attitude-behavior consistency is also affected by the specificity of the attitude and the behavior. Your attitudes and behaviors are more consistent with one another when they are at similar levels of specificity (Weigel, Vernon, & Tognacci, 1974). For example, your attitude toward safe driving might not predict whether you will obey the speed limit tomorrow morning, but it will predict your general tendency, over time, to engage in safe driving behaviors, such as checking your tire pressure, using turn signals, and obeying the speed limit.

The Influence of Behavior on Attitudes

In the mid 1950s, Leon Festinger (1919–1989) and his colleagues were intrigued by a sect whose members believed they would be saved by aliens in flying saucers at midnight prior to the day of a prophesied worldwide flood (Festinger, Riecken, & Schachter, 1956). But neither the aliens nor the flood ever arrived. Did the members lose their faith? Some did, but many reported that their faith was strengthened. They simply concluded that the aliens had rewarded their faith by saving the world from the flood. These members simply changed their belief in order to justify their action.

The ability of the sect's members to relieve the emotional distress they experienced when the prophecy failed to come true stimulated Festinger's interest in attitude change and his development of the **cognitive dissonance theory.** Cognitive dissonance is an unpleasant state of tension associated with increased physiological arousal (Harmon-Jones et al., 1996) and psychological arousal (Elliot & Devine, 1994), caused by the realization that one has beliefs that are inconsistent with each other or a belief that is inconsistent with one's behavior. This would occur in people who believe that smoking is dangerous yet find themselves to be smokers. We are motivated to reduce the unpleasant arousal

▲ **Richard Petty and John Cacioppo**
"There are only two fundamentally different 'routes' to changing a person's attitudes. One route, which we call the *central route*, emphasizes the information a person has about the person, object, or issue under consideration; and the other route, which we call the *peripheral route*, emphasizes just about anything else."

cognitive dissonance theory
Leon Festinger's theory that attitude change is motivated by the desire to relieve the unpleasant state of tension caused when one holds cognitions that are inconsistent with each other.

CHAPTER 17

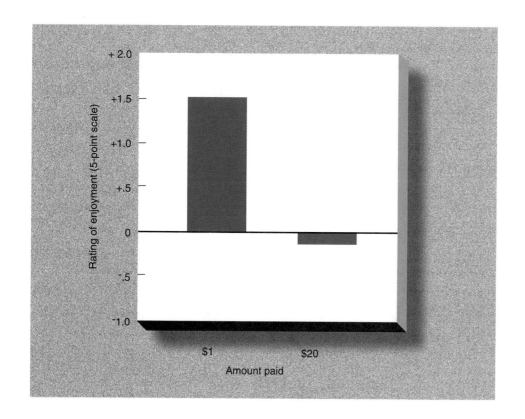

◀ FIGURE 17.4
Cognitive Dissonance
Subjects who were paid $1 for telling other people that a boring task was interesting later rated the task as more enjoyable than did subjects who were paid $20 for telling the same white lie (Festinger & Carlsmith, 1959).

associated with cognitive dissonance by making our cognitions consistent. Thus, a smoker might stop smoking, simply discount reports that link smoking to disease, or estimate that the risk is lower in his or her own case.

The theory of cognitive dissonance has practical applications in promoting positive behaviors. One study aroused cognitive dissonance in female swimmers who used their campus swimming pool by making them feel hypocritical about their showering habits. This was done by getting some of the subjects to recall times when they wasted water while showering, make a public commitment to conserve water, and urge others to take shorter showers. This inconsistency between their beliefs and their behavior was expected to arouse cognitive dissonance and, as a consequence, make them change their behavior. The results supported this, because subjects in the hypocrisy condition took significantly shorter showers than subjects not in that condition. Subjects who were only reminded that they had wasted water or who only made the public proconservation statement did not reduce the amount of water they used when showering (Dickerson et al., 1992). According to cognitive dissonance theory, the subjects in the hypocrisy condition reduced their distress by changing their behavior.

The more we feel responsible for the inconsistencies between our cognitions, the stronger our feelings of cognitive dissonance will be and the more motivated we will be to change them. This was the finding of the first experimental study of cognitive dissonance (Festinger & Carlsmith, 1959). Students were asked to perform boring tasks, one of which was to arrange small spools on a tray, dump the tray, and arrange the spools again and again for half an hour. Each student was paid either $1 or $20 to tell the next student that the task was enjoyable. After the experiment was over, the students were asked to express their attitude toward the task. Their responses violated what common sense predicted. As shown in Figure 17.4, those who were paid less ($1) tended to rate the task as interesting, while those who were paid more ($20) tended to rate the task as boring.

What could account for this finding? According to the theory of cognitive dissonance, the students experienced unpleasant arousal because their claim that the task was interesting did not agree with their belief that the task was boring. But those who were paid $20 to lie about the task experienced weaker cognitive dissonance because they could justify their lies by attributing them to the large payment they received. In contrast, those

▲ **Leon Festinger (1919–1989)**
"The human organism tries to establish internal harmony, consistency, or congruity among his opinions, attitudes, knowledge, and values."

Social Behavior |

who were paid only $1 to lie experienced stronger cognitive dissonance because they could not attribute their lies to such a paltry sum. Consequently, those who were paid only $1 reduced the dissonance between their cognitions by changing their attitudes toward the task, rating it as more interesting than it actually was.

The cognitive dissonance interpretation of attitude change is still being challenged by other theories (Shultz & Lepper, 1996), most notably one put forth by Daryl Bem (1967). According to his **self-perception theory,** attitude change is not motivated by our need to reduce cognitive dissonance. Instead, we infer our attitudes from our behavior in the same way that we infer other people's attitudes from their behavior. When we observe people behaving under no apparent external constraints, we use the behavior to make inferences about their attitudes. Likewise, when the situation we are in does not place strong constraints on our behavior, we might infer our attitudes from our behavior. Perhaps self-perception theory explains why we tend to favor our home sports teams. Because of our proximity to them, we are more likely to attend our home teams' games, watch our home teams on television, and read about them in the newspaper. When we perceive ourselves engaging in these behaviors, we might infer that we like our home teams.

But how does self-perception theory explain why students who were paid $1 for lying showed greater attitude change than students who were paid $20? According to Bem, the students did not experience cognitive dissonance. Instead, they determined whether their behavior was attributable to themselves or to the situation. The students who were paid $20 attributed their behavior to being paid a relatively large sum of money. They had no reason to attribute their behavior to their attitude. In contrast, the students who were paid $1 could not attribute their behavior to such a small sum of money. Consequently, those students attributed their behavior to their attitude, perhaps saying to themselves, "If I told another student that the task was interesting and I was not induced to do so by a large amount of money, then the task must have been interesting to me."

Neither cognitive dissonance theory nor self-perception theory has emerged as the clearly superior explanation of the effect of behavior on attitudes. But each seems to be superior in certain circumstances. Cognitive dissonance theory seems to be better at explaining the effect of behavior on well-defined attitudes; self-perception theory seems to be better at explaining the effect of behavior on poorly defined attitudes (Chaiken & Baldwin, 1981).

Social Prejudice

Two decades ago, third-grade teacher Jane Elliott of Riceville, Iowa, gained national attention for a demonstration she gave of the devastating psychological effects of a particular kind of attitude: social prejudice. She divided her students, who all were white, into a blue-eyed group and a brown-eyed group. On the first day of the demonstration, Elliott declared that blue-eyed people were superior to brown-eyed people. The next day, she declared that brown-eyed people were superior to blue-eyed people.

Members of the superior group were given privileges, such as sitting where they wanted to in class, going to lunch early, and staying late at recess. Members of the inferior group were made to wear identification collars and were not permitted to play with members of the superior group. Elliott reported that during the two-day demonstration, students who were made to feel inferior became depressed and performed poorly on classwork (Leonard, 1970). If prejudice could have this effect in an artificial, temporary situation, imagine the effect that prejudice has on children who are its targets in everyday life.

Prejudice is a positive or negative attitude toward a person based on her or his membership in a particular group. The behavioral component of prejudice is *discrimination*, which involves treating persons differently, whether positively or negatively, based only on their group membership. For example, a study found that students who evaluated the applications of males and females favored females for jobs that required warmth and submission and males for jobs that required shrewdness and leadership. The jobs for which males were favored were also those for which high-achieving applicants were favored. This suggests that female applicants are more apt to be discriminated against when applying for higher-status jobs (Zebrowitz, Tenenbaum, & Goldstein, 1991).

---

self-perception theory
Daryl Bem's theory that when we are unsure of our attitudes we infer them from our own behavior.

prejudice
An attitude, usually negative, toward others, based on their membership in particular groups.

Factors That Promote Prejudice

What factors account for the origin and maintenance of prejudice? As with all attitudes, learning plays an important role. Parents, peers, and the media all provide input, informing us of the supposed characteristics of particular groups.

Research has been especially concerned with factors that promote prejudice. The horrors of Nazism in the 1930s and 1940s led to a major research program at the University of California at Berkeley aimed at identifying the personality characteristics associated with fascist tendencies (Adorno et al., 1950). Based on the results of tests and interviews with adult Californians, the researchers discovered what they called the *authoritarian personality*. People with an **authoritarian personality** tend to be obedient toward their superiors and domineering toward subordinates (*authoritarianism*), prejudiced in favor of their own groups and against other groups (*ethnocentrism*), and unwilling to admit their own faults but willing to place them on members of other groups (*projection*). Authoritarians tend to be prejudiced against other ethnic groups (Duckitt & Farre, 1994), as well as other out-groups, including AIDS victims (Cunningham et al., 1991), homosexuals (Haddock, Zanna, & Esses, 1993), and mental hospital patients (Morrison, de Man, & Drumheller, 1993).

As mentioned earlier in the chapter, one of the most important factors in interpersonal attraction is attitude similarity. Prejudiced people perceive stereotyped groups as having attitudes that are different from those of their own groups. In fact, when there is little or no pressure to discriminate, race or ethnicity is less important than attitude similarity in determining racial or ethnic discrimination (Insko, Nacoste, & Moe, 1983). In a study of this phenomenon, subjects were asked to choose a work partner. When they were given information about another's race and attitudes, their choices were influenced more by their similarity in attitudes than by their similarity in race (Rokeach & Mezei, 1966).

Factors That Reduce Prejudice

Social psychologists are also concerned with finding ways to reduce prejudice. But this is difficult, because people are hesitant to revise personal judgments that are based on stereotypes. We modify the stereotypes we hold only gradually through individual experiences and by creating subtypes to accommodate instances that we cannot easily assimilate. As mentioned earlier, we do not necessarily revise our stereotypes after experiencing a few dramatic exceptions to them (Weber & Crocker, 1983). Nonetheless, exceptions to stereotypes do make the out-group seem more variable, which tends to weaken the stereotypes somewhat (Hamburger, 1994).

In the 1950s, Gordon Allport (1954) insisted that prejudice could be reduced by increasing social contact between members of different social groups. At about the same time, in 1954, in the landmark case of *Brown v. Board of Education of Topeka*, the United States Supreme Court ruled that "separate but equal" schools did not provide black children with the same benefits as white children received. The Court's decision was influenced by research showing that segregated schools hurt the self-esteem of black children, increased racial prejudice, and encouraged whites to view blacks as inferior. For example,

authoritarian personality
A personality type marked by the tendency to obey superiors while dominating subordinates, to favor one's own group while being prejudiced against other groups, and to be unwilling to admit one's own faults while projecting them onto members of other groups.

▲ Mamie Phipps Clark and Kenneth B. Clark
Through their research, Kenneth B. Clark and Mamie Phipps Clark demonstrated the harmful effects of racial segregation. The U.S. Supreme Court cited their work in support of the landmark 1954 decision, *Brown v. Board of Education of Topeka, Kansas,* which outlawed segregation in public schools (Guthrie, 1976).

a study by Kenneth Clark and Mamie Phipps Clark found that black children believed white dolls were better than black ones and preferred to play with white ones (Clark & Clark, 1947). A published review of studies of self-concept in black children revealed that research findings differ according to whether the research was conducted before or after the civil rights movement of the 1960s. Earlier studies reported that blacks had lower self-esteem than whites; studies conducted after the civil rights movement have found that this is no longer true (Spurlock, 1986).

Events during the past three decades have shown that social contact alone might not produce the effects predicted by Allport and the Supreme Court. For contact between groups to reduce prejudice, the contact must be between group members of equal status (Spangenberg & Nel, 1983). If the contact is between group members of unequal status, then prejudice may actually increase. The effectiveness of equal-status contact in reducing racial prejudice was supported by a study of black children and white children who spent a week at a summer camp. The children were between 8 and 12 years old and were of equally low socioeconomic status. At the end of the week, children of both races had more positive attitudes toward children of the other race (Clore et al., 1978). Contact with members of an out-group can weaken stereotypes by increasing the perceived heterogeneity of that group (Lee & Ottati, 1993).

Another way to reduce prejudice is to promote intergroup cooperation (Desforges et al., 1991). Unfortunately, cooperative efforts do not always increase liking. If cooperative efforts fail, members of one group might attribute responsibility for this to members of the other group. And if cooperative efforts succeed, members of one group will attribute responsibility for the success to a favorable situation, rather than giving any credit to members of the other group (Brewer & Kramer, 1985). Thus, in certain situations, members of a cooperating group will be caught in a no-win situation.

STAYING ON TRACK: *Attitudes*

1. What is the difference between the central route and the peripheral route in persuasion?

2. What factors influence the consistency between attitudes and behaviors?

3. What does research say about the effect of contact between in-group members and out-group members on prejudice?

GROUP DYNAMICS: DO YOU BEHAVE THE SAME IN GROUPS AS YOU DO WHEN YOU'RE ALONE?

In everyday life we refer to any collection of people as a "group." But social psychologists favor a narrower definition of a **group** as a collection of two or more persons who interact and have mutual influence. Examples of groups include a sorority, a softball team, and the board of trustees of your school. In the late 1940s, hoping to understand the social factors that contributed to the Great Depression, the rise of European dictatorships, and World War II, social psychologists became more interested in studying the factors that affect relationships among members of groups (Zander, 1979). This remains an important area of research in social psychology, and includes the topics of *group decision making, group effects on performance,* and *social influence.*

Group Decision Making

As members of groups, we are often called upon to make group decisions. A family must decide which new house to buy, college administrators must decide which proposed new academic majors to approve, and government officials must decide on air pollution standards. Decisions made by groups are not simply the outcome of rational give-and-take, with the wisest decision automatically emerging. They are affected by other factors as well.

group
A collection of two or more persons who interact and have mutual influence on each other.

Group Polarization: Moving Toward Extreme Decisions

In the 1950s, social critic William H. Whyte (1956) claimed that groups, notably those within business and government organizations, tended to make safe, compromise decisions instead of risky, extreme decisions. Whyte assumed that this tendency explained why organizations failed to be as creative and innovative as individuals. In the 1960s, his view was challenged by studies that found a tendency for group decisions to be *riskier* than decisions made by individuals who composed those groups (Stoner, 1961). This tendency became known as the *risky shift* (Wallach, Kogan, & Bem, 1962).

But later research found that groups tend to make decisions in either a risky *or* a cautious direction, rather than in only a risky direction. The tendency for groups to make more-extreme decisions than their individual members would make is called **group polarization.** For example, when groups of high school students either high or low in racial prejudice discussed racial issues, groups that were low in prejudice became even less prejudiced and groups that were high in prejudice became even more prejudiced (Myers & Bishop, 1970).

What accounts for group polarization? *Persuasive-argumentation theory* assumes that group members who initially hold a moderate position about an issue will move in the direction of the most persuasive arguments, which will eventually move the group toward either a risky or a cautious decision (Mongeau & Garlick, 1988). Simply repeating an attitude over and over will tend to polarize a group in that direction (Brauer, Judd, & Gliner, 1995).

group polarization
The tendency for groups to make more-extreme decisions than their members would make as individuals.

Minority Influence: Sticking to Your Position Might Help

Does the majority always determine the outcome of group decision making? In general, the answer is yes. This tendency becomes stronger as the size of the majority increases relative to the size of the minority (Maass & Clark, 1984). The majority has the power to convince group members to go along with its decision, in part because of its ability to criticize and socially ostracize those who dissent. Yet, under certain circumstances, minorities may influence group decisions.

If you are part of a minority and wish to influence group decisions, you should follow several well-established principles. First, you must present rational, rather than emotional, reasons for your position. This means that you must take the central, rather than peripheral, route of persuasion to make the majority consider your position. If minority arguments are of relatively higher quality than majority arguments, the minority will be more likely to influ-

One of the most important situations in which group polarization is desirable is in jury deliberations. We expect the members of juries to start with neutral positions concerning the defendant and then, after deliberation, to move to a more extreme position—deciding that the defendant is either guilty or innocent.

▲ **Irving Janis (1918–1990)**
"I use the term *groupthink* as a quick and easy way to refer to a mode of thinking that people engage in when they are deeply involved in a cohesive in-group, when the members' strivings for unanimity override their motivation to realistically appraise alternative courses of action."

groupthink
The tendency of small, cohesive groups to place unanimity ahead of critical thinking in making decisions.

ence the majority (Garlick & Mongeau, 1993). Second, you must appear absolutely confident in your position, with no wavering at all. If you are unsure or apologetic about your position, majority members will discount it. Third, you must be consistent in your position over time to make the majority wonder if there might actually be something to what you're saying. Again, if you are inconsistent, your opponents will discredit you. In fact, a meta-analysis of 97 relevant research studies found that the ability of the minority to be consistent in its position is an especially powerful factor in minority influence (Wood et al., 1994). Fourth, try to bring at least one other person over to your side. A minority of two is much more credible and influential than a minority of one. Each of the two will embolden and give credibility to the other. Fifth, you must be patient. Though majorities might initially dismiss minority positions, the passage of time might make them privately ponder the evidence you have provided and gradually change their positions (Nemeth, 1986).

Groupthink: Premature Unanimity in Decision Making

On January 28, 1986, the space shuttle *Challenger* exploded shortly after taking off from Cape Canaveral, Florida, killing all of the crew members and shocking the millions of television viewers excited by the presence onboard of the first teacher-astronaut, Christa McAuliffe. The committee that investigated this tragedy reported that the explosion was caused by a faulty joint seal in one of the rocket boosters. The decision to launch the shuttle had been made despite warnings from engineers that the joint might fail in cold weather. This ill-fated decision has been attributed to *groupthink*, which in this case put safety second to currying favor with the public and Congress (Moorhead, Ference, & Neck, 1991).

The term **groupthink** (Janis, 1983), coined by psychologist Irving Janis (1918–1990), refers to a decision-making process in small, cohesive groups that places unanimity ahead of critical thinking and aims at premature consensus (McCauley, 1989). Notice that groupthink is a form of group polarization. Groupthink is promoted by several factors: a charismatic leader, feelings of invulnerability, discrediting of contrary evidence, fear of criticism for disagreeing, the desire to maintain group harmony, isolation from outside influences, and disparaging outsiders as incompetent. In criticizing the decision to launch the *Challenger*, Senator John Glenn of Ohio, the first American to orbit Earth, referred to feelings of invulnerability among the officials who made the decision: "The mindset of a few people in key positions at NASA had changed from an optimistic and supersafety conscious 'can do' attitude, when I was in the program, to an arrogant 'can't fail' attitude" (Zaldivar, 1986, p. 12–A). This was unfortunate, because having a devil's advocate in a group promotes consideration of alternatives (Valacich & Schwenk, 1995).

Janis's concept of groupthink has received support from experimental studies on group decision making. Groups with directive leaders consider fewer alternatives than do groups with leaders who encourage member participation, especially if the directive leader expresses her or his opinion early in deliberation (Leana, 1985). Group cohesiveness also has an effect. A meta-analysis of the effect of group cohesiveness on decision making found that if other conditions conducive to groupthink are present, group cohesiveness will promote groupthink; if those conditions are not present, cohesiveness will actually improve decision making (Mullen et al., 1994). Of course, the groupthink phenomenon does not always occur during group decision making, and when it does occur, it does not always produce negative outcomes (Aldag & Fuller, 1993). Though the concept of groupthink seems convincing, evidence for it has come primarily from after-the-fact interpretations of well-known, misguided group decisions. More experimental research is needed to determine whether groupthink is a robust phenomenon and, if it does exist, to identify the factors that account for it.

Group Effects on Performance

One of the first topics to be studied by social psychologists was the influence of groups on the task performances of their members. Social psychologists have been especially interested in studying the effects of *social facilitation* and *social loafing* on performance.

Social Facilitation: Being Motivated by Others

As described at the beginning of the chapter, a century ago Norman Triplett (1898) observed that people performed faster when competing against other people than when competing against a clock. Two decades later psychologist Floyd Allport (1920) found that people performed a variety of tasks better when working in the same room than when working in separate rooms. Allport called the improvement in performance caused by the presence of other people **social facilitation.**

But later studies found that the presence of others can sometimes *impair* performance. A review of 241 studies involving almost 24,000 subjects found that the presence of other people improves performance on simple or well-learned tasks and impairs performance on complex or poorly learned tasks (Bond & Titus, 1983). For example, in one study, children tried to balance on a teeterboard for as long as possible. Children who were highly skilled performed better in the presence of others; children who were poorly skilled performed better when alone (MacCracken & Stadulis, 1985). Even college students learning to use computers may perform better when working alone than when working in the presence of an instructor (Schneider & Shugar, 1990).

What would account for these findings? The most influential explanation for both social facilitation and social inhibition is the *drive theory* of Robert Zajonc (1965), which was derived from a motivational theory put forth by Clark Hull (1943). According to Zajonc the presence of other people increases physiological arousal, which energizes the performer's most likely responses to a task. For those who are good at a task, the most likely responses will be effective ones; consequently, those people will perform *better* in the presence of others. In contrast, for those who are not good at a task, the most well-learned responses will be ineffective ones; consequently, those people will perform *worse* in the presence of others. This has practical implications. When you are learning to perform a new task, whether playing golf or playing the piano, you should practice as much as possible alone before seeking to play in the presence of others. However, a study of performance on a sport-related task found that extraverts performed better than introverts in front of an audience (Graydon & Murphy, 1995). Perhaps the presence of an audience pushes extraverts to their optimal level of arousal, while pushing introverts (who normally are higher in arousal than extraverts) beyond that level.

Our drive level might increase in the presence of others because of *evaluation apprehension*. Consider a field study in which male and female runners were timed (without their being aware of it) as they ran along a 90-yard segment of a footpath. One third of the subjects ran alone, one third encountered a female facing them at the halfway point, and one third encountered a female seated with her back to them at the halfway point. Only the

social facilitation
The improvement in a person's task performance when in the presence of other people.

▲ **Social Facilitation and Social Inhibition**
Because of social facilitation, a professional bicycle racer may perform better in the presence of other people. In contrast, because of social inhibition, a child learning to ride a bicycle may perform better when practicing alone.

group that encountered a female facing them (putting her in a position to evaluate them) showed a significant acceleration between the first and second halves of the segment (Worringham & Messick, 1983).

Social Loafing: The Lazy Group

Social facilitation is concerned with the effects of others on individual performance. But what of the effect of working in a group that has a common goal? In the 1880s, a French agricultural engineer named Max Ringelmann found that people exerted less effort when working in groups than when working alone. He had men pull on a rope attached to a meter that measured the strength of their pull. As the number of men pulling increased from one to eight, the average strength of each man's pull decreased. Ringelmann attributed this to a loss of coordination when working with other people, a phenomenon that became known as the *Ringelmann effect* (Kravitz & Martin, 1986). His study was successfully replicated almost a century later, but the effect diminished markedly beyond a group size of three (Ingham et al., 1974).

More recently, the Ringelmann effect has been attributed to a decrease in the effort exerted by individuals when working together, a phenomenon known as **social loafing.** This supports the old saying, "Many hands make light the work." In one experiment, high school cheerleaders cheered either alone or in pairs. Sound-level recordings found that individual cheerleaders cheered louder when alone than when cheering with a partner (Hardy & Latané, 1988). Social loafing has often been demonstrated in sports, such as elite rowing (Anshel, 1995) and high school swimming (Miles & Greenberg, 1993). A meta-analysis of 78 studies found that social loafing has been demonstrated across many different cultures, though it is more common in relatively individualistic cultures, such as Canada and the United States (Karau & Williams, 1993).

According to the concept of *diffusion of responsibility*, social loafing occurs when group members feel anonymous; believing that their individual performances are dispensable, they are less motivated to exert their maximum effort. Because of this, committees are often inefficient in accomplishing their goals, each member expecting someone else to do the work. A good way to reduce social loafing is to convince group members that their individual efforts will be evaluated or that they will be held accountable (Weldon & Gargano, 1988). Social loafing can also be overcome when a task is important to an individual and that person believes other group members lack the ability to perform better (Karau & Williams, 1995).

Social Influence

The groups we belong to influence our behavior in ways that range from subtle prodding to direct demands. We are influenced by police, bosses, clergy, parents, spouses, teachers, physicians, advertisers, politicians, salespersons, and a host of other people. Among the most important kinds of social influence are *conformity*, *compliance*, and *obedience*.

Conformity: Going Along with the Group

Do you dress the way you do because your friends dress that way? Do you hold certain religious beliefs because your parents hold them? If you answered yes to these questions, your behavior exhibits **conformity,** which means behaving in accordance with real or imagined group pressure. For example, a study of more than 100 men and 100 women found that people eating in a cafeteria were more likely to select a dessert if a dining companion did so (Guarino, Fridrich, & Sitton, 1994).

The power of conformity was demonstrated in a classic series of experiments conducted by psychologist Solomon Asch in the 1950s. In a typical experiment, a male college student who had volunteered to be a research subject was told that he would be taking part in a study of visual perception. He was seated at a table with six other "subjects," who were actually the experimenter's confederates. As illustrated in Figure 17.5, the experimenter presented a series of trials in which he displayed two large white cards. One card contained three vertical lines of different lengths. The second card contained a single vertical line clearly equal in length to one of the three lines on the first card. On each of 18 trials, the participants were asked,

▲ **Social Loafing**
Because of social loafing, these children will probably exert less individual effort than they would if they pulled by themselves.

social loafing
A decrease in the individual effort exerted by group members when working together on a task.

conformity
Behaving in accordance with group expectations with little or no overt pressure to do so.

CHAPTER 17

(a)

(b)

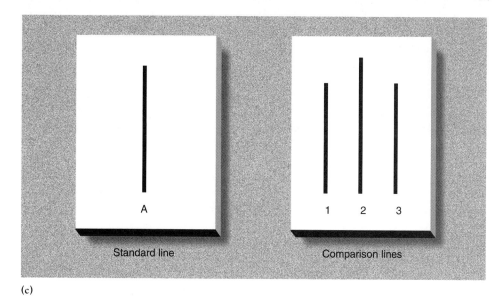

Standard line

Comparison lines

(c)

◄ **FIGURE 17.5**
The Asch Study
Subjects (a) in one of Solomon Asch's studies
(c) had to decide which of three lines was equal
in length to another line. The photograph
(b) shows the confusion of subject number 6
when other subjects chose the wrong line.

one person at a time, to choose the line on the first card that was the same length as the line on the second card. The lengths of the lines varied from trial to trial. On the first 2 trials each confederate chose the correct line. But on the third trial, and on 11 of the succeeding trials, the confederates chose a line that was clearly *not* the same length as the single line.

On the first few bogus trials, the subject appeared uncomfortable but usually chose the correct line. Yet, over the course of the 12 bogus trials, the subject sometimes conformed to the erroneous choices made by the confederates. The results indicated that, overall, the subjects conformed on 37 percent of the bogus trials. Three quarters of the subjects conformed on at least one bogus trial. In other versions of the experiment, Asch varied the number of confederates from one to fifteen persons. As illustrated in Figure 17.6, he found that the subjects' tendency to conform increased dramatically until there were three confederates, with additional confederates inducing smaller increases in conformity (Asch, 1955).

Though some attempts to replicate Asch's study have failed (Lalancette & Standing, 1990), his research has been successfully replicated in different cultures, including studies using American (Larsen, 1990), Dutch (Vlaander & Van Rooijen, 1985), Kuwaiti (Amir, 1984), or British (Nicholson, Cole, & Rocklin, 1985) subjects. But a meta-analysis of 133 studies from 17 countries that used Asch's line-judgment task found that conformity has declined since the 1950s. Collectivist countries tended to show greater conformity than individualistic countries (Bond & Smith, 1996). For example, Chinese college students tend to be more conforming than American college students (Zhang & Thomas, 1994).

In Asch's study, why did the subjects conform to the obviously erroneous judgments of strangers? A few claimed they really saw the lines as equal, and others assumed that the confederates knew something they did not. But their main reason for conforming was their need for social approval—they feared social rejection. The subjects found, as do many

▲ **Solomon Asch**
"How, and to what extent, do social forces
constrain people's opinions and attitudes?"

▶ Conformity
Conformity is a normal part of everyday life for
people in all walks of life, as shown in this
photograph of a high-society ball in Vienna.

people, that it is difficult to be the lone dissenter in a group. In variations of the experiment
in which one of the confederates joined the subject in dissenting, the subjects conformed
on less than one tenth, rather than on one third, of the bogus trials (Asch, 1955). Thus, as
in the case of minority influence, dissent is more likely when we have fellow dissenters.

Compliance: Responding Positively to Requests

We are continually bombarded with requests. A friend might want to borrow your car. A
professor might ask you to help move laboratory equipment. An advertiser might urge you
to purchase a particular deodorant. The process by which a person agrees to a request that
is backed by little or no threat of punishment is called **compliance.** As discussed in
Chapter 16, compliance is often life-saving when it comes to medical regimens, dieting,
and exercise. Two of the major means of inducing compliance are the *foot-in-the-door technique* and the *door-in-the-face technique*.

compliance
Behaving in accordance with a request
that is backed by little or no threat of
punishment.

The Foot-in-the-Door Technique. Years ago, it was common for salespersons to go
door-to-door trying to sell encyclopedias, vacuum cleaners, or other products. Every
salesperson knew that a person who complied with the small request to be permitted inside
to discuss or demonstrate a product would then be more likely to comply with the larger
request to purchase the product. This became known as the **foot-in-the-door technique**
(Dillard, 1991).

foot-in-the-door technique
Increasing the likelihood that someone
will comply with a request by first getting
them to comply with a smaller one.

This technique can produce extraordinary degrees of compliance. In one study, women
were surveyed by telephone to ask them questions about the brand of soap they used.
Three days later they were called again, as were a group of similar women who had not
received the first call. This time the caller asked each woman for permission to send a
team of men who would rummage through her cabinets to record the household items
that she used. Of those who had complied with the first (small) request, 53 percent agreed
to permit a team to visit their home. Of those who received only the second (large)
request, just 22 percent agreed to permit a team to visit their home (Freedman & Fraser,
1966). The foot-in-the-door technique has proved so effective that it has even been used
to encourage gynecological cancer check-ups (Dolin & Booth-Butterfield, 1995) and prevent drunk driving (Taylor & Booth-Butterfield, 1993).

Why is the foot-in-the-door technique effective? Self-perception theory, which assumes
that we infer our attitudes from observing our own behavior, provides an answer (Eisenberg
et al., 1987). If you freely comply with a small, worthwhile request, you will view yourself as

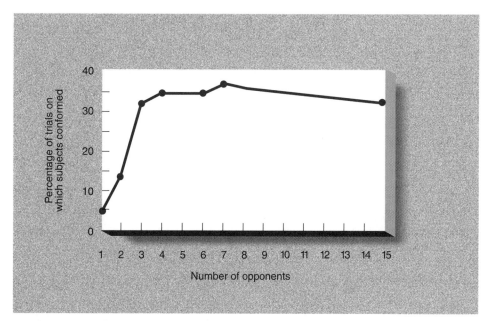

◀ **FIGURE 17.6**
Conformity and Group Size
Asch (1955) found that conformity increased dramatically as the number of opponents increased to three. Adding more than three opponents did little to increase conformity.

a person who has a positive attitude toward worthwhile requests. Because you wish to be consistent with your self-perception, you will be more likely to comply with other requests. Support for this explanation has been mixed (Dillard, 1990; Kilbourne, 1989).

The Door-in-the-Face Technique. Salespeople also know that those who refuse to purchase a particular item will be more likely to comply with a request to purchase a less expensive item. Fostering compliance by presenting a smaller request after a larger request has been denied is called the **door-in-the-face technique** (Dillard, 1991). We resort to this technique in our everyday lives in situations such as negotiating salaries (perhaps asking for several thousand dollars more than we expect), selling our homes (typically asking for 20 percent more than we will accept), or convincing professors to give us extra time to complete term papers (boldly asking for an extra week when we would gladly settle for two extra days). Even charities use the technique. In one study, potential volunteers were asked to commit themselves to serve as a Big Brother or Big Sister at a juvenile detention center for 2 hours a week for 2 years. After they all rejected this large request, they were subjected to a much smaller request to chaperon a group of low-income children on a single 2-hour visit to a zoo. The subjects were significantly more likely to comply with this request than were those who had not been asked earlier to serve as a Big Brother or Big Sister (Cialdini et al., 1975).

The door-in-the-face technique depends on social norms that require that concessions offered by one negotiating party be met by concessions from the other party. The willingness of one person to reduce the size of an initial request would be a concession, imposing social pressure on the person who had refused the first request to comply with the second one (Cann, Sherman, & Elkes, 1975). The foot-in-the door technique is generally more effective than the door-in-the-face technique (Fern, Monroe, & Avila, 1986).

Obedience: Following Orders

Would you assist in the cold-blooded murder of innocent people if your superior ordered you to? This question deals with the limits of **obedience**—the following of orders given by an authority. The limits of obedience were at the heart of the Nuremberg war crime trials held after World War II. The defendants were Nazis accused of crimes against humanity for their complicity in the executions of millions of innocent people during World War II, most notably the genocide of 6 million Jews. The defendants claimed that they were only following orders. The suprising extent to which people will obey orders to harm others was demonstrated in the following classic study.

▲ **The Foot-in-the-Door Technique**
If you have ever been in a major city or large airport, you have probably observed panhandlers use the foot-in-the-door technique. A panhandler might ask a passerby for a quarter to call home. If the person complies, the panhandler might then ask for a dollar for busfare home. A person who complies with the smaller request will be more likely to comply with the larger request than will one who is subjected only to the larger request.

door-in-the-face technique
Increasing the likelihood that someone will comply with a request by first getting them to reject a larger one.

obedience
Following orders given by an authority.

Social Behavior | **619**

▲ **Stanley Milgram (1933–1984)**
"A substantial proportion of people do what they are told to do, irrespective of the content of the act and without limitations of conscience, so long as they perceive that the command comes from a legitimate authority."

ANATOMY OF A CLASSIC RESEARCH STUDY

Would You Harm Someone Just Because an Authority Figure Ordered You To?

Rationale

Are people who obey orders to hurt innocent people unusually cruel, or are most human beings susceptible to obeying such orders? This question led psychologist Stanley Milgram (1933–1984) of Yale University to conduct perhaps the most famous—and controversial—of all psychology experiments (Milgram, 1963).

Method

Milgram's subjects were adult men who had responded to an advertisement for volunteers to participate in a study of the effects of punishment on learning. On arriving at the laboratory, each subject was introduced to a pleasant, middle-aged man who would also participate in the experiment. In reality, the man was a confederate of the experimenter. The experimenter asked both men to draw a slip of paper out of a hat to determine who would be the "teacher" and who would be the "learner." The drawing was rigged so that the subject was always the teacher.

The subject communicated with the learner over an intercom as the learner performed a memory task while strapped to an electrified chair in another room (Figure 17.7). The subject sat at a control panel with a series of switches with labels ranging from "Slight Shock" (15 volts) to "Danger: Severe Shock" (450 volts) in 15-volt increments. The experimenter instructed the subject to administer an increasingly strong electric shock to the learner's hand whenever he made an error. At higher shock levels, the learner cried out in pain or begged the teacher to stop. Many subjects responded to the learner's distress with sweating, trembling, and stuttering. If the subject hesitated to administer a shock, the experimenter might say, "You have no other choice, you must go on," and remind the teacher that he, the experimenter, was responsible for any ill effects. Note the similarity between this incremental approach and the foot-in-the-door technique (Gilbert, 1981). This approach is also used in the training of professional torturers and "brainwashers" (Gibson, 1991).

Results and Discussion

How far do you think you would have gone as the teacher in Milgram's study? Surveys of psychiatrists and Yale students had predicted that less than 2 percent of the subjects would reach the maximum level. To Milgram's surprise, two thirds of the subjects reached the maximum level of shock, and none stopped before reaching 300 volts—the point at which the learner frantically banged on the wall and stopped answering questions. (By the way, the learner never received a shock. In fact, his "responses" were played on a tape recorder.)

Could the prestige of Yale University and the apparent legitimacy of a laboratory study have affected the subjects? Milgram replicated the study in a run-down office building in Bridgeport, Connecticut. He did not wear a laboratory coat, and he made no reference to Yale. He obtained impressive results nonetheless. Of those who participated, 48 percent reached the maximum level of shock. Would physically separating the subject and the learner have an effect? Somewhat. Figure 17.8 shows that of the subjects who sat near the learner, 40 percent reached the maximum. Even when the subject had to force the learner's hand onto a shock grid, 30 percent still reached the maximum (Milgram, 1974). Milgram's original experiment has also been successfully replicated in other countries, which indicates that extreme obedience to authority is common across cultures (Shanab & Yahya, 1977).

Milgram's research has disturbing implications. The line that separates us from Nazi war criminals may be thinner than we would like to believe. Many of us, given orders by someone we consider to be a legitimate authority who we assume will be responsible for our actions, might be willing to harm an innocent person. Despite the insight it provided into the nature of obedience, Milgram's research provoked criticism, most notably from Diana Baumrind (1964). She claimed that Milgram's use of deception increased distrust of psychological

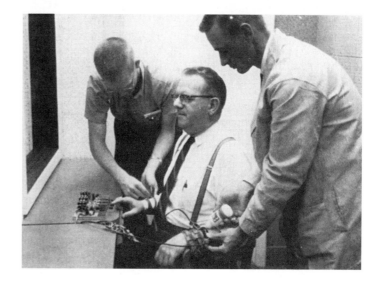

▲ FIGURE 17.7
Milgram's Study of Obedience
Stanley Milgram advertised for people who would be willing to take part in a study of memory. The photographs show the "shock generator" that he used and a subject helping the experimenter attach electrodes to the learner's arm.

Public Announcement

WE WILL PAY YOU $4.00 FOR ONE HOUR OF YOUR TIME

Persons Needed for a Study of Memory

*We will pay five hundred New Haven men to help us complete a scientific study of memory and learning. The study is being done at Yale University.

*Each person who participates will be paid $4.00 (plus 50c carfare) for approximately 1 hour's time. We need you for only one hour: there are no further obligations. You may choose the time you would like to come (evenings, weekdays, or weekends).

*No special training, education, or experience is needed. We want:

Factory workers	Businessmen	Construction workers
City employees	Clerks	Salespeople
Laborers	Professional people	White-collar workers
Barbers	Telephone workers	Others

All persons must be between the ages of 20 and 50. High school and college students cannot be used.

*If you meet these qualifications, fill out the coupon below and mail it now to Professor Stanley Milgram, Department of Psychology, Yale University, New Haven. You will be notified later of the specific time and place of the study. We reserve the right to decline any application.

*You will be paid $4.00 (plus 50c carfare) as soon as you arrive at the laboratory.

- -

TO:
PROF. STANLEY MILGRAM, DEPARTMENT OF PSYCHOLOGY, YALE UNIVERSITY, NEW HAVEN, CONN. I want to take part in this study of memory and learning. I am between the ages of 20 and 50. I will be paid $4.00 (plus 50c carfare) if I participate.

NAME (Please Print)......................................

ADDRESS ....

TELEPHONE NO. .... Best time to call you ....

AGE........OCCUPATION....................SEX......
CAN YOU COME:

WEEKDAYS .... EVENINGS ......WEEKENDS.........

---

researchers and that his subjects' self-esteem was damaged by the realization that they might harm an innocent person simply because an authority figure ordered them to.

In response to these criticisms, Milgram reported that 84 percent of the subjects in his study were debriefed, glad they had participated, that there was no evidence that any of them developed long-term emotional distress, and that the importance of the findings made the use of deception worthwhile (Milgram, 1964). Given today's increased concern with the rights of research subjects, partly in response to studies like Milgram's, it is unlikely that any researchers would replicate his studies.

Milgram's research still sparks interest today, particularly in regard to those who disobey despite threats to their life and well-being—such as those who smuggled slaves out of southern states via the underground railroad in the mid nineteenth century. One lesson is that those who resist early are more likely to maintain their defiance. For example, a reanalysis of audio recordings of subjects in one of Milgram's replications of his original study found that the sooner subjects resisted, the more likely they were to become defiant and refuse to give any more shocks (Modigliani & Rochat, 1995).

▲▲▲

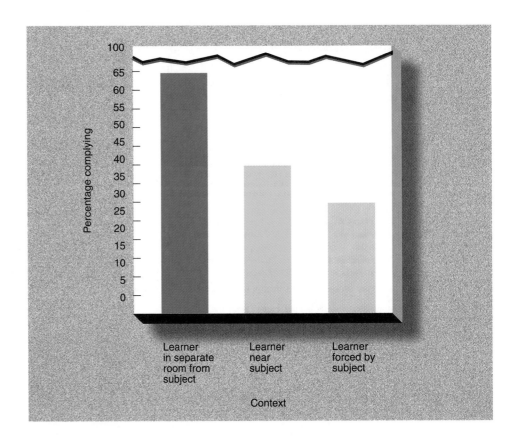

► FIGURE 17.8

Proximity and Obedience

Subjects in Milgram's studies were more willing to give maximum shocks when the subject and learner were in separate rooms. They were less willing when they sat near the learner. And they were the least willing when they had to force the learner's hand onto a shock grid.

STAYING ON TRACK: *Group Dynamics*

1. What factors promote group polarization in decision making?
2. What factors promote groupthink in decision making?
3. How would you reduce social loafing during group performance?
4. How would you use the door-in-the-face technique to get your psychology professor to postpone an exam until a week later?

PROSOCIAL BEHAVIOR: HELPING OTHER PEOPLE

On a spring day in 1986, 1-year-old Jennifer Kroll of West Chicago, Illinois, fell into her family's swimming pool. Jennifer's mother, after pulling Jennifer out of the pool and discovering that she was not breathing, ran outside and began screaming for help. Her screams were heard by James Patridge, who had been confined to a wheelchair since losing his legs in a land-mine explosion during the Vietnam War. Patridge responded by rolling his wheelchair toward the pool, until he encountered heavy brush, forcing him to crawl the final 20 yards. Patridge revived Jennifer by using cardiopulmonary resuscitation ("God's Hand," 1986). Patridge's heroic act led to offers of financial rewards, which he declined to accept, saying that saving Jennifer's life was reward enough.

Altruism: Selfless Helping

prosocial behavior
Behavior that helps others in need.

altruism
The helping of others without the expectation of a reward.

Patridge's act is an example of **prosocial behavior**—helping others in need. His behavior also is an example of **altruism**—helping others without the expectation of a reward in return. But are altruistic acts ever truly selfless? Perhaps people who engage in apparently altruistic behaviors do receive some kind of immaterial rewards. The most famous person to make this claim was Abraham Lincoln. During a train trip, Lincoln looked out his window and saw several piglets drowning. He ordered the train to stop so they could be saved. When praised for his action, Lincoln discounted altruism as his motive, claiming, instead, that his act was motivated by the selfish desire to avoid a guilty conscience (Batson et al., 1986).

Social psychologists interested in the study of altruism have been especially concerned with *empathy*, the ability to feel the emotions that someone else feels. Some researchers have found that prosocial behavior associated with feelings of empathy is truly altruistic (Batson & Shaw, 1991), while prosocial behavior associated with the desire to relieve one's own distress is not (Schroeder et al., 1988). Research studies on the role of empathy in prosocial behavior have provided contradictory findings. In one study, subjects completed a questionnaire that measured their level of sadness and their level of empathy for a person in need. The subjects were then given the opportunity to help the person. The results indicated that the subjects' willingness to help was related more to their sadness score than to their empathy score, indicating that they acted more out of a desire to reduce their own distress than out of a desire to reduce the distress of the other person. In fact, when the subjects were given a "mood fixing" placebo that allegedly (but not actually) made it impossible for them to alter their moods, fewer subjects were willing to help, even when they had high empathy scores (Cialdini et al., 1987). This study provided support for Robert Cialdini's **negative state relief theory** of prosocial behavior (Schaller & Cialdini, 1988).

But what of people whose prosocial behavior is associated with helpers' feelings of both distress and empathy? In an experiment, subjects were empathetically aroused and led to anticipate an imminent mood-enhancing experience. The experimenters reasoned that if the motivation to help were directed toward the goal of negative-state relief, then empathetically aroused individuals who anticipate mood-enhancement should help less than those who do not. The rate of helping among high-empathy subjects was no lower when they anticipated mood enhancement than when they did not. Regardless of anticipated mood enhancement, high-empathy subjects helped more than low-empathy subjects did. The results supported the empathy-altruism hypothesis (Batson et al., 1989). Research studies have produced inconsistent findings in regard to the existence of altruistic helping (Batson & Weeks, 1996; Cialdini & Fultz, 1990). So it is still unclear whether prosocial behavior is motivated more by empathy for others or by the desire to relieve one's own negative emotional states.

Bystander Intervention: Coming to the Rescue

Regardless of his motivation, James Patridge's rescue of Jennifer was an example of **bystander intervention**—helping someone who is in immediate need of aid. Interest in the study of bystander intervention was stimulated by a widely publicized tragedy in which bystanders did not try to save a woman's life. At 3:20 A.M. on March 13, 1964, a 28-year-old woman named Kitty Genovese was returning home from her job as a bar manager. As she neared her apartment building in the New York City borough of Queens, she was attacked by a mugger who repeatedly stabbed her. Thirty-eight of her neighbors reported that they had been awakened by her screams and had rushed to look out their windows, but had not seen the attack. The assailant left twice, returning each time to continue his attack until, 30 minutes after her ordeal had begun, Kitty Genovese died.

How would you have responded had you been one of her neighbors? The neighbors' responses might surprise you. At no time during these three separate attacks did any of the 38 persons try to help Kitty Genovese or even call the police. When questioned by police and reporters, the witnesses gave a variety of explanations for why they had not called the police. Their reasons included feeling tired, assuming it was a lovers' quarrel, and believing that "it can't happen here" (Gansberg, 1964). The murder of Kitty Genovese gained national attention, and the apparent apathy of her neighbors was taken as a sign of the callous, impersonal nature of the residents of big cities.

But social psychologists John Darley and Bibb Latané rejected this commonsense explanation as too simplistic. Instead, they conducted research studies to determine the factors that affect the willingness of bystanders to intervene in emergencies. This is important today, as it was when Kitty Genovese was murdered. In fact, a survey of more than

▲ Robert Cialdini
"An observer's heightened empathy for a sufferer brings with it increased personal sadness in the observer and . . . it is the egoistic desire to relieve the sadness, rather than the selfless desire to relieve the sufferer, that motivates helping."

negative state relief theory
The theory that we engage in prosocial behavior to relieve our own state of emotional distress at another's plight.

bystander intervention
The act of helping someone who is in immediate need of aid.

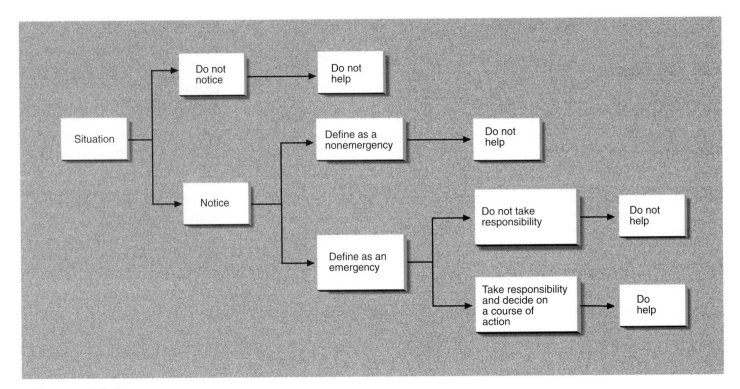

▲ FIGURE 17.9
Steps in Bystander Intervention
According to Bibb Latané and John Darley
(1968), bystanders go through certain steps
before intervening in emergencies. The
possibility of intervening can be inhibited at
any of these steps.

▲ Bibb Latané
"Even when bystanders to an emergency
cannot see or be influenced by each other, the
more bystanders who are present, the less likely
any one bystander will be to intervene and
provide aid."

500 undergraduates and faculty members found that only 25 percent of those who had
witnessed children being abused in public had ever intervened to help (Christy & Voight,
1994). Darley and Latané found that bystander intervention involves a series of steps,
which are presented in Figure 17.9. The intervention process can continue through each
of these steps or be halted at any one.

Noticing the Victim

To intervene in an emergency, you must first notice the event or the victim. James
Patridge heard the screams of Jennifer Kroll's mother, and neighbors heard the screams of
Kitty Genovese.

Interpreting the Situation as an Emergency

The same event can be interpreted as an emergency or as a nonemergency. James Patridge
was confronted by an unambiguous situation. He interpreted the screams of Jennifer's
mother as a sign that there was an emergency. In contrast, there was some ambiguity in
Kitty Genovese's situation. In fact, when there is an apparent confrontation between a
man and a woman, bystanders tend to assume that it is a lovers' quarrel rather than a true
emergency (Shotland & Straw, 1976). Because almost all of Kitty Genovese's neighbors
interpreted the situation as a nonemergency, at that point there was little likelihood that
any would help.

Taking Personal Responsibility

After interpreting the situation as an emergency, Patridge took responsibility for intervening. But not even those who may have interpreted Kitty Genovese's situation as an
emergency took responsibility for helping her. Darley and Latané discovered a surprising
reason for this. Contrary to what you might expect, as the number of bystanders *increases*,
the likelihood of a bystander's intervening *decreases*. Note that this is true only in situations involving strangers; in emergencies involving highly cohesive groups of people, such
as friends or relatives, the probability of intervention will increase as the number of
bystanders increases (Rutkowski, Gruder, & Romer, 1983).

The influence of the number of bystanders on bystander intervention was demonstrated
in an early study by Darley and Latané (1968). They had college students meet to discuss

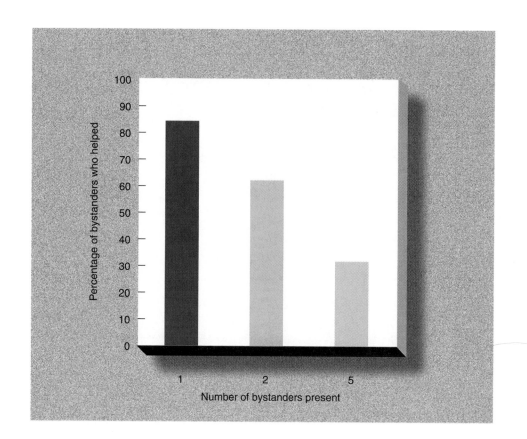

◄ **FIGURE 17.10**
Diffusion of Responsibility
Darley and Latané (1968) found that as the number of bystanders increased, the likelihood of any of them going to the aid of a woman apparently having an epileptic seizure decreased.

the problems they faced in attending school in New York City. Each student was led to a room and told to communicate with other students over an intercom. The students were told that there were two, three, or six students taking part in the discussion, but all of the other students were the experimenter's confederates; in fact, the remarks of the other students were tape recordings. Early in the session the subject (the nonconfederate) heard another student apparently having an epileptic seizure and crying out for help.

Figure 17.10 shows that of those subjects who believed they were a lone bystander, 85 percent sought help for the stricken person. Of those who believed they were one of two bystanders, 62 percent sought help. And of those who believed they were one of five bystanders, only 31 percent sought help. One reason for this is the diffusion of responsibility: As the number of bystanders increases, the responsibility felt by each one decreases. So the students who were exposed to the sounds of a mock epileptic seizure felt less responsibility for helping the victim when they believed other bystanders were present. In contrast to Kitty Genovese's neighbors, who assumed that other neighbors had been awakened, Patridge may have assumed that no one else could intervene, leaving him with the responsibility.

Deciding on a Course of Action

The decision to intervene depends, in part, on whether the bystander feels competent to meet the demands of the situation (Clark & Word, 1974). Patridge decided to wheel himself toward the pool and then crawl to it. Because Patridge had training in cardiopulmonary resuscitation, while Jennifer Kroll's mother did not, he felt more competent to try to revive Jennifer. Though none did so until after Kitty Genovese was dead, her neighbors might have at least considered calling the police when they heard her screams. A study that interviewed people who had intervened in violent crimes, such as muggings and armed robberies, found that they were usually larger and stronger than those who did not. Moreover, they typically were better trained to cope with crimes and emergencies, having had more police training or emergency medical training. Thus, they felt more competent to help (Huston et al., 1981).

Taking Action

Patridge believed that the potential benefits of intervention outweighed the potential costs. As discussed in Chapter 11, Abraham Maslow assumed that people are more motivated by the need for safety than by the need for self-esteem. This might explain why bystanders who believe that intervening in an emergency would place them in danger (as some may have believed in the case of Kitty Genovese) are less likely to intervene, even if failure to do so would lower their self-esteem. In fact, people who are more motivated by the need for safety are less likely to intervene in dangerous emergencies, such as explosions, than those who are more motivated by the need for self-esteem (Wilson & Petruska, 1984).

The characteristics of the victim also influence bystander intervention. One of the most important characteristics is the degree to which the victim appears responsible for his or her predicament. You might recognize this as an example of causal attribution. If we make dispositional attributions for a person's predicament, we will be less likely to help than if we make situational attributions for it (Weiner, 1980). We are more likely to help people in need when we perceive their situation to be the result of uncontrollable factors, such as a sudden illness, than when we perceive it to be the result of controllable factors, such as personal recklessness (Schmidt & Weiner, 1988).

As you can now appreciate, bystander intervention is not simply the product of a particular personality type. Instead, it is a complex process that depends on the interactions among characteristics of the victim, the bystander, and the situation.

STAYING ON TRACK: *Prosocial Behavior*

1. What research evidence supports the negative state relief theory of seemingly altruistic behavior?
2. What is the role of the diffusion of responsibility in bystander intervention?

AGGRESSION: HARMING OTHER PEOPLE

As much as human beings are capable of prosocial behavior, they are, unfortunately, just as capable of antisocial behavior. The most extreme form of antisocial behavior is **aggression,** which is verbal or physical behavior aimed at causing harm to another person. What accounts for the prevalence of aggression?

aggression
Behavior aimed at causing harm to another person.

Theories of Aggression

One class of theories views aggression as the product of physiology. A second class of theories views aggression as the product of experience. Obviously, both are important, as is their interaction.

Aggression as the Product of Physiology

The earliest theories of aggression claimed that it is instinctive. An *instinct* is an inborn tendency, unaffected by learning, to engage in a relatively complex behavior that characterizes members of a species—such as nest building in birds. After observing the extraordinary violence of World War I, Sigmund Freud concluded that human aggression is caused by an instinct that he called *Thanatos* (Greek for "death"). According to Freud, Thanatos causes a buildup of aggressive energy, which must be released periodically through a process called *catharsis*. This would prevent outbursts of extreme violence. You might experience catharsis by playing football, field hockey, or another aggressive sport.

Nobel Prize–winning ethologist Konrad Lorenz (1966) agreed with Freud that we have an instinct for aggression. He claimed that all animals have a powerful aggressive drive that, like the sex drive, promotes the survival of their species. But because animals have evolved natural weapons such as fangs and claws that can kill, they have also evolved ritualistic behaviors to inhibit aggression and prevent unnecessary injuries and deaths. In contrast, because human beings have not evolved natural weapons that can kill, they have not evolved ritualistic behaviors to inhibit aggression against their own species. As a consequence, human beings are less inhibited in using artificial weapons such as clubs, spears, guns, and missiles against one another. Lorenz, like Freud, believed that outbursts of aggression could be avoided only by providing outlets for the cathartic release of aggressive energy through means such as sports (Leakey & Lewin, 1977). But research has failed to support the belief that aggression can be reduced through catharsis. In fact, people who engage in aggression usually become *more* likely to engage in it (Geen, Stonner, & Shope, 1975).

The relatively new field called *sociobiology* (see Chapter 11) assumes there is a strong hereditary basis for aggression and other social behaviors (Wilson, 1975). Studies of twins have provided evidence supporting this. Psychologists who study twins might compare the aggressiveness of identical twins reared together to the aggressiveness of fraternal twins reared together. These researchers assume that if heredity plays a role in aggression, identical twins (who are genetically identical) will be more similar in aggressiveness than will fraternal twins (who are no more alike genetically than ordinary siblings). Twin studies have, indeed, found this, providing evidence for the hereditary basis of aggressiveness (Rushton et al., 1986). Of course, this does not rule out the possibility that identical twins are more similar in aggressiveness because they are treated more alike than fraternal twins are.

What might be the physiological means by which heredity affects aggression? Several brain structures play important roles, particularly structures in the limbic system, including the amygdala and the hypothalamus (Potegal et al., 1996). A review of brain-imaging studies using CT, MRI, and PET found a relationship between frontal lobe abnormalities and aggressiveness (Mills & Raine, 1994). Another factor is the sex hormone testosterone. Violent criminals have higher levels of testosterone than nonviolent criminals do (Rubin, Reinisch, & Haskett, 1981). Athletes who use anabolic steroids, which are synthetic derivatives of testosterone, become more aggressive (Gregg & Rejeski, 1990). Castration of male sex offenders lowers their testosterone levels and reduces their sex drive and sex-crime recidivism (Bradford, 1988). Female-to-male transsexuals, who undergo testosterone treatment, become more prone to anger and aggression after several months of hormone treatment (Van Goozen, Frijda, & Van de Poll, 1995). And male and female children prenatally exposed to testosterone because their mothers received a synthetic form of it during pregnancy are more aggressive than their same-sex siblings who were not exposed to it (Reinisch, 1981).

▲ **Catharsis and Violence**
According to Freud, both the participants and the spectators at this wrestling match should show a decrease in their tendencies toward violence as the result of catharsis. But research has found that, on the contrary, watching or taking part in violence will increase one's tendency to engage in it.

▲ **Konrad Lorenz (1903–1989)**
"Real beasts of prey, such as lions and wolves, that live in packs, have developed inhibitions because of their natural weapons. These inhibitions prevent their using these instruments of death against their own kind . . . . Mankind is different."

But some research has failed to find a relationship between testosterone levels and aggressiveness. One study found no relationship between increased testosterone levels in males during puberty and increased likelihood of aggression (Halpern et al., 1993). Other studies have found that males who receive testosterone injections might become more aggressive because of an expectancy effect—they act more aggressively simply because they believe they have received testosterone (Bjorkqvist et al., 1994). These negative findings have led some researchers to study the effect of experience on aggression (Albert, Walsh, & Jonik, 1993).

Aggression as the Product of Experience

While some researchers look to hereditary factors, most look to life experiences as the main determinants of aggression. In the late 1930s, a team of behaviorists concluded that aggression is caused by frustration (Dollard et al., 1939). This became known as the **frustration-aggression hypothesis.** We experience frustration when we are blocked from reaching a goal. But the frustration-aggression hypothesis is an inadequate explanation of aggression, because experiences other than frustration can cause aggression, and frustration does not always lead to it.

The inadequacies of the frustration-aggression hypothesis inspired psychologist Leonard Berkowitz to develop the *revised frustration-aggression hypothesis*. According to Berkowitz (1974), frustration does not directly provoke aggression. Instead, it directly provokes anger or another unpleasant emotion, such as anxiety or depression. The unpleasant emotion, in turn, will provoke aggression—particularly when stimuli (such as guns) that have been associated with aggression are present. Berkowitz demonstrated this in a study in which male college students gave electric shocks to other students to induce feelings of anger in the shock recipients. When students who had received shocks were given the opportunity to give shocks to those who had shocked them, they gave more shocks when an aggressive stimulus such as a revolver, rather than a neutral stimulus such as a badminton racket, was left on the table (Berkowitz & LePage, 1967). Though some studies have failed to support the revised frustration-aggression hypothesis (Buss, Booker, & Buss, 1972), many have found support for it (Dill & Anderson, 1995). Moreover, unexpected frustrations, because they evoke stronger unpleasant emotions, are more likely to provoke aggression than are expected frustrations (Berkowitz, 1989).

As described in Chapter 7, much of our behavior is the product of social learning by observing the behavior of others. Aggression is no exception to this. We can learn to be aggressive by observing people who act aggressively. For example, women who have observed their parents being aggressive are more likely to be aggressive themselves (White & Humphrey, 1994). In a classic experiment by Albert Bandura, children in a nursery school who observed an adult punching an inflated "Bobo doll" were more likely to engage in similar aggression against the Bobo doll than were children who had not observed the aggressive model (Bandura, Ross, & Ross, 1963). The observational learning of aggression is promoted by observing models who are rewarded for aggression and is inhibited by observing models who are punished for it.

▲ Leonard Berkowitz
"Frustrations generate aggressive inclinations to the degree that they arouse negative affect."

Television and Aggression

As you might expect, social learning theory predicts that televised violence will promote real-life violence. An early study of the effects of televised violence presented excerpts of the violent television show "The Untouchables" or nonviolent track-and-field events to children between 5 and 9 years old. Children who viewed the violent scenes were more likely to act aggressively toward another child and for a longer time (Liebert & Baron, 1972). In a more recent study, children's aggressiveness was considerably higher when they played with aggressive toys after watching an aggressive cartoon than after watching a neutral cartoon (Sanson & di Muccio, 1993).

Concern about the effects of televised violence on aggression is not new. It has existed ever since television became a popular medium in the 1950s (Carpenter, 1955). The first congressional report on the effects of television was a 1954 report on its impact on juvenile

delinquency. Since then, reports on the social effects of television have appeared every few years. Major reports, sponsored by the National Institute of Mental Health, on the social effects of television appeared in 1972 and 1982. Both reports found that violence on television led to aggressive behavior by children and adolescents and recommended a decrease in televised violence (Walsh, 1983). But critics of these reports claimed that the results of laboratory experiments on the effects of televised violence might not generalize to real life and that field studies on the effects of televised violence failed to control all of the other variables that might encourage violence (Fisher, 1983).

Psychologists themselves have not reached a consensus on the effects of televised violence. A recent meta-analysis found that there is a positive, significant correlation between television violence and aggressive behavior (Paik & Comstock, 1994). Another finding is that the relationship between televised violence and real-life aggression is bidirectional. This means that televised violence makes people more aggressive *and* that people who are aggressive choose to watch more televised violence (Wiegman, Kuttschreuter, & Baarda, 1992). Still another possibility is that both television watching and aggressiveness are influenced by a third factor—heredity. Though there is no "television-watching gene," the number of hours of television watched by children aged 3, 4, and 5 years has a hereditary basis (Plomin et al., 1990). Perhaps an inherited tendency to seek stimulation accounts for the positive correlation between television watching and aggressiveness. Of course, without additional evidence, this remains just a hypothesis.

Group Violence

In the year A.D. 59, opposing fans rioted at the Pompeii amphitheater during a gladiatorial contest, prompting the Roman Senate to ban such contests in Pompeii for 10 years. The twentieth century has also seen its share of riots at athletic events. In 1985 a riot at a soccer game in Brussels killed 38 people and injured more than 400 (Bredemeier & Shields, 1985).

What makes normally peaceful individuals become violent when they are in groups? We are usually aware of our own thoughts, feelings, and perceptions and are concerned about being socially evaluated. But when we are in groups, we might become less aware of ourselves and less concerned about being socially evaluated. Leon Festinger named this process

deindividuation
The process by which group members become less aware of themselves as individuals and less concerned about being socially evaluated.

deindividuation (Festinger, Pepitone, & Newcomb, 1952). As the result of deindividuation, our behavior might no longer be governed by our social norms, which in turn can lead to the loss of normal restraints against undesirable behavior, making us more likely to participate in group violence. Moreover, the anonymity provided by group membership can make us less concerned with the impression we make on other people, because we feel less accountable for our own actions (Prentice-Dunn & Rogers, 1982).

Even aggression by individuals who are not in groups is more likely when they feel anonymous. An experiment found that people driving convertibles with their tops up (high anonymity) will be more likely to honk their horns at cars that fail to proceed immediately at green lights than will people driving convertibles with their tops down (low anonymity). Those with tops up honk quicker, longer, and more frequently (Ellison et al., 1995).

Deindividuation is most likely when the group is large and when the group members feel anonymous and are emotionally aroused. This means that large groups of people, wearing masks, uniforms, or disguises and aroused by drugs, dancing, chanting, or oratory, will be more likely to engage in violence. These factors account for the use of hooded uniforms and frenzied meetings by members of the Ku Klux Klan.

STAYING ON TRACK: *Aggression*

1. What evidence is there for the role of testosterone in aggression?
2. What has research determined about the relationship between televised violence and real-life aggression?
3. What is the role of deindividuation in aggression?

THINKING ABOUT *Psychology*

Does Pornography Cause Aggression Against Women?

One of the most distressing social statistics concerning aggression is that one American woman in eight is raped during her lifetime, usually before the age of 18 ("Survey Finds Most Rape Victims Are Minors," 1992). This high incidence of sexual aggression has prompted researchers to study the factors that might promote it. One of the most controversial and extensively studied of these factors is **pornography**—sexually explicit material intended to incite sexual arousal.

pornography
Sexually explicit material intended to incite sexual arousal.

GOVERNMENT REPORTS ON PORNOGRAPHY AND AGGRESSION

In 1970, the President's Commission on Obscenity and Pornography concluded that exposure to pornography does not make men likely to commit sexual aggression. More recently, in ceremonies associated with the signing of the Child Protection Act of 1984, President Reagan announced his intention to sponsor a study of the effects of pornography. In 1985, he appointed an eleven-member commission headed by Attorney General Edwin Meese: the Attorney General's Commission on Pornography.

The commission's report, published in 1986, concluded that exposure to either violent or nonviolent pornography can cause aggression against women. Two members of the commission, Ellen Levine, editor of *Woman's Day*, and Judith Becker, a Columbia University

| CHAPTER   17

psychologist, wrote a dissenting opinion in which they claimed that the report incorrectly characterized the correlational evidence as supportive of a *causal* link between pornography and sexual aggression (Wilcox, 1987). You will recall that it is important to distinguish between causation and correlation when interpreting research findings. It is conceivable that pornography causes sexual aggression, that men who commit sexual aggression are more likely to seek pornography, or that some men have personal characteristics that make them enjoy pornography *and* commit sexual aggression.

The results of a 1986 conference sponsored by Surgeon General C. Everett Koop, "Report of the Surgeon General's Workshop on Pornography and Public Health" (Koop, 1987), were published several months after the attorney general's report. Unlike Meese, Koop, who also was morally appalled by pornography (but committed to objective scientific discourse), relied on testimony from some of the most eminent researchers in the field. Based on the data presented at the workshop, Koop concluded that children and adolescents who participate in the production of pornography experience adverse, enduring effects, such as eventual involvement in child prostitution. He also concluded that portrayals of rape as pleasurable for the victim increase the acceptance of coercion in sexual relations and might increase the incidence of rape by promoting the view that women enjoy being forced to have sex. Koop's report, unlike Meese's, did not conclude that nonviolent pornography *causes* aggression against women.

▲ **C. Everett Koop, Former Surgeon General**
"Pornography that portrays sexual aggression as pleasurable for the victim increases the acceptance of the use of coercion in sexual relations."

EMPIRICAL RESEARCH ON PORNOGRAPHY AND AGGRESSION

What kinds of research studies served as the bases for the Meese and Koop reports? Many have been conducted by Neil Malamuth, Edward Donnerstein, and their colleagues. They have found that violent sexual films, more than nonviolent sexual films, might stimulate aggression against women, as indicated by the following experiment.

ANATOMY OF A CONTEMPORARY RESEARCH STUDY

Do Pornographic Films Promote Aggression Against Women?

Rationale

The experiment examined several factors related to violence against women induced by erotic films (Donnerstein & Berkowitz, 1981). The study considered whether the films were violent or not and whether the victim seemed to enjoy being raped.

Method

Eighty male undergraduates were randomly assigned to one of four conditions in which they watched one of four films: a talk-show interview (neutral film); a young couple making love (erotic film); a woman enjoying being raped by two men (positive aggressive film); and a woman suffering during a rape by two men (negative aggressive film). Half of the men in each group had been insulted and angered by women confederates of the experimenter who pretended to be subjects in the study, and half had not been. The men were given the opportunity to retaliate against the confederates by giving them electric shocks when they made mistakes on a memory task. The intensity of the shock was used as a measure of aggression.

▲ **Neil Malamuth**
"The mass media can contribute to a cultural climate that is more accepting of aggression against women."

Results and Discussion

As shown in Figure 17.11, the results indicated that men who had seen the neutral or nonviolent erotic film displayed relatively little aggression. Both angered and nonangered men who had seen the film of the rape in which the woman enjoyed it displayed higher levels of aggression. And, of the men who had seen the rape during which the woman suffered, those who had been angered behaved more aggressively than those who had not. These results might also hold outside of the laboratory, because men who report that they are sexually

Pornography and Aggression
The results of the study by Donnerstein and Berkowitz (1981) showed that men who had been provoked and then watched an aggressive erotic film in which a woman acted as though she enjoyed being raped behaved the most aggressively toward women.

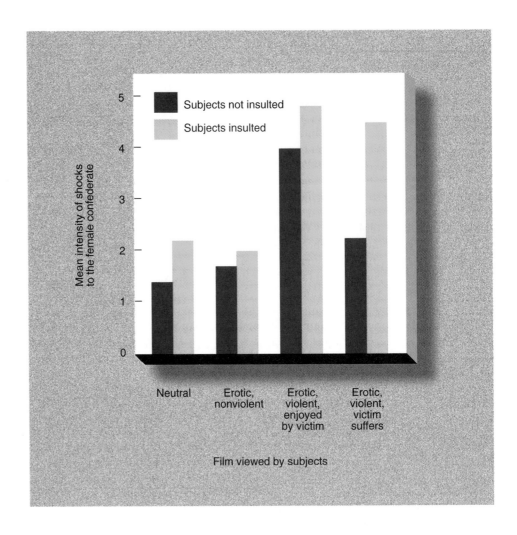

aroused by portrayals of sexual aggression against women are more likely to report that they would attack women (Malamuth, 1986). But a Canadian replication of this American reseach study found that exposure to violent pornography, even after provocation, did not increase the likelihood of aggression against women (Fisher & Grenier, 1994). Thus, research findings regarding the effect of violent pornography on male aggressiveness toward women appear to be inconsistent.

▲ ▲ ▲

Some research findings support the conclusions of the attorney general's commission (Page, 1990), but most findings are more consistent with those of the surgeon general's commission—though there is some evidence that nonviolent pornography causes sexual aggression against women (Allen et al., 1995). But there is stronger evidence that violent pornography, especially when it supports the myth that women enjoy being raped, causes aggression against women (Pollard, 1995). But this conclusion is based mainly on the results of laboratory experiments that have considered only short-term effects of violent pornography and that might not generalize outside of the laboratory. Regardless of this, repeated exposure to violent pornography does seem to desensitize viewers to real-life violence, such as domestic violence, against women, rating it as less severe and feeling less sympathy for victims. But sensitivity begins to rebound to normal levels once exposure to the materials is terminated (Mullin & Linz, 1995). Of course, whether violent erotic movies, such as the "teenage slasher" movies of the past decade, cause aggression against women is a scientific question. Whether such films are harmful in other ways is a legal, moral, social, and political dilemma.

1. What did the Koop report say about the relationship between pornography and aggression?

2. What have experiments found about the relationship between pornography and aggression?

 # CHAPTER SUMMARY

SOCIAL COGNITION

Social psychology is the field that studies behavior in its interpersonal context. The process by which we try to explain social behavior is called causal attribution. When you decide that a person is responsible for her or his own behavior, you are making a dispositional attribution. And when you decide that circumstances are responsible for a person's behavior, you are making a situational attribution.

Harold Kelley identified three factors that interact in determining whether we make dispositional or situational attributions: consistency, distinctiveness, and consensus. Bernard Weiner's more ambitious theory of attribution looks at the interaction of the internal-external, stable-unstable, and controllable-uncontrollable dimensions. Major biases in causal attribution include the fundamental attribution error, the actor-observer bias, and the self-serving bias.

Person perception is the process by which we make judgments about the personal characteristics of people. Sometimes we try to affect other people's perceptions of us by engaging in impression management. Person perception is also affected by social schemas, which comprise the presumed characteristics of a role, an event, a person, or a group. Social schemas that we believe can be applied to almost all members of a group are called stereotypes. Our first impressions play an important role in person perception, in some cases creating a self-fulfilling prophecy.

INTERPERSONAL ATTRACTION

Psychologists interested in studying social attraction are concerned with the factors that make us like or love other people. Liking depends on the factors of proximity, familiarity, physical attractiveness, similarity, and self-disclosure. Researchers who study love distinguish between passionate love and companionate love. According to Ellen Bersheid and Elaine Hatfield, romantic love depends on cultural support for the concept of romantic love, a state of physiological arousal, and the presence of an appropriate person to love. Sternberg's triangular theory of love has received little empirical evaluation. Among the most important factors in promoting love are similarity, self-disclosure, and equity.

ATTITUDES

Attitudes are evaluations of ideas, events, objects, or people. Attitudes have emotional, cognitive, and behavioral components. Classical conditioning, operant conditioning, and social learning theory explain how attitudes are learned. We are often subjected to persuasive messages aimed at getting us to change our attitudes. Persuasive messages can take a central route or a peripheral route. Persuasiveness depends on the message, the source, and the audience.

Sources that are more credible and attractive are more persuasive. Under certain circumstances, two-sided messages will be more effective than one-sided messages. The intelligence level of the receiver and the relevance of the message also determine the effectiveness of persuasive messages. But our attitudes might not always accurately predict our behavior.

Moreover, our behavior can sometimes affect our attitudes, a phenomenon that is explained by cognitive dissonance theory and self-perception theory.

Prejudice is a positive or negative attitude toward others based on their membership in particular groups. The behavioral component of prejudice is discrimination. Among the important factors promoting prejudice are stereotypes and the authoritarian personality. Prejudice can be reduced when there is equal-status contact and intergroup cooperation.

GROUP DYNAMICS

Psychologists interested in group dynamics study the effects of social relationships on thinking, feeling, and behaving. Decision making in groups can be affected by group polarization, which is the tendency for groups to make more-extreme decisions than their members would make as individuals. Group decisions are sometimes characterized by groupthink, in which group members place greater emphasis on unanimity than on critical thinking. Minorities can affect group decisions by being rational, confident, consistent, and patient.

Groups can affect task performance through social facilitation, which is the improvement of performance caused by the presence of other people. Our performance can also be affected by social loafing, which is the tendency of individuals to exert less effort when performing in groups.

Human relationships can involve conformity, compliance, and obedience. Conformity is behaving in accordance with group norms with little or no overt pressure to do so. Compliance is agreeing to a request that is backed by little or no threat of punishment. Two of the chief techniques for inducing compliance are the foot-in-the-door technique and the door-in-the-face technique. Obedience is following orders given by an authority. Stanley Milgram found that most people are all too willing to harm other people when ordered to do so by a legitimate authority figure.

PROSOCIAL BEHAVIOR

Prosocial behavior involves helping others in need. Altruism is helping others without the expectation of a reward in return. Some researchers have found that true altruism occurs only when prosocial acts are done out of empathy, rather than out of a desire to reduce one's own distress at the plight of another person. Other researchers have found, instead, that prosocial behavior is never truly altruistic—it always depends on the desire to reduce our own distress. Psychologists who study prosocial behavior are especially concerned with bystander intervention, the act of helping someone who is in immediate need of aid. Bystander intervention depends on noticing the victim, interpreting the situation as an emergency, taking personal responsibility, deciding on a course of action, and taking action to help.

AGGRESSION

Aggression is behavior aimed at causing harm to someone else. Some theories view aggression as biologically based, perhaps inborn. Sigmund Freud and Konrad Lorenz believed that aggression is instinctive, meaning that we have no choice but to engage in it periodically. Today most researchers reject the instinct theory of aggression but still study hormonal and hereditary influences on it. Most researchers look to life experiences as the main determinants of aggression. According to the frustration-aggression hypothesis, aggression becomes more likely after we have been blocked from reaching a goal. According to social learning theory, we can learn to be aggressive by observing people who act aggressively. Group violence is promoted by deindividuation, which is the loss of self-awareness and the feeling of anonymity that comes from being part of a group. The past two decades have seen a yet-unresolved controversy about the effects of televised violence on real-life aggression.

THINKING ABOUT PSYCHOLOGY: DOES PORNOGRAPHY CAUSE AGGRESSION AGAINST WOMEN

Pornography is sexually explicit material intended to provoke sexual arousal. Reports by the attorney general and the surgeon general of the United States published in 1986 and 1987 disagree about the effects of pornography on sexual aggression. Perhaps the only generally accepted finding is that violent pornography is more likely than nonviolent pornography to affect sexual aggression.

KEY CONCEPTS

social psychology 594

Social Cognition

social cognition 594
causal attribution 594
consistency 595
distinctiveness 595
consensus 595
fundamental attribution error 596
actor-observer bias 596
self-serving bias 597
person perception 597
impression management 597
social schema 598
stereotype 598
self-fulfilling prophecy 599

Interpersonal Attraction

passionate love 603
companionate love 603

Attitudes

attitude 604
persuasion 606
elaboration likelihood model 606
cognitive dissonance theory 608
self-perception theory 610
prejudice 610
authoritarian personality 611

Group Dynamics

group 612
group polarization 613

groupthink 614
social faclitation 615
social loafing 616
conformity 616
compliance 618
foot-in-the-door technique 618
door-in-the-face technique 619
obedience 619

Prosocial Behavior

prosocial behavior 622
altruism 622
negative state relief theory 623
bystander intervention 623

Aggression

aggression 626
frustration-aggression hypothesis 628
deindividuation 630

Does Pornography Cause Aggression Against Women?

pornography 630

KEY CONTRIBUTORS

Social Cognition

Harold Kelley 594
Bernard Weiner 596

Interpersonal Attraction

Elaine Hatfield 602
Ellen Berscheid 602

Attitudes

Leon Festinger 608
Kenneth Clark 612
Mamie Phipps Clark 612

Group Dynamics

Irving Janis 614
Robert Zajonc 615
Solomon Asch 616
Stanley Milgram 620
John Darley 623
Bibb Latané 623

Aggression

Sigmund Freud 627
Leonard Berkowitz 628
Albert Bandura 628

FOR MORE INFORMATION ON SOCIAL BEHAVIOR

FOR GENERAL WORKS ON SOCIAL BEHAVIOR

Gergen, K. J., & Gergen, M. M. (Eds.). (1984). *Historical social psychology*. Hillsdale, NJ: Erlbaum.
Lippa, R. A. (1994). *Introduction to social psychology* (2nd ed.). Pacific Grove, CA: Brooks/Cole.
Triandis, H. C. (1994). *Social behavior and culture*. New York: McGraw-Hill.

FOR MORE ON SOCIAL COGNITION

Fiske, S. T., & Taylor, S. E. (1991). *Social cognition*. New York: McGraw-Hill.
Hewstone, M. (1989). *Causal attribution: From cognitive processes to collective beliefs*. New York: Basil Blackwell.
Higgins, R. L., Snyder, C. R., & Berglas, S. (1990). *Self-handicapping*. New York: Plenum.

Schlenker, B. S., & Weigold, M. F. (1980). *Impression management: The self-concept*. Melbourne, FL: Krieger.
Snyder, M. (1987). *Public appearances/private realities: The psychology of self-monitoring*. New York: W. H. Freeman.
Zebrowitz, L. A. (1990). *Social perception*. Pacific Grove, CA: Brooks/Cole.

FOR MORE ON SOCIAL ATTRACTION

Derlega, V. J., Metts, S., Petronio, S., & Margulis, S. T. (1993). *Self-disclosure*. Newbury Park, CA: Sage.
Hatfield, E., & Rapson, R. L. (1993). *Love, sex, and intimacy: Their psychology, biology, and history*. New York: HarperCollins.

Hendrick, S. S., & Hendrick, C. (1992). *Liking, loving, and relating*. Pacific Grove, CA: Brooks/Cole.

Sternberg, R. J. (1988). *The triangle of love: Intimacy, passion, commitment*. New York: Basic Books.

FOR MORE ON ATTITUDES

Adorno, T. W., Frenkel-Brunswik, E., Levinson, D. J., & Sanford, R. N. (1950/1982). *The authoritarian personality*. New York: W. W. Norton.

Cialdini, R. B. (1994). *Influence: The new psychology of modern persuasion*. New York: Morrow.

Duckitt, J. (1992). *The social psychology of prejudice*. Westport, CT: Greenwood.

Eagly, A., Chaiken, S., & Youngblood, D. (Eds.). (1992). *The psychology of attitudes*. San Diego: Harcourt Brace Jovanovich.

Festinger, L. (1957). *A theory of cognitive dissonance*. Stanford, CA: Stanford University Press.

FOR MORE ON GROUP DYNAMICS

Forsyth, D. R. (1990). *Group dynamics*. Monterey, CA: Brooks/Cole.

Guerin, B. (1993). *Social facilitation*. New York: Cambridge University Press.

Janis, I. L. (1982). *Groupthink: Psychological studies of policy decisions and fiascoes* (2nd ed.). Boston: Houghton Mifflin.

Miller, A. G. (1986). *The obedience experiments: A case study of controversy in social science*. Westport, CT: Praeger.

Mugny, G., & Perez, J. A. (1991). *The social psychology of minority influence*. New York: Cambridge University Press.

Turner, J. C. (1991). *Social influence*. Belmont, CA: Brooks/Cole.

FOR MORE ON PROSOCIAL BEHAVIOR

Batson, C. D. (1991). *The altruism question: Toward a social-psychological answer*. Hillsdale, NJ: Erlbaum.

Clark, M. S. (Ed.). (1991). *Prosocial behavior*. Newbury Park, CA: Sage.

Kohn, A. (1990). *The brighter side of human nature: Altruism and empathy in everyday life*. New York: Basic Books.

Latané, B., & Darley, J. M. (1970). *The unresponsive bystander: Why doesn't he help?* Englewood Cliffs, NJ: Prentice Hall.

Piliavin, J. A., Dovidio, J. F., Gaertner, S. L., & Clark, R. D. (1981). *Emergency intervention*. New York: Academic Press.

FOR MORE ON AGGRESSION

Berkowitz, L. (1993). *Aggression: Its causes, consequences, and control*. New York: McGraw-Hill.

Ellis, L. (1989). *Theories of rape: Inquiries into the causes of sexual aggression*. New York: Taylor & Francis.

Geen, R. G. (1990). *Human aggression*. Monterey, CA: Brooks/Cole.

Liebert, R. M., & Sprafkin, J. (1988). *The early window: Effects of television on children and youth*. New York: Pergamon.

FOR MORE ON PORNOGRAPHY AND AGGRESSION

Donnerstein, E., Linz, D., & Penrod, S. (1986). *The question of pornography: Research findings and policy implications*. New York: Free Press.

Koop, C. E. (1987). Report of the Surgeon General's Workshop on Pornography and Public Health. *American Psychologist, 42*, 944–945.

Linz, D., Donnerstein, E., & Penrod, S. (1987). The findings and recommendations of the attorney general's commission on pornography. *American Psychologist, 42*, 946–953.

Zillmann, D., & Bryant, J. (Eds.). (1989). *Pornography: Research advances and policy considerations*. Hillsdale, NJ: Erlbaum.

FOR MORE ON CONTRIBUTORS TO THE STUDY OF SOCIAL BEHAVIOR

Evans, R. I. (1989). *Albert Bandura: The man and his ideas: A dialogue*. New York: Praeger.

Gay, P. (1988). *Freud: A life for our time*. New York: W. W. Norton.

Heider, F. (1983). *The life of a psychologist: An autobiography*. Lawrence: University of Kansas Press.

Rock, I. (Ed.). (1990). *The legacy of Solomon Asch: Essays in cognition and social psychology*. Hillsdale, NJ: Erlbaum.

Majoring in Psychology

Now that you know what psychologists do and some of the fields in which they specialize, you might be interested in pursuing a career in psychology. Table A.1 lists the many divisions of the American Psychological Association, providing further evidence of the diversity of pursuits available to budding psychologists. A career as a psychologist would potentially permit you to combine teaching, research, and practice in any variety of fields.

A major in psychology is particularly attractive because it is intrinsically interesting, provides marketable skills, and prepares students for further education or for employment (Lunneborg, 1978). No undergraduate major enhances one's ability to understand human and animal behavior more than psychology does. A major in psychology is also attractive because it does more than provide training in a narrow discipline aimed primarily at getting a first job. It improves personal and practical skills that make students more adaptable to many career opportunities. Students who major in psychology improve their abilities in writing, speaking, and problem solving. These students also learn to be open-minded skeptics capable of objectively evaluating claims made by scientists, advertisers, politicians, and people in everyday life. Most undergraduate psychology programs also provide experience in using statistics and computers.

BECOMING A PSYCHOLOGIST

If you decide to major in psychology as preparation for a career as a psychologist, you need to realize that the bachelor's degree is not adequate preparation; you must pursue graduate studies. Though psychologists might have a bachelor's degree in a field other than psychology, they usually have a bachelor's degree (B.A. or B.S.) in psychology. You would need 1 to 2 years of study beyond the bachelor's level to earn a master's degree (M.A., M.S., or M.Ed.). A master's degree usually requires advanced courses in psychology related to a field of specialization and completion of a written thesis or original research study. The most popular master's-level fields of specialization are clinical psychology, counseling psychology, and school psychology.

You would need 4 to 6 more years of study beyond the bachelor's level to earn a doctoral degree (Ph.D., Psy.D., or Ed.D.). The Ph.D. requires advanced courses in research methods, statistics, and a specialized field of study. It also requires completion of an ambitious original research project, which is then described in a written doctoral dissertation. The Psy.D. requires advanced courses in a particular field of study, usually clinical or counseling psychology, and an internship in an applied setting, such as a community mental health center. The Ph.D. indicates expertise in conducting research; the Psy.D. indicates expertise in providing therapy. But note that many psychologists who practice clinical or counseling psychology have a Ph.D., which means that they, too, are experts in providing therapy and have served an internship in an applied setting. Almost all states require that a person earn a doctoral degree, serve an internship, and pass a licensing exam to be licensed as a psychologist. The Ed.D. is normally offered by an education department and usually signifies expertise in relating psychology to education or counseling.

If you are considering a career in psychology, you should be aware of ways to make yourself more attractive to prospective graduate programs:

1. You must earn high grades—at least a B average for desirable graduate programs, and a B+ or A− average for the most competitive ones.

1.	General Psychology
2.	Society for the Teaching of Psychology
3.	Experimental Psychology
4.	No Division
5.	Evaluation, Measurement, and Statistics
6.	Behavioral Neuroscience and Comparative Psychology
7.	Developmental Psychology
8.	Society for Personality and Social Psychology
9.	Society for the Psychological Study of Social Issues (SPSSI)
10.	Psychology and the Arts
11.	No Division
12.	Clinical Psychology
13.	Consulting Psychology
14.	Society for Industrial and Organizational Psychology
15.	Educational Psychology
16.	School Psychology
17.	Counseling Psychology
18.	Psychologists in Public Service
19.	Military Psychology
20.	Adult Development and Aging
21.	Applied Experimental and Engineering Psychology
22.	Rehabilitation Psychology
23.	Society for Consumer Psychology
24.	Theoretical and Philosophical Psychology
25.	Experimental Analysis of Behavior
26.	History of Psychology
27.	Society for Community Research and Action: Division of Community Psychology
28.	Psychopharmacology and Substance Abuse
29.	Psychotherapy
30.	Psychological Hypnosis
31.	State Psychological Association Affairs
32.	Humanistic Psychology
33.	Mental Retardation and Developmental Disabilities
34.	Population and Environmental Psychology
35.	Psychology of Women
36.	Psychology of Religion
37.	Child, Youth, and Family Services
38.	Health Psychology
39.	Psychoanalysis
40.	Clinical Neuropsychology
41.	American Psychology-Law Society
42.	Psychologists in Independent Practice
43.	Family Psychology
44.	Society for the Psychological Study of Lesbian and Gay Issues
45.	Society for the Psychological Study of Ethnic Minority Issues
46.	Media Psychology
47.	Exercise and Sport Psychology
48.	Peace Psychology
49.	Group Psychology and Group Psychotherapy
50.	Addictions
51.	Society for the Psychological Study of Men and Masculinity

◀ TABLE A.1

Divisions of the American Psychological Association

2. You must perform well on the Graduate Record Examination (GRE), which is analogous to the SAT or ACT exam that you probably took for entrance into your undergraduate school. The GRE includes three subtests that measure verbal ability, mathematical ability, and reasoning ability, and an advanced test of general knowledge of psychology.

3. You might also be required to take the Miller Analogies Test, which assesses the ability to reason through the use of analogies.

4. You should perform research under faculty supervision and, preferably, present your findings at one of the many undergraduate psychology research conferences each spring. These conferences are announced in the *APA Monitor, American Psychologist*, and *Teaching of Psychology*, one or more of which should be available in your library or from a psychology faculty member.

5. You should serve an undergraduate internship in a setting geared to your career goals. You might even be able to serve a teaching internship under faculty supervision or a peer counseling internship sponsored by your campus counseling center.

6. You should get to know several psychology faculty members so that they provide advice and, eventually, write letters of recommendation for you. It is impossible for professors to write sterling letters for students they hardly know.

7. You should be active in your psychology club or Psi Chi (the national psychology honor society) chapter.

8. You should do summer work or volunteer work related to your career goals.

9. You should broaden yourself by taking courses in disciplines other than psychology. These might include courses in logic, writing, public speaking, and computer science.

10. You should discuss your career goals and graduate programs of interest with your faculty advisor. If you intend to proceed immediately to graduate school, you should begin considering graduate schools no later than your junior year.

You can get information about psychology and graduate training from psychological associations. These include the American Psychological Association, the American Psychological Society, the Canadian Psychological Association, regional associations, state associations, and local associations.

OTHER CAREER OPTIONS

Individuals who major in psychology might also choose to pursue graduate study in disciplines other than psychology. Many psychology majors pursue graduate study in law, medicine, computer science, or business administration. Of course, to pursue any of these careers, you should take courses that will prepare you for graduate study in your discipline of interest. For example, psychology majors who plan to attend medical school must also take courses in biology, chemistry, physics, and mathematics.

With proper course work and student teaching experience, you can become a high school teacher. The combination of a bachelor's degree in psychology, appropriate elective courses, and experience in a relevant setting can make a graduate attractive to prospective employers. If you major in psychology, it is advisable to minor in a discipline related to your career interests.

With a proper background, psychology majors can even compete with business majors. Business firms consider the following attributes for entry-level employees: first, technical skills such as accounting and interviewing skills; second, conceptual skills such as problem-solving ability and the ability to fit into the organization; third, social skills such as understanding human behavior; and fourth, communication skills such as writing, speaking, and listening (Carducci & Wheat, 1984). If you intend to enter the business world with a degree in psychology, you should consider taking courses in accounting, management, marketing, and other related areas. You might even serve as an undergraduate intern in a local business or industry and seek part-time and summer employment in a relevant setting.

Psychology majors are especially attractive to employers of all kinds because the psychology curriculum enhances their social, communication, and problem-solving skills. American Telephone and Telegraph (AT&T) has found that students with bachelor's degrees in liberal arts majors that provide a broad background—such as psychology, philosophy, history, and English—progress more rapidly in management than business or engineering majors (Candland, 1982).

 ## FOR MORE INFORMATION ON CAREERS IN PSYCHOLOGY

FOR MORE ON CAREERS IN PSYCHOLOGY

American Psychological Association. (Revised annually.) *Graduate study in psychology.* Washington, DC: Author.

American Psychological Association. (1993). *Getting in: A step-by-step plan for gaining admission to graduate school in psychology.* Washington, DC: Author.

Keith-Spiegel, P. (1990). *The complete guide to graduate school admission: Psychology.* Hillsdale, NJ: Erlbaum.

Keller, P. A. (Ed.). (1994). *Academic paths: Career decisions and experiences of psychologists.* Hillsdale, NJ: Erlbaum.

Kilburg, R. R. (Ed.). (1991). *How to manage your career in psychology.* Washington, DC: American Psychological Association.

Mayne, T., & Sayette, M. (1990). *Insider's guide to graduate programs in clinical psychology.* New York: Guilford.

Poe, R. E. (1990). Psychology careers material: Selected resources. *Teaching of Psychology, 17,* 175–178.

Rheingold, H. L. (1994). *The psychologist's guide to an academic career.* Washington, DC: American Psychological Association.

FOR MORE INFORMATION ON ANY ASPECT OF PSYCHOLOGY

American Psychological Association
750 First Street, NE
Washington, DC 20002-4242

American Psychological Society
1511 K Street, NW
Washington, DC 20005

Canadian Psychological Association
Chemin Vincent Road
Old Chelsea
Quebec JOX 2NO Canada

Statistics

▶ To understand God's thoughts we must study statistics; for these are the measure of his purpose. (Florence Nightingale, 1820–1910)

Most psychological research involves measurement, whether from a *case study* of a person with multiple personalities, a *naturalistic observational study* of chimpanzee parental behavior in the wild, a *survey study* of consumer product preferences, a *correlational study* of the relationship between aerobic exercise and well-being, or an *experimental study* on the effects of mood on memory. In each case, measurement yields a set of numbers, which are the findings, or *data*, produced by the research study. Though a simple perusal of a set of data may provide an appreciation of the gist of the research findings, such an approach to data analysis is too imprecise for science. The use of *statistics* provides a more precise approach. As discussed in Chapter 2, psychologists and other scientists use statistics to summarize data, find relationships between sets of data, and determine whether experimental manipulations have had a statistically significant effect.

The word **statistics** has two meanings: (1) the field that applies mathematical techniques to the organizing, summarizing, and interpreting of data, and (2) the actual mathematical techniques themselves. Knowledge of statistics has many practical benefits. Even a rudimentary knowledge of statistics will make you better able to evaluate statistical claims made by science reporters, weather forecasters, television advertisers, political candidates, government officials, and other persons who may use statistics in the information or arguments they present.

statistics

Mathematical techniques used to summarize research data or to determine whether the data support the researcher's hypothesis.

SCALES OF MEASUREMENT

Measurements are made on a variety of scales: *nominal scales, ordinal scales, interval scales,* and *ratio scales*. As one proceeds from the first to the last of these scales, their degree of precision increases; that is, they convey more and more information about what is being measured. Scales of measurement are important because they determine the kind of statistic that is appropriate to use with a particular kind of data.

Nominal Scales

A **nominal scale** of measurement is the simplest kind. It places objects, individuals, or characteristics into categories. Examples of nominal scales include telephone numbers, street address numbers, license plate numbers, team uniform numbers, and student identification numbers. Note that these numbers do not indicate magnitude. In fact, categorization by names instead of numbers also qualifies as nominal data. (The word *nominal* comes from the Latin word for "name.") For example, a developmental psychologist studying social changes during the undergraduate years might identify each class by its name (freshman, sophomore, junior, senior) or by a number (1 = freshman; 2 = sophomore; 3 = junior; 4 = senior). Similarly, consider the *DSM-IV*, which (as explained in Chapter 14) categorizes psychological disorders by both name and code number. For example, the code numbers for paranoid schizophrenia and agoraphobia (which are discussed in Chapter 14) are 295.30 and 300.22, respectively. Again, the numbers are just labels; they do not indicate the relative severity of the disorders.

nominal scale
A scale of measurement that places objects, individuals, or characteristics into categories.

Ordinal Scales

An **ordinal scale** indicates the relative magnitude of scores. The relative heights of your family members, the order in which runners finish in a race, and the daily major league baseball standings are ordinal data. They indicate rank position, but they do not tell how far apart one position is from another. Because ordinal data only represent ranks, equal differences between scores on an ordinal scale do not necessarily indicate equal differences in what they represent. For example, the difference in time between the second-place finisher and the fifth-place finisher in a race is not necessarily the same as the difference in time between the sixth-place finisher and the ninth-place finisher, even though in each case the racers finish three positions apart.

ordinal scale
A scale of measurement that indicates the relative, but not exact, magnitude of scores.

Interval Scales

An **interval scale,** like an ordinal scale, indicates relative magnitude. Unlike numbers on an ordinal scale, numbers on an interval scale indicate the exact magnitude of what they represent. Moreover, equal distances between numbers on an interval scale represent equal differences in magnitude. Consider temperature measured in degrees Fahrenheit or Centigrade. On either scale, the difference between 80 and 85 degrees is equivalent to the difference between 65 and 70 degrees. But interval scales have an arbitrary zero point. Though the zero point on the Centigrade scale is the point at which water freezes, it is not the lowest possible temperature. And the zero point on the Fahrenheit scale is just another point along the scale. Because interval scales lack a true zero point, it is meaningless to refer to ratios between scores on such scales. For example, 40 degrees Fahrenheit is not twice as hot as 20 degrees Fahrenheit. Because the lack of a true zero point is only a minor limitation, many statistics make use of interval data.

interval scale
A scale of measurement that indicates the exact magnitude of scores, but not their ratio to one another.

Ratio Scales

A **ratio scale** has all the characteristics of an interval scale, as well as a true zero point. This permits statements about the ratio of one score to another. For example, because weight loss falls on a ratio scale, it would be meaningful to say that a person who lost 8 pounds lost twice as much as a person who lost 4 pounds. Other variables that fall on ratio scales include time, height, and distance. Because it has a true zero point, the Kelvin scale of absolute temperature is also on a ratio scale. The same statistics are used with interval data and ratio data.

ratio scale
A scale of measurement that indicates the ratio of scores to one another.

Exam Scores				
83	81	90	82	83
89	81	80	90	80
88	90	88	92	88
90	93	89	84	94

Ungrouped Data		Grouped Data	
Score	Frequency	Score	Frequency
94	1	90–94	7
93	1	85–89	5
92	1	80–84	8
91	0		$N = \overline{20}$
90	4		
89	2		
88	3		
87	0		
86	0		
85	0		
84	1		
83	2		
82	1		
81	2		
80	2		
	$N = \overline{20}$		

REPRESENTATION OF DATA

Because a list of raw data may be difficult to interpret, psychologists prefer to represent their data in an organized way. Two of the most common ways are *frequency distributions* and *graphs*.

Frequency Distributions

Suppose that you had a set of 20 scores from a 100-point psychology exam. You might arrange them in a **frequency distribution,** which lists the frequency of each score or group of scores in a set of scores. Using the set of scores in Table B.1, you would set up a column that included the highest and lowest scores, as well as the possible scores in between. In this case, the highest score is 94 and the lowest is 80. You would then count the frequency of each score and list it in a separate column. The total of the frequencies in the distribution is symbolized by the letter N.

The frequency distribution might show a pattern in the set of scores that is not apparent when simply examining the individual scores. In this example (presented in Table B.1), the exam scores do not bunch up toward the lower, middle, or upper portions of the distribution. In some cases, when you have a relatively large number of scores, you might prefer to use a *grouped* frequency distribution. The scores would be grouped into intervals, and the frequency of scores in each internal would be listed in a separate column. The intervals can be of any size, but, for ease of construction, the lowest number in each interval should be a multiple of the interval size (with an interval size of 5 or 10 units most convenient to use). A grouped frequency distribution provides less-precise information than does an ungrouped one, because the individual scores are lost.

Graphs

If a picture is worth a thousand words, then a graph is worth several paragraphs in a research report. Because it provides a pictorial representation of the distribution of scores,

frequency distribution

A list of the frequency of each score or group of scores in a set of scores.

APPENDIX B

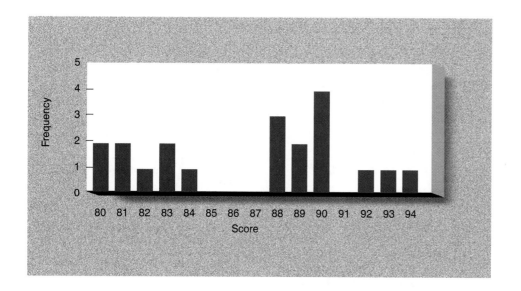

a graph can be an even more effective representation of research data than is a frequency distribution. Among the most common kinds of graphs are *pie graphs*, *frequency histograms*, *frequency polygons*, and *line graphs*.

Pie Graph

A simple, but visually effective, way of representing data is the **pie graph.** It represents data as percentages of a pie-shaped graph. The total of the slices of the pie must add up to 100 percent. Note that a pie graph is used in Figure 1.1 in Chapter 1 to represent the percentage of psychologists in major fields of psychology. The pie graph is especially useful with nominal data.

pie graph
A graph that represents data as percentages of a pie.

Frequency Histogram

Another approach to representing frequency data is the **frequency histogram,** which graphs frequencies as bars. In general, the scores are plotted on the *abscissa* (the horizontal axis) and the frequencies on the *ordinate* (the vertical axis). The width of the bars represents the intervals, and the height of the bars represents the frequency of scores in each interval. Figure B.1 is a frequency histogram of the exam scores in the ungrouped frequency distribution presented in Table B.1.

frequency histogram
A graph that displays the frequency of scores as bars.

Frequency Polygon

A **frequency polygon** serves the same purpose as a frequency histogram. As shown in Figure B.2, the frequency polygon is drawn by connecting the points, representing frequencies, located above the scores. Note that the polygon is completed by extending it to the abscissa one score below the lowest score and one score above the highest score in the distribution.

frequency polygon
A graph that displays the frequency of scores by connecting points representing them above each score.

An advantage of the frequency polygon over the frequency histogram is that it permits the plotting of more than one distribution on the same set of axes. Plotting more than one frequency historian on a set of axes would create a confusing graph. If more than one frequency polygon is plotted on a set of axes, they should be distinguished from one another. This can be done by drawing a different kind of line for each polygon (perhaps a solid line for one and a broken line for the other), drawing the lines in different colors (perhaps red for one polygon and blue for the other), or representing the points above the scores with geometric shapes (perhaps a circle for one polygon and a triangle for the other).

A graph in which scores bunch up toward either end of the abscissa (as shown in Figure B.3) is said to be *skewed*. The skewness of a graph is in the direction of its "tail." If the scores bunch up toward the high end, the graph has a **negative skew.** This might occur on an unusually easy exam. If the scores bunch up toward the low end, the graph has a **positive skew.** This might occur on an unusually difficult exam.

negative skew
A graph that has scores bunching up toward the positive end of the abscissa.

positive skew
A graph that has scores bunching up toward the negative end of the abscissa.

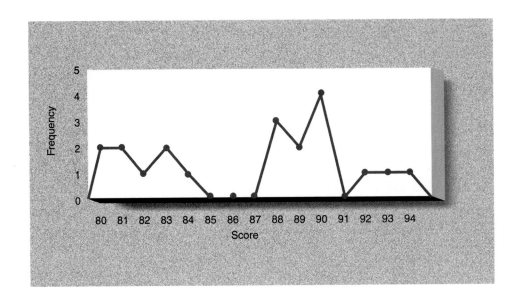

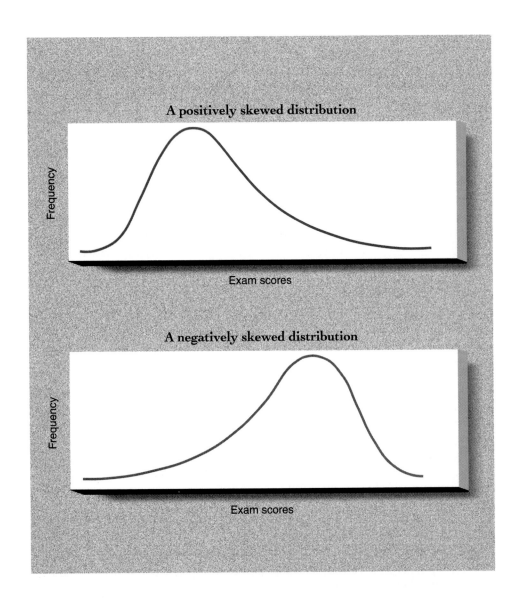

A positively skewed distribution

A negatively skewed distribution

APPENDIX B

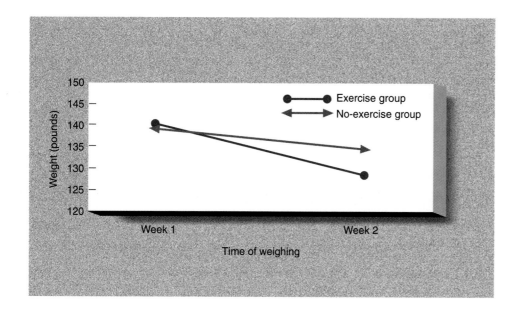

Line Graph

While pie graphs, frequency histograms, and frequency polygons are useful for plotting frequency data, a **line graph** is useful for plotting data generated by experiments. It uses lines to represent the relationship between independent and dependent variables. If you skim through this textbook, you will see several examples of line graphs. The graph shown in Figure B.4 represents the data from the experiment on exercise and weight loss discussed in Chapter 2.

line graph
A graph used to plot data showing the relationship between independent and dependent variables in an experiment.

DESCRIPTIVE STATISTICS

Suppose you gained access to the hundreds, or thousands, of high school grade point averages of all of the freshmen at your college or university. What is the most typical score? How similar are the scores? Simply scanning the scores would provide, at best, gross approximations of the answers to these questions. To obtain precise answers, psychologists use **descriptive statistics,** which include *measures of central tendency* and *measures of variability*.

descriptive statistics
Statistics that summarize research data.

Measures of Central Tendency

A measure of central tendency is a score that best represents a distribution of scores. The kind of measure that is appropriate depends on the scale of measurement that is used. The measures of central tendency include the *mode*, the *median*, and the *mean*.

Mode

The **mode** is the most frequently occurring score in a set of scores. In the frequency distribution of exam scores discussed, the mode is 90. If two scores occur equally often, the distribution is *bimodal*. Any distribution that has two or more scores that occur equally often is called *multimodal*. The mode can be used with any scale of measurement, but it is the only measure of central tendency that can be used with nominal data. For example, the mode would be the only acceptable measure of central tendency for determining the most common academic major at your school. The winner of a presidential primary election in which there are several candidates would represent the mode—the person selected by more voters than any other.

   The mode can also have practical benefits. Imagine a car dealership given the option of carrying a particular model, but limited to selecting just one color. The dealership owner would be wise to choose the mode—the color preferred by more people than any other.

mode
The score that occurs most frequently in a set of scores.

median

The middle score in a set of scores that have been ordered from lowest to highest.

Median

The **median** is the middle score in a distribution of scores that have been ranked in numerical order. If the median is located between two scores, it is assigned the value of the midpoint between them (for example, the median of 23, 34, 55, and 68 would equal 44.5). The median requires at least ordinal data; it would be impossible to find the median of data on a nominal scale. For example, since academic majors do not differ in magnitude, it would make no sense to ask what the median major is at a college. The median is the best measure of central tendency for skewed distributions, because it is unaffected by extreme scores. Note that in the example below the median is the same in both sets of exam scores, even though the second set contains an extreme score.

Exam A   23,   25,   **63,**   64,   67
Exam B   23,   25,   **63,**   64,   98

Mean

mean

The arithmetic average of a set of scores.

The **mean** is the arithmetic average, or simply the average, of a set of scores. You are probably more familiar with it than with the mode or the median. You encounter the mean in everyday life whenever you calculate your exam average, batting average, gas mileage average, or a host of other averages. The mean requires interval or ratio data.

The mean of a sample is calculated by adding all the scores and dividing by the number of scores. Unlike the median, the mean is affected by extreme scores. As shown below, one extreme score will pull the mean in its direction—especially if there are few scores in the set of scores. Thus, the mean may be a misleading statistic when used with a skewed distribution. For example, while the mean of the five exam scores below is 79, the median would be 93—a more satisfying estimate of the student's typical performance. In a symmetrical distribution the measures of central tendency are identical.

Exam Scores: 19,   92,   93,   94,   97

$$\overline{X} = \frac{\sum X}{N} = \frac{19 + 92 + 93 + 94 + 97}{5} = 79$$

When Disraeli pointed out the ease of lying with statistics, he might have been referring, in particular, to measures of central tendency. Suppose a baseball general manager is negotiating with an agent about a salary for a baseball catcher of average ability. Both might use a measure of central tendency to prove his own point, perhaps based on the salaries of the top seven catchers, as shown in Table B.2. The general manager might claim that a salary of $340,000 (the median) would provide the player with what he deserves—an average salary. The agent might counter that a salary of $900,000 (the mean) would provide the player with what he deserves—an average salary. Note that neither would technically be lying—they would simply be using statistics that favored their position. As Scottish writer Andrew Lang (1844–1912) warned, beware of anyone who "uses statistics as a drunken man uses lampposts—for support rather than for illumination."

Measures of Variability

A distribution of scores that contained scores that were all the same would have no variability. This is rare. Almost all distributions have variability; that is, they contain scores that differ from one another. Consider the members of your psychology class. They would vary on a host of measures, including height, weight, and grade point average. Measures of variability include the *range,* the *variance,* and the *standard deviation.*

Range

range

A statistic representing the difference between the highest and lowest scores in a set of scores.

The **range,** which requires at least ordinal data, is the difference between the highest and lowest scores in a distribution. This provides limited information, because distributions

Player	Salary
A	$200,000
B	$250,000
C	$290,000
D	$340,000
E	$550,000
F	$670,000
G	$4,000,000

in which scores bunch up toward the beginning, middle, or end of the distribution might have the same range. Of course the range is useful as a rough estimate of how a score compares with the highest and lowest in a distribution. For example, a student might find it useful to know whether he or she did near the best or the worst on an exam. The range of scores in the distribution of 20 grades in the earlier example in Table B.1 would be the difference between 94 and 80, or 14.

Variance

A more informative measure of variability is the **variance,** which represents the variability of scores around their group mean. Unlike the range, the variance takes into account every score in the distribution. Technically, the variance is the average of the squared deviations from the mean. The variance requires either interval or ratio data.

variance
A measure of variability indicating the average of the squared deviations from the mean.

Suppose you wanted to calculate the variance for the sets of 10-point quiz scores in Quiz A and Quiz B. First, find the group mean. Second, find the deviation of each score from the group mean. Note that deviation scores will be negative for scores that are below the mean. As a check on your calculations, the sum of the deviation scores should equal zero. Third, square the deviation scores. By squaring the scores, negative scores are made positive and extreme scores are given relatively more weight. Fourth, find the sum of the squared deviation scores. Fifth, divide the sum by the number of scores. This yields the variance. Note that the variance for Quiz A is larger than that for Quiz B, indicating the students were more varied in their performances on Quiz A.

Quiz A				Quiz B		
1, 2, 6, 8, 9				4, 5, 6, 7, 8		

$$\overline{X} = \frac{\Sigma X}{N} = \frac{1 + 2 + 6 + 8 + 9}{5} = \frac{26}{5} = 5.2 \qquad \overline{Y} = \frac{\Sigma Y}{N} = \frac{4 + 5 + 6 + 7 + 8}{5} = \frac{30}{5} = 6$$

Score	Deviation	Deviation^2		Score	Deviation	Deviation^2
1	−4.2	17.64		4	−2	4
2	−3.2	10.24		5	−1	1
6	.8	.64		6	0	0
8	2.8	7.84		7	1	1
9	3.8	14.44		8	2	4
		ΣDeviation^2 = 50.80				ΣDeviation^2 = 10

$$\text{Variance} = \frac{\Sigma \text{Deviation}^2}{N} = \frac{50.80}{5} = 10.16 \qquad \text{Variance} = \frac{\Sigma \text{Deviation}^2}{N} = \frac{10}{5} = 2$$

standard deviation

A statistic representing the degree of dispersion of a set of scores around their mean.

Standard Deviation

The **standard deviation,** or S is the square root of the variance. The standard deviation of Quiz A would be

$$S = \sqrt{S^2} = \sqrt{10.16} = 3.19.$$

The standard deviation of Quiz B would be

$$S = \sqrt{S^2} = \sqrt{2} = 1.414.$$

Why not simply use the variance? One reason is that, unlike the variance, the standard deviation is in the same units as the raw scores. This makes the standard deviation more meaningful. Thus, it would make more sense to discuss the variability of a set of IQ scores in IQ points than in squared IQ points. The standard deviation is used in the calculation of many other statistics.

The Normal Curve

normal curve

A bell-shaped graph representing a hypothetical frequency distribution for a given characteristic.

As illustrated in Figure B.5, the **normal curve** is a bell-shaped graph that represents a hypothetical frequency distribution in which the frequency of scores is greatest near the mean and progressively decreases toward the extremes. In essence, the normal curve is a smooth frequency polygon based on an infinite number of scores. The mean, median, and mode of a normal curve are the same. Many physical or psychological characteristics, such as height, weight, and intelligence, fall on a normal curve.

One useful characteristic of a normal curve is that certain percentages of scores fall at certain distances (measured in standard deviation units) from its mean. A special statistical table makes it a simple matter to determine the percentage of scores that fall above or below a particular score or between two scores on the curve. For example, about 68 percent of scores fall between plus and minus one standard deviation from the mean; about 95 percent fall between plus and minus two standard deviations from the mean; and about 99 percent fall between plus and minus three standard deviations from the mean.

For example, consider an IQ test, with a mean of 100 and a standard deviation of 15. What percentage of people score above 130? Because intelligence scores fall on a normal curve, about 95 percent of the scores fall within two standard deviations of the mean. Thus, about 5 percent fall more than two standard deviations from the mean. Because the normal curve is symmetrical, about 2.5 percent of the people would score above 130 (mentally gifted) and about 2.5 percent below 70 (mentally retarded). The precise percentages would be 2.14 percent above 130 and 2.14 percent below 70.

Standard Scores

Scores on a normal curve may be expressed in terms of their distance from the mean of the distribution in standard deviation units. These transformed scores are called standard scores, or *z scores*. One of the main advantages of z scores is that they permit scores on different distributions to be compared to each other. For example, which would be superior, a 73 on your biology exam or a 58 on your English exam? It would depend on the mean and standard deviation of each distribution of scores. The formula for a z score is

$$Z = \frac{X - \overline{X}}{S}$$

In the formula, X is a raw score, $\overline{X}$ is the mean of the set of scores containing the raw score, and S is the standard deviation of that set of scores. Suppose the mean for the biology score was 83 and the standard deviation was 5, while the mean for the English exam was 52 and the standard deviation was 3. The z score for your biology exam score would be

$$Z = \frac{73 - 83}{5} = -2$$

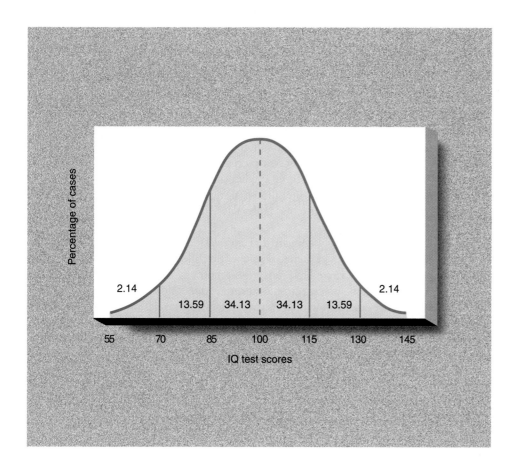

◄ FIGURE B.5
Normal Distribution, or Bell-Shaped Curve
This graph shows the normal distribution of
IQ scores as measured by the Wechsler Adult
Intelligence Scale. The normal distribution is
a type of bell-shaped frequency polygon in
which most of the scores are clustered around
the mean. The scores become less frequent the
farther they appear above or below the mean.

and the z score for your English exam score would be

$$Z = \frac{58 - 52}{3} = 2$$

Thus, the apparently inferior score of 58, being two standard deviations above its group mean, is actually superior to the score of 73, which is two standard deviations below its group mean.

If you took the SAT, a test that was designed to have a mean of 500 and a standard deviation of 100, you would be able to tell how well you performed relative to others. A score of 600 would yield a z score of 1. Because about 68 percent of the scores on a normal curve fall within 1 standard deviation of the mean, and the normal curve is symmetrical, about 34 percent of the scores fall between the mean and one standard deviation above the mean. Thus, about 84 percent (that is, 50 percent plus 34 percent) fall below a z score of 1.

Percentiles

Scores along the abscissa of the normal curve also represent **percentiles**—the scores at or below which particular percentages of scores fall. For example, the mode, median, and mean fall at the 50th percentile. While a z score of 1 would be equal to the 84th percentile, a z score of −1 would be equal to the 16th percentile.

CORRELATIONAL STATISTICS

So far, you have been reading about statistics that describe sets of data. In many research studies, psychologists rely on **correlational statistics,** which determine the relationship between two variables. Correlational statistics yield a number called the **coefficient of correlation.** The coefficient may vary from 0.00 to 1.00 or −1.00. In a positive correlation,

percentile
The score at or below which a particular percentage of scores fall.

correlational statistics
Statistics that determine the relationship between two variables.

coefficient of correlation
A number that represents the direction and strength of a correlation.

scores on two different distributions increase and decrease together. For example, there is a positive correlation between high school average and freshmen grade point average in college. In a negative correlation, as scores increase on one distribution they decrease on the other. For example, there is a negative correlation between absenteeism and course performance. The strength of a correlation depends on its size, not its sign. For example, a correlation of −.72 is stronger than a correlation of .53.

Correlational statistics are important because they permit us to determine the strength and direction of the relationship between different sets of data or to predict scores on one distribution based on our knowledge of scores on another. If the correlation between two sets of data were a perfect 1.00, we could predict one score from another with complete accuracy. But because correlations are almost always less than perfect, we predict one score from another only with a particular *probability* of being correct—the higher the correlation, the higher the probability.

It cannot be stressed strongly enough that correlation does not mean causation. For example, years ago, authorities presumed that autistic children, who have poor social and communication skills, were caused by "refrigerator mothers." Mothers of autistic children were aloof from them. This was taken as a sign that the children suffered from mothers who were emotionally cold. Knowing that this is simply a correlation, you might wonder whether causality was in the opposite direction. Perhaps autistic children, who do not respond to their mothers, cause their mothers to become aloof from them. Moreover, why would a mother have several normal children, then an autistic child, and then several more normal ones? It would be difficult to believe she was a warm parent to all but one. Today, evidence indicates that autism is a neurological problem that has nothing to do with the mother's emotionality.

As another example, though there is a positive correlation between smoking and cancer in human beings, this is not scientifically acceptable evidence that smoking *causes* cancer. Perhaps another factor (such as a level of stress tolerance) might make someone prone to both smoking and cancer, without smoking's necessarily causing cancer. Of course, correlation does not imply the *absence* of causation. For example, there may, indeed, be a causal relationship between smoking and cancer. The prudent thing would be to assume that there is.

Scatter Plots

Correlational data is graphed using a **scatter plot,** also known as a *scattergram* or *scatter diagram*. In a scatter plot, one variable is plotted on the abscissa and the other on the ordinate. Each subject's scores on both variables is indicated by a dot placed at the junction between those scores on the graph. This produces one dot for each subject. The pattern of the dots gives a rough impression of the size and direction of the correlation. In fact, a line drawn through the dots, or *line of best fit*, helps estimate this. The closer the dots lie to a straight line, the stronger the correlation. Figure B.6 illustrates several kinds of correlation.

Pearson's Product-Moment Correlation

The most commonly used correlational statistic is the **Pearson's product-moment correlation (Pearson's r),** named for the English statistician Karl Pearson. Pearson's r is used with interval or ratio data. One formula for calculating it is presented in Figure B.7. The example assesses the relationship between home runs and stolen bases by five baseball players during one month of a season.

INFERENTIAL STATISTICS

Inferential statistics help us determine whether the difference we find between our experimental and control groups is caused by the manipulation of the independent variable or by chance variation in the performances of the groups. If the difference has a low

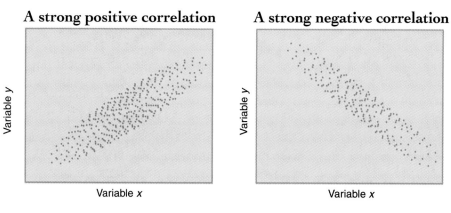

A strong positive correlation

Variable *y*

Variable *x*

A strong negative correlation

Variable *y*

Variable *x*

A moderate positive correlation

Variable *y*

Variable *x*

A moderate negative correlation

Variable *y*

Variable *x*

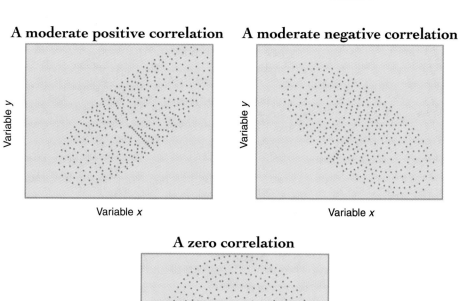

A zero correlation

Variable *y*

Variable *x*

probability of being caused by chance variation, we can feel confident in the inferences we make from our samples to the populations they represent.

Hypothesis Testing

In experiments, psychologists use inferential statistics to test the **null hypothesis.** This hypothesis states that the independent variable has no effect on the dependent variable. Consider an experimental study of the effect of overlearning on memory in college students. As discussed in Chapter 8, when we use overlearning, we study material until we know it perfectly—and then continue to study it some more. At the beginning of the experiment, the subjects would be selected from the same population (college students) and randomly assigned to either the experimental group (overlearning) or the control group (normal studying). Thus, the independent variable would be the method

null hypothesis

The prediction that the independent variable will have no effect on the dependent variable in an experiment.

Pearson's Product-Moment Correlation
This is a small negative correlation. It indicates that there is a slight tendency for stolen bases to decrease as home runs increase; that is, home-run hitters are somewhat less likely to steal bases.

Player	Home Runs (X)	Stolen Bases (Y)
A	8	3
B	2	6
C	1	2
D	5	1
E	6	3
	$\sum X = 22$	$\sum Y = 15$

$$r = \frac{\sum(\text{deviation from } \bar{X})(\text{deviation from } \bar{Y})}{N(S_X)(S_Y)}$$

Step 1: Calculate the means ($\bar{X}$ and $\bar{Y}$, respectively) of the two groups

$$\bar{X} = \frac{\sum X}{N} = \frac{22}{5} = 4.4 \qquad \bar{Y} = \frac{\sum Y}{N} = \frac{15}{5} = 3$$

Step 2: Find the deviation of each score from its mean

Deviation from X	Deviation from $\bar{Y}$
$8 - 4.4 = 3.6$	$3 - 3 = 0$
$2 - 4.4 = -2.4$	$6 - 3 = 3$
$1 - 4.4 = -3.4$	$2 - 3 = -1$
$5 - 4.4 = 0.6$	$1 - 3 = -2$
$6 - 4.4 = 1.6$	$3 - 3 = 0$

Step 3: Multiply the paired deviation scores

(Deviation from $\bar{X}$) (Deviation from $\bar{Y}$)

$$
\begin{aligned}
(3.6)(0) &= 0.0 \\
(-2.4)(3) &= -7.2 \\
(-3.4)(-1) &= 3.4 \\
(0.6)(-2) &= -1.2 \\
(1.6)(0) &= 0.0 \\
\hline
\sum &= -5.0
\end{aligned}
$$

Step 4: Calculate the standard deviations for both groups

$$S_X = \sqrt{\frac{\sum \text{Deviation}^2}{N}} \qquad S_Y = \sqrt{\frac{\sum \text{Deviation}^2}{N}}$$

1) Square the deviation scores

(Deviation from $\bar{X}$)^2	(Deviation from $\bar{Y}$)^2
$(3.6)^2 = 12.96$	$0^2 = 0$
$(-2.4)^2 = 5.76$	$3^2 = 9$
$(-3.4)^2 = 11.56$	$-1^2 = 1$
$(0.6)^2 = 0.36$	$-2^2 = 4$
$(1.6)^2 = 2.56$	$0^2 = 0$
$\sum(\text{Deviation from } \bar{X})^2 = 33.20$	$\sum(\text{Deviation from } \bar{Y})^2 = 14$

2) Substitute in the formula and calculate

$$S_X = \sqrt{\frac{33.20}{5}} \qquad S_Y = \sqrt{\frac{14}{5}}$$

$$S_X = 2.58 \qquad S_Y = 1.67$$

Step 5: Substitute in the correlation formula and calculate

$$r = \frac{-5}{5(2.58)(1.67)}$$

$$r = -0.23$$

of studying (overlearning versus normal studying). The dependent variable might be a 100-point exam on the material studied.

If the experimental manipulation has no effect, the experimental and control groups would not differ significantly in their performance on the exam. In that case, we would fail to reject the null hypothesis. If the experimental manipulation has an effect, the two groups would differ significantly in their performance on the exam. In that case, we would reject the null hypothesis. This would indirectly support the *research hypothesis*, which would predict that overlearning improves exam performance. But how large must a difference be between groups for it to be significant? To determine whether the difference between groups is large enough to minimize chance variation as an alternative explanation of the results, we must determine the *statistical significance* of the difference between them.

Statistical Significance

The characteristics of samples drawn from the population they represent will almost always vary somewhat from those of the true population. This is known as *sampling error*. Thus, a sample of five students taken from your psychology class (the population) would vary somewhat from the class means in age, height, weight, intelligence, grade point average, and other characteristics.

If we repeatedly took random samples of five students, we would continue to find that they differ from the population. But what of the difference between the means of two samples, presumably representing different populations, such as a population of students who practice overlearning and a population of students who practice normal study habits? How large would the differences have to be before we attributed them to the independent variable rather than to chance? In this example, how much difference in the performance of the experimental group and the control group would be needed before we could confidently attribute the difference to the practice of overlearning?

The larger the difference between the means of two samples, the less likely it would be attributable to chance. Psychologists typically accept a difference between sample means as statistically significant if it has a probability of less than 5 percent of occurring by chance. This is known as the .05 level of statistical significance. In regard to the example, if the difference between the experimental group and the control group has less than a 5 percent probability of occurring by chance, we would reject the null hypothesis. Our research hypothesis would be supported: overlearning is effective; the sample means of the experimental and control groups represent different populations (that is, the population that would be exposed to overlearning and the population that would not be exposed to it). Scientists who wish to use a stricter standard employ the .01 level of statistical significance. This means that a difference would be statistically significant if it had a probability of less than 1 percent of being obtained by chance alone.

The difference between the means of two groups will more likely be statistically significant under the following conditions:

1. When the samples are large.
2. When the difference between the means is large.
3. When the variability within the groups is small.

Note that **statistical significance** is a statement of probability. We can never be certain that what is true of our samples is true of the population they represent. This is one of the reasons why, as stressed in Chapter 2, all scientific findings are tentative. Moreover, *statistical* significance does not indicate *practical* significance. A statistically significant effect may be too small or be produced at too great a cost of time or money to be useful. What if those who practice overlearning must study an extra hour each day to improve their exam performance by a statistically significant, yet relatively small, 3 points. Knowing this, students might choose to spend their time in another way. As the American statesman Henry Clay (1777–1852) noted, in determining the importance of research findings, by themselves "statistics are no substitute for judgment."

When psychologists test the difference between the means of two sets of scores that are on interval or ratio scales, they often use a technique called the **t test.** When they wish to test the differences between the means of three or more such groups, they often use **analysis of variance,** which can also be used to compare two groups. The calculation of those statistics is covered in advanced courses in statistics and research methods.

statistical significance
A low probability (usually less than 5 percent) that the results of a research study are due to chance factors rather than to the independent variable.

***t* test**
A statistical technique used to determine whether the difference between two sets of scores is statistically significant.

analysis of variance
A statistical technique used to determine whether the difference between two or more sets of scores is statistically significant.

Summary

Scales of Measurement

Research data falls on one of four kinds of measurement scales. Nominal scales (such as the diagnoses of psychological disorders) classify data, but do not indicate magnitude. Ordinal scales (such as finishing positions in a race) rank data, but do not indicate exact magnitudes. Interval scales (such as temperature in degrees Fahrenheit) indicate exact magnitudes, but do not permit statements about the ratio of one score to another. Ratio scales (such as scores on an exam) permit statements about the ratio of one score to another.

Representation of Data

Data is often represented in frequency distributions, which indicate the frequency of each score in a set of scores. Psychologists also use graphs to represent data. These include pie graphs, frequency histograms, frequency polygons, and line graphs. Line graphs are important in representing the results of experiments, because they are used to illustrate the relationship between independent and dependent variables.

Descriptive Statistics

Descriptive statistics summarize and organize research data. Measures of central tendency represent the typical score in a set of scores. The mode is the most frequently occurring score, the median is the middle score, and the mean is the arithmetic average of the set of scores. Measures of variability represent the degree of dispersion of scores. The range is the difference between the highest and lowest scores. The variance is the average of the squared deviations from the mean of the set of scores. And the standard deviation is the square root of the variance.

Many kinds of measurements fall on a normal, or bell-shaped, curve. A certain percentage of scores fall below each point on the abscissa of the normal curve. Standard scores, such as the z score, represent points along the abscissa in standard deviation units. Percentiles identify the percentage of scores that fall below a particular score.

Correlational Statistics

Correlational statistics assess the relationship between two or more sets of scores. A correlation may be positive or negative and vary from 0.00 to plus or minus 1.00. The existence of a correlation does not necessarily mean that one of the correlated variables causes changes in the other. Nor does the existence of a correlation preclude that possibility. Correlations are commonly graphed on scatter plots. Perhaps the most common correlational technique is the Pearson's product-moment correlation.

Inferential Statistics

Inferential statistics permit experimenters to determine whether their findings can be generalized from their samples to the populations they represent. Consider a simple experiment in which an experimental group that is exposed to a condition is compared to a control group that is not. For the difference between the means of the two groups to be statistically significant, the difference must have a low probability (usually less than 5 percent) of occurring by normal random variation. When psychologists assess the difference between the two groups, they often use a statistic called the t test. When they assess the differences between more than two groups, they often use a statistic called analysis of variance.

 ## Key Concepts

statistics 640

Scales of Measurement

nominal scale 641
ordinal scale 641
interval scale 641
ratio scale 641

Representation of Data

frequency distribution 642
pie graph 643

frequency histogram 643
frequency polygon 643
negative skew 643
positive skew 643
line graph 645

Descriptive Statistics

descriptive statistics 645
mode 645
median 646
mean 646

Measures of Variability

range 646
variance 647
standard deviation 648
normal curve 648
percentile 649

Correlational Statistics

correlational statistics 649
coefficient of correlation 649

scatter plot 650
Pearson's product-moment correlation 650

Inferential Statistics

inferential statistics 650
null hypothesis 651
statistical significance 653
t test 653
analysis of variance 653

For More Information on Statistics

Cohen, J. (1990). Things I have learned so far. *American Psychologist, 45*, 1304–1312.

Comrey, A., Bott, P., & Lee, H. (1989). *Elementary statistics: A problem-solving approach.* Dubuque, IA: Wm. C. Brown.

Cowles, M. (1989). *Statistics in psychology: An historical perspective.* Hillsdale, NJ: Erlbaum.

Holmes, C. B. (1990). *The honest truth about lying with statistics.* Springfield, IL: Charles C Thomas.

Huff, C. (1954/1982). *How to lie with statistics.* New York: W. W. Norton.

Kimble, G. A. (1978). *How to use (and misuse) statistics.* Englewood Cliffs, NJ: Prentice Hall.

Stigler, S. M. (1986). *The history of statistics.* Cambridge, MA: Harvard University Press.

Tankard, J. W., Jr. (1984). *The statistical pioneers.* Cambridge, MA: Schenkman.

Yaremko, R. M., Harari, H., Harrison, R. C., & Lynn, E. (1982). *Reference handbook of research and statistical methods.* New York: Harper & Row.

Industrial/Organizational Psychology

PAUL LEVY, *THE UNIVERSITY OF AKRON*

Industrial/organizational (I/O) psychology is the application of psychological principles to the workplace. I/O psychologists study, among other things, the behaviors of employees and employers, the structure of organizations and organizational policies, complex processes of motivation and leadership, individual and organizational performance, and the match between people and jobs. Traditionally, industrial psychology and organizational psychology have been distinguished from one another by their content areas. Industrial psychology (sometimes called personnel psychology) has long been associated with job analysis, training, selection, and performance measurement and appraisal. Organizational psychology deals with motivation, work attitudes, and leadership, as well as organizational development, structure, and culture. The dichotomy, however, is in some sense a false one because the two areas largely overlap. In addition, most I/O psychologists are trained as exactly that—I/O psychologists—not as industrial psychologists only or organizational psychologists only. Finally, there is no broad line that divides workplace problems into organizational and industrial. For instance, a performance problem (i.e., industrial) may very likely be motivationally based (i.e., organizational). However, the distinction will be used here to be consistent with other treatments of the topic and largely to provide a framework for the discussion. *I* and *O* are put together into I/O for good reason—they are interdependent, related areas that form one subspecialty of psychology. Before we begin our discussion of these and other issues, we should consider the historical roots of the field.

ONE HUNDRED YEARS OF HISTORY

Although the field of I/O psychology is relatively young compared to other areas of psychology, its history is rich and interesting. (See Katzell & Austin, 1992, for a thorough review.)

Pre–World War I

The initial phase spans the period from the turn of the century to World War I. In 1901, Walter Dill Scott, a Northwestern professor and former student of Wilhelm Wundt, was invited to give a talk at the Agate Club in Chicago on the psychological aspects of advertising. Many refer to this as the beginning of business and industrial psychology, or what we now call I/O. Scott published *The Psychology of Advertising* in 1908. In 1915 the Division of Applied Psychology was established at Carnegie Tech (now Carnegie Mellon University), and in 1916 Scott became its first Professor of Applied Psychology. At about this same time Hugo Münsterberg (another Wundt student) moved to the United States and continued doing the applied work he had begun in Germany.

The World War I Years

The second period in the history of I/O psychology spans the World War I years through the 1920s. This is when I/O psychology really came of age. Walter Dill Scott and Walter VanDyke Bingham (who was the director of the program at Carnegie Tech) established a psychological program under the U.S. army's personnel officer. Their staff was responsible for such things as the development of personnel files for military personnel and performance rating forms. Another group of psychologists, led by Robert Yerkes (at that time the president of the American Psychological Association), worked for the government doing selection and placement of military personnel using their newly developed tools—the Army Alpha and Army Beta mental ability tests. It became very clear during this time that those who studied and practiced I/O psychology had a great deal to offer the military.

In 1921, Bruce V. Moore received from Carnegie Tech what is believed to be the first Ph.D. in industrial psychology. At this time I/O psychology began to expand beyond the academic and military realms into government and private industry. I/O psychologists

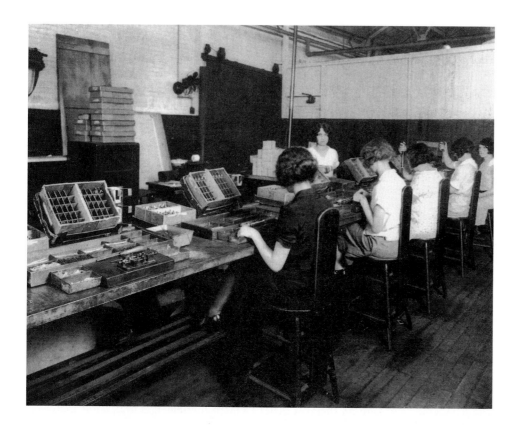

started consulting firms—such as the Scott Company (founded by Walter Dill Scott) and the Psychological Corporation, which still exists today, specializing in testing. Historians estimate that prior to 1917 there were fewer than ten I/O psychologists and that by 1929 there were about fifty, a very large increase in a little over 10 years.

The 1930s to World War II

The defining event of this next stage is what are collectively referred to as the Hawthorne Studies. These were a series of studies examining the impact of illumination on productivity conducted at the Western Electric Plant in Hawthorne, Illinois (Riggio, 1996). After observing employees' behaviors, researchers realized that social and psychological conditions of work were often more important than physical conditions (Roethlisberger & Dickson, 1939). As a result, the roles of team development, supervision, group process, worker morale, and other organizational phenomena began to play a much larger role in the I/O field. Many view this time period, and the Hawthorne Studies in particular, as the birth of organizational psychology.

World War II to the Mid 1960s

The World War II years were an important and dynamic time for the development of I/O psychology. Bingham and Scott were brought back to the military to help match recruits to jobs. Selection, placement, evaluation, and appraisal were all largely begun at this time, and there transpired a great refinement in the knowledge base in these areas and how best to apply them to specific situations. Organizational psychology became a more equal partner with industrial psychology and emphasized areas like organizational dynamics, work groups, and employee morale. As in the preceding period, there was more extension into industry and a great rise of consulting firms hired by industry for various purposes, as well as rapid growth in the number and diversity of graduate programs training I/O psychologists.

The Mid 1960s to the Present

One strong indication of the increasing role of organizational psychology is the fact that in 1970, Division 14 of the American Psychological Association changed its name from "Division of Business and Industrial Psychology" to "Division of Industrial and Organizational Psychology." Organizational psychology had truly arrived. During the last 30 years, the field of I/O has grown very rapidly, with more work in the traditional areas that we have already discussed as well as branching into new domains—such as the fairness of employment tests and the legal climate involved in personnel and labor law. Cognitive processes have become a strong area of research, as have motivation, organizational structure, and organizational systems. It is estimated that by 1939 there were fewer than 100 I/O psychologists (Katzell & Austin, 1992) in the world—and that their numbers grew to 760 by 1960, 2,000 by 1980, and an impressive 3,000 in the United States alone by 1990.

INDUSTRIAL PSYCHOLOGY

Industrial psychology is the older element of I/O and deals with the traditional personnel functions such as job analysis, testing, selection, and performance appraisal.

Job Analysis

job analysis

Defining a job in terms of the tasks and duties involved and the requirements needed to perform it.

job description

A written statement of what a job entails and how and why it is done.

The foundation for most of what is done in I/O psychology is the **job analysis**—the process of defining a job in terms of its component tasks or duties and then determining the requirements to perform them. A major element that emerges from a job analysis is the job description.

The **job description** is a written statement of what the jobholder does, how she does it, and why she does it (McCormick, 1979). These are often called the *task requirements*. This task information is used to determine the *people requirements*, or *KSAs* (i.e., knowledge, skills, and abilities), deemed necessary to do the job. These KSAs often serve as the minimally acceptable standards for recruitment, selection, and placement. A job description for a professor might resemble the following:

> ▶ A college professor teaches and mentors students, serves on various university and professional committees related to education issues, and demonstrates research scholarship through a program of published research in his or her chosen field. College professors usually work independently, in that a direct supervisor is not usually available to monitor their performance.

KSAs that are identified by a job analysis as instrumental to performing the job might include an ability to read and write at an advanced level (post college), an advanced degree (usually a Ph.D.), and an ability to relate to groups of people as well as to individuals on a one-to-one basis. The KSAs, or people requirements, constitute the *job specifications*.

There are many methods for gathering job analysis data. Job-oriented approaches usually involve a questionnaire, inventory, checklist, or some other standardized measure and are best suited for static jobs, which often involve manual labor. Worker-oriented approaches are often less standardized and emphasize the behaviors of an individual in a particular job. Jobs that involve a great deal of judgment and decision making are best suited to this approach. Job analysis data are usually provided by employees who currently hold the job, or by supervisors or trained job analysts. Supervisors and current jobholders—together termed subject matter experts (SME)—generally do the job analysis through questionnaires or interviews.

Selection

The area of selection and placement, one of the busiest areas in which I/O psychologists work, should be of interest to all of us because we have all, at one time or another, been

selected or rejected for a job, a school, or a team. Did you ever wonder why you were accepted by the college you are currently attending and why you weren't accepted by another college? How do colleges make those decisions? Typically, at the undergraduate level, colleges look at an applicant's SAT or ACT scores and high school GPA, the quality of the high school, and perhaps the applicant's extracurricular activities. In the world of I/O psychology, these are called tests or **predictors.** Have you ever applied for a job, but been told that you weren't hired because you didn't have enough experience, or did not have a college degree? Experience and education are two of the most common predictors used to select and place job applicants. To most, this doesn't sound like psychology, but it is at the core of I/O psychology: the recruitment, selection, and placement of employees into jobs that fit their interests, skills, and abilities.

predictors

Tests that measure the traits an employee needs in order to be successful at a job.

Validation

You have come across the term *validity* earlier in this book. **Validation** is the process that I/O psychologists use to demonstrate that their tests are accurate predictors of job success. For I/O psychologists, demonstrating the validity of our tests or predictors is of great importance. For instance, it makes sense to use tests of physical abilities (e.g., strength, speed, manual dexterity) to select people for the job of firefighter only if those measures predict success as a firefighter.

validation

A process that determines whether tests are accurate predictors of job success.

Where do predictors come from in the first place? Give yourself a bonus if you said *job analysis!* Remember, the job analysis results in a description of the job as well as information about what KSAs are required to perform the job. When we talk about the validity of employment selection tests, we are referring to how well the tests predict success on the job. Certainly, we wouldn't want to use tests of physical abilities like strength and running speed to select typists, but such tests might be valid for selecting firefighters. There are many different possible approaches to validation (Cascio, 1991), but the basic idea is to examine the relationship between individuals' scores on the predictors and job success, which we call the *criterion.* The strength of this relationship is called a validity coefficient and is indexed by a correlation. It provides information about how well the predictor relates to the criterion. These coefficients usually range from 0.00 (meaning no relationship) to 1.00 (meaning the predictor perfectly predicts the criterion), but seldom exceed .50. Let's talk about some of the common categories of predictors.

Ability Tests. Tests of cognitive abilities are frequently used in selection and include measures of general intellectual functioning such as the Wonderlic Personnel Test (Wonderlic, 1983), which assesses basic verbal and numerical abilities. In addition, tests of specific cognitive abilities, like mechanical comprehension and spatial ability, are also used as selection instruments for jobs like mechanic, draftsman, or engineer. Motor and physical abilities tests are often used for selecting individuals into jobs, like machine operator or assembler, that require a certain amount of physical dexterity. Validity coefficients for these types of tests are very good and range from about .40 to .55 (Hunter & Hunter, 1984), indicating that ability tests predict the criterion—job success—very well.

Personality Tests. Measures of individual attributes include tests that measure personality characteristics, such as sociability, conscientiousness, and openness, as well as interest inventories, which tap individuals' likes and dislikes regarding hobbies, recreational activities, and tasks. The notion here is that individuals who have particular personalities or interests might be best suited for a particular job or for all jobs. For instance, across all jobs, conscientiousness tends to be the best predictor in this category, with a validity coefficient around .22 (Barrick & Mount, 1991).

Work Sample Tests. Work sample tests measure the applicant's ability to perform brief examples of the critical tasks required on the job (Riggio, 1996). In other words, if we were interested in selecting a typist, we could give the applicants a work sample test that requires them to type something. Assessment centers use a standardized series of work sample tests and have become very popular ways of selecting managers and promoting employees into managerial positions. For instance, a prospective manager might be given an "in-basket" exercise in which he or she is presented with many and varied memoranda, letters, requests from supervisors and subordinates, and customer complaints. The assessee's job is to deal with these however she or he sees fit. The in-basket exercise seems to be a valid way of predicting managerial success, with validity coefficients among the best of all predictors, .54 (Hunter & Hunter, 1984).

Application Forms and Biodata. Many application forms ask applicants about their work history, education, and work or school accomplishments. Some research suggests that this type of information is among the best predictors of future job performance (Rothstein et al., 1990). The rationale behind this is the argument that past behavior is the best predictor of future behavior. In addition, biodata instruments are like application forms, but might also include more personal items related to the applicant's attitudes, values, and likes and dislikes (Owens, 1976). Of course, the biodata items must be validated against a performance criterion. In other words, if we are going to ask individuals about their likes and hobbies and use that information in hiring employees, we must ensure that responses to those items are related to job performance. Rothstein et al.'s (1990) recent meta-analysis (a statistical review of the literature) reported a validity coefficient of .33 for biodata.

Interviews. Interviews are among the most popular selection devices and are used across all job levels. In fact, it is estimated that over 80 percent of U.S. organizations use some type of interview process, and some estimates range as high as 99 percent (McDaniel et al., 1994). An interview is a procedure designed to predict future performance based on an applicant's oral responses to a series of oral questions. The rationale is that those conducting the interviews can gather information about applicants during the interview that enables accurate prediction of those applicants' future job performance. The validity of interviews for employee selection has been hotly debated for more than 30 years. A recent quantitative review of the literature uncovered a validity coefficient of .37 overall. This is strong evidence for the use of selection interviews in the hiring process (McDaniel et al., 1994).

Legal Implications

Legal issues have become a very large part of personnel selection as well as other areas within which I/O psychologists work. In 1964, Congress passed the Civil Rights Act, which included Title VII to protect individuals from discrimination in the arena of work. In particular, this act was intended to protect individuals from being discriminated against based on their ethnicity, gender, racial background, or religious preference (Riggio, 1996). In addition, other laws have helped prevent discrimination against those over 40 and the disabled, while the Civil Rights Act of 1991 has reaffirmed the major points of the earlier act and expanded some others. All of these pieces of legislation have led to more careful selection processes as well as the creation of the **EEOC** (Equal Employment Opportunity Commission) to ensure fair personnel practices. These laws are applicable not only to selection but also to other personnel practices, such as promotion decisions, firings, reductions in force (layoffs), and performance appraisal. Finally, as our society becomes more multicultural and diverse, the area of I/O psychology will continue to interface with the legal arena to ensure that no one's rights are trampled. Terms like *protected groups, adverse impact,* and *affirmative action* are as much a part of our language as I/O psychologists as they are a part of the political and legal lexicons.

EEOC
Equal Employment Opportunity Commission.

Performance Appraisal

In our discussion of the selection process, we focused on tests as predictors. These tests are usually employed to predict a *criterion.* As we noted earlier, the most typical criterion, and the one we will focus on in this section, is performance. **Performance appraisal** is the systematic review, evaluation, and feedback of an employee's job performance. Performance measures are often categorized as *judgmental* or *nonjudgmental.* Nonjudgmental performance criteria are largely objective, such as the number of units produced and the number of absences. In this appendix we will focus on judgmental measures of performance, which are somewhat subjective but are also the most commonly used, such as supervisor ratings of employee performance. At this point you should be asking yourself where these criteria come from. The answer, of course, is the job analysis. The job analysis identifies the important criteria for the job, which are then used as standards by which employees' performance can be judged.

performance appraisal
Systematic review, evaluation, and feedback regarding an employee's job performance.

Rating Formats

When it comes time for an evaluator to appraise another individual's performance, she or he typically uses some type of rating form. **Rating scales,** such as *graphic rating scales,* are probably the oldest format. These scales list a number of traits or behaviors (e.g., punctuality), and the rater is asked to judge how much of the particular trait the ratee possesses. These scales usually have some numerical and/or verbal anchors at various points along the scale, such as 1 labeled *very little,* 4 *an average amount,* and 7 *a great deal.*

rating scale
Any scale used for rating people or items.

Behaviorally Anchored Rating Scale (BARS) are similar to graphic rating scales except that they provide actual behavioral descriptions as anchors along the scale (Smith & Kendall, 1963). For instance, a 5-point BARS for "following procedures" might have as behavioral anchors at the two extremes "takes shortcuts at every opportunity" and "never deviates from the procedures set up for a particular task and follows the employee manual." A middle alternative might be "usually follows procedures, but occasionally skips steps in the process."

The final category of formats is called *employee comparison procedures.* Here, ratees are evaluated with respect to how they measure up to other employees. For example, in **rank-ordering** employees are ranked in comparison to each other from best to worst. A

rank-ordering
Rating individuals according to their standing in comparison to one another, from best to worst.

second example is *forced distribution*, in which raters are instructed to "force" a designated proportion of ratees into each of 5 to 7 categories. An analogous procedure is grading on the normal curve, where teachers assign grades based on meeting the normal curve percentages, such that 68 percent of the grades assigned are C's, 13.5 percent are B's, 13.5 percent are D's, 2.5 percent are A's, and 2.5 percent are F's.

Rating Errors

Evaluating another individual's performance accurately and fairly is not an easy thing to do. Many biases, both intentional and unintentional, can come into play. For instance, you might believe that you are fairly evaluating a co-worker and not even realize that you are allowing your close friendship to interfere with your objectivity. On the other hand, you might purposely give a co-worker a more favorable evaluation than you believe he deserves just because, like Jack Nicholson in *A Few Good Men,* you don't think he can handle the truth.

I/O psychologists have invested a great deal of research examining the various biases and errors that can take place in the performance appraisal process. For instance, one error that has received a great deal of attention is the **halo effect.** Halo effects can be positive or negative, but basically are specific ratings based on either a general evaluation of an individual or the belief that all of the dimensions of performance are related (Riggio, 1996). For example, sometimes a teacher might evaluate a student who is good in English as also being good in math and history, regardless of her actual ability in those areas.

Leniency is another common error in the appraisal process. The lenient rater tends to routinely give all workers very positive appraisals (Hauenstein, 1992). This is the teacher who gives everyone A's or the boss who rates all of her subordinates at the top of the rating scale. The rater who makes the **central tendency error** rates everyone in the middle. In this situation there appear to be no differences between employees regarding performance. Both leniency and the central tendency error can result in numerous organizational problems; because raters are not discriminating among employees, there is no basis in the appraisal data to make decisions about such things as raises or layoffs, since everyone is rated about the same.

New Wave Performance Appraisal

In a very influential paper, Landy and Farr (1980) noted that the appraisal research had been examining and emphasizing the role of rating formats and rater errors for years. They suggested a *cognitive process model* to direct future research. As a result, focus shifted from rating formats to the cognitive processing (e.g., encoding, storage, retrieval, and judgment) of raters. Many organizations do formal performance appraisals once or twice per year, with supervisors (or someone else) sitting down and evaluating the performance of all their subordinates. This means that the rater is required to recall and integrate information from a period of 6 to 12 months for a number of people and then objectively evaluate the performance of each. Research has indicated that, due to the limited information-processing capabilities of humans, this is very difficult to do and results in many of the errors and biases mentioned earlier.

Landy and Farr (1980) also suggest that we pay more attention to other, noncognitive elements of the appraisal process. Ilgen, Barnes-Farrell, and MeKellin (1993), in their recent review of the performance appraisal literature, argue that we have not learned as much from the appraisal literature of the last 15 years as we should have. They suggest that we pay more attention to the process aspect of appraisal as suggested by Landy and Farr. Many experts have begun to heed this advice by examining the context (social, legal, organizational, and political) in which the appraisal takes place (Levy & Steelman, in press; Murphy & Cleveland, 1995). Current and future trends in appraisal research include examining (1) how the relationship between the supervisor and the subordinate affects performance appraisal, (2) the role of rewards and motivation in the appraisal process, (3) the use of multiple feedback sources rather than just

---

halo effect
A type of rating bias in which the overall evaluation of an individual and other specific ratings are based on a single notable aspect of the individual's performance.

leniency
The tendency to rate too positively.

central tendency error
The tendency to rate everyone in the middle.

the supervisor in the appraisal process, and (4) the effect of employee participation on the appraisal process.

Training

We have talked abut selecting employees for jobs and evaluating their performance. The third large piece of industrial psychology is training employees. In fact, surveys routinely report that over 90 percent of all private companies utilize some formal training. Employees selected into a particular job might still need training to learn the job, and current employees often require training as their jobs change. The job analysis identifies what KSAs they must have to be able to perform the job, and this information can be used to determine which of these behaviors employees need to be trained in and how much training is required.

Needs Analysis

The first phase in any training program is to identify training needs through the use of a needs analysis. Typically, this is done at three levels. First, *organization analysis* answers the question, "Where in our organization is training needed?" This entails looking at the whole organization and perhaps breaking it down into departments or functional units, focusing on how resources are used to obtain goals. Second, *task analysis,* which is much like a job analysis, asks, "What jobs, tasks, or duties need improvement?" The organization looks at each job (separate from the person performing the job) to determine what the employee must do to adequately perform the job; this forms the basis for the content of training. Finally, *person analysis* asks, "Who needs the training?" At this stage of the needs analysis, the organization is interested in what particular employees need training and in what. This often involves evaluating the individual's performance.

Training Methods

There are many training programs and approaches available to organizations; we will look at a few of the basic approaches. First, *on-the-job* training is something that almost all trainees are exposed to at some point in their careers (Goldstein, 1993). Informally, this is often called "hands-on" training and involves new employees' learning how to do their job while actually working with an experienced employee doing the job. A second common approach to training is the *lecture method,* in which employees are taught about the job through lectures.

Programmed instruction (PI) is a self-instructional approach to training (Wexley & Latham, 1991). Typically, the material to be learned is broken down into small steps arranged in a logical sequence. Trainees work through these steps at their own pace; they are tested for knowledge after each step is completed, and provided with feedback on their performance. *Computer-assisted instruction* is a very similar process, but the trainee interacts with a computer. Computer technology allows for a version of this approach known as *adaptive training,* in which the training exercises or problems are adjusted as a result of the trainee's performance on previous exercises or problems. In this way, employees who are grasping the new material well can move on to more challenging material, while those who aren't can continue to focus on the areas where they are having problems.

Evaluation

The third phase of any training program is an evaluation of the effectiveness of that program. Kirkpatrick (1959) suggested four levels of criteria to consider in training evaluations. First, measures at the *reaction* level include what the trainees think or feel about the training program. Certainly, the organization wants to conduct a training program that the trainees like. The next level, *learning,* evaluates how much has been learned in the training program. This might involve a multiple-choice exam after the trainees have completed the program.

transfer
Bringing back to the job environment what was learned in training.

Kirkpatrick suggested that the *behavioral* level of criteria include measures of actual changes in performance back on the job. The issue here is **transfer**—bringing what was learned during the training program back to the actual job environment. The last level of criteria is commonly referred to as *results* and has to do with the utility of the training program for the organization. An evaluation at this level includes some sort of cost-benefit analysis. Let's assume that I liked the training, learned a great deal, and have been successfully using what I learned on the job (i.e., the reactions, learning, and behavioral criteria, respectively). The last questions from the organization's perspective are these: "Was the training worth it?" and "How useful was the training for our organization?" At the results level, effectiveness means that the expense of the training program was more than offset by benefits, such as improved performance, productivity, and profits.

ORGANIZATIONAL PSYCHOLOGY

Organizational psychology developed later than industrial psychology and stemmed from the human relations movement. It focuses on individual behavior and improving the well-being of employees.

Motivation

One of the most traditional areas of I/O psychology is the study of motivation. Work motivation has been defined in many ways, but Steers and Porter (1991) suggest that when we speak of work motivation we are primarily concerned with (1) what energizes human behavior, (2) what directs it, and (3) how it is maintained or sustained. Kanfer (1990) presents a useful framework for organizing motivational theories.

The Need-Motive-Value Perspective

Approaches to motivation from the need-motive-value perspective argue that individuals are motivated as a result of their personalities, dispositions, and values. Examples of theories that fall into this class are Maslow's hierarchy of needs and Alderfer's existence-relatedness-growth theory (ERG). Both of these theories hypothesize that behavior is naturally driven by a hierarchy of unmet needs. However, there has not been a great deal of research supporting the validity or usefulness of these approaches. Other examples of this category include intrinsic motivation and achievement motivation. These theories focus on a more narrowly defined set of psychological motives such as mastery and competence (Kanfer, 1990).

Cognitive Choice Theories

Cognitive processes involved in decision making and choice are the focus of the cognitive choice approach to motivation. The most famous theory of this type in the I/O literature is Vroom's expectancy-value theory (Vroom, 1964). According to Vroom, our behavior results from conscious choices among alternatives and these alternatives are evaluated with respect to three key concepts. First, **valence** is how much an individual values a particular outcome. Second, **instrumentality** is the extent to which an individual believes that attaining a particular outcome will lead to other positively valued outcomes. Finally, **expectancy** is the strength of an individual's belief about whether a particular outcome is attainable. Putting all of this together, Vroom suggests that individuals' beliefs about valances, instrumentalities, and expectancies interact psychologically to create a motivational force to act. Because motivation is a multiplicative function of the three factors, if any of them is zero there is no motivation to act. For instance, if I think that performing a certain task will lead to a *valued* outcome, and I believe that completing the task is *instrumental* in that it is likely to lead to other desired outcomes, but I *expect* that I cannot complete the task, I will not be motivated to attempt the task. On the other hand, if expectancy, valence, and instrumentality are high, this will be reflected in a strong motivational force to perform the task.

valence
How much value an individual places on a particular outcome.

instrumentality
The extent to which an individual believes that attaining a particular outcome will lead to other positively valued outcomes.

expectancy
The strength of the individual's beliefs about whether a particular outcome is attainable.

664 | APPENDIX C

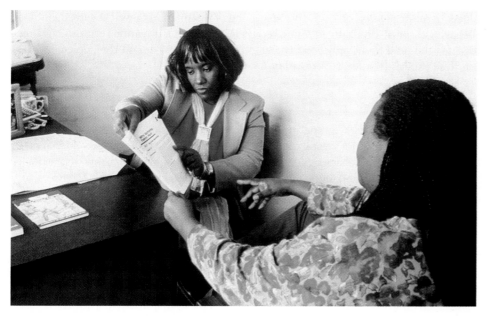

◄ **Goal Setting**
The effect of setting goals on performance is a major field of study within industrial/ organizational psychology. Workers who accept specific goals and receive feedback on their performance outperform those with nonspecific instructions to "do your best."

Self-Regulation/Metacognition Theories

Theories in the category of self-regulation/metacognition revolve around goal-directed behaviors. This approach to motivation differs from the other two paradigms because the notion here is that motivation is directly linked to self-regulation and that motivation is translated into behavior and performance as a result of self-governing cognitive mechanisms (Kanfer, 1990). This perspective explains how, once a goal is chosen, time and effort are allocated across various activities, all of which are directed toward attaining that goal. Note the distinction between the cognitive choice theories, which focus on making the choice to pursue an activity or goal, and the current theories, which describe the behaviors involved in attaining that goal. In other words, the former theories deal with intentions or choices, whereas the latter deal with volition or will (Lord & Levy, 1994).

The most researched theory of this type is **goal-setting theory.** Edwin Locke has spent nearly 30 years examining the effect of goals on performance (Locke & Latham, 1990). The most important conclusion from this huge literature is that individuals who (1) are assigned (or choose) difficult, specific goals, (2) accept them, and (3) receive feedback about their performance, outperform those who are aspiring to a "do your best" goal (Tubbs, 1986). This effect is consistently found in the laboratory setting and has been shown to be robust in real-world settings as well (Latham & Lee, 1986).

Bandura's (1986) social cognitive theory fits within this paradigm as well. Bandura views motivation as a function of the joint influence of self-efficacy expectations (self-perceptions of one's ability to complete a particular task) and reactions to discrepancies between current performance and some standard or goal. In other words, my motivation for a particular task is a result of my belief regarding how well I think I can do the task and how I tend to react to meeting or not meeting my goals. Another theory within this paradigm that is receiving a great deal of attention in the literature is control theory (Lord & Levy, 1994), according to which control systems (which are feedback loops) compare one's current or recent performance with a goal or standard. The individual is motivated to use the outcome of this comparison to reduce the discrepancy if one exists. For instance, let us suppose that my goal is to get an A in my introductory psychology course, but after the first two tests I have only a C. Obviously there is a discrepancy between my goal and the feedback that tells me that I am falling short of that goal. My motivation is reflected in my desire to reduce that discrepancy.

In sum, motivation is a very complex topic. Our thinking on the topic has evolved from a rather narrow focus on human needs to an emphasis on individual goals and the

goal-setting theory
The theory that performance is improved by setting specific goals.

effect of self-regulation on cognitive processing of information as well as subsequent task behavior (Kanfer, 1990). In addition, recent I/O work on motivation seems to have recognized the need to move beyond choice processes and to focus on the implementation of those choices (Kanfer, 1990; Lord & Levy, 1994).

Work Attitudes

Employees' attitudes, beliefs, and values have received a great deal of research attention from I/O psychologists, for several reasons. First, there seems to be a widespread assumption that attitudes lead to behaviors. In the world of work, it follows from this that attitudes toward one's work, organization, and supervisor should influence one's job behaviors and, therefore, performance. We will see shortly that it isn't so simple. Because of the complexities of human behavior (including motivation, performance, absence, and turnover), no one attitude is going to be strongly related to any one behavior. Certainly, one of the goals of any introductory psychology course is to demonstrate to students that human behavior is complex and determined by multiple causes. Second, for humanitarian reasons, organizations should be and are concerned with employees' attitudes. Working to improve employees' work attitudes is an important goal in itself. For these and other reasons, there is a great deal of research on work-related attitudes. Let's turn to some of that research.

Job Satisfaction

The most frequently studied job-related attitude is job satisfaction. Locke (1976) defined job satisfaction as a pleasurable, positive emotional state resulting from the appraisal of one's job or job experiences. There are certainly individual differences with respect to job satisfaction—some people tend to be more satisfied than others with their jobs (Staw & Ross, 1985)—but situational factors such as the work environment also seem to play a role (Gerhart, 1987; Newton & Keenan, 1991). In addition, the conceptualization of job satisfaction has been broadened to include multiple dimensions of job satisfaction. For instance, researchers and practitioners agree that workers' satisfaction can often differ as a function of the target. The important dimensions of job satisfaction include satisfaction with (1) the work itself, (2) the supervisor, (3) co-workers, (4) pay, and (5) growth opportunities.

Certainly, businesses need to turn a profit to survive, so they are almost always interested in the relationship between satisfaction and work outcomes. Research has examined the relationships among satisfaction and three work outcomes in particular: (1) performance, (2) absenteeism, and (3) turnover. Let's first look at the relationship between satisfaction and performance. Recent work in this area is somewhat mixed but generally identifies a small to moderate positive relationship ($r = .31$) between satisfaction and performance (Petty, McGee, & Cavender, 1984).

A model of absenteeism put forth by Steers and Rhodes (1978) suggests that satisfaction is one of a few key predictors of absenteeism. Although satisfaction is certainly an important part of the puzzle, it is far too simple to expect satisfaction to have a strong direct effect on absence, given the other variables involved—such as ability to attend work, motivation to attend work, and pressures to attend work. Despite the complexities involved, Scott and Taylor's (1985) quantitative review of the literature in this area reports a $-.29$ correlation between the two, indicating that more satisfied employees tend to be absent less often. Given the amount of money absenteeism costs organizations (as much as $40 billion per year) (Dalton & Mesch, 1991), the relation between satisfaction and absence continues to interest researchers and practitioners alike.

Finally, there is some support for the notion that job dissatisfaction leads to **turnover.** Carsten and Spector (1987) report a relationship in the range of $-.20$ to $-.30$, suggesting that dissatisfaction leads to turnover. Of course, turnover is much more complicated than this. For instance, voluntary turnover is initiated by the employee, and involuntary turnover is initiated by the organization (Wells & Muchinsky, 1985). Usually the best predictor of involuntary turnover is employee performance that results in being fired or laid off. Many researchers have put forth models of the voluntary turnover process, and most include job dissatisfaction as an important variable (Lee & Mitchell, 1994).

turnover

The ratio of new employees to established employees.

Organizational Commitment

The second most examined work-related attitude is organizational commitment (OC). This has traditionally been defined as the relative strength of an individual's identification with and involvement in a particular organization (Mowday, Steers, & Porter, 1979). Organizational commitment has been conceptualized as having three dimensions (Meyer, Allen, & Smith, 1993). **Affective commitment** is one's attitudinal attachment to the organization or wanting to remain a part of the organization. **Continuance commitment** has to do with the costs an individual perceives as being involved in leaving a job. For instance, one might experience continuance commitment because of the retirement benefits that one would lose by leaving the organization. **Normative commitment,** which is a much newer construct than the others and has not been as heavily researched, is defined as the felt obligation to stay with an organization (the feeling that one ought to remain).

Meyer et al. (1989) uncovered a .23 correlation between affective commitment and overall performance, but found a −.25 correlation between continuance commitment and overall performance. Thus, as Meyer et al. (1989) suggest, the relationship between commitment and performance depends on the nature of the commitment. People who are affectively committed to the organization, and *want* to remain, perform well. Those who are committed only because they don't want to lose benefits that they have built up (i.e., those who are continuance committed) don't perform very well; arguably, they just do enough to get by, while those who want to remain with the company do more than is required.

There has been very little research examining the role of OC in absenteeism. However, a meta-analysis of OC by Mathieu and Zajac (1990) reported only a small relationship between OC and absenteeism ($r = .10$). This is not surprising, though, given what we know about the complexities involved in absenteeism (Steers & Rhodes, 1978; Hackett, Bycio, & Guion, 1989). Based on the limited research to date, it appears that OC is not a very important predictor of absence frequency. A recent meta-analysis of the relationship between OC and turnover does find a moderate, negative relationship ($r = -.33$), indicating that OC is an important predictor of employees' likelihood of leaving their organization (Cohen, 1993).

affective commitment
Attitudinal attachment to the organization by which one is employed.

continuance commitment
The costs an employee perceives as being involved in leaving a job.

normative commitment
A felt obligation to stay with an organization.

Leadership

Yukl (1994) defines leadership as a social influence process through which an individual intentionally exerts influence over others to structure the behaviors and relationships in a group. It is commonly believed that effective leadership is vital for the survival and success of an organization.

Trait Theories

Trait theories were the earliest conceptualization of leadership. Trait theories argue that leader effectiveness is related to certain characteristics or traits common to all good leaders. It was assumed in the 1930s and 1940s that effective leaders were more intelligent, dominant, and aggressive than ineffective leaders or followers. However, results from over 100 studies showed that effective leaders were not necessarily more intelligent or aggressive (Stogdill, 1948). Some more recent and more sophisticated research has shown that some traits might still be important—such as behavioral flexibility, or the ability to recognize what subordinates need in a certain situation and to provide whatever that is (Zaccaro, Foti, & Kenny, 1991).

Behavior Theories

After the failure of the trait approach in the early 1950s, many researchers began studying what leaders actually do—that is, their behaviors. The most extensive program of research in this area was conducted at Ohio State University by Stogdill, Fleishman, Hemphill, and others. Questionnaires were developed for use in describing the behaviors of leaders. Two basic categories of leader behaviors emerged: consideration and initiating

consideration
The leadership characteristic of showing support, concern, and respect for subordinates.

initiating structure
The leadership characteristic of defining the roles of the leader and the subordinates in order to achieve the group's formal goals.

structure. **Consideration** is the leadership characteristic of showing support, concern, and respect for subordinates. **Initiating structure** is the leadership characteristic of defining the roles of the leader and of subordinates in order to achieve the group's formal goals. One of the more robust findings of these studies and other studies in this area is that subordinates are satisfied when leaders exhibit consideration behaviors. But critics have argued that this early work shows poor measurement qualities in the leadership questionnaires, methodological weaknesses that limit conclusions about causality, and a lack of attention to the situation in which the leadership takes place (Steers, Porter, & Bigley, 1996).

Situational Theories

In the 1960s, after some disappointment with both the trait perspective and the behavior perspective, researchers moved from a primary emphasis on the leader and began taking the situation into account. Fiedler's (1967) contingency theory argued that effective leadership is a joint function of the characteristics of the leader and features of the situation. The rationale behind this approach seems consistent with the direction in which psychology has moved over the last 30 years. Basically, Fiedler argued that a high-consideration leader will not be effective in all situations any more than a high-initiating-structure leader will. The interaction between the leader and the situation is what is most important. Although some of the specific predictions stemming from Fiedler's theory have not been supported (Riggio, 1996), and although researchers have criticized the measurement scales used in determining the leader characteristics and situation factors, Fiedler's work is important because his central idea has endured.

House (1971) presented a second situational theory, which he called path-goal theory. The premise is very simple: The main part of a leader's job is to help the work group achieve its goals, so the leader must adopt whatever approach will accomplish this end. Further, certain approaches are more appropriate in certain situations than in others. This theory is really based on an expectancy-theory conceptualization of motivation and emphasizes ways in which leaders can facilitate subordinates' performance by pointing out the instrumentalities of performance. They argued that the type of behavior exhibited by the leader should be contingent on the type of work task and characteristics of the subordinates. There has been some support for this model, but overall the results are mixed.

Newer Leadership Theories

Leader-member exchange (LMX) theory views leader effectiveness as a function of the quality of the interaction between the leader and a particular work group member (Dansereau, Graen, & Haga, 1975). The leader develops better relationships with some subordinates (the in-group) than she does with other subordinates (the out-group). In-group members have relationships with their supervisors that are characterized by mutual respect, loyalty, and trust, while out-group members do not have these positive experiences. In general, research has supported the prediction that in-group members do their jobs better and have more positive work-related attitudes, like job satisfaction, than out-group members (DeLuga & Perry, 1991).

Transformational leadership is one of the newest approaches to leadership. Bass (1985b) defines transformational leadership as occurring when a leader and follower interact in such a way as to raise one another to higher levels of motivation and morality than they would achieve separately. The goal of transformational leadership is to motivate workers to transcend their own self-interest. Based on a survey of chief executives, Bass (1985a) identified *charisma, individualized consideration,* and *intellectual stimulation* as the three major qualities of transformational leaders. *Transactional leadership*, on the other hand, is all about interactions for the purpose of exchanging valuable things. Here, leadership is based on a rational understanding of the task, as well as a clarifying of the role and task requirements of subordinates.

What exactly do transformational leaders do that makes them so special? Howell and Avolio (1993) suggest that transformational leaders concentrate their efforts on longer-term goals, place emphasis on developing and articulating a vision while inspiring followers to pursue it, change things in accordance with their vision rather than work within the preexisting boundaries of the organization, and coach followers to take on greater responsibility for their own and others' development. They inspire, they do not just motivate.

Although this approach to leadership is relatively new, research has supported its propositions. In fact, each of the three transformational leadership factors (charismatic leadership, individualized consideration, and intellectual stimulation) has been positively linked to work group performance (Howell & Avolio, 1993).

WHERE I/O PSYCHOLOGY IS GOING

Although this brief survey of the history of I/O psychology suggests that there has been a great deal of change over the past 100 years, it is fair to say that "you ain't seen nothing yet." The twenty-first century promises to be fast, frenzied, competitive, and turbulent. Dramatic changes are taking place in the world of work. Wayne Cascio, former president of the Society for Industrial and Organizational Psychology (SIOP), gave an excellent account of those changes and what the I/O field needs to do to keep up with them and to continue to make contributions to human welfare (Cascio, 1995). Some of his main points follow.

First, you hear the term **global competition** thrown about a great deal, and for good reason. U.S. businesses can no longer expect to freely and easily make a profit. Global competition will continue to make it absolutely necessary that we have a well-trained, competent workforce to compete favorably with the many countries that are now our competitors. Second, new technology has resulted in fewer jobs for workers, and organizations look, and will continue to look, significantly different than in the past. I/O psychology is important for helping the laid-off worker to be competitive for other jobs and helping those left behind to handle more diverse jobs.

Third, the latest trend in organizations is flatter organizational structures (this means that middle-level management is often cut out of the organization entirely) and empowered workers. No longer is it typical for organizations to have a manager for every 10 employees; rather, an upper-level manager might supervise 50 employees in teams of 10. Employees, or team members, are given greater responsibility for their performance as

global competition
Business competition among countries around the globe.

well as for setting objectives and decision making. Employees and teams manage themselves. I/O psychologists need to prepare current and future employees for this very different approach to organizational functioning.

Finally, the workplace is becoming more diverse in terms of race, gender, age, ethnicity, and culture. This diversity requires much more coordination and sensitivity to differences on the part of management and employees. Education and training in the world of work has become a very important area for I/O psychologists and will continue to grow in importance in the twenty-first century.

In sum, as American society and the American workplace change, the field of I/O psychology has potentially more to offer. As we traced the history and development of the field, we noted various areas in which I/O psychologists work. These areas (e.g., training, evaluation, appraisal, leadership, motivation) have been important to the world of work for many years, but now with the twenty-first century just around the corner and the workplace so very different from in the past, I/O psychology is poised to make a real difference.

▶ KEY CONCEPTS

Industrial Psychology

job analysis 658
job description 658
predictors 659
validation 659
EEOC 661

performance appraisal 661
rating scale 661
rank-ordering 661
halo effect 662
leniency 662
central tendency error 662
transfer 664

Organizational Psychology

valence 664
instrumentality 664
expectancy 664
goal-setting theory 665
turnover 666

affective commitment 667
continuance commitment 667
normative commitment 667
consideration 668
initiating structure 668
global competition 669

Chapter 1: The Nature of Psychology

Staying on Track: The History of Psychology
1. Historicism considers claims put forth by scientists in the context of the available knowledge, methods, and values of their times. In contrast, presentism sees the past in the context of current knowledge and beliefs. 2. Kant believed the mind could not be studied scientifically, partly because it could not be measured. 3. Functionalism stressed the importance of how the mind helps us adapt to reality, and it expanded the kinds of methods, subjects, and settings used in psychological research. 4. Psychic determinism is the belief that all behavior is influenced by psychological motives, often unconscious ones.

Staying on Track: Contemporary Psychological Perspectives
1. The humanistic perspective is called the third force because it was the first major alternative to the behavioral and psychoanalytic perspectives. 2. Like Gestalt psychologists, cognitive psychologists stress the active role of the mind in organizing perceptions, processing information, and interpreting experiences. Like behavioral psychologists, cognitive psychologists stress the need for objective, well-controlled, laboratory studies. 3. The social-cultural perspective is a reaction against the tendency to presume that psychological research findings in Western cultures are automatically generalizable to other cultures.

Staying on Track: Psychology as a Profession
1. Basic research aims at contributing to knowledge, and applied research aims at solving practical problems. 2. A psychiatrist is a physician who has served a residency in psychiatry, which takes a medical approach to the treatment of psychological disorders.

Staying on Track: What Role Did Women Play in the Growth of Psychology?
1. The chief obstacles were the notion of "separate spheres" for men and women and beliefs that women lacked the personal and intellectual abilities needed to profit from higher education. 2. The banning of women from the Experimentalists prevented women psychologists from "networking" and making the same useful professional connections as their male colleagues.

Chapter 2: Psychology as a Science

Staying on Track: Sources of Knowledge
1. The basic assumptions of science are that the universe is orderly, determinism is the best approach to explaining events, and skepticism is the proper scientific attitude. 2. Critical thinking is the systematic evaluation of claims by identifying the claim being made, examining evidence in support of the claim, and considering alternative explanations of the claim. 3. The steps in the scientific method include providing a rationale, conducting the study, analyzing the data, communicating the research findings, and replicating the study.

Staying on Track: Goals of Scientific Research
1. Scientists use operational definitions to provide precise, concrete definitions of events or characteristics in their research. 2. Science involves probabilistic prediction because so many variables are at work at any given time that it is usually impossible to be certain about the accuracy of one's predictions. 3. Scientific explanation in psychology involves the discovery of the causes of overt behaviors, mental experiences, and physiological changes.

Staying on Track: Methods of Psychological Research
1. An unbiased sample permits generalization of survey findings from the sample to the population. 2. The validity of a test is the extent to which a test measures what it is supposed to measure. 3. The independent variable is manipulated by the experimenter, who determines its values before the experiment begins. 4. Internal validity is the extent to which changes in the dependent variable are attributable to the independent variable.

Staying on Track: Statistical Analysis of Research Data
1. Measures of central tendency, which are used to represent a set of scores, include the mode, median, and mean. 2. Measures of variability, which are used to describe the degree of dispersion of a set of scores, include the range, the variance, and the standard deviation. 3. Statistical significance involves deciding whether the difference between group performances is of sufficiently low probability that it can be attributed to the independent variable.

Staying on Track: What Are the Ethics of Psychological Research
1. Critics argue that the methodological benefits of deception do not outweigh the mistrust of psychological research it might create and the distress it might cause in deceived subjects. 2. Debriefing involves informing subjects of the purpose of the research study in which they participated and any unusual aspects, such as the use of deception. 3. Animal rights advocates oppose all laboratory research using animals, regardless of its scientific merit or practical benefits. Animal welfare advocates would permit laboratory research on animals as long as the animals are given humane care and when the potential benefits of the research outweigh any pain and distress caused to the animals.

Chapter 3: Behavioral Neuroscience

Staying on Track: The Nervous System
1. Behavioral neuroscience studies the relationship between biological processes and psychological functions. 2. The nervous system is divided into the central nervous system (including the brain and spinal cord) and the peripheral nervous system (including the somatic nervous system and the autonomic nervous system).

Staying on Track: The Neuron
1. The major structures of the neuron are the cell body, the dendrites, and the axon. 2. Neural impulses depend on the flow of positively charged ions into the neuron, which produces an action potential.

Staying on Track: The Endocrine System
1. Whereas the endocrine glands secrete hormones into the bloodstream, exocrine glands secrete their chemicals into the body surface or into the body cavities. Moreover, endocrine secretions have many behavioral effects, but exocrine secretions have few. 2. Anabolic steroids promote muscular growth and endurance, but can provoke verbal and physical aggression.

Staying on Track: The Brain
1. The frontal lobes control movement, thinking, planning, and problem solving. 2. Phrenologists jump to conclusions about the relationship between the contours of the skull and the underlying brain structures, but phrenology did spark interest in research on the localization of brain functions. 3. Neural transplants achieve their beneficial effects by secreting neurotransmitters that the damaged region lacks, by forming new neural circuits to

replace damaged ones, and by secreting substances that promote neural regeneration. 4. The mind-brain problem in psychology considers whether mind and brain are composed of the same substance and how mind and brain are related

Staying on Track: Do the Cerebral Hemispheres Serve Different Functions?

1. Several cross-sectional studies indicate that left-handers die younger than right-handers, but critics argue that this is the result of prohibitions against left-handedness that made many left-handed children become right-handed decades ago. 2. When the corpus callosum is severed, the hemispheres can perform certain functions independently of each other, and sometimes one hemisphere does it better than the other.

Chapter 4: Human Development

Staying on Track: The Nature of Developmental Psychology

1. Because identical twins reared apart are psychologically more similar than nontwin siblings reared together, nature appears to play a stronger role than nurture in human development. 2. A cohort-sequential research design begins as a cross-sectional study by comparing different cohorts and then follows the cohorts longitudinally.

Staying on Track: Prenatal Development

1. Cell-adhesion molecules direct the movement of cells and determine which cells will adhere to one another, thereby determining the size, shape, and location of organs in the embryo. 2. The hallmarks of fetal alcohol syndrome are facial deformities and mental retardation.

Staying on Track: Infant and Child Development

1. Depth perception is present in human infants by 6 months of age, and generally it develops in animals about the time when they can move about on their own. 2. Piaget assumed that the child proceeds through qualitatively different stages of cognitive development during which cognitive schemas are altered by the processes of assimilation and accommodation. 3. Securely attached infants have more successful peer relationships and

more secure romantic attachments later in life. 4. Permissive parents set few rules and rarely punish misbehavior; authoritarian parents set strict rules and rely on punishment; and authoritative parents tend to be warm and loving, yet insist that their children behave appropriately. Authoritative parenting is the most successful, and the preferred, style of parenting.

Staying on Track: Adolescent Development

1. Cultural and historical factors that are unique to particular cohorts can make those cohorts somewhat different from cohorts that precede or succeed them. 2. The person who has reached the formal operational stage can apply abstract principles and make predictions about hypothetical situations. 3. The adolescent develops a sense of identity by adopting his or her own set of values and social behaviors. This is a normal part of finding answers to questions such as these: What do I believe is important? What are my goals in life?

Staying on Track: Adult Development

1. A reduction in caloric intake is associated with increased longevity. 2. Research indicates that fluid intelligence declines in old age but that crystallized intelligence does not. 3. Adults who achieve generativity become less self-absorbed and more concerned about being a productive worker, spouse, and parent.

Staying on Track: Are There Significant Psychological Sex Differences

1. The best-established psychological sex difference is that males score better than females on standardized tests in mathematics. 2. Some psychologists argue that sex differences are too small to have any practical meaning and that publicizing them might promote sex discrimination. Others insist that scientists are obliged to study topics even when their research findings might be disapproved of.

Chapter 5: Sensation and Perception

Staying on Track: Sensory Processes

1. Sensation is the process that detects stimuli from one's body or

environment. Perception is the process that organizes sensations into meaningful patterns. 2. Psychophysics is the study of the relationship between the physical characteristics of stimuli and the corresponding psychological responses to them. 3. Sensory adaptation is the tendency of sensory receptors to respond less and less to an unchanging stimulus.

Staying on Track: Vision

1. Light waves pass through the cornea, aqueous humor, pupil, lens, vitreous humor, and photoreceptors. 2. The trichromatic theory assumes that the retina has three kinds of receptors, each of which is maximally sensitive to red, green, or blue light. 3. These are the principles of proximity, closure, similarity, and continuity. 4. The binocular cues are retinal disparity and convergence.

Staying on Track: Hearing

1. The major structures are the pinna, auditory canal, tympanic membrane, eustachian tube, ossicles, oval window, cochlea, basilar membrane, hair cells, and auditory nerve. 2. The place theory assumes that particular points on the basilar membrane vibrate maximally in response to sound waves of particular frequencies. 3. Sound localization depends on sounds reaching one ear slightly before reaching the other, on sounds being slightly more intense at the closer ear, and on the irregular shape of the pinna altering sounds differently depending on their location.

Staying on Track: Chemical Senses

1. Pheromones are odorous chemicals that affect animals' behavior. 2. The stereochemical theory of smell assumes that smell receptors responsive to particular odors are sensitive to molecules of specific sizes, shapes, or electrical charges. 3. The enjoyment of flavors depends on not only the sense of taste but also the sense of smell, which is diminished by a head cold.

Staying on Track: Skin Senses

1. The blind person wears a camera on special eyeglasses and a computer-controlled electronic vest covered with a grid of tiny Teflon cones. Outlines of images provided by the camera are

impressed onto the skin by vibrations of the cones. 2. The gate-control theory of pain assumes that pain impulses from the limbs or body pass through a part of the spinal cord that provides a "gate" for pain impulses, perhaps involving substance P neurons. Stimulation of neurons that convey touch sensations "closes" the gate, preventing input from neurons that convey pain sensations. 3. If subjects are given naloxone and the pain-relieving technique becomes less effective, it is assumed that the technique depends on the release of endorphins, because naloxone blocks the effects of endorphins.

Staying on Track: Body Senses

1. The kinesthetic sense informs you of the position of your joints, the tension in your muscles, and the movement of your arms and legs. 2. One of the major theories of motion sickness holds that it is produced by a conflict between sensory input to the eyes and sensory input to the vestibular organs.

Staying on Track: Why Do Psychologists Discount ESP?

1. The four paranormal abilities are mental telepathy, clairvoyance, precognition, and psychokinesis. 2. The major shortcomings of paranormal research are that it may involve poorly controlled demonstrations, chance events, fraud, or magic. Moreover, paranormal events cannot be explained by any known physical processes.

Chapter 6: Consciousness

Staying on Track: The Nature of Consciousness

1. Both William James and James Joyce were interested in studying the stream of consciousness. 2. The "cocktail party phenomenon" involves being engrossed in one conversation at a party yet noticing when your name is mentioned in another conversation.

Staying on Track: Sleep

1. There is no scientific evidence supporting the belief that each of us is born with physical, emotional, and intellectual cycles that stay constant in length and govern us for the rest of our lives. 2. The night typically involves four or five cycles in which the sleeper descends into the depths of NREM sleep, ascends to lighter

stages of NREM sleep, and ends each cycle in REM sleep. During the second half of the night, the sleeper might not reach sleep deeper than stage 2 and will have longer REM periods. **3.** The length of sleep varies negatively with how long it takes animals to find their daily food and positively with how secure they are from attack when they sleep. **4.** Persons with sleep-onset insomnia should avoid ingesting caffeine or doing exercise too close to bedtime. They should also avoid napping during the day; go to bed only when they feel sleepy; refrain from eating, reading, watching television, or listening to music while in bed; and get out of bed instead of tossing and turning.

Staying on Track: *Dreams*
1. Among Calkins's findings were that we dream every night, that we have several dream periods each night, that we are more likely to dream during the second half of the night, that most dreams are mundane, that we can incorporate external stimuli into our dreams, that we can engage in "real thinking" while asleep, that we can control our dreams, and that dreams can disguise their true meanings. **2.** Freud believed that dreams are often disguised forms of wish fulfillment in which the manifest content of the dream symbolically represents its true meaning; its latent content.

Staying on Track: *Hypnosis*
1. During hypnotic induction you might have the subject focus on a spot on the ceiling. You might then suggest that the subject's eyelids are closing, feet are warming, muscles are relaxing, and breathing is slowing. You would gradually induce the subject to relinquish more and more control of his or her perceptions, thoughts, and behaviors to you. **2.** Hypnosis can help subjects recall memories but might make them overly confident in their recall of inaccurate "memories." **3.** Some researchers believe that hypnosis is merely a state of heightened suggestibility in which subjects are willing to act out the suggestions given by the hypnotist. They also note that motivated nonhypnotized people can often perform the same feats as hypnotized people.

Staying on Track: *Meditation*
1. You would practice the relaxation response by finding a quiet place to sit and repeat a sound, such as a number or a brief prayer, over and over again. **2.** Some research studies have found that meditation produces a unique physiological state, but others have found that it produces a state similar to simply relaxing with one's eyes closed.

Staying on Track: *Psychoactive Drugs*
1. The symptoms of drug dependency are tolerance and withdrawal symptoms. **2.** Cocaine is a stimulant drug that induces a relatively brief state of euphoria. It can cause addiction, paranoia, hallucinations, and sudden death from cardiac arrest. **3.** Marijuana alters sensory experiences and in higher doses can induce hallucinations. It impairs coordination, disrupts memory formation, and has been linked to amotivational syndrome.

Staying on Track: *Unconscious Influences*
1. Research indicates that although we might be able to perceive subliminal stimuli, we will not follow subliminal suggestions like obedient zombies. **2.** Subliminal psychodynamic activation presents emotionally charged subliminal messages to alter the recipient's moods and behaviors by stimulating unconscious fantasies.

Chapter 7: Learning

Staying on Track: *Classical Conditioning*
1. You would repeatedly turn on the can opener just before presenting the cat with food. Eventually the cat will come running at the sound of the can opener. **2.** Bernstein suggests offering patients unusual, strange-tasting food before they have chemotherapy so that they will associate their resulting nausea with that food instead of with more common, nutritious foods. **3.** Garcia found that rats have a tendency, apparently inborn, to associate nausea and dizziness with tastes, but not with sights and sounds, and to associate pain with sights and sounds, but not with tastes.

Staying on Track: *Operant Conditioning*
1. Thorndike, like Skinner, found that behavior can be changed by altering its consequences. **2.** You might train her by giving her a piece of cookie for looking at the tricycle, then for taking a step toward it, then for approaching it, then for touching it, then for sitting on it, and finally for peddling it. **3.** Both produce an increase in behavior, but whereas positive reinforcement involves the presentation of something appealing, negative reinforcement involves the removal of something unappealing.

Staying on Track: *Cognitive Learning*
1. According to the cognitive explanation, blocking occurs because a new neutral stimulus adds nothing to the predictability of the UCS. The existing CS already predicts the occurrence of the UCS. **2.** Latent learning and observational learning show that learning can take place without performing the relevant overt behavior.

Staying on Track: *Biofeedback*
1. If noncontingent feedback produces the same change in the relevant physiological response as contingent feedback, then the changes induced by biofeedback in that case would be attributable to a placebo effect. **2.** Biofeedback might produce physiological changes that are statistically significant but that are too small to be of practical significance.

Chapter 8: Memory

Staying on Track: *Information Processing and Memory*
1. Some psychologists note that normal memory processes, such as thinking more often and more elaborately about certain experiences, can explain so-called flashbulb memories. Moreover, there is evidence that people are more confident in their flashbulb memories, even though those might be no more accurate than normal memories. **2.** Sensory memory stores exact replicas of stimuli impinging on the senses for a brief period—from a fraction of second to several seconds. Short-term memory stores a limited amount of information in conscious awareness for about 20 seconds. And

long-term memory stores a virtually unlimited amount of information for up to a lifetime.

Staying on Track: *Sensory Memory*
1. By using partial report, Sperling demonstrated that iconic memory stores virtually all the information that strikes the photoreceptors, though the information fades so quickly that it seems that we store only a fraction of it. **2.** Echoic memory helps us store speech sounds long enough to blend them with subsequent speech sounds, thereby letting us perceive a meaningful sequence of sounds.

Staying on Track: *Short-Term Memory*
1. Research indicates that even when subjects are tested on their short-term memory for letters presented visually, their errors indicate that they confuse letters based on their sounds more than on their appearance. **2.** When they presented subjects with tyrigrams to recall and prevented rehearsal of them, they found that after about 20 seconds the subjects could not recall any trigrams.

Staying on Track: *Long-Term Memory*
1. Elaborative rehearsal involves processing the meaning of information instead of (as in maintenance rehearsal) its superficial qualities. **2.** Procedural memory includes memories of how to perform behaviors, whereas declarative memory includes memories of facts. **3.** In proactive interference, old memories interfere with new memories. In retroactive interference, new memories interfere with old ones. **4.** Memories encoded while a person is in a specific state (such as a psychoactive drug-induced state) will be recalled better when the person is again in that state. There is also research showing that our recall of information that has been encoded in a particular mood will be best when we are in that mood again.

Staying on Track: *Improving Your Memory*
1. You should set up a study schedule in a comfortable, nondistracting environment. You might also use the SQ3R method of studying. Other suggestions would be to use overlearning, distributed

practice, and mnemonic devices. 2. You would memorize a list of concrete nouns that rhyme with numbers 1, 2, 3, 4, and so on. You would then imagine the objects to be recalled interacting with the objects represented by the concrete nouns. Then simply recall the concrete nouns associated with each number. This should automatically make you recall the interacting object.

Staying on Track: The Biopsychology of Memory
1. After classically conditioning an eyeblink response in a rabbit, researchers found that electrical simulation of a tiny site in the cerebellum of the rabbit elicited the conditioned eye blink, and that destruction of the site eliminated it. 2. Since his hippocampus was removed decades ago, H. M. has been unable to form new long-term memories. 3. When subjects are given a drug that blocks the effects of acetylcholine, they have trouble forming new long-term declarative memories. Other evidence comes from the loss of memory in victims of Alzheimer's disease, which is associated with the destruction of acetylcholine neurons in the brain.

Staying on Track: Should We Trust Eyewitness Testimony?
1. Children are more susceptible to the effects of misleading information about events, which can distort their recall of them. The younger the child, the more likely this is to occur. 2. Loftus believes that biased or leading questions can alter witnesses' recall of past events.

Chapter 9: Thinking and Language

Staying on Track: Thinking
1. Cognitive psychology combines William James's concern with mental processes and John B. Watson's concern with observable behavior. 2. Research indicates that we can think and form memories while our speech muscles are paralyzed; therefore thinking does not depend on subvocal speech.

Staying on Track: Concept Formation
1. A logical concept is formed by identifying the specific features possessed by all things that the concept applies to. A natural

concept is formed through everyday experience rather than by testing hypotheses about particular features that are common to all members of the concept. 2. They have fuzzy borders because it is difficult to identify their defining features.

Staying on Track: Problem Solving
1. A heuristic can be more efficient, because it rules out many useless alternatives before they are even attempted. But unlike an algorithm, a heuristic does not guarantee a solution. 2. We sometimes are hindered by mental sets, which are commitments to problem-solving strategies that have succeeded in the past but that interfere with solving a problem that requires a new strategy.

Staying on Track: Creativity
1. Creative people tend to be above average in intelligence, prefer novelty, favor complexity, and make independent judgments. They are also able to combine verbal thinking and visual thinking, and reality-oriented thinking with imaginative thinking. 2. Amabile found that when students were given extrinsic reasons for writing poetry, they wrote less creative poems while there was no decline in the creativity in poems by students who wrote for intrinsic reasons.

Staying on Track: Decision Making
1. Utility is the value we assign to a given outcome, and probability is our estimate of the likelihood that a given alternative will lead to a particular outcome. We normally prefer outcomes of both high utility and high probability. 2. The availability heuristic is the tendency to estimate the probability of an event by how easily relevant instances of it come to mind.

Staying on Track: Artificial Intelligence
1. Expert systems are now using powerful computer programs that think more like world-class chess players, rather than simply relying on brute calculating speed. 2. Serial information processing involves processing information one step at a time. Parallel information processing involves processing different information simultaneously.

Staying on Track: The Structure of Language
1. Semanticity is the conveying of the thoughts of the communicator in a meaningful way to those who understand the language. Generativity is the combining of language symbols in novel ways, without being limited to a fixed number of combinations. Displacement is the use of language to refer to objects and events that are not present. 2. In terms of transformational grammar, language comprehension involves transforming the surface structure, which is the verbal message, into its deep structure, which is its meaning.

Staying on Track: The Acquisition of Language
1. Between 4 and 6 months of age, infants enter the babbling stage. When infants are about 1 year old, they begin to say their first words. Infants then begin using holophrastic speech, which is the use of single words to represent whole phrases or sentences. Next, in the two-word stage, infants use telegraphic speech. 2. Skinner believes that all aspects of language are learned. Chomsky believes that we have an inborn language mechanism that makes us sensitive to the rules of grammar.

Staying on Track: The Relationship Between Thinking and Language
1. In 1984 Orwell portrays a society in which the government changes the meaning of words or invents words to limit citizen's ability to think rebellious thoughts. 2. Research indicates that when male pronouns are used to represent people generically, those who read or hear them tend to take them to refer to males rather than to both males and females.

Staying on Track: Can Apes Use Language?
1. Some apes have been able to use words meaningfully, use words in novel ways, and use words to refer to things that are not physically present. 2. Some researchers believe that apes do not use language spontaneously but instead use it to get things they want or simply as responses to prompting by their trainers.

Chapter 10: Intelligence

Staying on Track: Intelligence Testing
1. An autistic savant is an autistic person with below-average intelligence but with an outstanding ability, typically in art, music, memory, or calculating. 2. Galton similarly assumed that people with superior physical abilities, especially sensory and motor abilities, are better adapted for survival and, therefore, more intelligent. 3. This ruling was based on a judge's finding that the use of IQ tests violated the civil rights of African American children, because a proportionately greater number of African American children than white children were being placed in classes for children with mental retardation.

Staying on Track: Extremes of Intelligence
1. The possible causes of mental retardation include hereditary defects, social-cultural deprivation, and brain damage. 2. The Studies of Genius have shown that mentally gifted children tend to become socially, physically, vocationally, and academically superior adults.

Staying on Track: Theories of Intelligence
1. Spearman found that intelligence depends on a general intelligence factor more than on separate kinds of intelligence. In contrast, Thurstone found that intelligence depends more on separate kinds of intelligence than on a general intelligence factor. 2. The seven types of intelligence are linguistic, logical-mathematical, spatial, musical, bodily-kinesthetic, intrapersonal, and interpersonal.

Staying on Track: Does Intelligence Depend More on Nature or on Nurture?
1. In intelligence, adopted children are more like their biological parents than like their adoptive parents. Moreover, identical twins reared apart are more alike in intelligence than ordinary siblings reared together are. 2. There is evidence that as the size of a family increases and the interval between births decreases, the intelligence of each subsequent child decreases, but there is also evidence that this does not always hold true.

| STAYING ON TRACK

Chapter 11: Motivation

Staying on Track: Sources of Motivation

1. Critics fear that acceptance of sociobiology would lend support to the status quo, making us less inclined to change what many people believe has been "ordained by God or nature," such as differences in the social status of men and women, blacks and whites, rich and poor. 2. According to Maslow, you must first satisfy your basic physiological needs before you will be motivated to meet your higher needs for safety and security, and so on up the hierarchy from the need for belongingness and love, through the need for esteem, and ultimately to the needs for self-actualization and transcendence.

Staying on Track: The Hunger Motive

1. Stimulation of the lateral hypothalamus provokes eating, and stimulation of the ventromedial hypothalamus inhibits eating. 2. The role of heredity in obesity has been supported by studies showing that the correlation in the amount of body fat between identical twins stays roughly the same whether they are reared together or apart. Moreover, adopted children are more similar in weight to their biological parents than to their adoptive parents. 3. Factors may include cultural emphasis on thinness in women, women's more distorted images of their bodies, brain malfunctions, hormone imbalances, and concerns about becoming a mature adult.

Staying on Track: The Sex Motive

1. Kinsey's surveys found that people engaged in more sex and a greater variety of sexual activities than was popularly believed. Sexual behavior, particularly women's, has become more liberal since Kinsey's time. But concerns about diseases such as genital herpes and AIDS have reduced the incidence of promiscuous behavior and unprotected sex. 2. The four phases of the human sexual response cycle are excitement, plateau, orgasm, and resolution. 3. Gender identity is one's self-perceived sex. Sexual orientation is one's interest in persons of one's own sex or of the other sex, or of both sexes.

Staying on Track: The Arousal Motive

1. According to the Yerkes-Dodson law, performance will be best at a moderate level of arousal. 2. Flotation REST has proved useful in reducing drug and alcohol use, tension headache, and high blood pressure.

Staying on Track: The Achievement Motive

1. Goals should be specific and challenging, and goal setting should include both short-term and long-term goals. 2. Overjustification theory assumes that an extrinsic reward decreases intrinsic motivation when a person attributes his or her performance to the extrinsic reward. Cognitive-evaluation theory holds that a reward perceived as providing information about a person's competence in an activity will increase her or his intrinsic motivation to perform that activity. But a reward perceived as an attempt to control a person's behavior will decrease that person's intrinsic motivation to perform that activity.

Staying on Track: What Is the Relationship Between Motivation and Sport?

1. An athlete might be underaroused or overaroused in practice and optimally roused during a competition—or optimally aroused during practice and underaroused or overaroused during a competition. 2. Opponents of much lower or much higher ability would not be a fair test of the athlete's ability.

Chapter 12: Emotion

Staying on Track: The Biopsychology of Emotion

1. Studies measuring brain activity or the effects of brain damage have found that increased activity in the left hemisphere is associated with positive emotions and increased activity in the right hemisphere is associated with negative emotions. 2. Endorphin levels rise markedly after activities that induce euphoria.

Staying on Track: The Expression of Emotion

1. Prosodic features of speech include rate, pitch, and loudness. 2. One line of research has found that even people who are blind from birth exhibit facial expressions for the basic emotions. A second line of research shows that young infants produce facial expressions for the basic emotions. Studies also show that facial expressions for the basic emotions are universal across cultures.

Staying on Track: The Experience of Emotion

1. Happiness is positively correlated with intelligence, social skills, and family support. Physical attractiveness has a low to moderate correlation with happiness. Our happiness also depends on comparisons we make between ourselves and others and between our current circumstances and our past circumstances. 2. According to the disparagement theory, we feel amused when humor makes us feel superior to other people. According to the incongruity theory, incongruous humor brings together incompatible ideas in a surprising outcome that violates our expectations. And according to the release theory, humor is a cathartic outlet for anxiety caused by repressed sexual or aggressive energy.

Staying on Track: Theories of Emotion

1. Evidence for the theory comes from studies finding different patterns of physiological responses for different emotions. Evidence against the theory includes the findings that we have poor ability to perceive many of the subtle physiological changes induced by the sympathetic nervous system, that different emotions are associated with the same pattern of physiological arousal, and that physiological changes dependent on the secretion of hormones by the adrenal glands are too slow to be the basis of all emotions. 2. When subjects alter their facial expressions, they report changes in their subjective emotional experience. 3. Subjects who experience unexplained arousal will experience negative emotions, regardless of their social context, thereby contradicting the theory. The only consistent finding in favor of the theory is that misattribution of physiological arousal to an outside source will intensify an emotional experience.

Staying on Track: Do Lie Detectors Tell the Truth?

1. Polygraph tests tend to be better at identifying guilty people than at identifying innocent ones; therefore they have the potential to harm the lives of the innocent. 2. The control-question test compares physiological responses to baseline control questions to physiological responses to relevant questions. In contrast, the Guilty Knowledge Test assesses whether the individual shows a physiological orienting response to relevant items related to the topic at hand.

Chapter 13: Personality

Staying on Track: The Psychoanalytic Approach to Personality

1. The Barnum effect demonstrates that useful personality descriptions must distinguish one person from another. 2. The id is unconscious, consists of our inborn biological drives, and demands immediate gratification. The ego directs us to express sexual and aggressive impulses in socially acceptable ways. The superego, our moral guide, counteracts the id, which is concerned only with immediate gratification, and the ego, which is concerned only with adapting to reality. 3. Adler assumed that because children feel small, weak, and dependent on others, they develop an inferiority complex. This motivates them to compensate by striving for superiority. 4. Jung claimed that archetypes influence our dreams, religious symbols, and artistic creations.

Staying on Track: The Dispositional Approach to Personality

1. Allport believed we are guided by the interaction among our cardinal traits, central traits, and secondary traits. 2. The MMPI was constructed by retaining only those questions that discriminate between people who differ on the characteristics of interest.

Staying on Track: The Behavioral Approach to Personality

1. It is different from operant conditioning theory in arguing that behavior is affected by cognitive processes. 2. Reciprocal determinism reflects Bandura's belief that neither personal dispositions nor environmental factors can by themselves explain behavior. Instead, Bandura assumes that personality traits, environmental

factors, and overt behavior affect one another. 3. In behavioral observation the subject is observed in real or simulated conditions related to work, school, recreation, or other situations of interest. In experience sampling, the subject carries a portable device that beeps at random times, and on hearing the beep the person reports her or his experiences and behaviors at that time.

Staying on Track: The Cognitive Approach to Personality
1. Kelly called our ability to apply different constructs to a given situation constructive alternativism. 2. The psychotherapist might use it to determine whether a client relies on too few or too many personal constructs in viewing other people.

Staying on Track: The Humanistic Approach to Personality
1. The humanistic approach tends to have a positive view of human nature, studies subjective mental experience, and assumes we have free will. 2. Some of the research topics include self-actualization, self-concept, self-handicapping, self-development, and self-esteem. 3. You would have the person sort the cards twice, first into piles of statements that are or are not characteristic of the actual self and then into piles of statements that are or are not characteristic of the ideal self.

Staying on Track: The Biopsychological Approach to Personality
1. One of the main problems is that raters have often related both the somatotypes and the temperaments of the subjects, permitting experimenter bias to creep in. 2. Researchers have found amazing similarities in the personalities of identical twins reared apart and reunited later in life.

Staying on Track: Is Personality Consistent?
1. Mischel found that the correlation between any two behaviors presumed to represent the same underlying personality trait rarely exceeded a relatively modest .30. 2. First, individuals do show consistency on certain traits. Second, cross-situational consistency in behavior depends on whether a person is a high self-monitor or a low self-monitor. Third, many of the studies that Mischel reviewed were guaranteed to find low cross-situational consistency, because they either correlated trait test scores with single instances of behaviors or correlated single instances of behaviors with each other. Psychologists have achieved greater success in demonstrating cross-situational consistency by using behavioral aggregation.

Chapter 14: Psychological Disorders

Staying on Track: The Nature of Psychological Disorders
1. If qualitative abnormality were sufficient, then people who achieve rare accomplishments would be considered psychologically disordered. By the criterion of quantitative abnormality, persons whose jobs involve repetitive behavior (such as handwashing, for doctors) would be considered disordered. Nonconformists would be considered psychologically disordered soley for opposing the status quo. 2. According to Rogers and Maslow, psychological disorders occur when people fail to reach their potential, perhaps because others, especially their parents, discourage them from expressing their true desires, thoughts, and interests. 3. Even though Rosenhan used deception in making believe that he and other individuals were suffering from schizophrenia in order to gain admission to mental hospitals, Spitzer argued that their admission was justified because their reported symptoms and their behaviors were consistent with typical symptoms of schizophrenia.

Staying on Track: Anxiety Disorders
1. An obsession is a persistent thought, whereas a compulsion is a persistent, repetitive behavior. 2. People who are prone to panic disorders often develop agoraphobia because they fear having a panic attack in public.

Staying on Track: Somatoform Disorders
1. A malingerer would have no physical ailment. A hypochondriac would exaggerate minor ailments. 2. This means that the person shows remarkable indifference to an apparently serious physical problem.

Staying on Track: Dissociative Disorders
1. Most of them have suffered physical and sexual abuse as young children. 2. Some psychologists believe that people suffering from multiple personalities are doing little more than role playing and do not, in fact, have more than one personality.

Staying on Track: Mood Disorders
1. Shneidman suggests that because suicide attempts are usually cries for help, the simple act of providing empathetic response can reduce the immediate likelihood of an actual attempt. Just talking about a problem might reduce its apparent dreadfulness and help the person realize that solutions other than suicide are possible and that his or her options include more than a choice between death and a hopeless, helpless life. An immediate goal should be to relieve the person's psychological pain by intervening, if possible, with those who might be contributing to the pain, whether friends, lovers, teachers, or family members. You should also encourage the person to seek professional help, even if you have to make the appointment for the person and accompany him or her to it. 2. The theory explains depression in terms of the attributions we make for events in our lives. According to this theory, depressed people attribute negative events in their lives to stable, global, internal factors. 3. People who constantly think about the sad state of their lives experience more severe and more chronic depression than people who take action to improve their lives or who distract themselves by pursuing enjoyable activities.

Staying on Track: Schizophrenia
1. The major symptoms of schizophrenia are hallucinations, problems maintaining attention, language disturbances, delusions, flat or inappropriate emotionality, unusual motor behavior, and social withdrawal. 2. First, drugs that are used to treat schizophrenia work by blocking dopamine receptors. Second, drugs such as amphetamines, which increase dopamine levels in the brain, can induce schizophrenic symptoms in normal people. Third, L-dopa, a drug used to treat Parkinson's disease because it increases dopamine levels in the brain, can induce schizophrenic symptoms in Parkinson's victims. 3. Positive symptoms are active symptoms, including hallucinations, delusions, thought disorders, and bizarre behaviors. Negative symptoms are passive symptoms, including mutism, apathy, flat affect, social withdrawal, intellectual impairment, poverty of speech, and inability to experience pleasure.

Staying on Track: Personality Disorders
1. People with antisocial personality disorder show an appalling lack of conscience and have no qualms about harming other people. 2. The unusually low level of arousal of people with an antisocial personality apparently motives them to engage in behaviors that increase their level of arousal, with a certain number of them choosing antisocial behaviors.

Staying on Track: Should We Retain the Insanity Defense?
1. The cognitive rule says that a person was insane at the time of a crime if the person did not know what he or she had done or did not know that it was wrong. The volitional rule says that the person was insane at the time of the crime if the person was not in voluntary control of his or her actions. 2. The American public was so appalled at his being judged insane and not responsible for his crime that it promoted legislators to pass new legislation.

Chapter 15: Therapy

Staying on Track: The History of Therapy
1. No, it might have been done for other purposes, perhaps medical, religious, or punitive. 2. Moral therapy used humane treatment, honest work, and pleasant recreation to promote mental well-being.

Staying on Track: The Psychoanalytic Orientation
1. In free association, the client is urged to report any thoughts or

feelings that come to mind—no matter how trivial or embarrassing they seem. This is supposed to reveal important information that can help the client gain self-knowledge. **2.** In the analysis of resistances, the psychoanalyst notes behaviors that interfere with therapeutic progress toward self-awareness. These resistances are interpreted to uncover the unconscious conflicts that underlie them.

Staying on Track: The Behavioral Orientation

1. You would first use progressive relaxation to train the person to relax. You would then set up a hierarchy of scenes related to oral presentation. Finally, you would have the person relax while first imagining low-anxiety scenes and gradually progressing to higher-anxiety scenes. **2.** You would give the students tokens for doing well in spelling and arithmetic and let them trade in the tokens for things or activities they enjoy.

Staying on Track: The Cognitive Orientation

1. Ellis assumes that maladaptive emotions and behaviors are caused by irrational thinking. Therefore, his therapeutic techniques are aimed at making his clients think more rationally. **2.** Beck assumes that depression is caused by negative beliefs about oneself, the world, and the future. Beck's cognitive therapy teaches clients to recognize their negative beliefs and replace them with positive beliefs.

Staying on Track: The Humanistic Orientation

1. Client-centered therapy strives to create greater congruence between the client's actual self and the client's public self by encouraging clients to express and accept their true feelings. The person-centered therapist promotes self-actualization through reflection of feelings, genuineness, accurate empathy, and unconditional positive regard. **2.** Irvin Yalom points to four issues that each of us must face: the inevitability of death, our responsibility for our own choices, the isolation of each person from all others, and the need to find meaning in life.

Staying on Track: The Social-Relations Orientation

1. TA assumes that there are basic roles we all play and that these are sometimes adaptive, sometimes maladaptive. TA teaches group members to recognize the roles they play in their interactions (their transactions, or the "games" they play), and to use this understanding to improve their social relations. **2.** Minuchin's therapy aims at achieving appropriate emotional boundaries between family members, so that there will be a balance between enmeshment and disengagement (especially between parent and child).

Staying on Track: The Biopsychological Orientation

1. Critics believe that ECT is dangerous because it can cause brain damage, memory loss, and other problems. Others say its dangers are outweighed by its ability to relieve depression and prevent suicide. **2.** The tricyclics increase the levels of serotonin and norepinephrine in the brain by preventing their re-uptake by brain neurons that release them.

Staying on Track: Community Mental Health

1. Four factors brought this movement about: (1) new drug treatments, (2) the underfunding and overcrowding of mental hospitals, (3) an increased concern for the legal rights of mental patients, and (4) the Community Mental Health Centers Act of 1963, which mandated the establishment of federally funded mental health centers in every community in the United States. **2.** Primary prevention helps prevent psychological disorders by fostering social support systems, eliminating sources of stress, and strengthening individuals' ability to deal with stressors.

Staying on Track: The Rights of the Therapy Client

1. The right to refuse treatment has led to some mental hospital patients not receiving necessary therapy. The right to receive treatment assures that patients who do not receive treatment must be released from custodial care. **2.** The *Tarasoff* decision has been praised because it might help protect individuals whom a therapy client has threatened to harm. It has been criticized because it might inhibit people who feel hostile toward others from dealing with those feelings honestly in therapy, and because it creates a legal obligation to inform that conflicts with the therapist's ethical obligation to maintain confidentiality.

Staying on Track: The Selection of a Therapist

1. Multimodal therapy was devised by Arnold Lazarus and is perhaps the best-known kind of eclectic therapy. It combines the techniques of BASIC ID. **2.** The college counseling center might be a good place to start. A friend, relative, or professor might be able to recommend a therapist or counseling center to you. Other potential sources of help or referral include community mental health associations. Many of these organizations, as well as private practitioners, are listed in the Yellow Pages.

Staying on Track: Is Psychotherapy Effective?

1. He found that about two thirds of people with psychological disorders improve with or without psychotherapy. **2.** The client's perception of therapist empathy has been consistently identified as an important factor in the effectiveness of psychotherapy. Personal warmth has also been found to be a factor that differentiates successful and unsuccessful therapists.

Chapter 16: Psychology and Health

Staying on Track: Stress and Illness

1. A century ago most people died young from infectious diseases. Today, with infectious diseases under control, people live longer and tend to succumb to behavior-related diseases, including cancer and cardiovascular disease. **2.** This is a disorder that appears months or years after a person experiences a traumatic event. It includes emotional, cognitive, and behavioral symptoms. **3.** Some studies have found that there is a stronger association between hassles and illness than between life changes and illness. Moreover, life changes might produce their negative effects by increasing daily hassles. **4.** In animal studies, when a neutral stimulus is paired with a drug that alters the immune response, the neutral stimulus will come to also alter the immune response.

Staying on Track: Factors That Moderate the Stress Response

1. Hardiness involves a sense of commitment, challenge, and control. **2.** Social support promotes health by reducing the effects of stressful life events, promoting recovery from illness, and increasing adherence to medical regimens.

Staying on Track: Coping with Stress

1. The study found that adolescents under high levels of stress who exercised regularly had a significantly lower incidence of illness than did adolescents who exercised little. **2.** The study found that the students who were not assigned to practice relaxation, compared to the students who were, displayed a significantly greater decrease in natural killer cell activity at final-exams time.

Staying on Track: Health-Impairing Habits

1. HIV is most commonly transmitted by transfusions of infected blood, the sharing of hypodermic needles by drug users, and unprotected anal and vaginal sex. **2.** Aerobic exercise boosts the immune response, boosts the basal metabolic rate, promotes weight control, and reduces the risk of cardiovascular disease. **3.** Dieting by itself slows the basal metabolic rate, cannot last a lifetime, promotes the loss of lean body tissue, and tends to result in greater weight gain from rebound eating when the diet ends.

Staying on Track: Reactions to Illness

1. Important factors include social support, explanatory style, and interpretation of symptoms. **2.** A study found a negative correlation between the perceived empathy of nurses and patient anger, anxiety, and depression. Patients who perceive a lack of empathy in their physicians are more likely to sue them for malpractice. And practitioners must communicate so that patients will adhere to medical regimens.

Staying on Track: Does Type A Behavior Promote Coronary Heart Disease?

1. The Type A behavior pattern involves being in a hurry, being competitive, doing several things at once, and harboring hostility. 2. Cynical hostility seems to be the symptom of Type A behavior that is most closely linked to coronary heart disease. 3. Parents of Type A children encourage them to try harder even when they do well and offer them few spontaneous positive comments. Type A children might be given no standards except "Do better," which makes it difficult for them to develop internal standards of achievement.

Chapter 17: Social Behavior

Staying on Track: Social Cognition
1. Self-serving bias is the tendency to make dispositional attributions for our own positive behaviors and situational attributions for our negative behaviors. 2. When we self-handicap, we lead others to believe that we are performing under a handicap. If we then do well, we look good to others. If we do poorly, others will attribute our poor performance to our "handicap." 3. This occurs because the social schema we have of the other person will make us act a certain way toward that person, which in turn can make the person respond in accordance with our expectations.

Staying on Track: Interpersonal Attraction
1. Evidence includes the fact that we like people more the more we

are exposed to them. We even like views of our own faces that we see in mirrors more than views of our faces as they are seen by other people. 2. Self-disclosure should be mutual and gradual. 3. Men offer financial status and seek physical attractiveness. Women seek financially well-off men and note their own physical attractiveness.

Staying on Track: Attitudes
1. A message that takes a central route relies on clear, explicit arguments about the issue at hand. A message that takes a peripheral route relies on factors other than the merits of the arguments, such as characteristics of the source or the situational context. 2. Attitudes that are strongly held or personally important are better predictors of behavior. Attitude-behavior consistency is also affected by the specificity of the attitude and the behavior. 3. For such contact to reduce prejudice, it must be between people of equal status.

Staying on Track: Group Dynamics
1. Persuasive arguments tend to move group members in their direction. Simply repeating arguments over and over is another factor. 2. Groupthink is promoted by several factors: a charismatic leader, feelings of invulnerability, discrediting of contrary evidence, fear of criticism for disagreeing, the desire to maintain group

harmony, isolation from outside influences, and disparaging outsiders as incompetent. 3. A good way to reduce social loafing is to convince group members that their individual efforts will be evaluated or that they will be held accountable. Social loafing can also be overcome when a task is important to an individual and that person believes other group members lack the ability to perform better. 4. You might ask for a two-week postponement, have it rejected, and then ask for a one-week postponement.

Staying on Track: Prosocial Behavior
1. Some research indicates that people will be more likely to help other people if they believe it will relieve their own negative feelings, such as guilt. 2. When strangers notice someone in trouble, as their number increases, their probability of helping decreases, apparently because each feels less responsible for helping.

Staying on Track: Aggression
1. Violent criminals have higher levels of testosterone than nonviolent criminals do. Athletes who use anabolic steroids become more aggressive. Castration of male sex offenders lowers their testosterone levels and reduces their sex drive and sex-crime recidivism. Female-to-male transsexuals who undergo testosterone treatment become more prone to

anger and aggression after several months of hormone treatment. And male and female children prenatally exposed to testosterone because their mothers received a synthetic form of it during pregnancy become more aggressive than their same-sex siblings who were not exposed to it. 2. There is a positive correlation between the two, but insufficient evidence to declare that this is a causal relationship. 3. When people feel anonymous, they are more likely to take part in group aggression.

Staying on Track: Does Pornography Cause Aggression Against Women?
1. Koop concluded that children and adolescents who participate in the production of pornography experience adverse, enduring negative effects, such as eventual involvement in child prostitution. He also concluded that portrayals of rape as being pleasurable for the victim increase the incidence of rape by promoting the view that women enjoy being forced to have sex. 2. They have found that violent sexual films, particularly those that portray the myth that women enjoy being raped, more than nonviolent sexual films, might stimulate aggression against women.

absolute threshold the minimum amount of stimulation that an individual can detect through a given sense. 153

accommodation 1. the cognitive process that revises existing schemas to incorporate new information. 2. the process by which the thickness of the lens in the eye changes to focus images of objects located at different distances from the eye. 119, 157

achievement motive the desire for mastery, excellence, and accomplishment. 397

achievement test a test that measures knowledge of a particular subject. 346

acronym a mnemonic device that involves forming a term from the first letters of a series of words that are to be recalled. 295

action potential a series of changes in the electrical charge across the axonal membrane that occurs after the axon has reached its firing threshold. 70

activation-synthesis theory the theory that dreams are the by-products of the mind's attempt to make sense of the spontaneous changes in physiological activity generated by the pons during REM sleep. 210

actor-observer bias the tendency of observers to make dispositional attributions for the behavior of others but to make situational attributions for their own behavior. 596

acupuncture a pain-relieving technique that relies on the insertion of fine needles into various sites on the body. 184

adaptation-level theory the theory that happiness depends on comparing one's present circumstances with one's past circumstances. 420

adolescence the transition period lasting from the onset of puberty to the beginning of adulthood. 130

adrenal glands endocrine glands that secrete hormones that regulate the excretion of minerals and the body's response to stress. 78

adulthood the period beginning when the individual assumes responsibility for her or his own life. 134

affective-commitment attitudinal attachment to the organization by which one is employed. 667

afterimage a visual image that persists after the removal of a visual stimulus. 163

age regression a hypnotic state in which the individual apparently behaves as she or he did as a child. 216

aggression behavior aimed at causing harm to another person. 626

agoraphobia a fear of being in public, usually because the person fears the embarrassment of a panic attack. 488

algorithm a problem-solving rule or procedure that, when followed step by step, assures that a correct solution will be found. 315

all-or-none law the principle that once a neuron reaches its firing threshold, a neural impulse travels at full strength along the entire length of its axon. 71

altruism the helping of others without the expectation of a reward. 622

Alzheimer's disease a brain disorder characterized by difficulty in forming new memories and by general mental deterioration. 74

amphetamines stimulants used to maintain alertness and wakefulness. 222

amygdala a limbic system structure that evaluates information from the immediate environment, contributing to feelings of fear, anger, or relief. 83

anal stage in Freud's theory, the stage of personality development, between ages 1 and 3, during which the child gains pleasure from defecation and faces a conflict over toilet training. 446

analysis of dreams in psychoanalysis, the process by which the therapist interprets the symbolic, manifest content of dreams to reveal their true, latent content to the client. 522

analysis of free associations in psychoanalysis, the process by which the therapist interprets the underlying meaning of the client's uncensored reports of anything that comes to mind. 521

analysis of resistances in psychoanalysis, the process by which the therapist interprets client behaviors that interfere with therapeutic progress toward uncovering unconscious conflicts. 522

analysis of transference in psychoanalysis, the process by which the therapist interprets the feelings expressed by the client toward the

therapist as being indicative of the feelings typically expressed by the client toward important people in his or her personal life. 522

analysis of variance a statistical technique used to determine whether the difference between two or more sets of scores is statistically significant. 653

analytic introspection a research method in which highly trained subjects report the contents of their conscious mental experiences. 9

anorexia nervosa an eating disorder marked by self-starvation. 384

antianxiety drugs psychoactive drugs, commonly known as minor tranquilizers, that are used to treat anxiety disorders. 541

antidepressant drugs psychoactive drugs that are used to treat major depression. 541

antimania drugs psychoactive drugs, most notably lithium carbonate, that are used to treat a bipolar disorder. 542

antipsychotic drugs psychoactive drugs, commonly known as major tranquilizers, that are used to treat schizophrenia. 542

antisocial personality disorder a personality disorder marked by impulsive, manipulative, often criminal behavior, without any feelings of guilt in the perpetrator. 507

anxiety disorder a psychological disorder marked by persistent anxiety that disrupts everyday functioning. 485

applied research research aimed at improving the quality of life and solving practical problems. 20

approach-approach conflict a conflict in which one must choose between two desirable courses of action. 560

approach-avoidance conflict a conflict in which one is faced by a course of action that has both desirable and undesirable qualities. 560

aptitude test a test designed to predict a person's potential to benefit from instruction in a particular academic or vocational setting. 347

archetypes in Jung's theory, inherited images that are passed down from our prehistoric ancestors and that reveal themselves as universal symbols in art, dreams, and religion. 449

archival research the systematic examination of collections of letters, manuscripts, tape recordings, video recordings, or other records. 45

arousal motive the motive to maintain an optimal level of physiological activation. 394

artificial intelligence (AI) the field that integrates computer science and cognitive psychology in studying information processing through the design of computer programs that appear to exhibit intelligence. 325

assertiveness training a form of social-skills training that teaches clients to express their feelings directly, instead of passively or aggressively. 535

assimilation the cognitive process that interprets new information in light of existing schemas. 119

association areas regions of the cerebral cortex that integrate information from the primary cortical areas and other brain areas. 84

atherosclerosis the narrowing of arteries caused by the accumulation of cholesterol deposits. 565

attention the process by which the individual focuses awareness on certain contents of consciousness while ignoring others. 197

attitude an evaluation, containing cognitive, emotional, and behavioral components, of an idea, event, object, or person. 604

audition the sense of hearing. 174

auditory cortex the area of the temporal lobes that processes sounds. 86, 175

auditory nerve the nerve that conducts impulses from the cochlea to the brain. 175

authoritarian personality a personality type marked by the tendency to obey superiors while dominating subordinates, to favor one's own group while being prejudiced against other groups, and to be unwilling to admit one's own faults while projecting them onto members of other groups. 611

authoritative parenting an effective style of parenting, in which the parent is warm and loving, yet sets well-defined limits that he or she enforces in an appropriate manner. 123

automatic processing information processing that requires less conscious awareness and mental effort, and that does not interfere with the performance of other ongoing activities. 226

autonomic nervous system the division of the peripheral nervous system that controls automatic, involuntary physiological processes. 67

autonomy versus shame and doubt Erikson's developmental stage in which success is achieved by gaining a degree of independence from one's parents. 122

availability heuristic in decision making, the tendency to estimate the probability of an event by how easily relevant instances of it come to mind. 324

aversion therapy a form of behavior therapy that inhibits maladaptive behavior by pairing a stimulus that normally elicits a maladaptive response with an unpleasant stimulus. 525

avoidance-avoidance conflict a conflict in which one must choose between two undesirable courses of action. 560

avoidance learning learning to prevent the occurrence of an aversive stimulus by giving an appropriate response to a warning stimulus. 251

axon the relatively long fiber of the neuron that conducts neural impulses to glands, muscles, or other neurons. 69

axonal conduction the transmission of a neural impulse along the length of an axon. 70

barbiturates depressants used to induce sleep or anesthesia. 221

basal metabolic rate the rate at which the body burns calories just to keep itself alive. 381

basic research research aimed at finding answers to questions out of theoretical interest or intellectual curiosity. 20

basilar membrane a membrane running the length of the cochlea that contains the auditory receptor (hair) cells. 175

behavioral contingencies relationships between behaviors and their consequences, such as positive reinforcement, negative reinforcement, extinction, and punishment. 246

behavioral genetics the study of the relationship between heredity and behavior. 107

behavioral neuroscience the field that studies the relationship between neurological and psychological processes. 21, 66

behavioral perspective the psychological viewpoint, descended from behaviorism, that stresses the importance of studying the effects of learning and environmental factors on overt behavior. 15

behavioral preparedness the degree to which members of a species are innately prepared to learn particular behaviors. 259

behaviorism the early school of psychology that rejected the study of mental processes in favor of the study of overt behavior. 11

behavior modification the application of the principles of operant conditioning to change maladaptive behaviors. 526

behavior therapy the therapeutic application of the principles of learning to change maladaptive behaviors. 522

binocular cues depth perception cues that require input from the two eyes. 167

biofeedback a form of operant conditioning that enables an individual either to learn to control a normally involuntary physiological process or to gain better control of a normally voluntary one when provided with visual or auditory information indicating the state of that process. 264

biological rhythms repeating cycles of physiological changes. 198

biopsychological perspective the psychological viewpoint that stresses the relationship of physiological factors to behavior and mental processes. 18

bipolar disorder a mood disorder marked by periods of mania alternating with longer periods of major depression. 497

blocking the process by which a neutral stimulus paired with a conditioned stimulus that already elicits a conditioned response fails to become a conditioned stimulus. 260

brain the structure of the central nervous system that is located in the skull and plays important roles in sensation, movement, and information processing. 67

brightness constancy the perceptual process that makes an object maintain a particular level of brightness despite changes in the amount of light reflected from it. 170

Broca's area the region of the frontal lobe responsible for the production of speech. 88

bulimia nervosa an eating disorder marked by binging and purging. 385

bystander intervention the act of helping someone who is in immediate need of aid. 623

caffeine a stimulant used to increase mental alertness. 222

cannabis sativa a hallucinogen derived from the hemp plant and ingested in the form of marijuana or hashish. 224

Cannon-Bard theory the theory that an emotion is produced when an event or object is perceived by the thalamus, which conveys this information simultaneously to the cerebral cortex and the skeletal muscles and autonomic nervous system. 424

case study an in-depth study of an individual. 41

catatonic schizophrenia a type of schizophrenia marked by unusual motor behavior, such as bizarre actions, extreme agitation, or immobile stupor. 503

catharsis in psychoanalysis, the release of repressed emotional energy as a consequence of insight into the unconscious causes of one's psychological problems. 521

causal attribution the cognitive process by which we infer the causes of both our own and other people's social behavior. 594

causation an effect of one or more variables on another variable. 46

central nervous system the division of the nervous system consisting of the brain and the spinal cord. 67

central tendency error the tendency to rate everyone in the middle. 662

cerebellum a hindbrain structure that controls the timing of well-learned movements. 81

cerebral cortex the outer covering of the forebrain. 84

cerebral hemispheres the left and right halves of the cerebrum. 84

cerebral palsy a movement disorder caused by brain damage and that is sometimes accompanied by mental retardation. 354

chaining an operant conditioning procedure used to establish a desired sequence of behaviors by positively reinforcing each behavior in the sequence. 248

childhood the period that extends from birth until the onset of puberty. 115

circadian rhythms twenty-four-hour cycles of physiological changes, most notably the sleep-wake cycle. 198

clairvoyance the alleged ability to perceive objects or events without any sensory contact with them. 188

classical conditioning a form of learning in which a neutral stimulus comes to elicit a response after being associated with a stimulus that already elicits that response. 237

clinical psychology the field that applies psychological principles to the prevention, diagnosis, and treatment of psychological disorders. 22

cocaine a stimulant used to induce mental alertness and euphoria. 222

cochlea the spiral, fluid-filled structure of the inner ear that contains the receptor cells for hearing. 175

coefficient of correlation 1. a statistic that assesses the degree of association between two or more variables. 2. A number that represents the direction and strength of a correlation. 54, 649

cognitive appraisal the subjective interpretation of the severity of a stressor. 570

cognitive-appraisal theory the theory that one's emotion at a given time depends on one's interpretation of the situation one is in. 431

cognitive dissonance theory Leon Festinger's theory that attitude change is motivated by the desire to relieve the unpleasant state of tension caused when one holds cognitions that are inconsistent with each other. 608

cognitive-evaluation theory the theory that a person's intrinsic motivation will increase when a reward is perceived as a source of information but will decrease when a reward is perceived as an attempt to exert control. 401

cognitive perspective the psychological viewpoint that favors the study of how the mind organizes perceptions, processes information, and interprets experiences. 17

cognitive psychology the field of psychology that studies how the mind organizes perceptions, processes information, and interprets experiences. 310

cognitive therapy a type of therapy, developed by Aaron Beck, that aims at eliminating exaggerated negative beliefs about oneself, the world, or the future. 530

cohort a group of people of the same age. 111

cohort-sequential research research that begins as a cross-sectional study of different cohorts and then follows the cohorts longitudinally. 112

collateral sprouting the process by which branches from the axons of nearby healthy neurons grow into the pathways normally occupied by the axons of damaged neurons. 91

collective unconscious in Jung's theory, the unconscious mind that is shared by all human beings and that contains archetypal images passed down from our prehistoric ancestors. 449

color blindness the inability to distinguish between certain colors, most often red and green. 163

companionate love love characterized by feelings of affection and commitment to a relationship with another person. 603

comparative psychology the field that studies similarities and differences in the physiology, behaviors, and abilities of different species of animals, including human beings. 21

compliance behaving in accordance with a request that is backed by little or no threat of punishment. 618

computed tomography (CT) a brain-scanning technique that relies on X rays to construct computer-generated images of the brain or body. 87

computer-assisted instruction the use of computer programs to provide programmed instruction. 257

concept a category of objects, events, qualities, or relations that share certain features. 311

concrete operational stage the Piagetian stage, extending from 7 to 12 years of age, during which the child learns to reason logically about objects that are physically present. 120

conditioned response (CR) in classical conditioning, the learned response given to a particular conditioned stimulus. 237

conditioned stimulus (CS) in classical conditioning, a neutral stimulus that comes to elicit a particular conditioned response after being paired with a particular unconditioned stimulus that already elicits that response. 237

conditioned taste aversion a taste aversion induced by pairing a taste with gastrointestinal distress. 242

conduction deafness hearing loss usually caused by blockage of the auditory canal, damage to the eardrum, or deterioration of the ossicles of the middle ear. 177

cones receptor cells of the retina that play an important role in daylight vision and color vision. 157

conflict the emotional state induced when one is torn between two or more potential courses of action. 560

confluence model the view that each child is born into an intellectual environment that is dependent on the intelligence levels of her or his parents and siblings, with the number of children and the interval between births affecting the intelligence of each successive child. 368

conformity behaving in accordance with group expectations with little or no overt pressure to do so. 616

confounding variable a variable whose unwanted effect on the dependent variable might be confused with that of the independent variable. 48

conscious mind the level of consciousness that includes the mental experiences that we are aware of at a given moment. 229

consciousness the awareness of one's own mental activity, including thoughts, feelings, and sensations. 196

consensus the extent to which, in a given situation, other people behave in the same way as the person being observed. 595

conservation the realization that changing the form of a substance does not change its amount. 120

consideration the leadership characteristic of showing support, concern and respect for subordinates. 668

consistency the extent to which a person behaves in the same way in a given situation on different occasions. 595

constructive alternativism the process by which a person applies personal constructs to a given situation. 461

constructive recall the distortion of memories by adding, dropping, or changing details to fit a schema. 284

context-dependent memory the tendency for recall to be best when the environmental context present during the encoding of a memory is also present during attempts at retrieving it. 290

continuance commitment the costs an employee perceives as being involved in leaving a job. 667

continuous schedule of reinforcement a schedule of reinforcement that provides reinforcement for each instance of a desired response. 249

control group the subjects in an experiment who are not exposed to the experimental condition of interest. 47

controlled processing information processing that involves conscious awareness and mental effort, and that interferes with the performance of other ongoing activities. 226

conventional level in Kohlberg's theory, the level of moral reasoning characterized by concern with upholding laws and conventional values and by favoring obedience to authority. 128

convergent thinking the cognitive process that focuses on finding conventional solutions to problems. 321

conversion disorder a somatoform disorder in which the person exhibits motor or sensory loss or the alteration of a physiological function without any apparent physical cause. 491

cornea the round, transparent area in the front of the sclera that allows light to enter the eye. 156

corpus callosum a thick bundle of axons that provides a means of communication between the cerebral hemispheres, which is severed in so-called split-brain surgery. 99

correlation the degree of relationship between two or more variables. 46

correlational research research that studies the degree of relationship between two or more variables. 46

correlational statistics statistics that determine the relationship between two variables. 649

counseling psychology the field that applies psychological principles to help individuals deal with problems of daily living, generally less severe ones than those treated by clinical psychologists. 22

counterconditioning a behavior therapy technique that applies the principles of classical conditioning to replace unpleasant emotional responses to stimuli with more pleasant ones. 523

creativity a form of problem solving that generates novel, socially valued solutions to problems. 319

critical period a period in childhood when experience with language produces optimal language acquisition. 332

cross-cultural psychology an approach that tries to determine the extent to which research findings about human psychology hold true across cultures. 19

cross-sectional research a research design in which groups of subjects of different ages are compared at the same point in time. 111

crystallized intelligence the form of intelligence that reflects knowledge acquired through schooling and in everyday life. 136, 360

cultural-familial retardation mental retardation apparently caused by social or cultural deprivation. 354

cultural psychology an approach that studies how cultural factors affect human behavior and mental experience. 19

dark adaptation the process by which the eyes become more sensitive to light when under low illumination. 161

daydreaming a state of consciousness that involves shifting attention from external stimuli to self-generated thoughts and images. 197

debriefing a procedure, after the completion of a research study, that informs subjects of the purpose of the study and aims to remove any physical or psychological distress caused by participation. 58

decay theory the theory that forgetting occurs because memories naturally fade over time. 286

decision making a form of problem solving in which one tries to make the best choice from among alternative judgments or courses of action. 323

declarative memory the long-term memory system that contains memories of facts. 279

deep structure the underlying meaning of a statement. 329

defense mechanism in Freud's theory, a process that distorts reality to prevent the individual from being overwhelmed by anxiety. 444

deindividuation the process by which group members become less aware

of themselves as individuals and less concerned about being socially evaluated. 630

deinstitutionalization the movement toward treating people with psychological disorders in community settings instead of mental hospitals. 543

déjà vu the feeling that one has experienced a present experience sometime in the past. 188

dendrites the branchlike structures of the neuron that receive neural impulses. 68

dependent variable a variable showing the effect of the independent variable. 47

depressants psychoactive drugs that inhibit activity in the central nervous system. 219

depth perception the perception of the relative distance of objects. 167

descriptive research research that involves the recording of behaviors that have been observed systematically. 40

descriptive statistics statistics that summarize research data. 53, 645

determinism the assumption that every event has physical, potentially measurable, causes. 34

developmental psychology the field that studies physical, cognitive, and psychosocial changes across the life span. 21, 106

diathesis-stress viewpoint the assumption that psychological disorders are consequences of the interaction of a biological, inherited predisposition (diathesis) and exposure to stressful life experiences. 482

difference threshold the minimum amount of change in stimulation that can be detected. 154

differential psychology the field of psychology that studies individual differences in intellectual, personality, and physical characteristics. 8, 348

discriminative stimulus in operant conditioning, a stimulus that indicates the likelihood that a particular response will be reinforced. 246

disorganized schizophrenia a type of schizophrenia marked by severe personality deterioration and extremely bizarre behavior. 503

disparagement theory the theory that humor is amusing when it makes one feel superior to other people. 421

displacement the characteristic of language marked by the ability to refer to objects and events that are not present. 327

dissociation a state in which the mind is split into two or more independent streams of consciousness. 215

dissociative disorder a psychological disorder in which thoughts, feelings, and memories become separated from conscious awareness. 492

dissociative identity disorder a dissociative disorder, more commonly known as multiple personality disorder, in which the person has two or more distinct personalities that alternate with one another. 493

distinctiveness the extent to which a person behaves in the same way across different situations. 595

distributed practice spreading out the memorization of information or the learning of a motor skill over several sessions. 293

divergent thinking the cognitive process by which an individual freely considers a variety of potential solutions to artistic, literary, scientific, or practical problems. 321

door-in-the-face technique increasing the likelihood that someone will comply with a request by first getting them to reject a larger one. 619

double-blind technique a procedure that controls experimenter bias and subject bias by preventing experimenters and subjects from knowing which subjects have been assigned to particular conditions. 51

Down syndrome a form of mental retardation, associated with certain physical deformities, that is caused by an extra, third chromosome on the 21st pair. 355

dream a storylike sequence of visual images, usually occurring during REM sleep. 207

drive a state of psychological tension induced by a need. 377

drive-reduction theory the theory that behavior is motivated by the need to reduce drives such as sex or hunger. 377

echoic memory auditory sensory memory, which lasts up to 4 or more seconds. 275

educational psychology the field that applies psychological principles to improving curriculum, teaching methods, and administrative procedures. 22

EEOC Equal Employment Opportunity Commission. 661

ego in Freud's theory, the part of the personality that helps the individual adapt to external reality by making compromises between the id, the superego, and the environment. 444

egocentrism the inability to perceive physical reality from the perspective of another person. 119

elaboration likelihood model a theory of persuasion that considers the extent to which messages take a central route or a peripheral route. 606

elaborative rehearsal actively organizing new information to make it more meaningful, and integrating it with information already stored in long-term memory. 278

Electra complex a term used by some psychoanalysts, but not by Freud, to refer to the Oedipus complex in females. 446

electroconvulsive therapy (ECT) a biomedical therapy that uses brief electric currents to induce brain seizures in victims of major depression. 540

electroencephalograph (EEG) a device used to record patterns of electrical activity produced by neuronal activity in the brain. 79

embryonic stage the prenatal period that lasts from the end of the second week through the eighth week. 113

emotion a motivated state marked by physiological arousal, expressive behavior, and mental experience. 410

empiricism the philosophical position that true knowledge comes through the senses. 6, 34

encoding the conversion of information into a form that can be stored in memory. 273

encoding specificity the principle that recall will be best when cues that were associated with the encoding of a memory are also present during attempts at retrieving it. 289

encounter group a derivative of humanistic group therapy in which group members learn to be themselves by openly expressing their true feelings to one another. 537

endocrine system glands that secrete hormones into the bloodstream. 76

endorphins neurotransmitters that play a role in pleasure, pain relief, and other functions. 74

engineering psychology the field that applies psychological principles to the design of equipment and instruments. 22

engram a memory trace in the brain. 297

environmental psychology the field that applies psychological principles to help improve the physical environment, including the design of buildings and the reduction of noise. 22

episodic memory the subsystem of declarative memory that contains memories of personal experiences tied to particular times and places. 280

equipotentiality the ability of more than one area of the brain to control a given function. 91

escape learning learning to perform a behavior that terminates an aversive stimulus, as in negative reinforcement. 251

ethology the study of animal behavior in the natural environment. 41

ethyl alcohol a depressant found in beverages and commonly used to reduce social inhibitions. 219

eugenics the practice of encouraging supposedly superior people to reproduce, while preventing supposedly inferior people from reproducing. 364

existential psychology a branch of humanistic psychology that studies how individuals respond to the basic philosophical issues of life, such as death, meaning, freedom, and isolation. 17

existential therapy a type of humanistic therapy that helps the client overcome emotional or behavioral problems by dealing with major philosophical issues in life, including death, freedom, isolation, and meaning. 533

expectancy 1. in achievement situations, the perceived probability of success in a particular area. 2. in I/O psychology, the strength of the individual's beliefs about whether a particular outcome is attainable. 399, 664

experimental group the subjects in an experiment who are exposed to the experimental condition of interest. 47

experimental method research that manipulates one or more variables, while controlling other factors, to determine the effects on one or more other variables. 47

experimental psychology the field primarily concerned with laboratory research on basic psychological processes, including perception, learning, memory, thinking, language, motivation, and emotion. 20

experimenter bias effect the tendency of experimenters to let their expectancies alter the way they treat their subjects. 49

expert system a computer program that displays expertise in a specific domain of knowledge. 325

explanatory style the tendency to explain events optimistically or pessimistically. 571

explicit memory conscious recollection of general information or personal experiences. 280

external validity the extent to which the results of a research study can be generalized to other people, animals, or settings. 51

extinction 1. in classical conditioning, the gradual disappearance of the conditioned response when the conditioned stimulus is repeatedly presented without being paired with the unconditioned stimulus. 2. in operant conditioning, the gradual disappearance of a response that is no longer followed by a reinforcer. 240, 252

extrasensory perception (ESP) the ability to perceive events without the use of sensory receptors. 187

extravert a person who is socially outgoing and prefers to pay attention to the external environment. 449

extrinsic motivation the desire to perform a behavior in order to obtain an external reward, such as praise, grades, or money. 400

eyewitness testimony witnesses' recollections about events, most notably about criminal activity. 301

facial-feedback theory the theory that particular facial expressions induce particular emotional experiences. 428

factor analysis a statistical technique that determines the degree of correlation between performances on various tasks to determine the extent to which they reflect particular underlying characteristics, which are known as factors. 359

family therapy a form of group therapy that encourages the constructive expression of feelings and the establishment of rules that family members agree to follow. 537

feature-detector theory the view that we construct our perceptions from neurons of the brain that are sensitive to specific features of stimuli. 166

feeling of control the degree to which a person feels in control over life's stressors. 571

fetal alcohol syndrome a disorder, marked by physical defects and mental retardation, that can afflict the offspring of women who drink alcohol during pregnancy. 114

fetal stage the prenatal period that lasts from the end of the eighth week through birth. 113

fight-or-flight response a state of physiological arousal that enables us to meet sudden threats by either confronting them or running away from them. 410

figure-ground perception the distinguishing of an object (the figure) from its surroundings (the ground). 165

fixation in Freud's theory, the failure to mature beyond a particular stage of psychosexual development. 446

fixed-interval schedule of reinforcement a partial schedule of reinforcement that provides reinforcement for the first desired response made after a set length of time. 250

fixed-ratio schedule of reinforcement a partial schedule of reinforcement that provides reinforcement after a set number of desired responses. 249

fixed-role therapy a kind of therapy, derived from Kelly's personality theory, that encourages clients to adopt roles that promote new, more adaptive personal constructs. 462

flashbulb memory a vivid, long-lasting memory of a surprising, important, emotionally arousing event. 272

flooding an extinction procedure in which a phobic client is exposed to a stimulus that evokes intense anxiety. 526

fluid intelligence the form of intelligence that reflects reasoning ability, memory capacity, and speed of information processing. 136, 360

foot-in-the-door technique increasing the likelihood that someone will comply with a request by first getting them to comply with a smaller one. 618

forensic psychology the field that applies psychological principles to improve the legal system, including the work of police and juries. 22

forgetting the failure to retrieve information from memory. 273

forgetting curve a graph showing that forgetting is initially rapid and then slows. 286

formal operational stage the Piagetian stage, beginning at about age 12, marked by the ability to use abstract reasoning and to solve problems by testing hypotheses. 131

fovea a small area at the center of the retina that contains only cones and provides the most acute vision. 158

framing effect in decision making, biases introduced into the decision-making process by presenting an issue or situation in a certain manner. 324

frequency distribution a list of the frequency of each score or group of scores in a set of scores. 642

frequency histogram a graph that displays the frequency of scores as bars. 643

frequency polygon a graph that displays the frequency of scores by connecting points representing them above each score. 643

frequency theory the theory of pitch perception that assumes that the basilar membrane vibrates as a whole in direct proportion to the frequency of the sound waves striking the eardrum. 176

frontal lobe a lobe of the cerebral cortex responsible for motor control and higher mental processes. 84

frustration the emotional state induced when one is blocked from reaching a goal. 559

frustration-aggression hypothesis the assumption that frustration causes aggression. 628

functional fixedness the inability to realize that a problem can be solved by using a familiar object in an unusual way. 318

functionalism the early school of psychology that studied how the conscious mind helps the individual adapt to the environment. 10

fundamental attribution error the bias to attribute other people's behavior to dispositional factors. 596

gate-control theory the theory that pain impulses can be blocked by the closing of a neuronal gate in the spinal cord. 184

gender identity a person's self-perceived sex. 391

gender roles the behaviors that are considered appropriate for females or males in a given culture. 125

gender-schema theory a theory of gender-role development that combines aspects of social learning theory and cognitive-developmental theory. 126

general adaptation syndrome as first identified by Hans Selye, the body's stress response, which includes the stages of alarm, resistance, and exhaustion. 565

generalized anxiety disorder an anxiety disorder marked by a persistent state of anxiety that exists independently of any particular stressful situation. 485

generativity the characteristic of language marked by the ability to combine words in novel, meaningful ways. 327

generativity versus stagnation Erikson's developmental stage in which success is achieved by becoming less self-absorbed and more concerned with the well-being of others. 139

genital stage in Freud's theory, the last stage of personality development, associated with puberty, during which the individual develops erotic attachments to others. 446

genotype an individual's genetic inheritance. 109

germinal stage the prenatal period that lasts from conception through the second week. 112

Gestalt psychology the early school of psychology that claimed that we perceive and think about wholes rather than simply about combinations of separate elements. 12

Gestalt therapy a type of humanistic therapy, developed by Fritz Perls, that encourages clients to become aware of their true feelings and to take responsibility for their own actions. 532

glial cell a kind of cell that provides a physical support structure for the neurons, supplies them with nutrition, removes neuronal metabolic waste materials, facilitates the transmission of messages by neurons, and helps regenerate damaged neurons in the peripheral nervous system. 68

global competition business competition among countries around the globe. 669

goal setting the establishment of a particular level of performance to achieve in the future. 399

goal setting theory the theory that performance is improved by setting specific goals. 665

gonads the male and female sex glands—the testes and the ovaries. 78, 386

grammar the set of rules that governs the proper use and combination of language symbols. 328

group a collection of two or more persons who interact and have mutual influence on each other. 612

group polarization the tendency for groups to make more-extreme decisions than their members would make as individuals. 613

groupthink the tendency of small, cohesive groups to place unanimity ahead of critical thinking in making decisions. 614

Guilty Knowledge Test a method that assesses lying by measuring physiological arousal in response to information that is relevant to a transgression and physiological arousal in response to information that is irrelevant to that transgression. 436

gustation the sense of taste, which detects molecules dissolved in the saliva. 181

hallucinogens psychoactive drugs that induce extreme alterations in consciousness, including visual hallucinations, a sense of timelessness, and feelings of depersonalization. 223

halo effect a type of rating bias in which the overall evaluation of an individual and other specific ratings are based on a single notable aspect of the individual's performance. 662

health psychology the field that applies psychological principles to the prevention and treatment of physical illness. 22, 558

hemispherectomy the surgical removal of an entire cerebral hemisphere, usually to treat uncontrollable epilepsy. 92

heritability the extent to which variability in a characteristic within a group can be attributed to heredity. 109, 365

heuristic a general principle or "rule of thumb" that guides problem solving, though it does not guarantee a correct solution. 316

hidden observer Ernest Hilgard's term for the part of the hypnotized person's consciousness that is not under the control of the hypnotist but is aware of what is taking place. 215

hierarchy of needs Abraham Maslow's arrangement of needs in the order of their motivational priority, ranging from physiological needs to the needs for self-actualization and transcendence. 378

higher-order conditioning in classical conditioning, the establishment of a conditioned response to a neutral stimulus that has been paired with an existing conditioned stimulus. 237

hippocampus a limbic system structure that contributes to the formation of memories. 83

historicism an approach to history that studies the past for its own sake, in the context of beliefs and knowledge that characterized the period being studied. 4

holophrastic speech the use of single words to represent whole phrases or sentences. 330

homeostasis a steady state of physiological equilibrium. 377

homosexuality a consistent preference for sexual relations with persons of one's own sex. 392

hormones chemicals, secreted by endocrine glands, that play a role in a variety of functions, including synaptic transmission. 76

hospice movement the movement to provide care for the terminally ill in settings that are as close as possible to everyday life, and that emphasizes the need to reduce pain and suffering. 140

humanistic perspective the psychological viewpoint that holds that the proper subject matter of psychology is the individual's subjective mental experience of the world. 17

hypermnesia the hypnotic enhancement of recall. 214

hyperopia visual farsightedness, which is caused by a shortened eyeball. 157

hypnosis an induced state of consciousness in which one person responds to suggestions by another person for alterations in perception, thinking, and behavior. 212

hypochondriasis a somatoform disorder in which the person interprets the slightest physical changes as evidence of a serious illness. 490

hypothalamus a forebrain structure that helps to regulate aspects of motivation and emotion, including eating, drinking, sexual behavior, body temperature, and stress responses, through its effects on the pituitary gland and the autonomic nervous system. 83

hypothesis a testable prediction about the relationship between two or more events or characteristics. 35

iconic memory visual sensory memory, which lasts up to about a second. 274

id in Freud's theory, the part of the personality that contains inborn biological drives and that seeks immediate gratification. 443

identity versus role confusion Erikson's developmental stage in which success is achieved by establishing a sense of personal identity. 132

illusory contours the perception of edges that do not actually exist, as though they were the outlines of real objects. 166

implicit memory recollection of previous experiences demonstrated through behavior, rather than through conscious, intentional remembering. 280

impression management the deliberate attempt to control the impression that others form of us. 597

incentive an external stimulus that pulls an individual toward a goal. 378

incentive value the perceived rewards that accompany success in a particular area. 399

incongruity theory the theory that humor is amusing when it brings together incompatible ideas in a surprising outcome that violates one's expectations. 422

independent variable a variable manipulated by the experimenter to determine its effect on another, dependent, variable. 47

industrial/organizational psychology the field that applies psychological principles to improve productivity in businesses, industries, and government agencies. 22

industry versus inferiority Erikson's developmental stage in which success is achieved by developing a sense of competency. 122

infancy the period that extends from birth through 2 years of age. 115

inferential statistics statistics used to determine whether changes in a dependent variable are caused by an independent variable. 56, 650

information-processing model the view that the processing of memories involves encoding, storage, and retrieval. 274

initiating structure the leadership characteristic of defining the roles of the leader and the subordinates in order to achieve the group's formal goals. 668

initiative versus guilt Erikson's developmental stage in which success is achieved by behaving in a spontaneous but socially appropriate way. 122

insanity a legal term attesting that a person is not responsible for his or her own actions, including criminal behavior. 509

insight an approach to problem solving that depends on mental manipulation of information rather than overt trial and error, and produces sudden solutions to problems. 315

insomnia chronic difficulty in either falling asleep or staying asleep. 206

instinct a relatively complex, inherited behavior pattern characteristic of a species. 376

instinctive drift the reversion of animals to behaviors characteristic of their species even when being reinforced for performing other behaviors. 259

instrumental conditioning a form of learning in which a behavior becomes more or less probable, depending on its consequences. 246

instrumentality the extent to which an individual believes that attaining a particular outcome will lead to other positively valued outcomes. 664

integrity versus despair Erikson's developmental stage in which success is achieved by reflecting back on a meaningful life. 140

intelligence the global capacity to act purposefully, to think rationally, and to deal effectively with the environment. 346

intelligence quotient (IQ) 1. originally, the ratio of mental age to chronological age; that is, MA/CA × 100. 2. today, the score on an intelligence test, calculated by comparing a person's performance to norms for her or his age group. 349

intelligence test a test that assesses overall mental ability. 347

interference theory the theory that forgetting results from some memories' interfering with the ability to remember other memories. 287

internal validity the extent to which changes in a dependent variable can be attributed to one or more independent variables rather than to a confounding variable. 48

interneuron a neuron that conveys messages between neurons in the brain or spinal cord. 68

interval scale a scale of measurement that indicates the exact magnitude of scores, but not their ratio to one another. 641

intimacy versus isolation Erikson's developmental stage in which success is achieved by establishing a relationship with a strong sense of emotional attachment and personal commitment. 137

intrinsic motivation the desire to perform a behavior for its own sake. 400

introvert a person who is socially reserved and prefers to pay attention to his or her private mental experiences. 449

in vivo desensitization a form of counterconditioning that trains the client to maintain a state of relaxation in the presence of anxiety-inducing stimuli. 525

iris the donut-shaped band of muscles behind the cornea that gives the eye its color and controls the size of the pupil. 156

James-Lange theory the theory that specific patterns of physiological changes evoke specific emotional experiences. 423

job analysis defining a job in terms of the tasks and duties involved and the requirements needed to perform it. 658

job description a written statement of what a job entails and how and why it is done. 658

just noticeable difference (JND) Weber and Fechner's term for the difference threshold. 154

kinesthetic sense the sense that provides information about the position of the joints, the degree of tension in the muscles, and the movement of the arms and legs. 185

language a formal system of communication involving symbols—whether spoken, written, or gestured—and rules for combining them. 326

latency stage in Freud's theory, the stage, between age 5 and puberty, during which there is little psychosexual development. 446

latent content Sigmund Freud's term for the true, though disguised, meaning of a dream. 209

latent learning learning that occurs without the reinforcement of overt behavior. 261

law of effect Edward Thorndike's principle that a behavior followed by a satisfying state of affairs is strengthened and a behavior followed by an annoying state of affairs is weakened. 245

lay psychology psychological beliefs based on common sense or folk wisdom. 32

learned helplessness a feeling of futility caused by the belief that one has little or no control over events in one's life, which might make one stop trying and develop feelings of depression. 257, 571

learning a relatively permanent change in knowledge or behavior resulting from experience. 236

leniency the tendency to rate too positively. 662

lens the transparent structure behind the pupil that focuses light onto the retina. 157

levels of processing theory the theory that the "depth" at which we process information determines how well it is encoded, stored, and retrieved. 279

libido Freud's term for the sexual energy of the id. 446

limbic system a group of forebrain structures that promote the survival of the individual and, as a result, the continuation of the species by their influence on emotion, motivation, and memory. 83

line graph a graph used to plot data showing the relationship between independent an dependent variables in an experiment. 645

linguistic relativity hypothesis Whorf's hypothesis that one's perception of the world is molded by one's language. 334

link method a mnemonic device that involves connecting, in sequence, images of items to be memorized, to make them easier to recall. 295

logical concept a concept formed by identifying the specific features possessed by all things that the concept applies to. 311

logotherapy a form of existential therapy, developed by Victor Frankl, that helps the client find meaning in life. 534

longitudinal research a research design in which the same group of subjects is tested or observed repeatedly over a period of time. 111

long-term memory the stage of memory that can store a virtually unlimited amount of information relatively permanently. 273

loudness perception the subjective experience of the intensity of a sound, which corresponds most closely to the amplitude of the sound waves composing it. 177

LSD a hallucinogen derived from a fungus that grows on rye grain. 223

lucid dreaming the ability to be aware that one is dreaming and to direct one's dreams. 209

magnetic resonance imaging (MRI) a brain-scanning technique that relies on strong magnetic fields to construct computer-generated images of the brain or body. 87

maintenance rehearsal repeating information to oneself to keep it in short-term memory. 277

major depression a mood disorder marked by depression so intense and prolonged that the person may be unable to function in everyday life. 494

mania a mood disorder marked by euphoria, hyperactivity, grandiose ideas, annoying talkativeness, unrealistic optimism, and inflated self-esteem. 497

manifest content Sigmund Freud's term for the verbally reported dream. 209

massed practice cramming the memorization of information or the learning of a motor skill into one session. 293

maturation the sequential unfolding of inherited predispositions in physical and motor development. 106

mean the arithmetic average of a set of scores. 53, 646

mean length of utterance (MLU) the average length of spoken statements, used as a measure of language development in children. 331

measurement the use of numbers to represent events or characteristics. 38

measure of central tendency a statistic that represents the "typical" score in a set of scores. 53

measure of variability a statistic describing the degree of dispersion in a set of scores. 54

median the middle score in a set of scores that have been ordered from lowest to highest. 53, 646

meditation a procedure that uses mental exercises to achieve a highly focused state of consciousness. 217

medulla oblongata (medulla) a hindbrain structure that regulates breathing, heart rate, blood pressure, and other life functions. 80

memory the process by which information is acquired, stored in the brain, later retrieved, and eventually possibly forgotten. 272

menarche the beginning of menstruation, usually occurring between the ages of 11 and 13. 131

mental giftedness intellectual superiority marked by an IQ above 130 and exceptionally high scores on achievement tests in specific subjects, such as mathematics. 356

mental retardation intellectual deficiency marked by an IQ below 70 and difficulties performing in everyday life. 353

mental set a tendency to use a particular problem-solving strategy that has succeeded in the past but that may interfere with solving a problem requiring a new strategy. 317

mental telepathy the alleged ability to perceive the thoughts of others without any sensory contact with them. 187

meta-analysis a technique that combines the results of many similar studies to determine the size and consistency of the effect of a particular kind of independent variable. 56

method of loci a mnemonic device in which items to be recalled are associated with landmarks in a familiar place and then recalled during a mental walk from one landmark to another. 294

method of savings the assessment of memory by comparing the time or number of trials needed to memorize a given amount of information and the time or number of trials needed to memorize it again at a later time. 284

mnemonic devices techniques for organizing information to be memorized to make it easier to remember. 294

mode the score that occurs most frequently in a set of scores. 53, 645

monocular cues depth perception cues that require input from only one eye. 168

mood disorder a psychological disorder marked by prolonged periods of extreme depression or elation, often unrelated to the person's current situation. 494

moon illusion the misperception that the moon is larger when it is at the horizon than when it is overhead. 171

moral therapy an approach to therapy, developed by Philippe Pinel, that provided mental patients with humane treatment. 519

morpheme the smallest meaningful unit of language. 328

motivation the psychological processes that arouse, direct, and maintain behavior toward a goal. 376

motor cortex the area of the frontal lobes that controls specific voluntary body movements. 84

motor neuron a neuron that sends messages from the central nervous system to smooth muscles, cardiac muscle, or skeletal muscles. 68

myelin a white fatty substance that forms sheaths around certain axons and increases the speed of neural impulses. 71

myopia visual nearsightedness, which is caused by an elongated eyeball. 157

narcolepsy a condition in which an awake person suffers from repeated, sudden, and irresistible REM sleep attacks. 206

nativism the philosophical position that heredity provides individuals with inborn knowledge and abilities. 5

natural concept a concept, typically formed through everyday experience, whose members possess some, but not all, of a common set of features. 312

naturalistic observation the recording of the behavior of subjects in their natural environments, with little or no intervention by the researcher. 40

need a motivated state caused by physiological deprivation, such as a lack of food or water. 377

negative correlation a correlation between two variables in which the variables tend to change in opposite directions. 46

negative reinforcement in operant conditioning, an increase in the probability of a behavior that is followed by the removal of an aversive stimulus. 251

negative skew a graph that has scores bunching up toward the positive end of the abscissa. 643

negative state relief theory the theory that we engage in prosocial behavior to relieve our own state of emotional distress at another's plight. 623

neglect syndrome a disorder, caused by damage to a parietal lobe, in which the individual acts as though the side of her or his world opposite to the damaged lobe does not exist. 66

neodissociation theory the theory that hypnosis induces a dissociated state of consciousness. 215

nerve a bundle of axons that conveys information to or from the central nervous system. 67

nerve deafness hearing loss caused by damage to the hair cells of the basilar membrane or the axons of the auditory nerve. 177

nervous system the chief means of communication in the body; the

system of neurons, along which messages are transmitted. 67

neural grafting the transplantation of brain tissue or, in some cases, adrenal gland tissue into the brain or spinal cord to restore functions lost because of brain damage. 92

neural plasticity the ability of the brain to alter its neuronal pathways. 91

neuron a cell specialized for the transmission of information in the nervous system. 67

neurosis a general category, no longer widely used, that comprises psychological disorders associated with maladaptive attempts to deal with anxiety but with relatively good contact with reality. 482

neurotransmitters chemicals secreted by neurons that provide the means of synaptic transmission. 72

nicotine a stimulant used to regulate physical and mental arousal. 222

nightmare a frightening REM dream. 208

night terror a frightening NREM experience, common in childhood, in which the individual may suddenly sit up, let out a bloodcurdling scream, speak incoherently, and quickly fall back to sleep, yet usually fails to recall it on awakening. 208

nominal scale a scale of measurement that places objects, individuals, or characteristics into categories. 641

norm a score, based on the test performances of large numbers of subjects, that is used as a standard for assessing the performances of test takers. 44

normal curve a bell-shaped graph representing a hypothetical frequency distribution for a given characteristic. 648

normative commitment a felt obligation to stay with an organization. 667

NREM sleep the stages of sleep not associated with rapid eye movements and marked by relatively little dreaming. 201

null hypothesis the prediction that the independent variable will have no effect on the dependent variable in an experiment. 651

obedience following orders given by an authority. 619

obesity a body weight more than 20 percent above the norm for one's height and build. 381

object permanence the realization that objects exist even when they are no longer visible. 119

observational learning learning a behavior by observing the consequences that others receive for performing it. 261

obsessive-compulsive disorder an anxiety disorder in which the person has recurrent, intrusive thoughts (obsessions) and recurrent urges to perform ritualistic actions (compulsions). 490

occipital lobe a lobe of the cerebral cortex responsible for processing vision. 86

Oedipus complex in Freud's theory, a conflict, during the phallic stage, between the child's sexual desire for the parent of the opposite sex and fear of punishment from the same-sex parent. 446

olfaction the sense of smell, which detects molecules carried in the air. 179

operant conditioning B. F. Skinner's term for instrumental conditioning, a form of learning in which a behavior becomes more or less probable, depending on its consequences. 246

operational definition the definition of behaviors or qualities in terms of the procedures used to measure them. 38

opiates depressant drugs, derived from opium, used to relieve pain or to induce a euphoric state of consciousness. 221

opponent-process theory of emotion the theory that the brain counteracts a strong positive or negative emotion by evoking an opposite emotional response. 427

opponent-process theory of vision the theory that color vision depends on red-green, blue-yellow, and black-white opponent processes in the brain. 163

optic chiasm the point under the frontal lobes at which some axons from each of the optic nerves cross over to the opposite side of the brain. 159

optic nerve the nerve, formed from the axons of ganglion cells, that carries visual impulses from the retina to the brain. 157

oral stage in Freud's theory, the stage of personality development, between birth and age 1 year, during which the infant gains pleasure from oral activities and faces a conflict over weaning. 446

ordinal scale a scale of measurement that indicates the relative, but not exact, magnitude of scores. 641

otolith organs the vestibular organs that detect horizontal or vertical linear movement of the head. 186

ovaries the female gonads, which secrete hormones that regulate the development of the female reproductive system and secondary sex characteristics. 78

overextension the tendency to apply a word to more objects or actions than it actually represents. 330

overjustification theory the theory that an extrinsic reward will decrease intrinsic motivation when a person attributes her or his performance to that reward. 401

overlearning studying material beyond the point of initial mastery. 293

overregularization the application of a grammatical rule without making necessary exceptions to it. 331

panic disorder an anxiety disorder marked by sudden, unexpected attacks of overwhelming anxiety, often associated with the fear of dying or "losing one's mind." 487

parallel processing the processing of different information simultaneously. 326

paranoid schizophrenia a type of schizophrenia marked by hallucinations, delusions, suspiciousness, and argumentativeness. 503

paraphilia a way of obtaining sexual gratification that violates legal or cultural norms concerning proper sex objects and sexual practices. 387

parapsychology the study of extrasensory perception, psychokinesis, and related phenomena. 187

parasympathetic nervous system the division of the autonomic nervous system that calms the body and serves maintenance functions. 67

parietal lobe a lobe of the cerebral cortex responsible for processing body sensations and perceiving spatial relations. 85

Parkinson's disease a degenerative disease of the dopamine pathway from the substantia nigra, which causes marked disturbances in motor behavior. 74

partial schedule of reinforcement a schedule of reinforcement that reinforces some, but not all, instances of a desired response. 249

participant modeling a form of social learning therapy in which the client learns to perform more-adaptive behaviors by first observing the therapist model the desired behaviors. 527

passionate love love characterized by intense emotional arousal and sexual feelings. 603

Pearson's product-moment correlation perhaps the most commonly used correlational statistic. 650

pegword method a mnemonic device that involves associating items to be recalled with objects that rhyme with the numbers 1, 2, 3, and so on, to make the items easier to recall. 295

percentile the score at or below which a particular percentage of scores fall. 649

perception the process that organizes sensations into meaningful patterns. 152

perception without awareness the unconscious perception of stimuli that normally exceed the absolute threshold but fall outside our focus of attention. 225

performance appraisal systematic review, evaluation, and feedback regarding an employee's job performance. 661

peripheral nervous system the division of the nervous system, composed of the nerves, that conveys sensory information to the central nervous system and motor commands from the central nervous system to the skeletal muscles and internal organs. 67

personal construct a hypothesis about social reality that is held by a person. 461

personality an individual's unique, relatively consistent pattern of thinking, feeling, and behaving. 442

personality disorder a psychological disorder characterized by enduring, inflexible, maladaptive patterns of behavior. 507

personality psychology the field that focuses on factors accounting for the differences in behavior and enduring personal characteristics among individuals. 21

personal unconscious in Jung's theory, the individual's own unconscious mind, which contains repressed memories. 448

person-centered therapy a type of humanistic therapy, developed by Carl Rogers, that helps clients find their own answers to their problems. 531

person perception the process of making judgments about the personal characteristics of others. 597

persuasion the attempt to influence the attitudes of other people. 606

phallic stage in Freud's theory, the stage of personality development, between ages 3 and 5, during which the child gains pleasure from the genitals and must resolve the Oedipus complex. 446

phase advance shortening the sleep-wake cycle, as occurs when traveling from west to east. 199

phase delay lengthening the sleep-wake cycle, as occurs when traveling from east to west. 200

phenomenological psychology a branch of humanistic psychology primarily concerned with the study of subjective mental experience. 17

phenotype the overt expression of an individual's genetic inheritance, which may also show the influence of the environment. 109

phenylketonuria (PKU) a hereditary enzyme deficiency that, if left untreated in the infant, causes mental retardation. 355

pheromones odorous chemicals secreted by an animal that affect the behavior of other animals. 180

phi phenomenon apparent motion caused by the presentation of different visual stimuli in rapid succession. 172

phobia an anxiety disorder marked by excessive or inappropriate fear. 487

phoneme the smallest unit of sound in a language. 328

phonology the study of the sounds that compose languages. 328

photopigments chemicals, including rhodopsin and iodopsin, that enable the rods and cones to generate neural impulses. 160

phrenology a discredited technique for determining intellectual abilities and personality traits by examining the bumps and depressions of the skull. 89

physiological reactivity the extent to which a person displays increases in heart rate, blood pressure, stress hormone secretion, and other physiological activity in response to stressors. 570

pie graph a graph that represents data as percentages of a pie. 643

pineal gland an endocrine gland that secretes a hormone that has a general tranquilizing effect on the body and that helps regulate biological rhythms. 199

pitch perception the subjective experience of the highness or lowness of a sound, which corresponds most closely to the frequency of the sound waves that compose it. 176

pituitary gland an endocrine gland that regulates many of the other endocrine glands by secreting hormones that affect the secretion of their hormones. 76

placebo an inactive substance that may induce some of the effects of the drug for which it has been substituted. 51, 184

place theory the theory of pitch perception that assumes that hair cells at particular points on the basilar membrane are maximally responsive to sound waves of particular frequencies. 176

pleasure principle the process by which the id seeks immediate gratification of its impulses. 443

polygraph test the "lie detector" test, which assesses lying by measuring changing patterns of physiological arousal in response to particular questions. 434

pons a hindbrain structure that regulates the sleep-wake cycle. 81

population a group of individuals who share certain characteristics. 43

pornography sexually explicit material intended to incite sexual arousal. 630

positive correlation a correlation in which variables tend to change values in the same direction. 46

positive reinforcement in operant conditioning, an increase in the probability of a behavior that is followed by a desirable consequence. 246

positive skew a graph that has scores bunching up toward the negative end of the abscissa. 643

positron-emission tomography (PET) a brain-scanning technique that produces color-coded pictures showing the relative activity of different brain areas. 87

postconventional level in Kohlberg's theory, the level of moral reasoning characterized by concern with obeying mutually agreed upon laws and by the need to uphold human dignity. 128

posthypnotic suggestions suggestions directing subjects to carry out particular behaviors or to have particular experiences after leaving hypnosis. 214

posttraumatic stress disorder a syndrome of physical and psychological symptoms that appears as a delayed response after exposure to an extremely emotionally distressing event. 562

pragmatics the relationship between language and its social context. 329

precognition the alleged ability to perceive events in the future. 188

preconscious mind the level of consciousness that contains feelings and memories that we are unaware of at the moment but can become aware of at will. 229

preconventional level in Kohlberg's theory, the level of moral reasoning characterized by concern with the consequences that behavior has for oneself. 128

predictors tests that measure the traits an employee needs in order to be successful at a job. 659

prejudice an attitude, usually negative, toward others, based on their membership in particular groups. 610

Premack principle the principle that a more probable behavior can be used as a reinforcer for a less probable one. 246

preoperational stage the Piagetian stage, extending from 2 to 7 years of age, during which the child's use of language becomes more sophisticated but the child has difficulty with the logical mental manipulation of information. 119

presentism an approach to history that studies the past in the context of current beliefs and knowledge. 4

pressure the emotional state induced when one is confronted by personal responsibilities that tax one's abilities. 559

primary cortical areas regions of the cerebral cortex that serve motor or sensory functions. 84

primary reinforcer in operant conditioning, an unlearned reinforcer, which satisfies a biological need such as air, food, or water. 246

proactive interference the process by which old memories interfere with the ability to remember new memories. 287

problem solving the thought process by which an individual overcomes obstacles to reach a goal. 313

procedural memory the long-term memory system that contains memories of how to perform particular actions or skills. 279

programmed instruction a step-by-step approach, based on operant conditioning, in which the learner proceeds at his or her own pace through more and more difficult material and receives immediate knowledge of the results of each response. 256

progressive relaxation a stress-reducing procedure that involves the successive tensing and relaxing of each of the major muscle groups of the body. 575

projective test a Freudian personality test based on the assumption that individuals project their unconscious feelings when responding to ambiguous stimuli. 450

prosocial behavior behavior that helps others in need. 622

prosopagnosia the inability to recognize faces, which is typically caused by damage to a region of the temporal and occipital lobes. 91

prototype the best representative of a concept. 312

psychiatry the field of medicine that diagnoses and treats psychological disorders by using medical or psychological forms of therapy. 22

psychic determinism the Freudian assumption that all human behavior is influenced by unconscious motives. 14

psychoactive drugs chemicals that induce changes in mood, thinking, perception, and behavior by affecting neuronal activity in the brain. 219

psychoanalysis 1. the early school of psychology that emphasized the importance of unconscious causes of behavior. 2. a type of psychotherapy, developed by Sigmund Freud, aimed at uncovering the unconscious causes of psychological disorders. 13, 521

psychoanalytic perspective the psychological viewpoint that is descended from psychoanalysis, but which places less emphasis on biological motives and more emphasis on the importance of interpersonal relationships. 16

psychodrama a form of psychoanalytic group therapy, developed by Jacob Moreno, that aims at achieving insight and catharsis through acting out real-life situations. 535

psychogenic amnesia a dissociative disorder marked by the inability to recall personally significant memories. 492

psychogenic fugue a dissociative disorder marked by the memory loss characteristic of psychogenic amnesia, the loss of one's identity, and fleeing from one's home. 492

psychokinesis (PK) the alleged ability to control objects with the mind alone. 188

psychological hardiness a personality characteristic—marked by feelings of commitment, challenge, and control—that promotes resistance to stress. 572

psychological test a formal sample of a person's behavior, whether written or performed. 44

psychology the science of behavior and mental processes. 4

psychoneuroimmunology the interdisciplinary field that studies the relationship between psychological factors and physical illness. 566

psychopathology the study of psychological disorders. 478

psychophysics the study of the relationship between the physical characteristics of stimuli and the conscious psychological experiences they produce. 8, 152

psychosis a general category, no longer widely used, that comprises severe psychological disorders associated with thought disturbances, bizarre behavior, severe disruption of social relations, and relatively poor contact with reality. 482

psychosurgery the treatment of psychological disorders by destroying brain tissue. 539

psychotherapy the treatment of psychological disorders through psychological, as opposed to biomedical, means, generally involving verbal interaction with a professional therapist. 520

puberty the period of rapid physical change that occurs during adolescence, including the development of the ability to reproduce sexually. 130

punishment in operant conditioning, the process by which an aversive stimulus decreases the probability of a response that precedes it. 252

pupil the opening at the center of the iris that controls how much light enters the eye. 156

random assignment the assignment of subjects to experimental and control conditions so that each subject is as likely to be assigned to one condition as to another. 49

random sampling the selection of a sample from a population so that each member of the population has an equal chance of being included. 43

range a statistic representing the difference between the highest and lowest scores in a set of scores. 54, 646

rank-ordering rating individuals according to their standing in comparison to one another, from best to worst. 661

rating scale any scale used for rating people or items. 661

rational-emotive behavior therapy (R-E-B-T) a type of cognitive therapy, developed by Albert Ellis, that treats psychological disorders by forcing the client to give up irrational beliefs. 529

rationalism the philosophical position that true knowledge comes through correct reasoning. 5

ratio scale a scale of measurement that indicates the ratio of scores to one another. 641

reality principle the process by which the ego directs the individual to express sexual and aggressive impulses in socially acceptable ways. 444

reciprocal determinism Bandura's belief that personality traits, environmental factors, and overt behavior affect each other. 458

reflex an automatic, involuntary motor response to sensory stimulation. 68

relaxation response a variation of transcendental meditation in which the individual may repeat a sound other than a mantra. 218

release theory the theory that humor is amusing when it relieves one's sexual or aggressive anxiety. 422

reliability the extent to which a test gives consistent results. 45

REM sleep the stage of sleep associated with rapid eye movements, an active brain-wave pattern, and vivid dreams. 201

replication the repetition of a research study, usually with some alterations in its subjects, methods, or setting, to determine whether the principles derived from that study hold up under similar circumstances. 35

representativeness heuristic in decision making, the assumption that a small sample is representative of its population. 323

repression the process by which emotionally threatening experiences are banished from the conscious mind to the unconscious mind. 288

resting potential the electrical charge of a neuron when it is not firing a neural impulse. 70

reticular formation a diffuse network of neurons, extending from the hindbrain through the midbrain and into the forebrain, that helps maintain vigilance and an optimal level of brain arousal. 81

retina the light-sensitive inner membrane of the eye that contains the receptor cells for vision. 157

retrieval the recovery of information from memory. 273

retroactive interference the process by which new memories interfere with the ability to remember old memories. 287

rods receptor cells of the retina that play an important role in night vision and peripheral vision. 157

saccadic movements continuous small darting movements of the eyes that bring new portions of scenes into focus on the foveae. 159

sample a group of subjects selected from a population. 43

scatter plot a graph of a correlational relationship. 650

schema a mental model incorporating the characteristics of particular persons, objects, events, or situations. 118

schema theory the theory that long-term memories are stored as parts of schemas, which are cognitive structures that organize knowledge about events or objects. 281

schizophrenia a class of psychological disorders characterized by grossly impaired social, emotional, cognitive, and perceptual functioning. 501

school psychology the field that applies psychological principles to improving the academic performance and social behavior of students in elementary, junior high, and high schools. 22

scientific method a source of knowledge based on the assumption that knowledge comes from the objective, systematic observation and measurement of particular variables and the events they affect. 35

scientific paradigm a model that determines the appropriate goals, methods, and subject matter of a science. 15

sclera the tough, white outer membrane of the eye. 156

seasonal affective disorder a mood disorder in which severe depression arises during a particular season, usually the winter. 494

secondary reinforcer in operant conditioning, a neutral stimulus that becomes reinforcing after being associated with a primary reinforcer. 246

self-actualization in Maslow's theory, the individual's predisposition to try to fulfill her or his potentials. 462

self-efficacy in Bandura's theory, a person's belief that she or he can perform behaviors that are necessary to bring about a desired outcome. 458

self-fulfilling prophecy the tendency for one person's expectations to influence another person to behave in accordance with them. 599

self-perception theory Daryl Bem's theory that when we are unsure of our attitudes we infer them from our own behavior. 610

self-serving bias the tendency to make dispositional attributions for one's successes and situational attributions for one's failures. 597

semanticity the characteristic of language marked by the use of symbols to convey thoughts in a meaningful way. 326

semantic memory the subsystem of declarative memory that contains general information about the world. 280

semantic network theory the theory that memories are stored as nodes interconnected by links that represent their relationships. 281

semantics the study of how language conveys meaning. 329

semicircular canals the curved vestibular organs of the inner ear that detect movements of the head in any direction. 186

sensate focusing a sex therapy technique that at first involves non-genital caressing and gradually progresses to sexual intercourse. 390

sensation the process that detects stimuli from the body or surroundings. 152

sensation seeking the extent to which an individual seeks sensory stimulation. 397

sensorimotor stage the Piagetian stage, from birth through the second year, during which the infant learns to coordinate sensory experiences and motor behavior. 118

sensory adaptation the tendency of the sensory receptors to respond less and less to a constant stimulus. 154

sensory deprivation the prolonged withdrawal of normal levels of external stimulation. 396

sensory memory the stage of memory that briefly, for at most a few seconds, stores exact replicas of sensations. 273

sensory neuron a neuron that sends messages from sensory receptors to the central nervous system. 68

sensory receptors specialized cells that detect stimuli and convert their energy into neural impulses. 152

sensory transduction the process by which sensory receptors convert stimuli into neural impulses. 152

serial-position effect the superiority of immediate recall for items at the beginning and end of a list. 284

serial processing the processing of information one step at a time. 326

set point a specific body weight that the brain tries to maintain through the regulation of diet, activity, and metabolism. 381

sexual dysfunction a chronic problem at one or more phases of the sexual response cycle. 390

sexual orientation one's sexual attraction toward persons of either one's own sex or the opposite sex. 391

sexual response cycle during sexual activity, the phases of excitement, plateau, orgasm, and resolution. 388

shape constancy the perceptual process that makes an object appear to maintain its normal shape regardless of the angle from which it is viewed. 170

shaping an operant conditioning procedure that involves the positive reinforcement of successive approximations of an initially improbable behavior to eventually bring about that behavior. 247

short-term memory the stage of memory that can store a few items of unrehearsed information for up to about 20 seconds. 273

signal-detection theory the theory holding that the detection of a stimulus depends on both the intensity of the stimulus and the physical and psychological state of the individual. 153

simple phobia a phobia of a specific object or situation. 487

size constancy the perceptual process that makes an object appear to remain the same size despite changes in the size of the image it casts on the retina. 169

skepticism an attitude that doubts all claims not supported by solid research evidence. 34

Skinner box an enclosure that contains a bar or key that can be pressed to obtain food or water, and that is used to study operant conditioning in rats, pigeons, or other small animals. 246

skin senses the senses of touch, temperature, and pain. 182

sleep apnea a condition in which a person awakens repeatedly in order to breathe. 206

smooth pursuit movements eye movements that track objects. 158

social attachment a strong emotional relationship between an infant and a caregiver. 121

social clock the major events that typically occur at certain times in the typical life cycle in a given culture. 130

social cognition the process of perceiving, interpreting, and predicting social behavior. 594

social-comparison theory the theory that happiness is the result of estimating that one's life circumstances are more favorable than those of others. 420

social-cultural perspective the psychological viewpoint that favors the scientific study of human behavior in its social-cultural context. 18

social facilitation the improvement in a person's task performance when in the presence of other people. 615

social learning theory a theory of gender-role development that assumes that people learn social behaviors mainly through observation and mental processing of information. 125, 262

social loafing a decrease in the individual effort exerted by group members when working together on a task. 616

social phobia a phobia of situations that involve public scrutiny. 488

social psychology the field that studies how people affect one another's thoughts, feelings, and behaviors. 21, 594

social schema a cognitive structure comprising the presumed characteristics of a role, an event, a person, or a group. 598

social-skills training a form of behavioral group therapy that improves the client's social relationships by improving her or his interpersonal skills. 535

social support the availability of support from other people, whether tangible or intangible. 573

sociobiology the study of the hereditary basis of human and animal social behavior. 377

soma the cell body, the neuron's control center. 68

somatic nervous system the division of the peripheral nervous system that sends messages from the sensory organs to the central nervous system and messages from the central nervous system to the skeletal muscles. 67

somatoform disorder a psychological disorder characterized by physical symptoms in the absence of disease or injury. 490

somatosensory cortex the area of the parietal lobes that processes information from sensory receptors in the skin. 85, 182

somatotype a person's body type, whether ectomorphic (thin), mesomorphic (muscular), or endomorphic (fat). 466

sound localization the process by which the individual determines the location of a sound. 178

spatial frequency filter theory the theory that visual perception depends on the detection and analysis of variations in patterns of light and dark. 166

spinal cord the structure of the central nervous system that is located in the spine and plays a role in body reflexes and in communicating information between the brain and the peripheral nervous system. 67

split-brain research research on hemispheric specialization that studies individuals whose corpus callosum has been severed. 99

spontaneous recovery 1. in classical conditioning, the reappearance after a period of time of a conditioned response that has been subjected to extinction. 2. in operant conditioning, the reappearance after a period of time of a behavior that has been subjected to extinction. 240, 252

spontaneous remission the improvement of some persons with psychological disorders without their undergoing formal therapy. 548

sport psychology the field that applies psychological principles to help amateur and professional athletes improve their performance. 22, 401

SQ3R method a study technique in which the student surveys, questions, reads, recites, and reviews course material. 292

standard deviation a statistic representing the degree of dispersion of a set of scores around their mean. 54, 648

standardization 1. a procedure assuring that a test is administered and scored in a consistent manner. 2. a procedure for establishing test norms by giving a test to large samples of people who are representative of those for whom the test is designed. 44

state-dependent memory the tendency for recall to be best when one's emotional or physiological state is the same during the recall of a memory as it was during the encoding of that memory. 291

statistical significance a low probability (usually less than 5 percent) that the results of a research study are due to chance factors rather than to the independent variable. 56, 653

statistics mathematical techniques used to summarize research data or to determine whether the data support the researcher's hypothesis. 35, 640

stereochemical theory the theory of olfaction and gustation that assumes that receptors are stimulated by molecules of particular sizes and shapes. 180

stereotype a social schema that incorporates characteristics, which may be positive or negative, supposedly shared by almost all members of a group. 598

stimulants psychoactive drugs that increase central nervous system activity. 222

stimulus discrimination in classical conditioning, giving a conditioned response to the conditioned stimulus but not to stimuli similar to it. 240

stimulus generalization in classical conditioning, giving a conditioned response to stimuli similar to the conditioned stimulus. 239

storage the retention of information in memory. 273

stress the physiological response of the body to physical and psychological demands. 558

stress-inoculation training a type of cognitive therapy, developed by Donald Meichenbaum, that helps clients change their pessimistic thinking into more positive thinking when in stressful situations. 527

stressor a physical or psychological demand that induces physiological adjustment. 558

structuralism the early school of psychology that sought to identify the components of the conscious mind. 9

subject bias the tendency of people who know they are subjects in a study to behave in a way other than they normally would. 49

subliminal perception the unconscious perception of stimuli that are too weak to exceed the absolute threshold for detection. 226

subliminal psychodynamic activation the use of subliminal messages to stimulate unconscious fantasies. 229

substantia nigra a midbrain structure that promotes smooth voluntary body movements. 81

superego in Freud's theory, the part of the personality that acts as a moral guide telling us what we should and should not do. 444

surface structure the word arrangements used to express thoughts. 329

survey a set of questions related to a particular topic of interest administered to a sample of people through an interview or questionnaire. 42

sympathetic nervous system the division of the autonomic nervous system that arouses the body to prepare it for action. 67

synapse the junction between a neuron and a gland, muscle, sensory organ, or another neuron. 72

synaptic transmission the conveying of a neural impulse between a neuron and a gland, muscle, sensory organ, or another neuron. 72

synesthesia the process in which an individual experiences sensations in one sensory modality that are characteristic of another. 224

syntax the rules that govern the acceptable arrangement of words in phrases and sentences. 328

systematic desensitization a form of counterconditioning that trains the client to maintain a state of relaxation in the presence of imagined anxiety-inducing stimuli. 524

taste buds structures lining the grooves of the tongue that contain the taste receptor cells. 181

tectum a midbrain structure that mediates reflexive responses to visual and auditory stimuli. 81

telegraphic speech speech marked by reliance on nouns and verbs, while omitting other parts of speech, including articles and prepositions. 330

temperament a person's characteristic emotional state, first apparent in early infancy and possibly inborn. 466

temporal lobe a lobe of the cerebral cortex responsible for processing hearing. 86

teratogen a noxious substance, such as a virus or drug, that can cause prenatal defects. 114

testes the male gonads, which secrete hormones that regulate the development of the male reproductive system and secondary sex characteristics. 78

thalamus a forebrain structure that acts as a sensory relay station for taste, body, visual, and auditory sensations. 82

theory an integrated set of statements that summarizes and explains research findings, and from which research hypotheses may be derived. 38

theory of multiple intelligences Howard Gardner's theory of intelligence, which assumes that the brain has evolved separate systems for seven kinds of intelligence. 362

thinking the mental manipulation of words and images, as in concept formation, problem solving, and decision making. 310

timbre the subjective experience that identifies a particular sound and corresponds most closely to the mixture of sound waves composing it. 177

tip-of-the-tongue phenomenon the inability to recall information that one knows has been stored in long-term memory. 289

token economy an operant conditioning procedure that uses tokens as positive reinforcers in programs designed to promote desirable behaviors, with the tokens later used to purchase desired items or privileges. 256, 526

trait a relatively enduring, cross-situationally consistent personality characteristic that is inferred from a person's behavior. 453

transactional analysis (TA) a form of psychoanalytic group therapy, developed by Eric Berne, that helps clients change their immature or inappropriate ways of relating to other people. 535

transcendental meditation (TM) a form of meditation in which the individual relaxes and repeats a sound called a mantra for two 20-minute periods a day. 218

transcutaneous electrical nerve stimulation (TENS) the use of electrical stimulation of sites on the body to provide pain relief, apparently by stimulating the release of endorphins. 184

transfer bringing back to the job environment what was learned in training. 664

transformational grammar the rules by which languages generate surface structures from deep structures, and deep structures from surface structures. 329

transitive inference the application of previously learned relationships to infer new relationships. 120

transsexualism a condition in which a genetic male or female has the gender identity of the opposite sex. 391

trephining an ancient technique in which sharp stones were used to chip holes in the skull, possibly to let out evil spirits that supposedly caused abnormal behavior. 518

trial and error an approach to problem solving in which the individual tries one possible solution after another until one works. 314

triarchic theory of intelligence Robert Sternberg's theory of intelligence, which assumes that there are three main kinds of intelligence: componential, experiential, and contextual. 361

trichromatic theory the theory that color vision depends on the relative degree of stimulation of red, green, and blue receptors. 162

trust versus mistrust Erikson's developmental stage in which success is achieved by having a secure social attachment with a caregiver. 121

t test a statistical technique used to determine whether the difference between two sets of scores is statistically significant. 653

turnover the ratio of new employees to established employees. 666

two-factor theory the theory that emotional experience is the outcome of physiological arousal and the attribution of a cause for that arousal. 429

tympanic membrane the eardrum; a membrane separating the outer and middle ears that vibrates in response to sound waves that strike it. 175

Type A behavior a syndrome—marked by impatience, hostility, and extreme competitiveness—that is associated with the development of coronary heart disease. 586

unconditioned response (UCR) in classical conditioning, an unlearned, automatic response to a particular unconditioned stimulus. 237

unconditioned stimulus (UCS) in classical conditioning, a stimulus that automatically elicits a particular unconditioned response. 237

unconscious mind the level of consciousness that contains thoughts, feelings, and memories that influence us without our awareness and that we cannot become aware of at will. 229

underextension the tendency to apply a word to fewer objects or actions than it actually represents. 330

undifferentiated schizophrenia a catchall category for cases that do not fall neatly into any single kind of schizophrenia. 503

valance how much value an individual places on a particular outcome. 664

validation a process that determines whether tests are accurate predictors of job success. 659

validity the extent to which a test measures what it is supposed to measure. 45

variable an event, behavior, or characteristic that has two or more values. 46

variable-interval schedule of reinforcement a partial schedule of reinforcement that provides reinforcement for the first desired response made after varying, unpredictable lengths of time. 250

variable-ratio schedule of reinforcement a partial schedule of reinforcement that provides reinforcement after varying, unpredictable numbers of desired responses. 250

variance a measure based on the average deviation of a set of scores from their group mean. 54, 647

vestibular sense the sense that provides information about one's position in space and helps in the maintenance of balance. 186

visible spectrum the portion of the electromagnetic spectrum that we commonly call light. 155

vision the sense that detects objects by the light reflected from them into the eyes. 155

visual cortex the area of the occipital lobes that processes visual input. 86, 160

visual illusion a misperception of physical reality usually caused by the misapplication of visual cues. 171

volley theory the theory of pitch perception that assumes that sound waves of particular frequencies induce auditory neurons to fire in volleys, with one volley following another. 177

Wada test a technique in which a cerebral hemisphere is anesthetized to assess hemispheric specialization. 97

Weber's law the principle that the amount of change in stimulation needed to produce a just noticeable difference is a constant proportion of the original stimulus. 154

Wernicke's area the region of the temporal lobe responsible for the comprehension of speech. 88

Yerkes-Dodson law the principle that the relationship between arousal and performance is best represented by an inverted U-shaped curve. 394

Abella, R., & Heslin, R. (1989). Appraisal processes, coping, and the regulation of stress-related emotions in a college examination. *Basic and Applied Social Psychology, 10*, 311–327.

Abelson, R. P. (1981). Psychological status of the script concept. *American Psychologist, 36*, 715–729.

Abend, S. M. (1993). An inquiry into the fate of the transference in psychoanalysis. *Journal of the American Psychoanalytic Association, 41*, 627–651.

Abernethy, E. M. (1940). The effect of changed environmental conditions upon the results of college examinations. *Journal of Psychology, 10*, 293–301.

Abrams, S. (1995). False memory syndrome versus total repression. *Journal of Psychiatry and Law, 23*, 283-293.

Abramson, L. Y., Seligman, M. E. P., & Teasdale, J. D. (1978). Learned helplessness in humans: Critique and reformulation. *Journal of Abnormal Psychology, 87*, 49–74.

Absher, J. R., & Cummings, J. L. (1995). Neurobehavioral examination of frontal lobe functions. *Aphasiology, 9*, 181–192.

Acker, M., & Davis, M. H. (1992). Intimacy, passion and commitment in adult romantic relationships: A test of the triangular theory of love. *Journal of Social and Personal Relationships, 9*, 21–50.

Adams, P. J., Katz, R. C., Beauchamp, K., & Cohen, E. (1993). Body dissatisfaction, eating disorders, and depression: A developmental perspective. *Journal of Child and Family Studies, 2*, 37–46.

Adams, P. R., & Adams, G. R. (1984). Mount Saint Helen's ashfall: Evidence for a disaster stress reaction. *American Psychologist, 39*, 252–260.

Adams, R. J., Courage, M. L., & Mercer, M. E. (1994). Systematic measurement of human neonatal color vision. *Vision Research, 34*, 1691–1701.

Adams, W. L., Garry, P. J., Rhyne, R., & Hunt, W. C. (1990). Alcohol intake in the healthy elderly: Changes with age in a cross-sectional and longitudinal study. *Journal of the American Geriatrics Society, 38*, 211–216.

Adelmann, P. K., & Zajonc, R. B. (1989). Facial efference and the experience of emotion. *Annual Review of Psychology, 40*, 249–289.

Adelson, B. (1984). When novices surpass experts: The difficulty of a task may increase with expertise. *Journal of Experimental Psychology: Learning, Memory, and Cognition, 10*, 483–495.

Ader, R., & Cohen, N. (1982). Behaviorally conditioned immunosuppression and murine systemic lupus erythematosus. *Science, 215*, 1534–1536.

Adler, A. (1927). *Understanding human nature*. New York: Greenberg.

Adler, K. A. (1994). Socialist influences on Alderian psychology. *Individual Psychology: Journal of Adlerian Theory, Research and Practice, 50*, 131–141.

Adler, T. (1989, November). Revision brings test "to the twenty-first century." *APA Monitor*, pp. 1, 6.

Adolphs, R., Tranel, D., Damasio, H., & Damasio, A. (1994). Impaired recognition of emotion in facial expressions following bilateral damage to the human amygdala. *Nature, 372*, 669–672.

Adorno, T. W., Frenkel-Brunswik, E., Levinson, D. J., & Sanford, R. N. (1950). *The authoritarian personality*. New York: Harper & Row.

Afnan, S. M. (1958/1980). *Avicenna: His life and works*. Westport, CT: Greenwood.

Aggleton, J. P. (1993). The contribution of the amygdala to normal and abnormal emotional states. *Trends in Neurosciences, 16*, 328–333.

Aggleton, J. P. (Ed.). (1992). *The amygdala: Neurobiological aspects of emotion, memory, and mental dysfunction*. New York: Wiley.

Aggleton, J. P., Kentridge, R. W., & Neave, N. J. (1993). Evidence for longevity differences between left handed and right handed men: An archival study of cricketers. *Journal of Epidemiology and Community Health, 47*, 206–209.

Aghajanian, G. K. (1994). Serotonin and the action of LSD in the brain. *Psychiatric Annals, 24*, 137–141.

Agmo, A., & Berendfeld, R. (1990). Reinforcing properties of ejaculation in the male rat: Role of opioids and dopamine. *Behavioral Neuroscience, 104*, 177–182.

Agnew, N. M., & Brown, J. L. (1989). Foundations for a model of knowing: I. Constructing reality. *Canadian Psychology, 30*, 152–167.

Agras, W. S. (1993). The diagnosis and treatment of panic disorder. *Annual Review of Medicine, 44*, 39–51.

Aguilar-Alonso, A. (1996). Personality and creativity. *Personality and Individual Differences, 21*, 959-969.

Aiken, L. R. (1982). *Psychological testing and assessment*. Boston: Allyn & Bacon.

Ainsworth, M. S. (1993). Attachment as related to mother-infant interaction. *Advances in Infant Research, 8*, 1–50.

Aisner, R., & Terkel, J. (1992). Ontogeny of pine cone opening behavior in the black rat, *Rattus rattus. Animal Behaviour, 44*, 327–336.

Akande, A. (1991). Perception of visual illusions in a sample of Nigerian children. *Perceptual and Motor Skills, 72*, 25–26.

Alba, J. W., & Hasher, L. (1983). Is memory schematic? *Psychological Bulletin, 93*, 203–231.

Albert, D. J., Walsh, M. L., & Jonik, R. H. (1993). Aggression in humans: What is its biological foundation? *Neuroscience and Biobehavioral Reviews, 17*, 405–425.

Alcock, J. E. (1991). On the importance of methodological skepticism. *New Ideas in Psychology, 9*, 151–155.

Aldag, R. J., & Fuller, S. R. (1993). Beyond fiasco: A reappraisal of the groupthink phenomenon and a new model of group decision processes. *Psychological Bulletin, 113*, 533–552.

Aldrich, M. S. (1992). Narcolepsy. *Neurology, 42*, 34–43.

Alexander, C. N., Robinson, P., & Rainforth, M. (1994). Treating and preventing alcohol, nicotine, and drug abuse through Transcendental Meditation: A review and statistical meta-analysis. *Alcoholism Treatment Quarterly, 11*, 13–87.

Alexander, C. N., Robinson, P., Orme-Johnson, D. W., & Schmeidler, R. H. (1994). The effects of transcendental meditation compared to other methods of relaxation and meditation in reducing risk factors, morbidity, and mortality. *Homeostasis in Health and Disease, 35*, 243–263.

Alexander, G. E., & Crutcher, M. D. (1990). Preparation for movement: Neural representations of intended direction in three motor areas of the monkey. *Journal of Neurophysiology, 64*, 133–150.

Alexander, L. B., Barber, J. P., Luborsky, L., & Crits-Christoph, P. (1993). On what bases do patients choose their therapists? *Journal of Psychotherapy Practice and Research, 2*, 135–146.

Alexander, P. E. (1993). Alprazolam-XR in the treatment of panic disorder: Results of a randomized, double-blind, fixed-dose, placebo-controlled multicenter study. *Psychiatric Annals, 23*, 14–18.

Alexopoulos, G. S., Inturrisi, C. E., Lipman, R., Frances, R., Haycox, J., Dougherty, J. H., & Rossier, J. (1983). Plasma immunoreactive beta-endorphin levels in depression: Effect of electroconvulsive therapy. *Archives of General Psychiatry, 40*, 181–183.

Alexy, B. B. (1991). Factors associated with participation or nonparticipation in a workplace wellness center. *Research in Nursing and Health, 14*, 33–40.

Algom, D., & Lubel, S. (1994). Psychophysics in the field: Perception and memory for labor pain. *Perception and Psychophysics, 55*, 133–141.

Allen, C. T., & Janiszewski, C. A. (1989). Assessing the role of contingency awareness in attitudinal conditioning with implications for advertising research. *Journal of Marketing Research, 26*, 30–43.

Allen, J. J., Iacono, W. G., Laravuso, J. J., & Dunn, L. A. (1995). An event-related potential investigation of posthypnotic recognition amnesia. Journal of Abnormal Psychology, 104, 421–430.

Allen, K. M., Blascovich, J., Tomaka, J., & Kelsey, R. M. (1991). Presence of human friends and pet dogs as moderators of autonomic responses to stress in women. *Journal of Personality and Social Psychology, 61*, 582–589.

Allen, M. (1993). Determining the persuasiveness of message sidedness: A prudent note about utilizing research summaries. *Western Journal of Communication, 57*, 98–103.

Allen, M. G. (1976). Twin studies of affective illness. *Archives of General Psychiatry, 33*, 1476–1478.

Allen, M. G. (1990). Group psychotherapy: Past, present, and future. *Psychiatric Annals, 20*, 358–361.

Allen, M., D'Alessio, D., & Brezgel, K. (1995). A meta-analysis summarizing the effects of pornography: II. Aggression after exposure. *Human Communication Research, 22*, 258–283.

Alliger, G. M., & Williams, K. J. (1993). Using signal-contingent experience sampling methodology to study work in the field: A discussion and illustration examining task perceptions and mood. *Personnel Psychology, 46*, 525–549.

Allport, F. H. (1920). The influence of the group upon association and thought. *Journal of Experimental Psychology, 3*, 159–182.

Allport, G. W. (1954). *The nature of prejudice*. Reading, MA: Addison-Wesley.

Allport, G. W. (1967). Autobiography. In E. G. Boring & G. Lindzey (Eds.), *A history of psychology in autobiography* (Vol. 5, pp. 1–25). New York: Appleton-Century-Crofts.

Aloise-Young, P. A., Graham, J. W., & Hansen, W. B. (1994). Peer influence on smoking initiation during early adolescence: A comparison of group members and group outsiders. *Journal of Applied Psychology, 79,* 281–287.

Alvarado, K. A., Templer, D. I., Bresler, C., & Thomas-Dobson, S. (1995). The relationship of religious variables to death depression and death anxiety. *Journal of Clinical Psychology, 51,* 202–204.

Amabile, T. M. (1985). Motivation and creativity effects of motivational orientation on creative writers. *Journal of Personality and Social Psychology, 48,* 393–399.

Amabile, T. M. (1989). *Growing up creative.* New York: Random House.

Amabile, T. M., Goldfarb, P., & Brackfield, S. C. (1990). Social influences on creativity: Evaluation, coaction, and surveillance. *Creativity Research Journal, 3,* 6–21.

Amato, P. R., & Keith, B. (1991). Parental divorce and the well-being of children: A meta-analysis. *Psychological Bulletin, 110,* 26–46.

Amemori, T., Ermakova, I. V., Buresova, O., & Zigova, T. (1989). Brain transplants enhance rather than reduce the impairment of spatial memory and olfaction in bulbectomized rats. *Behavioral Neuroscience, 103,* 61–70.

American Psychiatric Association. (1994). *Diagnostic and statistical manual of mental disorders* (4th ed.). Washington, DC: American Psychological Association.

Amir, S., & Stewart, J. (1996). Resetting of the circadian clock by a conditioned stimulus. *Nature, 379,* 542-545.

Amir, T. (1984). The Asch conformity effect: A study in Kuwait. *Social Behavior and Personality, 12,* 187–190.

Amirkhan, J. H., Risinger, R. T., & Swickert, R. J. (1995). Extraversion: A "hidden" personality factor in coping? *Journal of Personality, 63,* 189–212.

Amoore, J. E. (1963). Stereochemical theory of olfaction. *Nature, 198,* 271–277.

Anand, B. K., & Brobeck, J. R. (1951). Hypothalamic control of food intake in rats and cats. *Yale Journal of Biology and Medicine, 24,* 123–140.

Anastasi, A. (1958). Heredity, environment, and the question "How?" *American Psychologist, 65,* 197–208.

Anastasi, A. (1972). The cultivation of diversity. *American Psychologist, 27,* 1091–1099.

Anastasi, A. (1985). Psychological testing: Basic concepts and common misconceptions. In A. M. Rogers & C. J. Scheirer (Eds.), *The G. Stanley Hall Lecture Series* (Vol. 5, pp. 87–120). Washington, DC: American Psychological Association.

Anazonwu, C. O. (1995). Locus of control, academic self-concept, and attribution of responsibility for performance in statistics. *Psychological Reports, 77,* 367–370.

Andersen, A. E., & DiDomenico, L. (1992). Diet vs. shape content of popular male and female magazines: A dose-response relationship to the incidence of eating disorders? *International Journal of Eating Disorders, 11,* 283–287.

Andersen, A. E., Woodward, P. J., Spalder, A., & Koss, M. (1993). Body size and shape characteristics of personal ("in search of") ads. *International Journal of Eating Disorders, 14,* 111–115.

Andersen, B. L., Kiecolt-Glaser, J. K., & Glaser, R. A (1994). A biobehavioral model of cancer stress and disease course. *American Psychologist, 49,* 389–404.

Andersen, S. M., & Ross, L. (1984). Self-knowledge and social inference: I. The impact of cognitive/affective and behavioral data. *Journal of Personality and Social Psychology, 46,* 280–293.

Anderson, D. C., Crowell, C. R., Doman, M., & Howard, G. S. (1988). Performance posting, goal setting, and activity-contingent praise as applied to a university hockey team. *Journal of Applied Psychology, 73,* 87–95.

Anderson, J. R. (1983). Retrieval of information from long-term memory. *Science, 220,* 25–30.

Anderson, K. J., Revelle, W., & Lynch, M. J. (1989). Caffeine, impulsivity, and memory scanning: A comparison of two explanations for the Yerkes-Dodson effect. *Motivation and Emotion, 13,* 1–20.

Anderson, K. W., & Skidmore, J. R. (1995). Empirical analysis of factors in depressive cognition: The Cognitive Triad Inventory. *Journal of Clinical Psychology, 51,* 603–609.

Anderson, R. A., Baron, R. S., & Logan, H. (1991). Distraction, control, and dental stress. *Journal of Applied Social Psychology, 21,* 156–171.

Anderson, S. W., & Rizzo, M. (1994). Hallucinations following occipital lobe damage: The pathological activation of visual representations. *Journal of Clinical and Experimental Neuropsychology, 16,* 651–663.

Andrasik, F. (1990). Psychologic and behavioral aspects of chronic headache. *Neurologic Clinics, 8,* 961–976.

Andre, T. (1979). Does answering higher-level questions while reading facilitate productive learning? *Review of Educational Research, 49,* 280–318.

Andreasen, N. C., Arndt, S., Alliger, R., & Miller, D. (1995). Symptoms of schizophrenia: Methods, meanings, and mechanisms. *Archives of General Psychiatry, 52,* 341–351.

Andreasen, N. C., & Flaum, M. (1991). Schizophrenia: The characteristic symptoms. *Schizophrenia Bulletin, 17,* 27–49.

Andreasen, N. C., Flaum, M., Swayze, V. W., & Tyrrell, G. (1990). Positive and negative symptoms in schizophrenia: A critical reappraisal. *Archives of General Psychiatry, 47,* 615–621.

Andreassen, P. B. (1988). Explaining the price-volume relationship: The difference between price changes and changing prices. *Organizational Behavior and Human Decision Processes, 41,* 371–389.

Angst, J. (1993). Today's perspective on Kraepelin's nosology of endogenous psychoses. *European Archives of Psychiatry and Clinical Neuroscience, 243,* 164–170.

Anisfeld, M. (1991). Neonatal imitation. *Developmental Review, 11,* 60–97.

Ansbacher, H. L. (1990). Alfred Adler's influence on the three leading cofounders of humanistic psychology. *Journal of Humanistic Psychology, 30,* 45–53.

Anschutz, L., Camp, C. J., Markley, R. P., & Kramer, J. J. (1985). Maintenance and generalization of mnemonics for grocery shopping by older adults. *Experimental Aging Research, 11,* 157–160.

Anshel, M. H. (1995). Examining social loafing among elite female rowers as a function of task duration and mood. *Journal of Sport Behavior, 18,* 39–49.

Antoni, M. H., LaPerriere, A., Schneiderman, N., & Fletcher, M. A. (1991). Stress and immunity in individuals at risk for AIDS. *Stress Medicine, 7,* 35–44.

Ape language. (1981). *Science, 211,* 86–88.

Appelbaum, P. S., & Greer, A. (1994). Who's on trial? Multiple personalities and the insanity defense. *Hospital and Community Psychiatry, 45,* 965–966.

Appelbaum, P. S., & Gutheil, T. G. (1980). The Boston State Hospital case: "Involuntary mind control," the Constitution, and the "right to rot." *American Journal of Psychiatry, 137,* 720–723.

Ardila, A., Montanes, P., & Gempeler, J. (1986). Echoic memory and language perception. *Brain and Language, 29,* 134–140.

Arena, J. G., Bruno, G. M., Hannah, S. L., & Meador, K. J. (1995). A comparison of frontal electromyographic biofeedback training, and progressive muscle relaxation therapy in the treatment of tension headache. *Headache, 35,* 411-419.

Ariel, R., & Sadeh, M. (1996). Congenital visual agnosia and prosopagnosia in a child: A case report. *Cortex, 32,* 221-240.

Arnett, P. A., Howland, E. W., Smith, S. S., & Newman, J. P. (1993). Autonomic responsivity during passive avoidance in incarcerated psychopaths. *Personality and Individual Differences, 14,* 173–184.

Arntz, A., Lavy, E., Van den Berg, G., & Van Rijsoort, S. (1993). Negative beliefs of spider phobics: A psychometric evaluation of the Spider Phobia Beliefs Questionnaire. *Advances in Behaviour Research and Therapy, 15,* 257–277.

Aronson, S. C., Black, J. E., McDougle, C. J., & Scanley, B. E. (1995). Serotonergic mechanisms of cocaine effects in humans. *Psychopharmacology, 119,* 179–185.

Arterberry, M., Yonas, A., & Benson, A. S. (1989). Self–produced locomotion and the development of responsiveness to linear perspective and texture gradients. *Developmental Psychology, 25,* 976–982.

Arthur, W., Jr., & Graziano, W. G. (1996). The five-factor model, conscientiousness, and driving accident involvement. *Journal of Personality, 64,* 593–618.

Ary, D. V., Tildesley, E., Hops, H., & Andrews, J. A. (1993). The influence of parent, sibling, and peer modeling and attitudes on adolescent use of alcohol. *International Journal of the Addictions, 28,* 853–880.

Asbjornsen, A. E., & Hugdahl, K. (1995). Attentional effects in dichotic listening. *Brain and Language, 49,* 189-201.

Asch, S. E. (1955, November). Opinions and social pressure. *Scientific American,* pp. 31–35.

Aseltine, R. H., Jr. (1996). Pathways linking parental divorce with adolescent depression. *Journal of Health and Social Behavior, 37,* 133-148.

Aserinsky, E., & Kleitman, N. (1953). Regularly occurring periods of eye motility and concomitant phenomena during sleep. *Science, 118,* 273–274.

Aserinsky, E., Lynch, J. A., Mack, M. E., Tzankoff, S. P., & Hurn, E. (1985). Comparison of eye motion in wakefulness and REM sleep. *Psychophysiology, 22,* 1–10.

Ash, D. W., & Holding, D. H. (1990). Backward versus forward chaining in the acquisition of a keyboard skill. *Human Factors, 32,* 139–146.

Aslin, R. N., & Smith, L. B. (1988). Perceptual development. *Annual Review of Psychology, 39,* 435–474.

Asscheman, H., & Gorren, L. J. (1992). Hormone treatment in transsexuals. *Journal of Psychology and Human Sexuality, 5,* 39–54.

Astin, G. R., & Garber, H. (1982). *The rise and fall of national test scores.* New York: Academic Press.

Atkinson, D. R. (1983). Ethnic similarity in counseling psychology: A review of research. *Counseling Psychologist, 11,* 79–92.

Atkinson, J. W. (1981). Studying personality in the context of an advanced motivational psychology. *American Psychologist, 36,* 117–128.

Atkinson, J. W., & Litwin, G. H. (1960). Achievement motive and test anxiety concerned as motive to approach success and motive to avoid failure. *Journal of Abnormal and Social Psychology, 60,* 52–63.

Attie, I., & Brooks-Gunn, J. (1989). Development of eating problems in adolescent girls: A longitudinal study. *Developmental Psychology, 25,* 70–79.

Atwood, G. E., & Tomkins, S. S. (1976). On the subjectivity of personality theory. *Journal of the History of the Behavioral Sciences, 12,* 166–177.

Aydin, G. (1993). Is helpless explanatory style related to illness? *Psychology: A Journal of Human Behavior, 30,* 27–31.

Aydin, G., & Aydin, O. (1992). Learned helplessness and explanatory style in Turkish samples. *Journal of Social Psychology, 132,* 117–119.

Ayllon, T., & Azrin, N. H. (1968). *The token economy: A motivational system for therapy and rehabilitation.* New York: Appleton-Century-Crofts.

Babad, E., Bernieri, F., & Rosenthal, R. (1989). When less information is more informative: Diagnosing teacher expectations from brief samples of behavior. *British Journal of Educational Psychology, 59,* 281–295.

Bachiocco, V., Gentili, A., & Bortoluzzi, L. (1995). b-endorphin and "overt" pain measures in children. *Journal of Pain and Symptom Management, 10,* 1-3.

Bach-y-Rita, P. (1990). Brain plasticity as a basis for recovery of function in humans. *Neuropsychologia, 28,* 547–554.

Bachorowski, J. A., & Owren, M. J. (1995). Vocal expression of emotion: Acoustic properties of speech are associated with emotional intensity and context. *Psychological Science, 6,* 219–224.

Baddeley, A. D. (1982). Domains of recollection. *Psychological Review, 89,* 708–729.

Baddeley, A. D. (1994). The magical number seven: Still magic after all these years? *Psychological Review, 101,* 353–356.

Baer, J. (1996). The effects of task-specific divergent-thinking training. *Journal of Creative Behavior, 30,* 183-187.

Baer, L., Rauch, S. L., Ballantine, T., & Martuza, R. (1995). Cingulotomy for intractable obsessive-compulsive disorder: Prospective long-term follow-up of 18 patients. *Archives of General Psychiatry, 52,* 384–392.

Bahill, A. T., & LaRitz, T. (1984). Why can't batters keep their eyes on the ball? *American Scientist, 72,* 249–253.

Bahrick, H. P. (1984). Semantic memory content in permastore: Fifty years of memory for Spanish learned in school. *Journal of Experimental Psychology: General, 113,* 1–29.

Bahrick, H. P., Bahrick, P. O., & Wittlinger, R. P. (1975). Fifty years of memory for names and faces: A cross-sectional approach. *Journal of Experimental Psychology: General, 104,* 54–75.

Bahrick, H. P., Hall, L. K., & Berger, S. A. (1996). Accuracy and distortion in memory for high school grades. *Psychological Science, 7,* 265-271.

Bailey, J. M., Pillard, R. C., Neale, M. C., & Agyei, Y. (1993). Heritable factors influence sexual orientation in women. *Archives of general Psychiatry, 50,* 217–223.

Bailey, M. B., & Bailey, R. E. (1993). "Misbehavior": A case history. *American Psychologist, 48,* 1157–1158.

Baillargeon, R., & DeVos, J. (1991). Object permanence in young infants: Further evidence. *Child Development, 62,* 1227–1246.

Baird, J. C., & Wagner, M. (1982). The moon illusion: I. How high is the sky? *Journal of Experimental Psychology: General, 111,* 296–303.

Baird, J. C., Wagner, M., & Fuld, K. (1990). A simple but powerful theory of the moon illusion. *Journal of Experimental Psychology: Human Perception and Performance, 16,* 675–677.

Baisden, R. H. (1995). Therapeutic uses for neural grafts: Progress slowed but not abandoned. *Behavioral and Brain Sciences, 18,* 47-48, 90-107.

Baker, G. H. B. (1987). Psychological factors and immunity. *Journal of Psychosomatic Research, 31,* 1–10.

Baker, J. P. (1994). Outcomes of lithium discontinuation: A meta-analysis. *Lithium, 5,* 187–192.

Balaban, M. T. (1995). Affective influences on startle in five-month-old infants: Reactions to facial expressions of emotion. *Child Development, 66,* 28–36.

Balanovski, E., & Taylor, J. G. (1978). Can electromagnetism account for extrasensory phenomena? *Nature, 276,* 64–67.

Baldwin, B. A., de la Riva, C., & Ebenezer, I. S. (1990). Effects of intracerebroventricular injection of dynorphin, leumorphin, and a neoendorphin on operant feeding in pigs. *Physiology and Behavior, 48,* 821–824.

Baldwin, D., & Rudge, S. (1995). The role of serotonin in depression and anxiety. *International Clinical Psychopharmacology, 9,* 41–45.

Baldwin, E. (1993). The case for animal research in psychology. *Journal of Social Issues, 49,* 121–131.

Baldwin, M. W. (1954). Subjective measurements in television. *American Psychologist, 9,* 231–234.

Bales, J. (1986, September). Pastoral counseling. *APA Monitor,* p. 16.

Bales, J. (1988, August). Pre-work polygraph ban signed by Reagan. *APA Monitor,* p. 5.

Bales, J. (1988, March). Court rules no duty to commit in N.C. *APA Monitor,* p. 20.

Ball, C., Mann, L., & Stamm, C. (1994). Decision-making abilities of intellectually gifted and non-gifted children. *Australian Journal of Psychology, 46,* 13–20.

Ball, S. G., Baer, L., & Otto, M. W. (1996). Symptom subtypes of obsessive-compulsive disorder in behavioral treatment studies: A quantitative review. *Behaviour Research and Therapy, 34,* 47–51.

Bandura, A. (1965). Influence of model's reinforcement contingencies on the acquisition of imitative responses. *Journal of Personality and Social Psychology, 1,* 589–595.

Bandura, A. (1977). *Social learning theory.* Englewood Cliffs, NJ: Prentice Hall.

Bandura, A. (1982). Self-efficacy mechanism in human agency. *American Psychologist, 37,* 122–147.

Bandura, A. (1982). The psychology of chance encounters and life paths. *American Psychologist, 37,* 747–755.

Bandura, A. (1986). *Social foundations of thought and action: A social-cognitive theory.* Englewood Cliffs, NJ: Prentice Hall.

Bandura, A. (1989). Human agency in social cognitive theory. *American Psychologist, 44,* 1175–1184.

Bandura, A., Blanchard, E. B., & Ritter, B. (1969). The relative efficacy of desensitization and modeling approaches for inducing behavioral, affective, and attitudinal changes. *Journal of Personality and Social Psychology, 13,* 173–199.

Bandura, A., Reese, L., & Adams, N. E. (1982). Microanalysis of action and fear arousal as a function of differential levels of perceived self-efficacy. *Journal of Personality and Social Psychology, 43,* 5–21.

Bandura, A., Ross, D., & Ross, S. A. (1963). Imitation of film-mediated aggressive models. *Journal of Abnormal and Social Psychology, 66,* 3–11.

Bandura, A., & Schunk, D. H. (1981). Cultivating competence, self-efficacy, and intrinsic interest through proximal self-motivation. *Journal of Personality and Social Psychology, 41,* 586–598.

Banks, S. M., & Kerns, R. D. (1996). Explaining high rates of depression in chronic pain: A diathesis-stree framework. *Psychological Bulletin, 119,* 95–110.

Barber, N. (1994). Reducing fear of the laboratory rat: A participant modeling approach. *Teaching of Psychology, 21,* 228–230.

Barbut, M. (1993). Comments on a pseudo-mathematical model in social psychology. *European Journal of Social Psychology, 23,* 203–210.

Bard, P. (1934). On emotional experience after decortication with some remarks on theoretical views. *Psychological Review, 41,* 309–329.

Bargh, J. A. (1992). The ecology of automaticity: Toward establishing the conditions needed to produce automatic processing effects. *American Journal of Psychology, 105,* 181–199.

Baribeau-Braun, J., Picton, T. W., & Gosselin, J. Y. (1983). Schizophrenia: A neuropsychological evaluation of abnormal information processing. *Science, 219,* 874–876.

Barlow, D. H. (1986). Causes of sexual dysfunction: The role of anxiety and cognitive interference. *Journal of Consulting and Clinical Psychology, 54,* 140–148.

Barnes, M. L., & Rosenthal, R. (1985). Interpersonal effects of experimenter attractiveness, attire, and gender. *Journal of Personality and Social Psychology, 48,* 435–446.

Barnett, M. A., Quackenbush, S. W., & Sinisi, C. S. (1995). The role of critical experiences in moral development: Implications for justice and care orientations. *Basic and Applied Social Psychology, 17,* 137–152.

Barnett, S. K. (1984). The mentor role: A task of generativity. *Journal of Human Behavior and Learning, 1,* 15–18.

Barrett, P. T., Daum, I., & Eysenck, H. J. (1990). Sensory nerve conduction and intelligence: A methodological study. *Journal of Psychophysiology, 4,* 1–13.

Barrick, M. R., & Mount, M. K. (1991). The Big Five personality dimensions and job performance: A meta-analysis. *Personnel Psychology, 40,* 1–26.

Barrick, M. R., Mount, M. K., & Strauss, J. P. (1993). Conscientiousness and performance of sales representatives: Test of the mediating effects of goal setting. *Journal of Applied Psychology, 78,* 715–722.

Barron, F., & Harrington, D. M. (1981). Creativity, intelligence, and personality. *Annual Review of Psychology, 32,* 439–476.

Barsky, A. J., Coeytaux, R. R., Sarnie, M. K., & Cleary, P. D. (1993). Hypochondriacal patients' beliefs about good health. *American Journal of Psychiatry, 150,* 1085–1089.

Bartholomew, D. J. (1995). Spearman and the original and development of factor analysis. *British Journal of Mathematical and Statistical Psychology, 48,* 211-220.

Bartlett, F. C. (1932). *Remembering: A study in experimental and social psychology.* Cambridge, England: Cambridge University Press.

Bartlik, B. D., Kaplan, P., & Kaplan, H. S. (1995). Psychostimulants apparently reverse sexual dysfunction secondary to selective serotonin re-uptake inhibitors. *Journal of Sex and Marital Therapy, 21,* 264–271.

Bartoshuk, L. M. (1991). Sensory factors in eating behavior. *Bulletin of the Psychonomic Society, 29,* 250–255.

Bartoshuk, L. M., & Beauchamp, G. K. (1994). Chemical senses. *Annual Review of Psychology, 45,* 419–449.

Bartoshuk, L. M., Cain, W. S., & Pfaffmann, C. (1985). Taste and olfaction. In G. A. Kimble & K. Schlesinger (Eds.), *Topics in the history of psychology* (Vol. 1, pp. 221–260). Hillsdale, NJ: Erlbaum.

Bartusiak, M. (1980, November). Beeper man. *Discover,* p. 57.

Basadur, M. S., Wakabayashi, M., & Takai, J. (1992). Training effects on the divergent thinking attitudes of Japanese managers. *International Journal of Intercultural Relations, 16,* 329–345.

Bashore, T. R., & Rapp, P. E. (1993). Are there alternatives to traditional polygraph procedures? *Psychological Bulletin, 113,* 3–22.

Baskett, L. M. (1984). Ordinal position differences in children's family interactions. *Developmental Psychology, 20,* 1026–1031.

Basmajian, J. V. (1963). Control and training of individual motor units. *Science, 141,* 440–441.

Basmajian, J. V. (1988). Research foundations of EMG biofeedback in rehabilitation. *Biofeedback and Self-Regulation, 13,* 275–298.

Bass (1985a). *Leadership and performance beyond expectations.* New York: Free Press.

Bass (1985b). Leadership: Good, better, best. *Organizational Dynamics, 13,* 26–40.

Bassuk, E. L. (1984, July). The homelessness problem. *Scientific American,* pp. 40–45.

Bastiani, A. M., Rao, R., Weltzin, T., & Kaye, W. H. (1995). Perfectionism in anorixia nervosa. *International Journal of Eating Disorders, 17,* 147–152.

Basu, A. K. (1982). Comparison of four intelligence tests with culturally disadvantaged children. *International Newsletter: Educational Evaluation and Research, 21,* 18–19.

Batson, C. D., Batson, J. G., Griffitt, C. A., Barrientos, S., Brandt, J. R., Sprengelmeyer, P., & Bayly, M. J. (1989). Negative-state relief and the empathy-altruism hypothesis. *Journal of Personality and Social Psychology, 56,* 922–933.

Batson, C. D., Bolen, M. H., Cross, J. A., & Neuringer-Benefiel, H. E. (1986). Where is the altruism in the altruistic personality? *Journal of Personality and Social Psychology, 50,* 212–220.

Batson, C. D., & Shaw, L. L. (1991). Evidence for altruism: Toward a pluralism of prosocial motives. *Psychological Inquiry, 2*, 107–122.

Batson, C. D., & Weeks, J. L. (1996). Mood effects of unsuccessful helping: Another test of the empathy-altruism hypothesis. *Personality and Social Psychology Bulletin, 22*, 148–157.

Baum, A., Grunberg, N. E., & Singer, J. E. (1992). Biochemical measurements in the study of emotion. *Psychological Science, 3*, 56–60.

Baumeister, R. F. (1982). A self-presentational view of social phenomena. *Psychological Bulletin, 91*, 3–26.

Baumeister, R. F. (1984). Choking under pressure: Self-consciousness and paradoxical effects of incentives on skillful performance. *Journal of Personality and Social Psychology, 46*, 610–620.

Baumeister, R. F. (1988). Should we stop studying sex differences altogether? *American Psychologist, 43*, 1092–1095.

Baumeister, R. F. (1990). Suicide as escape from self. *Psychological Review, 97*, 90–113.

Baumeister, R. F., & Steinhilber, A. (1984). Paradoxical effects of supportive audiences on performance under pressure: The home field disadvantage in sports championships. *Journal of Personality and Social Psychology, 47*, 85–93.

Baumler, G. (1994). On the validity of the Yerkes-Dodson law. *Studia Psychologica, 36*, 205–209.

Baumrind, D. (1964). Some thoughts on ethics of research: After reading Milgram's "Behavioral Study of Obedience." *American Psychologist, 19*, 421–423.

Baumrind, D. (1983). Rejoinder to Lewis's reinterpretation of parental firm control effects: Are authoritative families really harmonious? *Psychological Bulletin, 94*, 132–142.

Baumrind, D. (1985). Research using intentional deception: Ethical issues revisited. *American Psychologist, 40*, 165–174.

Baxter, L. R. (1991). PET studies of cerebral function in major depression and obsessive-compulsive disorder: The emerging prefrontal cortex consensus. *Annals of Clinical Psychiatry, 3*, 103–109.

Bayley, N. (1955). On the growth of intelligence. *American Psychologist, 10*, 805–818.

Bayton, J. A. (1975). Francis Sumner, Max Meenes, and the training of black psychologists. *American Psychologist, 30*, 185–186.

Beail, N., & Parker, S. (1991). Group fixed-role therapy: A clinical application. *International Journal of Personal Construct Psychology, 4*, 85–95.

Beal, C. R., Schmitt, K. L., & Dekle, D. J. (1995). Eyewitness identification of children: Effects of absolute judgments, nonverbal response options, and event encoding. *Law and Human Behavior, 19*, 197–216.

Beatty, W. W. (1984). Discriminating drunkenness: A replication. *Bulletin of the Psychonomic Society, 22*, 431–432.

Beck, A. T. (1967). *Depression: Clinical, experimental and theoretical aspects.* New York: Harper & Row.

Beck, A. T., Rush, A. J., Shaw, B. F., & Emery, G. (1979). *Cognitive therapy of depression.* New York: Guilford.

Becker, J. B., Curran, E. J., & Freed, W. J. (1990). Adrenal medulla graft induced recovery of function in an animal model of Parkinson's disease: Possible mechanisms of action. *Canadian Journal of Psychology, 44*, 293–310.

Beckham, J. C., Keefe, F. J., Caldwell, D. S., & Brown, C. J. (1991). Biofeedback as a means to alter electromyographic activity in a total knee replacement patient. *Biofeedback and Self-Regulation, 16*, 23–35.

Becona, E., & Garcia, M. P. (1993). Nicotine fading and smokeholding methods to smoking cessation. *Psychological Reports, 73*, 779–786.

Beeghley, L., & Sellers, C. (1986). Adolescents and sex: A structural theory of premarital sex in the United States. *Deviant Behavior, 7*, 313–336.

Beers, C. W. (1908/1970). *A mind that found itself.* New York: Doubleday.

Beh, H. C. (1994). A survey of daytime napping in an elderly Australian population. *Australian Journal of Psychology, 46*, 100–106.

Behrend, D. A. (1988). Overextensions in early language comprehension: Evidence from a signal detection approach. *Journal of Child Language, 15*, 63–75.

Beiser, M., Shore, J. H., Peters, R., & Tatum, W. (1985). Does community care for the mentally ill make a difference? A tale of two cities. *American Journal of Psychiatry, 142*, 1047–1052.

Békésy, G. von (1957, August). The ear. *Scientific American,* pp. 66–78.

Bekoff, M., Gruen, L., Townsend, S. E., & Rollin, B. E. (1992). Animals in science: Some areas revisited. *Animal Behaviour, 44*, 473–484.

Belisle, M., Roskies, E., & Levesque, J. M. (1987). Improving adherence to physical activity. *Health Psychology, 6*, 159–172.

Bell, A. P., Weinberg, M. S., & Hammersmith, S. J. (1981). *Sexual preference: Its development in men and women.* Bloomington: Indiana University Press.

Bell, J. E., & Eisenberg, N. (1985). Life satisfaction in midlife childless and empty-nest men and women. *Lifestyles, 7*, 146–155.

Belmont, L., & Marolla, F. A. (1973). Birth order, family size, and intelligence. *Science, 182*, 1096–1101.

Belsky, J. (1988). The "effects" of infant day care reconsidered. *Early Childhood Research Quarterly, 3*, 235–272.

Belsky, J., & Pensky, E. (1988). Marital change across the transition to parenthood. *Marriage and Family Review, 12*, 133–156.

Bem, D. J. (1967). Self-perception: An alternative interpretation of cognitive dissonance phenomena. *Psychological Review, 74*, 183–200.

Bem, D. J., & Allen, A. (1974). On predicting some of the people some of the time: The search for cross-situational consistencies in behavior. *Psychological Review, 81*, 506–520.

Bem, D. J., & Honorton, C. (1994). Does psi exist? Replicable evidence for an anomalous process of information transfer. *Psychological Bulletin, 115*, 4–18.

Bem, S. L. (1981). Gender schema theory: A cognitive account of sex typing. *Psychological Review, 88*, 354–364.

Ben-Shlomo, Y., Smith, G. D., Shipley, M., & Marmot, M. G. (1993). Magnitude and causes of mortality differences between married and unmarried men. *Journal of Epidemiology and Community Health, 47*, 200-205.

Benbow, C. P. (1988). Sex differences in mathematical reasoning ability in intellectually talented preadolescents: Their nature, effect, and possible causes. *Behavioral and Brain Sciences, 11*, 169–232.

Benbow, C. P., Arjmand, O., & Walberg, H. J. (1991). Educational productivity predictors among mathematically talented students. *Journal of Educational Research, 84*, 215–223.

Benbow, C. P., & Stanley, J. C. (1983). Sex differences in mathematical reasoning ability: More facts. *Science, 222*, 1029–1031.

Bender, S. L., Ponton, L. E., Crittenden, M. R., & Word, C. O. (1995). For underprivileged children, standardized intelligence testing can do more harm than good: Reply. *Journal of Developmental and Behavioral Pediatrics, 16*, 428–430.

Benjamin, L. T., Durkin, M., Link, M., Vestal, M., & Acord, J. (1992). Wundt's American doctoral students. *American Psychologist, 47*, 123–131.

Benjamin, L. T., Jr. (1988). A history of teaching machines. *American Psychologist, 43*, 703–712.

Bennett, A.T.D., Cuthill, I. C., Partridge, J. C., & Maier, Erhard J. (1996). Ultraviolet vision and mate choice in zebra finches. *Nature, 380*, 433-435.

Bennett, T., Dittmar, C., & Raubach, S. (1991). Multiple sclerosis: Cognitive deficits and rehabilitation strategies. *Cognitive Rehabilitation, 9*, 18–23.

Bennett, W., & Gurin, J. (1982). *The dieter's dilemma.* New York: Basic Books.

Bensing, J. (1991). Doctor-patient communication and the quality of care. *Social Science and Medicine, 32*, 1301–1310.

Benson, H., Kornhaber, A., Kornhaber, C., & LeChanu, M. N. (1994). Increases in positive psychological characteristics with a new relaxation-response curriculum in high school students. *Journal of Research and Development in Education, 27*, 226–231.

Bentall, R. P. (1990). The illusion of reality: A review and integration of psychological research on hallucinations. *Psychological Bulletin, 107*, 82–95.

Bentall, R. P., & Pilgrim, D. (1993). Thomas Szasz, crazy talk and the myth of mental illness. *British Journal of Medical Psychology, 66*, 69–76.

Benton, D., Owens, D. S., & Parker, P. Y. (1994). Blood glucose influences memory and attention in young adults. *Neuropsychologia, 32*, 595–607.

Berenbaum, S. A., & Hines, M. (1992). Early androgens are related to childhood sex-typed toy preferences. *Psychological Science, 3*, 203–206.

Berenbaum, S. A., & Snyder, E. (1995). Early hormonal influences on childhood sex-typed activity and playmate preferences: Implications for the development of sexual orientation. *Developmental Psychology, 31*, 31–42.

Berg, J. H. (1984). Development of friendship between roommates. *Journal of Personality and Social Psychology, 46*, 346–356.

Berg, J. H., & McQuinn, R. D. (1986). Attraction and exchange in continuing and noncontinuing dating relationships. *Journal of Personality and Social Psychology, 50*, 942–952.

Berger, A. A. (1987). Humor: An introduction. *American Behavioral Scientist, 30*, 6–15.

Berger, R. E., & Persinger, M. A. (1991). Geophysical variables and behavior: LXVII. Quieter annual geomagnetic activity and larger effect size for experimental psi (ESP) studies over six decades. *Perceptual and Motor Skills, 73*, 1219–1223.

Berger, R. J., & Phillips, N. H. (1995). Energy conservation and sleep. *Behavioural Brain Research, 69*, 65-73.

Bergin, A. E., & Lambert, E. (1978). The evaluation of therapeutic outcome. In S. L. Garfield & A. E. Bergin (Eds.), *Handbook of psychotherapy and behavior change* (pp. 139–189). New York: Wiley.

Berko, J. (1958). The child's learning of English morphology. *Word, 14*, 150–177.

Berkowitz, L. (1974). Some determinants of impulsive aggression. *Psychological Review, 81*, 165–176.

Berkowitz, L. (1989). Frustration-aggression hypothesis: Examination and reformulation. *Psychological Bulletin, 106*, 59–73.

Berkowitz, L., & LePage, A. (1967). Weapons as aggression-eliciting stimuli. *Journal of Personality and Social Psychology, 7*, 202–207.

Berkowitz, M. W., Mueller, C. W., Schnell, S. V., & Padberg, U. (1986). Moral reasoning and judgments of aggression. *Journal of Personality and Social Psychology, 51*, 885–891.

Berman, S. M. W., & McCann, J. T. (1995). Defense mechanisms and personality disorders: An empirical test of Millon's theory. *Journal of Personality Assessment, 64*, 132–144.

Bermond, B., Fasotti, L., Nieuwenhuyse, B., & Schuerman, J. (1991). Spinal cord lesions, peripheral feedback, and intensities of emotional feelings. *Cognition and Emotion, 5*, 201–220.

Bernard, J. L. (1977). The significance for psychology of O'Connor v. Donaldson. *American Psychologist, 32*, 1085–1088.

Berndt, T. J. (1992). Friendship and friends' influence in adolescence. *Current Directions in Psychological Science, 1*, 156–159.

Berndt, T. J., & Hoyle, S. G. (1985). Stability and change in childhood and adolescent friendships. *Developmental Psychology, 21*, 1007–1015.

Berne, E. (1964). *Games people play*. New York: Grove.

Berninger, V. W. (1988). Development of operational thought without a normal sensorimotor stage. *Intelligence, 12,* 219–230.

Bernstein, I. L. (1978). Learned taste aversions in children receiving chemotherapy. *Science, 200,* 1302–1303.

Bernstein, I. L. (1991). Aversion conditioning in response to cancer and cancer treatment. *Clinical Psychology Review, 11,* 185–191.

Bernstein, J. J., & Goldberg, W. J. (1989). Graft-derived reafferentation of host spinal cord is not necessary for amelioration of lesion-induced deficits: Possible role of migrating grafted astrocytes. *Brain Research Bulletin, 22,* 139–146.

Bernstein, W. M., Stephan, W. G., & Davis, M. H. (1979). Explaining attributions for achievement: A path-analytic approach. *Journal of Personality and Social Psychology, 37,* 1810–1821.

Berquier, A., & Ashton, R. (1992). Characteristics of the frequent nightmare sufferer. *Journal of Abnormal Psychology, 101,* 246–250.

Berscheid, E., & Walster, E. (1974). A little bit about love. In T. L. Houston (Ed.), *Foundations of interpersonal attraction.* New York: Academic Press.

Bertelli, J. A., Orsal, D., & Mira, J. C. (1994). Median nerve neurotization by peripheral nerve grafts directly implanted into the spinal cord: Anatomical behavioural and electrophysiological evidences of sensorimotor recovery. *Brain Research, 644,* 150–159.

Bertenthal, B. I., Campos, J. J., & Kermoian, R. (1994). An epigenetic perspective on the development of self-produced locomotion and its consequences. *Current Directions in Psychological Science, 3,* 140–145.

Berti, G., & Berti, A. S. (1994). When an offspring dies: Logotherapy in bereavement groups. *International Forum for Logotherapy, 17,* 65–69.

Best, D. L., House, A. S., Barnard, A. E., & Spicker, B. S. (1994). Parent-child interactions in France, Germany, and Italy: The effects of gender and culture. *Journal of Cross Cultural Psychology, 25,* 181-193.

Beutler, L. E., & Consoli, A. J. (1993). Matching the therapist's interpersonal stance to clients' characteristics: Contributions from systematic eclectic psychotherapy. *Psychotherapy, 30,* 417–422.

Bexton, W. H., Heron, W., & Scott, T. H. (1954). Effects of decreased variation in the sensory environment. *Canadian Journal of Psychology, 8,* 70–76.

Bianchi, S. M. (1995). The changing demographic and socioeconomic characteristics of single parent families. *Marriage and Family Review, 20,* 71–97.

Bieliauskas, L. A., Counte, M. A., & Glandon, G. L. (1995). Inventorying stressing life events as related to health change in the elderly. *Stress Medicine, 11,* 93–103.

Binder, J. R., Rao, S. M., Hammeke, T. A., & Yetkin, F. Z. (1994). Functional magnetic resonance imaging of human auditory cortex. *Annals of Neurology, 35,* 662–672.

Birch, D. E. (1992). Duty to protect: Update and Canadian perspective. *Canadian Psychology, 33,* 94–104.

Birmaher, B., Rabin, B. S., Garcia, M. R., & Jain, U. (1994). Cellular immunity in depressed, conduct disorder, and normal adolescents: Role of adverse life events. *Journal of the American Academy of Child and Adolescent Psychiatry, 33,* 671–678.

Bishop, D. V. M. (1990). *Handedness and developmental disorder.* Oxford, England: Mac Keith Press.

Bjork, D. W. (1988). *William James: The center of his vision.* New York: Columbia University Press.

Bjork, E. L., & Cummings, E. M. (1984). Infant search errors: Stage of concept development or stage of memory development. *Memory and Cognition, 12,* 1–19.

Bjorklund, D. F., & Buchanan, J. J. (1989). Developmental and knowledge-base differences in the acquisition and extension of a memory strategy. *Journal of Experimental Child Psychology, 48,* 451–471.

Bjorkqvist, K., Nygren, T., Bjorklund, A.-C., & Bjorkqvist, S.-E. (1994). Testosterone intake and aggressiveness: Real effect or anticipation? *Aggressive Behavior, 20,* 17–26.

Black, D. W. (1982). Pathological laughter: A review of the literature. *Journal of Nervous and Mental Disease, 170,* 67–71.

Black, J. E., Isaacs, K. R., & Greenough, W. T. (1991). Usual vs. successful aging: Some notes on experiential factors. *Neurobiology of Aging, 12,* 325–328.

Blagrove, M., Alexander, C., & Horne, J. A. (1995). The effects of chronic sleep reduction on the performance of cognitive tasks sensitive to sleep deprivation. *Applied Cognitive Psychology, 9,* 21–40.

Blair, M. E., & Shimp, T. A. (1992). Consequences of an unpleasant experience with music: A second-order negative conditioning perspective. *Journal of Advertising, 21,* 35–43.

Blair, R. J. R., Jones, L., Clark, F., & Smith, M. (1995). Is the psychopath "morally insane"? *Personality and Individual Differences, 19,* 741–752.

Blakemore, C. (1977). *Mechanics of the mind.* New York: Cambridge University Press.

Blakemore, C., & Cooper, G. F. (1970). Development of the brain depends on the visual environment. *Nature, 228,* 477–478.

Blanchard, J. J., Kring, A. M., & Neale, J. M. (1994). Flat affect in schizophrenia: A test of neuropsychological models. *Schizophrenia Bulletin, 20,* 311–325.

Blaney, P. H. (1986). Affect and memory: A review. *Psychological Bulleting, 99,* 229–246.

Blankfield, R. P. (1991). Suggestion, relaxation, and hypnosis as adjuncts in the care of surgery patients: A review of the literature. *American Journal of Clinical Hypnosis, 33,* 172–186.

Blasco, R. D. (1994). Psychology and road safety. *Applied Psychology: An International Review, 43,* 313–322.

Blasi, A. (1980). Bridging moral cognition and moral action: A critical review of the literature. *Psychological Bulletin, 88,* 1–45.

Blaszczynski, A. P., & McConaghy, N. (1994). Antisocial personality disorder and pathological gambling. *Journal of Gambling Studies, 10,* 129–145.

Blatt, R., Peled, R., Gadoth, N., & Lavie, P. (1991). The value of sleep recording in evaluating somnambulism in young adults. *Electroencephalography and Clinical Neurophysiology, 78,* 407–412.

Blechman, E. A., Tinsley, B., Carella, E. T., & McEnroe, M. J. (1985). Childhood competence and behavior problems. *Journal of Abnormal Psychology, 94,* 70–77.

Blix, G. G., & Blix, A. G. (1995). The role of exercise in weight loss. *Behavioral Medicine, 21,* 31–39.

Block, J. (1995). A contrarian view of the five-factor approach to personality description. *Psychological Bulletin, 117,* 187–215.

Bloomquist, D. W. (1985). Teaching sensation and perception: Its ambiguous and subliminal aspects. In A. M. Rogers & C. J. Scheirer (Eds.), *The G. Stanley Hall Lecture Series* (Vol. 5, pp. 157–203). Washington, DC: American Psychological Association.

Boddington, S. J. A., & Lavender, A. (1995). Treatment models for couples therapy: A review of the outcome literature and the Dodo's verdict. *Sexual and Marital Therapy, 10,* 69–81.

Bohan, J. S. (1993). Women at center stage: A course about the women of psychology. *Teaching of Psychology, 20,* 74–79.

Bohannon, J. N., III, & Stanowicz, L. (1988). The issue of negative evidence: Adult responses to children's language errors. *Developmental Psychology, 24,* 684–689.

Boice, R. (1983). Observations skill. *Psychological Bulletin, 93,* 3–29.

Bolm-Audorff, U., Schwammle, J., Ehlenz, K., & Kaffarnik, H. (1989). Plasma level of catecholamines and lipids when speaking before an audience. *Work and Stress, 3,* 249–253.

Bond, C. F., Jr., & Titus, L. J. (1983). Social facilitation: A meta-analysis of 241 studies. *Psychological Bulletin, 94,* 265–292.

Bond, R., & Smith, P. B. (1996). Culture and conformity: A meta-analysis of studies using Asch's (1952b, 1956) line judgment task. *Psychological Bulletin, 119,* 111–137.

Bonds, D. R., & Crosby, L. O. (1986). "An adoption study of human obesity": Comment. *New England Journal of Medicine, 315,* 128.

Boneau, C. A. (1974). Paradigm regained? Cognitive behaviorism revisited. *American Psychologist, 29,* 297–309.

Boon, S., & Draijer, N. (1993). Multiple personality disorder in the Netherlands: A clinical investigation of 71 patients. *American Journal of Psychiatry, 150,* 489–494.

Bordage, G. (1987). The curriculum: Overloaded and too general? *Medical Education, 21,* 183–188.

Bordages, J. W. (1989). Self-actualization and personal autonomy. *Psychological Reports, 64,* 1263–1266.

Boring, E. G. (1950). *A history of experimental psychology.* New York: Appleton-Century-Crofts.

Borkovec, T. D., & Roemer, L. (1995). Perceived functions of worry among generalized anxiety disorder subjects: Distraction from more emotionally distressing topics? *Journal of Behavior Therapy and Experimental Psychiatry, 26,* 25–30.

Bors, D. A., & Forrin, B. (1995). Age, speed of information processing, recall, and fluid intelligence. *Intelligence, 20,* 229–248.

Botman, H. I., & Crovitz, H. F. (1989–1990). Dream reports and autobiographical memory. *Imagination, Cognition, and Personality, 9,* 213–224.

Bouchard, T. J., Jr. (1994). Genes, environment, and personality. *Science, 264,* 1700–1701.

Bouchard, T. J., Jr., Lykken, D. T., McGue, M., Segal, N. L., & Tellegen, A. (1990). Sources of human psychological differences: The Minnesota Study of Twins Reared Apart. *Science, 250,* 223–228.

Bouchard, T. J., Jr., & McGue, M. (1981). Familial studies of intelligence: A review. *Science, 212,* 1055–1059.

Bouchard, T. J., Jr., & McGue, M. (1990). Genetic and rearing environmental influences on adult personality: An analysis of adopted twins reared apart. *Journal of Personality, 58,* 263–292.

Bouton, M. E., & Swartzentruber, D. (1991). Sources of relapse after extinction in Pavlovian and instrumental learning. *Clinical Psychology Review, 11,* 123–140.

Bouzid, N., & Crawshaw, C. M. (1987). Massed versus distributed word processor training. *Applied Ergonomics, 18,* 220–222.

Bowd, A. D. (1990). A decade of debate on animal research on research in psychology: Room for consensus? *Canadian Psychologist, 31,* 74–82.

Bower, G. H. (1970). Analysis of a mnemonic device. *American Scientist, 58,* 496–510.

Bower, G. H. (1981). Mood and memory. *American Psychologist, 36,* 129–148.

Bower, G. H. (1993). The fragmentation of psychology? *American Psychologist, 48,* 905–907.

Bower, G. H., & Clark, M. C. (1969). Narrative stories as mediators for serial learning. *Psychonomic Science, 14,* 181–182.

Bower, G. H., & Mayer, J. D. (1989). In search of mood-dependent retrieval. *Bulletin of the Psychonomic Society, 4,* 121–156.

Bowers, K. S. (1994). A review of Ernest R. Hilgard's books on hypnosis, in commemoration of his 90th birthday. *Psychological Science, 5,* 186–189.

Bowers, L. B. (1990). Traumas precipitating female delinquency: Implications for assessment, practice, and policy. *Child and Adolescent Social Work Journal, 7,* 389–402.

Bowlby, J. (1988). *A secure base: Parent-child attachment and healthy human development.* New York: Basic Books.

Bowman, M. L. (1989). Testing individual differences in ancient China. *American Psychologist, 44,* 576–578.

Boyce, B. A. (1992). The effects of goal proximity on skill acquisition and retention of a shooting task in a field-based setting. *Journal of Sport and Exercise Psychology, 14,* 298–308.

Boyd, J. H. (1986). Use of mental health services for the treatment of panic disorder. *American Journal of Psychiatry, 143,* 1569–1574.

Boyd, J. H., & Crump, T. (1991). Westphal's agoraphobia. *Journal of Anxiety Disorders, 5,* 77–86.

Boyd, J. H., Rae, D. S., Thompson, J. W., & Burns, B. J. (1990). Phobia: Prevalence and risk factors. *Social Psychiatry and Psychiatric Epidemiology, 25,* 314–323.

Boylin, W., Gordon, S. K., & Nehrke, M. F. (1976). Reminiscing and ego integrity in institutionalized elderly males. *Gerontologist, 16,* 118–124.

Boynton, R. M. (1988). Color vision. *Annual Review of Psychology, 39,* 69–100.

Bozarth, J. D. (1990). The evolution of Carl Rogers as a therapist. *Person-Centered Review, 5,* 387–393.

Bozarth, J. D., & Brodley, B. T. (1991). Actualization: A functional concept in client-centered therapy. *Journal of Social Behavior and Personality, 6,* 45–59.

Brackbill, Y., & Nichols, P. L. (1982). A test of the confluence model of intellectual development. *Developmental Psychology, 18,* 192–198.

Bradbury, T. N., & Fincham, F. D. (1990). Attributions in marriage: Review and critique. *Psychological Bulletin, 107,* 3–33.

Bradford, J. M. (1988). Organic treatment of the male sexual offender. *Annals of the New York Academy of Sciences, 528,* 193–202.

Bradley, B. P., & Baddeley, A. D. (1990). Emotional factors in forgetting. *Psychological Medicine, 20,* 351–355.

Bradley, M. T., MacLaren, V. V., & Carle, S. B. (1996). Deception and nondeception in guilty knowledge and guilty actions polygraph tests. *Journal of Applied Psychology, 81,* 153–160.

Brady, D. R., & Mufson, E. J. (1990). Amygdaloid pathology in Alzheimer's disease: Qualitative and quantitative analysis. *Dementia, 1,* 5–17.

Brambilla, F., Brunetta, M., Draisci, A., & Peirone, A. (1995). T-lymphocyte concentrations of cholecystokinin-8 and beta-endorphin in eating disorders: II. Bulimia nervosa. *Psychiatry Research, 59,* 51–56.

Brauer, M., Judd, C. M., & Gliner, M. D. (1995). The effects of repeated expressions on attitude polarization during group discussions. *Journal of Personality and Social Psychology, 68,* 1014–1029.

Braungart, J. M., Plomin, R., DeFries, J. C., & Fulker, D. W. (1992). Genetic influence on tester-rated infant temperament as assessed by Bayley's Infant Behavior Record: Nonadaptive and adoptive siblings and twins. *Developmental Psychology, 28,* 40–47.

Breathnach, C. S. (1989). Validation of language localization by computer-assisted tomographic and topographic techniques. *Irish Journal of Psychological Medicine, 6,* 11–18.

Breathnach, C. S. (1992). Eduard Hitzig, neurophysiologist and psychiatrist. *History of Psychiatry, 3,* 329–338.

Breckler, S. J. (1984). Empirical validation of affect, behavior, and cognition as distinct components of attitude. *Journal of Personality and Social Psychology, 47,* 1191–1205.

Bredemeier, B. J., & Shields, D. L. (1985, October). Values and violence in sports today. *Psychology Today,* pp. 22–32.

Breier, A., & Paul, S. M. (1990). The GABA–sub(A)/benzodiazepine receptor: Implications for the molecular basis of anxiety. *Journal of Psychiatric Research, 24,* 91–104.

Breland, K., & Breland, M. (1961). The misbehavior of organisms. *American Psychologist, 16,* 681–684.

Brennan, J. L., & Andrews, G. (1990). An examination of defense style in parents who abuse children. *Journal of Nervous and Mental Disease, 178,* 592–595.

Bretherton, I. (1992). The origins of attachment theory: John Bowlby and Mary Ainsworth. *Developmental Psychology, 28,* 759–775.

Brewer, M. B., & Kramer, R. M. (1985). The psychology of intergroup attitudes and behavior. *Annual Review of Psychology, 36,* 219–243.

Brewin, C. R. (1985). Depression and causal attributions: What is their relation? *Psychological Bulletin, 98,* 297–309.

Brewin, C. R., Dalgleish, T., & Joseph, S. (1996). A dual representation theory of posttraumatic stress disorder. *Psychological Review, 103,* 670–686.

Brickman, P., Coates, D., & Janoff-Bulman, R. (1978). Lottery winners and accident victims: Is happiness relative? *Journal of Personality and Social Psychology, 36,* 917–927.

Briggs, K. C., & Myers, I. B. (1943). *Myers-Briggs type indicator.* Palo Alto, CA: Consulting Psychologists Press.

Brigham, C. C. (1923). *A study of American intelligence.* Princeton, NJ: Princeton University Press.

Brigham, C. C. (1930). Intelligence tests of immigrant groups. *Psychological Review, 37,* 158–165.

Brigham, T. A. (1989). On the importance of reorganizing the difference between experiments and correlational studies. *American Psychologist, 44,* 1077–1078.

Bringmann, M. W., Tyler, K. E., McAhren, P. E., Bringmann, W. G. (1989). A successful and unsuccessful replication of William Stern's eyewitness research. *Perceptual and Motor Skills, 69,* 619–625.

Bringmann, W. G., & Balk, M. M. (1992). Another look at Wilhelm Wundt's publication record. *History of Psychology Newsletter, 24,* 50–66.

Broberg, A. G., Wessels, H., Lamb, M. E., & Hwang, C. P. (1997). Effects of day care on the development of cognitive abilities in 8-year-olds: A longitudinal study. *Developmental Psychology, 33,* 62–69.

Broberg, D. J., & Bernstein, I. L. (1987). Candy as a scapegoat in the prevention of food aversions in children receiving chemotherapy. *Cancer, 60,* 2344–2347.

Brodnick, R. J., & Ree, M. J. (1995). A structural model of academic performance, socioeconomic status, and Spearman's g. *Educational and Psychological Measurement, 55,* 583–594.

Bromberg, W. (1954). *Man above humanity: A history of psychotherapy.* Philadelphia: Lippincott.

Brooks, K., & Siegel, M. (1991). Children as eyewitnesses: Memory, suggestibility, and credibility. *Australian Psychologist, 26,* 84–88.

Brooks-Gunn, J., & Furstenberg, F. F., Jr. (1989). Adolescent sexual behavior. *American Psychologist, 44,* 249–257.

Brooks-Gunn, J., Klebanov, P. K., & Duncan, G. J. (1996). Ethnic differences in children's intelligence test scores: Role of economic deprivation, home environment, and maternal characteristics. *Child Development, 67,* 396-408.

Brooks-Gunn, J., & Warren, M. P. (1989). Biological and social contributions to negative affect in young adolescent girls. *Child Development, 60,* 40–55.

Broota, A., Varma, R., & Singh, A. (1995). Role of relaxation in hypertension. *Journal of the Indian Academy of Applied Psychology, 21,* 29–36.

Brosschot, J. F., Benschop, R. J., Godaert, G. L. R., & Olff, M. (1994). Influence of life stress on immunological reactivity to mild psychological stress. *Psychosomatic Medicine, 56,* 216–224.

Broughton, R. (1990). The prototype concept in personality assessment. *Canadian Psychology, 31,* 26–37.

Broughton, R. S., & Perlstrom, J. R. (1992). PK in a competitive computer game: A replication. *Journal of Parapsychology, 56,* 291–305.

Brouwers, M., & Wiggum, C. D. (1993). Bulimia and perfectionism: Developing the courage to be imperfect. *Journal of Mental Health Counseling, 15,* 141–149.

Brown, A. S. (1991). A review of the tip-of-the-tongue experience. *Psychological Bulletin, 109,* 204–223.

Brown, D. M., Fuqua, J. W., & Otts, D. A. (1986). Helping reluctant readers "stick" to it. *Academic Therapy, 21,* 599–604.

Brown, J. D., & Siegel, J. M. (1988). Exercise as a buffer of life stress: A prospective study of adolescent health. *Health Psychology, 7,* 341–353.

Brown, R. (1973). *A first language: The early stages.* Cambridge, MA: Harvard University Press.

Brown, R., & Kulik, J. (1977). Flashbulb memories. *Cognition, 5,* 73–99.

Brown, W. J., & Basil, M. D. (1995). Media celebrities and public health: Responses to "Magic" Johnson's HIV disclosure and its impact on AIDS risk and high-risk behaviors. *Health Communication, 7,* 345–370.

Brownell, K. D. (1982). Obesity: Understanding and treating a serious, prevalent and refractory disorder. *Journal of Consulting and Clinical Psychology, 50,* 820–840.

Brownell, K. D. (1993). Whether obesity should be treated. *Health Psychology, 12,* 339–341.

Brownell, K. D., & Cohen, L. R. (1995). Adherence to dietary regimens: 1. An overview of research. *Behavioral Medicine, 20,* 149–154.

Brownell, K. D., & Wadden, T. A. (1991). The heterogeneity of obesity: Fitting treatments to individuals. *Behavior Therapy, 22,* 153–177.

Bruce, M. L., Takeuchi, D. T., & Leaf, P. J. (1991). Poverty and psychiatric status: Longitudinal evidence from the New Haven Epidemiologic Catchment Area study. *Archives of General Psychiatry, 48,* 470–474.

Brunello, N., Masotto, C., Steardo, L., & Markstein, R. (1995). New insights into the biology of schizophrenia through the mechanism of action of clozapine. *Neuropsychopharmacology, 13,* 177–213.

Bruner, J. S. (1956). Freud and the image of man. *American Psychologist, 11,* 463–466.

Bryden, M. P. (1993). Perhaps not so sinister [Review of *The left–hander syndrome*]. Contemporary Psychology, 38, 71–72.

Bryden, M. P., Ardila, A., & Ardila, O. (1993). Handedness in native Amazonians. *Neuropsychologia, 31,* 301–308.

Buchsbaum, M. S. (1990). The neuropsychiatric sequelae of mercury poisoning: The Mad Hatter's disease revisited. *Schizophrenia Bulletin, 16,* 379–389.

Buchsbaum, M. S., & Haier, R. J. (1983). Psychopathology: Biological approaches. *Annual Review of Psychology, 34,* 401–430.

Buck, R. (1980). Nonverbal behavior and the theory of emotion: The facial-feedback hypothesis. *Journal of Personality and Social Psychology, 38,* 811–824.

Buck, R. (1985). Prime theory: An integrated view of motivation and emotion. *Psychological Review, 92,* 389–413.

Bunge, M. (1992). The scientist's skepticism. *Skeptical Inquirer, 16,* 377–380.

Burchinal, M. R., Bryant, D. M., Lee, M. W., & Ramey, C. T. (1992). Early day care, infant-mother attachment, and maternal responsiveness in the infant's first year. *Early Childhood Research Quarterly, 3,* 383–396.

Burman, B., & Margolin, G. (1992). Analysis of the association between marital relationships and health problems: An interactional perspective. *Psychological Bulletin, 112,* 39–63.

Burnette, E. (1994, November). Psychology makes top 10 of country's hottest careers. *APA Monitor,* p. 10.

Burnette, M. M., & Adams, H. E. (1987). Detection of noncontingent feedback in EMG biofeedback. *Biofeedback and Self-Regulation, 12,* 281–293.

Busch, F. (1994). Some ambiguities in the method of free association and their implications for technique. *Journal of the American Psychoanalytic Association, 42,* 363–384.

Buss, A. R. (1976). Galton and the birth of differential psychology and eugenics: Social, political, and economic forces. *Journal of the History of the Behavioral Sciences, 12,* 47–58.

Buss, A., Booker, A., & Buss, E. (1972). Firing a weapon and aggression. *Journal of Personality and Social Psychology, 22,* 296–302.

Buss, D. M. (1985). Human mate selection. *American Scientist, 73,* 47–51.

Buss, D. M. (1988). The evolution of human intrasexual competition. *Journal of Personality and Social Psychology, 54,* 616–628.

Buss, D. M. (1990). Toward a biologically informed psychology of personality. *Journal of Personality, 58,* 1–16.

Buss, D. M. (1995). Psychological sex differences: Origins through sexual selection. *American Psychologist, 50,* 164–168.

Buss, D. M., & Barnes, M. (1986). Preferences in human mate selection. *Journal of Personality and Social Psychology, 50,* 559–570.

Buss, D. M., Larsen, R. J., Westen, D., & Semmelroth, J. (1992). Sex differences in jealousy: Evolution, physiology, and psychology. *Psychological Science, 3,* 251–255.

Butler, L. D., & Nolen-Hoeksema, S. (1994). Gender differences in responses to depressed mood in a college sample. *Sex Roles, 30,* 331–346.

Butschky, M. F., Bailey, D., Henningfield, J. E., & Pickworth, W. B. (1995). Smoking without nicotine delivery decreases withdrawal in 12-hour abstinent smokers. *Pharmacology, Biochemistry and Behavior, 50,* 91–96.

Button, E. (1983). Personal construct theory and psychological well-being. *British Journal of Medical Psychology, 56,* 313–321.

Buyer, L. S. (1988). Creative problem solving: A comparison of performance under different instructions. *Journal of Creative Behavior, 22,* 55–61.

Bwoers, K. S., & Farvolden, P. (1996). Revisiting a century-old Freudian slip–From suggestion disavowed to the truth repressed. *Psychological Bulletin, 119,* 355–380.

Byravan, A., & Ramanaiah, N. V. (1995). Structure of the 16 PF fifth edition from the perspective of the five-factor model. *Psychological Reports, 76,* 555–560.

Byrne, D., Ervin, C. R., & Lamberth, J. (1970). Continuity between the experimental study of attraction and real-life computer dating. *Journal of Personality and Social Psychology, 16,* 157–165.

Byrne, D., & Kelley, K. C. (1981). *An introduction to personality.* Englewood Cliffs, NJ: Prentice Hall.

Byrne, R. C. (1990). The effectiveness of the Beginning Experience Workshop: A paraprofessional group marathon workshop for divorce adjustment. *Journal of Divorce, 13,* 101–120.

Byrne, W., Bleier, R., & Houston, L. (1988). Variations in human corpus callosum do not predict gender: A study using magnetic resonance imaging. *Behavioral Neuroscience, 102,* 222–227.

Cacioppo, J. T. (1994). Social neuroscience: Autonomic, neuroendocrine, and immune responses to stress. *Psychophysiology, 31,* 113–128.

Cacioppo, J. T., & Berntson, G. G. (1992). Social psychological contributions to the decade of the brain: Doctrine of multilevel analysis. *American Psychologist, 47,* 1019–1028.

Cacioppo, J. T., Marshall-Goodell, B. S., Tassinary, L. G., & Petty, R. E. (1992). Rudimentary determinants of attitudes: Classical conditioning is more effective when prior knowledge about the attitude stimulus is low than high. *Journal of Experimental Social Psychology, 28,* 207–233.

Cadoret, R. J., Yates, W. R., Troughton, E., & Woodworth, G. (1995). Adoption study demonstrating two genetic pathways to drug abuse. *Archives of General Psychiatry, 52,* 42–52.

Cadwallader, E. H. (1984). Values in Fritz Perls' Gestalt Therapy: On the dangers of half-truths. *Counseling and Values, 28,* 192–201.

Cahan, E. D., & White, S. H. (1992). Proposals for a second psychology. *American Psychologist, 47,* 224–235.

Cahill, L., Babinsky, R., Markowitsch, H. J., & McGaugh, J. L. (1995). The amygdala and emotional memory. *Nature, 377,* 295–296.

Cahill, L., Prins, B., Weber, M., & McGaugh, J. L. (1994). b-Adrenergic activation and memory for emotional events. *Nature, 371,* 702–704.

Calantone, R. J., & Warshaw, P. R. (1985). Negating the effects of fear appraisals in election campaigns. *Journal of Applied Psychology, 70,* 627–633.

Calkins, M. W. (1893). Statistics of dreams. *American Journal of Psychology, 5,* 311–343.

Calkins, M. W. (1901). *An introduction to psychology.* New York: Macmillan.

Calkins, M. W. (1906). A reconciliation between structural and functional psychology. *Psychological Review, 13,* 61–81.

Calkins, M. W. (1913). Psychology and the behaviorist. *Psychological Bulletin, 10,* 288–291.

Calkins, M. W. (1930). Mary Whiton Calkins. In C. Murchison (Ed.), *A history of psychology in autobiography* (Vol. 1, pp. 31–62). New York: Russell & Russell.

Camel, J. E., Withers, G. S., & Greenough, W. T. (1986). Persistence of visual cortex dendritic alterations induced by postweaning exposure to a "superenriched" environment in rats. *Behavioral Neuroscience, 100,* 810–813.

Cameron, L., Leventhal, E. A., & Leventhal, H. (1995). Seeking medical care in response to symptoms and life stress. *Psychosomatic Medicine, 57,* 37–47.

Cameron, M. J., & Cappello, M. J. (1993). "We'll cross that hurdle when we get to it": Teaching athletic performance within adaptive physical education. *Behavior Modification, 17,* 136–147.

Campbell, J. B., Tyrrell, D. J., & Zingaro, M. (1993). Sensation seeking among whitewater canoe and kayak paddlers. *Personality and Individual Differences, 14,* 489–491.

Campione, J. E., & Brown, A. L. (1979). Toward a theory of intelligence: Contributions from research with retarded children. *Intelligence, 2,* 279–304.

Candland, D. K. (1982). Selective pressure and the teaching of psychology: The fox and the hedgehog. *Teaching of Psychology, 9,* 20–23.

Canetto, S. S., & Lester, D. (1995). Gender and the primary prevention of suicide mortality. *Suicide and Life-Threatening Behavior, 25,* 58–69.

Cann, A., Sherman, S. J., & Elkes, R. (1975). Effects of initial request size and timing of a second request on compliance: The foot in the door and the door in the face. *Journal of Personality and Social Psychology, 32,* 774–782.

Cannon, D. S., & Baker, T. B. (1981). Emetic and electric shock alcohol aversion therapy: Assessment of conditioning. *Journal of Consulting and Clinical Psychology, 49,* 20–33.

Cannon, W. B. (1915/1989). *Bodily changes in pain, hunger, fear, and rage.* Birmingham, AL: Gryphon.

Cannon, W. B. (1927). The James-Lange theory of emotions: A critical examination and an alternative. *American Journal of Psychology, 39,* 106–124.

Cannon, W. B., & Washburn, A. L. (1912). An explanation of hunger. *American Journal of Physiology, 29,* 444–454.

Cantor, N. (1990). From thought to behavior: "Having" and "doing" in the study of personality and cognition. *American Psychologist, 45,* 735–750.

Caplan, L. J., & Barr, R. A. (1989). On the relationship between category intensions and extensions in children. *Journal of Experimental Child Psychology, 47,* 413–429.

Caplan, P. J., & Larkin, J. (1991). The anatomy of dominance and self-protection. *American Psychologist, 46,* 536.

Carducci, B. J., & Wheat, J. E. (1984, September). Business: An open door for psych majors. *APA Monitor,* p. 20.

Carlat, D. J., & Camargo, C. A. (1991). Review of bulimia nervosa in males. *American Journal of Psychiatry, 148,* 831–843.

Carlson, E. R. (1995). Evaluating the credibility of sources: A missing link in the teaching of critical thinking. *Teaching of Psychology, 22,* 39–41.

Carlson, E. T. (1981). The history of multiple personality in the United States: I. The beginnings. *American Journal of Psychiatry, 138,* 666–668.

Carlsson, A. (1988). The current status of the dopamine hypothesis of schizophrenia. *Neuropsycho-pharmacology, 1,* 179–186.

Carmichael, L., Hogan, H. P., & Walter, A. (1932). An experimental study of the effect of language on the reproduction of visually perceived form. *Journal of Experimental Psychology, 15,* 73–86.

Carmody, T. P. (1993). Nicotine dependence: Psychosocial approaches to the prevention of smoking relapse. *Psychology of Addictive Behaviors, 7,* 96–102.

Carney, R. N., & Levin, J. R. (1994). Combining mnemonic strategies to remember who painted what when. *Contemporary Educational Psychology, 19,* 323–339.

Carpenter, C. R. (1955). Psychological research using television. *American Psychologist, 10,* 606–610.

Carroll, J. M., & Russell, J. A. (1996). Do facial expressions signal specific emotions? Judging emotion from the face in context. *Journal of Personality and Social Psychology, 70,* 205–218.

Carskadon, M. A. (1990). Patterns of sleep and sleepiness in adolescents. *Pediatrician, 17,* 5–12.

Carson, R. C., & Butcher, J. N. (1992). *Abnormal psychology* (9th ed.). New York: HarperCollins.

Carsten, J. M., & Spector, P. E. (1987). Unemployment, job satisfaction, and employee turnover: A meta-analytic test of the Muchinsky Model. *Journal of Applied Psychology, 72,* 374–381.

Cartwright, R. D. (1978). *A primer on sleep and dreaming.* Reading, MA: Addison-Wesley.

Cartwright, R. D. (1991). Dreams that work: The relation of dream incorporation to adaptation to stressful events. Dreaming: *Journal of the Association for the Study of Dreams, 1,* 3–9.

Carver, C. S., & Ganellen, R. J. (1983). Depression and components of self-punitiveness: High standards, self-criticism, and overgeneralization. *Journal of Abnormal Psychology, 92,* 330–337.

Cascio, W. F. (1991). *Applied psychology in personnel management* (4th ed.). Englewood Cliffs, NJ: Prentice Hall.

Cascio, W. F. (1995). Whither industrial and organizational psychology in a changing work of work? *American Psychologist, 50,* 928–939.

Cash, T. F., & Derlega, V. J. (1978). The matching hypothesis: Physical attractiveness among same-sexed friends. *Personality and Social Psychology Bulletin, 4,* 240–243.

Cassidy, J., & Berlin, L. J. (1994). The insecure/ambivalent pattern of attachment: Theory and research. *Child Development, 65,* 971–981.

Casto, S. D., DeFries, J. C., & Fulker, D. W. (1995). Multivariate genetic analysis of Wechsler Intelligence Scale for Children–Revised (WISC-R) factors. *Behavior Genetics, 25,* 25–32.

Castro, J. M. de. (1993). Genetic influences on daily intake and meal patterns of humans. *Physiology and Behavior, 53,* 777–782.

Catania, J. A., Coates, T. J., & Kegeles, S. (1994). A test of the AIDS Risk Reduction Model: Psychosocial correlates of condom use in the AMEN cohort survey. *Health Psychology, 13,* 548–555.

Catania, J. A., Coates, T. J., Stall, R., & Bye, L. (1991). Changes in condom use among homosexual men in San Francisco. *Health Psychology, 10,* 190–199.

Catania, J. A., Gibson, D. R., Chitwood, D. D., & Coates, T. J. (1990). Methodological problems in AIDS behavioral research: Influences on measurement error and participation bias in studies of sexual behavior. *Psychological Bulletin, 108,* 339–362.

Catherwood, D. (1993). The haptic processing of texture and shape by 7- to 9-month-old infants. *British Journal of Developmental Psychology, 11,* 299–306.

Cattell, J. M. (1890). Mental tests and measurements. *Mind, 15,* 373–381.

Cattell, R. B. (1940). A culture free intelligence test: I. *Journal of Educational Psychology, 31,* 161–179.

Cattell, R. B. (1949). *Sixteen personality factor questionnaire.* Champaign, IL: Institute for Personality and Ability Testing.

Ceci, S. J., & Bruck, M. (1993). Suggestibility of the child witness: A historical review and synthesis. *Psychological Bulletin, 113,* 403–439.

Ceci, S. J., Huffman, M. L. C., & Smith, E. (1994). Repeatedly thinking about a non-event: Source misattributions among preschoolers. *Consciousness and Cognition: An International Journal, 3,* 388–407.

Ceci, S. J., & Liker, J. J. (1986). A day at the races: A study of IQ, expertise, and cognitive complexity. *Journal of Experimental Psychology: General, 115,* 255–266.

Ceci, S. J., Ross, D. F., & Toglia, M. P. (1987). Suggestibility of children's memory: Psychological implications. *Journal of Experimental Psychology: General, 116,* 38–49.

Cha, K., Horch, K. W., & Normann, R. A. (1992). Mobility performance with a pixelized vision system. *Vision Research, 32,* 1367–1372.

Chadwick, H. (1986). *Augustine.* New York: Oxford University Press.

Chaiken, S., & Baldwin, M. W. (1981). Affective-cognitive consistency and the effect of salient behavioral information on the self-perception of attitudes. *Journal of Personality and Social Psychology, 41,* 1–12.

Chandler, C. C. (1993). Accessing related events increases retroactive interference in a matching recognition test. *Journal of Experimental Psychology Learning, Memory, and Cognition, 19,* 967–974.

Charness, N. (1992). The impact of chess research on cognitive science. *Psychological Research, 54,* 4–9.

Chase, T. N., Metman, L. V., Bravi, D., & Roberts, J. W. (1995). Dopamine-receptor subtype-selective agonists in the treatment of Parkinson's disease. *Clinical Neuropharmacology, 18,* S207–S215.

Chase, W. G., & Simon, H. A. (1973). Perception in chess. *Cognitive Psychology, 4,* 55–81.

Chaudhari, N., Yang, H., Lamp, C., & Delay, E. (1996). The taste of monosodium glutamate: Membrane receptors in taste buds. *Journal of Neuroscience, 16,* 3817–3826.

Cheatham, S. K., Rucker, H. N., Polloway, E. A., & Smith, J. D. (1995). Savant syndrome: Case studies, hypotheses, and implications for special education. *Education and Training in Mental Retardation and Developmental Disabilities, 30,* 243–253.

Chen, C., Lee, S.-Y., & Stevenson, H. W. (1995). Response style and cross-cultural comparisons of rating scales among East Asian and North American students. *Psychological Science, 6,* 170–175.

Chen, C.Y., & Michael, W. B. (1993). Higher-order abilities conceptualized within Guilford's structure-of-intellect (SOI) model for a sample of United States Coast Guard Academy cadets: A reanalysis of an SOI data base. *Educational and Psychological Measurement, 53,* 941–950.

Chen, G.-M. (1995). Differences in self-disclosure patterns among Americans versus Chinese: A comparative study. *Journal of Cross-Cultural Psychology, 26,* 84–91.

Chen, S. H. A., & Bernard-Opitz, V. (1993). Comparison of personal and computer-assisted instruction for children with autism. *Mental Retardation, 31,* 368–376.

Cherry, E. C. (1953). Some experiments on the recognition of speech with one and two ears. *Journal of the Acoustical Society of America, 25,* 975–979.

Chi, M. T. H., & Koeske, R. D. (1983). Network representation of a child's dinosaur knowledge. *Developmental Psychology, 19,* 29–39.

Child, I. L. (1985). Psychology and anomalous observations: The question of ESP in dreams. *American Psychologist, 40,* 1219–1230.

Chipuer, H. M., Rovine, M. J., & Plomin, R. (1990). LISREL modeling: Genetic and environmental influences on IQ revisited. *Intelligence, 14,* 11–29.

Choi, P. Y. L., & Pope, H. G. (1994). Violence toward women and illicit androgenic-anabolic steroid use. *Annals of Clinical Psychiatry, 6,* 21–25.

Chrisler, J. C. (1988). Conditioning the instructor's behavior: A class project in psychology of learning. *Teaching of Psychology, 15,* 135–137.

Christensen, A. J., & Smith, T. W. (1993). Cynical hostility and cardiovascular reactivity during self-disclosure. *Psychosomatic Medicine, 55,* 193–202.

Christensen, A. J., & Smith, T. W. (1995). Personality and patient adherence: Correlates of the five-factor model in renal analysis. *Journal of Behavioral Medicine, 18,* 305–313.

Christensen, L. (1988). Deception in psychological research: When is its use justified? *Personality and Social Psychology Bulletin, 14,* 664–675.

Christianson, S. A., & Loftus, E. F. (1987). Memory for traumatic events. *Applied Cognitive Psychology, 1,* 225–239.

Christianson, S. A., & Nilsson, L. (1984). Functional amnesia as induced by a psychological trauma. *Memory and Cognition, 12,* 142–155.

Christopher, F. S., & Cate, R. M. (1985). Anticipated influences on sexual decision making for first intercourse. *Family Relations: Journal of Applied Family and Child Studies, 34,* 265–270.

Christy, C. A., & Voigt, H. (1994). Bystander responses to public episodes of child abuse. *Journal of Applied Social Psychology, 24,* 824–847.

Chwalisz, K., Diener, E., & Gallagher, D. (1988). Autonomic arousal feedback and emotional experience: Evidence from the spinal cord injured. *Journal of Personality and Social Psychology, 54,* 820–828.

Cialdini, R. B., & Fultz, J. (1990). Interpreting the negative mood-helping literature via "mega"-analysis: A contrary view. *Psychological Bulletin, 107,* 210–214.

Cialdini, R. B., Schaller, M., Houlihan, D., Arps, K., Fultz, J., & Beaman, A. L. (1987). Empathy-based helping: Is it selflessly motivated? *Journal of Personality and Social Psychology, 52,* 749–758.

Cialdini, R. B., Vincent, J. E., Lewis, S. J., Catalan, J., Wheeler, D., & Darley, B. L. (1975). Reciprocal concessions procedure for inducing compliance: The door-in-the-face technique. *Journal of Personality and Social Psychology, 31,* 206–215.

Cicerello, A., & Sheehan, E. P. (1995). Personal advertisements: A content analysis. *Journal of Social Behavior and Personality, 10,* 751–756.

Cicerone, C. M., & Hayhoe, M. M. (1990). The size of the pool for bleaching in human rod vision. *Vision Research, 30,* 693–697.

Cicerone, C. M., & Nerger, J. L. (1989). The density of cones in the fovea centralis of the human dichromat. *Vision Research, 29,* 1587–1595.

Cinciripini, P. M., Cinciripini, L. G., Wallfisch, A., & Haque, W. (1996). Behavior therapy and the transdermal nicotine patch: Effects on cessation outcome, affect, and coping. *Journal of Consulting Clinical Psychology, 64,* 314–323.

Clark, K. B., & Clark, M. P. (1947). Racial identification and preference in Negro children. In T. M. Newcomb & E. L. Hartley (Eds.), *Readings in social psychology* (pp. 169–178). New York: Holt.

Clark, L. A., Watson, D., & Reynolds, S. (1995). Diagnosis and classification of psychopathology: Challenges to the current system and future directions. *Annual Review of Psychology, 46,* 121–153.

Clark, M. E., & Hirschman, R. (1990). Effects of paced respiration on anxiety reduction in a clinical population. *Biofeedback and Self-Regulation, 15,* 273–284.

Clark, N. M., Nothwehr, F., Gong, M., & Evans, D. (1995). Physician-patient partnership in managing chronic illness. *Academic Medicine, 70,* 957–959.

Clark, R. D., & Word, L. E. (1974). Where is the apathetic bystander? Situational characteristics of the emergency. *Journal of Personality and Social Psychology, 29,* 279–287.

Clarke, D. (1991). Belief in the paranormal: A New Zealand survey. *Journal of the Society for Psychical Research, 57,* 412–425.

Clarke, J. M., & Zaidel, E. (1994). Anatomical-behavioral relationships: Corpus callosum morphometry and hemispheric specialization. *Behavioural Brain Research, 64,* 185–202.

Clarke, J. V., Nicol, C. J., Jones, R., & McGreevy, P. D. (1996). Effects of observational learning on food selection in horses. *Applied Animal Behaviour Science, 50,* 177-184.

Clarke, K. M., & Greenberg, L. S. (1986). Differential effects of the Gestalt two-chair intervention and problem solving in resolving decisional conflict. *Journal of Counseling Psychology, 33,* 11–15.

Cliffe, M. J. (1991). Behaviour modification by successive approximation: Saxon age examples from Bede. *British Journal of Clinical Psychology, 30,* 367–369.

Clifford, C. A., Murray, R. M., & Fulker, D. W. (1984). Genetic and environmental influences on obsessional traits and symptoms. *Psychological Medicine, 14,* 791–800.

Clore, G. L., Bray, R. M., Itkin, S. M., & Murphy, P. (1978). Interracial attitudes and behavior at a summer camp. *Journal of Personality and Social Psychology, 36,* 107–116.

Clum, G. A., & Knowles, S. L. (1991). Why do some people with panic disorders become avoidant? A review. *Clinical Psychology Review, 11,* 295–313.

Clutton–Brock, T. H., & Parker, G. A. (1995). Punishment in animal societies. *Nature, 373,* 209–216.

Cofer, C. N. (1985). Drives and motives. In G. A. Kimble & K. Schlesinger (Eds.), *Topics in the history of psychology* (Vol. 2, pp. 151–190). Hillsdale, NJ: Erlbaum.

Cogan, D., & Cogan, R. (1984). Classical salivary conditioning: An easy demonstration. *Teaching of Psychology, 11,* 170–171.

Cohen, A. (1993). Organizational commitment and turnover: A meta-analysis. *Academy of Management Journal, 36,* 1140–1157.

Cohen, D. B. (1979). Sleep and dreaming: *Origins, nature and functions.* New York: Pergamon.

Cohen, H. H., & Cohen, D. M. (1994). Psychophysical assessment of the perceived slipperiness of floor tile surfaces in a laboratory setting. *Journal of Safety Research, 25,* 19–26.

Cohen, J. (1994). The earth is round (*p* < .05). *American Psychologist, 49,* 997–1003.

Cohen, M. S., & Bookheimer, S. Y. (1994). Localization of brain function using magnetic resonance imaging. *Trends in Neurosciences, 17,* 268–277.

Cohen, N. J., & Squire, L. R. (1980). Preserved learning and retention of pattern-analyzing skill in amnesia: Dissociation of knowing how and knowing that. *Science, 210,* 207–210.

Coile, D. C., & Miller, N. E. (1984). How radical animal activists try to mislead humane people. *American Psychologist, 39,* 700–701.

Coke-Pepsi slugfest. (1976, July 26). *Time,* pp. 64–65.

Cole, J. D., & Kazarian, S. S. (1993). Predictive validity of the Level of Expressed Emotion (LEE) Scale: Readmission follow-up data for 1, 2, and 5-year periods. *Journal of Clinical Psychology, 49,* 216–218.

Cole, P. (1994). Resistance to awareness: A Gestalt therapy perspective. *Gestalt Journal, 17,* 71–94.

Colegrove, F. W. (1899). Individual memories. *American Journal of Psychology, 10,* 228–255.

Coleman-Mesches, K., & McGaugh, J. L. (1995). Differential involvement of the right and left amygdalae in expression of memory for aversively motivated training. *Brain Research, 670,* 75–81.

Coles, R. (1970). *Erik Erikson: The growth of his work*. Boston: Atlantic/Little, Brown.

Collaer, M. L., & Hines, M. (1995). Human behavioral sex differences: A role for gonadal hormones during early development? *Psychological Bulletin, 118*, 55–107.

Collins, A. M., & Loftus, E. F. (1975). A spreading-activation theory of semantic processing. *Psychological Review, 82*, 407–428.

Collins, N. L., & Miller, L. C. (1994). Self-disclosure and liking: A meta-analytic review. *Psychological Bulletin, 116*, 457–475.

Comrey, A. L., Michael, W. B., & Fruchter, B. (1988). J. P. Guilford (1897–1987). *American Psychologist, 43*, 1086–1087.

Connolly, M. B., Strupp, H. H. (1996). Cluster analysis of patient reported psychotherapy outcomes. *Psychotherapy Research, 6*, 30–42.

Connor, S. R. (1986). Measurement of denial in the terminally ill: A critical review. *Hospice Journal, 2*, 51–68.

Conrad, R. (1962). An association between memory errors and errors due to acoustic masking of speech. *Nature, 193*, 1314–1315.

Conway, M., & Ross, M. (1984). Getting what you want by revising what you had. *Journal of Personality and Social Psychology, 47*, 738–748.

Conway, M. A., Anderson, S. J., Larsen, S. F., & Donnelly, C. M. (1994). The formation of flashbulb memories. *Memory and Cognition, 22*, 326–343.

Cook, M., & Mineka, S. (1989). Observational conditioning of fear to fear-relevant versus fear-irrelevant stimuli in rhesus monkeys. *Journal of Abnormal Psychology, 98*, 448–459.

Coon, D. J. (1982). Eponymy, obscurity, Twitmyer, and Pavlov. *Journal of the History of the Behavioral Sciences, 18*, 255–262.

Coon, H., Fulker, D. W., DeFries, J. C., & Plomin, R. (1990). Home environment and cognitive ability of seven-year-old children in the Colorado Adoption Project: Genetic and environmental etiologies. *Developmental Psychology, 26*, 459–468.

Cooney, J. L., & Zeichner, A. (1985). Selective attention to negative feedback in Type A and Type B individuals. *Journal of Abnormal Psychology, 94*, 110–111.

Coons, P. M., & Milstein, V. (1992). Psychogenic amnesia: A clinical investigation of 25 cases. *Dissociation: Progress in the Dissociative Disorders, 5*, 73–79.

Cooper, G. D., Adams, H. B., & Scott, J. C. (1988). Studies in REST: I. Reduced environmental stimulation therapy (REST) and reduced alcohol consumption. *Journal of Substance Abuse Treatment, 5*, 61–68.

Coram, G. J. (1995). A Rorschach analysis of violent murderers and nonviolent offenders. *European Journal of Psychological Assessment, 11*, 81–88.

Corcoran, K., & Winsalde, W. J. (1994). Eavesdropping on the 50-minute hour: Managed mental health care and confidentiality. *Behavioral Sciences and the Law, 12*, 351–365.

Coren, S., & Halpern, D. F. (1991). Left-handedness: A marker for decreased survival fitness. *Psychological Bulletin, 109*, 90–106.

Cornell-Bell, A. H., Finkbeiner, M., Cooper, M. S., & Smith, S. J. (1990). Glutamate induces calcium waves in cultured astrocytes: Long-range glial signaling. *Science, 247*, 470–473.

Corr, C. A. (1993). Coping with dying: Lessons that we should and should not learn from the work of Elisabeth Kübler-Ross. *Death Studies, 17*, 69–83.

Corsini, R. J. (1995). Putting the "B" in RET: It had to be. *Journal of Rational-Emotive and Cognitive Behavior Therapy, 13*, 5–7.

Corter, J. E., & Gluck, M. A. (1992). Explaining basic categories: Feature predictability and information. *Psychological Bulletin, 111*, 291–303.

Costa-Miserachs, D., Portell-Cortes, I., Aldavert-Vera, L., & Torras-Garcia, M. (1994). Long-term memory facilitation in rats by posttraining epinephrine. *Behavioral Neuroscience, 108*, 469–474.

Cotgrove, A. J., Zirinsky, L., Black, D., & Weston, D. (1995). Secondary prevention of attempted suicide in adolescence. *Journal of Adolescence, 18*, 569–577.

Cousins, N. (1983). *The healing heart: Antidotes to panic and helplessness*. New York: W. W. Norton.

Cowan, N. (1988). Evolving conceptions of memory storage, selective attention, and their mutual constraints within the human information-processing systems. *Psychological Bulletin, 104*, 163–191.

Cowles, M. (1989). *Statistics in psychology: An historical perspective*. Hillsdale, NJ: Erlbaum.

Cowley, G. (1995, November 6). Melatonin mania. *Newsweek*, pp. 60–63.

Cox, B. J. (1996). The nature and assessment of catastrophic thoughts in panic disorder. *Behaviour Research and Therapy, 34*, 363–374.

Cox, G. L., & Merkel, W. T. (1989). A qualitative review of psychosocial treatments for bulimia. *Journal of Nervous and Mental Disease, 177*, 77–84.

Cox, W. J., & Kenardy, J. (1993). Performance anxiety, social phobia, and setting effects in instrumental music students. *Journal of Anxiety Disorders, 7*, 49–60.

Craft, S., Zallen, G., & Baker, L. D. (1992). Glucose and memory in mild senile dementia of the Alzheimer type. *Journal of Clinical and Experimental Neuropsychology, 14*, 253–267.

Craig, C. L. (1994). Limits to learning: Effects of predator pattern and colour on perception and avoidance-learning by prey. *Animal Behaviour, 47*, 1087–1099.

Craik, F. I. M., & Lockhart, R. S. (1972). Levels of processing: A framework for memory research. *Journal of Verbal Learning and Verbal Behavior, 11*, 671–684.

Craik, F. I. M., & Tulving, E. (1975). Depth of processing and the retention of words in episodic memory. *Journal of Experimental Psychology: General, 104*, 268–294.

Cramer, P., & Blatt, S. J. (1990). Use of the TAT to measure change in defense mechanisms following intensive psychotherapy. *Journal of Personality Assessment, 54*, 236–251.

Crandall, J. E. (1980). Adler's concept of social interest: Theory, measurement, and implications for adjustment. *Journal of Personality and Social Psychology, 39*, 481–495.

Crano, W. D., & Prislin, R. (1995). Components of vested interest and attitude-behavior consistency. *Basic and Applied Social Psychology, 17*, 1–21.

Cravens, H. (1992). A scientific project locked in time: The Terman Genetic Studies of Genius, 1920s–1950s. *American Psychologist, 47*, 183–189.

Crews, F. T. (1994). Amyloid-b protein disruption of cholinergic and growth factor phospholipase C signals could underlie cognitive and neurodegenerative aspects of Alzheimer's disease. *Neurobiology of Aging, 15*, S95–S96.

Crisp, A. H. (1986). The integration of "self-help" and "help" in the prevention of anorexia nervosa. *British Review of Bulimia and Anorexia Nervosa, 1*, 27–39.

Critelli, J. W., & Neumann, K. F. (1984). The placebo: Conceptual analysis of a construct in transition. *American Psychologist, 39*, 32–39.

Croce, R. V. (1986). The effects of EMG biofeedback on strength acquisition. *Biofeedback and Self-Regulation, 11*, 299–310.

Croce, R. V. (1990). Effects of exercise and diet on body composition and cardiovascular fitness in adults with severe mental retardation. *Education and Training in Mental Retardation, 25*, 176–187.

Crocker, J., Alloy, L. B., & Kayne, N. T. (1988). Attributional style, depression, and perceptions of consensus for events. *Journal of Personality and Social Psychology, 54*, 840–846.

Crohan, S. E. (1992). Marital happiness and spousal consensus on beliefs about marital conflict: A longitudinal investigation. *Journal of Social and Personal Relationships, 9*, 89–102.

Crook, T., & Eliot, J. (1980). Parental death during childhood and adult depression: A critical review of the literature. *Psychological Bulletin, 87*, 252–259.

Crowe, R. R. (1990). Panic disorder: Genetic considerations. *Journal of Psychiatric Research, 24*, 129–134.

Crundell, J. K. (1993). Fluoxetine and suicidal ideation: A review of the literature. *International Journal of Neuroscience, 68*, 73–84.

Culebras, A., & Moore, J. T. (1989). Magnetic resonance findings in REM sleep behavior disorder. *Neurology, 39*, 1519–1523.

Cunningham, J. A., Dollinger, S. J., Satz, M., & Rotter, N. S. (1991). Personality correlates of prejudice against AIDS victims. *Bulletin of the Psychonomic Society, 29*, 165–167.

Cunningham, M. R., Roberts, A. R., Barbee, A. P., & Druen, P. B. (1995). "Their ideas of beauty are, on the whole, the same as ours": Consistency and variability in the cross-cultural perception of female physical attractiveness. *Journal of Personality and Social Psychology, 68*, 261–279.

Cunningham, S. (1983, March). Superior court restarts electroshock in Berkeley. *APA Monitor*, p. 17.

Cunningham, S. (1985, July). Chimps use sign language to talk to each other. *APA Monitor*, p. 11.

Curcio, C. A., Sloan, K. R., Jr., Packer, O., Hendrickson, A. E., & Kalina, R. E. (1987). Distribution of cones in human and monkey retina: Individual variability and radial asymmetry. *Science, 236*, 579–582.

Curran, W., & Johnston, A. (1994). Integration of shading and texture cues: Testing the linear model. *Vision Research, 34*, 1863–1874.

Curzon, G. (1982). Transmitter amines in depression. *Psychological Medicine, 12*, 465–470.

Cushman, P. (1989). Iron fists/velvet gloves: A study of a mass marathon psychology training. *Psychotherapy, 26*, 23–39.

Cutting, J. E. (1987). Perception and information. *Annual Review of Psychology, 38*, 61–90.

Cytowic, R. E. (1989). Synesthesia and mapping of subjective sensory dimensions. *Neurology, 39*, 849–850.

Czeisler, C. A., Moore-Ede, M. C., & Coleman, R. M. (1982). Rotating shift work schedules that disrupt sleep are improved by applying circadian principles. *Science, 217*, 460–463.

Dahlstrom, W. G. (1993). Tests: Small samples, large consequences. *American Psychologist, 48*, 393–399.

Daigle, M. S., & Mishara, B. L. (1995). Intervention styles with suicidal callers at two suicide prevention centers. *Suicide and Life-Threatening Behavior, 25*, 261–275.

Dalton, D. R., & Mesch, D. J. (1991). On the extent and reduction of avoidable absenteeism: An assessment of absence policy provisions. *Journal of Applied Psychology, 76*, 810–817.

Dalton, J. H., Elias, M. J., & Beck, B. L. (1994). Transforming coverage of primary prevention in abnormal psychology courses. *Teaching of Psychology, 21*, 217–222.

Daly, M., & Wilson, M. (1990). Is parent-offspring conflict sex-linked? Freudian and Darwinian models. *Journal of Personality, 58*, 163–189.

Dance, K. A., & Neufeld, R. W. J. (1988). Aptitude-treatment interaction research in the clinical setting: A review of attempts to dispel the "patient uniformity" myth. *Psychological Bulletin, 104*, 192–213.

Dandoy, A. C., & Goldstein, A. G. (1990). The use of cognitive appraisal to reduce stress reactions: A replication. *Journal of Social Behavior and Personality, 5*, 275–285.

Danenberg, M. A., Loos-Cosgrove, M., & LoVerde, M. (1987). Temporary hearing loss and rock music. *Language, Speech, and Hearing Services in Schools, 18,* 267–274.

Daniels, M. (1982). The development of the concept of self-actualization in the writings of Abraham Maslow. *Current Psychological Reviews, 2,* 61–75.

Dansereau, F., Graen, G. B., & Haga, W. J. (1975). A vertical dyad linkage approach to leadership within formal organizations. *Organizational Behavior and Human Performance, 13,* 46–78.

Danziger, K. (1990). *Constructing the subject: Historical origins of psychological research.* New York: Cambridge University Press.

Danziger, K. (1994). Does the history of psychology have a future? *Theory and Psychology, 4,* 467–484.

Darch, C. B., Carnine, D. W., & Kameenui, E. J. (1986). The role of graphic organizers and social structure in content area instruction. *Journal of Reading Behavior, 18,* 275–295.

Darian-Smith, I. (1982). Touch in primates. *Annual Review of Psychology, 33,* 155–194.

Darley, J. M., & Fazio, R. H. (1980). Expectancy confirmation processes arising in the social interaction sequence. *American Psychologist, 35,* 867–881.

Darley, J. M., & Latané, B. (1968). Bystander intervention in emergencies: Diffusion of responsibilities. *Journal of Personality and Social Psychology, 8,* 377–383.

Darling, C. A., Davidson, J. K., & Cox, R. P. (1991). Female sexual response and the timing of partner orgasm. *Journal of Sex and Marital Therapy, 17,* 3–21.

Darling, C. A., Davidson, J. K., & Jennings, D. A. (1991). The female sexual response revisited: Understanding the multiorgasmic experience in women. *Archives of Sexual Behavior, 20,* 527–540.

Darling, N., & Steinberg, L. (1993). Parenting style as context: An integrative model. *Psychological Bulletin, 113,* 487–496.

Darwin, C. (1859/1975). *The origin of species.* New York: W. W. Norton.

Darwin, C. (1872/1965). *The expression of the emotions in man and animals.* Chicago: University of Chicago Press.

Daum, I., & Ackermann, H. (1994). Dissociation of declarative and nondeclarative memory after bilateral thalamic lesions: A case report. *International Journal of Neuroscience, 75,* 153–165.

Davey, G. C. L. (1995). Preparedness and phobias: Specific evolved associations or a generalized expectancy bias? *Behavioral and Brain Sciences, 18,* 289–325.

David, S. S., Foot, H. C., & Chapman, A. J. (1990). Children's sensitivity to traffic hazard in peripheral vision. *Applied Cognitive Psychology, 4,* 471–484.

Davidson, D. (1995). The representativeness heuristic and the conjunction fallacy effect in children's decision making. *Merrill Palmer Quarterly, 41,* 328–346.

Davidson, M., Stern, R. G., Bierer, L. M., & Horvath, T. B. (1991). Cholinergic strategies in the treatment of Alzheimer's disease. *Acta Psychiatrica Scandinavia, 83,* 47–50.

Davidson, R. J. (1992). Emotion and affective style: Hemispheric substrates. *Psychological Science, 3,* 39–43.

Davies, M., & White, P. A. (1994). Use of the availability heuristic by children. *British Journal of Developmental Psychology, 12,* 503–505.

Davies, P. T., & Cummings, E. M. (1994). Marital conflict and child adjustment: An emotional security hypothesis. *Psychological Bulletin, 116,* 387–411.

Davis, A., & Eels, K. (1953). *Davis-Eels games.* Yonkers, NY: World Book.

Davis, C., Kennedy, S. H., Ravelski, E., & Dionne, M. (1994). The role of physical activity in the development and maintenance of eating disorders. *Psychological Medicine, 24,* 957–967.

Davis, H., & Memmott, J. (1982). Counting behavior in animals: A critical evaluation. *Psychological Bulletin, 92,* 547–571.

Davis, J. M., Sargent, R. G., Brayboy, T. D., & Bartoli, W. P. (1992). Thermogenic effects of pre-prandial and post-prandial exercise in obese females. *Addictive Behaviors, 17,* 185–190.

Davis, J. O., & Phelps, J. A. (1995). Twins with schizophrenia: Genes or germs? *Schizophrenia Bulletin, 21,* 13–18.

Davis, J., Schiffman, H. R., & Greist–Bousquet, S. (1990). Semantic context and figure–ground organization. *Psychological Research, 52,* 306–309.

Davis, R. (1986). Knowledge-based systems. *Science, 231,* 957–963.

Davis, S. F., Huss, M. T., & Becker, A. H. (1995). Norman Triplett and the dawning of sport psychology. *Sport Psychologist, 9,* 366–375.

Davis, S. F., Thomas, R. L., & Weaver, M. S. (1982). Psychology's contemporary and all-time notables: Student, faculty, and chairperson viewpoints. *Bulletin of the Psychonomic Society, 20,* 3–6.

Day, N. L., & Richardson, G. A. (1994). Comparative teratogenicity of alcohol and other drugs. *Alcohol Health and Research World, 18,* 42-48.

DeAngelis, G. C., Ohzawa, I., & Freeman, R. D. (1995). Depth is encoded in the visual cortex by a specialized receptive field structure. *Nature, 352,* 156–159.

DeAngelis, G. C., Ohzawa, I., & Freeman, R. D. (1995). Neuronal mechanisms underlying stereopsis: How do simple cells in the visual cortex encode binocular disparity? *Perception, 24,* 3-31.

Deaux, K. (1985). Sex and gender. *Annual Review of Psychology, 36,* 49–81.

DeCarli, C., Kaye, J. A., Horwitz, B., & Rapoport, S. I. (1990). Critical analysis of the use of computer-assisted transverse axial tomography to study human brain in aging and dementia of the Alzheimer type. *Neurology, 40,* 872–883.

DeCarvalho, R. J. (1992). The institutionalization of humanistic psychology. *Humanistic Psychology, 20,* 124–135.

DeCharms, R., & Moeller, G. H. (1962). Values expressed in American children's readers: 1800–1950. *Journal of Abnormal and Social Psychology, 64,* 136–142.

Deci, E. L., Nezlek, J., & Sheinman, L. (1981). Characteristics of the rewarder and intrinsic motivation of the rewardee. *Journal of Personality and Social Psychology, 40,* 1–10.

Deckers, L., & Buttram, R. T. (1990). Humor as a response to incongruities within or between schemata. *Humor: International Journal of Humor Research, 3,* 53–64.

Deffner-Rappold, C., Azorlosa, J. L., & Baker, J. D. (1996). Acquisition and extinction of context-specific morphine withdrawal. *Psychobiology, 24,* 219-226.

DeLacoste-Utamsing, C., & Holloway, R. L. (1982). Sexual dimorphism in the human corpus callosum. *Science, 216,* 1431–1432.

Delahanty, D. L., Dougall, A. L., Hawken, L., & Trakowski, J. H. (1996). Time course of natural killer cell activity and lymphocyte proliferation in response to two acute stressors in healthy men. *Healthy Psychology, 14,* 357–371.

DeLuga, R. J., & Perry, J. T. (1991). The relationship of subordinate upward influencing behavior, satisfaction and perceived superior effectiveness with leader-member exchanges. *Journal of Occupational Psychology, 64,* 239–252.

Dember, W. N., & Bagwell, M. (1985). A history of perception. In G. A. Kimble & K. Schlesinger (Eds.), *Topics in the history of psychology* (Vol. 1, pp. 261–304). Hillsdale, NJ: Erlbaum.

Dembroski, T. M., & Costa, P. T., Jr. (1988). Assessment of coronary-prone behavior: A current overview. *Annals of Behavioral Medicine, 10,* 60–63.

Dement, W. C. (1960). The effect of dream deprivation. *Science, 131,* 1705–1707.

Dement, W. C., & Wolpert, E. (1958). The relation of eye movements, body motility, and external stimuli to dream content. *Journal of Experimental Psychology, 53,* 543–553.

Dempster, F. N. (1985). Proactive interference in sentence recall: Topic similarity effects and individual differences. *Memory and Cognition, 13,* 81–89.

Denmark, F. L. (1980). Psyche: From rocking the cradle to rocking the boat. *American Psychologist, 35,* 1057–1065.

Denmark, F. L. (1994). Engendering psychology. *American Psychologist, 49,* 329–334.

Dennerstein, L., Smith, A. M. A., & Morse, C. (1994). Psychological well-being, mid-life and the menopause. *Maturitas, 20,* 1–11.

Denney, N. W., Field, J. K., & Quadagno, D. (1984). Sex differences in sexual needs and desires. *Archives of Sexual Behavior, 13,* 233–245.

Dennis, D. L., Buckner, J. C., Lipton, F. R., & Levine, I. S. (1991). A decade of research and services for homeless mentally ill persons: Where do we stand? *American Psychologist, 46,* 1129–1138.

Deppe, R. K., & Harackiewicz, J. M. (1996). Self-handicapping and intrinsic motivation: Buffering intrinsic motivation from the threat of failure. *Journal Personality and Social Psychology, 70,* 868–876.

Desforges, D. M., Lord, C. G., Ramsey, S. L., Manson, J. A., van Leeuwen, M. D., West, S. C., & Lepper, M. R. (1991). Effects of structured cooperative contact on changing negative attitudes toward stigmatized social groups. *Journal of Personality and Social Psychology, 60,* 531–544.

Deuser, W. E., & Anderson, C. A. (1995). Controllability attributions and learned helplessness: Some methodological and conceptual problems. *Basic and Applied Social Psychology, 16,* 297-318.

de Valois, R. L., Abramov, I., & Jacobs, G. H. (1966). Analysis of response patterns of LGN cells. *Journal of the Optical Society of America, 56,* 966–977.

Devine, D., & Forehand, R. (1996). Cascading toward divorce: The roles of marital and child factors. *Journal of Consulting and Clinical Psychology, 64,* 424-427.

de Valois, R. L., & de Valois, K. K. (1980). Spatial vision. *Annual Review of Psychology, 31,* 309–341.

Devine, D. P., & Spanos, N. P. (1990). Effectiveness of maximally different cognitive strategies and expectancy in attenuation of reported pain. *Journal of Personality and Social Psychology, 58,* 672–678.

Deweer, B., Ergis, A. M., Fossati, P., & Pillon, B. (1994). Explicit memory, procedural learning and lexical priming in Alzheimer's disease. *Cortex, 30,* 113–126.

Dewsbury, D. A. (1990). Early interactions between animal psychologists and animal activists and the founding of the APA Committee on Precautions in Animal Experimentation. *American Psychologist, 45,* 315–327.

Dewsbury, D. A. (1996). Beatrix Tugendhat Gardner (1933-1995). *American Psychologist, 51,* 1332.

Diaconis, P. (1978). Statistical problems in ESP research. *Science, 201,* 131–136.

Diamond, M. (1993). Homosexuality and bisexuality in different populations. *Archives of Sexual Behavior, 22,* 291–310.

Diamond, M. C. (1988). *Enriching heredity: The impact of the environment on the anatomy of the brain.* New York: Free Press.

Diaz Soto, L. (1989). Relationship between home environment and intrinsic versus extrinsic orientation of higher achieving and lower achieving Puerto Rican children. *Educational Research Quarterly, 13,* 22–36.

Dickerson, C. A., Thibodeau, R., Aronson, E., & Miller, D. (1992). Using cognitive dissonance to encourage water conservation. *Journal of Applied Social Psychology, 22,* 841–854.

Dickerson, F., Ringel, N., Parente, F., & Boronow, J. (1994). Seclusion and restraint, assaultiveness, and patient performance in a token economy. *Hospital and Community Psychiatry, 45,* 168–170.

Dickey, R., & Stephens, J. (1995). Female-to-male transsexualism, heterosexual type: Two cases. *Archives of Sexual Behavior, 24,* 439–445.

Dickson, D. (1984). Edinburgh sets up parapsychology chair. *Science, 223,* 1274.

Diener, E. (1984). Subjective well-being. *Psychological Bulletin, 95,* 542–575.

Diener, E., Colvin, C. R., Pavot, W. G., & Allman, A. (1991). The psychic costs of intense positive affect. *Journal of Personality and Social Psychology, 61,* 492–503.

Diener, E., Diener, M., & Diener, C. (1995). Factors predicting the subjective well-being of nations. *Journal of Personality and Social Psychology, 69,* 851–864.

Diener, E., & Fujita, F. (1995). Resources, personal strivings, and subjective well-being: A nomothetic and idiographic approach. *Journal of Personality and Social Psychology, 68,* 926–935.

Diener, E., Sandvik, E., Seidlitz, L., & Diener, M. (1993). The relationship between income and subjective well-being: Relative or absolute? *Social Indicators Research, 28,* 195–223.

Diener, E., Wolsic, B., & Fujita, F. (1995). Physical attractiveness and subjective well-being. *Journal of Personality and Social Psychology, 69,* 120–129.

Dill, J. C., & Anderson, C. A. (1995). Effects of frustration justification on hostile aggression. *Aggressive Behavior, 21,* 359–369.

Dillard, J. P. (1990). Self-inference and the foot-in-the-door technique: Quantity of behavior and attitudinal mediation. *Human Communication Research, 16,* 422–447.

Dillard, J. P. (1991). The current status of research on sequential-request compliance techniques. *Personality and Social Psychology Bulletin, 17,* 283–288.

DiMatteo, M. R., Reiter, R. C., & Gambone, J. C. (1994). Enhancing medication adherence through communication and informed collaborative choice. *Health Communication, 6,* 253–265.

DiMatteo, M. R., Sherbourne, C. D., Hays, R. D., & Ordway, L. (1993). Physicians' characteristics influence patients' adherence to medical treatment: Results from the Medical Outcomes Study. *Health Psychology, 12,* 93–102

Dindia, K., & Allen, M. (1992). Sex differences in self-disclosure: A meta-analysis. *Psychological Bulletin, 112,* 106–124.

Dishman, R. J., & Gettman, L. R. (1980). Psychobiologic influences on exercise adherence. *Journal of Sport Psychology, 2,* 295–310.

Dixon, N. F., & Henley, S. H. (1991). Unconscious perception: Possible implications of data from academic research for clinical practice. *Journal of Nervous and Mental Disease, 179,* 243–252.

Doane, J. A., West, K. L., Goldstein, M. J., Rodnick, E. H., & Jones, J. E. (1981). Parental communication deviance and affective style: Predictors of subsequent schizophrenia spectrum disorders in vulnerable adolescents. *Archives of General Psychiatry, 38,* 679–685.

Dobson, K. S., & Pusch, D. (1995). A test of the depressive realism hypothesis in clinically depressed subjects. *Cognitive Therapy and Research, 19,* 179–194.

Dockery, T. M., & Bedeian, A. G. (1989). "Attitudes versus actions": LaPiere's (1934) classic study revisited. *Social Behavior and Personality, 17,* 9–16.

Doell, R. G. (1995). Sexuality in the brain. *Journal of Homosexuality, 28,* 345–354.

Dolce, J. J., & Raczynski, J. M. (1985). Neuromuscular activity and electromyography in painful backs: Psychological and biomechanical models in assessment and treatment. *Psychological Bulletin, 97,* 502–520.

Dolin, D. J., & Booth-Butterfield, S. (1995). Foot-in-the-door and cancer prevention. *Health Communication, 7,* 55–66.

Dollard, J., Doob, I. W., Miller, N. E., Mowrer, O. H., & Sears, R. R. (1939). *Frustration and aggression.* New York: McGraw-Hill.

Dollard, J., & Miller, N. E. (1950). *Personality and psychotherapy.* New York: McGraw-Hill.

Dolliver, R. H. (1995). Carl Rogers's personality theory and psychotherapy as a reflection of his life and personality. *Journal of Humanistic Psychology, 35,* 111–128.

Domino, G. (1992). Cooperation and competition in Chinese and American children. *Journal of Cross Cultural Psychology, 23,* 456–467.

Donaldson, K. D. (1976). *Insanity inside out: The personal story behind the landmark Supreme Court decision.* New York: Crown.

Donderi, D. C. (1994). Visual acuity, color vision, and visual search performance at sea. *Human Factors, 36,* 129–144.

Donnerstein, E. I., & Berkowitz, L. (1981). Victim reactions in aggressive erotic films as a factor in violence against women. *Journal of Personality and Social Psychology, 41,* 710–724.

Douglas, S. (1993). The authentic Fritz. *Gestalt Journal, 16,* 125–136.

Doyle, A. C. (1930). *The complete Sherlock Holmes.* Garden City, NY: Doubleday.

Doyle, J. (1995). *The male experience* (3rd ed.). Madison, WI: Brown & Benchmark.

Dracup, K., Moser, D. K., Eisenberg, M., & Meischke, H. (1995). Causes of delay in seeking treatment for heart attack symptoms. *Social Science and Medicine, 40,* 379–392.

Dray, A., & Perkins, M. (1993). Bradykinin and inflammatory pain. *Trends in Neurosciences, 16,* 99–104.

Drevets, W. C., Burton, H., Videen, T. O., & Snyder, A. Z. (1995). Blood flow changes in human somatosensory cortex during anticipated stimulation. *Nature, 373,* 249–252.

Drigotas, S. M. (1993). Similarity revisited: A comparison of similarity-attraction versus dissimilarity-repulsion. *British Journal of Social Psychology, 32,* 365–377.

Driskell, J. E., Willis, R. P., & Copper, C. (1992). Effect of overlearning on retention. *Journal of Applied Psychology, 77,* 615–622.

Droste, C., Greenlee, M. W., Schreck, M., & Roskamm, H. (1991). Experimental pain thresholds and plasma beta-endorphin levels during exercise. *Medicine and Science in Sports and Exercise, 23,* 334–342.

Dubner, R., & Bennett, G. J. (1983). Spinal and trigeminal mechanisms of nociception. *Annual Review of Neuroscience, 6,* 381–418.

Duckitt, J., & Farre, B. (1994). Right-wing authoritarianism and political intolerance among Whites in the future majority-rule South Africa. *Journal of Social Psychology, 134,* 735–741.

Duckro, P. N. (1991). Biofeedback in the management of headache: II. *Headache Quarterly, 2,* 17–22.

Duckworth, J. C. (1991). The Minnesota Multiphasic Personality Inventory-2: A review. *Journal of Counseling and Development, 69,* 564–567.

Dudycha, G. J. (1936). An objective study of punctuality in relation to personality and achievement. *Archives of Psychology, 29,* 1–53.

Duke, M., & Nowicki, S. (1986). *Abnormal psychology.* San Diego: Harcourt Brace Jovanovich.

Dunbar-Jacob, J., Dwyer, K., & Dunning, E. J. (1991). Compliance with antihypertensive regimen: A review of the research in the 1980s. *Annals of Behavioral Medicine, 13,* 31–39.

Duncan, J., Burgess, P., & Emslie, H. (1995). Fluid intelligence after frontal lobe lesions. *Neuropsychologia, 33,* 261–268.

Duncan, N. C. (1991). CAI-enhanced exam performance in a research design course. *Behavior Research Methods, Instruments, and Computers, 23,* 324–327.

Dunn, J. (1993). Psychic conflict and the external world in Freud's theory of the instinctual drives in light of his adherence to Darwin. *International Journal of Psychoanalysis, 74,* 231–240.

Dunn, R. L., & Schwebel, A. I. (1995). Meta-analytic review of marital therapy outcome research. *Journal of Family Psychology, 9,* 58–68.

Durbin, D. L., Darling, N., Steinberg, L., & Brown, B. B. (1993). Parenting style and peer group membership among European-American adolescents. *Journal of Research on Adolescence, 3,* 87–100.

Dutton, D. G., & Aron, A. P. (1974). Some evidence for heightened sexual attraction under conditions of high anxiety. *Journal of Personality and Social Psychology, 30,* 510–517.

Duyme, M. (1988). School success and social class: An adoption study. *Developmental Psychology, 24,* 203–209.

Dvir, T., Eden, D., & Banjo, M. L. (1995). Self-fulfilling prophecy and gender: Can women be Pygmalion and Galatea? *Journal of Applied Psychology, 80,* 253–270.

Dworkin, B. R., & Miller, N. E. (1986). Failure to replicate visceral learning in the acute curarized rat preparation. *Behavioral Neuroscience, 100,* 299–314.

Dwyer, T. (1986, June 15). How the will to win drove an athlete to the edge. *Philadelphia Inquirer,* pp. 1-A, 8-A.

Dykema, J., Bergbower, K., & Peterson, C. (1995). Pessimistic explanatory style, stress, and illness. *Journal of Social and Clinical Psychology, 14,* 357–371.

Eagly, A. H. (1984). Gender and social influence: A social psychological analysis. *American Psychologist, 38,* 971–981.

Eagly, A. H. (1994). On comparing women and men. *Feminism and Psychology, 4,* 513–522.

Eagly, A. H. (1995). The science and politics of comparing women and men. *American Psychologist, 50,* 145–158.

Eagly, A. H., & Steffen, V. J. (1986). Gender and aggressive behavior: A meta-analytic review of the social psychological literature. *Psychological Bulletin, 100,* 309–330.

Eagly, A. H., & Warren, R. (1976). Intelligence, comprehension, and opinion change. *Journal of Personality and Social Psychology, 44,* 226–242.

Eastman, C. I., Stewart, K. T., Mahoney, M. P., & Liu, L. (1994). Dark goggles and bright light improve circadian rhythm adaptation to night-shift work. *Sleep, 17,* 535–543.

Ebbeck, V., & Weiss, M. R. (1988). The arousal-performance relationship: Task characteristics and performance measures in track and field athletics. *Sport Psychologist, 2,* 13–27.

Ebbinghaus, H. (1885/1913). *Memory: A contribution to experimental psychology.* New York: Columbia University Press.

Eccles, A., Wilde, A., & Marshall, W. L. (1988). In vivo desensitization in the treatment of recurrent nightmares. *Journal of Behavior Therapy and Experimental Psychiatry, 19,* 285–288.

Ecenbarger, W. (1987, June 4). The forgotten sense. *Philadelphia Inquirer Magazine,* pp. 24–26, 34–35.

Eckerman, C. O., Davis, C. C., & Didow, S. M. (1989). Toddlers' emerging ways of achieving social coordinations with a peer. *Child Development, 60,* 440–453.

Eckert, E. D., Bouchard, T. J., Bohlen, J., & Heston, L. L. (1986). Homosexuality in monozygotic twins reared apart. *British Journal of Psychiatry, 148,* 421–425.

Edeline, J. M., & Weinberger, N. M. (1991). Subcortical adaptive filtering in the auditory system: Associative receptive field plasticity in the dorsal medial geniculate body. *Behavioral Neuroscience, 105,* 154–175.

Edelman, G. M (1984, April). Cell adhesion molecules: A molecular basis for animal form. *Scientific American,* pp. 118–129.

Edelmann, R. J., & Golombok, S. (1989). Stress and reproductive failure. *Journal of Reproductive and Infant Psychology, 7,* 79–86.

Edinger, J. D., & Radtke, R. A. (1993). Use of in vivo desensitization to treat a patient's claustrophobic response to nasal CPAP. *Sleep, 16,* 678–680.

Edwards, D., & Kern, R. (1996). The implications of teachers' social interest on classroom behavior. *Individual Psychology: Journal of Adlerian Theory, Research and Practice, 51,* 67–73.

Egan, K. J., Carr, J. E., Hunt, D. D., & Adamson, R. (1988). Endogenous opiate system and systematic desensitization. *Journal of Consulting and Clinical Psychology, 56,* 287–291.

Egeland, J. A., Gerhard, D. S., Pauls, D. L., Sussex, J. N., Kidd, K. K., Allen, C. R., Hostetter, A. M., & Housman, D. E. (1987). Bipolar affective disorders linked to DNA markers on chromosome 11. *Nature, 325,* 783–787.

Ehara, T. H. (1980, December). On the electronic chess circuit. *Science 80,* pp. 78, 80.

Ehrlichman, H., & Halpern, J. N. (1988). Affect and memory: Effects of pleasant and unpleasant odors on retrieval of happy and unhappy memories. *Journal of Personality and Social Psychology, 55,* 769–779.

Eich, E., Macaulay, D., & Ryan, L. (1994). Mood-dependent memory for events of the personal past. *Journal of Experimental Psychology General, 123,* 201–215.

Eich, J. E. (1980). The cue-dependent nature of state-dependent retrieval. *Memory and Cognition, 8,* 157–173.

Eich, J. E. (1995). Searching for mood-dependent memory. *Psychological Science, 6,* 67–75.

Eich, J. E., Weingartner, H., Stillman, R. C., & Gillin, J. C. (1975). State-dependent accessibility of retrieval cues in the retention of a categorized list. *Journal of Verbal Learning and Verbal Behavior, 14,* 408–417.

Eichenbaum, H. (1997). Declarative memory: Insights from cognitive neurobiology. *Annual Review of Psychology, 48,* 547-572.

Eichhorn, S. K. (1982). Congenital cytomegalovirus infection: A significant cause of deafness and mental deficiency. *American Annals of the Deaf, 127,* 838–843.

Eisdorfer, C. (1983). Conceptual models of aging: The challenge of a new frontier. *American Psychologist, 38,* 197–202.

Eisen, S. V. (1979). Actor-observer differences in information inference and casual attribution. *Journal of Personality and Social Psychology, 37,* 261–272.

Eisenberg, N., & Lennon, R. (1983). Sex differences in empathy and related capacities. *Psychological Bulletin, 94,* 100–131.

Eisenberg, N., Cialdini, R. B., McCreath, H., & Shell, R. (1987). Consistency-based compliance: When and why do children become vulnerable? *Journal of Personality and Social Psychology, 52,* 1174–1181.

Eisenman, R. (1993). Belief that drug usage in the United States is increasing when it is really decreasing: An example of the availability heuristic. *Bulletin of the Psychonomic Society, 31,* 249–252.

Eiser, J. R., Eiser, C., Sani, F., & Sell, L. (1995). Skin cancer attitudes: A cross-national comparison. *British Journal of Social Psychology, 34,* 23–30.

Eison, A. S., & Eison, M. S. (1994). Serotonergic mechanisms in anxiety. *Progress in Neuropsychopharmacology and Biological Psychiatry, 18,* 47–62.

Ekman, P. (1992a). An argument for basic emotions. *Cognition and Emotion, 6,* 169–200.

Ekman, P. (1992b). Facial expressions of emotion: New findings, new questions. *Psychological Science, 3,* 34–38.

Ekman, P. (1993). Facial expression and emotion. *American Psychologist, 48,* 384–392.

Ekman, P., Davidson, R. J., & Friesen, W. V. (1990). The Duchenne smile: Emotional expression and brain physiology: 2. *Journal of Personality and Social Psychology, 58,* 342–353.

Ekman, P., & Friesen, W. V. (1971). Constants across cultures in the face and emotion. *Journal of Personality and Social Psychology, 17,* 124–129.

Ekman, P., Friesen, W. V., & Bear, J. (1984, May). The international language of gestures. *Psychology Today,* pp. 64–69.

Ekman, P., Friesen, W. V., O'Sullivan, M., Chan, A., Diacoyanni-Tarlatzis, I., Heider, K., Krause, R., LeCompte, W. A., Pitcairn, T., Ricci-Bitti, P. E., Scherer, K., Tomita, M., & Tzavaras, A. (1987). Universals and cultural differences in the judgments of facial expressions of emotion. *Journal of Personality and Social Psychology, 53,* 712–717.

Ekman, P., & Heider, K. G. (1988). The universality of a contempt expression: A replication. *Motivation and Emotion, 12,* 303–308.

Ekman, P., Levenson, R. W., & Friesen, W. V. (1983). Autonomic nervous system activity distinguishes among emotions. *Science, 221,* 1208–1210.

Ekman, P., & O'Sullivan, M. (1991). Who can catch a liar? *American Psychologist, 46,* 913–920.

Elaad, E. (1990). Detection of guilty knowledge in real-life criminal investigations. *Journal of Applied Psychology, 75,* 521–529.

Elaad, E. (1994). The accuracy of human decisions and objective measurements in psychophysiological detection of knowledge. *Journal of Psychology, 128,* 267–280.

El-Feky, H. A. (1991). Patterns of parental control in Kuwaiti society. *International Journal of Psychology, 26,* 485–495.

Elkins, R. L. (1987). An experimenter effect on place avoidance learning of selectively-bred taste-aversion prone and resistant rats. *Medical Science Research: Psychology and Psychiatry, 15,* 1181–1182.

Ellenberger, H. F. (1970). *The discovery of the unconscious: The history and evolution of dynamic psychiatry.* New York: Basic Books.

Elliot, A. J., & Devine, P. G. (1994). On the motivational nature of cognitive dissonance: Dissonance as psychological discomfort. *Journal of Personality and Social Psychology, 67,* 382–394.

Elliott, R. (1988). Tests, abilities, race, and conflict. *Intelligence, 12,* 333–350.

Ellis, A. (1962). *Reason and emotion in psychotherapy.* New York: Lyle Stuart.

Ellis, A. (1996). The treatment of morbid jealousy: A rational-emotive behavior therapy approach. *Journal of Cognitive Psychotherapy, 10,* 23–33.

Ellis, H. C. (1987). Recent developments in human memory. In V. P. Makosy (Ed.), *The G. Stanley Hall Lecture Series* (Vol. 7, pp. 161–206). Washington, DC: American Psychological Association.

Ellis, J. B., & Range, L. M. (1989). Characteristics of suicidal individuals: A review. *Death Studies, 13,* 485–500.

Ellis, L. (1987). Relationships of criminality and psychopathy with eight other apparent behavioral manifestations of sub-optimal arousal. *Personality and Individual Differences, 8,* 905–925.

Ellis, L., & Ames, M. A. (1987). Neurohormonal functioning and sexual orientation: A theory of homosexuality-heterosexuality. *Psychological Bulletin, 101,* 233–258.

Ellison, P. A., Govern, J. M., Petri, H. L., & Figler, M. H. (1995). Anonymity and aggressive driving behavior: A field study. *Journal of Social Behavior and Personality, 10,* 265–272.

Ellison, W. J. (1987). State execution of juveniles: Defining "youth" as a mitigating factor for imposing a sentence of less than death. *Law and Psychology Review, 11,* 1–38.

Elmore, R. T., Jr., Wildman, R. W., II, & Westefeld, J. S. (1980). The use of systematic desensitization in the treatment of blood phobia. *Journal of Behavior Therapy and Experimental Psychiatry, 11,* 277–279.

Emmelkamp, P. M., & Beens, H. (1991). Cognitive therapy with obsessive-compulsive disorder: A comparative evaluation. *Behaviour Research and Therapy, 29,* 293–300.

Emonson, D. L., & Vanderbeek, R. D. (1995). The use of amphetamines in U.S. Air Force tactical operations during Desert Shield and Storm. *Aviation, Space, and Environmental Medicine, 66,* 260–263.

Endler, N. S. (1988). The origins of electroconvulsive therapy (ECT). *Convulsive Therapy, 4,* 5–23.

Engels, G. I., Garnefski, N., & Diekstra, R. F. W. (1993). Efficacy of rational-emotive therapy: A quantitative analysis. *Journal of Consulting and Clinical Psychology, 61,* 1083–1090.

Epstein, R. (1991). Skinner, creativity, and the problem of spontaneous behavior. *Psychological Science, 2,* 362–370.

Epstein, R., Kirshnit, C. E., Lanza, R. P., & Rubin, L. C. (1984). "Insight" in the pigeon: Antecedents and determinants of an intelligent performance. *Nature, 308,* 61–62.

Epstein, S. (1994). Integration of the cognitive and the psychodynamic unconscious. *American Psychologist, 49,* 709–724.

Epstein, S., & Feist, G. J. (1988). Relation between self-and other-acceptance and its moderation by identification. *Journal of Personality and Social Psychology, 54,* 309–315.

Epstein, S., & O'Brien, E. J. (1985). The person-situation debate in historical and current perspective. *Psychological Bulletin, 98,* 513–537.

Epstein, W., & Hatfield, G. (1994). Gestalt psychology and the philosophy of mind. *Philosophical Psychology, 7,* 163–181.

Erdelyi, M. H. (1992). Psychodynamics and the unconscious. *American Psychologist, 47,* 784–787.

Erel, O., & Burman, B. (1995). Interrelatedness of marital relations and parent-child relations: A meta-analytic review. *Psychological Bulletin, 118,* 108–132.

Ericsson, K. A., & Polson, P. G. (1988). An experimental analysis of the mechanisms of a memory skill. *Journal of Experimental Psychology: Learning, Memory, and Cognition, 14,* 305–316.

Erikson, E. (1963). *Childhood and society.* New York: W. W. Norton.

Erlenmeyer-Kimling, L., Folnegovic, Z., Hrabak-Zerjavic, V., & Borcic, B. (1994). Schizophrenia and prenatal exposure to the 1957 A2 influenza epidemic in Croatia. *American Journal of Psychiatry, 151,* 1496–1498.

Erwin, P. G. (1994). Effectiveness of social skills training with children: A meta-analytic study. *Counseling Psychology Quarterly, 7,* 305–310.

Eslinger, P. J., Damasio, A. R., & Van Hoesen, G. W. (1982). Olfactory dysfunction in man: Anatomical and behavioral aspects. *Brain and Cognition, 1,* 259–285.

Estrada, C. A., Isen, A. M., & Young, M. J. (1994). Positive affect improves creative problem solving and influences reported source of practice satisfaction in physicians. *Motivation and Emotion, 18,* 285–299.

Evans, D. L., Leserman, J., Perkins, D. O., & Stern, R. A. (1995). Stress-associated reductions of cytotoxic T lymphocytes and natural killer cells in asymptomatic HIV infection. *American Journal of Psychiatry, 152,* 543–550.

Ewald, H., Mors, O., Flint, T., & Koed, K. (1995). A possible locus for manic depressive illness on chromosome 16p13. *Psychiatric Genetics, 5,* 71–81.

Ewin, D. M. (1994). Many memories retrieved with hypnosis are accurate. *American Journal of Clinical Hypnosis, 36,* 174–176.

Eysenck, H. J. (1982). *Personality, genetics, and behavior: Selected papers.* New York: Praeger.

Eysenck, H. J. (1988). Skinner, Skinnerism, and the Skinnerian in psychology. *Counseling Psychology Quarterly, 1,* 299–301.

Eysenck, H. J. (1990). Genetic and environmental contributions to individual differences: The three major dimensions of personality. *Journal of Personality, 58,* 245–261.

Eysenck, H. J. (1994). Cancer, personality and stress: Prediction and prevention. *Advances in Behaviour Research and Therapy, 16,* 167–215.

Eysenck, H. J. (1994). The outcome problem in psychotherapy: What have we learned? *Behaviour Research and Therapy, 32,* 477–495.

Eysenck, H. J., Wakefield, J. A., Jr., & Friedman, A. F. (1983). Diagnosis and clinical assessment: The DSM-III. *Annual Review of Psychology, 34,* 167–193.

Eysenck, S. B., Barrett, P. T., & Barnes, G. E. (1993). A cross-cultural study of personality: Canada and England. *Personality and Individual Differences, 14,* 1–9.

Fagan, M. M., & Ayers, K. (1982). The life of a police officer: A developmental perspective. *Criminal Justice and Behavior, 9,* 273–285.

Fagan, T. K. (1992). Compulsory schooling, child study, clinical psychology, and special education: Origins of school psychology. *American Psychologist, 47,* 236–243.

Fagerstrom, K. O., Schneider, N. G., & Lunell, E. (1993). Effectiveness of nicotine patch and nicotine gum as individual versus combined treatments for tobacco withdrawal symptoms. *Psychopharmacology, 111,* 271–277.

Faith, M. S., Wong, F. Y., & Carpenter, K. M. (1995). Group sensitivity training: Update, meta-analysis, and recommendations. *Journal of Counseling Psychology, 42,* 390–399.

Falbo, T., & Polit, D. F. (1986). Quantitative review of the only-child literature: Research evidence and theory development. *Psychological Bulletin, 100,* 176–189.

Falk, J. L. (1994). The discriminative stimulus and its reputation: Role in the instigation of drug abuse. *Experimental and Clinical Psychopharmacology, 2,* 43–52.

Fallon, A. E., & Rozin, P. (1985). Sex differences in perceptions of desirable body shape. *Journal of Abnormal Psychology, 94,* 102–105.

Fancher, R. E. (1979). *Pioneers of psychology.* New York: W. W. Norton.

Fancher, R. E. (1984). Not Conley, but Burt and others: A reply. *Journal of the History of the Behavioral Sciences, 20,* 186.

Fancher, R. E. (1987). Henry Goddard and the Kallikak family photographs: "Conscious skulduggery" or "Whig history"? *American Psychologist, 42,* 585–590.

Fancher, R. E. (1990). *Pioneers of psychology.* New York: W. W. Norton.

Faraone, S. V. (1982). Psychiatry and political repression in the Soviet Union. *American Psychologist, 37,* 1105–1112.

Farr, C. B. (1994). Benjamin Rush and American psychiatry. *American Journal of Psychiatry, 151,* 65–73.

Farrimond, T. (1990). Effect of alcohol on visual constancy values and possible relation to driving performance. *Perceptual and Motor Skills, 70,* 291–295.

Farthing, G. W., Venturino, M., & Brown, S. W. (1984). Suggestion and distraction in the control of pain: Test of two hypotheses. *Journal of Abnormal Psychology, 93,* 266–276.

Faust, J., Olson, R., & Rodriguez, H. (1991). Same-day surgery preparation: Reduction of pediatric patient arousal and distress through participant modeling. *Journal of Consulting and Clinical Psychology, 59,* 475–478.

Fava, G. A., Grandi, S., Canestrari, R., & Grasso, P. (1991). Mechanisms of change of panic attacks with exposure treatment of agoraphobia. *Journal of Affective Disorders, 22,* 65–71.

Fava, M., Littman, A., & Halperin, P. (1987). Neuroendocrine correlates of the Type A behavior pattern: A review and new hypotheses. *International Journal of Psychiatry in Medicine, 17,* 289–307.

Feder, H. H. (1984). Hormones and sexual behavior. *Annual Review of Psychology, 35,* 165–200.

Fehr, B., & Russell, J. A. (1984). Concept of emotion viewed from a prototypic perspective. *Journal of Experimental Psychology: General, 113,* 464–486.

Fehr, B., & Russell, J. A. (1991). The concept of love viewed from a prototype perspective. *Journal of Personality and Social Psychology, 60,* 425–438.

Fein, D. (1990). Cerebral lateralization: A dominant question in developmental research [Review of *Brain lateralization in children: Developmental implications*]. *Contemporary Psychology, 35,* 676–677.

Feingold, A. (1994). Gender differences in personality: A meta-analysis. *Psychological Bulletin, 116,* 429–456.

Ferlazzo, F., Conte, S., & Gentilomo, A. (1993). Event-related potentials and recognition memory within the "levels of processing" framework. *Neuroreport: An International Journal for the Rapid Communication of Research in Neuroscience, 4,* 667-670.

Fern, E. F., Monroe, K. B., & Avila, R. A. (1986). Effectiveness of multiple request strategies: A synthesis of research results. *Journal of Marketing Research, 23,* 144–152.

Fernandez, F., Turon, J., Siegfried, J., & Meermann, R. (1995). Does additional body therapy improve the treatment of anorexia nervosa? A comparison of two approaches. *Eating Disorders: The Journal of Treatment and Prevention, 3,* 158–164.

Ferrari, M. (1996). Observing the observer: Self-regulation in the observational learning of motor skills. *Developmental Review, 16,* 203-240.

Ferris, A. M., & Duffy, V. B. (1989). Effect of olfactory deficits on nutritional status: Does age predict persons at risk? *Annals of the New York Academy of Sciences, 561,* 113–123.

Festinger, L., & Carlsmith, J. M. (1959). Cognitive consequences of forced compliance. *Journal of Abnormal and Social Psychology, 58,* 203–210.

Festinger, L., Pepitone, A., & Newcomb, T. (1952). Some consequences of deindividuation in a group. *Journal of Abnormal and Social Psychology, 47,* 382–389.

Festinger, L., Riecken, H. W., & Schachter, S. (1956). *When prophecy fails.* New York: Harper & Row.

Festinger, L., Schachter, S., & Back, K. (1950). *Social pressures in informal groups: A study of a housing community.* Stanford, CA: Stanford University Press.

Fiedler, F. E. (1967). *A theory of leader effectiveness.* New York: McGraw-Hill.

Field, T. M. (1991). Quality infant day-care and grade school behavior and performance. *Child Development, 62,* 863–870.

Field, T. M., Woodson, R., Greenberg, R., & Cohen, D. (1982). Discrimination and imitation of facial expressions by neonates. *Science, 218,* 179–181.

Filsinger, E. E., Braun, J. J., Monte, W. C., & Linder, D. E. (1984). Human (*Homo sapiens*) responses to the pig (*Sus scrofa*) sex pheromone 5 alpha-androst-16-en-3-one. *Journal of Comparative Psychology, 98,* 219–222.

Findley, M. J., & Cooper, H. M. (1983). Locus of control and academic achievement: A literature review. *Journal of Personality and Social Psychology, 44,* 419–427.

Fine, A., Meldrum, B. S., & Patel, S. (1990). Modulation of experimentally induced epilepsy by intracerebral grafts of fetal GABAergic neurons. *Neuropsychologia, 28,* 627–634.

Fink, M. (1984). Meduna and the origins of convulsive therapy. *American Journal of Psychiatry, 141,* 1034–1041.

Finkelstein, P., Wenegrat, B., & Yalom, I. (1982). Large group awareness training. *Annual Review of Psychology, 33,* 515–539.

Fiore, M. C., Smith, S. S., Jorenby, D. E., & Baker, T. B. (1994). The effectiveness of the nicotine patch for smoking cessation: A meta-analysis. *JAMA: Journal of the American Medical Association, 271,* 1940–1947.

Fiorentini, A., Berardi, N., & Maffei, L. (1995). Nerve growth factor preserves behavioral visual acuity in monocularly deprived kittens. *Visual Neuroscience, 12,* 51–55.

Fiorito, G., & Scotto, P. (1992). Observational learning in *Octopus vulgaris*. *Science, 256,* 545–547.

Fischer, K. W., & Silvern, L. (1985). Stages and individual differences in cognitive development. *Annual Review of Psychology, 36,* 613–648.

Fisher, C. B., & Fyrberg, D. (1994). Participant partners: College students weight the costs and benefits of deceptive research. *American Psychologist, 49,* 417–427.

Fisher, E. B., Delamater, A. M., Bertelson, A. D., & Kirkley, B. G. (1982). Psychological factors in diabetes and its treatment. *Journal of Consulting and Clinical Psychology, 50,* 993–1003.

Fisher, K. (1983, February). TV violence. *APA Monitor,* pp. 7, 9.

Fisher, K. (1984, April). Strangler's mind becomes a trap for psychologists. *APA Monitor,* pp. 10–11, 13.

Fisher, K. (1985, November). Duty to warn: Where does it end? *APA Monitor,* pp. 24–25.

Fisher, K. (1986, March). Animal research: Few alternatives seen for behavioral studies. *APA Monitor,* pp. 16–17.

Fisher, S., & Greenberg, R. P. (1985). *The scientific credibility of Freud's theories and therapy.* New York: Columbia University Press.

Fisher, S. K., & Ciuffreda, K. J. (1989). The effect of accommodative hysteresis on apparent distance. *Ophthalamic and Physiological Optics, 9,* 184–190.

Fisher, W. A., & Grenier, G. (1994). Violent pornography, antiwoman thoughts, and antiwoman acts: In search of reliable effects. *Journal of Sex Research, 31,* 23–38.

Fiske, D. W., Conley, J. J., & Goldberg, L. R. (1987). E. Lowell Kelly (1905–1986). *American Psychologist, 42,* 511–512.

Flannagan, D. A., & Blick, K. A. (1989). Levels of processing and the retention of word meanings. *Perceptual and Motor Skills, 68,* 1123–1128.

Flavell, J. H. (1996). Piaget's legacy. *Psychological Science, 7,* 200-203.

Flay, B. R. (1985). Psychosocial approaches to smoking prevention: A review of findings. *Health Psychology, 4,* 449–488.

Flett, G. L., Hewitt, P. L., Blankstein, K. R., & Dynin, C. B. (1994). Dimensions of perfectionism and Type A behaviour. *Personality and Individual Differences, 16,* 477–485.

Flor-Henry, P. (1983). Mood, the right hemisphere and the implications of spatial information-perceiving systems. *Research Communications in Psychology, Psychiatry, and Behavior, 8,* 143–170.

Flynn, J. R. (1987). Massive IQ gains in 14 nations: What IQ tests really measure. *Psychological Bulletin, 101,* 171–191.

Foerstl, J. (1989). Early interest in the idiot savant. *American Journal of Psychiatry, 146,* 566.

Fogarty, G. J. (1994). Using the Personal Orientation Inventory to measure change in student self-actualization. *Personality and Individual Differences, 17,* 435–439.

Foley, J. M. (1988). Experiments on human pattern vision. *Hiroshima Forum for Psychology, 13,* 51–61.

Folkes, V. S. (1982). Forming relationships and the matching hypothesis. *Personality and Social Psychology Bulletin, 8,* 631–636.

Folkes, V. S. (1988). The availability heuristic and perceived risk. *Journal of Consumer Research, 15,* 13–23.

Foltin, R. W., Fischman, M. W., & Levin, F. R. (1995). Cardiovascular effects of cocaine in humans: Laboratory studies. *Drug and Alcohol Dependence, 37,* 193–210.

Fontaine, K. R., & Shaw, D. F. (1995). Effects of self-efficacy and dispositional optimism on adherence to step aerobic exercise classes. *Perceptual and Motor Skills, 81,* 251–255.

Fontana, A., & Rosenheck, R. (1994). Posttraumatic stress disorder among Vietnam theater veterans: A causal model of etiology in a community sample. *Journal of Nervous and Mental Disease, 182,* 677–684.

Fontana, D. J., Inouye, G. T., & Johnson, R. M. (1994). Linopirdine (DuP 996) improves performance in several tests of learning and memory by modulation of cholinergic neurotransmission. *Pharmacology, Biochemistry and Behavior, 49,* 1075–1082.

Foote, D. (1995, January 30). "Any old day . . ." *Newsweek*, p. 28.

Ford, B. D. (1993). Emergenesis: An alternative and a confound. *American Psychologist, 48,* 1294.

Foreyt, J. P. (1987). Issues in the assessment and treatment of obesity. *Journal of Consulting and Clinical Psychology, 55,* 677–684.

Foreyt, J. P., & Goodrick, G. K. (1994). Impact of behavior therapy on weight loss. *American Journal of Health Promotion, 8,* 466–468.

Forgays, D. G., & Forgays, D. K. (1994). The use of flotation isolation to modify important Type A components in young adults. *Journal of Environmental Psychology, 14,* 47–55.

Forgays, D. K. (1996). The relationship between Type A parenting and adolescent perceptions of family environment. *Adolescence, 31,* 841–862.

Forster, J., & Schwartz, T. (1994). Constructing and measuring self-esteem. *Journal of Constructivist Psychology, 7,* 163–175.

Forsyth, D. R., Pope, W. R., & McMillan, J. H. (1985). Students' reactions after cheating: An attributional analysis. *Contemporary Educational Psychology, 10,* 72–82.

Fortmann, S. P., & Killen, J. D. (1995). Nicotine gum and self-help behavioral treatment for smoking relapse prevention: Results from a trial using population-based recruitment. *Journal of Consulting and Clinical Psychology, 63,* 460–468.

Fowles, D. C. (1992). Schizophrenia: Diathesis-stress revisited. *Annual Review of Psychology, 43,* 303–336.

Fox, J. L. (1984). The brain's dynamic way of keeping in touch. *Science, 225,* 820–821.

Fox, L. H. (1981). Identification of the academically gifted. *American Psychologist, 36,* 1103–1111.

Fox, N. A., & Davidson, R. J. (1988). Patterns of brain electrical activity during facial signs of emotion in 10-month-old infants. *Developmental Psychology, 24,* 230–236.

Fox, S. E., & Burns, D. J. (1993). The mere exposure effect for stimuli presented below recognition threshold: A failure to replicate. *Perceptual and Motor Skills, 76,* 391–396.

Frances, A., Mack, A., First, M. B., & Jones, C. (1995). DSM-IV: Issues in development. *Psychiatric Annals, 25,* 15–19.

Frank, M. G., & Ekman, P. (1993). Not all smiles are created equal: The differences between enjoyment and nonenjoyment smiles. *Humor: International Journal of Humor Research, 6,* 9–26.

Frankel, R. M. (1995). Emotion and the physician-patient relationship. *Motivation and Emotion, 19,* 163–173.

Frankl, V. E. (1961). Logotherapy and the challenge of suffering. *Review of Existential Psychology and Psychiatry, 1,* 3–7.

Franzek, E., & Beckmann, H. (1996). Gene-environment interaction in schizophrenia: Season-of-birth effect reveals etiologically different subgroups. *Psychopathology, 29,* 14–26.

Frasciello, L. M., & Willard, S. G. (1995). Anorexia nervosa in males: A case report and review of the literature. *Clinical Social Work Journal, 23,* 47–58.

Frederick, C. M., & Ryan, R. M. (1995). Self-determination in sport: A review using cognitive evaluation theory. *International Journal of Sport Psychology, 26,* 5–23.

Frederiksen, N. (1986). Toward a broader conception of human intelligence. *American Psychologist, 41,* 445–452.

Free, N. K., Green, B. L., Grace, M. C., Chernus, L. A., & Whitman, R. M. (1985). Empathy and outcome in brief focal dynamic therapy. *American Journal of Psychiatry, 142,* 917–921.

Free, N. K., Winget, C. N., & Whitman, R. M. (1993). Separation anxiety in panic disorder. *American Journal of Psychiatry, 150,* 595–599.

Freedman, J. L. (1984). Effect of television violence on aggressiveness. *Psychological Bulletin, 96,* 227–246.

Freedman, J. L., & Fraser, S. C. (1966). Compliance without pressure. *Journal of Personality and Social Psychology, 4,* 195–202.

Freivalds, A., & Horii, K. (1994). An oculomotor test to measure alcohol impairment. *Perceptual and Motor Skills, 78,* 603–610.

Freud, S. (1900/1990). *The interpretation of dreams.* New York: Basic Books.

Freud, S. (1901/1965). *Psychopathology of everyday life.* New York: W. W. Norton.

Freud, S. (1901/1990). *Psychopathology of everyday life.* New York: Gryphon.

Freud, S. (1905). *Jokes and their relationship to the unconscious.* London: Hogarth Press.

Freud, S. (1914/1957). On the history of the psychoanalytic movement. In J. Strachey (Ed.), *The standard edition of the complete psychological works of Sigmund Freud* (Vol. 14, pp. 7–66). London: Hogarth Press.

Freud, S. (1917/1963). Mourning and melancholia. In J. Strachey (Ed.), *The standard edition of the complete psychological works of Sigmund Freud* (Vol. 14, pp. 243–258). London: Hogarth Press.

Freud, S. (1974). *Cocaine papers* (R. Byck, Ed.). New York: Stonehill.

Frezza, M., di Padova, C., Pozzato, G., Terpin, M., Baraona, E., & Lieber, C. S. (1990). High blood alcohol levels in women: The role of decreased gastric alcohol dehydrogenase activity and first-pass metabolism. *New England Journal of Medicine, 322,* 95–99.

Frick, R. W. (1985). Communicating emotion: The role of prosodic features. *Psychological Bulletin, 97,* 412–429.

Fried, P. A., & Watkinson, B. (1990). Thirty-six and forty-eight-month neurobehavioral follow-up of children prenatally exposed to marijuana, cigarettes, and alcohol. *Journal of Developmental and Behavioral Pediatrics, 11,* 49–58.

Fried, R. (1990). Integrating music in breathing training and relaxation: II. Applications. *Biofeedback and Self-Control, 12,* 171–177.

Friedman, M., & Rosenman, R. H. (1959). Association of specific overt behavior pattern with blood and cardiovascular findings. *Journal of the American Medical Association, 169,* 1286–1296.

Friedman, M., & Rosenman, R. H. (1974). *Type A behavior and your heart.* New York: Knopf.

Friedman, R. C., & Downey, J. (1993). Neurobiology and sexual orientation: Current relationships. *Journal of Neuropsychiatry and Clinical Neurosciences, 5,* 131–153.

Frisch, K. von. (1974). Decoding the language of a bee. *Science, 185,* 663–668.

Fritsch, G., & Hitzig, E. (1870/1960). On the electrical excitability of the cerebrum. Springfield, IL: Charles C. Thomas.

Fromm, E. (1941). *Escape from freedom.* New York: Holt, Rinehart & Winston.

Fromm, E. (1956). *The art of loving.* New York: Harper & Row.

Fuchs-Beauchamp, K. D., Karnes, M. B., & Johnson, L. J. (1993). Creativity and intelligence in preschoolers. *Gifted Child Quarterly, 37,* 113–117.

Fujita, K., Blough, D. S., & Blough, P. M. (1993). Effects of the inclination of context lines on perception of the Ponzo illusion by pigeons. *Animal Learning and Behavior, 21,* 29–34.

Fukuda, T., Kanada, K., & Saito, S. (1990). An ergonomic evaluation of lens accommodation related to visual circumstances. *Ergonomics, 33,* 811–831.

Fulker, D. W., DeFries, J. C., & Plomin, R. (1988). Genetic influence on general mental ability increases between infancy and middle childhood. *Nature, 336,* 767–769.

Furedy, J. J. (1987). Specific versus placebo effects in biofeedback training: A critical perspective. *Biofeedback and Self-Regulation, 12,* 169–184.

Furnham, A., & Thompson, J. (1991). Personality and self-reported delinquency. *Personality and Individual Differences, 12,* 585–593.

Furstenberg, F. F., & Teitler, J. O. (1994). Reconsidering the effects of marital disruption: What happens to children of divorce in early adulthood? *Journal of Family Issues, 15,* 173–190.

Furumoto, L. (1980). Mary Whiton Calkins (1863–1930). *Psychology of Women Quarterly, 5,* 55–68.

Furumoto, L. (1988). Shared knowledge: The experimentalists, 1904–1929. In J. G. Morawski (Ed.), *The rise of experimentation in American psychology* (pp. 94–113). New Haven, CT: Yale University Press.

Furumoto, L. (1992). Joining separate spheres: Christine Ladd-Franklin, woman-scientist (1847–1930). *American Psychologist, 47,* 175–182.

Gabrieli, J. D. E., Fleischman, D. A., Keane, M. M., & Reminger, S. L. (1995). Double dissociation between memory systems underlying explicit and implicit memory in the human brain. *Psychological Science, 6,* 76-82.

Gaffan, E. A., Tsaousis, J., & Kemp-Wheeler, S. M. (1995). Researcher allegiance and meta-analysis: The case of cognitive therapy for depression. *Journal of Consulting and Clinical Psychology, 63,* 966–980.

Gainotti, G. (1993). The riddle of the right hemisphere's contribution to the recovery of language. *European Journal of Disorders of Communication, 28,* 227–246.

Galambos, N. L. (1992). Parent-adolescent relations. *Current Directions in Psychological Science, 1,* 146–149.

Galanter, E. (1962). *New directions in psychology.* New York: Holt, Rinehart & Winston.

Galef, B. G., Jr. (1980). Diving for food: Analysis of a possible case of social learning in wild rats (*Rattus norvegicus*). *Journal of Comparative and Physiological Psychology, 94,* 416–425.

Galef, B. G., Jr. (1993). Functions of social learning about food: A causal analysis of effects of diet novelty on preference transmission. *Animal Behaviour, 46,* 257-265.

Gallagher, B. J., McFalls, J. A., & Vreeland, C. N. (1993). Preliminary results from a national survey of psychiatrists concerning the etiology of male homosexuality. *Psychology: A Journal of Human Behavior, 30,* 1–3.

Gallup, G. G., Jr., & Suarez, S. D. (1985). Alternatives to the use of animals in psychological research. *American Psychologist, 40,* 1104–1111.

Galton, F. (1869). *Hereditary genius.* London: Macmillan.

Ganchrow, J. R., Steiner, J. E., & Daher, M. (1983). Neonatal facial expressions in response to different qualities and intensities of gustatory stimuli. *Infant Behavior and Development, 6,* 189–200.

Gandour, J., Larsen, J., Dechongkit, S., & Ponglorpisit, S. (1995). Speech prosody in affective contexts in Thai patients with right hemisphere lesions. *Brain and Language, 51,* 422–443.

Gangestad, S., & Snyder, M. (1985). "To carve nature at its joints": On the existence of discrete classes in personality. *Psychological Review, 92,* 317–349.

Ganley, R. M. (1989). Emotion and eating in obesity: A review of the literature. *International Journal of Eating Disorders, 8,* 343–361.

Gansberg, M. (1964, March 27). Thirty-seven who saw murder didn't call the police. *New York Times,* pp. 1, 38.

Garcia, E. E. (1990). A brief note on "Jekyll and Hyde" and MPD. *Dissociation: Progress in the Dissociative Disorders, 3,* 165–166.

Garcia, J. (1981). Tilting at the paper mills of academe. *American Psychologist, 36,* 149–158.

Garcia, J., Kimeldorf, D. J., Hunt, E. L., & Davies, B. P. (1956). Food and water consumption of rats during exposure to gamma radiation. *Radiation Research, 4,* 33–41.

Garcia, J., & Koelling, R. A. (1966). The relation of cue to consequence in avoidance learning. *Psychonomic Science, 4,* 123–124.

Gard, T. (1993). Transactional analysis for battered women. *Transactional Analysis Journal, 23*, 152–157.

Gardner, D. G. (1986). Activation theory and task design: An empirical test of several new predictions. *Journal of Applied Psychology, 71*, 414–418.

Gardner, H. (1983). *Frames of mind: The theory of multiple intelligences.* New York: Basic Books.

Gardner, H. (1985). *The mind's new science: A history of the cognitive revolution.* New York: Basic Books.

Gardner, R. A., & Gardner, B. T. (1969). Teaching sign language to a chimpanzee. *Science, 165*, 664–672.

Gardner, R. A., Gardner, B. T., & Van Cantfort, T. E. (Eds.). (1989). *Teaching sign language to chimpanzees.* Albany: State University of New York Press.

Garfield, S. L. (1983). Effectiveness of psychotherapy: The perennial controversy. *Professional Psychology, 14*, 35–43.

Garfield, S. L. (1992). Comments on "Retrospect: Psychology as a profession" by J. McKeen Cattell (1937). *Journal of Consulting and Clinical Psychology, 60*, 9–15.

Garlick, R., & Mongeau, P. A. (1993). Argument quality and group member status as determinants of attitudinal minority influence. *Western Journal of Communication, 57*, 289–308.

Garonzik, R. (1989). Hand dominance and implications for left-handed operation of controls. *Ergonomics, 32*, 1185–1192.

Garrett, T. J., Selnow, G., Dobkin, J. F., & Healton, C. (1990). Computer-assisted instruction in AIDS infection control for physicians. *Teaching and Learning in Medicine, 2*, 215-218.

Garrison, D. W., & Foreman, R. D. (1994). Decreased activity of spontaneous and noxiously evoked dorsal horn cells during transcutaneous electrical nerve stimulation (TENS). *Pain, 58*, 309–315.

Gastil, J. (1990). Generic pronouns and sexist language: The oxymoronic character of masculine generics. *Sex Roles, 23*, 629–643.

Gathercole, S. E., & Conway, M. A. (1988). Exploring long-term modality effects: Vocalization leads to best retention. *Memory and Cognition, 16*, 110–119.

Gauld, A. O. (1990). The early history of hypnotic skin marking and blistering. *British Journal of Experimental and Clinical Hypnosis, 7*, 139–152.

Gauthier, J., Cote, G., & French, D. (1994). The role of home practice in the thermal biofeedback treatment of migraine headache. *Journal of Consulting and Clinical Psychology, 62*, 180-184.

Gawin, F. H. (1991). Cocaine addiction: Psychology and neurophysiology. *Science, 251*, 1580–1586.

Gay, P. (1988). *Freud: A life for our time.* New York: W. W. Norton.

Gay, V. (1986). Augustine: The reader as self-object. *Journal for the Scientific Study of Religion, 25*, 64–76.

Gazzaniga, M. S. (1967, August). The split brain in man. *Scientific American*, pp. 24–29.

Gazzaniga, M. S. (1983). Right hemisphere language following brain bisection: A 20-year perspective. *American Psychologist, 38*, 525–537.

Gebhardt, D. L., & Crump, C. E. (1990). Employee fitness and wellness programs in the workplace. *American Psychologist, 45*, 262–272.

Geen, R. G. (1984). Preferred stimulation levels in introverts and extraverts: Effects on arousal and performance. *Journal of Personality and Social Psychology, 46*, 1303–1312.

Geen, R. G., Stonner, D., & Shope, G. L. (1975). The facilitation of aggression by aggression: Evidence against the catharsis hypothesis. *Journal of Personality and Social Psychology, 31*, 721–726.

Geffen, G., & Quinn, K. (1984). Hemispheric specialization and ear advantages in processing speech. *Psychological Bulletin, 96*, 273–291.

Gelb, S. A. (1986). Henry H. Goddard and the immigrants, 1910–1917: The studies and their social context. *Journal of the History of the Behavioral Sciences, 22*, 324–332.

Geller, L. (1982, Spring). The failure of self-actualization theory: A critique of Carl Rogers and Abraham Maslow. *Journal of Humanistic Psychology, 22*, 56–73.

Gelman, D., Foote, D., Barrett, T., & Talbot, M. (1992, February 24). Born or bred? *Newsweek*, pp. 46–53.

Gendlin, E. T. (1988). Obituary: Carl Rogers (1902–1987). *American Psychologist, 43*, 127–128.

Genuis, M. L. (1995). The use of hypnosis in helping cancer patients control anxiety, pain, and emesis: A review of recent empirical studies. *American Journal of Clinical Hypnosis, 37*, 316-325.

Gerhart, B. (1987). How important are dispositional factors as determinants of job satisfaction? Implications for job design and other personnel programs. *Journal of Applied Psychology, 72*, 366–373.

Gerrard, M. (1987). Sex, sex guilt, and contraceptive use revisited: The 1980s. *Journal of Personality and Social Psychology, 52*, 975–980.

Gerwood, J. B. (1994). Meaning and love in Viktor Frankl's writing: Reports from the Holocaust. *Psychological Reports, 75*, 1075–1081.

Gescheider, G. A., Beiles, E. J., Checkosky, C. M., & Bolanowski, S. J. (1994). The effects of aging on information-processing channels in the sense of touch: II. Temporal summation in the P channel. *Somatosensory and Motor Research, 11*, 359–365.

Geschwind, N. (1979, September). Specializations of the human brain. *Scientific American*, pp. 180–199.

Gfellner, B. M., & Hundleby, J. D. (1994). Developmental and gender differences in drug use and problem behaviour during adolescence. *Journal of Child and Adolescent Substance Abuse, 3*, 59–74.

Gibbons, B. (1986). The intimate sense of smell. *National Geographic, 170*, 324–361.

Gibbs, E. D., Teti, D. M., & Bond, L. A. (1987). Infant-sibling communication: Relationships to birth-spacing and cognitive and linguistic development. *Infant Behavior and Development, 10*, 307–323.

Gibson, E. J., & Walk, R. D. (1960, April). The visual cliff. *Scientific American*, pp. 67–71.

Gibson, H. B. (1991). Can hypnosis compel people to commit harmful, immoral and criminal acts? A review of the literature. *Contemporary Hypnosis, 8*, 129–140.

Gibson, J. J. (1979). *The ecological approach to visual perception.* Boston: Houghton Mifflin.

Giesler, G. J., Katter, J. T., & Dado, R. J. (1994). Direct spinal pathways to the limbic system for nociceptive information. *Trends in Neurosciences, 17*, 244–250.

Gilchrist, H., Povey, R., Dickinson, A., & Povey, R. (1995). The Sensation Seeking Scale: Its use in a study of the characteristics of people choosing "adventure holidays." *Personality and Individual Differences, 19*, 513–516.

Giles, D. E., & Shaw, B. F. (1987). Beck's cognitive theory of depression: Convergence of constructs. *Comprehensive Psychiatry, 28*, 416–427.

Gill, D. (1980). *Quest: The life of Elisabeth Kübler-Ross.* New York: Harper & Row.

Gillam, B. (1980, January). Geometrical illusions. *Scientific American*, pp. 102–111.

Gillam, B. (1992). The status of perceptual grouping 70 years after Wertheimer. *Australian Journal of Psychology, 44*, 157–162.

Gilligan, C. (1982). *In a different voice: Psychological theory and women's development.* Cambridge, MA: Harvard University Press.

Gilovich, T., Vallone, R., & Tversky, A. (1985). The hot hand in basketball: On misperception of random sequences. *Cognitive Psychology, 17*, 295–314.

Gingerich, W. J. (1990). Expert systems: New tools for professional decision-making. *Computers in Human Services, 6*, 219–230.

Giovannini, D., & Ricci Bitti, P. E. (1981). Culture and sex effect in recognizing emotions by facial and gestural cues. *Italian Journal of Psychology, 8*, 95–102.

Gisiner, R., & Schusterman, R. J. (1992). Sequence, syntax, and semantics: Responses of a language-trained sea lion (Zalophus californianus) to novel sign combinations. *Journal of Comparative, 106*, 78–91.

Glanzman, D. L. (1995). The cellular basis of classical conditioning in Aplysia californica: It's less simple than you think. *Trends in Neurosciences, 18*, 30-35.

Glaser, R., Rice, J., Speicher, C. E., Stout, J. C., & Kiecolt-Glaser, J. K. (1986). Stress depresses interferon production by leukocytes concomitant with a decrease in natural killer cell activity. *Behavioral Neuroscience, 100*, 675–678.

Glass, A. L., & Waterman, D. (1988). Predictions of movie entertainment value and the representativeness heuristic. *Applied Cognitive Psychology, 2*, 173–179.

Glassman, R. B., Garvey, K. J., Elkins, K. M., & Kasal, K. L. (1994). Spatial working memory score of humans in a large radial maze, similar to published score of rats, implies capacity close to the magical number 7 ± 2. *Brain Research Bulletin, 34*, 151–159.

Glen, L., & Anderson, J. A. (1989). Medication and the elderly: A review. *Journal of Geriatric Drug Therapy, 4*, 59–89.

Glenn, S. S., & Ellis, J. (1988). Do the Kallikaks look "menacing" or "retarded"? *American Psychologist, 43*, 742–743.

Glennon, R. A. (1990). Do classical hallucinogens act as 5-HT-sub-2 agonists or antagonists? *Neuropsychopharmacology, 3*, 509–517.

Glick, P., Gottesman, D., & Jolton, J. (1989). The fault is not in the stars: Susceptibility of skeptics and believers in astrology to the Barnum effect. *Personality and Social Psychology Bulletin, 15*, 572–583.

Gliedman, J. (1983, November). Interview with Noam Chomsky. *Omni*, pp. 112–118, 171–174.

Glisky, E. L. (1992). Computer-assisted instruction for patients with traumatic brain injury: Teaching of domain-specific knowledge. *Journal of Head Trauma Rehabilitation, 7*, 1-12.

Gloor, P. (1994). Is Berger's dream coming true? *Electroencephalography and Clinical Neurophysiology, 90*, 253–266.

Glucksberg, S., & Danks, J. H. (1968). Effects of discriminative labels and of nonsense labels upon availability of novel functions. *Journal of Verbal Learning and Verbal Behavior, 7*, 72–76.

Glueckauf, R. L., & Quittner, A. L. (1992). Assertiveness training for disabled adults in wheelchairs: Self-report, role-play, and activity pattern outcomes. *Journal of Consulting and Clinical Psychology, 60*, 419–425.

Goddard, H. H. (1912). *The Kallikak family: A study in the heredity of feeble-mindedness.* New York: Macmillan.

Goddard, H. H. (1917). Mental tests and the immigrant. *Journal of Delinquency, 2*, 243–277.

Goddard, M. J. (1997). Spontaneous recovery in US extinction. *Learning and Motivation, 28*, 118-128.

Godden, D. R., & Baddeley, A. D. (1975). Context-dependent memory in two natural environments: On land and under water. *British Journal of Psychology, 66*, 325–331.

Godemont, M. (1992). Six hundred years of family care in Geel, Belgium: 600 years of familiarity with madness in town life. *Community Alternatives: International Journal of Family Care, 4*, 155–168.

Godin, G., Desharnais, R., Valois, P., & Bradet, R. (1995). Combining behavioral and motivational dimensions to identify and characterize the stages in the process of adherence to exercise. *Psychology and Health, 10*, 333–344.

"God's hand": Legless veteran crawls to save life of a baby. (1986, June 6). *Philadelphia Inquirer*, pp. 1A, 24A.

Goebel, B. L., & Boeck, B. E. (1987). Ego integrity and fear of death: A comparison of institutionalized and independently living older adults. *Death Studies, 11*, 193–204.

Goebel, B. L., & Brown, D. R. (1981). Age differences in motivation related to Maslow's need hierarchy. *Developmental Psychology, 17*, 809–815.

Goisman, R. M. (1983). Therapeutic approaches to phobia: A comparison. *American Journal of Psychotherapy, 37*, 227–234.

Gold, J. M., & Rogers. J. D. (1995). Intimacy and isolation: A validation study of Erikson's theory. *Journal of Humanistic Psychology, 35*, 78-86.

Gold, M. S., Pottash, A. L. C., Sweeney, D. R., Martin, D. M., & Davies, R. K. (1980). Further evidence of hypothal-amic-pituitary dysfunction in anorexia nervosa. *American Journal of Psychiatry, 137*, 101–102.

Goldbloom, D. S., & Garfinkel, P. E. (1990). The serotonin hypothesis of bulimia nervosa: Theory and evidence. *Canadian Journal of Psychiatry, 35*, 741–744.

Goldfried, M. R., Greenberg, L. S., & Marmar, C. (1990). Individual psychotherapy: Process and outcome. *Annual Review of Psychology, 41*, 659–688.

Goldin-Meadow, S., & Mylander, C. (1983). Gestural communication in deaf children: Noneffect of parental input on language development. *Science, 221*, 372–373.

Goldman, D. L. (1990). Dorothea Dix and her two missions of mercy in Nova Scotia. *Canadian Journal of Psychiatry, 35*, 139–143.

Goldman, M., & Fordyce, J. (1983). Prosocial behavior as affected by eye contact, touch, and voice expression. *Journal of Social Psychology, 121*, 125–129.

Goldstein, A. (1980). Thrills in response to music and other stimuli. *Physiological Psychology, 8*, 126–129.

Goldstein, I. L. 91993). *Training in organizations* (3rd ed.). Pacific Grove, CA: Brooks/Cole.

Goldstein, S. R., & Hall, D. (1990). Variable ratio control of the spitting response in the archer fish (*Toxotes jaculator*). *Journal of Comparative Psychology, 104*, 373–376.

Gonzalez, R. (1989). Ministering intelligence: A Venezuelan experience in the promotion of cognitive abilities. *International Journal of Mental Health, 18*, 5–18.

Goodall, J. (1990). *Through a window: My thirty years with the chimpanzees of Gombe.* Boston: Houghton Mifflin.

Goodenough, F. L. (1932). Expression of the emotions in a blind-deaf child. *Journal of Abnormal and Social Psychology, 27*, 328–333.

Goodman, E. S. (1980). Margaret F. Washburn (1871–1939): First woman Ph.D. in psychology. *Psychology of Women Quarterly, 5*, 69–80.

Goodwin, C. J. (1985). On the origins of Titchener's experimentalists. *Journal of the History of the Behavioral Sciences, 21*, 383–389.

Goodwin, C. J. (1987). In Hall's shadow: Edmund Clark Sanford (1859–1924). *Journal of the History of the Behavioral Sciences, 23*, 153–168.

Gorczynski, R. M. (1990). Conditioned enhancement of skin allografts in mice. *Brain, Behavior and Immunity, 4*, 85–92.

Gordon, B. N., & Follmer, A. (1994). Developmental issues in judging the credibility of children's testimony. *Journal of Clinical Child Psychology, 23*, 283–294.

Gordon, C. M., & Carey, M. P. (1995). Penile tumescence monitoring during morning naps to assess male erectile functioning: An initial study of healthy men of varied ages. *Archives of Sexual Behavior, 24*, 291–307.

Gordon, I. E., & Earle, D. C. (1992). Visual illusions: A short review. *Australian Journal of Psychology, 44*, 153–156.

Gorelick, P. B., & Ross, E. D. (1987). The aprosodias: Further functional-anatomical evidence for the organization of affective language in the right hemisphere. *Journal of Neurology, Neurosurgery, and Psychiatry, 50*, 553–560.

Gorman, J. (1985, February). My fair software. *Discover*, pp. 64–65.

Gosnell, B. A., & Hsiao, S. (1984). Effects of cholecystokinin on taste preference and sensitivity in rats. *Behavioral Neuroscience, 98*, 452–460.

Gosselin, P., Kirouac, G., & Dore, F. Y. (1995). Components and recognition of facial expression in the communication of emotion by actors. *Journal of Personality and Social Psychology, 68*, 83–96.

Gotlib, I. H., & Robinson, L. A. (1982). Responses to depressed individuals: Discrepancies between self-report and observer-rated behavior. *Journal of Abnormal Psychology, 91*, 231–240.

Gottesman, I. L., & Shields, J. (1982). *Schizophrenia: The epigenetic puzzle.* Cambridge, MA: Cambridge University Press.

Gould, S. J. (1981). *The mismeasure of man.* New York: W. W. Norton.

Graaf, C. de, Polet, P., & van Staveren, W. A. (1994). Sensory perception and pleasantness of food flavors in elderly subjects. *Journals of Gerontology, 49*, P93–P99.

Graffin, N. F., Ray, W. J., & Lundy, R. (1995). EEG concomitants of hypnosis and hypnotic susceptibility. *Journal of Abnormal Psychology, 104*, 123–131.

Graham, J. R. (1991). Comments on Duckworth's review of the Minnesota Multiphasic Personality Inventory–2. *Journal of Counseling and Development, 69*, 570–571.

Graham, K. S., & Hodges, J. R. (1997). Differentiating the roles of the hippocampus complex and the neocortex in long-term memory storage: Evidence from the study of semantic dementia and Alzheimer's disease. *Neuropsychology, 11*, 77-89.

Gratzer, T. G., & Matas, M. (1994). The right to refuse treatment: Recent Canadian developments. *Bulletin of the American Academy of Psychiatry and the Law, 22*, 249–256.

Graves, R., & Landis, T. (1990). Asymmetry in mouth opening during different speech tasks. *International Journal of Psychology, 25*, 179–189.

Gravitz, M. A. (1995). First admission (1846) of hypnotic testimony in court. *American Journal of Clinical Hypnosis, 37*, 326–330.

Graw, P., Krauchi, K., Wirz-Justice, A., & Poldinger, W. (1991). Diurnal variation of symptoms in seasonal affective disorder. *Psychiatry Research, 37*, 105–111.

Gray, J. T., Neisser, U., Shapiro, B. A., & Kouns, S. (1991). Observational learning of ballet sequences: The role of kinematic information. *Ecological Psychology, 3*, 121–134.

Gray, P. H. (1980). Behaviorism: Some truths that need telling, some errors that need correcting. *Bulletin of the Psychonomic Society, 15*, 357–360.

Graydon, J., & Murphy, T. (1995). The effect of personality on social facilitation whilst performing a sports related task. *Personality and Individual Differences, 19*, 265–267.

Greca, A. M. la. (1993). Social skills training with children: Where do we go from here? *Journal of Clinical Child Psychology, 22*, 288–298.

Green, A. J., & Gilhooly, K. J. (1990). Individual differences and effective learning procedures: The case of statistical computing. *International Journal of Man-Machine Studies, 33*, 97–119.

Green, C. D., & Powell, R. (1990). Comment on Kimble's generalism. *American Psychologist, 45*, 556–557.

Green, J. A., & Shellenberger, R. D. (1986). Biofeedback research and the ghost in the box: A reply to Roberts. *American Psychologist, 41*, 1003–1005.

Greenberg, L. S., & Dompierre, L. M. (1981). Specific effects of Gestalt two-chair dialogue on intrapsychic conflict in counseling. *Journal of Counseling Psychology, 28*, 288–294.

Greenblatt, D. J., Shader, R. I., & Abernethy, D. R. (1983). Drug therapy: Current status of benzodiazepines. *New England Journal of Medicine, 309*, 354–358.

Greendale, G. A., & Judd, H. L. (1993). The menopause: Health implications and clinical management. *Journal of the American Geriatrics Society, 41*, 426–436.

Greene, E., Flynn, M. S., & Loftus, E. F. (1982). Inducing resistance to misleading information. *Journal of Verbal Learning and Verbal Behavior, 21*, 207–219.

Greene, R. L. (1987). Effects of maintenance rehearsal on human memory. *Psychological Bulletin, 102*, 403–413.

Greenlee, R. W. (1990). The unemployed Appalachian coal miner's search for meaning. *International Forum for Logotherapy, 13*, 71–75.

Greenlees, I. A., & McGrew, W. C. (1994). Sex and age differences in preferences and tactics of mate attraction: Analysis of published advertisements. *Ethology and Sociobiology, 15*, 59–72.

Greeno, C. G., & Wing, R. R. (1994). Stress-induced eating. *Psychological Bulletin, 115*, 444–464.

Greeno, J. G. (1980). Psychology of learning, 1960–1980: One participant's observations. *American Psychologist, 35*, 713–728.

Greenwald, A. G., Spangenberg, E. R., Pratkanis, A. R., & Eskenazi, J. (1991). Double-blind tests of subliminal self-help audiotapes. *Psychological Science, 2*, 119–122.

Gregg, E., & Rejeski, W. J. (1990). Social psychobiologic dysfunction associated with anabolic steroid abuse: A review. *Sport Psychologist, 4*, 275–284.

Gregory, R. L. (1991). Putting illusions in their place. *Perception, 20*, 1–4.

Greskoo, R. B., & Karlsen, A. (1994). The Norwegian program for the primary, secondary, and tertiary prevention of eating disorders. *Eating Disorders: The Journal of Treatment and Prevention, 2*, 57–63.

Grey, W. (1994). Philosophy and the paranormal. Part 1: The problem of "psi." *Skeptical Inquirer, 18*, 142–149.

Griffiths, M. D., & Dancaster, I. (1995). The effect of Type A personality on physiological arousal while playing computer games. *Addictive Behaviors, 20*, 543–548.

Griffiths, P., Paterson, L., & Harvie, A. (1995). Neuropsychological effect of subsequent exposure to phenylalanine in adolescents and young adults with early-treated phenylketonuria. *Journal of Intellectual Disability Research, 39*, 365–372.

Gross, M., & Lavie, P. (1994). Dreams in sleep apnea patients. *Dreaming: Journal of the Association for the Study of Dreams, 4*, 195–204.

Grossberg, I. N., & Cornell, D. G. (1988). The relationship between personality adjustment and high intelligence: Terman versus Hollingworth. *Exceptional Children, 55*, 266–272.

Grossberg, S., & Merrill, J. W. L. (1996). The hippocampus and cerebellum in adaptively timed learning, recognition, and movement. *Journal of Cognitive Neuroscience, 8*, 257-277.

Grosz, R. D. (1990). Suicide: Training the resident assistant as an interventionist. *Journal of College Student Psychotherapy, 4*, 179–194.

Grove, W. M., Eckert, E. D., Heston, L., & Bouchard, T. J. (1990). Heritability of substance abuse and antisocial behavior: A study of monozygotic twins reared apart. *Biological Psychiatry, 27*, 1293–1304.

Grych, J. H., & Fincham, F. D. (1992). Interventions for children of divorce: Toward greater integration of research and action. *Psychological Bulletin, 111*, 434–454.

Guarino, M., Fridrich, P., & Sitton, S. (1994). Male and female conformity in eating behavior. *Psychological Reports, 75*, 603–609.

Guastello, S. J., Guastello, D. D., & Craft, L. L. (1989). Assessment of the Barnum effect in computer-based test interpretations. *Journal of Psychology, 123*, 477–484.

Guilford, J. P. (1959). Three faces of intellect. *American Psychologist, 14*, 469–479.

Guilford, J. P. (1980). Fluid and crystallized intelligences: Two fanciful concepts. *Psychological Bulletin, 88*, 406–412.

Guilford, J. P. (1984). Varieties of divergent production. *Journal of Creative Behavior, 18*, 1–10.

Guilford, J. P. (1985). The structure of intellect model. In B. B. Wolman (Ed.), *Handbook of Intelligence* (pp. 225–266). New York: Wiley.

Gulevich, G., Dement, W., & Johnson, L. (1966). Psychiatric and EEG observations on a case of prolonged (264 hours) wakefulness. *Archives of General Psychiatry, 15*, 29–35.

Gunderson, V. M., Yonas, A., Sargent, P. L., & Grant-Webster, K. S. (1993). Infant macaque monkeys respond to pictorial depth. *Psychological Science, 4*, 93–98.

Gunstream, J. D., Castro, G. A., & Walters, E. T. (1995). Retrograde transport of plasticity signals in Aplysia sensory neurons following axonal injury. *Journal of Neuroscience, 15*, 439–448.

Gunzburger, D. (1995). Acoustic and perceptual implications of the transsexual voice. *Archives of Sexual Behavior, 24*, 339–348.

Gustafson, R. (1993). Conditioning treatment of children's bedwetting: A follow-up and predictive study. *Psychological Reports, 72*, 923–930.

Gustavson, C. R., Garcia, J., Hawkins, W. G., & Rusiniak, K. W. (1974). Coyote predation control by aversive conditioning. *Science, 184*, 581–583.

Guthrie, E. V. (1976). *Even the rat was white: A historical view of psychology.* New York: Harper & Row.

Haaga, D. A. F., & Beck, A. T. (1995). Perspectives on depressive realism: Implications for cognitive theory of depression. *Behaviour Research and Therapy, 33*, 41–48.

Haber, R. N. (1980). How we perceive depth from flat pictures. *American Scientist, 68*, 370–380.

Hackett, G. (1985). Role of mathematics self-efficacy in the choice of math-related majors of college women and men: A path analysis. *Journal of Counseling Psychology, 32*, 47–56.

Hackett, R. D., Bycio, P., & Guion, R. M. (1989). Absenteeism among hospital nurses: An idiographic-longitudinal analysis. *Academy of Management Journal, 32*, 424–453.

Haddock, G., Zanna, M. P., & Esses, V. M. (1993). Assessing the structure of prejudicial attitudes: The case of attitudes toward homosexuals. *Journal of Personality and Social Psychology, 65*, 1105–1118.

Hagopian, L. P., Farrell, D. A., & Amari, A. (1996). Treating total liquid refusal with backward chaining and fading. *Journal of Applied Behavior Analysis, 29*, 573-575.

Haimov, I., & Lavie, P. (1996). Melatonin—A soporific hormone. *Current Directions in Psychological Science, 5*, 106-111.

Hale, M., Jr. (1980). *Hugo Münsterberg: The origins of applied psychology.* Philadelphia: Temple University Press.

Hall, C. S. (1966). *The meaning of dreams.* New York: McGraw–Hill.

Hall, G. S. (1904). *Adolescence.* New York: Appleton.

Hallenbeck, B. A., & Kauffman, J. M. (1995). How does observational learning affect the behavior of students with emotional or behavioral disorders? A review of research. *Journal of Special Education, 29*, 45-71.

Halling, S., & Nill, J. D. (1995). A brief history of existential-phenomenological psychiatry and psychotherapy. *Journal of Phenomenological Psychology, 66*, 1179–1184.

Halpern, C. T., Udry, J. R., Campbell, B., & Suchindran, C. (1993). Relationships between aggression and pubertal increases in testosterone: A panel analysis of adolescent males. *Social Biology, 40*, 8–24.

Halpern, D. F. (1992). *Sex differences in cognitive abilities* (2nd ed.). Hillsdale, NJ: Erlbaum.

Halpern, D. F., & Coren, S. (1988). Do right-handers live longer? *Nature, 333*, 213.

Halpern, D. F., & Coren, S. (1993). Left-handedness and life span: A reply to Harris. *Psychological Bulletin, 114*, 235–241.

Halpern, L., Blake, R., & Hillerbrand, J. (1986). Psychoacoustics of a chilling sound. *Perception and Psychophysics, 39*, 77–80.

Hama, A. T., & Sagen, J. (1993). Reduced pain-related behavior by adrenal medullary transplants in rats with experimental painful peripheral neuropathy. *Pain, 52*, 223–231.

Hamburg, D. A. (1982). Health and behavior. *Science, 217*, 399.

Hamburger, Y. (1994). The contact hypothesis reconsidered: Effects of the atypical outgroup member on the outgroup stereotype. *Basic and Applied Social Psychology, 15*, 339–358.

Hamer, D. H., Hu, S., Magnuson, V. L., & Hu, N. (1993). A linkage between DNA markers on the X chromosome and male sexual orientation. *Science, 261*, 321–327.

Hamill, R., Decamp Wilson, T., & Nisbett, R. E. (1980). Insensitivity to sample bias: Generalizing from atypical cases. *Journal of Personality and Social Psychology, 39*, 578–589.

Hamilton, M. C. (1988). Using masculine generics: Does generic he increase male bias in the user's imagery? *Sex Roles, 19*, 785–799.

Hanna, E., & Meltzoff, A. N. (1993). Peer imitation by toddlers in laboratory, home, and day-care contexts: Implications for social learning and memory. *Developmental Psychology, 29*, 701–710.

Hannah, M. T., Domino, G., Figueredo, A. J., & Hendrickson, R. (1996). The prediction of ego integrity in older persons. *Educational and Psychological Measurement, 56*, 930-950.

Hansen, C. H., & Hansen, R. D. (1988). Finding the face in the crowd: An anger superiority effect. *Journal of Personality and Social Psychology, 54*, 917–924.

Hanson, R. K. (1990). The psychological impact of sexual assault on women and children: A review. *Annals of Sex Research, 3*, 187–232.

Harbin, G., Durst, L., & Harbin, D. (1989). Evaluation of oculomotor response in relationship to sports performance. *Medicine and Science in Sports and Exercise, 21*, 258–262.

Hardaway, R. A. (1990). Subliminally activated symbiotic fantasies: Fact and artifacts. *Psychological Bulletin, 107*, 177–195.

Hardy, C. J., & Latané, B. (1988). Social loafing in cheerleaders: Effects of team membership and competition. *Journal of Sport and Exercise Psychology, 10*, 109–114.

Hare, R. D., McPherson, L. M., & Forth, A. E. (1988). Male psychopaths and their criminal careers. *Journal of Consulting and Clinical Psychology, 56*, 710–714.

Hargadon, R., Bowers, K. S., & Woody, E. Z. (1995). Does counterpain imagery mediate hypnotic analgesia? *Journal of Abnormal Psychology, 104*, 508–516.

Harlow, H. F., & Zimmerman, R. R. (1959). Affectional responses in the infant monkey. *Science, 130*, 421–432.

Harlow, J. M. (1993). Recovery from the passage of an iron bar through the head. *History of Psychiatry, 4*, 271–281.

Harmon-Jones, E., Brehm, J. W., Greenberg, J., & Simon, L. (1996). Evidence that the production of aversive consequences is not necessary to create cognitive dissonance. *Journal of Personality and Social Psychology, 70*, 5–16.

Harrington, D. M., Block, J. H., & Block, J. (1987). Testing aspects of Carl Rogers' theory of creative environments: Child-rearing antecedents of creative potential in young adolescents. *Journal of Personality and Social Psychology, 52*, 851–856.

Harris, B. (1979). Whatever happened to Little Albert? *American Psychologist, 34*, 151–160.

Harris, K. M., & Kater, S. B. (1994). Dendritic spines: Cellular specializations imparting both stability and flexibility to synaptic function. *Annual Review of Neuroscience, 17*, 341–371.

Harris, L. J. (1993). Do left-handers die sooner than right-handers? Commentary on Coren and Halpern's (1991) "Left-handedness: A marker for decreased survival fitness." *Psychological Bulletin, 114*, 203–234.

Harris, M. J. (1994). Self-fulfilling prophecies in the clinical context: Review and implications for clinical practice. *Applied and Preventive Psychology, 3*, 145–158.

Harris, M. J., & Rosenthal, R. (1985). Mediation of interpersonal expectancy effects: Thirty-one meta-analyses. *Psychological Bulletin, 97*, 363–386.

Harris, R. J., Schoen, L. M., & Hensley, D. L. (1992). A cross-cultural study of story memory. *Journal of Cross Cultural Psychology, 23*, 133–147.

Harris, R. L., Ellicott, A. M., & Holmes, D. S. (1986). The timing of psychosocial transitions and changes in women's lives: An examination of women aged 45 to 60. *Journal of Personality and Social Psychology, 51*, 409–416.

Harrison, A. A. (1969). Exposure and popularity. *Journal of Personality, 37*, 359–377.

Harrison, A. A. (1977). Let's make a deal: An analysis of revelations and stipulations in lonely hearts advertisements. *Journal of Personality and Social Psychology, 35*, 257–264.

Harrison, D. W., Gavin, M. R., & Isaac, W. (1988). A portable biofeedback device for autonomic responses. *Journal of Psychopathology and Behavioral Assessment, 10*, 217–224.

Hart, S. D., Knapp, P. R., & Hare, R. D. (1988). Performance of male psychopaths following conditional release from prison. *Journal of Consulting and Clinical Psychology, 56*, 227–232.

Hartley, D., Roback, H. B., & Abramowitz, S. I. (1976). Deterioration effects in encounter groups. *American Psychologist, 31*, 247–255.

Hartley, J., & Homa, D. (1981). Abstraction of stylistic concepts. *Journal of Experimental Psychology: Human Learning and Memory, 7*, 33–46.

Hartshorne, H., & May, M. A. (1928). *Studies in deceit.* New York: Macmillan.

Hartup, W. W. (1989). Social relationships and their developmental significance. *American Psychologist, 44*, 120–126.

Hasenfratz, M., Bunge, A., Dal Pra, G., & Battig, K. (1993). Antagonistic effects of caffeine and alcohol on mental performance parameters. *Pharmacology, Biochemistry, and Behavior, 46*, 463–465.

Hasselmo, M. E., & Bower, J. M. (1993). Acetylcholine and memory. *Trends in Neurosciences, 16*, 218–222.

Hassett, J. (1978). *A primer of psychophysiology.* San Francisco: Freeman.

Hatfield, E. (1988). Passionate and companionate love. In R. J. Sternberg & M. L. Barnes (Eds.), *The psychology of love.* New Haven, CT: Yale University Press.

Hatfield, E., & Sprecher, S. (1995). Men's and women's preferences in marital partners in the United States, Russia, and Japan. *Journal of Cross-Cultural Psychology, 26*, 728–750.

Hathaway, S. R., & McKinley, J. C. (1943). *Minnesota Multiphasic Personality Inventory.* New York: Psychological Corporation.

Hattori, N. (1995). "The pleasure of your Bedlam": The theatre of madness in the Renaissance. *History of Psychiatry, 6,* 283–308.

Hatzichristou, D. G., Bertero, E. B., & Goldstein, I. (1994). Decision making in the evaluation of impotence: The patient profile-oriented algorithm. *Sexuality and Disability, 12,* 29–37.

Hauenstein, N. M. A. (1992). An information-processing approach to leniency in performance judgments. *Journal of Applied Psychology, 77,* 485–493.

Hawkes, N. (1979). *Tracing Burt's descent to scientific fraud. Science, 205,* 673–675.

Hawkins, M. J., Hawkins, W. E., & Ryan, E. R. (1989). Self-actualization as related to age of faculty members at a large midwestern university. *Psychological Reports, 65,* 1120–1122.

Hawton, K., Catalan, J., Martin, P., & Fagg, J. (1986). Long-term outcome of sex therapy. *Behaviour Research and Therapy, 24,* 665–675.

Hayden, T., & Mischel, W. (1976). Maintaining trait consistency in the resolution of behavioral inconsistency: The wolf in sheep's clothing? *Journal of Personality, 44,* 109–132.

Hayes, C. (1951). *The ape in our house.* New York: Harper & Row.

Hayes, D. S., Chemelski, B. E., & Palmer, M. (1982). Nursery rhymes and prose passages: Preschoolers' liking and short-term retention of story events. *Developmental Psychology, 18,* 49–56.

Hayes, R. L., Pechura, C. M., Katayama, Y., Povlishuck, J. T., Giebel, M. L., & Becker, D. P. (1984). Activation of pontine cholinergic sites implicated in unconsciousness following cerebral concussions in the cat. *Science, 223,* 301–303.

Hayflick, L. (1980, January). The cell biology of human aging. *Scientific American,* pp. 58–65.

Hays, J. R. (1989). The role of *Addington v. Texas* on involuntary civil commitment. *Psychological Reports, 65,* 1211–1215.

Hayslip, B., Jr., & Leon, J. (1992). *Hospice care.* Newbury Park, CA: Sage.

Haywood, H. C., Meyers, C. E., & Switzky, H. N. (1982). Mental retardation. *Annual Review of Psychology, 33,* 309–342.

Hazelrigg, P. J., Cooper, H., & Strathman, A. J. (1991). Personality moderators of the experimenter expectancy effect: A reexamination of five hypotheses. *Personality and Social Psychology Bulletin, 17,* 569–579.

Hearne, K. M. (1989). A nationwide mass dream-telepathy experiment. *Journal of the Society for Psychical Research, 55,* 271–274.

Hearnshaw, L. S. (1979). *Cyril Burt: Psychologist.* Ithaca: Cornell University Press.

Hearnshaw, L. S. (1985). Francis Bacon: Harbinger of scientific psychology. *Revista de Historia de la Psicologia, 6,* 5–14.

Heath, A. C., Kendler, K. S., Eaves, L. J., & Martin, N. G. (1990). Evidence for genetic influences on sleep disturbance and sleep pattern in twins. *Sleep, 13,* 318–335.

Heatherton, T. F., Polivy, J., & Herman, C. P. (1989). Restraint and internal responsiveness: Effects of placebo manipulation of hunger state on eating. *Journal of Abnormal Psychology, 98,* 89–92.

Heatherton, T. F., Polivy, J., & Herman, C. P. (1990). Dietary restraint: Some current findings and speculations. *Psychology of Addictive Behaviors, 4,* 101–106.

Hebb, D. O. (1955). Drives and the CNS (conceptual nervous system). *Psychological Review, 62,* 243–254.

Hebb, D. O. (1958). The motivating effects of exteroceptive stimulation. *American Psychologist, 13,* 109–113.

Hechinger, N. (1981, March). Seeing without eyes. *Science 81,* pp. 38–43.

Hedges, L. V. (1987). How hard is hard science, how soft is soft science? The empirical cumulativeness of research. *American Psychologist, 42,* 443–455.

Heffner, H. E. (1983). Hearing in large and small dogs: Absolute thresholds and size of the tympanic membrane. *Behavioral Neuroscience, 97,* 310–318.

Heider, F. (1944). Social perception and phenomenal causality. *Psychological Review, 51,* 358–374.

Heitzmann, C. A., & Kaplan, M. (1988). Assessment of methods for measuring social support. *Health Psychology, 7,* 75–109.

Heller, W. (1993). Neuropsychological mechanisms of individual differences in emotion, personality, and arousal. *Neuropsychology, 7,* 476–489.

Hellige, J. B. (1993). Unity of thought and action: Varieties of interaction between the left and right cerebral hemispheres. *Current Directions in Psychological Science, 2,* 21–25.

Hellstrom, A., & Tekle, J. (1994). Person perception through facial photographs: Effects of glasses, hair, and beard on judgments of occupation and personal qualities. *European Journal of Social Psychology, 24,* 693–705.

Helmes, E., & Reddon, J. R. (1993). A perspective on developments in assessing psychopathology: A critical review of the MMPI and MMPI-2. *Psychological Bulletin, 113,* 453–471.

Helmreich, R. L., Spence, J. T., Beane, W. E., Lucker, G. W., & Matthews, K. A. (1980). Making it in academic psychology: Demographic and personality correlates of attainment. *Journal of Personality and Social Psychology, 39,* 896–908.

Hendrick, C. (1990). Replications, strict replications, and conceptual replications: Are they important? *Journal of Social Behavior and Personality, 5,* 41–49.

Hendrick, S., Hendrick, C., Slapion-Foote, M., & Foote, F. (1985). Gender differences in sexual attitudes. *Journal of Personality and Social Psychology, 48,* 1630–1642.

Hendrickson, K. M., McCarty, T., & Goodwin, J. M. (1990). Animal alters: Case reports. *Dissociation: Progress in the Dissociative Disorders, 3,* 218–221.

Hendrixson, L. L. (1989). Care versus justice: Two moral perspectives in the Baby "M" surrogacy case. *Journal of Sex Education and Therapy, 15,* 247–256.

Henle, M. (1978). Gestalt psychology and gestalt therapy. *Journal of the History of the Behavioral Sciences, 14,* 23–32.

Henle, M. (1978). One man against the Nazis: Wolfgang Kohler. *American Psychologist, 33,* 939–944.

Henle, M. (1993). Man's place in nature in the thinking of Wolfgang Kohler. *Journal of the History of the Behavioral Sciences, 29,* 3–7.

Hennessey, B. A., & Zbikowski, S. M. (1993). Immunizing children against the negative effects of reward: A further examination of intrinsic motivation training techniques. *Creativity Research Journal, 6,* 297–307.

Hennig, J., Laschefski, U., & Opper, C. (1994). Biopsychological changes after bungee jumping: b-Endorphin immunoreactivity as a mediator of euphoria? *Neuropsychobiology, 29,* 28–32.

Hennrikus, D. J., Jeffery, R. W., & Lando, H. A. (1995). The smoking cessation process: Longitudinal observations in a working population. *Preventive Medicine: An International Journal Devoted to Practice and Theory, 24,* 235–244.

Herbert, T. B., & Cohen, S. (1993). Depression and immunity: A meta-analytic review. *Psychological Bulletin, 113,* 472–486.

Herbert, W. (1983). MMPI: Redefining normality for modern times. *Science News, 134,* 228.

Herbert, W. (1983). Remembrance of things partly. *Science News, 124,* 378–381.

Hergenhahn, B. R. (1984). *An introduction to theories of personality.* Englewood Cliffs, NJ: Prentice Hall.

Herkenhahn, M., Lynn, A. B., deCosta, B. R., & Richfield, E. K. (1991). Neuronal localization of cannabinoid receptors in the basal ganglia of the rat. *Brain Research, 547,* 267–274.

Herman, C. P., Olmsted, M. P., & Polivy, J. (1983). Obesity, externality, and susceptibility to social influence: An integrated analysis. *Journal of Personality and Social Psychology, 45,* 926–934.

Herman, K. C., & Usita, P. M. (1994). Predicting Big Brothers/Big Sisters volunteer attrition with the 16 PF. *Child and Youth Care Forum, 23,* 207–211.

Herman, L. M., Kuczaj, S. A., & Holder, M. D. (1993). Responses to anomalous gestural sequences by a language-trained dolphin: Evidence for processing of semantic relations and syntactic information. *Journal of Experimental Psychology: General, 122,* 184–194.

Hermann, D. H. (1990). Autonomy, self determination, the right of involuntarily committed persons to refuse treatment, and the use of substituted judgment in medication decisions involving incompetent persons. *International Journal of Law and Psychiatry, 4,* 361–385.

Herning, R. I. (1985). Cocaine increases EEG beta: A replication of Hans Berger's historic experiments. *Electroencephalography and Clinical Neurophysiology, 60,* 470–477.

Herrero, J. V., & Hillix, W. A. (1990). Hemispheric performance in detecting prosody: A competitive dichotic listening task. *Perceptual and Motor Skills, 71,* 479–486.

Herrick, C., Kvale, J. K., & Goodykoontz, L. G. (1991). Resolving faculty conflict: Application of a psychotherapeutic model in an encounter group process. *Journal for Specialists in Group Work, 16,* 32–39.

Herringer, L. G. (1993). Consistency and variability in two personality traits over time and across situations. *Psychological Reports, 73,* 355–362.

Herrnstein, R. J., Nickerson, R. S., de Sanchez, M., & Swets, J. A. (1986). Teaching thinking skills. *American Psychologist, 41,* 1279–1289.

Hersen, M., Kazdin, A. E., & Bellack, A. S. (Eds.). (1983). *The clinical psychology handbook.* New York: Pergamon.

Herz, R. S., & Cupchik, G. C. (1992). An experimental characterization of odor-evoked memories in humans. *Chemical Senses, 17,* 519–528.

Herz, R. S., & Engen, T. (1996). Odor memory: Review and analysis. *Psychonomic Bulletin and Review, 3,* 300-313.

Herzog, H. A., Jr. (1995). Has public interest in animal rights peaked? *American Psychologist,50,* 945–947.

Hesse, H. (1930/1968). *Narcissus and Goldmund.* New York: Farrar, Straus & Giroux.

Hetherington, A. W., & Ranson, S. W. (1942). The spontaneous activity and food intake of rats with hypothalamic lesions. *American Journal of Physiology, 136,* 609–617.

Hewson-Bower, B., & Drummond, P. D. (1996). Secretory immunoglobulin A increases during relaxation in children with and without recurrent upper respiratory tract infections. *Journal of Developmental and Behavioral Pediatrics, 17,* 311–316.

Heyes, C. M., Dawson, G. R., & Nokes, T. (1992). Imitation in rats: Initial responding and transfer evidence. *Quarterly Journal of Experimental Psychology Comparative and Physiological Psychology, 45B,* 229–240.

Hiatt, S. W., Campos, J. J., & Emde, R. N. (1980). Facial patterning and infant emotional expression: Happiness, surprise, and fear. *Annual Progress in Child Psychiatry and Child Development,* 95–121.

Hicks, R. A., Johnson, C., & Pellegrini, R. J. (1992). Changes in the self-reported consistency of normal habitual sleep duration of college students (1978 and 1992). *Perceptual and Motor Skills, 75,* 1168–1170.

Hicks, R. A., Johnson, C., Cuevas, T., & Debaro, D. (1994). Do right-handers live longer? An updated assessment of baseball player data. *Perceptual and Motor Skills, 78,* 1243–1247.

Higashiyama, A., & Kitano, S. (1991). Perceived size and distance of persons in natural outdoor settings: The effects of familiar size. *Psychologia: An International Journal of Psychology in the Orient, 34*, 188–199.

Higgins, E. T. (1987). Self-discrepancy: A theory relating self and affect. *Psychological Review, 94*, 319–340.

Higgins, E. T. (1990). Self-state representations: Patterns of interconnected beliefs with specific holistic meanings and importance. *Bulletin of the Psychonomic Society, 28*, 248–253.

Higgins, J. E., & Endler, N. S. (1995). Coping, life stress, and psychological and somatic distress. *European Journal of Personality, 9*, 253–270.

High, D. M. (1992). Research with Alzheimer's disease subjects: Informed consent and proxy decision making. *Journal of the American Geriatrics Society, 40*, 950–957.

Hilgard, E. R. (1973). A neodissociative interpretation of pain reduction in hypnosis. *Psychological Review, 80*, 403–419.

Hilgard, E. R. (1978, January). Hypnosis and consciousness. *Human Nature*, pp. 42–49.

Hilgard, E. R. (1987). *Psychology in America: A historical survey*. San Diego: Harcourt Brace Jovanovich.

Hilgard, E. R. (1993). Which psychologists prominent in the second half of this century made lasting contributions to psychological theory? *Psychological Science, 4*, 70–80.

Hilgard, E. R., Leary, D. E., & McGuire, G. R. (1991). The history of psychology: A survey and critical assessment. *Annual Review of Psychology, 42*, 79–107.

Hill, C. E., & Stephany, A. (1990). Relation of nonverbal behavior to client reactions. *Journal of Counseling Psychology, 37*, 22–26.

Hill, D. W., Hill, C. M., Fields, K. L., & Smith, J. C. (1993). Effects of jet lag on factors related to sport performance. *Canadian Journal of Applied Physiology, 18*, 91–103.

Hill, R. D., Allen, A. C., & McWhorter, P. (1991). Stories as a mnemonic aid for older learners. *Psychology and Aging, 6*, 484–486.

Hillbrand, M., & Waite, B. M. (1994). The everyday experience of an institutionalized sex offender: An idiographic application of the experience sampling method. *Archives of Sexual Behavior, 23*, 453–463.

Hillson, T. R., & Martin, R. A. (1994). What's so funny about that?: The domains-interaction approach as a model of incongruity and resolution in humor. *Motivation and Emotion, 18*, 1–29.

Hilsenroth, M. J., Hibbard, S. R., Nash, M. R., & Handler, L. (1993). A Rorschach study of narcissism, defense, and aggression in borderline, narcissistic, and Cluster C personality disorders. *Journal of Personality Assessment, 60*, 346–361.

Hilts, V. L. (1982). Obeying the laws of hereditary descent: Phrenological views on inheritance and eugenics. *Journal of the History of the Behavioral Sciences, 18*, 62–77.

Hinchy, J., Lovibond, P. F., & Ter-Horst, K. M. (1995). Blocking in human electrodermal conditioning. *Quarterly Journal of Experimental Psychology Comparative and Physiological Psychology, 48*, 2–12.

Hindeland, M. J. (1971). Edward Bradford Titchener: A pioneer in perception. *Journal of the History of the Behavioral Sciences, 7*, 23–28.

Hiramoto, R. N., Hiramoto, N. S., Solvason, H. B., & Ghanta, V. K. (1987). Regulation of natural immunity (NK activity) by conditioning. *Annals of the New York Academy of Sciences, 496*, 545–552.

Hirsch, H. V. B., & Spinelli, D. N. (1970). Visual experience modifies distribution of horizontally and vertically oriented receptive fields in cats. *Science, 168*, 869–871.

Hirsh, I. J. (1996). Auditory psychophysics and perception. *Annual Review of Psychology, 47*, 461–484.

Hobson, J. A. (1985, November/December). Can psychoanalysis be saved? *Sciences*, pp. 52–58.

Hobson, J. A. (1988). *The dreaming brain*. New York: Basic Books.

Hobson, J. A., & McCarley, R. W. (1977). The brain as a dream state generator: An activation-synthesis hypothesis of the dream process. *American Journal of Psychiatry, 134*, 1335–1348.

Hodgins, H. S., & Zuckerman, M. (1990). The effect of nonverbal sensitivity on social interaction. *Journal of Nonverbal Behavior, 14*, 155–170.

Hoemann, H. W., & Keske, C. M. (1995). Proactive interference and language change in hearing adult students of American Sign Language. *Sign Language Studies, 86*, 45–61.

Hoff-Ginsberg, E. (1986). Function and structure in maternal speech: Their relation to the child's development of syntax. *Developmental Psychology, 22*, 155–163.

Hoffman, C., Lau, I., & Johnson, D. R. (1986). The linguistic relativity of person cognition: An English-Chinese comparison. *Journal of Personality and Social Psychology, 51*, 1097–1105.

Hoffman, L. W. (1991). The influence of the family environment on personality: Accounting for sibling differences. *Psychological Bulletin, 110*, 187–203.

Hoffman, N. (1995). The social "instinct." *Journal of the American Academy of Psychoanalysis, 23*, 197–206.

Hofmann, A. (1983). *LSD: My problem child*. Los Angeles: Tarcher.

Hofsten, C. (1983). Eye-hand coordination in the newborn. *Developmental Psychology, 18*, 450–461.

Hofsten, C. von, Kellman, P., & Putaansuu, J. (1992). Young infants' sensitivity to motion parallax. *Infant Behavior and Development, 15*, 245–264.

Holden, C. (1980, November). Twins reunited: More than the faces are familiar. *Science 80*, pp. 55–59.

Holden, C. (1983). Insanity defense reexamined. *Science, 222*, 994–995.

Holden, C. (1986). Depression research advances, treatment lags. *Science, 233*, 723–726.

Holden, C. (1986). Researchers grapple with problems of updating classic psychological test. *Science, 233*, 1249–1251.

Holden, C. (1987). Animal regulations: So far, so good. *Science, 238*, 880–882.

Holden, C. (1987). The genetics of personality. *Science, 237*, 598–601.

Holland, L. N., Goldstein, B. D., & Aronstam, R. S. (1993). Substance P receptor desensitization in the dorsal horn: Possible involvement of receptor-G protein complexes. *Brain Research, 600*, 89–96.

Hollender, M. H. (1983). The 51st landmark article. *Journal of the American Medical Association, 250*, 228–229.

Hollins, M., Delemos, K. A., & Goble, A. K. (1991). Vibrotactile adaptation on the face. *Perception and Psychophysics, 49*, 21–30.

Hollway, W. (1994). Beyond sex differences: A project for feminist psychology. *Feminism and Psychology, 4*, 538–546.

Holmes, D. S. (1984). Meditation and somatic arousal reduction: A review of the experimental evidence. *American Psychologist, 39*, 1–10.

Holmes, M. (1986, August 3). 20 years ago, the Texas tower massacre. *Philadelphia Inquirer*, p. 3E.

Holmes, T. H., & Rahe, R. H. (1967). The Social Readjustment Rating Scale. *Journal of Psychosomatic Research, 11*, 213–218.

Holroyd, J. (1996). Hypnosis treatment of clinical pain: Understanding why hypnosis is useful. *International Journal of Clinical and Experimental Hypnosis, 44*, 33-51.

Holst, V. F., & Pezdek, K. (1992). Scripts for typical crimes and their effects on memory for eyewitness testimony. *Applied Cognitive Psychology, 6*, 573–587.

Holtgraves, T., & Skeel, J. (1992). Cognitive biases in playing the lottery: Estimating the odds and choosing the numbers. *Journal of Applied Social Psychology, 22*, 934–952.

Homa, D. (1983). An assessment of two extraordinary speed-readers. *Bulletin of the Psychonomic Society, 21*, 123–126.

Homant, R. J., Kennedy, D. B., & Howton, J. D. (1993). Sensation seeking as a factor in police pursuit. *Criminal Justice and Behavior, 20*, 293–305.

Honchar, M. P., Olney, J. W., & Sherman, W. R. (1983). Systematic cholinergic agents induce seizures and brain damage in lithium-treated rats. *Science, 220*, 323–325.

Honts, C. R., Hodes, R. L., & Raskin, D. C. (1985). Effects of physical countermeasures on the physiological detection of deception. *Journal of Applied Psychology, 70*, 177–187.

Hood, K. (1995. Social psychology and sociobiology: Which is the metatheory? *Psychological Inquiry, 6*, 54–56.

Hope, D. A., & Mindell, J. A. (1994). Global social skill ratings: Measures of social behavior or physical attractiveness? *Behaviour Research and Therapy, 32*, 463–469.

Hope, D. A., Gansler, D. A., & Heimberg, R. G. (1989). Attentional focus and causal attributions in social phobia: Implications from social psychology. *Clinical Psychology Review, 9*, 49–60.

Hopkins, J. R. (1995). Erik Homburger Erikson (1902–1994). *American Psychologist, 50*, 796–797.

Hoppe, R. B. (1988). In search of a phenomenon: Research in parapsychology [Review of *Foundations of parapsychology*]. *Contemporary Psychology, 33*, 129–130.

Hoptman, M. J., & Davidson, R. J. (1994). How and why do the two cerebral hemispheres interact? *Psychological Bulletin, 116*, 195–219.

Hormuth, S. E. (1986). The sampling of experiences in situ. *Journal of Personality, 54*, 262–293.

Horn, J. L., & Cattell, R. C. (1966). Refinement and test of the theory of fluid and crystallized general intelligences. *Journal of Educational Psychology, 57*, 253–270.

Horn, J. L., & Donaldson, G. (1976). On the myth of individual decline in adulthood. *American Psychologist, 31*, 701–719.

Horne, J. A., & Reyner, L. A. (1996). Counteracting driver sleepiness: Effects of napping, caffeine, and placebo. *Psychophysiology, 33*, 306-309.

Horner, M. D. (1990). Psychobiological evidence for the distinction between episodic and semantic memory. *Neuropsychology Review, 1*, 281–321.

Horney, K. (1926/1967). The flight from womanhood. In K. Horney, *Feminine psychology* (H. Kelman, Ed. pp. 54–70). New York: W. W. Norton.

Horney, K. (1937). *The neurotic personality of our time*. New York: W. W. Norton.

Hornstein, G. A. (1992). The return of the repressed: Psychology's problematic relations with psychoanalysis, 1909–1960. *American Psychologist, 47*, 254–263.

Horowitz, F. D. (1992). John B. Watson's legacy: Learning and environment. *Developmental Psychology, 28*, 360–367.

Houlihan, D., Schwartz, C., Miltenberger, R., & Heuton, D. (1993). The rapid treatment of a young man's balloon (noise) phobia using in vivo flooding. *Journal of Behavior Therapy and Experimental Psychiatry, 24*, 233–240.

House, R. J. (1971). A path-goal theory of leadership. *Administrative Science Quarterly, 16*, 321–338.

Hovland, C. I., Lumsdaine, A., & Sheffield, F. (1949). *Experiments on mass communication*. Princeton, NJ: Princeton University Press.

Howard, K. I., Kopta, S. M., Krausse, M. S., & Orlinsky, D. E. (1986). The dose-effect relationship in psychotherapy. *American Psychologist, 41*, 159–164.

Howe, M. J., & Smith, J. (1988). Calendar calculating in "idiot savants": How do they do it? *British Journal of Psychology, 79*, 371–386.

Howell, J. M., & Avolio, B. J. (1993). Transformational leadership, transactional leadership, locus of control, and support for innovation: Key predictors of consolidated-business-unit performance. *Journal of Applied Psychology, 78,* 891–902.

Hsu, F. H., Anantharaman, R., Campbell, M., & Nowatzyk, A. (1990, October). A grandmaster chess machine. *Scientific American,* pp. 44–50.

Hsu, L. G., Chester B. E., & Santhouse, R. (1990). Bulimia nervosa in eleven sets of twins: A clinical report. *International Journal of Eating Disorders, 9,* 275–282.

Hsu, L. G., & Sobkiewicz, T. A. (1991). Body image disturbance: Time to abandon the concept for eating disorders? *International Journal of Eating Disorders, 10,* 15–30.

Hubel, D. H., & Wiesel, T. N. (1979, September). Brain mechanisms of vision. *Scientific American,* pp. 130–144.

Huber, S. J., Shulman, H. G., Paulson, G. W., & Shuttleworth, E. C. (1989). Dose-dependent memory impairment in Parkinson's disease. *Neurology, 39,* 438–440.

Hudak, M. A. (1993). Gender-schema theory revisited: Men's stereotypes of American women. *Sex Roles, 28,* 279–293.

Hudesman, J., Page, W., & Rautiainen, J. (1992). Use of subliminal stimulation to enhance learning mathematics. *Perceptual and Motor Skills, 74,* 1219–1224.

Hugdahl, K., Satz, P., Mitrushina, M., & Miller, E. N. (1993). Left-handedness and old age: Do left-handers die earlier? *Neuropsychologia, 31,* 325–333.

Hughes, D. (1990). Participant modeling as a classroom activity. *Teaching of Psychology, 7,* 238–240.

Hughes, J., Smith, T. W., Kosterlitz, H. W., Fothergill, L. A., Morgan, B. A., & Morris, H. R. (1975). Identification of two related pentapeptides from the brain with potent opiate agonistic activity. *Nature, 258,* 577–579.

Hughes, J. R., Gust, S. W., Skoog, K., & Keenan, R. (1991). Symptoms of tobacco withdrawal: A replication and extension. *Archives of General Psychiatry, 48,* 52–59.

Hughes, J. R., Higgins, S. T., & Bickel, W. K. (1994). Nicotine withdrawal versus other drug withdrawal syndromes: Similarities and dissimilarities. *Addiction, 89,* 1461–1470.

Hughes, J. R., Higgins, S. T., Bickel, W. K., Hunt, W. K., Fenwick, J. W., Gulliver, S. B., & Mireault, G. C. (1991). Caffeine self-administration, withdrawal, and adverse effects among coffee drinkers. *Archives of General Psychiatry, 48,* 611–617.

Hull, C. L. (1943). *Principles of behavior.* New York: Appleton-Century-Crofts.

Hull, J. G., & Bond, C. F., Jr. (1986). Social and behavioral consequences of alcohol consumption and expectancy: A meta-analysis. *Psychological Bulletin, 99,* 347–360.

Hulme, C., & Roodenrys, S. (1995). Verbal working memory development and its disorders. *Journal of Child Psychology and Psychiatry and Allied Disciplines, 36,* 373–398.

Humphrey, D. H., & Dahlstrom, W. G. (1995). The impact of changing from the MMPI to the MMPI-2 on profile configurations. *Journal of Personality Assessment, 64,* 428–439.

Humphreys, M. S., & Revelle, W. (1984). Personality, motivation, and performance: A theory of the relationship between individual differences and information processing. *Psychological Review, 91,* 153–184.

Hunt, E., & Agnoli, F. (1991). The Whorfian hypothesis: A cognitive psychology perspective. *Psychological Review, 98,* 377–389.

Hunt, J. M. (1979). Psychological development: Early experience. *Annual Review of Psychology, 30,* 103–143.

Hunter, I. M. L. (1993). Heritage from the wild boy of Aveyron. *Early Child Development and Care, 95,* 143–155.

Hunter, J. E., & Hunter, R. F. (1984). Validity and utility of alternative predictors of job performance. *Psychological Bulletin, 96,* 72–98.

Hur, J., & Osborne, S. (1993). A comparison of forward and backward chaining methods used in teaching corsage making skills to mentally retarded adults. *British Journal of Developmental Disabilities, 39,* 108–117.

Hurford, J. R. (1991). The evolution of the critical period for language acquisition. *Cognition, 40,* 159–201.

Hurst, L. C., & Mulhall, D. J. (1988). Another calendar savant. *British Journal of Psychiatry, 152,* 274–277.

Husain, S. A. (1990). Current perspective on the role of psychosocial factors in adolescent suicide. *Psychiatric Annals, 20,* 122–127.

Huston, A. C., Watkins, B. A., & Kunkel, E. (1989). Public policy and children's television. *American Psychologist, 44,* 424–433.

Huston, T. L., Ruggiero, M., Conner, R., & Geis, G. (1981). Bystander intervention into crime: A study based on naturally-occurring episodes. *Social Psychology Quarterly, 44,* 14–23.

Hutchins, C. M. (1981, October). The acoustics of violin plates. *Scientific American,* pp. 170–174, 177–180, 182–186.

Huttenlocher, P. R. (1990). Morphometric study of human cerebral cortex development. *Neuropsychologia, 28,* 517–527.

Hyde, J. S. (1984). Children's understanding of sexist language. *Developmental Psychology, 20,* 697–706.

Hyde, J. S., Fennema, E., & Lamon, S. J. (1990). Gender differences in mathematics performance: A meta-analysis. *Psychological Bulletin, 107,* 139–155.

Hyde, J. S., & Linn, M. C. (1988). Gender differences in verbal ability: A meta-analysis. *Psychological Bulletin, 104,* 56–69.

Hyde, J. S., & Plant, E. A. (1995). Magnitude of psychological gender differences: Another side of the story. *American Psychologist, 50,* 159–161.

Hyman, R. (1994). Anomaly or artifact? Comments on Bem and Honorton. *Psychological Bulletin, 115,* 19–24.

Hyman, R. B. (1988). Four stages of adulthood: An exploratory study of growth patterns of inner-direction and time-competence in women. *Journal of Research in Personality, 22,* 117–127.

Hynan, D. J. (1990). Client reasons and experiences in treatment that influence termination of psychotherapy. *Journal of Clinical Psychology, 46,* 891–895.

Iancu, I., Spivak, B., Ratzoni, G., & Apter, A. (1994). The sociocultural theory in the development of anorexia nervosa. *Psychopathology, 27,* 29–36.

Ichikawa, M., & Saida, S. (1996). How is motion disparity integrated with binocular disparity in depth perception? *Perception and Psychophysics, 58,* 271-282.

Ilgen, D. R., Barnes-Farrell, J. L., & McKellin, D. B. (1993). Performance appraisal process research in the 1980s: What has it contributed to appraisals in use? *Organizational Behavior and Human Decisions Processes, 54,* 321–368.

Immergluck, L. (1964). Determinism-freedom in contemporary psychology: An ancient problem revisited. *American Psychologist, 19,* 270–281.

Ingelfinger, F. J. (1944). The late effects of total and subtotal gastrectomy. *New England Journal of Medicine, 231,* 321–327.

Ingham, A. G., Levinger, G., Graves, J., & Peckham, V. (1974). The Ringelmann effect: Studies of group size and group performance. *Journal of Experimental Social Psychology, 10,* 371–384.

Inglis, A., & Greenglass, E. R. (1989). Motivation for marriage among women and men. *Psychological Reports, 65,* 1035–1042.

Inkson, K., & Paterson, J. (1993). Organizational behavior in New Zealand, 1987–1992: A review. *New Zealand Journal of Psychology, 22,* 54–66.

Inoki, R., Hayashi, T., Kudo, T., & Matsumoto, K. (1978). Effects of aspirin and morphine on the release of a bradykinin-like substance into the subcutaneous perfusate of the rat paw. *Pain, 5,* 53–63.

Inoue, S., Honda, K., & Komoda, Y. (1995). Sleep as neuronal detoxification and restitution. *Behavioural Brain Research, 69,* 91-96.

Insko, C. A., Nacoste, R. W., & Moe, J. L. (1983). Belief congruence and racial discrimination: Review of the evidence and critical evaluation. *European Journal of Social Psychology, 13,* 153–174.

Ironson, G., Schneiderman, H., Kumar, M., & Antoni, M. H. (1994). Psychosocial stress, endocrine and immune response in HIV-1 disease. *Homeostasis in Health and Disease, 35,* 137–148.

Irwin, D. E. (1996). Integrating information across saccadic eye movements. *Current Directions in Psychological Science, 5,* 94-100.

Irwin, M., Mascovich, A., Gillin, J. C., & Willoughby, R. (1994). Partial sleep deprivation reduced natural killer cell activity in humans. *Psychosomatic Medicine, 56,* 493–498.

Ispa, J. M., Thornburg, K. R., & Gray, M. M. (1990). Relations between early childhood care arrangements and college students' psychosocial development and academic performance. *Adolescence, 25,* 529–542.

Ito, M. (1993). Movement and thought: Identical control mechanisms by the cerebellum. *Trends in Neurosciences, 16,* 448–450.

Iversen, I. H. (1992). Skinner's early research: From reflexology to operant conditioning. *American Psychologist, 47,* 1318–1328.

Iversen, I. H. (1993). Techniques for establishing schedules with wheel running as reinforcement in rats. *Journal of the Experimental Analysis of Behavior, 60,* 219–238.

Izard, C. E. (1990a). Facial expressions and the regulation of emotions. *Journal of Personality and Social Psychology, 58,* 487–498.

Izard, C. E. (1990b). The substrates and functions of emotion feelings: William James and current emotion theory. *Personality and Social Psychology Bulletin, 16,* 626–635.

Izard, C. E. (1993). Four systems for emotion activation: Cognitive and noncognitive processes. *Psychological Review, 100,* 68–90.

Izard, C. E., & Haynes, O. M. (1988). On the form and universality of the contempt expression: A challenge to Ekman and Friesen's claim of discovery. *Motivation and Emotion, 12,* 1–16.

Izard, C. E., Huebner, R. R., Risser, D., McGinnes, G. C., & Dougherty, L. M. (1980). The young infant's ability to produce discrete emotion expressions. *Developmental Psychology, 16,* 132–140.

Jacklin, C. N. (1989). Female and male: Issues of gender. *American Psychologist, 44,* 127–133.

Jackson, C., Bee-Gates, D. J., & Henriksen, L. (1994). Authoritative parenting, child competencies, and initiation of cigarette smoking. *Health Education Quarterly, 21,* 103–116.

Jackson, H. C., & Nutt, D. J. (1990). Does electroconvulsive shock therapy work through opioid mechanisms? *Human Psychopharmacology Clinical and Experimental, 5,* 3–23.

Jackson, L. A., Hunter, J. E., & Hodge, C. N. (1995). Physical attractiveness and intellectual competence: A meta-analytic review. *Social Psychology Quarterly, 58,* 108–122.

Jackson, R. R., & Wilcox, R. S. (1993). Spider flexibly chooses aggressive mimicry signals for different prey by trial and error. *Behavior, 127,* 21–36.

Jackson, S. W. (1994). Catharsis and abreaction in the history of psychological healing. *Psychiatric Clinics of North America, 17,* 471–491.

Jacob, R. G., Wing, R. R., & Shapiro, A. P. (1987). The behavioral treatment of hypertension: Long-term effects. *Behavior Therapy, 18,* 325–352.

Jacobs, G. D., Rosenberg, P. A., Friedman, R., & Matheson, J. (1993). Multifactor behavioral treatment of chronic sleep-onset insomnia using stimulus control and the relaxation response: A preliminary study. *Behavior Modification, 17,* 498–509.

Jacobs, G. H., Neitz, M., Deegan, J. F., & Neitz, J. (1996). Trichromatic colour vision in New World monkeys. *Nature, 382,* 156-158.

Jacobs, W. J., & Blackburn, J. R. (1995). A model of Pavlovian conditioning: Variations in representations of the unconditional stimulus. *Integrative Physiological and Behavioral Science, 30,* 12–33.

Jacobsen, P. B., Bovbjerg, D. H., Schwartz, M. D., & Hudis, C. A. (1995). Conditioned emotional distress in women receiving chemotherapy for breast cancer. *Journal of Consulting and Clinical Psychology, 63,* 108–114.

Jacobson, E. (1929/1974). *Progressive relaxation.* Chicago: University of Chicago Press.

James, W. (1884). What is an emotion? *Mind, 9,* 188–205.

James, W. (1890/1991). *The principles of psychology* (2 vols.). Cambridge, MA: Harvard University Press.

James, W. (1902/1992). *The varieties of religious experience.* New York: Gryphon.

Jamieson, D. G., & Morosan, D. E. (1986). Training non-native speech contrasts in adults: Acquisition of the English *O-O* contrast by Francophones. *Perception and Psychophysics, 40,* 205–215.

Janis, I. L. (1983). *Groupthink: Psychological studies of policy decisions and fiascoes.* Boston: Houghton Mifflin.

Janowiak, J. J., & Hackman, R. (1994). Meditation and college students' self-actualization and rated stress. *Psychological Reports, 75,* 1007–1010.

Jansson, L., & Ost, L. G. (1982). Behavioral treatments for agoraphobia: An evaluative review. *Clinical Psychology Review, 2,* 311–336.

Janzen, L. A., Nanson, J. L., & Block, G. W. (1995). Neuropsychological evaluation of preschoolers with fetal alcohol syndrome. *Neurotoxicology and Teratology, 17,* 273–279.

Jemmott, J. B., & Locke, S. E. (1984). Psychosocial factors, immunologic mediation, and human susceptibility to infectious diseases: How much do we know? *Psychological Bulletin, 95,* 78–108.

Jemmott, J. B., & Magloire, K. (1988). Academic stress, social support, and secretory immunoglobulin A. *Journal of Personality and Social Psychology, 55,* 803–810.

Jenkins, J. G., & Dallenbach, K. M. (1924). Oblivescence during sleep and waking. *American Journal of Psychology, 35,* 605–612.

Jensen, A. J. (1969). How much can we boost IQ and scholastic achievement? *Harvard Educational Review, 39,* 1–123.

Jensen, A. R. (1980). *Bias in mental testing.* New York: Free Press.

Jensen, J. P., Bergin, A. E., & Greaves, D. W. (1990). The meaning of eclecticism: New survey and analysis of components. *Professional Psychology: Research and Practice, 21,* 124–130.

Jernigan, T. L., Salmon, D. P., Butters, N., & Hesselink, J. R. (1991). Cerebral structure on MRI: 2. Specific changes in Alzheimer's and Huntington's diseases. *Biological Psychiatry, 29,* 68–81.

Jocklin, V., McGue, M., & Lykken, D. T. (1996). Personality and divorce: A genetic analysis. *Journal of Personality and Social Psychology, 71,* 288–299.

Johnson, C., & Flach, A. (1985). Family characteristics of 105 patients with bulimia. *American Journal of Psychiatry, 142,* 1321–1324.

Johnson, J. S., & Newport, E. L. (1989). Critical period effects in second language learning: The influence of maturational state on the acquisition of English as a second language. *Cognitive Psychology, 21,* 60–99.

Johnson, R. C., McClearn, G. E., Yuen, S., Nagoshi, C. T., Ahern, F. M., & Cole, R. E. (1985). Galton's data a century later. *American Psychologist, 40,* 875–892.

Johnston, M., & Vogele, C. (1993). Benefits of psychological preparation for surgery: A meta-analysis. *Annals of Behavioral Medicine, 15,* 245–256.

Johnstone, V., & Alsop, B. (1996). Human signal-detection performance: Effects of signal presentation probabilities and reinforcer distributions. *Journal of the Experimental Analysis of Behavior, 66,* 243-263.

Jonas, G. (1972). *Visceral learning: Toward a science of self-control.* New York: Viking.

Jones, E. E. (1985). *History of social psychology.* In G. A. Kimble & K. Schlesinger (Eds.), *Topics in the history of psychology* (Vol. 2, pp. 371–407). Hillsdale, NJ: Erlbaum.

Jones, L. (1900). Education during sleep. *Suggestive Therapeutics, 8,* 283–285.

Jones, L. A. (1986). Perception of force and weight: Theory and research. *Psychological Bulletin, 100,* 29–42.

Jones, L. V. (1984). White-black achievement differences: The narrowing gap. *American Psychologist, 39,* 1207–1213.

Jones, M. C. (1924). The elimination of children's fears. *Journal of Experimental Psychology, 7,* 383–390.

Jones, M. M. (1980). Conversion disorder: Anachronism or evolutionary form? A review of the neurologic, behavioral, and psychoanalytic literature. *Psychological Bulletin, 87,* 427–441.

Jorgensen, R. S., Nash, J. K., Lasser, N. L., Hymowitz, N., & Langer, A. W. (1988). Heart rate acceleration and its relationship to total serum cholesterol, triglycerides, and blood pressure. *Psychophysiology, 25,* 39–44.

Joubert, P. H., & Van Os, B. E. (1989). The effect of hypnosis, placebo, paracetamol, and naloxone on the response to dental pulp stimulation. *Current Therapeutic Research, 46,* 774–781.

Joyce, J. (1916/1967). *A portrait of the artist as a young man.* New York: Viking.

Ju, J. J. (1982). Counselor variables and rehabilitation outcomes: A literature overview. *Journal of Applied Rehabilitation Counseling, 13,* 28–31, 43.

Judge, S. J., & Cumming, B. G. (1986). Neurons in the monkey mibrain with activity related to vergence eye movement and accommodation. *Journal of Neurophysiology, 55,* 915–930.

Julien, R. M. (1981). *A primer of drug action.* San Francisco: Freeman.

Jung, C. G. (1959/1969). *Flying saucers: A modern myth of things seen in the sky.* New York: Signet.

Jussim, L. (1991). Social perception and social reality: A reflection-construction model. *Psychological Review, 98,* 54–73.

Kaas, J. H. (1987). The organization of neocortex in mammals: Implications for theories of brain function. *Annual Review of Psychology, 38,* 129–151.

Kahan, T. L., & LaBerge, S. (1994). Lucid dreaming as metacognition: Implications for cognitive science. *Consciousness and Cognition: An International Journal, 3,* 246–264.

Kahneman, D. (1991). Judgment and decision making: A personal view. *Psychological Science, 2,* 142–145.

Kahneman, D., & Tversky, A. (1973). On the psychology of prediction. *Psychological Review, 80,* 237–251.

Kahneman, D., & Tversky, A. (1982, January). The psychology of preferences. *Scientific American,* pp. 160–173.

Kaiser, M. K., Montegut, M. J., & Proffitt, D. R. (1995). Rotational and translational components of motion parallax: Observers' sensitivity and implications for three-dimensional computer graphics. *Journal of Experimental Psychology: Applied, 1,* 321-331.

Kaitz, M., & Eidelman, A. I. (1992). Smell-recognition of newborns by women who are not mothers. *Chemical Senses, 17,* 222–229.

Kalichman, S. C., & Rompa, D. (1995). Sexual sensation seeking and sexual compulsivity scales: Reliability, validity, and predicting HIV risk behavior. *Journal of Personality Assessment, 65,* 586–601.

Kalmun, A. J. (1982). Electric and magnetic field detection in elasmobranch fishes. *Science, 218,* 916–918.

Kamin, L. (1969). Predictability, surprise, attention, and conditioning. In B. Campbell & R. Church (Eds.), *Punishment and aversive behavior.* New York: Appleton-Century-Crofts.

Kamin, L. J. (1974). *The science and politics of IQ.* New York: Wiley.

Kamins, M. A., & Assael, H. (1987). Two-sided versus one-sided appeals: A cognitive perspective on argumentation, source derogation, and the effect of disconfirming trial on belief change. *Journal of Marketing Research, 24,* 29–39.

Kamiya, J. (1969). Operant control of the EEG alpha rhythm and some of its reported effects on consciousness. In C. Tart (Ed.), *Altered states of consciousness* (pp. 489–501). New York: Wiley.

Kandel, E. R., & Schwartz, J. H. (1982). Molecular biology of learning: Modulation of transmitter release. *Science, 218,* 433–443.

Kandel, E., Mednick, S. A., Kirkegaard-Sorensen, L., Hutchings, B., Knop, J., Rosenberg, R., & Schulsinger, R. (1988). IQ as a protective factor for subjects at high risk for antisocial behavior. *Journal of Consulting and Clinical Psychology, 56,* 224–226.

Kanekar, S. (1976). Observational learning of attitudes: A behavioral analysis. *European Journal of Social Psychology, 6,* 5–24.

Kanfer, R. (1990). Motivation theory and industrial organizational psychology. In M. E. Dunnette and L. M. Hough (Eds.), *Handbook of industrial and organizational psychology* (2nd ed., pp. 75–124). Palo Alto: Consulting Psychologists Press.

Kanner, A. D., Coyne, J. C., Schaefer, C., & Lazarus, R. S. (1981). Comparisons of two modes of stress measurement: Daily hassles and uplifts versus major life events. *Journal of Behavioral Medicine, 4,* 1–39.

Kao, E. C., Ngan, P. W., Wilson, S., & Kunovich, R. (1990). Wire-bending test as a predictor of preclinical performance by dental students. *Perceptual and Motor Skills, 71,* 667–673.

Kaplan, B. J., & Shayne, V. T. (1993). Unsafe sex: Decision-making biases and heuristics. *AIDS Education and Prevention, 5,* 294–301.

Kaplan, D. M. (1993). What is sublimated in sublimation? *Journal of the American Psychoanalytic Association, 41,* 549–570.

Kaplan, R. M., & Saccuzzo, D. P. (1982). *Psychological testing: Principles, applications, and issues.* Belmont, CA: Brooks/Cole.

Karau, S. J., & Williams, K. D. (1993). Social loafing: A meta-analytic review and theoretical integration. *Journal of Personality and Social Psychology, 65,* 681–706.

Karau, S. J., & Williams, K. D. (1995). Social loafing: Research findings, implications, and future directions. *Current Directions in Psychological Science, 4,* 134–140.

Karlsson, I. (1993). Neurotransmitter changes in aging and dementia. *Nordic Journal of Psychiatry, 47,* 41–44.

Karney, B. R., & Bradbury, T. N. (1995). The longitudinal course of marital quality and stability: A review of theory, methods, and research. *Psychological Bulletin, 118,* 3–34.

Kastner, J., Gottlieb, B. W., Gottlieb, J., & Kastner, S. (1995). Use of incentive structure in mainstream classes. *Journal of Educational Research, 89,* 52–57.

Katz, J. (1984). Symptom prescription: A review of the clinical outcome literature. *Clinical Psychology Review, 4,* 703–717.

Katz, R. J., Lott, M., Landau, P., & Waldmeier, P. (1993). A clinical test of noradrenergic involvement in the therapeutic mode of action of an experimental antidepressant. *Biological Psychiatry, 33,* 261–266.

Katzell, R. A., & Austin, J. T. (1992). From then to now: The development of industrial-organizational psychology in the United States. *Journal of Applied Psychology, 77,* 803–835.

Kaufman, J., & Cicchetti, D. (1989). Effects of maltreatment on school-age children's socioemotional development: Assessments in a day-camp setting. *Developmental Psychology, 25,* 516–524.

Kaufman, J., & Zigler, E. (1987). Do abused children become abusive parents? *American Journal of Orthopsychiatry, 57,* 186–192.

Kaufman, L., & Rock, I. (1962, July). The moon illusion. *Scientific American,* pp. 120–130.

Kazdin, A. E. (1982). Symptom substitution, generalization, and response covariation: Implications for psychotherapy outcome. *Psychological Bulletin, 91,* 349–365.

Keck, P. E., & McElroy, S. L. (1993). Current perspectives on treatment of bipolar disorder with lithium. *Psychiatric Annals, 23,* 64–69.

Keesey, R. E., & Powley, T. L. (1986). The regulation of body weight. *Annual Review of Psychology, 37,* 109–133.

Keith, J. R., & McVety, K. M. (1988). Latent place learning in a novel environment and the influences of prior training in rats. *Psychobiology, 16,* 146–151.

Keller, F. S. (1991). Burrhus Frederic Skinner (1904–1990). *Journal of the History of the Behavioral Sciences, 27,* 3–6.

Kelley, H. H. (1950). The warm-cold variable in first impressions of personality. *Journal of Personality, 18,* 431–439.

Kelley, H. H. (1973). The processes of causal attributions. *American Psychologist, 28,* 107–128.

Kelley, H. H. (1992). Common-sense psychology and scientific discovery. *Annual Review of Psychology, 43,* 1–23.

Kellogg, W. N., & Kellogg, L. A. (1933). *The ape and the child.* New York: McGraw-Hill.

Kelly, G. A. (1963). *A theory of personality: The psychology of personal constructs.* New York: W. W. Norton.

Kelly, G. F. (1996). Using meditative techniques in psychotherapy. *Journal of Humanistic Psychology, 36,* 49–66.

Kelly, J. A. (1986). Psychological research and the rights of animals: Disagreement with Miller. *American Psychologist, 41,* 839–841.

Kelly, J. B., & Kavanagh, G. L. (1994). Sound localization after unilateral lesions of inferior colliculus in the ferret (*Mustela putorius*). *Journal of Neurophysiology, 71,* 1078–1087.

Kelly, M. P., Strassberg, D. S., & Kircher, J. R. (1990). Attitudinal and experiential correlates of anorgasmia. *Archives of Sexual Behavior, 19,* 165–177.

Kelly, R. B., Zyzanski, S. J., & Alemagno, S. A. (1991). Prediction of motivation and behavior change following health promotion: Role of health beliefs, social support, and self-efficacy. *Social Science and Medicine, 32,* 311–320.

Kelsoe, J. R., Kristbjanarson, H., Bergesch, P., & Shilling, P. (1993). A genetic linkage study of bipolar disorder and 13 markers on chromosome 11 including the D-sub-2 dopamine receptor. *Neuropsychopharmacology, 9,* 293–301.

Kendler, K. S., Walters, E. E., Truett, K. R., & Heath, A. C. (1995). A twin-family study of self-report symptoms of panic-phobia and somatization. *Behavior Genetics, 25,* 499–515.

Kendrick, K. M., & Baldwin, B. A. (1987). Cells in temporal cortex of conscious sheep can respond preferentially to the sight of faces. *Science, 236,* 448–450.

Kenrick, D. T., & Dantchik, A. (1983). Interactionism, idiographics, and the social psychological invasion of personality. *Journal of Personality, 51,* 286–307.

Kenrick, D. T., & Funder, D. C. (1988). Profiting from controversy: Lessons from the person-situation debate. *American Psychologist, 43,* 23–34.

Kent, R. J., & Allen, C. T. (1994). Competitive interference effects in consumer memory for advertising: The role of brand familiarity. *Journal of Marketing, 58,* 97–105.

Kerr, G., & Goss, J. (1996). The effects fo a stress management program on injuries and stress levels. *Journal of Applied Sport Psychology, 8,* 109–117.

Kershner, J. R., & Ledger, G. (1985). Effect of sex, intelligence, and style of thinking on creativity: A comparison of gifted and average IQ children. *Journal of Personality and Social Psychology, 48,* 1033–1040.

Kessler, R. C. (1994). The National Comorbidity Survey of the United States. *International Review of Psychiatry, 6,* 365–376.

Kessler, S. (1984). The myth of mythical disease [Review of *Schizophrenia: Medical diagnosis or moral verdict?*]. *Contemporary Psychology, 29,* 380–381.

Kety, S. S., Wender, P. H., Jacobsen, B., & Ingraham, L. J. (1994). Mental illness in the biological and adoptive relatives of schizophrenic adoptees: Replication of the Copenhagen study in the rest of Denmark. *Archives of General Psychiatry, 51,* 442–455.

Kiecolt-Glaser, J. K., & Glaser, R. (1995). Psychoneuroimmunology and health consequences: Data and shared mechanisms. *Psychosomatic Medicine, 57,* 269–274.

Kiecolt-Glaser, J. K., Glaser, R., Strain, E. C., Stout, J. C., Tarr, K. L., Holliday, J. E., & Speicher, C. E. (1986). Modulation of cellular immunity in medical students. *Journal of Behavioral Medicine, 9,* 5–21.

Kiernan, B. D., Dane, J. R., Phillips, L. H., & Price, D. D. (1995). Hypnotic analgesia reduces R–III nociceptive reflex: Further evidence concerning the multifactorial nature of hypnotic analgesia. *Pain, 60,* 39–47.

Kihlstrom, J. F., & Couture, L. J. (1992). Awareness and information processing in general anesthesia. *Journal of Psychopharmacology, 6,* 410–417.

Kihlstrom, J. F., & McConkey, K. M. (1990). William James and hypnosis: A centennial reflection. *Psychological Science, 1,* 174–178.

Kilborn, L. C., & Labbe, E. E. (1990). Magnetic resonance imaging scanning procedures: Development of phobic response during scan and at one-month follow-up. *Journal of Behavioral Medicine, 13,* 391–401.

Kilbourne, B. K. (1989). A cross-cultural investigation of the foot-in-the-door compliance induction procedure. *Journal of Cross-Cultural Psychology, 20,* 3–38.

Killackey, H. P. (1990). Neocortical expansion: An attempt toward relating phylogeny and ontogeny. *Journal of Cognitive Neuroscience, 2,* 1–17.

Killian, G. A., Holzman, P. S., Davis, J. M., & Gibbons, R. (1984). Effects of psychotropic medication on selected cognitive and perceptual measures. *Journal of Abnormal Psychology, 93,* 58–70.

Kilmann, P. R., Boland, J. P., Norton, S. P., & Davidson, E. (1986). Perspectives of sex therapy outcome: A survey of AASECT providers. *Journal of Sex and Marital Therapy, 12,* 116–138.

Kilmann, P. R., & Sotile, W. M. (1976). The marathon encounter group: A review of the outcome literature. *Psychological Bulletin, 83,* 827–850.

Kim, J. J., DeCola, J. P., Landeira-Fernandez, J., & Fanselow, M. S. (1991). N-methyl-D-aspartate receptor antagonist APV blocks acquisition but not expression of fear conditioning. *Behavioral Neuroscience, 105,* 126–133.

Kimball, M. M. (1989). A new perspective on women's math achievement. *Psychological Bulletin, 105,* 198–214.

Kimble, D. P. (1990). Functional effects of neural grafting in the mammalian central nervous system. *Psychological Bulletin, 108,* 462–479.

Kimble, G. A. (1981). Biological and cognitive constraints on learning. In L. T. Benjamin, Jr. (Ed.), *The G. Stanley Hall Lecture Series* (Vol. 1, pp. 11–60). Washington, DC: American Psychological Association.

Kimble, G. A. (1989). Psychology from the standpoint of a generalist. *American Psychologist, 44,* 491–499.

Kimura, D., & Hampson, E. (1994). Cognitive pattern in men and women is influenced by fluctuations in sex hormones. *Current Directions in Psychological Science, 3,* 57–61.

King, D. B., Raymond, B. L., & Simon-Thomas, J. A. (1995). History of sport psychology in cultural magazines of the Victorian era. *Sport Psychologist, 9,* 376–390.

King, D. B., & Viney, W. (1992). Modern history of pragmatic and sentimental attitudes toward animals and the selling of comparative psychology. *Journal of Comparative Psychology, 106,* 190–195.

Kinsey, A. C., Pomeroy, W. D., & Martin, C. E. (1948). *Sexual behavior in the human male.* Philadelphia: Saunders.

Kinsey, A. C., Pomeroy, W. D., Martin, C. E., & Gebhard, T. H. (1953). *Sexual behavior in the human female.* Philadelphia: Saunders.

Kirkpatrick, D. L. (1959). Techniques for evaluating training programs. I. *Journal of the American Society of Training Directors, 13,* 3–9, 21–26.

Kirkpatrick, D. L. (1960). Techniques for evaluating training programs. II. *Journal of the American Society of Training Directors, 14,* 13–18, 28–32.

Kirmeyer, S. L., & Biggers, K. (1988). Environmental demand and demand engineering behavior: An observational analysis of the Type A patterns. *Journal of Personality and Social Psychology, 54,* 997–1005.

Kirsch, I. (1996). Hypnotic enhancement of cognitive-behavioral weight loss treatments: Another meta-reanalysis. *Journal of Consulting and Clinical Psychology, 64,* 517-519.

Kirsch, I., & Lynn, S. J. (1995). The latered state of hypnosis: Changes in the theoretical landscape. *American Psychologist, 50,* 846–848.

Klar, Y., Mendola, R., Fisher, J. D., & Silver, R. C. (1990). Characteristics of participants in a large group awareness training. *Journal of Consulting and Clinical Psychology 58,* 99–108.

Klein, P., & Westcott, M. R. (1994). The changing character of phenomenological psychology. *Canadian Psychology, 35,* 133–158.

Klein, S. B. (1982). *Motivation: Biosocial approaches.* New York: McGraw-Hill.

Kleinmuntz, B., & Szucko, J. J. (1984a). A field study of the fallibility of polygraph lie detection. *Nature, 308,* 449–450.

Kleinmuntz, B., & Szucko, J. J. (1984b). Lie detection in ancient and modern times: A call for contemporary scientific study. *American Psychologist, 39,* 766–776.

Klepac, R. K. (1986). Fear and avoidance of dental treatment in adults. *Annals of Behavioral Medicine, 8,* 17–22.

Klesges, R. C., Ward, K. D., & DeBon, M. (1996). Smoking cessation: A successful behavioral/pharmacologic interface. *Clinical Psychology Review, 16,* 479–496.

Klimesch, W., Schimke, H., & Schwaiger, J. (1994). Episodic and semantic memory: An analysis in the EEG theta and alpha band. *Electroencephalography and Clinical Neurophysiology, 91,* 428–441.

Klonoff, E. A., Janata, J. W., & Kaufman, B. (1986). The use of systematic desensitization to overcome resistance to magnetic resonance imaging (MRI) scanning. *Journal of Behavior Therapy and Experimental Psychiatry, 17,* 189–192.

Klonoff, E. A., & Moore, D. J. (1986). "Conversion reactions" in adolescents: A biofeedback-based operant approach. *Journal of Behavior Therapy and Experimental Psychiatry, 17,* 179–184.

Klosterhalfen, W., & Klosterhalfen, S. (1983). A critical analysis of the animal experiments cited in support of learned helplessness. *Psychologische Beitrage, 25,* 436–458.

Kluft, R. P. (1987). An update on multiple personality disorder. *Hospital and Community Psychiatry, 38,* 363–373.

Kluger, M. A., Jamner, L. D., & Tursky, B. (1985). Comparison of the effectiveness of biofeedback and relaxation training on handwarming. *Psychophysiology, 22,* 162–166.

Klüver, H., & Bucy, P. C. (1937). "Psychic blindness" and other symptoms following bilateral temporal lobectomy in rhesus monkeys. *American Journal of Physiology, 119,* 352–353.

Knapp, T. J., & Shodahl, S. A. (1974). Ben Franklin as a behavior modifier: A note. *Behavior Therapy, 5,* 656–660.

Knight, I. F. (1984). Freud's "Project": A theory for studies on hysteria. *Journal of the History of the Behavioral Sciences, 20,* 340–358.

Knouse, S. B. (1994). Impressions of the resume: The effects of applicant education, experience, and impression management. *Journal of Business and Psychology, 9,* 33–45.

Knudsen, E. I. (1981, December). The hearing of the barn owl. *Scientific American,* pp. 112–113, 115–116, 118–125.

Kobasa, S. C., Maddi, S. R., & Kahn, S. (1982). Hardiness and health: A prospective study. *Journal of Personality and Social Psychology, 42,* 168–177.

Koenigsberger, L. (1906/1965). *Hermann von Helmholtz.* New York: Dover.

Kohlberg, L. (1981). *Essays on moral development.* New York: Harper & Row.

Kohler, W. (1925). *The mentality of apes.* New York: Harcourt Brace Jovanovich.

Kohler, W. (1959). Gestalt psychology today. *American Psychologist, 14,* 727–734.

Kohnken, G., & Maass, A. (1988). Eyewitness testimony: False alarms on biased instructions. *Journal of Applied Psychology, 73,* 363–370.

Kokkinidis, L., & Anisman, H. (1980). Amphetamine models of paranoid schizophrenia: An overview and elaboration of animal experimentation. *Psychological Bulletin, 88,* 551–579.

Kolata, G. (1985). Why do people get fat? *Science, 227,* 1327–1328.

Kolata, G. (1987). Associations or rules in learning language? *Science, 237,* 133–134.

Kolb, B. (1989). Brain development, plasticity, and behavior. *American Psychologist, 44,* 1203–1212.

Koop, C. E. (1987). Report of the Surgeon General's Workshop on Pornography and Public Health. *American Psychologist, 42,* 944–945.

Koopmans, J. R., Boomsma, D. I., Heath, A. C., & and van Doornen, L. J. P. (1995). A multivariate genetic analysis of sensation seeking. *Behavior Genetics, 25,* 349-356.

Kopelman, M. D., Christensen, H., Puffett, A., & Stanhope, N. (1994). The great escape: A neuropsychological study of psychogenic amnesia. *Neuropsychologia, 32,* 675–691.

Kopf, S. R., & Baratti, C. M. (1996). Memory modulation by post-training glucose or insulin remains evident at long retention intervals. *Neurobiology of Learning and Memory, 65,* 189-191.

Koppe, S. (1983). The psychology of the neuron: Freud, Cajal, and Golgi. *Scandinavian Journal of Psychology, 24,* 1–12.

Korn, J. H., Davis, R., & Davis, S. F. (1991). Historians' and chairpersons' judgments of eminence among psychologists. *American Psychologist, 46,* 789–792.

Korpi, E. R. (1994). Role of GABA-sub(A) receptors in the actions of alcohol and in alcoholism: Recent advances. *Alcohol and Alcoholism, 29,* 115–129.

Korsnes, M. S., Magnussen, S., & Reinvang, I. (1996). Serial position effects in visual short-term memory or words and abstract spatial patterns. *Scandinavian Journal of Psychology, 37,* 62-73.

Kothera, L., Fudin, R., & Nicastro, R. (1990). Effects of subliminal psychodynamic activation on dart-throwing performance: Another nonreplication. *Perceptual and Motor Skills, 71,* 1015–1022

Kozar, B., Whitfield, K. E., Lord, R. H., & Mechikoff, R. A. (1993). Timeouts before free-throws: Do the statistics support the strategy? *Perceptual and Motor Skills, 76,* 47–50

Krafka, C., & Penrod, S. (1985). Reinstatement of context in a field experiment on eyewitness identification. *Journal of Personality and Social Psychology, 49,* 58–69.

Kramer, D. E., & Bayern, C. D. (1984). The effects of behavioral strategies on creativity training. *Journal of Creative Behavior, 18,* 23–24.

Kramer, T. H., Buckhout, R., Eugenio, P., & Cohen, R. (1985). Presence of malice: Scientific evaluation of reader response to innuendo. *Bulletin of the Psychonomic Society, 23,* 61–63.

Krantz, D. S., Contrada, R. J., Hill, D. R., & Friedler, E. (1988). Environmental stress and biobehavioral antecedents of coronary heart disease. *Journal of Consulting and Clinical Psychology, 56,* 333–341.

Krantz, D. S., & Manuck, S. B. (1984). Acute psychophysiologic reactivity and risk of cardiovascular disease: A review and methodologic critique. *Psychological Bulletin, 96,* 435–464.

Kraus, S. J. (1995). Attitudes and the prediction of behavior: A meta-analysis of the empirical literature. *Personality and Social Psychology Bulletin, 21,* 58–75.

Kravitz, D. A., & Martin, B. (1986). Ringelmann rediscovered: The original article. *Journal of Personality and Social Psychology, 50,* 936–941.

Krechevsky, M., & Gardner, H. (1990). Approaching school intelligently: An infusion approach. *Contributions to Human Development, 21,* 79–94.

Kremer, J. F., & Dietzen, L. L. (1991). Two approaches to teaching accurate empathy to undergraduates: Teacher-intensive and self-directed. *Journal of College Student Development, 32,* 69–75.

Kreppner, K. (1992). William L. Stern, 1871–1938: A neglected founder of developmental psychology. *Developmental Psychology, 28,* 539–547.

Kretschmer, E. (1925). *Physique and character.* New York: Harcourt, Brace.

Krinsky, R., & Krinsky, S. G. (1996). Pegword mnemonic instruction: Retrieval times and long-term memory performance among fifth-grade children. *Contemporary Educational Psychology, 21,* 193-207.

Krippner, S. (1993). The Maimonides ESP-dream studies. *Journal of Parapsychology, 57,* 39–54.

Krippner, S. (1995). Psychical research in the postmodern world. *Journal of the American Society for Psychical Research, 89,* 1–18.

Krippner, S., Braud, W., Child, I. L., & Palmer, J. (1993). Demonstration research and meta-analysis in parapsychology. *Journal of Parapsychology, 57,* 275–286.

Krueger, J. (1996). Personal beliefs and cultural stereotypes about racial characteristics. *Journal of Personality and Social Psychology, 71,* 536–548.

Krupa, D. J., Thompson, J. K., & Thompson, R. F. (1993). Localization of a memory trace in the mammalian brain. *Science, 260,* 989–991.

Kübler-Ross, E. (1969). *On death and dying.* New York: Macmillan.

Kübler-Ross, E. (1974). *Questions and answers on death and dying.* New York: Macmillan.

Kubovy, M., & Wagemans, J. (1995). Grouping by proximity and multistability in dot lattices: A quantitative Gestalt theory. *Psychological Science, 6,* 225–234.

Kugel, W. (1990–1991). Amplifying precognition: Two experiments with roulette. *European Journal of Parapsychology, 8,* 85–97.

Kuhlman, T. L. (1985). A study of salience and motivational theories of humor. *Journal of Personality and Social Psychology, 49,* 281–286.

Kuhn, T. S. (1970). *The structure of scientific revolutions.* Chicago: University of Chicago Press.

Kukla, A. (1989). Nonempirical issues in psychology. *American Psychologist, 44,* 785–794.

Kulik, J. A., & Mahler, H. I. M. (1987). Effects of preoperative roommate assignment and preoperative anxiety and recovery from coronary-bypass surgery. *Health Psychology, 6,* 525–543.

Kumar, K. B., Ramalingam, S., & Karanth, K. S. (1994). Phenytoin and phenobarbital: A comparison of their state-dependent effects. *Pharmacology, Biochemistry, and Behavior, 47,* 951–956.

Kunda, Z., & Oleson, K. C. (1995). Maintaining stereotypes in the face of disconfirmation: Constructing grounds for subtyping deviants. *Journal of Personality and Social Psychology, 68,* 565–579.

Kunda, Z., & Schwartz, S. H. (1983). Undermining intrinsic moral motivation: External reward and self-presentation. *Journal of Personality and Social Psychology, 45,* 763–771.

Kunugi, H., Nanko, S., Takei, N., & Saito, K. (1995). Schizophrenia following in utero exposure to the 1957 influenza epidemics in Japan. *American Journal of Psychiatry, 152,* 450–452.

Kurtz, L. (1995). Coping processes and behavioral outcomes in children of divorce. *Canadian Journal of School Psychology, 11,* 52-64.

Kurzweil, R. (1985). What is artificial intelligence anyway? *American Scientist, 73,* 258–264.

Kusseling, F. S., Shapiro, M. F., Greenberg, J. M., & Wenger, N. S. (1996). Understanding why heterosexual adults do not practice safer sex: A comparison of two samples. *AIDS Education and Prevention, 8,* 247–257.

Kyllo, L. B., & Landers, D. M. (1995). Goal setting in sport and exercise: A research synthesis to resolve the controversy. *Journal of Sport and Exercise Psychology, 17,* 117–137.

Labbate, L. A., Fava, M., Oleshansky, M., & Zoltec, J. (1995). Physical fitness and perceived stress: Relationships with coronary artery disease risk factors. *Psychosomatics, 36,* 555–560.

Ladouceur, R. (1983). Participant modeling with or without cognitive treatment for phobias. *Journal of Consulting and Clinical Psychology, 51,* 942–944.

Ladouceur, R., & Gros-Louis, Y. (1986). Paradoxical intention versus stimulus control in the treatment of severe insomnia. *Journal of Behavior Therapy and Experimental Psychiatry, 17,* 267–269.

Laing, R. D. (1967). *The politics of experience.* New York: Ballantine Books.

Lalancette, M. F., & Standing, L. G. (1990). Asch fails again. *Social Behavior and Personality, 18,* 7–12.

Lam, R. W., Zis, A. P., Grewal, A., & Delgado, P. L. (1996). Effects of rapid tryptophan depletion in patients with seasonal affective disorder in remission after light therapy. *Archives of General Psychiatry, 53,* 41–44.

Lamb, H. R. (1993). Lessons learned from deinstitutionalization in the U.S. *British Journal of Psychiatry, 162,* 587–592.

Lamb, M. E. (1996). Effects of nonparental child care on child development: An update. *Canadian Journal of Psychiatry, 41,* 330-342.

Lambert, M. J. (1989). The individual therapist's contribution to psychotherapy process and outcome. *Clinical Psychology Review, 9,* 469–485.

Lambert, N. M. (1981). Psychological evidence in Larry P. v. Wilson Riles. *American Psychologist, 36,* 937–952.

Lamme, V. A. F. (1995). The neurophysiology of figure-ground segregation in primary visual cortex. *Journal of Neuroscience, 15,* 1605–1615.

Lancaster, L., Royal, K. E., & Whiteside, H. D. (1995). Attitude similarity and evaluation of a women's athletic team. *Journal of Social Behavior and Personality, 10,* 885–890.

Landers, S. (1987, December). Aversive device sparks controversy. *APA Monitor,* p. 15.

Landesman, S., & Ramey, C. (1989). Developmental psychology and mental retardation: Integrating scientific principles with treatment practices. *American Psychologist, 44,* 409–415.

Landolt, H. P., Werth, E., Borbely, A. A., & Dijk, D. J. (1995). Caffeine intake (200 mg) in the morning affects human sleep and EEG power spectra at night. *Brain Research, 675,* 67–74.

Landy, F. J. (1992). Hugo Münsterberg: Victim or visionary? *Journal of Applied Psychology, 77,* 787–802.

Landy, F. J., & Farr, J. L. (1980). Performance rating. *Psychological Bulletin, 87,* 72–107.

Lang, P. J. (1994). The varieties of emotional experience: A meditation on James-Lange theory. *Psychological Review, 101,* 211–221.

Langenbucher, J. W., & Nathan, P. E. (1983). Psychology, public policy, and the evidence for alcohol intoxication. *American Psychologist, 38,* 1070–1077.

Langlois, J. H., Ritter, J. M., Casey, R. J., & Sawin, D. B. (1995). Infant attractiveness predicts maternal behaviors and attitudes. *Developmental Psychology, 31,* 464–472.

Langone, J. (1983, September). B. F. Skinner: Beyond reward and punishment. *Discover,* pp. 38–46.

LaPiere, R. T. (1934). Attitudes versus action. *Social Forces, 13,* 230–237.

La Pointe, F. H. (1970). Origin and evolution of the term "psychology." *American Psychologist, 25,* 640–646.

Larsen, K. S. (1990). The Asch conformity experiment: Replication and transhistorical comparisons. *Journal of Social Behavior and Personality, 5,* 163–168.

Larson, G. E., & Saccuzzo, D. P. (1989). Cognitive correlates of general intelligence: Toward a process theory of *g. Intelligence, 13,* 5–31.

Lashley, K. S (1950). In search of the engram. In *Symposium of the Society for Experimental Biology* (Vol. 4, pp. 454–482). New York: Cambridge University Press.

Latané, B., & Darley, J. M. (1968). Group inhibition of bystander intervention in emergencies. *Journal of Personality and Social Psychology, 10,* 215–221.

Latham, G. P., & Lee, T. W. (1986). Goal setting. In E. A. Locke (Ed.), *Generalizing form laboratory to field settings* (pp. 101–117). Lexington, MA: Heath.

Latimer, P. R. (1995). Tardive dyskinesia: A review. *Canadian Journal of Psychiatry, 40,* S49–S54.

Lattal, K. A. (1995). Contingency and behavior analysis. *Behavior Analyst, 18,* 209-224.

Laurence, J. R., & Perry, C. (1983). Hypnotically created memory among highly hypnotizable subjects. *Science, 222,* 523–524.

Laver, A. B. (1972). Precursors of psychology in ancient Egypt. *Journal of the History of the Behavioral Sciences, 8,* 181–195.

Lavoisier, P., Aloui, R., Schmidt, M. H., & Watrelot, A. (1995). Clitoral blood flow increases following vaginal pressure stimulation. *Archives of Sexual Behavior, 24,* 37–45.

Lazarus, A. A. (1989). Brief psychotherapy: The multimodal model. *Professional Psychology, 26,* 6–10.

Lazarus, A. A., & Lazarus, C. N. (1986). Reactions from a multimodal perspective. *International Journal of Eclectic Psychotherapy, 5,* 328–330.

Lazarus, R. S. (1993). From psychological stress to the emotions: A history of changing outlooks. *Annual Review of Psychology, 44,* 1–21.

Lazarus, R. S. (1993a). Coping theory and research: Past, present, and future. *Psychosomatic Medicine, 55,* 234–247.

Lazarus, R. S. (1995). Cognition and emotion from the RET viewpoint. *Journal of Rational-Emotive and Cognitive Behavior Therapy, 13,* 29–54.

Lazarus, R. S., DeLongis, A., Folkman, S., & Gruen, R. (1985). Stress and adaptational outcomes: The problem of confounded measures. *American Psychologist, 40,* 770–779.

Leaf, R. C., Krauss, D. H., Dantzig, S. A., & Alington, D. E. (1992). Educational equivalents of psychotherapy: Positive and negative mental health benefits after group therapy exercises by college students. *Journal of Rational Emotive and Cognitive Behavior Therapy, 10,* 189–206.

Leakey, R. E., & Lewin, R. (1977, November). Is it our culture, not our genes, that makes us killers? *Smithsonian,* pp. 56–64.

Leana, C. R. (1985). A partial test of Janis' groupthink model: Effects of group cohesiveness and leader behavior on defective decision making. *Journal of Management, 11,* 5–17.

Leary, M. R., & Kowalski, R. M. (1990). Impression management: A literature review and two-component model. *Psychological Bulletin, 107,* 34–47.

Lebow, J. (1982). Consumer satisfaction with mental health treatment. *Psychological Bulletin, 91,* 244–259.

LeDoux, J. E. (1986). Sensory systems and emotion: A model of affective processing. *Integrative Psychiatry, 4,* 237–243.

LeDoux, J. E. (1995). Emotion: Clues from the brain. *Annual Review of Psychology, 46,* 209–235.

LeDoux, J. E., Romanski, L., & Xagoraris, A. (1989). Indelibility of subcortical emotional memories. *Journal of Cognitive Neuroscience, 1,* 238–243.

Lee, G. P., Loring, D. W., Meader, K. J., & Brooks, B. B. (1990). Hemispheric specialization for emotional expression: A reexamination of results from intracarotid administration of sodium amobarbital. *Brain and Cognition, 12,* 267–280.

Lee, J.-H., & Beitz, A. J. (1992). Electroacupuncture modifies the expression of c-fos in the spinal cord induced by noxious stimulation. *Brain Research, 577,* 80–91.

Lee, S., & Crockett, M. S. (1994). Effect of assertiveness training on levels of stress and assertiveness experienced by nurses in Taiwan, Republic of China. *Issues in Mental Health Nursing, 15,* 419–432.

Lee, T. W., & Mitchell, T. R. (1994). An alternative approach: The unfolding model of voluntary employee turnover. *Academy of Management Review, 19,* 51–89.

Lee, V. E., Brooks-Gunn, J., Schnur, E., & Liaw, F. R. (1990). Are Head Start effects sustained? A longitudinal follow-up comparison of disadvantaged children attending Head Start, no preschool, and other preschool programs. *Child Development, 61,* 495–507.

Lee, V. E., & Loeb, S. (1995). Where do Head Start attendees end up? One reason why preschool effects fade out. *Educational Evaluation and Policy Analysis, 17,* 62–82.

Lee, Y. T., & Ottati, V. (1993). Determinants of in-group and out-group perceptions of heterogeneity: An investigation of Sino-American stereotypes. *Journal of Cross-Cultural Psychology, 24,* 298–318.

Lei, T. (1994). Being and becoming moral in a Chinese culture: Unique or universal? *Cross-Cultural Research: The Journal of Comparative Social Science, 28,* 58–91.

Leibowitz, H. W. (1996). The symbiosis between basic and applied research. *American Psychologist, 51,* 366-370.

Leibowitz, H. W., & Pick, H. A., Jr. (1972). Cross-cultural and educational aspects of the Ponzo perspective illusion. *Perception and Psychophysics, 12,* 430–432.

Leigh, P. N., & Ray-Chaudhuri, K. (1994). Motor neuron disease. *Journal of Neurosurgery and Psychiatry, 57,* 886–896.

Leikin, L., Firestone, P., & McGrath, P. (1988). Physical symptom reporting in Type A and Type B children. *Journal of Consulting and Clinical Psychology, 56,* 721–726.

Leitenberg, H. (1995). Cognitive-behavioural treatment of bulimia nervosa. *Behaviour Change, 12,* 81–97.

Lemere, F. (1993). "Homeless mentally ill or mentally ill homeless?" Comment. *American Journal of Psychiatry, 150,* 989.

Leonard, J. (1970, May 8). Ghetto for blue eyes in the classroom. *Life,* p. 16.

Lepper, M. R., Greene, D., & Nisbett, R. E. (1973). Undermining children's intrinsic interest with extrinsic reward: A test of the "overjustification" hypothesis. *Journal of Personality and Social Psychology, 28,* 129–137.

Lerman, D. C., & Iwata, B. A. (1995). Prevalence of the extinction burst and its attenuation during treatment. *Journal of Applied Behavior Analysis, 28,* 93–94.

Lerman, D. C., & Iwata, B. A. (1996). Developing a technology for the use of operant extinction in clinical settings: An examination of basic and applied research. *Journal of Applied Behavior Analysis, 29,* 345-382.

Lerner, B. S., & Locke, E. A. (1995). The effect of goal setting, self-efficacy, competition, and personal trials on the performance of an endurance task. *Journal of Sport and Exercise Psychology, 17,* 138–152.

Lescaudron, L., & Stein, D. G. (1990). Functional recovery following transplants of embryonic brain tissue in rats with lesions of visual, frontal and motor cortex: Problems and prospects for future research. *Neuropsychologia, 28,* 588–599.

Leslie, K., & Ogilvie, R. (1996). Vestibular dreams: The effect of rocking on dream mentation. Dreaming: *The Journal of the Association for the Study of Dreams, 6,* 1-16.

Lester, D. (1990). Maslow's hierarchy of needs and personality. *Personality and Individual Differences, 11,* 1187–1188.

Lester, D. (1993). The effectiveness of suicide prevention centers. *Suicide and Life-Threatening Behavior, 23,* 263–267.

Lester, D. (1995). Myths about childhood suicide. *Psychological Reports, 77,* 330.

Lester, D., Kaminsky, S., & McGovern, M. (1993). Sheldon's theory of personality in young children. *Perceptual and Motor Skills, 77,* 1330.

Lester, D., & Wosnack, K. (1990). An exploratory test of Sheldon's theory of personality in neonates. *Perceptual and Motor Skills, 71,* 1282.

Leung, J. (1994). Treatment of post-traumatic stress disorder with hypnosis. *Australian Journal of Clinical and Experimental Hypnosis, 22,* 87–96.

LeVay, S. (1991). A difference in hypothalamic structure between heterosexual and homosexual men. *Science, 253,* 1034–1037.

Levenson, J. L., & Bemis, C. (1991). The role of psychological factors in cancer onset and progression. *Psychosomatics, 32,* 124–132.

Levenson, R. W., Carstensen, L. L., Friesen, W. V., & Ekman, P. (1991). Emotion, physiology, and expression in old age. *Psychology and Aging, 6,* 28–35.

Levenson, R. W., Ekman, P., Heider, K., & Friesen, W. V. (1992). Emotion and autonomic nervous system activity in the Minangkabau of West Sumatra. *Journal of Personality and Social Psychology, 62,* 972–988.

Leventhal, H., & Tomarken, A. J. (1986). Emotion: Today's problems. *Annual Review of Psychology, 37,* 565–610.

Levin, E. D., Westman, E. C., Stein, R. M., & Carnahan, E. (1994). Nicotine skin patch treatment increases abstinence, decreases withdrawal symptoms, and attenuates rewarding effects of smoking. *Journal of Clinical Psychopharmacology*, 14, 41–49.

Levin, I. P., & Gaeth, J. (1988). How consumers are affected by the framing of attribute information before and after consuming the product. *Journal of Consumer Research*, 15, 374–378.

Levin, I. P., Schnittjer, S. K., & Thee, S. L. (1988). Information framing effects in social and personal decisions. *Journal of Experimental Social Psychology*, 24, 520–529.

Levine, J. S., & MacNichol, E. F., Jr. (1982, February). Color vision in fishes. *Scientific American*, pp. 140–149.

Levine, M. (1976). The academic achievement test: Its historical context and social functions. *American Psychologist*, 31, 228–238.

Levine, S. B., Risen, C. B., & Althof, S. E. (1990). Essay on the diagnosis and nature of paraphilia. *Journal of Sex and Marital Therapy*, 16, 89–102.

Levinson, D. J. (1978). *The seasons of a man's life*. New York: Knopf.

Levinson, D. J. (1986). A conception of adult development. *American Psychologist*, 41, 3–13.

Levinson, S. E., & Liberman, M. Y. (1981, April). Speech recognition by computer. *Scientific American*, pp. 64–76.

Levinthal, C. F. (1988). *Messengers of paradise*. New York: Anchor/Doubleday.

Levitt, E. E. (1983). Estimating the duration of sexual behavior: A laboratory analog study. *Archives of Sexual Behavior*, 12, 329–335.

Levitt, M. J., Weber, R. A., & Clark, M. C. (1986). Social network relationships as sources of maternal support and well-being. *Developmental Psychology*, 22, 310–316.

Levitz-Jones, E. M., & Orlofsky, J. L. (1985). Separation-individuation and intimacy capacity in college women. *Journal of Personality and Social Psychology*, 49, 156–169.

Levy, J. (1983). Language, cognition, and the right hemisphere: A response to Gazzaniga. *American Psychologist*, 38, 538–541.

Levy, J. (1985, May). Right brain, left brain: Fact and fiction. *Psychology Today*, pp. 38–39.

Levy, P. E., & Steelman, L. A. (in press). Performance appraisal for team-based organizations: A prototypical multiple rater system. In M. Beyerlein (Ed.), *Advances in interdisciplinary studies of work teams: Team implementation Issues* (Vol. 4). Greenwich, CT: JAI Press.

Lewicki, P. (1985). Nonconscious biasing effects of single instances on subsequent judgments. *Journal of Personality and Social Psychology*, 48, 563–574.

Lewin, K. (1935). *A dynamic theory of personality*. New York: McGraw-Hill.

Lewin, R. (1988). Cloud over Parkinson's therapy. *Science*, 240, 390–392.

Lewis, D. (1899/1983). The gynecologic consideration of the sexual act. *Journal of the American Medical Association*, 250, 222–227.

Lewis, J. (1981). *Something hidden: A biography of Wilder Penfield*. New York: Doubleday.

Lewis, S., & Cooper, C. L. (1983). The stress of combining occupational and parental roles: A review of the literature. *Bulletin of the British Psychological Society*, 36, 341–345.

Li, A. K. F. (1994). A response to Janzen, Paterson, and Paterson: "School psychology and violence prevention in schools." *Canadian Journal of School Psychology*, 10, 105–107.

Li, Z. (1996). A theory of the visual motion coding in the primary visual cortex. *Neural Computation*, 8, 705-730.

Lieberman, D. A. (1979). Behaviorism and the mind: A (limited) call for a return to introspection. *American Psychologist*, 34, 319–333.

Liebert, R. M., & Baron, R. A. (1972). Some immediate effects of television violence on children's behavior. *Developmental Psychology*, 6, 469–475.

Lief, H. I., & Hubschman, L. (1993). Orgasm in the postoperative transsexual. *Archives of Sexual Behavior*, 22, 145–155.

Liegois, M. J. (1899). The relation of hypnotism to crime. *Suggestive Therapeutics*, 6, 18–21.

Lightdale, J. R., & Prentice, D. A. (1994). Rethinking sex differences in aggression: Aggressive behavior in the absence of social roles. *Personality and Social Psychology Bulletin*, 20, 34–44.

Lin, E. H., & Peterson, C. (1990). Pessimistic explanatory style and response to illness. *Behaviour Research and Therapy*, 28, 243–248.

Lindsay, D. S. (1993). Eyewitness suggestibility. *Current Directions in Psychological Science*, 2, 86–89.

Lindsay, D. S. (1994). Contextualizing and clarifying criticisms of memory work. *Consciousness and Cognition: An International Journal*, 3, 426–437.

Lindsay, D. S., & Jacoby, L. I. (1994). Stroop process dissociations: The relationship between facilitation and interference. *Journal of Experimental Psychology: Human Perception and Performance*, 20, 219-234.

Lindvall, O., Brundin, P., Widner, H., Rehncrona, S., Gustavii, B., Frackowiak, R., Leenders, K. L., Sawle, G., Rothweel, J. C., Marsden, C. D., & Bjorklund, A. (1990). Grafts of fetal dopamine neurons survive and improve motor function in Parkinson's disease. *Science*, 247, 574–577.

Link, S. W. (1994). Rediscovering the past: Gustav Fechner and signal detection theory. *Psychological Science*, 5, 335–340.

Linn, R. L. (1982). Admissions testing on trial. *American Psychologist*, 37, 279–291.

Lipman, J. J., Miller, B. E., Mays, K. S., & Miller, M. N. (1990). Peak B endorphin concentration in cerebrospinal fluid: Reduced in chronic pain patients and increased during the placebo response. *Psychopharmacology*, 102, 112–116.

Litt, M. D., Nye, C., & Shafer, D. (1995). Preparation for oral surgery: Evaluating elements of coping. *Journal of Behavioral Medicine*, 18, 435–459.

Livingstone, M., & Hubel, D. (1988). Segregation of form, color, movement, and depth: Anatomy, physiology, and perception. *Science*, 240, 740–749.

Llorente, M. D., Currier, M. B., Norman, S. E., & Mellman, T. A. (1992). Night terrors in adults: Phenomenology and relationship to psychopathology. *Journal of Clinical Psychiatry*, 53, 392–394.

Lloyd, M. A., & Appel, J. B. (1976). Signal detection theory and the psychophysics of pain: An introduction and review. *Psychosomatic Medicine*, 38, 79–94.

LoBello, S. G., & Gulgoz, S. (1991). Factor analysis of the Wechsler Preschool and Primary Scale of Intelligence Revised. *Psychological Assessment*, 3, 130–132.

Locke, E. A. (1976). The nature and causes of job satisfaction. In M. Dunnette (Ed.), *Handbook of industrial and organizational psychology* (pp. 1297–1349). Rand McNally: Chicago.

Locke, E. A., & Latham, G. P. (1985). The application of goal setting to sports. *Journal of Sport Psychology*, 7, 205–222.

Locke, E. A., & Latham, G. P. (1990). *A theory of goal-setting and task performance*. Englewood Cliffs, NJ: Prentice Hall.

Locke, J. (1690/1959). *An essay concerning human understanding*. New York: Dover.

Lockhart, R. S., & Craik, F. I. (1990). Levels of processing: A retrospective commentary on a framework for memory research. *Canadian Journal of Psychology*, 44, 87–112.

Locurto, C. (1990). The malleability of IQ as judged from adoption studies. *Intelligence*, 14, 275–292.

Locurto, C. (1991). Beyond IQ in preschool programs? *Intelligence*, 15, 295–312.

Loeb, G. E. (1985, February). The functional replacement of the ear. *Scientific American*, pp. 104–111.

Loeber, R., & Dishion, T. (1983). Early predictors of male delinquency: A review. *Psychological Bulletin*, 94, 68–99.

Loehlin, J. C., Horn, J. M., & Willerman, L. (1990). Heredity, environment, and personality change: Evidence from the Texas Adoption Project. *Journal of Personality*, 58, 221–243.

Loehlin, J. C., Horn, J. M., & Willerman, L. (1994). Differential inheritance of mental abilities in the Texas Adoption Project. *Intelligence*, 19, 325–336.

Loeser, J. D., Henderlite, S. E., & Conrad, D. A. (1995). Incentive effects of workers' compensation benefits: A literature synthesis. *Medical Care Research and Review*, 52, 34–59.

Loftus, E. F. (1993a). Psychologists in the eyewitness world. *American Psychologist*, 48, 550–552.

Loftus, E. F. (1993b). The reality of repressed memories. *American Psychologist*, 48, 518–537.

Loftus, E. F., & Burns, T. E. (1982). Mental shock can produce retrograde amnesia. *Memory and Learning*, 10, 318–323.

Loftus, E. F., & Hoffman, H. G. (1989). Misinformation and memory: The creation of new memories. *Journal of Experimental Psychology: General, 118*, 100–104.

Loftus, E. F., & Palmer, J. C. (1974). Reconstruction of automobile destruction: An example of the interaction between language and memory. *Journal of Verbal Learning and Verbal Behavior*, 13, 585–589.

Loftus, G. R., Duncan, J., & Gehrig, P. (1992). On the time course of perceptual information that results from a brief visual presentation. *Journal of Experimental Psychology: Human Perception and Performance*, 18, 530–549.

Lonner, W. J., & Malpass, R. S. (Eds.). (1994). *Psychology and culture*. Boston: Allyn & Bacon.

Lonnqvist, J., Sihvo, S., Syvalahti, E., & Kiviruusu, O. (1994). Moclobemide and fluoxetine in atypical depression: A double-blind trial. *Journal of Affective Disorders*, 32, 169–177.

Loomis, A. L., Harvey, E. N., & Hobart, G. A. (1937). Electrical potentials of the human brain. *Journal of Experimental Psychology*, 21, 127–144.

Loomis, M., & Saltz, E. (1984). Cognitive styles as predictors of artistic styles. *Journal of Personality*, 52, 22–35.

Lopes, L. L. (1981). Decision making in the short run. *Journal of Experimental Psychology: Human Learning and Memory*, 7, 377–385.

LoPiccolo, J., & Stock, W. E. (1986). Treatment of sexual dysfunction. *Journal of Consulting and Clinical Psychology*, 54, 158–167.

Lord, C. G. (1982). Predicting behavioral consistency from an individual's perception of situational similarities. *Journal of Personality and Social Psychology*, 42, 1076–1088.

Lord, R. G., & Levy, P. E. (1994). Control theory: Moving from cognition to action. *Applied Psychology: An international Review*, 43, 335–367.

Lorenz, K. Z. (1966). *On aggression*. New York: Harcourt Brace Jovanovich.

Lorig, T. S., Herman, K. B., Schwartz, G. E., & Cain, W. S. (1990). EEG activity during administration of low-concentration odors. *Bulletin of the Psychonomic Society*, 28, 405–408.

Loring, D. W., Meador, K. J., Lee, G. P., & King, D. W. (Eds.). (1991). *Amobarbitol effects and lateralized brain function: The Wada test*. New York: Springer-Verlag.

Loring, D. W., & Sheer, D. E. (1984). Laterality of 40 Hz EEG and EMG during cognitive performance. *Psychophysiology*, 21, 34–38.

Lottes, I. L. (1993). Nontraditional gender roles and the sexual experiences of heterosexual college students. *Sex Roles*, 29, 645–669.

Lovass, O. I. (1987). Behavioral treatment and normal educational and intellectual functioning in young autistic children. *Journal of Consulting and Clinical Psychology*, 55, 3–9.

Lu, Z. L., Williamson, S. J., & Kaufman, L. (1992). Behavioral lifetime of human auditory sensory memory predicted by physiological measures. *Science, 258,* 1668–1670.

Lubar, J. F. (1991). Discourse on the development of EEG diagnostics and biofeedback for attention-deficit/hyperactivity disorders. *Biofeedback and Self-Regulation, 16,* 201–225.

Lubek, I., Innis, N. K., Kroger, R. O., McGuire, G. R., Stam, H. J., & Herrmann, T. (1995). Faculty genealogies in five Canadian universities: Historiographical and pedagogical concerns. *Journal of the History of the Behavioral Sciences, 31,* 52–72.

Luborsky, L., Chandler, M., Auerbach, A. H., Cohen, J., & Bachrach, H. M. (1971). Factors influencing the outcome of psychotherapy: A review of quantitative research. *Psychological Bulletin, 75,* 145–185.

Luchins, A. (1946). Classroom experiments on mental sets. *American Journal of Psychology, 59,* 295–298.

Lundquist, L. O. (1995). Facial EMG reactions to facial expressions: A case of facial emotional contagion? *Scandinavian Journal of Psychology, 36,* 130–141.

Lundstrom, B., Pauly, I. B., & Walinder, J. (1984). Outcome of sex reassignment surgery. *Acta Psychiatrica Scandinavica, 70,* 289–294.

Lunneborg, P. W. (1978). *Why study psychology?* Monterey, CA: Brooks/Cole.

Lutz, J., Means, L. W., & Long, T. E. (1994). Where did I park? A naturalistic study of spatial memory. *Applied Cognitive Psychology, 8,* 439–451.

Lydon, J. E., Jamieson, D., & Zanna, M. P. (1988). Interpersonal similarity and the social and intellectual dimensions of first impressions. *Social Cognition, 6,* 269–286.

Lykken, D. T. (1974). Psychology and the lie detector industry. *American Psychologist, 29,* 725–739.

Lykken, D. T. (1981). *A tremor in the blood: Uses and abuses of the lie detector.* New York: McGraw-Hill.

Lykken, D. T. (1982). Research with twins: The concept of emergenesis. *Psychophysiology, 19,* 361–373.

Lykken, D. T. (1988). Detection of guilty knowledge: A comment on Forman and McCauley. *Journal of Applied Psychology, 73,* 303–304.

Lykken, D. T., Bouchard, T. J., Jr., McGue, M., & Tellegen, A. (1993). Heritability of interests: A twin study. *Journal of Applied Psychology, 78,* 649–661.

Lykken, D. T., McGue, M., Tellegen, A., & Bouchard, T. J., Jr. (1992). Emergenesis: Genetic traits that may not run in families. *American Psychologist, 47,* 1565–1577.

Lyness, S. C. (1993). Predictors of differences between Type A and B individuals in heart rate and blood pressure reactivity. *Psychological Bulletin, 114,* 266–295.

Lynn, R. (1982). IQ in Japan and the United States shows a growing disparity. *Nature, 297,* 222–223.

Lynn, R., & Wilson, R. G. (1990). Reaction times, movement times and intelligence among Irish nine-year-olds. *Irish Journal of Psychology, 11,* 329–341.

Lynn, S. J., Rhue, J. W., & Weekes, J. R. (1990). Hypnotic involuntariness: A social-cognitive analysis. *Psychological Review, 97,* 169–184.

Lysle, D. T., Cunnick, J. E., & Maslonek, K. A. (1991). Pharmacological manipulation of immune alterations induced by an aversive conditioned stimulus: Evidence for a-adrenergic receptor-mediated Pavlovian conditioning process. *Behavioral Neuroscience, 105,* 443–449.

Lytton, H., & Romney, D. M. (1991). Parents' differential socialization of boys and girls: A meta-analysis. *Psychological Bulletin, 109,* 267–296.

Lyubomirsky, S., & Nolen-Hoeksema, S. (1993). Self-perpetuating properties of dysphoric rumination. *Journal of Personality and Social Psychology, 65,* 339–349.

Maass, A., & Clark, R. D. (1984). Hidden impact of minorities: Fifteen years of minority influence research. *Psychological Bulletin, 95,* 428–450.

Maccoby, E. E., & Jacklin, C. N. (1974). *The psychology of sex differences* (2 vols.). Stanford, CA: Stanford University Press.

MacCracken, M. J., & Stadulis, R. E. (1985). Social facilitation of young children's dynamic balance performance. *Journal of Sport Psychology, 7,* 150–165.

MacFarlane, J. G., Cleghorn, J. M., Brown, G. M., & Streiner, D. L. (1991). The effects of exogenous melatonin on the total sleep time and daytime alertness of chronic insomniacs: A preliminary study. *Biological Psychiatry, 30,* 371–376.

MacGregor, M. W. (1996). Multiple personality disorder: Etiology, treatment, and treatment techniques from a psychodynamic perspective. *Psychoanalytic Psychology, 13,* 389–402.

Mack, A., Heuer, F., Villardi, K., & Chambers, D. (1985). The dissociation of position and extent in Muller-Lyer figures. *Perception and Psychophysics, 37,* 335–344.

Mack, S. (1981). Novel help for the handicapped. *Science, 212,* 26–27.

Mackenzie, B. (1984). Explaining race differences in IQ: The logic, the methodology, and the evidence. *American Psychologist, 39,* 1214–1233.

Macklin, M. C. (1994). The effects of an advertising retrieval cue on young children's memory and brand evaluations. *Psychology and Marketing, 11,* 291–311.

Macklin, W. R. (1996, February 18). Kasparov is the victor in man-vs-machine match. *Philadelphia Inquirer,* pp. B1–B4.

Macklis, R. M., & Macklis, J. D. (1992). Historical and phrenologic reflections on the nonmotor functions of the cerebellum: Love under the tent? *Neurology, 42,* 928–932.

MacLean, H. N. (1993). *Once upon a time: A true story of memory, murder, and the law.* New York: HarperCollins.

MacLeod, C. M. (1988). Forgotten but not gone: Savings for pictures and words in long-term memory. *Journal of Experimental Psychology: Learning, Memory, and Cognition, 14,* 195–212.

MacMillan, H. L., & Thomas, B. H. (1993). Public health nurse home visitation for the tertiary prevention of child

MacNiven, E. (1994). Increased prevalence of left-handedness in victims of head trauma. *Brain Injury, 8,* 457–462.

Madigan, M. W., & O'Hara, R. (1992). Short-term memory at the turn of the century: Mary Whiton Calkins's memory research. *American Psychologist, 47,* 170–174.

Madrazo, I., Drucker-Colin, R., Diaz, V., Martinez-Mata, J., Torres, C., & Becerril, J. J. (1987). Open microsurgical autograft of adrenal medulla to the right caudate nucleus in two patients with intractable Parkinson's disease. *New England Journal of Medicine, 316,* 831–834.

Maher, W. B., & Maher, B. A. (1985). Psychopathology: I. From ancient times to the 18th century. In G. A. Kimble & K. Schlesinger (Eds.), *Topics in the history of psychology* (Vol. 2, pp. 251–294). Hillsdale, NJ: Erlbaum.

Mahowald, M. B. (1989). Neural fetal tissue transplantation: Should we do what we can do? *Neurologic Clinics, 7,* 745–757.

Maier, N. R. (1931). Reasoning in humans. *Journal of Comparative Psychology, 12,* 181–194.

Main, M., & George, C. (1985). Responses of abused and disadvantaged toddlers to distress in agemates: A study in the day-care setting. *Developmental Psychology, 21,* 407–412.

Malamuth, N. M. (1986). Predictors of naturalistic sexual aggression. *Journal of Personality and Social Psychology, 50,* 953–962.

Malarkey, W. B., Kiecolt-Glaser, J. K., Pearl, D., & Glaser, R. (1994). Hostile behavior during marital conflict alters pituitary and adrenal hormones. *Psychosomatic Medicine, 56,* 41–51.

Malarkey, W. B., Pearl, D. K., Demers, L. M., & Kiecolt-Glaser, J. K. (1995). Influence of academic stress and season on 24-hour mean concentrations of ACTH, cortisol, and b-endorphin. *Psychoneuroendocrinology, 20,* 499–508.

Malinowski, C. I., & Smith, C. P. (1985). Moral reasoning and moral conduct: An investigation prompted by Kohlberg's theory. *Journal of Personality and Social Psychology, 49,* 1016–1027.

Mancia, M. (1995). One possible function of sleep: To produce dreams. *Behavioural Brain Research, 69,* 203-206.

Mandai, O., Guerrien, A., Sockeel, P., & Dujardin, K. (1989). REM sleep modifications following a Morse code learning session in humans. *Physiology and Behavior, 46,* 639–642.

Mandel, D. R., Jusczyk, P. W., & Pisoni, D. B. (1995). Infants' recognition of the sound patterns of their own names. *Psychological Science, 6,* 314–317.

Mandl, G. (1985). Responses of visual cells in cat superior colliculus to relative pattern movement. *Vision Research, 25,* 267–281.

Mangalmurti, V. S. (1994). Psychotherapists' fear of Tarasoff: All in the mind? *Journal of Psychiatry and Law, 22,* 379–409.

Manicas, P. T., & Secord, P. F. (1983). Implications for psychology of the new philosophy of science. *American Psychologist, 38,* 399–413.

Mann, C. C. (1994). Behavioral genetics in transition. *Science, 264,* 1686–1689.

Manning, B. H. (1990). A categorical analysis of children's self-talk during independent school assignments. *Journal of Instructional Psychology, 17,* 208–217.

Manning, C. A., Parsons, M. W., & Gold, P. E. (1992). Anterograde and retrograde enhancement of 24-hour memory by glucose in elderly humans. *Behavioral and Neural Biology, 58,* 125–130.

Mansfield, J. G. (1979). Dose-related effects of ethanol on avoidance-avoidance conflict behavior in the rat. *Psychopharmacology, 66,* 67–71.

Maragos, W. F., Greenamyre, J. T., Penney, J. B., & Young, A. B. (1987). Glutamate dysfunction in Alzheimer's disease: A hypothesis. *Trends in Neuroscience, 10,* 65–68.

Maranto, G. (1984, December). Aging: Can we slow the inevitable? *Discover,* pp. 17–21.

Marchand, S., Charest, J., Li, J., & Chenard, J. R. (1993). Is TENS purely a placebo effect? A controlled study on chronic low back pain. *Pain, 54,* 99–106.

Marcus, G. F. (1995). Children's overregularization of English plurals: A quantitative analysis. *Journal of Child Language, 22,* 447–459.

Marcus, G. F., Pinker, S., Ullman, M., Hollander, M., Rosen, T. J., & Ku, F. (1992). *Overregularization in language acquisition.* Chicago: University of Chicago Press.

Maren, S., & Baudry, M. (1995). Properties and mechanisms of long-term synaptic plasticity in the mammalian brain: Relationships to learning and memory. *Neurobiology of Learning and Memory, 63,* 1–18.

Margalit, M. (1995). Effects of social skills training for students with an intellectual disability. *International Journal of Disability, Development and Education, 42,* 75–85.

Margiotta, E. W., Davilla, D. A., & Hicks, R. A. (1990). Type A-B behavior and the self-report of daily hassles and uplifts. *Perceptual and Motor Skills, 70,* 777–778.

Margo, G. M., Greenberg, R. P., Fisher, S., & Dewan, M. (1993). A direct comparison of the defense mechanisms of non-depressed people and depressed psychiatric inpatients. *Comprehensive Psychiatry, 34,* 65–69.

Margolis, R. B., & Mynatt, C. R. (1986). The effects of external and self-administered reward on high base rate behavior. *Cognitive Therapy and Research, 10,* 109–122.

Marken, R. S., & Powers, W. T. (1989). Random-walk chemotaxis: Trial and error as a control process. *Behavioral Neuroscience, 103*, 1348–1355.

Markman, H. J., Leber, B. D., Cordova, A. D., & St. Peters, M. (1995). Behavioral observation and family psychology: Strange bedfellows or happy marriage?: Comment on Alexander et al. (1995). *Journal of Family Psychology, 9*, 371–379.

Markovic, B. M., Dimitrijevic, M., & Jankovic, B. D. (1993). Immunomodulation by conditioning: Recent developments. *International Journal of Neuroscience, 71*, 231–249.

Marks, I. M. (1995). Advances in behavioral-cognitive therapy of social phobia. *Journal of Clinical Psychiatry, 56*, 25–31.

Markus, E., Lange, A., & Pettigrew, T. F. (1990). Effectiveness of family therapy: A meta-analysis. *Journal of Family Therapy, 12*, 205–221.

Marlowe, C. M., Schneider, S. L., & Nelson, C. E. (1996). Gender and attractiveness biases in hiring decisions: Are more experienced managers less biased? *Journal of Applied Psychology, 81*, 11–21.

Marshall, G. D., & Zimbardo, P. G. (1979). Affective consequences of inadequately explained physiological arousal. *Journal of Personality and Social Psychology, 37*, 970–988.

Marshall, M. (1990). The theme of quantification and the hidden Weber in the early work of Gustav Theodor Fechner. *Canadian Psychology, 31*, 45–53.

Marsland, A. L., Manuck, S. B., Fazzari, T. V., & Stewart, C. J. (1995). Stability of individual differences in cellular immune responses to acute psychological stress. *Psychosomatic Medicine, 57*, 295–298.

Martin, J. E., & Dubbert, P. M. (1985). Exercise in hypertension. *Annals of Behavioral Medicine, 7(1)*, 13–18.

Martin, M. A. (1985). Students' applications of self-questioning study techniques: An investigation of their efficacy. *Reading Psychology, 6*, 69–83.

Martin, R. A., Kuiper, N. A., Olinger, L. J., & Dance, K. (1993). Humor, coping with stress, self-concept, and psychological well-being. *Humor: International Journal of Humor Research, 6*, 89–104.

Martinez, J. L., Jr., & Derrick, B. E. (1996). Long-term potentiation and learning. *Annual Review of Psychology, 47*, 173–203.

Martinot, J. L., Hardy, P., Feline, A., & Huret, J. D. (1990). Left prefrontal glucose hypometabolism in the depressed state: A confirmation. *American Journal of Psychiatry, 147*, 1313–1317.

Marx, J. L. (1980). Ape-language controversy flares up. *Science, 207*, 1330–1332.

Maser, J. D., Kaelber, C., & Weise, R. E. (1991). International use and attitudes toward DSM-III and DSM-III-R: Growing consensus in psychiatric classification. *Journal of Abnormal Psychology, 100*, 271–279.

Maslow, A. H. (1970). *Motivation and personality*. New York: Harper & Row.

Masoro, E. J., Shimokawa, I., Higami, Y., & McMahan, C. A. (1995). Temporal pattern of food intake not a factor in the retardation of aging processes by dietary restriction. *Journals of Gerontology: Series A: Biological Sciences and Medical Sciences, 50A*, B48–B53.

Massaro, D. W. (1991). Psychology as a cognitive science. *Psychological Science, 2*, 302–307.

Masserano, J. M., Takimoto, G. S., & Weiner, N. (1981). Electroconvulsive shock increases tyrosine hydroxylase activity via the brain and adrenal gland of the rat. *Science, 214*, 662–665.

Masters, K. S. (1992). Hypnotic susceptibility, cognitive dissociation, and runner's high in a sample of marathon runners. American *Journal of Clinical Hypnosis, 34*, 193–201.

Masters, W. H., & Johnson, V. E. (1966, 1970). *Human sexual inadequacy*. Boston: Little, Brown.

Matese, M., Matson, J. L., & Sevin, J. (1994). Comparison of psychotic and autistic children using behavioral observation. *Journal of Autism and Developmental Disorders, 24*, 83–94.

Mathieu, J. E., & Zajac, D. M. (1990). A review and meta-analysis of the antecedents, correlates, and consequences of organizational commitment. *Psychological Bulletin, 108*, 171–194.

Matlock, J. G. (1991). Records of the Parapsychology Laboratory: An inventory of the collection in the Duke University library. *Journal of Parapsychology, 55*, 301–314.

Matson, J. L., DiLorenzo, T. M., & Esveldt-Dawson, K. (1981). Independence training as a method of enhancing self-help skills acquisition of the mentally retarded. *Behaviour Research and Therapy, 19*, 399–405.

Matsumoto, D. (1987). The role of facial response in the experience of emotion: More methodological problems and a meta-analysis. *Journal of Personality and Social Psychology, 52*, 769–774.

Matsumoto, D. (1992). More evidence for the universality of a contempt expression. *Motivation and Emotion, 16*, 363–368.

Matsumoto, D. (1994). *Cultural influences on research methods and statistics*. Pacific Grove, CA: Brooks/Cole.

Matt, G. E., Vazquez, C., & Campbell, W. K. (1992). Mood-congruent recall of affectively toned stimuli: A meta-analytic review. *Clinical Psychology Review, 12*, 227–255.

Matthews, D. B., Best, P. J., White, A. M., Vandergriff, J. L., & Simon, P. E. (1996). Ethanol impairs spatial cognitive processing: New behavioral and electrophysiological findings. *Current Directions in Psychological Science, 5*, 111–115.

Matthews, K. A., & Woodall, K. L. (1988). Childhood origins of overt Type A behaviors and cardiovascular reactivity to behavioral stressors. *Annals of Behavioral Medicine, 10*, 71–77.

Mattingley, J. B., Bradshaw, J. L., & Phillips, J. G. (1992). Reappraising unilateral neglect. *Australian Journal of Psychology, 44*, 163–169.

Maugh, T. (1982). *The scent makes sense. Science, 215*, 1224.

Maurino, D. E. (1994). Cross–cultural perspectives in human factors training: Lessons from the ICAO human factors program. *International Journal of Aviation Psychology, 4*, 173–181.

Mautner, B. (1991). Freud's Irma dream: A psychoanalytic interpretation. *International Journal of Psycho-Analysis, 72*, 275–286.

May, R. (1982, Summer). The problem of evil: An open letter to Carl Rogers. *Journal of Humanistic Psychology*, pp. 10–21.

Mayberry, J. S., & Eichen, E. B. (1991). The long-lasting advantage of learning sign language in childhood: Another look at the critical period for language acquisition. *Journal of Memory and Language, 30*, 486–512.

Mayrhauser, R. T. von. (1989). Making intelligence functional: Walter Dill Scott and applied psychological testing in World War I. *Journal of the History of the Behavioral Sciences, 25*, 60–72.

Mazzella, R., & Feingold, A. (1994). The effects of physical attractiveness, race, socioeconomic status, and gender of defendants and victims on judgments of mock jurors: A meta-analysis. *Journal of Applied Social Psychology, 24*, 1315–1344.

McAdams, D. P., de St. Aubin, E., & Logan, R. L. (1993). Generativity among youth, midlife, and older adults. *Psychology and Aging, 8*, 221–230.

McAleney, P. J., Barabasz, A., & Barabasz, M. (1990). Effects of flotation restricted environmental stimulation on intercollegiate tennis performance. *Perceptual and Motor Skills, 71*, 1023–1028.

McAllister, D. E., & McAllister, W. R. (1994). Extinction and reconditioning of classically conditioned fear before and after instrumental learning: Effects of depth of fear extinction. *Learning and Motivation, 25*, 339–367.

McAllister, H. A. (1996). Self-serving bias in the classroom: Who shows it? Who knows it? *Journal of Educational Psychology, 88*, 123–131.

McAuley, E. (1985). Modeling and self-efficacy: A test of Bandur's model. *Journal of Sport Psychology, 7*, 283–295.

McAuley, E., Poag, K., Gleason, A., & Wraith, S. (1990). Attrition from exercise programs: Attributional and affective perspectives. *Journal of Social Behavior and Personality, 5*, 591–602.

McCabe, M. P. (1994). The influence of the quality of relationship on sexual dysfunction. *Australian Journal of Marriage and Family, 15*, 2–8.

McCammon, S., Durham, T. W., Allison, E. J., & Williamson, J. E. (1988). Emergency workers' cognitive appraisal and coping with traumatic events. *Journal of Traumatic Stress, 1*, 353–372.

McCann, B. S., & Matthews, K. A. (1988). Influences of potential for hostility, Type A behavior, and parental history of hypertension on adolescents' cardiovascular responses during stress. *Psychophysiology, 25*, 503–511.

McCanne, T. R., & Anderson, J. A. (1987). Emotional responding following experimental manipulation of facial electromyographic activity. *Journal of Personality and Social Psychology, 52*, 759–768.

McCarthy, G. W., & Craig, K. (1995). Flying therapy for flying phobia. *Aviation, Space, and Environmental Medicine, 66*, 1179–1194.

McCarthy, T. (1981). Freud and the problem of sexuality. *Journal of the History of the Behavioral Sciences, 17*, 332–339.

McCauley, C. (1989). The nature of social influence in groupthink: Compliance and internalization. *Journal of Personality and Social Psychology, 57*, 250–260.

McCauley, C., & Forman, R. F. (1988). A review of the Office of Technology Assessment report on polygraph validity. *Basic and Applied Social Psychology, 9*, 73–84.

McCauley, C., Woods, K., Coolidge, C., & Kulick W. (1983). More-aggressive cartoons are funnier. *Journal of Personality and Social Psychology, 44*, 817–823.

McClane, W. E., & Singer, D. D. (1991). The effective use of humor in organizational development. *Organization Development Journal, 9*, 67–72.

McClelland, D. C. (1985). How motives, skills, and values determine what people do. *American Psychologist, 40*, 812–825.

McClelland, J. L., McNaughton, B. L., & O'Reilly, R. C. (1995). Why there are complementary learning systems in the hippocampus and neocortex: Insights from the successes and failures of connectionist models of learning and memory. *Psychological Review, 102*, 419–437.

McCloskey, M., & Egeth, H. E. (1983). Eyewitness identification: What can a psychologist tell a jury? *American Psychologist, 38*, 550–563.

McCloskey, M., Wible, C. G., & Cohen, N. J. (1988). Is there a special flashbulb-memory mechanism? *Journal of Experimental Psychology: General, 117*, 171–181.

McConaghy, N., & Blaszcynski, A. (1991). Initial stages of validation by penile volume assessment that sexual orientation is distributed dimensionally. *Comprehensive Psychiatry, 32*, 52–58.

McConkey, K. M. (1995). Hypnosis, memory, and the ethics of uncertainty. *Australian Psychologist, 30*, 1–10.

McConnell, J. V., Cutter, R. L., & NcNeil, E. B. (1958). Subliminal stimulation: An overview. *American Psychologist, 13*, 229–242.

McConnell, J. V., Jacobson, A. L., & Kimble, D. P. (1959). The effects of regeneration upon retention of a conditioned response in the planarian. *Journal of Comparative and Physiological Psychology, 52*, 1–5.

McConnell, R. A., & Clark, T. K. (1991). National Academy of Sciences' opinion on parapsychology. *Journal of the American Society for Psychical Research, 85*, 333–365.

McCormick, E. J. (1979). *Job analysis: Methods and applications*. New York: AMACON.

McCormick, N. B., & Jones, A. J. (1989). Gender differences in flirtation. *Journal of Sex Education and Therapy, 15*, 271–282.

McCrae, R. R., & Costa, P. T. (1991). Adding Liebe and Arbeit: The full five-factor model and well-being. *Personality and Social Psychology Bulletin, 17*, 227–232.

McCrae, R. R., & Costa, P. T. (1995). Trait explanations in personality psychology. *European Journal of Personality, 9*, 231–252.

McCrea, D. A. (1992). Can sense be made of spinal interneuron circuits? *Behavioral and Brain Sciences, 15*, 633–643.

McDaniel, M. A., Whetzel, D. L., Schmidt, F. L., & Maurer, S. D. (1994). The validity of employment interviews: A comprehensive review and meta-analysis. *Journal of Applied Psychology, 79*, 599–616.

McDougall, W. (1908). *Social psychology*. New York: G. Putnam & Sons.

McFarlane, A. C., & Brooks, P. M. (1990). Psychoimmunology and rheumatoid arthritis: Concepts and methodologies. *International Journal of Psychiatry in Medicine, 20*, 307–322.

McGaha, A. C., & Korn, J. H. (1995). The emergence of interest in the ethics of psychological research with humans. *Ethics and Behavior, 5*, 147-159.

McGee, R. A., & Wolfe, D. A. (1991). Psychological maltreatment: Toward an operational definition. *Development and Psychopathology, 3*, 3–18.

McGrady, A., Turner, J. W., Fine, T. H., & Higgins, J. T. (1987). Effects of biobehaviorally assisted relaxation training on blood pressure, plasma renin, cortisol, and aldosterone levels in borderline essential hypertension. *Clinical Biofeedback and Health, 10*, 16–25.

McGreevy, M. A., Steadman, H. J., & Callahan, L. A. (1991). The negligible effects of California's 1982 reform of the insanity defense test. *American Journal of Psychiatry, 148*, 744–750.

McGue, M., Bacon, S., & Lykken, D. T. (1993). Personality stability and change in early adulthood: A behavioral genetic analysis. *Developmental Psychology, 29*, 96–109.

McGue, M., & Lykken, D. T. (1992). Genetic influence on risk of divorce. *Psychological Science, 3*, 368–373.

McGuigan, F. J. (1970). Covert oral behavior during the silent performance of language tasks. *Psychological Bulletin, 74*, 309–326.

McGuire, B. (1990). Post-traumatic stress disorder: A review. *Irish Journal of Psychology, 11*, 1–23.

McKelvie, S. J. (1990). Student acceptance of a generalized personality description: Forer's graphologist revisited. *Journal of Social Behavior and Personality, 5*, 91–95.

McKinney, M., & Richelson, E. (1984). The coupling of the neuronal muscarinic receptor to responses. *Annual Review of Pharmacology and Toxicology, 24*, 121–146.

McMinn, M. R. (1984). Mechanisms of energy balance in obesity. *Behavioral Neuroscience, 98*, 375–393.

McNally, R. J. (1987). Preparedness and phobia: A review. *Psychological Bulletin, 101*, 283–303.

McNally, R. J. (1990). Psychological approaches to panic disorder: A review. *Psychological Bulletin, 108*, 403–419.

McNeal, E. T., & Cimbolic, P. (1986). Antidepressants and biochemical theories of depression. *Psychological Bulletin, 99*, 361–374.

McNish, K. A., Betts, S. L., Brandon, S. E., & Wagner, A. R. (1997). Divergence of conditioned eyeblink and conditioned fear in backward Pavlovian training. *Animal Learning and Behavior, 25*, 43-52.

McPherson, K. S. (1985). On intelligence testing and immigration legislation. *American Psychologist, 40*, 242–243.

McReynolds, P. (1989). Diagnosis and clinical assessment: Current status and major issues. *Annual Review of Psychology, 40*, 83–108.

McWilliams, R., Nietupski, J., & Hamre-Nietupski, S. (1990). Teaching complex activities to students with moderate handicaps through the forward chaining of shorter total cycle response sequences. *Education and Training in Mental Retardation, 25*, 292–298.

McWilliams, S. A., & Tuttle, R. J. (1973). Long-term psychological effects of LSD. *Psychological Bulletin, 79*, 341–351.

Meana, M., & Binik, Y. M. (1994). Painful coitus: A review of female dyspareunia. *Journal of Nervous and Mental Disease, 182*, 264–272.

Medin, D. L. (1989). Concepts and conceptual structure. *American Psychologist, 44*, 1469–1481.

Mednick, S. A. (1962). The associative basis of the creative process. *Psychological Review, 69*, 220–232.

Mednick, S. A., Huttunen, M. O., & Machon, R. A. (1994). Prenatal influenza infections and adult schizophrenia. *Schizophrenia Bulletin, 20*, 263–267.

Meehan, J. W., & Day, R. H. (1995). Visual accomodation as a cue for size. *Ergonomics, 38*, 1239-1249.

Meehl, P. E. (1956). Wanted: A good cookbook. *American Psychologist, 11*, 263–272.

Meeker, W. B., & Barber, T. X. (1971). Toward an explanation of stage hypnosis. *Journal of Abnormal Psychology, 77*, 61–70.

Meichenbaum, D. (1985). *Stress-inoculation training*. New York: Pergamon Press.

Meichenbaum, D. H., Bowers, K. S., & Ross, R. R. (1969). A behavioral analysis of teacher expectancy effect. *Journal of Personality & Social Psychology, 13*, 306–316.

Meissner, W. W. (1996). Empathy in the therapeutic alliance. *Psychoanalytic Inquiry, 16*, 39–53.

Melanoma risk and socio-economic class. (1983). *Science News, 124*, 232.

Melton, G. B., & Grey, J. N. (1988). Ethical dilemmas in AIDS research: Individual privacy and public health. *American Psychologist, 43*, 60–64.

Meltzer, H. Y. (1995). Multiple-outcome criteria in schizophrenia; An overview of outcome with clozapine. *European Psychiatry, 10*, 19S–25S.

Melzack, R. (1993). Pain: Past, present and future. *Canadian Journal of Experimental Psychology, 47*, 615–629.

Melzack, R., & Wall, P. D. (1965). Pain mechanisms: A new theory. *Science, 150*, 971–979.

Mendelson, W. B., Maczaj, M., & Holt, J. (1991). Buspirone administration to sleep apnea patients. *Journal of Clinical Psychopharmacology, 11*, 71–72.

Mengel, M. K. C., Stiefenhofer, A. E., Jyvasjarvi, E., & Kniffki, K. D. (1993). Pain sensation during cold stimulation of the teeth: Differential reflection of Ad and C fibre activity? *Pain, 55*, 159–169.

Merckelbach, H., Arntz, A., & de Jong, P. (1991). Conditioning experiences in spider phobics. *Behaviour Research and Therapy, 29*, 333–335.

Merckelbach, H., Muris, P., & Kop, W. J. (1994). Handedness, symptom reporting, and accident susceptibility. *Journal of Clinical Psychology, 50*, 389–392.

Merewether, F. C., & Alpert, M. (1990). The components and neuroanatomical bases of prosody. *Journal of Communication Disorders, 23*, 325–336.

Merikangas, K. R. (1993). Genetic epidemiologic studies of affective disorders in childhood and adolescence. *European Archives of Psychiatry and Clinical Neuroscience, 243*, 121–130.

Merikle, P. M. (1992). Perception without awareness: Critical issues. *American Psychologist, 47*, 792–795.

Mersch, P. P., Emmelkamp, P. M., & Lips, C. (1991). Social phobia: Individual response patterns and the long-term effects of behavioral and cognitive interventions. A follow-up study. *Behaviour Research and Therapy, 29*, 357–362.

Mertens, D. M., & Rabiu, J. (1992). Combining cognitive learning theory and computer assisted instruction for deaf learners. *American Annals of the Deaf, 137*, 399–403.

Mervis, J. (1984, March). Council ends forums trial, opens way for new divisions. *APA Monitor*, pp. 10–11.

Mervis, J. (1986, July). NIMH data point way to effective treatment. *APA Monitor*, pp. 1, 13.

Messer, W. S., & Griggs, R. A. (1989). Student belief and involvement in the paranormal and performance in introductory psychology. *Teaching of Psychology, 16*, 187–191.

Messick, S. (1995). Validity of psychological assessment. *American Psychologist, 50*, 741–749.

Messick, S., & Jungeblut, A. (1981). Time and method in coaching for the SAT. *Psychological Bulletin, 89*, 191–196.

Messier, C., Durkin, T., Mrabet, O., & Destrade, C. (1990). Memory-improving action of glucose: Indirect evidence for a facilitation of hippocampal acetylcholine synthesis. *Behavioural Brain Research, 39*, 135–143.

Metcalfe, J., & Wiebe, D. (1987). Intuition in insight and noninsight problem solving. *Memory and Cognition, 15*, 238–246.

Mewaldt, S. P., Ghoneim, M. M., Choi, W. W., & Korttila, K. (1988). Nitrous oxide and human state-dependent memory. *Pharmacology, Biochemistry, and Behavior, 30*, 83–87.

Meyer, D. R., Gurklis, J. A., & Cloud, M. D. (1985). An equipotential function of the cerebral cortex. *Physiological Psychology, 13*, 48–50.

Meyer, J. P., Allen, N. J., & Smith, C. A. (1993). Commitment to organizations and occupations: Extension and test of a three-component conceptualization. *Journal of Applied Psychology, 78*, 538–551.

Meyer, J. P., Paunonen, S. V., Gellatly, I. R., Goffin, R. D., & Jackson, D. N. (1989). Organizational commitment and job performance: It's the nature of the commitment that counts. *Journal of Applied Psychology, 74*, 152–156.

Meyer-Bahlburg, H. F. L., Ehrhardt, A. A., Rosen, L. R., & Gruen, R. S. (1995). Prenatal estrogens nad the development of homosexual orientations. *Developmental Psychology, 31*, 12–21.

Miczek, K. A., Thompson, M. L., & Shuster, L. (1982). Opioid-like analgesia in defeated mice. *Science, 215*, 1520–1523.

Middleton, J. A. (1995). A study of intrinsic motivation in the mathematics classroom: A personal constructs approach. *Journal for Research in Mathematics Education, 26*, 254–279.

Mikulincer, M., & Peer-Goldin, I. (1991). Self-congruence and the experience of happiness. *British Journal of Social Psychology, 30*, 21–35.

Milan, R. J., Kilmann, P. R., & Boland, J. P. (1988). Treatment outcome of secondary orgasmic dysfunction: A two- to six-year follow-up. *Archives of Sexual Behavior, 17*, 463–480.

Miles, J. A., & Greenberg, J. (1993). Using punishment threats to attenuate social loafing effects among swimmers. *Organizational Behavior and Human Decision Processes, 56*, 246–265.

Milgram, S. (1963). Behavioral study of obedience. *Journal of Abnormal and Social Psychology, 67*, 371–378.

Milgram, S. (1964). Issues in the study of obedience: A reply to Baumrind. *American Psychologist, 19*, 848–852.

Milgram, S. (1974). *Obedience to authority*. New York: Harper & Row.

Miller, D. L., & Kelley, M. L. (1994). The use of goal setting and contingency contracting for improving children's homework performance. *Journal of Applied Behavior Analysis, 27*, 73–84.

Miller, E. (1996). Phrenology, neuropsychology and rehabilitation. *Neuropsychological Rehabilitation, 6,* 245-255.

Miller, E. M. (1994). Intelligence and brain myelination: A hypothesis. *Personality and Individual Differences, 17,* 803-832.

Miller, G. A. (1956). The magical number seven, plus or minus two: Some limits on our capacity for processing information. *Psychological Review, 63,* 81-97.

Miller, G. A. (1990). The place of language in a scientific psychology. *Psychological Science, 1,* 7-14.

Miller, H. L., Chaplin, W. F., & Coombs, D. W. (1990). Cause and correlation: One more time. *Psychological Reports, 66,* 1293-1294.

Miller, J. (1991). Threshold variability in subliminal perception experiments: Fixed threshold estimates reduce power to detect subliminal effects. *Journal of Experimental Psychology Human Perception and Performance, 17,* 841-851.

Miller, L. L., & Branconnier, R. J. (1983). Cannabis: Effects on memory and the cholinergic limbic system. *Psychological Bulletin, 93,* 441-456.

Miller, M. G. (1984). Oral somatosensory factors in dietary self-selection in rats. *Behavioral Neuroscience, 98,* 416-423.

Miller, N. E. (1985). The value of behavioral research on animals. *American Psychologist, 40,* 423-440.

Miller, N. E. (1992). Introducing and teaching much-needed understanding of the scientific process. *American Psychologist, 47,* 848-850.

Miller, N. S., & Gold, M. S. (1994). LSD and Ecstasy: Pharmacology, phenomenology, and treatment. *Psychiatric Annals, 24,* 131-133.

Miller, R. R., Barnet, R. C., & Grahame, N. J. (1995). Assessment of the Rescorla-Wagner model. *Psychological Bulletin, 117,* 363-386.

Miller, T. Q., Turner, C. W., Tindale, R. S., Posavac, E. J., & Dugoni, B. L. (1991). Reasons for the trend toward null findings in research on Type A behavior. *Psychological Bulletin, 110,* 469-485.

Mills, S., & Raine, A. (1994). Neuroimaging and aggression. *Journal of Offender Rehabilitation, 21,* 145-158.

Milne, J. (1995). An analysis of the law of confidentiality with special reference to the counseling of minors. *Australian Psychologist, 30,* 169-174.

Milton, M. (1994). The case for existential therapy in HIV-related psychotherapy. *Counseling Psychology Quarterly, 7,* 367-374.

Mineka, S., & Cook, M. (1993). Mechanisms involved in the observational conditioning of fear. *Journal of Experimental Psychology General, 122,* 23-38.

Miner, C. M., & Davidson, J. R. T. (1995). Biological characterization of social phobia. *European Archives of Psychiatry and Clinical Neuroscience, 244,* 304-308.

Minuchin, S. (1974). *Families and family therapy.* Cambridge, MA: Harvard University Press.

Mio, J. S., & Graesser, A. C. (1991). Humor, language, and metaphor. *Metaphor and Symbolic Activity, 6,* 87-102.

Mirsky, A. F., Yardley, S. L., & Jones, B. P., & Walsh, D. (1995). Analysis of the attention deficit in schizophrenia: A study of patients and their relatives in Ireland. *Journal of Psychiatric Research, 29,* 23-42.

Mischel, W., & Peake, P. J. (1982). Beyond déjà vu in the search for cross-situational consistency. *Psychological Review, 89,* 730-755.

Miserandino, M. (1991). Memory and the seven dwarfs. *Teaching of Psychology, 18,* 169-171.

Mishkin, M., & Appenzeller, T. (1987). The anatomy of memory. *Scientific American,* pp. 80-89.

Mita, T. H., Dermer, M., & Knight, J. (1977). Reversed facial images and the mere-exposure hypothesis. *Journal of Personality and Social Psychology, 35,* 597-601.

Mitchell, P., Mackinnon, A. J., & Waters, B. (1993). The genetics of bipolar disorder. *Australian and New Zealand Journal of Psychiatry, 27,* 560-580.

Mitchell, P., Waters, B., Morrison, N., & Shine, J. (1991). Close linkage of bipolar disorder to chromosome 11 markers is excluded in two large Australian pedigrees. *Journal of Affective Disorders, 21,* 23-32.

Mitler, M. M., Hajdukovic, R., & Erman, M. K. (1993). Treatment of narcolepsy with methamphetamine. *Sleep, 16,* 306-317.

Modestin, J., Ammann, R., & Wurmle, O. (1995). Season of birth: Comparison of patients with schizophrenia, affective disorders and alcoholism. *Acta Psychiatrica Scandinavica, 91,* 140-143.

Modigliani, A., & Rochat, F. (1995). The role of interaction sequences and the timing of resistance in shaping obedience and defiance to authority. *Journal of Social Issues, 51,* 107-123.

Mohr, D. C. (1995). Negative outcome in psychotherapy: A critical review. *Clinical Psychology: Science and Practice, 2,* 1-27.

Moller, A. T., & Botha, H. C. (1996). Effects of a group rational-emotive behavior therapy program on the Type A behavior pattern. *Psychological Reports, 78,* 947-961.

Monahan, J. (1993). Limiting therapist exposure to Tarasoff liability: Guidelines for risk containment. *American Psychologist, 48,* 242-250.

Money, J. (1986). *Venuses penuses: Sexology, sexosophy, and exigency theory.* Buffalo, NY: Prometheus.

Money, J. (1987). Sin, sickness, or status? Homosexual gender identity and psychoneuroendocrinology. *American Psychologist, 42,* 384-399.

Money, J. (1994). The concept of gender identity disorder in childhood and adolescence after 39 years. *Journal of Sex and Marital Therapy, 20,* 163-177.

Mongeau, P. A., & Garlick, R. (1988). Social comparison and persuasive arguments as determinants of group polarization. *Communication Research Reports, 5,* 120-125.

Moniz, E. (1937/1994). Prefrontal leucotomy in the treatment of mental disorders. *American Journal of Psychiatry, 151,* 237-239.

Monroe, S. M. (1982). Life events and disorder: Event-symptom associations and the course of disorder. *Journal of Abnormal Psychology, 91,* 14-24.

Monroe, S. M., & Simons, A. D. (1991). Diathesis-stress theories in the context of life stress research: Implications for the depressive disorders. *Psychological Bulletin, 110,* 406-425.

Monson, T. C., Hesley, J. W., & Chernick, L. (1982). Specifying when personality traits can and cannot predict behavior: An alternative to abandoning the attempt to predict single-act criteria. *Journal of Personality and Social Psychology, 43,* 385-399.

Montag, I., & Comrey, A. L. (1987). Internality and externality as correlates of involvement in fatal driving accidents. *Journal of Applied Psychology, 72,* 339-343.

Monte, C. F. (1980). *Beneath the mask: An introduction to theories of personality.* New York: Holt, Rinehart & Winston.

Montgomery, G., & Kirsch, I. (1996). Mechanisms of placebo pain reduction: An empirical investigation. *Psychological Science, 7,* 174-176.

Montgomery, R. W. (1993). The ancient origins of cognitive therapy: The reemergence of stoicism. *Journal of Cognitive Psychotherapy, 7,* 5-19.

Monti, P. M., Curran, J. P., Corriveau, D. P., DeLancey, A. L., & Hagerman, S. M. (1980). Effects of social skills training groups and sensitivity training groups with psychiatric patients. *Journal of Consulting and Clinical Psychology, 48,* 241-248.

Monti, P. M., Gulliver, S., & Myers, M. G. (1994). Social skills training for alcoholics: Assessment and treatment. *Alcohol and Alcoholism, 29,* 627-637.

Montour, K. (1977). William James Sidis: The broken twig. *American Psychologist, 32,* 265-279.

Moore, J. (1990). On mentalism, privacy, and behaviorism. *Journal of Mind and Behavior, 11,* 19-36.

Moore, M. (1984). Sex and acknowledgments: A nonreactive study. *Sex Roles, 10,* 1021-1031.

Moore, T. E. (1995). Subliminal self-help auditory tapes: An empirical test of perceptual consequences. *Canadian Journal of Behavioural Science, 27,* 9-20.

Moorhead, G., Ference, R., & Neck, C. P. (1991). Group decision fiascoes continue: Space shuttle Challenger and a revised groupthink framework. *Human Relations, 44,* 539-550.

Moran, M. G. (1991). Psychological factors affecting pulmonary and rheumatologic diseases: A review. *Psychosomatics, 32,* 14-23.

Morawski, J. G. (1982). Assessing psychology's moral heritage through our neglected utopias. *American Psychologist, 37,* 1082-1095.

Mordkoff, J. T., Yantis, S., & Egeth, H. E. (1990). Detecting conjunctions of color and form in parallel. *Perception and Psychophysics, 48,* 157-168.

Moreland, R. L., & Zajonc, R. B. (1982). Exposure effects in person perception: Familiarity, similarity, and attraction. *Journal of Experimental Social Psychology, 18,* 395-415.

Moretti, M. M., & Higgins, E. T. (1990). Relating self-discrepancy to self-esteem: The contribution of discrepancy beyond actual-self ratings. *Journal of Experimental Social Psychology, 26,* 108-123.

Morgan, C., & Murray, H. A. (1935). A method of investigating fantasies. *Archives of Neurology and Psychiatry, 4,* 310-329.

Morgan, W. G. (1995). Origin and history of the thematic apperception test images. *Journal of Personality Assessment, 65,* 237-254.

Morisse, D., Batra, L., Hess, L., & Silverman, R. (1996). A demonstration of a token economy for the real world. *Applied and Preventive Psychology, 5,* 41-46.

Morley, J. E., & Levine, A. S. (1980). Stress-induced eating is mediated through endogenous opiates. *Science, 209,* 1259-1261.

Moroff, S. V. (1986). Qualitative and ethical issues in quantitative clinical decision making. *New York Journal of Medicine, 86,* 250-253.

Morris, S. (1980, April). Interview: James Randi. *Omni,* pp. 76-78, 104, 106, 108.

Morris, W., & Morris, M. (1985). *Harper dictionary of contemporary usage.* New York: Harper & Row.

Morrison, A. R. (1983, April). A window on the sleeping brain. *Scientific American,* pp. 94-102.

Morrison, M., de Man, A. F., & Drumheller, A. (1993). Correlates of socially restrictive and authoritarian attitudes toward mental patients in university students. *Social Behavior and Personality, 21,* 333-338.

Morrongiello, B. A., Fenwick, K. D., & Chance, G. (1990). "Sound localization acuity in very young infants: An observer-based testing procedure": Correction. *Developmental Psychology, 26,* 1003.

Morrongiello, B. A., Fenwick, K. D., Hillier, L., & Chance, G. (1994). Sound localization in newborn human infants. *Developmental Psychobiology, 27,* 519-538.

Mortimer, R. G., & Fell, J. C. (1989). Older drivers: Their night fatal crash involvement and risk. *Accident Analysis and Prevention, 21,* 273-282.

Moruzzi, G., & Magoun, H. W. (1949). Brain-stem reticular formation and activation of the EEG. *Electroencephalography and Clinical Neurophysiology, 1,* 455-473.

Moscicki, E. K. (1995). Epidemiology of suicide. *International Psychogeriatrics, 7,* 137-148.

Moscovitch, M. (1995). Recovered consciousness: A hypothesis concerning modularity and episodic memory. *Journal of Clinical and Experimental Neuropsychology, 17,* 276–290.

Moscovitch, M., & Behrmann, M. (1994). Coding of spatial information in the somatosensory system: Evidence from patients with neglect following parietal lobe damage. *Journal of Cognitive Neuroscience, 6,* 151–155.

Moses, L. N. (1989). The Zelig syndrome. *Issues in Ego Psychology, 12,* 117–126.

Moskowitz, D. S., & Schwarz, J. C. (1982). Validity comparison of behavior counts and ratings by knowledgeable informants. *Journal of Personality and Social Psychology, 42,* 518–528.

Mowday, R. T., Steers, R. M., & Porter, L. W. (1979). The measurement of organizational commitment. *Journal of Vocational Behavior, 14,* 224–247.

Mowrer, O. H. (1947). On the dual nature of learning: A reinterpretation of "conditioning" and "problem solving." *Harvard Educational Review, 17,* 102–148.

Mowrer, O. H., & Mowrer, W. M. (1938). Enuresis: A method for its study and treatment. *American Journal of Orthopsychiatry, 8,* 436–559.

Muehlbach, M. J., & Walsh, J. K. (1995). The effects of caffeine on simulated night-shift work and subsequent daytime sleep. *Sleep, 18,* 22–29.

Mueller, C. G. (1979). Some origins of psychology as a science. *Annual Review of Psychology, 30,* 9–29.

Mullen, B., Anthony, T., Salas, E., & Driskell, J. E. (1994). Group cohesiveness and quality of decision making: An integration of tests of the groupthink hypothesis. *Small Group Research, 25,* 189–204.

Mullen, B., Futrell, D., Stairs, D., Tice, D. M., Baumeister, R. F., Dawson, K. E., Radloff, C. E., Goethals, G. R., Kennedy, J. G., & Rosenfeld, P. (1986). Newscasters' facial expressions and voting behavior of viewers: Can a smile elect a president? *Journal of Personality and Social Psychology, 51,* 291–295.

Mulligan, T., & Moss, C. R. (1991). Sexuality and aging in male veterans: A cross-sectional study of interest, ability, and activity. *Archives of Sexual Behavior, 20,* 17–25.

Mullin, C. R., & Linz, D. (1995). Desensitization and resensitization to violence against women: Effects of exposure to sexually violent films on judgments of domestic violence victims. *Journal of Personality and Social Psychology, 69,* 449–459.

Mullington, J., & Broughton, R. (1993). Scheduled naps in the management of daytime sleepiness in narcolepsy-cataplexy. *Sleep, 16,* 444–456.

Mullins, L. L., & Olson, R. A. (1990). Familial factors in the etiology, maintenance, and treatment of somatoform disorders in children. *Family Systems Medicine, 8,* 159–175.

Mumford, M. D., & Gustafson, S. B. (1988). Creativity syndrome: Integration, application, and innovation. *Psychological Bulletin, 103,* 27–43.

Munley, P. H., & Zarantonello, M. M. (1990). A comparison of MMPI profile types with corresponding estimated MMPI-2 profiles. *Journal of Clinical Psychology, 46,* 803–811.

Münsterberg, H. (1908). *On the witness stand.* New York: Doubleday.

Murphy, G. L., & Medin, D. L. (1985). The role of theories in conceptual coherence. *Psychological Review, 92,* 289–316.

Murphy, K. R., & Cleveland, J. N. (1995). *Understanding performance appraisal: Social, organizational, and goal-based perspectives.* Thousand Oak, CA: Sage.

Murphy, S. T., & Zajonc, R. B. (1993). Affect, cognition, and awareness: Affective priming with optimal and suboptimal stimulus exposures. *Journal of Personality and Social Psychology, 64,* 723–739.

Murray, B. (1995, June). Undergrad research brings psychology to life. APA *Monitor,* p. 41.

Murray, D. J. (1990). Fechner's later psychophysics. *Canadian Psychology, 31,* 54–60.

Murray, J. B. (1995). Evidence for acupuncture's analgesic effectiveness and proposals for the physiological mechanisms involved. *Journal of Psychology, 129,* 443-461.

Murray, H. A. (1938). *Explorations in personality.* New York: Oxford University Press.

Murray, J. B. (1990). Review of research on the Myers-Briggs Type Indicator. *Perceptual and Motor Skills, 70,* 1187–1202.

Murray, R. P., Johnston, J. J., Dolce, J. J., & Lee, W. W. (1995). Social support for smoking cessation and abstinence: The Lung Health Study. *Addictive Behaviors, 20,* 159–170.

Murstein, B. (1972). Physical attractiveness and marital choice. *Journal of Personality and Social Psychology, 22,* 8–12.

Murtagh, D.R.R., & Greenwood, K. M. (1995). Identifying effective psychological treatments for insomnia: A metaanalysis. *Journal of Consulting and Clinical Psychology, 63,* 79-89.

Murtha, T. C., Kanfer, R., & Ackerman, P. L. (1996). Toward an interactionist taxonomy of personality and situations: An integrative situational-dispositional representations of personality traits. *Journal of Personality and Social Psychology, 71,* 193–207.

Musick, P. L. (1976). Primitive percepts and collective creativity. *Art Psychotherapy, 3,* 43–50.

Myers, D. G., & Bishop, G. D. (1970). Discussion effects on racial attitudes. *Science, 169,* 778–779.

Myerscough, R., & Taylor, S. (1985). The effects of marijuana on human physical aggression. *Journal of Personality and Social Psychology, 49,* 1541–1546.

Myrtek, M. (1995). Type A behavior pattern, personality factors, disease, and physiological reactivity: A meta-analytic update. *Personality and Individual Differences, 18,* 491–502.

Najavits, L. M., & Strupp, H. H. (1994). Differences in the effectiveness of psychodynamic therapists: A process-outcome study. *Psychotherapy, 31,* 114–123.

Nakagawa, Y., & Iwasaki, T. (1996). Ethanol-induced state-dependent learning is mediated by 5-hydroxytryptamine-sub-3 receptors but not by N-methyl-D-aspartate receptor complex. *Brain Research, 706,* 227-232.

Nakano, T., Shimomura, T., Takahashi, K., & Ikawa, S. (1993). Platelet substance P and 5-hydroxytryptamine in migraine and tension-type headache. *Headache, 33,* 528–532.

Nakayama, K. (1994). James J. Gibson: An appreciation. *Psychological Review, 101,* 329–335.

Narens, L., & Mausfeld, R. (1992). On the relationship of the psychological and the physical in psychophysics. *Psychological Review, 99,* 467–479.

NAS calls tests fair but limited. (1982, April). APA *Monitor,* p. 2.

Nash, M. (1987). What, if anything, is regressed about hypnotic age regression? A review of the empirical literature. *Psychological Bulletin, 102,* 42–52.

Natsoulas, T. (1994-95). The stream of consciousness: VIII. James's ejective consciousness (First Part). *Imagination, Cognition and Personality, 14,* 333-352.

Navarro, M., Fernandex-Ruiz, J. J., de Miguel, R., & Hernandez, M. L. (1993). Motor disturbances induced by an acute dose of d-sup-9-tetrahydrocannabinol: Possible involvement of nigrostriatal dopaminergic alterations. *Pharmacology, Biochemistry, and Behavior, 45,* 291–298.

Navon, D. (1974). Forest before trees: The precedence of global features in visual perception. *Cognitive Psychology, 9,* 353–383.

Neimeyer, G. J. (1984). Cognitive complexity and marital satisfaction. *Journal of Social and Clinical Psychology, 2,* 258–263.

Neimeyer, G. J. (1989). Applications of repertory grid technique to vocational assessment. *Journal of Counseling and Development, 67,* 585–589.

Neimeyer, R. A. (1983). Toward a personal construct conceptualization of depression and suicide. *Death Education, 7,* 127–173.

Neisser, U. (1981). John Dean's memory: A case study. *Cognition, 9,* 1–22.

Neisser, U. (1984). Interpreting Harry Bahrick's discovery: What confers immunity against forgetting? *Journal of Experimental Psychology: General, 113,* 32–35.

Neisser, U., & Becklen, R. (1975). Selective looking: Attending to visually specified events. *Cognitive Psychology, 7,* 480–494.

Neisser, U., Boodoo, G., Bouchard, T. J., Jr., Boykin, T. J., Brody, N., Ceci, S. J., Halpern, D. F., Loehlin, J. C., Perloff, R., Sternberg, R. J., & Urbina, S. (1996). Intelligence: Knowns and unknowns. *American Psychologist, 51,* 77-101.

Nelson, E. S., Karr, K. M., & Coleman, P. K. (1995). Relationships among daily hassles, optimism and reported physical symptoms. *Journal of College Student Psychotherapy, 10,* 11–26.

Nelson, K. E. (1977). Facilitating children's syntax acquisition. *Developmental Psychology, 18,* 101–107.

Nelson, M. O. (1991). Another look at masculine protest. *Individual Psychology: Journal of Adlerian Theory, Research, and Practice, 47,* 490–497.

Nelson, P. L. (1994). Cannabis amotivational syndrome and personality trait absorption: A review and reconceptualization. *Imagination, Cognition, and Personality, 14,* 43–58.

Nelson, T. O. (1996). Consciousness and metacognition. *American Psychologist, 51,* 102-116.

Nelson, T. O., Leonesio, R. J., Shimamura, A. P., Landwehr, R. F., & Narens, L. (1982). Overlearning and the feeling of knowing. *Journal of Experimental Psychology: Learning, Memory, and Cognition, 8,* 279–288.

Nemeth, C. J. (1986). Differential contributions of majority and minority influence. *Psychological Review, 93,* 23–32.

Nenty, H. J. (1986). Cross-culture bias analysis of Cattell Culture-Fair Intelligence Test. *Perspectives in Psychological Researches, 9,* 1–16.

Nevo, O. (1985). Does one ever really laugh at one's own expense? *Journal of Personality and Social Psychology, 49,* 799–807.

Nevo, O., & Nevo, B. (1983). What do you do when asked to answer humorously? *Journal of Personality and Social Psychology, 44,* 188–194.

Newberry, K. J., Reckers, P. M., & Wyndelts, R. W. (1993). An examination of tax practitioner decisions: The role of preparer sanctions and framing effects associated with client condition. *Journal of Economic Psychology, 14,* 439–452.

Newcomb, A. F., & Bagwell, C. L. (1995). Children's friendship relations: A meta-analytic review. *Psychological Bulletin, 117,* 306–347.

Newcomb, A. F., Bukowski, W. M., & Pattee, L. (1993). Children's peer relations: A meta-analytic review of popular, rejected, neglected, controversial, and average sociometric status. *Psychological Bulletin, 113,* 99–128.

Newell, A., & Simon, H. (1972). *Human problem solving.* Englewood Cliffs, NJ: Prentice Hall.

Newman, B., O'Grady, M. A., Ryan, C. S., & Hemmes, N. S. (1993). Pavlovian conditioning of the tickle response of human subjects: Temporal and delay conditioning. *Perceptual and Motor Skills, 77,* 779–785.

Newman, E. A., & Hartline, P. H. (1982, March). The infrared "vision" of snakes. *Scientific American,* pp. 116–124, 127.

Newman, J., & Layton, B. D. (1984). Overjustification: A self-perception perspective. *Personality and Social Psychology Bulletin, 10,* 419–425.

Newton, J., Toby, O., & Spence, S. H. (1995). Cognitive-behavioral therapy versus EMG biofeedback in the treatment of chronic low back pain. *Behaviour Research and Therapy, 33,* 691–697.

Newton, T., & Deenan, T. (1991). Further analyses of the dispositional argument in organizational behavior. *Journal of Applied Psychology, 76,* 781–787.

Nicholls, J. G. (1972). Creativity in the person who will never produce anything original or useful: The concept of creativity as a normally distributed trait. *American Psychologist, 27,* 717–727.

Nicholls, J. G. (1984). Achievement motivation: Conceptions of ability, subjective experience, task choice, and performance. *Psychological Review, 91,* 328–346.

Nichols, M. P., & Efran, J. S. (1985). Catharsis in psychotherapy: A new perspective. *Psychotherapy, 22,* 46–58.

Nicholson, N., Cole, S. G., & Rocklin, T. (1985). Conformity in the Asch situation: A comparison between contemporary British and U.S. university students. *British Journal of Social Psychology, 24,* 59–63.

Nickerson, R. S., & Adams, M. J. (1979). Long-term memory for a common object. *Cognitive Psychology, 11,* 287–307.

Nicki, R. M., Remington, R. E., & MacDonald, G. A. (1984). Self-efficacy, nicotine-fading/self-monitoring and cigarette-smoking behaviour. *Behaviour Research and Therapy, 22,* 477–485.

Nicol, S. E., & Gottesman, I. I. (1983). Clues to the genetics and neurobiology of schizophrenia. *American Scientist, 71,* 398–404.

Nicoll, R. A., & Madison, D. V. (1982). General anesthetics hyperpolarize neurons in the vertebrate nervous system. *Science, 217,* 1055–1057.

Nides, M., Rakos, R. F., Gonzales, D., & Murray, R. P. (1995). Predictors of initial smoking cessation and relapse through the first 2 years of the Lung Health Study. *Journal of Consulting and Clinical Psychology, 63,* 60–69.

Nides, M., Rand, C., Dolce, J., & Murray, R. (1994). Weight gain as a function of smoking cessation and 2-mg nicotine gum use among middle-aged smokers with mild lung impairment in the first 2 years of the Lung Health Study. *Health Psychology, 13,* 354–361.

Nielsen, T. A. (1993). Changes in the kinesthetic content of dreams following somatosensory stimulation of leg muscles during REM sleep. *Dreaming: Journal of the Association for the Study of Dreams, 3,* 99–113.

Nigg, J. T., & Goldsmith, H. H. (1994). Genetics of personality disorders: Perspectives from personality and psychopathology research. *Psychological Bulletin, 115,* 346–380.

Nikkhah, G., Bentlage, C., Cunningham, M. G., & Bjorklund, A. (1994). Intranigral fetal dopamine grafts induce behavioral compensation in the rat Parkinson model. *Journal of Neuroscience, 14,* 3449–3461.

Nisbett, R. E., & Ross, L. (1980). *Human inference: Strategies and shortcomings of social judgment.* Englewood Cliffs, NJ: Prentice Hall.

Nissen, M. J., Knopman, D. S., & Schacter, D. L. (1987). Neurochemical dissociation of memory systems. *Neurology, 37,* 789–794.

Nolen-Hoeksema, S. (1994). An interactive model for the emergence of gender differences in depression in adolescence. *Journal of Research on Adolescence, 4,* 519–534.

Nolen-Hoeksema, S., & Girgus, J. S. (1994). The emergence of gender differences in depression during adolescence. *Psychological Bulletin, 115,* 424–443.

Nolen-Hoeksema, S., Girgus, J. S., & Seligman, M. E. (1992). Predictors and consequences of childhood depressive symptoms: A 5-year longitudinal study. *Journal of Abnormal Psychology, 101,* 405–422.

Nolen-Hoeksema, S., & Morrow, J. (1993). Effects of rumination and distraction on naturally occurring depressed mood. *Cognition and Emotion, 7,* 561–570.

Nolen-Hoeksema, S., Morrow, J., & Fredrickson, B. L. (1993). Response styles and the duration of episodes of depressed mood. *Journal of Abnormal Psychology, 102,* 20–28.

Nopoulos, P., Torres, I., Flaum, M., & Andreasen, N. C. (1995). Brain morphology in first-episode schizophrenia. *American Journal of Psychiatry, 152,* 1721–1723.

Norcross, J. C., Strausser, D. J., & Faltus, F. J. (1988). The therapist's therapist. *American Journal of Psychotherapy, 42,* 53–66.

Nordstrom, R., Lorenzi, P., & Hall, R. V. (1990). A review of public posting of performance feedback in work settings. *Journal of Organizational Behavior Management, 11,* 101–123.

Norman, R. M., & Malla, A. K. (1993). Stressful life events and schizophrenia: I. A review of the research. *British Journal of Psychiatry, 162,* 161–166.

Norris, F. H., & Uhl, G. A. (1993). Chronic stress as a mediator of acute stress: The case of Hurricane Hugo. *Journal of Applied Social Psychology, 23,* 1263–1284.

Norris, N. P. (1978). Fragile subjects. *American Psychologist, 33,* 962–963.

Norton, E. M., Durlak, J. A., & Richards, M. H. (1989). Peer knowledge of and reactions to adolescent suicide. *Journal of Youth and Adolescence, 18,* 427–437.

Nosofsky, R. M. (1991). Relation between the rational model and the context model of categorization. *Psychological Science, 2,* 416–421.

Notz, W. W. (1975). Work motivation and the negative effects of extrinsic rewards: A review with implications for theory and practice. *American Psychologist, 30,* 884–891.

Nowicki, S., & Duke, M. P. (1992). The association of children's nonverbal decoding abilities with their popularity, locus of control, and academic achievement. *Journal of Genetic Psychology, 153,* 385–393.

Nunn, J., & Hodges, H. (1994). Cognitive deficits induced by global cerebral ischaemia: Relationship to brain damage and reversal by transplants. *Behavioural Brain Research, 65,* 1–31.

Nyklicek, I., Vingerhoets, A. J. J. M., & Van Heck, G. L. (1996). Hypertension and objective and self-reported stressor exposure: A review. *Journal of Psychosomatic Research, 40,* 585–601.

O'Carroll, R. E., Masterton, G., Dougall, N., & Ebmeier, K. P. (1995). The neuropsychiatric sequelae of mercury poisoning: The Mad Hatter's disease revisited. *British Journal of Psychiatry, 167,* 95–98.

O'Connell, A. N., & Russo, N. F. (Eds.). (1990). *Women in psychology: A bio-bibliographic sourcebook.* New York: Greenwood.

O'Connor, B. P., & Molly, K. (1991). A test of the intellectual cycle of the popular biorhythm theory. *Journal of Psychology, 125,* 291–299.

O'Connor, K. P. (1981). The intentional paradigm and cognitive psychophysiology. *Psychophysiology, 18,* 121–128.

O'Connor, N., & Hermelin, B. (1992). Do young calendrical calculators improve with age? *Journal of Child Psychology and Psychiatry and Allied Disciplines, 33,* 907–912.

O'Connor, P. J., Lewis, R. D., & Kirchner, E. M. (1995). Eating disorder symptoms in female college gymnasts. *Medicine and Science in Sports and Exercise, 27,* 550–555.

O'Donnell, I., Farmer, R., & Catalan, J. (1993). Suicide notes. *British Journal of Psychiatry, 163,* 45–48.

O'Halloran, C. M., & Altmaier, E. M. (1995). The efficacy of preparation for surgery and invasive medical procedures. *Patient Education and Counseling, 25,* 9–16.

O'Leary, A. (1985). Self-efficacy and health. *Behaviour Research and Therapy, 23,* 437–451.

O'Leary, A. (1990). Stress, emotion, and human immune function. *Psychological Bulletin, 108,* 363–382.

O'Leary, K. D., & Smith, D. A. (1991). Marital interactions. *Annual Review of Psychology, 42,* 191–212.

O'Neil, W. M. (1995). American behaviorism: A historical and critical analysis. *Theory and Psychology, 5,* 285–305.

O'Neill, M., & Kempler, B. (1969). Approach and avoidance responses of the hysterical personality to sexual stimuli. *Journal of Abnormal Psychology, 74,* 300–305.

Oakhill, J. (1993). Children's difficulties in reading comprehension. *Educational Psychology Review, 5,* 223–237.

Ochs, E. P., Meana, M., Pare, L., & Mah, K. (1994). Learning about sex outside the gutter: Attitudes toward a computer sex-expert system. *Journal of Sex and Marital Therapy, 20,* 86–102.

Oden, G. C. (1984). Dependence, independence, and emergence of word features. *Journal of Experimental Psychology: Human Perception and Performance, 10,* 394–405.

Oden, M. H. (1968). The fulfillment of promise: 40-year followup of the Terman gifted group. *Genetic Psychology Monographs, 77,* 3–93.

Ogden, J., & Ward, E. (1995). Help-seeking behavior in sufferers of vaginismus. *Sexual and Marital Therapy, 10,* 23–30.

Ogden, J. A. (1989). Visuospatial and other "right-hemispheric" functions after long recovery periods in left-hemispherectomized subjects. *Neuropsychologia, 27,* 765–776.

Ogilvie, R. D., McDonagh, D. M., Stone, S. N., & Wilkinson, R. T. (1988). Eye movements and the detection of sleep onset. *Psychophysiology, 25,* 81–91.

Ogloff, J. R., & Otto, R. K. (1991). Are research participants truly informed? Readability of informed consent forms used in research. *Ethics and Behavior, 1,* 239–252.

Ohira, H., & Kurono, K. (1993). Facial feedback effects on impression formation. *Perceptual and Motor Skills, 77,* 1251–1258.

Ohman, A., Erixon, G., & Lofberg, I. (1975). Phobias and preparedness: Phobic versus neutral pictures as conditioned stimuli for human autonomic responses. *Journal of Abnormal Psychology, 84,* 41–45.

Okagaki, L., & Sternberg, R. J. (1993). Parental beliefs and children's school performance. *Child Development, 64,* 36–56.

Okogbaa, O., Shell, R. L., & Filipusic, D. (1994). On the investigation of the neurophysiological correlates of knowledge worker mental fatigue using the EEG signal. *Applied Ergonomics, 25,* 355–365.

Okwumabua, T. M. (1985). Psychological and physical contributions to marathon performance: An exploratory investigation. *Journal of Sport Behavior, 8,* 163–171.

Olds, J. (1956, October). Pleasure centers in the brain. *Scientific American,* pp. 105–116.

Olds, J., & Milner, P. (1954). Positive reinforcement produced by electrical stimulations of septal area and other regions of rat brain. *Journal of Comparative and Physiological Psychology, 47,* 419–427.

Oller, D. K., & Eilers, R. E. (1988). The role of audition in infant babbling. *Child Development, 59,* 441–449.

Olmo, R. J., & Stevens, G. L. (1984, August). Chess champs: Introverts at play. *Psychology Today,* pp. 72, 74.

Olson, J. K. (1995). Relationships between nurse-expressed empathy, patient-perceived empathy and patient distress. *IMAGE: Journal of Nursing Scholarship, 27,* 317–322.

Olympia, D. E., Sheridan, S. M., Jenson, W. R., & Andrews, D. (1994). Using student-managed interventions to increase homework completion and accuracy. *Behavior Analysis in School Psychology, 27,* 85–99.

Onstad, S., Skre, I., Torgersen, S., & Kringlen, E. (1991). Twin concordance for DSM-III-R schizophrenia. *Acta Psychiatrica Scandinavica, 83,* 395–401.

Oosterveld, W. J. (1987). The combined effect of Cinnarizine and domperidone on vestibular susceptibility. *Aviation, Space, and Environmental Medicine, 58,* 218–223.

Oppliger, P. A., & Sherblom, J. C. (1992). Humor: Incongruity, disparagement, and David Letterman. *Communication Research Reports, 9,* 99–108.

Organ, D. W., & Hui, C. T. (1995). Time pressure, Type A syndrome, and organizational citizenship behavior: A field study replication of Hui, Organ, and Crocker (1994). *Psychological Reports, 77,* 179–185.

Orne, M. T. (1951). The mechanisms of hypnotic age regression: An experimental study. *Journal of Abnormal and Social Psychology, 46,* 213–225.

Orne, M. T., Dinges, D. F., & Orne, E. C. (1984). On the differential diagnosis of multiple personality in the forensic context. *International Journal of Clinical and Experimental Hypnosis, 32,* 118–169.

Orne, M. T., & Evans, F. J. (1965). Social control in the psychological experiment: Antisocial behavior and hypnosis. *Journal of Personality and Social Psychology, 1,* 189–200.

Orwell, G. (1949). *1984.* New York: Harcourt Brace Jovanovich.

Osberg, T. M. (1993). Psychology is not just common sense: An introductory psychology demonstration. *Teaching of Psychology, 20,* 110–111.

Osberger, M. J., Maso, M., & Sam, L. K. (1993). Speech intelligibility of children with cochlear implants, tactile aids, or hearing aids. *Journal of Speech and Hearing Research, 36,* 186–203.

Ost, L. G. (1985). Ways of acquiring phobias and outcome of behavioral treatments. *Behaviour Research and Therapy, 23,* 683–689.

Overton, D. A. (1991). Historical context of state dependent learning and discriminative drug effects. *Behavioural Pharmacology, 2,* 253–264.

Owens, R. A. (1976). Background data. In M. D. Dunnette (Ed.), *Handbook of industrial and organizational psychology.* Chicago: Rand McNally.

Ozbay, H., Goka, E., Ozturk, E., & Gungor, S. (1993). Therapeutic factors in an adolescent psychodrama group. *Journal of Group Psychotherapy, Psychodrama, and Sociometry, 46,* 3–11.

Paddock, J. R., & Nowicki, S. (1986). Paralanguage and the interpersonal impact of dysphoria: It's not what you say but how you say it. *Social Behavior and Personality, 14,* 29–44.

Page, S. (1990). The turnaround on pornography research: Some implications for psychology and women. *Canadian Psychology, 31,* 359–367.

Page, S., & Tyrer, J. (1995). Gender and prediction of Gilligan's justice and care orientations. *Journal of College Student Psychotherapy, 10,* 43–56.

Paik, H., & Comstock, G. (1994). The effects of television violence on antisocial behavior: A meta-analysis. *Communication Research, 21,* 516–546.

Paikoff, R. L., & Brooks-Gunn, J. (1991). Do parent-child relationships change durng puberty? *Psychological Bulletin, 110,* 47–66.

Pallast, E. G. M., Jongbloet, P. H., Straatman, H. M., & Zielhuis, G. A. (1994). Excess seasonality of births among patients with schizophrenia and seasonal ovopathy. *Schizophrenia Bulletin, 20,* 269–276.

Palmer, J. A., Honorton, C., & Utts, J. (1989). Reply to the National Research Council Study on parapsychology. *Journal of the American Society for Psychical Research, 83,* 31–49.

Parham, K., & Willott, J. F. (1990). Effects of inferior colliculus lesions on the acoustic startle response. *Behavioral Neuroscience, 104,* 831–840.

Paris, J. (1996). Antisocial personality disorder: A biopsychosocial model. *Canadian Journal of Psychiatry, 41,* 75–80.

Park, B., & Rothbart, M. (1982). Perception of out-group homogeneity and levels of social categorization: Memory for the subordinate attributes of in-group and out-group members. *Journal of Personality and Social Psychology, 42,* 1051–1068.

Park, D. C., Smith, A. D., & Cavanaugh, J. C. (1990). Metamemories of memory researchers. *Memory and Cognition, 18,* 321–327.

Parker, K. (1983). A meta-analysis of the reliability and validity of the Rorschach. *Journal of Personality Assessment, 47,* 227–231.

Parker, K. C. H., Hanson, R. K., & Hunsley, J. (1988). MMPI, Rorschach, and WAIS: A meta-analytic comparison of reliability, stability, and validity. *Psychological Bulletin, 103,* 367–373.

Parker, S. (1990). A note on the growth of the use of statistical tests in perception and psychophysics. *Bulletin of the Psychonomic Society, 28,* 565–566.

Parrott, A. C. (1995). Smoking cessation leads to reduced stress, but why? *International Journal of the Addictions, 30,* 1509–1516.

Parsons, M. W., & Gold, P. E. (1992). Glucose enhancement of memory in elderly humans: An inverted-U dose-response curve. *Neurobiology of Aging, 13,* 401–404.

Parten, M. B. (1932). Social participation among pre-school children. *Journal of Abnormal and Social Psychology, 27,* 243–269.

Paterson, R. J., & Neufeld, R. W. J. (1995). What are my options: Influences of choice availability on stress and the perception of control. *Journal of Research in Personality, 29,* 145–167.

Pattatucci, A. M. L., & Hamer, D. H. (1995). Development and familiality of sexual orientation in females. *Behavior Genetics, 25,* 407–420.

Patterson, C. H. (1989). Eclecticism in psychotherapy: Is integration possible? *Psychotherapy, 26,* 157–161.

Patterson, F. G., Patterson, L. H., & Brentari, D. K. (1987). Language in child, chimp, and gorilla. *American Psychologist, 42,* 270–272.

Patton, J. E., Routh, D. K., & Stinard, T. A. (1986). Where do children study? Behavioral observations. *Bulletin of the Psychonomic Society, 24,* 439–440.

Paul, S. M., Hulihan-Giblin, B., & Skolnick, P. (1982). (+)-amphetamine binding to rat hypothalamus: Relation to anorexic potency of phenylethylamines. *Science, 218,* 487–490.

Paulsen, F. (1899/1963). *Immanuel Kant: His life and doctrine.* New York: Ungar.

Paunonen, S. V., Keinonen, M., Trzebinski, J., & Forsterling, F. (1996). The structure of personality in six cultures. *Journal of Cross-Cultural Psychology, 27,* 339–353.

Pavlov, I. P. (1928). *Lectures on conditioned reflexes.* New York: Liveright.

Pears, R., & Bryant, P. E. (1990). Transitive inferences by young children about spatial position. *British Journal of Psychology, 81,* 497–510.

Peeples, E. E. (1990). Training, certification, and experience of handwriting analysts. *Perceptual and Motor Skills, 70,* 1219–1226.

Peeters, M. C. W., Buunk, B. P., & Schaufeli, W. B. (1995). A microanalysis exploration of the cognitive appraisal of daily stressful events at work: The role of controllability. *Anxiety, Stress and Coping: An International Journal, 8,* 127–139.

Penfield, W. (1975). *The mystery of the mind.* Princeton, NJ: Princeton University Press.

Pennebaker, J. W., & Watson, D. (1988). Blood pressure estimation and beliefs among normotensives and hypertensives. *Health Psychology, 7,* 309–328.

Pepitone, A. (1981). Lessons from the history of social psychology. *American Psychologist, 36,* 972–985.

Peretz, I., Kolinsky, R., Tramo, M., & Labrecque, R. (1994). Functional dissociations following bilateral lesions of auditory cortex. *Brain, 117,* 1283–1301.

Perkins, K. A., Grobe, J. E., D'Amico, D., & Fonte, C. (1996). Low-dose nicotine nasal spray use and effects during initial smoking cessation. *Experimental and Clinical Psychopharmacology, 4,* 157–165.

Perlow, M. J., Freed, W. J., Hoffer, B. J., Seiger, A., Olson, L., & Wyatt, R. J. (1979). Brain grafts reduce motor abnormalities produced by destruction of nigrostriatal dopamine system. *Science, 204,* 643–647.

Perls, F. (1972). Interview with Frederick Perls. In A. Bry (Ed.), *Inside psychotherapy* (pp. 58–70). New York: Basic Books.

Perls, F. (1973). *The Gestalt approach and eyewitness to therapy.* Palo Alto, CA: Science & Behavior Books.

Perosa, S. L., & Perosa, L. M. (1993). Relationships among Minuchin's structural family model, identity achievement, and coping style. *Journal of Counseling Psychology, 40,* 479–489.

Perry, P. J. (1996). Pharmacotherapy for major depression with melancholic features: Relative efficacy of tricyclic versus selective serotonin reuptake inhibitor antidepressants. *Journal of Affective Disorders, 39,* 1–6.

Persad, E. (1990). Electroconvulsive therapy in depression. *Canadian Journal of Psychiatry, 35,* 175–182.

Pert, C. B., & Snyder, S. H. (1973). Opiate receptor: Demonstration in nervous tissue. *Science, 179,* 1031–1034.

Pervin, L. A. (1994). A critical analysis of current trait theory. *Psychological Inquiry, 5,* 103–113.

Peters, R., & McGee, R. (1982). Cigarette smoking and state-dependent memory. *Psychopharmacology, 76,* 232–235.

Peters, R. D. (1994). Better Beginnings, Better Futures: A community-based approach to primary prevention. *Canadian Journal of Community Mental Health, 13,* 183–188.

Peterson, B. E., & Stewart, A. J. (1996). Antecedents and contexts of generativity motivation at midlife. *Psychology and Aging, 11,* 21-33.

Peterson, C., & Barrett, L. C. (1987). Explanatory style and academic performance among university freshmen. *Journal of Personality and Social Psychology, 53,* 603–607.

Peterson, C., Seligman, M. E. P., & Vaillant, G. E. (1988). Pessimistic explanatory style is a risk factor for physical illness: A 35-year longitudinal study. *Journal of Personality and Social Psychology, 55,* 23–27.

Peterson, I. (1983). Playing chess bit by bit. *Science News, 124,* 236–237.

Peterson, L. R., & Peterson, M. (1959). Short-term retention of individual verbal items. *Journal of Experimental Psychology, 58,* 193–198.

Peterson, M. A., & Gibson, B. S. (1994). Must figure-ground organization precede object recognition? An assumption in peril. *Psychological Science, 5,* 253–259.

Petronis, K. R., Samuels, J. F., Moscicki, E. K., & Anthony, J. C. (1990). An epidemiologic investigation of potential risk factors for suicide attempts. *Social Psychiatry and Psychiatric Epidemiology, 25,* 193–199.

Pettersen, L., Yonas, A., & Fisch, R. O. (1980). The development of blinking in response to impending collision in preterm, full-term, and postterm infants. *Infant Behavior and Development, 3,* 155–165.

Petty, M. M., McGee, G. W., & Cavender, J. W. (1984). A meta-analysis of relationships between individual job satisfaction and individual performance. *Academy of Management Review, 9,* 712–721.

Petty, R. E., & Cacioppo, J. T. (1981). *Attitudes and persuasion: Classic and contemporary approaches.* Dubuque, IA: Wm. C. Brown.

Petty, R. E., & Cacioppo, J. T. (1990). Involvement and persuasion: Tradition versus integration. *Psychological Bulletin, 107,* 367–374.

Petty, R. E., Cacioppo, J. T., & Goldman, R. (1981). Personal involvement as a determinant of argument-based persuasion. *Journal of Personality and Social Psychology, 41,* 847–855.

Pezdek, K., & Greene, J. (1993). Testing eyewitness memory: Developing a measure that is more resistant to suggestibility. *Law and Human Behavior, 17,* 361–369.

Phelps, M. E., & Mazziotta, J. C. (1985). Positron-emission tomography: Human brain function and biochemistry. *Science, 228,* 799–809.

Philipp, E., Pirke, K. M., Kellner, M. B., & Krieg, J. C. (1991). Disturbed cholecystokinin secretion in patients with eating disorders. *Life Sciences, 48,* 2443–2450.

Phillips, D. P., & Brugge, J. F. (1985). Progress in neurophysiology of sound localization. *Annual Review of Psychology, 36,* 245–274.

Phillips, R. D., Wagner, S. H., Fells, C. A., & Lynch, M. (1990). Do infants recognize emotion in facial expressions? Categorical and "metaphorical" evidence. *Infant Behavior and Development, 13,* 71–84.

Phillips, W. M. (1981). The minimax problem of personal construct organization and schizophrenic thought disorder. *Journal of Clinical Psychology, 37,* 692–698.

Piaget, J. (1932). *The moral judgment of the child.* New York: Harcourt, Brace & World.

Piaget, J. (1952). *The origins of intelligence in children.* New York: International Universities Press.

Pierce, E. F., Eastman, N. W., Tripathi, H. L., & Olson, K. G. (1993). b–Endorphin response to endurance exercise: Relationship to exercise dependence. *Perceptual and Motor Skills, 77,* 767–770.

Piliavin, J. A., Callero, P. L., & Evans, E. E. (1982). Addiction to altruism: Opponent-process theory and habitual blood donation. *Journal of Personality and Social Psychology, 43,* 1200–1213.

Pillow, D. R., Zautra, A. J., & Sandler, I. (1996). Major life events and minor stressors: Identifying mediational links in the stress process. *Journal of Personality and Social Psychology, 70,* 381–394.

Piner, K. E., & Kahle, L. R. (1984). Adapting to the stigmatizing label of mental illness: Foregone but not forgotten. *Journal of Personality and Social Psychology, 47,* 805–811.

Pines, M. (1981, September). The civilizing of Genie. *Psychology Today,* pp. 28–34.

Piper, A. (1993). Tricyclic antidepressants versus electroconvulsive therapy: A review of the evidence for efficacy in depression. *Annals of Clinical Psychiatry, 5,* 13–23.

Plass, J. A., & Hill, K. T. (1986). Children's achievement strategies and test performance: The role of time pressure, evaluation, anxiety, and sex. *Developmental Psychology, 22,* 31–36.

Plomin, R. (1994). Nature, nurture, and social development. *Social Development, 3,* 37–53.

Plomin, R. (1995). Molecular genetics and psychology. *Current Directions in Psychological Science, 4,* 111–117.

Plomin, R., Corley, R., DeFries, J. C., & Fulker, D. W. (1990). Individual differences in television viewing in early childhood: Nature as well as nurture. *Psychological Science, 1,* 371–377.

Plomin, R., Loehlin, J. C., & DeFries, J. C. (1985). Genetic and environmental components of "environmental" influences. *Developmental Psychology, 21,* 394–402.

Plotkin, W. B. (1979). The alpha experience revisited: Biofeedback in the transformation of psychological state. *Psychological Bulletin, 86,* 1132–1148.

Plous, S. (1991) An attitude survey of animal rights activists. *Psychological Science, 2,* 192–196.

Plug, C., & Ross, H. E. (1994). The natural moon illusion: A multifactor angular account. *Perception, 23,* 321–333.

Plutchik, R. (1980, February). A language for the emotions. *Psychology Today,* pp. 68–78.

Podlesny, J. A., & Raskin, D. C. (1978). Effectiveness of techniques and physiological measures in the detection of deception. *Psychophysiology, 15,* 344–359.

Poincaré, H. (1948, August). Mathematical creation. *Scientific American,* pp. 14–17.

Polkinghorne, D. E. (1992). Research methodology in humanistic psychology. *Humanistic Psychologist, 20,* 218–242.

Pollack, M. H., Otto, M. W., Kaspi, S. P., & Hammerness, P. G. (1994). Cognitive behavior therapy for treatment-refractory panic disorder. *Journal of Clinical Psychiatry, 55,* 200–205.

Pollak, G. D., Wenstrup, J. J., & Fuzessey, Z. M. (1986). Auditory processing in the mustache bat's inferior colliculus. *Trends in Neurosciences, 9,* 556–561.

Pollard, P. (1995). Pornography and sexual aggression. *Current Psychology: Developmental, Learning, Personality, Social, 14,* 200–221.

Polster, E., & Polster, M. (1993). Frederick Perls: Legacy and invitation. *Gestalt Journal, 16,* 23–25.

Pomerleau, O. F. (1995). Individual differences in sensitivity to nicotine: Implications of genetic research on nicotine dependence. *Behavior Genetics, 25,* 161–177.

Poole, D. A., & White, L. T. (1993). Two years later: Effect of question repetition and retention interval on the eyewitness testimony of children and adults. *Developmental Psychology, 29,* 844–853.

Poppen, P. J. (1994). Adolescent contraceptive use and communication: Changes over a decade. *Adolescence, 29,* 503–514.

Popplestone, J. A., & McPherson, M. W. (1976). Ten years at the Archives of the History of American Psychology. *American Psychologist, 31,* 533–534.

Post, R. B., Lott, L. A., Beede, J. I., & Maddock, R. J. (1994). The effect of alcohol on the vestibulo-ocular reflex and apparent concomitant motion. *Journal of Vestibular Research, Equilibrium, and Orientation, 4,* 181–187.

Postman, L. (1985). Human learning and memory. In G. A. Kimble & K. Schlesinger (Eds.), *Topics in the history of psychology* (Vol. 1, pp. 69–134). Hillsdale, NJ: Erlbaum.

Potegal, M., Hebert, M., DeCoster, M., & Meyerhoff, J. L. (1996). Brief, high-frequency stimulation of the corticomedial amygdala induces a delayed and prolonged increase of aggressiveness in male Syrian golden hamsters. *Behavioral Neuroscience, 110,* 401–412.

Potgieter, J. R., & Venter, R. E. (1995). Relationship between adherence to exercise and scores on extraversion and neuroticism. *Perceptual and Motor Skills, 81,* 520–522.

Poulson, R. L. (1990). Mock juror attribution of criminal responsibility: Effects of race and the guilty but mentally ill (GBMI) verdict option. *Journal of Applied Social Psychology, 20,* 1596–1611.

Powell, D. J., & Fuller, R. W. (1983). Marijuana and sex: Strange bedpartners. *Journal of Psychoactive Drugs, 15,* 269–280.

Powell, S. (1993). Electra: The dark side of the moon. *Journal of Analytical Psychology, 38,* 155–173.

Prasinos, S., & Tittler, B. I. (1981). The family relationships of humor-oriented adolescents. *Journal of Personality, 47,* 295–305.

Pratkanis, A. R. (1992). The cargo-cult science of subliminal persuasion. *Skeptical Inquirer, 16,* 260–272.

Premack, D. (1965). Reinforcement theory. In D. Levine (Ed.), *Nebraska symposium on motivation* (pp. 123–188). Lincoln: University of Nebraska Press.

Premack, D. (1971). Language in chimpanzee? *Science, 172,* 808–822.

Prentice, D. A. (1994). Do language reforms change our way of thinking? *Journal of Language and Social Psychology, 13,* 3-19.

Prentice-Dunn, S., & Rogers, R. W. (1982). Effects of public and private self-awareness on deindividuation and aggression. *Journal of Personality and Social Psychology, 3,* 503–513.

Pribram, K. H. (1985, September). "Holism" could close cognition era. *APA Monitor,* pp. 5–6.

Price, R., & Gottesman, I. I. (1991). Body fat in identical twins reared apart: Roles for genes and environment. *Behavior Genetics, 21,* 1–7.

Price-Williams, E., Gordon, W., & Ramirez, M. (1969). Skill and conservation: A study of pottery-making children. *Developmental Psychology, 1,* 769.

Priester, J. R., & Petty, R. E. (1995). Source attributions and persuasion: Perceived honesty as a determinant of message scrutiny. *Personality and Social Psychology Bulletin, 21,* 637–654.

Pritchard, W. S., Robinson, J. H., deBethizy, J. D., & Davis, R. A. (1995). Caffeine and smoking: Subjective, performance, and psychophysiological effects. *Psychophysiology, 32,* 19–27.

Prochaska, J. O. (1984). *Systems of psychotherapy: A transtheoretical approach.* Homewood, IL: Dorsey.

Proeve, M. (1995). A multimodal therapy approach to treatment of borderline personality disorder: A case study. *Psychological Reports, 76,* 587–592.

Program power. (1981, April). *Scientific American,* pp. 83–85.

Prud'homme, M. J. L., Cohen, D. A. D., & Kalaska, J. F. (1994). Tactile activity in primate primary somatosensory cortex during active arm movements: Cytoarchitectonic distribution. *Journal of Neurophysiology, 71,* 173–181.

Psychic Abscam. (1983, March). *Discover,* pp. 10, 13.

A psychic Watergate. (1981, June). *Discover,* p. 8.

Puccio, G. J. (1991). William Duff's eighteenth century examination of original genius and its relationship to contemporary creativity research. *Journal of Creative Behavior, 25,* 1–10.

Puente, A. E. (1995). Roger Wolcott Sperry (1913–1994). *American Psychologist, 50,* 940–941.

Pullum, G. K. (1991). *The great Eskimo vocabulary hoax.* Chicago: University of Chicago Press.

Purdy, J. E., Harriman, A., & Molitorisz, J. (1993). Contributions to the history of psychology: XCV. Possible relations between theories of evolution and animal learning. *Psychological Reports, 73,* 211–223.

Purghe, F., & Coren, S. (1992). Subjective contours 1900–1990: Research trends and bibliography. *Perception and Psychophysics, 51,* 291–304.

Purifoy, F. E., Grodsky, A., & Giambra, L. M. (1992). The relationship of sexual daydreaming to sexual activity, sexual drive, and sexual attitudes for women across the life-span. *Archives of Sexual Behavior, 21,* 369–385.

Putnam, D. E., Finney, J. W., Barkley, P. L., & Bonner, M. J. (1994). Enhancing commitment improves adherence to a medical regimen. *Journal of Consulting and Clinical Psychology, 62,* 191–194.

Quinn, R. H. (1993). Confronting Carl Rogers: A developmental-interactional approach to person-centered therapy. *Journal of Humanistic Psychology, 33,* 6–23.

Rabin, J., & Wiley, R. (1994). Switching from forward-looking infrared to night vision goggles: Transitory effects on visual resolution. *Aviation, Space, and Environmental Medicine, 65,* 327–329.

Rabinowitz, F. E. (1994). The impact of an interpersonal encounter-group class for North American college students studying abroad. *Journal for Specialists in Group Work, 19,* 38–42.

Rabinowitz, F. M. (1984). The heredity-environment controversy: A Victorian legacy. *Canadian Psychology, 25,* 159–166.

Rachman, S. (1991). Neo-conditioning and the classical theory of fear acquisition. *Clinical Psychology Review, 11,* 155–173.

Rachman, S. J. (1993). Statistically significant difference or probable nonchance difference. *American Psychologist, 48,* 1093.

Raeburn, J. M., Atkinson, J. M., Dubignon, J. M., & Fitzpatrick, J. (1994). Superhealth Basic: Development and evaluation of a low-cost community-based lifestyle change programme. *Psychology and Health, 9,* 383–395.

Ragland, D. R., & Brand, R. J. (1988). Type A behavior and mortality from coronary heart disease. *New England Journal of Medicine, 318,* 65–69.

Raglin, J. S., & Turner, P. E. (1993). Anxiety and performance in track and field athletes: A comparison of the inverted-U hypothesis with Zone of Optimal Function theory. *Personality and Individual Differences, 14,* 163–171.

Rainey, D. W. (1994). Assaults on umpires: A statewide survey. *Journal of Sport Behavior, 17,* 148–155.

Rainwater, N., Sweet, A. A., Elliott, L., & Bowers, M. (1988). Systematic desensitization in the treatment of needle phobias for children with diabetes. *Child and Family Behavior Therapy, 10,* 19–31.

Raloff, J. (1982). Noise can be hazardous to your health. *Science News, 121,* 377–381.

Ramachandran, V. S. (1992). Filling in gaps in perception: Part I. *Current Directions in Psychological Science, 1,* 199–205.

Ramón y Cajal, S. (1937/1966). *Recollections of my life.* Cambridge, MA: MIT Press.

Rapee, R. M. (1991). Generalized anxiety disorder: A review of clinical features and theoretical concepts. *Clinical Psychology Review, 11,* 419–440.

Rapp, D. (1988). The reception of Freud by the British press: General interest and literary magazines, 1920–1925. *Journal of the History of the Behavioral Sciences, 24,* 191–201.

Raskin, D. C., & Podlesny, J. A. (1979). Truth and deception: A reply to Lykken. *Psychological Bulletin, 86,* 54–59.

Rasmussen, S. A. (1993). Genetic studies of obsessive-compulsive disorder. *Annals of Clinical Psychiatry, 5,* 241–247.

Rasmussen, S. A., & Eisen, J. L. (1990). Epidemiology of obsessive-compulsive disorder. *Journal of Clinical Psychiatry, 51,* 10–13.

Ratner, H. H., Schell, D. A., Crimmins, A., Mittelman, D., & Baldinelli, L. (1987). Changes in adults' prose recall: Aging or cognitive demands? *Developmental Psychology, 23,* 521–525.

Ratner, S. C., Karon, B. P., VandenBos, G. R., & Denny, M. R. (1981). The adaptive significance of the catatonic stupor in humans and animals from an evolutionary perspective. Academic *Psychology Bulletin, 3,* 273–279.

Ravelli, G. P., Stein, Z. A., & Susser, M. W. (1976). Obesity in young men after famine exposure in utero in early infancy. *New England Journal of Medicine, 295,* 349–353.

Rawdon, V. A., Willis, F. N., & Ficken, E. J. (1995). Locus of control in young adults in Russia and the United States. *Perceptual and Motor Skills, 80,* 599–604.

Ray, C. G., & Finley, J. K. (1994). Did CMHCs fail or succeed? Analysis of the expectations and outcomes of the community mental health movement. *Administration and Policy in Mental Health, 21,* 283–293.

Ray, O. (1983). *Drugs, society, and human behavior.* St. Louis: Mosby.

Rayner, K. (1993). Eye movements in reading: Recent developments. *Current Directions in Psychological Science, 2,* 81–85.

Read, M. S. (1982). Malnutrition and behavior. *Applied Research in Mental Retardation, 3,* 279–291.

Read, P. P. (1974). *Alive: The story of the Andes survivors.* Philadelphia: Lippincott.

Rebeta, J. L., Brooks, C. I., O'Brien, J. P., & Hunter, G. A. (1993). Variations in trait-anxiety and achievement motivation of college students as a function of classroom seating position. *Journal of Experimental Education, 61,* 257–267.

Redd, W. H., Jacobsen, P. B., Die-Trill, M., Dermatis, H., McEvoy, M., & Holland, J. C. (1987). Cognitive/attentional distraction in the control of conditioned nausea in pediatric cancer patients receiving chemotherapy. *Journal of Consulting and Clinical Psychology, 55,* 391–395.

Reddy, A. V., & Reddy, P. B. (1983). Creativity and intelligence. *Psychological Studies, 28,* 20–24.

Redfern, S., Dancey, C. P., & Dryden, W. (1993). Empathy: Its effect on how counsellors are perceived. *British Journal of Guidance and Counselling, 21,* 300–309.

Reed, T. E. (1993). Effect of enriched (complex) environment on nerve conduction velocity: New data and review of implications for the speed of information processing. *Intelligence, 17,* 533–540.

Reeder, K., & Shapiro, J. (1993). Relationships between early literate experience and knowledge and children's linguistic pragmatic strategies. *Journal of Pragmatics, 19,* 1–22.

Rees, L. (1983). The development of psychosomatic medicine during the past 25 years. *Journal of Psychosomatic Medicine, 27,* 157–164.

Reese, E. P. (1986). Learning about teaching from teaching about learning: Presenting behavioral analysis in an introductory survey course. In V. P. Makosky (Ed.), *The G. Stanley Hall Lecture Series* (Vol. 6, pp. 65–127). Washington, DC: American Psychological Association.

Reese, H. W., & Fremouw, W. J. (1984). Normal and normative ethics in behavioral sciences. *American Psychologist, 39,* 863–876.

Reilly, R. R., & Chao, G. R. (1982). Validity and fairness of some alternative employee selection procedures. *Personnel Psychology, 35,* 1–62.

Reiman, E. M., Fusselman, M. J., Fox, P. T., & Raichle, M. E. (1989). Neuroanatomical correlates of anticipatory anxiety. *Science, 243,* 1071–1074.

Reiman, E. M., Raichle, M. E., Butler, F. K., Herscovitch, P., & Robins, E. (1984). A focal brain abnormality in panic disorder, a severe form of anxiety. *Nature, 310,* 683–685.

Reinisch, J. M. (1981). Prenatal exposure to synthetic progestins increases potential for aggression in humans. *Science, 211,* 1171–1173.

Reis, S. (1989). Reflections on policy affecting the education of gifted and talented students: Past and future perspectives. *American Psychologist, 44,* 399–408.

Reisenzein, R. (1983). The Schachter theory of emotion: Two decades later. *Psychological Bulletin, 94,* 239–264.

Reitman, J. S. (1974). Without surreptitious rehearsal, information in short-term memory decays. *Journal of Verbal Learning and Verbal Behavior, 13,* 365–377.

Rejeski, J., Gregg, E., Thompson, A., & Berry, M. (1991). The effects of varying doses of acute aerobic exercise on psychophysiological stress responses in highly trained cyclists. *Journal of Sport and Exercise Psychology, 13,* 188–199.

Renik, O. (1995). The role of an analyst's expectations in clinical technique: Reflections on the concept of resistance. *Journal of the American Psychoanalytic Association, 43,* 83–94.

Renner, J. W., Abraham, M. R., Grzybowski, E. B., & Marek, E. A. (1990). Understandings and misunderstandings of eighth graders of four physics concepts found in textbooks. *Journal of Research in Science Teaching, 27,* 35–54.

Rennie, D. L. (1994). Clients' accounts of resistance in counselling: A qualitative analysis. *Canadian Journal of Counselling, 28,* 43–57.

Rescorla, R. A. (1968). Probability of shock in the presence and absence of CS in fear conditioning. *Journal of Comparative and Physiological Psychology, 66,* 1–5.

Rescorla, R. A. (1988). Pavlovian conditioning: It's not what you think it is. *American Psychologist, 43,* 151–160.

Rescorla, R. A., & Holland, P. C. (1982). Behavioral studies of associative learning in animals. *Annual Review of Psychology, 33,* 265–308.

Reynaert, C., Janne, P., Bosly, A., & Staquet, P. (1995). From health locus of control to immune control: Internal locus of control has a buffering effect on natural killer cell activity decrease in major depression. *Acta Psychiatrica Scandinavica, 92,* 294–300.

Rheingold, H. L., & Adams, J. L. (1980). The significance of speech to newborns. *Developmental Psychology, 16,* 397–403.

Rhodes, N., & Wood, W. (1992). Self-esteem and intelligence affect influenceability: The mediating role of message reception. *Psychological Bulletin, 111,* 156–171.

Rhodewalt, F., & Hill, S. K. (1995). Self-handicapping in the classroom: The effects of claimed self-handicaps on responses to academic failure. *Basic and Applied Social Psychology, 16,* 397–416.

Rhodewalt, F., Sanbonmatsu, D. M., Tschanz, B., & Feick, D. L. (1995). Self-handicapping and interpersonal trade-offs: The effects of claimed self-handicaps on observers' performance evaluations and feedback. *Personality and Social Psychology Bulletin, 21,* 1042–1050.

Ricci, L. C., & Wellman, M. M. (1990). Monoamines: Biochemical markers of suicide? *Journal of Clinical Psychology, 46,* 106–116.

Rice, M. L. (1989). Children's language acquisition. *American Psychologist, 44,* 149–156.

Richardson, J. T. E., & Zucco, G. M. (1989). Cognition and olfaction: A review. *Psychological Bulletin, 105,* 352–360.

Rickabaugh, C. A. (1993). The psychology portfolio: Promoting writing and critical thinking about psychology. *Teaching of Psychology, 20,* 170–172.

Rickard, N. S., & Ng, K. T. (1995). Blockade of metabotropic glutamate receptors prevents long-term memory consolidation. *Brain Research Bulletin, 36,* 355–359.

Rieber, R. W. (Ed.). (1980). *Wilhelm Wundt and the making of a scientific psychology.* New York: Plenum.

Rierdan, J., & Koff, E. (1985). Premenarcheal predictors of the experience of menarche: A prospective study. *Journal of Adolescent Health Care, 11,* 404–407.

Riggio, R. E. (1996). *Introduction to industrial/organizational psychology* (2nd ed.). New York: HarperCollins.

Riggs, L. A. (1985). Sensory processes: Vision. In G. A. Kimble & K. Schlesinger (Eds.), *Topics in the history of psychology* (Vol. 1, pp. 165–220). Hillsdale, NJ: Erlbaum.

Rilling, M. (1996). The mystery of the vanished citations: James McConnell's forgotten 1960s quest for planarian learning, a biochemical engram, and celebrity. *American Psychologist, 51,* 589–598.

Rinaldi, R. C. (1987). Patient-therapist personality similarity and the therapeutic relationship. *Psychotherapy in Private Practice, 5,* 11–29.

Rinn, W. E. (1984). The neuropsychology of facial expression: A review of the neurological and psychological mechanisms for producing facial expressions. *Psychological Bulletin, 95,* 52–77.

Riordan, C. A., & Tedeschi, J. T. (1983). Attraction in aversive environments: Some evidence for classical conditioning and negative reinforcement. *Journal of Personality and Social Psychology, 44,* 683–692.

Risch, N., Squires-Wheeler, E., & Keats, B. J. B. (1993). Male sexual orientation and genetic evidence. *Science, 262,* 2063–2065.

Rittenhouse, C. D., Stickgold, R., & Hobson, J. A. (1994). Constraint on the transformation of characters, objects, and settings in dream reports. *Consciousness and Cognition: An International Journal, 3,* 100–113.

Rivera-Tovar, L. A., & Jones, R. T. (1990). Effect of elaboration on the acquisition and maintenance of cardiopulmonary resuscitation. *Journal of Pediatric Psychology, 15,* 123–138.

Rivinus, T. M. (1990). The deadly embrace: The suicidal impulse and substance use and abuse in the college student. *Journal of College Student Psychotherapy, 4,* 45–77.

Roback, H. B., & Shelton, M. (1995). Effects of confidentiality limitations on the psychotherapeutic process. *Journal of Psychotherapy Practice and Research, 4,* 185–193.

Robert, M. (1990). Observational learning in fish, birds, and mammals: A classified bibliography spanning over 100 years of research. *Psychological Record, 40,* 289–311.

Roberts, A. H. (1985). Biofeedback: Research, training, and clinical roles. *American Psychologist, 40,* 938–941.

Roberts, J. E., & Schuele, C. M. (1990). Otitis media and later academic performance: The linkage and implications for intervention. *Topics in Language Disorders, 11,* 43–62.

Roberts, M. C., & Fanurik, D. (1986). Rewarding elementary school children for their use of safety belts. *Health Psychology, 5,* 185–196.

Roberts, P., & Newton, P. M. (1987). Levinsonian studies of women's adult development. *Psychology and Aging, 2,* 154–163.

Roberts, S. J. (1988). Social support and help seeking: Review of the literature. *Advances in Nursing Science, 10,* 1–11.

Robertson, H. A. (1992). Dopamine receptor interactions: Some implications for the treatment of Parkinson's disease. *Trends in Neurosciences, 15,* 201–206.

Robins, L. N., Helzer, J. E., Weissman, M. M., Orvaschel, H., Gruenberg, E., Burke, J. D., Jr., & Regier, D. A. (1984). Lifetime prevalence of specific psychiatric disorders in three sites. *Archives of General Psychiatry, 41,* 949–958.

Robins, R. W., & Craik, K. H. (1994). A more appropriate test of the Kuhnian displacement thesis. *American Psychologist, 49,* 815–816.

Robinson, F. P. (1970). *Effective study.* New York: Harper & Row.

Rock, I., Gopnik, A., & Hall, S. (1994). Do young children reverse ambiguous figures? *Perception, 23,* 635–644.

Rockwell, T. (1979). Pseudoscience or pseudocriticism? *Journal of Parapsychology, 43,* 221–231.

Rodgers, C. D., Paterson, D. H., Cunningham, D. A., & Noble, E. G. (1995). Sleep deprivation: Effects on work capacity, self-paced walking, contractile properties and perceived exertion. *Sleep, 18,* 30–38.

Rodgers, J. E. (1982, June). The malleable memory of eyewitnesses. *Science, 82,* pp. 32–35.

Rodgers, J. L. (1988). Birth order, SAT, and confluence: Spurious correlations and no causality. *American Psychologist, 43,* 476–477.

Rodgers, R., & Hunter, J. E. (1991). Impact of management by objectives on organizational productivity. *Journal of Applied Psychology, 76,* 322–336.

Rodin, J. (1981). Current status of the internal-external hypothesis for obesity: What went wrong? *American Psychologist, 36,* 361–372.

Rodin, J. (1985). Insulin levels, hunger, and food intake: An example of feedback loops in body weight regulation. *Health Psychology, 4,* 1–23.

Rodin, J. (1986). Aging and health: Effects of the sense of control. *Science, 233,* 1271–1276.

Roe, C. A. (1995). Pseudopsychics and the Barnum effect *European Journal of Parapsychology, 11,* 76–91.

Roethlisberger, F. J., & Dickson, E. J. (1939). *Management and the worker.* Cambridge: Harvard University Press.

Rogers, C. R. (1951). *Client-centered therapy.* Boston: Houghton Mifflin.

Rogers, C. R. (1957). The necessary and sufficient conditions of therapeutic personality change. *Journal of Consulting Psychology, 21,* 95–103.

Rogers, C. R. (1968). Interpersonal relationships. *Journal of Applied Behavioral Science, 4,* 1–12.

Rogers, C. R. (1985). Toward a more human science of the person. *Journal of Humanistic Psychology, 25,* 7–24.

Rogers, R. (1987). APA's position on the insanity defense: Empiricism versus emotionalism. *American Psychologist, 42,* 840–848.

Rogers, R. C. (1985). The chemical senses. *Science, 229,* 374–375.

Rogers, R. L., Meyer, J. S., & Mortel, K. F. (1990). After reaching retirement age physical activity sustains cerebral perfusion and cognition. *Journal of the American Geriatrics Society, 38,* 123–128.

Rogers, R., Duncan, J. C., Lynett, E., & Sewell, K. W. (1994). Prototypical analysis of antisocial personality disorder: DSM-IV and beyond. *Law and Human Behavior, 18,* 471–484.

Rogoff, B., & Chavajay, P. (1995). What's become of research on the cultural basis of cognitive development? *American Psychologist, 50,* 459–477.

Roig, M. (1993). Summarizing parapsychology in psychology textbooks: A rejoinder to Kalat and Kohn. *Teaching of Psychology, 20,* 174–175.

Rokeach, M. (1964/1981). *The three Christs of Ypsilanti.* New York: Columbia University Press.

Rokeach, M., & Mezei, L. (1966). Race and shared belief as factors in social choice. *Science, 151,* 167–172.

Rolnick, A., & Bles, W. (1989). Performance and well-being under tilting conditions: The effects of visual reference and artificial horizon. *Aviation, Space, and Environmental Medicine, 60,* 779–785.

Rolnick, A., & Lubow, R. E. (1991). Why is the driver rarely motion sick? The role of controllability in motion sickness. *Ergonomics, 34,* 867–879.

Rondall, J. A. (1994). Pieces of minds in psycholinguistics: Steven Pinker, Kenneth Wexler, and Noam Chomsky. *International Journal of Psychology, 29,* 85–104.

Rook, K. S., Catalano, R., & Dooley, D. (1989). The timing of major life events: Effects of departing from the social clock. *American Journal of Community Psychology, 17,* 233–258.

Rorer, L. G., & Widiger, T. A. (1983). Personality structure and assessment. *Annual Review of Psychology, 34,* 431–463.

Rosch, E. (1975). Cognitive representations of semantic categories. *Journal of Experimental Psychology: General, 104,* 192–233.

Rose, J. E., & Fantino, E. (1978). Conditioned reinforcement and discrimination in second-order schedules. *Journal of the Experimental Analysis of Behavior, 29,* 393–418.

Roseman, I. J., Dhawan, N., Rettek, S. I., & Naidu, R. K. (1995). Cultural differences and cross-cultural similarities in appraisals and emotional responses. *Journal of Cross-Cultural Psychology, 26,* 23–48.

Rosen, D. H., Smith, S. M., Huston, H. L., & Gonzalez, G. (1991). Empirical study of associations between symbols and their meanings: Evidence of collective unconscious (archetypal) memory. *Journal of Analytical Psychology, 36,* 211–228.

Rosenbaum, M. E. (1986). The repulsion hypothesis: On the nondevelopment of relationships. *Journal of Personality and Social Psychology, 51,* 1156–1166.

Rosenfeld, J. P., & Xia, L. Y. (1993) Reversible tetracaine block of rat periaqueductal gray (PAG) decreases baseline tail-flick latency and prevents analgesic effects of met-enkephalin injections in nucleus paragigantocellularis (PGC). *Brain Research, 605,* 57–66.

Rosenhan, D. L. (1973). On being sane in insane places. *Science, 179,* 250–258.

Rosenman, R. H., Brand, R. J., Jenkins, D., Friedman, M., Straus, R., & Wurm, M. (1975). Coronary heart disease in the Western Collaborative Group Study: Final follow-up experience of 8½ years. *Journal of the American Psychological Association, 233,* 872–877.

Rosenthal, R. (1995). Ethical issues in psychological science: Risk, consent, and scientific quality. *Psychological Science, 6,* 322–323.

Rosenthal, R., & Fode, K. L. (1963). The effect of experimenter bias on the performance of the albino rat. *Behavioral Science, 8,* 183–189.

Rosenthal, R., & Jacobson, L. (1968). *Pygmalion in the classroom.* New York: Holt, Rinehart & Winston.

Rosenzweig, M. R. (1996). Aspects of the search for neural mechanisms of memory. *Annual Review of Psychology, 47,* 1–32.

Rosenzweig, M. R., & Bennett, E. L. (1996). Psychobiology of plasticity: Effects of training and experience on brain and behavior. *Behavioural Brain Research, 78,* 57-65.

Ross, D. (1972). *G. Stanley Hall: The psychologist as prophet.* Chicago: University of Chicago Press.

Ross, E. D., Edmondson, J. A., Seibert, G. B., & Homan, R. W. (1988). Acoustic analysis of affective prosody during right-sided Wada test: A within-subjects verification of the right hemisphere's role in language. *Brain and Language, 33,* 128–145.

Ross, M. J., & Berger, R. S. (1996). Effects of stress inoculation training on athletes' postsurgical pain and rehabilitation after orthopedic injury. *Journal of Consulting and Clinical Psychology, 64,* 406–410.

Rossi, A. F., Rittenhouse, C. D., & Paradiso, M. A. (1996). The representation of brightness in primary visual cortex. *Science, 273,* 1104-1107.

Rossi, A. M., & Seiler, W. J. (1989–1990). The comparative effectiveness of systematic desensitization and an integrative approach in treating public speaking anxiety: A literature review and a preliminary investigation. *Imagination, Cognition, and Personality, 9,* 49–66.

Rossi, B., & Creatti, L. (1993). The sensation seeking in mountain athletes as assessed by Zuckerman's Sensation Seeking Scale. *International Journal of Sport Psychology, 24,* 417–431.

Rossi, F. (1988, November 8). Stress test. *Philadelphia Inquirer,* pp. 1E, 10E.

Roth, T. (1995). An overview of the report of the National Commission on Sleep Disorders Research. *European Psychiatry, 10,* 109s-113s.

Rothbaum, B. O., & Foa, E. B. (1991). Exposure treatment of PTSD concomitant with conversion mutism: A case study. *Behavior Therapy, 22,* 449–456.

Rothblum, E. D. (1990). Psychological factors in the Antarctic. *Journal of Psychology, 124,* 253–273.

Rothman, A. J., & Salovey, P. (1997). Shaping perceptions to motivate healthy behavior: The role of message framing. *Psychological Bulletin, 121,* 3-19.

Rothstein, H. R., Schmidt, F. L., Erwin, F. W., Owens, W. A., & Sparks, C. P. (1990). Biographical data in employment selection: Can validities be made generalizable? *Journal of Applied Psychology, 75,* 175–184.

Rotter, J. B. (1966). Generalized expectancies for internal versus external control of reinforcement. *Psychological Monographs, 80.*

Rotter, J. B. (1990). Internal versus external control of reinforcement: Case history of a variable. *American Psychologist, 45,* 489–493.

Rotton, J., & Kelly, I. W. (1985). Much ado about the full moon: A meta-analysis of lunar-lunacy research. *Psychological Bulletin, 97,* 286–306.

Roug, L., Landberg, I., & Lundberg, L. J. (1989). Phonetic development in early infancy: A study of four Swedish children during the first eighteen months of life. *Journal of Child Language, 16,* 19–40.

Routh, D. K. (1969). Conditioning of vocal response differentiation in infants. *Developmental Psychology, 1,* 219–226.

Rowan, A., & Shapiro, K. J. (1996). Animal rights, a bitten apple. *American Psychologist, 51*, 1183-1184.

Rowsell, H. C. (1988). The status of animal experimentation in Canada. *International Journal of Psychology, 23*, 377–381.

Roy, M.-A., Neale, M. C., Pedersen, N. L., & Mathe, A. A. (1995). A twin study of generalized anxiety disorder and major depression. *Psychological Medicine, 25*, 1037–1049.

Roy-Byrne, P. P., Uhde, T. W., Holcomb, H. H., & Thompson, K. (1987). Effects of diazepam on cognitive processes in normal subjects. *Psychopharmacology, 91*, 30–33.

Royer, J. M., Greene, B. A., & Anzalone, S. J. (1994). Can U.S. developed CAI work effectively in a developing country? *Journal of Educational Computing Research, 10*, 41–61.

Rozin, P., & Fallon, A. E. (1987). A perspective on disgust. *Psychological Review, 94*, 23–41.

Rozin, P., & Zellner, D. (1985). The role of Pavlovian conditioning in the acquisition of food likes and dislikes. *Annals of the New York Academy of Sciences, 443*, 189–202.

Rubin, J. R., Provenzano, F. J., & Luria, Z. (1974). The eye of the beholder: Parents' views on sex of newborns. *American Journal of Orthopsychiatry, 44*, 512–519.

Rubin, L. C., & Mills, M. J. (1983). Behavioral precipitants to civil commitment. *American Journal of Psychiatry, 140*, 603–606.

Rubin, R. T., Reinisch, J. M., & Haskett, R. F. (1981). Postnatal gonadal steroid effects on human behavior. *Science, 211*, 1318–1324.

Rubin, Z. (1985). Deceiving ourselves about deception: Comment on Smith and Richardson's "Amelioration of deception and harm in psychological research." *Journal of Personality and Social Psychology, 48*, 252–253.

Ruch, W., McGhee, P. E., & Hehl, F. J. (1990). Age differences in the enjoyment of incongruity-resolution and nonsense humor during adulthood. *Psychology and Aging, 5*, 348–355.

Ruda, M. A. (1982). Opiates and pain pathways: Demonstration of enkephalin synapses on dorsal horn projection neurons. *Science, 215*, 1523–1525.

Ruffin, C. L. (1993). Stress and health: Little hassles vs. major life events. *Australian Psychologist, 28*, 201–208.

Ruffman, T. K., & Olson, D. R. (1989). Children's ascriptions of knowledge to others. *Developmental Psychology, 25*, 601–606.

Rumbaugh, D. M., Gill, T. V., & von Glasersfeld, E. C. (1973). Reading and sentence completion by a chimpanzee (*Pan*). *Science, 182*, 731–733.

Rummel, A., & Feinberg, R. (1988). Cognitive Evaluation Theory: A meta-analytic review of the literature. *Social Behavior and Personality, 16*, 147–164.

Runco, M. A. (1993). Divergent thinking, creativity, and giftedness. *Gifted Child Quarterly, 37*, 16-22.

Rury, J. L. (1988). Race, region, and education: An analysis of black and white scores on the 1917 Army Alpha Intelligence Test. *Journal of Negro Education, 57*, 51–65.

Rushton, J. P. (1990). Creativity, intelligence, and psychoticism. *Personality and Individual Differences, 11*, 1291–1298.

Rushton, J. P., Fulker, D. W., Neale, M. C., Nias, D. K. B., & Eysenck, H. J. (1986). Altruism and aggression: The heritability of individual differences. *Journal of Personality and Social Psychology, 50*, 1192–1198.

Russell, J. A. (1991). In defense of a prototype approach to emotion concepts. *Journal of Personality and Social Psychology, 60*, 37–47.

Russell, J. A. (1995). Facial expressions of emotion: What lies beyond minimal universality? *Psychological Bulletin, 118*, 379–391.

Russell, J. A., & Fehr, B. (1987). Relativity in the perception of emotion in facial expressions. *Journal of Experimental Psychology: General, 116*, 223–237.

Russell, J. A., & Fehr, B. (1994). Fuzzy concepts in a fuzzy hierarchy: Varieties of anger. *Journal of Personality and Social Psychology, 67*, 186–205.

Russell, M. J. (1976). Human olfactory communication. *Nature, 260*, 520–522.

Rust, J., Golombok, S., & Collier, J. (1988). Marital problems and sexual dysfunction: How are they related? *British Journal of Psychiatry, 152*, 629–631.

Rutkowski, G. K., Gruder, C. L., & Romer, D. (1983). Group cohesiveness, social norms, and bystander intervention. *Journal of Personality and Social Psychology, 44*, 545–552.

Ryan, C. S., Judd, C. M., & Park, B. (1996). Effects of racial stereotypes on judgments of individuals: The moderating role of perceived group variability. *Journal of Experimental Social Psychology, 32*, 71–103.

Ryan, E. D. (1980). Attribution, intrinsic motivation, and athletics: A replication and extension. In C. H. Nadeau, W. R. Halliwell, K. M. Newell, & G. C. Roberts (Eds.), *Psychology of motor behavior and sport–1979* (pp. 19–26). Champaign, IL: Human Kinetics.

Ryan, R. H., & Geiselman, R. E. (1991). Effects of biased information on the relationship between eyewitness confidence and accuracy. *Bulletin of the Psychonomic Society, 29*, 7–9.

Rychlak, J. F. (1988). *The psychology of rigorous humanism*. New York: New York University Press.

Saal, F. E., Johnson, C. B., & Weber, N. (1989). Friendly or sexy? It may depend on whom you ask. *Psychology of Women Quarterly, 13*, 263–276.

Sabourin, M. E., Cutcomb, S. D., Crawford, H. J., & Pribram, K. (1990–1991). EEG correlates of hypnotic susceptibility and hypnotic trance: Spectral analysis and coherence. *International Journal of Psychophysiology, 10*, 125–142.

Sackeim, H. A. (1994). Central issues regarding the mechanisms of action of electroconvulsive therapy: Directions for future research. *Psychopharmacology Bulletin, 30*, 281–308.

Sacks, O. (1985). *The man who mistook his wife for a hat and other clinical tales*. New York: Summit.

Safford, F. (1991). Humor as an aid in gerontological education. *Gerontology and Geriatrics Education, 11*, 27–37.

Sagen, J., Pappas, G. D., & Perlow, M. J. (1986). Adrenal medullary tissue transplants in the rat spinal cord reduce pain sensitivity. *Brain Research, 384*, 189–194.

Salovey, P., & Haar, M. D. (1990). The efficacy of cognitive-behavior therapy and writing process training for alleviating writing anxiety. *Cognitive Therapy and Research, 14*, 513–526.

Salter, A. (1949). *Conditioned reflex therapy*. New York: Creative Age Press.

Salthouse, T. A. (1991). Mediation of adult age differences in cognition by reductions in working memory and speed of processing. *Psychological Science, 2*, 179–183.

Salzinger, K. (1994). The one with the most citations wins. *American Psychologist, 49*, 816.

Samelson, F. (1981). Struggle for scientific authority: The reception of Watson's behaviorism, 1913–1920. *Journal of the History of the Behavioral Sciences, 17*, 399–425.

Samelson, F. (1992). Rescuing the reputation of Sir Cyril Burt. *Journal of the History of the Behavioral Sciences, 28*, 221-233.

Samms, M., Hari, R., Rif, J., & Knuutila, J. (1993). The human auditory sensory memory trace persists about 10 sec: Neuromagnetic evidence. *Journal of Cognitive Neuroscience, 5*, 363–370.

Samuels, C. A., Butterworth, G., Roberts, T., & Graupner, L. (1994). Facial aesthetics: Babies prefer attractiveness to symmetry. *Perception, 23*, 823–831.

Sanderson, W. C., Beck, A. T., & McGinn, L. K. (1994). Cognitive therapy for generalized anxiety disorder: Significance of comorbid personality disorders. *Journal of Cognitive Psychotherapy, 8*, 13–18.

Sandford, D. A., Elzinga, R. H., & Grainger, W. (1987). Evaluation of a residential behavioral program for behaviorally disturbed, mentally retarded young adults. *American Journal of Mental Deficiency, 91*, 431–434.

Sanghvi, C. (1995). Efficacy of study skills training in managing study habits and test anxiety of high test anxious students. *Journal of the Indian Academy of Applied Psychology, 21*, 71-75.

Sanson, A., & di Muccio, C. (1993). The influence of aggressive and neutral cartoons and toys on the behaviour of preschool children. *Australian Psychologist, 28*, 93–99.

Santucci, A. C., Gluck, R., Kanof, P. D., Haroutunian, V. (1993). Induction of memory and cortical cholinergic neurochemical recovery with combined fetal transplantation and GM1 treatments in rats with lesions of the NBM. *Dementia, 4*, 273–281.

Sanua, V. C. (1994). Quo vadis APA? Inroads of the medical model. *Humanistic Psychologist, 22*, 3–27.

Sappington, A. A. (1990). Recent psychological approaches to the free will versus determinism issue. *Psychological Bulletin, 108*, 19–29.

Sarason, S. (1984). If it can be studied or developed, should it be? *American Psychologist, 39*, 477–485.

Satir, V., Bitter, J. R., & Krestensen, K. K. (1988). Family reconstruction: The family within–A group experience. *Journal for Specialists in Group Work, 13*, 200–208.

Satow, R., & Rector, J. (1995). Using Gestalt graphology to identify entrepreneurial leadership. *Perceptual and Motor Skills, 81*, 263–270.

Saucier, G., & Goldberg, L. R. (1996). Evidence for the Big Five in analyses of familiar English personality adjectives. *European Journal of Personality, 10*, 61–77.

Saudino, K. J., & Plomin, R. (1996). Personality and behavioral genetics: Where have we been and where are we going? *Journal of Research in Personality, 30*, 335-347.

Saunders, D. M., Fisher, W. A., Hewitt, E. C., & Clayton, J. P. (1985). A method for empirically assessing volunteer selection effects: Recruitment procedures and responses to erotica. *Journal of Personality and Social Psychology, 49*, 1703–1712.

Saunders, T., Driskell, J. E., Johnston, J. H., & Salas, E. (1996). The effect of stress inoculation training on anxiety and performance. *Journal of Occupational Health Psychology, 1*, 170–186.

Savage-Rumbaugh, E. S. (1987). Communication, symbolic communication, and language: Reply to Seidenberg and Petitto. *Journal of Experimental Psychology: General, 116*, 288–292.

Savage-Rumbaugh, E. S. (1990). Language acquisition in a nonhuman species: Implications for the innateness debate. *Developmental Psychobiology, 23*, 599–620.

Savage-Rumbaugh, E. S., McDonald, K., Sevcik, R. A., Hopkins, W. D., & Rupert, E. (1986). Spontaneous symbol acquisition and communicative use by pygmy chimpanzees (*Pan paniscus*). *Journal of Experimental Psychology: General, 115*, 211–235.

Savage-Rumbaugh, E. S., Murphy, J., Sevcik, R. A., & Brakke, K. E.. (1993). Language comprehension in ape and child. *Monographs of the Society for Research in Child Development, 58* (3/4), v–221.

Savage-Rumbaugh, E. S., Rumbaugh, D. M., Smith, S. T., & Lawson, J. (1980). Reference: The linguistic essential. *Science, 210*, 922–925.

Saxe, L. (1994). Detection of deception: Polygraph and integrity tests. *Current Directions in Psychological Science, 3*, 69–73.

Saxe, L., Dougherty, D., & Cross, T. (1985). The validity of polygraph testing: Scientific analysis and public controversy. *American Psychologist, 40*, 355–366.

Sayette, M. A., & Mayne, T. J. (1990). Survey of current clinical and research trends in clinical psychology. *American Psychologist, 45,* 1263–1266.

Scarborough, E., & Furumoto, L. (1987). *Untold lives: The first generation of American women psychologists.* New York: Columbia University Press.

Scarborough, H. S., Rescorla, L., Tager-Flusberg, H., & Fowler, A. E. (1991). The relation of utterance length to grammatical complexity in normal and language-disordered groups. *Applied Psycholinguistics, 12,* 23–45.

Scarr, S. (1985). Constructing psychology: Making facts and fables for our times. *American Psychologist, 40,* 499–512.

Scarr, S. (1988). Race and gender as psychological variables: Social and ethical issues. *American Psychologist, 43,* 56–59.

Scarr, S. (1995). Psychology will be truly evolutionary when behavior genetics is included. *Psychological Inquiry, 6,* 68-71.

Scarr, S., & Carter-Saltzman, L. (1979). Twin method: Defense of a critical assumption. *Behavior Genetics, 9,* 527–542.

Scarr, S., Phillips, D., & McCartney, K. (1990). Facts, fantasies, and the future of child care in the United States. *Psychological Science, 1,* 26–35.

Scarr, S., & Weinberg, R. A. (1976). IQ test performance of black children adopted by white families. *American Psychologist, 31,* 726–739.

Scarr, S., & Weinberg, R. A. (1983). The Minnesota Adoption Studies: Genetic differences and malleability. *Child Development, 54,* 260–267.

Schaal, B. (1988). Olfaction in infants and children: Developmental and functional perspectives. *Chemical Senses, 13,* 145–190.

Schachter, S. (1971). Some extraordinary facts about obese humans and rats. *American Psychologist, 26,* 129–144.

Schachter, S. (1982). Recidivism and self-cure of smoking and obesity. *American Psychologist, 37,* 436–444.

Schachter, S., & Singer, J. E. (1962). Cognitive, social and physiological determinants of emotional state. *Psychological Review, 69,* 379–399.

Schacter, D. L. (1983). Amnesia observed: Remembering and forgetting in a natural environment. *Journal of Abnormal Psychology, 92,* 236–242.

Schacter, D. L. (1992). Understanding implicit memory: A cognitive neuroscience approach. *American Psychologist, 47,* 559–569.

Schafe, G. E., Sollars, S. I., & Bernstein, I. L. (1995). The CS-US interval and taste aversion learning: A brief look. *Behavioral Neuroscience, 109,* 799–802.

Schaie, K. W. (1989). Perceptual speed in adulthood: Cross-sectional and longitudinal studies. *Psychology and Aging, 4,* 443–453.

Schaie, K. W., & Hertzog, C. (1983). Fourteen-year cohort-sequential analyses of adult intellectual development. *Developmental Psychology, 19,* 531–543.

Schaie, K. W., Labouvie, G. V., & Barrett, T. J. (1973). Selective attrition effects in a 14-year study of adult intelligence. *Journal of Gerontology, 28,* 328–334.

Schaller, M., & Cialdini, R. B. (1988). The economics of empathic helping: Support for a mood management motive. *Journal of Experimental Social Psychology, 24,* 163–181.

Scherer, K. R., & Wallbott, H. G. (1994). Evidence for universality and cultural variation of differential emotion

Schiff, M., Duyme, M., Dumaret, A., & Tomkiewicz, S. (1982). How much could we boost scholastic achievement and IQ scores? A direct answer from a French adoption study. *Cognition, 12,* 165–196.

Schiffman, S. S., Suggs, M. S., & Sattely-Miller, E. A. (1995). Effect of pleasant odors on mood of males at midlife: Comparison of African-American and European-American men. *Brain Research Bulletin, 36,* 31–37.

Schildkraut, J. J., Kopin, I. J., Schanberg, S. M., & Durell, J. (1995). Norepinephrine metabolism and psychoactive drugs in the endogenous depressions. *Pharmacopsychiatry, 28,* 24–37.

Schill, T., & O'Laughlin, M. S. (1984). Humor preference and coping with stress. *Psychological Reports, 55,* 309–310.

Schilling, R. F., & Weaver, G. E. (1983). Effects of extraneous verbal information on memory for telephone numbers. *Journal of Applied Psychology, 68,* 559–564.

Schlebusch, L., & Cassidy, M. J. (1995). Stress, social support and biopsychosocial dynamics in HIV-AIDS. *South African Journal of Psychology, 25,* 27–30.

Schleifer, L. M., & Amick, B. C. (1989). System response time and method of pay: Stress effects in computer-based tasks. *International Journal of Human-Computer Interaction, 1,* 23–39.

Schleifer, S. J., Keller, S. E., Camerino, M., Thornton, J. C., & Stein, M. (1983). Suppression of lymphocytic stimulation following bereavement. *Journal of the American Medical Association, 250,* 374–377.

Schlenker, B. R., Phillips, S. T., Boniecki, K. A., & Schlenker, D. R. (1995). Championship pressures: Choking or triumphing in one's own territory? *Journal of Personality and Social Psychology, 68,* 632–643.

Schlesinger, K. (1985). Behavioral genetics and the nature-nurture question. In G. A. Kimble & K. Schlesinger (Eds.), *Topics in the history of psychology* (Vol. 2, pp. 19–62). Hillsdale, NJ: Erlbaum.

Schmeidler, G. R. (1985). Belief and disbelief in psi. *Parapsychology Review, 16,* 1–4.

Schmidt, G., & Weiner, B. (1988). An attribution-affect-action theory of behavior: Replications of judgments of help-giving. *Personality and Social Psychology Bulletin, 14,* 610–621.

Schmidt, H. G., & Boshuizen, H. P. (1993). On acquiring expertise in medicine. *Educational Psychology Review, 5,* 205–221.

Schmidt, S. R., & Bohannon, J. N. (1988). In defense of the flashbulb-memory hypothesis: A comment on McCloskey, Wible, and Cohen (1988). *Journal of Experimental Psychology: General, 117,* 332–335.

Schnaiberg, A., & Goldenberg, S. (1989). From empty nest to crowded nest: The dynamics of incompletely launched young adults. *Social Problems, 36,* 251–269.

Schneider, C. J. (1987). Cost effectiveness of biofeedback and behavioral medicine treatments: A review of the literature. *Biofeedback and Self-Regulation, 12,* 71–92.

Schneider, F., Gur, R. E., Mozley, L. H., & Smith, R. J. (1995). Mood effects on limbic blood flow correlate with emotional self-rating: A PET study with oxygen-15 labeled water. *Psychiatry Research: Neuroimaging, 61,* 265–283.

Schneider, H. G., & Shugar, G. J. (1990). Audience and feedback effects in computer learning. *Computers in Human Behavior, 6,* 315–321.

Schneider, W., & Shiffrin, R. M. (1977). Controlled and automatic human information processing: I. Detection, search, and attention. *Psychological Review, 84,* 1–66.

Schneider, W. H. (1992). After Binet: French intelligence testing, 1900–1950. *Journal of the History of the Behavioral Sciences, 28,* 111–132.

Schoeneman, T. J., & Rubanowitz, D. E. (1985). Attributions in the advice columns: Actors and observers, causes and reasons. *Personality and Social Psychology Bulletin, 11,* 315–325.

Schonemann, P. H., & Schonemann, R. D. (1994). Environmental versus genetic models for Osborne's personality data on identical and fraternal twins. *Cahiers de Psychologie, 13,* 141–167.

Schroeder, D. A., Dovidio, J. F., Sibicky, M. E., Matthews, L. L., & Allen, J. L. (1988). Empathic concern and helping behavior: Egoism or altruism? *Journal of Experimental Social Psychology, 24,* 333–353.

Schoen, L. M. (1996). Mnemopoly: Board games and mnemonics. *Teaching of Psychology, 23,* 30-32.

Schroth, M. L. (1991). Dyadic adjustment and sensation seeking compatability. *Personality and Individual Differences, 12,* 467–471.

Schroth, M. L. (1995). A comparison of sensation seeking among different groups of athletes and nonathletes. *Personality and Individual Differences, 18,* 219–222.

Schrut, A. H. (1994). The Oedipus complex: Some observations and questions regarding its validity and universal existence. *Journal of the American Academy of Psychoanalysis, 22,* 727–751.

Schull, W. J., Norton, S., & Jensh, R. P. (1990). Ionizing radiation and the developing brain. *Neurotoxicology and Teratology, 12,* 249–260.

Schulz, P., & Kaspar, C. H. (1994). Neuroendocrine and psychological effects of restricted environmental stimulation technique in a flotation tank. *Biological Psychology, 37,* 161–175.

Schulz, R., & Curnow, C. (1988). Peak performance and age among superathletes: Track and field, swimming, baseball, tennis, and golf. *Journal of Gerontology, 43,* 113–120.

Schuster, B., Forsterling, F., & Weiner, B. (1989). Perceiving the causes of success and failure: A cross-cultural examination of attributional concepts. *Journal of Cross-Cultural Psychology, 20,* 191–213.

Schwartz, B. L., & Smith, S. M. (1997). The retrieval of related information influences tip-of-the-tongue states. *Journal of Memory and Language, 36,* 68-86.

Schwartz, P. J., Brown, C., Wehr, T. A., & Rosenthal, N. E. (1996). Winter seasonal affective disorder: A follow-up study of the first 59 patients of the National Institute of Mental Health Seasonal Studies Program. *American Journal of Psychiatry, 153,* 1028–1036.

Schwarz, T., Loewenstein, J., & Isenberg, K. E. (1995). Maintenance ECT: Indications and outcome. *Convulsive Therapy, 11,* 14–23.

Schwolow, R., Wilckens, E., & Roth, N. (1988). Effect of transcutaneous nerve stimulation (TENS) on dental pain: Comparison of psychophysical and neurophysiological data and application in dentistry. *Activitas Nervosa Superior, 30,* 129–130.

Scott, D., & Willits, F. K. (1994). Environmental attitudes and behavior: A Pennsylvania survey. *Environment and Behavior, 26,* 239–260.

Scott, K. G., & Carran, D. T. (1987). The epidemiology and prevention of mental retardation. *American Psychologist, 42,* 801–804.

Scott, K. D., & Taylor, G. S. (1985). An examination of conflicting findings on the relationship between job satisfaction and absenteeism: A meta-analysis. *Academy of Management Journal, 28,* 599–612.

Scoville, W. B., & Milner, B. (1957). Loss of recent memory after bilateral hippocampal lesions. *Journal of Neurology, Neurosurgery, and Psychiatry, 20,* 11–21.

Sears, D. O. (1986). College sophomores in the laboratory: Influences of a narrow data base on social psychology's view of human nature. *Journal of Personality and Social Psychology, 51,* 515–530.

Sears, R. R. (1977). Source of life satisfaction of the Terman gifted men. *American Psychologist, 32,* 119–128.

Sechrest, L. (1984). Review of The development and application of social language theory: Selected papers. *Journal of the History of the Behavioral Sciences, 20,* 228–230.

Sedlacek, K., & Taub, E. (1996). Biofeedback treatment of Raynaud's disease. *Professional Psychology: Research and Practice, 27,* 548-553.

Seeman, J. (1990). Theory as autobiography: The development of Carl Rogers. *Person-Centered Review, 5*, 373–386.

Segal, J., & Luce, G. G. (1966). *Sleep*. New York: Arena Books.

Segal, M. W. (1974). Alphabet and attraction: An unobtrusive measure of the effect of propinquity in a field setting. *Journal of Personality and Social Psychology, 30*, 654–657.

Segall, M. H., Dasen, P. R., Berry, J. W., & Poortinga, Y. H. (1990). *Human behavior in global perspective: An introduction to cross-cultural psychology*. New York: Pergamon.

Seligman, M. E. P. (1970). On the generality of the laws of learning. *Psychological Review, 77*, 406–418.

Seligman, M. E. P. (1971). Phobias and preparedness. *Behavior Therapy, 2*, 307–320.

Seligman, M. E. P. (1989). Research in clinical psychology: Why is there so much depression today? In I. S. Cohen (Ed.), *The G. Stanley Hall Lecture Series* (Vol. 9, pp. 75–96). Washington, DC: American Psychological Association.

Seligman, M. E. P., & Maier, S. F. (1967). Failure to escape traumatic shock. *Journal of Experimental Psychology, 74*, 1–9.

Selye, H. (1936). A syndrome produced by diverse nocuous agents. *Nature, 138*, 32.

Selye, H. (1980). The stress concept today. In I. L. Kutash, L. B. Schlesinger, & Associates (Eds.), *Handbook on stress and anxiety* (pp. 127–143). San Francisco: Jossey-Bass.

Senkfor, A. J., & Williams, J. M. (1995). The moderating effects of aerobic fitness and mental training on stress reactivity. *Journal of Sport Behavior, 18*, 130–156.

Serebriakoff, V. (1985). *Mensa: The society for the highly intelligent*. New York: Stein & Day.

Serok, S., & Levi, N. (1993). Application of Gestalt therapy with long-term prison inmates in Israel. *Gestalt Journal, 16*, 105–127.

Seroussi, D.–E. (1995). Heuristic hypotheses in problem solving: An example of conceptual issues about scientific procedures. *Science Education, 79*, 595–609.

Seto, M. C., Lalumiere, M. L., & Quinsey, V. L. (1995). Sensation seeking and males' sexual strategy. *Personality and Individual Differences, 19*, 669–675.

Severi, B. (1994). Parapsychological publications in non–parapsychology journals. *European Journal of Parapsychology, 10*, 104–129.

Seyfarth, R. M., Cheney, D. L., & Marler, P. (1980). Monkey responses to three different alarm calls: Evidence for predator classification and semantic communication. *Science, 210*, 801–803.

Seymour, G. O., Stahl, J. M., Levine, S. L., & Ingram, J. L. (1994). Modifying law enforcement training simulators for use in basic research. *Behavior Research Methods, Instruments and Computers, 26*, 266–268.

Sforza, E., & Lugaresi, E. (1995). Daytime sleepiness and nasal continuous positive airway pressure therapy in obstructive sleep apnea syndrome patients: Effects of chronic treatment and one-night therapy withdrawal. *Sleep, 18*, 195–201.

Shaffer, J. W., Graves, P. L., Swank, R. T., & Pearson, T. A. (1987). Clustering of personality traits in youth and the subsequent development of cancer among physicians. *Journal of Behavioral Medicine, 10*, 441–447.

Shafran, R., Watkins, E., & Charman, T. (1996). Guilt in obsessive-compulsive disorder. *Journal of Anxiety Disorders, 10*, 509–516.

Shah, M., & Jeffery, R. W. (1991). Is obesity due to overeating and inactivity, or to a defective metabolic rate? A review. *Annals of Behavioral Medicine, 13*, 73–81.

Shaham, Y., Singer, J. E., & Schaeffer, M. H. (1992). Stability/instability of cognitive strategies across tasks determine whether stress will affect judgmental processes. *Journal of Applied Social Psychology, 22*, 691–713.

Shanab, M. E., & Yahya, K. A. (1977). A behavioral study of obedience in children. *Journal of Personality and Social Psychology, 35*, 530–536.

Shapiro, C. M., Bortz, R., Mitchell, D., Bartel, P., & Jooste, P. (1981). Slow-wave sleep: A recovery period after exercise. *Science, 214*, 1253–1254.

Shapiro, D. A. (1995). Finding out how psychotherapies help people change. *Psychotherapy Research, 5*, 1–21.

Shapiro, J. K. (1995). Dr. Kohlberg goes to Washington: Using congressional debates to teach moral development. *Teaching of Psychology, 22*, 244–247.

Shapley, R. (1990). Visual sensitivity and parallel retinocortical channels. *Annual Review of Psychology, 41*, 635–658.

Sharp, C. W., & Freeman, C. P. (1993). The medical complications of anorexia nervosa. *British Journal of Psychiatry, 162*, 452–462.

Sharpe, D., Adair, J. G., & Roese, N. J. (1992). Twenty years of deception research: A decline in subjects' trust? *Personality and Social Psychology Bulletin, 18*, 585–590.

Sharpsteen, D. J. (1993). Romantic jealousy as an emotion concept: A prototype analysis. *Journal of Social and Personal Relationships, 10*, 69–82.

Shaughnessy, M. F., & Nystul, M. S. (1985). Preventing the greatest loss—suicide. *Creative Child and Adult Quarterly, 10*, 164–169.

Shavitt, S., Swan, S., Lowrey, T. M., & Wanke, M. (1994). The interaction of endorser attractiveness and involvement in persuasion depends on the goal that guides message processing. *Journal of Consumer Psychology, 3*, 137–162.

Shea, M. T., Elkin, I., Imber, S. D., & Sotsky, S. M. (1992). Course of depressive symptoms over follow-up: Findings from the National Institute of Mental Health Treatment of Depression Collaborative Research Program. *Archives of General Psychiatry, 49*, 782–787.

Shearn, D. W. (1962). Operant conditioning of heart rate. *Science, 137*, 530–531.

Sheehan, P. W., & Tilden, J. (1983). Effects of suggestibility and hypnosis on accurate and distorted retrieval from memory. *Journal of Experimental Psychology: Learning, Memory, and Cognition, 9*, 283–293.

Shefler, G., Dasberg, H., & Ben-Shakhar, G. A. (1995). A randomized controlled outcome and follow-up study of Mann's time-limited psychotherapy. *Journal of Consulting and Clinical Psychology, 63*, 585–593.

Sheldon, W. H., & Stevens, S. S. (1942). *The varieties of temperament: A psychology of constitutional differences*. New York: Harper.

Shell, D. F., Colvin, C., & Bruning, R. H. (1995). Self-efficacy, attribution, and outcome expectancy mechanisms in reading and writing achievement: Grade-level and achievement-level differences. *Journal of Educational Psychology, 87*, 386–398.

Shettleworth, S. J., & Juergensen, M. R. (1980). Reinforcement of the organization of behavior in golden hamsters: Brain stimulation reinforcement for seven action patterns. *Journal of Experimental Psychology: Animal Behavior Processes, 6*, 352–375.

Shevrin, H., & Dickman, S. (1980). The psychological unconscious: A necessary assumption for all psychological theory? *American Psychologist, 35*, 421–434.

Shields, S. A. (1975). Functionalism, Darwinism, and the psychology of women: A study in social myth. *American Psychologist, 30*, 737–754.

Shiffman, S., Paty, J. A., Gnys, M., & Kassel, J. D. (1995). Nicotine withdrawal in chippers and regular smokers: Subjective and cognitive effects. *Health Psychology, 14*, 301–309.

Shiffrin, R. M., & Atkinson, R. C. (1969). Storage and retrieval processes in long-term memory. *Psychological Review, 76*, 179–193.

Shiraishi, T. (1990). CCK as a central satiety factor: Behavioral and electrophysiological evidence. *Physiology and Behavior, 48*, 879–885.

Shneidman, E. (1987, March). At the point of no return. *Psychology Today*, pp. 54–58.

Shneidman, E. S. (1994). Clues to suicide reconsidered. *Suicide and Life-Threatening Behavior, 24*, 395–397.

Shockley, W. (1972). Dysgenics, geneticity, raceology: A challenge to the intellectual responsibility of educators. *Phi Delta Kappan, 53*, 297–307.

Short, R. H., & Hess, G. C. (1995). Fetal alcohol syndrome: Characteristics and remedial implications. *Developmental Disabilities Bulletin, 23*, 12–29.

Shostrom, E. L. (1962). *Personal orientation inventory*. San Diego: EDITS.

Shotland, R. L., & Straw, M. J. (1976). Bystander response to an assault: When a man attacks a woman. *Journal of Personality and Social Psychology, 34*, 990–999.

Shultz, T. R., & Lepper, M. R. (1996). Cognitive dissonance reduction as constraint satisfaction. *Psychological Review, 103*, 219–240.

Shurcliff, A. (1968). Judged humor, arousal, and the relief theory. *Journal of Personality and Social Psychology, 8*, 360–363.

Shweder, R. A., & Sullivan, M. A. (1993). Cultural psychology: Who needs it? *Annual Review of Psychology, 44*, 497–521.

Siberstein, A. (1988). An Aristotlean resolution of the idiographic versus nomothetic tension. *American Psychologist, 43*, 425–430.

Siegel, J. M., & Brown, J. D. (1988). A prospective study of stressful circumstances, illness symptoms, and depressed mood among adolescents. *Developmental Psychology, 24*, 715–721.

Siegel, S., Hinson, R., Krank, M. D., & McCully, J. (1982). Heroin overdose death: Contribution of drug-associated environmental cues. *Science, 216*, 436–437.

Sierra-Honigmann, A. M., Carbone, K. M., & Yolken, R. H. (1995). Polymerase chain reaction (PCR) search for viral nucleic acid sequences in schizophrenia. *British Journal of Psychiatry, 166*, 55–60.

Silbersweig, D. A., Stern, E., Frith, C., & Cahill, C. (1995). A functional neuroanatomy of hallucinations in schizophrenia. *Nature, 378*, 176–179.

Silinsky, E. M. (1989). Adenosine derivatives and neuronal function. *Seminars in the Neurosciences, 1*, 155–165.

Silva, J. M., III, & Weinberg, R. S. (1984). *Psychological foundations of sport*. Champaign, IL: Human Kinetics.

Silver, E., Cirincione, C., & Steadman, H. J. (1994). Demythologizing inaccurate perceptions of the insanity defense. *Law and Human Behavior, 18*, 63–70.

Silverstein, L. B. (1991). Transforming the debate about child care and maternal employment. *American Psychologist, 46*, 1025–1032.

Simon, H. A. (1995). The information-processing theory of mind. *American Psychologist, 50*, 505–506.

Simon, N. (1979). Kaspar Hauser's recovery and autopsy: A perspective on neurological and sociological requirements for language development. *Annual Progress in Child Psychiatry and Child Development*, 215–224.

Simons, A. D., Garfield, S. L., & Murphy, G. E. (1984). The process of change in cognitive therapy and pharmacotherapy for depression. *Archives of General Psychiatry, 41*, 45–51.

Simons, R. L., Whitbeck, L. B., Conger, R. D., & Wu, C. I. (1991). Intergenerational transmission of harsh parenting. *Developmental Psychology, 27*, 159–171.

Simonton, D. K. (1988). Age and outstanding achievement: What do we know after a century of research? *Psychological Bulletin, 104*, 251–267.

Simpson, B. A. (1986). The polygraph: Concept, usage, and validity. *Psychology: A Quarterly Journal of Human Behavior, 23*, 42–45.

Simpson, J. A. (1990). Influence of attachment styles on romantic relationships. *Journal of Personality and Social Psychology, 59,* 971–980.

Singer, A. G., & Macrides, F. (1990). Aphrodisin: Pheromone or transducer? *Chemical Senses, 15,* 199–203.

Singer, J. L., & Kolligian, J., Jr. (1987). Personality: Developments in the study of private experience. *Annual Review of Psychology, 38,* 533–574.

Sinson, J. C. (1994). Normalization and community integration of adults with severe mental handicap relocated to group homes. *Journal of Developmental and Physical Disabilities, 6,* 255-270.

Sizemore, C. C., & Huber, R. J. (1988). The 22 faces of Eve. *Individual Psychology: Journal of Adlerian Theory, Research, and Practice, 44,* 53–62.

Skinner, B. F. (1938). *The behavior of organisms.* New York: Appleton-Century-Crofts.

Skinner, B. F. (1945, October). Baby in a box. *Ladies Home Journal,* pp. 30–31.

Skinner, B. F. (1948). *Walden Two.* New York: Macmillan.

Skinner, B. F. (1953). *Science and human behavior.* New York: Macmillan.

Skinner, B. F. (1956). A case history in scientific method. *American Psychologist, 11,* 221–233.

Skinner, B. F. (1957). *Verbal behavior.* New York: Appleton-Century-Crofts.

Skinner, B. F. (1960). Pigeons in a pelican. *American Psychologist, 15,* 28–37.

Skinner, B. F. (1974). *About behaviorism.* New York: Knopf.

Skinner, B. F. (1983). Switching answers on multiple-choice questions: Shrewdness or shibboleth? *Teaching of Psychology, 10,* 220–222.

Skinner, B. F. (1984). The shame of American education. *American Psychologist, 39,* 947–954.

Skinner, B. F. (1986). What is wrong with daily life in the Western world? *American Psychologist, 41,* 220–222.

Skinner, B. F. (1989). Teaching machines. *Science, 243,* 1535.

Slagg, N. B., Lyons, J. S., Cook, J. A., & Wasmer, D. J. (1994). A profile of clients served by a mobile outreach program for homeless mentally ill persons. *Hospital and Community Psychiatry, 45,* 1139–1141.

Slater, A. (1992). The visual constancies in early infancy. *Irish Journal of Psychology, 13,* 412–425.

Slifer, K. J., Babbitt, R. L., & Cataldo, M. D. (1995). Simulation and counterconditioning as adjuncts to pharmacotherapy for invasive pediatric procedures. *Journal of Developmental and Behavioral Pediatrics, 16,* 133–141.

Smith, B. M., Schumaker, J. B., Schaeffer, J., & Sherman, J. A. (1982). Increasing participation and improving the quality of discussion in seventh-grade social studies classes. *Journal of Applied Behavior Analysis, 15,* 97–110.

Smith, B., Munday, R., & Windham, R. (1995). Prediction of teachers' use of technology based on personality type. *Journal of Instructional Psychology, 22,* 281–285.

Smith, B. H. (1997). An analysis of blocking in odorant mixtures: An increase but not a decrease in intensity of reinforcement produces unblocking. *Behavioral Neuroscience, 111,* 57-69.

Smith, C. (1996). Sleep states, memory processes and synaptic plasticity. *Behavioural Brain Research, 78,* 49-56.

Smith, C. A., & Ellsworth, P. C. (1985). Patterns of cognitive appraisal in emotion. *Journal of Personality and Social Psychology, 48,* 813–838.

Smith, D. (1982). Trends in counseling and psychotherapy. *American Psychologist, 37,* 802–809.

Smith, D. G., Standing, L., & de Man, A. (1992). Verbal memory elicited by ambient odor. *Perceptual and Motor Skills, 74,* 339–343.

Smith, H. F. (1995). Introduction: Gedo and Freud on working through. *Journal of the American Psychoanalytic Association, 43,* 331–392.

Smith, H. V. (1992). Is there a magical number 7 ± 2? The role of exposure duration and information content in immediate recall. *Irish Journal of Psychology, 13,* 85–97.

Smith, J. A. (1995). Guidelines, standards, and perspectives in exercise immunology. *Medicine and Science in Sports and Exercise, 27,* 497–506.

Smith, J. D. (1988). Fancher on Gould, Goddard, and historical interpretation: A reply. *American Psychologist, 43,* 744–745.

Smith, J. W., & Frawley, P. J. (1993). Treatment outcome of 600 chemically dependent patients treated in a multimodal inpatient program including aversion therapy and pentothal interviews. *Journal of Substance Abuse Treatment, 10,* 359–369.

Smith, L. T. (1974). The interanimal transfer phenomenon: A review. *Psychological Bulletin, 81,* 1078–1095.

Smith, M. B. (1986). The plausible assessment report: A phrenological example. *Professional Psychology: Research and Practice, 17,* 294–295.

Smith, M. C. (1983). Hypnotic memory enhancement of witnesses: Does it work? *Psychological Bulletin, 94,* 387–407.

Smith, M. L., Glass, G. V., & Miller, T. I. (1980). *The benefits of psychotherapy.* Baltimore: Johns Hopkins University Press.

Smith, P. C., & Kendall, L. M. (1963). Retranslation of expectations: An approach to the construction of unambiguous anchors for rating scales. *Journal of Applied Psychology, 47,* 149–155.

Smith, P. F. (1995). Cannabis and the brain: Recent developments. *New Zealand Journal of Psychology, 24,* 5-12.

Smith, P. F., & Curthoys, I. S. (1989). Mechanisms of recovery following unilateral labyrinthectomy: A review. *Brain Research Reviews, 14,* 155–180.

Smith, R. H., Diener, E., & Wedell, D. H. (1989). Intrapersonal and social comparison determinants of happiness: A range-frequency analysis. *Journal of Personality and Social Psychology, 56,* 317–325.

Smith, S. M. (1984). A comparison of two techniques for reducing context-dependent forgetting. *Memory and Cognition, 12,* 477–482.

Smith, S. M., Brown, H. O., Toman, J. E. P., & Goodman, L. S. (1947). The lack of cerebral effects of d-tubercurarine. *Anesthesiology, 8,* 1–14.

Smith, S. M., & Vela, E. (1992). Environmental context-dependent eyewitness recognition. *Applied Cognitive Psychology, 6,* 125–139.

Smith, S. S., & Richardson, D. (1983). Amelioration of deception and harm in psychological research: The important role of debriefing. *Journal of Personality and Social Psychology, 44,* 1075–1082.

Smith, T., Snyder, C. R., & Perkins, S. C. (1983). The self-serving function of hypochondriacal complaints: Physical symptoms as self-handicapping strategies. *Journal of Personality and Social Psychology, 44,* 787–797.

Smith, T. E., Bellack, A. S., & Liberman, R. P. (1996). Social skills training for schizophrenia: Review and future directions. *Clinical Psychology Review, 16,* 599–617.

Smith, W. P., Compton, W. C., & West, W. B. (1995). Meditation as an adjunct to a happiness enhancement program. *Journal of Clinical Psychology, 51,* 269–273.

Snaith, P., Tarsh, M. J., & Reid, R. W. (1993). Sex reassignment surgery: A study of 141 Dutch transsexuals. *British Journal of Psychiatry, 162,* 681–685.

Snarey, J. R., Reimer, J., & Kohlberg, L. (1985). Development of social-moral reasoning among kibbutz adolescents: A longitudinal cross-cultural study. *Developmental Psychology, 21,* 3–17.

Sno, H. N., Schalken, H. F., & de Jonghe, F. (1992). Empirical research on déjà vu experiences: A review. *Behavioural Neurology, 5,* 155–160.

Snodgrass, S. R. (1994). Cocaine babies: A result of multiple teratogenic influences. *Journal of Child Neurology, 9,* 227-233.

Snow, C. E. (1981). The uses of imitation. *Journal of Child Language, 8,* 205–212.

Snyder, B. K., Roghmann, K. J., & Sigal, L. H. (1993). Stress and psychosocial factors: Effects on primary cellular immune response. *Journal of Behavioral Medicine, 16,* 143–161.

Snyder, M. (1983). The influence of individuals on situations: Implications for understanding the links between personality and social behavior. *Journal of Personality, 51,* 497–516.

Snyderman, M., & Herrnstein, R. J. (1983). Intelligence tests and the Immigration Act of 1924. *American Psychologist, 38,* 986–995.

Sogon, S., & Izard, C. E. (1987). Sex differences in emotion recognition by observing body movements: A case of American students. *Japanese Psychological Research, 29,* 89–93.

Sokal, M. M. (1992). Origins and early years of the American Psychological Association, 1890-1906. *American Psychologist, 47,* 111–121.

Sokolov, E. N., & Izmailov, C. A. (1988). Three-stage model of color vision. *Sensory Systems, 2,* 314–320.

Solcova, I., & Sykora, J. (1995). Relation between psychological hardiness and physiological response. *Homeostasis in Health and Disease, 36,* 30–34.

Solomon, P. R., & Morse, D. L. (1981). Teaching the principles of operant conditioning through laboratory experience: The rat olympics. *Teaching Psychology, 8,* 111–112.

Solomon, R. L. (1980). The opponent-process theory of acquired motivation: The costs of pleasure and the benefits of pain. *American Psychologist, 35,* 691–712.

Solomon, S., & Guglielmo, K. M. (1985). Treatment of headache by transcutaneous electrical stimulation. *Headache, 25,* 12–15.

Solomon, S. D. (1982). Individual versus group therapy: Current status in the treatment of alcoholism. *Advances in Alcohol and Substance Abuse, 2,* 69–86.

Solowij, N., Michie, P. T., & Fox, A. M. (1995). Differential impairments of selective attention due to frequency and duration of cannabis use. *Biological Psychiatry, 37,* 731–739.

Solvason, H. B., Ghanta, V. K., & Hiramoto, R. N. (1993). The identity of the unconditioned stimulus to the central nervous system is interferon-b. *Journal of Neuroimmunology, 45,* 75–81.

Sommers, S. (1984). Reported emotions and conventions of emotionality among college students. *Journal of Personality and Social Psychology, 46,* 207–215.

Sondhaus, E., & Finger, S. (1988). Aphasia and the CNS from Imhotep to Broca. *Neuropsychology, 2,* 87–110.

Sonstroem, R. J., & Bernardo, P. (1982). Intraindividual pregame state anxiety and basketball performance: A re-examination of the inverted-U curve. *Journal of Sport Psychology, 4,* 235–245.

Spangenberg, J., & Nel, E. M. (1983). The effect of equal-status contact on ethnic attitudes. *Journal of Social Psychology, 121,* 173–180.

Spangler, W. D. (1992). Validity of questionnaire and TAT measures of need for achievement: Two meta-analyses. *Psychological Bulletin, 112,* 140–154.

Spanos, N. P., & Bures, E. (1993–1994). Pseudomemory responding in hypnotic, task-motivated and simulating subjects: Memory distortion or reporting bias? *Imagination, Cognition and Personality, 13,* 303–310.

Spanos, N. P., Burgess, C. A., & Perlini, A. H. (1991–1992). Compliance and suggested deafness in hypnotic and nonhypnotic subjects. *Imagination, Cognition and Personality, 11,* 211–223.

Spanos, N. P., & Hewitt, E. C. (1980). The hidden observer in hypnotic analgesia: Discovery or experimental creation? *Journal of Personality and Social Psychology, 49,* 1201–1214

Spanos, N. P., McNeil, C., & Stam, H. J. (1982). Hypnotically "reliving" a prior burn: Effects on blister formation and localized skin temperature. *Journal of Abnormal Psychology, 91,* 303–305.

Spanos, N., Weekes, J. R., & Bertrand, L. (1983). Multiple personality: A social psychological perspective. *Journal of Abormal Psychology, 94,* 362–376.

Spector, I. P., & Carey, M. P. (1990). Incidence and prevalence of the sexual dysfunctions: A critical review of the empirical literature. *Archives of Sexual Behavior, 19,* 389–408.

Speisman, J. C., Lazarus, R. S., Mordkoff, A., & Davison, L. (1964). Experimental reduction of stress based on ego-defense theory. *Journal of Abnormal and Social Psychology, 68,* 367–380.

Spengler, F., Godde, B., & Dinse, H. R. (1995). Effects of ageing on topographic organization of somatosensory cortex. *Neuroreport: An International Journal for the Rapid Communication of Research in Neuroscience, 6,* 469–473.

Sperling, G. (1960). The information available in brief visual presentations. *Psychological Monographs, 74* (498).

Sperry, R. W. (1982). Some effects of disconnecting the cerebral hemispheres. *Science, 217,* 1223–1226.

Sperry, R. W. (1993). The impact and promise of the cognitive revolution. *American Psychologist, 48,* 878–885.

Spiegel, D., Cutcomb, S., Ren, C., & Pribram, K. (1985). Hypnotic hallucination alters evoked potentials. *Journal of Abnormal Psychology, 94,* 249–255.

Spiess, W. F., Geer, J. H., & O'Donohue, W. T. (1984). Premature ejaculation: Investigation of factors in ejaculatory latency. *Journal of Abnormal Psychology, 93,* 242–245.

Spillmann, J., & Spillmann, L. (1993). The rise and fall of Hugo Munsterberg. *Journal of the History of the Behavioral Sciences, 29,* 322–338.

Spitzer, R. L. (1975). On pseudoscience in science, logic in remission, and psychiatric diagnosis: A critique of Rosenhan's "On being sane in insane places." *Journal of Abnormal Psychology, 84,* 442–452.

Sprecher, S. (1989). The importance to males and females of physical attractiveness, earning potential, and expressiveness in initial attraction. *Sex Roles, 21,* 591–607.

Spring, B., Chiodo, J., & Bowen, D. J. (1987). Carbohydrates, tryptophan, and behavior: A methodological review. *Psychological Bulletin, 102,* 234–256.

Springer, S. P., & Deutsch, G. (1993). *Left brain, right brain* (4th ed.). New York: W. H. Freeman.

Spurlock, J. (1986). Development of self-concept in Afro-American children. *Hospital and Community Psychiatry, 37,* 66–70.

Spyer, K. M. (1989). Neural mechanisms involved in cardiovascular control during affective behavior. *Trends in Neurosciences, 12,* 506–513.

Staats, A. W. (1993). Personality theory, abnormal psychology, and psychological measurement: A psychological behaviorism. *Behavior Modification, 17,* 8–42.

Staats, A. W. (1994). Psychological behaviorism and behaviorizing psychology. *Behavior Analyst, 17,* 93–114.

Stafford-Clark, D. (1965). *What Freud really said.* New York: Schocken Books.

Stairs, A. (1992). Self-image, world-image: Speculations on identity from experiences with Inuit. *Ethos, 20,* 116–126.

Stallone, T. M. (1993). The effects of psychodrama on inmates within a structured residential behavior modification program. *Journal of Group Psychotherapy, Psychodrama, and Sociometry, 46,* 24–31.

Stanard, R., & Hazler, R. (1995). Legal and ethical implications of HIV and duty to warn for counselors: When does Tarasoff apply? *Journal of Counseling and Development, 73,* 397–400.

Stankov, L., & Chen, K. (1988). Can we boost fluid and crystallized intelligence? A structural modelling approach. *Australian Journal of Psychology, 40,* 363–376.

Stapleton, J. A., Russell, M. A. H., Feyerabend, C., & Wiseman, S. M. (1995). Dose effects and predictors of outcome in a randomized trial of transdermal nicotine patches in general practice. *Addiction, 90,* 31–42.

Stapp, J., Tucker, A. M., & VandenBos, G. R. (1985). Census of psychological personnel: 1983. *American Psychologist, 40,* 1317–1351.

Stark, E. (1981, September). Pigeon patrol. *Science 81,* pp. 85–86.

Staw, B. M., & Ross, J. (1985). Stability in the midst of change: A dispositional approach to job attitudes. *Journal of Applied Psychology, 70,* 469–480.

Steblay, N.–M., & Bothwell, R. K. (1994). Evidence for hypnotically refreshed testimony: The view from the laboratory. *Law and Human Behavior, 18,* 635–651.

Steele, C. M., & Josephs, R. A. (1990). Alcohol myopia: Its prized and dangerous effects. *American Psychologist, 45,* 921–933.

Steele, R. J., Stewart, M. G., & Rose, S. P. R. (1995). Increases in NMDA receptor binding are specifically related to memory formation for a passive avoidance task in the chick: A quantitative autoradiographic study. *Brain Research, 674,* 352–356.

Steers, R. M., & Porter, L. W. (Eds.). (1991). *Motivation and work behavior* (5th ed.). New York: McGraw-Hill.

Steers, R. M., Porter, L. W., & Bigley, G. A. (Eds.). (1996). *Motivation and leadership at work* (6th ed.). New York: McGraw-Hill.

Steers, R. M., & Rhodes, S. R. (1978). Major influences on employee attendance: A process model. *Journal of Applied Psychology, 63,* 391–407.

Stein, D. M., & Lambert, M. J. (1995). Graduate training in psychotherapy: Are therapy outcomes enhanced? *Journal of Consulting and Clinical Psychology, 63,* 182–196.

Steinberg, L., Lamborn, S. D., Dornbusch, S. M., & Darling, N. (1992). Impact of parenting practices on adolescent achievement: Authoritative parenting, school achievement, and encouragement to succeed. *Child Development, 63,* 1266–1281.

Steinbrueck, S. M., Maxwell, S. E., & Howard, G. S. (1983). A meta-analysis of psychotherapy and drug therapy in the treatment of unipolar depression with adults. *Journal of Consulting and Clinical Psychology, 51,* 856–863.

Steiner, S. S., & Dince, W. M. (1981). Biofeedback efficacy studies: A critique of critiques. *Biofeedback and Self-Regulation, 6,* 275–288.

Stelmack, R. M. (1990). Biological bases of extraversion: Psychophysiological evidence. *Journal of Personality, 58,* 293–311.

Stelmack, R. M., & Stalikas, A. (1991). Galen and the humour theory of temperament. *Personality and Individual Differences, 12,* 255–263.

Stemberger, R. T., Turner, S. M., Beidel, D. C., & Calhoun, K. S. (1995). Social phobia: An analysis of possible developmental factors. *Journal of Abnormal Psychology, 104,* 526–531.

Stemmer, N. (1990). Skinner's *Verbal Behavior,* Chomsky's review, and mentalism. *Journal of the Experimental Analysis of Behavior, 54,* 307–315.

Stephan, W. G., Stephan, C. W., & de Vargas, M. C. (1996). Emotional expression in Costa Rica and the United States. *Journal of Cross-Cultural Psychology, 27,* 147–160.

Steptoe, A., Moses, J., Edwards, S., & Mathews, A. (1993). Exercise and responsivity to mental stress: Discrepancies between the subjective and physiological effects of aerobic training. *International Journal of Sport Psychology, 24,* 110–129.

Stern, R. M., & Koch, K. L. (1996). Motion sickness and differential susceptibility. *Current Directions in Psychological Science, 5,* 115-120.

Sternberg, D. E., Van Kammen, D. P., Lerner, P., & Bunney, W. E. (1982). Schizophrenia: Dopamine beta-hydroxylase activity and treatment response. *Science, 216,* 1423–1425.

Sternberg, R. J. (1986). A triangular theory of love. *Psychological Review, 93,* 119–135.

Sternberg, R. J. (1994). Experimental approaches to human intelligence. *European Journal of Psychological Assessment, 10,* 153–161.

Sternberg, R. J., & Clinkenbeard, P. B. (1995). The triarchic model applied to identifying, teaching, and assessing gifted children. *Roeper Review, 17,* 255–260.

Sternberg, R. J., Conway, B. E., Ketron, J. L., & Bernstein, M. (1981). People's conceptions of intelligence. *Journal of Personality and Social Psychology, 41,* 37–55.

Sternberg, R. J., & Wagner, R. K. (1993). The g-ocentric view of intelligence and job performance is wrong. *Current Directions in Psychological Science, 2,* 1–5.

Sterrenberg, P., & Thunnissen, M. M. (1995). Transactional analysis as a cognitive treatment for borderline personality disorder. *Transactional Analysis Journal, 25,* 221–227.

Stevens, C. K., & Kristof, A. L. (1995). Making the right impression: A field study of applicant impression management during job interviews. *Journal of Applied Psychology, 80,* 587–606.

Stevens, J. C. (1989). Food quality reports from noninstitutionalized aged. *Annals of the New York Academy of Sciences, 561,* 87–93.

Stevens, J. C., Cain, W. S., & Oatley, M. W. (1989). Aging speeds olfactory adaptation and slows recovery. *Annals of the New York Academy of Sciences, 561,* 323–325.

Stewart, M. G., Lowdnes, M., Hunter, A., & Doubell, T. (1992). Memory storage in chicks involves an increase in dendritic spine number and synaptic density. *Brain Dysfunction, 5,* 50–64.

Stiles, W. B., Shapiro, D. A., & Elliott, R. (1986). Are all psychotherapies equivalent? *American Psychologist, 41,* 165–180.

St. Lawrence, J. S., & Madakasira, S. (1992). Evaluation and treatment of premature ejaculation: A critical review. *International Journal of Psychiatry in Medicine, 22,* 77–97.

Stogdill, R. M. (1948). Personal factors associated with leadership: A survey of the literature. *Journal of Psychology, 25,* 35–71.

Stolerman, I. P., & Jarvis, M. J. (1995). The scientific case that nicotine is addictive. *Psychopharmacology, 117,* 2–10.

Stone, A. A., Bovbjerg, D. H., Neale, J. M., & Napoli, A. (1992). Development of common cold symptoms following experimental rhinovirus infection is related to prior stressful life events. *Behavioral Medicine, 18,* 115–120.

Stone, A. A., & Brownell, K. D. (1994). The stress-eating paradox: Multiple daily measurements in adult males and females. *Psychology and Health, 9,* 425–436.

Stone, A. A., Cox, D. S., Valdimarsdottir, H., Jandorf, L., & Neale, J. M. (1987). Evidence that secretory IgA antibody is associated with daily mood. *Journal of Personality and Social Psychology, 52,* 988–993.

Stone, A. A., Hedges, S. M., Neale, J. M., & Satin, M. S. (1985). Prospective and cross-sectional mood reports offer no evidence of a "blue Monday" phenomenon. *Journal of Personality and Social Psychology, 49,* 129–134.

Stoner, J. A. F. (1961). *A comparison of individual and group decisions involving risk* [Unpublished master's thesis, Massachusetts Institute of Technology].

Stoney, C. M., Davis, M. C., & Matthews, K. A. (1987). Sex differences in physiological responses to stress and in coronary heart disease: A causal link? *Psychophysiology, 24,* 127–131.

Storms, M. D. (1981). A theory of erotic orientation development. *Psychological Review, 88,* 340–353.

Strack, F., Schwarz, N., Chassein, B., & Kern, D. (1990). Salience of comparison standards and the activation of social norms: Consequences for judgements of happiness and their communication. *British Journal of Social Psychology, 29,* 303–314.

Strange, W., & Dittmann, S. (1984). Effects of discrimination training on the perception of r-l by Japanese adults learning English. *Perception and Psychophysics, 36*, 131–145.

Strassman, R. J. (1984). Adverse reactions to psychedelic drugs: A review of the literature. *Journal of Nervous and Mental Disease, 172*, 577–595.

Stratton, G. M. (1917). The mnemonic feat of the "Shass Pollak." *Psychological Review, 24*, 244–247.

Strauman, T. J., & Higgins, E. T. (1988). Self-discrepancies as predictors of vulnerability to distinct syndromes of chronic emotional distress. *Journal of Personality, 56*, 246–253, 685–707.

Straus, M. A. (1991). Discipline and deviance: Physical punishment of children and violence and other crime in adulthood. *Social Problems, 38*, 133–154.

Straus, M. A., & Kantor, G. K. (1994). Corporal punishment of adolescents by parents: A risk factor in the epidemiology of depression, suicide, alcohol abuse, child abuse, and wife beating. *Adolescence, 29*, 543–561.

Strayer, D. L., & Kramer, A. F. (1990). Attentional requirements of automatic and controlled processing. *Journal of Experimental Psychology Learning, Memory, and Cognition, 16*, 67–82.

Strecher, V. J., Seijts, G. H., Kok, G. J., & Latham, G. P. (1995). Goal setting as a strategy for health behavior change. *Health Education Quarterly, 22*, 190–200.

Streitmatter, J. (1993). Gender differences in identity development: An examination of longitudinal data. *Adolescence, 28*, 55–66.

Stretch, R. H. (1991). Psychosocial readjustment of Canadian Vietnam veterans. *Journal of Consulting and Clinical Psychology, 59*, 188–189.

Strichartz, A. F., & Burton, R. V. (1990). Lies and truth: A study of the development of the concept. *Child Development, 61*, 211–220.

Stricker, E. M., & McCann, M. J. (1985). Visceral factors in the control of food intake. *Brain Research Bulletin, 14*, 687–692.

Stricker, E. M., & Verbalis, J. G. (1987). Biological bases of hunger and satiety. *Annals of Behavioral Medicine, 9*, 3–8.

Strickland, B. R. (1989). Internal-external control expectancies: From contingency to creativity. *American Psychologist, 44*, 1–12.

Strickland, B. R. (1995). Research on sexual orientation and human development: A commentary. *Developmental Psychology, 31*, 137–140.

Striegel-Moore, R. H., Silberstein, L. R., & Rodin, J. (1986). Toward an understanding of risk factors in bulimia. *American Psychologist, 41*, 246–263.

Strober, M., & Humphrey, L. L. (1987). Familial contributions to the etiology and course of anorexia nervosa and bulimia. *Journal of Consulting and Clinical Psychology, 55*, 654–659.

Stroebe, M. S. (1994). The broken heart phenomenon: An examination of the mortality of bereavement. *Journal of Community and Applied Social Psychology, 4*, 47–61.

Stroebe, M. S., & Stroebe, W. (1983). Who suffers more? Sex differences in health risks of the widowed. *Psychological Bulletin, 93*, 279–301.

Stunkard, A. J., Stinnett, J. L., & Smoller, J. W. (1986). Psychological and social aspects of the surgical treatment of obesity. *American Journal of Psychiatry, 143*, 417–429.

Sturgeon, R. S., Cooper, L. M., & Howell, R. J. (1989). Pupil response: A psychophysiological measure of fear during analogue desensitization. *Perceptual and Motor Skills, 69*, 1351–1367.

Stuss, D. T., Gow, C. A., & Hetherington, C. R. (1992). "No longer Gage": Frontal lobe dysfunction and emotional changes. *Journal of Consulting and Clinical Psychology, 60*, 349–359.

Subotnik, R, F., Karp, D. E., & Morgan, E. R. (1989). High IQ children at midlife: An investigation into the generalizability.

Sue, S., & Okazaki, S. (1990). Asian-American educational achievements: A phenomenon in search of an explanation. *American Psychologist, 45*, 913–920.

Suedfeld, P. (1990). Restricted environmental stimulation and smoking cessation: A 15-year progress report. *International Journal of the Addictions, 25*, 861–888.

Suedfeld, P., & Bruno, T. (1990). Flotation REST and imagery in the improvement of athletic performance. *Journal of Exercise and Exercise Psychology, 12*, 82–85.

Suedfeld, P., & Coren, S. (1989). Perceptual isolation, sensory deprivation, and REST: Moving introductory psychology texts out of the 1950s. *Canadian Psychology, 30*, 17–29.

Suh, E., Diener, E., & Fujita, F. (1996). Events and subjective well-being: Only recent events matter. *Journal of Personality and Social Psychology, 70*, 1091–1102.

Suler, J. R. (1980). Primary process thinking and creativity. *Psychological Bulletin, 88*, 144–165.

Sullins, E. S., Hernandez, D., Fuller, C., & Tashiro, J. S. (1995). Predicting who will major in a science discipline: Expectancy-value theory as part of an ecological model for studying academic communities. *Journal of Research in Science Teaching, 32*, 99–119.

Sullivan, H. S. (1953). *An interpersonal theory of psychiatry*. New York: W. W. Norton.

Sulloway, F. J. (1979). *Freud: Biologist of the mind*. New York: Basic Books.

Sumino, R., & Dubner, R. (1981). Response characteristics of specific thermoreceptive afferents innervating monkey facial skin and their relationship to human thermal sensitivity. *Brain Research Reviews, 3*, 105–122.

Superkids?: A sperm bank for Nobelists. (1980, March 10). *Time*, p. 49.

Survey finds most rape victims are minors: Many are under 10. (1992, April 26). *Philadelphia Inquirer*, p. A-6.

Sussan, T. A. (1990). How to handle the process litigation effectively under the Education for All Handicapped Children Act of 1975. *Journal of Reading, Writing, and Learning Disabilities International, 6*, 63–70.

Swain, J. J., Allard, G. B., & Holborn, S. W. (1982). The good toothbrushing game: A school-based dental hygiene program for increasing the toothbrushing effectiveness of children. *Journal of Applied Behavior Analysis, 15*, 171–176.

Swann, W. B., Jr., Hixon, J. G., & De La Ronde, C. (1992). Embracing the bitter "truth": Negative self–concepts and marital commitment. *Psychological Science, 3*, 118–121.

Swayze, V. W. (1995). Frontal leukotomy and related psychosurgical procedures in the era before antipsychotics (1935–1954): A historical overview. *American Journal of Psychiatry, 152*, 505–515.

Sweat, J. A., & Durm, M. W. (1993). Psychics: Do police departments really use them? *Skeptical Inquirer, 17*, 141–158.

Sweeney, P. D., Anderson, K., & Bailey, S. (1986). Attributional style in depression: A meta-analytic review. *Journal of Personality and Social Psychology, 50*, 974–991.

Swenson, C. R. (1994). Freud's "Anna O.": Social work's Bertha Pappenheim. *Clinical Social Work Journal, 22*, 149–163.

Swenson, R. S., Danielsen, E. H., Klausen, B. S., & Erlich, E. (1989). Deficits in beam-walking after neonatal motor cortical lesions are not spared by fetal cortical transplants in rats. *Journal of Neural Transplantation, 1*, 129–133.

Swiatek, M. A. (1993). A decade of longitudinal research on academic acceleration through the study of mathematically precocious youth. *Roeper Review, 15*, 120–124.

Swiezy, N. B., Matson, J. L., & Box, P. (1992). The Good Behavior Game: A token reinforcement system for preschoolers. *Child and Family Behavior Therapy, 14*, 21–32.

Swindale, N. V. (1982). The development of columnar systems in the mammalian visual cortex: The role of innate and environmental factors. *Trends in Neurosciences, 5*, 235–241.

Syvalahti, E. K. G. (1994). Biological factors in schizophrenia: Structural and functional aspects. *British Journal of Psychiatry, 164*, 9–14.

Szasz, T. (1960). The myth of mental illness. *American Psychologist, 15*, 113–118.

Szasz, T. (1980). "J'Accuse": Psychiatry and the diminished American capacity for justice. *Journal of Mind and Behavior, 1*, 111–120.

Szymanski, S., Kane, J. M., & Lieberman, J. A. (1991). A selective review of biological markers in schizophrenia. *Schizophrenia Bulletin, 17*, 99–111.

Taal, E., Rasker, J. J., Seydel, E. R., & Wiegman, O. (1993). Health status, adherence with health recommendations, self-efficacy and social support in patients with rheumatoid arthritis. *Patient Education and Counseling, 20*, 63–76.

Taddese, A., Nah, S.–Y., & McCleskey, E. W. (1995). Selective opioid inhibition of small nociceptive neurons. *Science, 270*, 1366-1369.

Takagi, M., Toda, H., Yoshizawa, T., & Hara, N. (1992). Ocular convergence-related neuronal responses in the lateral suprasylvian area of alert cats. *Neuroscience Research, 15*, 229–234.

Takahata, Y., Hasegawa, T., & Nishida, T. (1984). Chimpanzee predation in the Mahale Mountains from August 1979 to May 1982. *International Journal of Primatology, 5*, 213–233.

Takeuchi, A. H., & Hulse, S. H. (1993). Absolute pitch. *Psychological Bulletin, 113*, 345–361.

Talcott, G. W., Fiedler, E. R., Pascale, R. W., & Klesges, R. C. (1995). Is weight after smoking cessation inevitable? *Journal of Consulting and Clinical Psychology, 63*, 313–316.

Taller, A. M., Asher, D. M., Pomeroy, K. L., & Eldadah, B. A. (1996). Search for viral nucleic acid sequences in brain tissues of patients with schizophrenia using nested polymerase chain reaction. *Archives of General Psychiatry, 53*, 32–40.

Tam, W.-C. C., & Sewell, K. W. (1995). Seasonality of birth in schizophrenia in Taiwan. *Schizophrenia Bulletin, 21*, 117–127.

Tan, D. T. Y., & Singh, R. (1995). Attitudes and attraction: A developmental study of the similarity-attraction and dissimilarity-repulsion hypotheses. *Personality and Social Psychology Bulletin, 21*, 975–986.

Tan, E. M., Lam, R. W., & Levitt, A. J. (1995). Treatment of seasonal affective disorder: A review. *Canadian Journal of Psychiatry, 40*, 457–466.

Tang, S. H., & Hall, V. C. (1995). The overjustification effect: A meta-analysis. *Applied Cognitive Psychology, 9*, 365–404.

Tang, T. L., & Hammontree, M. L. (1992). The effects of hardiness, police stress, and life stress on police officers' illness and absenteeism. *Public Personnel Management, 21*, 493–510.

Tankard, J. W. (1984). *The statistical pioneers*. Cambridge, MA: Schenkman.

Tarchanoff, J. R. (1885/1973). Über die willkurliche acceleration der herzschlage beim menschen (Voluntary acceleration of the heart beat in man). *Pflugers Archives, 35*, 109–135. (Reprinted from *Biofeedback and self–control*, pp. 3–20, by D. Shapiro et al., Eds., 1972, Chicago: Aldine-Atherton.)

Tarricone, B. J., Simon, J. R., Li, Y. J., & Low, W. C. (1996). Neural grafting of cholinergic neurons in the hippocampal formation. *Behavioural Brain Research, 74*, 25-44.

Tateyama, M., Asai, M., Kamisada, M., & Hashimoto, M. (1993). Comparison of schizophrenic delusions between Japan and Germany. *Psychopathology, 26*, 151–158.

Tauer, C. A. (1994). The NIH trials of growth hormone for short stature. *IRB: A Review of Human Subjects Research, 16*, 1–9.

Taulbee, P. (1983). Solving the mystery of anxiety. *Science News, 124*, 45.

Taylor, E. (1990). William James on Darwin: An evolutionary theory of consciousness. *Annals of the New York Academy of Sciences, 602*, 7–33.

Taylor, R. L. (1990). The *Larry P.* decision a decade later: Problems and future directions. *Mental Retardation, 28*, iii–vi.

Taylor, S., & Goritsas, E. (1994). Dimensions of identity diffusion. *Journal of Personality Disorders, 8*, 229–239.

Taylor, S. E. (1989). *Positive illusions: Creative self-deception and the healthy mind.* New York: Basic Books.

Taylor, S. E., & Brown, J. D. (1988). Illusion and well-being: A social psychological perspective on mental health. *Psychological Bulletin, 103*, 193–210.

Taylor, T., & Booth-Butterfield, S. (1993). Getting a foot in the door with drinking and driving: A field study of healthy influence. *Communication Research Reports, 10*, 95–101.

Teaching a machine the shades of gray. (1981). *Science News, 119*, 38–39.

Teasdale, N., Forget, R., Bard, C., & Paillard, J. (1993). The role of proprioceptive information for the production of isometric forces and for handwriting tasks. *Acta Psychologica, 82*, 179–191.

Teicher, M. H., Glod, C., & Cole, J. O. (1990). Emergence of intense suicide preoccupation during fluoxetine treatment. *American Journal of Psychiatry, 147*, 207–210.

Teichman, Y., & Teichman, M. (1990). Interpersonal view of depression: Review and integration. *Journal of Family Psychology, 3*, 349–367.

Teigen, K. H. (1984). A note on the origin of the term "nature and nurture": Not Shakespeare and Galton, but Mulcaster. *Journal of the History of the Behavioral Sciences, 20*, 363–364.

Teigen, K. H. (1994). Yerkes-Dodson: A law for all seasons. *Theory and Psychology, 4*, 525–547.

Telch, C. F., & Telch, M. J. (1985). Psychological approaches for enhancing coping among cancer patients: A review. *Clinical Psychology Review, 5*, 325–344.

Tellegen, A., Lykken, D. T., Bouchard, T. J., Jr., Wilcox, K. J., Segal, N. L., & Rich, S. (1988). Personality similarity in twins reared apart and together. *Journal of Personality and Social Psychology, 54*, 1031–1039.

Tenzer, S. (1989). Fat acceptance therapy (F.A.T.): A non-dieting group approach to physical wellness, insight and self-acceptance. *Women and Therapy, 8*, 39–47.

Terman, L. M. (1917). The intelligence quotient of Francis Galton in childhood. *American Journal of Psychology, 28*, 209–215.

Terman, L. M. (1918). Expert testimony in the case of Alberto Flores. *Journal of Delinquency, 3*, 145–164.

Terrace, H. S. (1985). In the beginning was the "name." *American Psychologist, 40*, 1011–1028.

Terrace, H. S., Petitto, L. A., Sanders, R. J., & Bever, T. G. (1979). Can an ape create a sentence? *Science, 206*, 891–902.

Thearle, M. J. (1993). The rise and fall of phrenology in Australia. *Australian and New Zealand Journal of Psychiatry, 27*, 518–525.

Theorell, T., Blomkvist, V., Jonsson, H., & Schulman, S. (1995). Social support and the development of immune function in human immunodeficiency virus infection. *Psychosomatic Medicine, 57*, 32–36.

Thomas, E. (1988). Forebrain mechanisms in the relief of fear: The role of the lateral septum. *Psychobiology, 16*, 36–44.

Thomas, H. (1993). A theory explaining sex differences in high mathematical ability has been around for some time. *Behavioral and Brain Sciences, 16*, 187–189.

Thomas, L. (1981, December). On the need for asylums. *Discover*, pp. 68, 71.

Thomas, R. E., Vaidya, S. C., Herrick, R. T., & Congleton, J. (1993). The effects of biofeedback on carpal tunnel syndrome. *Ergonomics, 36*, 353–361.

Thompson, B. (1994). The pivotal role of replication in psychological research: Empirically evaluating the replicability of sample results. *Journal of Personality, 62*, 157–176.

Thompson, J. K., Coovert, M. D., Richards, K. J., & Johnson, S. (1995). Development of body image, eating disturbance, and general psychological functioning in female adolescents: Covariance structure modeling and longitudinal investigations. *International Journal of Eating Disorders, 18*, 221–236.

Thompson, P. B., & Lambert, J. V. (1995). Touch sensitivity through latex examination gloves. *Journal of General Psychology, 122*, 47-58.

Thompson, R. F. (1991). Are memory traces localized or distributed? *Neuropsychologia, 29*, 571–582.

Thorndike, E. L. (1898). Animal intelligence: An experimental study of the associative processes in animals. *Psychological Review Monograph Supplement, 2* (8).

Thorndike, E. L. (1961). Edward Lee Thorndike. In C. Murchison (Ed.), *A history of psychology in autobiography* (Vol. 1, pp. 263–270). New York: Russell & Russell.

Thorpe, S. J., & Salkovskis, P. M. (1995). Phobia beliefs: Do cognitive factors play a role in specific phobias? *Behaviour Research and Therapy, 33*, 805–816.

Thurman, C. W. (1985). Effectiveness of cognitive-behavioral treatments in reducing Type A behavior among university faculty one year later. *Journal of Counseling Psychology, 32*, 445–448.

Thurstone, L. L. (1938). *Primary mental abilities.* Chicago: University of Chicago Press.

Tiefer, L. (1994). Sex is not a natural act. *Zeitschrift fur Sexualforschung, 7*, 36–42.

Tiffany, S. T., Martin, E. M., & Baker, T. B. (1986). Treatments for cigarette smoking: An evaluation of the contributions of aversion and counseling procedures. *Behaviour Research and Therapy, 24*, 437–452.

Tilley, A. J., & Empson, J. A. (1978). REM sleep and memory consolidation. *Biological Psychology, 6*, 293–300.

Timberlake, W., & Farmer-Dougan, V. A. (1991). Reinforcement in applied settings: Figuring out ahead of time what will work. *Psychological Bulletin, 110*, 379–391.

Timberlake, W., & Melcer, T. (1988). Effects of poisoning on predatory andingestive behavior toward artificial prey in rats (*Rattus norvegicus*). *Journal of Comparative Psychology, 102*, 182–187.

Timm, H. W. (1982). Effect of altered outcome expectancies stemming from placebo and feedback treatments on the validity of the guilty knowledge technique. *Journal of Applied Psychology, 67*, 391–400.

Todd, J. T., & Morris, E. K. (1992). Case histories in the great power of steady misrepresentation. *American Psychologist, 47*, 1441–1453.

Todd, L. K. (1996). A computer-assisted expert system for clinical diagnosis of eating disorders: A potential tool for practitioners. *Professional Psychology: Research and Practice, 27*, 184-187.

Tolman, E. C. (1932). *Purposive behavior in animals and man.* New York: Appleton-Century-Crofts.

Tolman, E. C., & Honzik, C. H. (1930). Introduction and removal of reward, and maze performance in rats. *University of California Publications in Psychology, 4*, 257–275.

Tomarken, A. J., Mineka, S., & Cook, M. (1989). Fear-relevant selective associations and covariation bias. *Journal of Abnormal Psychology, 98*, 381–394.

Torgersen, S. (1983). Genetic factors in anxiety disorders. *Archives of General Psychiatry, 40*, 1085–1089.

Torgersen, S. (1986). Genetics of somatoform disorders. *Archives of General Psychiatry, 43*, 502–505.

Torgersen, S. (1989). Genetics of panic disorder. *Psychiatria Fennica, (Supplement)*, 29–34.

Torri, G., Cecchettin, M., Bellometti, S. &, Galzigna, L. (1995). Analgesic effect and beta-endorphin and substance P levels in plasma after short-term administration of a ketoprofen-lysine salt or acetylsalicylic acid in patients with osteoarthrosis. *Current Therapeutic Research, 56*, 62–69.

Toufexis, A. (1990, December 17). Drowsy America. *Time*, pp. 78–85.

Towbin, A. (1978). Cerebral dysfunctions related to perinatal organic damage: Clinical-neuropathologic correlations. *Journal of Abnormal Psychology, 87*, 617–635.

Towell, A., Muscat, R., & Willner, P. (1989). Noradrenergic receptor interactions in feeding elicited by stimulation of the paraventricular hypothalamus. *Pharmacology, Biochemistry, and Behavior, 32*, 133–139.

Tranel, D. (1995). Where did my arm go? [Review of *Unilateral neglect: Clinical and experimental studies*]. *Contemporary Psychology, 40*, 885–887.

Tranel, D., & Damasio, A. R. (1985). Knowledge without our awareness: An automatic index of facial recognition by prosopagnosics. *Science, 228*, 1453–1454.

Traskman, L., Asberg, M., Bertilsson, L., & Sjostrand, L. (1981). Monoamine metabolites in CSF and suicidal behavior. *Archives of General Psychiatry, 38*, 631–636.

Treasure, D. C., Monson, J., & Lox, C. L. (1996). Relationship between self-efficacy, wrestling performance, and affect prior to competition. *Sport Psychologist, 10*, 73–83.

Triandis, H. C. (1990). Theoretical concepts that are applicable to the analysis of ethnocentrism. In R. W. Brislin (Ed.), *Applied cross-cultural psychology* (pp. 34–55). Newbury Park, CA: Sage.

Trice, A. D., & Ogden, E. P. (1987). Informed consent: 9. Effects of the withdrawal clause in longitudinal research. *Perceptual and Motor Skills, 65*, 135–138.

Tripathy, S. P., Levi, D. M., Ogmen, H., & Harden, C. (1995). Perceived length across the physiological blind spot. *Visual Neuroscience, 12*, 385–402.

Triplet, R. G. (1992). Discriminatory biases in the perception of illness: The application of availability and representativeness heuristics to the AIDS crisis. *Basic and Applied Social Psychology, 13*, 303–322.

Triplett, N. (1898). The dynamogenic factors in pacemaking and competition. *American Journal of Psychology, 9*, 507–553.

Troster, H., & Bambring, M. (1992). Early social-emotional development in blind infants. *Child Care, Health and Development, 18*, 207–227.

Trotter, R. J. (1981). Psychiatry for the 80's. *Science News, 119*, 348–349.

Trotter, R. J. (1986, August). Three heads are better than one. *Psychology Today*, pp. 56–62.

Truax, C. B. (1966). Reinforcement and nonreinforcement in Rogerian psychotherapy. *Journal of Abnormal Psychology, 71*, 1–9.

Trujillo, C. M. (1983). The effect of weight training and running exercise intervention programs on the self-esteem of college women. *International Journal of Sport Psychology, 14*, 162–173.

Tubbs, M. E. (1986). Goal setting: A meta-analytic examinations of the empirical evidence. *Journal of Applied Psychology, 71*, 474–483.

Tucker, L. A. (1982). Effect of a weight training program on the self-concept of college males. *Perceptual and Motor Skills, 54*, 1055–1061.

Tucker, L. A. (1983). Muscular strength: A predictor of personality in males. *Journal of Sports Medicine and Physical Fitness, 23*, 213–220.

Tucker, L. A., Aldana, S. G., & Friedman, G. M. (1990). Cardiovascular fitness and absenteeism in 8,301 employed adults. *American Journal of Health Promotion, 5*, 140–145.

Tucker, W. H. (1994). Fact and fiction in the discovery of Sir Cyril Burt's flaws. *Journal of the History of the Behavioral Sciences, 30*, 335–347.

Tulsky, F. N. (1986, March 28). $988,000 is awarded in suit over lost psychic power. *Philadelphia Inquirer*, p. 1–A.

Tulving, E. (1985). How many memory systems are there? *American Psychologist, 40*, 385–398.

Tulving, E. (1993). What is episodic memory? *Current Directions in Psychological Science, 2*, 67–70.

Tulving, E., & Thomson, D. M. (1973). Encoding specificity and retrieval processes in episodic memory. *Psychological Review, 80*, 352–373.

Turk, D. C. (1994). Perspectives on chronic pain: The role of psychological factors. *Current Directions in Psychological Science, 3*, 45–48.

Turkheimer, E. (1991). Individual and group differences in adoption studies of IQ. *Psychological Bulletin, 110*, 392–405.

Turkington, C. (1984, August). Supportive homes few, barriers many. *APA Monitor*, pp. 20, 22.

Turnbull, C. M. (1961). Some observations regarding the experiences of the Bambuti Pygmies. *American Journal of Psychology, 74*, 304–308.

Turner, S. M., Beidel, D. C., Cooley, M. R., & Woody, S. R. (1994). A multicomponent behavioral treatment for social phobia: Social effectiveness therapy. *Behaviour Research and Therapy, 32*, 381–390.

Turner, S. M., Beidel, D. C., & Costello, A. (1987). Psychopathology in the offspring of anxiety disorder patients. *Journal of Consulting and Clinical Psychology, 55*, 229–235.

Turner, S. M., Beidel, D. C., Long, P. J., & Greenhouse, J. (1992). Reduction of fear in social phobics: An examination of extinction patterns. *Behavior Therapy, 23*, 389–403.

Tversky, A., & Kahneman, D. (1973). Availability: A heuristic for judging frequency and probability. *Cognitive Psychology, 5*, 207–232.

Type A: A change of heart and mind. (1984). *Science News, 126*, 109.

Tyson, P. D., & Sobschak, K. B. (1994). Perceptual responses to infant crying after EEG biofeedback assisted stress management training: Implications for physical child abuse. *Child Abuse and Neglect, 18*, 933–943.

Uchino, B. N., Cacioppo, J. T., & Keicolt-Glaser, J. K. (1996). The relationship between social support and physiological processes: A review with emphasis on underlying mechanisms and implications for health. *Psychological Bulletin, 119*, 488–531.

Ullman, M., Krippner, S., & Vaughan, A. (1973). *Dream telepathy*. New York: Macmillan.

Ullmann, L. P., & Krasner, L. (1975). *Psychological approaches to abnormal behavior*. Englewood Cliffs, NJ: Prentice Hall.

Ulrich, R. E., Stachnik, T. J., & Stainton, N. R. (1963). Student acceptance of generalized personality interpretations. *Psychological Reports, 13*, 831–834.

Underwood, G. (1994). Subliminal perception on TV. *Nature, 370*, 103.

Unger, G., Desiderio, D. M., & Parr, W. (1972). Isolation, identification and synthesis of a specific-behavior-inducing brain peptide. *Nature, 238*, 198–202.

Ungs, T. J., & Sangal, S. P. (1990). Perception of near-earth altitudes by pilots: Ascending versus descending over both a land and water surface. *Aviation, Space, and Environmental Medicine, 61*, 1098–1101.

Usher, J. A., & Neisser, U. (1993). Childhood amnesia and the beginnings of memory for four early life events. *Journal of Experimental Psychology General, 122*, 155–165.

Vaillant, G. E. (1992). The historical origins and future potential of Sigmund Freud's concept of the mechanisms of defense. *International Review of Psychoanalysis, 19*, 35–50.

Vaillant, G. E., & Milofsky, E. (1980). Natural history of male psychological health: 9. Empirical evidence for Erikson's model of the life cycle. *American Journal of Psychiatry, 137*, 1348–1359.

Valacich, J. S., & Schwenk, C. (1995). Devil's advocate and dialectical inquiry effects on face-to-face and computer-mediated group decision making. *Organizational Behavior and Human Decision Processes, 63*, 158–173.

Valenstein, E. S. (1980). *The psychosurgery debate*. San Francisco: Freeman.

Valentine, C. W. (1930). The innate bases of fear. *Journal of Genetic Psychology, 37*, 485–497.

Vance, E. B., & Wagner, N. N. (1976). Written descriptions of orgasm: A study of sex differences. *Archives of Sexual Behavior, 5*, 87–98.

VanderZee, K. I., Buunk, B. P., DeRuiter, J. H., & Tempelaar, R. (1996). Social comparison and the subjective well-being of cancer patients. *Basic and Applied Social Psychology, 18*, 453–468.

Van Doornen, L. J. P., & van Blokland, R. (1987). Serum-cholesterol: Sex specific psychological correlates during rest and stress. *Journal of Psychosomatic Research, 31*, 239–249.

Van Elteren, M. (1992). Kurt Lewin as filmmaker and methodologist. *Canadian Psychology, 33*, 599–608.

Van Goozen, S. H. M., Frijda, N. H., & Van de Poll, N. E. (1995). Anger and aggression during role-playing: Gender differences between hormonally treated male and female transsexuals and controls. *Aggressive Behavior, 21*, 257–273.

VanHelder, W. P., Kofman, E., & Tremblay, M. S. (1991). Anabolic steroids in sport. *Canadian Journal of Sport Sciences, 16*, 248–257.

Vargas, E. A., & Vargas, J. S. (1991). Programmed instruction: What it is and how to do it. *Journal of Behavioral Education, 1*, 235–251.

Vein, A. M., Sidorov, A. A., Martazaev, M. S., & Karlov, A. V. (1991). Physical exercise and nocturnal sleep in healthy humans. *Human Physiology, 17*, 391–397.

Veissier, I. (1993). Observational learning in cattle. *Applied Animal Behaviour Science, 35*, 235–243.

Veliz, J., & James, W. S. (1987). Medicine court: Rogers in practice. *American Journal of Psychiatry, 144*, 62–67.

Venn, J. (1984). Family etiology and remission in a case of psychogenic fugue. *Family Process, 23*, 429–435.

Veroff, J., Depner, C., Kulka, R., & Douvan, E. (1980). Comparison of American motives: 1957 versus 1976. *Journal of Personality and Social Psychology, 39*, 1249–1262.

Vessey, J. A., Carlson, K. L, & McGill, J. (1994). Use of distraction with children during an acute pain experience. *Nursing Research, 43*, 369–372.

Vetter, H. J. (1969). *Language behavior and psychopathology*. Chicago: Rand McNally.

Vicente, K. J. (1994). A pragmatic conception of basic and applied research: Commentary on Hoffman and Deffenbacher (1993). *Ecological Psychology, 6*, 65–81.

Vicente, K. J., & Brewer, W. F. (1993). Reconstructive remembering of the scientific literature. *Cognition, 46*, 101–128.

Vickers, J. N. (1992). Gaze control in putting. *Perception, 21*, 117–132.

Vincent, K. R. (1991). Black/white IQ differences: Does age make the difference? *Journal of Clinical Psychology, 47*, 266–270.

Viney, L. L. (1991). The personal construct theory of death and loss: Toward a more individually oriented grief therapy. *Death Studies, 15*, 139–155.

Viney, W. (1989). The cyclops and the twelve-eyed toad: William James and the unity-disunity problem in psychology. *American Psychologist, 44*, 1261–1265.

Viney, W. (1990). The tempering effect of determinism in the legal system: A response to Rychlak and Rychlak. *New Ideas in Psychology, 8*, 31–42.

Viney, W. (1993). *A history of psychology: Ideas and context*. Boston: Allyn & Bacon.

Viney, W., & Bartsch, K. (1984). Dorothea Lynde Dix: Positive or negative influence on the development of treatment for the mentally ill. *Social Science Journal, 21*, 71–82.

Vlaander, G. P., & Van Rooijen, L. (1985). Independence and conformity in Holland: Asch's experiment three decades later. *Gedrag: Tijdschrift voor Psychologie, 13*, 49–55.

Voeller, B. (1991). AIDS and heterosexual anal intercourse. *Archives of Sexual Behavior, 20*, 233–276.

Vokey, J. R., & Read, J. D. (1985). Subliminal messages: Between the devil and the media. *American Psychologist, 40*, 1231–1239.

Volling, B. L., & Feagans, L. V. (1995). Infant day care and children's social competence. *Infant Behavior and Development, 18*, 177–188.

Vonnegut, M. (1974, April). Why I want to bite R. D. Laing. *Harper's Magazine*, pp. 90–92.

Vonnegut, M. (1975). *The Eden express*. New York: Bantam Books.

Voyer, D., Voyer, S., & Bryden, M. P. (1995). Magnitude of sex differences in spatial abilities: A meta-analysis and consideration of critical variables. *Psychological Bulletin, 117*, 250–270.

Vroom, V. H. (1964). *Work and motivation*. New York: Wiley.

Vrooman, J. R. (1970). *René Descartes: A biography*. New York: Putnam.

Wadden, T. A., Foster, G. D., & Letizia, K. A. (1994). One-year behavioral treatment of obesity: Comparison of moderate and severe caloric restriction and the effects of weight maintenance therapy. *Journal of Consulting and Clinical Psychology, 62*, 165–171.

Wade, N. J. (1994). Hermann von Helmholtz (1821–1894). *Perception, 23*, 981–989.

Wagner, A. M., & Houlihan, D. D. (1994). Notes and shorter communications: Sensation seeking and trait anxiety in hang-glider pilots and golfers. *Personality and Individual Differences, 16*, 975–977.

Wagstaff, G. F., Vella, M., & Perfect, T. (1992). The effect of hypnotically elicited testimony on jurors' judgments of guilt and innocence. *Journal of Social Psychology, 132*, 591–595.

Waid, W. M., & Orne, M. T. (1982). The physiological detection of deception. *American Scientist, 70*, 402–409.

Waid, W. M., Wilson, S. K., & Orne, M. T. (1981). Cross-modal physiological effects of electrodermal ability in the detection of deception. *Journal of Personality and Social Psychology, 40*, 1118–1125.

Wald, G. (1964). The receptors of human color vision. *Science, 145*, 1007–1017.

Waldhauser, F., Saletu, B., & Trinchard, L. I. (1990). Sleep laboratory investigations on hypnotic properties of melatonin. *Psychopharmacology, 100*, 222–226.

Waldrop, M. M. (1984, June). Astrology is off target. *Science, 84*, pp. 80, 82.

Walk, R. D., & Homan, C. P. (1984). Emotion and dance in dynamic light displays. *Bulletin of the Psychonomic Society, 22*, 437–440.

Walker, E., Hoppes, E., Emory, E., Mednick, S., & Schulsinger, F. (1981). Environmental factors related to schizophrenia in psychophysiologically labile high-risk males. *Journal of Abnormal Psychology, 90*, 313–320.

Walker, L. J. (1984). Sex differences in the development of moral reasoning: A critical review. *Child Development, 55*, 677–691.

Walker, L. J. (1986). Experiential and cognitive sources of moral development in adulthood. *Human Development, 29*, 113–124.

Walker, L. J. (1989). A longitudinal study of moral reasoning. *Child Development*, 60, 157–166.

Wallabaum, A. B., Rzewnicki, R., Steele, H., & Suedfeld, P. (1991). Progressive muscle relaxation and restricted environmental stimulation therapy for chronic tension headache: A pilot study. *International Journal of Psychosomatics*, 38, 33–39.

Wallace, A. (1986). *The prodigy*. New York: Dutton.

Wallace, B., & Kokoszka, A. (1995). Fluctuations in hypnotic susceptibility and imaging ability over a 16-hour period. *International Journal of Clinical and Experimental Hypnosis*, 43, 20–33.

Wallace, C. S., Kilman, V. L., Withers, G. S., & Greenough, W. T. (1992). Increases in dendritic length in occipital cortex after 4 days of differential housing in weanling rats. *Behavioral and Neural Biology*, 58, 64-68.

Wallace, R. E. (1988). Abolish the duty to protect: It's time to release the scapegoats. *Psychotherapy in Private Practice*, 6, 55–63.

Wallace, R. K., & Benson, H. (1972, February). The physiology of meditation. *Scientific American*, pp. 84–90.

Wallach, H., & Marshall, F. J. (1986). Shape constancy in pictorial representation. *Perception and Psychophysics*, 39, 233–235.

Wallach, M. A., Kogan, N., & Bem, D. J. (1962). Group influence on individual risk taking. *Journal of Abnormal and Social Psychology*, 65, 75–86.

Waller, N. G., Kojetin, B. A., Bouchard, T. J., & Lykken, D. T. (1990). Genetic and environmental influences on religious interests, attitudes, and values: A study of twins reared apart and together. *Psychological Science*, 1, 138–142.

Wallis, C. (1984, June 11). Unlocking pain's secrets. *Time*, pp. 58–66.

Walsh, D. M., Liggett, C., Baxter, D., & Allen, J. M. (1995). A double-blind investigation of the hypoalgesic effects of transcutaneous electrical nerve stimulation upon experimentally induced ischaemic pain. *Pain*, 61, 39–45.

Walsh, J. (1981). A plenipotentiary for human intelligence. *Science*, 214, 640–641.

Walsh, J. (1983). Wide world of reports. *Science*, 214, 640–641.

Walsh, J. J., Wilding, J. M., & Eysenck, M. W. (1994). Stress responsivity: The role of individual differences. *Personality and Individual Differences*, 16, 385–394.

Walster, E., Aronson, V., Abrahams, D., & Rottman, L. (1966). Importance of physical attractiveness in dating behavior. *Journal of Personality and Social Psychology*, 4, 508–516.

Walters, G. C., & Grusec, J. E. (1977). *Punishment*. San Francisco: Freeman.

Waltz, D. L. (1982, October). Artificial intelligence. *Scientific American*, pp. 118–133.

Wang, J. J., & Kaufman, A. S. (1993). Changes in fluid and crystallized intelligence across the 20- to 90-year age range in the K-BIT. *Journal of Psycheducational Assessment*, 11, 29–37.

Wang, J. Q., Mao, L., & Han, J.–S. (1992). Comparison of the antinociceptive effects induced by electroacupuncture and transcutaneous electrical nerve stimulation in the rat. *International Journal of Neuroscience*, 65, 117–129.

Wang, M. Q., Nicholson, M. E., Mahoney, B. S., & Li, Y. (1993). Proprioceptive responses under rising and falling BACs: A test of Mellanby effect. *Perceptual and Motor Skills*, 77, 83–88.

Wang, X. T., & Johnston, V. S. (1995). Perceived social context and risk preference: A re-examination of framing effects in a life-death decision problem. *Journal of Behavioral Decision Making*, 8, 279–293.

Wankel, L. M. (1993). The importance of enjoyment to adherence and psychological benefits from physical activity. Special Issue: Exercise and psychological well being. *International Journal of Sport Psychology*, 24, 151–169.

Ward, N. J., & Parkes, A. (1994). Head-up displays and their automotive application: An overview of human factors issues affecting safety. *Accident Analysis and Prevention*, 26, 703–717.

Washburn, D. A., Rumbaugh, D. M., & Putney, R. T. (1994). Apparatus as milestones in the history of comparative psychology. *Behavior Research Methods, Instruments and Computers*, 26, 231-235.

Washburn, M. F. (1908). *The animal mind: A textbook of comparative psychology*. New York: Macmillan.

Washburn, M. F. (1916). *Movement and mental imagery*. Boston: Houghton Mifflin.

Wasserman, E. A. (1997). What's elementary about associative learning? *Annual Review of Psychology*, 48, 573-607.

Watanabe, S., & Bruera, E. (1994). Corticosteroids as adjuvant analgesics. *Journal of Pain and Symptom Management*, 9, 442–445.

Watkins, P. C., Vache, K., Verney, S. P., & Mathews, A. (1996). Unconscious mood-congruent memory bias in depression. *Journal of Abnormal Psychology*, 105, 34-41.

Watkins, C. E., Jr., Lopez, F. G., Campbell, V. L., & Himmell, C. D. (1986). Counseling psychology and clinical psychology: Some preliminary comparative data. *American Psychologist*, 41, 581–584.

Watkins, J. G. (1984). The Bianchi (L.A. Hillside Strangler) case: Sociopath or multiple personality? *International Journal of Clinical and Experimental Hypnosis*, 32, 67–101.

Watkins, J. G. (1989). Hypnotic hypermnesia and forensic hypnosis: A cross-examination. *American Journal of Clinical Hypnosis*, 32, 71–83.

Watson, J. B. (1913). Psychology as the behaviorist views it. *Psychological Review*, 20, 158–177.

Watson, J. B. (1930). *Behaviorism*. New York: W. W. Norton.

Watson, J. B., & Rayner, R. (1920). Conditioned emotional reactions. *Journal of Experimental Psychology*, 3, 1–14.

Watten, R. G., Lie, I., & Birketvedt, O. (1994). The influence of long-term visual near-work on accommodation and vergence: A field study. *Journal of Human Ergology*, 23, 27–39.

Watts, B. L. (1982). Individual differences in circadian activity rhythms and their effects on roommate relationships. *Journal of Personality*, 50, 374–384.

Watts, R. E., & Holden, J. M. (1994). Why continue to use "fictional finalism?" *Individual Psychology: Journal of Adlerian Theory, Research and Practice*, 50, 161–163.

Weaver, C. A. (1993). Do you need a "flash" to form a flashbulb memory? *Journal of Experimental Psychology: General*, 122, 39–46.

Weaver, J. B., Masland, J. L., Kharazmi, S., & Zillman, D. (1985). Effect of alcoholic intoxication on the appreciation of different types of humor. *Journal of Personality and Social Psychology*, 49, 781–787.

Webb, C. (1977). The use of myoelectric facial feedback in teaching facial expression to the blind. *Biofeedback and Self-Regulation*, 2, 147–160.

Webb, E. J., Campbell, D. T., Schwartz, R. D., & Sechrest, L. (1966). *Unobtrusive measures: Nonreactive research in the social sciences*. Chicago: Rand McNally.

Webb, W. B. (1981). An essay on consciousness. *Teaching of Psychology*, 8, 15–19.

Webb, W. B. (1985). Sleep and dreaming. In G. A. Kimble & K. Schlesinger (Eds.), *Topics in the history of psychology* (Vol. 2, pp. 191–217). Hillsdale, NJ: Erlbaum.

Webb, W. B. (1992). *Sleep: The gentle tyrant* (2nd ed.). Boston: Anker.

Webb, W. B., & Agnew, H. W., Jr. (1974). Sleeping and waking in a time-free environment. *Aerospace Medicine*, 45, 617–622.

Weber, J. M., Klesges, R. C., & Klesges, L. M. (1988). Dietary restraint and obesity: Their effects on dietary intake. *Journal of Behavioral Medicine*, 11, 185–199.

Weber, R., & Crocker, J. (1983). Cognitive processes in the revision of stereotype beliefs. *Journal of Personality and Social Psychology*, 45, 961–977.

Webster, S., & Coleman, S. R. (1992). The reception of Clark L. Hull's behavior theory, 1943–1960. *Psychological Reports*, 70, 1063–1071.

Wechsler, D. (1958). *Measurement and appraisal of adult intelligence*. Baltimore: Williams & Wilkins.

Weekes, J. R., Lynn, S. J., Green, J. P., & Brentar, J. T. (1992). Pseudomemory in hypnotized and task-motivated subjects. *Journal of Abnormal Psychology*, 101, 356–360.

Wegner, D. M., Schneider, D. J., Carter, S. R., III, & White, T. L. (1987). Paradoxical effects of thought suppression. *Journal of Personality and Social Psychology*, 53, 5–13.

Weigel, R. H., Vernon, D. T. A., & Tognacci, L. N. (1974). Specificity of the attitude as a determinant of attitude-behavior congruence. *Journal of Personality and Social Psychology*, 30, 724–728.

Weinberg, R. A. (1989). Intelligence and IQ: Landmark issues and great debates. *American Psychologist*, 44, 98–104.

Weinberg, R. S., Burton, D., Yukelson, D., & Weigand, D. (1993). Goal setting in competitive sport: An exploratory investigation of practices of collegiate athletes. *Sport Psychologist*, 7, 275–289.

Weinberg, R. A., Scarr, S., & Waldman, I. D. (1992). The Minnesota Transracial Adoption Study: A follow-up of IQ test performance at adolescence. *Intelligence*, 16, 117–135.

Weinberg, R. S., & Weigand, D. (1993). Goal setting in sport and exercise: A reaction to Locke. *Journal of Sport and Exercise Psychology*, 15, 88–96.

Weinberger, D. R., Goldberg, T. E., & Tamminga, C. A. (1995). Prefrontal leukotomy. *American Journal of Psychiatry*, 152, 330–331.

Weinberger, J., & Silverman, L. H. (1990). Testability and empirical verification of psychoanalytic dynamic propositions through subliminal psychodynamic activation. *Psychoanalytic Psychology*, 7, 299–339.

Weiner, B. (1980). A cognitive (attribution)-emotion-action model of motivated behavior: An analysis of judgments of help-giving. *Journal of Personality and Social Psychology*, 39, 186–200.

Weiner, B. (1985a). An attributional theory of achievement motivation and emotion. *Psychological Review*, 92, 548–573.

Weiner, B. (1985b). "Spontaneous" causal thinking. *Psychological Bulletin*, 97, 74–84.

Weiner, B., Figueroa-Munoz, A., & Kakihara, C. (1991). The goals of excuses and communication strategies related to causal perceptions. *Personality and Social Psychology Bulletin*, 17, 4–13.

Weiner, D. B. (1992). Philippe Pinel's "Memoir on Madness" of December 11, 1794: A fundamental text of modern psychiatry. *American Journal of Psychiatry*, 149, 725–732.

Weinstein, L., & Almaguer, L. L. (1987). "I'm bored!" *Bulletin of the Psychonomic Society*, 25, 389–390.

Weinstein, N. D. (1984). Reducing unrealistic optimism about illness susceptibility. *Health Psychology*, 3, 431–457.

Weir, P. (1990). Hypnosis and the treatment of burned patients: A review of the literature. *Australian Journal of Clinical Hypnotherapy and Hypnosis*, 11, 11–15.

Weisberg, R. W. (1992). Metacognition and insight during problem solving: Comment on Metcalfe. *Journal of Experimental Psychology: Learning, Memory, and Cognition*, 18, 426–431.

Weisburd, S. (1984). Whales and dolphins use magnetic "roads." *Science News*, 126, 391.

Weiskrantz, L. (1995). Blindsight: Not an island unto itself. *Psychological Science*, 4, 146–151.

Weisman, J. (1988, November 19–25). Remembering JFK: Our first TV president. *TV Guide*, pp. 2–4, 6–8.

Weiss, J. M. (1972, June). Psychological factors in stress and disease. *Scientific American*, pp. 104–113.

Weiss, M. G. (1995). Eating disorders and disordered eating in different cultures. *Psychiatric Clinics of North America, 18*, 537–553.

Weiss, S. J., Panlilio, L. V., & Schindler, C. W. (1993). Single-incentive selective associations produced solely as a function of compound-stimulus conditioning context. *Journal of Experimental Psychology Animal Behavior Processes, 19*, 284-294.

Weissman, M. M. (1990). The hidden patient: Unrecognized panic disorder. *Journal of Clinical Psychiatry, 51*, 5–8.

Weisz, J. R., Weiss, B., Han, S. S., & Granger, D. A. (1995). Effects of psychotherapy with children and adolescents revisited: A meta-analysis of treatment outcome studies. *Psychological Bulletin, 117*, 450–468.

Weitzenhoffer, A. M., & Hilgard, E. R. (1962). *Stanford Scale of Hypnotic Susceptibility, Form C.* Palo Alto, CA: Consulting Psychologists Press.

Weldon, E., & Gargano, G. M. (1988). Cognitive loafing: The effects of accountability and shared responsibility on cognitive effort. *Personality and Social Psychology Bulletin, 14*, 159–171.

Weller, L., & Weller, A. (1995). Menstrual synchrony: Agenda for future research. *Psychoneuroendocrinology, 20*, 377–383.

Wells, D. L., & Muchinsky, P. M. (1985). Performance antecedents of voluntary and involuntary turnover managerial turnover. *Journal of Applied Psychology, 70*, 329–336.

Wells, G. L., & Lindsay, R. C. L. (1985). Methodological notes on the accuracy-confidence relation in eyewitness identification. *Journal of Applied Psychology, 70*, 413–419.

Wenderoth, P. (1994). On the relationship between the psychology of visual perception and the neurophysiology of vision. *Australian Journal of Psychology, 46*, 1–6.

Wertheimer, M. (1978). Humanistic psychology and the humane but tough-minded psychologist. *American Psychologist, 33*, 739–745.

Wertheimer, M., & King, D. B. (1994). Max Wertheimer's American sojourn, 1933–1943. *History of Psychology Newletter, 26*, 3–15.

Wever, E. G., & Bray, C. W. (1937). The perception of low tones and the resonance volley theory. *Journal of Psychology, 3*, 101–114.

Wexley, K. N., & Latham, G. P. (1991). *Developing and training human resources in organizations* (2nd ed.). New York: HarperCollins.

Wheeler, R. E., Davidson, R. J., & Tomarken, A. J. (1993). Frontal brain asymmetry and emotional reactivity: A biological substrate of affective style. *Psychophysiology, 30*, 82–89.

Wheldall, K., & Benner, H. (1993). Conservation without conversation revisited: A replication and elaboration of the Wheldall-Poborca findings on the non-verbal assessment of conservation of liquid quantity. *Educational Psychology, 13*, 49–58.

Whishaw, I. Q. (1991). Latent learning in a swimming pool place task by rats: Evidence for the use of associative and not cognitive mapping processes. *Quarterly Journal of Experimental Psychology: Comparative and Physiological Psychology, 43*, 83–103.

Whissell, C. M. (1984). Emotion: A classification of current literature. *Perceptual and Motor Skills, 59*, 599–609.

Whitbourne, S. K., & Hulicka, I. M. (1990). Ageism in undergraduate psychology texts. *American Psychologist, 45*, 1127–1136.

White, G. L., Fishbein, S., & Rutstein, J. (1981). Passionate love and the misattribution of arousal. *Journal of Personality, 41*, 56–62.

White, J. W., & Humphrey, J. A. (1994). Women's aggression in heterosexual conflicts. *Aggressive Behavior, 20*, 195–202.

White, S. H. (1990). Child study at Clark University. *Journal of the History of the Behavioral Sciences, 26*, 131–150.

White, S. H. (1994). Hilgard's vision of psychology's history. *Psychological Science, 5*, 192–194.

Whitehurst, G. J., Falco, F. L., Lonigan, C. J., Fischel, J. E., DeBaryshe, B. D., Valdez-Menchaca, M. C., & Caulfield, M. (1988). Accelerating language development through picture book reading. *Developmental Psychology, 24*, 552–559.

Whitlock, F. A. (1987). Addiction. In R. L. Gregory (Ed.), *Oxford companion to the mind* (pp. 3–5). New York: Oxford University Press.

Whorf, B. L. (1956). Science and linguistics. In J. B. Carroll (Ed.), *Language, thought, and reality: Selected writings of Benjamin Lee Whorf* (pp. 202–219). Cambridge, MA: MIT Press.

Whyte, W. H. (1956). *The organization man.* New York: Simon & Schuster.

Wicker, F. W., Barron, W. L., & Willis, A. C. (1980). Disparagement humor: Dispositions and resolutions. *Journal of Personality and Social Psychology, 39*, 701–709.

Widiger, T. A., & Trull, T. J. (1991). Diagnosis and clinical assessment. *Annual Review of Psychology, 42*, 109–133.

Widmeyer, W. N., & Loy, J. W. (1988). When you're hot, you're hot: Warm-cold effects in first impressions of persons and teaching effectiveness. *Journal of Educational Psychology, 80*, 118–121.

Wiebe, D. J., & McCallum, D. M. (1986). Health practices and hardiness as mediators in the stress-illness relationship. *Health Psychology, 5*, 425–438.

Wiegman, O., Kuttschreuter, M., & Baarda, B. (1992). A longitudinal study of the effects of television viewing on aggressive and prosocial behaviours. *British Journal of Social Psychology, 31*, 147–164.

Wightman, D. C., & Lintern, G. (1984, August). Part-task training of tracking in manual control. *NAVTRAEQUIPCEN* (Technical Report 81-C 0105 2).

Wilcox, B. L. (1987). Pornography, social science, and politics: When research and ideology collide. *American Psychologist, 42*, 941–943.

Wilcox, J. A. (1990). Fluoxetine and bulimia. *Journal of Psychoactive Drugs, 22*, 81–82.

Wilding, J., Rashid, W., Gilmore, D., & Valentine, E. (1986). A comparison of two mnemonic methods in learning medical information. *Human Learning: Journal of Practical Research and Applications, 5*, 211–217.

Williams, C. D. (1959). The elimination of tantrum behavior by extinction procedures. *Journal of Abnormal and Social Psychology, 59*, 269.

Williams, J., Merritt, J., Rittenhouse, C., & Hobson, J. A. (1992) Bizarreness in dreams and fantasies: Implications for the activation-synthesis hypothesis. *Consciousness and Cognition: An International Journal, 1*, 172–185.

Williams, R. B., Jr., Kuhn, C. M., Melosh, W., White, A. D., & Schonberg, S. M. (1982). Type A behavior and elevated physiological and neuroendocrine responses to cognitive tasks. *Science, 218*, 483–485.

Williams, S. L., & Kinney, P. J. (1991). Performance and nonperformance strategies for coping with acute pain: The role of perceived self-efficacy, expected outcomes, and attention. *Cognitive Therapy and Research, 15*, 1–19.

Williams, S. L., Turner, S. M., & Peer, D. F. (1985). Guided mastery and performance desensitization treatments for severe acrophobia. *Journal of Consulting and Clinical Psychology, 53*, 237–247.

Wilson, C., Boni, N., & Hogg, A. (1997). The effectiveness of task clarification, positive reinforcement and corrective feedback in changing courtesy among police staff. *Journal of Organizational Behavior Management, 17*, 65-99.

Wilson, E. J., & Sherrell, D. L. (1993). Source effects in communication and persuasion research: A meta-analysis of effect size. *Journal of the Academy of Marketing Science, 21*, 101–112.

Wilson, E. O. (1975). *Sociobiology: The new synthesis.* Cambridge, MA: Harvard University Press.

Wilson, G. D. (1987). Male-female differences in sexual activity, enjoyment, and fantasies. *Personality and Individual Differences, 8*, 125–127.

Wilson, G. T. (1994). Behavioral treatment of obesity: Thirty years and counting. *Advances in Behaviour Research and Therapy, 16*, 31–75.

Wilson, J. P., & Petruska, R. (1984). Motivation, model attributes, and prosocial behavior. *Journal of Personality and Social Psychology, 46*, 458–468.

Wilson, J. R. (1967). *The mind.* New York: Time.

Wilson, R. A. (1994). Logotherapy in the classroom. *International Forum for Logotherapy, 17*, 32–41.

Wilson, T. D. (1994). The proper protocol: Validity and completeness of verbal reports. *Psychological Science, 5*, 249–252.

Wilson-Barnett, J. (1994). Preparing patients for invasive medical and surgical procedures: III. Policy implications for implementing specific psychological interventions. *Behavioral Medicine, 20*, 23–26.

Winders, S. E., & Grunberg, N. E. (1989). Nicotine, tobacco smoke, and body weight: A review of the animal literature. *Annals of Behavioral Medicine, 11*, 125–133.

Windholz, G. (1992). Pavlov's conceptualization of learning. *American Journal of Psychology, 105*, 459–469.

Windholz, G., & Kuppers, J. R. (1990). Pavlov and the Nobel Prize award. *Pavlovian Journal of Biological Science, 25*, 155–162.

Winefield, A. H. (1982). Methodological difficulties in demonstrating learned helplessness in humans. *Journal of General Psychology, 107*, 255–266.

Winn, K. I., Crawford, D. W., & Fischer, J. L. (1991). Equity and commitment in romance versus friendship. *Journal of Social Behavior and Personality, 6*, 301–314.

Winter, D. A. (1993). Slot rattling from law enforcement to lawbreaking: A personal construct theory exploration of police stress. *International Journal of Personal Construct Psychology, 6*, 253–267.

Winton, W. M. (1990). Jamesian aspects of misattribution research. *Personality and Social Psychology Bulletin, 16*, 652–664.

Wisely, D. W., Masur, F. T., & Morgan, S. B. (1983). Psychological aspects of severe burn injuries in children. *Health Psychology, 2*, 45–72.

Wissink, L. M. (1994). A validation of transactional analysis in increasing self-esteem among participants in a self-reparenting program. *Transactional Analysis Journal, 24*, 189–196.

Wittchen, H. U., Zhao, S., Kessler, R. C., & Eaton, W. W. (1994). DSM-III-R generalized anxiety disorder in the National Comorbidity Survey. *Archives of General Psychiatry, 51*, 355–364.

Wixted, J. T. (1991). Conditions and consequences of maintenance rehearsal. *Journal of Experimental Psychology: Learning, Memory, and Cognition, 17*, 963–973.

Wixted, J. T., & Ebbesen, E. B. (1991). On the form of forgetting. *Psychological Science, 2*, 409–415.

Wogalter, M. S., & Laughery, K. R. (1996). Warning! Sign and label effectiveness. *Current Directions, 5*, 33-37.

Wojcikiewicz, A., & Orlick, T. (1987). The effects of post-hypnotic suggestion and relaxation with suggestion on competitive fencing anxiety and performance. *International Journal of Sport Psychology, 18*, 303–313.

Wolfe, D. A., Mendes, M. G., & Factor, D. (1984). A parent-administered program to reduce children's television viewing. *Journal of Applied Behavior Analysis, 17*, 267–272.

Wolfe, J. (1936). Effectiveness of token rewards for chimpanzees. *Comparative Psychology Monographs, 12* (5).

Wolfe, T. (1979). *The right stuff.* New York: Bantam Books.

Wolfensberger, W. (1972). *Normalization.* Toronto: National Institute on Mental Retardation.

Wolkowitz, O. M., Gertz, B., Weingartner, H., & Beccaria, L. (1990). Hunger in humans induced by MK 329, a specific peripheral-type cholecystokinin receptor antagonist. *Biological Psychiatry, 28*, 169–173.

Wollen, K. A., Weber, A., & Lowry, D. H. (1972). Bizarreness versus interaction of mental images as determinants of learning. *Cognitive Psychology, 3*, 518–523.

Wolpe, J. (1958). *Psychotherapy by reciprocal inhibition.* Stanford, CA: Stanford University Press.

Wolpe, J. (1988). Obituary: Mary Cover Jones 1896–1987. *Journal of Behavior Therapy and Experimental Psychiatry, 19*, 34.

Wolpin, M., Marston, A., Randolph, C., & Clothier, A. (1992). Individual difference correlates of reported lucid dreaming frequency and control. *Journal of Mental Imagery, 16*, 231–236.

Wonderlic, E. F. (1983). *Wonderlic Personnel test.* Northfield, IL: Wonderlic.

Wong, E. V., Kenwrick, S., Willems, P., & Lemmon, V. (1995). Mutations in the cell adhesion molecule L1 cause mental retardation. *Trends in Neurosciences, 18*, 168–172.

Wood, J. M., Bootzin, R. R., & Kihlstrom, J. F. (1992). Implicit and explicit memory for verbal information presented during sleep. *Psychological Science, 3*, 236–239.

Wood, J. M., Bootzin, R. R., Rosenhan, D., Nolen-Hoeksema, S., & Jourden, F. (1992). Effects of the 1989 San Francisco earthquake on frequency and content of nightmares. *Journal of Abnormal Psychology, 101*, 219–224.

Wood, N., & Cowan, N. (1995). The cocktail party phenomenon revisited: How frequent are attention shifts to one's name in an irrelevant auditory channel? *Journal of Experimental Psychology Learning, Memory, and Cognition, 21*, 255–260.

Wood, W., & Eagly, A. H. (1981). Stages in the analysis of persuasive messages: The role of causal attributions and message comprehension. *Journal of Experimental and Social Psychology, 40*, 246–259.

Wood, W., Lundgren, S., Ouellette, J. A., & Busceme, S. (1994). Minority influence: A meta-analytic review of social influence processes. *Psychological Bulletin, 115*, 323–345.

Woodruff-Pak, D. S. (1993). Eyeblink classical conditioning in H. M.: Delay and trace paradigms. *Behavioral Neuroscience, 107*, 911–925.

Worringham, C. J., & Messick, D. M. (1983). Social facilitation of running: An unobtrusive study. *Journal of Social Psychology, 121*, 23–29.

Wright, A. A., Cook, R. G., Rivera, J. J., & Shyan, M. R. (1990). Naming, rehearsal, and interstimulus interval effects in memory processing. *Journal of Experimental Psychology: Learning, Memory, and Cognition, 16*, 1043–1059.

Wu, J. C., Maguire, G., Riley, G., & Fallon, J. (1995). A positron emission tomography (-sup-1-sup-8F) deoxyglucose study of developmental stuttering. *Neuroreport: An International Journal for the Rapid Communication of Research in Neuroscience, 6*, 501–505.

Wurtz, R. H., Goldberg, M. E., & Robinson, D. L. (1982, June). Brain mechanisms of visual attention. *Scientific American*, pp. 124–135.

Wyatt, J. W. (1993). Identical twins, emergenesis, and environments. *American Psychologist, 48*, 1294–1295.

Wyatt, J. W., Posey, A., Walker, W., & Seamonds, C. (1984). Natural levels of similarities between identical twins and between unrelated people. *Skeptical Inquirer, 9*, 62–66.

Wynn, K. (1995). Infants possess a system of numerical knowlege. *Current Directions in Psychological Science, 4*, 172–177.

Yaccarino, M. E. (1993). Using Minuchin's structural family therapy techniques with Italian-American families. *Contemporary Family Therapy: An International Journal, 15*, 459–466.

Yalom, I. D. (1980). *Existential psychotherapy.* New York: Basic Books.

Yap, J. N. (1988). The effects of hospitalization and surgery on children: A critical review. *Journal of Applied Developmental Psychology, 9*, 349–358.

Yarmey, A. D. (1973). I recognize your face but I can't remember your name: Further evidence on the tip-of-the-tongue phenomenon. *Memory and Cognition, 1*, 287–290.

Yerkes, R. M., & Dodson, J. D. (1908). The relation of strength of stimulus to rapidity of habit-formation. *Journal of Comparative Neurology and Psychology, 18*, 459–482.

Yoshioka, T., Dow, B. M., & Vautin, R. G. (1996). Neuronal mechanisms of color categorization in areas V1, V2 and V4 of macaque monkey visual cortex. *Behavioural Brain Research, 76*, 51-70.

Young, A. W., & Ellis, H. D. (1989). Childhood prosopagnosia. *Brain and Cognition, 9*, 16–47.

Young, L. D., Richter, J. E., Bradley, L. A., & Anderson, K. O. (1987). Disorders of the upper gastrointestinal system: An overview. *Annals of Behavioral Medicine, 9 (3)*, 7–12.

Young, R. L., & Nettelbeck, T. (1995). The abilities of a musical savant and his family. *Journal of Autism and Developmental Disorders, 25*, 231–248.

Youngren, M. A., & Lewinsohn, P. M. (1980). The functional relation between depression and problematic interpersonal behavior. *Journal of Abnormal Psychology, 89*, 333–341.

Yu, S., & Ho, I. K. (1990). Effects of acute barbiturate administration, tolerance and dependence on brain GABA system: Comparison to alcohol and benzodiazepines. *Alcohol, 7*, 261–272.

Yukl, G. (1994). *Leadership in organizations* (3rd ed.). Englewood Cliffs, NJ: Prentice Hall.

Zaccaro, S. J., Foti, R. J., & Kenny, D. A. (1991). Self-monitoring and trait-based variance in leadership: An investigation of leader flexibility across multiple group situations. *Journal of Applied Psychology, 76*, 308–315.

Zahn, B. S., & Schug, S. E. (1993). The Survivors Project: A multimodal therapy program for adolescents in residential treatment who have survived child sexual abuse. *Residential Treatment for Children and Youth, 11*, 65–88.

Zajonc, R. B. (1965). Social facilitation. *Science, 149*, 269–274.

Zajonc, R. B. (1976). Family configuration and intelligence. *Science, 192*, 227–236.

Zajonc, R. B. (1984). On the primacy of affect. *American Psychologist, 39*, 117–123.

Zajonc, R. B. (1985). Emotion and facial efference: A theory revisited. *Science, 228*, 15–21.

Zajonc, R. B. (1986). The decline and rise of scholastic aptitude scores: A prediction derived from the confluence model. *American Psychologist, 41*, 862–867.

Zajonc, R. B. (1993). The confluence model: Differential or difference equation. *European Journal of Social Psychology, 23*, 211–215.

Zaldivar, R. A. (1986, June 10). Panel faults NASA on shuttle. *Philadelphia Inquirer*, pp. 1-A, 12-A.

Zander, A. (1979). The psychology of group processes. *Annual Review of Psychology, 30*, 417–451.

Zebrowitz, L. A., Tenenbaum, D. R., & Goldstein, L. H. (1991). The impact of job applicants' facial maturity, gender, and academic achievement on hiring recommendations. *Journal of Applied Social Psychology, 21*, 525–548.

Zentall, T. R., Sutton, J. E., & Sherburne, L. M. (1996). True imitative learning in pigeons. *Psychological Science, 7*, 343-346.

Zhang, J., & Thomas, D. L. (1994). Modernization theory revisited: A cross-cultural study of adolescent conformity to significant others in mainland China, Taiwan, and the USA. *Adolescence, 29*, 885-903.

Zigler, E., Abelson, W. D., Trickett, P. K., & Seitz, V. (1982). Is an intervention program necessary in order to improve economically disadvantaged children's IQ scores? *Child Development, 33*, 340–348.

Zimmer, J. W., & Hocevar, D. J. (1994). Effects of massed versus distributed practice of test taking on achievement and test anxiety. *Psychological Reports, 74*, 915–919.

Zimmerman, G., L., Legge, G. E., & Cavanagh, P. (1995). Pictorial depth cues: A new slant. *Journal of the Optical Society of America–A, 12*, 17–26.

Zimmerman, M. (1983). Methodological issues in the assessment of life events: A review of issues and research. *Clinical Psychology Review, 3*, 339–370.

Zimpfer, D. G. (1991). Groups for grief and survivorship after bereavement: A review. *Journal for Specialists in Group Work, 16*, 46–55.

Zisook, S., Byrd, D., Kuck, J., & Jeste, D. V. (1995).Command hallucinations in outpatients with schizophrenia. *Journal of Clinical Psychiatry, 56*, 462–465.

Zisook, S., Shuchter, S. R., Irwin, M., & Darko, D. F. (1994). Bereavement, depression, and immune function. *Psychiatry Research, 52*, 1–10.

Ziv, A. (1987). The effect of humor on aggression catharsis in the classroom. *Journal of Psychology, 121*, 359–364.

Zola-Morgan, S. M., & Squire, L. R. (1990). The primate hipppocampal formation: Evidence for a time-limited role in memory storage. *Science, 250*, 288–290.

Zucker, G. S., & Weiner, B. (1993). Conservatism and perceptions of poverty: An attributional analysis. *Journal of Applied Social Psychology, 23*, 925–943.

Zuckerman, M. (1990). The psychophysiology of sensation seeking. *Journal of Personality, 58*, 313–345.

Zuckerman, M., Koestner, R., DeBoy, T., Garcia, T., Maresca, B. C., & Sartoris, J. M. (1988). To predict some of the people some of the time: A reexamination of the moderator variable approach in personality theory. *Journal of Personality and Social Psychology, 54*, 1006–1019.

Zuckerman, M., Kuhlman, D. M., & Camac, C. (1988). What lies beyond E and N? Factor analyses of scales believed to measure basic dimensions of personality. *Journal of Personality and Social Psychology, 54*, 96–107.

Zuckerman, M., Ulrich, R. S., & McLaughlin, J. (1993). Sensation seeking and reactions to nature paintings. *Personality and Individual Differences, 15*, 563–576.

Zuniga, J. R., Davis, S. H., Englehardt, R. A., & Miller, I. J. (1993). Taste performance on the anterior human tongue varies with fungiform taste bud density. *Chemical Senses, 18*, 449–460.

Zuroff, D. C. (1986). Was Gordon Allport a trait theorist? *Journal of Personality and Social Psychology, 51*, 983–1000.

Zuwerink, J. R., & Devine, P. G. (1996). Attitude importance and resistance to persuasion: It's not just the thought that counts. *Journal of Personality and Social Psychology, 70*, 931–944.

Zweigenhaft, R. L. (1977). The empirical study of signature size. *Social Behavior and Personality, 5*, 177–185.

Zwislocki, J. J. (1981). Sound analysis in the ear: A history of discoveries. *American Scientist, 69*, 184–192.

CREDITS

Photographs

Table of Contents

p. vii: Charles Olson, Recognition, 1993. Acrylic/Canvas 84" x 60", Collection of the Artist and Denise Bibro Fine Art, NYC; **p. viii:** Listen to Living by Roberto Sebastian Antonio Matta Echaurren. 1941. Oil on Canvas, 29 1/2 x 37 3/8" (74.9 x 94.9 cm). The Museum of Modern Art, New York. Inter-American Fund. Photograph © 1997 The Museum of Modern Art, New York.; **p. ix:** Edward Potthast, Children at Shore. Dr. Spencer H. Gross, Pamela G. Fisher, and Lawrence E. Gross.; **p. x:** Henri Rousseau. The Sleeping Gypsy. 1897. Oil on canvas, 51" x 6'7". Collection, The Museum of Modern Art, New York. Gift of Mrs. Simon Guggenheim.; **p. xi:** Buste D'Homme Au Chapeau by Pablo Picasso, Spanish, Christie's Images, London/Superstock; **p. xii:** © 1998 Romare Bearden Foundation/Licensed by VAGA, New York, NY; **p. xiii:** Girl Before a Mirror, by Pablo Picasso. Boisgeloup, March 1932. 64 x 51 1/4" (162.3 x 130.2 cm). Oil on canvas. The Museum of Modern Art, New York. Gift of Mrs. Simon Guggenheim. Photograph © 1997 The Museum of Modern Art, New York.; **p. xiv:** The Armour by Gayle Ray. American/Superstock; **p. xv:** Summer by Eric Isenburger. Private Collection/Superstock; **p. xvi:** Claude Monet. Boulevard des Capucines. 1873. Oil on canvas. 31 3/4" x 23 13/16". The Nelson-Atkins Museum of Art, Kansas City, Missouri. Purchase: Kenneth A. and Helen F. Spencer Foundation Acquisition Fund.

Chapter 1

Opener: Charles Olson, Recognition, 1993. Acrylic/Canvas 84" x 60", Collection of the Artist and Denise Bibro Fine Art, NYC; **p. 5:** © Daniel Wray/The Image Works; **p. 6:** © The The Granger Collection; **p. 7 top:** © The Granger Collection; **p. 7 bottom:** © The Granger Collection; **p. 8 top:** National Library of Medicine; **p. 8 bottom:** © Archives of the History of American Psychology, University of Akron, Akron, OH; **p. 9:** © National Library of Medicine; **p. 10 top:** © Dover Publications, Inc.; **p. 10 bottom:** © National Library of Medicine; **p. 11 top:** Archives of the History of American Psychology, University of Akron, Akron, OH; **p. 11 bottom:** Howard University/Photo, Scurlock Studios; **p. 12 top:** © Culver Pictures; **p. 12 bottom:** ©

Archives of the History of American Psychology, University of Akron, Akron, OH; **p. 14:** © Archives of the History of American Psychology, Seymour Wapner Gift, Permission Clark University Archives; **p. 16 top:** © Christopher S. Johnson/Stock, Boston; **p. 16 bottom:** © The Wellcome Institute Library, London; **p. 17:** © Corbis/Bettmann; **p. 18 top:** © Courtesy, Dr. Herbert Simon; **p. 18 bottom:** Courtesy, Roger Sperry; **p. 19:** Courtesy, Dr. Harry Triandis; **figure 1.2a:** © Lawrence Migdale/Photo Researchers; **figure 1.2b:** © Lawrence Migdale/Photo Researchers; **figure 1.3 a,b:** © David Frazier Photolibrary; **figure 1.3c:** © Bill Auth/Uniphoto; **p. 23:** Courtesy of Florence L. Denmark/Photo by Robert Wesner; **p. 24:** Courtesy, Laurel Furumoto; **p. 25:** Courtesy, Evan Calkins.

Chapter 2

Opener: Grafismo by Joaquin Torres-Garcia, Uruguayan, Christie's Images, New York/Superstock; **p. 32:** © 1995, Newsweek, Inc. all rights reserved. Reprinted by permission.; **p. 33 top:** © David Frazier Photolibrary; **p. 33 bottom:** National Library of Medicine; **p. 37:** © David Frazier Photolibrary; **p. 41:** © Penelope Breese/Gamma Liaison; **p. 42 top:** © Olivier Blaise/Gamma Liaison; **p. 42 bottom:** © Photofest; **p. 44 top:** © Corbis/Bettmann; **p. 44 margin:** © Laura Dwight; **p. 47:** c David Frazier Photolibrary; **p. 50:** Courtesy, Robert Rosenthal; **p. 51:** Courtesy, David Matsumoto; **p. 59:** Courtesy, Dr. Diana Baumrind; **p. 60:** © Paul Conklin; **p. 61:** © Matt Meadows/Peter Arnold.

Chapter 3

Opener: Listen to Living by Roberto Sebastian Antonio Matta Echaurren. 1941. Oil on Canvas, 29 1/2 x 37 3/8" (74.9 x 94.9 cm). The Museum of Modern Art, New York. Inter-American Fund. **p. 64:** Photograph © 1997 The Museum of Modern Art, New York.; **p. 66:** © The The Granger Collection; **p. 68:** © G. Pace/Sygma; **p. 69:** 3.2b: © Biophoto Associates/Photo Researchers; **p. 72 top:** © Historical Pictures/Stock Montage; **p. 72 bottom:** © Mary Evans Picture Library; **p. 73:** © Don M. Goode/Photo Researchers; **p. 74:** © Doug Mills/AP/Wide World Photos; **p. 75 top:** © Jules Asher; **p. 75 bottom:** © AP/Anders Krusberg/Wide World Photos; **p. 79:** © A. Glauberman/Photo Researchers; **p. 80:** © The McGraw-Hill Companies, Inc. /Karl Rubin photogra-

pher; **p. 82:** National Library of Medicine; **p. 85:** © Corbis/Bettmann; **p. 86:** © Penfield Archive/Montreal Neurological Institute; **p. 87:** Courtesy of Drs. Michael Phelps and John Mazziotta, UCLA School of Medicine.; **p. 88 top:** © Corbis/Bettmann; **p. 88 bottom:** © Dr. Francis Schiller; **p. 90:** © Corbis/Bettmann; **p. 91:** © Fred McConnaughey/Photo Researchers; **p. 93:** © Courtesy, Jacqueline Sagen; **p. 97:** © Courtesy, Stanley Coren; **p. 97:** © Courtesy, Diane Halpern; **p. 98:** Courtesy of Drs. John Mazziotta and Michael Phelps, UCLA School of Medicine; **p. 99:** Wurtz, Scientific American, June 1982.; **p. 100:** © Fred Hossler/Visuals Unlimited; **p. 100:** Courtesy, Jerre Levy.

Chapter 4

Opener: Edward Potthast, Children at Shore. **p. 104:** Dr. Spencer H. Gross, Pamela G. Fisher, and Lawrence E. Gross.; **p. 106:** © Archives of the History of American Psychology, Akron, OH; **p. 107:** Courtesy, Wendy Hill/Photo by Dennis Connors/Lafayette College; **p. 111:** © Courtesy, Robert Plomin; **p. 113 top left:** © Petit Format/Photo Researchers; **p. 113 top right:** © Petit Format/Photo Researchers; **p. 113 bottom left:** © Petit Format/Photo Researchers; **p. 113 bottom right:** © Petit Format/Photo Researchers; **p. 114:** Courtesy, University of Washington; **p. 114 top left:** Scala/Art Resource, NY; **p. 114 top right:** Scala/Art Resource, NY; **p. 116:** Courtesy, Tiffany Field; **p. 116:** Courtesy, Tiffany Field; **p. 116:** Courtesy, Tiffany Field; **p. 116:** Courtesy, Tiffany Field; **p. 116:** Courtesy, Tiffany Field; **p. 116:** Courtesy, Tiffany Field; **p. 117 left:** © Enrico Ferorelli; **p. 117 right:** © Enrico Ferorelli; **p. 118:** © Yves De Braine/Black Star; **p. 119 left:** © Doug Goodman/Monkmeyer; **p. 119 right:** © Doug Goodman/Monkmeyer; **p. 120 left:** © Laura Dwight/Peter Arnold; **p. 120 center:** © Laura Dwight/Peter Arnold; **p. 120 right:** © Laura Dwight/Peter Arnold; **p. 121:** Harlow Primate Laboratory, University of Wisconsin; **p. 122:** © Daniel Grogan; **p. 123:** © David Frazier Photolibrary; **p. 125 top left:** © Laura Dwight; **p. 125 top right:** © Laura Dwight; **p. 125:** Courtesy, Eleanor Maccoby; **p. 126:** © David Strickler/The Picture Cube; **p. 128 top left:** © Corbis/Bettmann; **p. 128 top right:** © Wide World Photos; **p.128:** © Harvard University Archives; **p. 129:** © Keith

Carter Photography; **p. 131:** © Estate of Sybil Shelton/Peter Arnold; **p. 132:** © Corbis/Bettmann; **p. 133 top left:** © Lisa Law/The Image Works; **p. 133 top right:** © Topham/The Image Works; **p. 135 top:** Courtesy, Gregg Amore; **p. 135 bottom left:** © Jaye R. Phillips/The Picture Cube; **p. 135 bottom right:** © Mark Antman/The Image Works; **p. 136:** © Toni Michaels; **p. 140:** © Bob Daemmrich/The Image Works; **p. 141 top left:** © Corbis/Bettmann; **p. 141 top right:** © Corbis/Bettmann; **p. 141:** © Corbis/Bettmann; **p. 142:** © Frank Siteman/The Picture Cube.

Chapter 5

Opener: © 1998 Estate of Grant Wood/Licensed by VAGA, New York, NY; **p. 152:** © Personality Photos; **p. 153:** From Dallenbach, K.M. (1951). A puzzle Picture with a New Principle of Concealment. American Journal of Psychology, 54, 431-433.; **p. 154:** © David Grossman/Photo Researchers; **p. 162:** © Villafuerte/TexaStock; **p. 164:** Fritiz Goreau/LIFE Magazine © 1944 Time, Inc.; **p. 165:** Sunday Afternoon on the Island of La Grande Jatte, 1984-86, by Georges Seurat. Oil on Canvas, 207.6 x 308 cm. Helen Birch Bartlett Memorial Collection, Art Institute of Chicago.; **p. 165:** Courtesy, Kaiser Porcelain, Ltd.; **p. 167:** © Ira Wyman/Sygma; **p. 168:** © The The Granger Collection; **p. 169:** © Wayne Sorce; **p. 170 top left:** © Digital Stock/Animals; **p. 170 top right:** © Digital Stock/Roads & Structures; **p. 170 middle left:** © Digital Stock/Roads & Structures; **p. 170 middle right:** © Digital Stock/Flowers; **p. 170 bottom left:** Jean-Claude LeJeune; **p. 170 bottom right:** © Jean-Claude LeJeune; **p. 171:** © Arthur Sirdofsky; **p. 172 left:** © Mark Antman/The Image Works; **p. 172 right:** © Mark Antman/The Image Works; **p. 174:** © Van Bucher/Photo Researchers; **p. 176:** © AP/Wide World Photos; **p. 178:** © T. Orban/Sygma; **p. 180 top:** © Louie Psihoyos/Contact Press Images; **p. 180 bottom:** Courtesy, Linda Bartoshuk; **p. 182:** © Christopher Springmann; **p. 184:** Courtesy, Ronald Melzack.; **p. 185 top:** © Willie Hill, Jr./The Image Works; **p. 185 bottom:** © David Frazier Photolibrary; **TA5.15:** © The Granger Collection.

Chapter 6

Opener: Henri Rousseau. The Sleeping Gypsy. 1897. Oil on canvas, 51" x 6'7". **p. 194:** Collection, The Museum of

Modern Art, New York. Gift of Mrs. Simon Guggenheim.; **p. 196:** AP/Wide World Photos; **p. 197:** Courtesy, Eric Klinger; **p. 198:** © David Frazier Photolibrary; **p. 200:** © Susan Leavines/Photo Researchers; **p. 201:** © Richard T. Nowitz/Photo Researchers; **p. 204:** © D. Wells/The Image Works; **p. 205:** © Orlando Sentinel; **p. 209:** Henry Fuseli, "The Nightmare," © 1781, oil on canvas, Detroit Institute of Arts, Gift of Mr. and Mrs. Bert L. Smokler and Mr. and Mrs. Lawrence A. Fleischman.; **p. 210 top:** © Corbis/Bettmann; **p. 210 left:** © Rush-Presbyterian-St. Luke's Medical Center, Photo by Rona Talcott; **p. 212:** National Library of Medicine; **p. 213:** © AP/Gary C. Klein/Wide World Photos; **p. 215:** © Corbis/Bettmann; **p. 216:** Courtesy, E.R. Hilgard; Stanford University; **p. 218:** © Toni Michaels/The Image Works; **p. 219:** © Stanford News Service, photo by L.A. Cicero; **p. 221:** © Corbis/Bettmann; **p. 222:** Courtesy, The Coca-Cola Company; **p. 223:** © Corbis/Bettmann; **p. 223 top left:** Ronald K. Siegel; **p. 223 top center:** Ronald K. Siegel; **p. 223 top right:** Ronald K. Siegel; **p. 227 top:** © David Frazier Photolibrary; **p. 227 bottom:** © Toni Michaels; **p. 229:** © Corbis/Bettmann.

Chapter 7

Opener: Henry O. Tanner. "The Banjo Lesson" (1893), oil on canvas, 4'1/2" x 3'11". **p. 234:** Hampton University Museum,, Hampton, VA.; **p. 237:** © Corbis/Bettmann; **p. 239:** © Mark Henley/Impact Photos; **p. 242:** Courtesy of Professor Benjamin Harris.; **p. 243:** Photo by Irwin Bernstein ; **p. 245:** Archives of the History of American Psychology; **p. 247:** © Richard Wood/The Picture Cube; **p. 249 a-d:** © Robert W. Kelley/Life Magazine © 1952 Time Inc.; **p. 250 top:** © Jeff Greenberg/Unicorn Stock Photos; **p. 250:** © Arni Katz/Unicorn Stock Photos; **p. 254:** © Gerald Davis/Woodfin Camp & Associates; **p. 256:** © Rita Nannini/Photo Researchers; **p. 257:** © AP/Wide World Photos; **p. 258:** © Skjold Photographs; **p. 260:** Courtesy, Robert Rescorla; **p. 262:** Courtesy, Albert Bandura; **p. 263:** Courtesy, Albert Bandura; **p. 264:** © Russ Kinne/Comstock; **p. 265:** Courtesy, Neal Miller.

Chapter 8

Opener: Salvador Dali. The Persistence of Memory, 1931, oil on canvas, 9 1/2 x 13". **p. 270:** Collection, The Museum of Modern Art, New York. Given anonymously. © 1993 Demart Pro Arte, Geneva / ARS. N.Y.; **p. 273:** © Sylvia Johnson/Woodfin Camp & Associates; **p. 275:** © Jake Evans/Tony Stone Images; **p. 276:** Courtesy, Dr. George Sperling; **p. 279:** Courtesy, Endel Tulving; **p. 283:** Courtesy, Ulric Neisser; **p. 285:** Archives of the History of American Psychology; **p. 289:** © Corbis/Bettmann; **p. 291:** © Culver Pictures; **p. 292:** Courtesy, Gordon Bower; **p. 293:** © UPI/Corbis-Bettmann; **p. 294 top left:** © Corel/Food; **p. 194 top**

right, center right, bottom right: © Corel/Interior Design; **p. 294 center left, bottom left:** © Toni Michaels; **p. 297:** © Archives of the History of American Psychology, Akron, OH; **p. 299:** Courtesy, V.A. Medical Center, San Diego; **p. 300:** © Mimi Forsyth/Monkmeyer Press; **p. 302 left:** © Corbis/Bettmann; **p. 302 right:** © Corbis/Bettmann; **p. 305:** Courtesy, Elizabeth Loftus. Photo by Alex-Mares-Manton.

Chapter 9

Opener: Buste D'Homme Au Chapeau by Pablo Picasso, **p. 308:** Spanish, Christie's Images, London/Superstock; **p. 310:** © Archives of the History of American Psychology, Akron, OH; **p. 311 top left:** © Kathy Tarantola/Picture Cube; **p. 311 top right:** © Owen Franken/Stock Boston; **p. 311 bottom left:** © Susan McCartney/Photo Researchers; **p. 311 bottom right:** © Michael Collier/Stock Boston; **p. 313 top left:** © Larry Kokvoord/The Image Works; **p. 313 bottom left:** © Kevin Vandivier/TexaStock; **p. 313 top right:** © James Feeney/The Picture Cube; **p. 313 bottom right:** © Digital Stock; **p. 314 top left:** © Giraudon/Art Resource, NY; **p. 314 bottom left:** Giraudon/Art Resource, NY; **p. 314 top center:** © Erich Lessing/Art Resource, NY; **p. 314 bottom center:** © Giraudon/Art Resource, NY; **p. 314 top right:** © Scala/Art Resource, NY; **p. 314 bottom right:** © Giraudon/Art Resource, NY; **p. 315:** © Archives of the History of American Psychology, Akron, OH; **p. 316 top a-c:** © Superstock; **p. 316 bottom a-c:** © Normal Baxley/@1984/Discover Magazine; **p. 317:** © Paul Hein/Unicorn Stock Photos; **p. 319:** © Robert Kusel; **p. 321:** Courtesy, Dr. Teresa M. Amabile; **p. 323 top:** Courtesy, Amos Tversky; **p. 323 bottom:** Courtesy, Daniel Kahneman; **p. 326:** © Reuters/Barbara L. Johnson/Archive Photos; **p. 327:** © Bachman/Uniphoto; **p. 332:** © Ira Wyman/Sygma; **p. 332 right:** Museum of Modern Art Film Stills Library; **p. 333 top:** Skjold Photographs; **p. 333 bottom:** Courtesy, Noam Chomsky; **p. 338:** © The Granger Collection; **p. 339 top:** Dr. R. Allen Gardner; **p. 339 bottom:** © Susan Kuklin/Photo Researchers; **p. 340 top:** © Dr. Ronald Cohn/Gorilla Foundation.; **p. 340 center:** © Language Research Center/Georgia State University; **p. 340 bottom:** © Language Research Center/Georgia State University; **p. 341:** © Language Research Center/Georgia State University.

Chapter 10

Opener: Shakespeare in his Study by Michelle Puleo. **p. 344:** American/Superstock; **p. 346:** © Gamma Liaison; **p. 347:** © Archives of the History of American Psychology; **p. 347 top a,b:** © University College London; **p. 348 top:** © Corbis/Bettmann; **p. 348 bottom:** © Corbis/Bettmann; **p. 349 a,b:** National Archives; **p. 355 top:** © J. Kent

Gidley/University of Alabama; **p. 355 bottom:** © Ron Davis/Shooting Star; **p. 356:** © Corbis/Bettmann; **p. 357:** © Alan Carey/The Image Works; **p. 357 bottom:** Courtesy, News and Publication Service, Stanford University; **p. 358:** © Margot Ganitsas/The Image Works; **p. 361:** Courtesy, Dr. Heather Cattell; **p. 362 bottom:** Courtesy, Dr. Howard Gardner/Photo by Gail Zucker; **p. 362 top left:** © Kolvoord/TexaStock; **p. 362 top left center:** © Corbis/Bettmann; **p. 362 top right center:** © Corbis/Bettmann; **p. 362 top right:** © Dave Samble/Sygma; **p. 364:** © Brown Brothers; **p. 366 left:** © Edward L. Miller/Stock Boston; **p. 366 right:** © Philip Jon Bailey/The Picture Cube; **p. 368:** Courtesy, Dr. Robert Zajonc; **p. 370:** © Paul Conklin/Uniphoto.

Chapter 11

Opener: © 1998 Romare Bearden Foundation/Licensed by VAGA, New York, NY; **p. 376:** © The Philadelphia Inquirer/Charles Fox; **p. 377 right:** © Archives of the History of American Psychology; **p. 377 left:** © Don & Esther Phillips/Tom Stack & Associates; **p. 377 center:** © Andrew Brilliant/The Picture Cube; **p. 378 top:** Courtesy, Edward O. Wilson; **p. 378 bottom:** Archives of the History of American Psychology; **p. 380:** © Kindra Clineff/The Picture Cube; **p. 381:** From Teitelbaum, P. Appetyite, Proceedings of the American Philosophical Society, 1964, 108, 464-473.; **p. 383:** Courtesy, Judith Rodin; **p. 385:** © Steve Schapiro/Sygma; **p. 388:** Reprinted by permission of The Kinsey Institute for Research in Sex, Gender, and Reproduction, Inc./Photo: Dellenback; **p. 389:** © Corbis/Bettmann; **p. 391 a,b:** © AP/Wide World Photos; **p. 392 a-d:** © Corbis/Bettmann; **p. 394:** Courtesy, Dr. John Money; **p. 398:** Reprinted by permission of the publishers from Henry A. Murray, THEMATIC APPERCEPTION TEST, Cambridge, Mass.: Harvard University Press, Copyright © 1943 by the President and Fellows of Harvard College; © 1971 by Henry A. Murray.; **p. 399 top:** Courtesy, Mrs. Henry A. Murray.; **p. 399 bottom:** © Harvard University Archives; **p. 400 top left:** © Dana Fineman/Sygma; **p. 400 top left center:** © Micheline Pelletier/Sygma; **p. 400 top right center:** © Paula Lerner/Woodfin Camp & Associates; **p. 400 top right:** © Wide World Photos; **p. 400 bottom:** Courtesy, Edwin Locke; **p. 401:** Courtesy, Edward Deci; **p. 402 bottom:** Courtesy, Dr. Richard Suinn; **p. 402 top left:** © Gerard Schachmes/Sygma; **p. 402 top center:** Patrick Durand/Sygma; **p. 402 top right:** © Haruyoshi Yamazucki/Sygma; **p. 403 top:** © Corbis/Bettmann; **p. 403 bottom:** © John Ficara/Woodfin Camp & Associates.

Chapter 12

Opener: Tahitian Idyll by Paul Gaugin. **p. 408:** French. Narodni Gallery, Prague, Czechoslovakia/Superstock; **p. 412:** © Dr.

Richard J. Davidson, William James Professor of Psychology and Psychiatry. Courtesy of University of Wisconsin News Service.; **p. 414:** © Uniphoto; **p. 416 left:** © Toni Michaels/The Image Works; **p. 416 center:** © Toni Michaels/The Image Works; **p. 416 right:** © Toni Michaels; **p. 418 top:** © Dave Bartruff/Stock Boston; **p. 418 center:** © Digital Stock/Indigenous People; **p. 418 bottom:** © Digital Stock/Babies & Children; **p. 419:** © David Burnett/Contact Stock Images; **p. 420 top:** Courtesy, Robert Plutchik; **p. 420 bottom:** Courtesy, Prof. Edward Diener; **p. 421:** © Corbis/Bettmann; **p. 422 top:** © Suzie Bleeden/Globe Photos; **p. 422 center:** © Corbis/Bettmann; **p. 422 bottom:** © Jan-Olaf Fritz/Shooting Star; **p. 427:** Courtesy, Richard L. Solomon; **p. 428:** © Corel/Winter Sports; **p. 429 top:** Courtesy, Dr. Paul Ekman; **p. 429 bottom:** Courtesy, Office of Public Information, Columbia University; **p. 431 bottom:** Courtesy, Richard S. Lazarus; **p. 431 top:** © Mark Antman/The Image Works; **p. 433:** © Paul Conklin; **p. 437:** Courtesy, Dr. David T. Lykken.

Chapter 13

Opener: Girl Before a Mirror, by Pablo Picasso. Boisgeloup, March 1932. 64 x 51 1/4" (162.3 x 130.2 cm). Oil on canvas. The Museum of Modern Art, New York. Gift of Mrs. Simon Guggenheim. **p. 440:** Photograph © 1997 The Museum of Modern Art, New York.; **p. 443:** © Mary Evans Picture Library; **p. 447 second from top:** © Mark M. Walker/The Picture Cube; **p. 447 third from top:** © MacDonald/The Picture Cube; **p. 448 left:** © Corbis/Bettmann; **p. 448 center:** © Historical Pictures/Stock Montage, Inc.; **p. 448 right:** © Rene Burri/Magnum Photos; **p. 447 right:** © Corbis/Bettmann; **p. 449 top left:** Courtesy of Lucasfilm Ltd./Photo, Museum of Modern Art Film Stills Archive; **p. 449 top right:** Courtesy of Lucasfilm Ltd./Photo, Museum of Modern Art Film Stills Archive; **p. 449 right:** © Y. Karsh/Woodfin Camp & Associates; **p. 450 top:** C.G. Jung, The Archetypes and the Collective Unconscious, Bollingen Series XXm, 1969, Princeton University Press.; **p. 450 center:** C.G. Jung, The Archetypes and the Collective Unconscious, Bollingen Series XXm, 1969, Princeton University Press.; **p. 450 bottom:** © Will & Deni McIntyre/Photo Researchers; **p. 451:** © The The Granger Collection; **p. 452 left:** Museum of Modern Art Film Stills Archive; **p. 452 center:** © Personality Photos; **p. 452 right:** © Personality Photos; **p. 453:** © Archives of the History of American Psychology, Akron, OH; **p. 454:** © Corbis/Bettmann; **p. 459:** NASA; **p. 460:** © Courtesy, Julian Rotter; **p. 461:** Ralph Norman/Brandeis University Photography Department; **p. 463:** National Library of Medicine; **p. 467 left:** © Dana Fineman/Sygma; **p. 467 center:** © Frank Trapper/Sygma; **p. 467 right:** © Laura Lungo/Gamma

Liaison; **p. 468 top:** © Enrico Ferorelli; **p. 469:** Courtesy, Dr. Thomas J. Bourchard, Jr.; **p. 471 top:** © Personality Photos; **p. 471 bottom:** Courtesy, Walter Mischel.

Chapter 14

Opener: Vincent van Gogh. Self Portrait Dedicated to Paul Gauguin. 1888. oil on canvas, 60.3 x 49.4 cm. **p. 476:** Courtesy of the Fogg Art Museum, Harvard University Art Museums, Cambridge, MA. Bequest - Collection of Maurice Wertheim, Class of 1906.; **p. 479 right:** © AP/Wide World Photos; **p. 479 left:** © Corbis/Bettmann; **p. 481:** © Corbis/Bettmann; **p. 482:** © The The Granger Collection; **p. 484:** Courtesy, Dr. David Rosenhan; **p. 485:** © Corbis/Bettmann; **p. 487 top:** Courtesy, Samuel Turner; **p. 487 bottom:** Scala/Art Resource, NY; **p. 489:** © Jean Gaumy/Magnum Photos; **p. 493 top left:** Museum of Modern Art Film Stills Archive; **p. 493 top right:** Museum of Modern Art Film Stills Library; **p. 493 bottom left:** Museum of Modern Art Film Stills Library; **p. 493 bottom right:** AP/Wide World Photos; **p. 495 left:** © Robin Thomas; **p. 495 right:** Courtesy, Dr. Norman E. Rosenthal/NIMH; **p. 496:** © Reuters/Lee Celano/Archive Photos; **p. 497 left:** © Corbis/Bettmann; **p. 497 center:** © Kathy Banks/Sygma; **p. 497 right:** © Corbis/Bettmann; **p. 498:** Courtesy of Drs. Lewis Baxter and Michael Phelps, UCLA School of Medicine.; **p. 499:** Courtesy, Dr. Peter Lewinsohn; **p. 500:** Courtesy, Dr. Lauren Alloy; **p. 502 a-d:** © Derek Bayes/Life Magazine © Time Warner.; **p. 503:** © Grunnitus/Monkmeyer Press; **p. 505 top:** © Alexander Tsiaras/Science Source/Photo Researchers; **p. 505 bottom:** Courtesy, Dr. Daniel R. Weinberger; **p. 506:** Courtesy, Nancy Andreasen; **p. 508:** © AP/Wide World Photos; **p. 509 right:** © Courtesy, Robert Hare; **p. 509 left:** © Wide World Photos; **p. 511:** Courtesy, Martin Orne.

Chapter 15

Opener: The Armour by Gayle Ray. **p. 516:** American/Superstock; **p. 518:** Courtesy, National Museum of Denmark; **p. 519 left:** © Corbis/Bettmann; **p. 519 top right:** © Historical Pictures/Stock Montage; **p. 520 top left center:** © Corbis/Bettmann; **p. 520 top right center:** © Corbis/Bettmann; **p. 520 top right:** National Library of Medicine; **p. 519 bottom right:** © National Portrait Gallery, Smithsonian Institution/Art Resource, NY; **p. 520 top left:** © The The Granger Collection; **p. 521 top left:** © Andrew Schwebel; **p. 520 bottom left:** © The Archives of the American Psychiatric Association; **p. 521 top right:** © Corbis/Bettmann; **p. 521 bottom right:** © Ann Chwatsky/Picture Cube; **p. 524 left:** Courtesy, Joseph Wolpe; **p. 524 right:** © Archives of the History of American Psychology; **p. 525:** © Jacques M. Chenet/Woodfin Camp & Associates;

p. 526: Johns Hopkins University; **p. 528:** Courtesy, Albert Bandura; **p. 530:** Courtesy, Albert Ellis; **p. 531:** Courtesy, Aaron T. Beck; **p. 533:** © Esalen Institute/Paul Herbert, photographer; **p. 534:** © Harvard University Archives; **p. 535:** © Grove/Atlantic, Inc.; **p. 536:** © Joe Sohm/Stock Boston; **p. 537 top:** © Frank Pedrick/The ImageWorks; **p. 537 bottom:** © Karen R. Preuss/The Image Works; **p. 540:** © Will McIntyre/Photo Researchers; **p. 544:** © Mark Antman/The Image Works; **p. 550:** Courtesy, Lester Luborsky.

Chapter 16

Opener: Summer by Eric Isenburger. **p. 556:** Private Collection/Superstock; **p. 558:** © MacDonald/The Picture Cube; **p. 559:** © Paul John Miller; **p. 561:** Courtesy, Dr. Richard Rahe; **p. 565 top:** © RBP/Custom Medical Stock Photo; **p. 565 bottom:** © Roseman/Custom Medical Stock Photo; **p. 564 top:** © Sygma; **p. 564 bottom:** © AP/Wide World Photos; **p. 571:** Courtesy, Dr. Shelley Taylor; **p. 572:** Courtesy, Suzanne Kobasa; **p. 575 top:** University of Chicago Library, Special Collections; **p. 575 bottom:** Courtesy, Janice Kiecolt-Glaser.; **p. 577 top left:** © Lee Corkran/Sygma; **p. 577 top right:** © Brian Reynolds/Sygma; **p. 577 bottom left:** Ralph Domingue/Globe Photros; **p. 577 bottom right:** © Bill Nation/Sygma; **p. 578:** © Stan Gelberg/Globe Photos; **p. 581 left:** Scala/Art Resource, NY; **p. 581 center:** © AP/Wide World Photos; **p. 581 right:** © AP/Wide World Photos; **p. 582:** © Corbis/Bettmann; **p. 583 left:** © Corbis/Bettmann; **p. 583 right:** © Wide World Photos; **p. 586:** © Corbis/Bettmann; **p. 587:** © Tomas Del Amo/Index Stock/Profiles West; **p. 588:** Courtesy, Dr. Redford Williams; **p. 589:** Courtesy, Karen Matthews.

Chapter 17

Opener: Claude Monet. Boulevard des Capucines. 1873. Oil on canvas. 31 3/4" x 23 13/16". **p. 592:** The Nelson-Atkins Museum of Art, Kansas City, Missouri. Purchase: Kenneth A. and Helen F. Spencer Foundation Acquisition Fund.; **p. 595:** Courtesy, Dr. Harold Kelley; **p. 596:** Courtesy, Bernard Weiner; **p. 597:** © Chet Seymour/The Picture Cube; **p. 599 top:** © Hangarter/The Picture Cube; **p. 599 bottom:** © Alan Carey/The Image Works; **p. 600:** © Bob Daemmrich/The Image Works; **p. 601 left:** © Alan Carey/The Image Works; **p. 601 center:** © Skjold/The Image Works; **p. 601 right:** © Charles Gatewood/The Image Works; **p. 603 top:** Courtesy, Ellen Berscheid; **p. 603 bottom:** Courtesy, Elaine Hatfield; **p. 604:** © Skjold Photographs; **p. 606:** © Robert Kusel/Tony Stone Images; **p. 607:** © AP/Wide World Photos; **p. 608 top:** Courtesy, Prof. Richard E. Petty; **p. 608 bottom:** Courtesy, John Cacioppo; **p. 609:** © Karen Zebulon/New School for Social Research; **p. 611 left:** © Rick

Friedman/The Picture Cube; **p. 611 right:** © Larry Kolvoord/The Image Works; **p. 612:** Courtesy, Northside Center for Child Development, NYC; **p. 613:** © MacDonald/The Picture Cube; **p. 614 right:** © John Neubauer/Uniphoto; **p. 614 left:** Courtesy, Yale University, Office of Public Information; **p. 615 bottom:** © David Frazier Photolibrary; **p. 615 top:** © Alan Carey/The Image Works; **p. 616:** © Bob Daemmrich/The Image Works; **p. 618:** © R. Holzbachova/P. Benet; **p. 617 top left:** © William Vandivert; **p. 617 top right:** © William Vandivert; **p. 617 bottom right:** Courtesy, Florence M. Asch; **p. 619:** © Alan Carey/The Image Works; **p. 621 b,c:** From film OBEDIENCE copyright 1965 Stanley Milgram; distributed by Penn State Media Sales. Photo courtesy Mrs. Alexandra Milgram; **p. 620:** Courtesy, Alexandra Milgram/Photo by Eric Kroll; **p. 623:** Courtesy, Prof. Robert Cialdini; **p. 624:** Courtesy, Bibb Latane; **p. 626:** © Bill Perry/Gannett News Service; **p. 627 top:** © AP/Wide World Photos; **p. 627 bottom:** © Sybille Kalas; **p. 628:** Courtesy, University of Wisconsin, Madison; **p. 629:** © Corbis/Bettmann; **p. 631 top:** © Pamela Price; **p. 631 bottom:** Courtesy, Dr. Neil Malamuth.

Appendix C

p. 657: Property of AT&T Archives. Reprinted with permission of AT&T.; **p. 659:** © Corel/People; **p. 665:** © Michael Newman/PhotoEdit; **p. 668:** © Digital Stock/Business & Industry.

Line Art, Excerpts

Chapter 1

Figure 1.1: Source: Data from National Science Foundation, *Special Analyses of the Data from 1973-1991: Survey of Doctoral Recipients*, 1994.

Chapter 2

Figure 2.2: Source: Data from Rosenthal and Fode, "The Effect of Experimenter Bias on the Performance of the Albino Rat" in *Behavioral Science*, 8:183-189, 1963.

Chapter 3

Figure 3.3: From Kurt Schlesinger and Philip M. Groves, *Psychology: A Dynamic Science*. Copyright © 1976 Wm. C. Brown Communications, Inc., Dubuque, Iowa. Reprinted by permission of the author. **Figure 3.15:** From S. Coren and D. Halpern, "Left Handedness: A Marker for Decreased Survival Fitness" in *Psychological Bulletin*, 109: 91. Copyright © 1991 by the American Psychological Association. Reprinted with permission.

Chapter 4

Figure 4.9: Source: Data from J. M. Tanner, et al., "Standards from Birth to Maturity for Height, Weight, Height Velocity, and Weight Velocity" in *Archives of Diseases in Childhood*, British Medical Association, London, England, 1966. **Figure 4.10:** Source: Data from D. K.

Simonton, "Age and Outstanding Achievement: What Do We Know after a Century of Research?" in *Psychological Bulletin*, 104:251-267, American Psychological Association, 1988.

Chapter 5

Figure 5.2: From John W. Santrock, *Psychology: The Science of Mind and Behavior*, 3d ed. Copyright © 1991 The McGraw-Hill Companies, Inc. All Rights Reserved. Reprinted by permission. **Figure 5.3:** From David Shier, et al., *Hole's Human Anatomy & Physiology*, 7th ed. Copyright © 1996 The McGraw-Hill Companies, Inc. All Rights Reserved. Reprinted by permission. **Figure 5.9:** From G. Wald and P. K. Brown, "Human Color Vision and Color Blindness" in *Cold Spring Harbor Laboratory Symposia on Quantitative Biology*, 30:351. Copyright © 1965 Cold Spring Harbor. Reprinted by permission. **Figure 5.15:** From Bradley and Petry, "Organizational Determinants of Subjective Contour" in *American Journal of Psychology*, 90:253-262. Copyright © 1970 by the Board of Trustees of the University of Illinois. Used with the permission of the University of Illinois Press. **Figure 5.18:** From Benjamin B. Lahey, *Psychology: An Introduction*, 3d ed. Copyright © 1989 The McGraw-Hill Companies, Inc. All Rights Reserved. Reprinted by permission. **Figure 5.21:** From John W. Santrock, *Psychology: The Science of Mind and Behavior*, 5th ed. Copyright © 1997 The McGraw-Hill Companies, Inc. All Rights Reserved. Reprinted by permission. **Figure 5.22:** From John W. Santrock, *Psychology: The Science of Mind and Behavior*, 3d ed. Copyright © 1991 The McGraw-Hill Companies, Inc. All Rights Reserved. Reprinted by permission.

Chapter 6

Figure 6.1: From W. B. Webb and H. W. Agnew, Jr., "Sleeping and Waking in a Time-Free Environment" in *Airspace Medicine*, 45:617-622. Copyright © 1974 Aerospace Medical Association, Washington, DC. Reprinted by permission. **Figure 6.3:** From R. D. Cartwright, *A Primer on Sleep and Dreaming*. Copyright © 1978 Addison-Wesley Publishing Company, Reading, MA. Reprinted by permission of the author. **Figure 6.6:** From Spanos and Hewitt, *Journal of Personality and Social Psychology*, 39:1209. Copyright © 1980 by the American Psychological Association. Reprinted with permission.

Chapter 7

Figure 7.3: Source: Data from Ilene L. Bernstein, "Learned Taste Aversions in Children Receiving Chemotherapy" in *Science*, 200:1302-1303, American Association for the Advancement of Science, 1978. **Figure 7.6:** From Benjamin B. Lahey, *Psychology: An Introduction*, 5th ed. Copyright © 1995 The McGraw-Hill Companies, Inc. All Rights Reserved. Reprinted by permission. **Figure 7.7:** From M. C. Roberts and D. Fanurick,

"Rewarding Elementary Schoolchildren for their Use of Safety Belts" in *Health Psychology*, 5:192. Copyright © 1986 Lawrence Erlbaum Associates, Inc., Mahwah, NJ. Reprinted by permission. **Figure 7.8:** From E. C. Tolman and C. H. Honzik, "Introduction and Removal of the Reward and Maze Performance in Rats" in *University of California Publications in Psychology*, 4:257-275. Copyright © 1930 University of California Press, Berkeley, CA. Reprinted by permission.

Chapter 8

Figure 8.2: G. Sperling, *Psychological Monographs*, 74 (whole no. 498), 1960. **Figure 8.3:** Source: L. R. Peterson and M. J. Peterson, "Short-Term Retention of Individual Items" in *Journal of Experimental Psychology*, 58:193-198, 1959. **Figure 8.4:** From R. S. Nickerson and M. J. Adams, *Cognitive Psychology*, 11:297. Copyright © 1979 Academic Press. **Figure 8.5:** Source: Data from F. I. M. Craik and E. Tulving, *Journal of Experimental Psychology: General*, 104:268-294, American Psychological Association, 1975. **Figure 8.7:** From A. M. Collins and E. F. Loftus, "A Spreading Activation Theory of Semantic Processing" in *Psychological Review*, 82:407-428. Copyright © 1975 by the American Psychological Association. Reprinted with permission. **Figure 8.9:** Source (top): Hermann Ebbinghaus, *Uber das Cedachnis (On Memory)*, 1885. **Figure 8.10:** Source: J. G. Jenkins and K. M. Dallenbach, "Obliviscence During Sleeping and Waking" in *American Journal of Psychology*, 35:605-612, 1924. **Figure 8.12:** Adapted from D. R. Godden and A. D. Baddeley, "Context-Dependent Memory in Two Natural Environments: On Land and Under Water" in *British Journal of Psychology*, 66:325-331. Copyright © 1975 British Psychological Society, Leicester, England. Reprinted by permission. **Figure 8.15:** From G. H. Bower and M. C. Clark, "Narrative Stories as Mediators for Serial Learning" in *Psychonomic Science*, 14:181-182. Copyright © 1969 The Psychonomic Society, Inc. Reprinted by permission of the Psychonomic Society, Inc. **Figure 8.18:** Source: Data from E. F. Loftus and J. C. Palmer, "Reconstruction of Automobile Destruction: An Example of the Interaction Between Language and Memory" in *Journal of Verbal Learning and Verbal Behavior*, 13:585-589, American Psychological Association, 1974.

Chapter 9

Figure 9.1: From Benjamin B. Lahey, *Psychology: An Introduction*, 3d ed. Copyright © 1989 The McGraw-Hill Companies, Inc. All Rights Reserved.

Reprinted by permission. **Figure 9.6:** Source: Abraham S. Luchins, "Mechanization in Problem-Solving: The Effect of Einstellung" in *Psychological Monographs*, 6 (whole no. 248), 1942. **Figure 9.11:** Source: Data from the Nobel Foundation, 1974. **Figure 9.12:** From Roger Brown, et. al., "The Child's Grammar from I-III" in *Minnesota Symposium on Child Psychology*, Vol. 2, John P. Hill (ed.). Copyright © 1969 University of Minnesota Press, Minneapolis, MN. Reprinted by permission. **Figure 9.13:** Source: L. Carmichael, et. al., "An Experimental Study of the Effect of Language on the Reproduction of Visually Perceived Form" in *Journal of Experimental Psychology*, 15:73-86, 1932.

Chapter 10

Figure 10.2: A5 taken from the Raven *Standard Progressive Matrices*. Reprinted by permission of J. C. Raven Limited. **Figure 10.3:** Source: J. P. Guilford, "Three Faces of Intellect" in *American Psychologist*, 14:469-479, 1959. **Figure 10.4:** From J. L. Horn and G. Donaldson, "On the Myth of Intellectual Decline in Adulthood" in *American Psychologist*, 31:701-719. Copyright © 1976 by the American Psychological Association. Reprinted with permission. **Figure 10.5:** Source: Data from T. J. Bouchard, et al., "Familial Studies of Intelligence: A Review" in *Science*, 212:1055-1059, AAAS, 1981. **Figure 10.6:** From R. B. Zajonc, "The Decline and Rise of Scholastic Aptitude Scores: A Prediction Derived from the Confluence Model" in *American Psychologist*, 41:862-867. Copyright © 1986 by the American Psychological Association. Reprinted with permission.

Chapter 11

Figure 11.2: This diagram was taken from *Foundations of Experimental Psychology* (C. Murchison, ed.), 1929, and is reprinted by permission of Clark University Press. **Figure 11.4:** Source: Data from *New England Journal of Medicine*, 314:193-198, Massachusetts Medical Society, 1986. **Figure 11.5:** From A. J. Stunkard, et al., "Use of the Danish Adoption Register for the Study of Obesity and Thinness" in The Genetics of Neurological and Psychiatric Disorders, S. Kety (ed.). Copyright © 1983 Lippincott-Raven Publishers, Philadelphia, PA. **Figure 11.6:** Copyright © Masters and Johnson Institute. Reprinted by permission. **Figure 11.8:** Source: Data from R. de Charms and G. H. Moeller, "Values Expressed in American Children's Readers: 1800-1950" in *Journal of Abnormal and Social Psychology*, 64:136-142, American Psychological Association, 1962. **Figure 11.10:** From

D. C. Anderson, et al., "Performance Posing, Goal Setting, and Activity-Contingent Praise as Applied to a University Hockey Team" in *Journal of Applied Psychology*, 73:87-95. Copyright © 1988 by the American Psychological Association. Reprinted with permission.

Chapter 12

Figure 12.6: Reprinted with permission from P. Ekman, et al., "Autonomic Nervous System Activity Distinguishers Among Emotions" in *Science*, 221: 1208-1210. Copyright 1983 American Association for the Advancement of Science. **Figure 12.8:** From R. L. Solomon, "The Opponent-Process Theory of Acquired Motivation: The Costs of Pleasure and Benefits of Pain" in *American Psychologist*, 35:691-712. Copyright © 1980 by the American Psychological Association. Reprinted with permission. **Figure 12.12:** From J. C. Speisman, et al., "Experimental Reduction of Stress Based on Ego-Defense Theory" in *Journal of Abnormal and Social Psychology*, 68:367-380. Copyright © 1964 by the American Psychological Association. Reprinted with permission. **Figure 12.14:** Source: Data from B. Kleinmuntz and J. Szucko, "A Field Study of the Fallibility of Polygraph Lie Detection" in *Nature*, 308:449-450, Macmillan Magazine Ltd., 1984.

Chapter 13

Figure 13.7: Adapted from R. B. Cattell, "Personality Pinned Down" in *Psychology Today*. Copyright © 1973 Institute for Personality and Ability Testing, Inc., Champaign, IL. Reprinted by permission of the author.

Chapter 14

Figure 14.1: Source: Data from L. N. Robins, et al., "Lifetime Prevalence of Specific Psychiatric Disorders in Three Sites" in *Archives of General Psychiatry*, 41:949-958, American Medical Association, 1984. **Figure 14.4:** Source: Data from I. I. Gottesman and J. Shields, *Schizophrenia: The Epigenetic Puzzle*, Cambridge University Press, 1982. **p. 501:** Source: *Harper's Weekly*, December 10, 1881.

Chapter 15

Figure 15.3: From A. Bandura, et al., "The Relative Efficacy of Desensitization and Modeling Approaches for Inducing Behavioral, Affective, and Attitudinal Changes" in *Journal of Personality and Social Psychology*, 13:173-199. Copyright © 1969 by the American Psychological Association. Reprinted with permission. **Figure 15.8:** Source: Data from Mary Lee Smith, et al., *The Benefits of Psychotherapy*, The John Hopkins University Press,

1981. **Figure 15.9:** From K. I. Howard, et al., "The Dose-Effect Relationship In Psychotherapy" in *American Psychologist*, p. 160. Copyright © 1986 by the American Psychological Association. Reprinted with permission.

Chapter 16

Figure 16.1: From Benjamin B. Lahey, *Psychology: An Introduction*, 5th ed. Copyright © 1995 The McGraw-Hill Companies, Inc. All Rights Reserved. Reprinted by permission. **Figure 16.7:** Source: Data from the University of Michigan. **Figure 16.9:** Source: Data from W. H. Redd, et al., "Cognitive/Attentional Distraction in the Control of Conditional Nausea in Pediatric Cancer Patients Receiving Chemotherapy" in *Journal of Consulting and Clinical Psychology*, 55:391-395, American Psychological Association, 1987.

Chapter 17

Figure 17.4: Source: Data from L. Festinger and J. M. Carlsmith, "Cognitive Consequences of Forced Compliance" in *Journal of Abnormal and Social Psychology*, 58, American Psychological Association, 1959. **Figure 17.5:** Source (line art): Solomon E. Asch , "Studies of Independence and Conformity: A Minority of One Against a Unanimous Majority" in *Psychological Monographs* 90 (whole no. 416), 1956. **Figure 17.7:** "PUBLIC ANNOUNCE-MENT" figure from *Obedience to Authority* by STANLEY MILGRAM. Copyright © 1974 by Stanley Milgram. Reprinted by permission of HarperCollins Publishers, Inc. **Figure 17.8:** Source: Data from Stanley Milgram, "Some Conditions of Obedience and Disobedience to Authority" in *Human Relations*, Vol. 18, No. 1, 1965, pp. 57-75; and Stanley Milgram, *Obedience to Authority* Harper & Row, Publishers, 1974, p. 35. **Figure 17.9:** Source: Data from Bibb Latane and John M. Darley, "Group Inhibition of Bystander Intervention in Emergencies" in *Journal of Personality and Social Psychology*, 10:215-221, American Psychological Association, 1968. **Figure 17.10:** From J. M. Darley and B. Latane, "Bystander Intervention in Emergencies: Diffusion of Responsibility" in *Journal of Personality and Social Psychology*, 8:377-383. Copyright © 1968 by the American Psychological Association. Reprinted with permission. **Figure 17.11:** From E. Donnerstein and L. Berkowitz, "Victim Reactions in Aggressive Erotic Films as a Factor in Violence against Women" in *Journal of Personality and Social Psychology*, 41:710-724. Copyright © 1981 by the American Psychological Association. Reprinted with permission.

Leung, J., 574
LeVay, S., 393
Levenson, J.L., 420, 569
Levenson, R.W., 423, 424, 428
Leventhal, E.A., 583
Leventhal, H., 413, 583
Levesque, J.M., 578
Levi, N., 533
Levin, E.D., 579
Levin, F.R., 223
Levin, I.P., 324
Levin, J.R., 294
Levine, A.S., 383
Levine, E., 631
Levine, J.S., 162
Levine, M., 348
Levine, R., 558
Levine, S.B., 387
Levinson, D.J., 134, 139
Levinson, S.E., 329
Levinthal, C.F., 75, 221
Levitt, E.E., 389
Levitt, M.J., 138
Levitz-Jones, E.M., 137
Levy, D., 325
Levy, J., 98, 100
Lewicki, P., 324
Lewin, K., 13, 560
Lewin, R., 93, 627
Lewinsohn, P.M., 499
Lewis, C., 402
Lewis, D., 387
Lewis, J., 186, 452, 468
Lewis, R.D., 385
Lewis, S., 560
Li, A.K.F., 22
Li, Z., 160
Liberman, M.Y., 329
Liberman, R.P., 535
Lie, I., 167
Lieberman, D.A., 10
Lieberman, J.A., 504
Liebert, R.M., 628
Lief, H.I., 392
Liegois, M.J., 214
Lightdale, J.R., 144
Liker, J.J., 359
Lin, E.H., 583
Lincoln, A., 378, 462, 622–623
Lindsay, D.S., 226, 289, 304
Lindsay, R.C.L., 303
Lindvall, O., 93
Linn, M.C., 143
Linn, R.L., 351
Lintern, G., 249
Linz, D., 632
Lipman, J.J., 184
Lips, C., 530
Litt, M.D., 584
Littman, A., 588
Litwin, G.H., 403
Livingstone, M., 160
Llorente, M.D., 208
Lloyd, M.A., 154
LoBello, S.G., 350
Locke, E.A., 399, 400, 404
Locke, J., 6–7, 33–34, 183, 196, 236, 241
Locke, S.E., 567
Lockhart, R.S., 279
Locurto, C., 368, 369
Loeb, G.E., 179
Loeb, S., 369

Loeber, R., 133
Loehlin, J.C., 107, 367, 467
Loeser, J.D., 378
Loewi, O., 72
Lofberg, I., 488
Loftus, E.F., 281, 282, 288, 289, 302, 303, 304, 305
Loftus, G.R., 275
Logan, H., 185
Logan, R.L., 139
Lombroso, C., 433
Long, T.E., 40
Lonner, W.J., 18
Lonnqvist, J., 51
Loomis, A.L., 201
Loomis, M., 451
Loos-Cosgrove, M., 177
Lopes, L.L., 323
Lopez, N., 402
LoPiccolo, J., 391
Lord, C.G., 471
Lorenz, K.Z., 627
Lorenzi, P., 399
Lorig, T.S., 179
Loring, D.W., 97
Lottes, I.L., 388
Louis XVI, King of France, 212
Lovass, O.I., 526
LoVerde, M., 177
Lovibond, P.F., 260
Lowenstein, J., 540
Lowry, D.H., 295
Lox, C.L., 459
Loy, J.W., 599
Lu, Z.L., 276
Lubar, J.F., 265
Lubek, I., 10
Lubel, S., 153
Luborsky, L., 550, 551
Lubow, R.E., 186
Luce, G.G., 196
Luchins, A., 317, 318
Lugaresi, E., 206
Lumsdaine, A., 607
Lundberg, L.J., 330
Lundqvist, L.O., 417
Lundstrom, B., 392
Lundy, R., 216
Lunell, E., 580
Luria, Z., 125
Lutz, J., 40
Lydon, J.E., 602
Lykken, D.T., 107, 110, 111, 366, 434, 436, 437, 467
Lynch, M.J., 395
Lyness, S.C., 588
Lynn, R., 348, 370
Lynn, S.J., 213, 217
Lysle, D.T., 568
Lytton, H., 125
Lyubomirsky, S., 500

Maass, A., 304, 613
Macaulay, D., 291
Maccoby, E.E., 125, 142
MacCracken, M.J., 615
MacDonald, G.A., 580
MacFarlane, J.G., 56, 199
MacGregor, M.W., 494
Machon, R.A., 505
Mack, A., 173
Mack, S., 256
Mackenzie, B., 351
Mackinnon, A.J., 497

Macklin, M.C., 283
Macklin, W.R., 326
Macklis, J.D., 89
Macklis, R.M., 89
MacLaren, V.V., 437
MacLean, H.N., 288
MacLeod, C.M., 285
MacMillan, H.L., 544
MacNichol, E.F., Jr., 162
MacNiven, E., 96
Macrides, F., 180
Maczaj, M., 206
Madakasira, S., 390
Maddi, S.R., 572
Madigan, M.W., 284
Madison, D.V., 70
Madrazo, I., 93
Maffei, L., 172
Magloire, K., 574
Magnussen, S., 284
Magoun, H.W., 81
Maher, B.A., 518
Maher, W.B., 518
Mahler, H.I.M., 584
Mahowald, M.B., 93
Maier, N.R., 318
Maier, S.F., 257
Main, M., 122
Malamuth, N.M., 631, 632
Malarkey, W.B., 78, 565
Malinowski, C.I., 129
Malla, A.K., 504
Malpass, R.S., 18
Mancia, M., 209
Mandai, O., 210
Mandel, D.R., 118
Mandl, G., 168
Mangalmurti, V.S., 546
Manicas, P.T., 38
Mann, C.C., 108
Mann, L., 362
Manning, B.H., 459
Manning, C.A., 301
Mansfield, J.G., 560
Manson, C., 508
Manuck, S.B., 566, 570
Mao, L., 184
Maragos, W.F., 300
Maranto, G., 135
Marchand, S., 184
Marcus, G.F., 331, 332
Maren, S., 83
Margalit, M., 535
Margiotta, E.W., 587
Margo, G.M., 500
Margolin, G., 137
Margolis, R.B., 400
Mariotte, E., 159
Marken, R.S., 314
Markman, H.J., 459
Markovic, B.M., 568
Marks, I.M., 527
Markus, E., 538
Marler, P., 327
Marlowe, C.M., 601
Marmar, C., 522
Marolla, F.A., 368
Marshall, F.J., 170
Marshall, G.D., 431
Marshall, M., 8
Marshall, W.L., 525
Marsland, A.L., 567
Martin, B., 616

Martin, C.E., 388
Martin, E.M., 580
Martin, J.E., 577
Martin, M.A., 292
Martin, R.A., 421, 422
Martinez, J.L., Jr., 297
Martinot, J.L., 498
Marx, J.L., 340
Maser, J.D., 484
Masloneck, K.A., 568
Maslow, A.H., 17, 378, 462, 482
Masoro, E.J., 135
Massaro, D.W., 310
Masserano, J.M., 541
Masters, K.S., 215
Masters, W.H., 388–389, 390, 391
Masur, F.T., 584
Matas, M., 545
Matese, M., 459
Matlock, J.G., 188
Matson, J.L., 256, 355, 459
Matsumoto, D., 51, 418, 428
Matt, G.E., 292
Matthews, D.B., 219
Matthews, K.A., 588, 589, 620
Mattingley, J.B., 98
Maugh, T., 181
Maurino, D.E., 22
Mausfeld, R., 8
Mautner, B., 522
Maxwell, S.E., 542
May, M.A., 471, 472
May, R., 465
Mayberry, J.S., 332
Mayer, J.D., 292
Mayne, T.J., 558
Mayrhauser, R.T. von, 349
Mazzella, R., 601
Mazziotta, J.C., 87, 98, 498
McAdams, D.P., 139
McAleney, P.J., 403
McAllister, D.E., 241
McAllister, H.A, 597
McAllister, W.R., 241
McAuley, E., 527, 577
McCabe, M.P., 390
McCallum, D.M., 573
McCammon, S., 431
McCann, B.S., 588
McCann, J.T., 445
McCann, M.J., 379
McCanne, T.R., 429
McCarley, R.W., 210
McCarthy, G.W., 525
McCarthy, T., 443
McCartney, K., 124
McCarty, T., 493
McCauley, C., 422, 437, 614
McClane, W.E., 421
McClelland, D.C., 397, 398
McClelland, J.L., 298
McCleskey, E.W., 184
McCloskey, M., 272, 305
McConaghy, N., 394
McConkey, K.M., 214, 217
McConnell, J.V., 227, 299
McConnell, R.A., 188
McCormick, N.B., 40
McCrae, R.R., 453, 457
McCrea, D.A., 68
McDonnell, J., 189
McDougall, W., 99, 376, 377
McElroy, S.L., 542

McFalls, J.A., 393
McFarlane, A.C., 569
McGaha, A.C., 58
McGaugh, J.L., 297
McGee, R.A., 38, 291
McGhee, P.E., 422
McGill, J., 185
McGinn, L.K., 531
McGovern, M., 469
McGrady, A., 396
McGrath, P., 588
McGreevy, M.A., 512
McGrew, W.C., 604
McGue, M., 107, 111, 366, 367, 467
McGuigan, F.J., 310
McGuire, B., 562
McGuire, G.R., 4
McKelvie, S.J., 450
McKinley, J.C., 454
McKinney, M., 300
McLaughlin, J., 397
McMinn, M.R., 582
McNally, R.J., 487, 488
McNaughton, B.L., 298
McNeal, E.T., 498
McNeil, C., 213
McNeil, E.B., 227
McNish, K.A., 239
McPherson, K.S., 365
McPherson, L.M., 508
McPherson, M.W., 45
McQionn, R.D., 604
McReynolds, P., 483
McVety, K.M., 261
McWhorter, P., 295
McWilliams, R., 248
McWilliams, S.A., 224
Meana, M., 390
Means, L.W., 40
Medin, D.L., 312
Mednick, S.A., 322, 323, 505
Meduna, L. von, 540
Meehan, J.W., 168
Meehl, P.E., 442
Meeker, W.B., 215
Meese, E., 630–631
Meichenbaum, D.H., 52, 527
Meissner, W.W., 532
Melcer, T., 243
Meldrum, B.S., 92
Melton, G.B., 58
Meltzer, H.Y., 542
Meltzoff, A.N., 262
Melzack, R., 184
Memmott, J., 337
Mendel, G., 108
Mendelson, W.B., 206
Mendes, M.G., 256
Mengel, M.K.C., 183
Mercer, M.E., 162
Merckelbach, H., 97, 262
Merewether, F.C., 415
Merikangas, K.R., 497
Merikle, P.M., 225
Merkel, W.T., 386
Merrill, J.W.L., 81
Mersch, P.P., 530
Mertens, D.M., 257
Mervis, J., 511, 549
Mesmer, A., 212
Messer, W.S., 187
Messick, D.M., 616
Messick, S., 45, 351

Messier, C., 301
Metcalfe, J., 315
Mewaldt, S.P., 291
Meyer, D.R., 90
Meyer, J.S., 136
Meyer-Bahlburg, H.F.L., 393
Meyers, C.E., 353
Mezei, L., 611
Michael, W.B., 360
Michie, P.T., 224
Miczek, K.A., 75
Middleton, J.A., 461
Mikulincer, M., 464
Milan, R.J., 391
Miles, J.A., 616
Milgram, S., 620, 621
Miller, D.L., 399
Miller, E.M., 71, 90
Miller, G.A., 276, 334
Miller, H.L., 47
Miller, J., 227
Miller, L.C., 602
Miller, L.L., 74
Miller, M.G., 379
Miller, N.E., 33, 59, 60, 61, 264, 265, 560
Miller, N.S., 224
Miller, R.R., 260
Miller, T.I., 56, 549, 550
Miller, T.Q., 586
Mills, M.J., 546
Mills, S., 627
Milne, J., 546
Milner, B., 83, 298
Milner, P., 83
Milofsky, E., 120
Milstein, V., 492
Milton, M., 534
Mindell, J.A., 435
Mineka, S., 263, 487
Miner, C.M., 488
Minuchin, S., 537
Mio, J.S., 422
Mira, J.C., 92
Mirsky, A.F., 502
Mischel, W., 458, 470–471
Miserandino, M., 289
Mishra, B.L., 496
Mita, T.H., 601
Mitchell, P., 497, 498
Mitler, M.M., 207
M'Naghten, D., 509–510
Modestin, J., 505
Modigliani, A., 621
Moe, J.L., 611
Moeller, G.H., 397, 398
Mohr, D.C., 551
Molitorisz, J., 236
Moller, A.T., 589
Molly, K., 198
Monahan, J., 546
Mondale, W., 418, 419
Money, J., 387, 392, 394
Mongeau, P.A., 613, 614
Moniz, E., 539
Monrie, M., 581
Monroe, K.B., 619
Monroe, S.M., 482, 562
Monson, J., 459
Monson, T.C., 472
Montag, I., 460
Montanes, P., 276
Monte, C.F., 449

Montegut, M.J., 168
Montesquieu, C., 420
Montgomery, G., 184
Montgomery, R.W., 527
Monti, P.M., 535, 537
Montour, K., 356
Moore, D.J., 491
Moore, J.T., 12, 81
Moore, M., 46
Moore, T.E., 228
Moore-Ede, M.C., 200
Moorhead, G., 614
Moran, M.G., 565
Morawski, J.G., 12
Mordkoff, J.T., 326
Morel, B., 501
Moreland, R.L., 600
Moreno, J., 535
Moretti, M.M., 464
Morgan, C., 398, 399, 450
Morgan, E.R., 358
Morgan, S.B., 584
Morgan, W.G., 450
Morisse, D., 258, 526
Morley, J.E., 383
Moroff, S.V., 323
Morosan, D.E., 328
Morris, E.K., 12
Morris, M., 446, 518
Morris, S., 189
Morris, W., 446, 518
Morrison, A.R., 205
Morrison, M., 611
Morrison, T., 400
Morrongiello, B.A., 118, 178
Morrow, J., 500
Morse, C., 135
Morse, D.L., 249
Mortel, K.F., 136
Mortimer, R.G., 161
Moruzzi, G., 81
Moscicki, E.K., 299, 495
Moscone, G., 510–511
Moscovitch, M., 98
Moses, A.M., 141
Moses, L.N., 449
Moskoowitz, D.S., 459
Moss, C.R., 112
Mother Teresa, 453, 454
Mount, M.K., 399
Mowrer, O.H., 239, 252
Mowrer, W.M., 239
Muehlbach, M.J., 222
Mueller, C.G., 12
Mufson, E.J., 297
Mulhall, D.J., 346
Mullen, B., 418, 615
Mulligan, T., 112
Mullin, C.R., 632
Mullington, J., 207
Mullins, L.L., 491
Mumford, M.D., 319
Munch, E., 503
Munday, R., 454
Munley, P.H., 456
Münsterberg, H., 11, 25, 301
Muris, P., 97
Murphy, E., 422
Murphy, G.E., 501
Murphy, G.L., 312
Murphy, S.T., 432
Murphy, T., 615
Murray, B., 36, 452

Murray, D.J., 153
Murray, H.A., 397, 398, 399, 450
Murray, J.B., 184, 454
Murray, R.M., 490
Murray, R.P., 580
Murstein, B., 604
Murtagh, D.R.R., 206
Murtha, T.C., 472
Muscat, R., 380
Musick, P.L., 449
Myers, D.G., 613
Myers, I.B., 454
Myers, M.G., 535
Myerscough, R., 224
Mylander, C., 334
Mynatt, C.R., 400
Myrtek, M., 588

Nacoste, R.W., 611
Nah, S.Y., 184
Najavits, L.M., 552
Nakagawa, Y., 291
Nakano, T., 74
Nakayama, K., 164
Nanson, J.L., 354
Narens, L., 8
Nash, M., 216
Nason, S., 287–288
Nathan, P.E., 36
Natsoulas, T., 196
Navarro, M., 224
Navon, D., 165
Navratilova, M., 392
Neale, J.M., 503
Neave, N.J., 45
Neck, C.P., 614
Nehrke, M.F., 140
Neimeyer, G.J., 461
Neimeyer, R.A., 499
Neisser, U., 198, 283, 284, 298, 352
Nel, E.M., 612
Nelson, C.E., 601
Nelson, E.S., 563
Nelson, K.E., 333
Nelson, M.O., 448
Nelson, P.L., 224
Nelson, T.O., 198, 293
Nemeth, C.J., 614
Nenty, H.J., 352
Nerger, J.L., 163
Nettelbeck, T., 346
Neufeld, R.W.J., 551, 571
Neumann, K.F., 549
Nevo, B., 422
Nevo, O., 422
Newcomb, A.F., 124
Newcomb, T., 630
Newell, A., 315
Newman, B., 238
Newman, E.A., 155
Newman, J., 401
Newport, E.L., 333
Newton, P.M., 139
Nezlek, J., 401
Ng, K.T., 74
Nicastro, R., 230
Nicholls, J.G., 319, 403
Nichols, M.P., 531
Nichols, P.L., 368
Nicholson, N., 617
Nickerson, R.S., 278
Nicki, R.M., 580
Nicol, S.E., 505
Nicoll, R.A., 70

on schizophrenia, 506
Behavioral preparedness, 259, 526
Behaviorism, 11–12, 15
Behavior modification, 258, 526–527
Behavior therapy, 522–527
    classical-conditioning therapies,
        523–526
    group, 535–536
    operant-conditioning therapies,
        526–527
    social learning therapies, 527
Belongingness needs, 378
Benzodiazepines, 541
Beta rhythm, 80
Beta waves, 201
Bias(es)
    in causal attribution, 596–597
    experimenter, 49–51
    in intelligence testing, 351–352,
        364–365
    in questioning eyewitnesses,
        303–305
    subject, 49
Biased samples, 43–44
Bimodal distribution, 645
Binet-Simon scale, 348
Binocular cues, 167
Biofeedback, 264–267
    applications of, 265–266
    definition of, 264
    historical background of, 265
    research on, 266–267
Biological constraints
    on classical conditioning, 244
    on operant conditioning, 258–259
Biological rhythms, 198
    sleep-wake cycle and, 198–200
Biomedical model of health and
    illness, 558
Biopsychological approach to
    personality, 465–470
    heredity and, 467
    personality assessment and, 467–469
    physique and, 466–467
    status of, 469–470
Biopsychological perspective, 18
    on mood disorders, 497–498
    on psychological disorders, 480
    on schizophrenia, 504–506
Biopsychological theories of emotion,
    423–427
Biopsychological therapy, 538–542
    drug therapy, 541–542
    electroconvulsive therapy,
        540–541
    psychosurgery, 539
Biopsychosocial model of health and
    illness, 558
Bipolar cells, 157
Bipolar disorder, 497
Bisexuals, 392
Blacks
    bias in intelligence testing of,
        351–352
    prejudice against, 610–612
Blocking, 260
B-lymphocytes, 567
Bodily-kinesthetic intelligence, 362
Body movements, emotional
    expression and, 415–416
Body senses, 185–187
Borderline personality disorder, 507, 508
Bottom-up processing, 165

Brain, 67, 78–100
    emotion and, 412–413
    functions of, 78–89
    hemispheric specialization and,
        94–100
    hunger and, 380–381
    localization of functions in, 89–91
    memory and, 296–299
    mind versus, 93–94
    plasticity of, 91–93
    vision and, 159–160
Brain damage
    hemispheric specialization and, 98
    neural grafting to treat, 92–93
    psychosurgical, 539
Brain stem, 82
Brightness constancy, 170
Brightness of light, 156
Broca's aphasia, 88
Broca's area, 88–89
Brown v. Board of Education of
    Topeka, 611
Bulimia nervosa, 385–386
Bystander intervention, 623–626

Caffeine, 220, 222
Cancer, stress and, 569
Cannabis sativa, 220, 224
Cannon-Bard theory of emotion,
    424–425
Cardinal traits, 453
Case studies, 41–42, 640
Catatonic excitement, 503
Catatonic schizophrenia, 503
Catatonic stupor, 503
Catharsis, 520
Cattell Culture Fair Intelligence
    Test, 352
Causal attribution, 594–597
    biases in, 596–597
    dimensions of, 596
    principles of, 594–595
Causation, 46
    inferential statistics and, 56–57
Cell-adhesion molecules, 113
Cell body, 68
Central nervous system, 67
Central tendency error, 662
Central tendency measures, 53–54,
    645–646
Central traits, 453
Cerebellum, 81
Cerebral cortex, 84–89
Cerebral hemispheres, 84
Cerebral palsy, 354
Cerebrotonia, 466
C fibers, 183
Chaining, 248–249
Challenge, psychological hardiness
    and, 572
Chemical senses, 179–181
Chemistry
    of emotion, 413–414
    of memory, 299–301
Childhood
    children as eyewitnesses and,
        302–303
    definition of, 115
    development during. See
        Infant/child development;
        Psychosocial development
Child psychology, 106
Child rearing. See also Parenting

operant conditioning for, 256
Chimpanzees, language acquisition by,
    338–339, 340–341
Chloride, neural impulses and, 70
Cholecystokinin, hunger and, 379–380
Choline, memory and, 300
Chromosomes, 108
Circadian rhythms, 198–200
Circumspection phase of constructive
    alternativism, 461
Clairvoyance, 188
Classical conditioning, 236–245
    acquisition in, 237–239
    applications of, 240–243
    biological constraints on, 244
    extinction in, 240
    higher-order, 238
    of immune responses, 568–569
    stimulus generalization and
        stimulus discrimination in,
        239–240
Classical-conditioning therapies,
    523–526
Claustrophobia, 487
Client-centered therapy, 531
Clients
    effectiveness of therapy and,
        551–552
    rights of, 545–546
Clinical psychologists, 547
Clinical psychology, 21–22
Closure principle, 165
Cocaine, 220, 222–223
Cochlea, 175
Cochlear implants, 177
Coefficient of correlation, 54, 649
Cognition
    hypnosis and, 214
    social, 594–599
Cognitive appraisal, stress and, 570–571
Cognitive-appraisal theory of emotion,
    431–433
Cognitive approach to personality,
    460–462
    personal-construct theory, 460–461
    personality assessment and, 461
    status of, 462
Cognitive-behavioral assessment, of
    personality, 459–460
Cognitive-behavioral therapies, 527,
    529–531
    cognitive therapy, 530–531
    rational-emotive behavior therapy,
        529–530
    stress-inoculation training, 527, 529
Cognitive development
    during adolescence, 131–132
    during adulthood, 136
    during infancy and childhood,
        118–120
    sex differences in, 142–143
Cognitive dissonance theory, 608–610
Cognitive-evaluation theory, 401
Cognitive learning, 259–263
    associative, 259–260
    latent, 260–261
    observational, 261–263
Cognitive perspective, 17–18
    on psychological disorders, 480,
        481–482
    on schizophrenia, 506
Cognitive psychology, 310. See also
    Thinking

Cognitive rule for determining
    insanity, 510
Cognitive theories of emotion,
    429–433
Cognitive therapy, 530–531
Cognitive triad, 499
Cognitive viewpoint on mood
    disorders, 499–501
Cohorts, 111
Cohort-sequential research, 112
Cold pressor test, 215
Collateral sprouting, 91
Collective unconscious, 448
Color blindness, 163–164
Color vision, 162–164
Commitment
    love and, 603
    psychological hardiness and, 572
Common sense, 32–33
Community mental health, 543–545
Community Mental Health Centers
    Act of 1963, 543
Companionate love, 603
Comparative psychology, 21
Compensation as defense mechanism,
    445, 446
Complementary transactions, 535
Compliance, 618–619
Componential intelligence, 361
Compulsions, 490
Computed tomography (CT), 87
Computer-assisted instruction, 257
Computer programs, artificial
    intelligence and, 325–326
Concept(s), 311–313
    logical, 311–312
    natural, 312–313
Conception, 112
Concrete operational stage, 118, 120
Conditional positive regard, 482
Conditioned reinforcers, 246
Conditioned response (CR), 237–241
Conditioned stimulus (CS), 237–241
Conditioned taste aversion, 242–243
Conditioning. See also Classical condi-
    tioning; Operant conditioning
    instrumental, 246
Conditions of worth, 463
Conduction deafness, 177
Cones, 157, 158
Confidentiality, 545–546
Conflict, 560–561
Confluence model, 368
Conformity, 616–618
Confounding variables, 48–49
Conscious mind, 229, 443
Consciousness, 194–231. See also
    Dreams; Hypnosis; Meditation;
    Psychoactive drugs; Sleep;
    Unconscious mind
    definition of, 196
    flight of, 197
    focusing of, 197–198
    personality and, 443
    stream of, 10, 196–197
Consensus, causal attribution and, 595
Consent, informed, 58
Conservation during concrete
    operational stage, 120
Consideration, 668
Consistency, causal attribution and, 595
Constitutional theory of personality,
    466–467

Excitement phase of sexual response cycle, 389
Exercise, stress and, 574, 577–578
Exhaustion, stage of, 565
Existential psychology, 17
Existential therapy, 533–534
Exocrine glands, 76
Expectancy, 399, 664
Experience
  phenomenological, 462
  vicarious, self-efficacy and, 459
  visual perception and, 171–174
Experience-sampling method, 459
Experiential intelligence, 361
Experimental group, 47
Experimentalists, 24
Experimental method, 47–48
Experimental psychology, 20
Experimental research, 47–52, 640
  experimental method for, 47–48
  external validity and, 51–52
  internal validity and, 48–51
Experimenter bias effect, 49–51
Expert opinion, 33
Expert systems, 325
Explanation as research goal, 39
Explanatory style, stress and, 571
Explicit memory, 280
Expressed emotion, 506
External auditory canal, 175
External validity, 51–52
Extinction, 240
  in behavior modification, 526–527
  in operant conditioning, 252, 253
Extracellular fluid, 70
Extrasensory perception (ESP), 187–190
  alleged abilities and, 187–188
  research on, 188–190
Extraversion, 452, 457
Extraverts, 449
Extrinsic motivation, 400
Eye, 156–159
Eyewitness testimony, 301–305
  bias questions and, 303–305
  of children, 302–303

Facial expressions, 416–418
Facial-feedback theory of emotion, 428–429
Factor analysis, 359
  theories of intelligence and, 359–361
Fallopian tubes, 112
Familiarity, liking and, 600–601
Family studies
  of intelligence, 366–368
  nature-nurture issue and, 109–111
Family therapy, 537–538
Farsightedness, 157
Feature-doctor theory, 166
Feelings
  of control, stress and, 571–572
  reflection of, 531–532
Fetal alcohol syndrome, 114, 354
Fetal stage, 113–114
Fetishism, 387
Fictional finalism, 448
Field experiments, 35–36
Fight-or-flight response, 410, 412
Figure-ground perception, 164–166
Firing threshold, 70, 72
Fitness, stress and, 577–578

Five-factor theory of personality, 457
Fixation, 446
Fixed-interval schedules of reinforcement, 250
Fixed-ratio schedules of reinforcement, 249–250
Fixed-role therapy, 462
Flashbulb memories, 272
Flooding, 526–527
Flotation restricted environmental stimulation (REST), 396
Fluid intelligence, 136, 360–361
Foot-in-the-door technique, 618–619
Forebrain, functions of, 82–89
Forensic psychology, 22
Forgetting, 273, 284–292. See also Amnesia
  cue dependence and, 289–292
  interference and, 287
  motivation and, 287–289
  trace decay and, 286
Forgetting curve, 286
Formal operational stage, 118, 131–132
Form perception, 164–166
Fovea, 158
Framing effects, 324–325
Fraternal twins, 110
Free associations, analysis of, 521–522
Frequency distributions, 642
Frequency histogram, 643
Frequency of sound waves, 174
Frequency polygon, 643
Frequency theory of pitch perception, 176–177
Freudian slips, 443
Frontal lobe, 84
Frustration-aggression hypothesis, 628
Frustration as stressor, 559
Fugue, psychogenic, 492
Functional fixedness, 318
Functionalism, 10–11, 15
Functional MRI, 88
Fundamental attribution error, 596

g (general intelligence factor), 359
Gamma aminobutyric acid (GABA), 74
Gays, 392
Gender identity, 391–392
  disorders of, 391–392
Gender roles, 125
  development of, 125–126
Gender-schema theory, 126
General adaptation syndrome, 565
General intelligence factor (g), 359
Generalized anxiety disorder, 485–487
Generativity, language and, 327
Generativity versus stagnation stage, 121, 139
Genetics. See also Heredity; Nature-nurture issue
  behavioral, 107–109
Genital herpes, mental retardation due to, 354
Genital stage, 446, 447
Genius. See Mental giftedness
Genotype, 109
Geriatric population, psychosocial development of, 140–141
Germinal stage, 112
Gestalt psychology, 12–13, 15
Gestalt therapy, 532–533
Glial cells, 68

Global competition, 669
Glucose, memory and, 300–301
Glutamic acid, 74
Goal setting, 399–400
Goal setting theory, 665
Gonads, 77, 78, 386
Gorillas, language acquisition by, 339–340
Gradient as monocular cue, 169
Grammar, 328
  transformational, 329
Graphology, 449–450
Graphs, 642–645
Gray matter, 71
Group(s)
  definition of, 612
  performance and, 615–616
  violence in, 629–630
Group decision making, 612–615
  group polarization and, 613
  groupthink and, 614–615
  minority influence and, 613–614
Group polarization, 613
Group therapy, 534–537
  behavioral, 535–536
  humanistic, 536–537
  psychoanalytic, 535
Groupthink, 614–615
Growth hormone, 77
Guilty but mentally ill rule, 511–512
Guilty Knowledge Test, 436–437
Gustation, 181

Hair cells of inner ear, 175
Halfway houses, 544
Hallucinations, 501–502
Hallucinogens, 220, 223–224
Halo effect, 662
Hammer (malleus), 175
Handwriting analysis, 449–450
Happiness, 420
Hashish, 224
Head movement sense, 186–187
Health, 556–590
  fitness and, 577–578
  nutrition and, 580–582
  smoking and, 578–580
  stress and. See Stress
  unsafe sexual practices, 576–577
Health psychology, 22, 558
Hearing, 174–179. See also Auditory perception
  auditory system and, 174–175
Helplessness, learned, 257–258
  stress and, 571–572
Hemispherectomy, 92
Hemispheric specialization, 94–100
  evidence from damaged brain, 98
  evident from intact brain, 97
  split-brain studies of, 98–100
Heredity. See also Behavioral genetics; Nature-nurture issue
  intelligence and, 365–366
  mood disorders and, 497–498
  motivation and, 376–377
  personality and, 467
  schizophrenia and, 504–505
  sex differences and, 144–145
Heritability, 109
Herpes, mental retardation due to, 354
Heuristics
  decision making and, 323–324
  problem solving and, 316–317

Hidden observer, 215
Hierarchy of needs, 378
Higher-order conditioning, 238
Hindbrain, functions of, 80–81
Hippocampus, 83–84
Historicism, 4
Histrionic personality disorder, 508
HIV (human immunodeficiency virus), 569
Holophrastic speech, 330
Homeostasis, 377
Homosexuality, 392–394
  AIDS and, 576–577
Hormones, 76–78
  memory and, 300
  during puberty, 131
Hospice movement, 140–141
Human immunodeficiency virus (HIV), 569
Humanistic approach to personality, 462–465
  personality assessment and, 464
  self-actualization theory, 462
  self theory, 463–464
  status of, 464–465
Humanistic perspective, 17
  on mood disorders, 501
  on psychological disorders, 480, 482
  on schizophrenia, 506–507
Humanistic therapy, 531–534
  existential therapy, 533–534
  Gestalt therapy, 532–533
  group, 536–537
  person-centered therapy, 531–532
Human subjects, ethical treatment of, 58–59
Humor, 421–422
Humors, 466
Hunger, 378–386
  bodily factors regulating, 379–380
  brain factors regulating, 380–381
  eating disorders and, 383–386
  environmental factors regulating, 381
  obesity and, 381–383
Hypermnesia, 214
Hyperopia, 157
Hypnosis, 212–217
  as altered state of consciousness, 215–216
  effects of, 213–215
  induction and susceptibility for, 212–213
  as normal state of consciousness, 216–217
Hypochondriasis, 490–491
Hypothalamus, 76, 77, 83
  drives and, 377
  emotion and, 412
  hunger and, 380–381
Hypotheses, 35
  testing, 651–653
Hypoxia, mental retardation due to, 354
Hysteria, 491

Iconic memory, 274
Id, 443–444
Ideal self, 463–464, 465
Identical twins, 110
Identification, psychosexual development of personality and, 446

Identified patient, 537
Identity disorder, 493–494
Identity versus role confusion stage, 121, 132
Idiot savants, 346
Illness, 582–586. *See also specific illnesses*
  general adaptation syndrome and, 565
  mental retardation due to, 354
  promoting adherence to medical regimens and, 585
  relieving patient distress and, 584–585
  seeking treatment for, 583
  stress and. *See* Stress
  type A behavior and, 586–589
Illusions, visual, 170–171, 173–174
Illusory contours, 166
Imaginal flooding, 526
Immigrants, intelligence testing of, 364–365
Immigration Act of 1924, 365
Immune function, stress and, 566–569
Implicit memory, 280
Impression management, 597
Incentives, 377, 378
Incentive value, 399
Incongruity theory of humor, 422
Incus, 175
Independent variable, 47
Industrial/organizational psychology, 22, 656–670
Industry versus inferiority stage, 121, 122
Infancy, 115
Infant/child development, 115–129
  cognitive, 118–120
  perceptual, 116–118
  physical, 115–116
  psychosocial. *See* Psychosocial development
Infectious disease, stress and, 566–569
Inferences, unconscious, visual perception and, 164
Inferential statistics, 56–57, 650–652
  hypothesis testing and, 651–653
  statistical significance and, 650–654
Inferiority complex, 448
Influence, 616–621
  compliance and, 618–619
  conformity and, 616–618
  obedience and, 619
Information processing
  automatic and controlled, 226
  bottom-up and top-down, 165
  memory and, 273–274
  parallel and serial, 326
Information-processing model of memory, 274
Informed consent, 58
In-groups, 598
Inhibitory neurotransmitters, 73
Initiating structure, 668
Initiative versus guilt stage, 121, 122
Inner ear, 175
Insanity
  definition of, 509–510
  moral, 507
Insanity defense, 509–512
  alternative to, 511–512
  controversy over, 510–511
  nature of, 509–510

Insecurely attached infants, 122
Insight, 315
Insomnia, 206
Instinct(s), 376–377
Instinctive drift, 259
Instrumental conditioning, 246
Instrumentality, 664
Insulin, hunger and, 380
Integrity versus despair stage, 121, 140
Intellectualization, as defense mechanism, 445
Intelligence, 344–371. *See also* Mental giftedness; Mental retardation
  artificial, 325–326
  bodily-kinesthetic, 362
  componential, 361
  contextual, 361
  crystallized, 136, 360–361
  definition of, 346
  enhancing, 369–371
  experiential, 361
  factor-analytic theories of, 359–361
  family studies of, 366–368
  fluid, 136, 360–361
  interpersonal, 362
  intrapersonal, 362
  linguistic, 362
  logical-mathematical, 362
  musical, 362
  nature-nurture issue and, 363–371
  spatial, 362
  theory of multiple intelligences and, 362–363
  triarchic theory of, 361–362
Intelligence quotient (IQ), 349–350
  mental retardation and, 353–354
Intelligence testing, 346–353
  bias in, 364–365
  historical background of, 347–350
  reliability of tests for, 350–351
  validity of tests for, 351–353
Interference theory of forgetting, 287
Interferon, 569
Internal-external dimension of causal attribution, 596
Internal-External Locus of Control Scale, 459–460
Internal validity, 48–51
Interneurons, 68
Interpersonal attraction. *See* Liking; Love
Interpersonal intelligence, 362
Interposition as monocular cue, 168
Interval scales, 641
Intimacy, love and, 603
Intimacy versus isolation stage, 121, 137
Intracellular fluid, 70
Intrapersonal intelligence, 362
Intrinsic motivation, 400–401
Introspection, analytic, 9–10
Introverts, 449
In vivo desensitization, 525
In vivo flooding, 526
Iodopsin, 160
Ion channels, 70
IQ (intelligence quotient), 349–350
  mental retardation and, 353–354
Iris, 156

James-Lange theory of emotion, 423–424
Jet lag, 199–200

Job analysis, 658
Job description, 658
Just noticeable difference (jnd), 152–154

Kidneys, 77
Kinesthetic sense, 185
Knowledge, sources of, 32–37

La belle indifference, 491
Language, 326–341
  definition of, 326
  structure of, 328–330
  thinking related to, 334–337
Language acquisition, 330–334
  by apes, 337–341
  critical period for, 332–333
  stages in, 330–332
  theories of, 333–334
Latency stage, 446, 447
Latent content of dreams, 209, 522
Latent learning, 260–261
Lateral hypothalamus (LH), hunger and, 380–381
Law of effect, 245
Lay psychology, 32–33
L-dopa
  Parkinson's disease and, 82
  schizophrenia and, 505
Leading questions, eyewitness testimony and, 303–305
Learned helplessness, 257–258
  stress and, 571–572
Learning, 234–268
  associative, cognitive factors in, 259–260
  avoidance, 251–252
  biofeedback as means of, 264–267
  cognitive. *See* Cognitive learning
  conditioning and. *See* Classical conditioning; Operant conditioning
  definition of, 236
  escape, 251
  latent, 260–261
  observational, 261–263
  social learning theory and, 262
Leniency, 662
Lens, 157
Lesbians, 392
Leucotomy, 539
Levels of processing theory of long-term memory, 279
LH (lateral hypothalamus), hunger and, 380–381
Libido, 446
Lie detectors, 433–437
  alternative to, 436–437
  issues with, 435–436
  procedure using, 434
Life changes as stressors, 561–563
Life scripts, 535
Liking, 600–602
  familiarity and, 600–601
  physical attractiveness and, 601–602
  proximity and, 600
  self-disclosure and, 602
  similarity and, 602
Limbic system, 83, 180
  emotion and, 412
Line graphs, 645
Linear perspective, 168–169
Linguistic intelligence, 362

Linguistic relativity hypothesis, 334–337
  sexist language and, 336–337
Link method, 295
Listening, dichotic, 226
Lithium carbonate, 542
Lobotomy, 539
Locus of control, 459–460
Logic, 33
Logical concepts, 311–312
Logical-mathematical intelligence, 362
Logotherapy, 534
Longitudinal research, 111
Long-term memory, 273, 278–292
  encoding and, 278–279
  forgetting and, 284–292
  retaining, 279–283
  retrieving, 283–284
Loudness perception, 177
Love, 602–604
  companionate, 603
  passionate, 603
  promoting, 604
  theories of, 602–604
Love needs, 378
LSD (lysergic acid diethylamide), 220, 223–224
Lucid dreaming, 209
Lunacy, 480
Lysergic acid diethylamide (LSD), 220, 223–224

Magnetic resonance imaging (MRI), 87–88
Mainstreaming, 355
Maintenance rehearsal, 277, 278
Major depression, 478, 494–496
Maladaptiveness as criterion for psychological disorders, 479
Malingering, 490
Malleus, 175
Malnutrition, mental retardation due to, 354
Management by objectives, 399–400
Mania, 497
  drug therapy for, 542
Manic depression, 497
Manifest content of dreams, 209, 522
MAO inhibitors, 541
Marijuana, 224
Marriage, 121, 137
  divorce and, 137–138
Masculine protest, 448
Massed practice, 293
Mathematical abilities, sex differences in, 143
Maturation, 106
Mean, 53, 646
Mean length of utterance (MLU), 331
Measurement, 38
Measurement scales, 640–641
Measures of central tendency, 53–54, 646
Measures of variability, 54, 646–648
Median, 53, 646
Medical model, 481
Meditation, 217–219
  effects of, 218
  practices used for, 217–218
Medulla oblongata, 80
Melatonin, 32, 199

Memory(ies), 270–306. See also
    Amnesia; Forgetting
  brain and, 296–299
  chemistry of, 299–301
  context-dependent, 290
  declarative, 279–280
  definition of, 272
  dreaming as aid to, 210
  echoic, 275–276
  episodic, 280
  explicit, 280
  eyewitness testimony and, 301–305
  flashbulb, 272
  iconic, 274
  implicit, 280
  improving, 292–296
  information processing and, 273–274
  long-term. See Long-term memory
  mood-congruent, 291–292
  mood-dependent, 291
  procedural, 279, 280
  semantic, 280
  sensory, 273, 274–276
  short-term (working), 273, 276–278
  state-dependent, 291
Menarche, 131
Mental age, 348–349
Mental giftedness, 356–358
  genetic studies of, 357
  Study of Mathematically
    Precocious Youth and, 358
Mental retardation, 114, 353–356
  causes of, 354–355
  classification of, 353–354
  education of persons with, 355–356
Mental sets, 317
Mental telepathy, 187–188
Mental tests, 8, 348
Mere exposure effect, 602
Mescaline, 223
Mesmerism, 212
Mesomorphs, 466–467
Message, persuasion and, 607
Meta-analysis, 56
Method of loci, 294
Method of savings, 284–285
Midbrain, functions of, 81–82
Middle ear, 175
Mild retardation, 353
Mind-brain problem, 93–94
Minnesota Multiphasic Personality
  Inventory (MMPI), 454–456
Minority influence, group decision
  making and, 613–614
MLU (mean length of utterance), 331
MMPI (Minnesota Multiphasic
  Personality Inventory), 454–456
Mnemonic devices, 292, 294–295
Mode, 53, 645
Modeling, participant, 527
Moderate retardation, 353
Monochromats, 164
Monocular cues, 168–169
Monozygotic twins, 110
Mood-congruent memory, 291–292
Mood-dependent memory, 291
Mood disorders, 494–501
  behavioral viewpoint on causes
    of, 499
  biopsychological viewpoint on
    causes of, 497–498

bipolar disorder, 497
  cognitive viewpoint on causes of, 499–501
  humanistic viewpoint on causes
    of, 501
  major depression, 494–496
  psychoanalytic viewpoint on causes
    of, 498–499
Moon illusion, 171, 172
Moral development, 126–129
Moral insanity, 507
Moral therapy, 519
Morphemes, 328
Morphine, 221
Motion parallax, 168
Motion sickness, 186–187
Motivated forgetting, 287–289
Motivation, 374–406. See also
    Achievement motive; Hunger;
    Sexual behavior
  arousal motive and, 394–397
  definition of, 376
  intrinsic and extrinsic, 400–401
  sources of, 376–378
  sport and, 401–405
Motor cortex, 84
Motor homunculus, 85
Motor neurons, 68
Motor theory of thinking, 310
Movement senses, 185–187
MRI (magnetic resonance imaging), 87–88
Müller-Lyer illusion, 173
Multimodal therapy, 547–548
Multiple intelligences, theory of, 362–363
Multiple personality, 41–42
Multiple sclerosis, 71
Musical intelligence, 362
Myelin, 71
Myelin sheath, 72
Myers-Briggs Type Indicator, 454
Myopia, 157

Narcissistic personality disorder, 508
Narcolepsy, 206–207
Narrative method, 295
Nativism, 5
Natural concepts, 312–313
Naturalistic observation, 40–41, 640
Natural killer cells, 569
Natural selection, 8, 106
Nature-nurture issue, 7, 106–111
  behavioral genetics and, 107–109
  intelligence and, 363–371
  language acquisition and, 333–334
  relative studies and, 109–111
Nearsightedness, 157
Needs, 377
  for achievement, 398–399
  hierarchy of, 378
Negative correlation, 46, 54, 55
Negative punishment, 252
Negative reinforcement, 251–252, 253
Negative skew, 643
Negative state relief theory, 623
Negative symptoms of
  schizophrenia, 505
Negative transference, 522
Neglect syndrome, 66
Neodissociation theory of hypnosis, 215
Neo-Freudians, 447–448
Neologisms, 502

Nerve(s), 67
Nerve deafness, 177
Nervous system, 67–68
Neural grafting, 92–93
Neural impulses, 69–72
Neural plasticity, 91–93
Neuromodulators, 75
Neuron(s), 67, 68–76
  communication between, 72–76
  neural impulses and, 69–72
  types of, 68
Neuronal membrane, 70
Neuropeptides, 74–76
Neuroscience. See Brain; Nervous
    system; Neuron(s)
  behavioral. See Behavioral
    neuroscience
Neuroses, 482
Neuroticism, 452, 457
Neurotransmitters, 72–76
  memory and, 299–300
  mood disorders and, 497–498
Nicotine, 220, 222
Nicotine chewing gum, 579, 580
Nicotine fading, 580
Nicotine patches, 579–580
Nightmares, 208
Night terrors, 208
N-methyl-D-aspartate (NMDA)
  receptors, 300
Nociception, 183–185
Nociceptors, 183
Nocturnal enuresis, 239
Nodes of Ranvier, 71
Nominal scales, 641
Nondirective therapy, 531
Norepinephrine, 77
  emotion and, 410
  mood disorders and, 497–498
Normal curve, 648–649
Normative commitment, 667
Norms, 44
NREM sleep, 201–203
Null hypothesis, 651
Nutrition, 580–582
  inadequate, mental retardation due
    to, 354

Obedience, 619
Obesity, 381–383
Objective personality tests
  (inventories), 454
Object permanence, 119
Observation
  behavioral, 459
  naturalistic, 40–41
  unsystematic, 33–34
Observational learning, 261–263
Obsessions, 489–490
Obsessive-compulsive disorder, 489–490
Obsessive-compulsive personality
  disorder, 508
Occipital lobes, 86
  vision and, 160
Odors, 180
Oedipus complex, 446
Older adults, psychosocial
  development of, 140–141
Olfaction, 179–181
Olfactory nerves, 180
Openness to experience, 457
Operant conditioning, 245–259

applications of, 254–258
  biological constraints on, 258–259
  extinction in, 252, 253
  negative reinforcement in, 251–252, 253
  positive reinforcement in, 246–251, 253
  punishment in, 252–253
Operant conditioning theory of
  personality, 457
Operant-conditioning therapies, 526–527
Operation(s), intelligence and, 360
Operational definitions, 38
Opiates, 220, 221
Opponent-process theory
  of color vision, 163
  of emotion, 426–427
Optic chiasm, 159–160
Optic nerves, 157
Oral-aggressive personality, 446
Oral-dependent personality, 446
Oral stage, 446, 447
Ordinal scales, 641
Organizational psychology, 22
Orgasmic dysfunction, 390
Orgasm phase of sexual response
  cycle, 389
Otis-Lennon Mental Abilities
  tests, 349
Otolith organs, 186
Ought self, 465
Outer ear, 174–175
Out-groups, 598
Oval window, 175
Ovaries, 77, 78
Overcompensation, 448
Overextension, 330
Overjustification theory, 401
Overlearning, 293
Overregularization, 331
Ovum, 112

Pain, 183–185
  factors inducing, 183–184
  relief of, 184–185
Pancreas, 77
Panic attacks, 487
Panic disorder, 478, 487
Papillae, 181
Paradoxical intention, 206
Parallel processing, 326
Paranoid personality disorder, 508
Paranoid schizophrenia, 503
Paranormal abilities, 187–190
  alleged, 187–188
  research on, 188–190
Paraphilias, 387
Paraprofessionals, 547
Parapsychology, 187
Parasympathetic nervous system, 67, 410
Parenting
  adult psychosocial development
    and, 138
  styles of, 122–124
Parietal lobe, 85
Parkinson's disease, 74, 81–82, 93
Partial schedules of reinforcement, 249
Participant modeling, 527
Passion, love and, 603
Passionate love, 603
Passivity, 536

Psychoneuroimmunology, 566–569
Psychopathy, 507–509
Psychophysics, 8, 152–154
Psychoses, 482–483. *See also*
    Schizophrenia
    drug therapy for, 542
Psychosexual theory of personality,
    443–446
    defense mechanisms and, 444–446
    levels of consciousness and, 443
    personality formation and, 446
    structure of personality and,
        443–444
Psychosocial development
    during adolescence, 132–134
    during adulthood, 136–141
    early attachment and, 121–122
    gender roles and, 125–126
    identity achievement and,
        132–133
    during infancy and childhood,
        120–129
    marriage and, 137–138
    moral development and, 126–129
    parenthood and, 138
    parenting and, 122–124
    peer relationships and, 124–125,
        133–134
    sex differences in, 143–144
Psychosurgery, 539
Psychotherapy, 520. *See also*
    Effectiveness of psychotherapy;
    Therapy
    evaluation of, 549
Psychoticism, 452
Puberty, 130–131
Punishment, 252–253
    in behavior modification, 526
Pupils, 156–157
Pygmalion effect, 50

Q-sort, 464

Race
    bias in intelligence testing and,
        351–352
    prejudice and, 610–612
Random assignment, 49
Random sampling, 43
Range, 54, 646
Rank ordering, 661
Rapid smoking, 580
Rating scale, 661
Ratio scales, 641
Rational-emotive behavior therapy
    (R-E-B-T), 529–530
Rational-emotive therapy (R-E-T), 529
Rationalism, 5
Rationalization as defense
    mechanism, 445
Raven Progressive Matrices, 352
Reaction formation, 445–446
Reality principle, 444
Reasoning, 33
R-E-B-T (rational-emotive behavior
    therapy), 529–530
Recall, constructive, 284
Recall tests, 285
Recency effect, 284
Receptor sites, 73
Recessive genes, 109
Reciprocal determinism, 458
Recognition tests, 285

Recovered memory syndrome, 289
Reflection of feelings, 531–532
Reflexes, 68
Refractory phase of sexual response
    cycle, 389
Regression as defense mechanism, 445
Rehearsal
    elaborative, 278
    maintenance, 277, 278
Reinforcement. *See* Negative rein-
    forcement; Positive reinforcement
Reinforcement theory of mood
    disorders, 499
Relative size as monocular cue, 168
Relaxation
    progressive, 524, 575
    stress and, 574–575
Relaxation response, 218
Relearning, 284–285
Release theory of humor, 422
Reliability
    of diagnoses, 484
    of intelligence tests, 350–351
    of tests, 45
REM sleep, 201–203, 211
Replication, 35
Repolarization of neurons, 72
Representativeness heuristic, 323–324
Repression, 288, 443, 444–445
REP Test (Role Construct Repertory
    Test), 461
Research
    on ape acquisition of language,
        339–341
    applied, 20
    basic, 20
    on biofeedback, 266–267
    correlational, 46–47
    descriptive. *See* Descriptive
        research
    in developmental psychology,
        111–112
    ethics of, 57–61
    experimental. *See* Experimental
        research
    goals of, 37–40
    on intelligence, 365–368
    paranormal, 188–190
    on pornography and aggression,
        631–633
    scientific method for, 34–37
    statistical analysis for. *See* Statistics
Research hypothesis testing, 651–653
Resistance, stage of, 565
Resistances, analysis of, 522
Resolution phase of sexual response
    cycle, 389
Response
    conditioned, 237–241
    unconditioned, 237–238, 241
Responsibility
    bystander intervention and,
        624–625
    diffusion of, 616
REST (restricted environmental stim-
    ulation), 396
Resting potentials, 70
Restricted environmental stimulation
    (REST), 396
R-E-T (rational-emotive therapy),
    529–530
Reticular formation, 81
Retina, 157

Retrieval, 273
    of long-term memories, 283–284
Retroactive interference, 287
Re-uptake, 73
Rhodopsin, 160
Ribonucleic acid (RNA), 108
Ringelmann effect, 616
Risky shift, 613
RNA (ribonucleic acid), 108
Rods, 157–158
*Rogers v. Commissioner of Mental
    Health,* 545
Role Construct Repertory Test (REP
    Test), 461
Role reversal, 535
Romantic love. *See* Love
Rorschach test, 450
Rubella, mental retardation
    due to, 354
Rumination theory of mood
    disorders, 500

Saccadic movements, 159
Sadomachism, 387
Safety needs, 378
Samples, 43–44
    biased, 43–44
Saturation of light, 156
Scatter plots (scatter diagrams; scatter-
    grams), 650
Schema theory of long-term memory,
    281, 283
Schizoid personality disorder, 508
Schizophrenia, 74, 501–507
    behavioral viewpoint on causes
        of, 506
    biopsychological viewpoint on
        causes of, 504–506
    characteristics of, 501–503
    cognitive viewpoint on causes
        of, 506
    drug therapy for, 542
    humanistic viewpoint on causes of,
        506–507
    psychoanalytic viewpoint on causes
        of, 506
    types of, 503
Schizotypal personality disorder, 508
School psychology, 22
Schools of psychology, 9–15. *See also*
    specific schools
Scientific method, 34–37
    assumptions and, 34–35
    steps in, 35–36
Scientific paradigm, 15
Sclera, 156
Scotophobin, 299
Seasonal affective disorder, 494–495
Secondary cognitive appraisal, 570
Secondary prevention, 544
Secondary reinforcers, 246
Securely attached infants, 122
Security needs, 378
Selective permeability of neuronal
    membrane, 70
Self-actualization, therapeutic
    promotion of, 531–532
Self-actualization needs, 378
Self-actualization theory of
    personality, 462
Self-disclosure, liking and, 602
Self-efficacy, 458–459
    stress and, 571

Self-fulfilling prophecy, 49–50, 599
Self-handicapping, 491
Self-help groups, 537
Selfless helping, 622–623
Self-management programs, for
    smoking cessation, 580
Self-monitoring, personality
    consistency and, 471
Self-perception theory, 610
Self-serving bias, 597
Self theory of personality, 463–464
Semanticity, 326–327
Semantic memory, 280
Semantic network theory of long-term
    memory, 281
Semantics, 329
Semicircular canals, 186
Sensate focusing, 390
Sensation, 152–187. *See also*
    specific senses
    definition of, 152
    sensory adaptation and, 154–155
    sensory thresholds and, 152–154
Sensation seeking, 397
Sensitivity groups, 536–537
Sensorimotor stage, 118–119
Sensory adaptation, 154–155
Sensory data, 33–34
Sensory deprivation, 395–396
Sensory memory, 273, 274–276
Sensory neurons, 68
Sensory receptors, 152
Sensory registers, 273
Sensory transduction, 152
Septum, 412
Serial-position effect, 284
Serial processing, 326
Serotonin, mood disorders and, 497–498
Serotonin re-uptake inhibitors, 542
Set point, 381
Severe retardation, 354
Sex differences, 141–145
    cognitive, 142–143
    physiological explanations for,
        144–145
    psychosocial, 143–144
    social-cultural explanations
        for, 145
Sexist language, linguistic relativity
    hypothesis and, 336–337
Sex therapy, 390–391
Sexual behavior, 386–394
    gender identity and, 391–392
    physiological factors in, 386
    psychological factors in, 387–389
    sexual dysfunctions and, 390–391
    sexual orientation and, 392–394
    unsafe practices and, 576–577
Sexual dysfunctions, 390–391
Sexual orientation, 391, 392–394
Sexual response cycle, 388–389
Shading patterns, 169
Shape constancy, 170
Shaping, 247–248
Short-term memory, 273, 276–278
Signal-detection theory, 153–154
Significance, statistical, 653
Similarity, liking and, 602
Similarity principle, 165
Simple phobias, 487
Situational attribution, 594
16 Personality Factor Questionnaire
    (16PF), 456

SUBJECT INDEX